NX 2506 Black Book

By
Gaurav Verma
Matt Weber
(CADCAMCAE Works)

Edited by
Kristen

ISBN # 978-1-77459-208-3

NOTICE TO THE READER

Publisher does not warrant or guarantee any of the products described in the text or perform any independent analysis in connection with any of the product information contained in the text. Publisher does not assume, and expressly disclaims, any obligation to obtain and include information other than that provided to it by the manufacturer.

The reader is expressly warned to consider and adopt all safety precautions that might be indicated by the activities herein and to avoid all potential hazards. By following the instructions contained herein, the reader willingly assumes all risks in connection with such instructions.

The Publisher makes no representation or warranties of any kind, including but not limited to, the warranties of fitness for a particular purpose or merchantability, nor are any such representations implied with respect to the material set forth herein, and the publisher takes no responsibility with respect to such material. The publisher shall not be liable for any special, consequential, or exemplary damages resulting, in whole or part, from the reader's use of, or reliance upon, this material.

DEDICATION

To teachers, who make it possible to disseminate knowledge
to enlighten the young and curious minds
of our future generations

To students, who are the future of the world

THANKS

To my friends and colleagues

To my family for their love and support

Training and Consultant Services

At CADCAMCAE WORKS, we provide effective and affordable one to one online training on various software packages in Computer Aided Design(CAD), Computer Aided Manufacturing(CAM), Computer Aided Engineering (CAE), Computer programming languages(C/C++, Java, .NET, Android, Javascript, HTML and so on). The training is delivered through remote access to your system and voice chat via Internet at any time, any place, and at any pace to individuals, groups, students of colleges/universities, and CAD/CAM/CAE training centers. The main features of this program are:

Training as per your need

Highly experienced Engineers and Technician conduct the classes on the software applications used in the industries. The methodology adopted to teach the software is totally practical based, so that the learner can adapt to the design and development industries in almost no time. The efforts are to make the training process cost effective and time saving while you have the comfort of your time and place, thereby relieving you from the hassles of traveling to training centers or rearranging your time table.

Software Packages on which we provide basic and advanced training are:

CAD/CAM/CAE: CATIA, Creo Parametric, Creo Direct, SolidWorks, Autodesk Inventor, Solid Edge, UG NX, AutoCAD, AutoCAD LT, EdgeCAM, MasterCAM, SolidCAM, DelCAM, BOBCAM, UG NX Manufacturing, UG Mold Wizard, UG Progressive Die, UG Die Design, SolidWorks Mold, Creo Manufacturing, Creo Expert Machinist, NX Nastran, Hypermesh, SolidWorks Simulation, Autodesk Simulation Mechanical, Creo Simulate, Gambit, ANSYS and many others.

Computer Programming Languages: C++, VB.NET, HTML, Android, Javascript and so on.

Game Designing: Unity.

Civil Engineering: AutoCAD MEP, Revit Structure, Revit Architecture, AutoCAD Map 3D and so on.

We also provide consultant services for Design and development on the above mentioned software packages

For more information you can mail us at:
cadcamcaeworks@gmail.com

Table of Contents

Chapter 3 : Sketching Practical and Practice

Chapter 4 : 3D Modeling

Chapter 5 : 3D Modeling-II

Chapter 6 : 3D Modeling - III

Chapter 7 : Rendering and 3D Modeling Practice

Chapter 8 : Curve Sketching

Chapter 10 : Surface Editing

Chapter 11 : Assembly

Chapter 12 : Drawing and Practice

Preface

NX 2506 is an advanced, integrated CAD/CAM/CAE solution that combines high-end parametric and direct modeling capabilities with comprehensive engineering analysis and manufacturing tools. It seamlessly unifies three-dimensional (3D) design with drafting and documentation workflows, while covering the entire product development cycle from concept to production. Continuous advancements have strengthened its position as a full-scale PLM-driven platform, enabling efficient collaboration and data management. The software delivers powerful simulation and validation tools with streamlined usability, and its deep integration with manufacturing modules ensures a highly efficient transition from design to machining. Driven by industry requirements and user feedback, NX 2506 provides a robust yet intuitive environment that enhances productivity from the outset.

The **NX 2506 Black Book** is the 1st edition of our series on Siemens NX. The book follows a step by step methodology. In this book, we have tried to give real-world examples with real challenges in designing. We have tried to bridge the gap between academic use and industrial use of NX. The book covers almost all the information required by a beginner to learn applications of the NX. The book covers Sketching, Basic 3D modeling, Advanced 3D modeling, Curve Sketching, Basic Surfacing, Advanced Surfacing, Basic and Advanced Assembly, and Drafting (Drawing). Some of the salient features of this book are :

In-Depth explanation of concepts

Every new topic of this book starts with the explanation of the basic concepts. In this way, the user becomes capable of relating the things with real world.

Topics Covered

Every chapter starts with a list of topics being covered in that chapter. In this way, the user can easy find the topic of his/her interest easily.

Instruction through illustration

The instructions to perform any action are provided by maximum number of illustrations so that the user can perform the actions discussed in the book easily and effectively. There are about 1590 illustrations that make the learning process effective.

Tutorial point of view

At the end of concept's explanation, the tutorial make the understanding of users firm and long lasting. Almost each chapter of the book has tutorials that are real world projects. Moreover most of the tools in this book are discussed in the form of tutorials.

Project

Projects and exercises are provided to students for practicing.

For Faculty

If you are a faculty member, then you can ask for video tutorials on any of the topic, exercise, tutorial, or concept. As faculty, you can register on our website to get electronic desk copies of our latest books, self-assessment, and solution of practical. Faculty resources are available in the **Faculty Member** page of our website (**www.cadcamcaeworks.com**) once you login. Note that faculty registration approval is manual and it may take two days for approval before you can access the faculty website.

Formatting Conventions Used in the Text

All the key terms like name of button, tool, drop-down etc. are kept bold.

Free Resources

Link to the resources used in this book are provided to the users via email. To get the resources, mail us at ***cadcamcaeworks@gmail.com*** with your contact information. With your contact record with us, you will be provided latest updates and informations regarding various technologies. The format to write us mail for resources is as follows:

Subject of E-mail as ***Application for resources of .... book***.
Also, given your information like
Name:
Course pursuing/Profession:
Contact Address:
E-mail ID:

Note: We respect your privacy and value it. If you do not want to give your personal informations then you can ask for resources without giving your information.

About Authors

The author of this book, Matt Weber, has written more than 15 books on CAD/CAM/CAE available in market. He has coauthored SolidWorks Simulation, SolidWorks Electrical, SolidWorks Flow Simulation, and SolidWorks CAM Black Books. The author has hands on experience on almost all the CAD/CAM/CAE packages. If you have any query/doubt in any CAD/CAM/CAE package, then you can contact the author by writing at cadcamcaeworks@gmail.com

The author of this book, Gaurav Verma, has written and assisted in more than 19 titles in CAD/CAM/CAE which are already available in market. He has authored Solid Edge Black Book, SolidWorks Black Book, Autodesk Fusion Black Book, AutoCAD Electrical Black Book, Autodesk Revit Black Books, and so on. He has provided consultant services to many industries in US, Greece, Canada, and UK. He has assisted in preparing many Government aided skill development programs. He has been speaker for Autodesk University. He has assisted in preparing AutoCAD Electrical course for Autodesk Design Academy. He has worked on Sheetmetal, Forging, Machining, and Casting designs in Design and Development departments of various manufacturing firms.

For Any query or suggestion

If you have any query or suggestion, please let us know by mailing us on ***cadcamcaeworks@gmail.com***. Your valuable constructive suggestions will be incorporated in our books and your name will be addressed in special thanks area of our books on your confirmation.

Chapter 1

Starting with NX

Topics Covered

The major topics covered in this chapter are:

- ***Introduction to Siemens NX***
- ***Interface Elements***
- ***First Screen Tools***
- ***File Menu***
- ***Customizing Interface***

INTRODUCTION

NX is one of the most advanced CAD, CAM, and CAE tool available in the market. Various functions that NX is capable to perform are given next.

- 2D Drafting
- 3D Parametric Modeling
- 3D Synchronous Modeling
- Sheet Metal Design
- Mesh Modeling
- Assembly
- Layout Design
- Mold Design
- Electrode Design
- Press Die Design
- Machining
- Additive Manufacturing
- Electrical Harness and Cable Design
- Pipe and Tube Routing
- Logical Routing
- HVAC Design
- Motion, Simulation, and Analysis
- Welding Design
- Shape Studio
- PCB Design
- Mechatronics Design
- Knowledge Fusion and so on.

NX is a good choice if you are manufacturing some complex parts and assemblies in industry. NX was developed by Unigraphics and I-deas back in 1980s. Since then the software is under constant development. Now the software is offered by Siemens and hence called Siemens NX. The latest additions in the software are Convergent Modeling, Topology Optimization, Lattice Design, Design Checker, and so on.

While going through this book, you will learn about various applications of the software.

DOWNLOADING AND INSTALLING NX STUDENT VERSION

- Open your web browser and visit the link https://trials.sw.siemens.com/nx-student-edition/
- Click on the **Create a Siemens account** link button below **Log In to Siemens** button on this webpage to create a new account if you are not a user already. The **Create account** page will be displayed; refer to Figure-1.

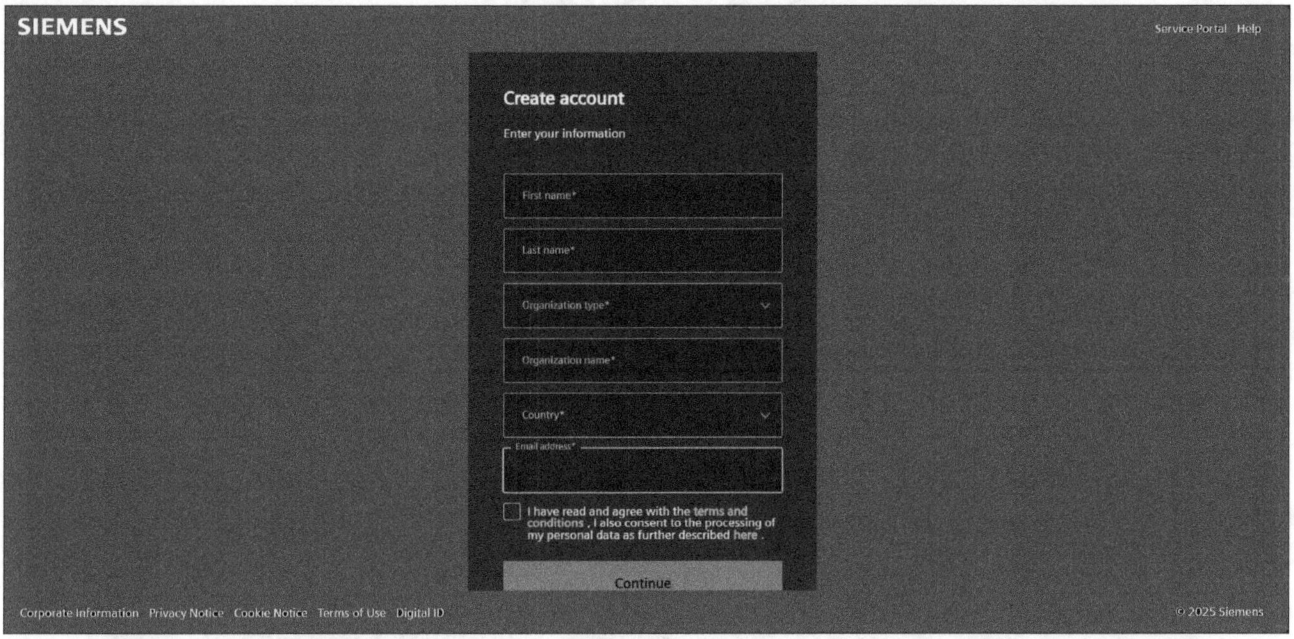

Figure-1. Create account web page

- Specify name, email address, and other details on this page; select the check box, and click on the **Continue** button. The page to specify password for your account will be displayed.
- Enter desired password and click on the **Create account** button to create the account. Now you can use this information to login to account and start trial. Alternatively, you can use Sign in with Google or Sign in with LinkedIn to start your trial.
- Once you have logged in to your account, click on the Download your software button from webpage being displayed. The webpage with links to your download will be displayed; refer to Figure-2.
- Click on the zip file link button to download the software zip file.

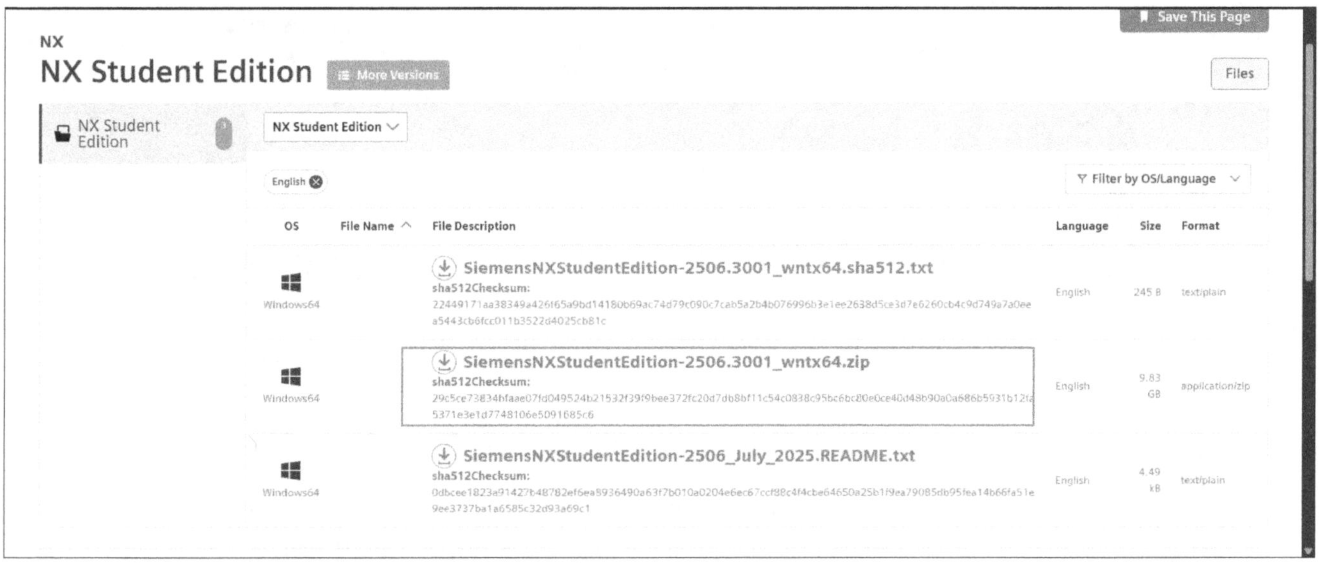

Figure-2. Download option for NX Student Edition

- Extract the downloaded zip file at desired location and then double-click on the Setup.exe file from the extracted directory. Follow the instructions shown in the installation dialog box and Install the software.

STARTING NX

After installing the NX software, follow the steps given next.

- Click on the **Start** button and type **NX**. The list of applications with name starting from NX will be displayed; refer to Figure-3.

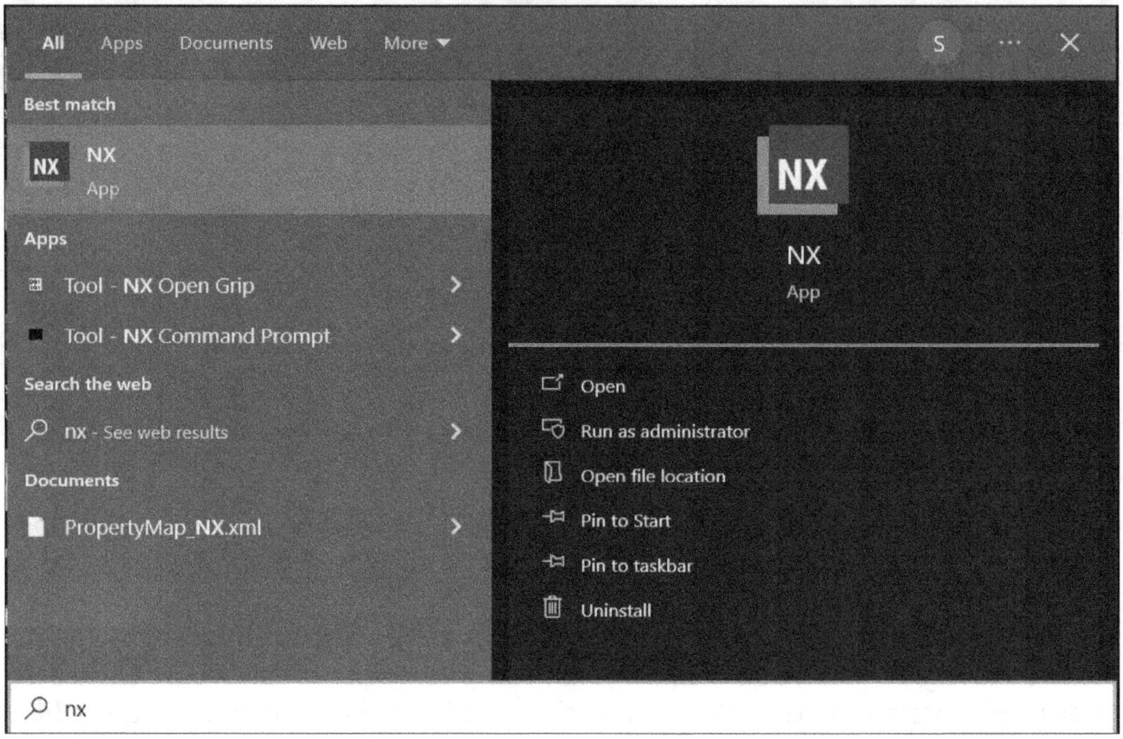

Figure-3. Start menu

- Click on NX from the list. The initial screen of NX will be displayed; refer to Figure-4.

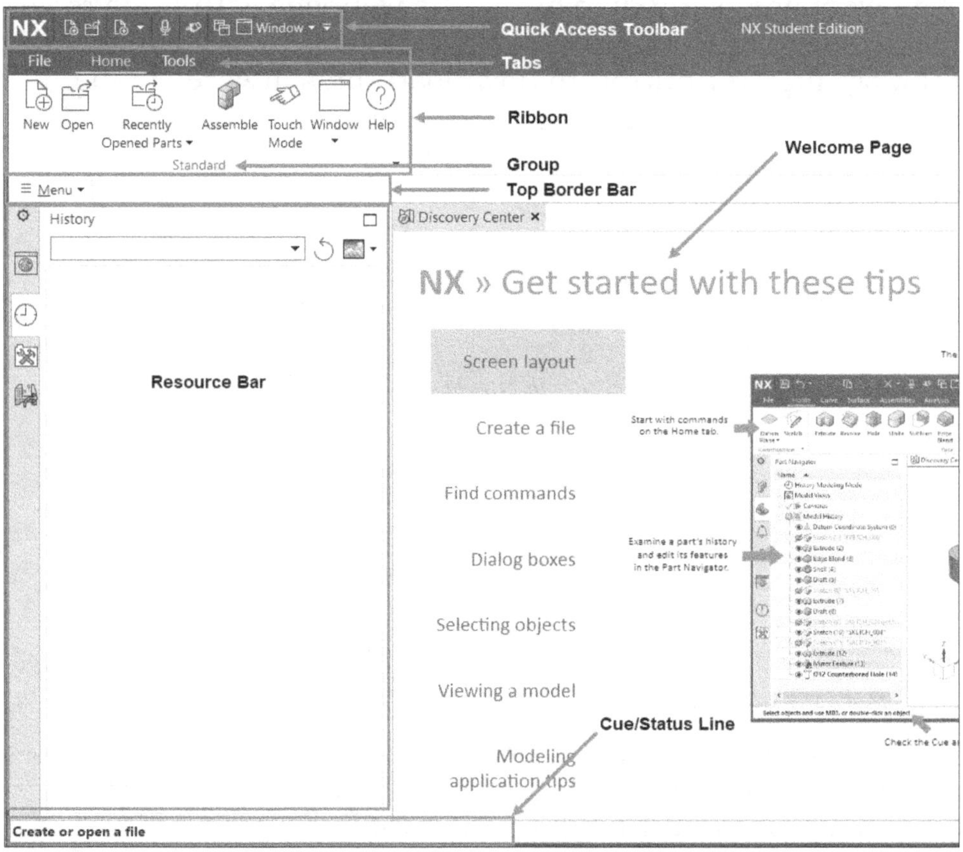

Figure-4. Initial screen of UG NX

STARTING NEW PART FILE

- Click on the **New** tool from the **Standard** group of the **Home** tab in the **Ribbon**. The **New** dialog box will be displayed; refer to Figure-5.

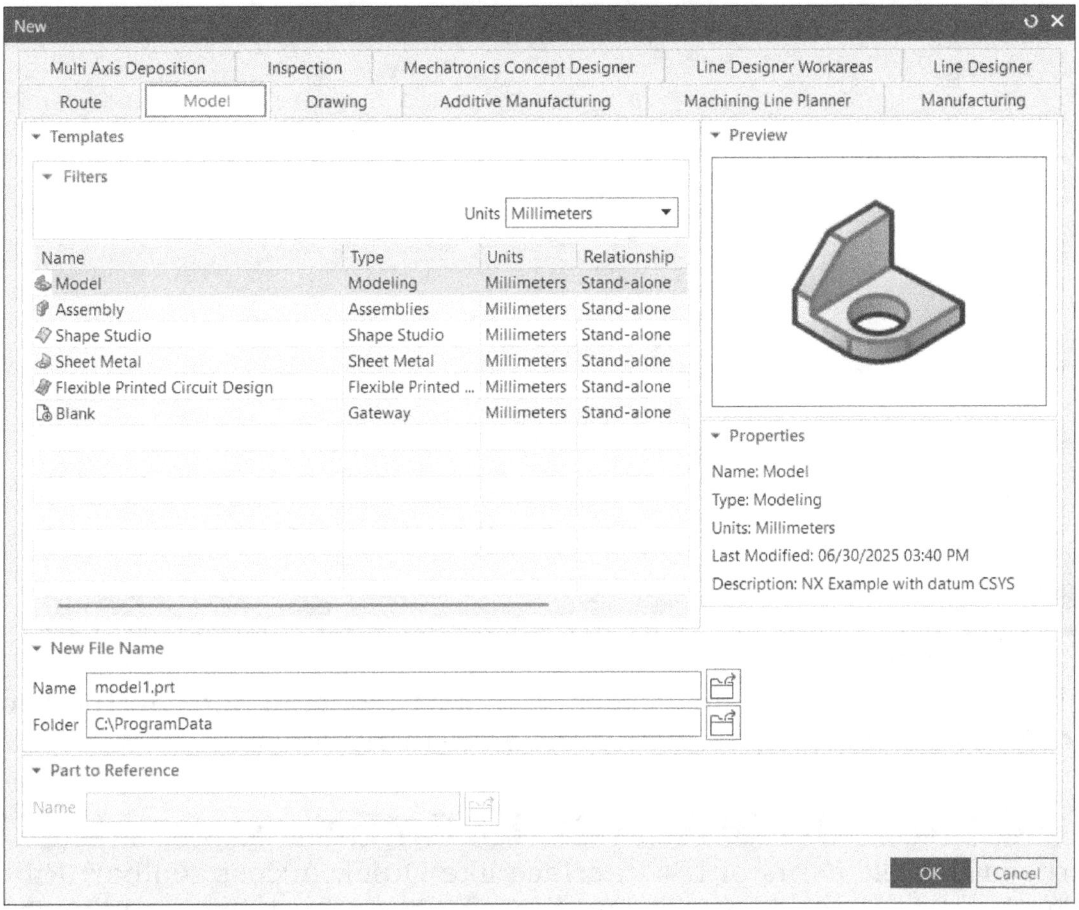

Figure-5. New dialog box

- Make sure the **Model** tab is selected in the dialog box and you have selected **Model** option from the **Templates** area to create a new part file.
- Select desired unit from the **Units** drop-down.
- Click in the **Name** edit box and specify desired name for part file.
- Click in the **Folder** edit box and specify the location of file. You can also use **Browse** button next to the edit box and select desired location for the file.
- After setting desired parameters, click on the **OK** button. The user interface to start a new part will be displayed; refer to Figure-6.

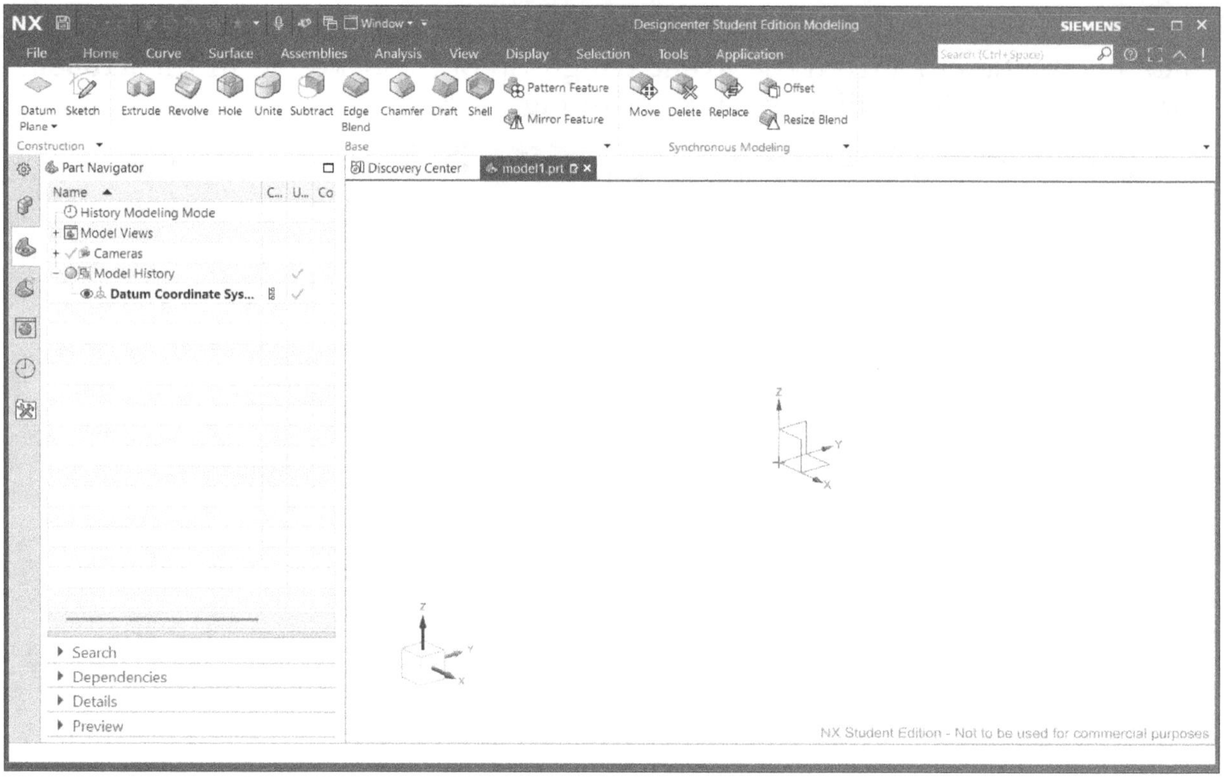

Figure-6. NX modeling environment

We will learn more about the tools related to part modeling later in the book. Now, we will discuss the interface elements and **File** menu tools.

INTERFACE ELEMENTS

There are various elements of NX interface like Quick Access toolbar, Ribbon bar, Menus, and so on. These elements and their functions are discussed next.

Quick Access Toolbar

The **Quick Access Toolbar** is available at the top in application window; refer to Figure-7. There are various tools like New, Open, Touch Mode, and so on.

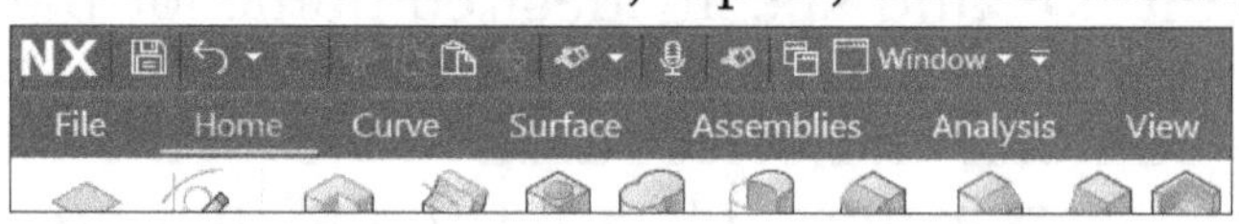

Figure-7. Quick Access toolbar

Click on the **Touch Mode** toggle button from the **Quick Access toolbar** to activate or deactivate touch mode in application. Select **Speech Recognition** toggle button (needs separate license) if you want to activate commands by speaking through Microphone of computer.

If you have more than one windows open in the application like 5 different parts open then select desired window from **Window** flyout in the QAT (**Quick Access Toolbar**).

Ribbon

Ribbon is a place in interface that holds all the important tools. The **Ribbon** is divided into **Tabs** which are further divided into **Groups**. Each group holds tools of similar functioning; refer to Figure-8. For example, the **Direct Sketch** group shown in Figure-8 holds the tools related to sketching.

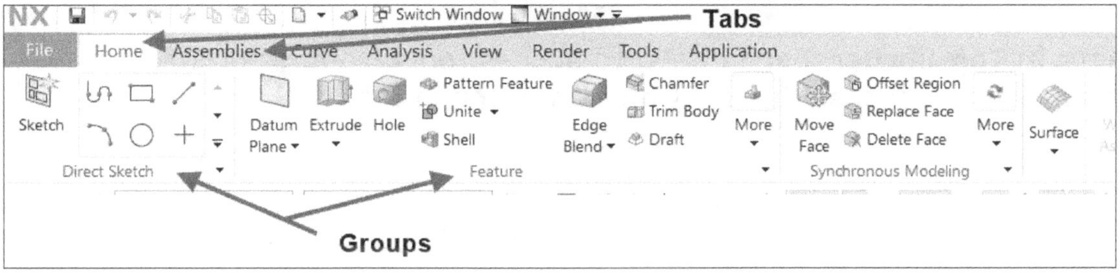

Figure-8. Ribbon

Note that the terminology discussed here is important to follow this book effectively while learning. Throughout the book, we will ask you to select the tool based on this terminology like we will ask you to click on the **Hole** tool from **Feature** group in **Home** tab of the **Ribbon**. Also, all the key terms of software will be in bold font.

Top Border Bar

The **Top Border Bar** is used to access menus, selection filter options, snap options, and view options; refer to Figure-9. To display **Top Border Bar**, you need to activate the **Advanced** role of user interface. To do so, click on the **Roles** tab from the **Resource Bar** at the left in the application window and select the **Role Advanced** button from the **Content** folder in the **Roles** tab; refer to Figure-10.

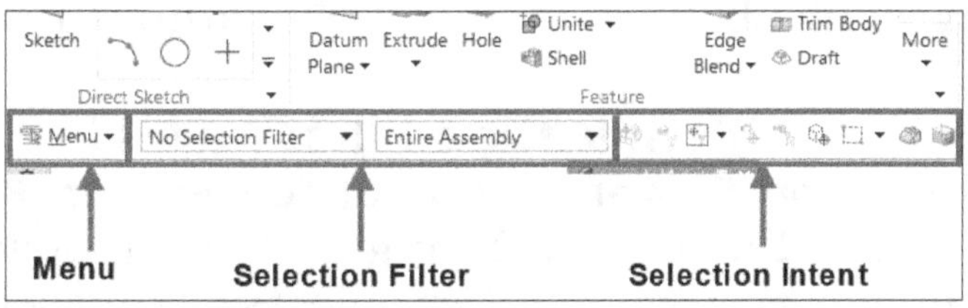

Figure-9. Top Border Bar

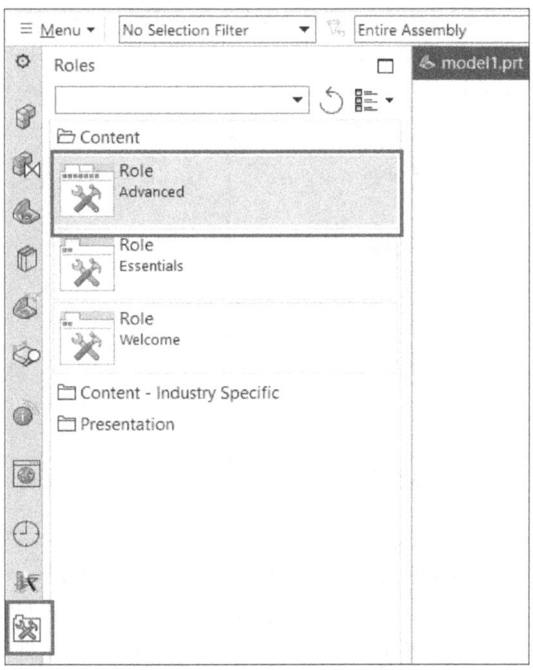

Figure-10. Role Advanced option

Menu

The Menu in **Top Border Bar** is used to access tools from different menus. Click on the **Menu** button to access different menus; refer to Figure-11.

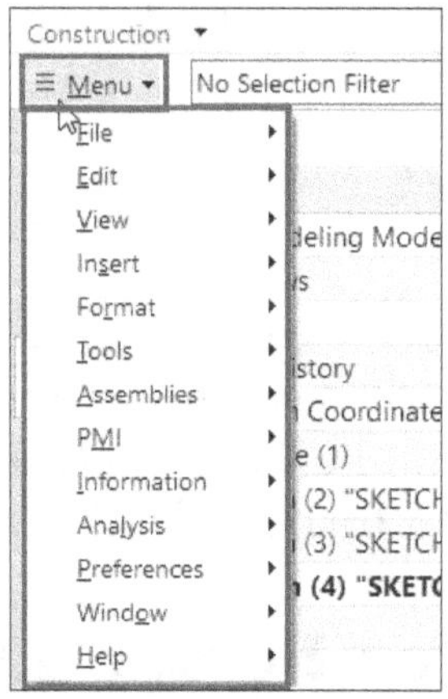

Figure-11. Menus

Hover the cursor on any of the menu to display list of related tools. Click on the tool from menu to activate it. The tools which are in the menus can also be accessed from the **Ribbon**. **Ribbon** is latest way to select tools and **Menus** are relatively older way. But if you are more comfortable with menus then you can access the tools using menus. In this book, we will describe both the ways of activating a tool.

Selection Filter

The options in the **Selection Filter** section of **Top Border Bar** are used to define what objects can be selected by cursor from graphics window. For example, if you want to select only sketches and ignore other objects during selection then select the **Sketch** option from **Type Filter** drop-down in **Top Border Bar**; refer to Figure-12. By default, **No Selection Filter** option is selected in the **Type Filter** drop-down and so you can select any type of object.

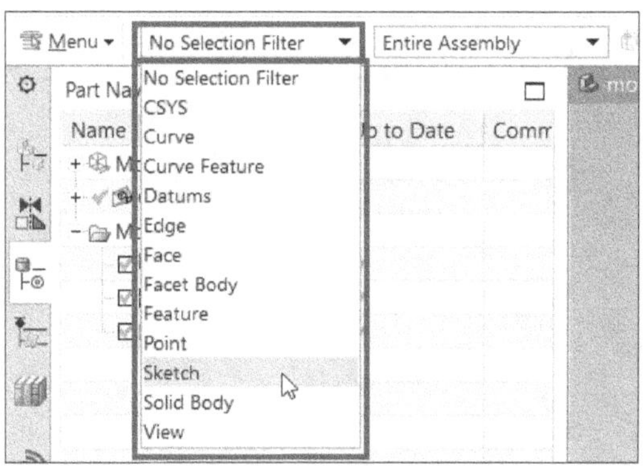

Figure-12. Sketch option in Type Filter drop-down

Select desired option from **Selection Scope** drop-down to define the scope of selection; refer to Figure-13. Select the **Entire Assembly** option if you want all the parts/components of assembly to be selectable. Select the **Within Work Part and Components** option if you want entities of current part to be selectable along with related components. Select the **Within Work Part Only** option if you want only current part to be selectable.

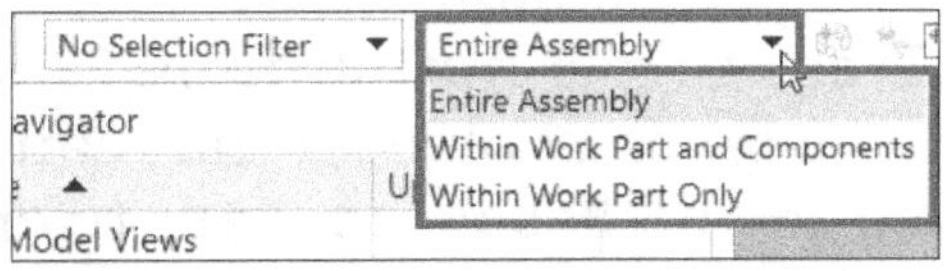

Figure-13. Selection Scope drop-down

Selection Intent

The options in **Selection Intent** section of **Top Border Bar** are used to define how entities can be selected from graphics window. For example, you can use 3D Box selection or 2D rectangle selection to select the objects. Various tools in this section are discussed next.

Allow Automatic Work Part Change

Set the **Allow Automatic Work Part Change** toggle button to **ON** if you want the work part to be automatically changed when select a reference from the parts in drawing area.

Create Interpart Link

The **Create Interpart Link** toggle button in **Top Border Bar** is used to create a wave linked part while performing boolean or other operations. This button gets activated during other operations when a wave link part can be created. Like in Figure-14, we are performing a boolean operation between two components of an assembly and **Create Interpart Link** toggle button is available to select. Select this toggle button to create an interpart link. The benefit of activating this button is that if you modify the tool body then the target body will automatically change based on the changed made to their inter link location. Like, if you later modify the height of boss feature tool body then the depth of slot will automatically change.

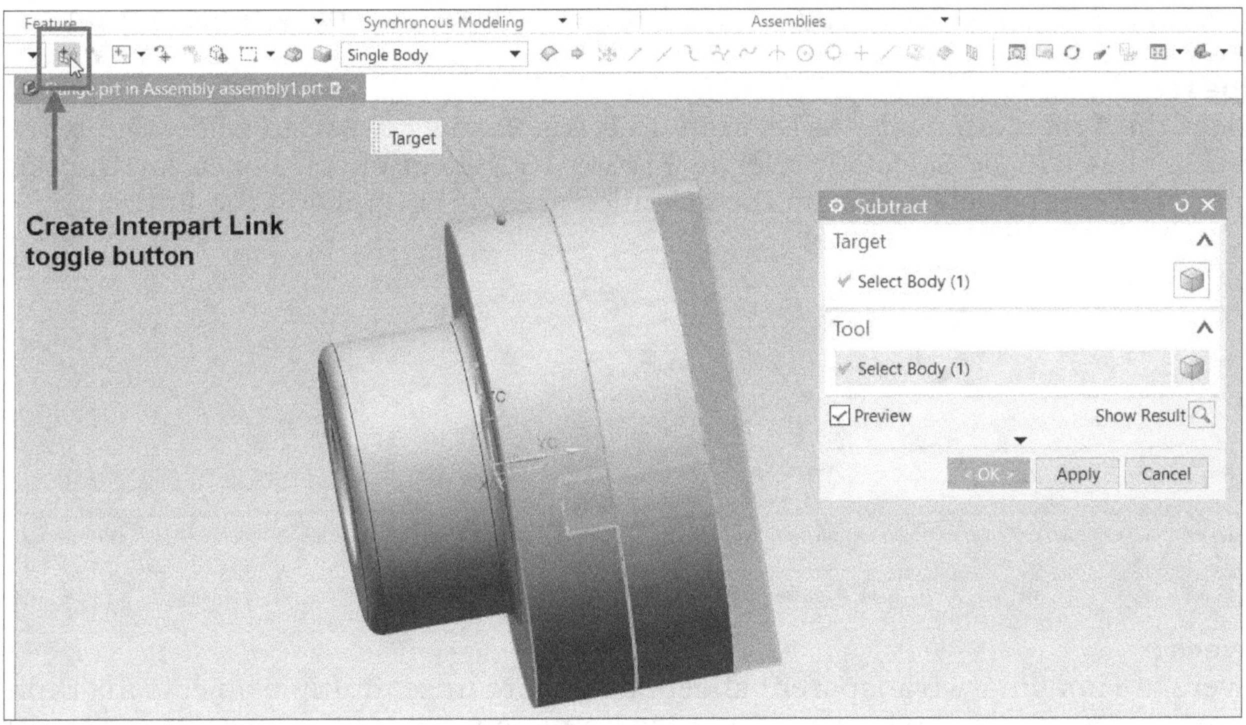

Figure-14. Creating interpart link

You will learn more about linking later in this book.

Selection Filters

Click on the **Selection Filters** toggle button from Top Border Bar to set various selection filters that narrow the types of objects that can be selected. The **Selection Filters** tab will be displayed in the **Resource Bar**; refer to Figure-15. When there are multiple objects with overlapping sections and you want to select a specific type of object like point or edge then these selection filters are very useful.

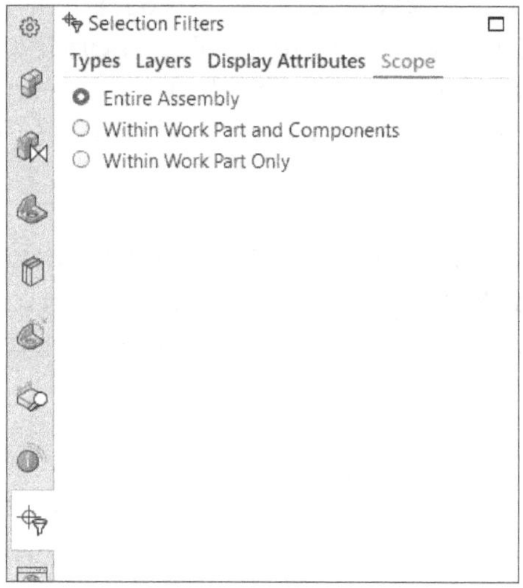

Figure-15. Selection Filters tab

Scope:

By default, the **Scope** tab is selected in the **Selection Filters Resource Bar**. Select desired ratio button to define the scope of applied selection filters. If you want to perform selection in current working part then select **Within Work Part Only** radio button. If you want to perform selection in current work part as well as its components then select the **Within Work Part and Components** radio button. If you want to make selection from whole assembly then select the **Entire Assembly** radio button.

Types:

Select the **Types** tab in the **Selection Filters Resource Bar** to select the types of objects that can be selected; refer to Figure-16. Select check boxes for the object types that can be selected from the graphics area after applying the filters.

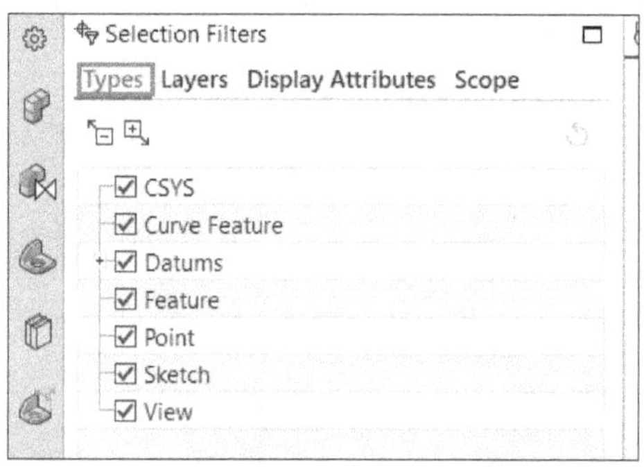

Figure-16. Types tab

Layers:

Layers are imaginary transparent sheet used to organize multiple objects in graphics area. Objects are placed on multiple layers which are stacked one over the other in the graphics area. For example, sketches will be created in one layer and solid bodies will be created on another layer. You can show, hide, color, and assign various properties to layers; and those properties will be assigned to all the objects on that layer. Select check boxes for desired layers (types of objects) from the **Layers** tab in the **Selection Filters Resource Bar** that you want to select.

Display Attributes:

The options in **Display Attributes** tab are used to set selection filter based on color, line style, and thickness of lines; refer to Figure-17.

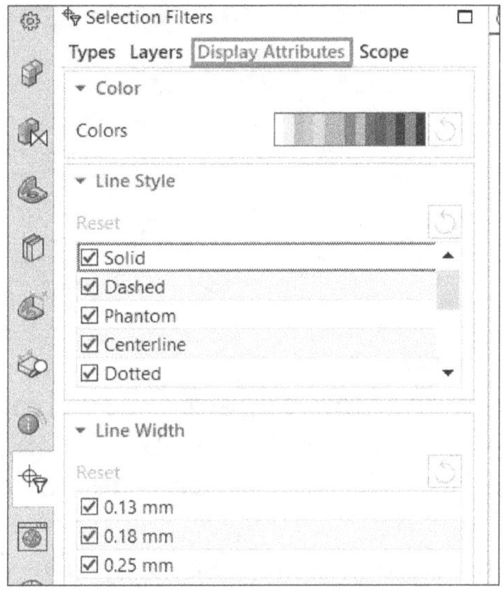

Figure-17. Display Attributes tab

Deselect All

The **Deselect All** button in **Top Border Bar** is active only when you have selected objects from graphics window. Click on the **Deselect All** button to deselect all the selected entities.

3D Box Selection

The **3D Box Selection** button is used to draw a 3D box. The objects inside the box will be selected automatically. The procedure to use this tool is given next.

- Click on the **3D Box Selection** button from the **Top Border Bar**. The **3D Box Selection** dialog box will be displayed; refer to Figure-18.

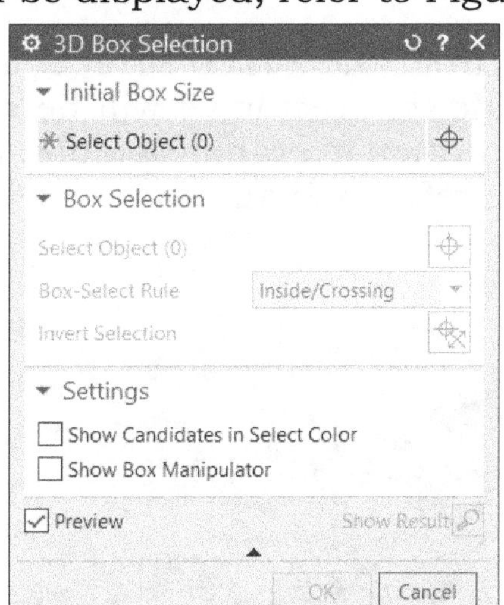

Figure-18. 3D Box Selection dialog box

- Select the objects around which you want to create the box and then click on the **Select Object** selection button in **Box Selection** area of the dialog box. Drag handles will be displayed on the box to define its size; refer to Figure-19.

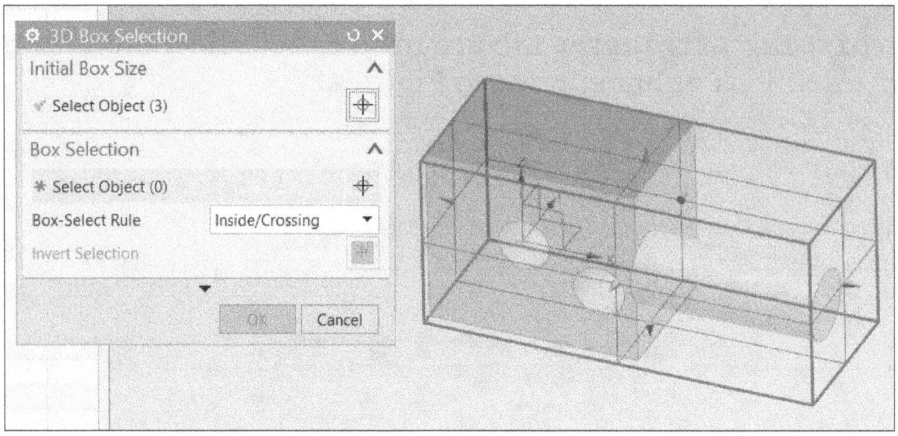

Figure-19. Preview of 3D selection box

- Select desired option from the **Box-Select Rule** drop-down. Select the **Inside/Crossing** option if you want to select the objects that are either inside the box or they are touching the box. Select the **Inside** option if you want to select the objects that are inside the box.
- Expand the **Settings** rollout to modify settings for 3D selection and select the **Show Candidates in Select Color** check box to select only those objects whose color are set in color filter.
- Select the **Show Box Manipulator** check box to display 3D manipulator for modifying orientation of 3D box.
- Click on the **Show Results** button to check which objects will get selected by current 3D box. Click on the **OK** button to perform selection.

Multi-Select Gesture drop-down

The options in **Multi-Select Gesture** drop-down of **Top Border Bar** are used to define how multiple bodies can be selected. There are three options in this drop-down; Rectangle, Lasso, and Circle.

Rectangle Multi-Selection

Select the **Rectangle** option from the **Multi-Select Gesture** drop-down to create a rectangle. The objects inside this rectangle will be selected. To draw a selection rectangle, click at an empty location in graphic window and drag the cursor to define other corner of the rectangle; refer to Figure-20.

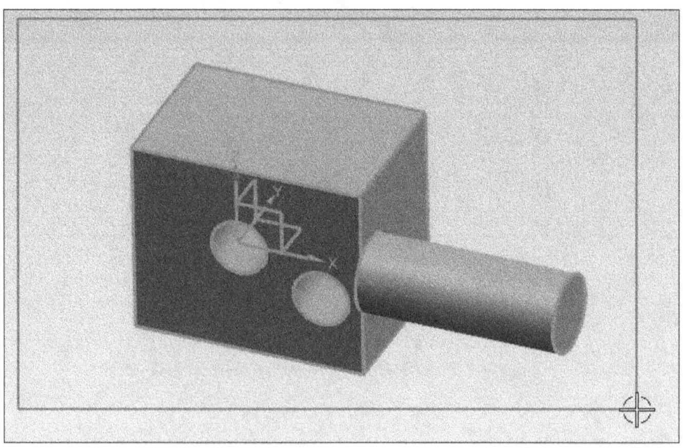

Figure-20. Selection rectangle

Lasso Selection

Select the **Lasso** option from the **Multi-Select Gesture** drop-down to create a free hand boundary. The objects inside the boundary will be selected. To perform lasso selection, click at desired location and drag the cursor at desired locations to form a lasso boundary; refer to Figure-21.

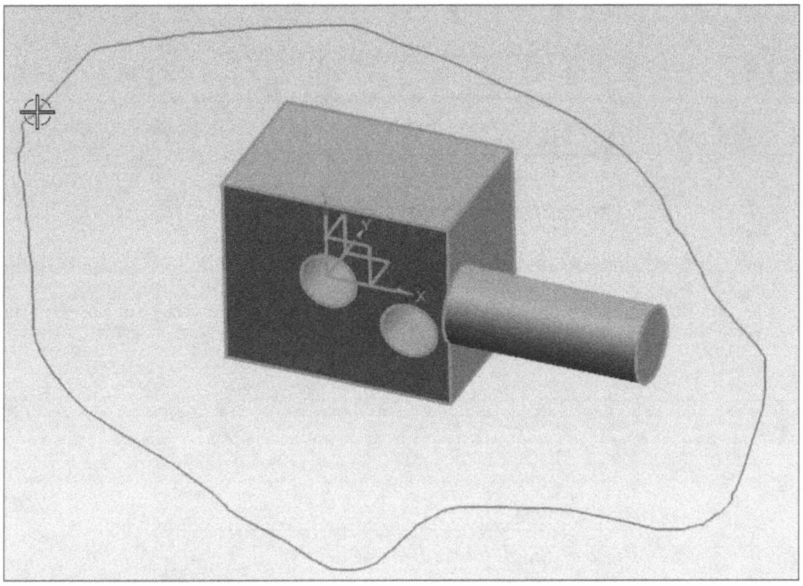

Figure-21. Lasso selection

Circle Selection

Select the **Circle** option from the **Multi-Select Gesture** drop-down to create circular boundary to select objects. The objects inside the boundary will be selected automatically. To perform circular selection, click at desired location to be used as center for selection of circle and then drag the cursor to define diameter of the circle.

Allow Selection of Hidden Wireframe

Select the **Allow Selection of Hidden Wireframe** toggle button to allow selection of hidden edges. This means even if the edges are not displayed, you can still select them if you can guess their exact location and click there.

Highlight Hidden Edges

The **Highlight Hidden Edges** toggle button is used to enable or disable automatic highlighting of hidden edges whenever you move the cursor over them. Generally, **Allow Selection of Hidden Wireframe** and **Highlight Hidden Edges** toggle buttons are active together when you want to select hidden edges.

Resource Bar

The **Resource Bar** is used to access different navigator. The resource bar is available at the left in the application window; refer to Figure-22. Click on desired tab in the left of **Resource Bar** to open respective navigator. The applications of different tabs of **Resource Bar** are given next.

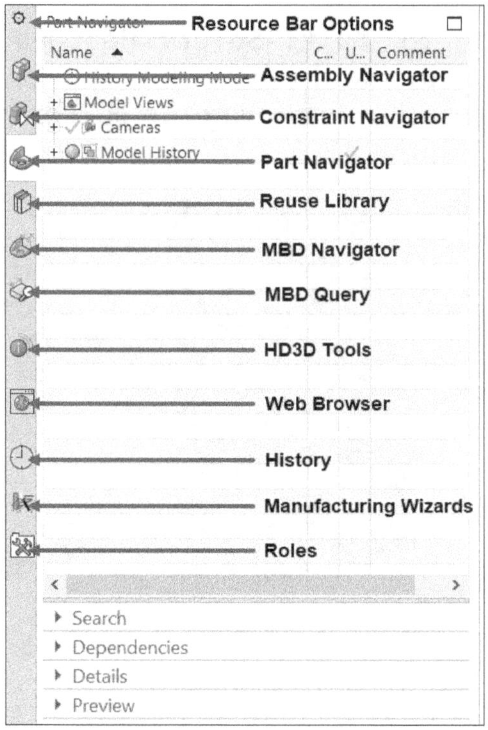

Figure-22. Resource Bar

Assembly Navigator

Assembly Navigator is used to manage components of assembly; refer to Figure-23. Click on the **+** sign adjacent to **Constraints** in the **Assembly Navigator** to check various constraints applied to components in the assembly. Select or clear the check boxes in **Assembly Navigator** to display or hide parts of the assembly. You will learn more about assembly later in this book.

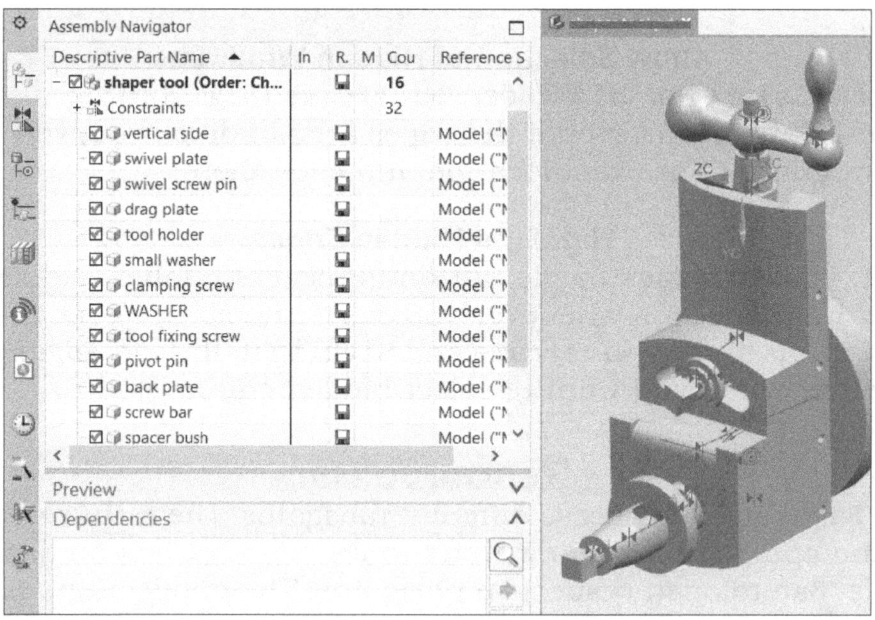

Figure-23. Assembly Navigator

Constraint Navigator

The **Constraint Navigator** is used to check and modify assembly constraints applied to the model; refer to Figure-24. You will learn more about constraints later in the book.

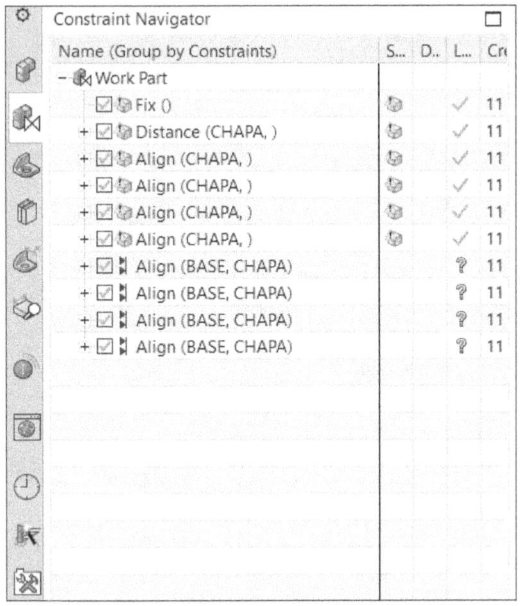

Figure-24. Constraint Navigator

Part Navigator

Part Navigator is used to access features used in creating the part. The **Part Navigator** records all the operations performed to create a part; refer to Figure-25. You can edit any feature of the part by double-clicking on it in **Part Navigator**. Using options in the **Model Views** node, you can switch between various orientations. The **Links** section shows various objects linked to current model. The **History Modeling Mode** defines that all features are parametrically saved with history.

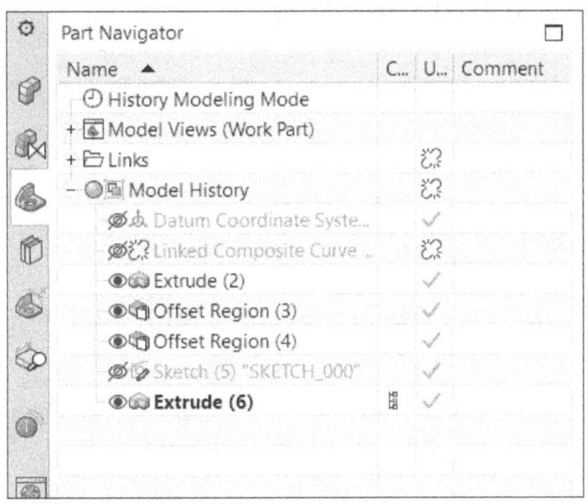

Figure-25. Part Navigator

Reuse Library Tab

The options in **Reuse Library** tab of **Resource Bar** are used to store commonly used objects in a library and then insert them in the model when required; refer to Figure-26.

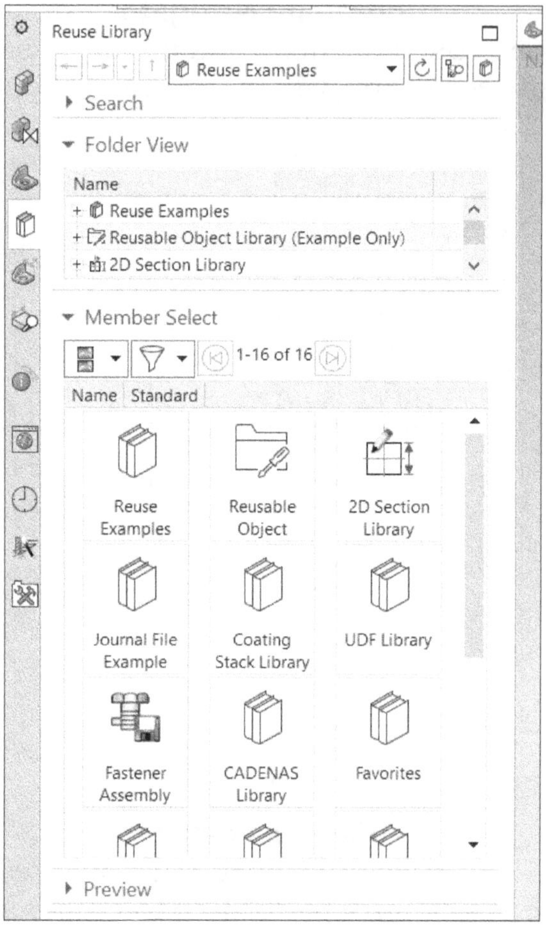

Figure-26. Reuse Library

MBD Navigator

The options in **MBD Navigator** are used to manage annotation planes and PMI annotations of the model; refer to Figure-27.

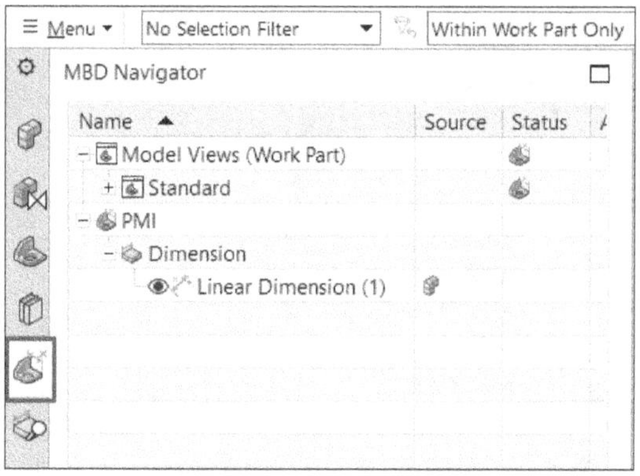

Figure-27. MBD Navigator

MBD Query

The options in **MBD Query** tab of **Resource Bar** are used to search and analyze dimensions using text based or rule based queries; refer to Figure-28.

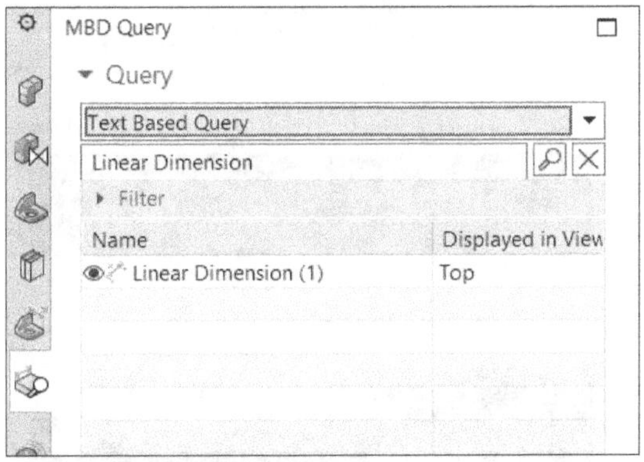

Figure-28. MBD Query

HD3D Tools

The options in **HD3D Tools** tab of **Resource Bar** are used to perform various validations and checks on the model; refer to Figure-29.

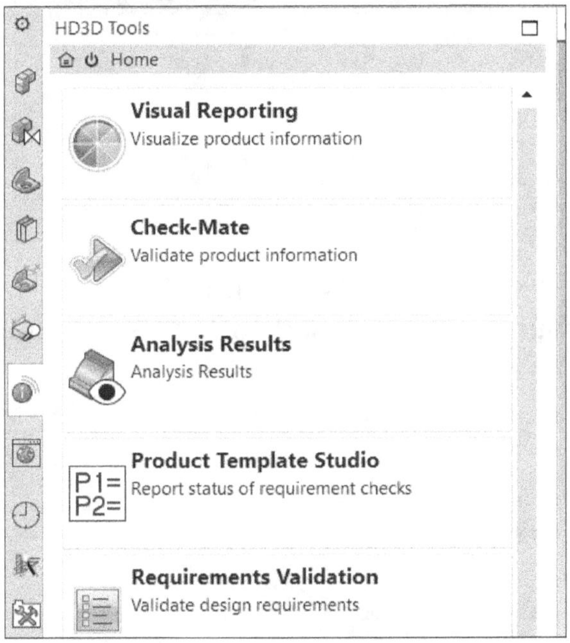

Figure-29. HD3D Tools tab

Web Browser

The **Web Browser** tab in **Resource Bar** is used to access web browser inside NX; refer to Figure-30.

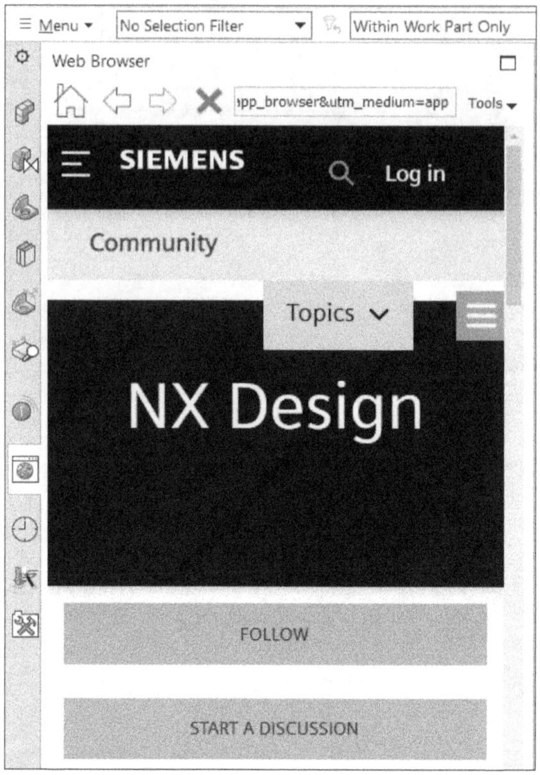

Figure-30. Web Browser

History Tab

The **History** tab of **Resource Bar** is used to browse through earlier opened parts; refer to Figure-31.

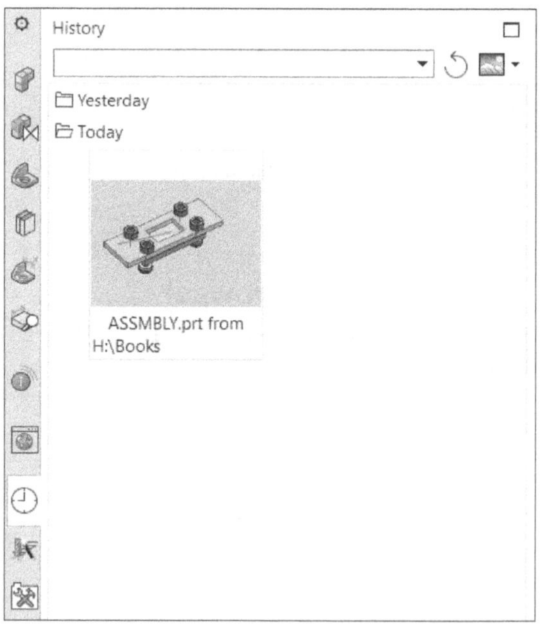

Figure-31. History tab

Manufacturing Wizards Tab

The **Manufacturing Wizards** tab of **Resource Bar** is used to access different wizards for performing manufacturing operations; refer to Figure-32.

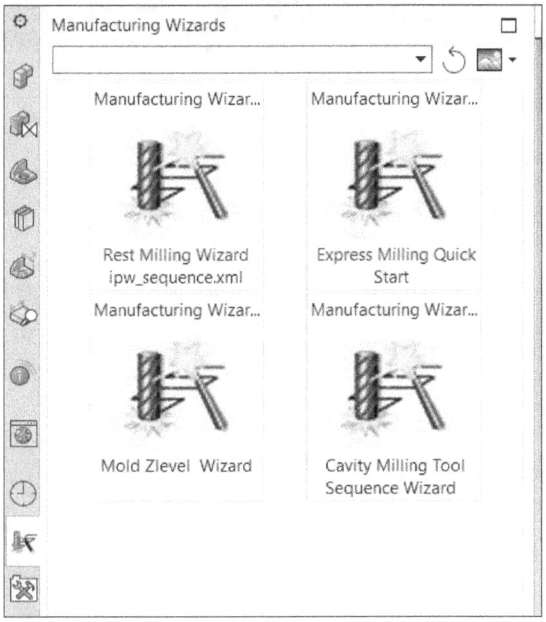

Figure-32. Manufacturing Wizards

Roles Tab

The **Roles** tab in **Resource Bar** is used to activate different user interfaces like you can activate interface for Touch panel, Tablet, 4K Monitor, and so on; refer to Figure-33.

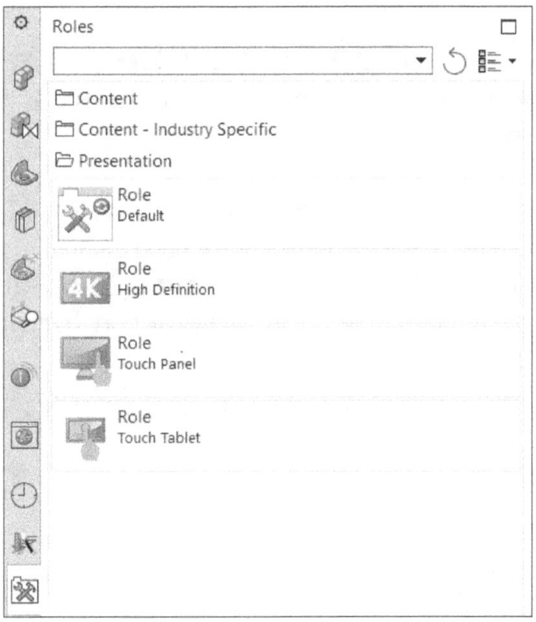

Figure-33. Roles tab

FILE MENU

File menu is an important component of user interface. This menu is used to access tools and options related to overall function of files and software; refer to Figure-34. Various tools and options of **File** menu are discussed next.

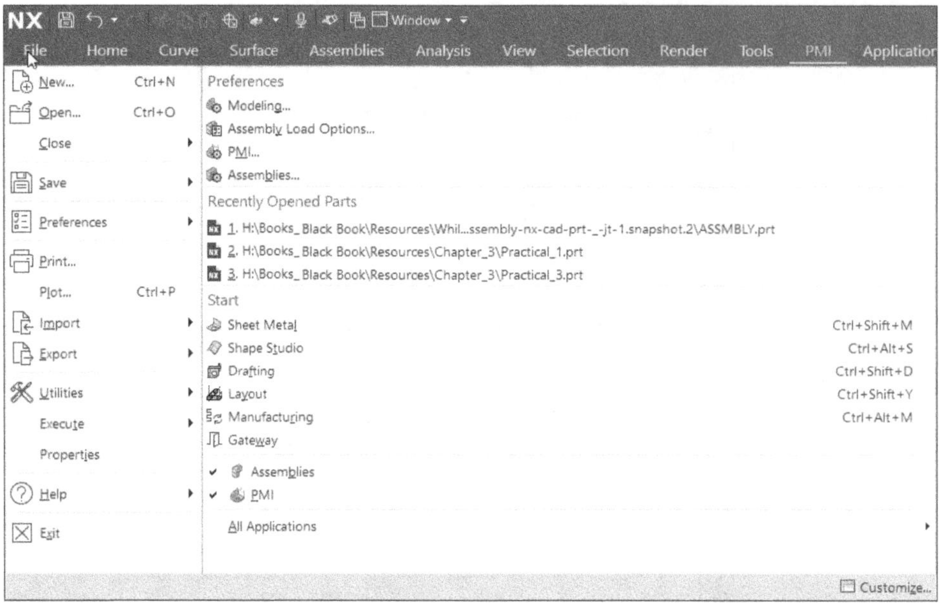

Figure-34. File menu

Starting New File

The **New** tool in **File** menu is used to start a new file. On clicking this tool, the **New** dialog box will be displayed. The options of this dialog box have already been discussed.

Opening a File

The **Open** tool is used to open different types of CAD files earlier created. The procedure to use this tool is given next.

- Click on the **Open** tool from the **File** menu or press **CTRL+O** from keyboard. The **Open** dialog box will be displayed; refer to Figure-35.
- Select desired format from the **Files of type** drop-down at the bottom in the dialog box; refer to Figure-36. The files of selected format will be displayed in the dialog box.

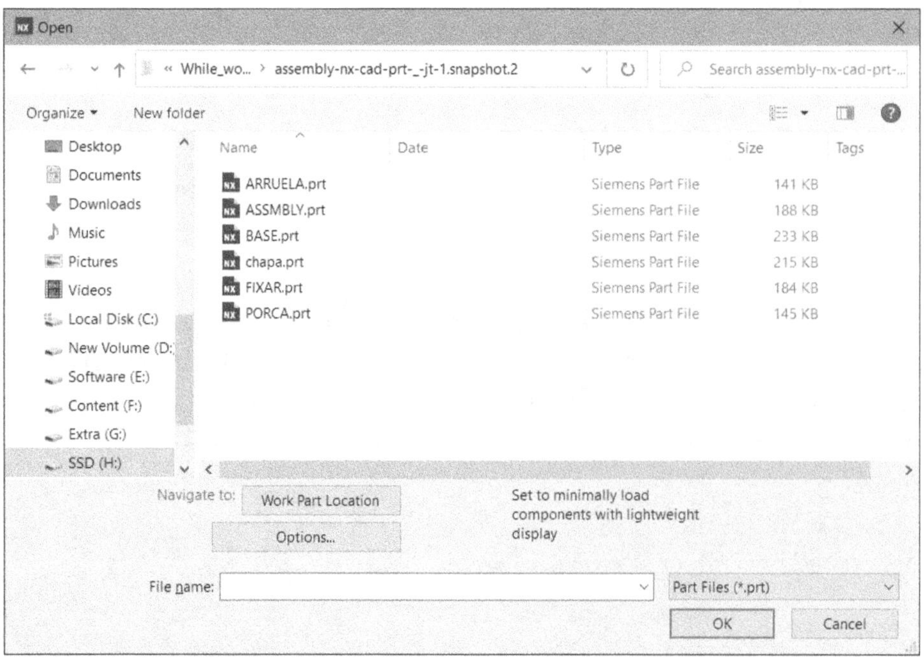

Figure-35. Open dialog box

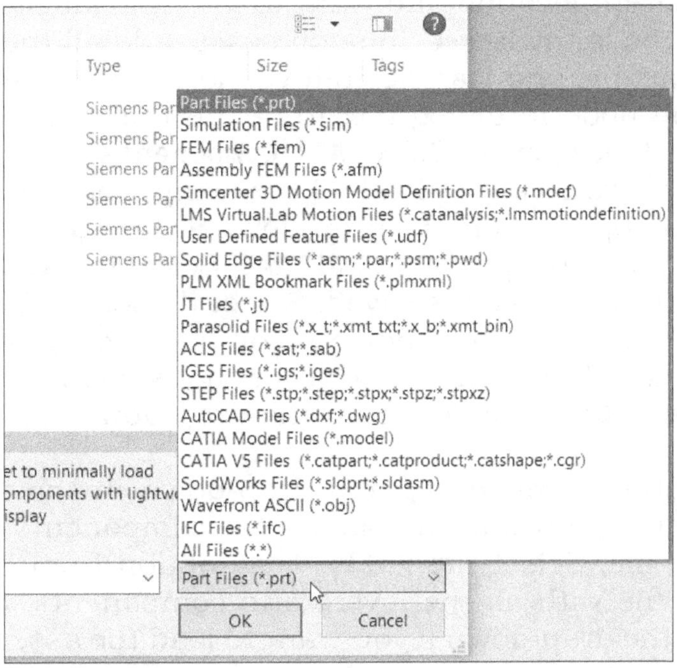

Figure-36. Files of type drop-down

- Select desired file from the dialog box. You can browse through the folder using the basic Windows functions. You can also use the **Work Part Location** button from the dialog box to open your default working directory for design files.

Options

- Click on the **Options** button at the bottom in the dialog box to modify options related to current file format being opened. The **Assembly Load Options** dialog box with related options will be displayed; refer to Figure-37 for NX part.

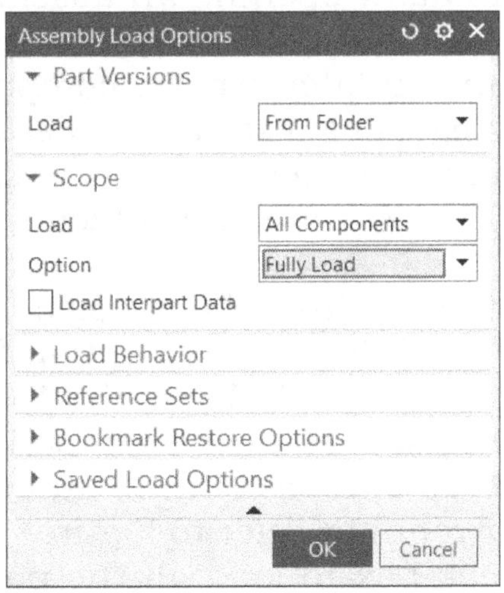

Figure-37. Assembly Load Options

- Select desired option from the **Load** drop-down in the **Part Versions** rollout of the dialog box to define which version of part will be loaded when opening the file. Select the **As Saved** option from the drop-down to load latest saved version of the part file. Select the **From Folder** option from the drop-down to load desired version of the part file from current folder. Select the **From Search Folders** option to load the version of file from current session folders and the folders added in search folder list. This option is useful when you have saved multiple versions of the part at different location and want to load the latest version of file but do not know which one is the latest. In such cases, add all the locations where you have saved the part file and load desired version from the list box.

- Expand the **Scope** node in dialog box to define the detail level upto which the current part file will be opened. Select **All Components** option from the **Load** drop-down in this node if you want to load all the components of the assembly. Select the **Structure Only** option from the drop-down if you want to load assembly parts and not their components to reduce load time. Select the **As Saved** option from the drop-down to load the file as it is saved. Select the **Re-evaluate Last Component Group** option from the **Load** drop-down if you want to open only those part files and components which were included in previous component group. Select the **Specify Component Group** option from the drop-down to select the component from the group.
- Select desired option from the **Option** drop-down in the **Scope** node of dialog box to define whether you want to load all the components of file or you want to partially load the file. Select the **Fully Load** option from the drop-down if you want to load the file with all the layers and components. Select the **Partially Load** option from the drop-down if you want to load the assembly constraints and keep the component hidden. You can later select the components to be displayed from the **Assembly Navigator Resource Bar**. Select the **Fully Load - Lightweight Display** option to open the model in higher level. In this way, small components are combined in the display and less CPU resources are taken by software to open the file fast. This option is useful in opening big assemblies. Similarly, you can use **Partially Load - Lightweight Display** option to load the file partially and with low level accuracy. Select the **Minimally Load - Lightweight Display** option to load only bodies which are in active reference set.
- Expand **Load Behavior** node from the dialog box to define how missing parts of assembly will be interpreted. Select the **Allow replacement** check box from the **Load Behavior** node to allow opening an assembly file which does not have original components but the first component of assembly has name matching to original component. You can later replace component parts with other parts. Select the **Generate Missing Part Family Members** check box to automatically generate missing part from the related part family like bolts and nuts. Select the **Cancel Load on Failure** check box to cancel loading of assembly file if it has a missing component.
- Expand the **Reference Sets** node from the dialog box to set the reference set to be loaded when opening the file. Select desired option from the reference sets list to load respective set; refer to Figure-38. Select the **Apply to All Assembly Levels** check box to apply reference sets to all the components in assembly.
- Expand the **Bookmark Restore Options** node to automatically restore parts loaded in earlier session of the current file; refer to Figure-39. Select the **Load All Parts in Previous Session** check box to load all the parts as they were in previous session. Select desired option from the **Parts to Load** drop-down to define whether to load visible parts in previous session or to load parts earlier loaded in previous session. Select the **Restore Load State** and **Restore Reference Sets** check boxes to restore respective settings when opening the part file.

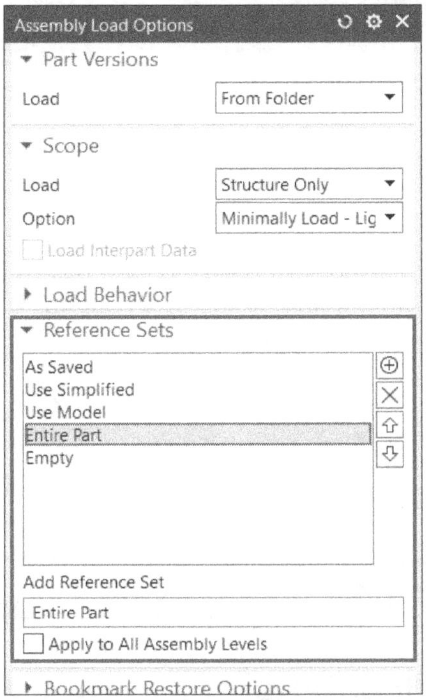

Figure-38. Reference Sets list

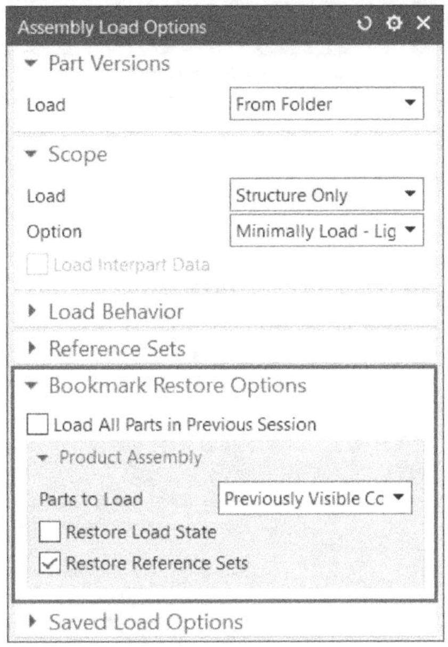

Figure-39. Bookmark Restore Options node

- Expand the **Saved Load Options** node to save and load default settings. Select the **Save as Default** button from the node to save current settings as default settings. Select the **Restore Default** button from the node to load default settings.
- Set desired parameters in dialog box and click on the **OK** button. Note that the **Options** dialog box can be vary depending on file formats. Like if we are opening a file with IGES format then the **Options** dialog box is shown as in Figure-40.

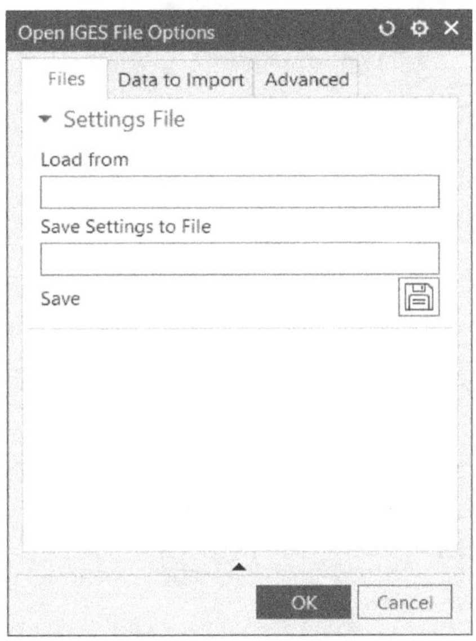

Figure-40. Open IGES File Options dialog box

- After selecting the file and specifying desired parameters in the **Open** dialog box, click on the **OK** button. The file will be opened.

Closing Files

The options in **Close** cascading menu are used to close files with different approaches; refer to Figure-41.

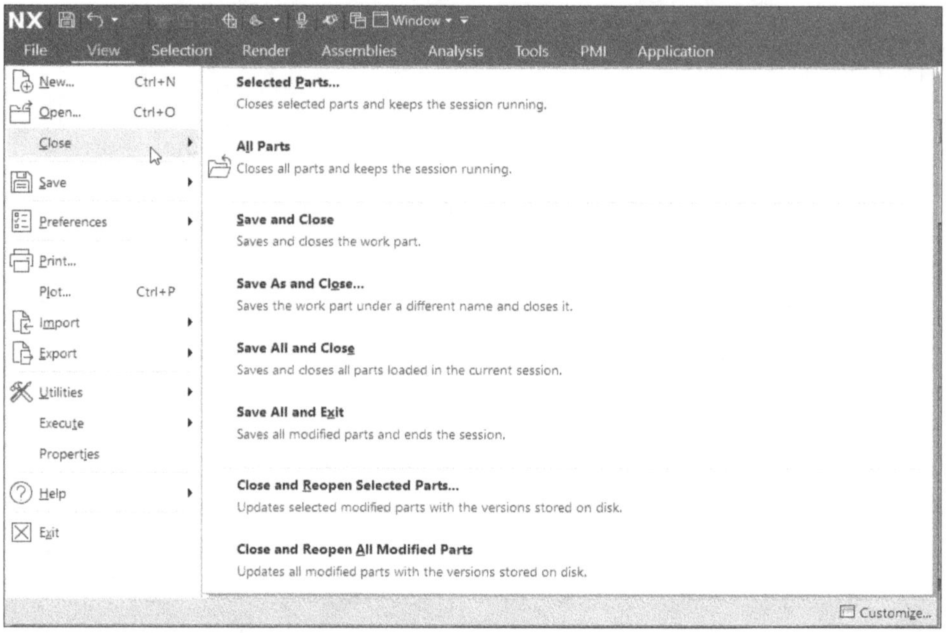

Figure-41. Close options

Closing Selected Parts

Select the **Selected Parts** option from the cascading menu if you want to close only selected parts from the list. The procedure is given next.

- Click on the **Selected Parts** option from the **Close** cascading menu of the **File** menu. The **Close Part** dialog box will be displayed; refer to Figure-42.

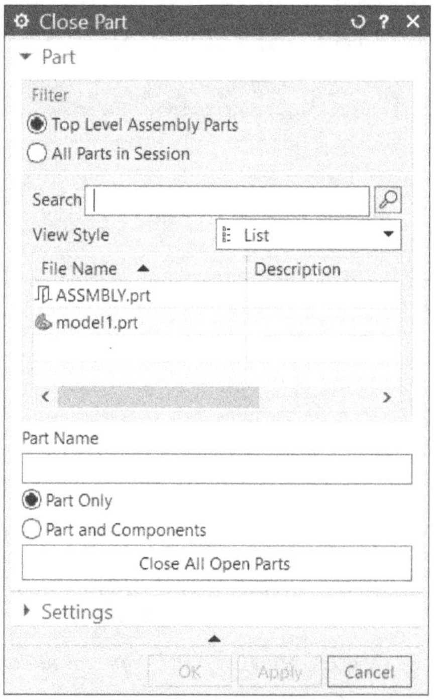

Figure-42. Close Part dialog box

- By default **Top Level Assembly Parts** radio button is selected in the dialog box and so only top level assemblies are displayed in the list box. Select the **All Parts in Session** radio button from the dialog box to display all the parts in the list which are currently open in the session.
- Select the parts to be closed from the list while holding the **CTRL** key. Note that you can also use the **Part Name** edit box to select parts to be closed. Type the name of part to be closed in the edit box and then press **TAB** to exit.

- Expand the **Settings** node at the bottom in the dialog box and select the **Force Close if Modified** check box to forcefully close the current open modified files without saving them.
- After setting desired parameters, click on the **OK** button from the dialog box. The selected parts will be closed.

Closing All Parts

The **All Parts** option in **Close** cascading menu is used to close all the parts currently open in application. The procedure to use this tool is given next.

- Click on the **All Parts** option from the **Close** cascading menu in **File** menu. All the parts currently open will be closed. If there are any unsaved changes in the files then **Close All Files** dialog box will be displayed; refer to Figure-43.

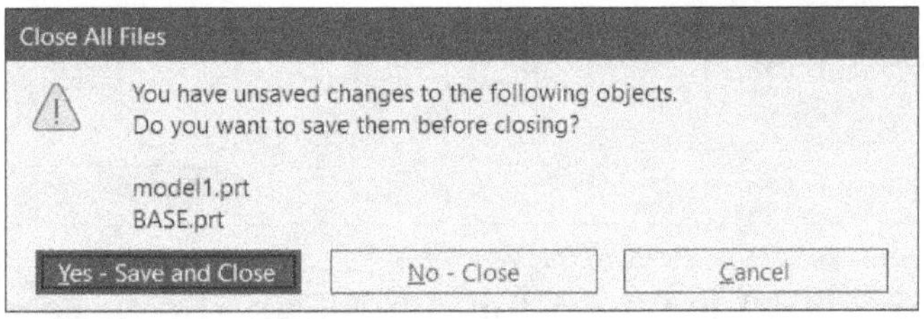

Figure-43. Close All Files dialog box

- Click on the **Yes-Save and Close** button to save the files before closing them. If you do not want to save changes then click on the **No-Close** button. If you do not want to close files then click on the **Cancel** button.

You can use the other options in the **Close** cascading menu in the same way.

Saving Files

There are various options to save files in the **Save** cascading menu of the **File** menu; refer to Figure-44. These options are discussed next.

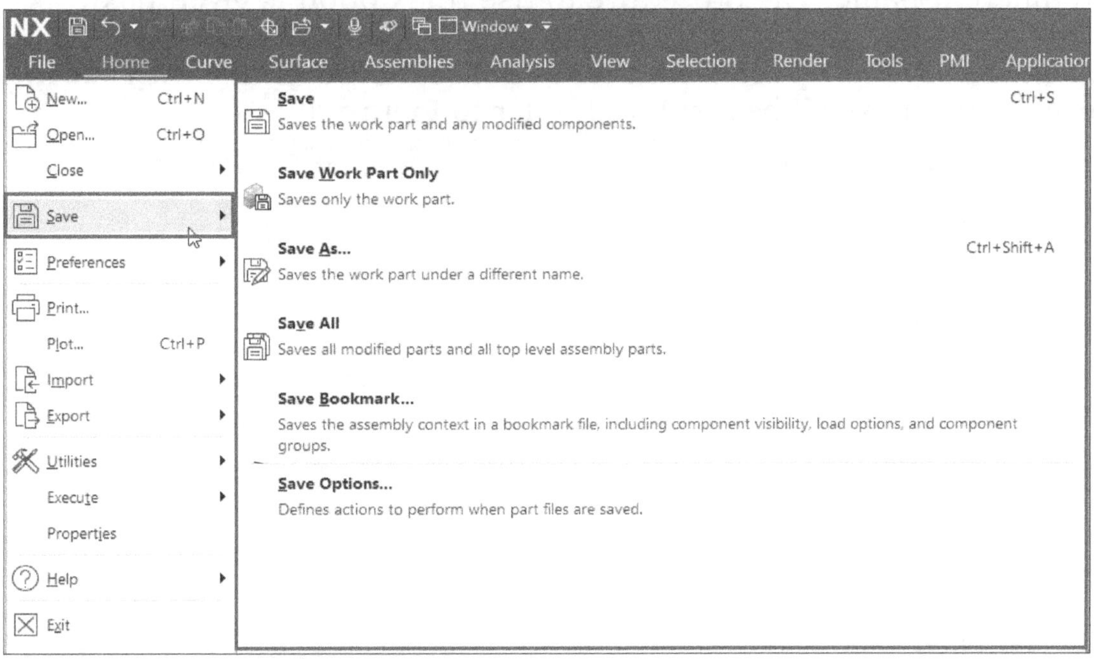

Figure-44. Save cascading menu

Saving File

The **Save** option in the **Save** cascading menu is used to save current file. The procedure to save files is given next.

- Click on the **Save** tool from the **Save** cascading menu of the **File** menu. If you have earlier saved the file then the version of file will be updated. If you are saving the file for the first time then the **Name Parts** dialog box will be displayed; refer to Figure-45.

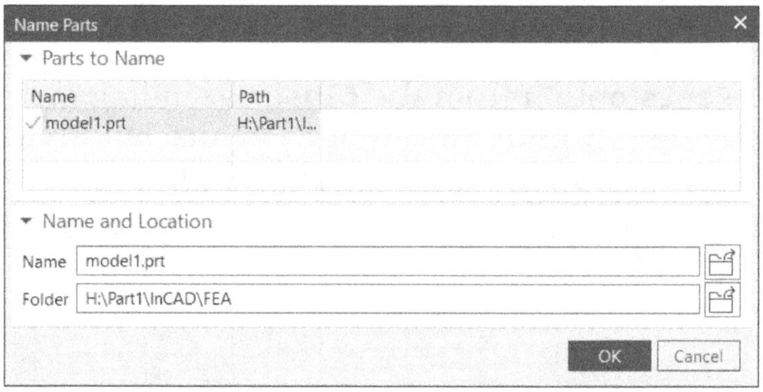

Figure-45. Name Parts dialog box

- Specify desired name and location for the file in the **Name** and **Folder** edit boxes of the dialog box, respectively.
- After specifying the parameters, click on the **OK** button to save the file.

Saving Work Parts only

Suppose you are working on an assembly file and editing a part of the assembly. If you want to save only the part on which you are working and not the whole assembly then you can use **Save Work Parts Only** option.

Saving File with Different Name

The **Save As** option in **Save** cascading menu of **File** menu is used to save the current file with different name. The procedure to use this option is given next.

- Click on the **Save As** option from the **Save** cascading menu of the **File** menu. The **Save As** dialog box will be displayed; refer to Figure-46.

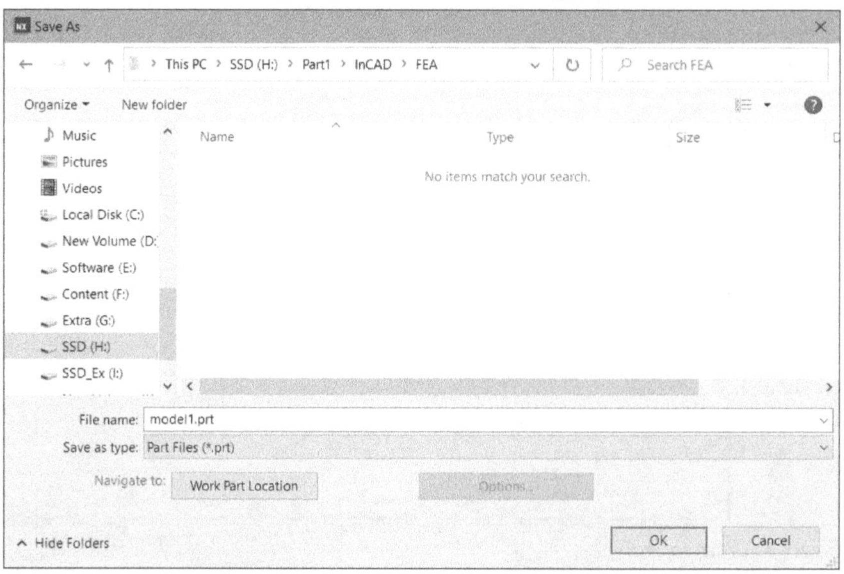

Figure-46. Save As dialog box

- Specify desired name for the file in **File name** edit box and click on the **OK** button.

Similarly, you can use the **Save All** and **Save Bookmark** options of the **Save** cascading menu.

Defining Save Options

The **Save Options** tool in **Save** cascading menu of **File** menu is used to define the options for saving file in NX part format (default format of UG NX). The procedure to use this tool is given next.

- Click on the **Save Options** tool from the **Save** cascading menu of the **File** menu before saving the file. The **Save Options** dialog box will be displayed; refer to Figure-47.

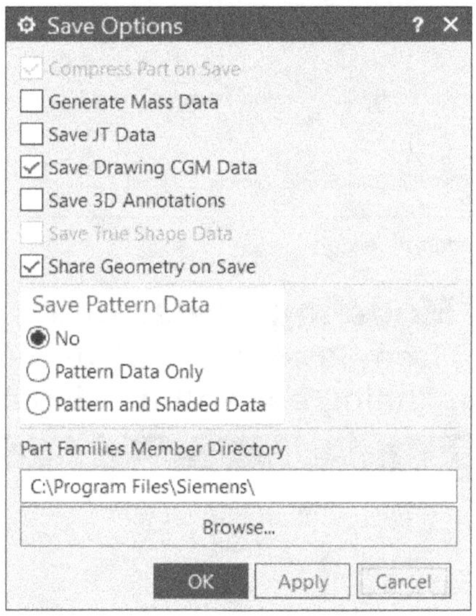

Figure-47. Save Options dialog box

- Select the check boxes as required. For example, if you want to include mass data while saving the file then select the **Generate Mass Data** check box.
- Use the **Part Families Member Directory** edit box to define the location where you want to save current and subsequent files.
- After specifying desired parameters, click on the **OK** button to define default save options for saving files in default format.

Preference Setting

The **Preferences** option in **File** menu are used to modify the application interface and behavior as per the user's requirement; refer to Figure-48. Some of the important preference settings are discussed next. You will learn about other preference settings whenever needed during the course of this book.

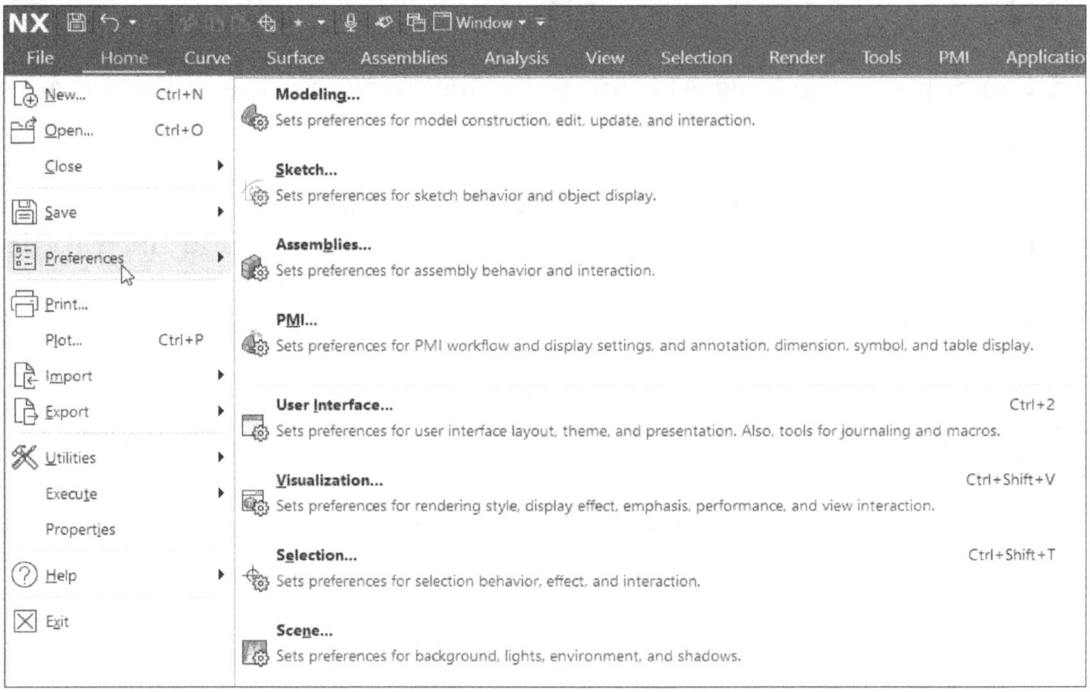

Figure-48. Preferences cascading menu

Modeling Preferences

- Click on the **Modeling** tool from **Preferences** cascading menu of the **File** menu. The **Modeling Preferences** dialog box will be displayed; refer to Figure-49.

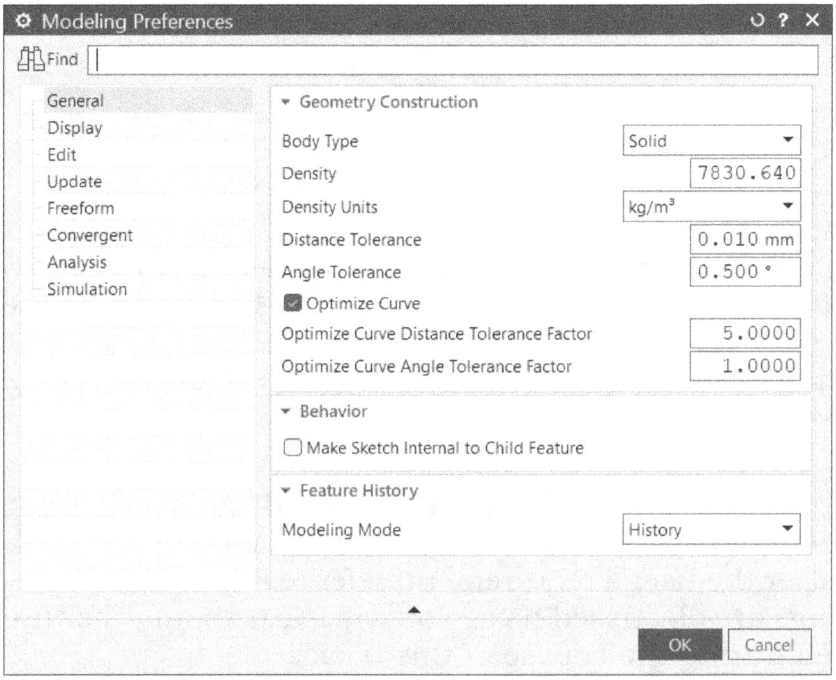

Figure-49. Modeling Preferences dialog box

- Select the **Solid** option from **Body Type** drop-down of the dialog box to save parts as solid objects. Select the **Sheet** option to create sheet (surface) parts.
- Specify desired value of density in the **Density** edit box. Click in the **Density Units** drop-down and select desired unit to define density of material. This value will be used to calculate mass of part.

- Specify desired value of tolerance in **Distance Tolerance** and **Angle Tolerance** edit boxes. These values are used to define the accuracy up to which model can be created.
- Select the **Optimize Curve** check box to optimize the curves in sketches further by factors specified in edit boxes below it.
- Select the **Make Sketches Internal to Child Features** check box to make sketches and datums child features wherever possible.
- Expand the **Feature History** node to define whether modeling history is to be recorded or not. Select the **History Free** option from the **Modeling Mode** drop-down if you want to perform freeform modeling.
- Select the **Display** option from left in the dialog box to define how new faces and geometries will be displayed in the model.
- Select the **Inherit from Body** option from the **New Face** drop-down to apply same display properties to new face as its body. Select the **Inherit Object Preferences** option from the **New Face** drop-down if you want to copy properties of object preferences. Similarly, select desired option from the **Face Modified by Boolean** drop-down to define properties of faces generated by performing boolean operations.
- Select desired option from the **Link and Extract Geometry** drop-down to define how lined and extracted objects will be displayed.
- Specify desired value of number of grid lines in **U** and **V** edit boxes to generate specified number of grid lines on all new surfaces and faces.

Now, we will define only those options which are commonly used when creating models.

- Click on the **Update** option from the left area in the dialog box. The options will be displayed as shown in Figure-50.

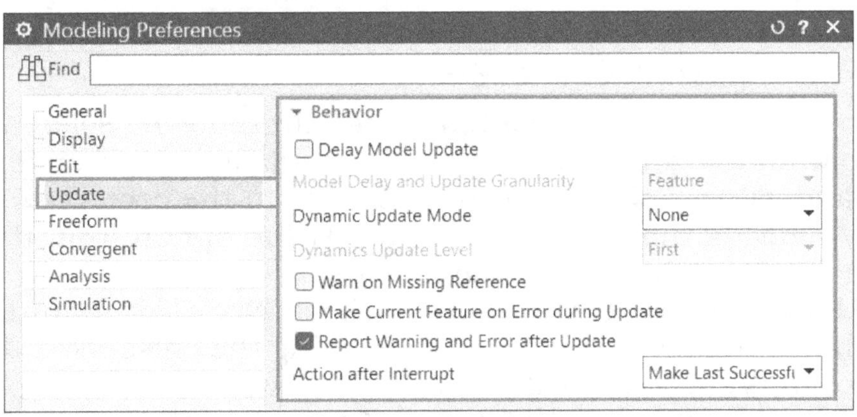

Figure-50. Update tab in Modeling Preferences dialog box

- Select the **Continuous** option from **Dynamic Update Mode** drop-down to update the model dynamically when you drag any curve to modify in the base sketches. Select the **Incremental** option from the drop-down if you want to update the model only when you have stopped moving the control point of curve.
- Select the **Warn on Missing References** check box to display a warning when a reference sketch or feature (based on which other features are created in the model) is missing.
- Select the **Make Current Feature on Error during Update** check box if you want to stop updating model when an error occurs in a feature of model.

- Select the **Make Last Successful Feature Content** option from the **Action after Interrupt** drop-down to load last successful content if new changes fail. Select the **Undo** option from the drop-down to undo recently made changes.
- Click on the **OK** button from the dialog box to apply the settings.

Sketch Preferences

The **Sketch** option in **Preferences** cascading menu is used to define preferences for sketching in NX. The procedure to modify sketching options is given next.

- Click on the **Sketch** tool from the **Preferences** cascading menu of the **File** menu. The **Sketch Preferences** dialog box will be displayed; refer to Figure-51.

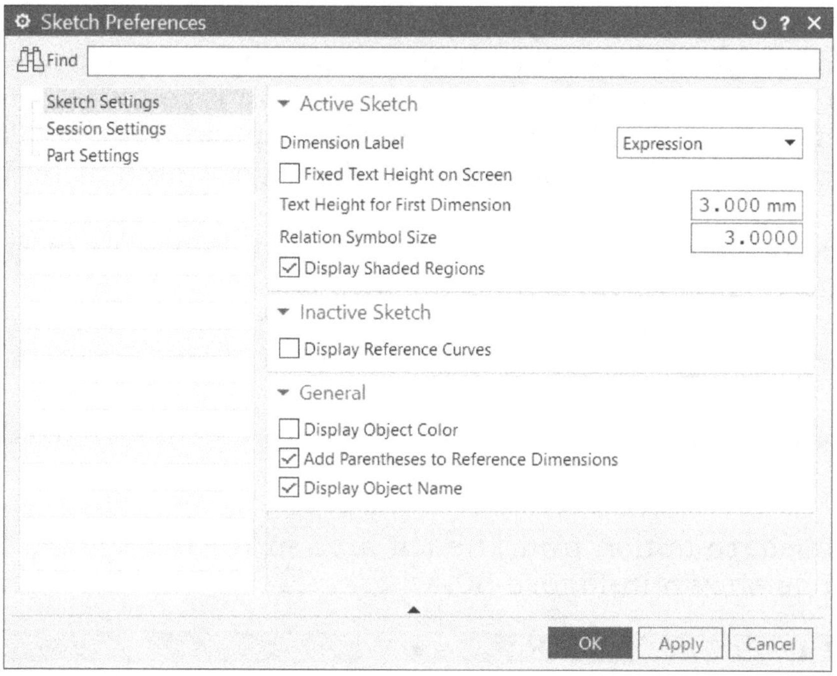

Figure-51. Sketch Preferences dialog box

- Select desired option from **Dimension Label** drop-down. Select the **Expression** option if you want to display expression (if formula is applied on dimension) along with name and value. Select the **Name** option from the drop-down if you want to display only name of dimension. Select the **Value** option from the drop-down if you want to display only value of the dimension.
- Select the **Fixed Text Height on Screen** check box if you want the text to be of fixed size while zooming the sketch. On selecting the check box, the **Text Height** edit box below this check box will become active where you can specify the height of text. Clear the **Fixed Text Height on Screen** check box if you want to scale the text height based on zoom operation.
- Select the **Display Shaded Regions** check box to display closed sketch regions as shaded in the sketch.
- Select the **Display Reference Curves** check box to display the reference curves of currently inactive sketch.
- Select the **Add Parentheses to Reference Dimensions** check box to automatically add brackets to reference dimensions.
- Select the **Session Settings** option from the left area in the dialog box to define automatic constraint and dimension creation settings.

Session Settings

Click on the **Session Settings** option from the dialog box to display settings related to snapping and task environment; refer to Figure-52.

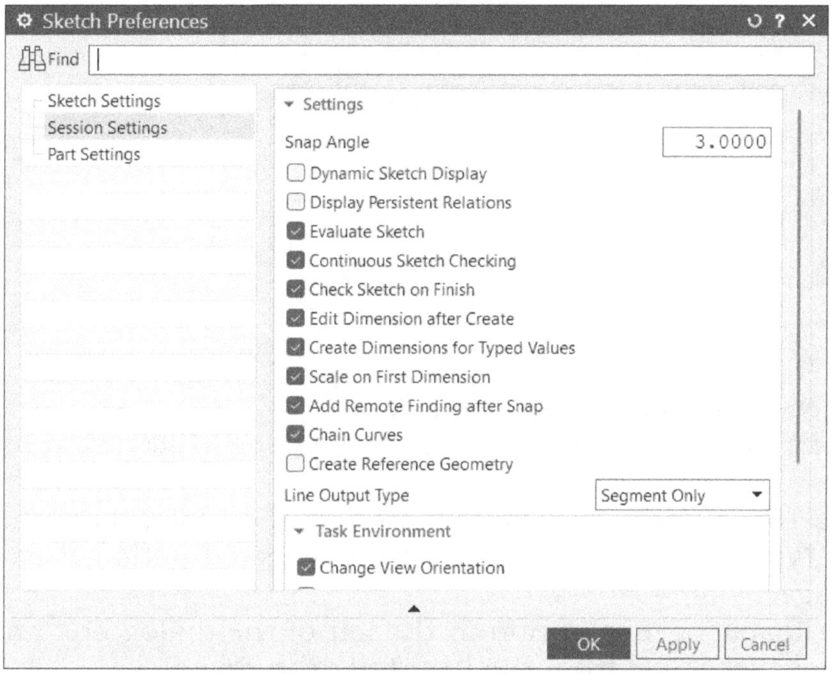

Figure-52. Session Settings page in Sketch Preferences dialog box

- Specify desired value of snap angle in the **Snap Angle** edit box. If the angle of a line relative to the horizontal or vertical reference is less than or equal to the **Snap Angle** value, the line is automatically snapped to the vertical or horizontal position.
- Select the **Dynamic Sketch Display** check box if you do not want to display constraints and vertices of very small sketch sections.
- Select the **Display Persistent Relations** check box if you want to display initial constraints on sketches automatically.
- Select the **Evaluate Sketch** check box if you want to use only fully defined sketches.
- Select the **Edit Dimension after Create** check box to display edit boxes after creating dimension.
- Select the **Create Dimensions for Typed Values** check box to automatically generate dimensions on specifying size parameters of the sketch entity.
- Select the **Scale on First Dimension** check box to scale the drawing area after specifying first dimension.
- Select the **Change View Orientation** check box if you want to place orient view to sketching plane automatically. If the sketching plane does not become parallel to screen automatically then press **SHIFT+F8**.
- Click on the **OK** button from the dialog box to apply the settings.

User Interface Preferences

The **User Interface** option in **Preferences** cascading menu is used to modify the interface of UG NX based on user's requirements. The procedure to define these options is given next.

- Click on the **User Interface** option from the **Preferences** cascading menu of the **File** menu. The **User Interface Preferences** dialog box will be displayed; refer to Figure-53.

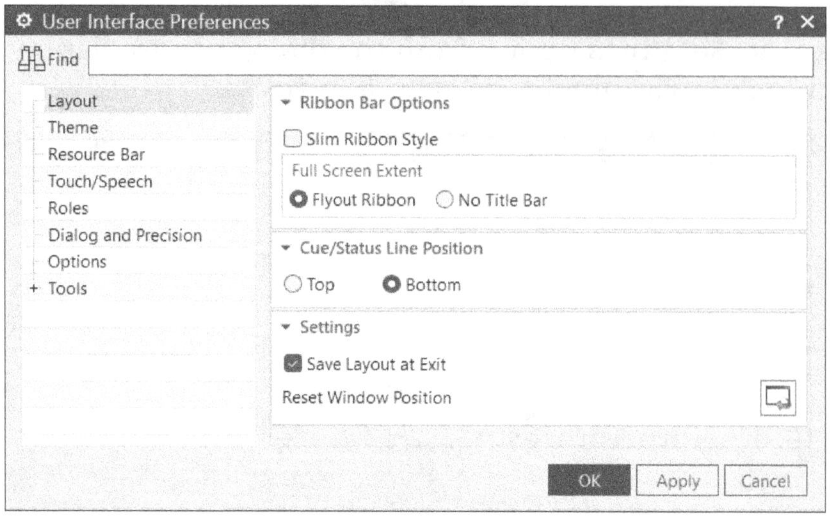

Figure-53. User Interface Preferences dialog box

- Select the **Slim Ribbon Style** check box to make the **Ribbon** slim so that it occupies less space.
- Click on the **Theme** option at the left area in the dialog box and select desired theme from **Type** drop-down. Based on the selected option, the color scheme of NX will change.
- Click on the **Resource Bar** option in the left of the dialog box and select desired position of **Resource Bar** from the **Display** drop-down.
- Click on the **Touch/Screen** option at the left in the dialog box to define options for touch enabled devices; refer to Figure-54.

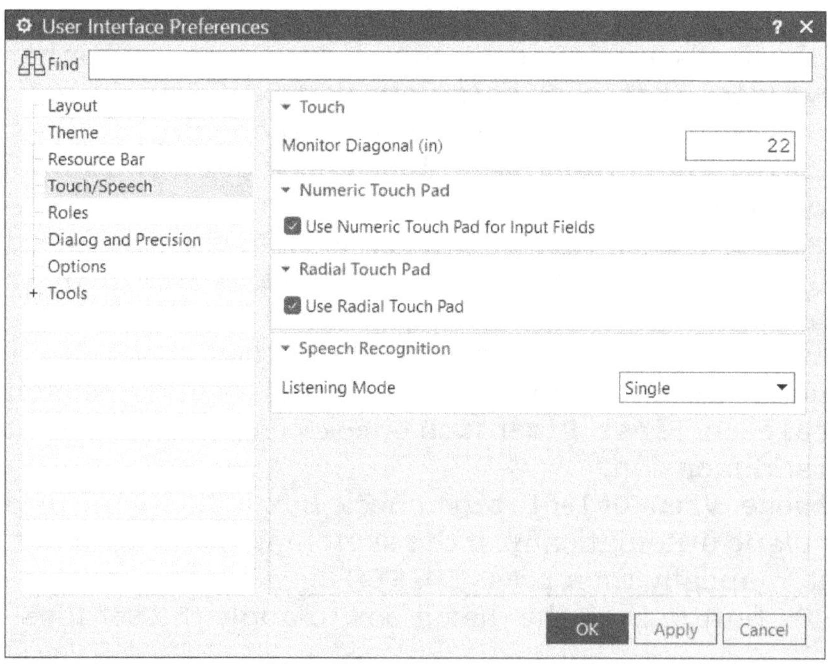

Figure-54. Interface options for touch devices

- Click on the **Options** option from the left in the dialog box and specify the decimal places up to which you want to give inputs while creating model in the **Decimal Places** edit box.
- Click on the **OK** button from the dialog box to apply the settings.

Background Preference

The **Scene** option in **Preferences** cascading menu is used to define color of background in UG NX. The procedure is given next.

- Click on the **Scene** option from the **Preferences** cascading menu of the **File** menu. The **Scene Preferences** dialog box will be displayed; refer to Figure-55.

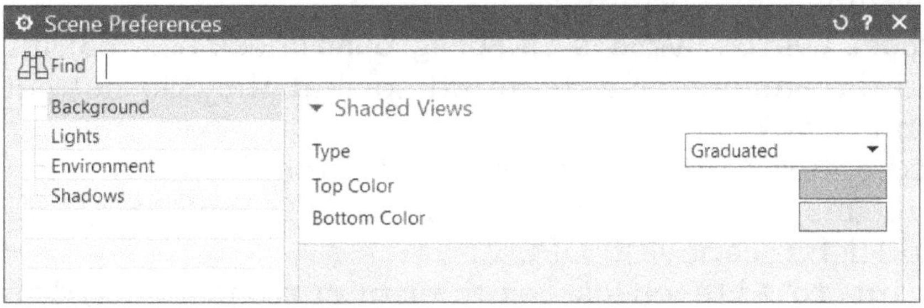

Figure-55. Scene Preferences dialog box

- Click on the color boxes and select desired colors for background.
- After setting desired colors, click on the **OK** button.

Printing Model

The **Print** tool in **File** menu is used to print the model or drawing currently displayed in graphics window. The procedure to use this tool is given next.

- Click on the **Print** tool from the **File** menu. The **Print** dialog box will be displayed; refer to Figure-56.

Figure-56. Print dialog box

- Select desired printer from the **Printer** drop-down.
- Expand the **Settings** node and set desired number of copies to be printed in the **Copies** spinner.
- Set desired value in **Scale Factor** edit box to increase or decrease size of printed model.
- Select desired option from **Output** drop-down. Select the **Color Wireframe** option from the drop-down if you want to create a print of model in colored wireframe. Select the **Black and White Wireframe** option from the drop-down if you want to create a print of model in Black & white wireframe mode. Select the **Shaded** option from the drop-down if you want to create a print of shaded model.

- Select the **White Background** check box to create print of model with white background. This check box is active only if **Shaded** option is selected in the **Output** drop-down.
- Select the **Export Raster Images in Drawing** check box to print the raster images contained in selected drawing/model.
- Select the **Export Shaded Geometry as Wireframe** check box to convert shaded views in wireframe while printing.
- Select the **Export Custom Symbols in Foreground** check box to print all annotations, symbols, and dimensions in foreground so that they do not get hidden behind the model while printing.
- Select desired option from the **Image Resolution** drop-down to define quality of print. Draft means 75 DPI (Dots Per Inch), Low means 180 DPI, Medium means 300 DPI, and High means 400 DPI.
- Select the **Print to File** check box to print current model/drawing to a file.
- After setting desired parameters, click on the **OK** button to create the print.

Plotting Model/Drawing

The **Plot** tool in **File** menu is used to plot current model or drawing in different image formats. The procedure to use this tool is given next.

- Click on the **Plot** tool from the **File** menu. The **Plot** dialog box will be displayed; refer to Figure-57.

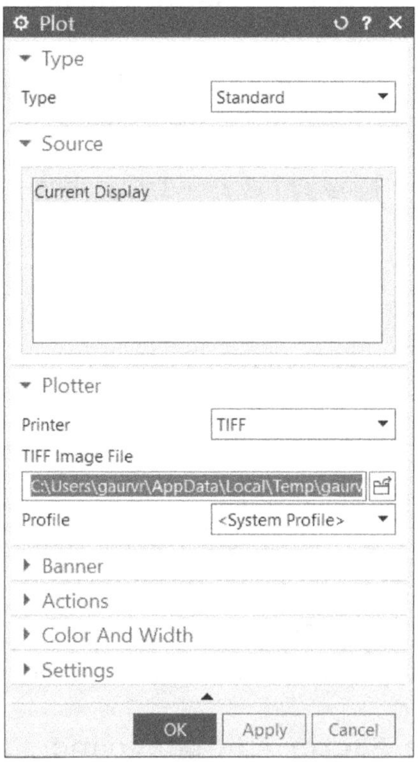

Figure-57. Plot dialog box

- Select desired image format from the **Printer** drop-down.
- Specify the location of file to be plotted in the edit box below it.
- Set the other parameters to define quality of image and click on the **OK** button to plot the file.

Importing Files

The options in **Import** cascading menu of the **File** menu are used to import files created in other software into current model. Some of the important options in this cascading menu are discussed next. You can apply the same procedure to other options.

Importing IGES file

The **IGES** tool in **Import** cascading menu of the **File** menu is used to import IGES format model in current graphics window. The procedure is given next.

- Click on the **IGES** tool from **Import** cascading menu of the **File** menu. The **Import from IGES Options** dialog box will be displayed; refer to Figure-58.

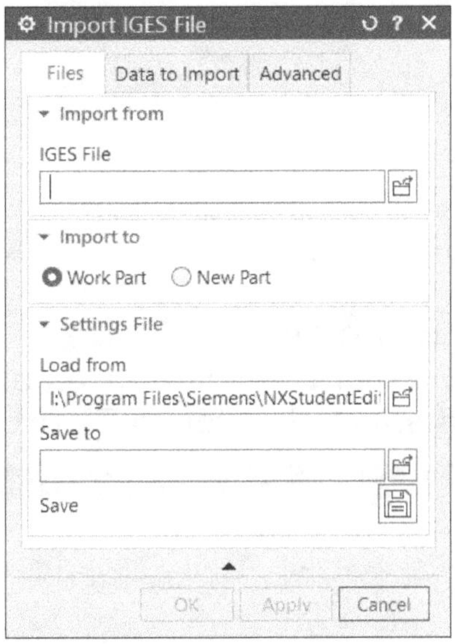

Figure-58. Import IGES File dialog box

- Click on the **Browse** button next to **IGES File** edit box and select desired IGES file to be imported.
- Select desired option from the **Import to Part** rollout. Select the **Work Part** radio button to use imported model as current work part. Select the **New Part** radio button to import the model as a new part.
- Click on the **Data to Import** tab and select the check boxes for objects you want to import from IGES file.
- Click on the **Advanced** tab and apply desired tweaks to the imported geometry.
- Click on the **OK** button from the dialog box. The part will be imported in the graphics window.

Exporting Model to Different Formats

The tools in **Export** cascading menu are used to export the model in graphics window to different formats; refer to Figure-59. Some of the tools in this cascading menu are discussed next. You can apply the same procedure to other tools.

Figure-59. Export cascading menu

Exporting to STL file

- Click on the **STL** tool from **Export** cascading menu of the **File** menu. The **STL Export** dialog box will be displayed; refer to Figure-60.

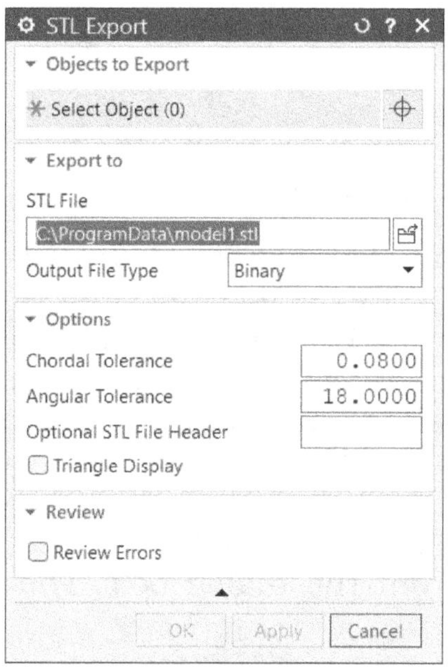

Figure-60. STL Export dialog box

- Select desired objects to be exported from the graphics area.
- Set desired location in the **STL File** edit box to define where you want to save the file.
- Select desired option from the **Output File Type** drop-down to define whether you want to save the STL file in binary format or text (ASCII) format.
- Select the **Triangle Display** check box to display model in triangulated form.
- Set the other parameters as discussed earlier and click on the **OK** button. The file will be created.

Exporting Model/Drawing to Image Format

- Click on the **Image** tool from the **Export** cascading menu of the **File** menu. The **Export Image** dialog box will be displayed; refer to Figure-61.

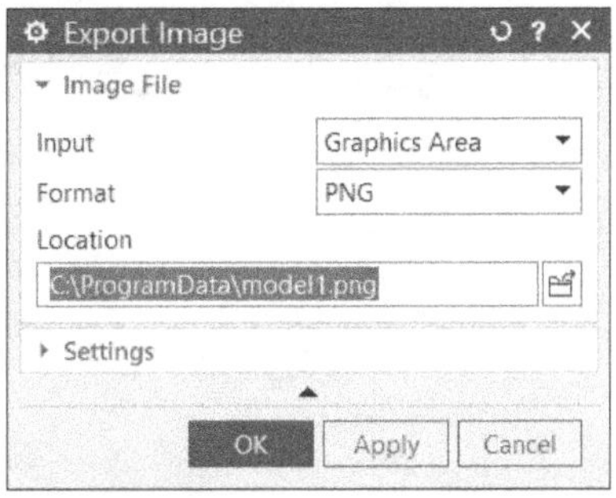

Figure-61. Export Image dialog box

- Select desired option from **Input** drop-down. If you want to export the objects displayed in graphics area then select the **Graphics Area** option. If you want to define a specific which should be exported as image then select the **Region** option and draw a box; refer to Figure-62.
- Select desired format for image from the **Format** drop-down.
- Click in the **Location** edit box and specify the location of file to be exported.
- Expand the **Settings** rollout and specify desired background color.
- After setting desired parameters, click on the **OK** button to export the file.

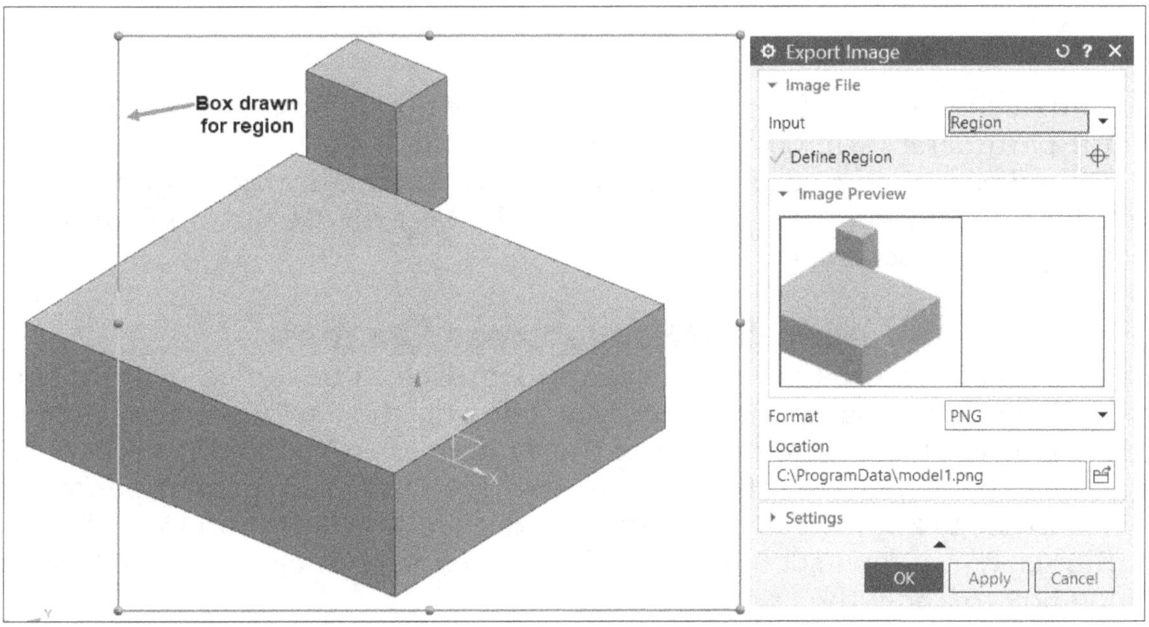

Figure-62. Drawing box for region

Utilities

The tools in **Utilities** cascading menu are used to customize various default modeling parameters. Some of the commonly used utilities are discussed next.

Modifying Customer Defaults

The **Customer Defaults** tool is used to modify the default parameters of software as per customer's requirement. The procedure to use this tool is given next.

- Click on the **Customer Defaults** tool from the **Utilities** cascading menu of **File** menu. The **Customer Defaults** dialog box will be displayed; refer to Figure-63.

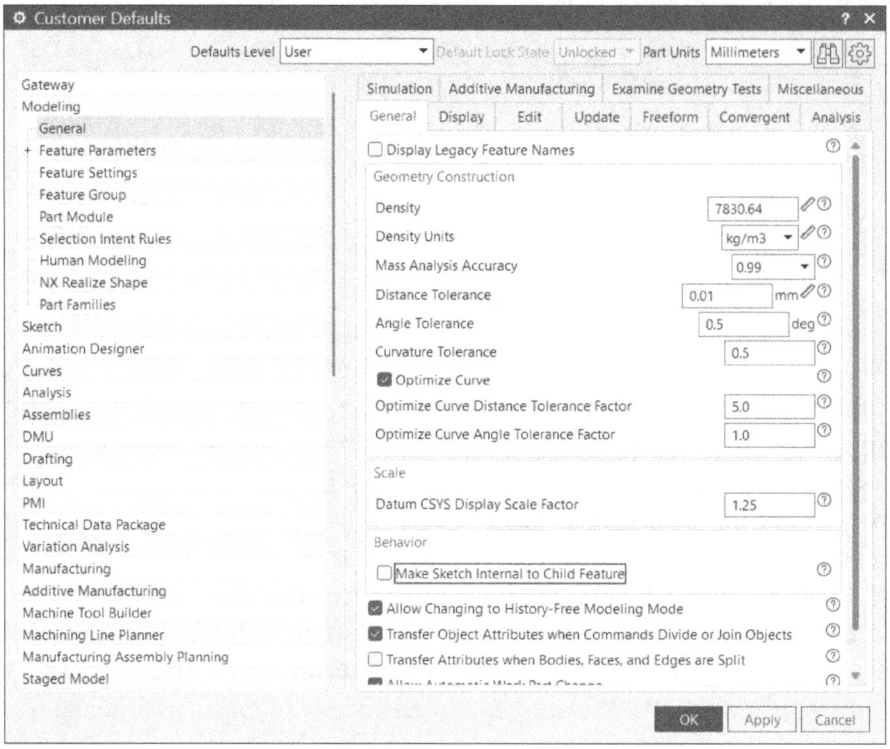

Figure-63. Customer Defaults dialog box

- Click on desired option from the left area of the dialog box. The options to modify default parameters will be displayed in the right.
- Set desired parameters as discussed earlier. We will modify these options whenever required during the course of this book. Click on the **OK** button from the dialog box to apply the settings.

Activating Early Access Features

The Early Access features are experimental features to be added later in the main software. To enable/disable these features, click on the **Early Access Feature** tool from the **Utilities** cascading menu of the **File** menu. The **Early Access Feature** dialog box will be displayed; refer to Figure-64. To activate any experimental feature, right-click in the **State** field for the feature and select the **On** option from the shortcut menu. Similarly, you can set **Off** option for any feature. Click on the **OK** button from the dialog box to apply the changes.

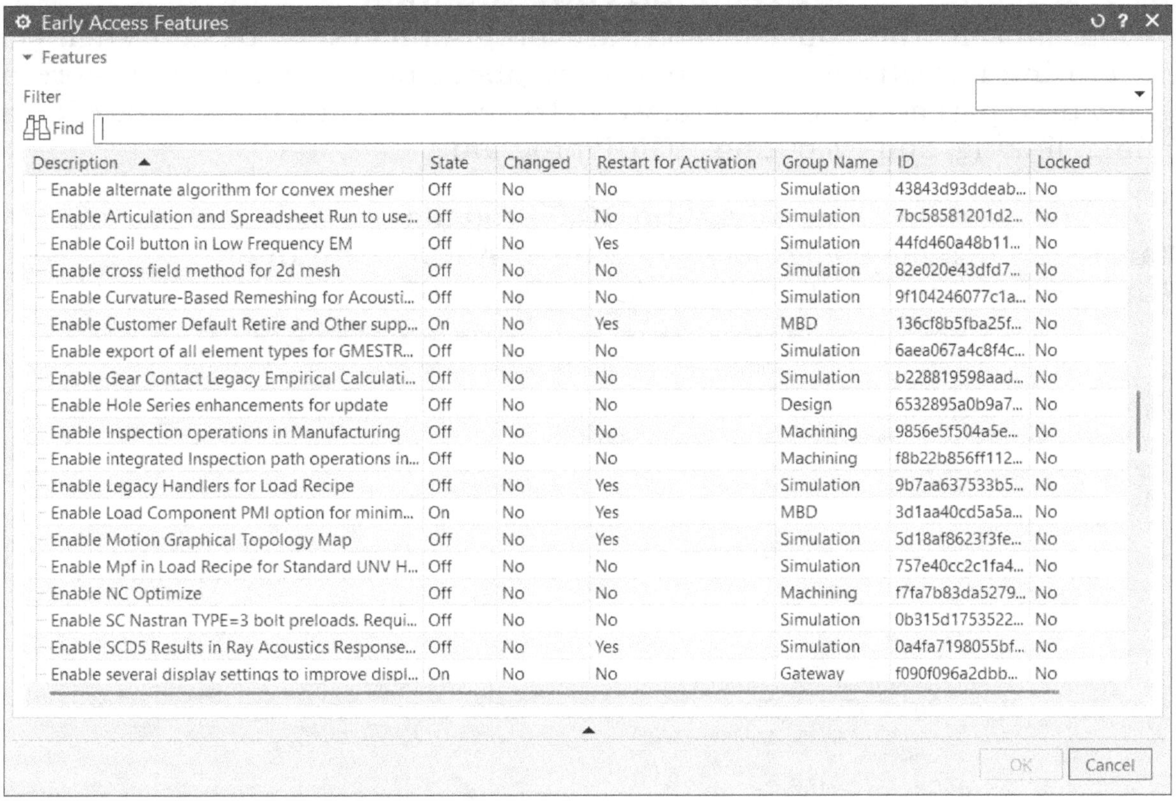

Figure-64. Early Access Features dialog box

Similarly, you can use the other options in this cascading menu.

Executing External Programs/Scripts in NX

The options in **Execute** cascading menu of the **File** menu are used to execute external programs or scripts; refer to Figure-65. Here, we will discuss to execute a GRIP program provided as sample by Siemens. You can apply the same procedure for other options in the cascading menu.

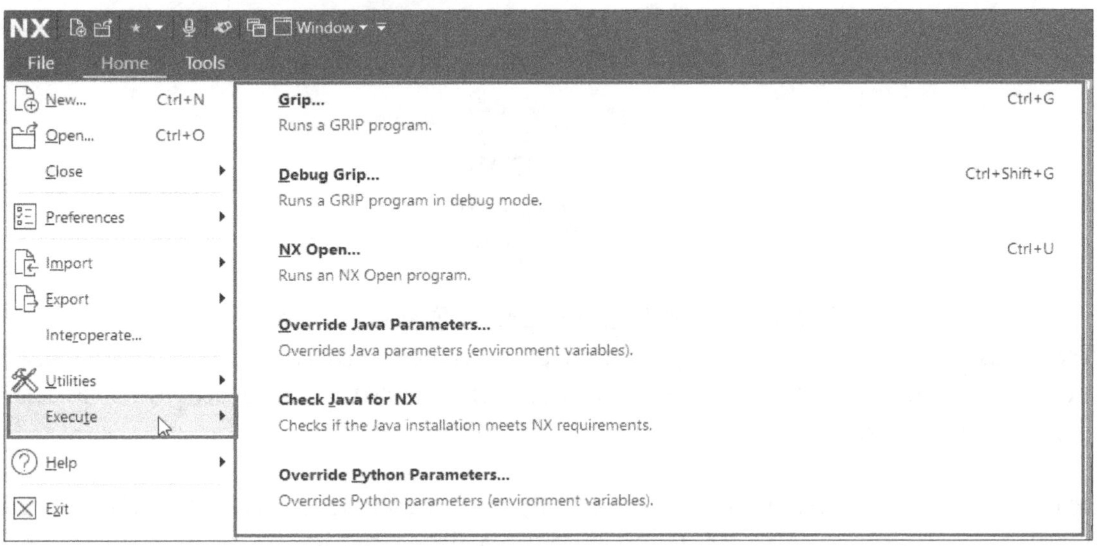

Figure-65. Execute cascading menu

Executing GRIP program

This topic falls in the court of software programmers as design engineers in manufacturing industry are less concerned about programming and more about designing their part accurately. Here, we will discuss only the basic steps of creating, compiling, linking, and executing a GRIP program.

Creating GRIP Program

- Start a new text file using Notepad or other ASCII Text Editor.
- Write down the code in the text; refer to Figure-66.

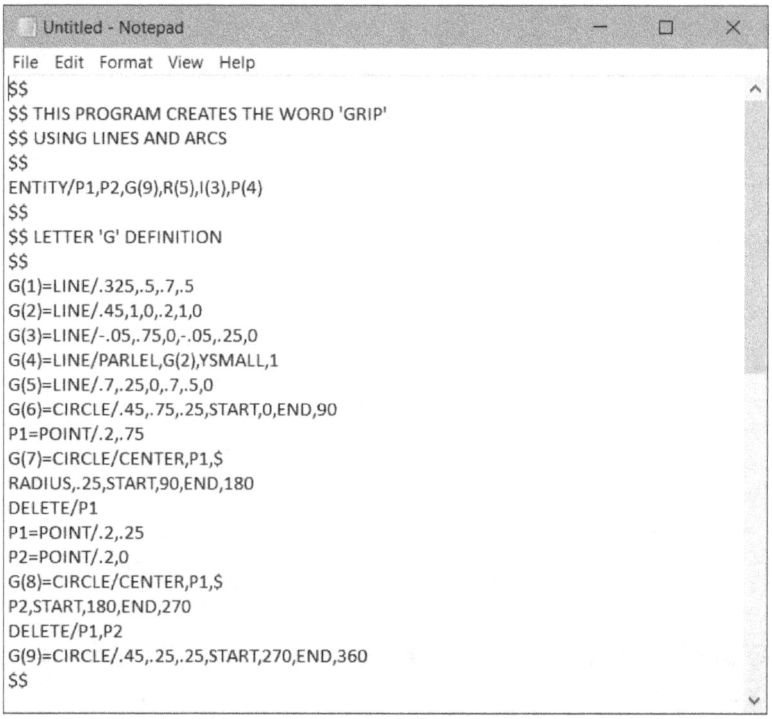


```
$$
$$ THIS PROGRAM CREATES THE WORD 'GRIP'
$$ USING LINES AND ARCS
$$
ENTITY/P1,P2,G(9),R(5),I(3),P(4)
$$
$$ LETTER 'G' DEFINITION
$$
G(1)=LINE/.325,.5,.7,.5
G(2)=LINE/.45,1,0,.2,1,0
G(3)=LINE/-.05,.75,0,-.05,.25,0
G(4)=LINE/PARLEL,G(2),YSMALL,1
G(5)=LINE/.7,.25,0,.7,.5,0
G(6)=CIRCLE/.45,.75,.25,START,0,END,90
P1=POINT/.2,.75
G(7)=CIRCLE/CENTER,P1,$
RADIUS,.25,START,90,END,180
DELETE/P1
P1=POINT/.2,.25
P2=POINT/.2,0
G(8)=CIRCLE/CENTER,P1,$
P2,START,180,END,270
DELETE/P1,P2
G(9)=CIRCLE/.45,.25,.25,START,270,END,360
$$
```

Figure-66. Program typed in Notepad

- After writing the code, save this file with name **Sample.grs** at desired location. (Note: Save the file in a folder with smaller path like in D drive or E drive as it will be easier to call file while compiling). Note that GRIP is a very old language. You can use below QR code for more details.

Compiling the Program Source File

If you are totally unaware of programming then you should know that compiling is used to convert source file into machine readable format. The steps to compile GRIP source file are discussed next.

- Click on the **Start** button and type **GRIP**. Various applications with the name will be displayed. Click on the **NX Open Grip** application icon; refer to Figure-67. The **NX Open Grip** command window will be displayed; refer to Figure-68.

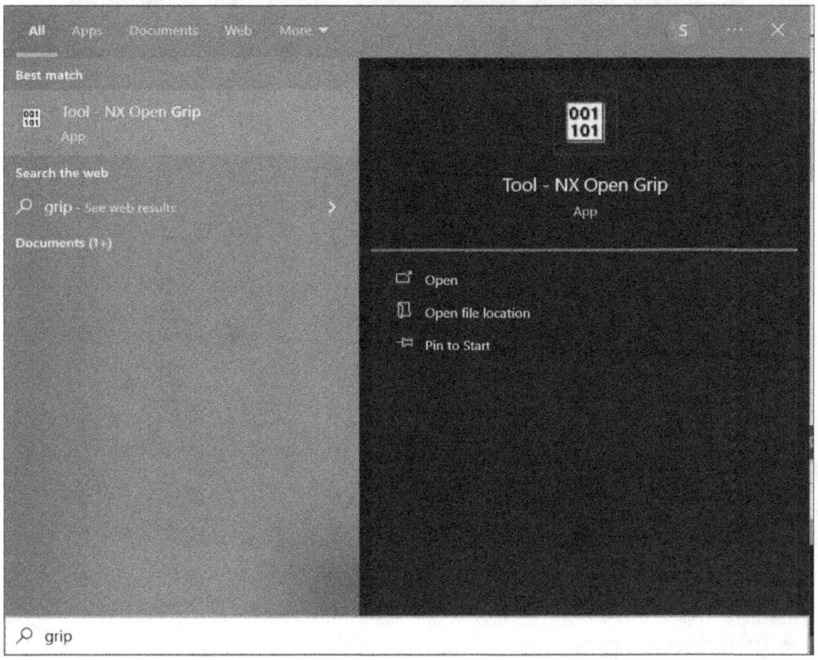

Figure-67. NX Open Grip icon

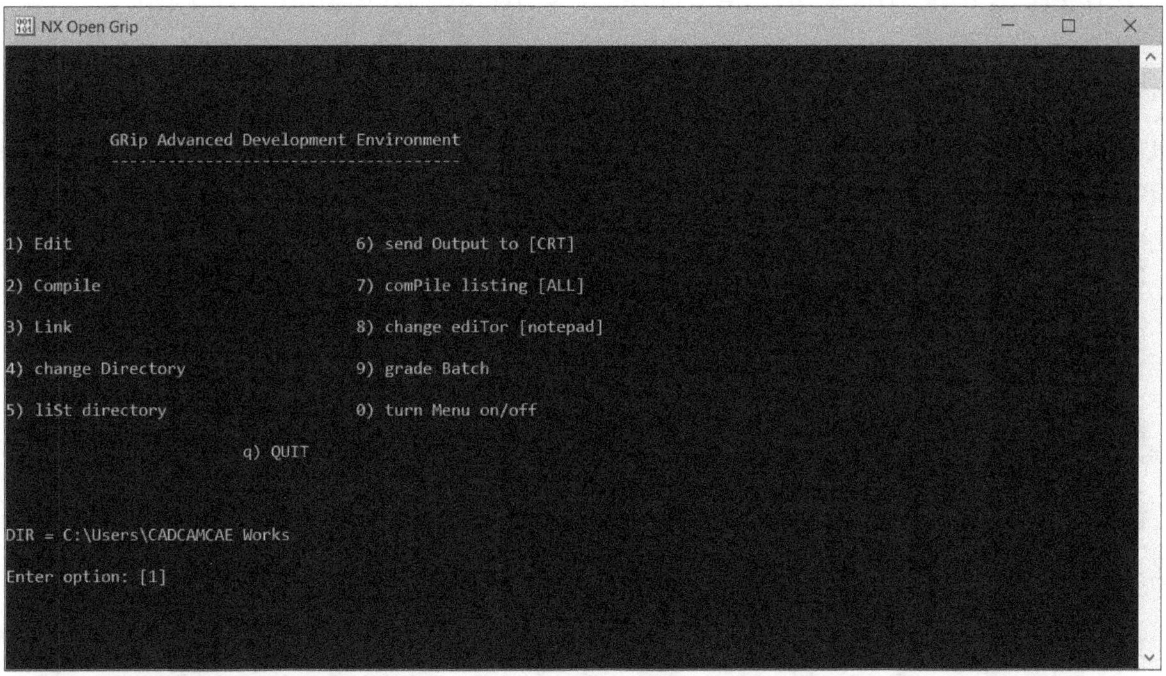

Figure-68. NX Open Grip window

- Type **2** in the command window and press **ENTER**. You will be prompted to specify location of source file.
- Type the full location of GRIP code source file; refer to Figure-69 and press **ENTER**. Once the compiling is successfully completed, the message will be displayed ***1 GRIP PROGRAM COMPILED WITHOUT ERROR.

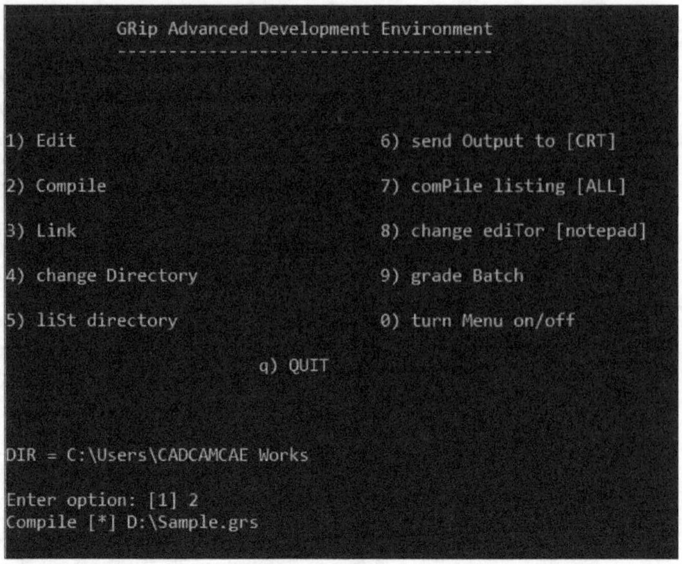

Figure-69. Specifying location of source file to compiler

- Press **ENTER** to return to main page. A *.gri format file will be created in the same location where you have placed the code file.

Now we need to link this *.gri file to create software readable program.

- Type **3** in the command window and press **ENTER** to start linking.
- Now, specify the location of **Sample.gri** file in the command prompt and press **ENTER**. Once the linking is successful, the command window will be displayed as shown in Figure-70.

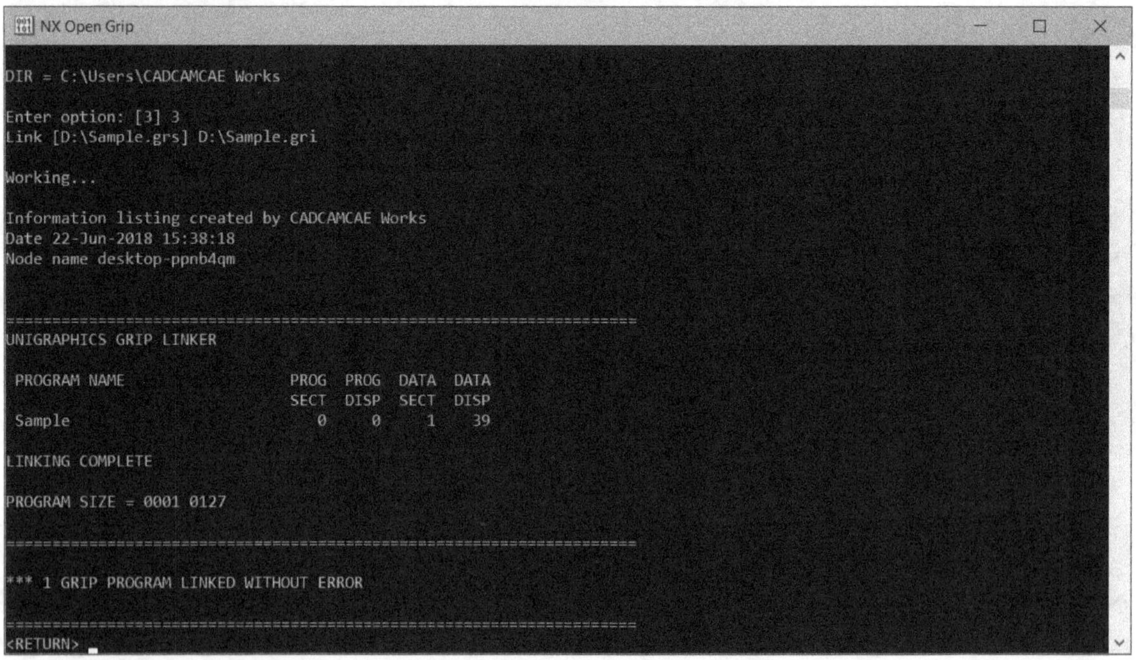

Figure-70. Linking GRIP file

- Press **ENTER** at the command prompt. **Sample.grx** file will be created which NX can read to perform operation.
- Type **q** at the command prompted and press **ENTER** to exit the Command Window.

Executing GRIP program

- Click on the **Grip** tool from **Execute** cascading menu of the **File** menu. The **Execute GRIP** dialog box will be displayed. Select the **Sample.grx** file earlier created and click on the **OK** button from the dialog box.
- Once the program is executed, the output will be displayed in the graphics window; refer to Figure-71.

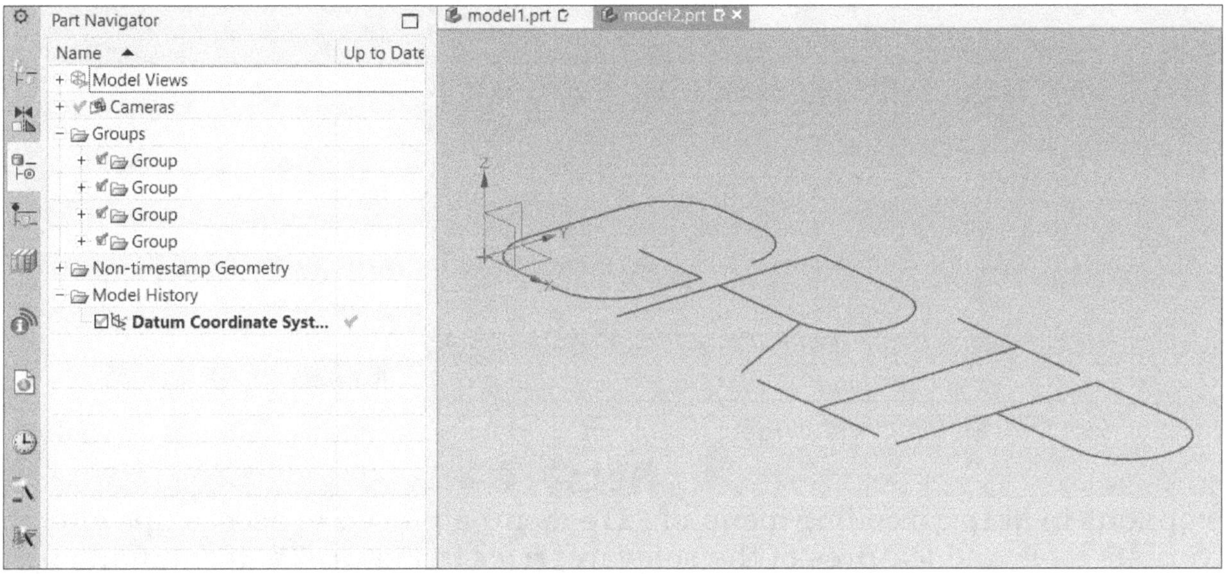

Figure-71. Output of Sample program

Checking Properties

The **Properties** tool in **File** menu is used to check different properties of the model. The procedure to use this tool is given next.

- Click on the **Properties** tool from the **File** menu. The **Displayed Part Properties** dialog box will be displayed; refer to Figure-72.

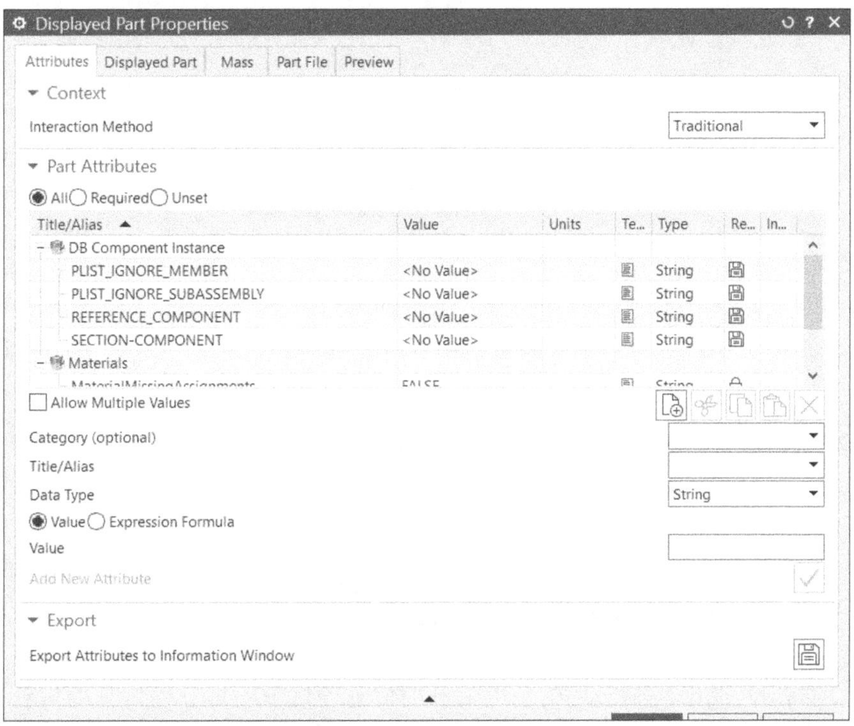

Figure-72. Displayed Part Properties dialog box

- Most of the time we are required to check the mass of part during manufacturing. Click on the **Mass** tab in the dialog box and click on the **Update Mass Properties Now** button. The mass of part will be displayed; refer to Figure-73.
- Similarly, check the other parameters of the part and click on the **OK** button to exit.

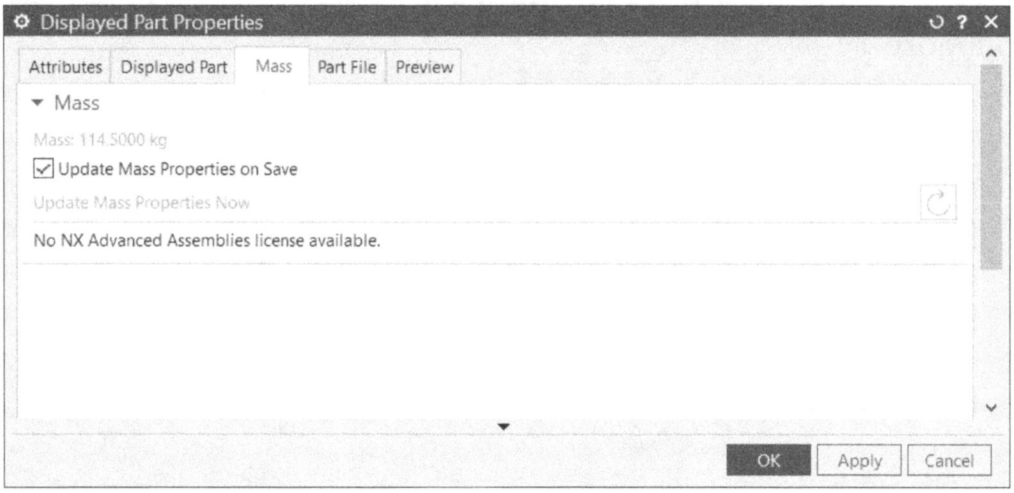

Figure-73. Checking mass of part

Help

The options in **Help** cascading menu of **File** menu are used to access tips and notes on various tools and features of the software; refer to Figure-74. If you find any tool or topic not discussed in this book then you can search it in Help database of NX.

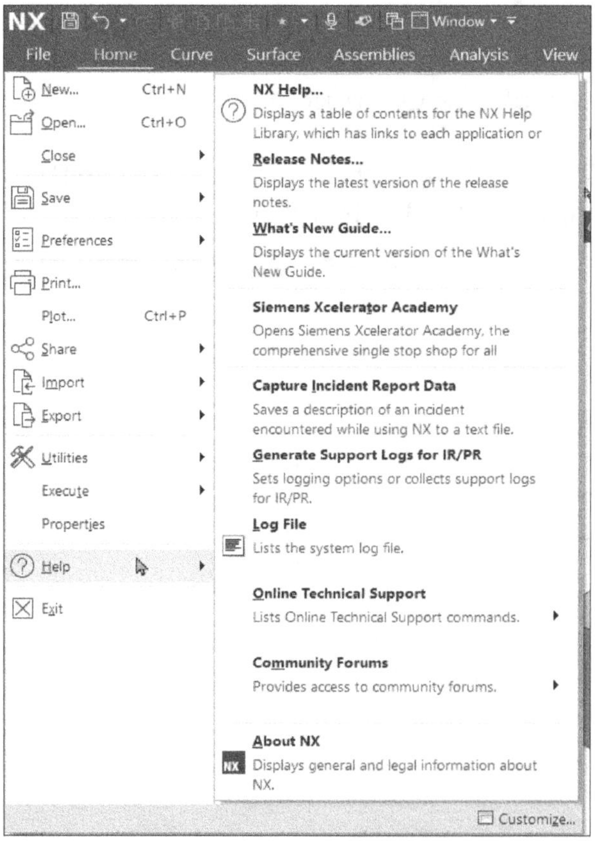

Figure-74. Help cascading menu

CUSTOMIZING INTERFACE

The **Customize** tool at the bottom right in **File** menu is used to customize the interface of UG NX; refer to Figure-75. Using this tool, you can add or remove tools from **Menus**, **Ribbon**, **Quick Access Toolbar**, and other interface sections. The procedure to use this tool is given next.

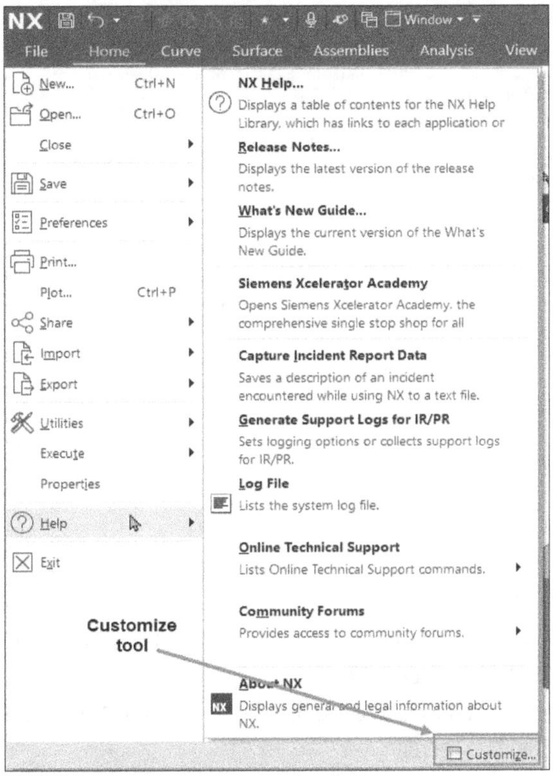

Figure-75. Customize tool in File menu

- Click on the **Customize** tool from the bottom right in the **File** menu. The **Customize** dialog box will be displayed; refer to Figure-76.

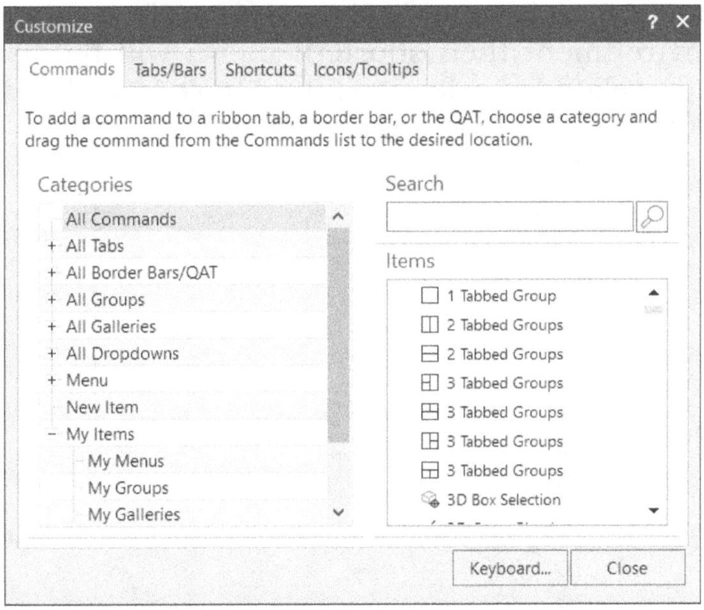

Figure-76. Customize dialog box

- Select the tool in **Item** list box in the dialog box and drag it to desired location in **Ribbon**, **Menu**, or **Quick Access Toolbar**; refer to Figure-77.

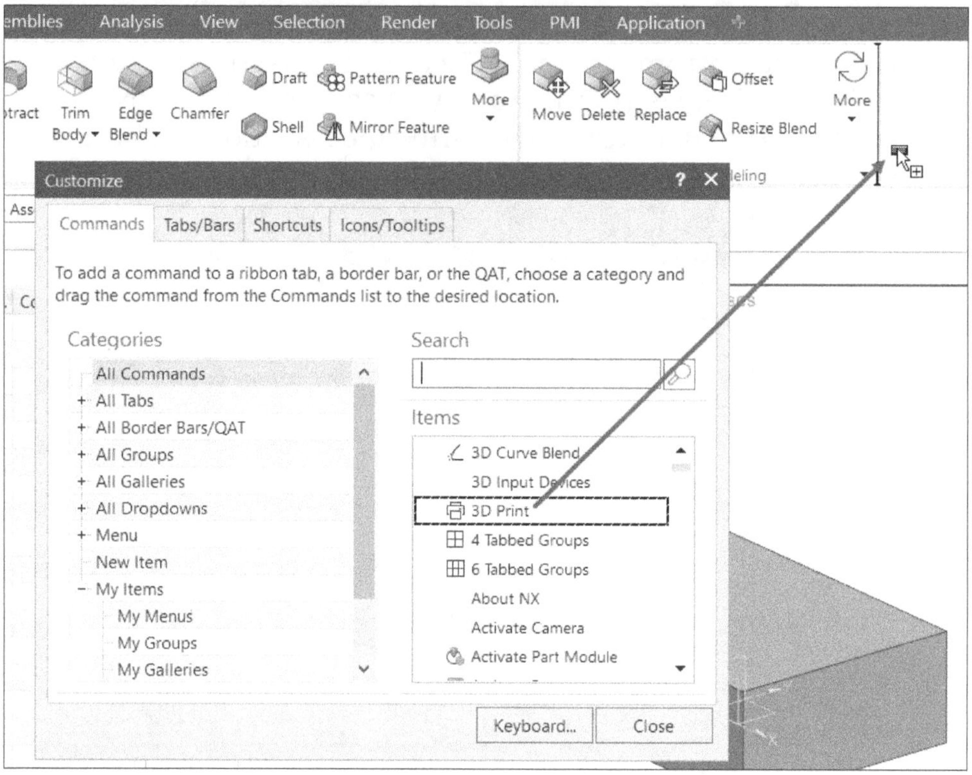

Figure-77. Dragging tool to Ribbon

- Click on the **Tabs/Bars** tab in the dialog box and select the check boxes for tabs that you want to display in **Ribbon**.
- Similarly, set the other customizing options in other tabs of the dialog box and then click on the **Close** button.

RIGHT-CLICK SHORTCUT MENU

The right-click shortcut menu in Modeling environment is used to access selection filters, orientation related and context related tools. If you right-click in the empty area in Modeling environment then shortcut menu will be displayed as shown in Figure-78. The options related to selection filters have already been discussed. Other options of this shortcut menu are discussed next.

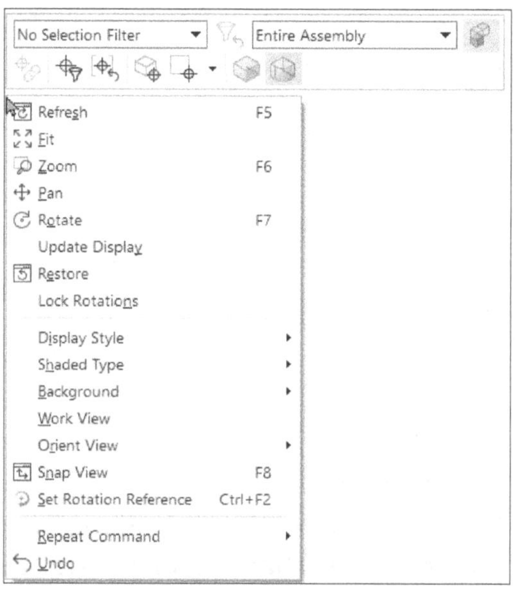

Figure-78. Right-click shortcut menu

Orientation Options

This section of shortcut menu contains quick orientation modification options like Zoom, Fit, Refresh etc.

Refresh

The **Refresh** option in shortcut menu is used to update the graphics view of model after performing changes if they have not been updated automatically. You can press **F5** key to do the same.

Fit

The **Fit** option in shortcut menu is used to fit the display of all the models available in current design inside the current viewable window. This option is useful when due to view rotation or other operations, you are not able to find your design in graphics area. Press **ESC** to exit.

Zoom

The **Zoom** option in shortcut menu is used to zoom in on specific area of model by drawing rectangular window; refer to Figure-79. You can Scroll Up using Mouse wheel to do the same and Scroll Down Mouse wheel to zoom out. Alternatively, Hold **CTRL+MMB** (Middle Mouse Button) and drag upward to zoom in or drag downward to zoom out. Press **ESC** to exit.

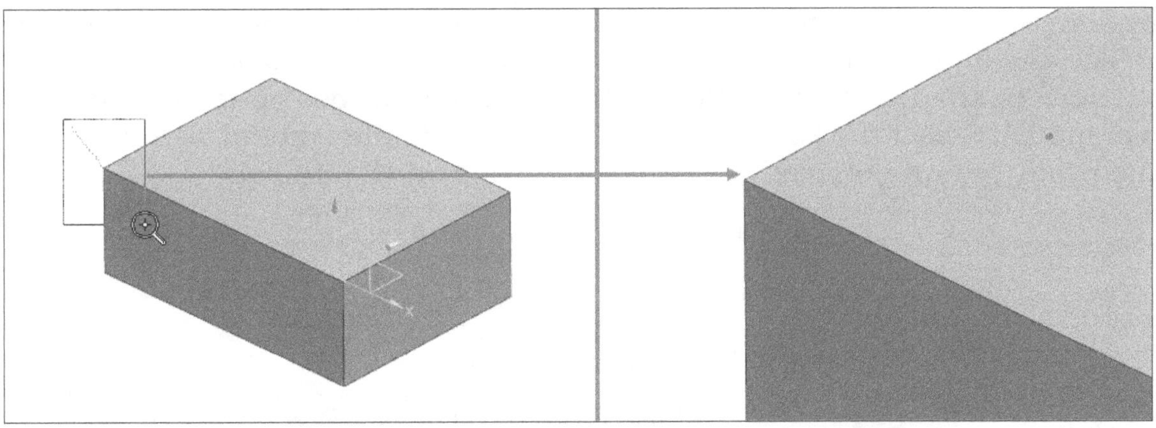

Figure-79. Zooming in on model

Pan

The **Pan** option in shortcut menu is used to move the model view in current plane. After selecting this option, hold the **LMB** (Left Mouse Button) and drag to move the model view. You can also perform this operation by holding **SHIFT+MMB** or **MMB+RMB** (Right Mouse Button) and dragging the cursor. Press **ESC** to exit.

Rotate

The **Rotate** option in shortcut menu is used to rotate model view about model's geometric center. After selecting this option, drag the cursor to rotate model view. Alternatively, you can hold the MMB and drag cursor to perform same operation.

Update Display

If you have performed changed the display properties of model (face color change, line thickness change etc.) and they have not been reflected in the display then you can use this **Update Display** option to apply these changes.

Restore

The **Restore** option is used to revert back to earlier selected standard view after you have performed rotation or zoom operations.

Lock Rotations

Select the **Lock Rotations** toggle option to stop unintentional view rotations.

Display Styles

The options in **Display Styles** cascading menu of right-click shortcut menu are used to switch between various display styles like Shaded, Wireframe, and Studio; refer to Figure-80. Select the **Shaded** option if you want to display 3D model surfaces in smooth colored shades with lighting. Select the **Wireframe** option if you want to display skeleton of 3D model. Select the **Studio** option to display model view in high quality realistic surface texture.

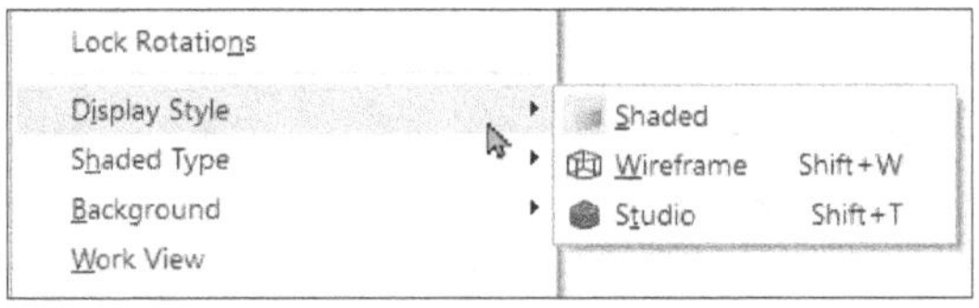

Figure-80. Display Style cascading menu

Shaded Type

The options in **Shaded Type** cascading menu are used to switch between various model face shading conditions; refer to Figure-81. Select the **Shaded** option to generate smooth surface shades of model. Select the **Partially Shaded** option to display hidden edges of model. Select the **Face Analysis** option to display model surfaces with color scheme produced on performing surface analysis on the model.

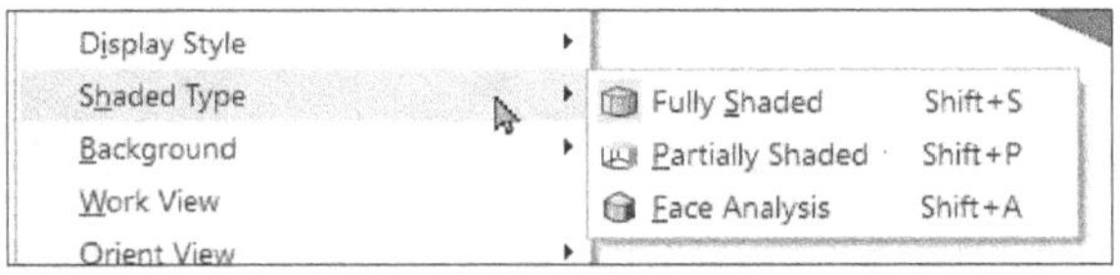

Figure-81. Shaded Type cascading menu

Background

The options in the **Background** cascading menu are used to switch between various color schemes of background in the graphics area; refer to Figure-82. Select desired option from the cascading menu to change the background color.

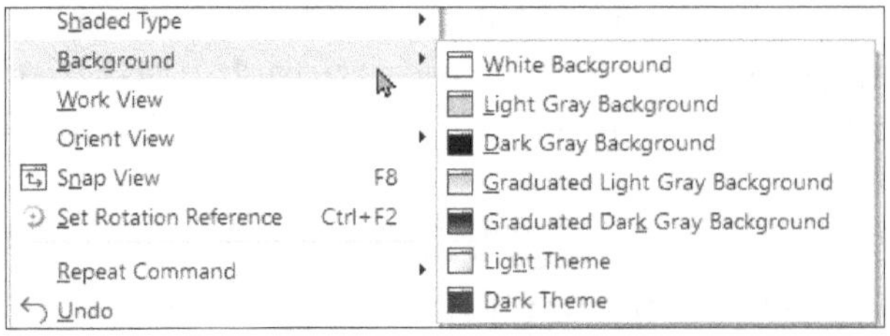

Figure-82. Background cascading menu

Work View

The **Work View** option in shortcut menu is used to set current view as work view. A work view defines orientation of new sketches and other modeling directions.

Orient View

The options in the **Orient View** cascading menu are used to change the view orientation of the model; refer to Figure-83. Select desired option to change the orientation. Generally, you will be switching between Isometric, Top, and Front views when creating 3D Models. Use the shortcut keys **End** for Isometric view, **CTRL+ALT+T** for Top view, and **CTRL+ALT+F** for front view.

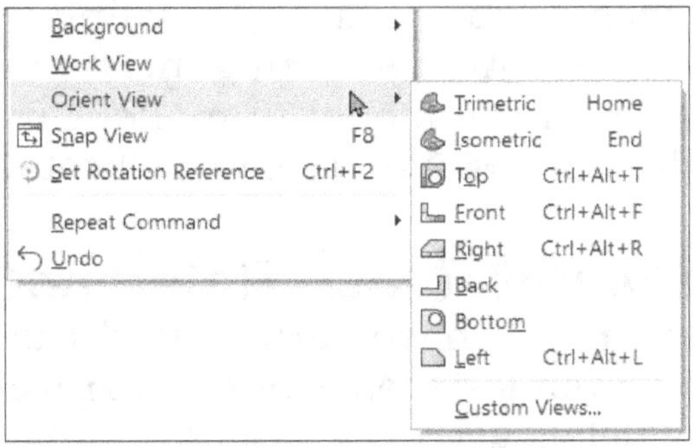

Figure-83. Orient View cascading menu

Creating and Selecting Custom Views

Rotate, pan, and zoom the model in desired orientation for which you want to create a custom view and then **Add View** option from shortcut menu displayed on right-clicking on **Model Views** node in the **Part Navigator**; refer to Figure-84. A new view will be added and activated as Work view; refer to Figure-85. If you now select the **Custom Views** option from the **Orient View** cascading menu in the right-click shortcut menu; refer to Figure-83 then option to selected newly created custom view will be displayed in the **Orient View** window; refer to Figure-86. Click **Close** to exit window.

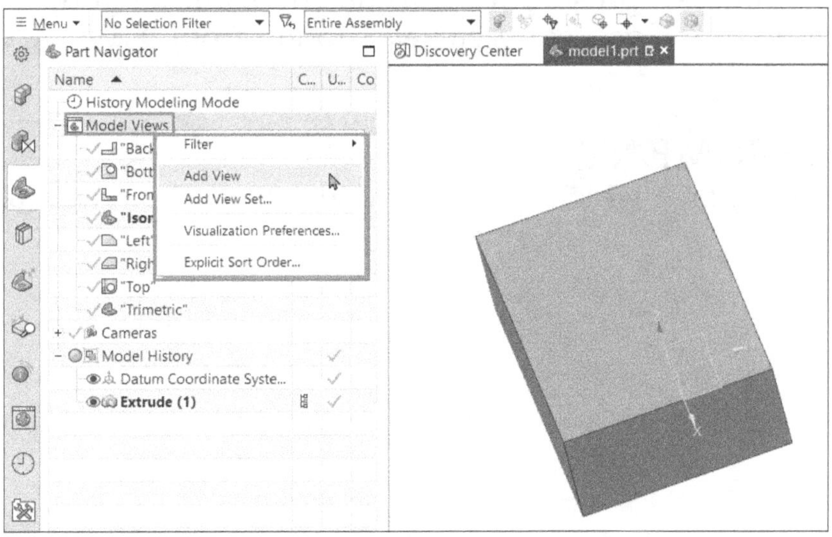

Figure-84. Model Views shortcut menu

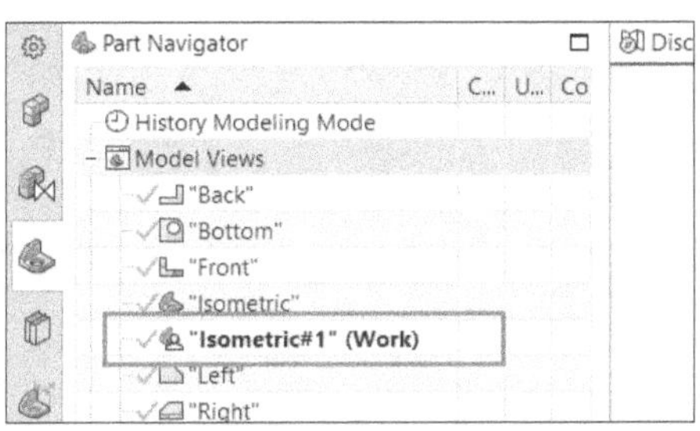

Figure-85. New custom view added

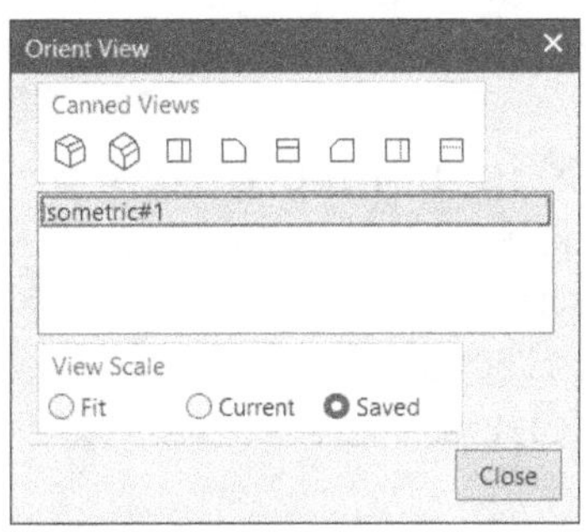

Figure-86. Orient View window

Snap View

The **Snap View** option is used to switch to nearest orthographic view (Front, Left, Top, etc.) after you have rotated the model view. You can also use **F8** key to do the same operation. This option is extensively used for orientation when creating 3D model.

Set Rotation Reference

The **Set Rotation Reference** option is used to define center point of rotation for rotate operation earlier discussed. After selecting this option from right-click shortcut menu, select desired point from the model to make it rotation center. Now, if you rotate the model view by dragging **MMB** then view will rotate about selected point.

Clear Rotation Reference

This option is displayed when you have earlier used the **Set Rotation Reference** option. Select the **Clear Rotation Reference** option to revert back to geometric center as center for rotation of model view.

Repeat Command

The **Repeat Command** cascading menu in right-click shortcut menu shows last 10 commands/tools that you have used recently. You can select desired command from cascading menu to reactivate it.

Undo and Redo

The **Undo** option in shortcut menu is used to revert the latest operation performed in graphics area. You can press **CTRL+Z** to do the same. If you want to revert the effects of **Undo** option then you can use **Redo** option from **Quick Access Toolbar** or press **CTRL+Y**.

SELF-ASSESSMENT

Q1. In the New dialog box, which tab should be selected to create a part file?
A. Drafting
B. Assembly
C. Model
D. Sheet

Q2. Which interface element is located at the top and contains tools like New and Open?
A. Ribbon
B. Menu Bar
C. Quick Access Toolbar
D. Resource Bar

Q3. Ribbon in NX is divided into:
A. Panels and Tools
B. Tabs and Groups
C. Windows and Sections
D. Layers and Menus

Q4. Which bar provides access to menus, filters, and snap options?
A. Ribbon
B. Resource Bar
C. Top Border Bar
D. Status Bar

Q5. How can Top Border Bar be displayed?
A. By restarting NX
B. By activating Advanced role
C. By opening file
D. By saving project

Q6. Which option allows selecting only specific object types like sketches?
A. Selection Scope
B. Type Filter
C. Intent Filter
D. Display Filter

Q7. Which option allows selection from entire assembly?
A. Work Part Only
B. Within Component
C. Entire Assembly
D. Local Part

Q8. Selection Intent is used to define:
A. File size
B. Selection method
C. View type
D. Layer color

Q9. What does “Allow Automatic Work Part Change” do?
A. Saves file automatically
B. Changes work part automatically
C. Deletes part
D. Locks part

Q10. Create Interpart Link is used for:
A. Saving file
B. Linking parts
C. Deleting objects
D. Viewing model

Q11. Which tool helps to narrow object selection types?
A. Selection Filters
B. Ribbon
C. Menu
D. Navigator

Q12. Layers in NX are:
A. Solid objects
B. Transparent sheets
C. Tools
D. Commands

Q13. Which option helps select objects based on color or line style?
A. Layers
B. Display Attributes
C. Scope
D. Types

Q14. What does Deselect All button do?
A. Deletes objects
B. Selects all objects
C. Deselects selected objects
D. Hides objects

Q15. 3D Box Selection is used to:
A. Create cube
B. Select objects in a box
C. Draw sketch
D. Edit part

Q16. Which option selects objects inside or touching the box?
A. Inside
B. Crossing
C. Inside/Crossing
D. Outside

Q17. Lasso selection is used to:
A. Draw straight line
B. Create free-hand boundary
C. Delete objects
D. Rotate view

Q18. Assembly Navigator is used to:
A. Create sketch
B. Manage components
C. Add dimensions
D. Save file

Q19. Part Navigator records:
A. Colors
B. Operations performed
C. File size
D. Views

Q20. Reuse Library is used to:
A. Delete objects
B. Store commonly used objects
C. Print drawing
D. Export file

Q21. Web Browser tab is used to:
A. Draw model
B. Access internet
C. Create sketch
D. Apply material

Q22. File menu is used for:
A. Drawing only
B. File operations
C. Coloring
D. Rendering

Q23. Shortcut key to open a file is:
A. CTRL+N
B. CTRL+S
C. CTRL+O
D. CTRL+P

Q24. Which option is used to close only selected parts from the list?
A. All Parts
B. Selected Parts
C. Save As
D. Close All

Q25. Which dialog box appears when you select “Selected Parts” option?
A. Save As dialog box
B. Close Part dialog box
C. Print dialog box
D. Preferences dialog box

Q26. By default, which radio button is selected in Close Part dialog box?
A. All Parts in Session
B. Selected Parts Only
C. Top Level Assembly Parts
D. Close All

Q27. Which key is used to select multiple parts in the list?
A. ALT
B. SHIFT
C. CTRL
D. TAB

Q28. What is the function of "Force Close if Modified" option?
A. Saves file automatically
B. Closes file after saving
C. Forcefully closes without saving
D. Renames file

Q29. What happens if there are unsaved changes while closing all parts?
A. Files are deleted
B. Close All Files dialog box appears
C. System shuts down
D. Nothing happens

Q30. When saving a file for the first time, which dialog box appears?
A. Close Part
B. Name Parts
C. Print
D. Preferences

Q31. What does "Save Work Parts Only" option do?
A. Saves entire assembly
B. Saves only current working part
C. Deletes other parts
D. Closes file

Q32. Which option is used to save file with different name?
A. Save
B. Save All
C. Save As
D. Export

Q33. Save Options tool is used for?
A. Printing file
B. Defining save settings
C. Closing file
D. Importing file

Q34. Which check box is used to include mass data while saving?
A. Include Data
B. Generate Mass Data
C. Save Mass
D. Mass Option

Q35. Preferences option is used to?
A. Save files
B. Modify interface and behavior
C. Print files
D. Import files

Q36. In Modeling Preferences, which option saves parts as solid objects?
A. Sheet
B. Solid
C. Curve
D. Surface

Q37. Density value is used to calculate?
A. Volume
B. Length
C. Mass
D. Area

Q38. Dynamic Update Mode "Continuous" means?
A. Update after stop
B. No update
C. Dynamic update while dragging
D. Manual update

Q39. Sketch Preferences are used for?
A. Printing
B. Importing
C. Defining sketch settings
D. Exporting

Q40. Which option displays only value of dimension?
A. Name
B. Expression
C. Value
D. Label

Q41. Fixed Text Height on Screen option does what?
A. Changes color
B. Fixes text size while zooming
C. Deletes text
D. Rotates text

Q42. Snap Angle is used to?
A. Rotate model
B. Snap lines to horizontal/vertical
C. Delete sketch
D. Save sketch

Q43. User Interface Preferences are used to?
A. Modify interface
B. Delete files
C. Export files
D. Import files

Q44. Slim Ribbon Style option does what?
A. Expands ribbon
B. Makes ribbon slim
C. Deletes ribbon
D. Locks ribbon

Q45. Scene option is used to?
A. Print model
B. Change background color
C. Save file
D. Import file

Q46. Print tool is used to?
A. Save file
B. Print model/drawing
C. Export file
D. Import file

Q47. Plot tool is used to?
A. Delete file
B. Plot model in image format
C. Close file
D. Rename file

Q48. IGES tool is used for?
A. Export file
B. Import IGES file
C. Print file
D. Save file

Q49. What is the primary purpose of the right-click shortcut menu in the Modeling environment?
A. To create new models
B. To access selection filters and context-related tools
C. To delete components
D. To export files

Q50. Which section of the shortcut menu contains options like Zoom, Fit, and Refresh?
A. Display Styles
B. Orientation Options
C. Background
D. Work View

Q51. Which option is used to update the graphics view when changes are not automatically reflected?
A. Restore
B. Refresh
C. Fit
D. Zoom

Q52. What is the shortcut key for the Refresh option?
A. F2
B. F5
C. F8
D. ESC

Q53. What does the Fit option do?
A. Rotates the model
B. Fits all models within the current viewable window
C. Deletes unwanted parts
D. Changes display color

Q54. Which key is used to exit the Fit operation?
A. F5
B. CTRL
C. ESC
D. ALT

Q55. How can you zoom in using the mouse wheel?
A. Scroll down
B. Scroll up
C. Double click
D. Hold SHIFT

Q56. Which key combination allows zooming using mouse dragging?
A. CTRL + MMB
B. SHIFT + LMB
C. ALT + RMB
D. CTRL + LMB

Q57. What does the Pan option do?
A. Rotates the model
B. Moves the model view in the current plane
C. Zooms the model
D. Deletes view

Q58. Which combination can also perform Pan operation?
A. CTRL + LMB
B. SHIFT + MMB
C. ALT + RMB
D. CTRL + RMB

Q59. What is the function of the Rotate option?
A. Moves the model
B. Rotates model about geometric center
C. Zooms in
D. Changes background

Q60. Which mouse action performs rotation without selecting the Rotate option?
A. LMB drag
B. MMB drag
C. RMB drag
D. Scroll

Q61. When should you use Update Display?
A. To rotate model
B. To apply display property changes not yet reflected
C. To zoom out
D. To create sketch

Q62. What does the Restore option do?
A. Deletes last action
B. Reverts to earlier selected standard view
C. Saves file
D. Locks rotation

Q63. What is the purpose of Lock Rotations?
A. Enable rotation
B. Prevent unintentional rotations
C. Zoom faster
D. Change view

Q64. Which display style shows only skeleton of 3D model?
A. Shaded
B. Studio
C. Wireframe
D. Face Analysis

Q65. Which display style provides realistic surface texture?
A. Wireframe
B. Studio
C. Shaded
D. Partial

Q66. Which Shaded Type shows hidden edges of model?
A. Shaded
B. Face Analysis
C. Partially Shaded
D. Studio

Q67. Which option displays surface analysis color scheme?
A. Shaded
B. Wireframe
C. Face Analysis
D. Studio

Q68. What is the function of Background option?
A. Change model geometry
B. Change background color scheme
C. Rotate model
D. Zoom model

Q69. What does Work View define?
A. Background color
B. Orientation of sketches and modeling directions
C. File format
D. Rendering speed

Q70. Which shortcut key is used for Isometric view?
A. CTRL+ALT+T
B. CTRL+ALT+F
C. End
D. F8

Q71. Which shortcut key is used for Top view?
A. End
B. CTRL+ALT+T
C. CTRL+ALT+F
D. F5

Q72. Which shortcut key is used for Front view?
A. CTRL+ALT+F
B. CTRL+ALT+T
C. End
D. ESC

Q73. What is the purpose of Snap View?
A. Delete model
B. Switch to nearest orthographic view
C. Save file
D. Rotate continuously

Q74. Which key performs Snap View operation?
A. F5
B. F8
C. ESC
D. CTRL

Q75. What does Set Rotation Reference do?
A. Changes background
B. Defines rotation center point
C. Deletes model
D. Zooms model

Q76. What happens after using Clear Rotation Reference?
A. Model resets
B. Rotation center returns to geometric center
C. File closes
D. Zoom resets

Q77. What does Repeat Command menu show?
A. Saved files
B. Last 10 used commands
C. Deleted commands
D. Hidden commands

Q78. What is the shortcut for Undo?
A. CTRL+Y
B. CTRL+Z
C. CTRL+X
D. CTRL+S

Q79. What is the shortcut for Redo?
A. CTRL+Z
B. CTRL+X
C. CTRL+Y
D. CTRL+R

Chapter 2

Sketching

Topics Covered

The major topics covered in this chapter are:

- ***Starting Sketch***
- ***Sketch Curve Creation Tools***
- ***Curve Editing Tools***
- ***Dimensioning Tools***
- ***Geometric Constraints***

INTRODUCTION

In this chapter, we will learn about creating sketches. Sketches are the base features for most of the Parametric CAD software. There are various tools named similar to geometries entities like line, circle, spline, round, and so on. These tools when used together form a meaningful sketch. There is no separate environment in NX to create sketches. You can create sketches in Modeling, Sheetmetal, Assembly, and many other environments. We will discuss the sketching tools inside Modeling environment. You will find the same tools in other environments.

STARTING A SKETCH

- After starting NX and click on the **New** button from **Standard** group in the **Ribbon**. The **New** dialog box will be displayed.
- Specify desired name and location of file, and double-click on **Model** template in the **Templates** area. The Modeling environment will be displayed with three default planes in the graphics area; refer to Figure-1.

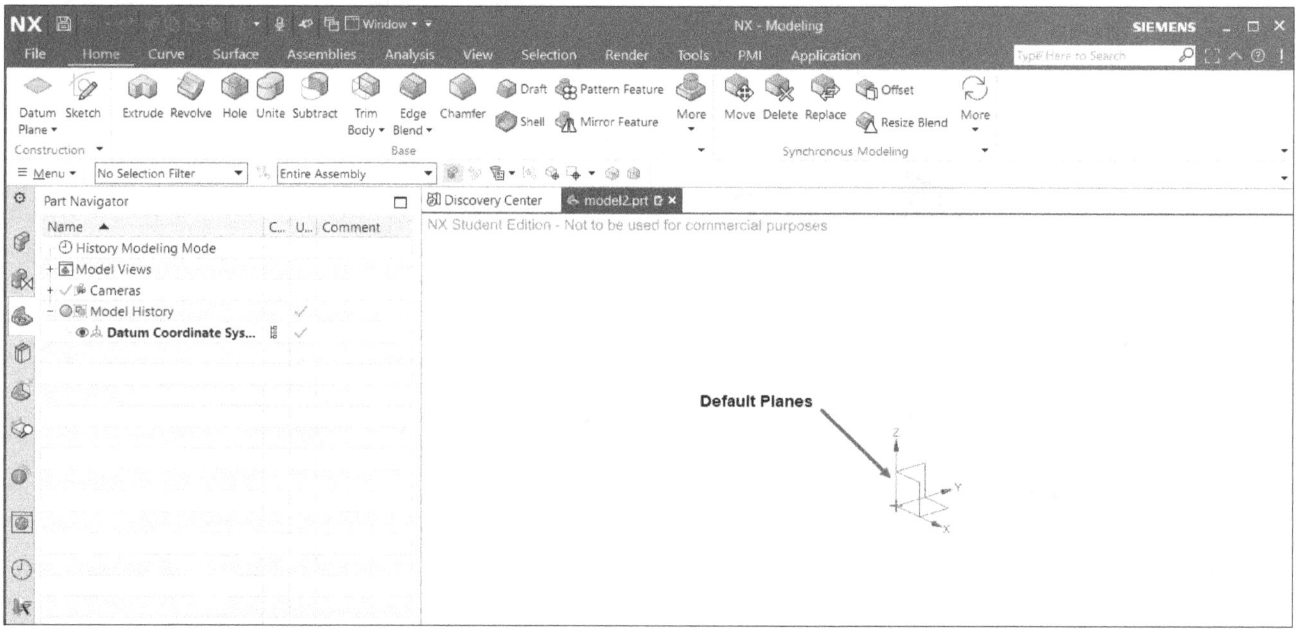

Figure-1. Modeling environment with default planes

- Click on the **Sketch** button from the **Construction** group in **Home** tab of the **Ribbon**. The **Create Sketch** dialog box will be displayed and you will be asked to select a sketching plane; refer to Figure-2.

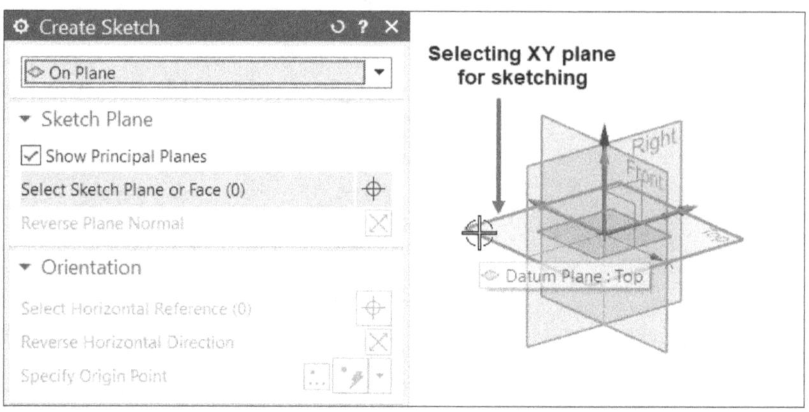

Figure-2. Selecting plane for sketching

- Select desired plane from the graphics window and click on the **OK** button. The sketching tools will become active in the **Home** tab of **Ribbon**.

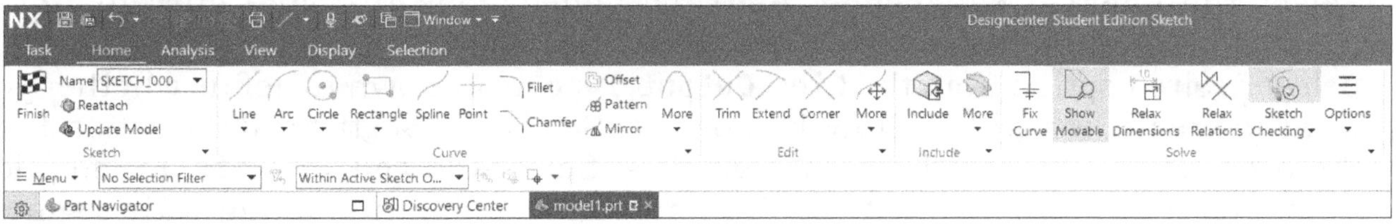

Figure-3. Direct Sketch group

Various tools in **Curve** group are discussed next.

CREATING LINES

The **Line** tool in the **Curve** group is used to create a string of lines. The procedure to use this tool is given next.

- After activating the sketch, click on the **Line** tool from the **Curve** group in the **Home** tab of **Ribbon**. The **Line** dialog box will be displayed; refer to Figure-4 and you will be asked to specify starting point for line. You can also activate this tool by pressing **Z** key from keyboard.

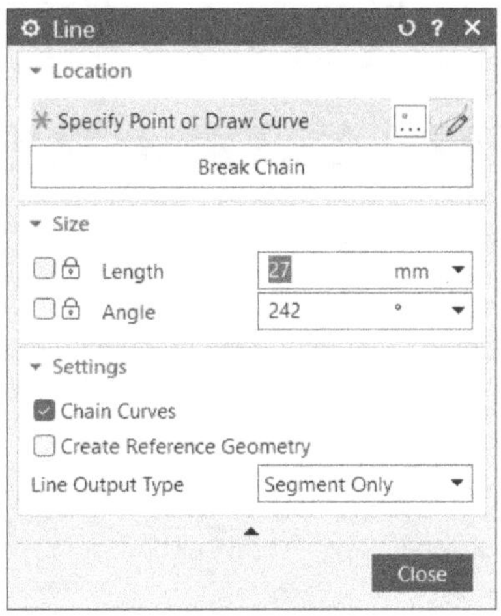

Figure-4. Line dialog box

- Click at desired location to specify starting point of line.
- Specify desired values of length and angle of line in respective edit boxes of the **Size** rollout. X and Y coordinate values in respective edit boxes of dynamic input box or click at desired location to define end point of the line. Press **TAB** to switch between two input boxes; refer to Figure-5.

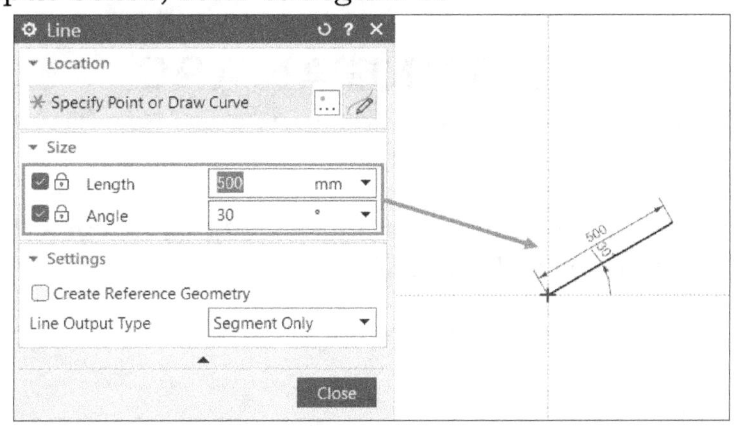

Figure-5. Creating line

- Select the **Chain Curves** check box to enable continuous line creation after specifying end point of line.
- Select the **Create Reference Geometry** check box to make current line a construction geometry.
- Select desired option from the **Line Output Type** drop-down to define whether you want to create line with infinite line or not. Select the **Segment Only** option from the drop-down to create lines in segments. Select the **Add Infinite Line** option from the drop-down to create an infinite construction line along with segment of line. Select the **Infinite Line Only** option from the drop-down to create only infinite construction line.
- Select the **Break Chain** button from the **Location** rollout after creating chain of lines to start a new chain.
- After setting desired parameters, click on the **Close** button to exit the tool.

CREATING LINE FROM MIDPOINT

The **Line from Midpoint** tool is used to create a line by specifying midpoint and end point of the line segment. The procedure is given next.

- Click on the **Line from Midpoint** tool from the **Line** drop-down in the **Curve** panel of **Home** tab in the **Ribbon**. The **Line From Midpoint** dialog box will be displayed; refer to Figure-6.

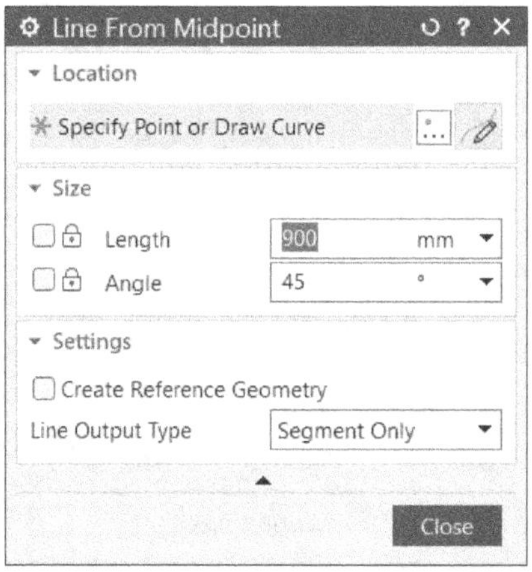

Figure-6. Line From Midpoint dialog box

- Set the parameters as discussed earlier in the dialog box and click at desired location to place the line.
- After setting desired parameters and creating line, click on the **Close** button.

CREATING AN ARC

The **Arc** tool is used to create geometric arc in the sketch. The procedure to create arc is given next.

- Click on the **Arc** tool from the **Curve** panel in the **Home** tab of **Ribbon**. The **Arc** dialog box will be displayed; refer to Figure-7.

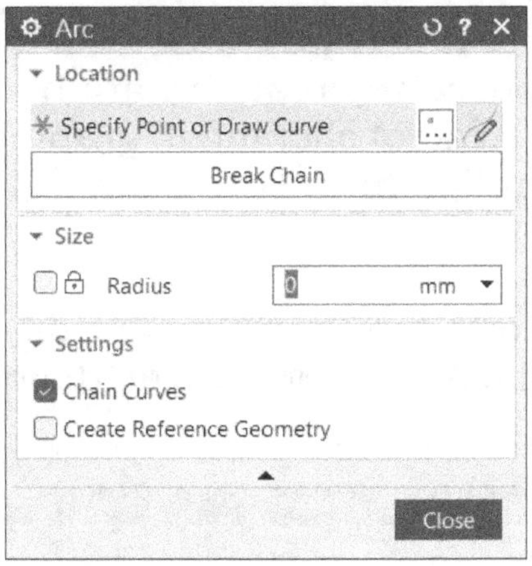

Figure-7. Arc dialog box

- Click at desired location to specify start point of arc. You will be asked to specify end point of the arc.
- Click at desired location to specify the end point of arc. You will be asked to specify a point on circumference of arc or value of radius in **Radius** edit box in the dialog box.
- Enter desired radius value in the edit box or click in the graphics area to define radius of arc; refer to Figure-8.

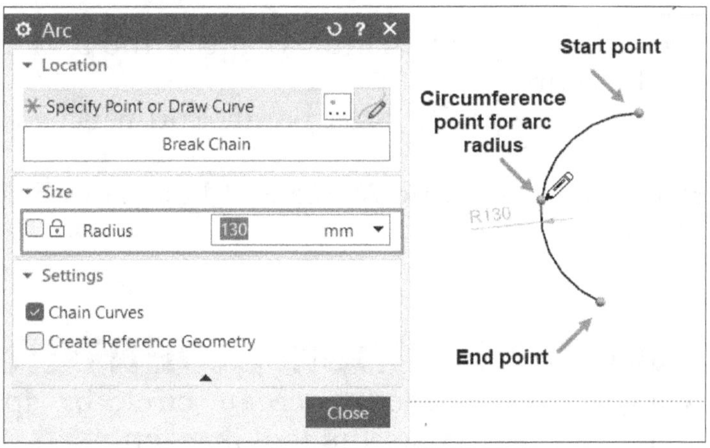

Figure-8. Defining arc points

- Set the other options as discussed earlier in the dialog box and press **ESC** key to exit the tool.

Tip: When you draw an arc starting from another arc or line and you follow the curvature of that arc/line after specifying the start point then a tangential arc is created automatically; refer to Figure-9.

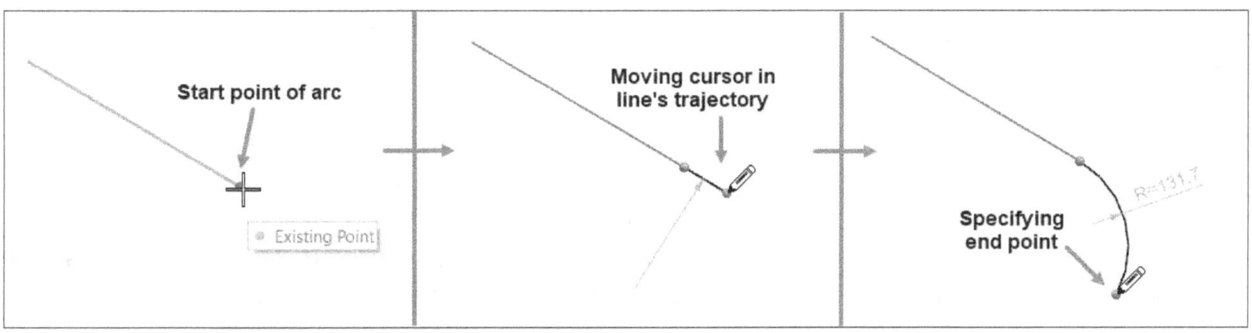

Figure-9. Creating tangential arc

CREATING ARC USING CENTER

The **Arc from Center** tool is used to create an arc by specifying center point, start point and end point of arc. Instead of clicking in graphics area for end point, you can specify radius and angle of end point in edit boxes of the dialog box. The procedure to use this tool is given next.

- Click on the **Arc from Center** tool from the **Arc** drop-down in the **Curve** panel of **Home** tab in the **Ribbon**. The **Arc From Center** dialog box will be displayed; refer to Figure-10.

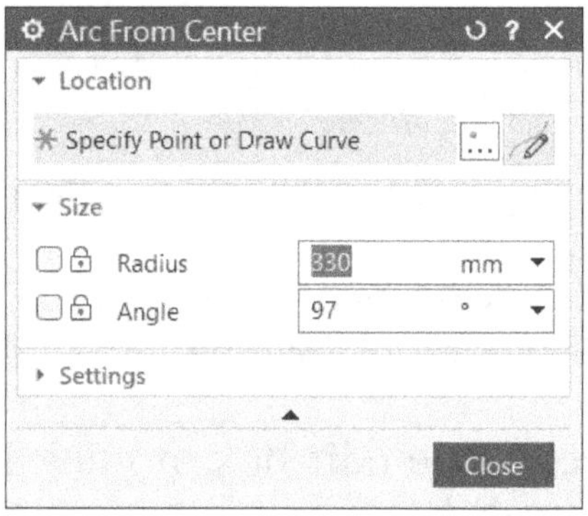

Figure-10. Arc From Center dialog box

- Click at desired location to specify center point of the arc. You will be asked to specify start point of the arc.
- Click at desired location to specify start point. You will be asked to specify end point of the arc.
- Set desired values in the **Radius** and **Angle** edit boxes or click at desired location to define end point of arc.
- Press **ESC** to exit the tool.

CREATING CIRCLE USING CENTER POINT

The **Circle** tool in **Curve** group is used to create circle by specifying center and diameter/radius. The procedure to use this tool is given next.

- Click on the **Circle** tool from the **Curve** group in the **Home** tab of the **Ribbon**. The **Circle** dialog box will be displayed and you will be asked to specify the center point of the circle; refer to Figure-11.

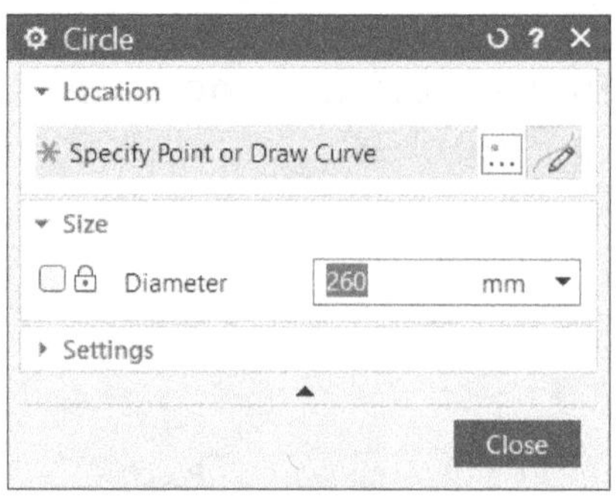

Figure-11. Circle dialog box

- Click at desired location to specify center point of the circle. You will be asked to specify circumferential point or diameter of the circle.

- Click at desired location in graphics area to define diameter of the circle or enter desired diameter value of circle in the **Diameter** edit box of the dialog box; refer to Figure-12.

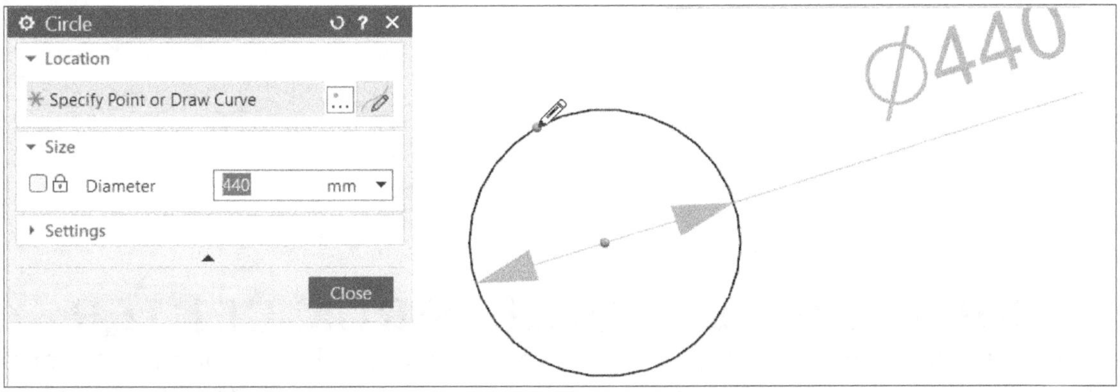

Figure-12. Creating circle

- Set the other parameters as discussed earlier and click on the **Close** button to exit the dialog box.

CREATING CIRCLE BY 3 POINTS

The **Three Point Circle** tool is used to create a circle by specifying 3 circumferential points. The procedure to use this tool is given next.

- Click on the **Three Point Circle** tool from the **Circle** drop-down of the **Curve** panel of **Home** tab in the **Ribbon**. You will be asked to specify first point of the circle.
- One by one click at three points to create the circle; refer to Figure-13. The circle will be created. Press **ESC** to exit the tool.

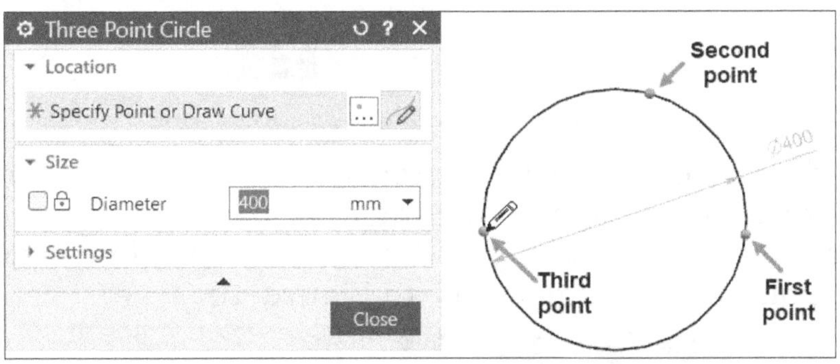

Figure-13. Creating three point circle

CREATING RECTANGLE BY TWO CORNER POINTS

The **Rectangle** tool is used to create rectangle by specifying two diagonal corner points. The procedure to create rectangle is given next.

- Click on the **Rectangle** tool from **Curve** group in **Home** tab of the **Ribbon**. The **Rectangle** dialog box will be displayed; refer to Figure-14 and you will be asked to specify first point of rectangle.
- Click at desired location to specify start point of rectangle. You will be asked to specify other diagonal corner point of the rectangle.
- Set desired values of width and height of rectangle or click at desired location to create the rectangle.

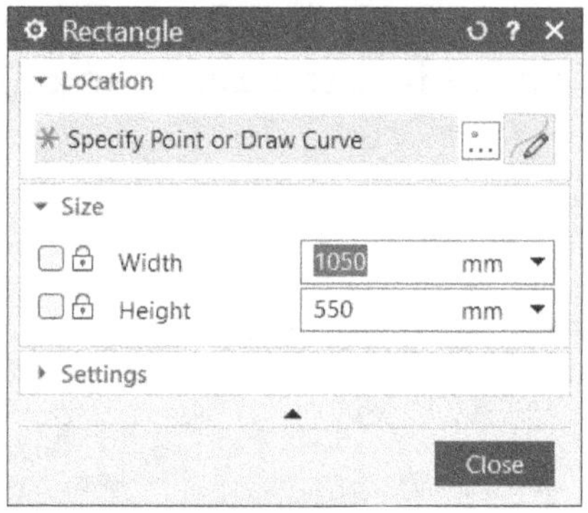

Figure-14. Rectangle dialog box

CREATING RECTANGLE FROM CENTER

The **Rectangle from Center** tool is used to create rectangle by specify center point of rectangle and points on side of rectangle. The procedure to use this tool is given next.

- Click on the **Rectangle from Center** tool from the **Rectangle** drop-down in the **Curve** panel of **Home** tab in the **Ribbon**. The **Rectangle from Center** dialog box will be displayed; refer to Figure-15.

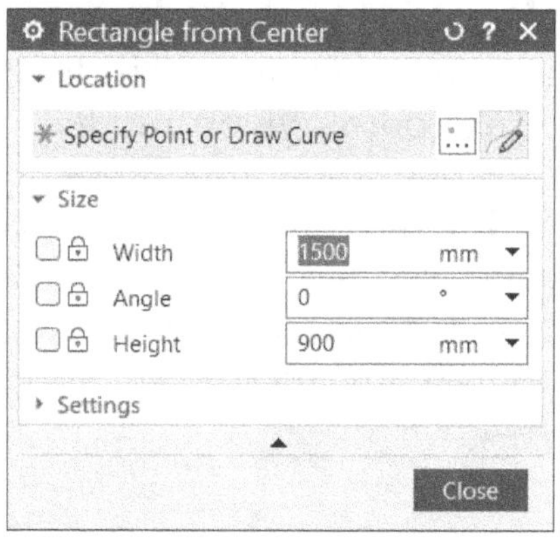

Figure-15. Rectangle from Center dialog box

- Click at desired location to specify center point of rectangle. You will be asked to specify end point of center line of rectangle.
- Click at desired location to specify end point of center line. You will be asked to specify corner point of rectangle; refer to Figure-16.

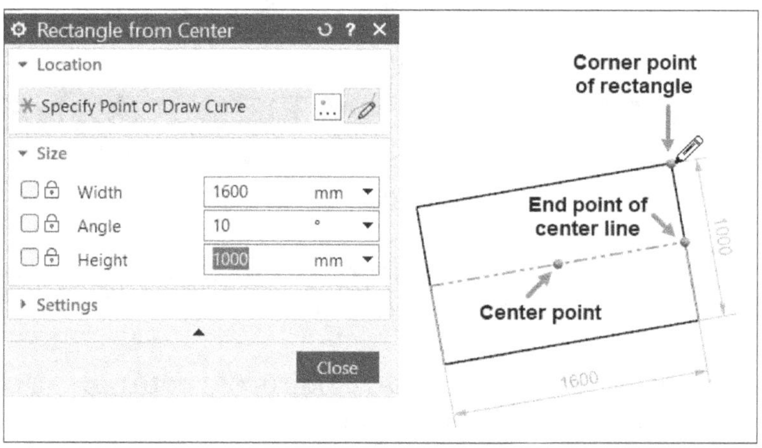

Figure-16. Creating rectangle from center

- Click at desired location to create the rectangle.

- You can create rectangle by specifying desired parameters in the edit boxes of **Size** rollout to define width, height and orientation angle of rectangle. After specifying these parameters, click at desired location to place the rectangle.

CREATING RECTANGLE BY 3 POINTS

The **Rectangle by Three Points** tool is used to create a rectangle by specifying three corner points of rectangle. The procedure to use this tool is given next.

- Click on the **Rectangle by Three Points** tool from the **Rectangle** drop-down in the **Curve** panel of **Home** tab in the **Ribbon**. The **Rectangle by Three Points** dialog box will be displayed; refer to Figure-17.

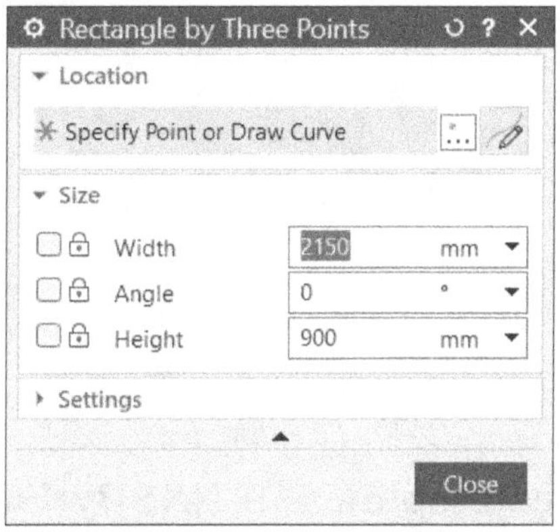

Figure-17. Rectangle by Three Points dialog box

- Click at desired location to define start point of base line of rectangle. The end point of base line will get attached to cursor and you will be asked to specify the width, height, and angle for the rectangle.
- Click to specify end point of base line. You will be asked to define height of the rectangle.
- Click at desired location to define height and side of rectangle; refer to Figure-18.

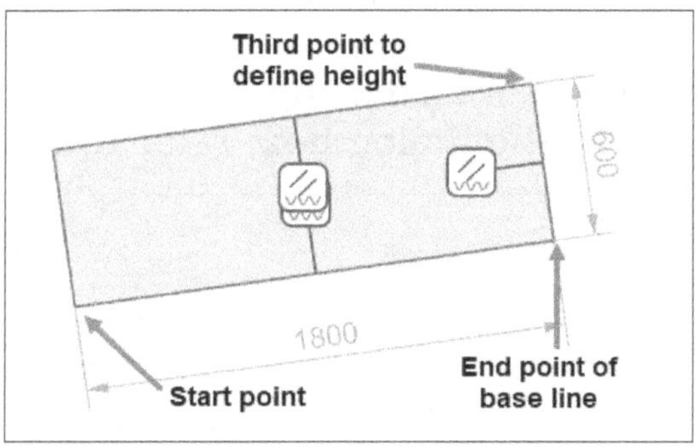

Figure-18. Creating rectangle by three points

- After creating rectangle, press **ESC** to exit the tool.

The other options are same as discussed earlier.

CREATING STUDIO SPLINE

The **Spline** tool from **Curve** group of **Ribbon** is used to create splines in the sketch. Splines are generally used in reverse engineering applications. The procedure to use this tool is given next.

- Click on the **Spline** tool from the **Curve** group of the **Home** tab in the **Ribbon**. The **Studio Spline** dialog box will be displayed; refer to Figure-19.

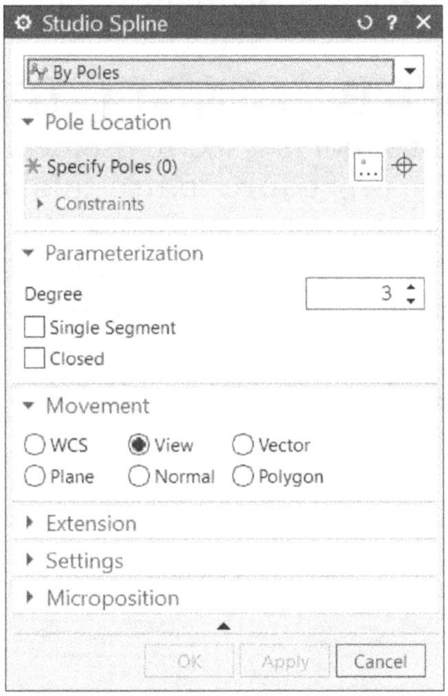

Figure-19. Studio Spline dialog box

There are two methods to create splines in NX; By Poles and Through Points. We will first discuss the method to create spline by using poles and then we will discuss the method of using points.

Creating Spline by Poles

- By default, the **By Poles** option is selected in the drop-down at the top in the dialog box. If not selected in your case, then select the **By Poles** option. The **Studio Spline** dialog box should display as shown in Figure-19.
- Click in the graphics window at desired locations or points to specify control points for spline.
- Specify the number of degrees for creating the spline curve in **Degree** edit box of **Parameterization** rollout in the dialog box; refer to Figure-20.

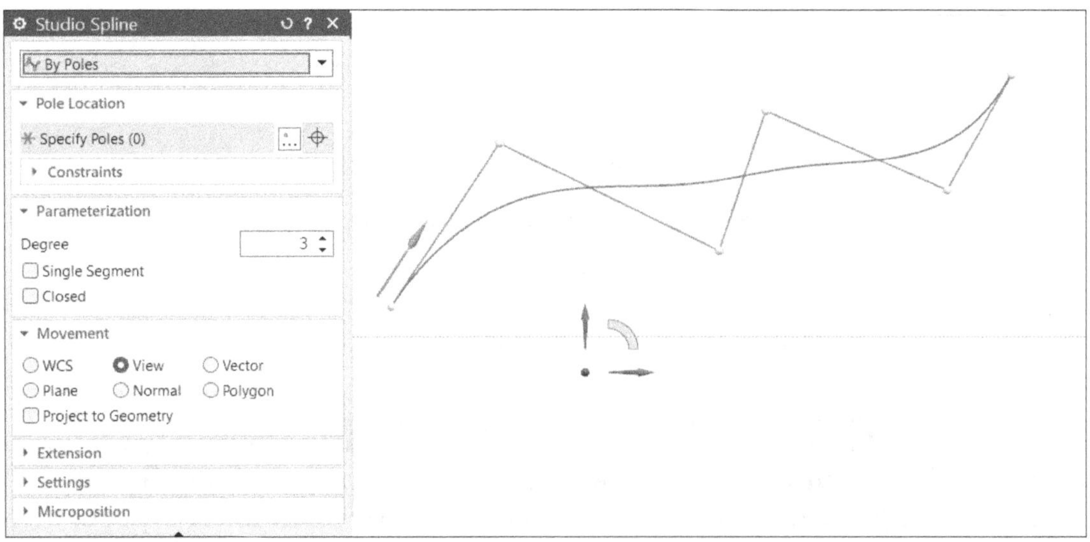

Figure-20. Creating spline using poles

- Select the **Single Segment** check box to create a spline controlled by poles and one degree lesser than the value specified in the **Degree** edit box.
- Select the **Closed** check box to connect the starting and end points of spline; refer to Figure-21.

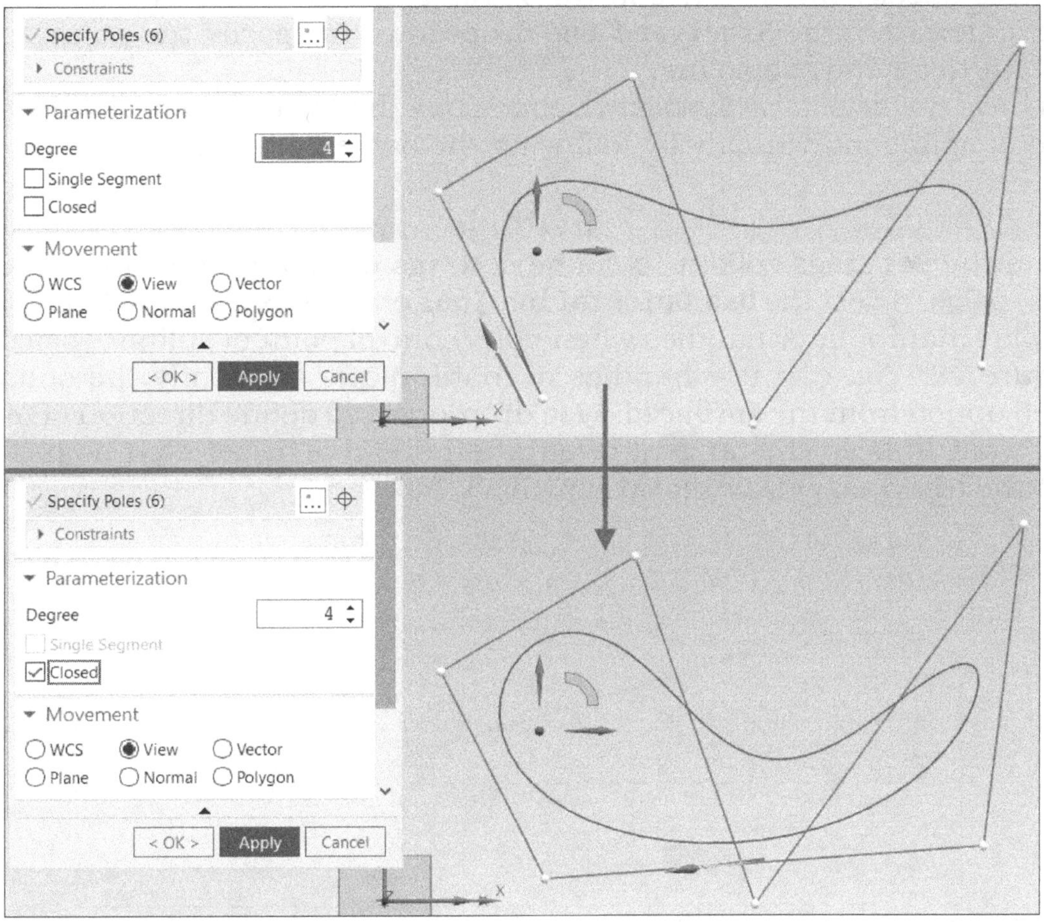

Figure-21. Creating closed spline

- Select desired movement option from the **Movement** rollout of the dialog box to define in which direction the spline poles/points can move when you drag them.

Extension Options

- Expand the **Extension** rollout to specify distance by which you want to extend the spline at its end points. The options will be displayed as shown in Figure-22.

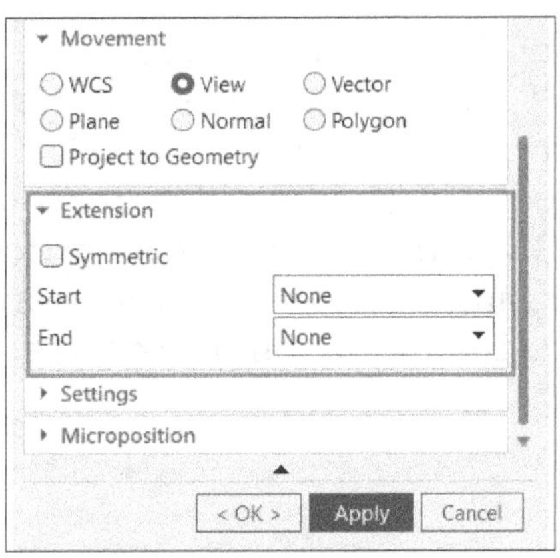

Figure-22. Extension rollout

- Select the **Symmetric** check box from the **Extension** rollout if you want to extend the start point and end point of spline by equal distance. The **Start** and **End** drop-downs will be replaced by a single drop-down named **Start and End**. Select **By Value** option from the **Start and End** drop-down to extend the spline by specified value and specify the distance in the **Value** edit box below drop-down. Select **By Point** option from the **Start and End** drop-down to specify the point upto which you want to extend the spline.
- If you have not select the **Symmetric** check box then you can specify the extension length of spline individually by following the same method.

Settings

- Expand the **Settings** rollout to define settings of manipulator for spline control points/poles. Select the **Use Orientation Tool** check box from the **Settings** rollout to display manipulator handles when pole/control point of spline is selected; refer to Figure-23. You can use handles of manipulator to modify the spline. Select desired option from the **Inferred Type** drop-down to define direction of movement. If you want to keep the tangent orientation of curve at selected point fixed then select the **Fix Tangent Orientation** check box.

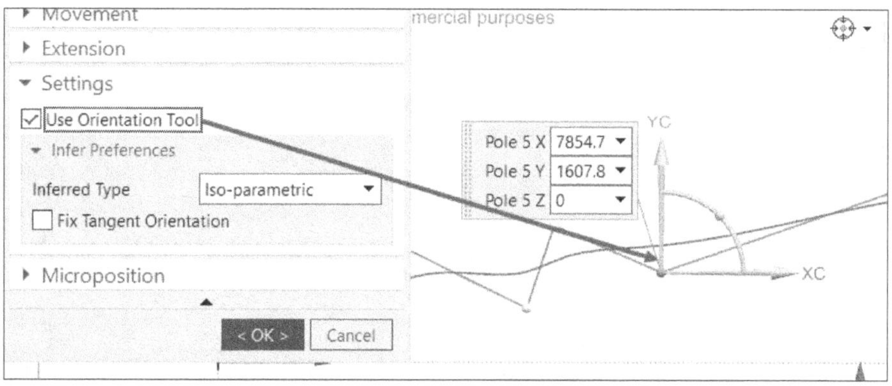

Figure-23. Orientation tool

Microposition Options

- Expand the **Microposition** rollout to define parameters for reducing movement of cursor when modifying position of control point/pole. Select the **Rate** check box and set desired value using the slider to define the amount by which cursor movement will be reduced.
- After setting desired parameters and performing the manipulation, click on the **OK** button from the dialog box to create the spline.

Note that if you are using points of other curves to create splines then options to define curvature of spline will be displayed just after clicking on the points; refer to Figure-24. Select desired curvature option from G1, G2, and G3. Select G1 option to create tangent curve. Select G2 to align 2 control vertices of spline with select end point curvature. Select G3 to align 4 control vertices of spline. Select G0 which is generally default option to make straight connection. You can also select desired curvature option from **Constraints** sub-rollout of **Pole Location** rollout in the dialog box; refer to Figure-25.

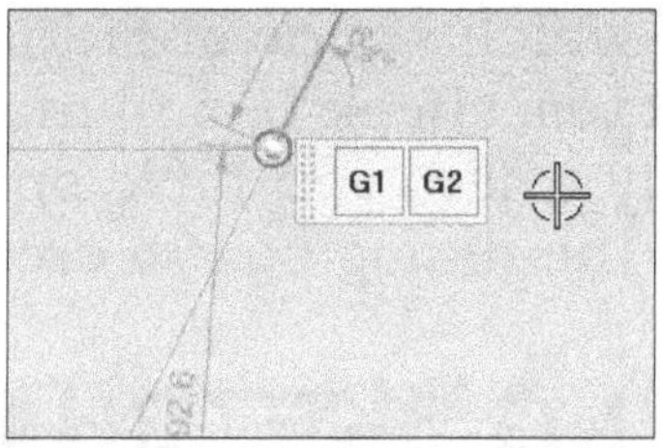

Figure-24. Options displayed for curvature

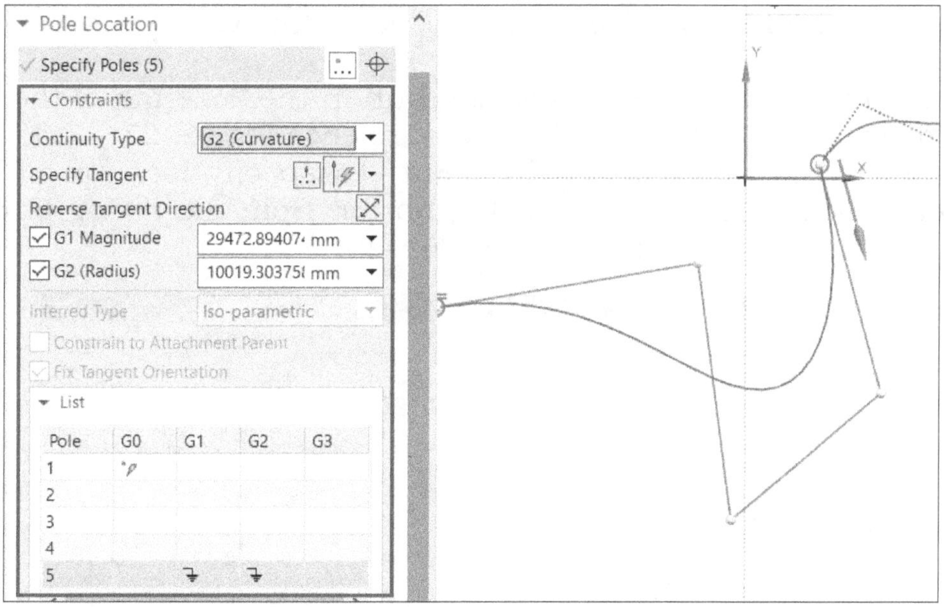

Figure-25. Constraints sub-rollout

- Click on the **OK** button from the dialog box to create the spline.

Creating Spline Through Points

- Select the **Through Points** option from the drop-down at the top in the **Studio Spline** dialog box. The options in the dialog box will be displayed as shown in Figure-26.

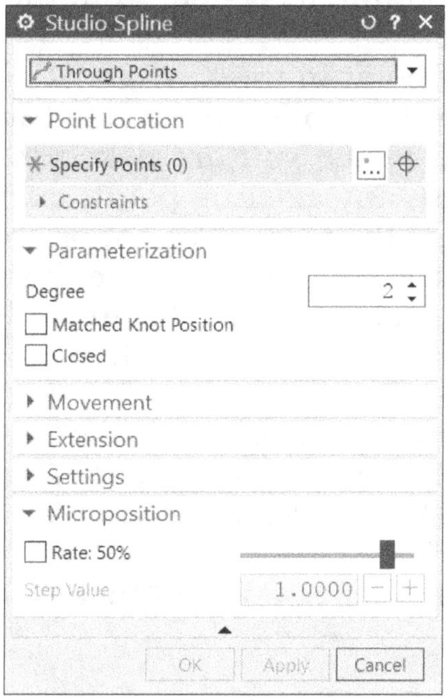

Figure-26. Studio Spline dialog box with Through Points options

- Click on the points through which spline should pass.
- Select the **Match Knot Position** check box to match degree with knot positions. This option places knots only where you have specified the defining points.
- Click on the **OK** button from the dialog box to create the spline.

CREATING SKETCH POINTS

The **Point** tool in **Curve** group is used to create points in sketch. Points are mainly used as reference for other sketch entities. The procedure to use this tool is given next.

- Click on the **Point** tool from the **Curve** group in the **Home** tab of the **Ribbon**. The **Sketch Point** dialog box will be displayed; refer to Figure-27.
- Click at desired location to specify point. To specify location of point using parameters, click on the **Point Dialog** button from the dialog box. The **Point** dialog box will be displayed; refer to Figure-28.

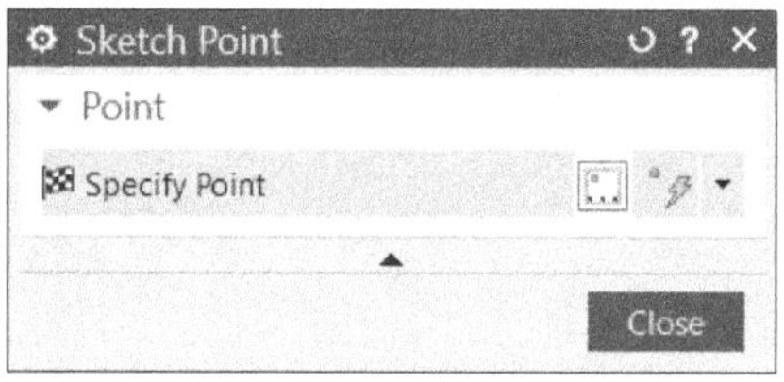

Figure-27. Sketch Point dialog box

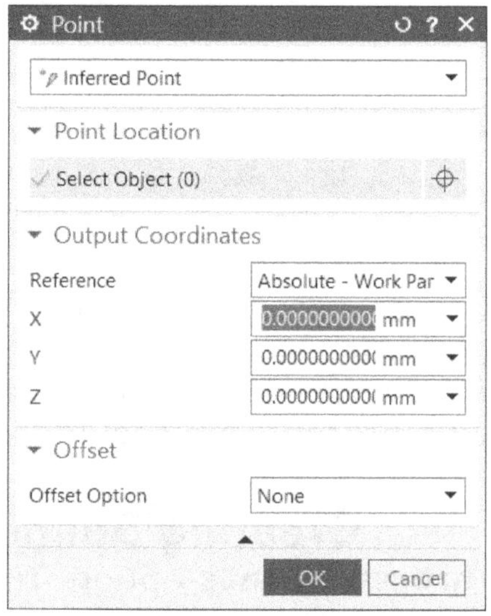

Figure-28. Point dialog box

- Select desired reference coordinate system from the **Reference** drop-down in the dialog box.
- Specify the coordinates of point in the **X**, **Y**, and **Z** edit boxes.
- In our case, **Cursor Location** option is selected in the **Type** drop-down at the top in the dialog box and hence you are asked to click for specifying location of point. If you want to use any existing point, curve, other geometry to specify location of point then select the respective option from the drop-down and select the references; refer to Figure-29. For example, if you want to create a quadrant point on circle then select the **Quadrant Point** option from the **Type** drop-down in the dialog box and then click on the circle near desired quadrant point. The point will be created.
- Click on the **OK** button from the **Point** dialog box after specifying location of point. The **Sketch Point** dialog box will be displayed. You can select the same options from **Type** drop-down in **Sketch Point** dialog box which were available in **Type** drop-down of **Point** dialog box.
- After creating desired points, click on the **Close** button to exit the tool.

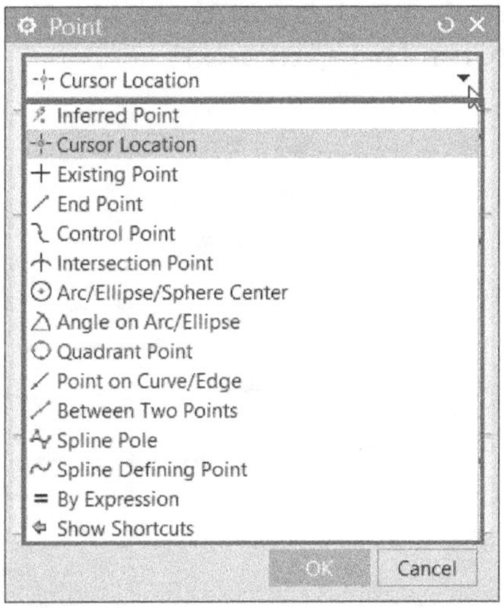

Figure-29. Type drop-down

APPLYING CHAMFER

Chamfer is applied in the sketch to bevel sharp corners formed by two lines. The procedure to apply chamfer is given next.

- Click on the **Chamfer** tool from the **Curve** group in the **Home** tab of the **Ribbon**. The **Chamfer** dialog box will be displayed; refer to Figure-30.
- Select the **Trim Input Curves** check box if you want to trim the lines where chamfer is being created.
- Select the **Symmetric** option from **Chamfer** drop-down if you want to create a chamfer which has equal distance in both sides. The **Distance** edit box will be displayed below the drop-down to specify the distance.
- Select the **Asymmetric** option from the **Chamfer** drop-down if you want to specify different distance values for both sides of chamfer. The **Distance 1** and **Distance 2** edit boxes will be displayed. Specify desired values of distances in both the edit boxes. Note that **Distance 1** is the distance of chamfer along first selected line.

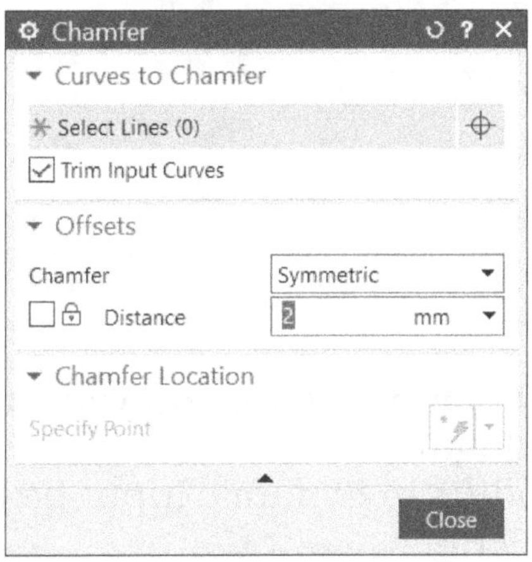

Figure-30. Chamfer dialog box

- Select the **Offset and Angle** option from the **Chamfer** drop-down if you want to specify distance and angle to define chamfer. The **Distance** and **Angle** edit boxes will be displayed below the drop-down. Set desired values for distance and angle. Note that both the distance and angle are measured from first selected line.
- After specifying desired values for chamfer, make sure to select the lock check boxes otherwise the chamfer will move with cursor.

- Select the two lines intersecting at a point where you want to apply chamfer. The chamfer will be created; refer to Figure-31.

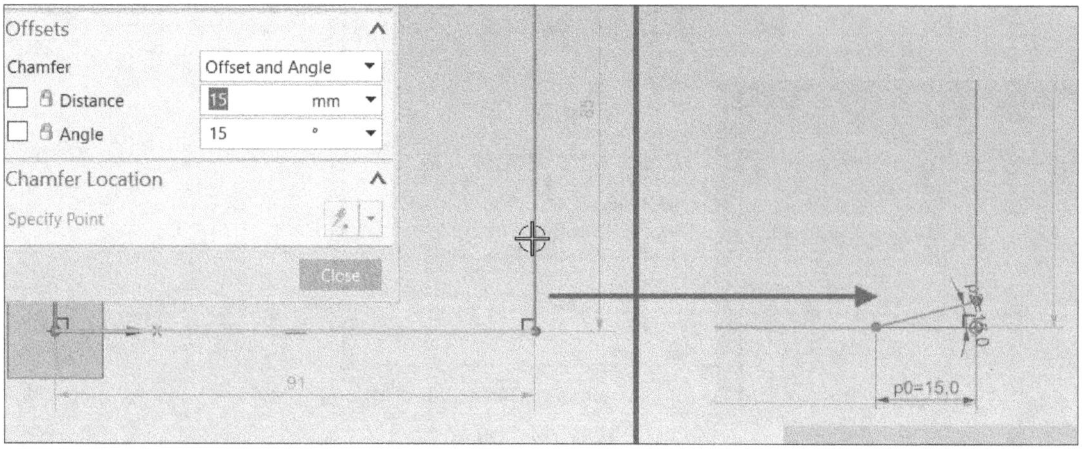

Figure-31. Creating chamfer

- Select other two lines in a set to create another chamfer. You can create as many chamfers as you want by selecting line sets. You can also modify the value of chamfer before selecting lines.
- Click on the **Close** button to exit the tool.

APPLYING FILLET

The **Fillet** tool is used to apply fillet/round between two or three curves. The procedure to use this tool is given next.

- Click on the **Fillet** tool from the **Curve** group in the **Home** tab of the **Ribbon**. The **Fillet** dialog box will be displayed; refer to Figure-32.

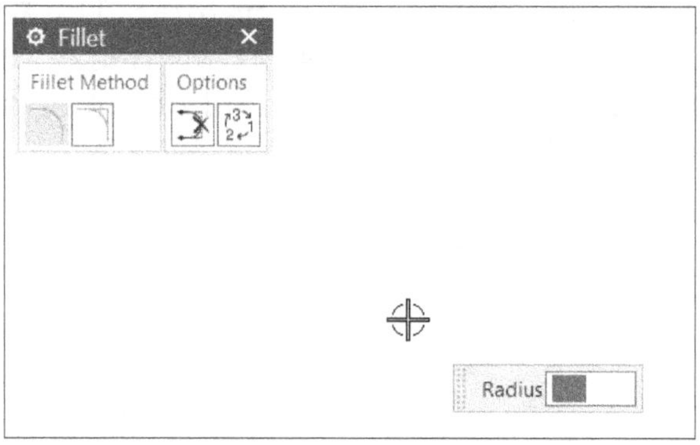

Figure-32. Fillet dialog box

- Select two sketch curves between which you want to apply fillet. Preview of fillet will be displayed; refer to Figure-33.
- Specify desired value of radius in dynamic input box and press **TAB**. The specified radius will get fixed for fillet.
- Now, click on desired side of selected curves to create fillet.
- Press Middle mouse button or press **ESC** to exit the tool.

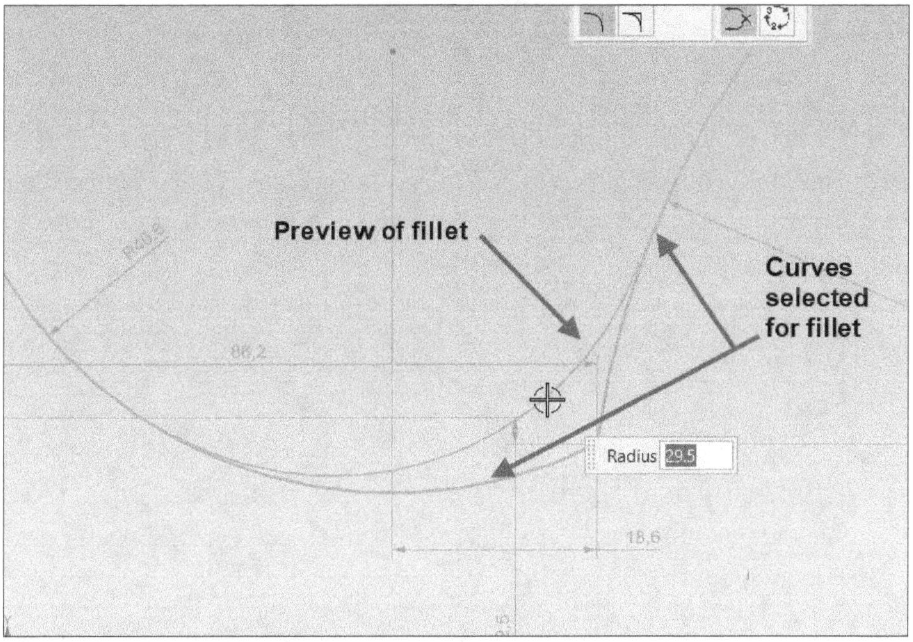

Figure-33. Preview of fillet

OFFSETTING CURVES

The **Offset** tool in the **Curve** group is used to create copy of selected curves at specified distance. The procedure to use this tool is given next.

- Click on the **Offset** tool from the **Curve** group in the **Home** tab of the **Ribbon**. The **Offset Curve** dialog box will be displayed; refer to Figure-34 and you will be asked to select the curves to be offsetted.

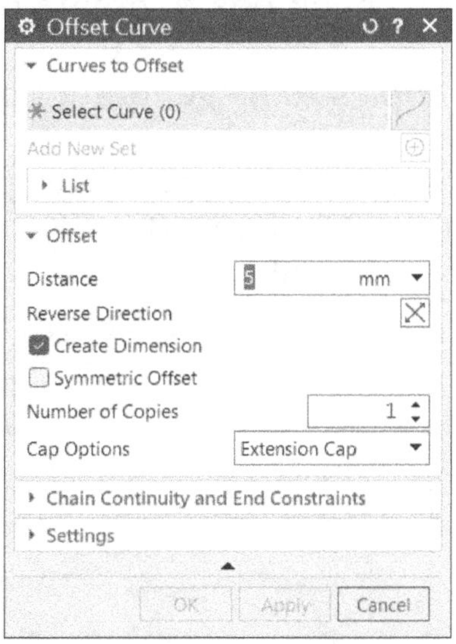

Figure-34. Offset Curve dialog box

- Select all the curves to be offsetted. Note that on selecting a curve of any chain, the software will automatically select the chain. If you want to select a single curve of curve chain then click in the **Curve Rule** drop-down below **Ribbon** in drawing area and select the **Single Curve** option; refer to Figure-35. Select the **Tangent Curves** option from this drop-down if you want to select all the curves that are tangent to selected curve. Select the **Curves in Group** option if you want to select group of select curve.
- On selecting the curve, preview of offsetted curves will be displayed; refer to Figure-36.

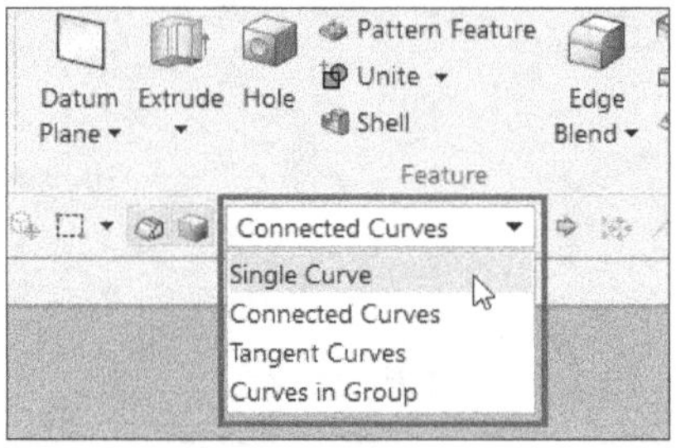

Figure-35. Curve Rule drop-down

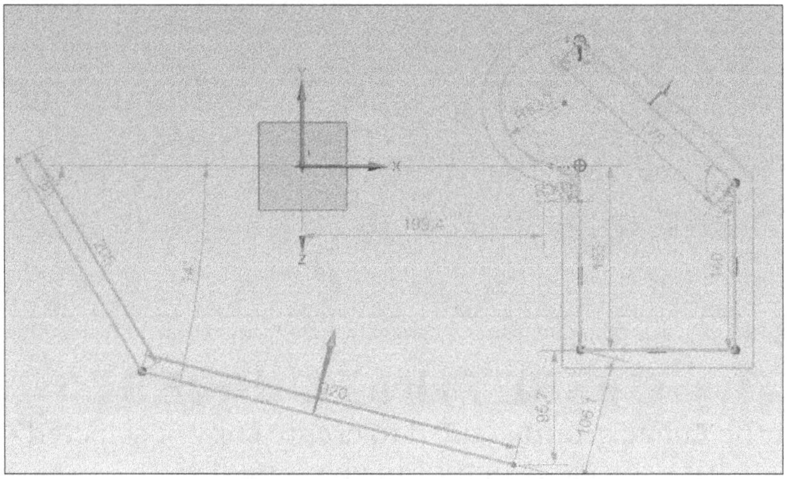

Figure-36. Preview of offsetted curves

- Specify desired value of offset distance in the **Distance** edit box.
- Click on the **Reverse Direction** button in the dialog box to flip the direction of offset.
- Select the **Symmetric Offset** check box to create offset on both sides of selected curves.
- Specify desired number of copies to be generated by specified distance in **Number of Copies** spinner.
- Select the **Arc Cap** option from the **Cap Options** drop-down if you want the corners to be in the form of arcs; refer to Figure-37. Select the **Extension Cap** option if you do not want to change corner style.

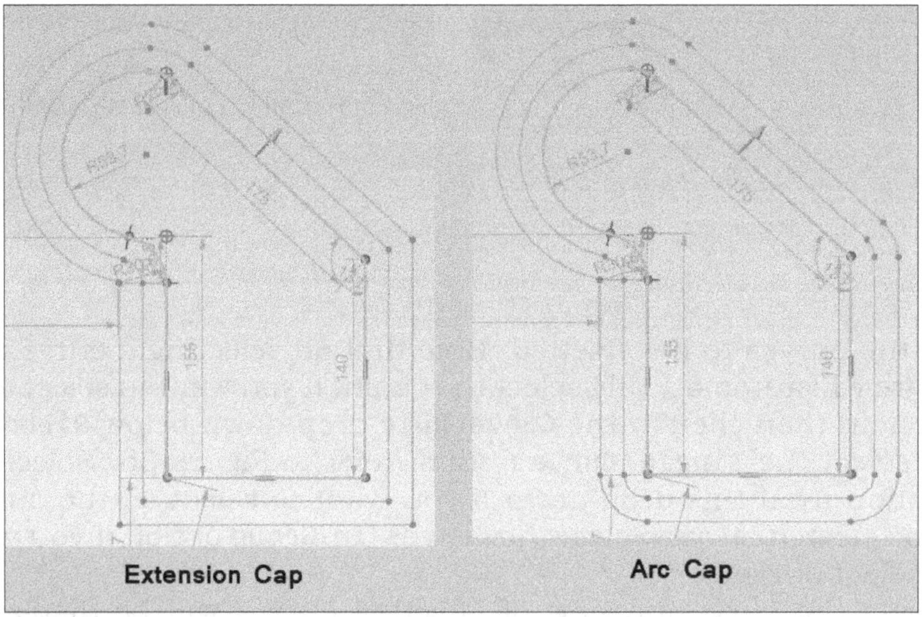

Figure-37. Cap options

- Expand the **Chain Continuity and End Constraints** rollout to define conditions for chain continuity of offset curves. Select the **Show Corners** check box if you want to display corners and select the **Show Ends** check box to display ends in the offsetted curves.
- Select the **Convert Input Curves to Reference** check box from the **Settings** rollout if you want to convert selected curves into reference curve. Select the **Create Persistent Relation** check box to create fixed relations between original curve and offset curve.
- Set desired number of degrees in the **Degree** edit box if you are offsetting studio spline.
- Click on the **OK** button to create offset copies of selected curves.

CREATING PATTERNS OF CURVES

The **Pattern** tool is used to create multiple copies of selected curves based on specified conditions. There are three types of patterns that can be created in NX during sketching; **Linear Pattern**, **Circular Pattern**, and **General Pattern**. The procedure to use this tool is given next.

- Click on the **Pattern** tool from the **Curve** group of the **Home** tab in the **Ribbon**. The **Pattern Curve** dialog box will be displayed; refer to Figure-38 and you will be asked to select the curves to be patterned.

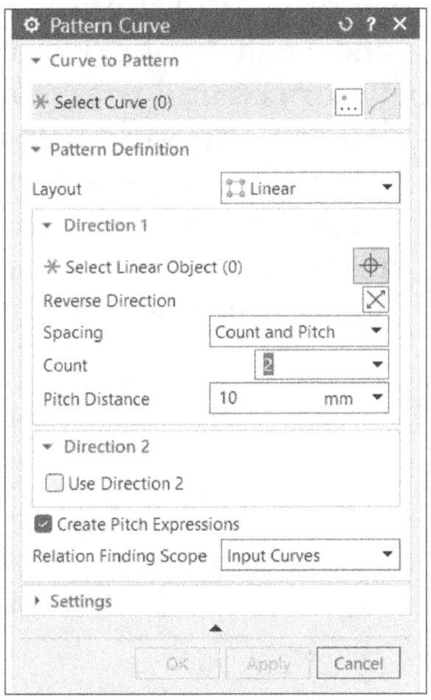

Figure-38. Pattern Curve dialog box

- Click on the curve to be patterned from the drawing area.

Creating Linear Pattern

- Select the **Linear** option from the **Layout** drop-down in the **Pattern Definition** rollout of the dialog box to create copies in X and Y directions.
- Click on the **Select Linear Object** selection button from the **Direction 1** sub-rollout. You will be asked to select direction reference.
- Select the axis, plane, or curve to be used as reference for linear direction. Preview of the pattern will be displayed; refer to Figure-39.

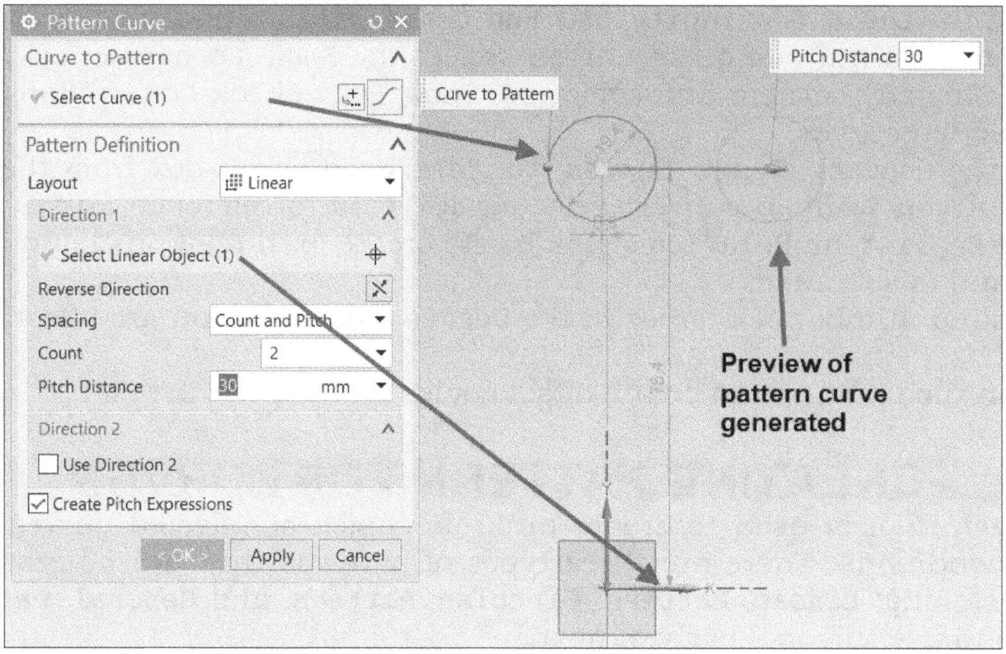

Figure-39. Preview of pattern curve

- Select the **Count and Pitch** option from the **Spacing** drop-down if you want to specify number of instances and distance between the two instances of selected curve. Select the **Count and Span** option from the **Spacing** drop-down if you want to specify number of instances and total distance within which the pattern will be created. Select the **Pitch and Span** option from the drop-down if you want to specify distance between two instances and the total span within which the pattern will be created. On selecting desired option in this drop-down, the respective edit boxes will become available below the drop-down.
- Specify desired parameters in edit boxes below the **Spacing** drop-down.
- To create pattern in second direction, select the **Use Direction 2** check box from **Direction 2** rollout in the dialog box and specify the parameter as discussed earlier; refer to Figure-40.

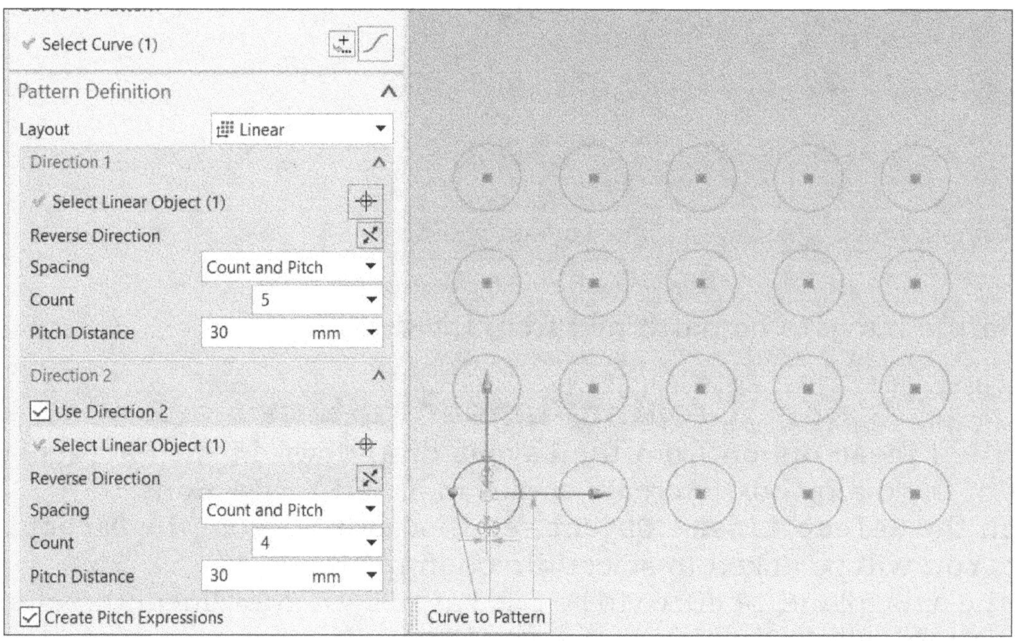

Figure-40. Preview of linear pattern in two directions

- Select the **Create Pitch Expressions** check box if you want to create an expression of pitch and pattern count while creating the pattern.
- Select the **Input Curves** option from the **Relation Finding Scope** drop-down if you want to create pitch expressions by using selected curves (used for creating pattern). Select the **No Finding to Pattern** option if you do not want to use original curve or pattern instances for creation pitch expressions. Select the **Selected Instances** option if you want to use only selected pattern instances for creating pitch expressions. Select the **All of Pattern** option from the drop-down if you want to use all the instances of current and earlier created patterns for creating pitch expression.
- Click on the **OK** button from the dialog box to create the pattern and exit the dialog box.

Creating Circular Pattern

- Select the **Circular** option from the **Layout** drop-down in **Pattern Curve** dialog box. The options in the dialog box will be displayed as shown in Figure-41.

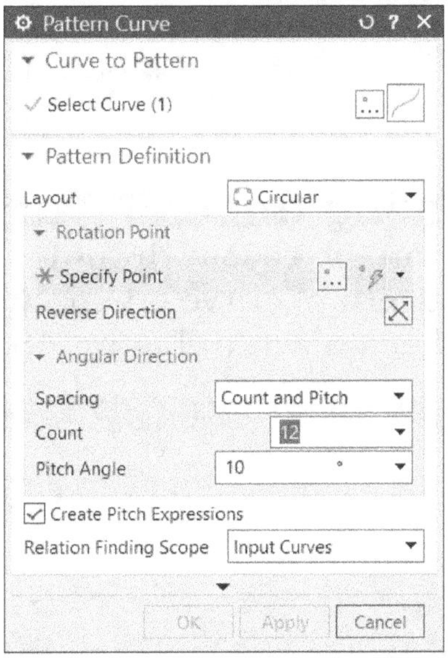

Figure-41. Pattern Curve dialog box for circular pattern

- Select the curves that you want to pattern in circular layout.
- Click on the **Specify Point** selection button from the **Rotation Point** section of **Pattern Definition** rollout and click on the point that you want to use as center for circular pattern. Preview of circular pattern will be displayed; refer to Figure-42.

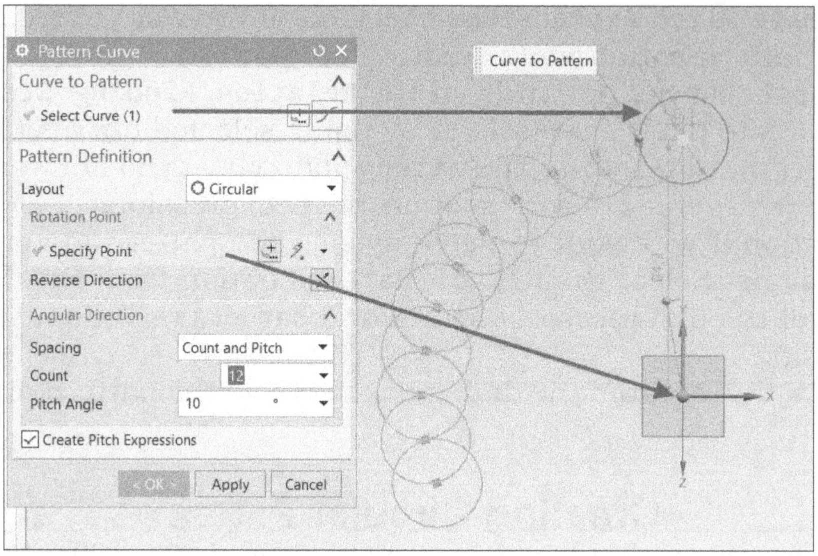

Figure-42. Preview of circular pattern

- Select desired option from **Spacing** drop-down and set desired parameters in edit boxes below the drop-down as discussed earlier.
- After setting the parameters, click on the **OK** button to create pattern and exit the dialog box.

Creating General Pattern

- Select the **General** option from the **Layout** drop-down in the **Pattern Curve** dialog box if you want to create pattern of curve on specified points. The options in the dialog box will be displayed as shown in Figure-43.

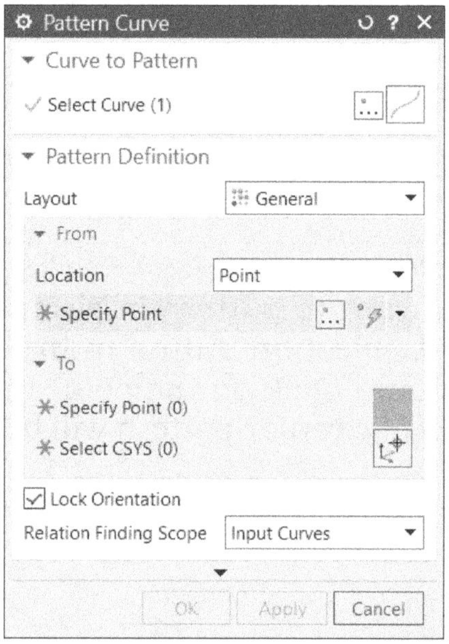

Figure-43. Pattern Curve dialog box for general pattern

- Select the curves to be patterned from the drawing area.
- Click on the **Specify Point** option from the **From** section in **Pattern Definition** rollout of the dialog box. You will be asked to specify the location which you want to use as reference point for creating pattern instances.

- Click on the **Specify Point** option from the **To** section in the **Pattern Definition** rollout and click at the locations where you want to create pattern instances; refer to Figure-44.

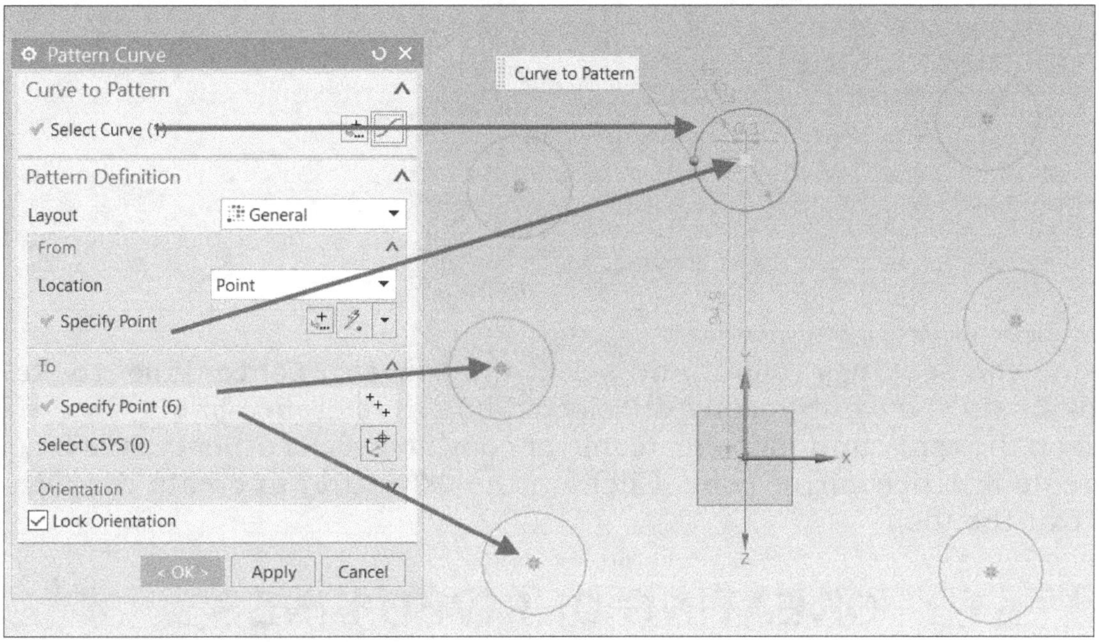

Figure-44. Preview of general pattern

- Click on the **OK** button from the dialog box to create the pattern and exit the dialog box.

MIRRORING CURVES

The **Mirror** tool in **Curve** group is used to create mirror copy of selected curves. The procedure to use this tool is given next.

- Click on the **Mirror** tool from the **Curve** group in the **Home** tab of **Ribbon**. The **Mirror Curve** dialog box will be displayed; refer to Figure-45.

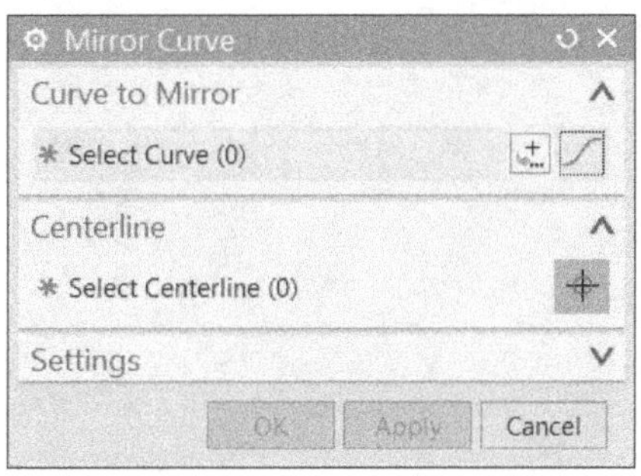

Figure-45. Mirror Curve dialog box

- Select the curves to be mirror copied.
- Click on the **Select Centerline** selection button from the **Centerline** rollout and select the line, axis, face, or plane to be used as centerline reference for mirroring. Preview of mirror will be displayed; refer to Figure-46.

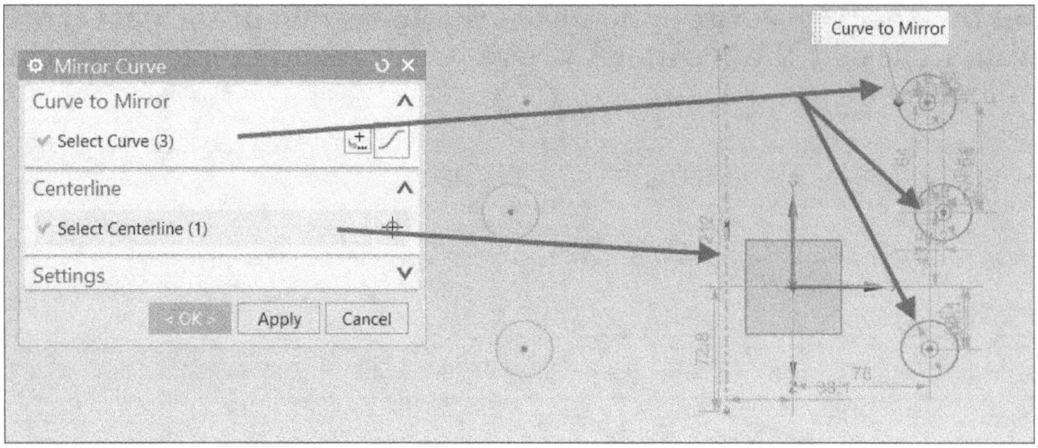

Figure-46. Preview of mirror curves

- Expand the **Settings** rollout and select the **Convert Centerline to Reference** check box if you want to convert selected line to reference line.
- Click on the **Apply** button to create mirror copy and select other curves & centerline to create another mirror copy. Click on the **OK** button to create the mirror copy and exit the tool.

CREATING DERIVED LINES

The **Derived Lines** tool in expanded **Sketch Curve** toolbox is used to offset selected lines or create a bisector line between two selected lines. The procedure to use this tool is given next.

- Click on the **Derived Lines** tool from the **More** drop-down of **Curve** group in the **Ribbon**. You will be asked to select a reference line.
- Select the line to be copied and offsetted. The offset copy will get attached to cursor; refer to Figure-47.

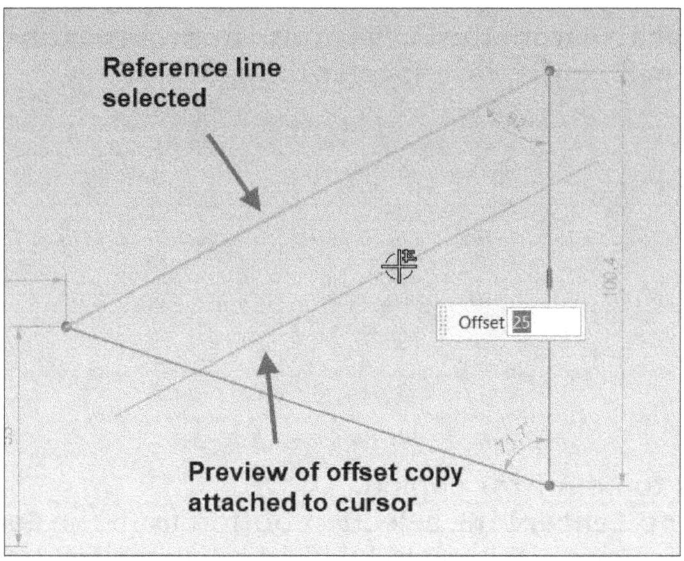

Figure-47. Preview of offsetted line

- Click at desired location to place the offsetted line or enter desired values in the input box.

- If you want to create a bisector line then select the other line without placing the offset line. Preview of bisector will be displayed; refer to Figure-48. Specify the length of bisector line by clicking at desired location or by entering the value in **Length** input box.

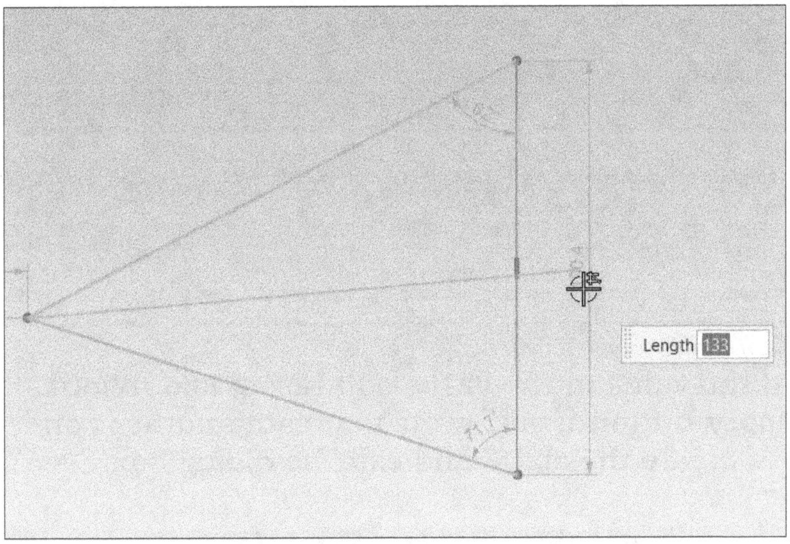

Figure-48. Preview of bisector line

- Press **ESC** to exit the tool.

CREATING CONIC CURVE

The **Conic** tool in the **More** drop-down of **Ribbon** is used to create conic curves with specified rho value. The procedure to use this tool is given next.

- Click on the **Conic** tool from the **More** drop-down of **Curve** group in the **Home** tab of the **Ribbon**. The **Conic** dialog box will be displayed; refer to Figure-49.

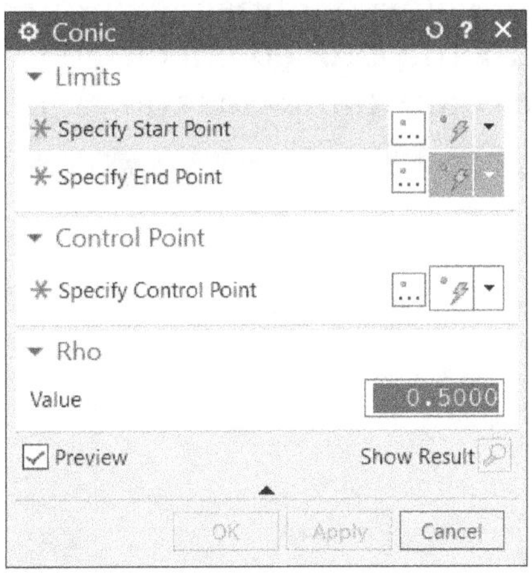

Figure-49. Conic dialog box

- Click at desired locations to specify start point, end point, and control point; refer to Figure-50.

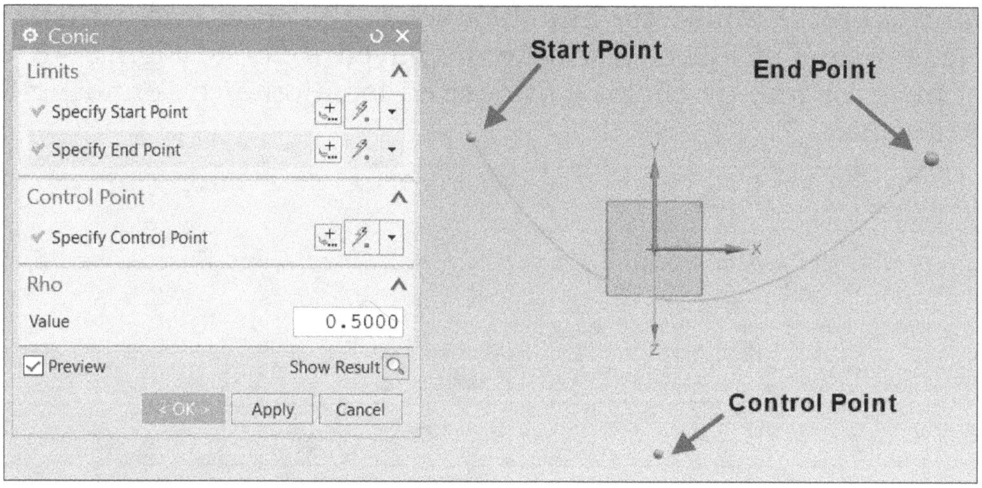

Figure-50. Specifying points for conic curve

- Specify desired rho value in the **Value** edit box of **Rho** rollout.
- Click on the **Apply** button if you want to create another conic curve or click on the **OK** button to create the curve and exit the dialog box.

CREATING ELLIPSE

The **Ellipse** tool in the **More** drop-down of **Curve** group is used to create ellipse in the sketch. The procedure to use this tool is given next.

- Click on the **Ellipse** tool from the **More** drop-down in the **Curve** group of the **Home** tab in the **Ribbon**. The **Ellipse** dialog box will be displayed; refer to Figure-51.
- Click at desired location to specify center of the ellipse. Preview of the ellipse will be displayed.
- Specify the value of major radius, minor radius, and rotation angle in respective edit boxes of the dialog box.
- By default, a full 360 degree closed ellipse is created. If you want to create a half or quarter ellipse then clear the **Closed** check box from the **Limits** rollout in the dialog box and specify the angle limits for the ellipse.

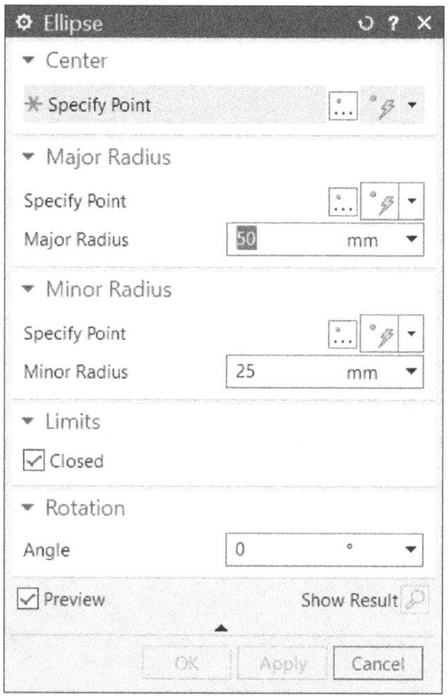

Figure-51. Ellipse dialog box

- After setting desired parameters, click on the **Apply** button if you want to create another ellipse and click on the **OK** button to create the ellipse and exit the dialog box.

CREATING SLOT

The **Slot** tool is used to create a closed loop slot in the graphics area. The procedure to use this tool is given next.

- Click on the **Slot** tool from the **More** drop-down in the **Curve** group of **Home** tab in the **Ribbon**. The **Slot** dialog box will be displayed; refer to Figure-52 and you will be asked to specify start point of centerline of slot.

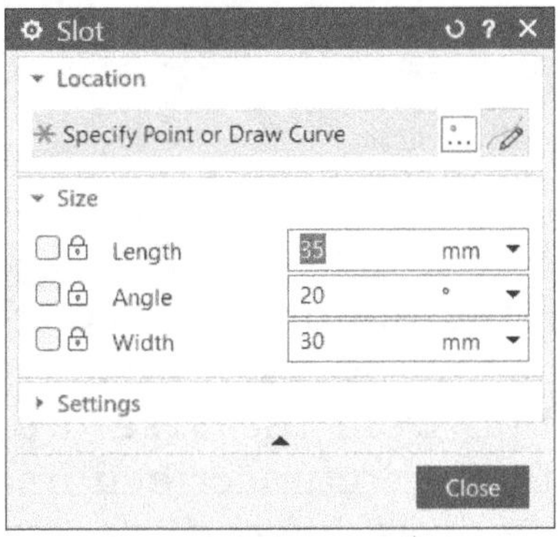

Figure-52. Slot dialog box

- Set desired values of length, width, and angle of slot in respective edit boxes of the **Size** rollout to define size of slot.
- After setting desired parameters, click at desired location to place the slot.
- Press **ESC** to exit the tool.

CREATING POLYGON

The **Polygon** tool is used to create polygon of desired number of sides. The procedure to use this tool is given next.

- Click on the **Polygon** tool from the **More** drop-down in the **Curve** group of the **Home** tab in the **Ribbon**. The **Polygon** dialog box will be displayed; refer to Figure-53.

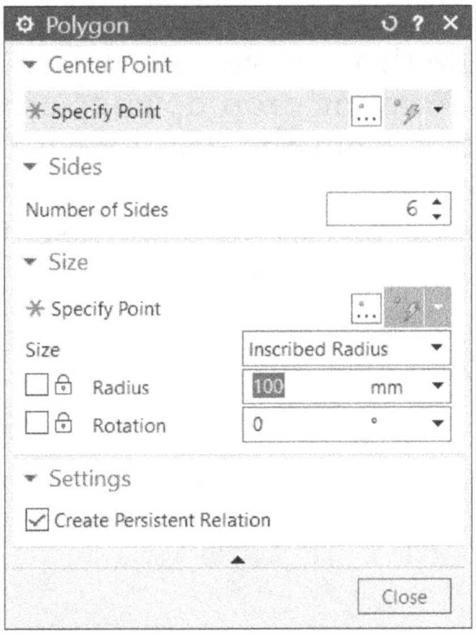

Figure-53. Polygon dialog box

- Click at desired location to place center point of the polygon. You will be asked to specify radius and rotation angle for polygon; refer to Figure-54.

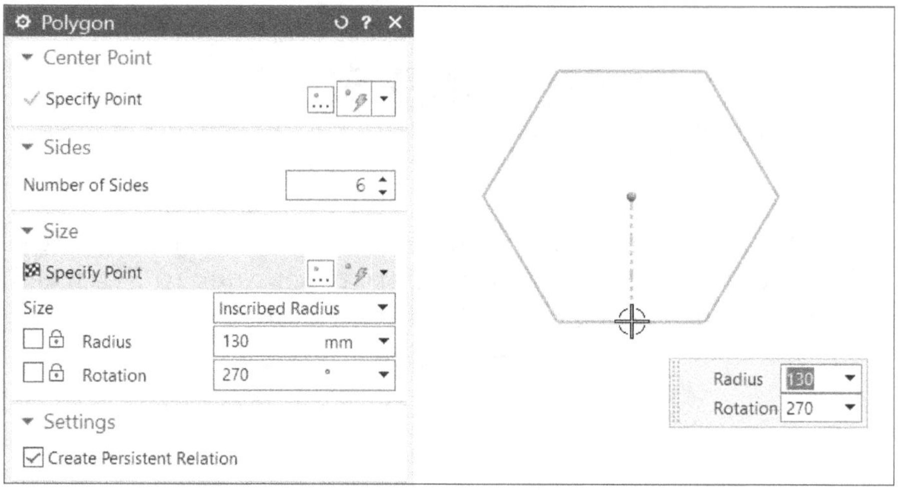

Figure-54. Creating polygon

- By default, **Inscribed Radius** option is selected in the **Size** drop-down and hence, you are asked to specify radius of inscribed imaginary circle. Select the **Circumscribed Radius** option from the **Size** drop-down if you want to create polygon by specifying radius of circumscribed imaginary circle. Select the **Side Length** option from the **Size** drop-down if you want to specify length of side of the polygon.
- After setting desired option in the drop-down, specify the parameters for polygon in respective edit boxes of the dialog box and press **ENTER**. The polygon will be created.
- Click on the **Close** button from the dialog box to exit the tool or press **ESC**.

FITTING CURVES

The **Fit Curve** tool is used to create various curves like spline, line, circle, and ellipse using selected points/vertices. The procedure to use this tool is given next.

- Click on the **Fit Curve** tool from the **More** drop-down in the **Curve** group of **Home** tab in the **Ribbon**. The **Fit Curve** dialog box will be displayed; refer to Figure-55.
- Select desired option from the drop-down at the top in the dialog box. Select the **Fit Spline** option from the drop-down to create a spline using selected points. Select the **Fit Line** option from the drop-down to create line using selected points. Select the **Fit Circle** option from the drop-down to create circle using selected points. Select the **Fit Ellipse** option from the drop-down to create an ellipse using selected points. The procedure to use these options is given next.

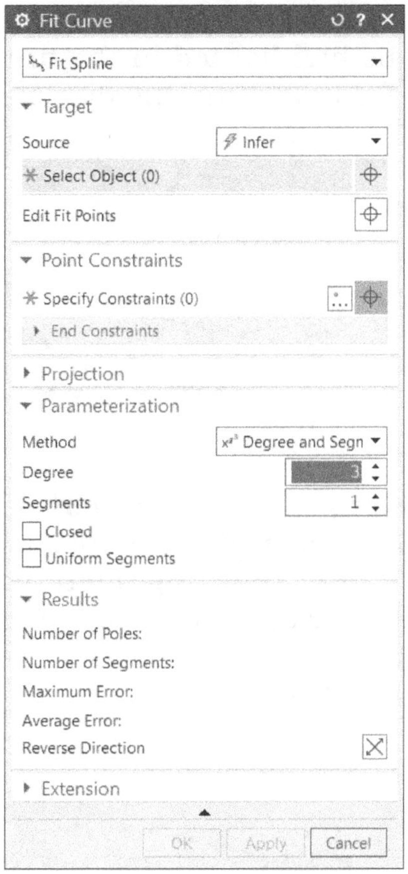

Figure-55. Fit Curve dialog box

Fitting Spline on Points

- Select the **Fit Spline** option from the drop-down to fit spline on selected points. The options will be displayed as shown in Figure-56.
- Select the **Specified points** option from the **Source** drop-down to use selected points for creating spline. Select the **Chained Points** option from the **Source** drop-down to use chain of points selected from drawing area. Select the **Curve** option from the drop-down to use selected curve as reference for generating spline. Select the **Infer** option from the **Source** drop-down to automatically select option from the drop-down based on selected entity from the drawing area. After selecting desired option, select the points/curves from drawing area. Preview of spline will be displayed; refer to Figure-56.

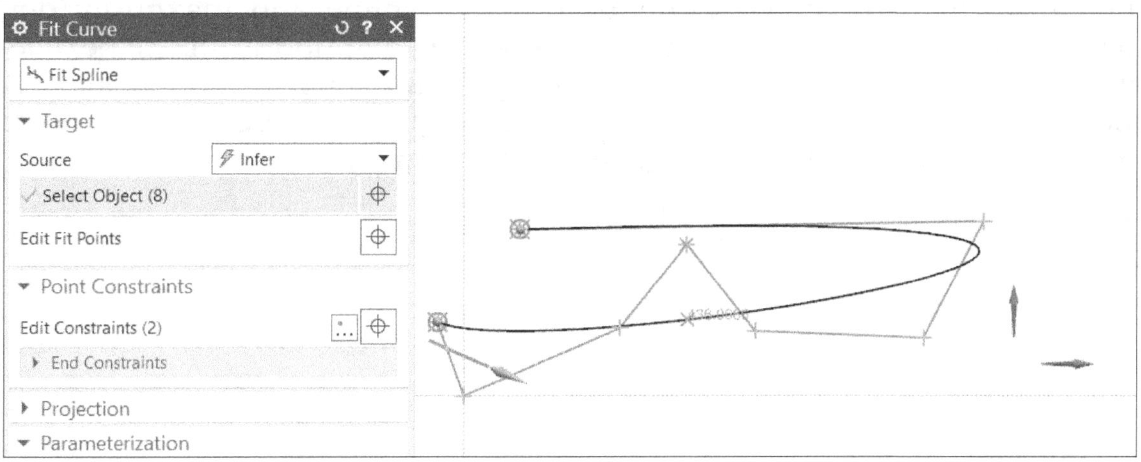

Figure-56. Preview of fit spline

- If you want to modify the position of fit points then click on the **Edit Fit Points** button. The fit points will be highlighted in the drawing area. Select a point and drag it to desired location for modifying the curve; refer to Figure-57.

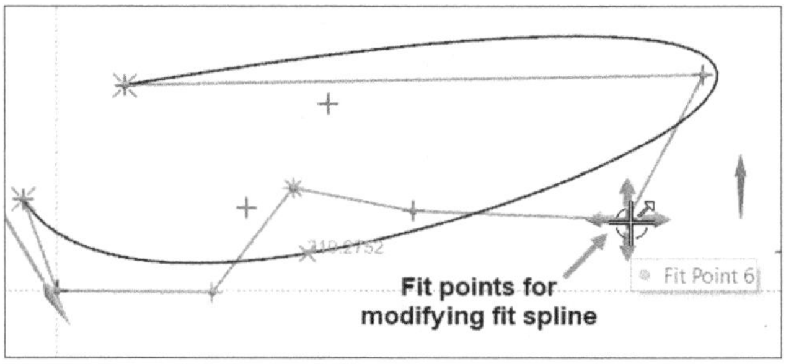

Figure-57. Fit point highlighted

- Expand the **End Constraints** rollout from **Point Constraints** section in the dialog box and select the **Start** or **End** radio button to define the point whose end conditions will be modified. After selecting the radio button, click on the **Specify Tangent** selection button and select reference curve (line) to be used as tangency reference; refer to Figure-58.

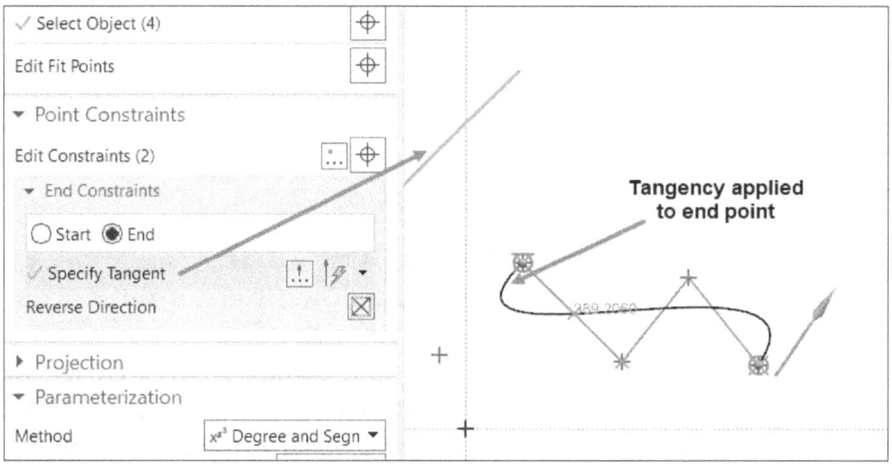

Figure-58. Tangency applied to point

- Expand the **Parameterization** rollout to define the method and degree of freedom for spline. Select **Degree and Segments** option from the **Method** drop-down in **Parameterization** rollout to create spline by specifying the polynomial order of spline and number of segments to be created. Select the **Degree and Tolerance** option from the drop-down to define order of spline and maximum deviation allowed from fit points. Select the **Template Curve** option from the **Method** drop-down to use selected curve as template for generating new curve passing through fit points; refer to Figure-59. Select the **Keep Template Curve Selected** check box to keep the template curve after generating fit curve.

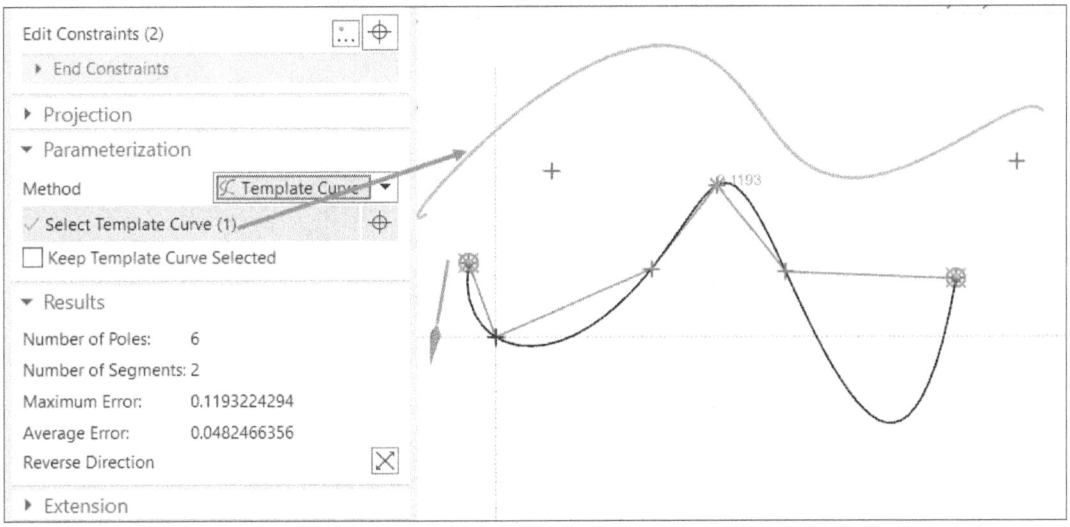

Figure-59. Using template curve

- Using the options in **Extension** rollout, you can extend the start or end points of the spline.
- After setting parameters, click on the **Apply** button to create the fit spline.

Fitting Line on Points

- Select the **Fit Line** option from the drop-down at the top in the **Fit Curve** dialog box. The **Fit Curve** dialog box will be displayed as shown in Figure-60.
- Select the points to be used for fitting line from drawing area. Preview of line will be displayed.

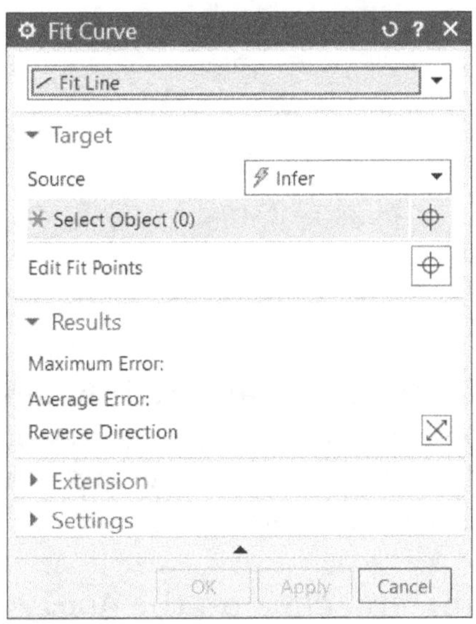

Figure-60. Fit Line options

- Set the parameters as discussed earlier and click on the **Apply** button to create the line.

Fitting Circle on Points

- Select the **Fit Circle** option from the drop-down at the top in the dialog box. The options will be displayed as shown in Figure-61.

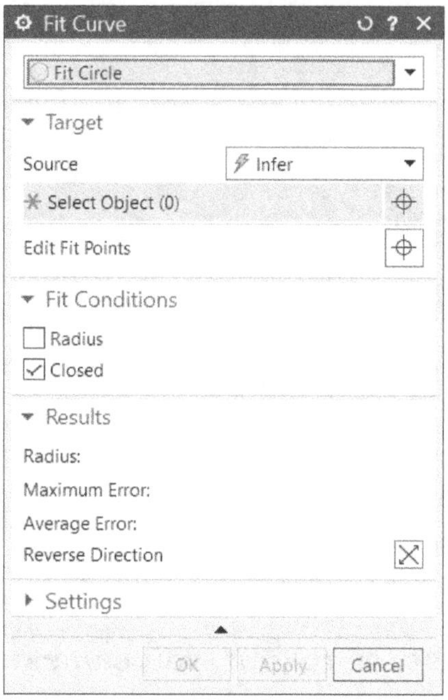

Figure-61. Fit Circle options

- Select the points from the drawing area. Preview of fit circle will be displayed; refer to Figure-62.

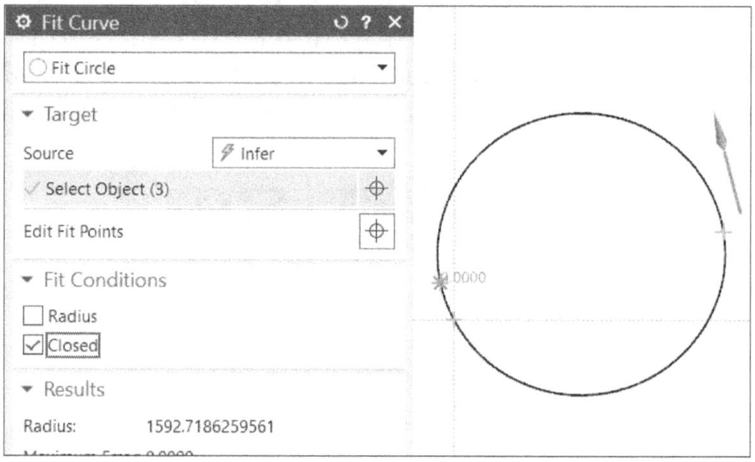

Figure-62. Preview of fit circle

- Clear the **Closed** check box to create an arc instead of full circle.
- Select the **Radius** check box to specify the radius of fit circle/arc manually.
- Expand the **Settings** rollout and select the **Automatic Point Rejection** check box to define the maximum limit from tentative fit curve upto which points will be considered for fitting.
- After setting desired parameters, click on the **Apply** button to create the fit circle.

Similarly, you can use **Fit Ellipse** option to create fit ellipse.

OPTIMIZING CURVES

The **Optimize Curve** tool is used to optimize imported curve based on specified distance and angle threshold. The procedure to use this tool is given next.

- Click on the **Optimize Curve** tool from the **More** drop-down in the **Curve** group of **Home** tab in the **Ribbon**. The **Optimize 2D Curve** dialog box will be displayed; refer to Figure-63.

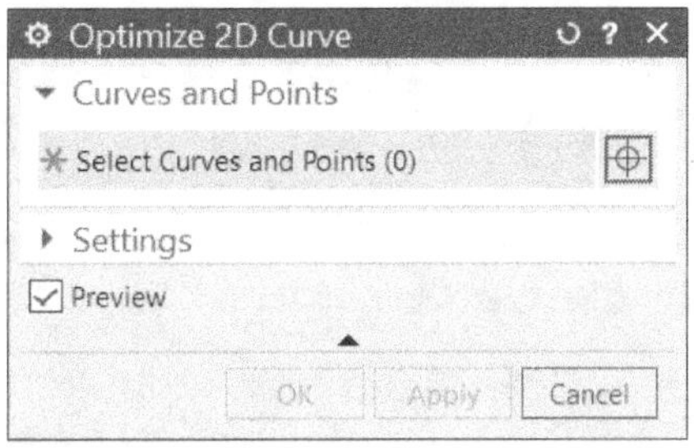

Figure-63. Optimize 2D Curve dialog box

- Select the curves/points to be optimized from the drawing area.
- Expand the **Settings** rollout in the dialog box and specify optimization tolerance in the **Distance Threshold** and **Angle Threshold** edit boxes.
- Set the other parameters as discussed earlier and click on the **OK** button to apply optimization.

TRIMMING GEOMETRIC ENTITIES

The **Trim** tool in **Edit** group is used to trim extra portion of sketch entities. The procedure to use this tool is given next.

- Click on the **Trim** tool from the **Edit** group in the **Home** tab of the **Ribbon**. The **Trim** dialog box will be displayed; refer to Figure-64 and you will be asked to select the entities to be trimmed.

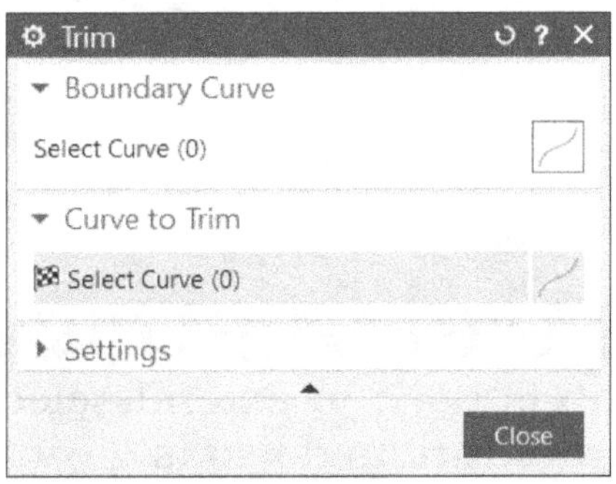

Figure-64. Trim dialog box

- Hover the cursor on entity to check what portion of the entity will be removed. The trim portion will be highlighted in red color.
- Click on the entity to remove it.
- If you want to explicitly define the portion to be removed then click on the **Select Curve** selection button in **Boundary Curve** rollout and select the entity to be used as boundary reference. Note that the boundary curve (or its extension) should intersect with the curve to be trimmed; refer to Figure-65.
- Expand the **Settings** rollout and select the **Trim to Extension** check box to extend the boundary curve for trimming curve at possible intersection; refer to Figure-66.
- After trimming desired geometric entities, press Middle Mouse Button (MMB) or click on the **Close** button from the dialog box.

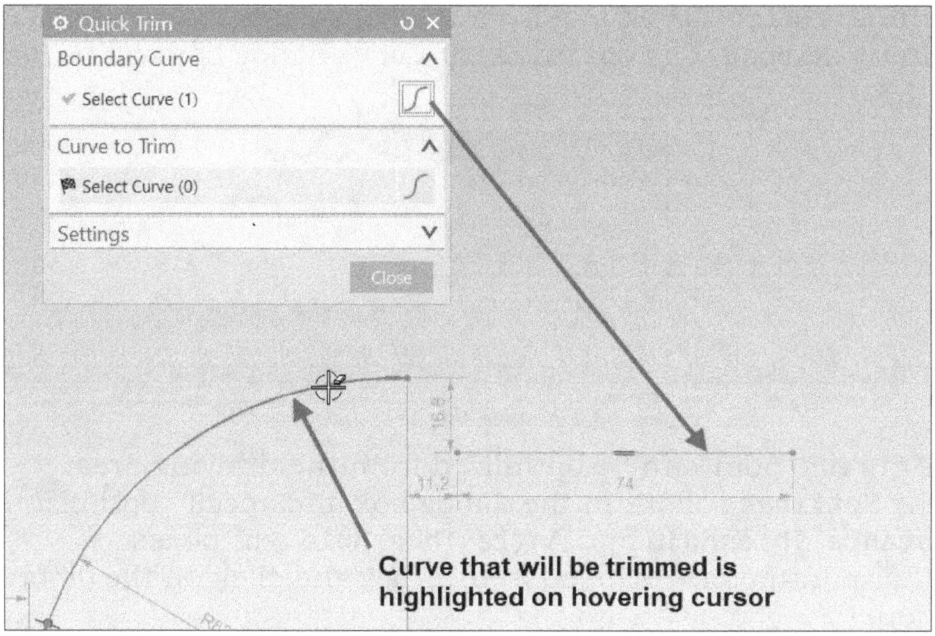

Figure-65. Trimming curve using boundary curve

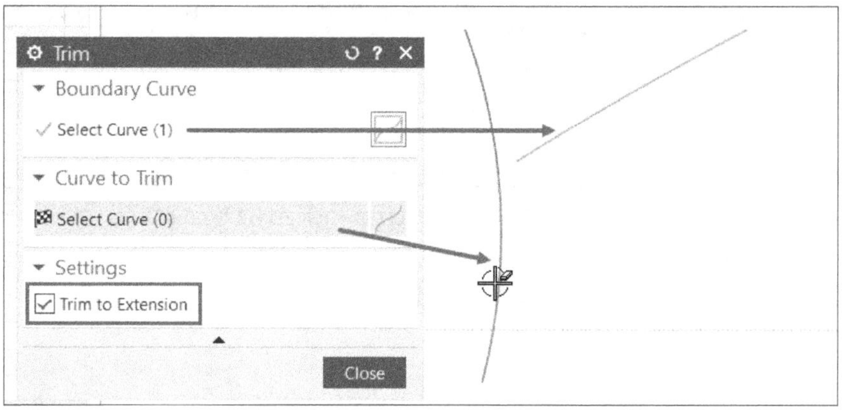

Figure-66. Using trim to extension check box

EXTENDING GEOMETRIC ENTITIES

The **Extend** tool in **Edit** group is used to extend selected geometry up to the next intersecting geometry. The procedure to do so is given next.

- Click on the **Extend** tool from the **Edit** group in the **Home** tab of the **Ribbon**. The **Extend** dialog box will be displayed; refer to Figure-67 and you will be asked to select the entity.

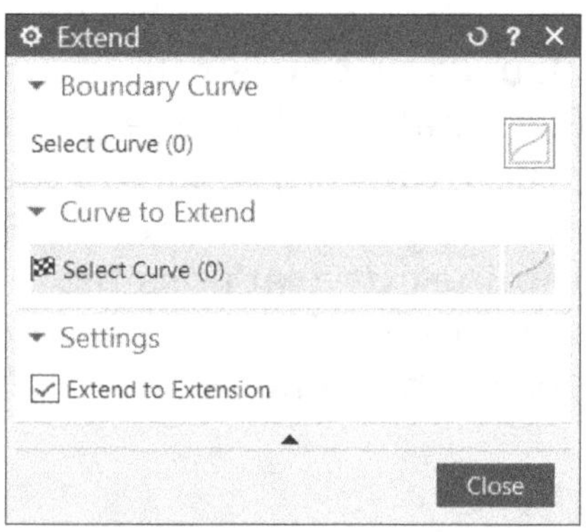

Figure-67. Quick Extend dialog box

- Hover the cursor on entity that you want to extend. Preview of extended curve will be displayed; refer to Figure-68.

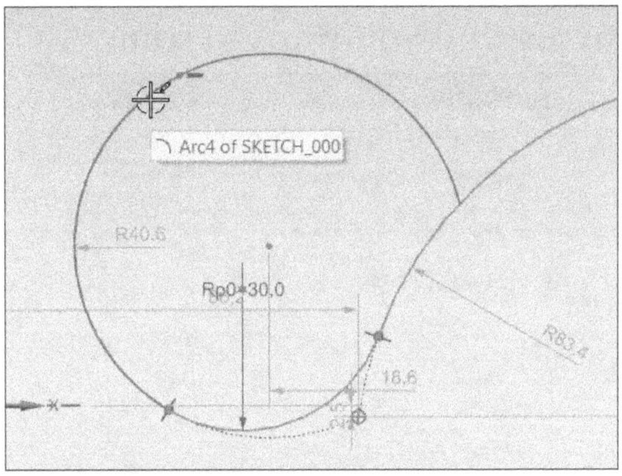

Figure-68. Preview of extended curve

- You can use the boundary curve in the same way as discussed for **Trim** tool.
- Select the curve to be extended and click on the **Close** button to exit the dialog box.

CONNECTING CURVES (CORNER)

The **Corner** tool in **Edit** group is used to extend or trim two curves at a corner point. The procedure to use this tool is given next.

- Click on the **Corner** tool from the **Edit** group of **Home** tab in the **Ribbon**. The **Corner** dialog box will be displayed; refer to Figure-69.

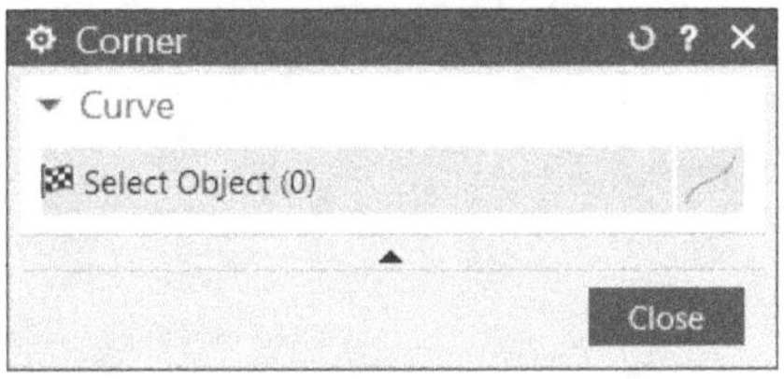

Figure-69. Corner dialog box

- Select two curves which you want to extend or trim to form corner point. The curves will extend or trim based on scenario to make corner; refer to Figure-70.

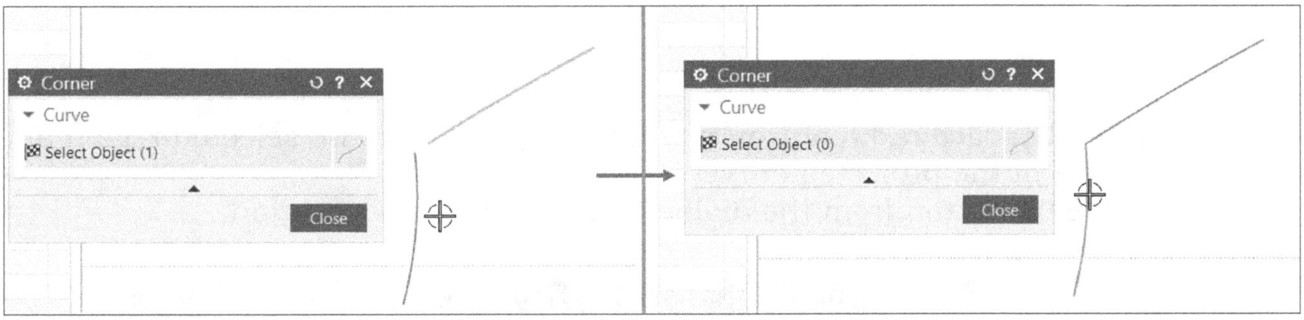

Figure-70. Extending curves to form corner

- Press **MMB** or click on the **Close** button from the dialog box.

TRIMMING ASSOCIATIVE CURVE

The associative curves are the curves generated by projecting edges of part or curves in another sketch. The **Trim Associative Curve** tool is used to trim associative curves. The procedure to use this tool is given next.

- Click on the **Trim Associative Curve** tool from the **More** drop-down in **Edit** group of the **Home** tab of the **Ribbon**. The **Trim Associative Curve** dialog box will be displayed; refer to Figure-71.
- Select the projected curves that you want to trim.

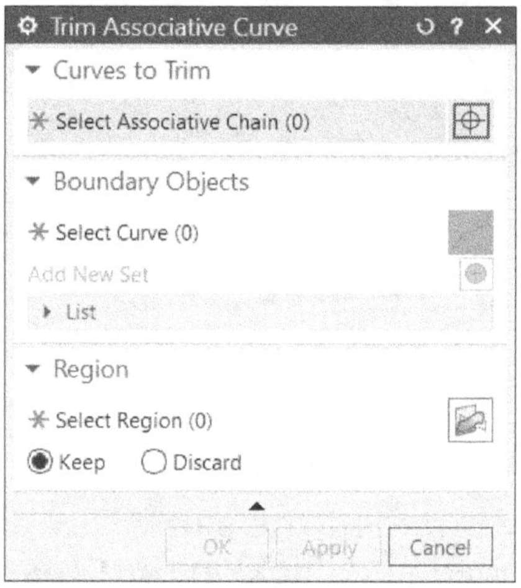

Figure-71. Trim Associative Curve dialog box

- Click on the **Select Curve** button in the **Boundary Objects** rollout and select the curve that you want to use as boundary for trimming projected curves.
- Click on the **Select Region** button from the **Region** rollout and select the region of projected curve that you want to keep; refer to Figure-72.

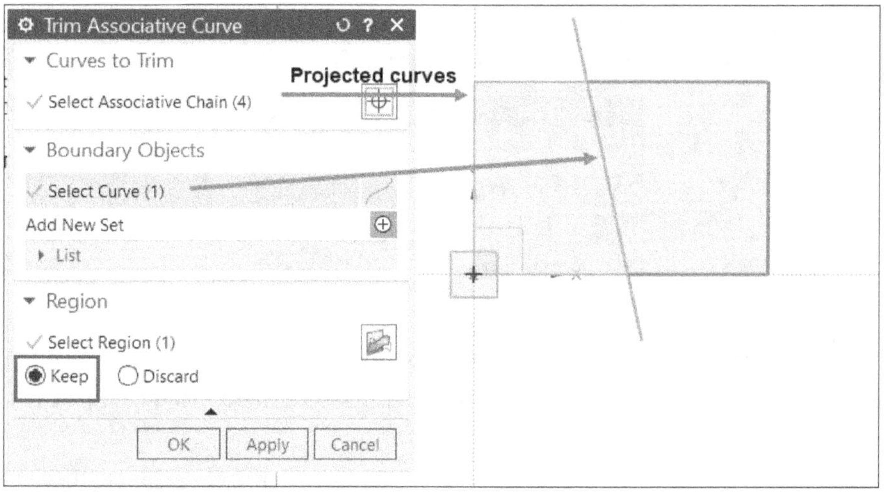

Figure-72. Selecting region to be kept

- Click on the **Discard** radio button if you want to discard the selected region and keep the rest of the projected curve.
- Click on the **OK** button from the dialog box to apply the operation.

MOVING CURVES

The **Move Curve** tool in **More** drop-down of **Edit** group is used to move selected curves at desired location. While moving the curves, this tool also accommodates the constraints applied to the curves. The procedure to use this tool is given next.

- Click on the **Move Curve** tool from **More** drop-down of **Edit** group in the **Home** tab of the **Ribbon**. The **Move Curve** dialog box will be displayed; refer to Figure-73.

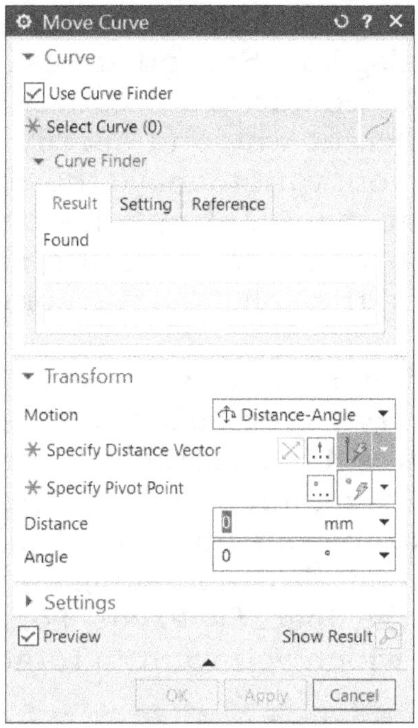

Figure-73. Move Curve dialog box

- Select the curves that you want to move. A dynamic handle will be displayed on curve to facilitate movement; refer to Figure-74.

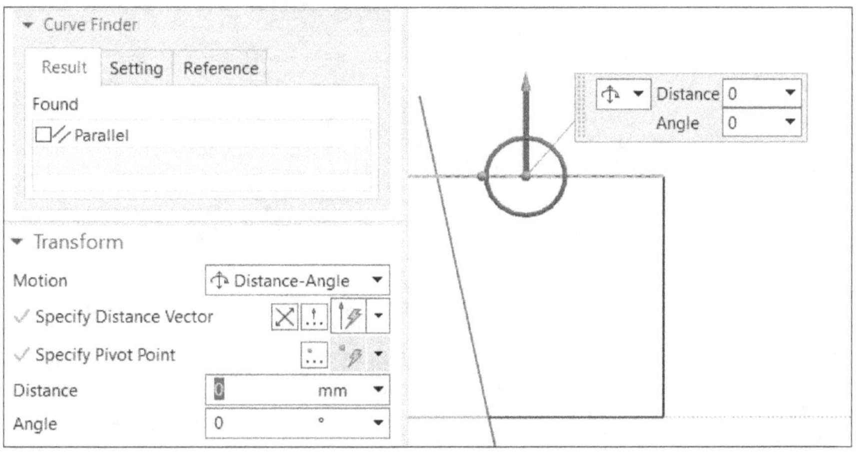

Figure-74. Handle displayed for moving curve

- Drag the arrow handle to move the curve. Drag the dot on circular handle in direction to rotate the curve. You can also specify desired values in dynamic input boxes instead of dragging handles to move curves; refer to Figure-75.

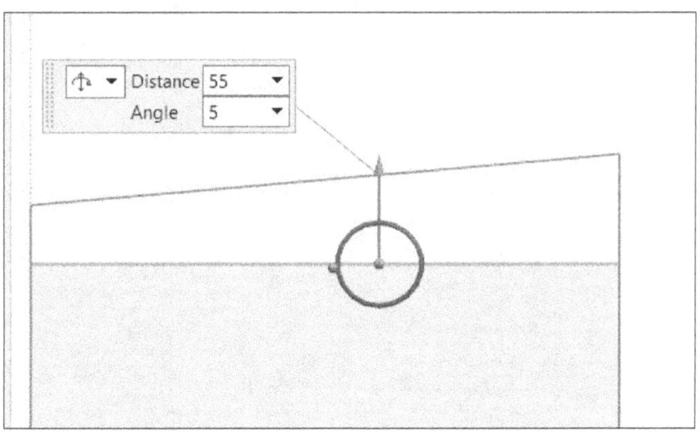

Figure-75. Moving curve

- By default, the **Distance-Angle** option is selected in the **Motion** drop-down of **Transform** rollout in the dialog box. So, you are asked to specify the distance and angle values for moving selected curve. Select desired option from the drop-down to move the curve in a different way and specify respective parameters in the dialog box. For example, if you want to move the curve by selecting From and To points then select the **Point to Point** option from the **Motion** drop-down. You will be asked to select the from point. Click at a point on curve from where you want to move the cursor and then click on the point where you want to place the curve; refer to Figure-76.
- If you have selected any option that allows to specify distance or angle then **Specify Distance Vector** and **Specify Pivot Point** options will be available in the dialog box. Click on the **Specify Direction Vector** option and select a reference to define direction of movement (selecting line will make the direction along selected line, selecting a plane will make the direction perpendicular to plane, selecting two points will make the movement direction along an imaginary line joining the two points, and so on). Select the **Specify Pivot Point** option from the dialog box and select the point about which you want to rotate the selected curves.

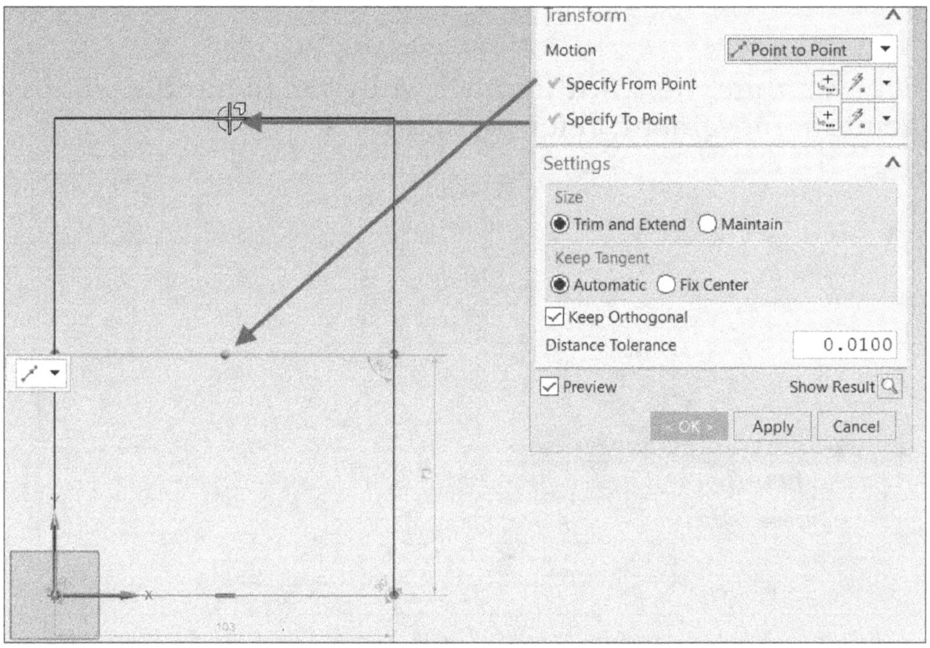

Figure-76. Moving curve by specifying points

- Click on the **Settings** button in the dialog box to expand **Settings** rollout. The options to tweak the movement of curve will be displayed; refer to Figure-77.

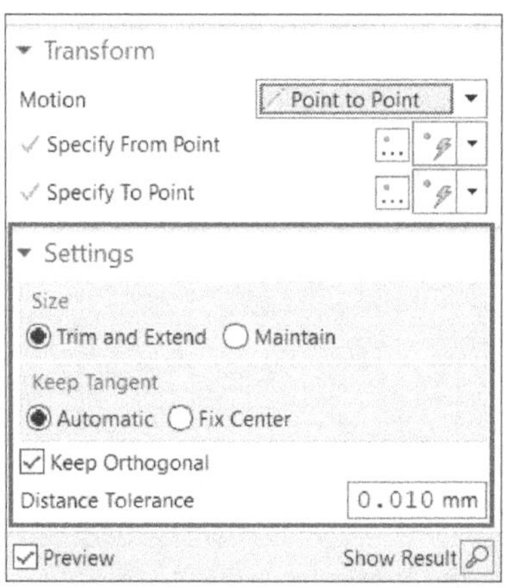

Figure-77. Settings rollout in Move Curve dialog box

- Select the **Trim and Extend** radio button if you want to trim or extend adjacent curves while moving the curve. Select the **Maintain** radio button if the adjacent curves to be of original size.
- Select the **Automatic** radio button from the **Keep Tangent** area if you want the centers of fillets move as the curves move. Select the **Fix Center** radio button from the **Keep Tangent** area if you want the centers of fillets to be fixed while the curves move.
- Clear the **Keep Orthogonal** check box if you want the adjacent sides to move in any direction possible for moving the curve otherwise the adjacent sides will move in orthogonal directions only.

Curve Finder

The options in **Curve Finder** rollout are used to find the curves similar to select curves. The procedure to find curves is given next.

- Select the **Use Curve Finder** check box if not selected by default.
- Expand the **Curve Finder** rollout and options based on selected curves will be displayed; refer to Figure-78.

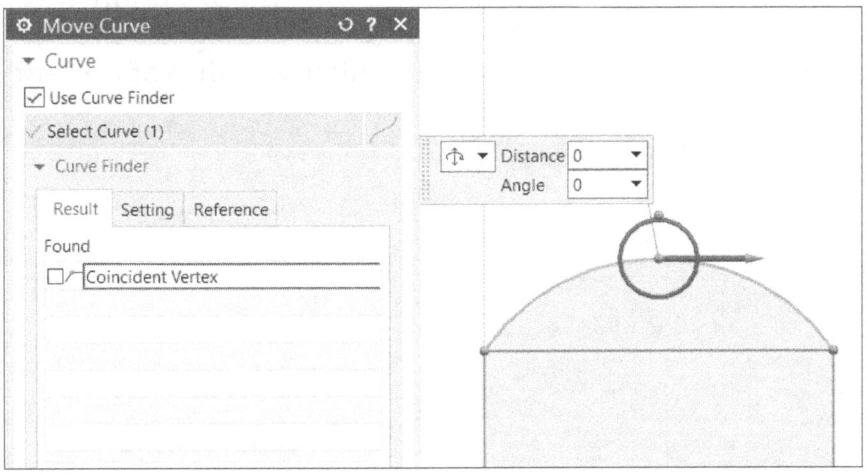

Figure-78. Options in Curve Finder rollout

- Select the check boxes for parameters by which you want to select the other curves. For example, in our case, if we select the **Coincident Vertex** check box then all the curves on which the select curve has vertices will be selected. Similarly, if you select the **Parallel** check box from the list then all the curves that are parallel to any of the selected curve will get selected.
- Now, move the curves as required and then click on the **OK** button.

MOVING CURVE BY OFFSET

The **Offset Move Curve** tool is used to move the curve at a specified offset distance. The procedure to use this tool is given next.

- Click on the **Offset Move Curve** tool from the **More** drop-down in **Edit** group of the **Home** tab in the **Ribbon**. The **Offset Move Curve** dialog box will be displayed; refer to Figure-79.

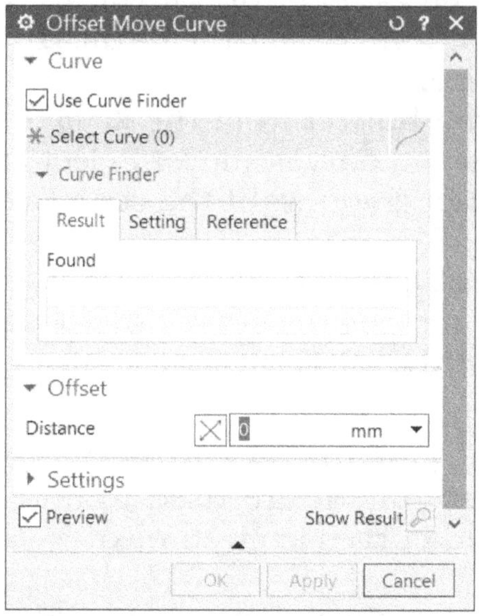

Figure-79. Offset Move Curve dialog box

- Select the curves that you want to move by offset.
- Click on the **Reverse Direction** button to flip the direction where offset curves will be generated from the **Offset** rollout of the dialog box.
- Click in the **Distance** edit box and specify desired value of distance by which you want to move the curves.

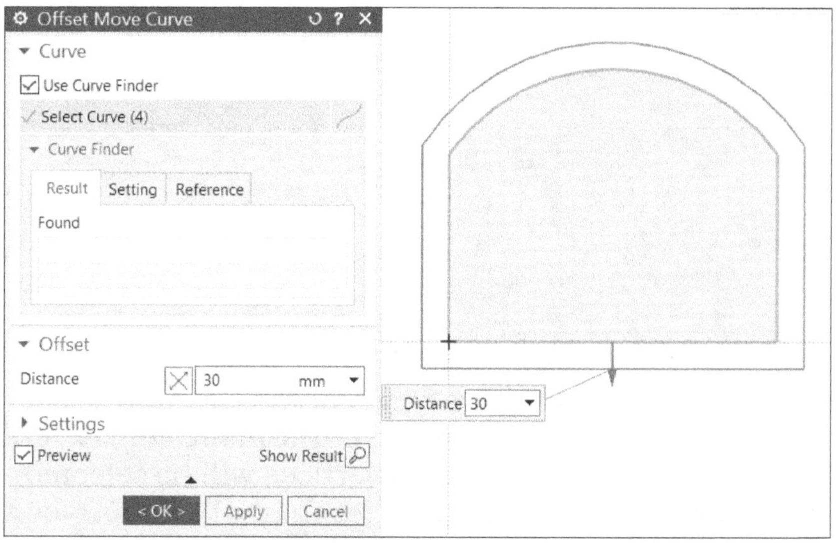

Figure-80. Preview of offset move curve

- Use the **Curve Finder** to find and select other curves as discussed earlier. Preview of the offset move will be displayed.
- Click on the **OK** button from the dialog box to move curves by offset.

SCALING CURVES

The **Scale Curve** tool in **More** drop-down of the **Edit** group is used to increase or decrease the size of curves based on specified scale factor. The procedure to use this tool is given next.

- Click on the **Scale Curve** tool from **More** drop-down of the **Edit** group in the **Home** tab of the **Ribbon**. The **Scale Curve** dialog box will be displayed; refer to Figure-81.

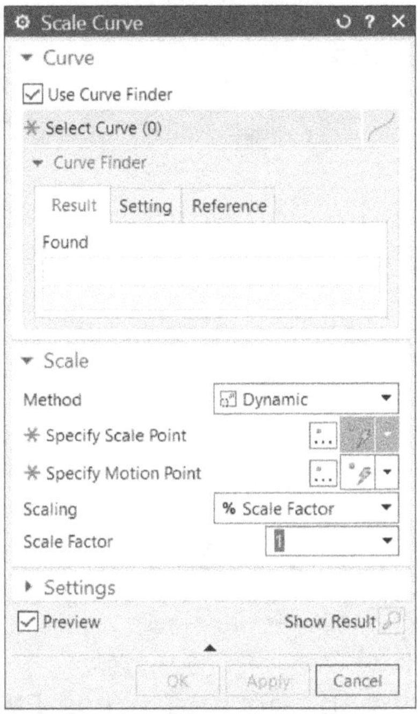

Figure-81. Scale Curve dialog box

- Select the curves that you want to scale up/down. Use the **Curve Finder** if needed.
- Click in the **Method** drop-down of **Scale** rollout and select desired option to define scaling method.

Scaling with Dynamic Method

- Select the **Dynamic** option from the **Method** drop-down. The options of **Scale** rollout will be displayed as shown in Figure-81.
- Click on the **Specify Scale Point** selection button from the **Scale** rollout and select the point to be used as reference for scaling.
- Click on the **Specify Motion Point** selection button from the **Scale** rollout and select the point to be moved dynamically for scaling.
- Drag the handle to point to scale up/down the curves. The curves will increase or decrease in size accordingly.
- Select the **%Scale Factor** option from the **Scaling** drop-down in **Scale** rollout if you want to specify scale factor. Note that instead of dragging the handle, you can specify the scale value in edit box below **Scaling** drop-down.

Scaling with Dimension Method

- Select the **Dimension** option from the **Method** drop-down. You will be asked to select the dimension to be used as scale; refer to Figure-82.

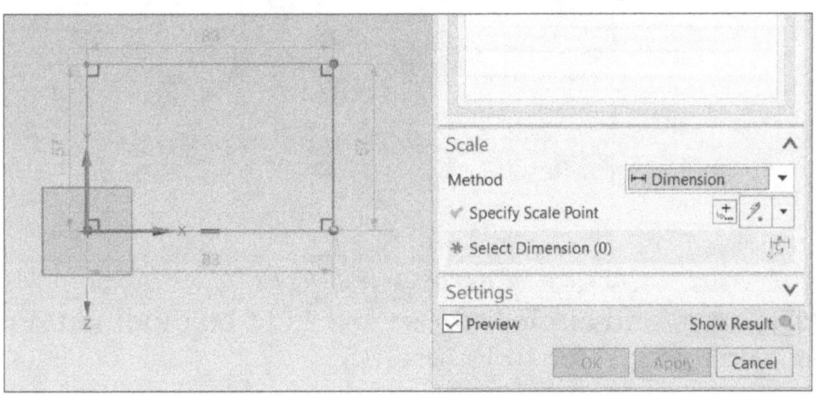

Figure-82. Options to scale using dimensions

- Select the dimension that you want to use as reference. A dynamic edit box will be displayed; refer to Figure-83.

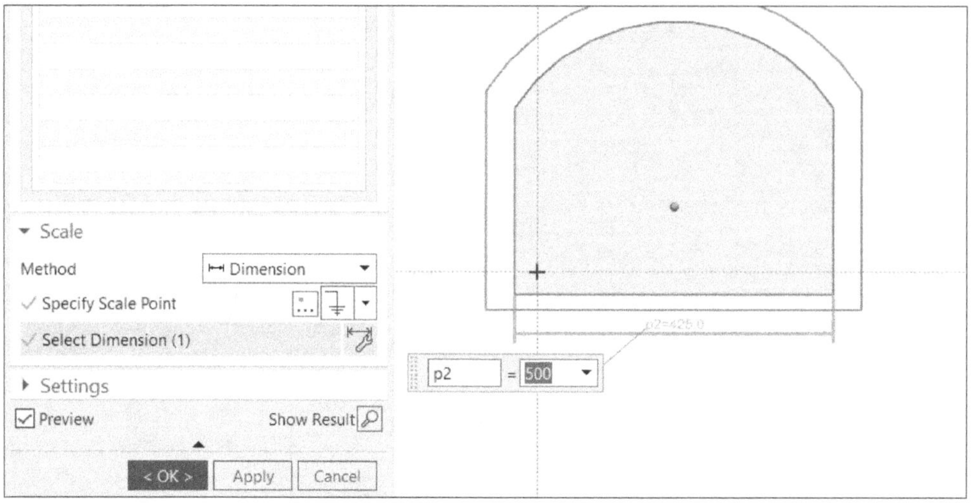

Figure-83. Dimension to scale curves

- Specify desired value for dimension and press **ENTER**. Preview of scaled curves will be displayed.
- Click on the **OK** button from the dialog box.

RE-SIZING CURVES

The **Resize Curve** tool is used to re-define size of circles, arcs, and fillets in the sketch. This tool is very useful in making size of selected fillets, arcs, or circles equal. The procedure to use this tool is given next.

- Click on the **Resize Curve** tool from the **More** drop-down in the **Edit** group of the **Home** tab in the **Ribbon**. The **Resize Curve** dialog box will be displayed; refer to Figure-84.

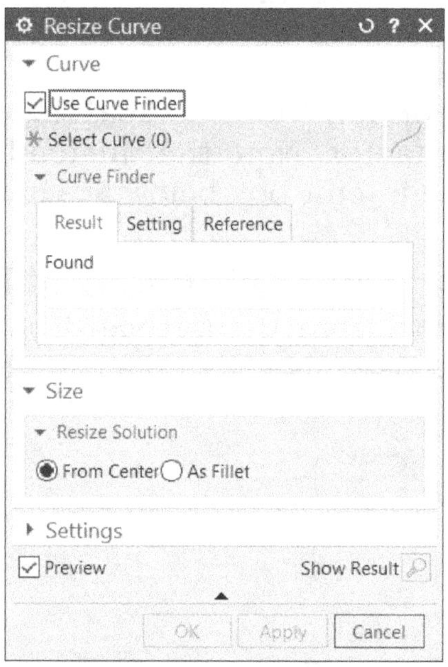

Figure-84. Resize Curve dialog box

- Select the fillets, arcs, and circles whose size is to be modified. Preview of re-sized curves will be displayed; refer to Figure-85.

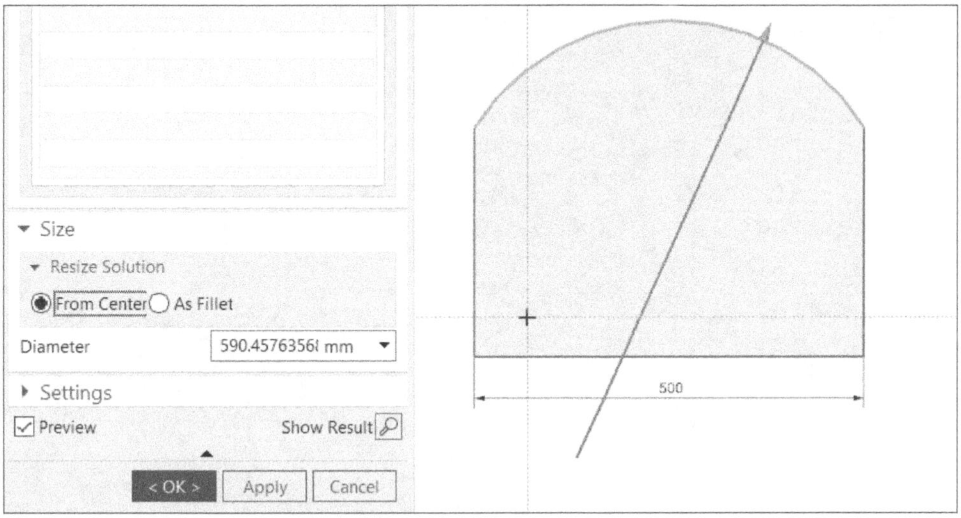

Figure-85. Preview of resized curves

- Click in the **Radius/Diameter** edit box of **Size** rollout in the dialog box and specify desired value for re-sizing selected curves.
- Select the **As Fillet** radio button from the **Size** rollout if you want to resize selected curves as fillets. This option will keep the adjacent curves fixed. Select the **From Center** radio button if you want to specify diameter for re-sizing and want the centers of curves to move.
- Use the **Curve Finder** as discussed earlier to select more curves based on relations.
- Click on the **OK** button to perform re-sizing.

RE-SIZING CHAMFER CURVES

The **Resize Chamfer Curve** tool is used to modify size of multiple selected chamfers and make them uniform. The procedure to use this tool is given next.

- Click on the **Resize Chamfer Curve** tool from the **More** drop-down in the **Edit** group of the **Home** tab in the **Ribbon**. The **Resize Chamfer Curve** dialog box will be displayed; refer to Figure-86.

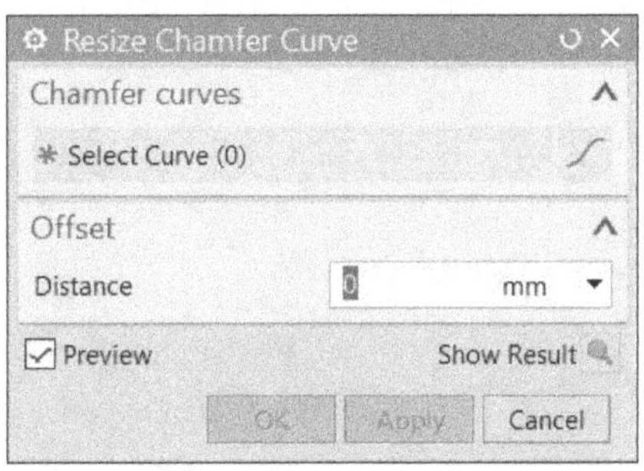

Figure-86. Resize Chamfer Curve dialog box

- Select the chamfers to be re-sized. The preview of chamfer resize will be displayed; refer to Figure-87.

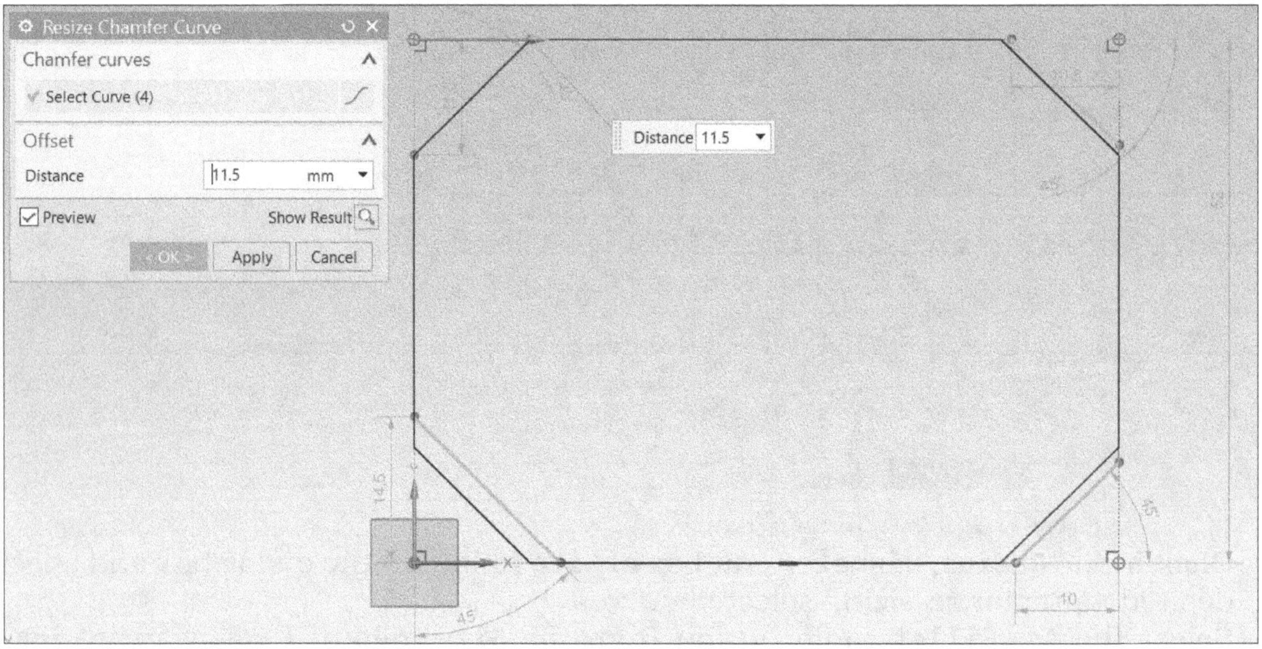

Figure-87. Preview of resized chamfers

- Specify desired value of chamfer in **Distance** edit box.
- Click on the **OK** button from the dialog box to modify chamfers.

DELETING CURVES

The **Delete Curve** tool is used to delete selected curves. This tool is available in the **More** drop-down of the **Edit** group in the **Home** tab of the **Ribbon**. The procedure to use this tool is given next.

- Click on the **Delete Curve** tool from the **More** drop-down in the **Edit** group of the **Home** tab in the **Ribbon**. The **Delete Curve** dialog box will be displayed and you will be asked to select the curves.
- Select the curves that you want to be deleted. The preview of sketch after deleting the curves will be displayed; refer to Figure-88.

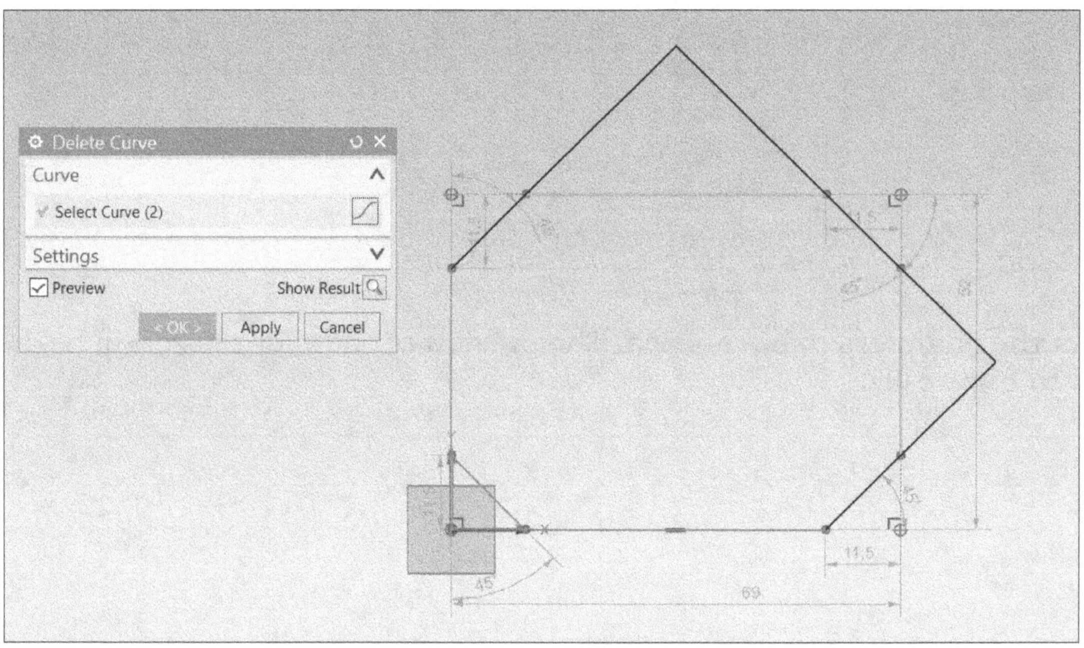

Figure-88. Deleting curves

- If you do not want the near by geometries to heal the sketch after deleting selected curves then clear the **Heal** check box from **Settings** rollout in the **Delete Curve** dialog box.
- Click on the **OK** button from the dialog box to apply the changes.

CONVERTING CURVES TO REFERENCES

Reference curves are those curves that help to create geometry/sketch but do not represent any feature of sketch or model. The procedure to convert selected curves to references is discussed next.

- Select the curve(s) that you want to convert to references and right-click on them. A shortcut menu will be displayed; refer to Figure-89.

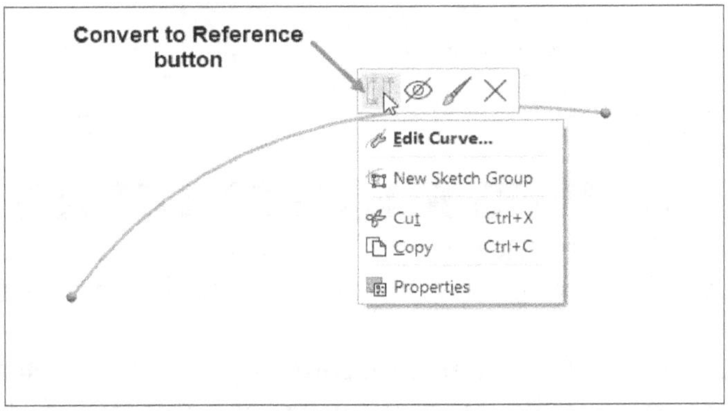

Figure-89. Shortcut menu for curve

- Click on the **Convert to Reference** option from the shortcut menu. The selected curves will be converted to references.

In **Menu**, this tool is available as **Menu->Tools->Sketch->Convert To/From Reference**.

Command Finder

You can also access tools from **Command Finder** at the top-right corner of application window; refer to Figure-90. To activate a tool, type few keywords of the tool name and press **ENTER**. The **Command Finder** dialog box will be displayed; refer to Figure-91. Click on desired command in the dialog box to activate the tool.

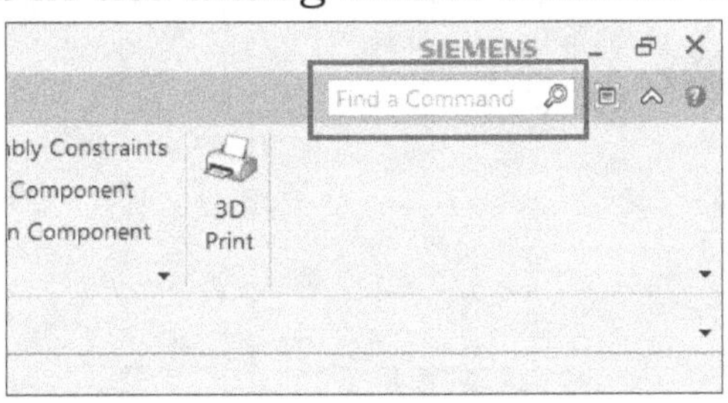

Figure-90. Command Finder

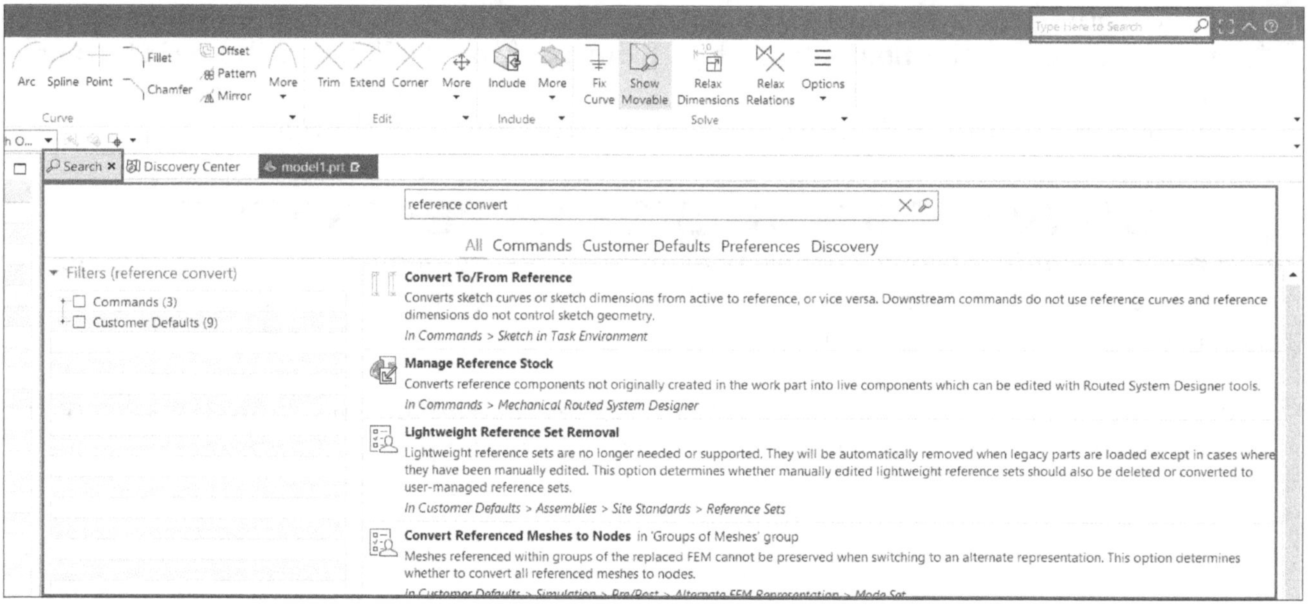

Figure-91. Command Finder dialog box

INCLUDING CURVES FROM EXTERNAL OBJECTS

The **Include** tool is used to include curves from external objects in current sketch as reference geometry. The procedure to use this tool is given next.

- Click on the **Include** tool from the **Include** group in the **Home** tab of the **Ribbon**. The **Include** dialog box will be displayed; refer to Figure-92.

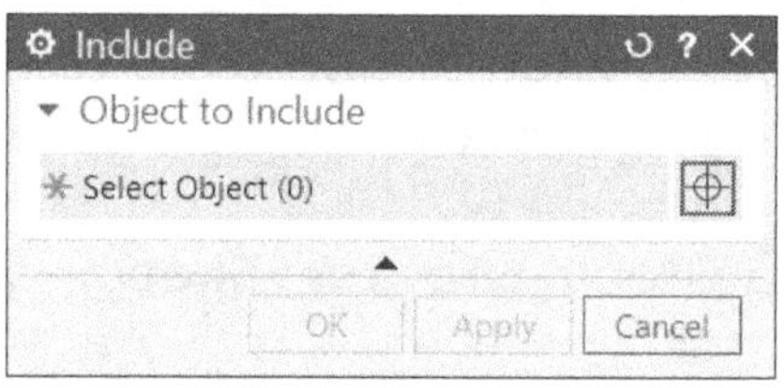

Figure-92. Include dialog box

- Select the edges of the model to be included in the current sketch; refer to Figure-93 and click on the **OK** button. The edges will be projected as reference curve.

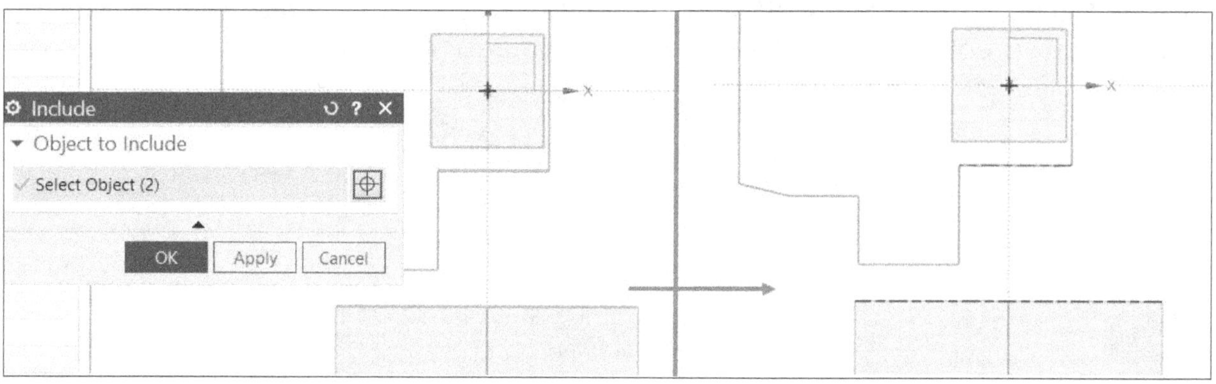

Figure-93. Including curves in sketch

PROJECTING CURVES

The **Project Curve** tool is used to project edges, curves, and points of other external features/sketches on the current sketching plane. In simple words, if you want to use edges, curves, or points of other sketches of solid/surface features then you can use this tool. The procedure to use this tool is discussed next.

- Click on the **Project Curve** tool from the **More** drop-down of **Include** group in the **Home** tab of **Ribbon**. The **Project Curve** dialog box will be displayed; refer to Figure-94.

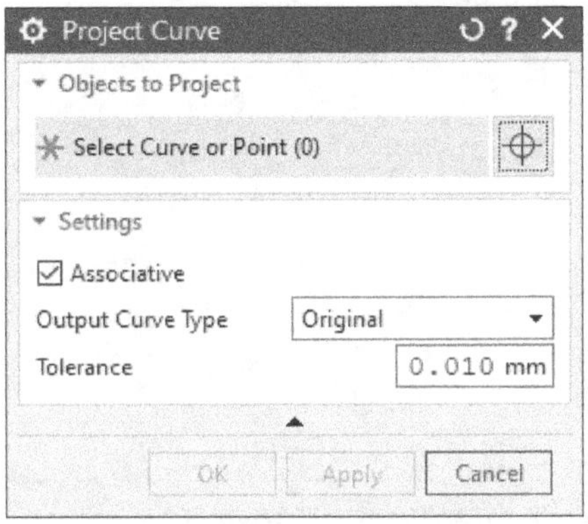

Figure-94. Project Curve dialog box

- Select the curves, edges, faces, points, or vertices to be projected on the sketching plane. Preview of the projected edges/points will be displayed; refer to Figure-95.

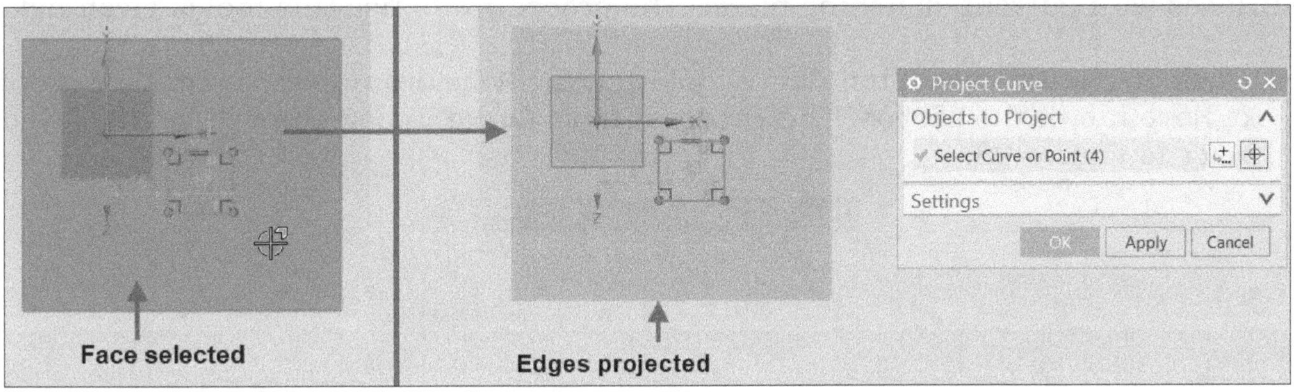

Figure-95. Projecting edges of a face

- Click on the **OK** button from the dialog box to create projected curves.

CREATING INTERSECTION POINT

The **Intersection Point** tool is used to generate point where an external curve intersects with current sketch plane. The procedure to use this tool is given next.

- Click on the **Intersection Point** tool from the **More** drop-down in the **Include** group of **Home** tab in the **Ribbon**. The **Intersection Point** dialog box will be displayed; refer to Figure-96.

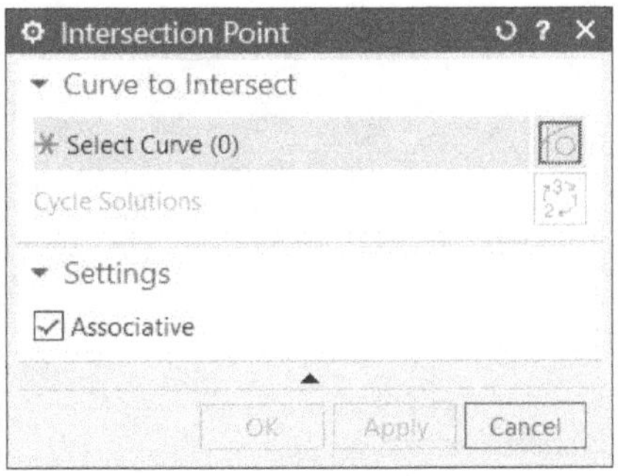

Figure-96. Intersection Point dialog box

- Select the external curves whose intersection point is to be projected on the current sketching plane.

- Click on the **OK** button to create the point; refer to Figure-97.

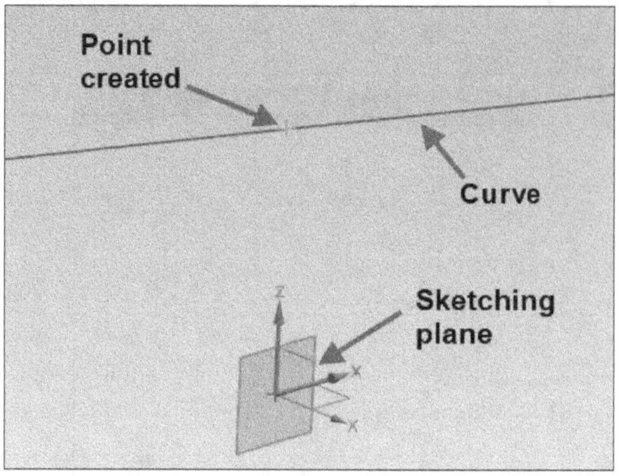

Figure-97. Creating intersection point

CREATING INTERSECTION CURVES

The **Intersection Curve** tool is used to generate curves at the intersection of solids/ surfaces with current sketching plane. The procedure to use this tool is given next.

- Click on the **Intersection Curve** tool from the **More** drop-down in **Include** group of **Home** tab in the **Ribbon**. The **Intersection Curve** dialog box will be displayed; refer to Figure-98.

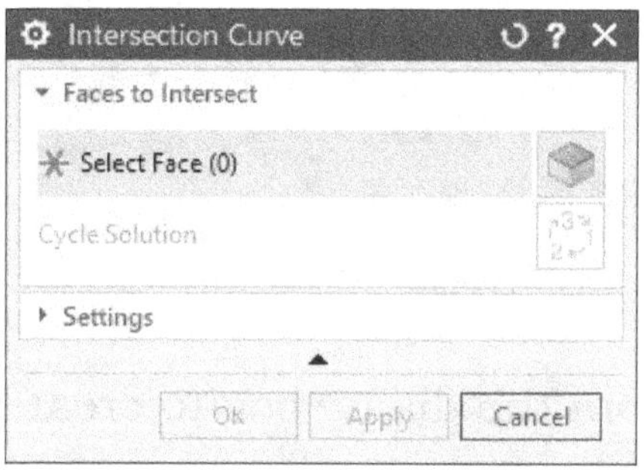

Figure-98. Intersection Curve dialog box

- Select the faces that are to be projected at intersection with sketching plane. Preview of the intersection curves will be displayed; refer to Figure-99.

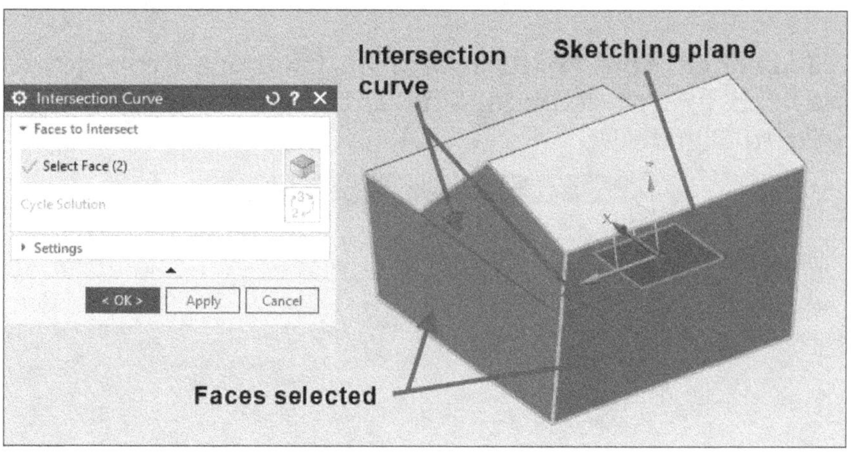

Figure-99. Creating intersection curve

- Expand the **Settings** rollout and select the **Join Curves** check box to join the intersection curves if they are connected at end points.

- Select the **Ignore Holes** check box if you do not want to generate curve on the hole edges when there is a hole at intersection of faces. In this case, you will be asked to select the side of hole for generating respective intersection curve and **Cycle Solution** button will be displayed in the dialog box; refer to Figure-100. Click on the **Cycle Solution** button to switch between intersection curves.

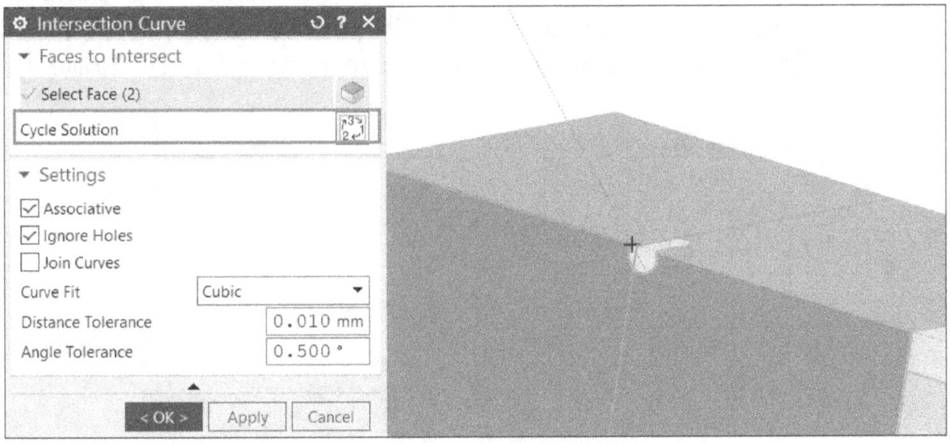

Figure-100. Cycle Solution button

- Set the other parameters as discussed earlier and click on the **OK** button from the dialog box to create the intersection curves.

Similarly, you can use the **Intersection Point** tool to generate intersection point of two edges in the current sketch.

ADDING EXISTING CURVES TO SKETCH

The **Add Curves** tool in the **More** drop-down is used to extract existing curves in current sketch plane which are coplanar. The procedure to use this tool is given next.

- Click on the **Add Curves** tool from the **More** drop-down of **Include** group in the **Home** tab of the **Ribbon**. The **Add Curve** dialog box will be displayed; refer to Figure-101.

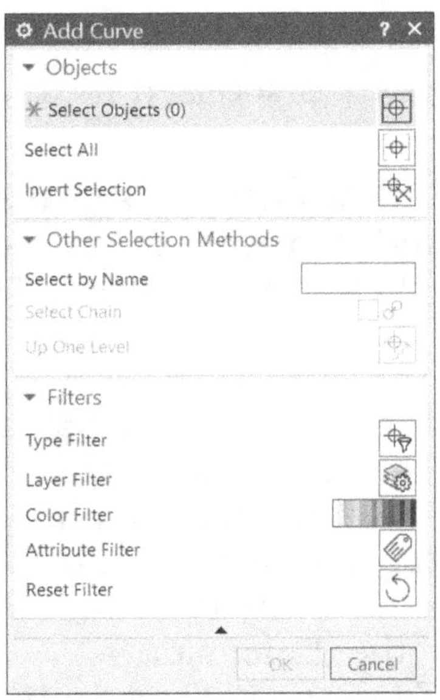

Figure-101. Add Curve dialog box

- Set desired filters in the **Filters** rollout and click on the **Select All** button from the **Objects** rollout of the dialog box to select all the objects in graphics window.
- Click on the **OK** button from the dialog box.

APPLYING DIMENSIONS

Dimension is an important aspect of engineering drawings. Without dimensions, there is no meaning of drawing for engineers. By default, the **Dimension** drop-down is not displayed in the **Ribbon**. To display the drop-down, select the **Dimensions Drop-down** option from the **Solve Group** cascading menu of the **Ribbon Options** drop-down at the right in the **Ribbon**; refer to Figure-102. The tools to apply dimensions will be available in **Rapid Dimension** drop-down of **Solve** group in the **Home** tab of **Ribbon**; refer to Figure-103.

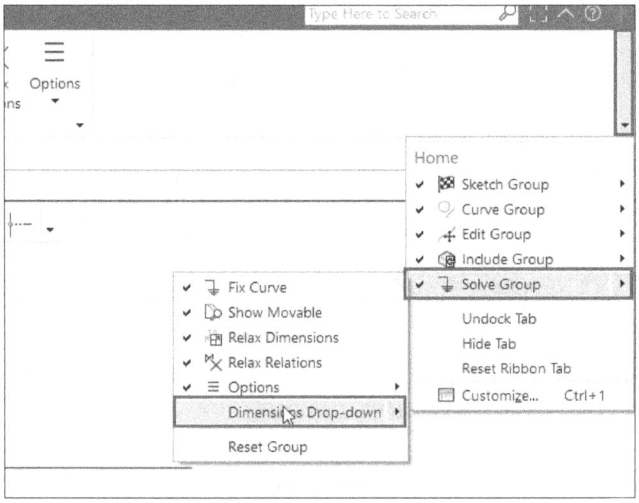

Figure-102. Dimensions drop-down option

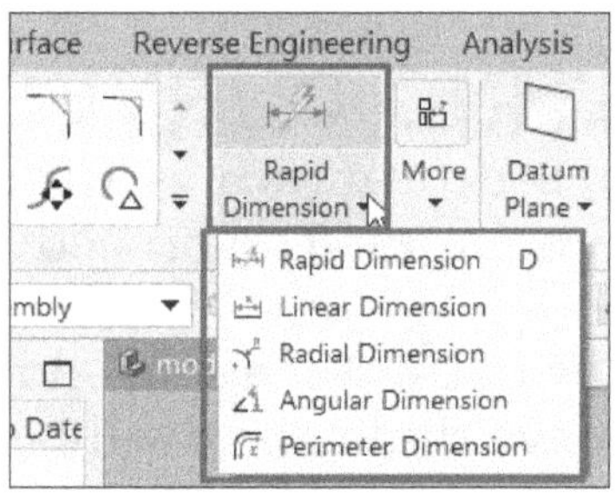

Figure-103. Rapid Dimension drop-down

Various tools of this drop-down are discussed next.

Rapid Dimensioning

The **Rapid Dimension** tool in **Rapid Dimension** drop-down is used to apply different types of dimensions to the sketching entities. The procedure to apply rapid dimensioning is given next.

- Click on the **Rapid Dimension** tool from the **Rapid Dimension** drop-down in the **Solve** group of the **Ribbon**. The **Rapid Dimension** dialog box will be displayed and you will be asked to select the entities to be dimensioned; refer to Figure-104.
- Select the **Place Automatically** check box if you do not want to specify the position of dimension after selecting the entity to be dimensioned. Clear this check box if you want to manually place the dimension.
- Select the **Inferred** option from the **Method** drop-down of **Measurement** rollout to automatically select the type of dimensioning based on selected entity.

- Select the **Reference** check box from the **Driving** rollout to make the current dimension as reference dimension. On selecting this check box, the dimension will be enclosed in brackets; refer to Figure-105.
- Select the **Expression** check box to display the expression value of the dimension so that you can later use this value in equations.

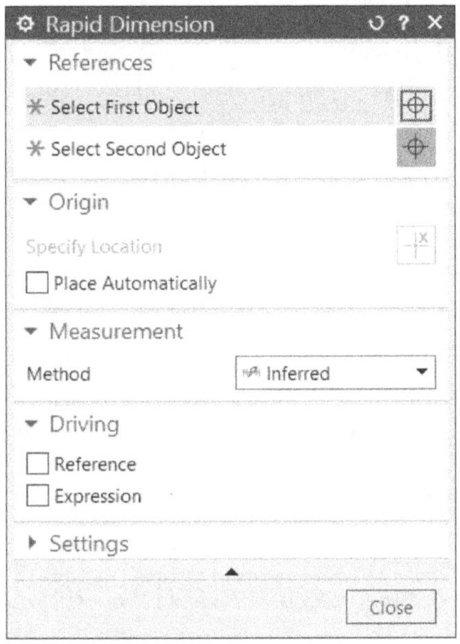

Figure-104. Rapid Dimension dialog box

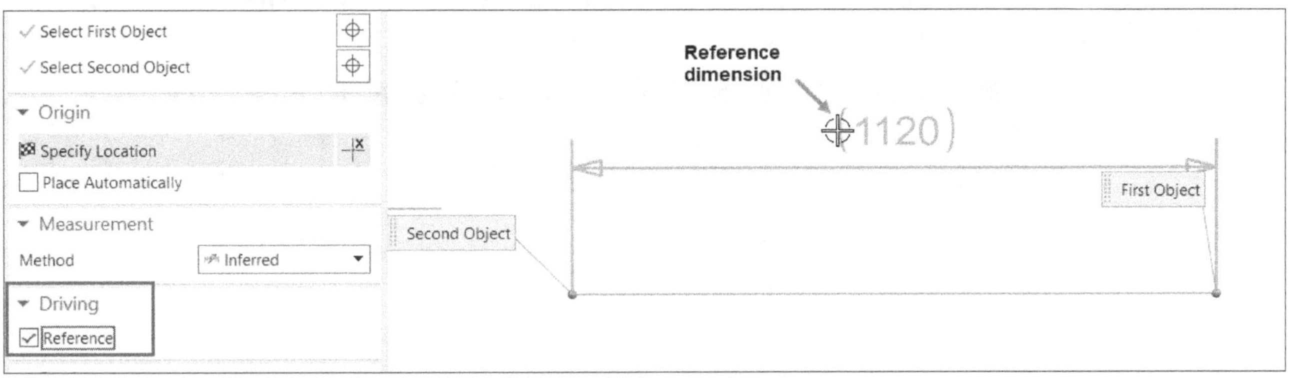

Figure-105. Creating reference dimension

Settings Parameters

- Expand the **Settings** rollout to specify dimension settings. The options will be displayed as shown in Figure-106.

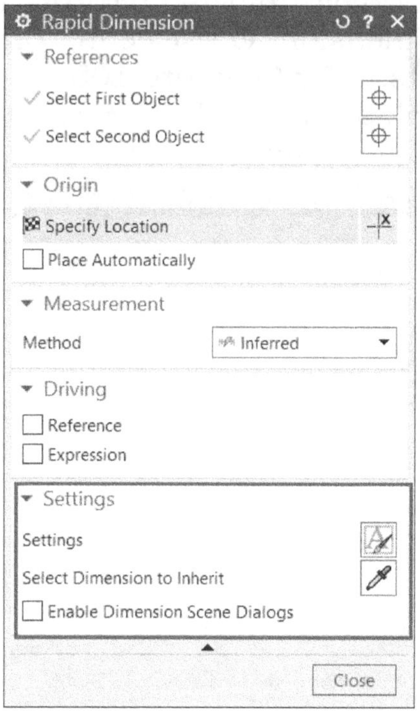

Figure-106. Settings rollout in Rapid Dimension dialog box

- Click on the **Settings** button from the **Settings** rollout in the dialog box to modify rapid dimension settings. The **Rapid Dimension Settings** dialog box will be displayed; refer to Figure-107.

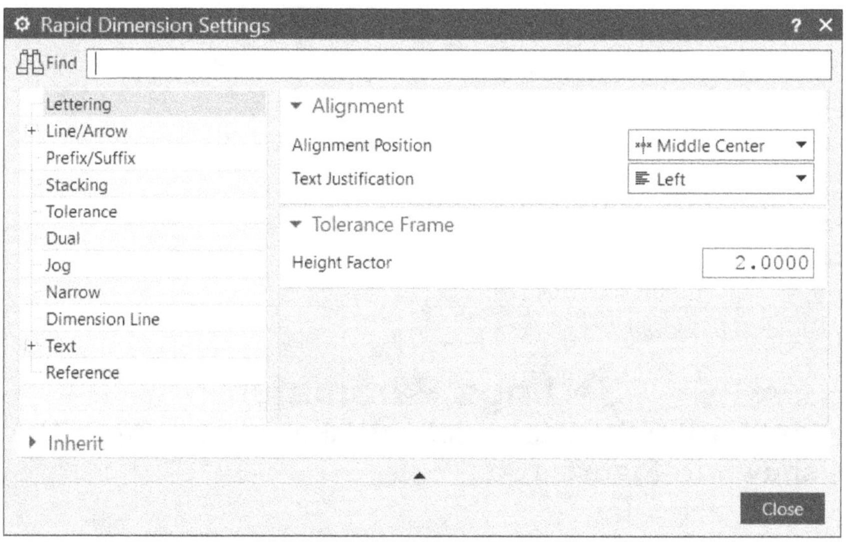

Figure-107. Rapid Dimension Settings dialog box

- Select the **Lettering** option from the left in the dialog box to set alignment position of dimension text and justification of text in respective drop-downs. Set desired value in the **Height Factor** edit box to increase/decrease the height of tolerance frame by respective factor.
- Select the **Arrowhead** option from the left area in the dialog box to define shape and size of arrow heads in dimension; refer to Figure-108.

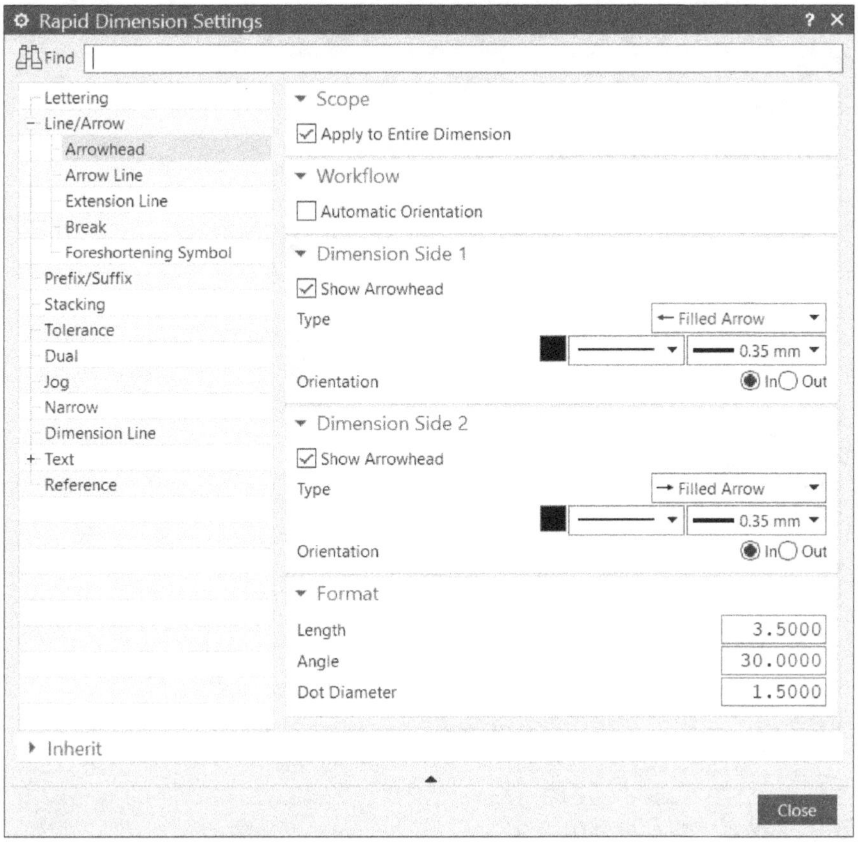

Figure-108. Arrowhead options

- Select the **Apply to Entire Dimension** check box to apply the modifications of current dialog box to all the dimensions in drawing area.
- Select the **Automatic Orientation** check box to automatically set whether arrowhead will be created inside the extension lines of dimension or outside the extension lines of dimension. On selecting this check box, the **Orientation** radio buttons will not be displayed in **Dimension Side 1** and **Dimension Side 2** rollouts.
- Select the **Show Arrowhead** check box from the **Dimension Side 1** rollout to display arrowhead in dimension. Select desired option from the **Type** drop-down to define shape of the arrowhead. Click on the **Object Color** button from the **Dimension Side 1** rollout to change the color of arrowheads.
- Select desired line style and thickness of line from respective drop-downs in the rollout.
- Similarly, you can set arrowhead parameters for dimension side 2.
- Specify desired values in the **Length**, **Angle**, and **Dot Diameter** edit boxes to define angle of arrowhead and size of arrowhead, respectively.
- Select the **Arrow Line** option from the left area in the dialog box, the options will be displayed as shown in Figure-109.

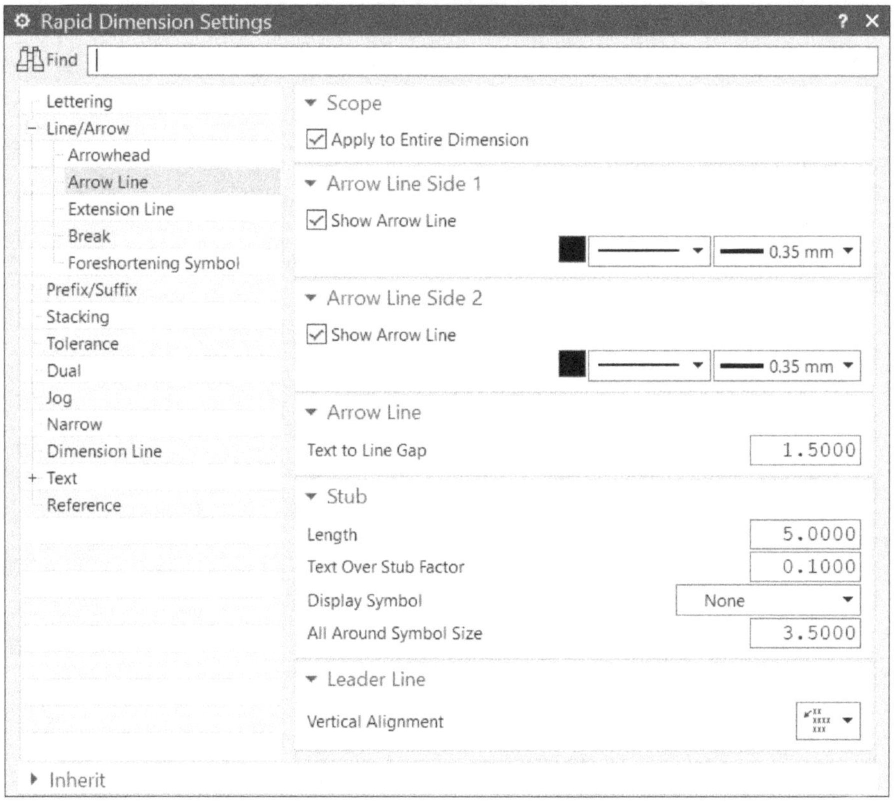

Figure-109. Arrow Line options

- Set the parameters for arrow line like color, style, and thickness of arrow line as discussed earlier.
- Specify desired value in the **Text Over Stub Factor** edit box to define distance between text and stub line when text over leader stub is active.
- Select desired option from the **Vertical Alignment** drop-down to define the location of text with respect to leader end.
- Similarly, you can set parameters for extension line, break, and foreshortening symbols from respective pages in the dialog box.
- Select the **Prefix/Suffix** option from the left area in the dialog box to add prefix/ suffix symbols in the dimension text line for radial dimensions like radius, diameter, and so on; refer to Figure-110. Select desired option from the **Location** drop-down to define the position where you want to place the symbol. Select desired option from the **Diameter Symbol** drop-down to define symbol for prefix/suffix. Set desired value in the **Text Gap** edit box to define distance between symbol and dimension text.

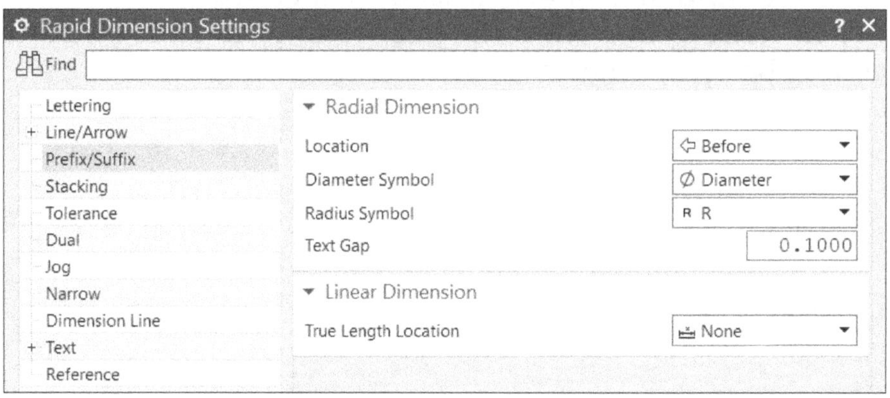

Figure-110. Prefix Suffix options

- Select the **Stacking** option from the left area to define how text and symbols will be stacked over one another in creating dimensions; refer to Figure-111.

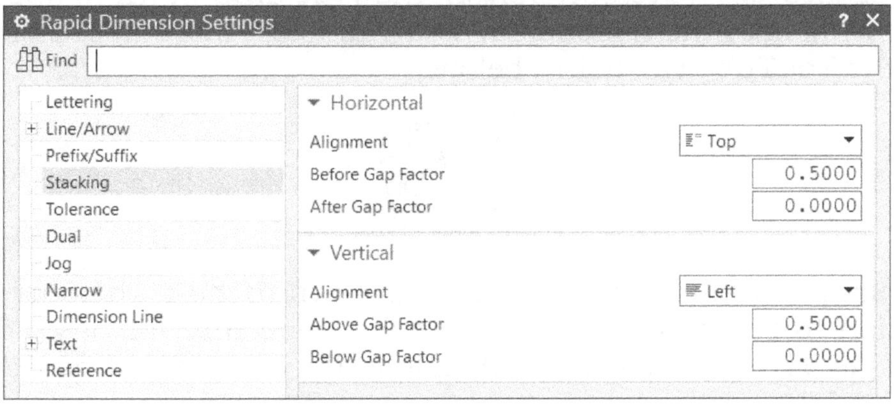

Figure-111. Stacking option

- Select desired option from the **Alignment** drop-downs to define the horizontal and vertical alignment of dimension text stacked over one another.
- Similarly, specify gap factors in respective edit boxes.
- Select the **Tolerance** option from the left area in the dialog box to define tolerance style of dimensioning; refer to Figure-112.

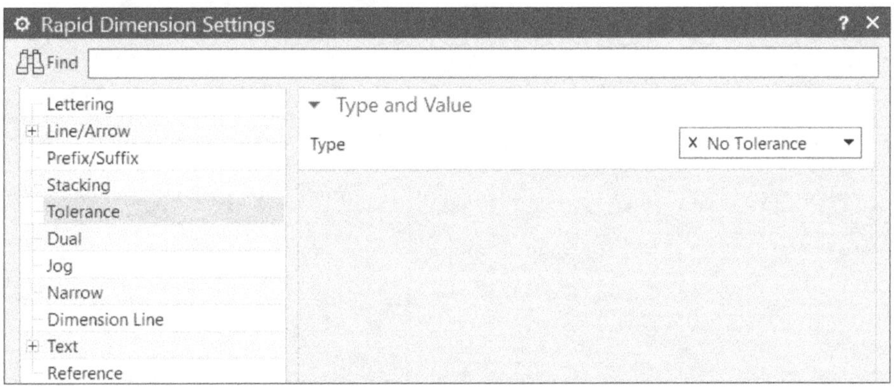

Figure-112. Tolerance options

- Select the **No Tolerance** option from the **Type** drop-down if you do not want to apply tolerance in dimensioning.
- Select the **Equal Bilateral Tolerance** option from the **Type** drop-down if you want to apply equal positive and negative tolerances to the dimension. Specify desired precision level of tolerances in the **Decimal Places** spinner. Specify the tolerance value in the **Tolerance** edit box to apply it to dimension. Select desired option from the **Text Position** drop-down to define where will the tolerance text be placed with respect to dimension line. Select the **Show Leading Zeros** check box to display 0 before dimension text decimal separator. Select the **Convert Tolerance when Changing Units** check box to automatically convert tolerance value based on change in unit.
- Select the **Bilateral Tolerance** option from the **Type** drop-down if you want to apply different tolerance values in positive and negative directions. On selecting this option, the **Upper Tolerance** and **Lower Tolerance** edit boxes will be available to specify positive and negative tolerances, respectively.
- Select the **Unilateral +** option from the **Type** drop-down to set only positive tolerance to the dimension.

- Select the **Unilateral -** option from the **Type** drop-down to set only negative tolerance to the dimension.
- Select the **Limits and Fits** option from the **Type** drop-down to apply limits & fits tolerance symbols to the dimension. You can learn more about limit and fits by scanning the YouTube video link below.

- Select the **Basic** option from the **Type** drop-down to make the current dimension as dimension to be used as exact reference. Note that for basic dimension, no tolerance is explicitly specified yet their tolerance is defined based on boundary dimensions of the part.
- Select the **Dual** option from the left area to define parameters for displaying dimensions in two different units; refer to Figure-113. Set the parameters in page as discussed earlier. Note that **Dual** option is not available when **Limits and Fits** option is selected in **Tolerance** page of the dialog box.

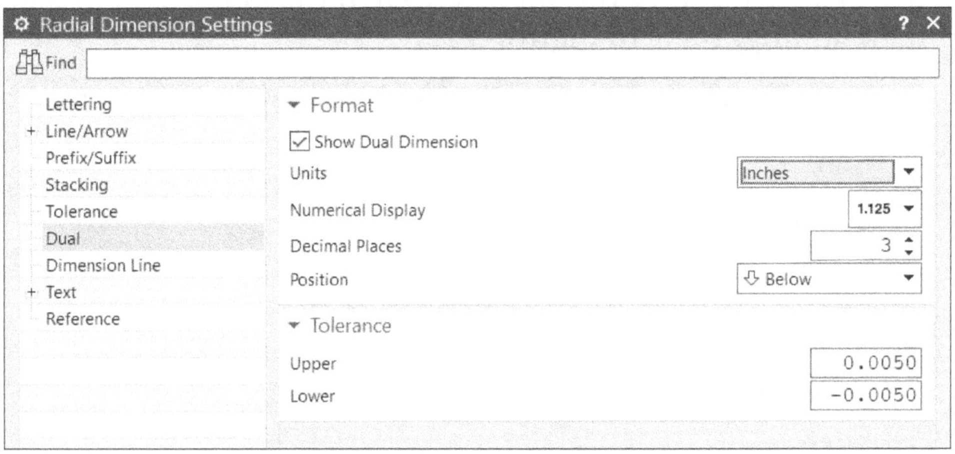

Figure-113. Dual setting page

- Select the **Text** option from the left area and specify the parameters related to dimension text as discussed earlier.
- Select the **Dimension Line** option from left area to define how dimension lines will be generated.
- Similarly, set other parameters and click on the **Close** button to exit the dialog box.
- Click on the **Select Dimension to Inherit** button from the **Rapid Dimension** dialog box if you want to use already existing dimension as reference style to create new dimension.
- Click on the **Enable Dimension Scene Dialogs** check box to enable input box for defining tolerance, text style, and so on; refer to Figure-114.

The procedure to apply dimensions to various entities are discussed next.

Dimensioning a Line

- Click on the line to be dimensioned. The length dimension of line will get attached to cursor; refer to Figure-115.

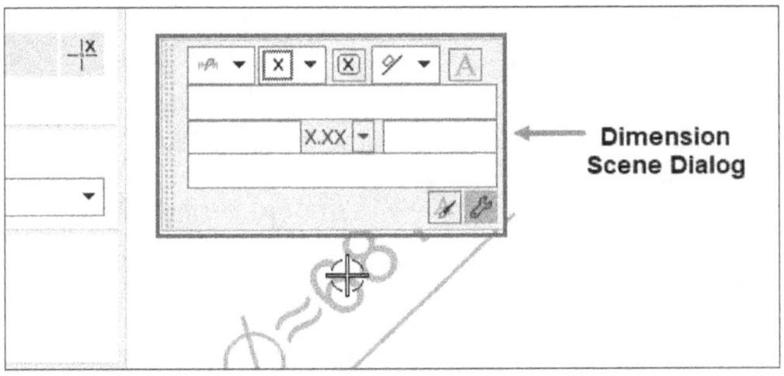

Figure-114. Dimension Scene Dialog

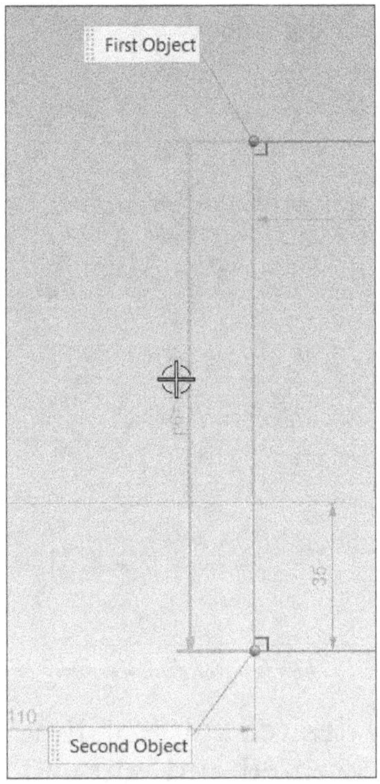

Figure-115. Dimensioning a line

- Click at desired location to place the dimension. You will be asked to specify length of the line. Enter desired value in dynamic input box and then select the next entity to be dimensioned.

Dimensioning Inclined Line

- Click on the inclined line near the middle. The dimension will get attached to the cursor; refer to Figure-116.

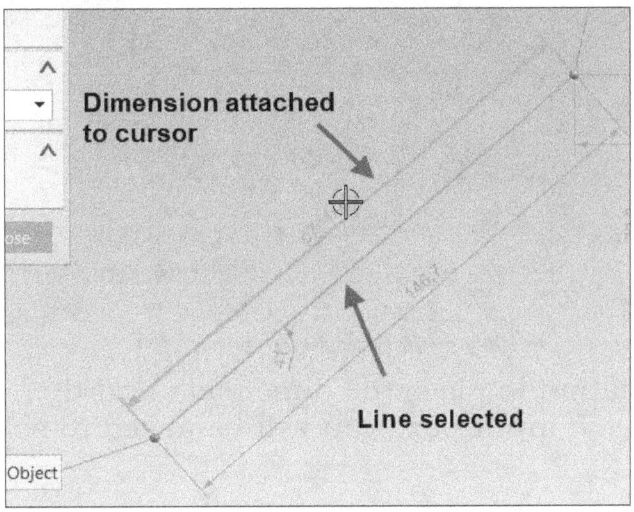

Figure-116. Preview of inclined dimension

- Move the cursor perpendicular to line from the mid-point and click at desired location to place inclined dimension. If you want to specify horizontal dimension then move the cursor along Y axis and click when horizontal dimension is displayed; refer to Figure-117. Similarly, if you want to create vertical dimension then move the along X axis and click when the vertical dimension is displayed; refer to Figure-118.

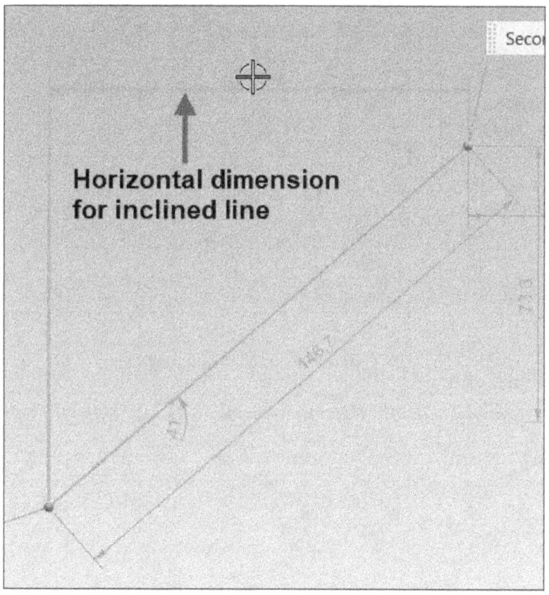

Figure-117. Horizontal dimensioning of inclined line

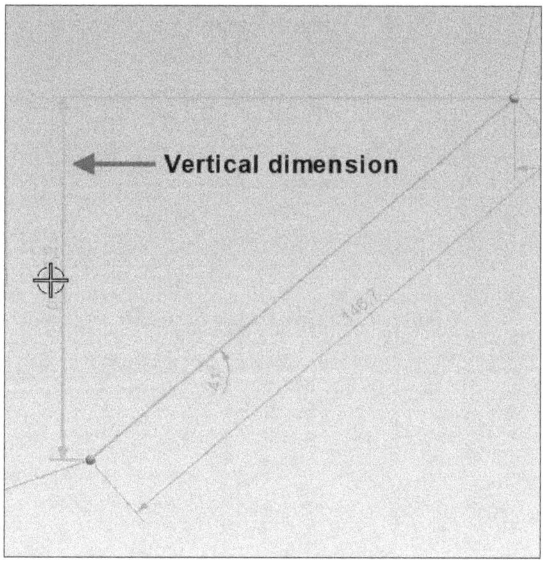

Figure-118. Vertical dimensioning of inclined line

- Specify desired value of dimension in the input box and press **ENTER**. The dimension will be created and you will be asked to select the next entity.

Dimensioning a Circle

- Click on the circumference of a circle to apply diameter dimension. The diameter dimension will get attached to the cursor; refer to Figure-119.

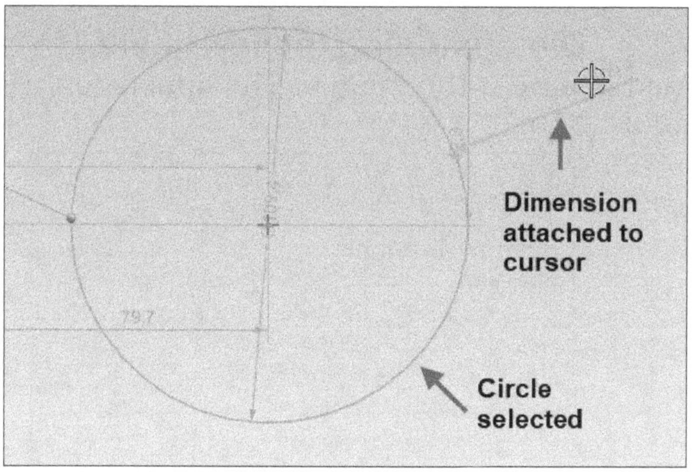

Figure-119. Applying diameter dimension

- Click at desired location to place the dimension and then enter desired value of dimension in dynamic input box. You will be asked to select the next entity for dimensioning.

Dimensioning an Arc

- Click on one of the end point of arc. The radius dimension will get attached to the cursor; refer to Figure-120.

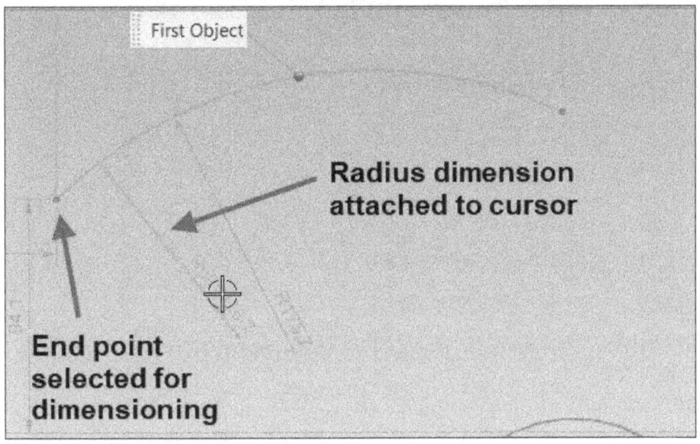

Figure-120. Applying radius dimension to arc

- Click at desired location to place the dimension and enter desired value of dimension in dynamic input box. You will be asked to select the next entity.

Creating Arc Angle Dimension

There is no direct method in NX to create arc angle dimension but we can create angular dimension between two lines. So, we will first create reference lines connecting the end points of arc with center; refer to Figure-121. Now, click on the **Rapid Dimension** tool and select the two reference lines created earlier. Preview of angular dimension will be displayed; refer to Figure-122.

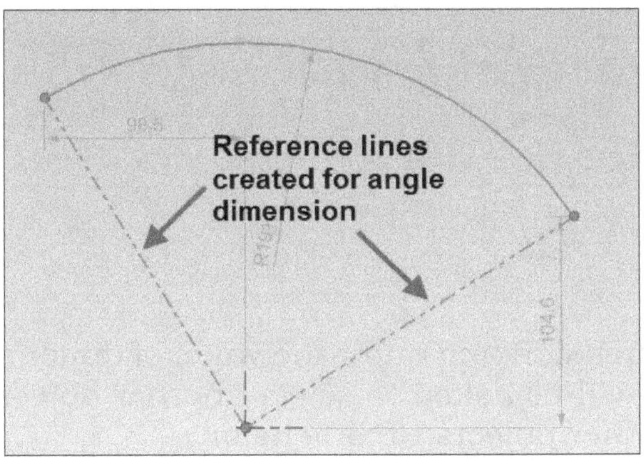

Figure-121. Lines created for angular dimension

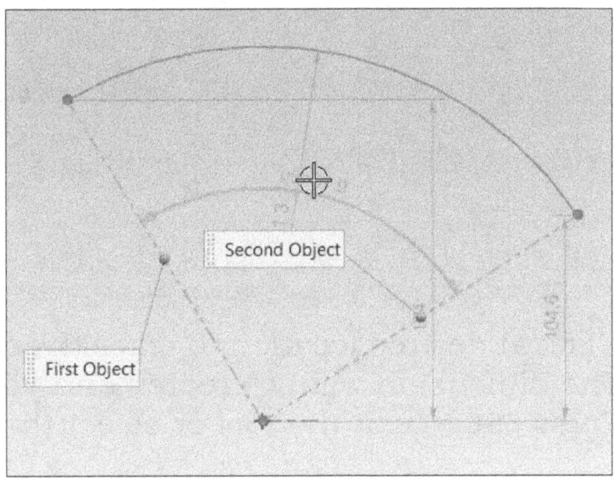

Figure-122. Preview of angle dimension

Click at desired location to place the dimension and enter desired value.

Linear Dimensioning

The **Linear Dimension** tool in **Rapid Dimension** drop-down is used to create straight dimensions like horizontal dimension, vertical dimension, and inclined dimension. The procedure to use this tool is discussed next.

- Click on the **Linear Dimension** tool from the **Rapid Dimension** drop-down in the **Solve** group of the **Home** tab in **Ribbon**. The **Linear Dimension** dialog box will be displayed and you will be asked to select the objects to be dimensioned; refer to Figure-123.
- Select the lines or end points of curves to create linear dimensions. The dimension will get attached to cursor; refer to Figure-124.

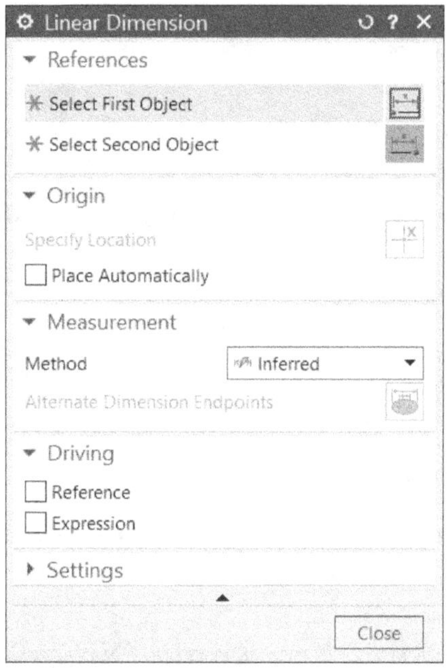

Figure-123. Linear Dimension dialog box

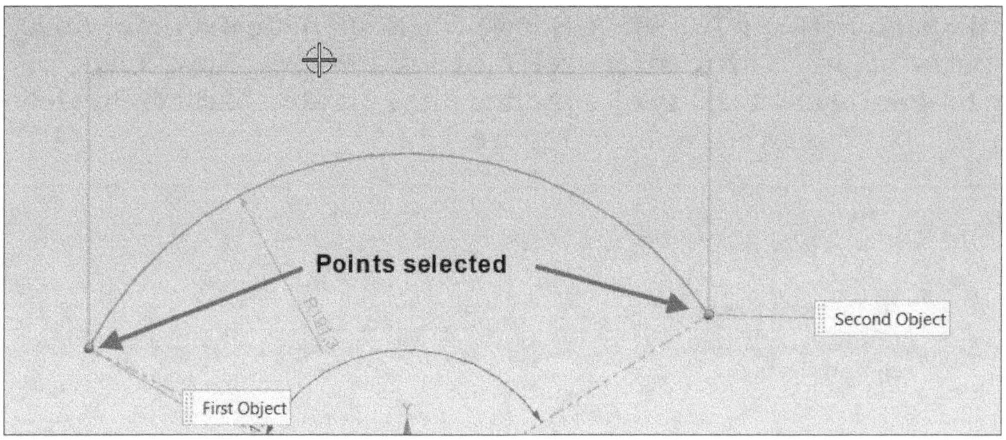

Figure-124. Preview of linear dimension

- Click at desired location to place the dimension and enter the value of dimension. The dimension will be created and you will be asked to select another objects.
- Press **ESC** to exit the tool or select the other objects to dimension.

Radial Dimensioning

The **Radial Dimension** tool in **Rapid Dimension** drop-down is used to create diameter or radius dimensions on selected curves. The procedure to use this tool is given next.

- Click on the **Radial Dimension** tool from the **Rapid Dimension** drop-down in **Solve** group of the **Home** tab in **Ribbon**. The **Radial Dimension** dialog box will be displayed; refer to Figure-125.
- Select the arc or circle to be dimensioned. If you have selected an arc then radius dimension will get attached and if you have selected a circle then diameter dimension will get attached to cursor.
- If you want to create radius dimension for circle then select the **Radius** option from **Method** drop-down in **Measurement** rollout of the dialog box and then select the circle. Similarly, if you want to apply diameter dimension to an arc then select the **Diameter** option from the **Method** drop-down in **Measurement** rollout and then select the arc.

- After selecting object, click at desired location to place the dimension and enter desired value in dynamic input box.
- Press **ESC** to exit the tool.

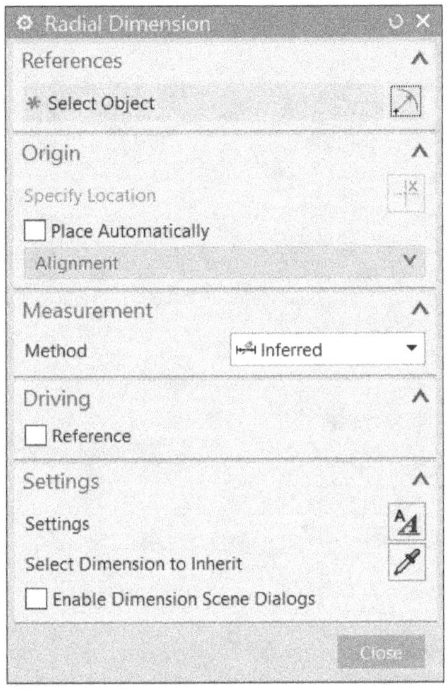

Figure-125. Radial Dimension dialog box

- To convert a diameter dimension to radial dimension or vice-versa, select the dimension from drawing area and right-click on it. A shortcut menu will be displayed; refer to Figure-126.

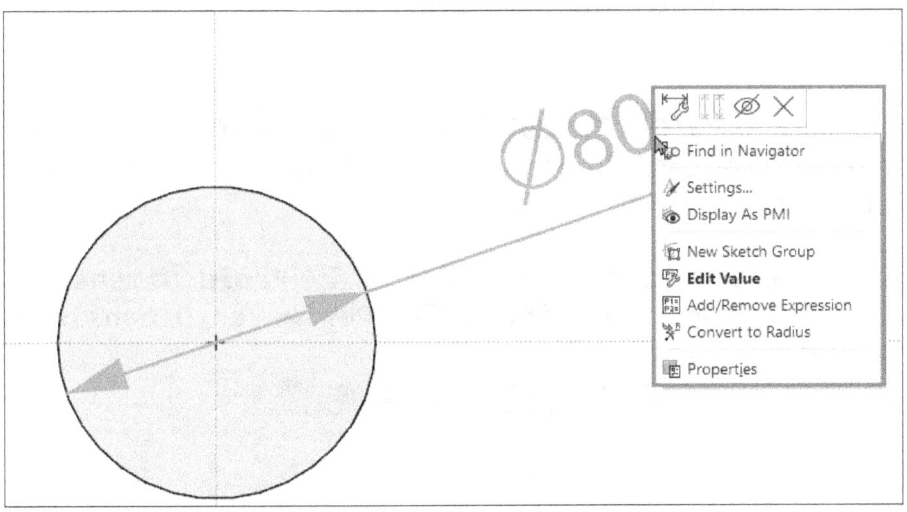

Figure-126. Radial dimension shortcut menu

- Select the **Convert to Radius** option from the shortcut menu. The diameter dimension will convert to radius dimension. Similarly, you can do vice-versa.

Angular Dimensioning

The **Angular Dimension** tool in **Rapid Dimension** drop-down is used to create angular dimension between two selected lines. The procedure to use this tool is given next.

- Click on the **Angular Dimension** tool from the **Rapid Dimension** drop-down in the **Curve** group of **Home** tab in the **Ribbon**. The **Angular Dimension** dialog box will be displayed; refer to Figure-127.

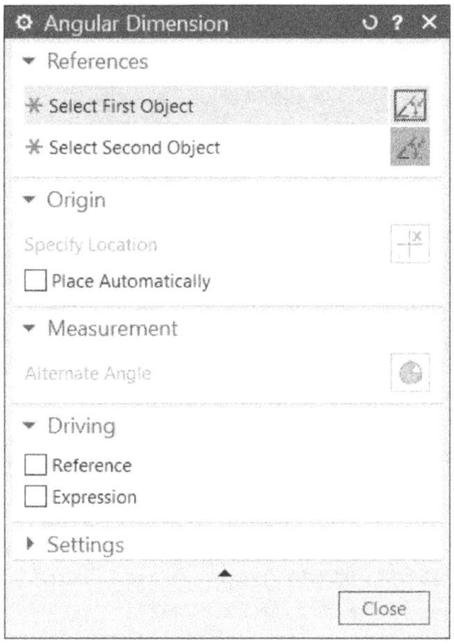

Figure-127. Angular Dimension dialog box

- Click on the first line and then second line to create angular dimension. The dimension will get attached to cursor.
- Click at desired location to place the dimension and enter desired angle value in dynamic edit box. The dimension will be created and you will be asked to select other lines for creating next angular dimension.
- Press **ESC** to exit to tool.

Perimeter Dimensioning

The **Perimeter Dimension** tool is used to constrain perimeter of selected objects. The procedure to use this tool is given next.

- Click on the **Perimeter Dimension** tool from the **Rapid Dimension** drop-down in the **Curve** group of **Home** tab in **Ribbon**. The **Perimeter Dimension** dialog box will be displayed; refer to Figure-128.

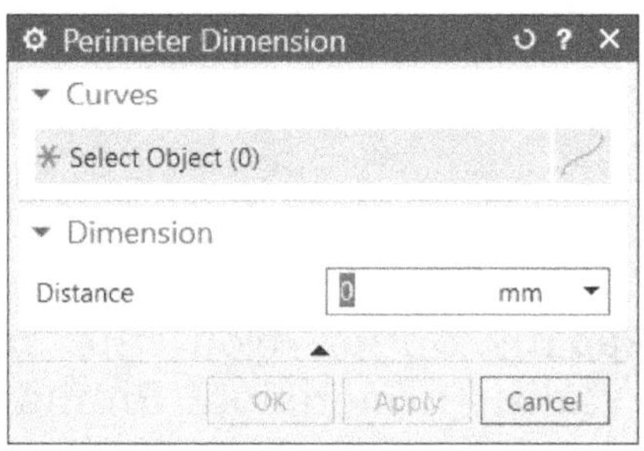

Figure-128. Perimeter Dimension dialog box

- Select the curve whose perimeter is to be specified. The value of perimeter of selected object will be displayed in the **Distance** edit box of the dialog box.
- Specify desired value of perimeter and click on the **OK** button to constrain the perimeter & exit the dialog box.

GEOMETRIC CONSTRAINTS

The **Geometric Constraints** are used to apply different constraints to the sketch entities so that the sketch retains specified shape. Like, you can make two lines parallel to each other. The tools to apply geometric constraints are available in the **Sketch Scene Bar**; refer to Figure-129.

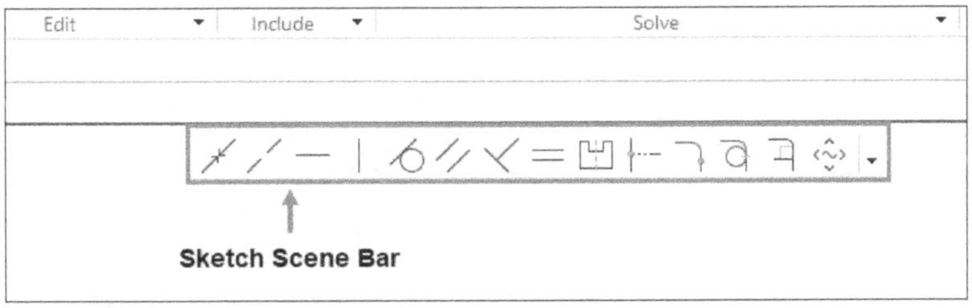

Figure-129. Sketch Scene Bar

Various constraints available in this dialog box are discussed next.

Applying Coincident Constraint

The **Coincident** constraint is used to make two selected vertices or points, coincide at same location. The procedure to apply this constraint is given next.

- Click on the **Make Coincident** button from the **Sketch Scene Bar**. The **Make Coincident** dialog box will be displayed; refer to Figure-130 and you will be asked to select objects to be made coincident.

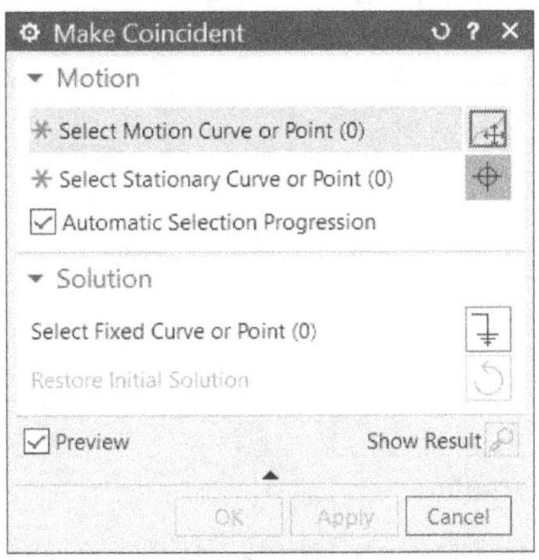

Figure-130. Make Coincident dialog box

- Select vertex/point of first object and then select vertex/point of second object. The preview of coincident points/vertices will be displayed; refer to Figure-131.
- Click on the **Apply** button to apply the constraint and start over. Click on the **OK** button from the dialog box to apply constraint and exit the dialog box.

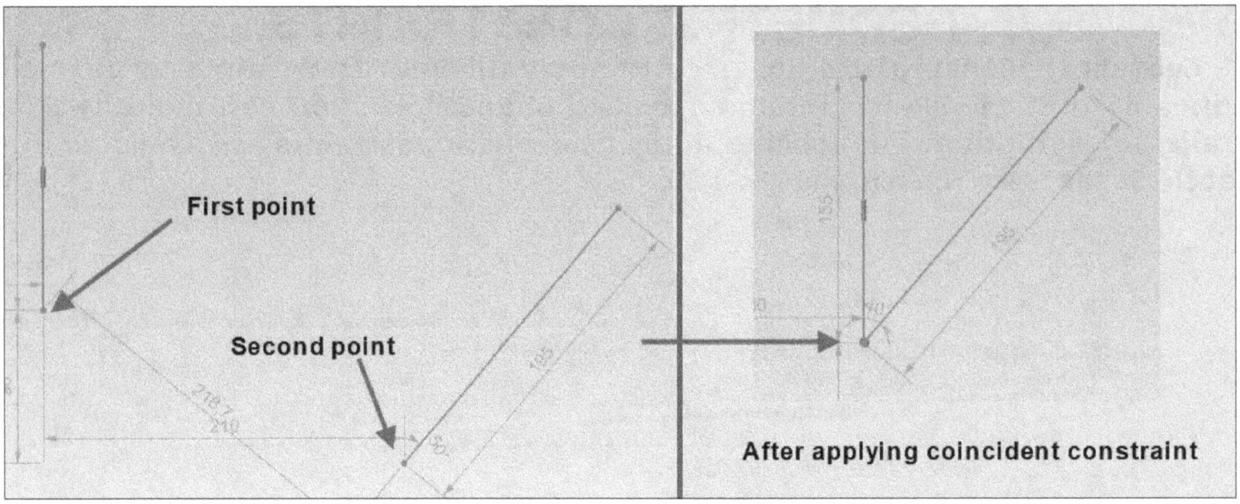

Figure-131. Applying coincident constraint

Applying Tangent Constraint

The **Tangent** constraint is used to make selected entity tangent to another entity. The procedure to apply this constraint is given next.

- Click on the **Tangent** button from the **Constraint** rollout in **Geometric Constraints** dialog box. You will be asked to select objects.
- Select the two objects to which you want to apply tangent constraint. The constraint will be applied to them; refer to Figure-132.

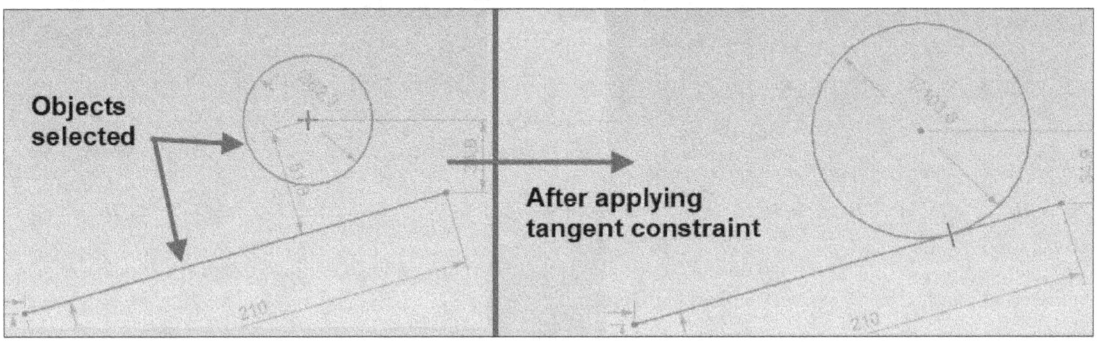

Figure-132. Applying tangent constraint

Applying Parallel Constraint

The **Parallel** constraint is used to make two selected lines parallel to each other. The procedure to apply this constraint is given next.

- Click on the **Make Parallel** button from the **Sketch Scene Bar**. The **Make Parallel** dialog box will be displayed; refer to Figure-133 and you will be asked to select objects.
- Select two lines which you want to make parallel. The constraint will be applied to them; refer to Figure-134. Click on the **OK** button to apply constraint.

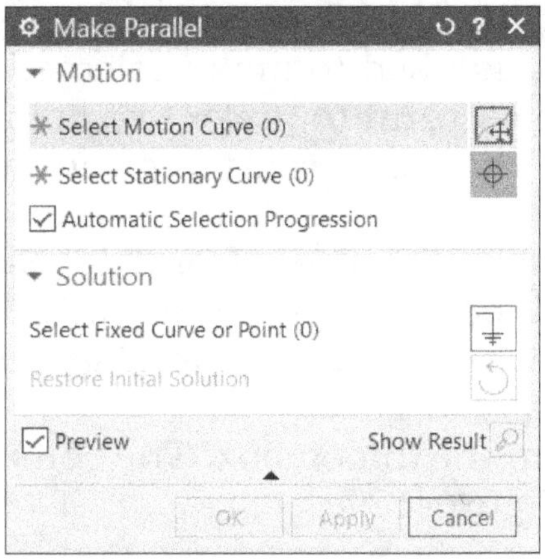

Figure-133. Make Parallel dialog box

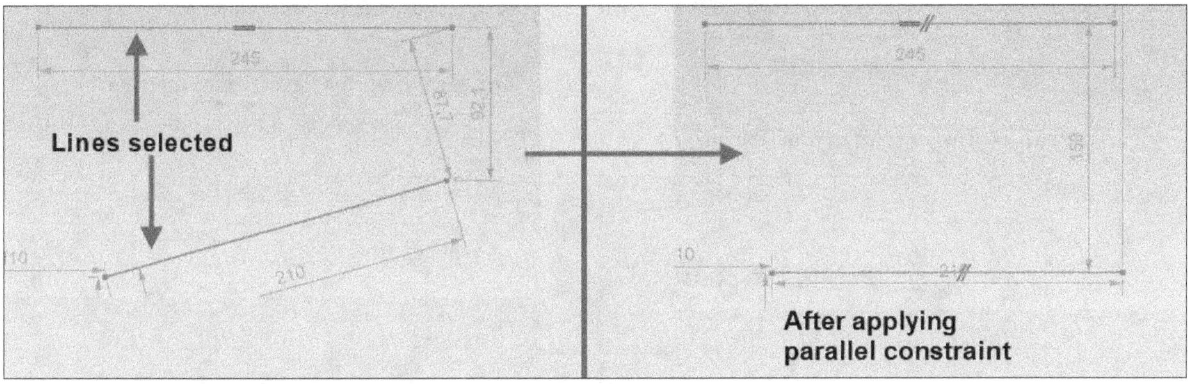

Figure-134. Applying parallel constraint

Applying Perpendicular Constraint

The **Perpendicular** constraint is used to make one object perpendicular to another object. The procedure to apply **Perpendicular** constraint is given next.

- Click on the **Make Perpendicular** button from the **Sketch Scene Bar**. The **Make Perpendicular** dialog box will be displayed and you will be asked to select objects.
- Select the two lines or curves which you want to make perpendicular. The constraint will be applied to them; refer to Figure-135. Click on the **OK** button to apply constraint.

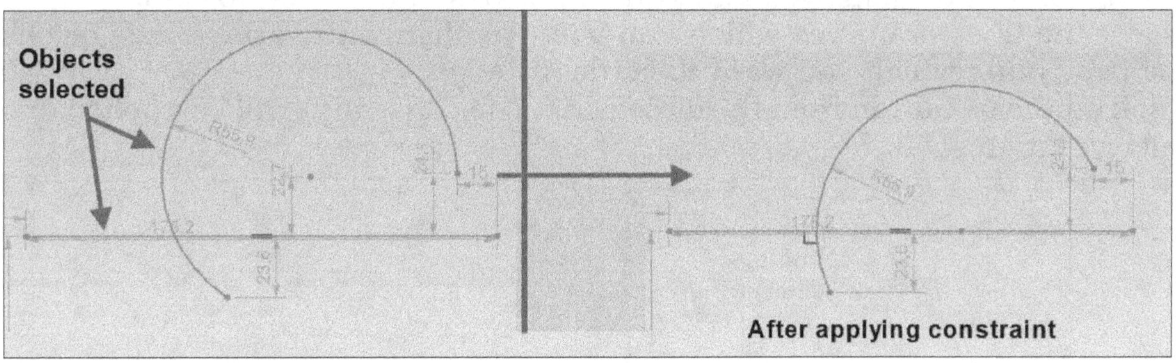

Figure-135. Applying perpendicular constraint

Applying Horizontal Constraint

The **Horizontal** constraint is used to make selected lines aligned with horizontal axis. You can also use this constraint to make two points aligned in same horizontal axis. The procedure to apply this constraint is given next.

- Click on the **Make Horizontal** button from the **Sketch Scene Bar**. The **Make Horizontal** dialog box will be displayed and you will be asked to select objects.
- Select the lines or curves which you want to align with horizontal axis or click on two points to be horizontally aligned.
- Click on the **OK** button from the dialog box. The constraint will be applied to them; refer to Figure-136 and Figure-137.

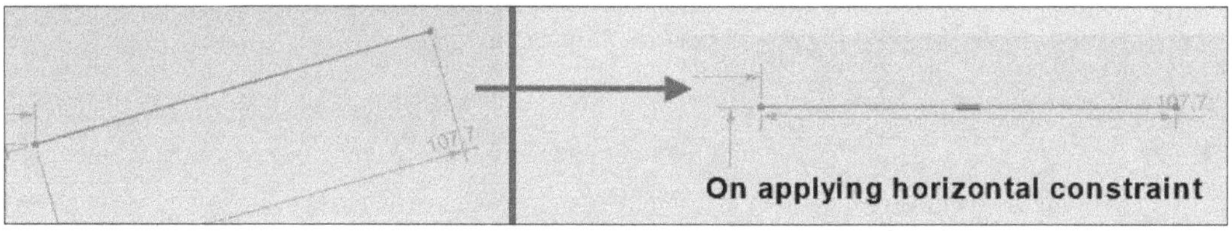

Figure-136. Applying horizontal constraint

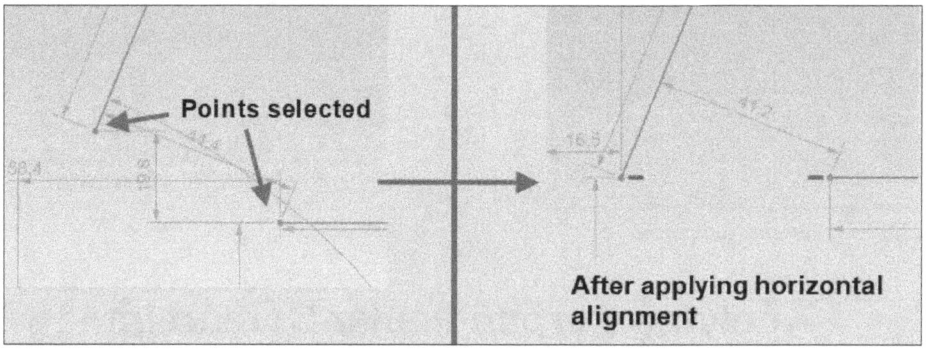

Figure-137. Applying horizontal alignment

Applying Vertical Constraint

The **Vertical** constraint is used to make selected lines aligned with vertical axis of sketch. You can also use this constraint to make two points aligned in same vertical axis. The procedure to apply this constraint is given next.

- Click on the **Make Vertical** button from the **Sketch Scene Bar**. The **Make Vertical** dialog box will be displayed and you will be asked to select objects.
- Select the lines or curves which you want to align with vertical axis or click on the two points which you want to vertically align.
- Click on the **OK** button from the dialog box. The constraint will be applied to them; refer to Figure-138.

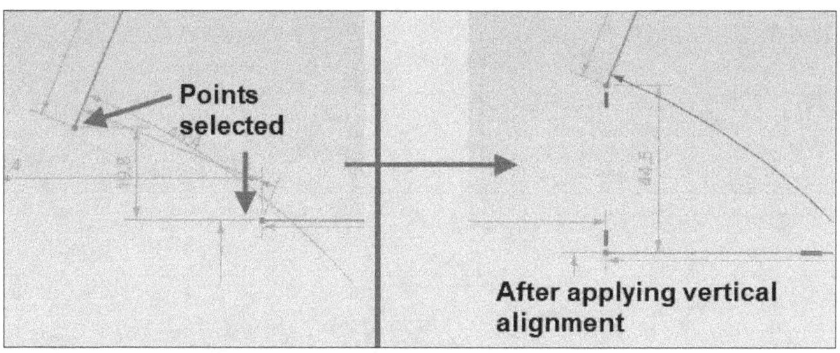

Figure-138. Applying vertical alignment

Applying Midpoint Constraint

The **Midpoint** constraint is used to place selected vertex/point on the midpoint of another selected curve. The procedure to use this tool is given next.

- Click on the **Make Midpoint Aligned** button from the **Sketch Scene Bar**. The **Make Midpoint Aligned** dialog box will be displayed and you will be asked to select objects.
- Select the point/vertex of object and then select the curve on whose midpoint you want to place the vertex/point. Preview of constraint will be displayed; refer to Figure-139. Click on the **OK** button to apply constraint.

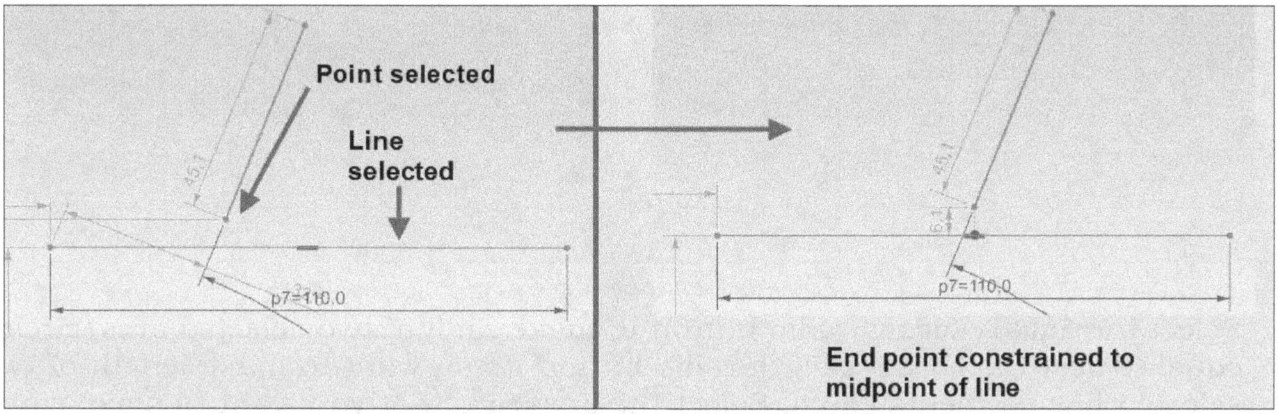

Figure-139. Applying midpoint constraint

Applying Collinear Constraint

The **Collinear** constraint is used to make two or more lines collinear. The procedure to apply this constraint is given next.

- Click on the **Make Collinear** button from the **Sketch Scene Bar**. The **Make Collinear** dialog box will be displayed and you will be asked to select objects.
- Select the lines that you want to make collinear. Preview of constraint will be displayed; refer to Figure-140. Click on the **OK** button to apply constraint.

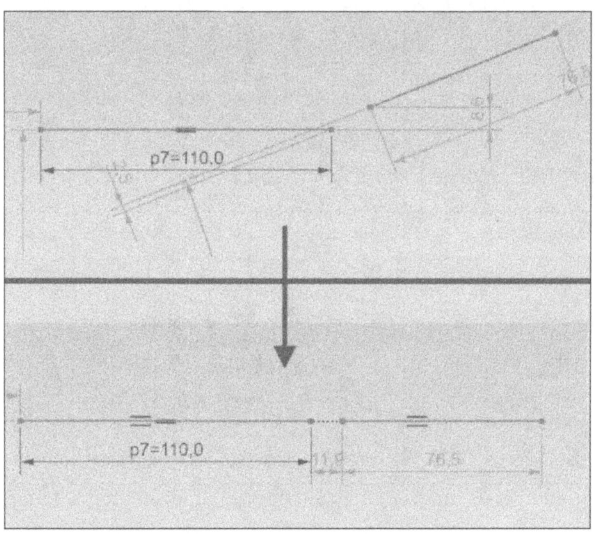

Figure-140. Applying collinear constraint

Applying Equal Constraint

The **Equal** constraint [=] is used to make two selected lines/arcs/circles of same size. The procedure to apply equal length constraint is given next.

- Click on the **Make Equal** button from the **Sketch Scene Bar**. The **Make Equal** dialog box will be displayed; refer to Figure-141 and you will be asked to select objects.

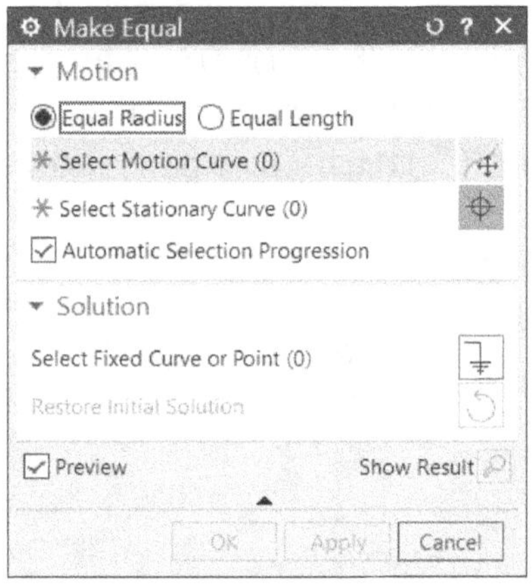

Figure-141. Make Equal dialog box

- Select the **Equal Radius** radio button to make radii of two selected arcs/circles equal. Select the **Equal Length** radio button if you want to make length of two selected line segments equal. Select the lines/arc that you want to make equal in length/radii. Preview of equal constraint will be displayed; refer to Figure-142 and Figure-143.

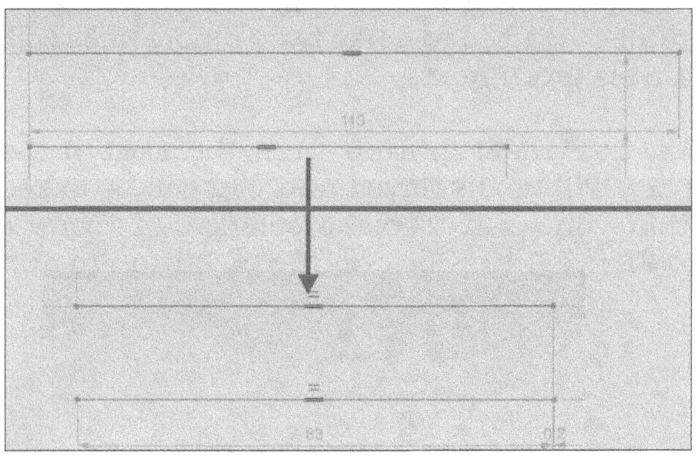

Figure-142. Applying equal length constraint

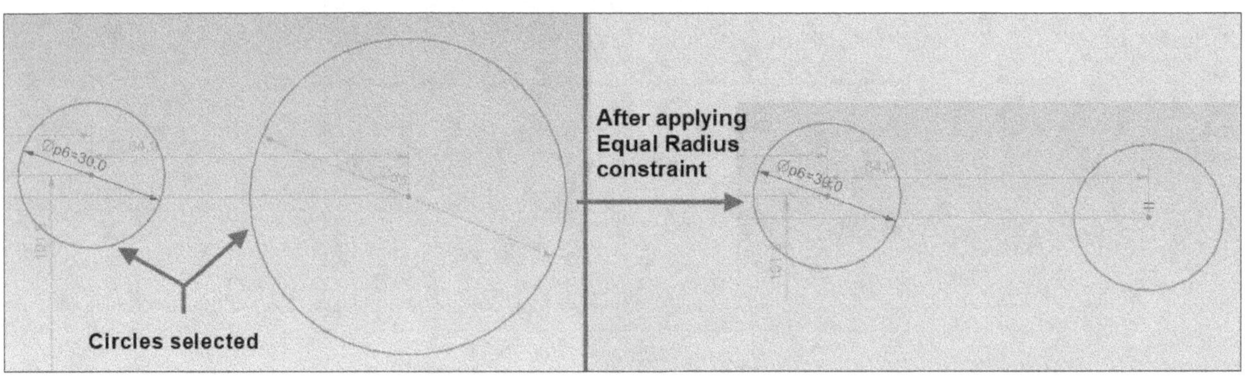

Figure-143. Applying equal radius constraint

- Click on the **OK** button to apply constraint.

Applying Symmetric Constraint

The **Symmetric** constraint is used to make two selected entities mirror copy with respect to selected symmetry line. The procedure to apply this constraint is given next.

- Click on the **Make Symmetric** button from the **Sketch Scene Bar**. The **Make Collinear** dialog box will be displayed; refer to Figure-144 and you will be asked to select objects.

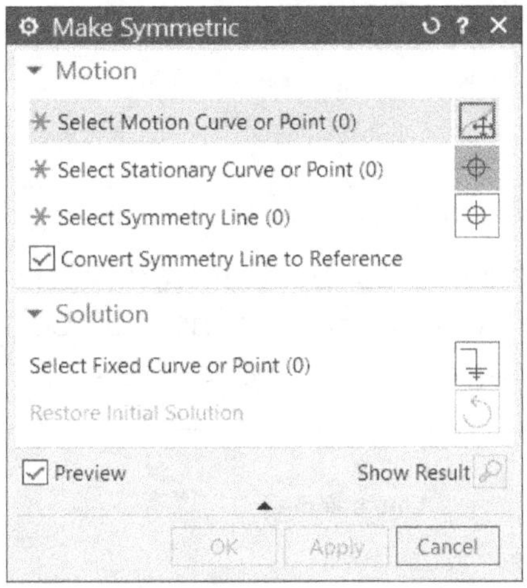

Figure-144. Make Symmetric dialog box

- Select the two objects (lines, arcs, circles, and so on) to be made symmetric and then select the symmetry line. Preview of constraint will be displayed; refer to Figure-145. Click on the **OK** button to apply constraint.

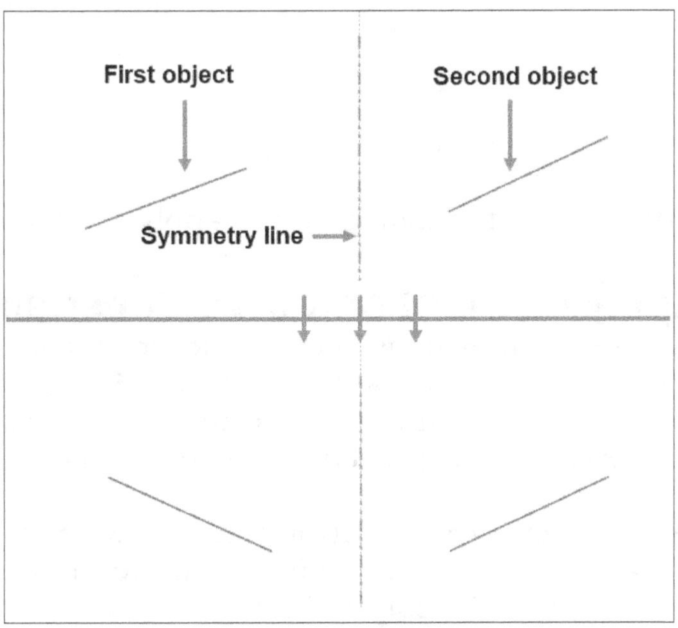

Figure-145. Applying symmetric constraint

Applying Midpoint Aligned Constraint

The **Make Midpoint Aligned** tool is used to align selected line/object with mid point of another entity. The procedure to use this tool is given next.

- Click on the **Make Midpoint Aligned** tool from the **Sketch Scene Bar**. The **Make Midpoint Aligned** dialog box will be displayed; refer to Figure-146 and you will be asked to select objects.

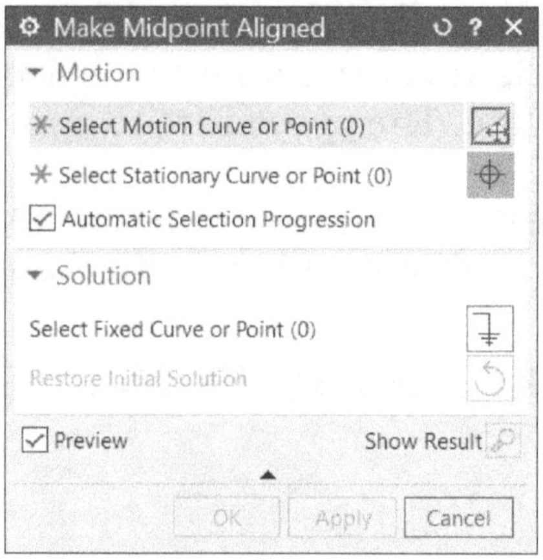

Figure-146. Make Midpoint Aligned dialog box

- Select the point of line/object to be aligned with mid point of another entity and then select the entity whose mid point will be used as reference. Preview of alignment will be displayed; refer to Figure-147.

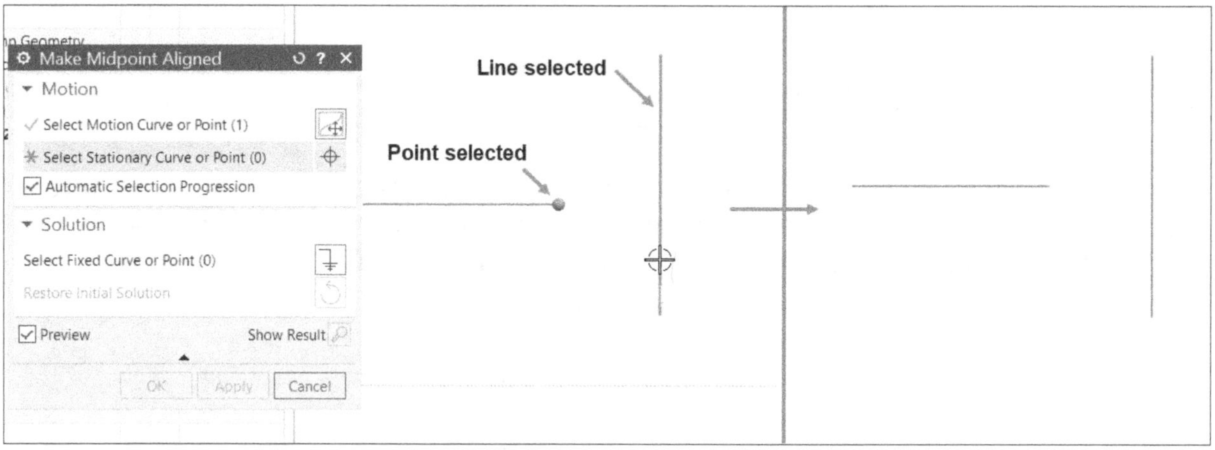

Figure-147. Preview of midpoint aligned

- Click on the **OK** button from the dialog box to apply the changes.

Applying Point on Curve Constraint

The **Point on String** constraint is used to restrict the movement of selected point on selected curve. This option is available in **Sketch Scene Bar** when the **Create Persistent Relations** toggle button is selected in the **Options** drop-down of **Solve** group in the **Home** tab of **Ribbon**. The procedure to apply this constraint is given next.

- Click on the **Make Point on String** button from the **Sketch Scene Bar**. The **Make Point on String** dialog box will be displayed; refer to Figure-148 and you will be asked to select the objects to be constrained.
- Click on the point/vertex and then click on the curve. Preview of constraint will be displayed; refer to Figure-149.

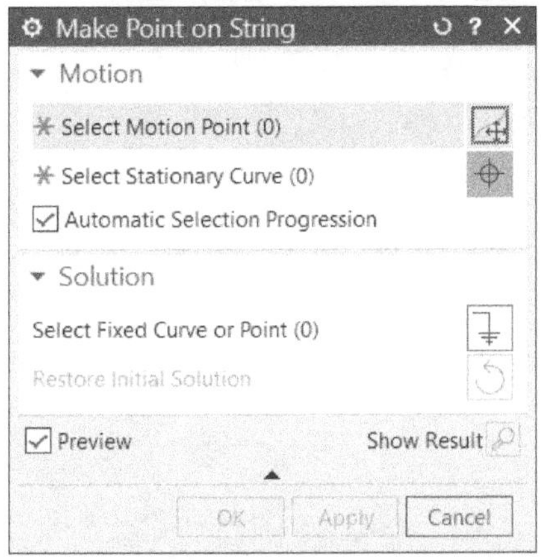

Figure-148. Make Point on String dialog box

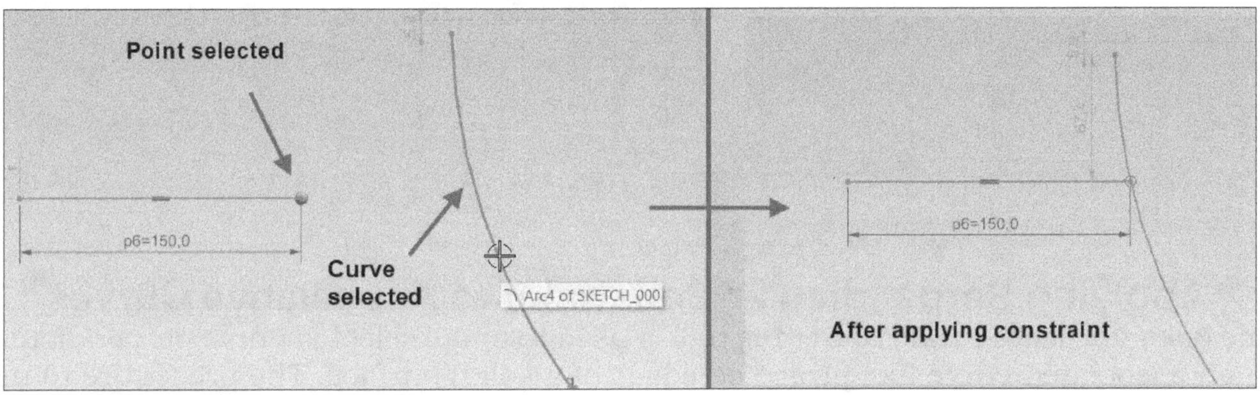

Figure-149. Applying point on curve constraint

Applying Tangent Constraint to Associative Curves

The **Make Tangent to String** tool is used to make selected curve tangent to an associated curve like projected edges of a solid/surface. The procedure to use this tool is given next.

- Click on the **Make Tangent to String** tool from the **Sketch Scene Bar**. The **Make Tangent to String** dialog box will be displayed; refer to Figure-150.

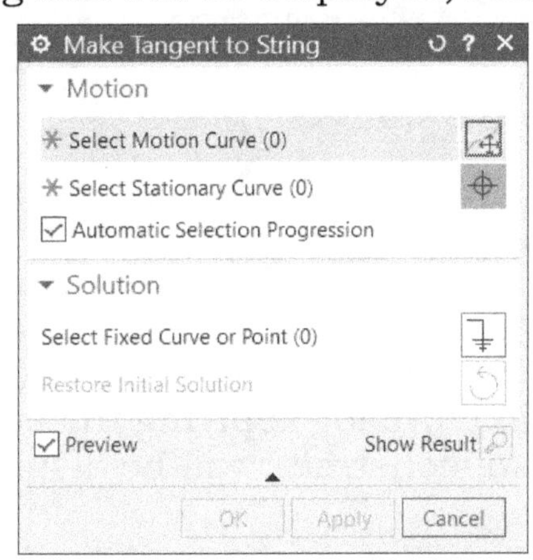

Figure-150. Make Tangent to String dialog box

- Select the curve which you want to move while applying the constraint and then select the associative curve. Preview of constraint will be displayed; refer to Figure-151.
- Click on the **OK** button from the dialog box to apply the constraint.

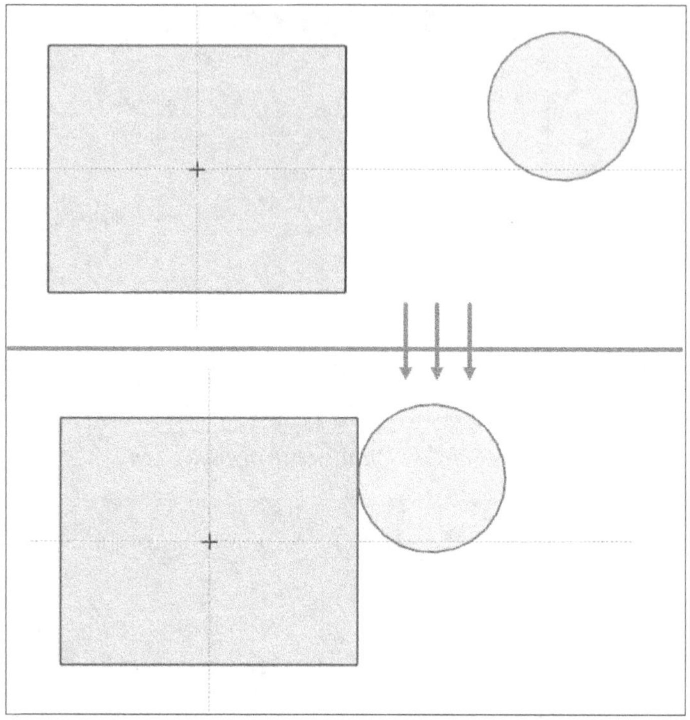

Figure-151. Applying constraint

Applying Perpendicular Constraint to Associative Curves

The **Make Perpendicular to String** tool is used to make selected curve perpendicular to an associated curve like projected edges of a solid/surface. The procedure to use this tool is given next.

- Click on the **Make Perpendicular to String** tool from the **Sketch Scene Bar**. The **Make Perpendicular to String** dialog box will be displayed; refer to Figure-152.

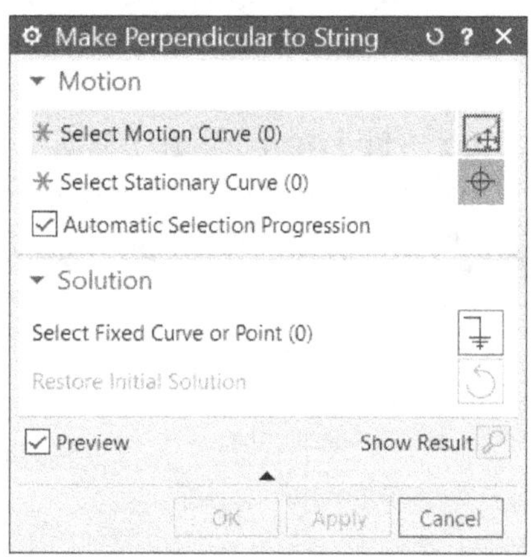

Figure-152. Make Perpendicular to String dialog box

- Select the curve which will move for applying the constraint and then select the associated curve. Preview of constraint will be displayed; refer to Figure-153.

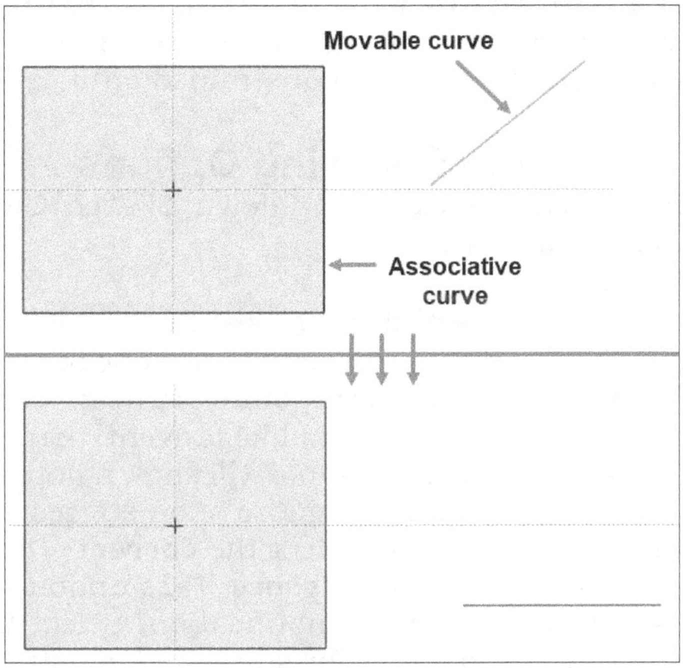

Figure-153. Applying perpendicular to string constraint

- Click on the **OK** button from the dialog box to apply the constraint.

Make Uniform Scale

The **Make Uniform Scale** tool is used to make a spline scale uniformly when using **Scale Curve** tool later. After selecting the spline to which you want to apply the constraint, click on the **Make Uniform Scale** tool from the **Sketch Scene Bar**.

Creating Persistent Relation

The **Create Persistent Relations** tool is used to activate mode in which you can create permanent relations and use the Make commands of constraints.

Fixing Curves

The **Fix Curve** tool is used to make selected curves fixed at their location so that they do not move accidently. To make a curve fixed, click on the **Fix Curve** tool from the **Solve** group in the **Home** tab of the **Ribbon**, select the curve(s) to be fixed, and click on the **OK** button.

Showing Movable Entities

Select the **Show Movable Entities** toggle button from **Solve** group in the **Home** tab of **Ribbon** to display entities which can be moved dynamically in brown color. Note that in this case, fully defined sketch entities will be displayed in black color. When this button is toggle ON then you can easily identify the sketch entities which are to be dimensioned for making fully defined sketch.

Relaxing Dimensions for Dynamic Modifications

Select the **Relax Dimensions** toggle button from the **Solve** group in **Home** tab of **Ribbon** to allow dynamic modification of dimensioned entities by dragging or based on applied constraints.

Relaxing Relations for Dynamic Modifications

Select the **Relax Relations** toggle button from the **Solve** group in the **Home** tab of the **Ribbon** to allow dynamic modifications of constrained entities in the sketch.

Sketch Checking Options

There are two tools in **Sketch Checking** drop-down; **Sketch Checking** and **Checking Settings**. These tools are discussed next.

Sketch Checking

The **Sketch Checking** tool is used to continuously run checks on the movable curves in the current sketch. If two curves or curve points are near each other in such a way that there is possibility of applying constraint like tangent, perpendicular, horizontal, and so on; then activating **Sketch Checking** tool will show a notification at such places in the sketch. You can decide to apply or ignore such suggestions by right-clicking on the notification; refer to Figure-154. Select the **Correct This** option if you want to apply suggested constraint. Select the **Ignore This** option if you do not want to apply suggested constraint and clear the notification. Select the **Deactivate this Check** option if you do not want to check for suggested constraint anymore.

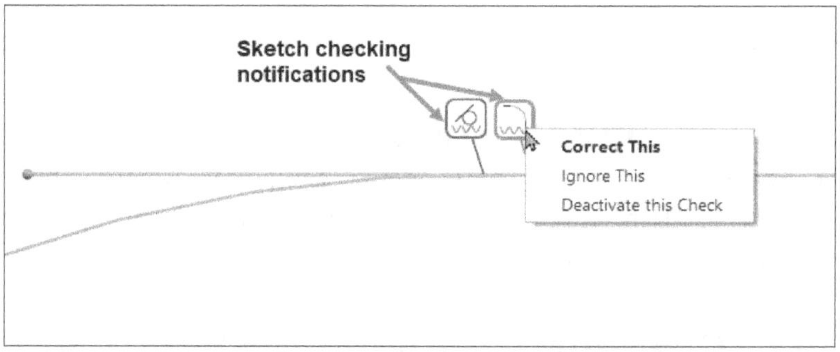

Figure-154. Sketch Checking shortcut menu

Checking Settings

The **Checking Settings** tool is used to define which constraints will be checked and what will be the check criteria. The procedure to use this tool is given next.

- Click on the **Checking Settings** tool from the **Sketch Checking** drop-down in **Solve** group of **Home** tab in the **Ribbon**. The **Sketch Checking Settings** dialog box will be displayed; refer to Figure-155.
- Select check boxes for constraints that you want to be checked actively in the sketch from the **Active Checks** section of the dialog box.
- Select the **Display Size** option from the **Check Measurement** drop-down to consider displayed size of sketch entities for measurement. The displayed size also considers zoom level so if you have zoomed in by 4x or more than 0.1 inch actual gap will be like 0.4 inch displayed gap. Select the **Model Size** option if you want to consider actual size of entities for measurement.
- Set desired values in the **Distance Checks**, **Angular Checks**, **Tiny Curves Check**, and **Tangent at Vertex Check** edit boxes to define the limit below which gap will be considered for applying constraint check notification.
- Click on the **OK** button from the dialog box to apply the check settings.

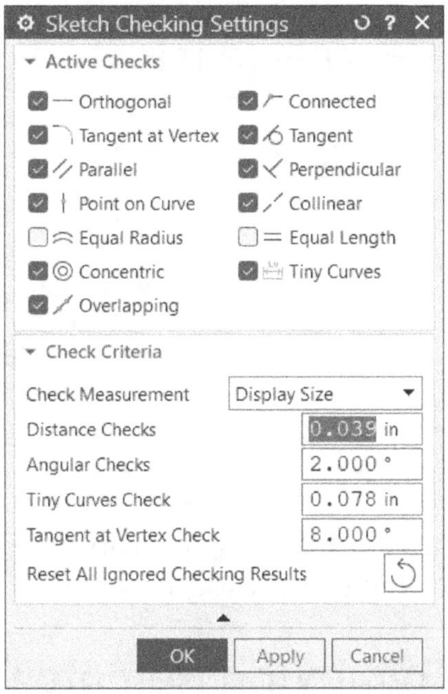

Figure-155. Sketch Checking Settings dialog box

Defining Work Region

The **Work Region** tool is used to define the region in sketch which can be modified. Using this tool ensures that rest of the sketch is not modified unintentionally. The procedure to use this tool is given next.

- Click on the **Work Region** tool from the **Options** drop-down in the **Home** tab of the **Ribbon**. The **Work Region** dialog box will be displayed; refer to Figure-156.

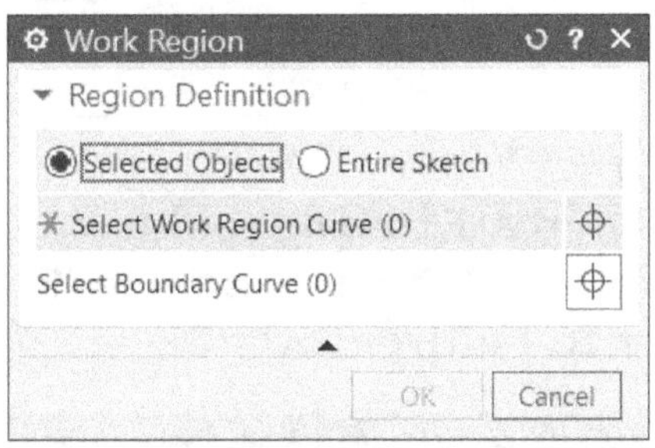

Figure-156. Work Region dialog box

- Select the **Selected Objects** radio button and select the section of sketch which you want to allow for modification by using window selection; refer to Figure-157.

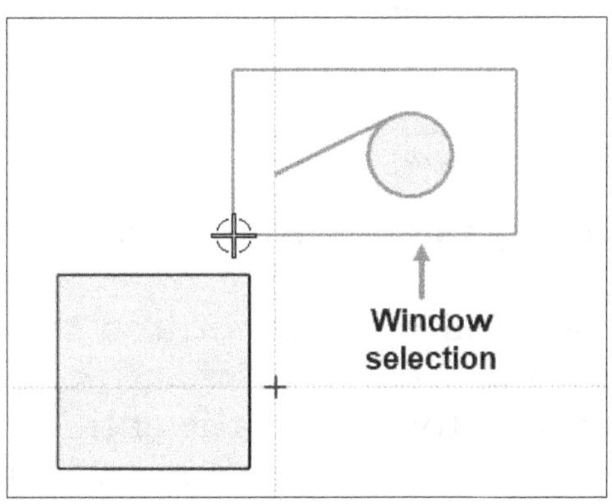

Figure-157. Making window selection

- Click on the **OK** button from the dialog box to apply changes. On doing so, rest of the sketch gets inactive; refer to Figure-158.

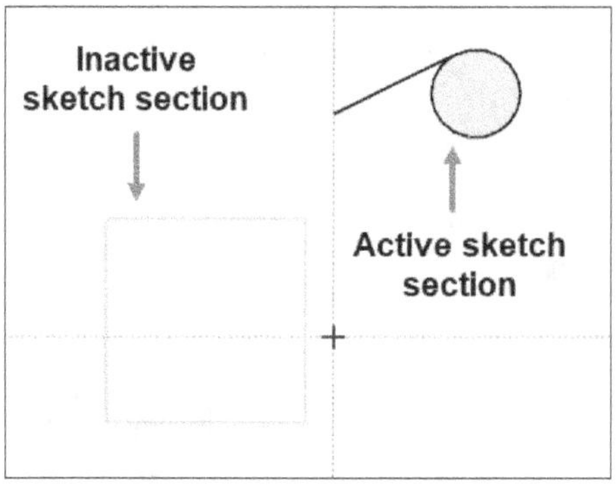

Figure-158. After defining work region

- To exit this mode, activate the **Work Region** tool again, select the **Entire Sketch** radio button from the **Work Region** dialog box, and click on the **OK** button.

Adding/Removing Remote Finding

The **Add/Remove Remote Finding** tool is used to add/remove relation lines displayed on applied constraints where entity is not directly linked to related object; refer to Figure-159. The procedure to use this tool is given next.

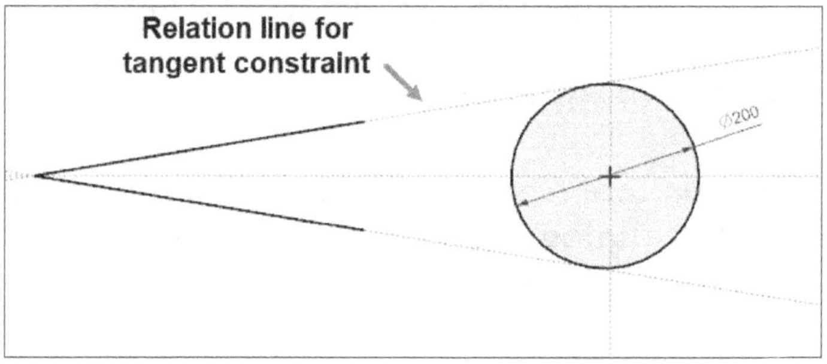

Figure-159. Relation line

- Click on the **Add/Remove Remote Finding** tool from the **Options** drop-down in the **Solve** group of **Home** tab in the **Ribbon**. The **Add/Remove Remote Finding** dialog box will be displayed; refer to Figure-160.

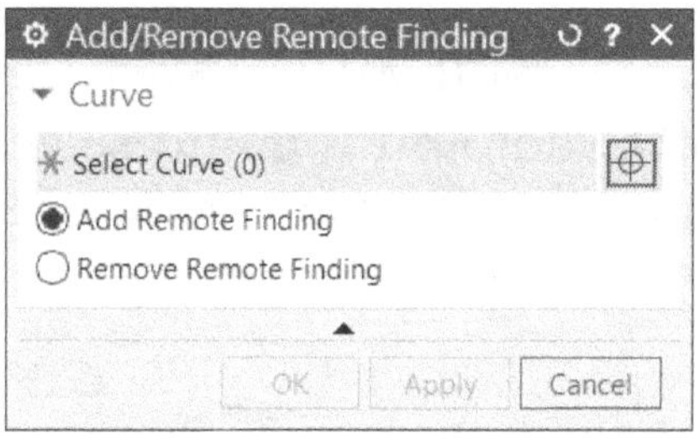

Figure-160. Add/Remove Remote Finding dialog box

- Select the **Add Remote Finding** radio button to display the relation lines of selected entities.
- Select the **Remove Remote Finding** radio button to remove the relation lines of selected entities from drawing area.
- After selected desired radio button, select the entities whose relations lines are to be added/removed and click on the **OK** button; refer to Figure-161.

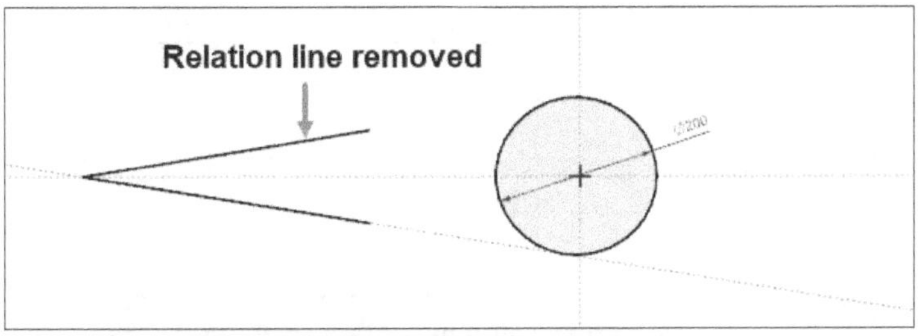

Figure-161. After removing relation line

Enabling Rotation and Dragging of Sketch Entities

The **Rotate Drag** tool is used to enable/disable rotation and dragging of selected sketch entities. The procedure to use this tool is given next.

- Click on the **Rotate Drag** tool from the **Options** drop-down in the **Solve** group of **Home** tab in the **Ribbon**. The rotation handle will be displayed at the origin; refer to Figure-162.

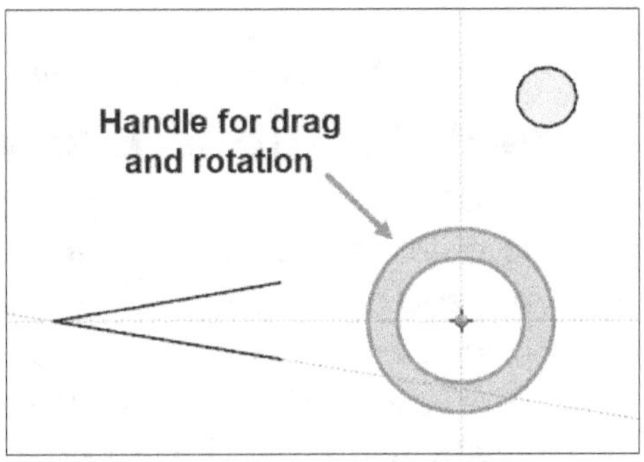

Figure-162. Handle for drag and rotation

- Select the entity to be rotated or scaled and drag it in the drawing area.
- Click again on the tool to exit.

Creating Persistent Relations

There are two ways in which relations can be used in sketching; using them to temporarily align entities and using them to permanently relate the sketch entities. If the **Create Persistent Relations** toggle button is not selected in the **Options** drop-down of **Home** tab in the **Ribbon** then temporary relations are created which can be modified simply by dragging the entities. Select this toggle button to apply permanent relations. Note that on selecting this toggle button, more buttons become available in the **Sketch Scene Bar**.

Displaying Persistent Relations

The **Display Persistent Relations** toggle button is used to display/hide persistent relations in the drawing area. Select the **Display Persistent Relations** toggle button from the **Options** drop-down in the **Solve** group of **Home** tab in the **Ribbon**. Symbol of applied relation will be displayed in the drawing area; refer to Figure-163.

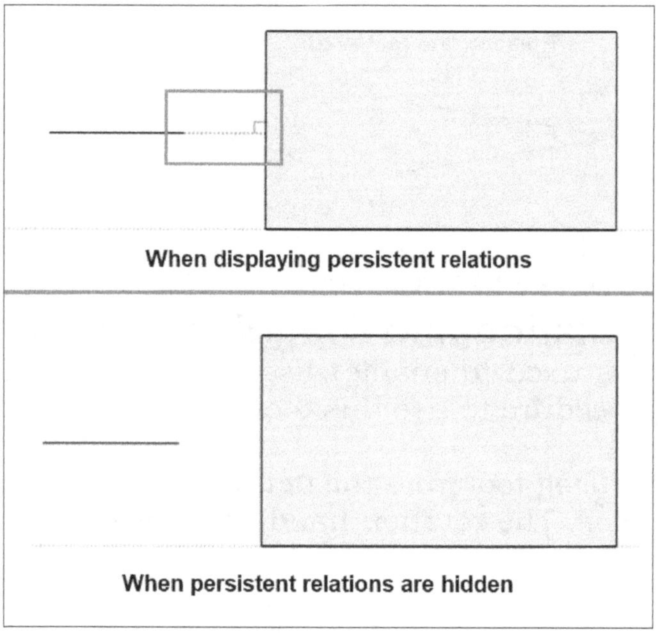

Figure-163. Showing and hiding persistent relations

Persistent Relations Browser

The **Persistent Relations Browser** is used to analyze persistent relations applied in the active sketch. Click on the **Persistent Relations Browser** tool from the **Options** drop-down in the **Solve** group of **Home** tab in the **Ribbon**. The **Persistent Relations Browser** will be displayed; refer to Figure-164. By default, the **Relations** radio button is selected in the **Top-level Node Objects** section of the dialog box so all the relations applied in active sketch are displayed in the dialog box. Select the **Curves** radio button from the **Top-level Node Objects** section of the dialog box to check the curves in sketch which are not fully constrained. Click on the **Close** button to exit the dialog box.

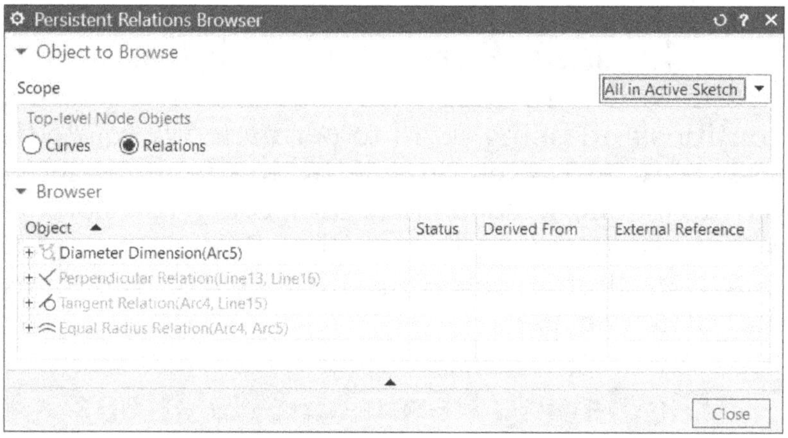

Figure-164. Persistent Relations Browser

Ignoring Relations

The **Ignore Relation** tool is used to remove selected relations and dimensions from persistent relation finder results and allow dynamic modifications of the related entities. The procedure to use this tool is given next.

- Click on the **Ignore Relation** tool from the **Options** drop-down in the **Solve** group of **Home** tab in the **Ribbon**. The **Ignore Relation** dialog box will be displayed; refer to Figure-165.

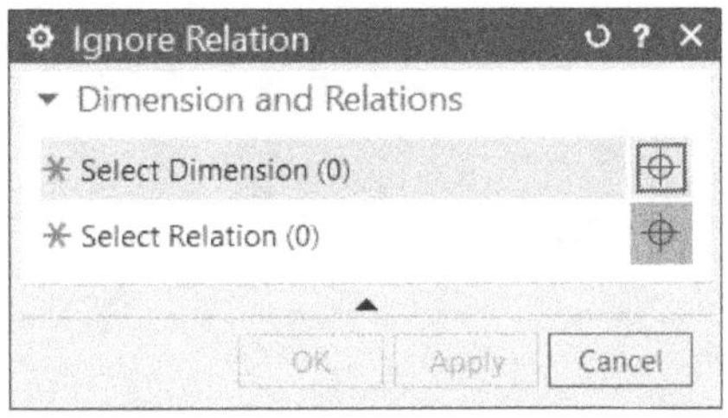

Figure-165. Ignore Relation dialog box

- Select desired relations and dimensions from the drawing area and click on the **OK** button to ignore them.

SELF-ASSESSMENT

Q1. Which tool is used to create a string of lines in NX?
A. Arc
B. Line
C. Circle
D. Spline

Q2. Which key is used to switch between input boxes while creating a line?
A. CTRL
B. SHIFT
C. TAB
D. ALT

Q3. What does the Chain Curves option do?
A. Deletes curves
B. Enables continuous line creation
C. Changes color
D. Rotates line

Q4. Which option creates construction geometry?
A. Infinite Line Only
B. Create Reference Geometry
C. Segment Only
D. Chain Curves

Q5. Which option creates only infinite construction line?
A. Segment Only
B. Add Infinite Line
C. Infinite Line Only
D. Chain Curves

Q6. What is created when following curvature of another arc?
A. Straight arc
B. Tangential arc
C. Broken arc
D. Infinite arc

Q7. Spline tool is mainly used in?
A. Drafting
B. Reverse engineering
C. Printing
D. Assembly

Q8. Default spline creation method is?
A. Through Points
B. By Poles
C. By Curve
D. By Lines

Q9. Closed option in spline does what?
A. Deletes spline
B. Closes start and end points
C. Changes color
D. Rotates spline

Q10. G1 curvature option represents?
A. Straight line
B. Tangent curve
C. High curvature
D. No connection

Q11. Point tool is used to?
A. Draw line
B. Create reference points
C. Create arc
D. Create circle

Q12. Chamfer is used to?
A. Round corners
B. Bevel sharp corners
C. Extend lines
D. Offset curves

Q13. Fillet tool is used to?
A. Cut lines
B. Round between curves
C. Extend lines
D. Copy curves

Q14. Offset tool is used to?
A. Delete curves
B. Create copies at distance
C. Rotate curves
D. Mirror curves

Q15. Symmetric Offset option creates?
A. One side offset
B. Both sides offset
C. No offset
D. Random offset

Q16. Pattern tool is used to?
A. Delete objects
B. Create multiple copies
C. Save file
D. Import file

Q17. Which pattern type creates copies in X and Y direction?
A. Circular
B. Linear
C. General
D. Random

Q18. Circular Pattern requires?
A. Center point
B. Line
C. Radius only
D. Angle only

Q19. General Pattern is based on?
A. Radius
B. Points
C. Angles
D. Lines

Q20. Derived Lines tool is used for?
A. Drawing circles
B. Offset and bisector lines
C. Creating arcs
D. Deleting curves

Q21. The Conic tool is used to create curves with which parameter?
A. Radius
B. Diameter
C. Rho value
D. Angle

Q22. In the Conic tool, which points must be specified?
A. Center only
B. Start, end, and control point
C. Two endpoints only
D. Radius and angle

Q23. The Ellipse tool is available in which group?
A. Edit
B. Include
C. Curve
D. Solve

Q24. What is the first step in creating an ellipse?
A. Specify radius
B. Specify center point
C. Specify angle
D. Select curve

Q25. By default, an ellipse is created as:
A. Half ellipse
B. Quarter ellipse
C. Open ellipse
D. Full 360 degree closed ellipse

Q26. Which option must be cleared to create a partial ellipse?
A. Apply
B. Closed
C. Radius
D. Angle

Q27. Slot tool is used to create:
A. Open curve
B. Straight line
C. Closed loop slot
D. Arc

Q28. Polygon tool is used to create:
A. Circles
B. Arcs
C. Multi-sided shapes
D. Lines

Q29. Default polygon option uses:
A. Circumscribed radius
B. Side length
C. Inscribed radius
D. Diameter

Q30. Which option allows defining polygon using side length?
A. Inscribed Radius
B. Circumscribed Radius
C. Side Length
D. Diameter

Q31. Fit Curve tool is used to create curves using:
A. Dimensions
B. Selected points/vertices
C. Angles
D. Colors

Q32. Which option creates spline using points?
A. Fit Line
B. Fit Circle
C. Fit Spline
D. Fit Ellipse

Q33. Which source option automatically selects based on entity?
A. Curve
B. Infer
C. Points
D. Chain

Q34. Which option is used to modify fit points?
A. Edit Fit Points
B. Modify Curve
C. Adjust Line
D. Move Point

Q35. Fit Circle tool can create arc by:
A. Selecting arc tool
B. Clearing Closed check box
C. Increasing radius
D. Using spline

Q36. Optimize Curve tool works based on:
A. Color and layer
B. Distance and angle threshold
C. Radius only
D. Length only

Q37. Trim tool is used to:
A. Extend curves
B. Delete extra portions
C. Move curves
D. Scale curves

Q38. Trim preview shows removable portion in:
A. Blue
B. Green
C. Red
D. Yellow

Q39. Extend tool extends geometry up to:
A. Infinite length
B. Next intersecting geometry
C. Midpoint
D. Origin

Q40. Corner tool is used to:
A. Rotate curves
B. Join curves at corner
C. Delete curves
D. Scale curves

Q41. Move Curve tool allows movement using:
A. Static input only
B. Dynamic handles
C. Color selection
D. Layers

Q42. Default motion option in Move Curve is:
A. Point to Point
B. Distance-Angle
C. Rotate Only
D. Scale

Q43. Offset Move Curve tool moves curves by:
A. Angle
B. Rotation
C. Offset distance
D. Scale factor

Q44. Scale Curve tool changes size using:
A. Color
B. Scale factor
C. Layer
D. Constraint

Q45. Delete Curve tool removes:
A. Points
B. Selected curves
C. Dimensions
D. Layers

Q46. Include tool is used to:
A. Delete curves
B. Import curves from external objects
C. Scale curves
D. Rotate curves

Q47. The Settings rollout is used to specify:
A. Geometry creation
B. Dimension settings
C. File settings
D. View settings

Q48. The Lettering option is used to control:
A. Line thickness
B. Text alignment and justification
C. Curve length
D. Radius

Q49. Height Factor is used to:
A. Change line thickness
B. Adjust tolerance frame height
C. Rotate text
D. Scale curve

Q50. Automatic Orientation option controls:
A. Text size
B. Arrowhead placement
C. Line color
D. Curve type

Q51. Which option displays arrowhead in dimension?
A. Show Arrowhead
B. Display Line
C. Show Curve
D. Apply Arrow

Q52. Arrow Line option is used to define:
A. Curve type
B. Arrow line properties
C. Text position
D. Radius

Q53. Text Over Stub Factor defines:
A. Text height
B. Distance between text and stub line
C. Line thickness
D. Curve angle

Q54. Prefix/Suffix option is used for:
A. Changing curve
B. Adding symbols to dimension text
C. Scaling curves
D. Rotating text

Q55. Stacking option controls:
A. Curve overlap
B. Text stacking alignment
C. Line thickness
D. Radius

Q56. Which tolerance type applies no tolerance?
A. Equal Bilateral
B. Bilateral
C. No Tolerance
D. Limits and Fits

Q57. Equal Bilateral Tolerance applies:
A. Only positive tolerance
B. Only negative tolerance
C. Equal positive and negative tolerance
D. No tolerance

Q58. Bilateral Tolerance allows:
A. Same tolerance
B. Different positive and negative tolerance
C. No tolerance
D. Fixed tolerance

Q59. Dual option is used to:
A. Create curves
B. Display dimensions in two units
C. Scale curves
D. Delete dimensions

Q60. Rapid Dimension tool is used to:
A. Delete dimensions
B. Apply different dimensions
C. Rotate curves
D. Scale objects

Chapter 3

Sketching Practical and Practice

Topics Covered

The major topics covered in this chapter are:

- ***Sketching Practical and Practice***

INTRODUCTION

In this chapter, we will work on creating sketches using the tools discussed earlier. We will use some basic engineering drawings as target for our practical and practice here.

PRACTICAL 1

In this practical, we will create sketch from the drawing given in Figure-1 using inches as unit of length.

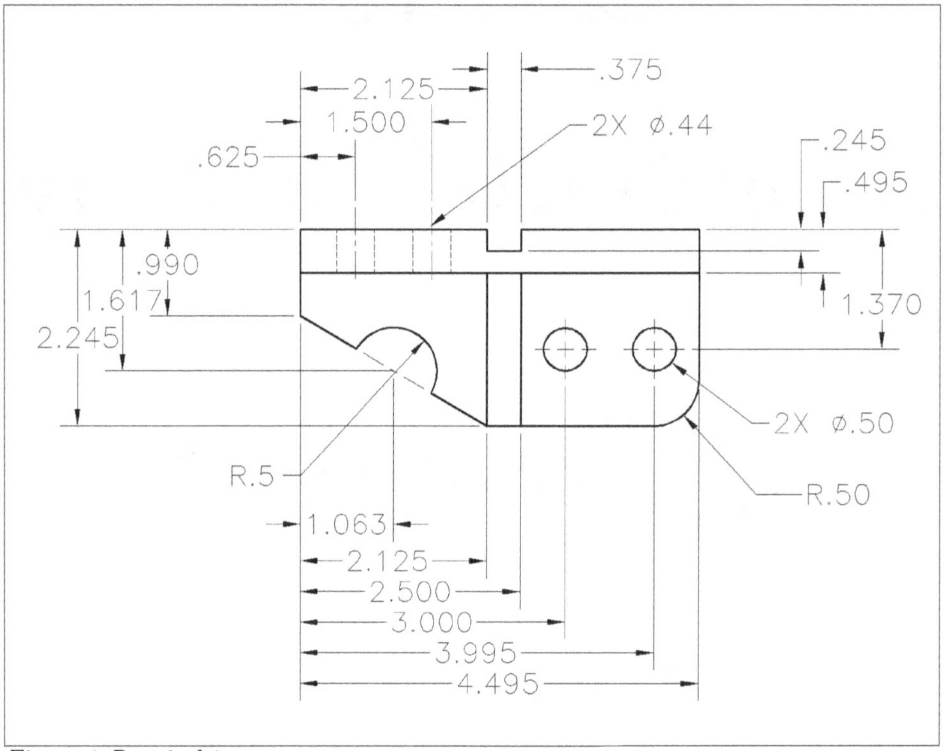

Figure-1. Practical 1

Starting Sketch

- Start NX by double-clicking on the icon from the desktop.
- Click on the **New** button from the **Quick Access Toolbar**. The **New** dialog box will be displayed.
- Select the **Model** option from **Templates** rollout of the dialog box and select the **Inches** option from the **Units** drop-down in the rollout.
- Specify desired name in the **Name** edit box and set desired location in **Folder** edit box of the dialog box.
- Click on the **OK** button from the **New** dialog box. The Modeling environment will be displayed.
- Click on the **Sketch** button from the **Construction** group of **Home** tab in the **Ribbon**. The **Create Sketch** dialog box will be displayed and you will be asked to select the sketching plane.
- Select the **TOP Plane** from the graphics area to select the plane.
- Click on the **Reverse Horizontal Direction** button from the **Orientation** rollout in the dialog box to flip the horizontal direction if needed and click on the **OK** button; refer to Figure-2. The sketching environment will be activated.

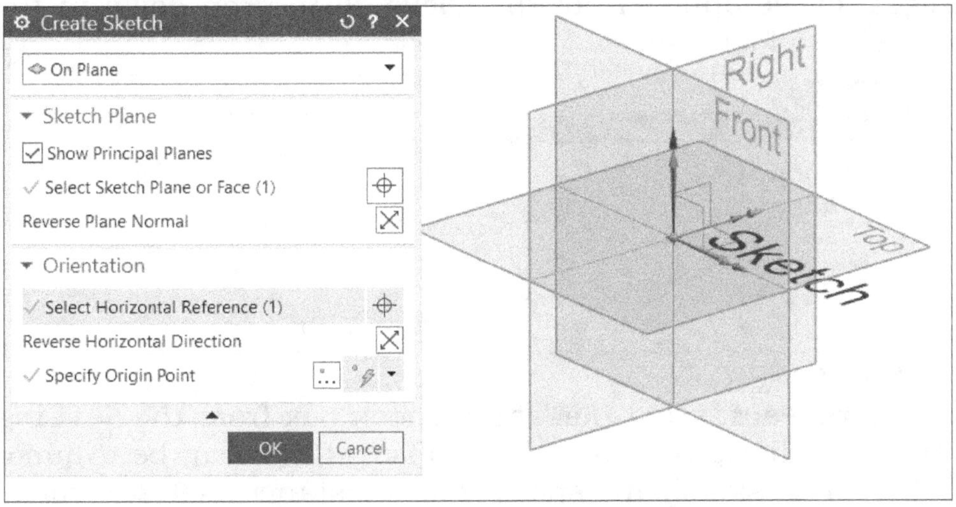

Figure-2. Selecting plane

Creating sketch boundaries

- Click on the **Line** tool from the **Curve** group in **Home** tab of the **Ribbon**. You are asked to specify the start point of the line.
- Click at the origin and then create the profile as shown in Figure-3.

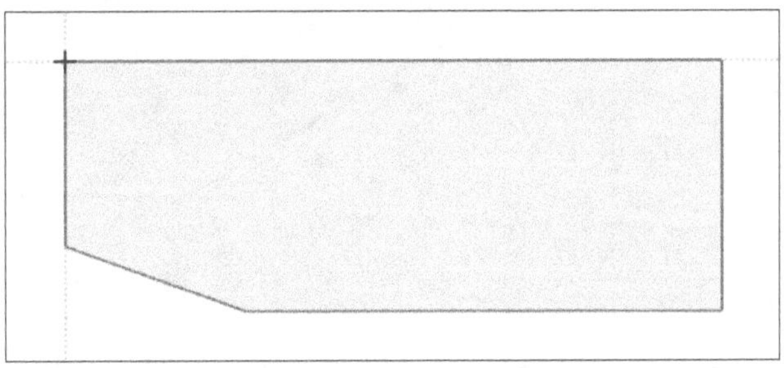

Figure-3. Profile for Practical 1

- Click on the **Rapid Dimension** tool from the **Direct Sketch** panel in the **Home** tab of **Ribbon**. The **Rapid Dimension** dialog box will be displayed.
- Apply the dimensions as shown in Figure-4.

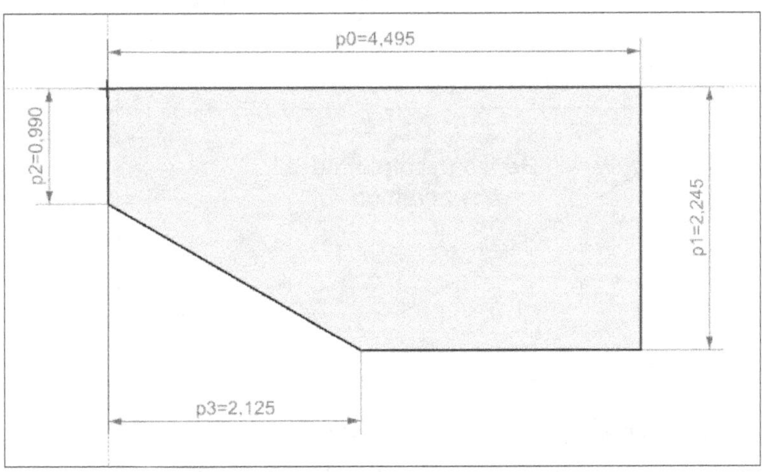

Figure-4. After applying dimensions

Creating Offset Lines

- Click on the **Offset** tool from the **Curve** group in the **Home** tab of the **Ribbon**. The **Offset Curve** dialog box will be displayed and you will be asked to select the curves.

- Select **Single Curve** option from the **Curve Rule** drop-down in the **Selection Scene Bar**; refer to Figure-5.

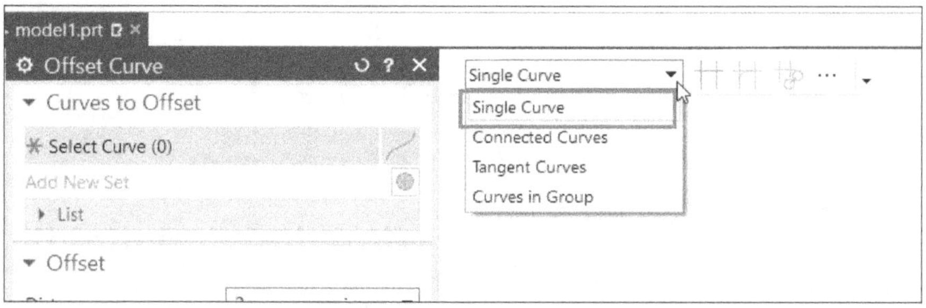

Figure-5. Single Curve option

- Clear the **Create Persistent Relation** check box from the **Settings** rollout in the **Offset Curve** dialog box so that the offset curves can be trimmed later.
- Select the top line of sketch and specify offset distance as **0.245**; refer to Figure-6.

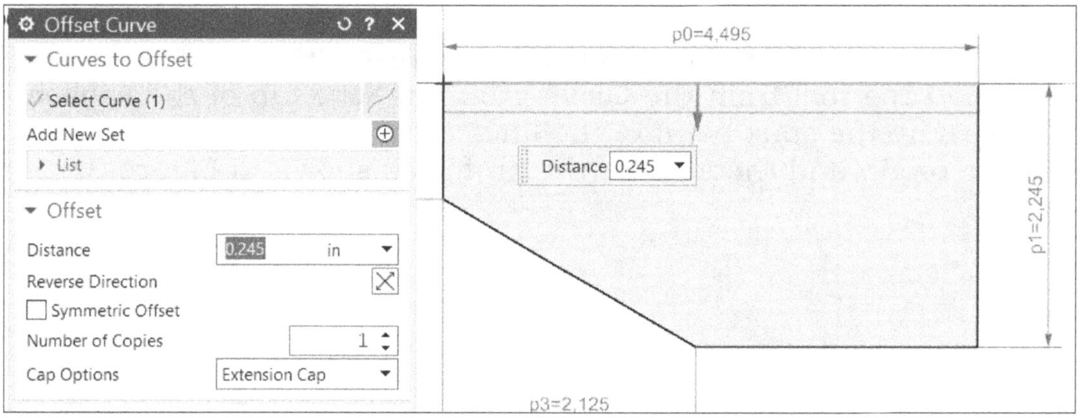

Figure-6. Offsetting a line

- Click on the **Apply** button to create the offset line. Now, specify the offset distance as **0.495** in the edit box and again click on the same line. Click on the **Apply** button to create offset line; refer to Figure-7.

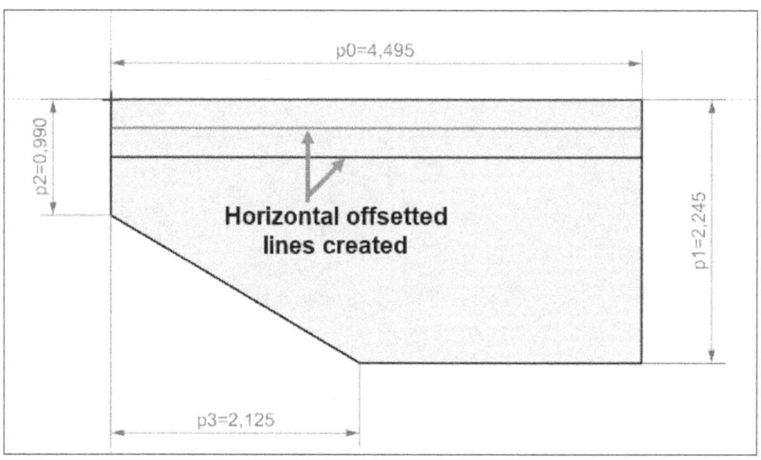

Figure-7. Creating offsetted horizontal lines

- Specify the distance as **2.125** in the **Distance** edit box and select the left line of boundary sketch; refer to Figure-8 (If your sketch does not update in offset distance automatically then press **TAB** once after specifying distance value). Click on the **Apply** button to create the offset line.

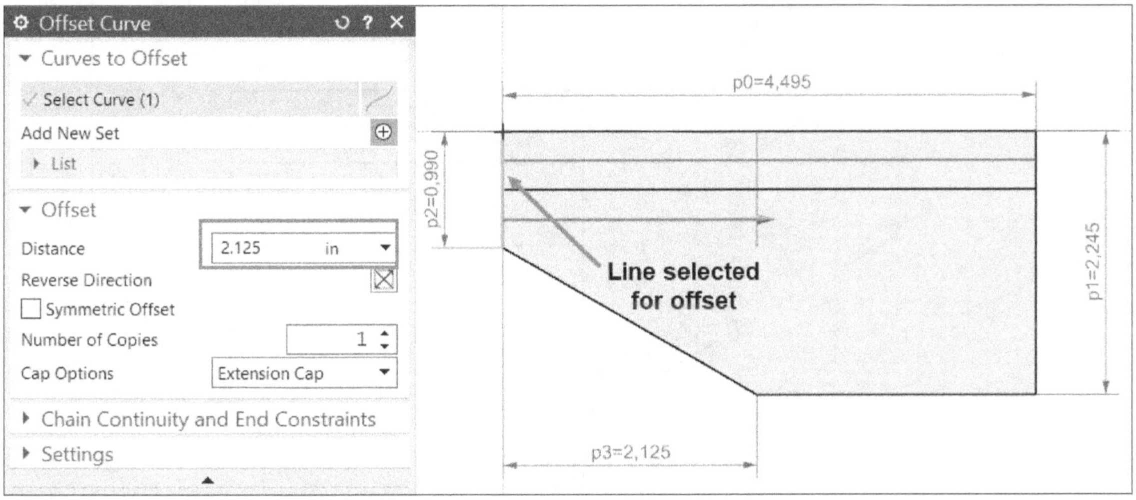

Figure-8. Line selected for offset

- Specify the offset distance as **2.500** in the **Distance** edit box and select the same vertical line. Preview of offset line will be displayed (Don't worry if lines are overlapping in preview, they get separated on creating offset). Click on the **OK** button to create the line. The sketch will be displayed as shown in Figure-9.

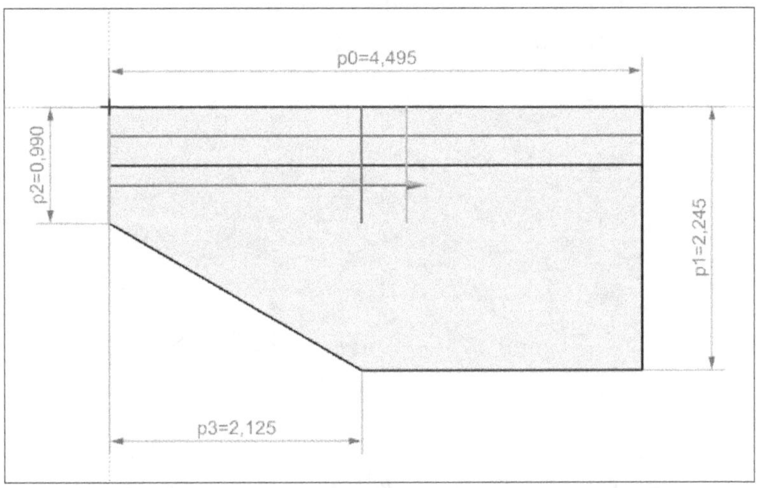

Figure-9. Sketch after offset

Extending and Trimming Lines

- Click on the **Extend** tool from the **Edit** group in **Home** tab of the **Ribbon**. The **Extend** dialog box will be displayed and you will be asked to select the curves to be extended.
- Select the vertical line offsetted at a distance of **2.125** and then select the next vertical line which was offsetted at a distance of **2.500**. The lines will be extended to next boundary.
- Click on the **Close** button from the dialog box to exit. The sketch should be displayed as shown in Figure-10.

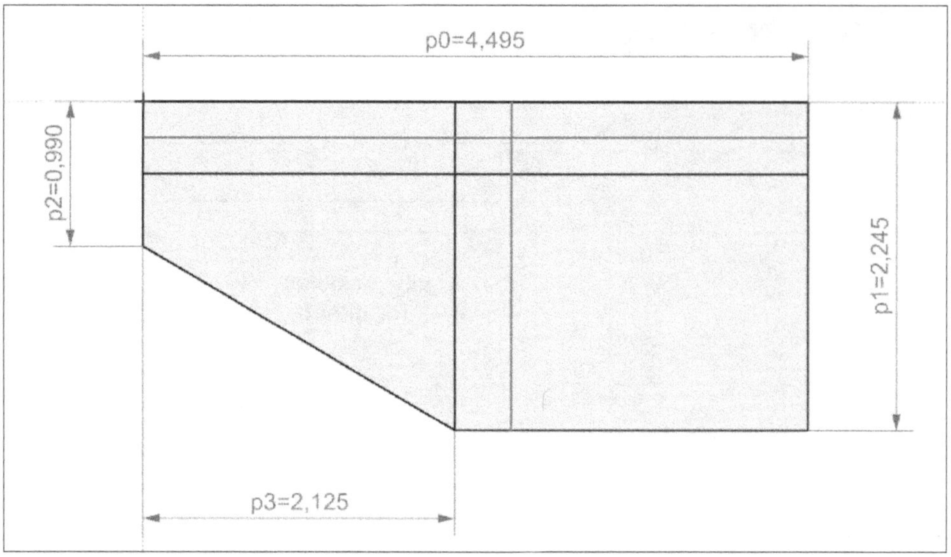

Figure-10. Sketching after extending lines

- Click on the **Trim** tool from the **Edit** group of **Home** tab in the **Ribbon**. The **Trim** dialog box will be displayed and you will be asked to select the entities to be trimmed.
- Click on the lines at the locations where numbers are marked in Figure-11 to trim extra entities. The sketch should display as shown in Figure-12. After trimming, click on the **Close** button from the dialog box.

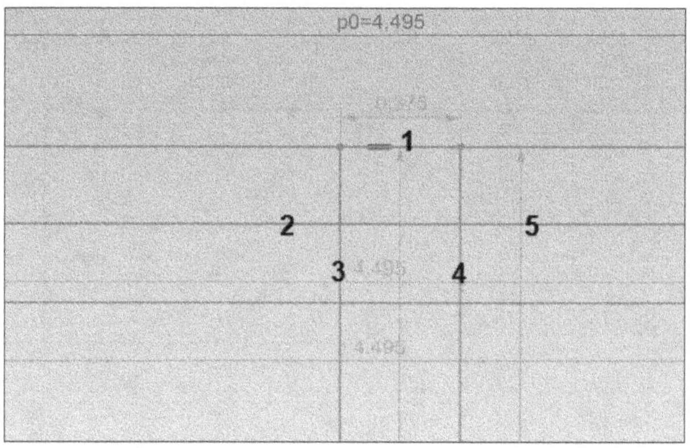

Figure-11. Entities to be trimmed

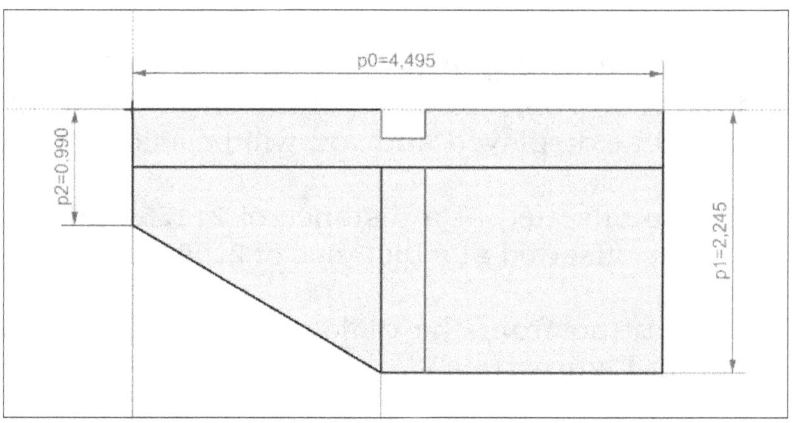

Figure-12. Sketch after trimming

Creating Circle and Pattern

- Click on the **Line** tool from the **Curve** group in the **Ribbon** and click at the mid point of inclined line. Input the parameters as shown in Figure-13. Note that you can specify these parameters in **Line** dialog box if you are not using input boxes.

- Press **ENTER** to create the line. Press **ESC** to exit the **Line** tool.

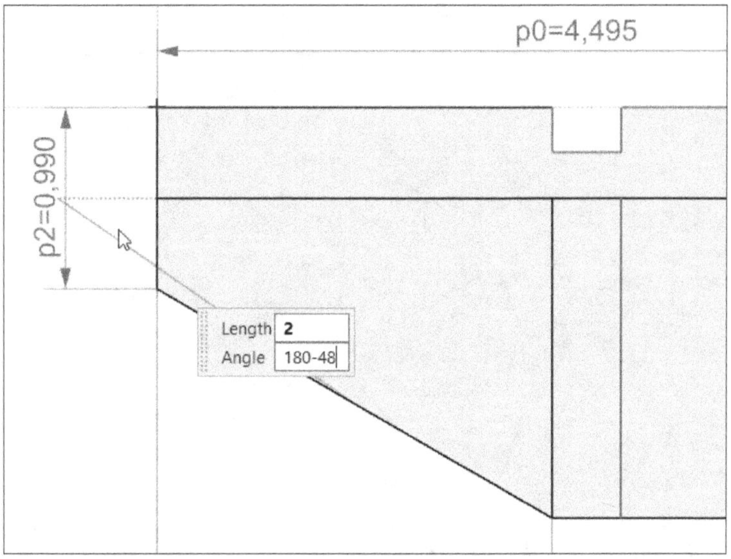

Figure-13. Parameters for creating line

- Select the **No Selection Filter** option from the **Type Filter** drop-down in **Top Border Bar** to enable selection of all entities and right-click on the recently created line. A shortcut menu will be displayed.
- Select the **Convert to Reference** option from the shortcut menu.
- Click on the **Circle** tool from the **Curve** group in **Ribbon** and create a circle of diameter **1.5** with center at the mid point of inclined line; refer to Figure-14.

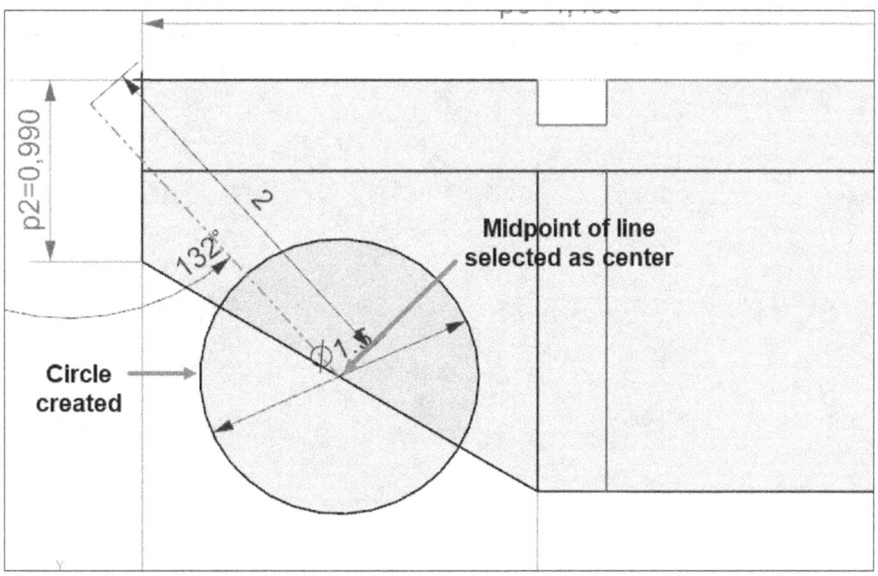

Figure-14. Circle to be created

- Type the diameter for a new circle as **0.2** in Diameter edit box of the Circle dialog box and press **TAB**. A smaller circle will get attached to cursor.
- Click at the location where circle and construction line intersects; refer to Figure-15. Press **ESC** twice to exit the **Circle** tool.

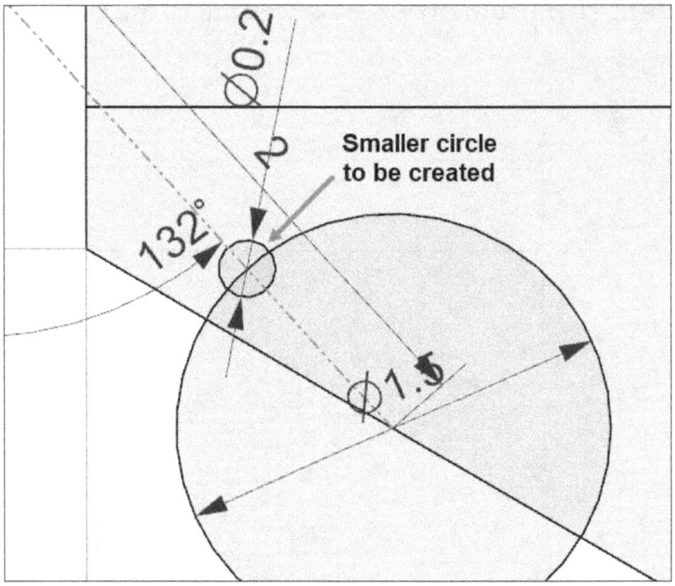

Figure-15. Smaller circle to be created

- Click on the **Pattern** tool from the **Curve** group in the **Ribbon**. The **Pattern Curve** dialog box will be displayed.
- Select the **Circular** option from the **Layout** drop-down in the dialog box and select the smaller circle.
- Click on the **Specify Point** selection button in the dialog box and then click on the midpoint of inclined line (which is also center of bigger circle). Preview of the circular pattern will be displayed; refer to Figure-16.

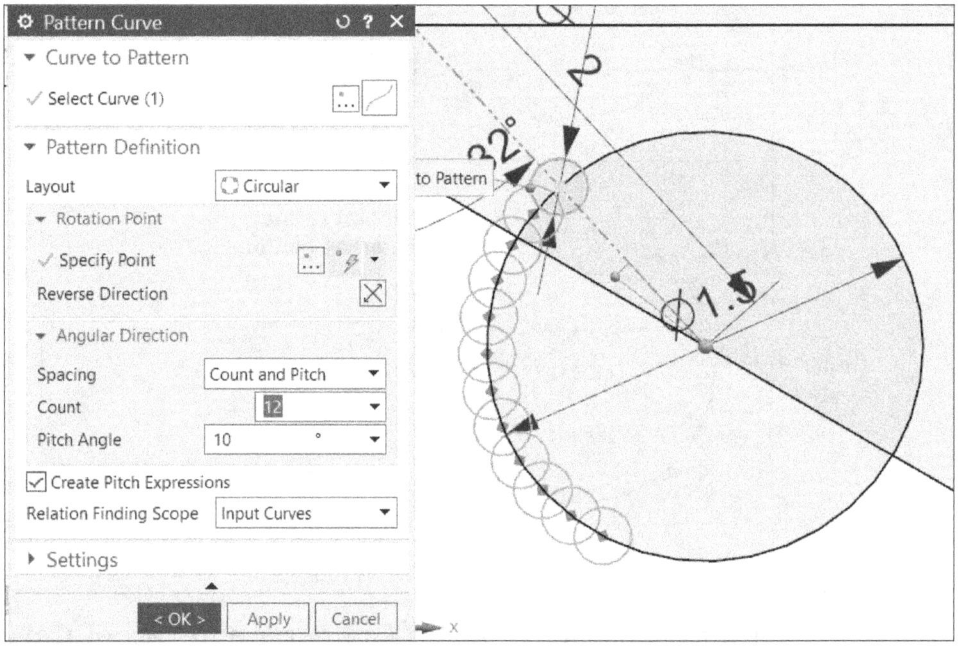

Figure-16. Preview of circular pattern

- Click on the **Reverse Direction** button and specify the parameters as shown in Figure-17 in the dialog box.
- Click on the **OK** button from the dialog box to create the pattern.
- Convert the bigger circle to reference as discussed earlier by using right-click shortcut menu.

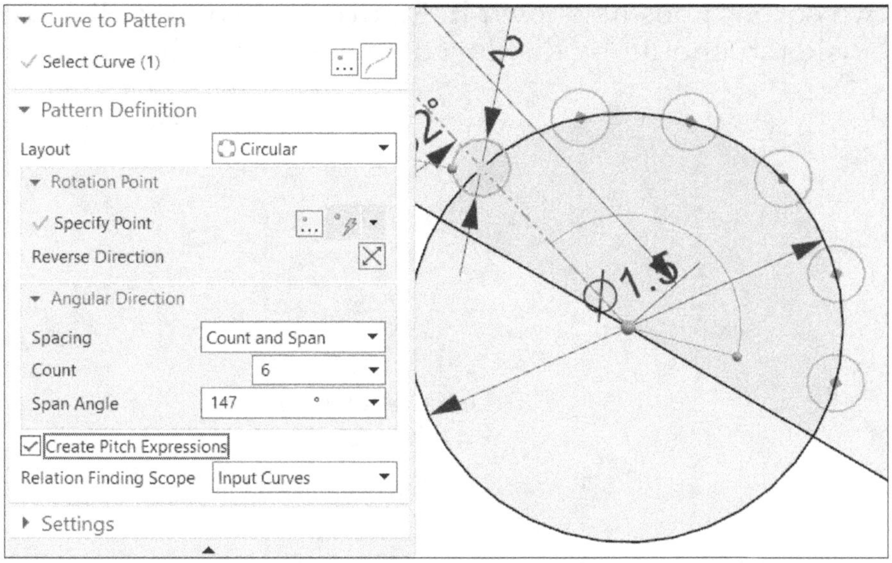

Figure-17. Specifying parameters for circular pattern

Creating other circles

- Click on the **Circle** tool from the **Curve** panel in the **Ribbon**. The **Circle** dialog box will be displayed.
- Make sure the **Circle by Center and Diameter** button is selected in the **Circle** dialog box and click on the mid point of inclined line. You will be asked to specify diameter of circle.
- Type **1** in the dynamic input box and press **ENTER**. The circle will be created.
- Now, type the diameter as **0.5** in dynamic input box and press **TAB**. Smaller circle will get attached to cursor.
- Click to place the circles as shown in Figure-18.

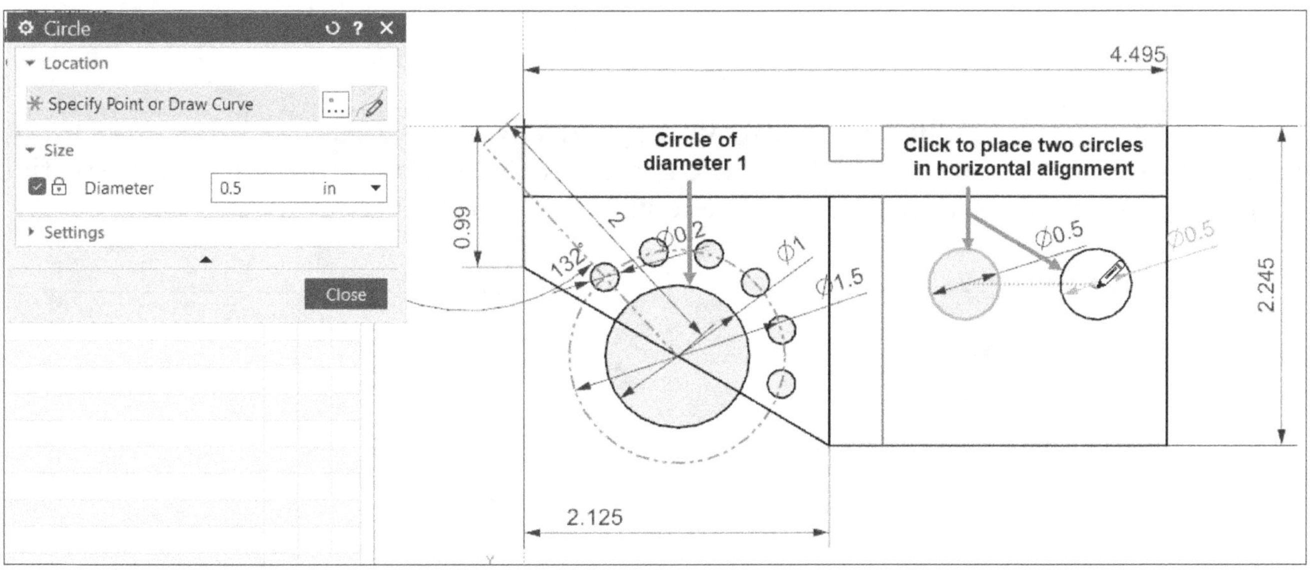

Figure-18. Creating circles

- Press **ESC** to exit the tool.

Applying Fillet

- Click on the **Fillet** tool from the **Curve** group in the **Ribbon** and specify the value of radius as **0.5** in the dynamic input box displayed.

- Select the two corner lines as shown in Figure-19 to apply fillet. Press **ESC** to exit the tool. The sketch should be displayed as shown in Figure-20 so far.

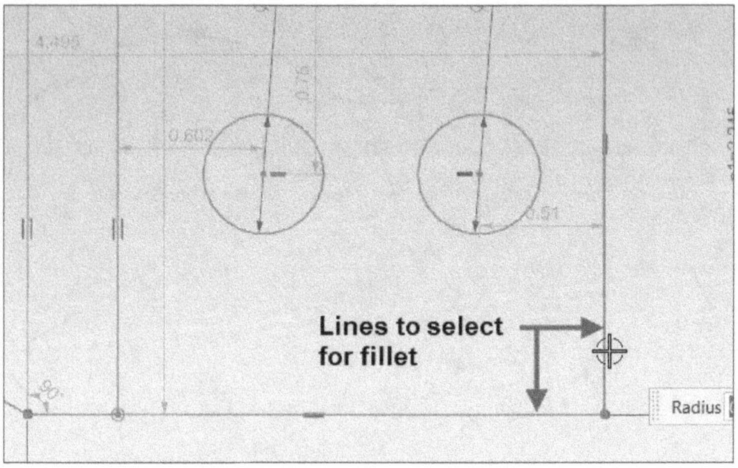

Figure-19. Applying fillet

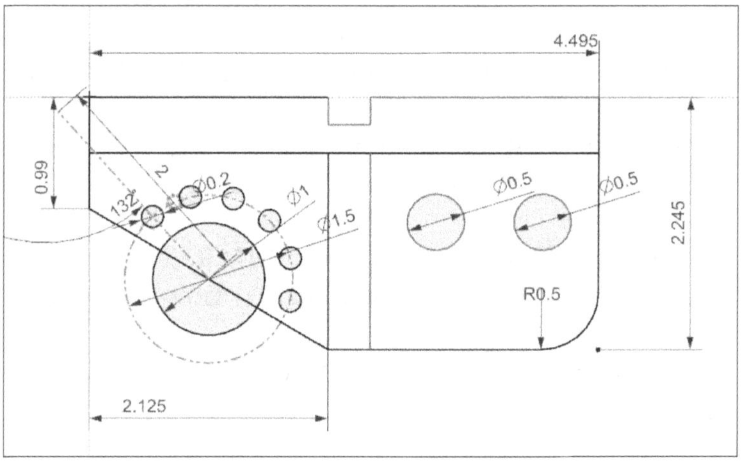

Figure-20. Sketch after applying fillet

Trimming and Applying Dimensions

- Click on the **Trim** tool from the **Edit** group in the **Ribbon** and select the entities marked by numbers in Figure-21. Press **ESC** to exit the tool.

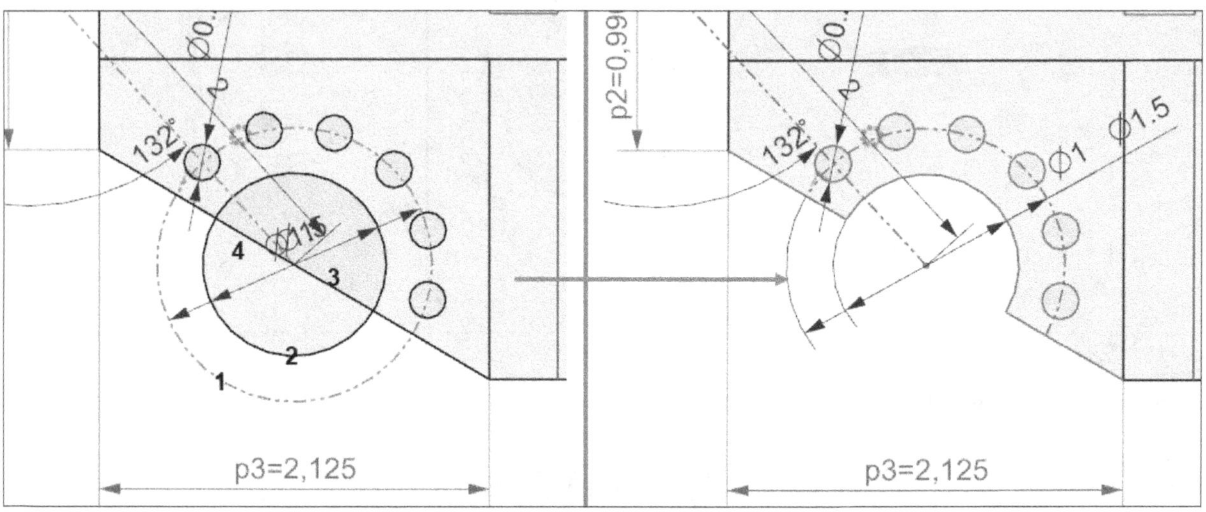

Figure-21. Trimming circles and lines

- Select the extra dimensions and delete them.

- Click on the **Rapid Dimension** tool from the **Solve** group in the **Home** tab of **Ribbon**. The **Rapid Dimension** dialog box will be displayed.
- Apply the dimensions as shown in Figure-22. Make sure to remove extra dimensions.

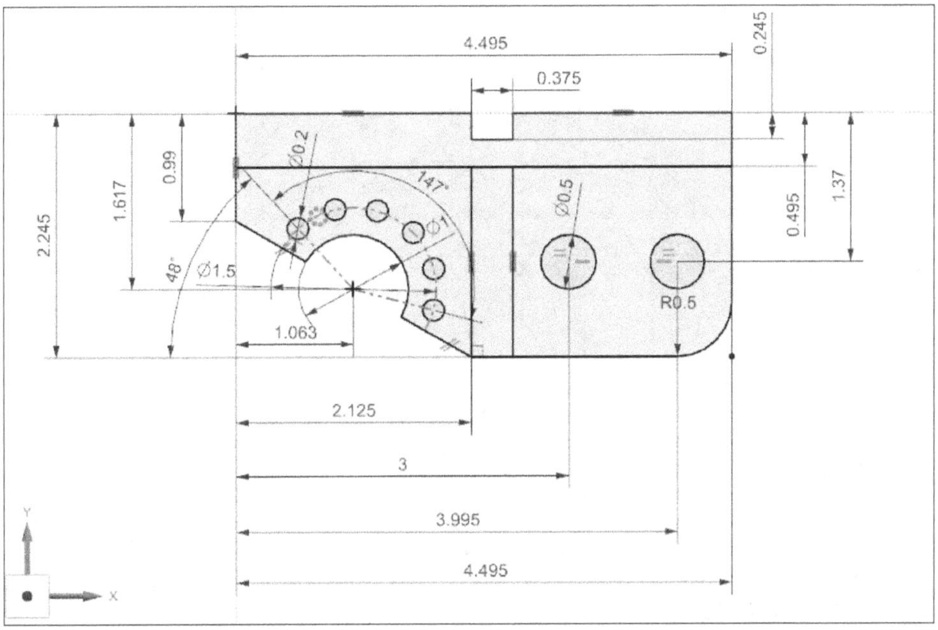

Figure-22. Sketch after applying dimensions

Note that by default, the names of dimensions are also displayed along with dimension values. To hide the names, click on the **Sketch** option from the **Preferences** cascading menu of **File** menu. Click on the **OK** button from the information box displayed. The **Sketch Preferences** dialog box will be displayed. Select the **Value** option from the **Dimension Label** drop-down in the **Active Sketch** section of **Sketch Settings** page; refer to Figure-23 and click on the **OK** button. Note that the changes will be applied once you restart NX with a new file.

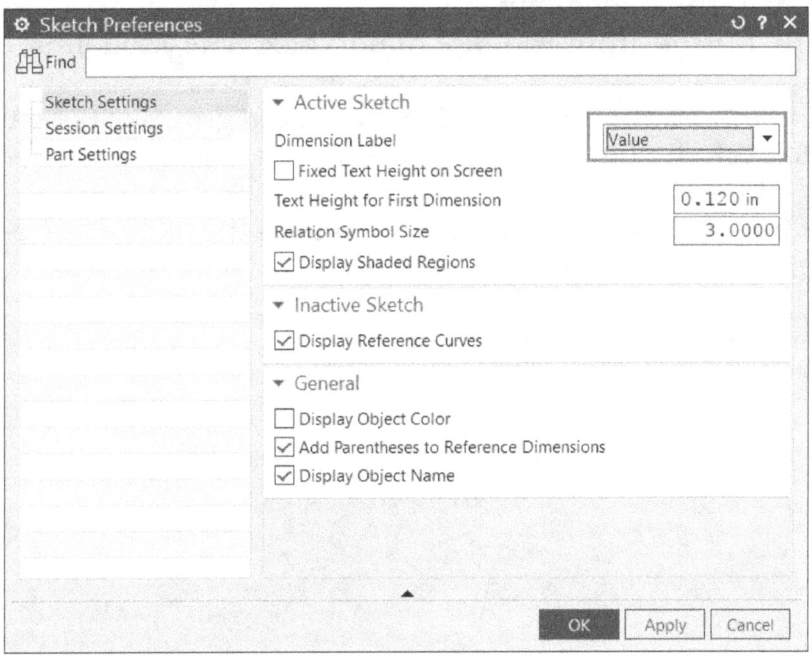

Figure-23. Sketch Preferences dialog box

- Save the file and close it.

Practical 2

Create the sketch as shown in Figure-24.

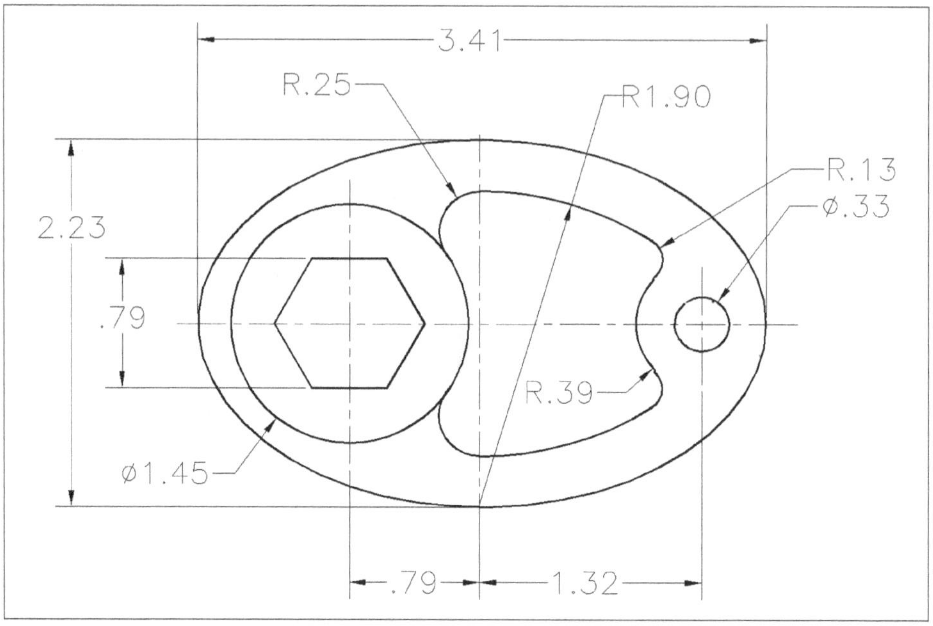

Figure-24. Practical 2

Starting Sketch

- Start NX by double-clicking on the icon from the desktop if not started yet.
- Click on the **New** button from the **Quick Access Toolbar**. The **New** dialog box will be displayed.
- Select the **Model** option from **Templates** rollout of the dialog box and select the **Inches** option from the **Units** drop-down in the rollout.
- Specify the name as **Practical 2** in the **Name** edit box and set desired location in **Folder** edit box of the dialog box.
- Click on the **OK** button from the **New** dialog box. The Modeling environment will be displayed.
- Click on the **Sketch** button from the **Construction** group of **Home** tab in the **Ribbon**. The **Create Sketch** dialog box will be displayed and you will be asked to select the sketching plane.
- Select the **TOP** from the graphics area and click on the **OK** button; refer to Figure-25. The sketching environment will be activated.

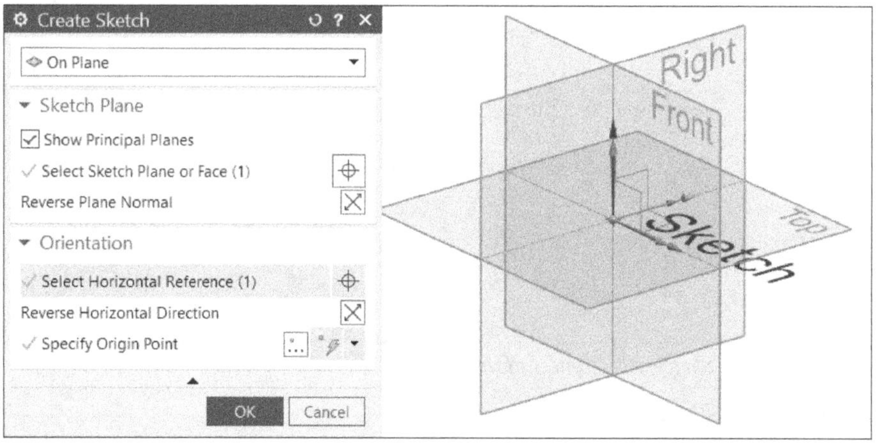

Figure-25. Selecting plane

Creating sketch boundaries

- Click on the **Ellipse** tool from the **More** drop-down in **Curve** panel of **Home** tab in the **Ribbon**. You will be asked to specify the center point of the ellipse.
- Click in the **Major Radius** edit box and enter the value as **3.41/2**.
- Click in the **Minor Radius** edit box of **Ellipse** dialog box and specify the value as **2.23/2**.
- Click at the origin to specify center point of ellipse. Preview of ellipse will be displayed; refer to Figure-26.

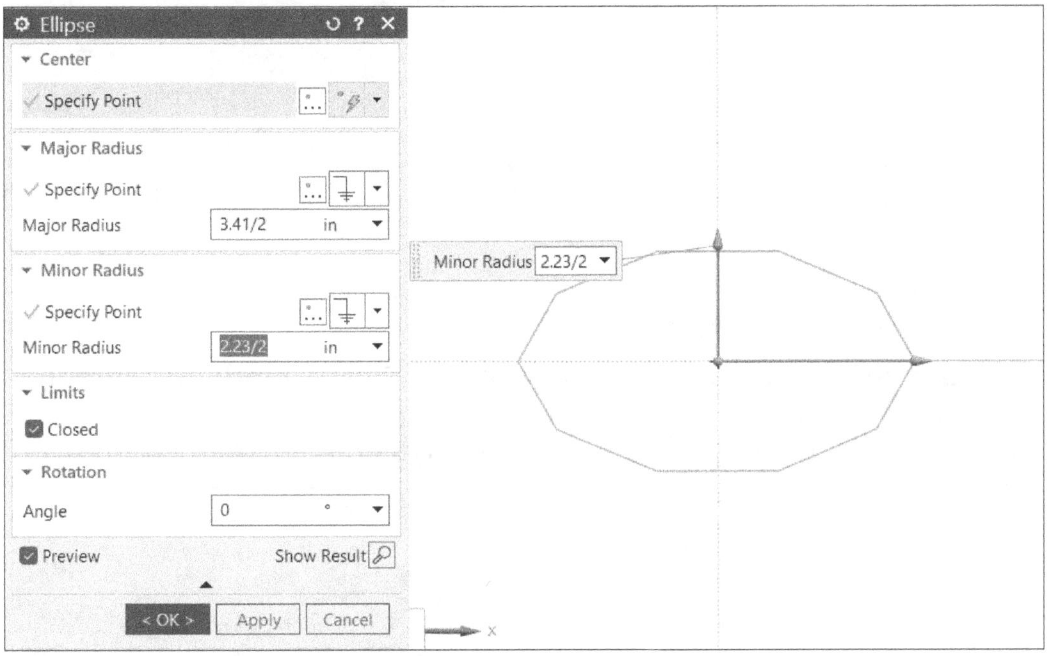

Figure-26. Preview of ellipse

- Click on the **OK** button from the dialog box to create the ellipse.

Creating Circles

- Click on the **Circle** tool from the **Curve** group in the **Home** tab of **Ribbon**. The **Circle** dialog box will be displayed.
- Click at a location in horizontal alignment with origin as shown in Figure-27 to place center of circle. You will be asked to specify diameter of circle.

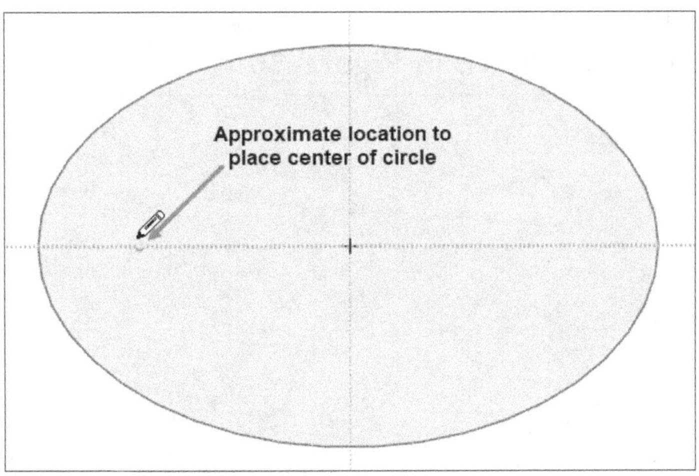

Figure-27. Placing center of circle

- Enter the diameter as **1.45** in the **Diameter** edit box. The circle will be created.
- Specify the diameter value as **0.33** in **Diameter** edit box and then press **TAB**. A smaller circle will get attached to cursor.
- Move the cursor to location as shown in Figure-28 and click to place it.

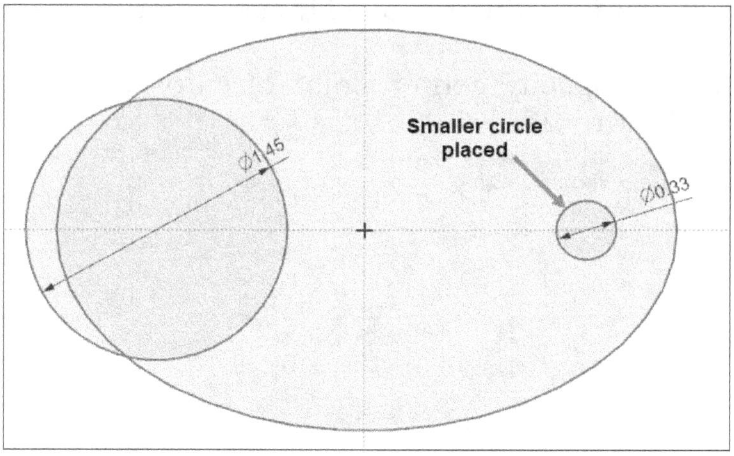

Figure-28. Placing smaller circle

- Type the diameter value as **0.39*2** and press **TAB**. A circle of diameter **0.78** will get attached to cursor.
- Click at the center of smaller circle to place this circle; refer to Figure-29.

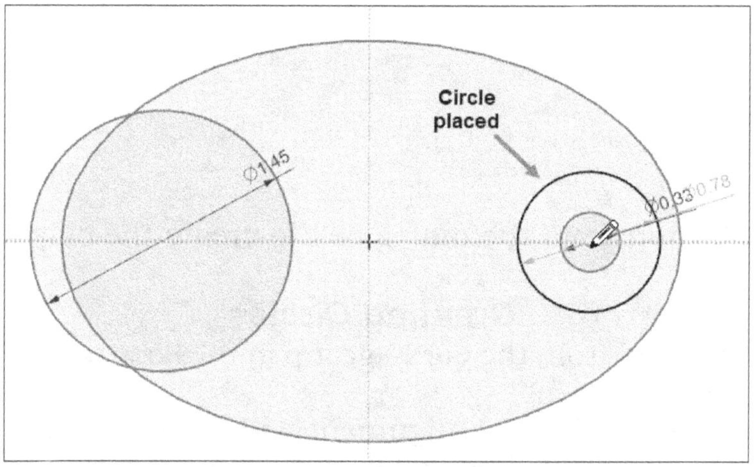

Figure-29. Circle placed

- Press **ESC** to exit the tool.
- Apply the dimensions as shown in Figure-30.

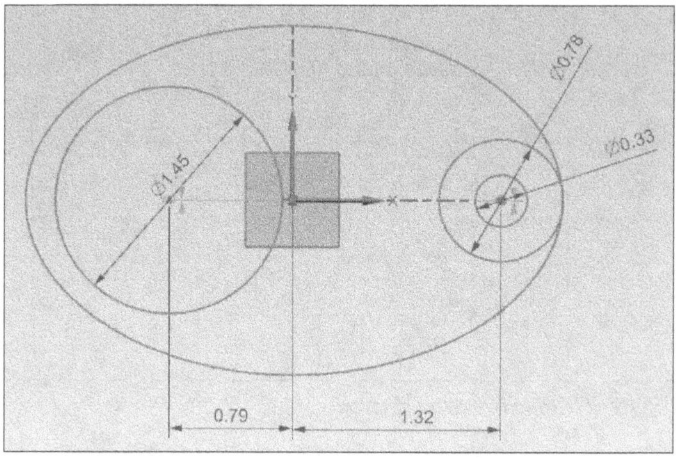

Figure-30. After dimensioning circles

Creating Arcs and Fillets

- Click on the **Arc from Center** tool from the **Arc** drop-down in the **Curve** group of the **Home** tab in the **Ribbon**. The **Arc From Center** dialog box will be displayed.
- Click on the bottom quadrant point of ellipse to define center point of arc.
- Specify the radius as **1.9** in dynamic input box and press **TAB**. You will be asked to specify start point of arc; refer to Figure-31.

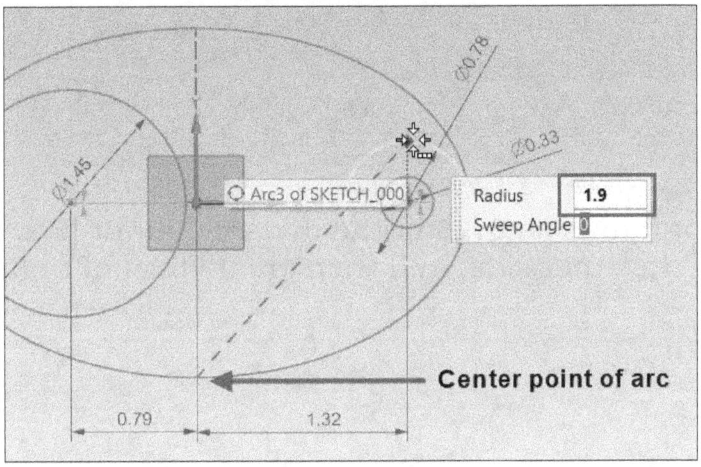

Figure-31. Specifying radius of circle

- Create an arc as shown in Figure-32. Press **ESC** to exit the tool.

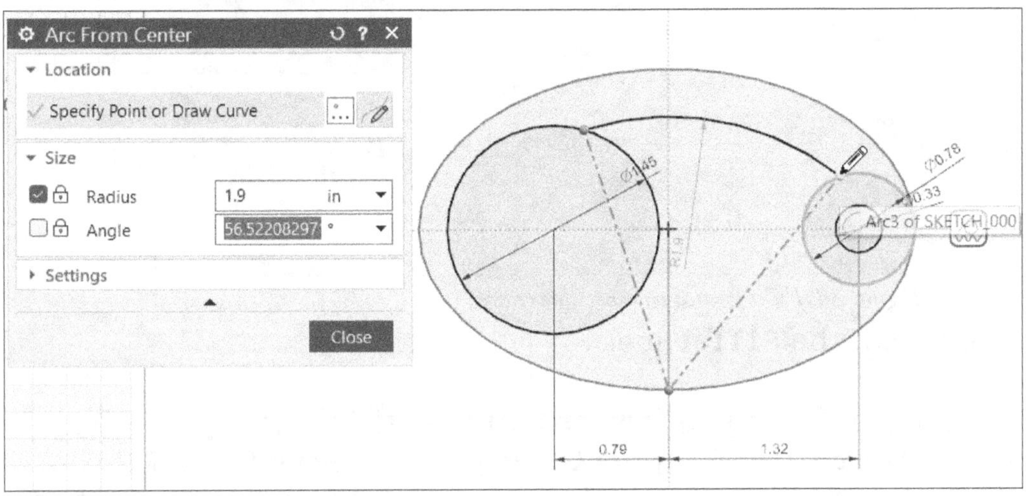

Figure-32. Creating arc

- Click on the **Fillet** tool from **Curve** group in the **Home** tab of **Ribbon**. The **Fillet** dialog box will be displayed.
- Click on the **Untrim** button from the **Fillet Method** section in the **Fillet** dialog box and select the entities as shown in Figure-33. You will be asked to specify the radius of fillet.

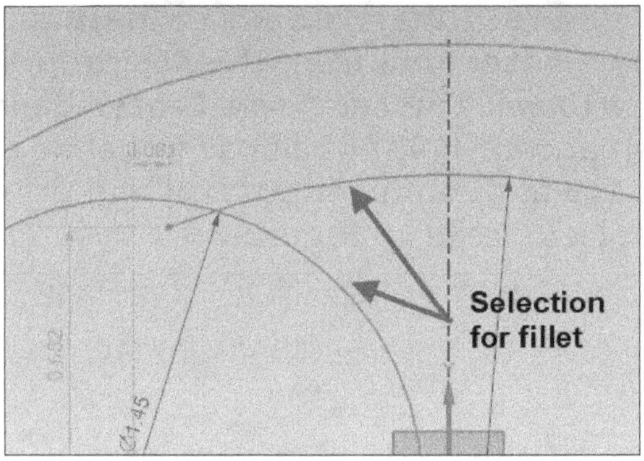

Figure-33. Selection for fillet

- Enter the value of radius as **0.25** in the dynamic input box. Similarly, select the arc and circle on the other side, and then create fillet of radius **0.13** as shown in Figure-34.

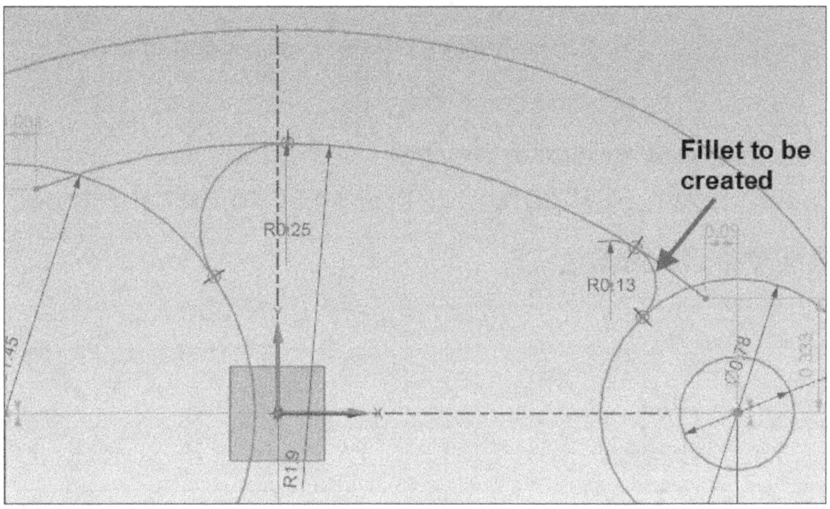

Figure-34. Fillet created on other side of arc

- Press **ESC** to exit the **Fillet** tool.

Creating Mirror Copy and Trimming

- Click on the **Mirror** tool from the **Curve** group in **Home** tab of **Ribbon**. The **Mirror Curve** dialog box will be displayed and you will be asked to select the curves to be mirrored.
- Select the arc and fillets recently created and click on the **Select Centerline** selection button in the dialog box. You will be asked to specify centerline reference for mirror.
- Click on the X-axis from graphics window. Preview of mirror copy will be displayed; refer to Figure-35.

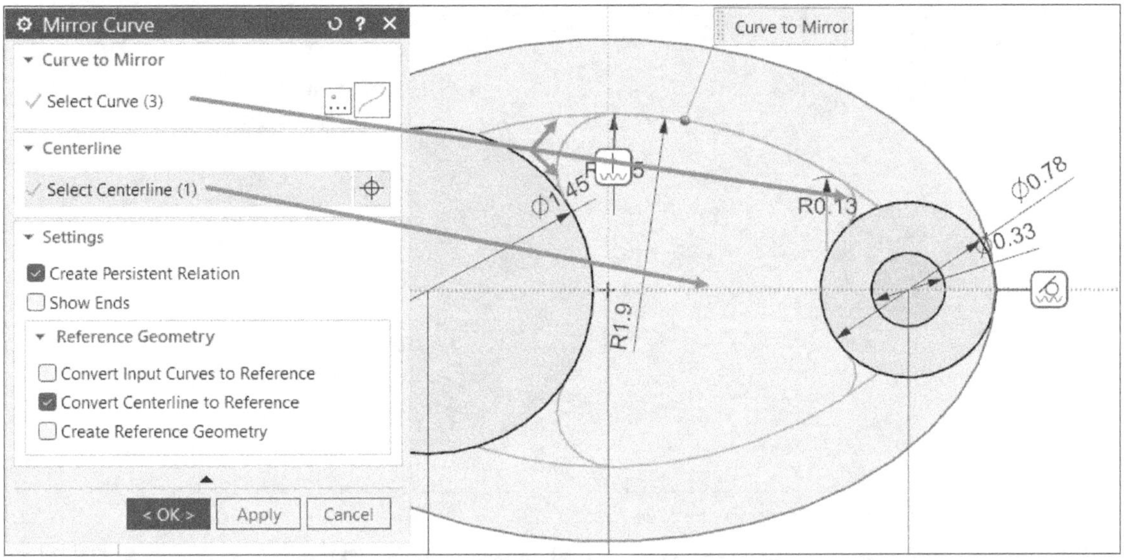

Figure-35. Preview of mirroring

- Click on the **OK** button from the dialog box to create the copy.
- Click on the **Trim** tool from the **Edit** group in **Home** tab of **Ribbon**. You will be asked to select the entities to be trimmed.
- Select the curves at locations marked with numbers in Figure-36. Note that the mirrored curves will be automatically trimmed if that does not happen then trim the mirrored curves as well. Press **ESC** to exit the tool.

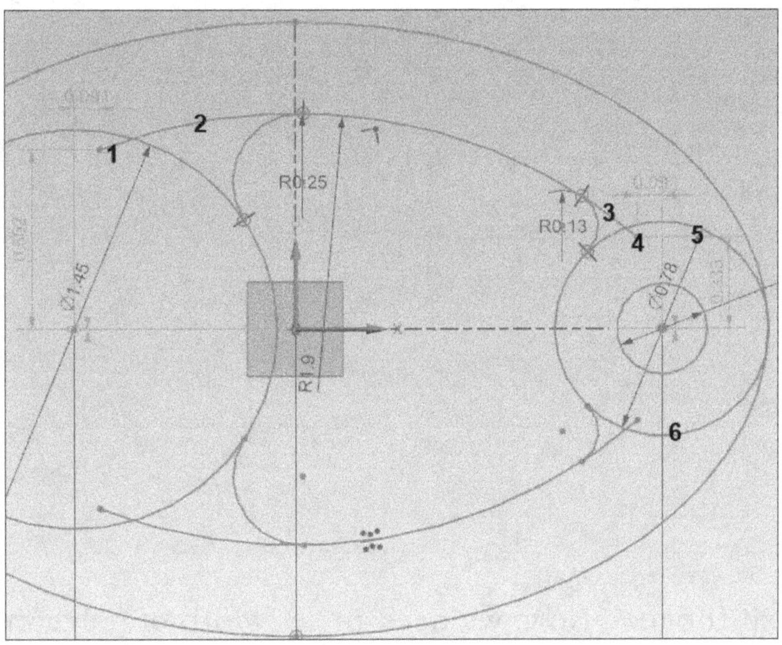

Figure-36. Curve locations for trimming

- Now, zoom in at the location where circle of diameter **0.78** touches the ellipse and delete the left over curve; refer to Figure-37. Press **ESC** to exit the tool.

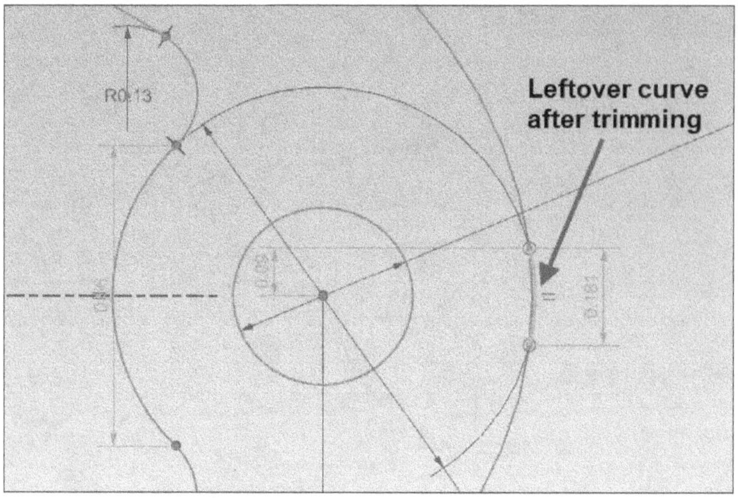

Figure-37. Extra curve to be deleted

Creating Hexagon and Applying Dimension

- Click on the **Polygon** tool from the **More** drop-down in the **Curve** group of **Home** tab in the **Ribbon**. The **Polygon** dialog box will be displayed and you will be asked to specify center point of polygon.
- Click at the center of circle whose diameter is **1.45**. You will be asked to specify the radius and angle for polygon.
- Specify the angle as **90** in the **Rotation** edit box of the dialog box and click when radius is approximately **0.4** in the **Radius** edit box; refer to Figure-38.

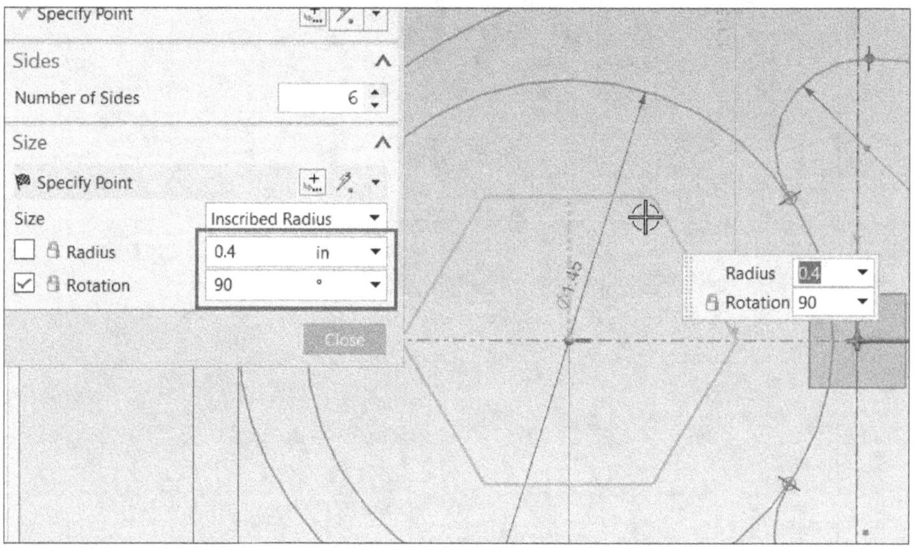

Figure-38. Creating hexagon

- Press **ESC** to exit the tool. Now, we need to set width of polygon as **0.79**.
- Click **Rapid Dimension** tool from the **Solve** group in the **Ribbon**. The **Rapid Dimension** dialog box will be displayed.
- Dimension the polygon and other entities of sketch as shown in Figure-39. Note that you need to create two reference lines (horizontal and vertical) to dimension ellipse. Apply necessary constraints as discussed earlier.

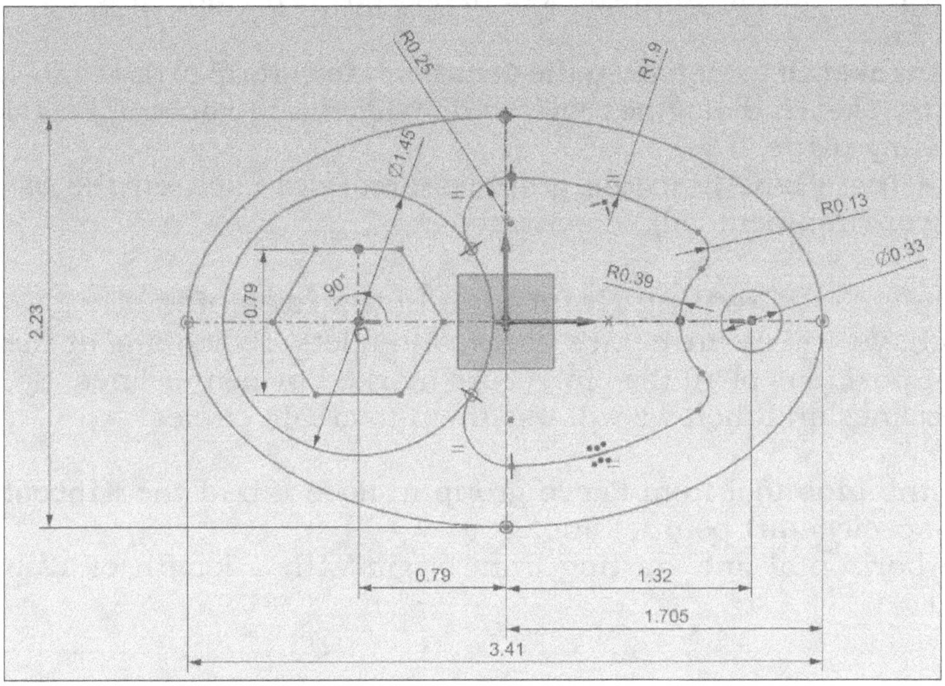

Figure-39. Sketch after dimensioning

PRACTICAL 3

Create the sketch as shown in Figure-40.

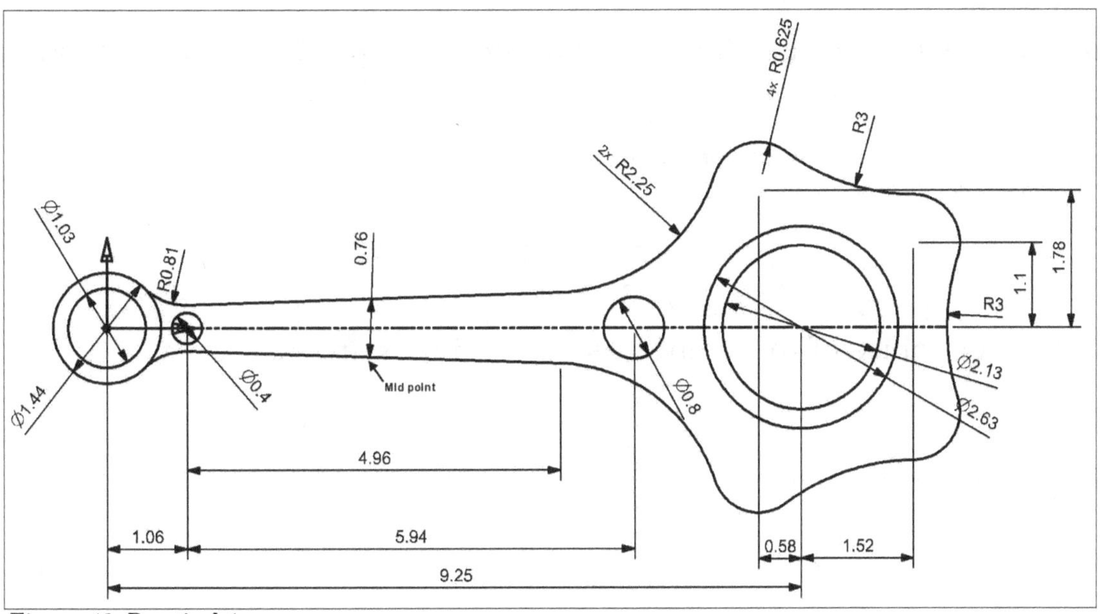

Figure-40. Practical 4

Starting Sketch

- Start NX by double-clicking on the icon from the desktop if not started yet.
- Click on the **New** button from the **Quick Access Toolbar**. The **New** dialog box will be displayed.
- Select the **Model** option from **Templates** rollout of the dialog box and select the **Inches** option from the **Units** drop-down in the rollout.
- Specify the name as **Practical 3** in the **Name** edit box and set desired location in **Folder** edit box of the dialog box.

- Click on the **OK** button from the **New** dialog box. The Modeling environment will be displayed.
- Click on the **Sketch** button from the **Construction** group of **Home** tab in the **Ribbon**. The **Create Sketch** dialog box will be displayed and you will be asked to select the sketching plane.
- Select the **Top Plane** from the graphics area and click on the **OK** button. The sketching environment will be activated.

Creating Reference Lines for Holes

In this sketch, we will create circles, lines, and fillets. By looking at the sketch, you can find that positions of all the circles are marked by center lines. So, we will first create center lines and then we will use them to create circles.

- Click on the **Line** tool from **Curve** group in **Home** tab of the **Ribbon**. You will be asked to specify start point of line.
- Create a horizontal line starting from origin with a length of **12** inch; refer to Figure-41.

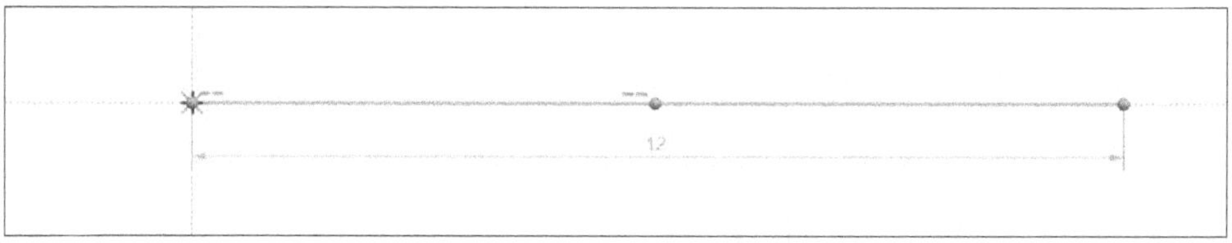

Figure-41. Horizontal line created

- Similarly, create a vertical line at the origin of length 2 inch; refer to Figure-42.

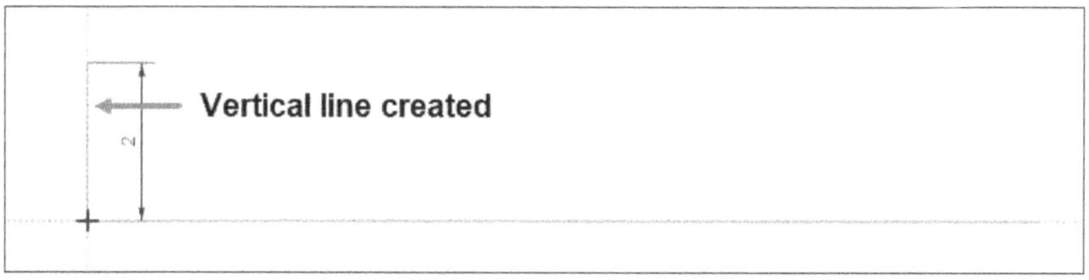

Figure-42. Vertical line created

- Create offset copies of these lines as shown in Figure-43.

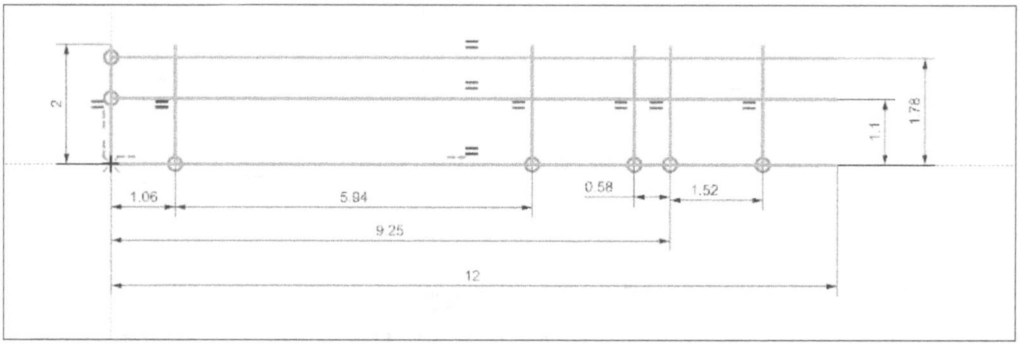

Figure-43. Offset copies of lines

- Select all the lines created and right-click on one of them. A shortcut menu will be displayed.
- Click on the **Convert to Reference** option from the shortcut menu to convert them into reference geometry; refer to Figure-44.

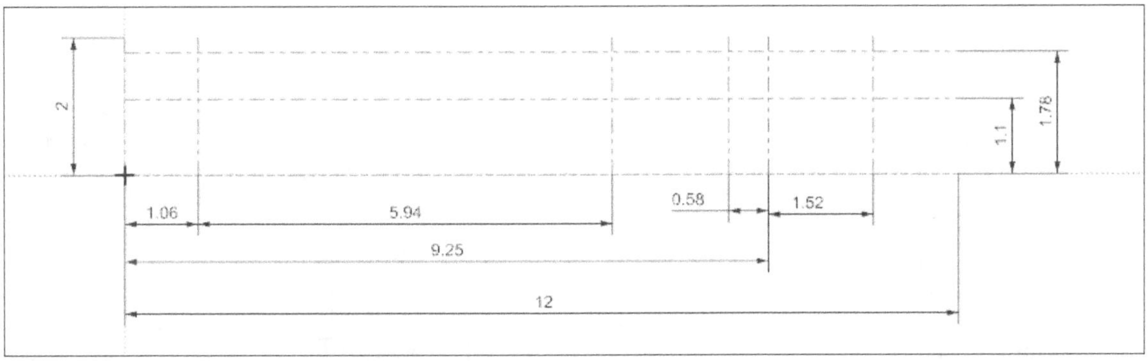

Figure-44. Converting lines to reference geometry

Creating Circles

- Click on the **Circle** tool from **Curve** group in the **Home** tab of the **Ribbon**. The **Circle** dialog box will be displayed and you will be asked to specify center point of circle.
- Create the circles as shown in Figure-45.

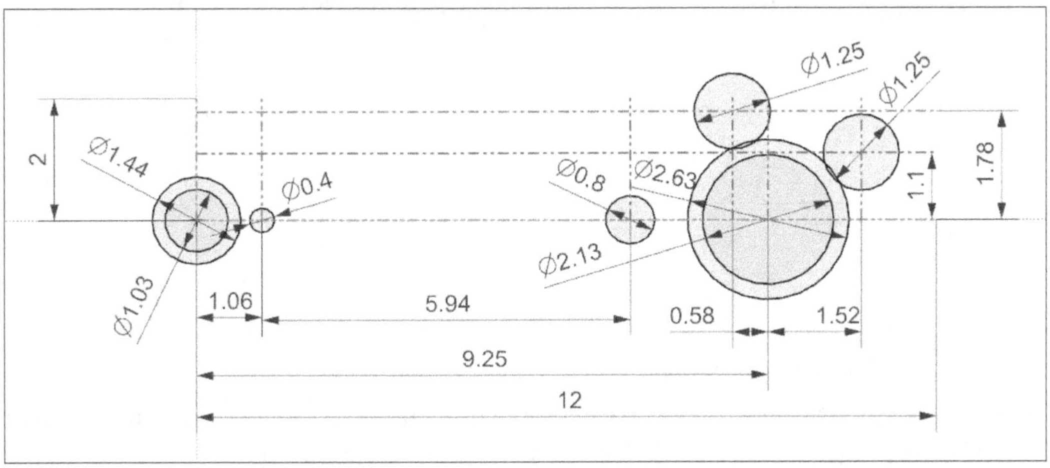

Figure-45. Sketch after creating circles

- Press **ESC** twice to exit the tool.

Creating Lines and Applying Fillet

- Click on the **Line** tool from the **Curve** panel in **Ribbon** and create a line joining circle of diameter **1.44** with circle of diameter **2.63**; refer to Figure-46. Note that you need to press and hold **ALT** key while creating the line so that it does not snap automatically to tangent points.

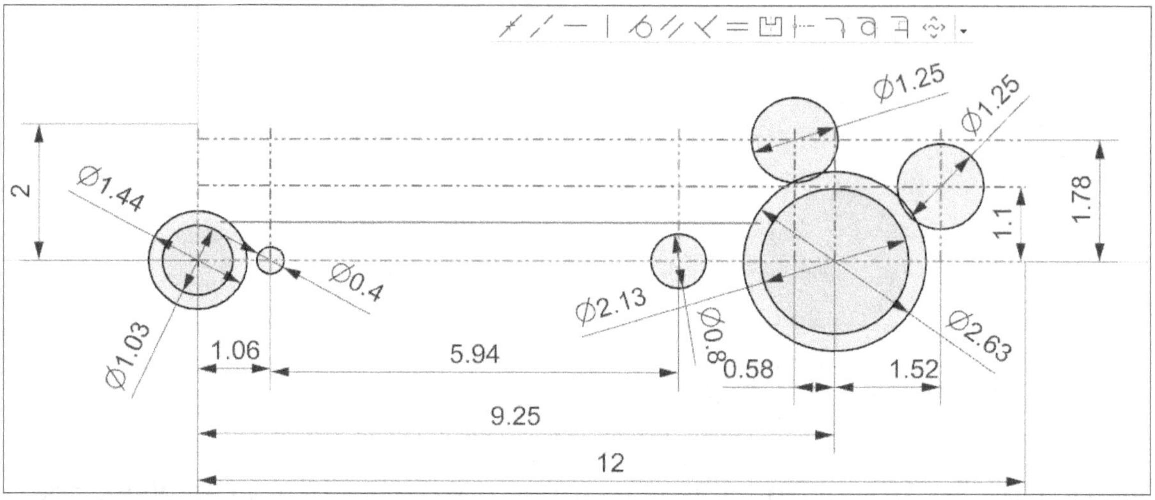

Figure-46. Line joining the circles

- Trim the extra portion of line by using **Trim** tool and specify the distance of line from horizontal centerline as **0.38**; refer to Figure-47.

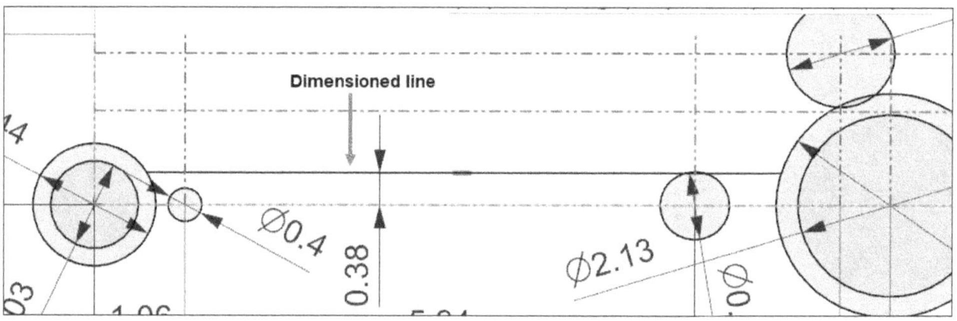

Figure-47. Line after dimensioning

- Click on the **Fillet** tool from the **Sketch Curve** toolbox in the **Direct Sketch** panel of **Ribbon**. The **Fillet** dialog box will be displayed.
- Select the **Untrim** button from the **Fillet Method** section of the **Fillet** dialog box and create the fillets as shown in Figure-48. Note that the selection sets for creating fillets are marked by numbers in the figure.

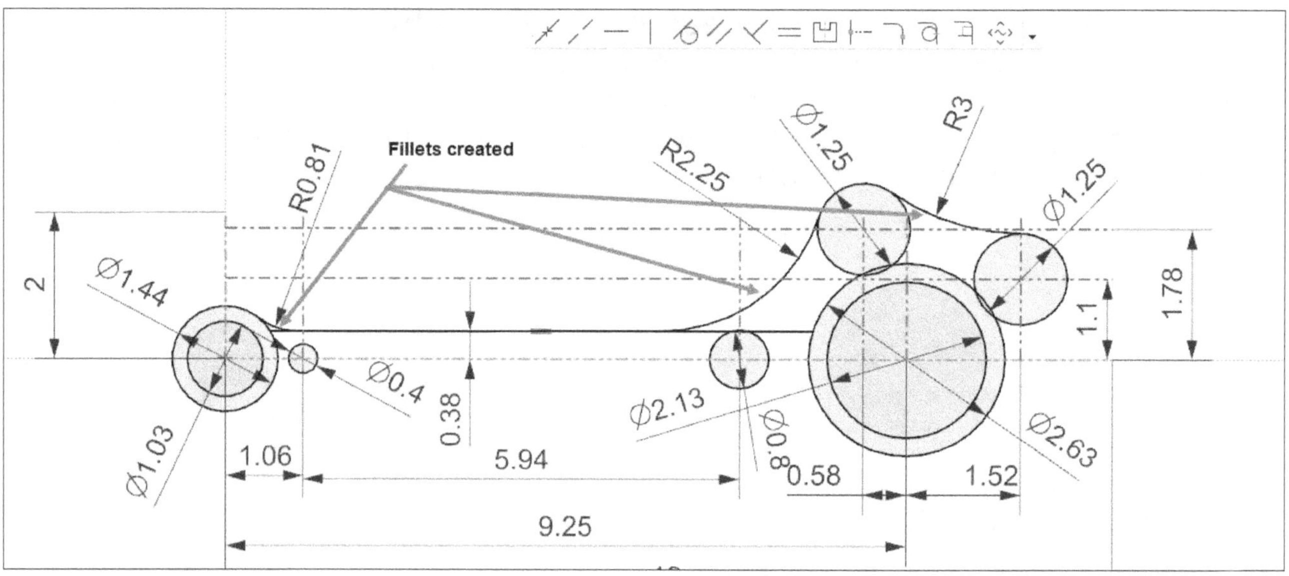

Figure-48. Creating fillets

Creating Mirror Copy

- Click on the **Mirror** tool from the **Curve** group in the **Home** tab of **Ribbon**. The **Mirror Curve** dialog box will be displayed.
- Select the recently created fillets and their connected circles/lines; refer to Figure-49.

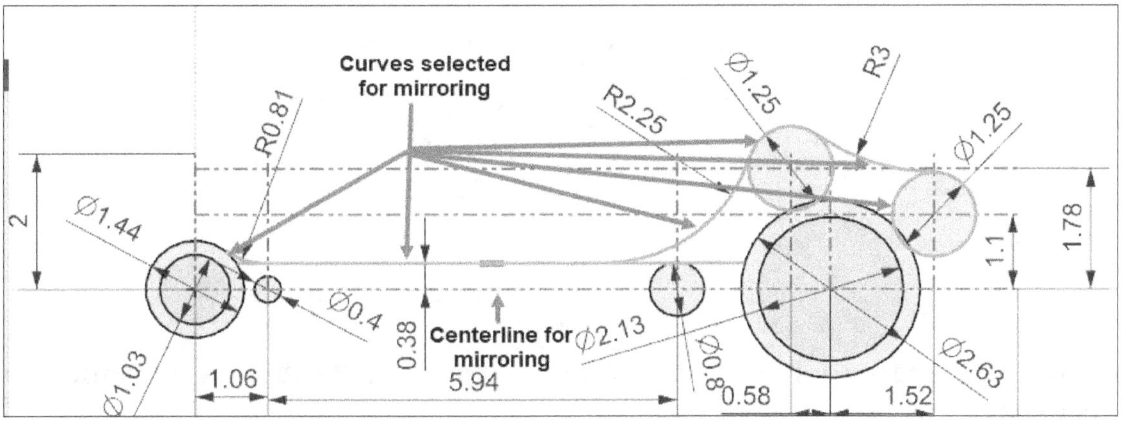

Figure-49. Selecting curves for mirroring

- Click on the **Select Centerline** selection button from the **Centerline** rollout in the dialog box and select the centerline as shown in Figure-49. Preview of mirror feature will be displayed; refer to Figure-50.

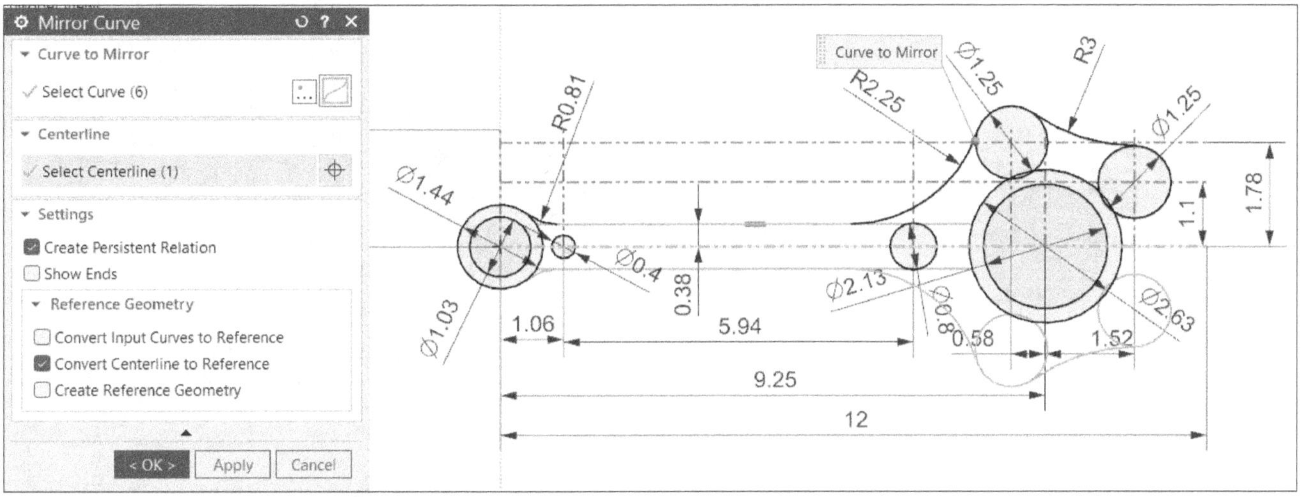

Figure-50. Preview of mirrored curves

- Click on the **OK** button from the dialog box to create the feature.

Creating Last Fillet and Trimming

- Click on the **Fillet** tool from the **Curve** group in the **Ribbon** and create the fillet of radius **3** as shown in Figure-51.

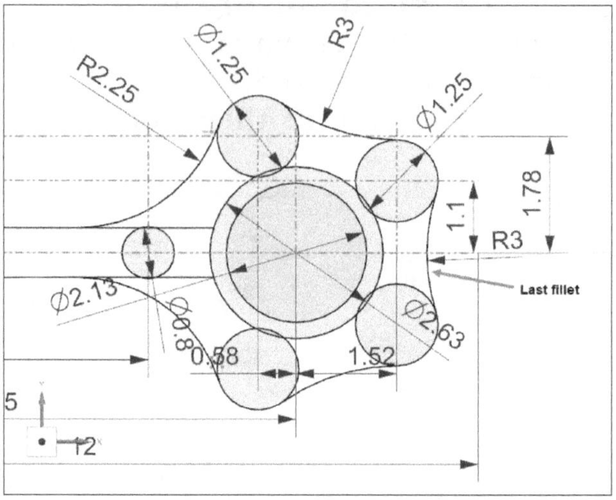

Figure-51. Last fillet to be created

- Click on the **Trim** tool from the **Curve** group in **Ribbon** and remove all the unnecessary entities.
- Delete the earlier created lines and re-apply the dimensions so that the sketch is displayed as shown in Figure-52.

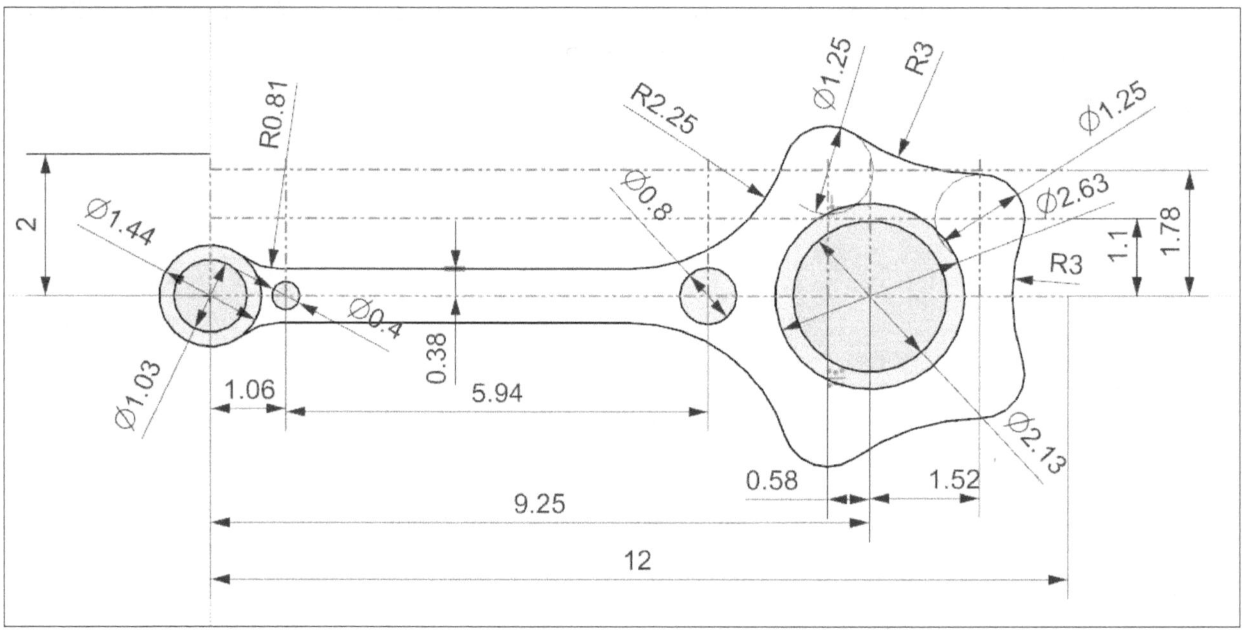

Figure-52. Final sketch for practical 3

PRACTICAL 4

Create the sketch as shown in Figure-53.

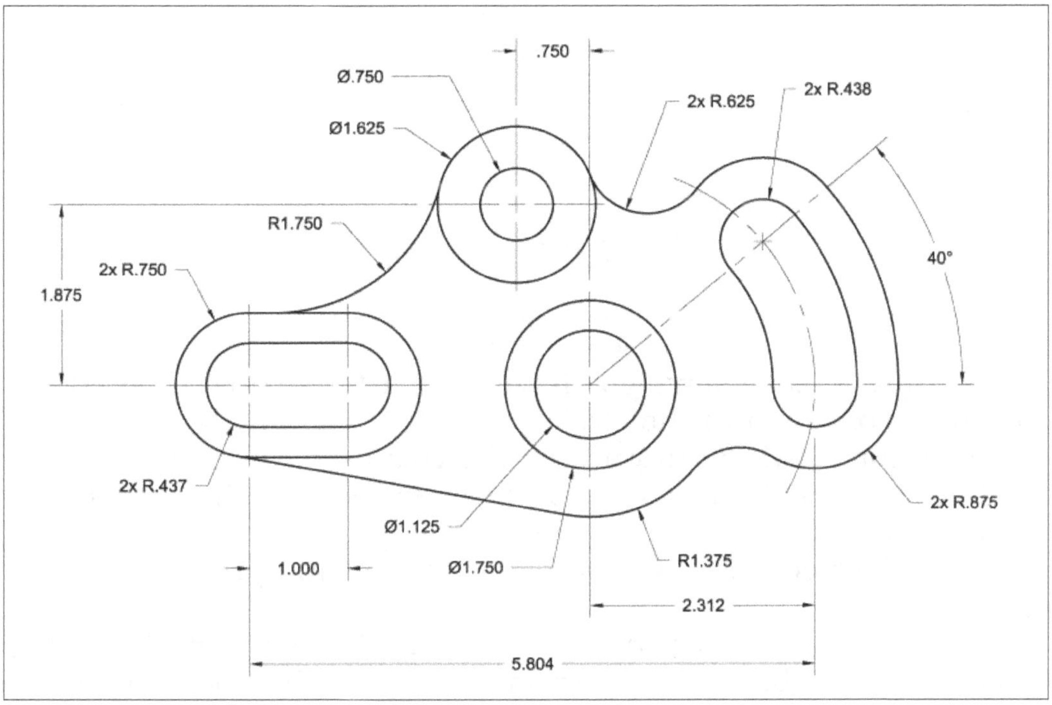

Figure-53. Practical 4

Starting Sketch

- Start NX by double-clicking on the icon from the desktop if not started yet.
- Click on the **New** button from the **Quick Access Toolbar**. The **New** dialog box will be displayed.
- Select the **Model** option from **Templates** rollout of the dialog box and select the **Inches** option from the **Units** drop-down in the rollout.
- Specify the name as **Practical 4** in the **Name** edit box and set desired location in **Folder** edit box of the dialog box.
- Click on the **OK** button from the **New** dialog box. The Modeling environment will be displayed.
- Click on the **Sketch** tool from the **Construction** panel of **Home** tab in the **Ribbon**. The **Create Sketch** dialog box will be displayed and you will be asked to select the sketching plane.
- Select the **Top Plane** from the graphics area and click on the **OK** button. The sketching environment will be activated.

Creating Circles

- Click on the **Circle** tool from the **Curve** group in the **Home** tab of the **Ribbon**. The **Circle** dialog box will be displayed.

- Create two circles of diameter **1.125** and **1.750** with their centers at the origin; refer to Figure-54.

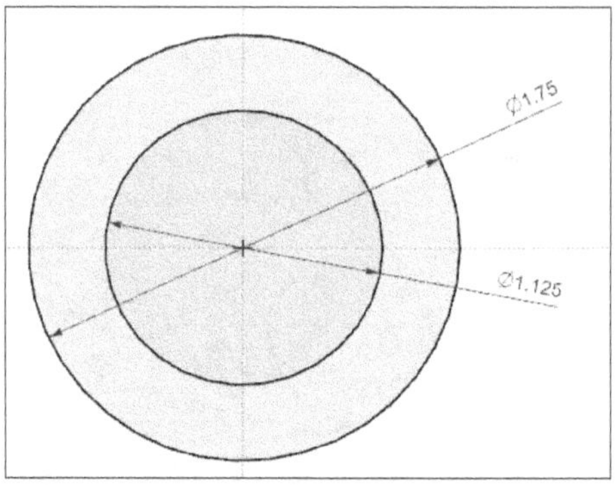

Figure-54. Base circles created

- Click on the **Circle** tool again if you have exit the tool. You will be asked to specify the coordinates of center of the circle.
- Click on the **Point Dialog** button from the **Location** rollout in the **Circle** dialog box to define location of center of circle by specified coordinates. The Point dialog box will be displayed.
- Type **-0.75** in the **X** edit box of dynamic input box and press **TAB**. You will asked to specify value of Y.
- Type **1.875** in the **Y** edit box and click on the **OK** button from the dialog box. The **Circle** dialog box will be displayed again and you will be asked to specify diameter of circle.
- Enter the diameter value as **0.750** in the input box. The circle will be created; refer to Figure-55. Create another circle of diameter **1.625** on the same center where circle of diameter **0.750** was created; refer to Figure-56. Press **ESC** to exit the **Circle** tool.

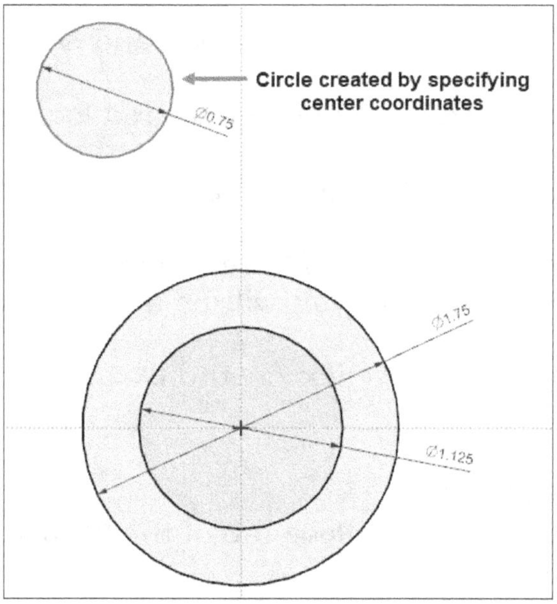

Figure-55. Circle to be created by center coordinates

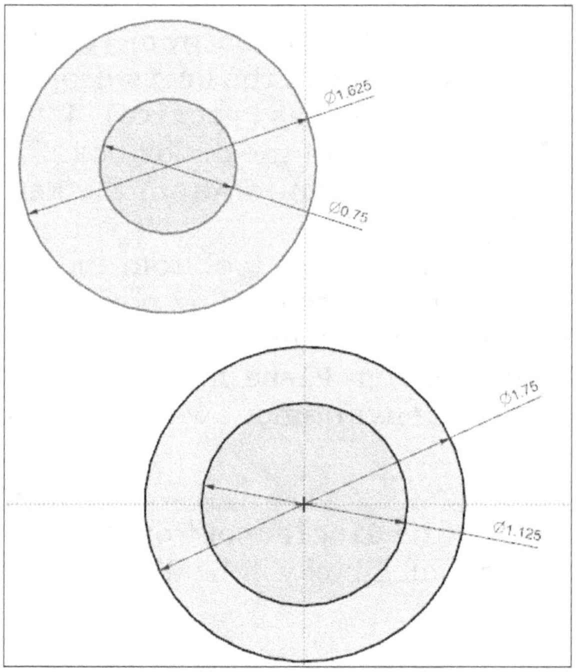

Figure-56. Circles created

Creating Angular Slot

Till this version of software, there is no direct tool to create angular slots in sketch. So, we will use arcs and circles to create slots in NX.

- Click on the **Arc from Center** tool from the **Curve** group of **Home** tab in the **Ribbon**. The **Arc** dialog box will be displayed.
- Create an arc as shown in Figure-57.

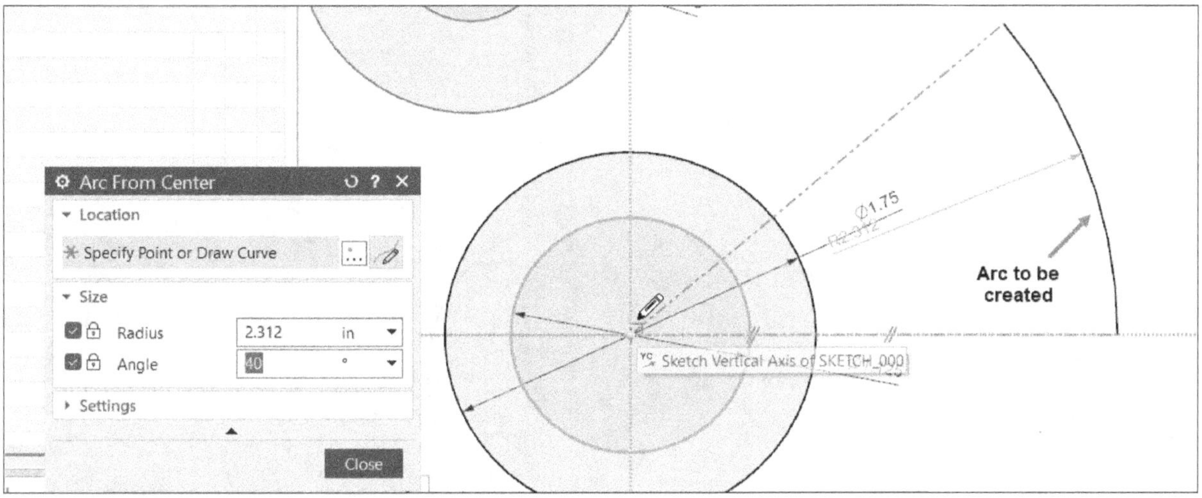

Figure-57. Arc to be created

- Press **ESC** to exit the **Arc** tool.
- Click on the **Offset** tool from **Curve** group in the **Home** tab of **Ribbon**. The **Offset Curve** dialog box will be displayed.
- Set the parameters as shown in Figure-58 and select the recently created arc. Preview of slot arcs will be displayed; refer to Figure-58.

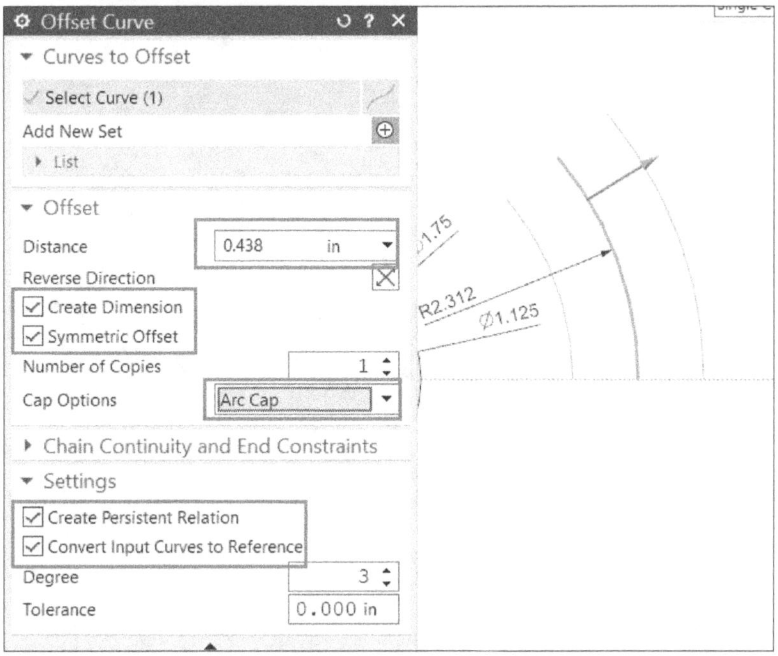

Figure-58. Preview of slot arcs

- Click on the **OK** button to create the offset copies.
- Click on the **Arc** tool from the **Curve** panel in the **Home** tab of **Ribbon**. You will be asked to specify start point of arc.
- Create an arc joining two end points of offsetted arcs; refer to Figure-59.
- Similarly, create the same arc on other end points of offsetted arcs to complete the slot; refer to Figure-60.

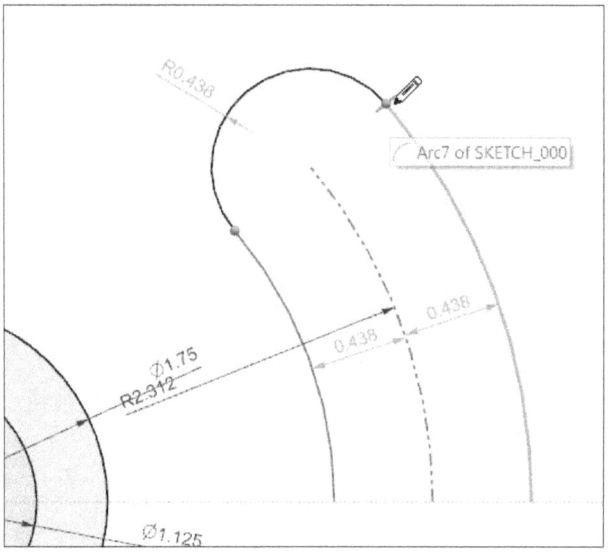

Figure-59. Arc at end points of other arcs

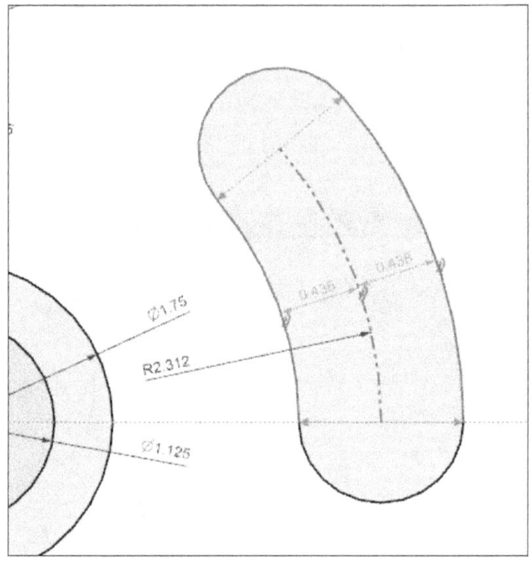

Figure-60. Slot created

- Offset the slot outward by **0.437** (radius of outer slot - radius of inner slot); refer to Figure-61. Note that you need to select only three sides of slot to offset and parameters should be same as shown in Figure-61.

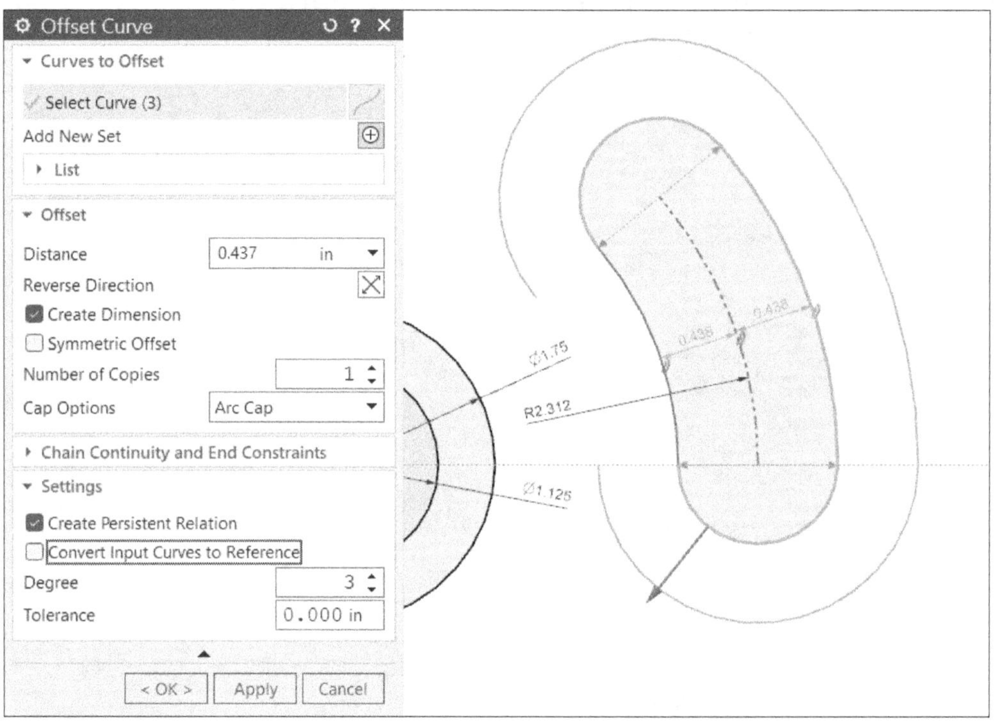

Figure-61. Preview of offsetted slot

- Click on the **OK** button from the **Offset Curve** dialog box to create the offset.

Creating Straight Slot

- Click on the **Line** tool from the **Curve** group in the **Ribbon** and create a line as shown in Figure-62.

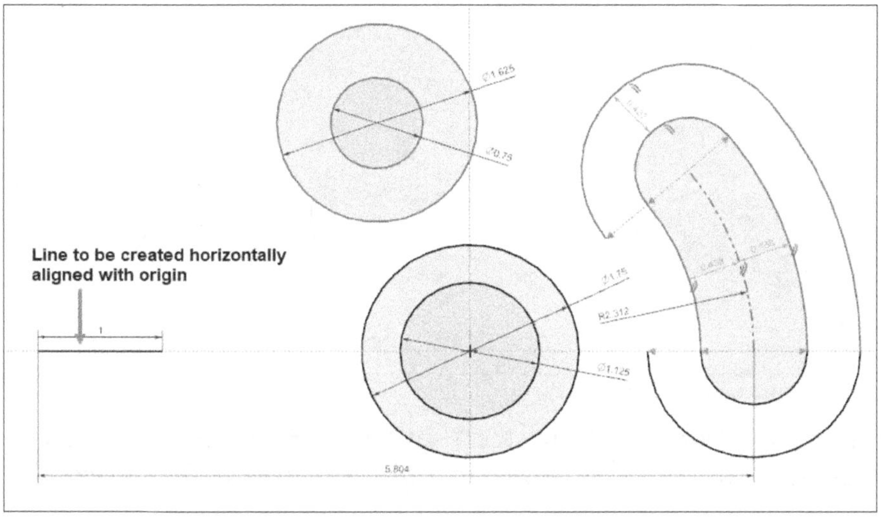

Figure-62. Centerline for slot

- Offset this line by parameters as shown in Figure-63.

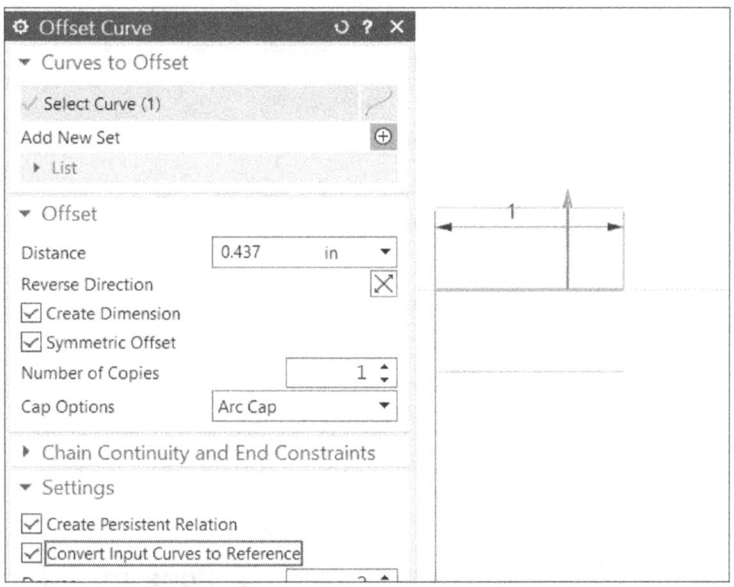

Figure-63. Preview of line offset

- Join the end points of offsetted lines by using tangent arcs; refer to Figure-64.

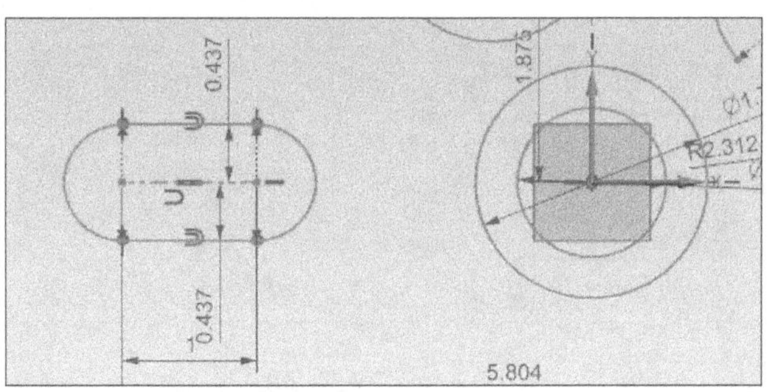

Figure-64. Straight slot after creating tangent arcs

- Create an offset copy of this slot at a distance of **0.313** outward (Radius of outer slot - radius of inner slot); refer to Figure-65.

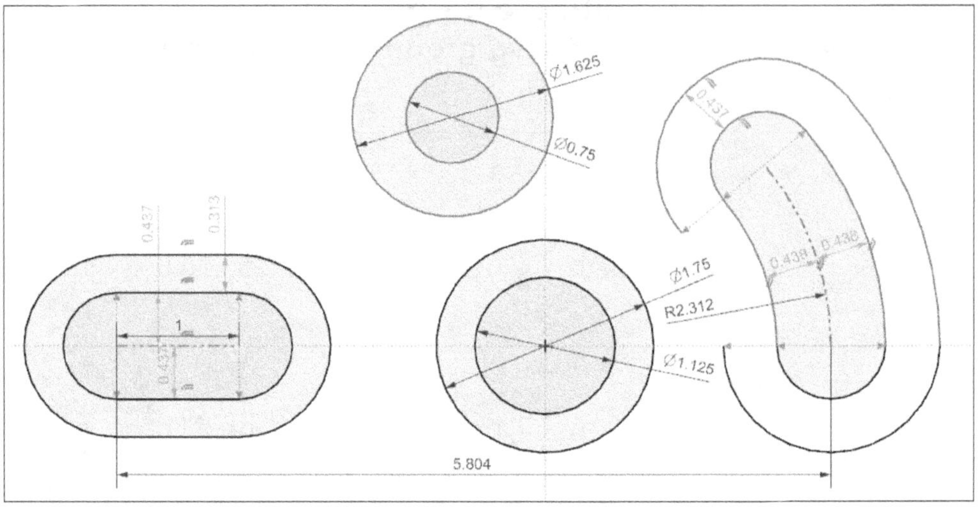

Figure-65. After creating offset copy of slot

Tip: Use **Increase** and **Decrease** buttons in **Text Size** panel of **Display** tab in the **Ribbon** to change size of dimensions being shown in graphics area.

Creating Outer Boundary of Sketch

- Click on the **Arc from Center** tool from the **Curve** group in **Home** tab of **Ribbon** and create an arc of radius **1.375** as shown in Figure-66.

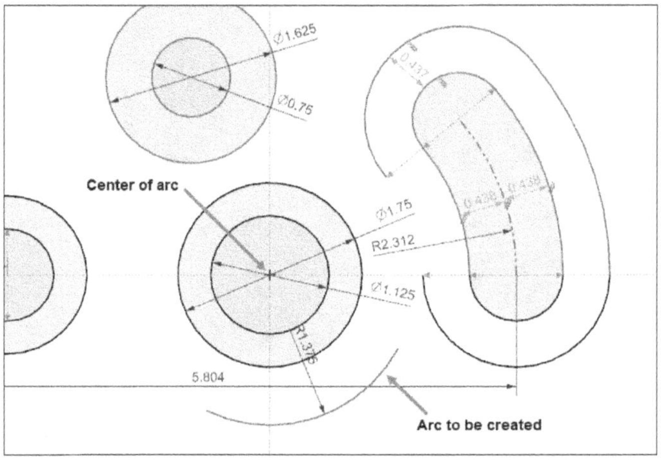

Figure-66. Arc to be created

- Click on the **Line** tool from the **Curve** group in **Home** tab of **Ribbon** and create a line joining slot with recently created arc as shown in Figure-67.

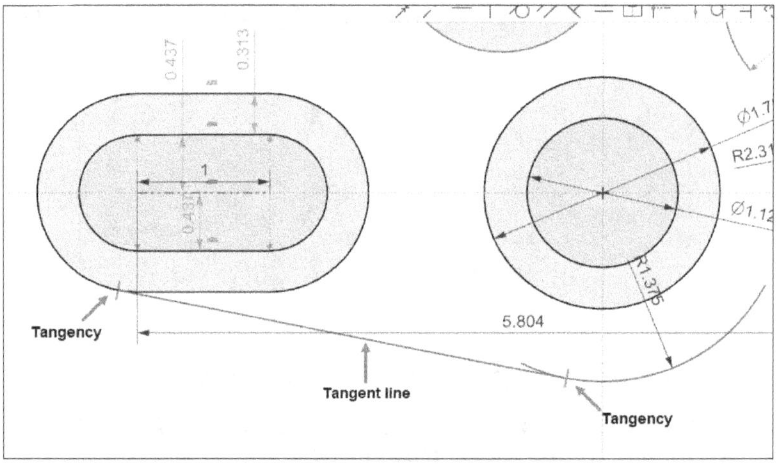

Figure-67. Line joining slot with arc

- Click on the **Fillet** tool from **Sketch Curve** toolbox and create the untrimmed fillets as shown in Figure-68.

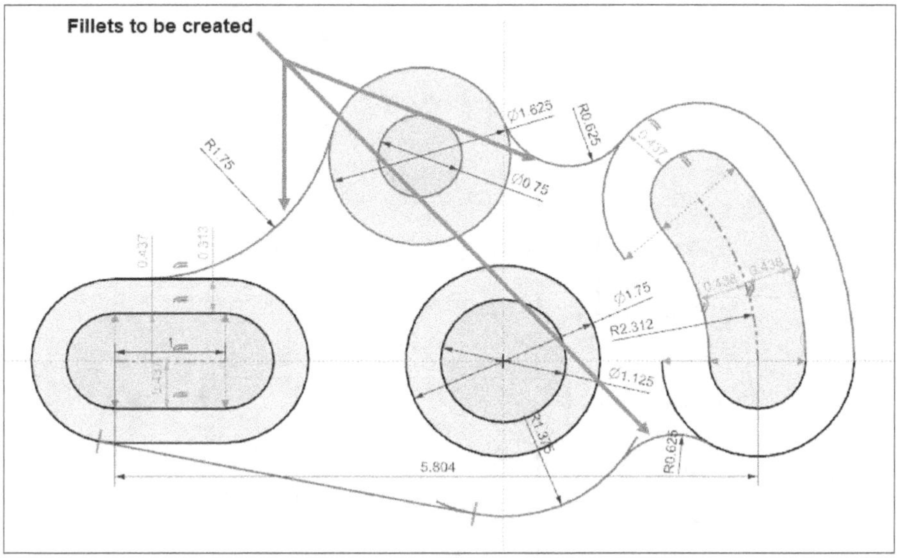

Figure-68. Fillets to be created

- Click on the **Trim** tool from the **Curve** group in **Home** tab of **Ribbon** and remove the extra entities of sketch. After removing extra entities and applying dimensions, the sketch should display as shown in Figure-69.

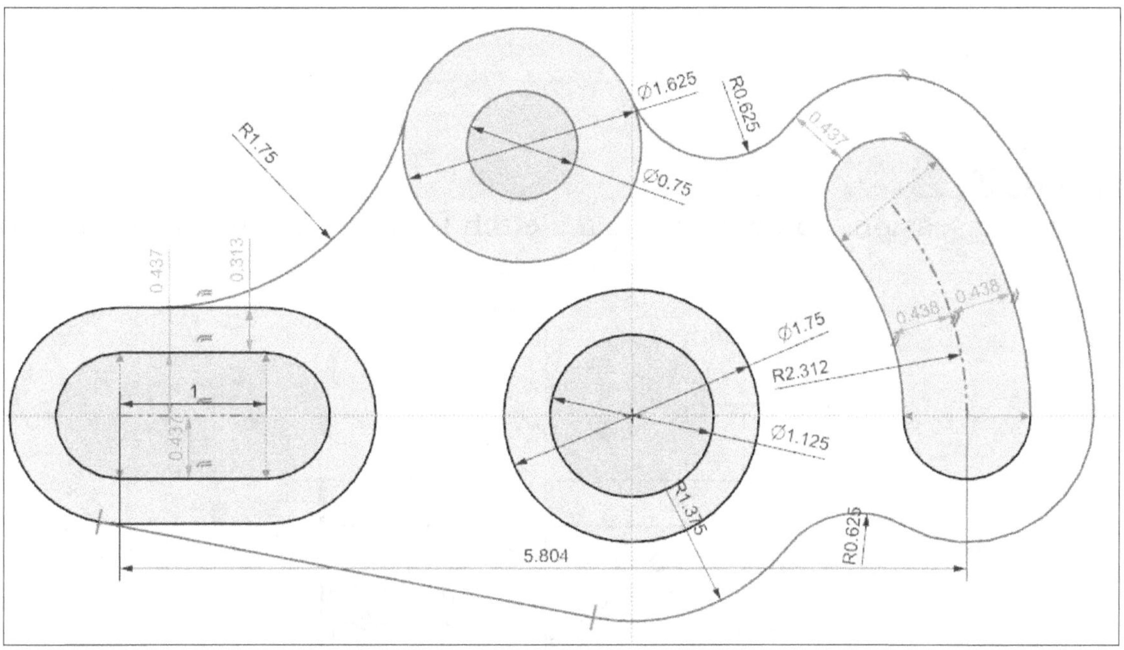

Figure-69. Sketch after trimming and dimensioning

PRACTICE 1

In this practice session, you will create a sketch for the drawing given in Figure-70.

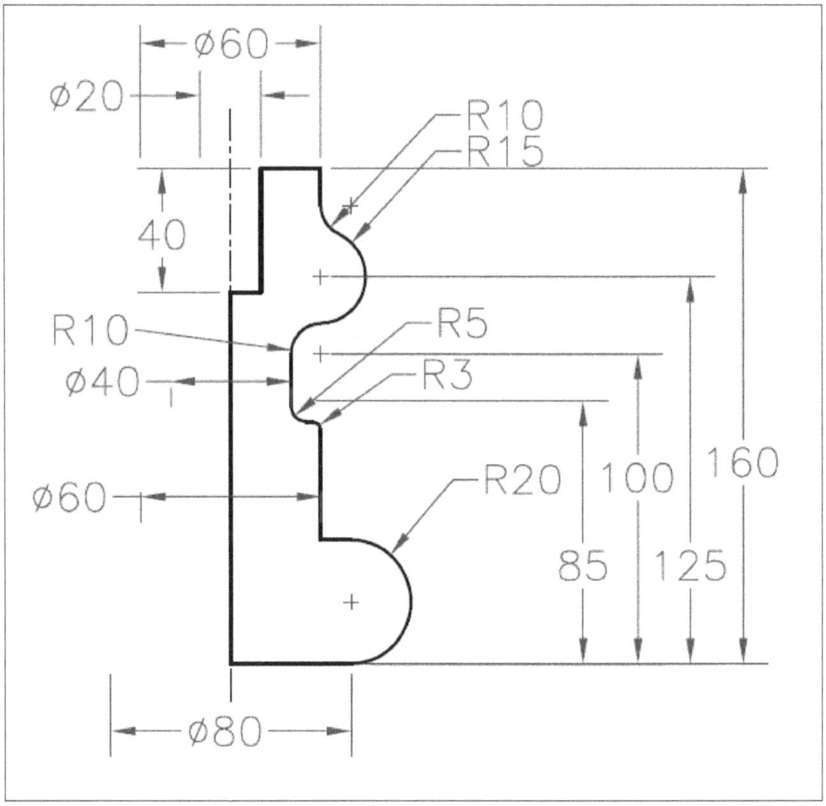

Figure-70. Practice 1

PRACTICE 2

In this practice session, you will create a sketch for the drawing given in Figure-71.

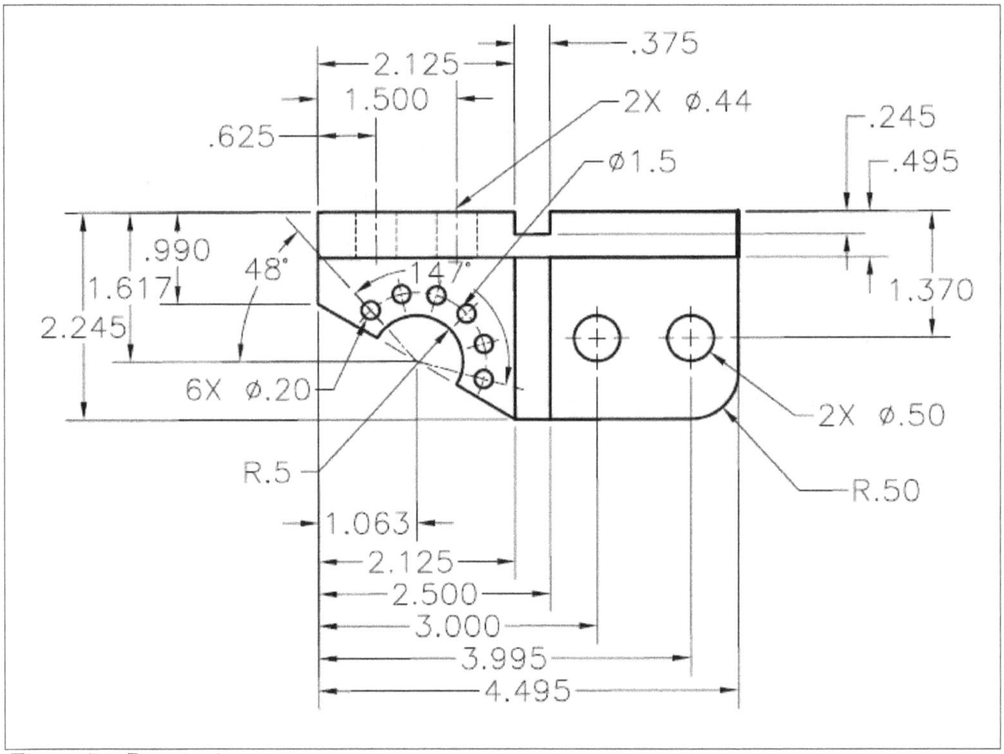

Figure-71. Practice 2

Practice 3

In this practice session, you will create a sketch for the drawing given in Figure-72.

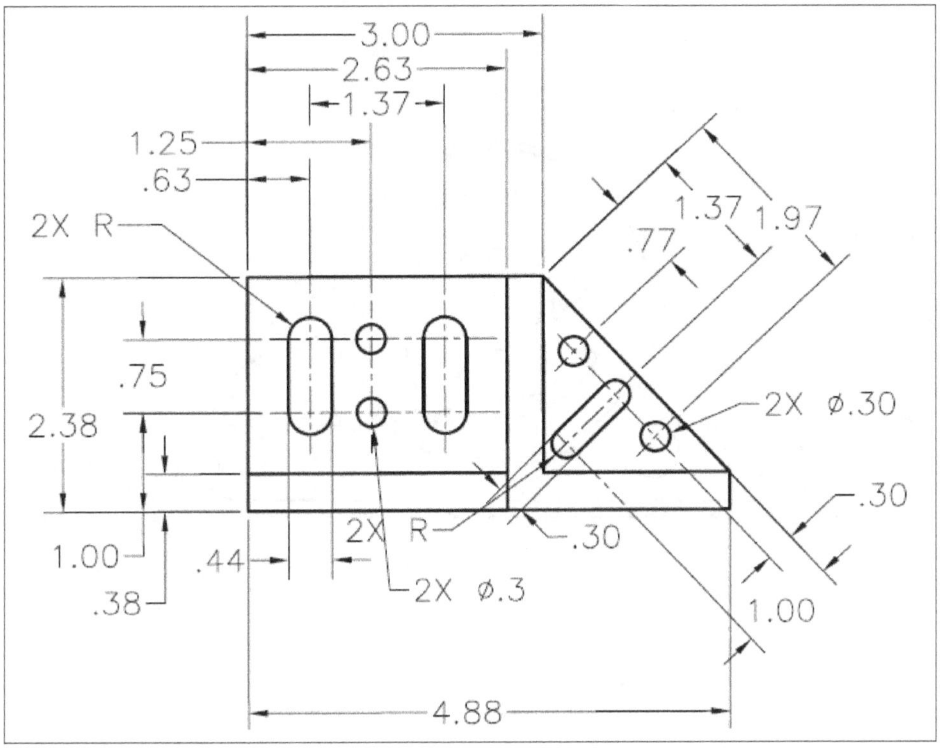

Figure-72. Practice 3

Practice 4

In this practice session, you will create a sketch for the drawing given in Figure-73.

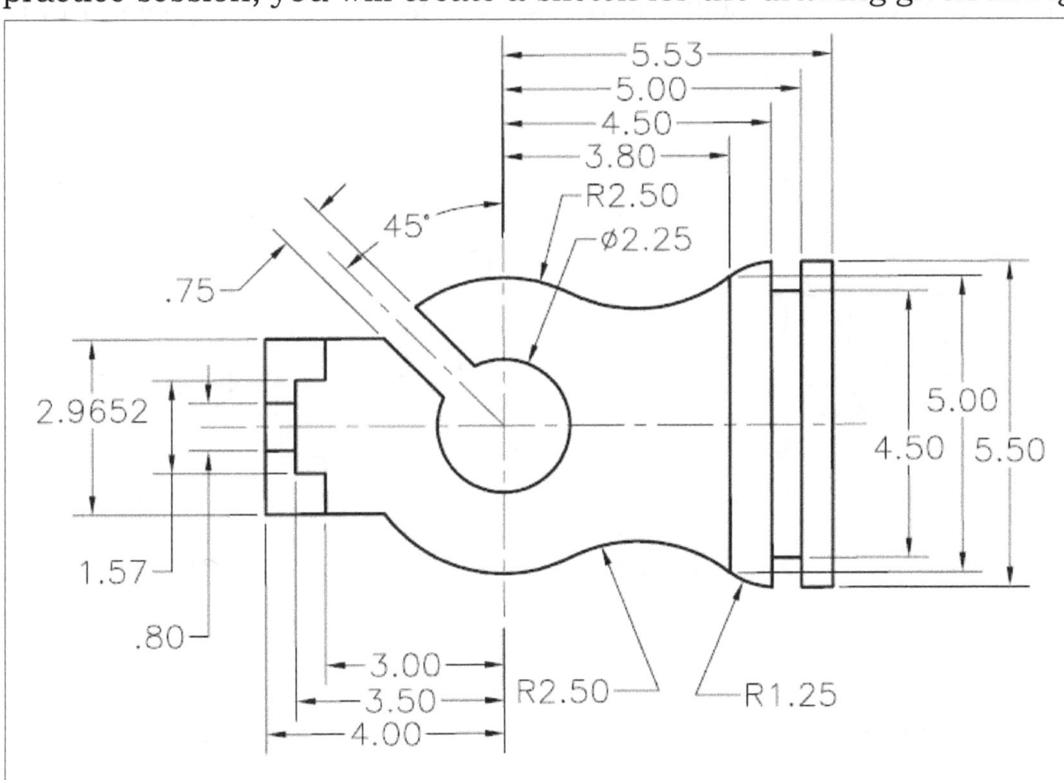

Figure-73. Practice 4

PRACTICE 5

In this practice session, you will create a sketch for the drawing given in Figure-74.

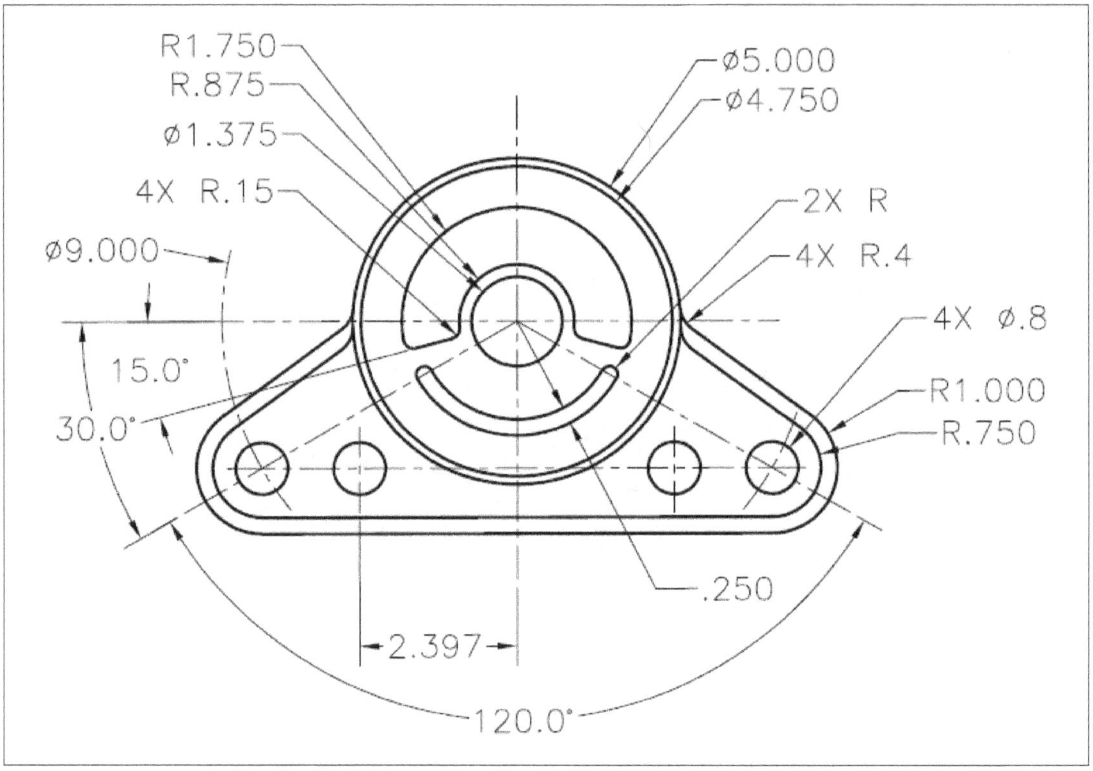

Figure-74. Practice 5

PRACTICE 6

In this practice session, you will create a sketch for the drawing given in Figure-75.

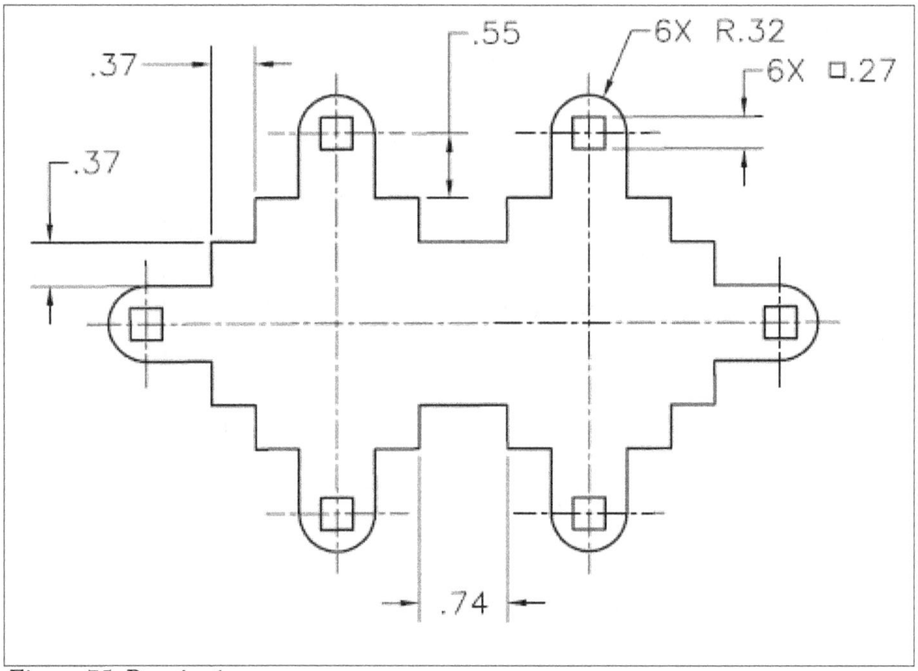

Figure-75. Practice 6

Chapter 4

3D Modeling

Topics Covered

The major topics covered in this chapter are:

- ***Extrude***
- ***Datum Feature***
- ***Revolve***
- ***Sweep Features***

INTRODUCTION TO 3D MODELING

In previous chapters, we have worked on sketching tools to create sketches based on given drawings. These sketches are the base features for 3D features like extrude, revolve, sweep, and so on. In today's CAD packages, our aim is to create exact digital replica of real world object that we can use to manufacture. In this chapter, we will work on some of the 3D modeling tools that convert the sketch features into 3D objects.

EXTRUDE FEATURE

The extrude feature is used to add material to the sketch while moving it along any vector. The procedure to create extrude feature in NX is given next.

- Click on the **Extrude** tool from the **Extrude** drop-down in **Feature** panel of the **Home** tab in **Ribbon**. The **Extrude** dialog box will be displayed; refer to Figure-1.

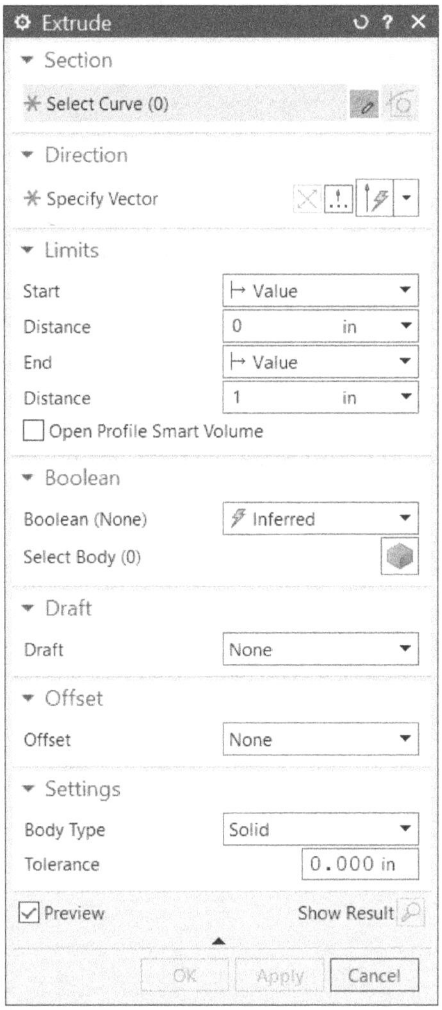

Figure-1. Extrude dialog box

- Select the closed loop sketch to be extruded or click on the **Sketch Section** button from the **Section** rollout in the dialog box if you want to create the sketch. On selecting the sketch, preview of extrude feature will be displayed; refer to Figure-2.

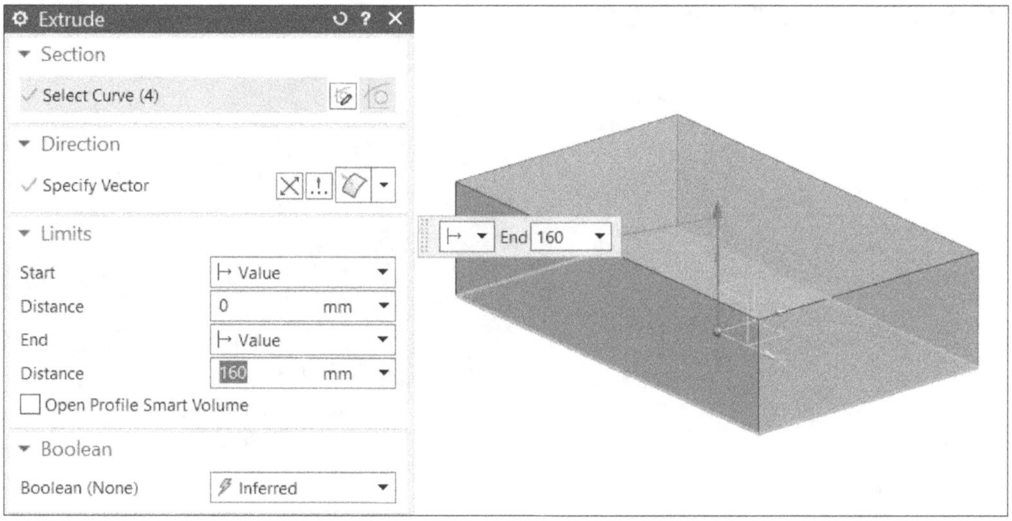

Figure-2. Preview of extrude feature

- Click on the **Specify Vector** selection button in the **Direction** rollout and select the reference for direction of extrusion. By default, the direction of extrusion is perpendicular to sketching plane.
- Click on the **Reverse Direction** button from **Direction** rollout to reverse the direction of extrude feature.
- Click on the **Vector Dialog** button from the **Direction** rollout to manually define reference for direction vector. The **Vector** dialog box will be displayed; refer to Figure-3. You will learn about parameters of this dialog box later in this book.

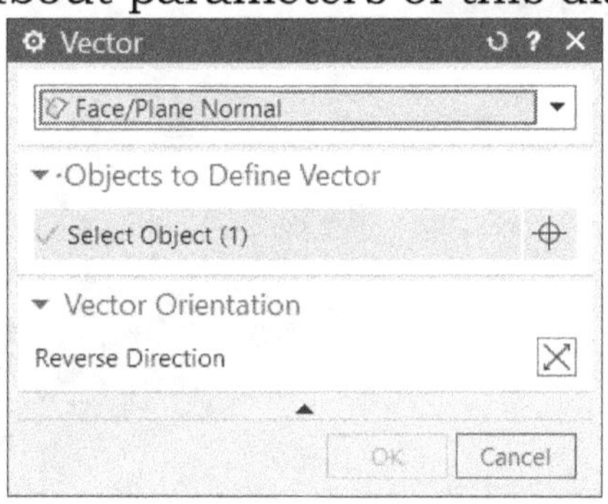

Figure-3. Vector dialog box

Extrude by Distance Values

- Select the **Value** option from the **Start** drop-down in **Limits** rollout if you want the extrude feature to start at specified distance from sketching plane. Specify desired value in **Distance** edit box below the drop-down and press **TAB**. Preview of feature will be displayed; refer to Figure-4.

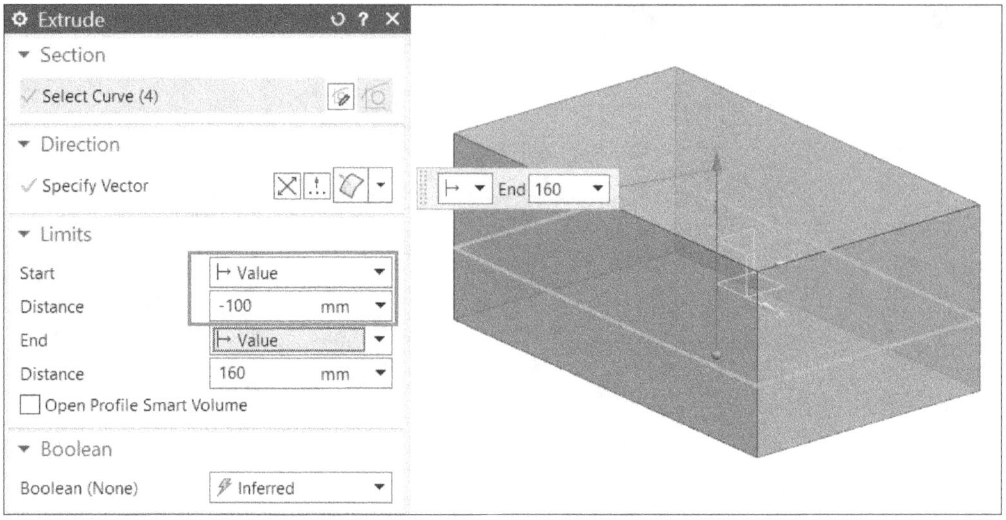

Figure-4. Specifying starting distance for extrude

- Similarly, select the **Value** option from **End** drop-down and specify desired distance value up to which you want to extrude the feature in **Distance** edit box.

Symmetric Extrude

- Select the **Symmetric Value** option from the **Start** or **End** drop-down to create extrude feature of equal length on both sides of sketch plane; refer to Figure-5.

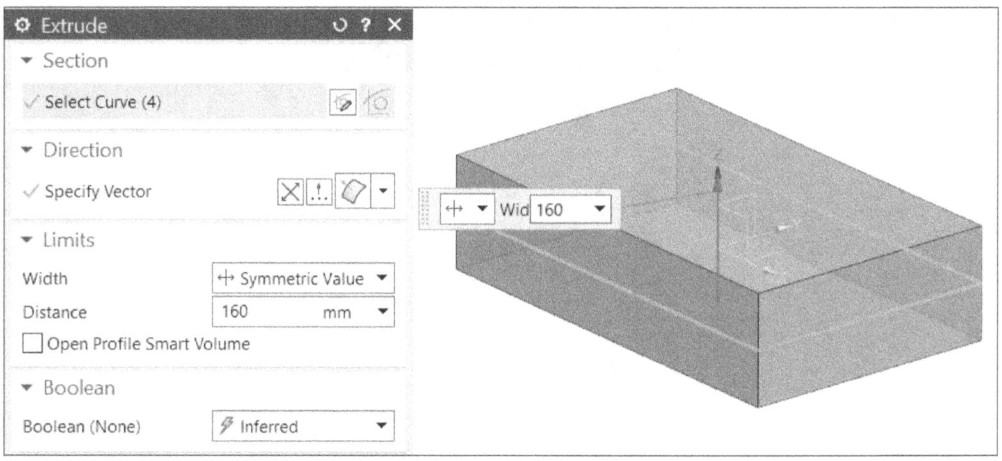

Figure-5. Preview of symmetric extrude

Extrude Until Next

- If there is any other feature created along the direction in which you are extruding the current sketch then you can select the **Until Next** option from the **End** drop-down. The extrude feature will be created up to next feature; refer to Figure-6. Similarly, you can set **Until Next** option for **Start** drop-down.

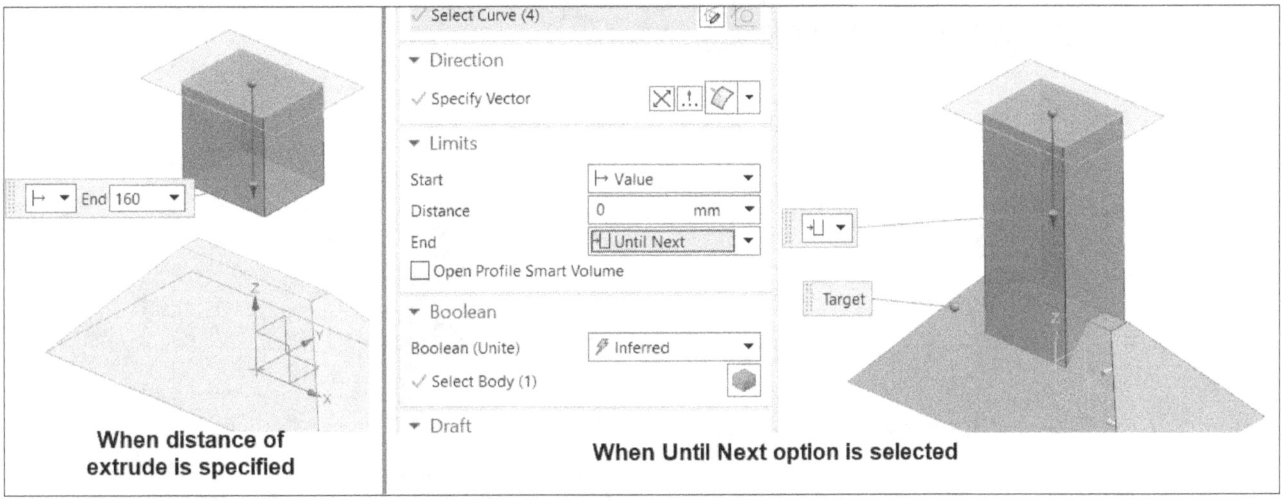

Figure-6. Extruding with Until next option

Extrude Until Selected

- Select the **Until Selected** option from the **End** drop-down if you want to select a reference face, plane, or body to define the distance of extrude; refer to Figure-7.

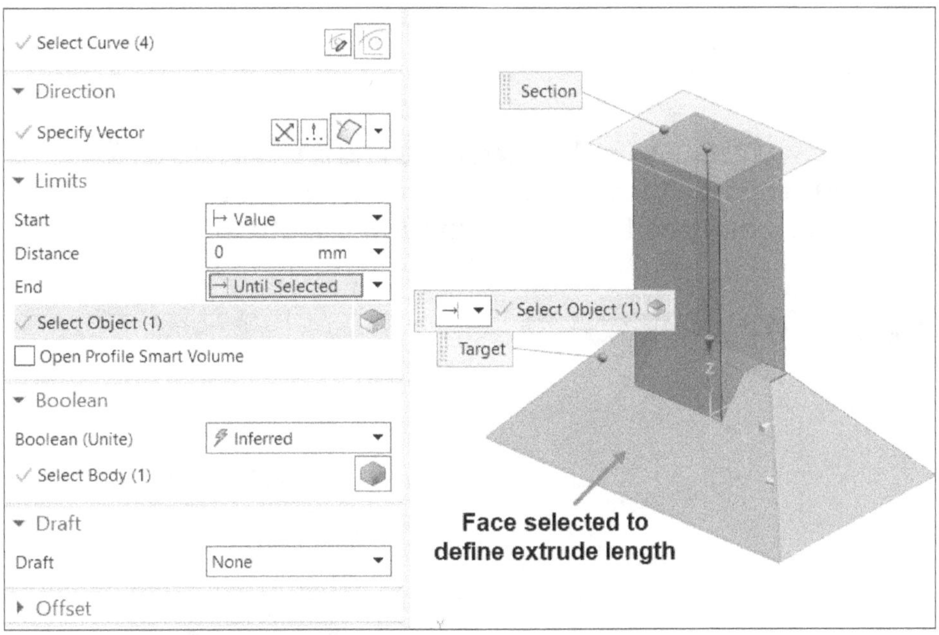

Figure-7. Extrude with Until Selected option

Extrude Until Extended

- Select the **Until Extended** option from the **End** drop-down if you want to extrude the sketch up to selected face, plane, or body and the extrude feature can be trimmed to fullfil specified conditions; refer to Figure-8. Note that you can use planar face as reference of distance but you can not use B-spline surface as reference for extrude distance.

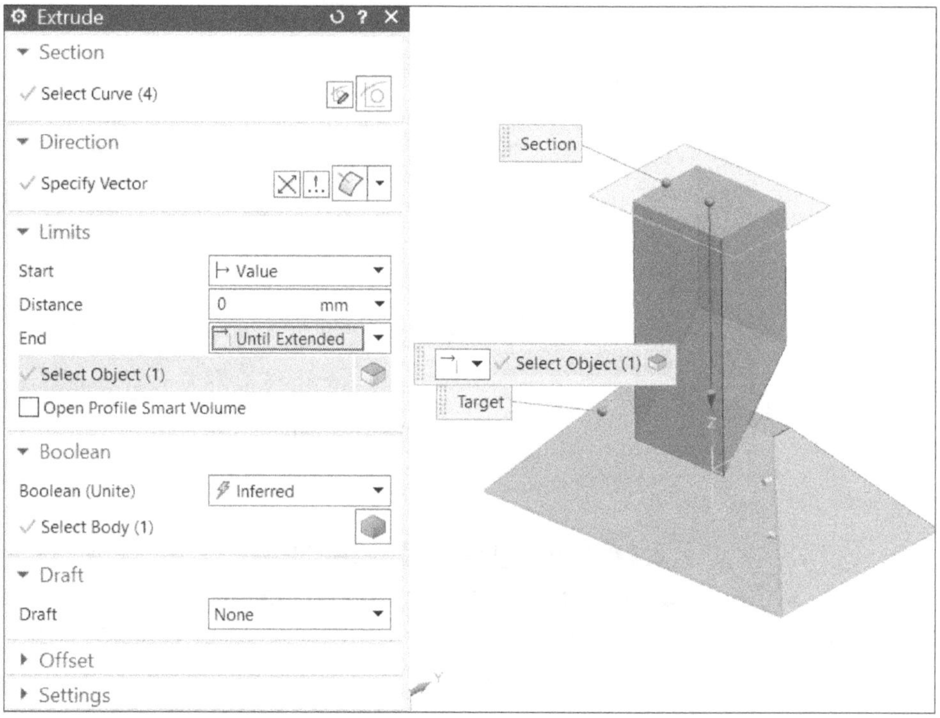

Figure-8. Extrude with Until Extended option

Extrude Using Offset from Selected

- Select the **Offset from Selected** option from the **End** drop-down to create extrude feature which ends at specified offset distance from selected extrude reference; refer to Figure-9.

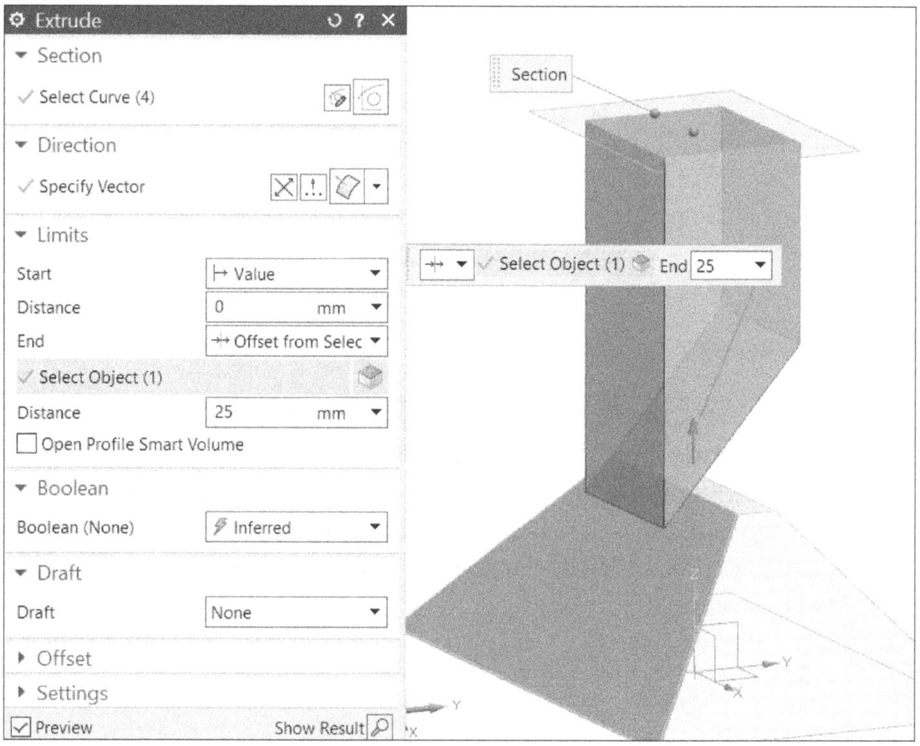

Figure-9. Extrude with Offset from Selected option

Extrude Through All

- Select the **Through All** option from the **End** drop-down to create extrude feature up to the last face/plane/body along the extrude direction; refer to Figure-10.

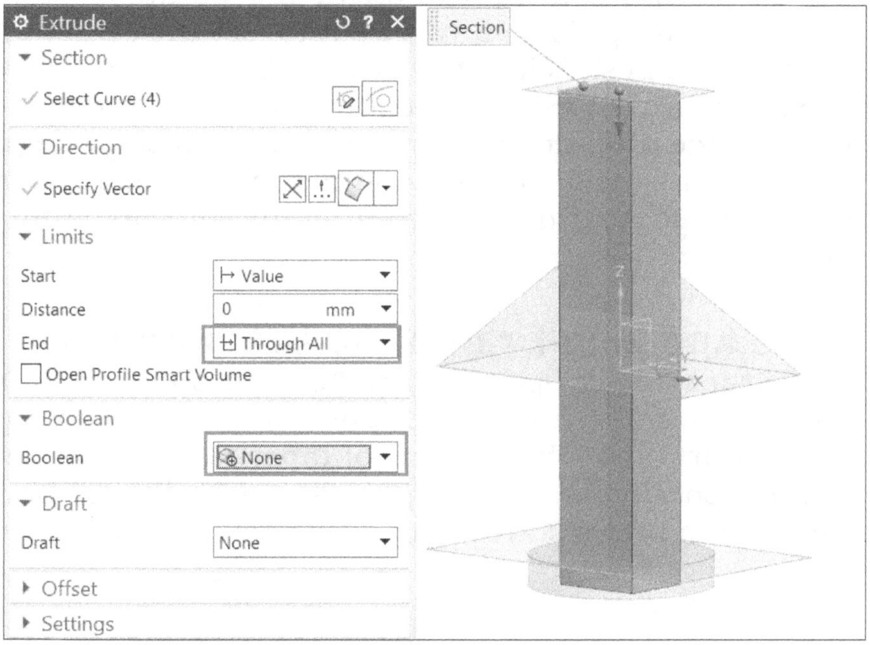

Figure-10. Extrude with Through All option

Using Open Profile Smart Volume

- Select the **Open Profile Smart Volume** check box if you want to use open profile and boundaries of nearby bodies to create a smart extrude volume. Refer to Figure-11. Note that to use this option, there must be solid boundaries near the open profile.

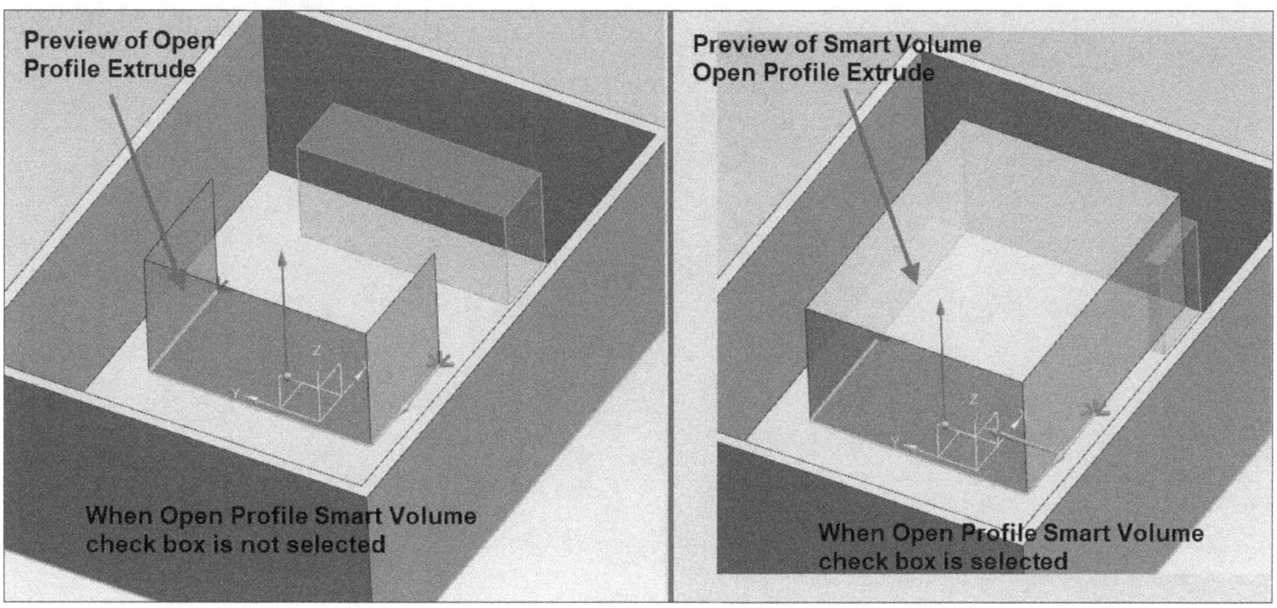

Figure-11. Creating open profile smart volume

Boolean Operations

There are mainly 4 options in **Boolean** drop-down of **Boolean** rollout in the dialog box to perform boolean operations; **None**, **Unite**, **Subtract**, and **Intersect**. Select the **None** option from the drop-down if you want to create a separate extruded body. Select the **Unite** option from the drop-down if you want to join the current extrude feature with nearby connected bodies. Select the **Subtract** option from the drop-down if you want to remove the current extruded feature from connected bodies. Select the **Intersect** option from the drop-down if you want to keep only the portion which is common between current extrude feature and nearby connected bodies. Select the **Inferred** option from the **Boolean** drop-down to let the software automatically decide most probable option.

Applying Draft while Extruding

- Select the **From Start Limit** option in the **Draft** drop-down of **Draft** rollout in the dialog box if you want to apply taper angle to the side faces extrude feature starting from the start face. The preview of taper feature will be displayed and you will be asked to specify the taper angle; refer to Figure-12. Note that the draft will start from location set as start point for extrude feature; refer to Figure-13.

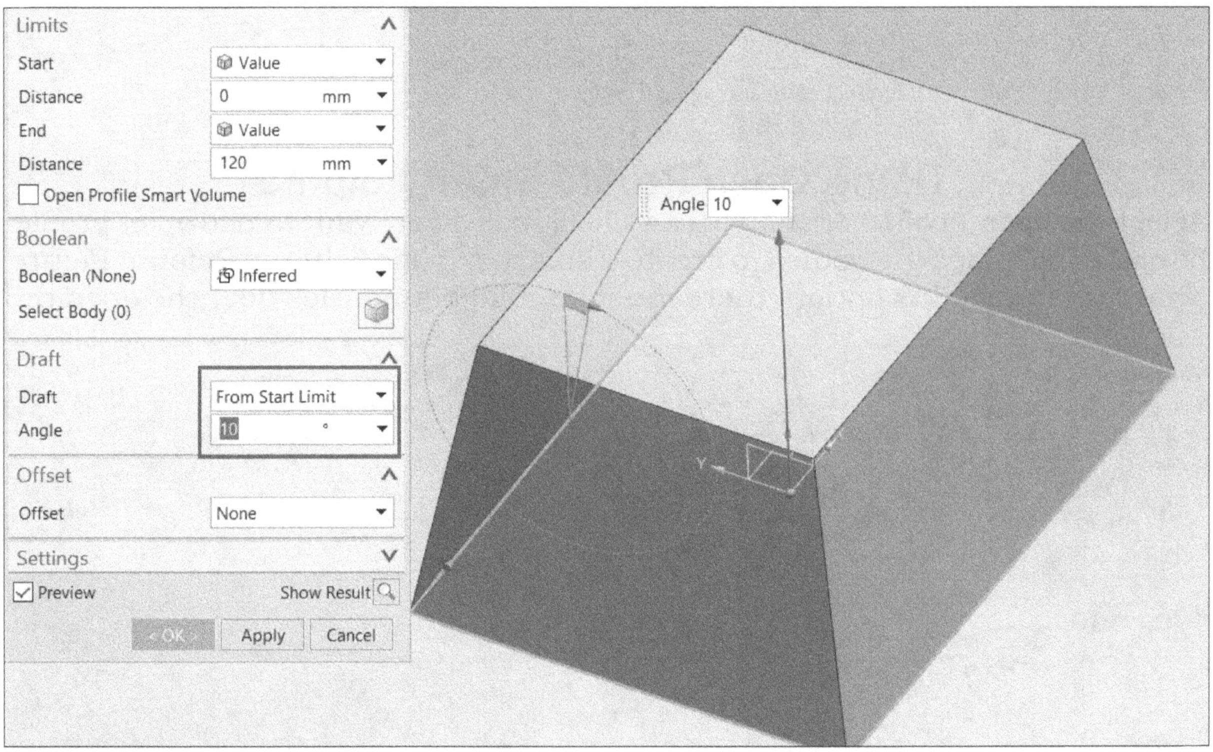

Figure-12. Preview of extrude-feature with draft

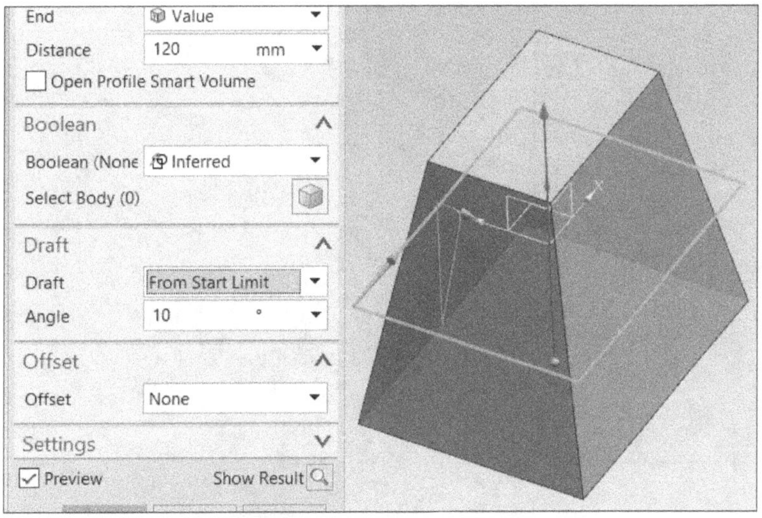

Figure-13. Draft using From Start Limit option

- Specify desired taper angle value in **Angle** edit box and press **TAB** to check the preview.
- Select the **From Section** option in **Draft** drop-down if you want to apply multiple drafts to the feature or want the specified draft angle to be at the section; refer to Figure-14.

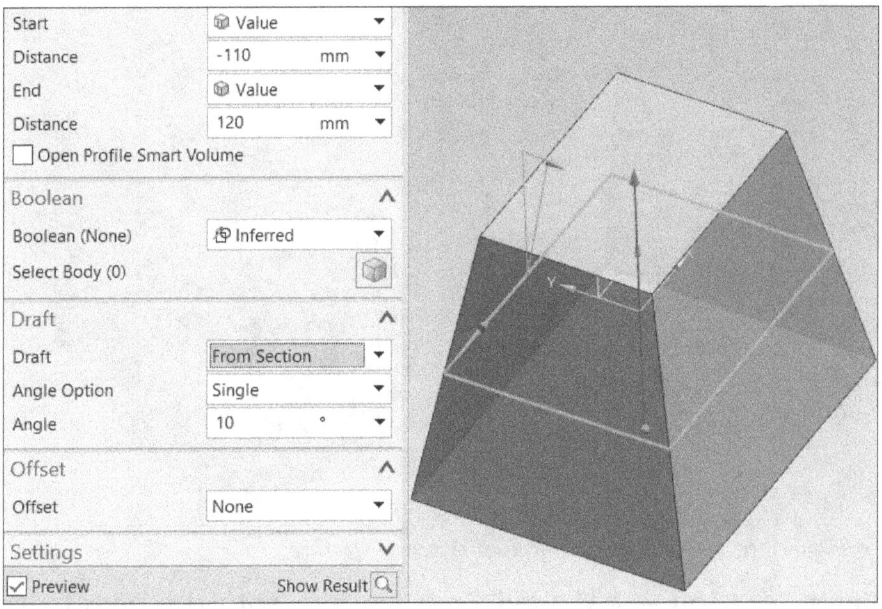

Figure-14. Draft using From Section option

- Select the **Multiple** option from the **Angle Option** drop-down if you want to apply different draft angles to different faces and specify the angle values in list box.
- Select the **From Section - Asymmetric Angle** option from the **Draft** drop-down if you want to specify different values of draft for faces above the section and faces below the section; refer to Figure-15. Note that this option is displayed when **Symmetric Value** option is selected for limits.

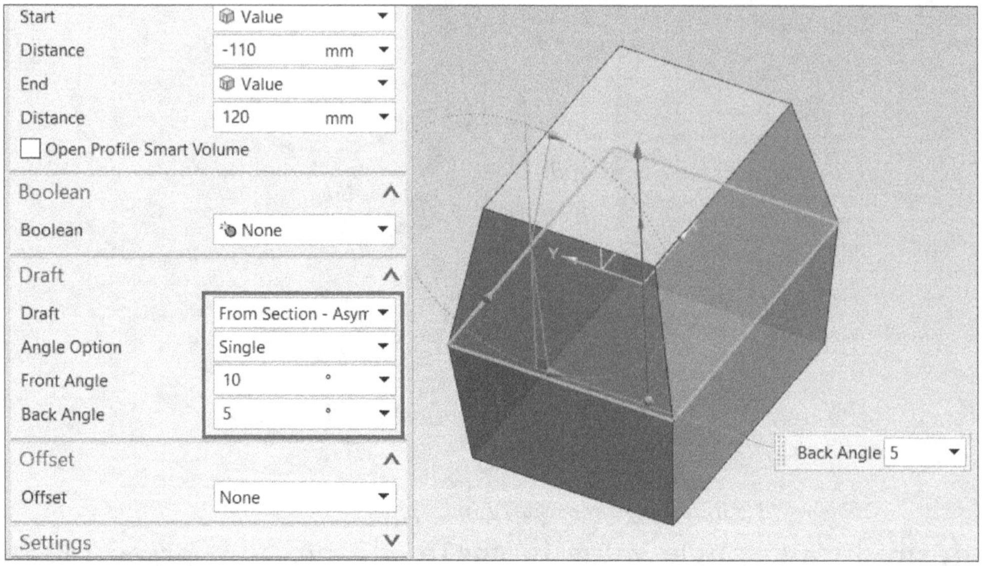

Figure-15. Applying asymmetric draft to extrude feature

- Select the **From Section - Symmetric Angle** option from the **Draft** drop-down if you want to apply same angle draft on both sides from section; refer to Figure-16.

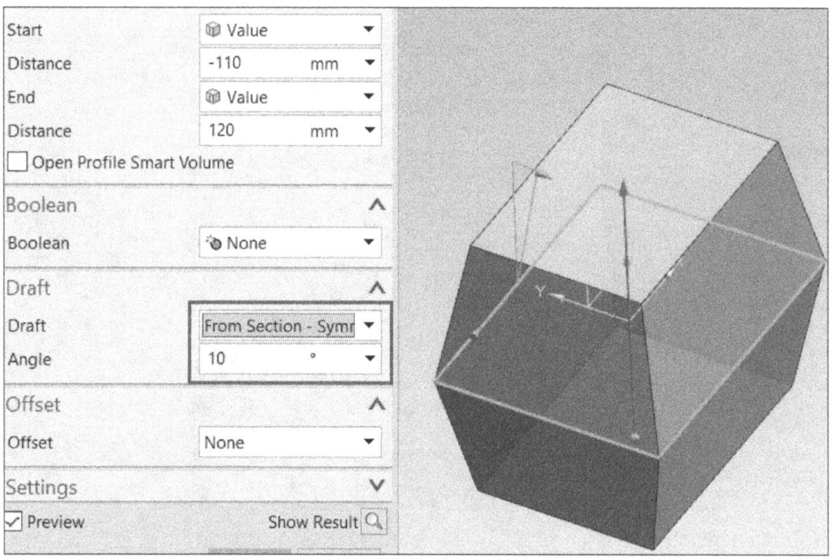

Figure-16. Applying symmetric draft to extrude feature

- Select the **From Section - Matched Ends** option from the **Draft** drop-down if you want to keep extrude feature section same at start and end locations after applying the symmetric draft; refer to Figure-17.

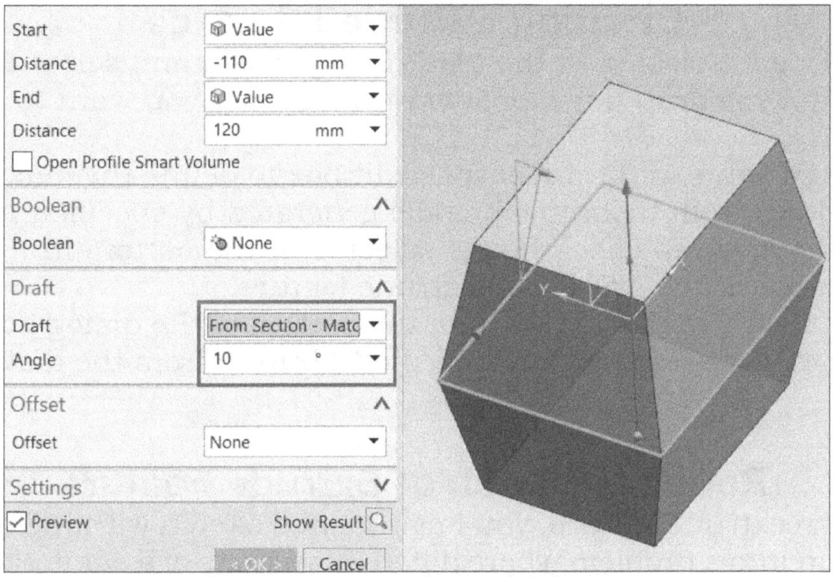

Figure-17. Applying matched ends with draft to extrude feature

Applying Offset while Extruding

- Select the **Single-Sided** option from the **Offset** drop-down if you want to increase the thickness of extrude feature by specified offset value.
- Select the **Two-Sided** option from the **Offset** drop-down if you want to create a thin feature of specified thickness; refer to Figure-18. Specify desired value of offset for both inside and outside of sketch section in respective edit boxes in the **Offset** rollout.

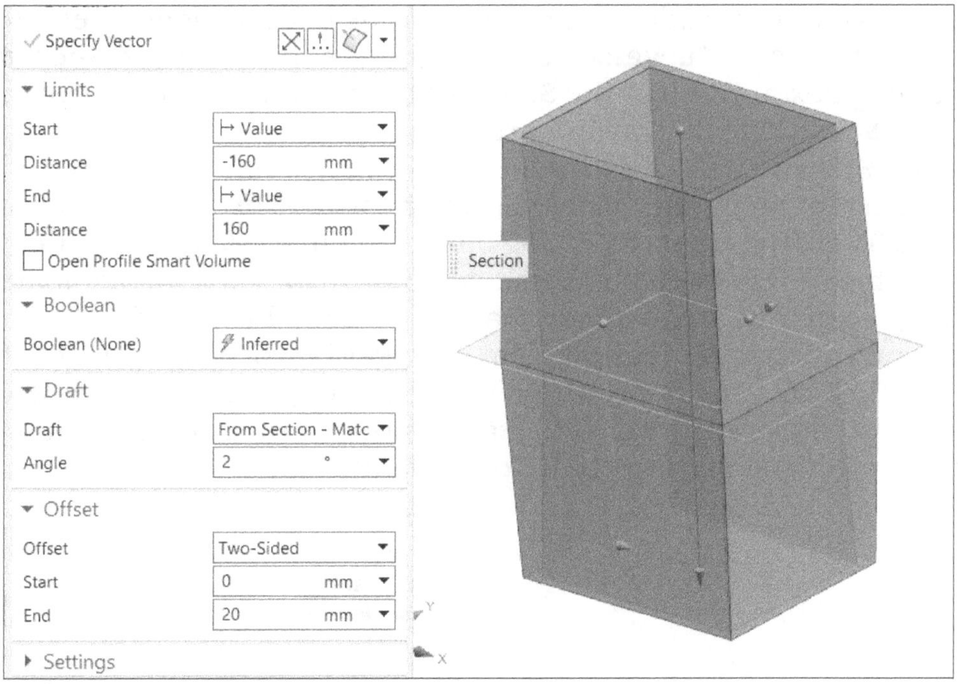

Figure-18. Specifying two sided offset extrude feature

- Select the **Symmetric** option from the **Offset** drop-down and specify the thickness for both sides of section.

Creating Extruded Surface

- Make sure **None** is selected in the **Offset** drop-down and select the **Sheet** option from the **Body Type** drop-down of **Settings** rollout if you want to create extruded surface.
- Specify desired value in the **Tolerance** edit box to define the maximum deviation allowed in model from theoretical model generated by specified parameters.
- Make sure the **Preview** check box is selected at the bottom in the dialog box so that you can check the preview of extrude feature.
- Click on the **Show Result** button from the bottom of the dialog box to check final result of the extrude feature. Click on the **OK** button from the dialog box to create the feature.

Reusing Sketch of Extrude Feature

While creating an extrude feature, you have created sketch within Extrude operation and you have run into a problem where different sections of a same sketch are needed to be extruded at different depths or locations. In such cases, you can follow the procedure given next.

- Click on the **Extrude** tool from the **Home** tab in **Ribbon**. The **Extrude** dialog box will be displayed.
- Select the face/plane on which you want to create the extrude feature. The sketching environment will be displayed.
- Create multiple closed sketch sections as needed; refer to Figure-19. After creating sketch, when you click on the **Finish** button from the **Ribbon** to exit sketching mode, the preview of extrude feature will include both the loops; refer to Figure-20.
- Make sure the **Select Curve** selection button is active in the **Section** rollout of **Extrude** dialog box and select the **Single Curve** option from the **Curve Rule** drop-down in the **Scene Bar** of drawing area.
- Hold the **SHIFT** key and select the curves of sections which you do not want to extrude at current step. The selected sections will be excluded; refer to Figure-21.
- Click on the **OK** button from the dialog box to create the feature. Notice that in **Part Navigator**, there is no sketch created separately for the extrude feature because sketch was created within extrude feature; refer to Figure-22.
- Right-click on the Extrude feature from **Part Navigator** and select the **Make Sketch External** option from the shortcut menu displayed; refer to Figure-23. The sketch will be separated from the extrude feature; refer to Figure-24. You can now use the sections of this sketch to create other features.

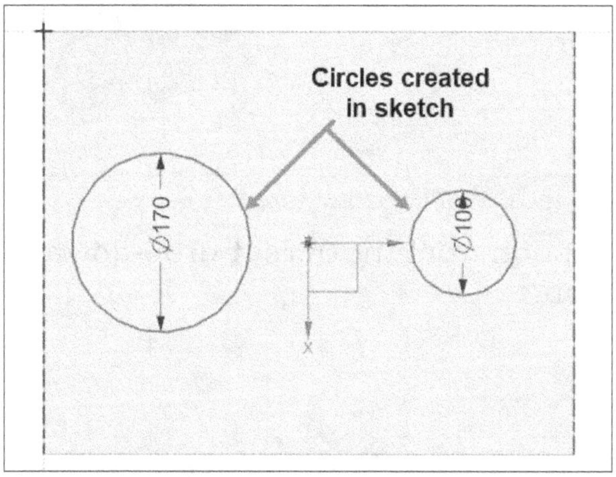

Figure-19. Sketch created

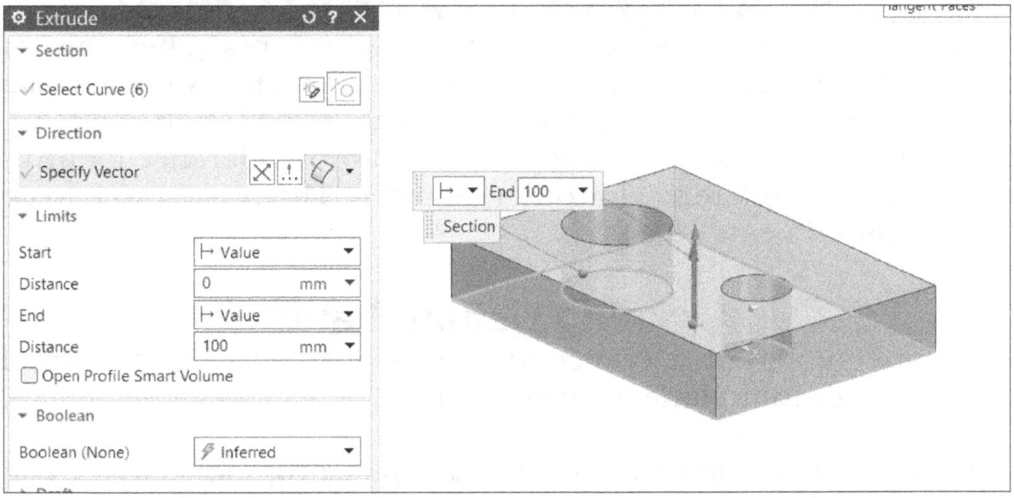

Figure-20. Preview of extrude

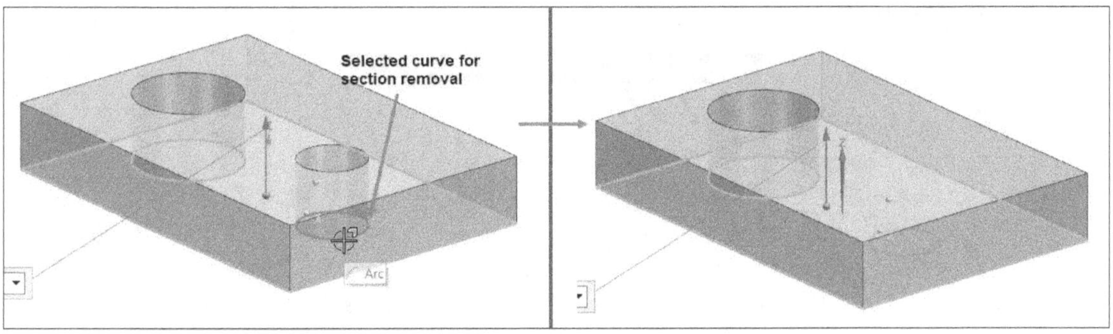

Figure-21. Excluding sections from extrude

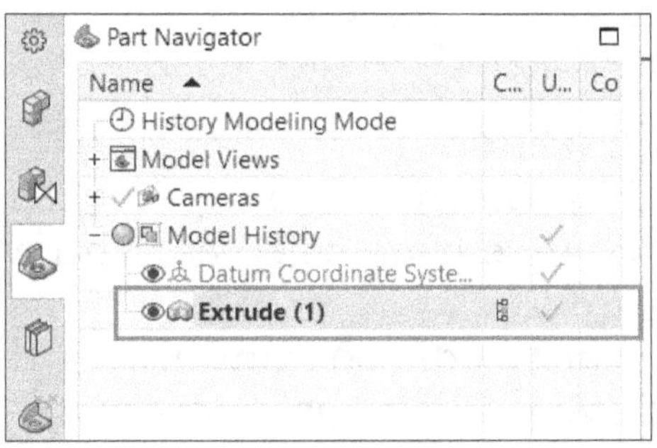

Figure-22. Extrude feature with in-built sketch

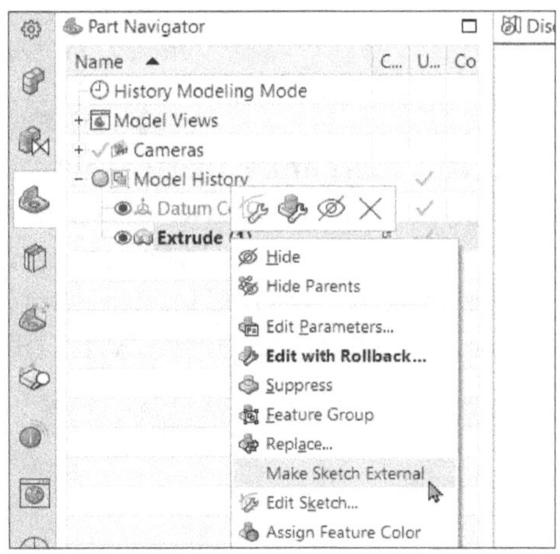

Figure-23. Shortcut menu for extrude

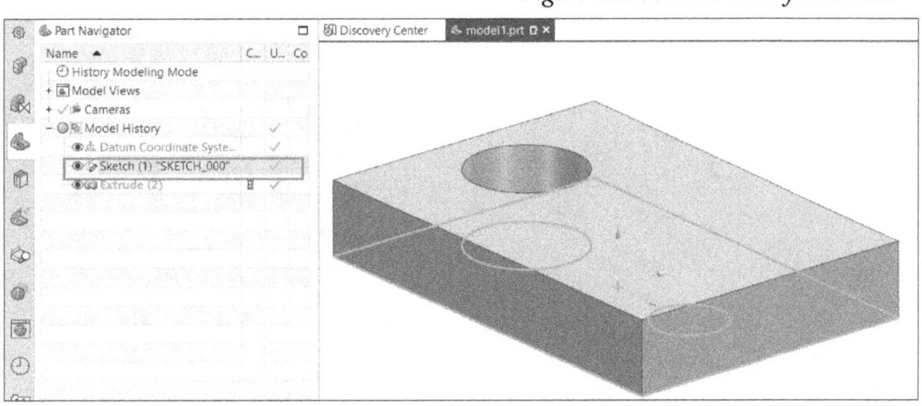

Figure-24. Sketch separated from extrude feature

CREATING DATUM FEATURES

Datum features are the references used to create features. There are mainly four datum features; plane, axis, coordinate system, and point. A datum plane acts as invisible base for other feature. A datum axis acts as direction reference for other features. A datum coordinate system acts as orientation reference for other features. A point acts as location reference for other features. The procedures to create these features are discussed next.

Creating Datum Plane

Datum planes are created in reference to other features like faces and planes. The procedure to create datum plane is given next.

- Click on the **Datum Plane** tool from the **Datum Plane** drop-down in the **Construction** group of the **Home** tab in **Ribbon**. The **Datum Plane** dialog box will be displayed; refer to Figure-25.

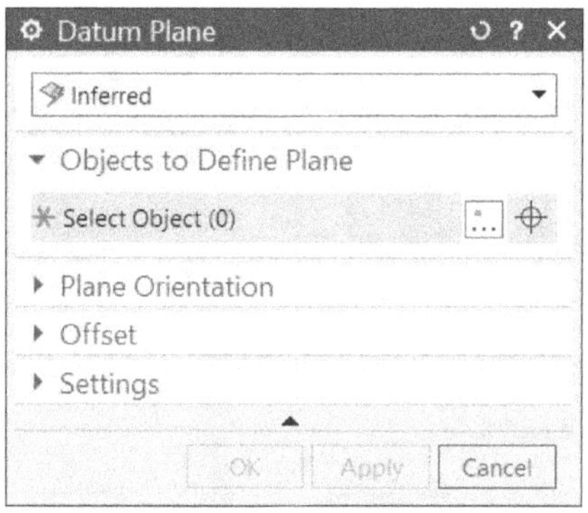

Figure-25. Datum Plane dialog box

Plane at a Distance

- Select the **At Distance** option from the drop-down at the top in the dialog box if you want to create a plane at specified distance from selected. You will be asked to specify distance for offset; refer to Figure-26.
- Specify desired distance value in the **Distance** edit box and select the reference face/plane. Preview of plane will be displayed. Click **Apply** to create the plane.

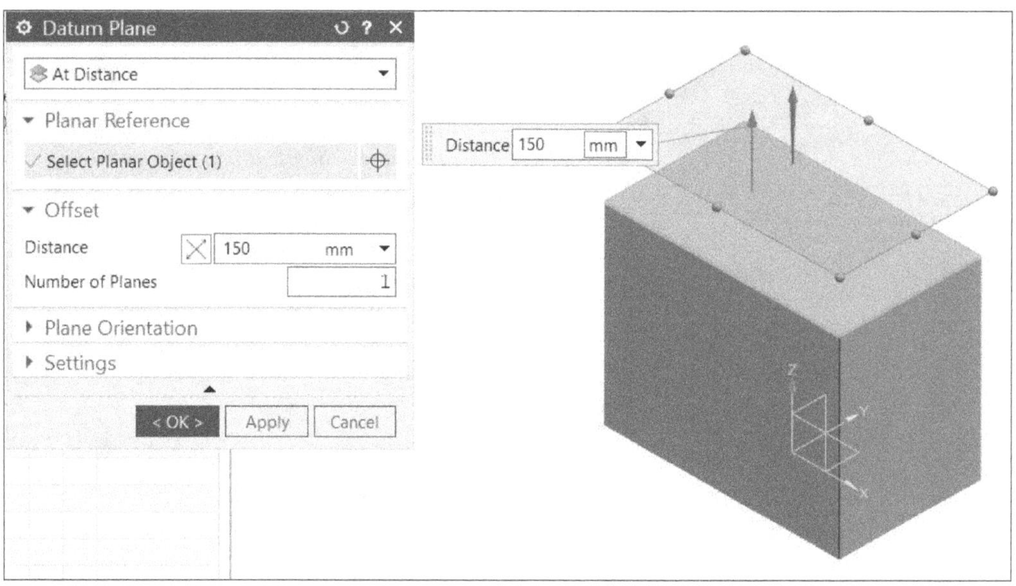

Figure-26. Datum plane at distance

Plane at an Angle

- Select the **At Angle** option from the top drop-down if you want to create a plane at an angle to selected face/plane. You will be asked to select a planar face/plane.
- Select the face at which you want to create the plane. You will be asked to select an axis for rotating plane.
- Select the axis. Preview of plane will be displayed; refer to Figure-27.
- Specify desired value of angle in the **Angle** edit box and click on the **OK** button to create the plane.

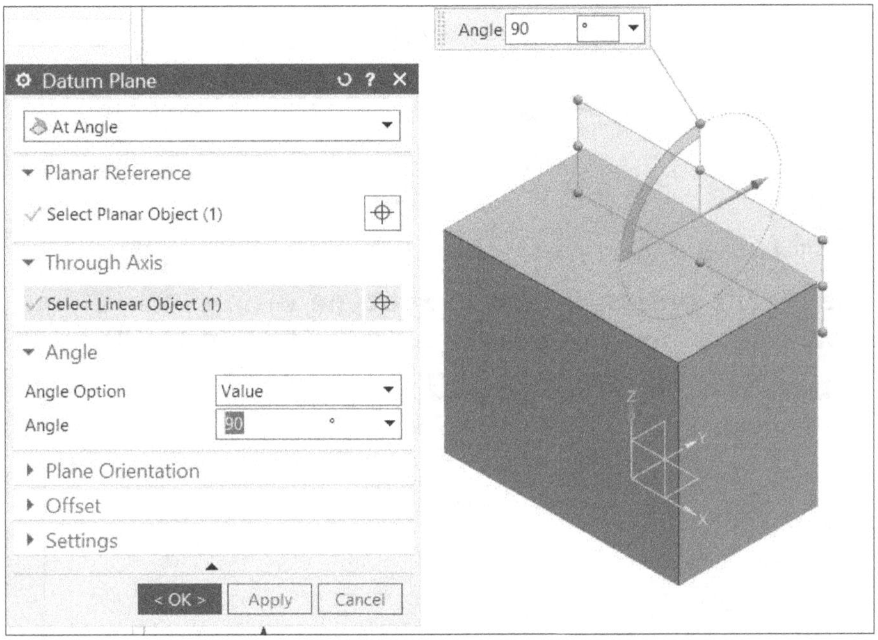

Figure-27. Preview of plane at an angle

Plane at Bisector

- Select the **Bisector** option from the drop-down at the top in the dialog box if you want to create a plane at the middle of two selected planar faces/planes. You will be asked to select two planar faces/planes.
- One by one, select two faces. Preview of bisector plane will be displayed; refer to Figure-28.

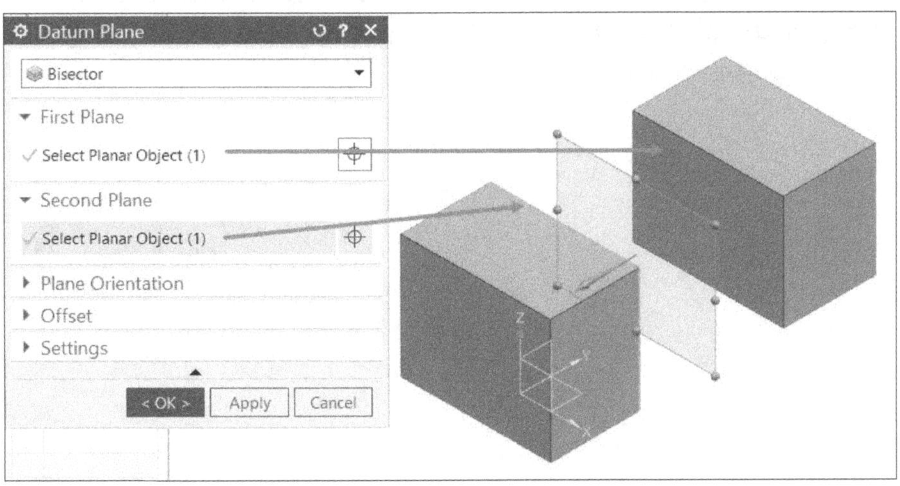

Figure-28. Preview of bisector plane

- Click on the **OK** button from the dialog box to create the plane.

Plane at Curves and Points

- Select the **Curves and Points** option from the drop-down at the top in the dialog box if you want to create a plane perpendicular to the selected curve at specified point.
- Select a point on the curve. Preview of the plane will be displayed; refer to Figure-29.

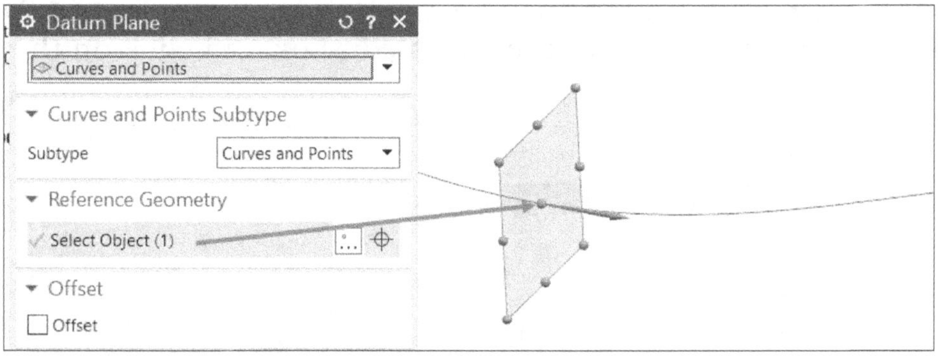

Figure-29. Preview of plane on curve

- Select the **One Point** option from the **Subtype** drop-down if you want to create plane at selected snap point of the curve; refer to Figure-30.

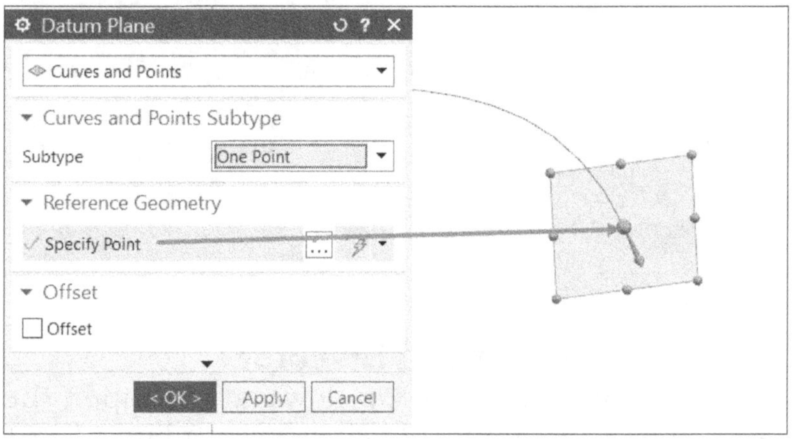

Figure-30. Preview of plane at one point

- Select the **Two Points** option from the **Subtype** drop-down if you want to create a plane passing through two selected points. You will be asked to select two points. Select desired two points. Preview of plane will be displayed at the first selected point and perpendicular to the imaginary line connecting two points; refer to Figure-31.

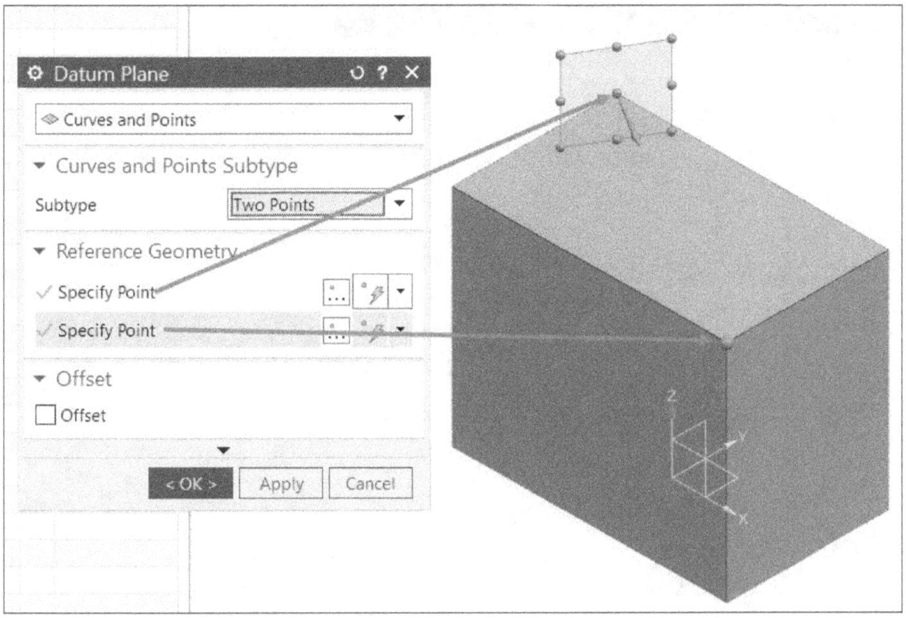

Figure-31. Preview of two point plane

- Select the **Three Points** option from the **Subtype** drop-down if you want to create a plane passing through selected three points. You will be asked to select the points. Select the three points. Preview of the plane will be displayed; refer to Figure-32.

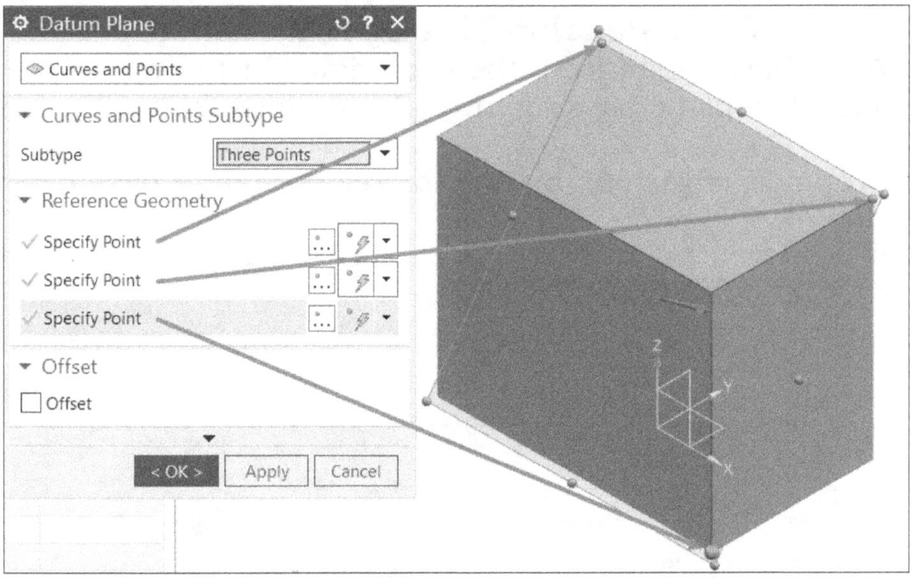

Figure-32. Plane passing through selected three points

- Select the **Point and Curve/Axis** option from the **Subtype** drop-down if you want to create a plane passing through a point and selected curve/axis; refer to Figure-33. Click on the **Alternate Solution** button in the **Plane Orientation** rollout of the dialog box to check different possible plane options if available.

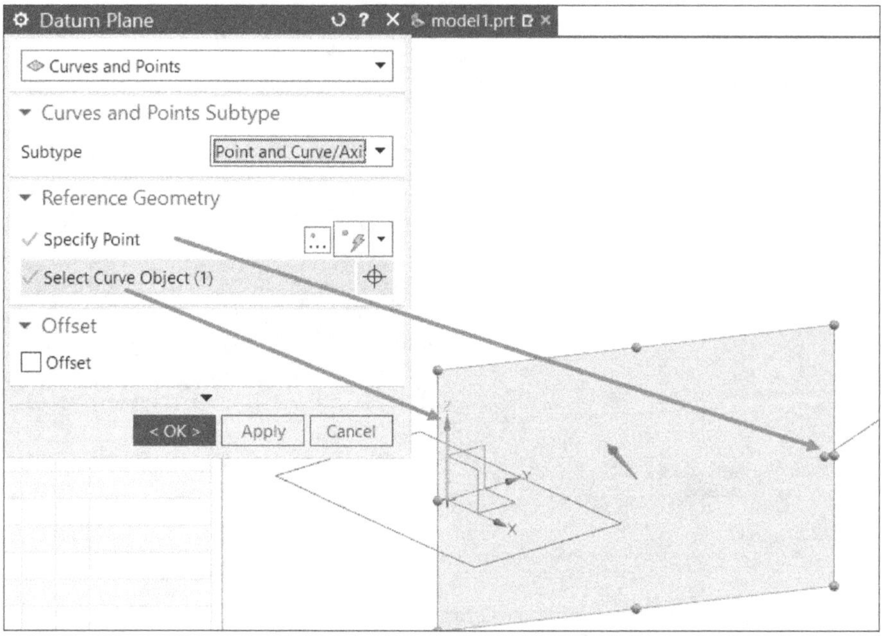

Figure-33. Plane passing through point and axis

- Select the **Point and Plane/Face** option from the **Subtype** drop-down if you want to create a plane passing through selected point and parallel to selected face/plane.

Plane Passing Through Two Lines

- Select the **Two Lines** option from the drop-down at the top in the dialog box if you want to create a plane passing through two lines. You will be asked to select two lines.
- Select the two lines/edges one by one to create a plane passing through them; refer to Figure-34.

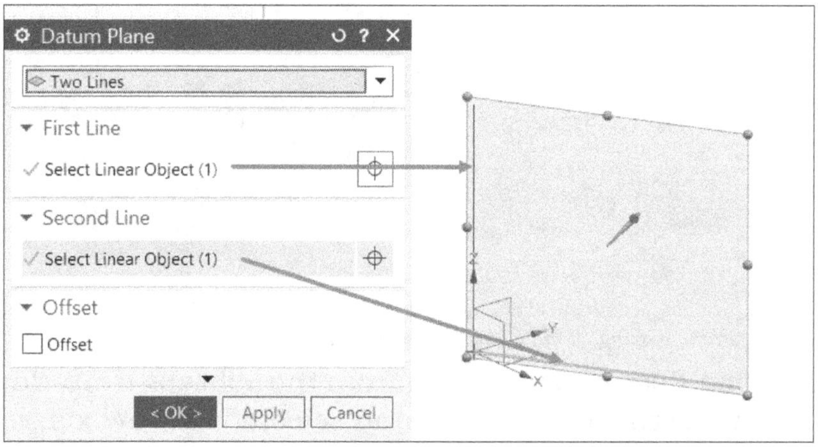

Figure-34. Plane passing through two lines

Creating Tangent Plane

- Select the **Tangent** option from the drop-down at the top in the dialog box to create a plane tangent to selected round face. On selecting the round face, preview of the tangent plane is displayed; refer to Figure-35.

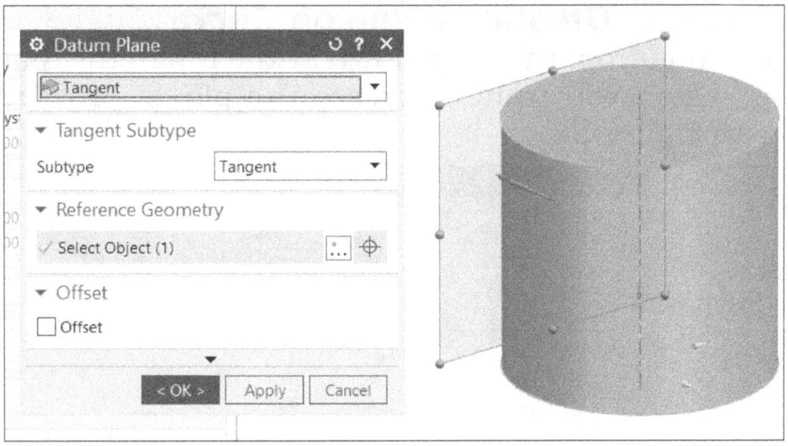

Figure-35. Preview of tangent plane

Creating Plane Through Object

- Select the **Through Object** option from the drop-down if you want to create a plane through axis of circular object or through curved face. On selecting the object, preview of plane passing through object will be displayed; refer to Figure-36.

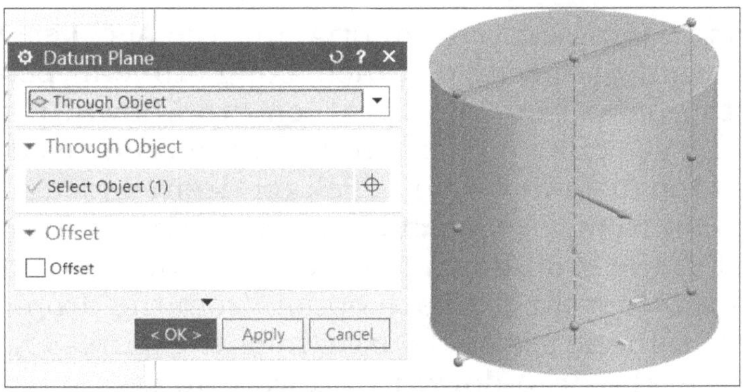

Figure-36. Plane passing through object

Creating Plane at a Point along Selected Direction

- Select the **Point and Direction** option from the drop-down at the top in the dialog box. You will be asked to specify point and direction vector.
- Select the point and direction vector for plane. Preview of plane will be displayed; refer to Figure-37.

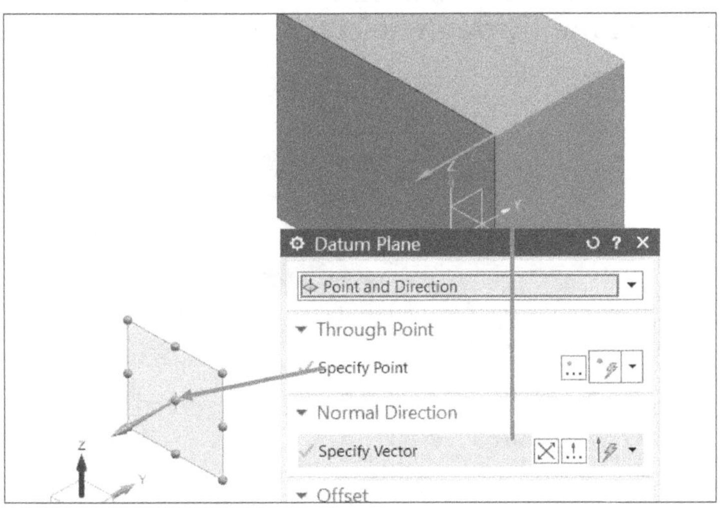

Figure-37. Preview of plane using point and direction vector

Creating Plane on Curve

- Select **On Curve** option from the drop-down at the top in the dialog box and select the curve along which you want to create the plane. Preview of plane will be displayed; refer to Figure-38.

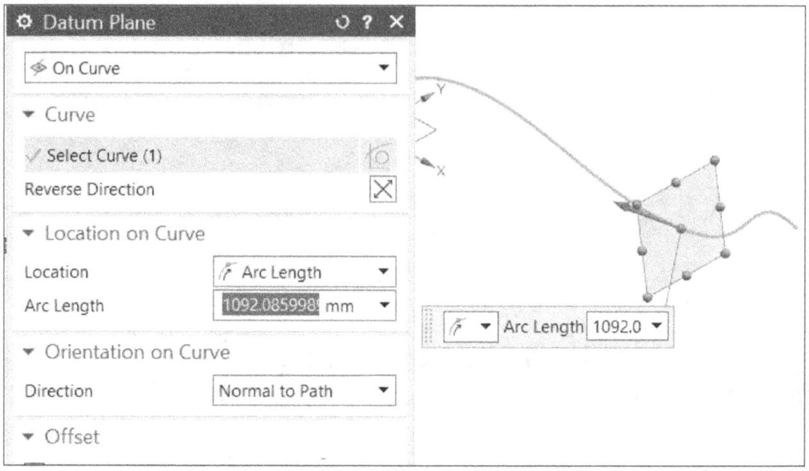

Figure-38. Preview of plane along curve

- Specify the distance along curve from origin in the **Arc Length** edit box to place the plane. If you want to specify distance along curve in percentage then select the **% Arc Length** option from the **Location** drop-down. If you want to specify location of plane by selecting a point on the curve then select the **Through Point** option from **Location** drop-down and click on desired location.
- Select desired option from the **Direction** drop-down. By default, **Normal to Path** option is selected in the drop-down and hence plane is created perpendicular to the curve. Select the **Tangent to Path** option from the drop-down if you want to create plane tangent to the selected curve; refer to Figure-39. Select the **Binormal to Path** option from the drop-down if you want to create a plane perpendicular to both normal plane of curve and tangent plane of curve; refer to Figure-40. Select the **Relative to Object** option from the **Direction** drop-down if you want to select direction reference for plane; refer to Figure-41. Select the **Normal to Vector** option from the drop-down if you want to create plane perpendicular to selected vector; refer to Figure-42. Select the **Parallel to Vector** option from the **Direction** drop-down if you want to create plane parallel to selected vector; refer to Figure-43. Select the **Through Axis** option from the **Direction** drop-down if you want to create plane through selected axis; refer to Figure-44.

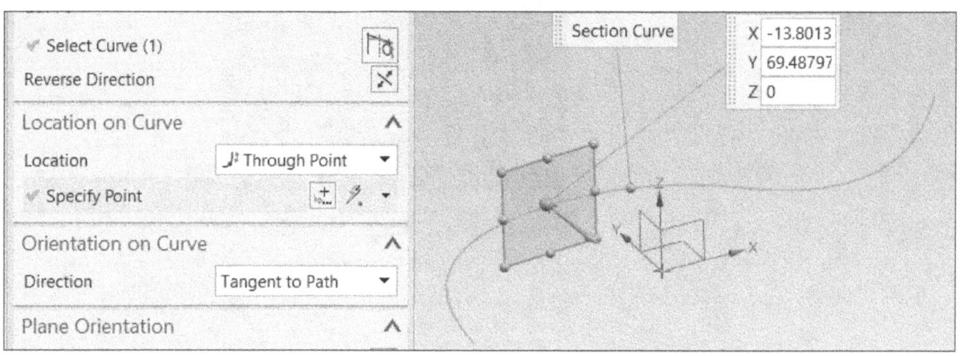

Figure-39. Tangent to path plane

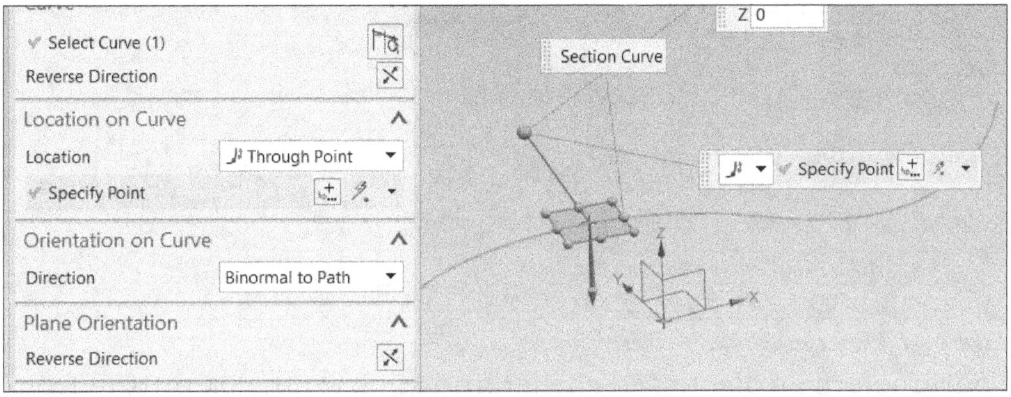

Figure-40. Plane binormal to curve

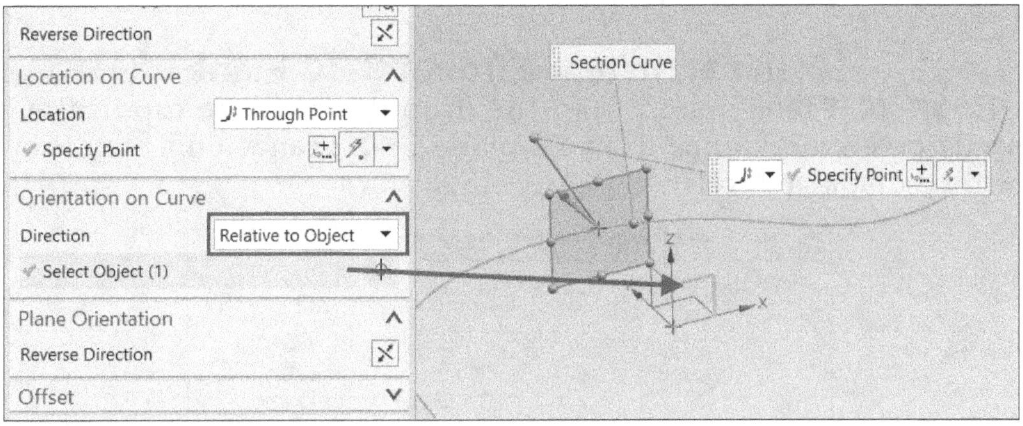

Figure-41. Plane on curve relative to object

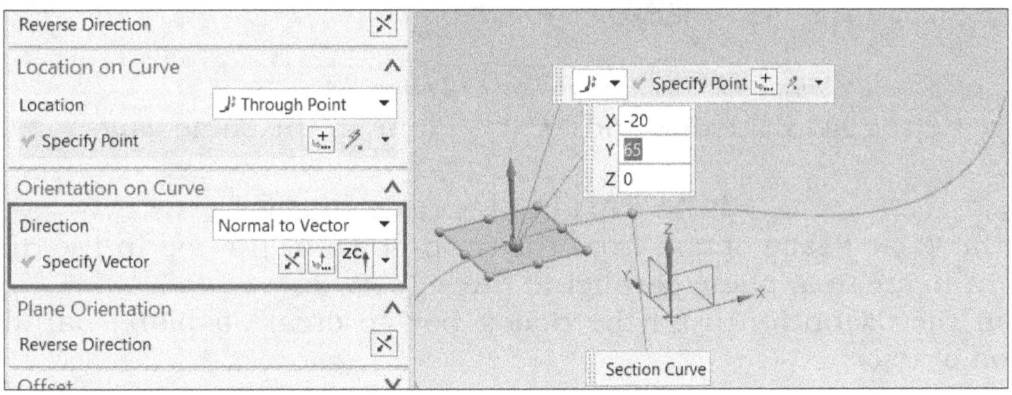

Figure-42. Plane normal to vector on curve

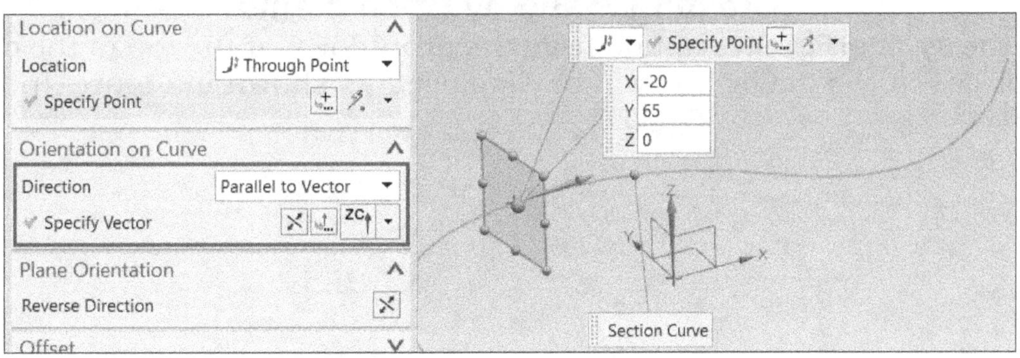

Figure-43. Parellel to vector on curve

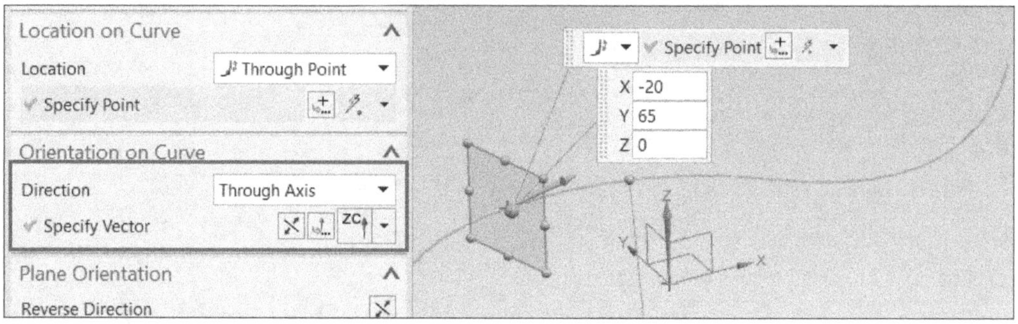

Figure-44. Plane through axis on curve

- Set the parameters as discussed earlier and click on the **OK** button from the dialog box to create the plane.

Plane at Distance from YC-ZC Plane

- Select the **YC-ZC Plane** option from the drop-down at the top in the dialog box and specify desired distance from YZ plane in **Distance** edit box. Preview of the plane will be displayed; refer to Figure-45.

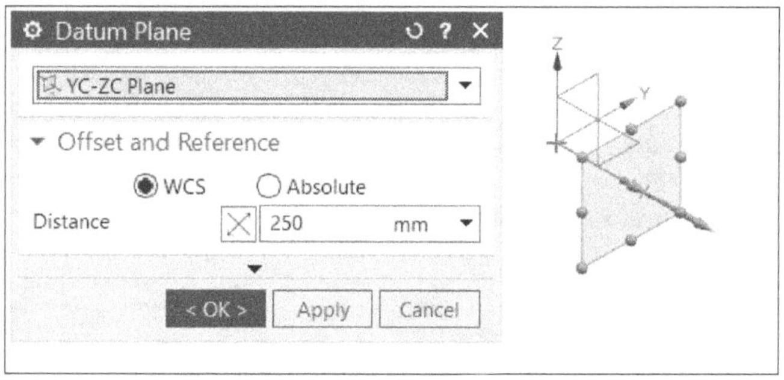

Figure-45. Plane at distance from YZ plane

You can create the XC-ZC Plane and XC-YC Plane in the same ways.

Plane Parallel to View Plane

- Select the **View Plane** option from the drop-down at the top in the dialog box if you want to create a plane parallel to the screen.
- Click on the **OK** button from the dialog box to create a plane parallel to view direction of user.

Creating Plane by Coefficients

- Select the **By Coefficients** option from the drop-down at the top in the dialog box. The options in the dialog box will be displayed as shown in Figure-46.

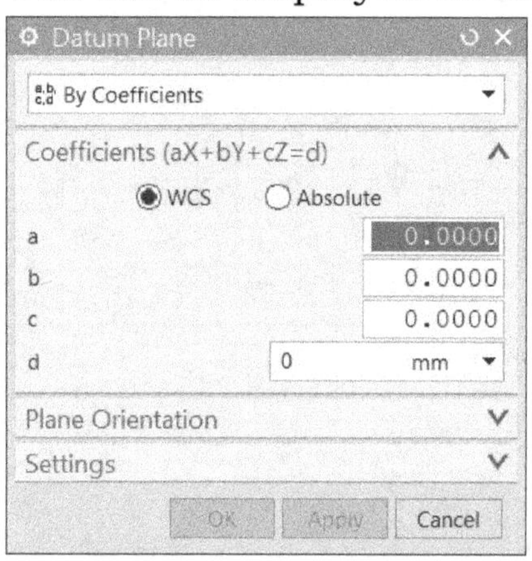

Figure-46. Datum Plane dialog box for By Coefficients option

- Set desired parameters in the **a**, **b**, and **c** edit boxes to define coordinates along different axes. Set desired value in **d** edit box to define offset distance. Preview of plane will be displayed; refer to Figure-47.

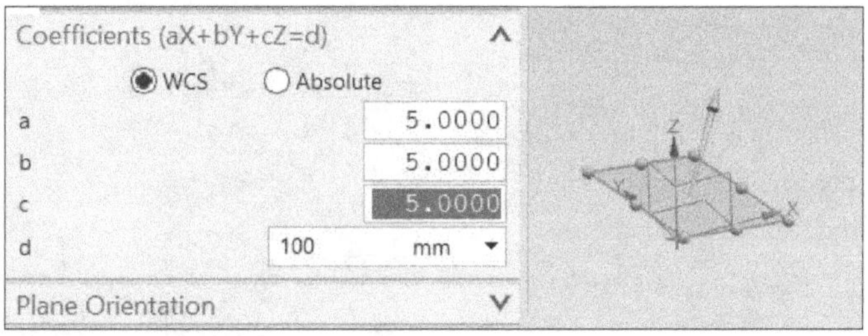

Figure-47. Preview of plane by coefficients

- After setting desired parameters, click on the **OK** button from the dialog box to create the plane.

Creating Datum Axis

Datum axis is used as reference of direction for other features. The **Datum Axis** tool in **Datum Plane** drop-down is used to create axes of different types. The procedure to create datum axis is given next.

- Click on the **Datum Axis** tool from the **Datum Plane** drop-down in the **Construction** panel of **Home** tab in the **Ribbon**. The **Datum Axis** dialog box will be displayed; refer to Figure-48.

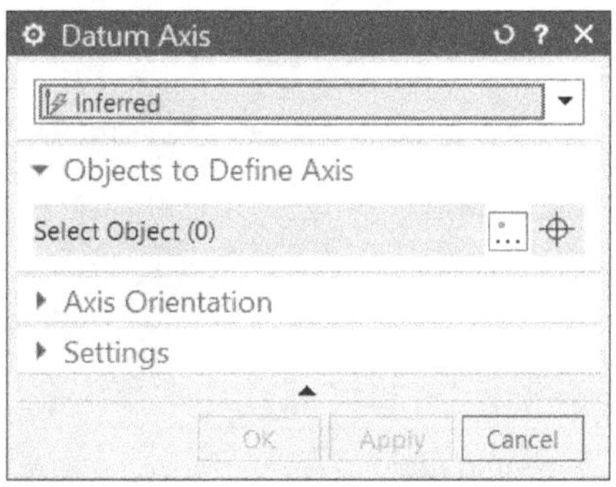

Figure-48. Datum Axis dialog box

Creating Axis at Intersection of Two Faces/Planes

- Select the **Intersection** option from the drop-down at the top in the dialog box. You will be asked to select two faces/planes.
- Select the two intersecting faces/planes. Preview of axis will be displayed; refer to Figure-49.

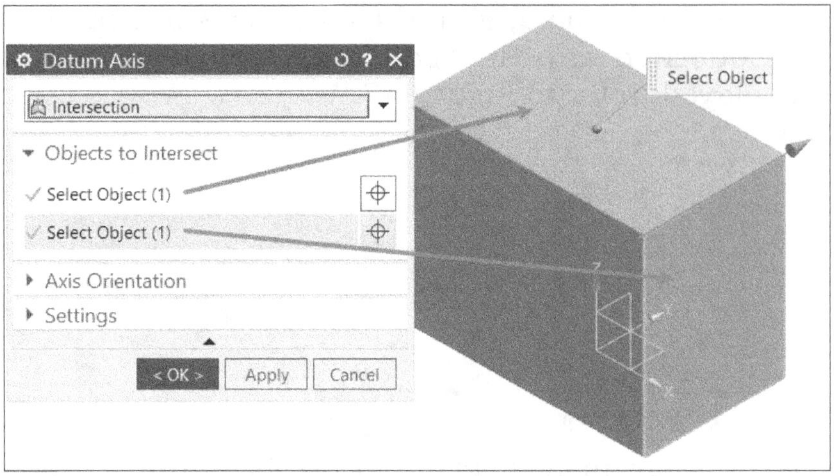

Figure-49. Preview of intersecting axis

- Click on the **Reverse** button in the **Axis Orientation** rollout to reverse the direction of axis. Click on the **OK** button to create the axis.

Creating Axis at an Edge or Axis

- Select the **Curve/Face Axis** option from the drop-down at the top in the dialog box and select an edge or round face. Preview of axis will be displayed; refer to Figure-50.

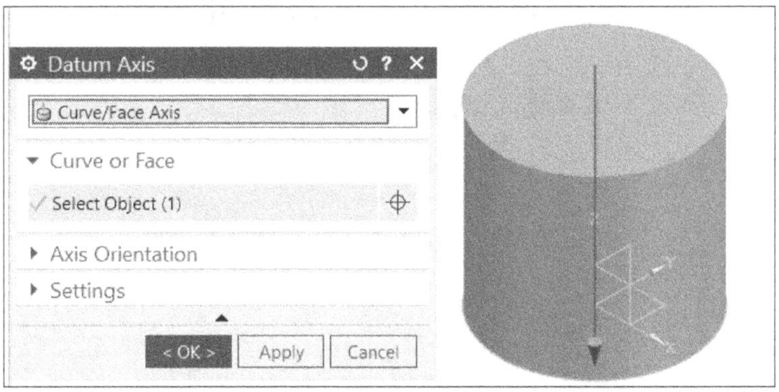

Figure-50. Axis for round face

Creating Axis on Curve

- Select the **On Curve Vector** option from the drop-down at the top in the dialog box. You will be asked to select the curve on which you want to create the axis.
- Select desired curve on which you want to create the axis. Preview of the axis will be displayed; refer to Figure-51.

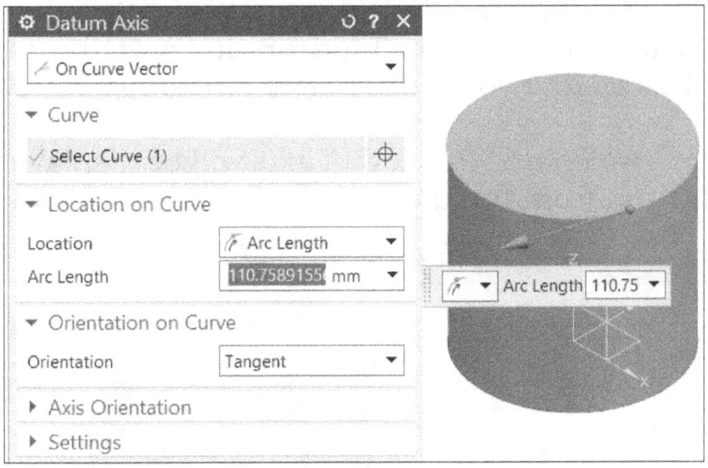

Figure-51. Preview of axis on curve

- Set desired location of axis using the options in the **Location on Curve** rollout of the dialog box.
- Select desired option from the **Orientation** drop-down to define the orientation of axis. By default, the **Tangent** option is selected in the drop-down. Note that the options in this drop-down work in the same way as they do for datum plane.

Creating Axis along X, Y, or Z

- Select the **XC-axis**, **YC-axis**, or **ZC-axis** option from the drop-down at the top in the dialog box if you want to create an axis along X, Y, or Z axis. Preview of the axis will be displayed.

Creating Axis using Point and Direction

- Select the **Point and Direction** option from the drop-down at the top in the **Datum Axis** dialog box if you want to create an axis by specifying a point and direction of axis. You will be asked to select a point where you want the axis to be located.
- Click at desired location or point. You will be asked to specify direction vector.
- Select desired direction reference to define direction of axis. Preview of the axis will be displayed; refer to Figure-52.

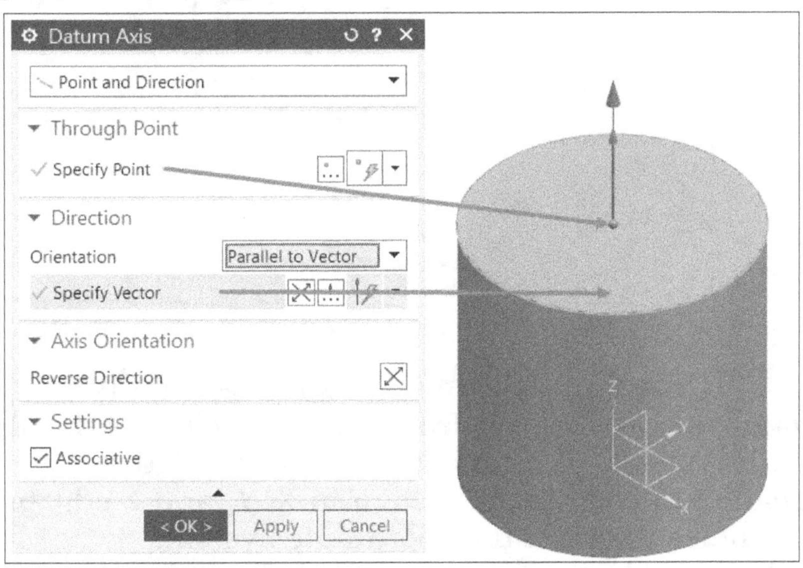

Figure-52. Preview of axis using point and direction

Creating Axis using Two Points

- Select the **Two Points** option from the drop-down at the top in the dialog box. You will be asked to select two points passing through which the axis should be created.
- One by one click on two points. Preview of axis will be displayed; refer to Figure-53.
- Click on the **OK** button from the dialog box to create the axis.

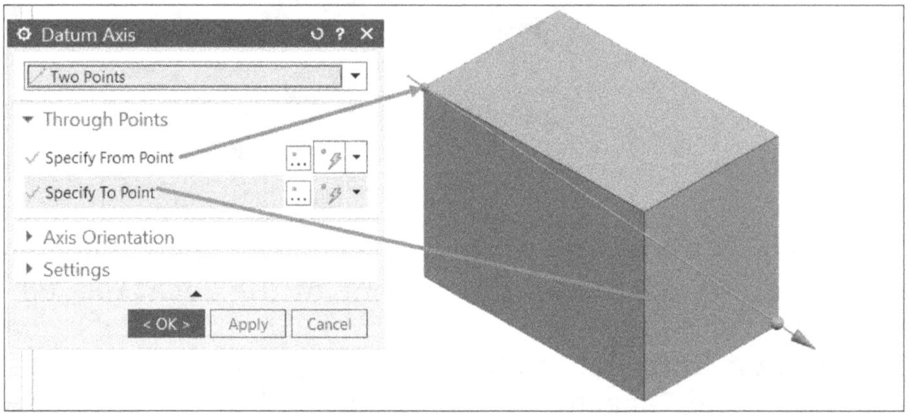

Figure-53. Datum axis passing through points

Creating Datum Coordinate System

The Datum Coordinate System is used as reference for creating sketches and features in NX. A coordinate system acts as origin and defines directions of axes. The procedure to create datum coordinate system is discussed next.

- Click on the **Datum CSYS** tool from the **Datum Plane** drop-down in the **Construction** panel of **Home** tab in the **Ribbon**. The **Datum CSYS** dialog box will be displayed; refer to Figure-54.

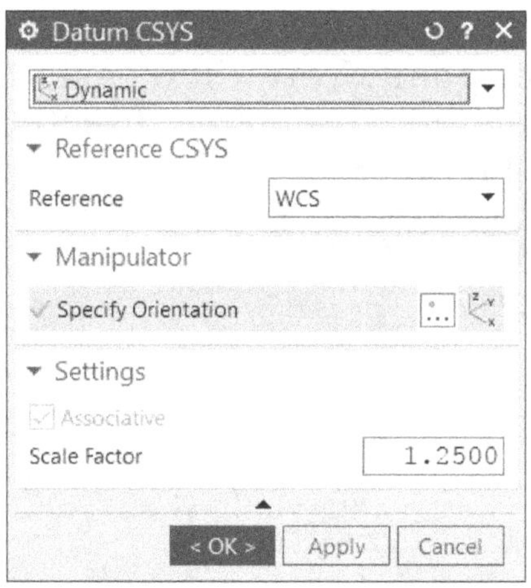

Figure-54. Datum CSYS dialog box

Creating Datum CSYS Dynamically

- Select the **Dynamic** option from the drop-down at the top in the dialog box. Preview of the coordinate system will be displayed; refer to Figure-55.
- Specify the location of coordinate system in **X**, **Y**, and **Z** edit boxes and use the rotation drag handles to orient the coordinate system.
- Specify desired scale value in the **Scale Factor** edit box to increase or decrease the display size of coordinate system.
- Click on the **OK** button from the dialog box to create the coordinate system.

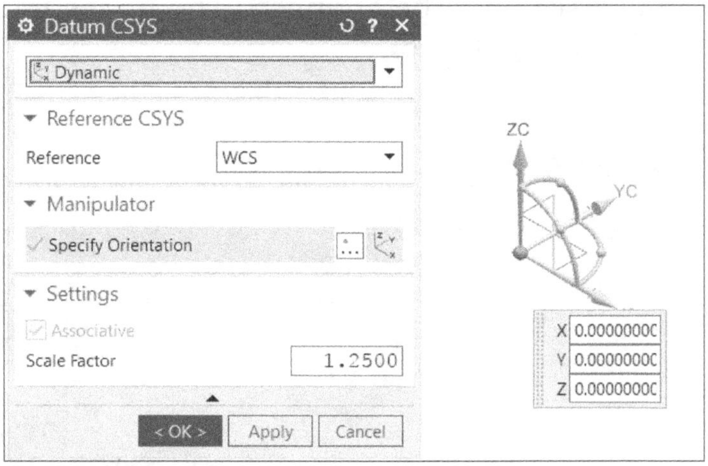

Figure-55. Preview of dynamic coordinate system

You can use the other options to create coordinate system in the same way as discussed for planes and axes.

Adding More tools in Construction panel

There are various other tools available to create datum features in NX which are generally hidden from **Ribbon**. To display these tools, click on the **Group Options** button from the **Construction** group in **Home** tab of **Ribbon** and select check boxes for the tools you want to add from the **Datum Drop-Down** cascading menu; refer to Figure-56.

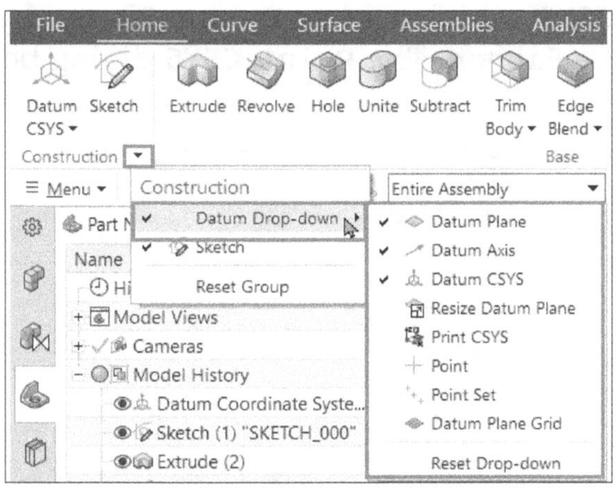

Figure-56. Options to add in Construction group

Resizing Datum Plane

The **Resize Datum Plane** tool is used to change the size of selected datum plane. The procedure to use this tool is given next.

- Click on the **Resize Datum Plane** tool from the **Datum Plane** drop-down in the **Construction** group in **Home** tab of **Ribbon**. The **Resize Datum Plane** dialog box will be displayed; refer to Figure-57.

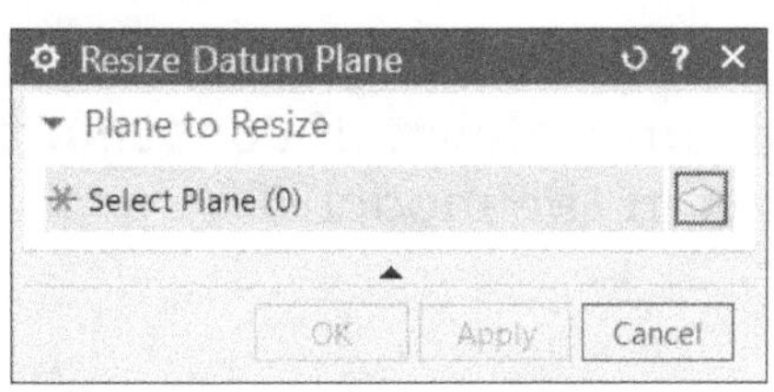

Figure-57. Resize Datum Plane dialog box

- Select the plane whose size is to be changed. The nodes to modify size of plane will be displayed; refer to Figure-58.

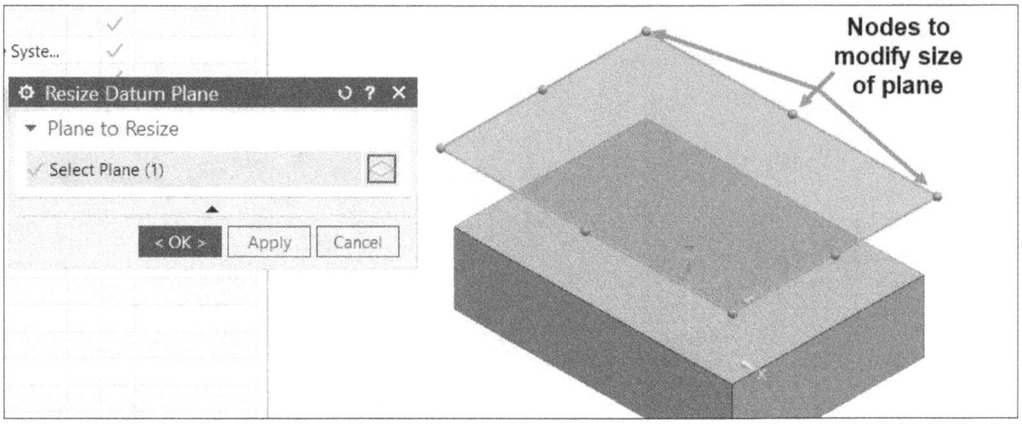

Figure-58. Nodes to modify size of plane

- Drag the nodes to modify size of plane and click on the **OK** button to apply changes.

Creating Print Coordinate System

The **Print CSYS** tool in **Datum Plane** drop-down is used to define orientation of model for 3D printing or performing additive manufacturing. Note that you must have separate license of Additive Manufacturing for using this tool. The procedure to use this tool is given next.

- Click on the **Print CSYS** tool from the **Datum Plane** drop-down in the **Feature** panel of **Home** tab in the **Ribbon**. The **Print CSYS** dialog box will be displayed; refer to Figure-59.

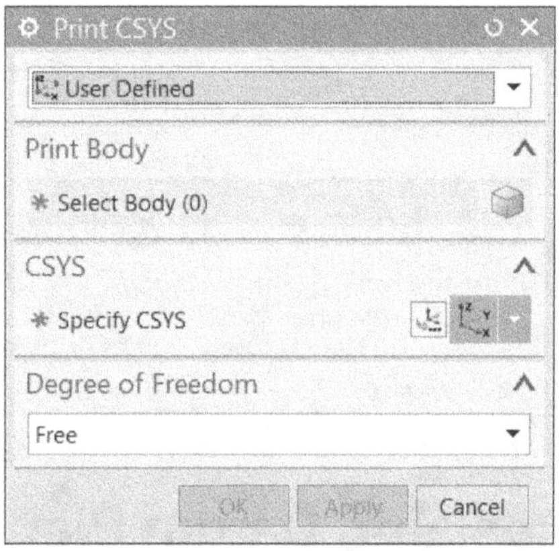

Figure-59. Print CSYS dialog box

- Select the model to be 3D printed.
- Click on the **Specify CSYS** selection button in the **CSYS** rollout and set the orientation of model as desired for 3D printing.
- Click on the **OK** button to create the coordinate system.

Creating Point

The **Point** tool in **Datum Plane** drop-down of **Construction** group in the **Home** tab of **Ribbon** is used to create points in the model. The procedure to create point is given next.

- Click on the **Point** tool in **Datum Plane** drop-down of **Construction** group in the **Home** tab of **Ribbon**. The **Point** dialog box will be displayed; refer to Figure-60. You can also access this tool from the **Base** panel of the **Curve** tab in the **Ribbon**.

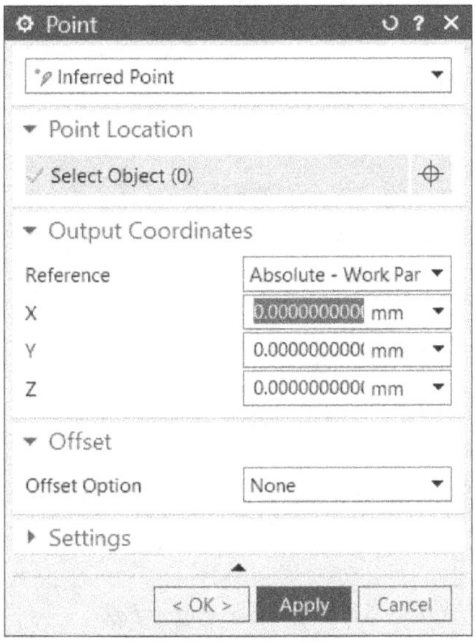

Figure-60. Point dialog box

- By default, the **Inferred Point** option is selected in the drop-down at the top in the dialog box. Hence, points are created automatically based on selection.
- Select desired option from the **Reference** drop-down to define reference about which coordinates of point will be specified.
- Specify the coordinates for the point in edit boxes of the dialog box or you can click at desired snap points to define location of points.
- Click on the **OK** button from the dialog box to create the points.

You can use the other options in the **Point** dialog box in the same way as discussed for datum plane or axis.

Creating Point Set

The **Point Set** tool is used to create multiple points on the curves, splines, face, and so on. The procedure to create point set is given next.

- Click on the **Point Set** tool from the **Datum Plane** drop-down in the **Construction** group of **Home** tab in the **Ribbon**. The **Point Set** dialog box will be displayed; refer to Figure-61.

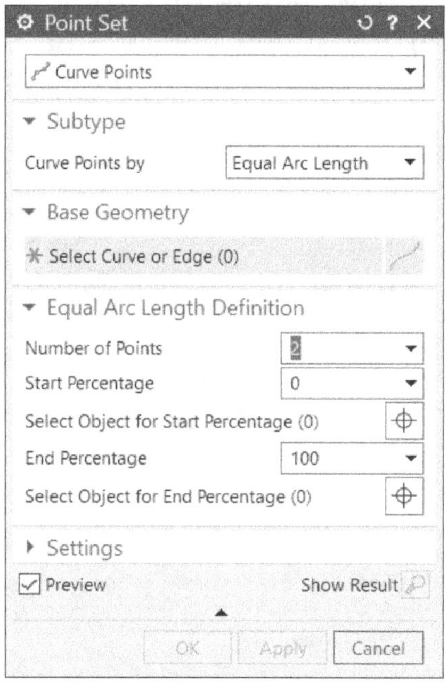

Figure-61. Point Set dialog box

Creating Point Set on Curve

- Select the **Curve Points** option from the drop-down at the top in the dialog box. The options in the dialog box will be displayed as shown in Figure-61.
- Select the edge or curve on which you want to create point set. Preview of points will be displayed; refer to Figure-62.

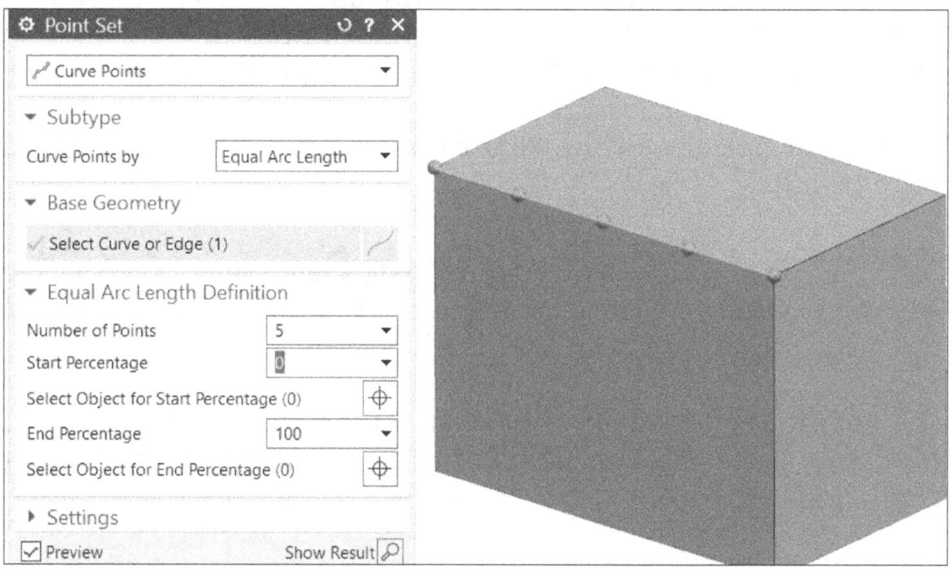

Figure-62. Preview of point set

- Select the **Equal Arc Length** option from the **Curve Points by** drop-down in the **Subtype** rollout if you want to create points at equal distance on the curve. The **Equal Arc Length Definition** rollout will be displayed. Specify the number of points to be created in the point set in **Number of Points** edit box. Set desired starting and end location of points in **Start Percentage** and **End Percentage** edit boxes, respectively.

- Select the **Equal Parameters** option from the **Curve Points by** drop-down to create points at equal distance on curve. The options for **Equal Parameters** are same as for **Equal Arch Length**.
- Select the **Geometric Progression** option from the **Curve Points** by drop-down if you want to increase or decrease distance between curve points by specified multiplication value. Most of the options are same as discussed for **Equal Arc Length**. Click in the **Ratio** edit box and specify distance multiplication factor for geometric progression. Preview of point set will be displayed; refer to Figure-63.

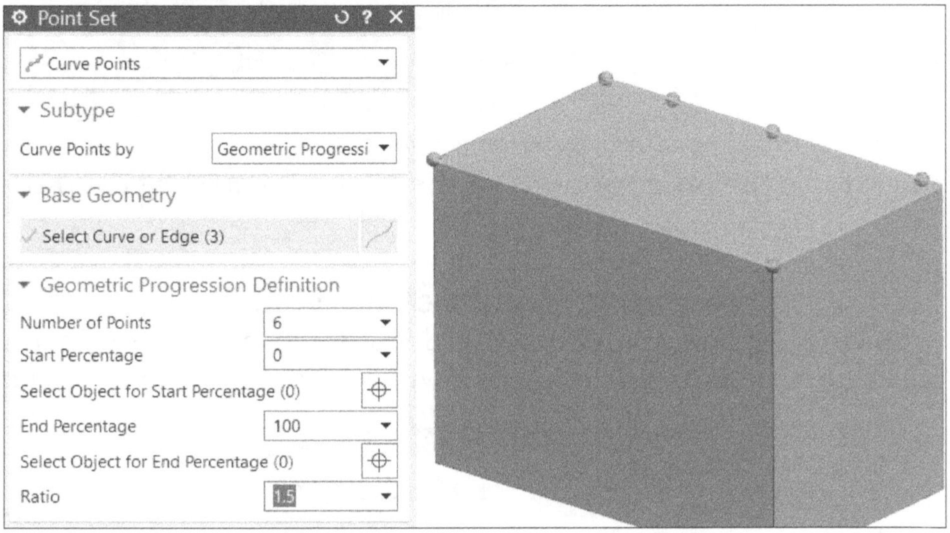

Figure-63. Point set using geometric progression

- Select the **Chordal Tolerance** option from the **Curve Points by** drop-down if you want to create points at specified distance along the selected curves. Specify desired value in **Chordal Tolerance** edit box. Preview of point set will be displayed; refer to Figure-64.

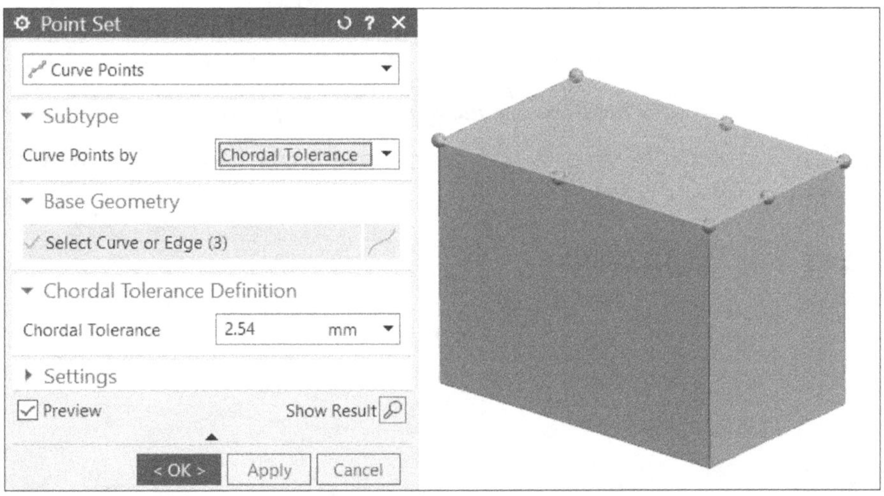

Figure-64. Point set using chordal tolerance option

- Select the **Incremental Arc Length** option from the **Curve Points by** drop-down if you want to create points at specified distance on the curve. Preview of the points will be displayed; refer to Figure-65. Specify desired distance in the **Arc Length** edit box.

Figure-65. Preview of point set using incremental arc length

Similarly, you can use the other options of the **Curve Points by** drop-down to create points.

Creating Point Set on Spline

- Select the **Spline Points** tool from the drop-down at the top in the **Point Set** dialog box. The options in the dialog box will be displayed as shown in Figure-66.

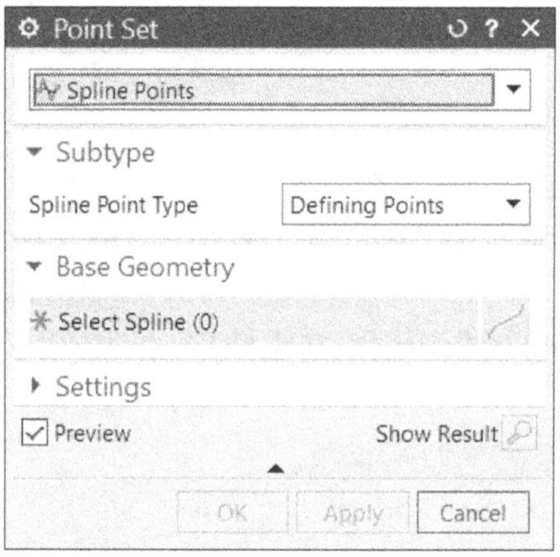

Figure-66. Point Set dialog box for spline points

- Select the spline on which you want to create point set. Preview of point set will be displayed; refer to Figure-67.

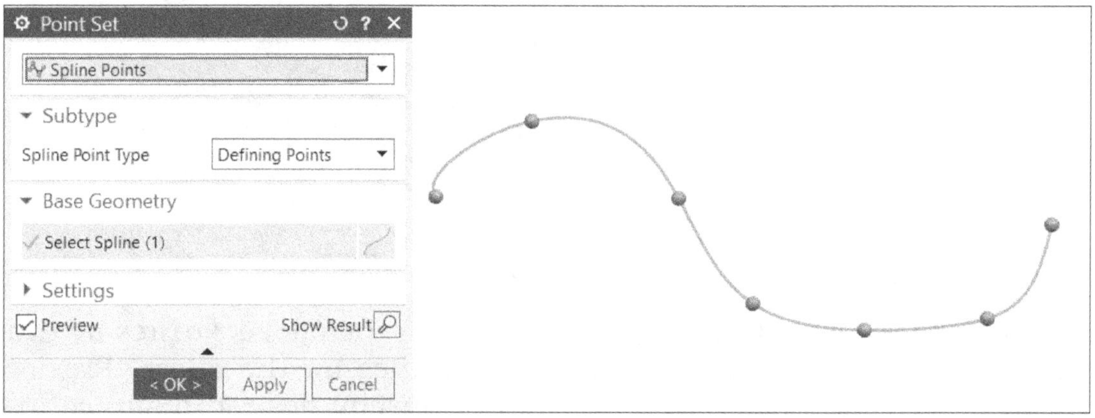

Figure-67. Preview of spline point set

- Select desired option from the **Spline Point Type** drop-down to define what type of spline points are to be created. Select the **Defining Points** option from the drop-down if you want to create points on definition points of spline. Select the **Knot Points** option from the drop-down to create points on knot locations of splines. Select the **Poles** option from the drop-down if you want to create points on the pole locations of spline.
- Click on the **OK** button from the dialog box to create the point.

Creating Face Points

- Select the **Face Points** option from the drop-down at the top in the **Point Set** dialog box. The options in the dialog box will be displayed as shown in Figure-68.

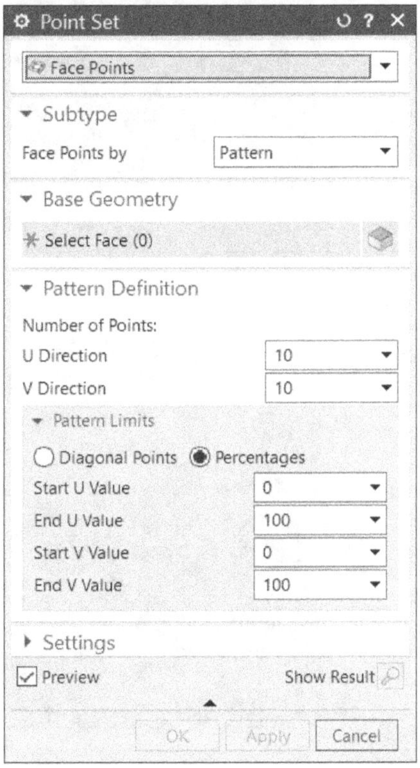

Figure-68. Point Set dialog box for face points

- Select the face on which you want to create point set. Since the **Pattern** option is selected by default in **Face Points by** drop-down, the preview of point set will be displayed with pattern; refer to Figure-69.
- Set desired number of points along u and v directions in the **U Direction** and **V Direction** edit boxes, respectively.
- Set desired limits of pattern in the edit boxes of **Pattern Limits** sub-rollout.
- Select the **Face Percentage** option from the **Face Points by** drop-down if you want to create points by specifying location point in percentage along u and v edge of the face; refer to Figure-70. Click on the **Add New Set** button from the **Face Parameter Percentage Definition** rollout in the dialog box.
- Select the **B-Surface Poles** option from the **Face Points by** drop-down to generation points on B-surface.

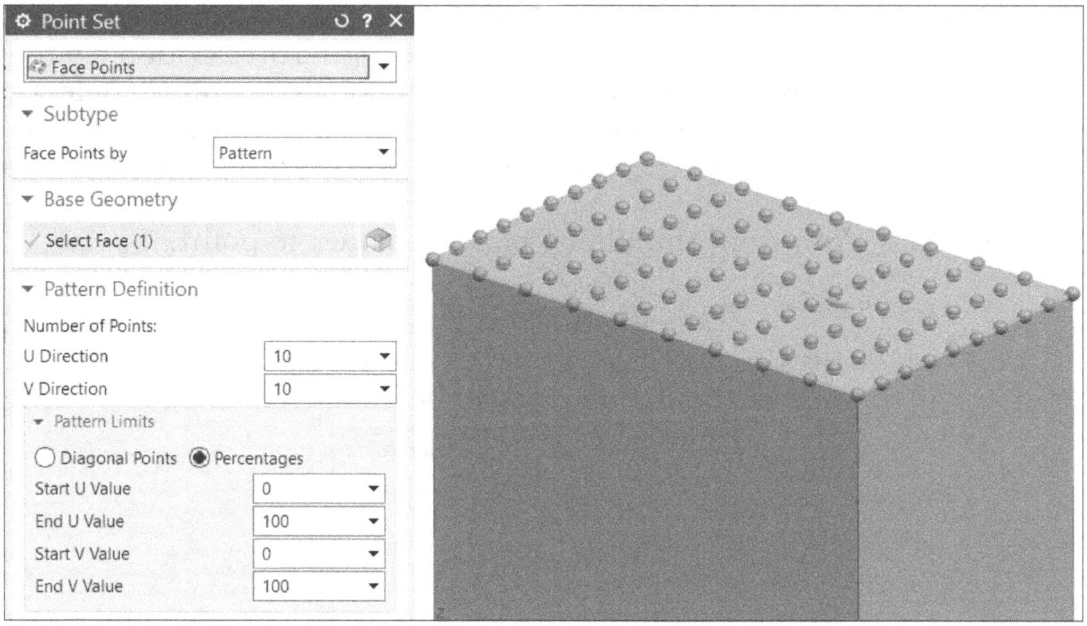

Figure-69. Preview of face point set

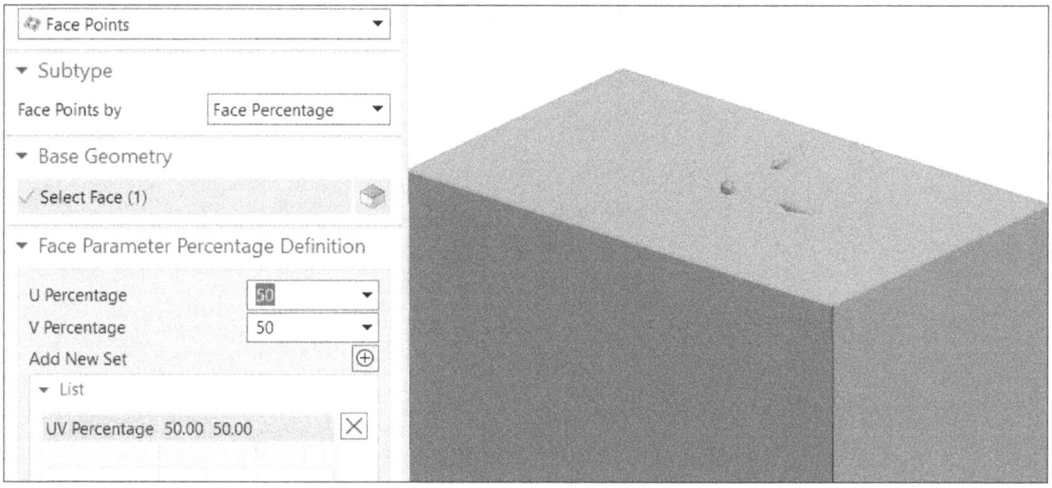

Figure-70. Point by face percentage

- Select the **Intersection Points** option from the **Point Sets** drop-down in the dialog box if you want to create points at intersection of selected faces and selected curves; refer to Figure-71.

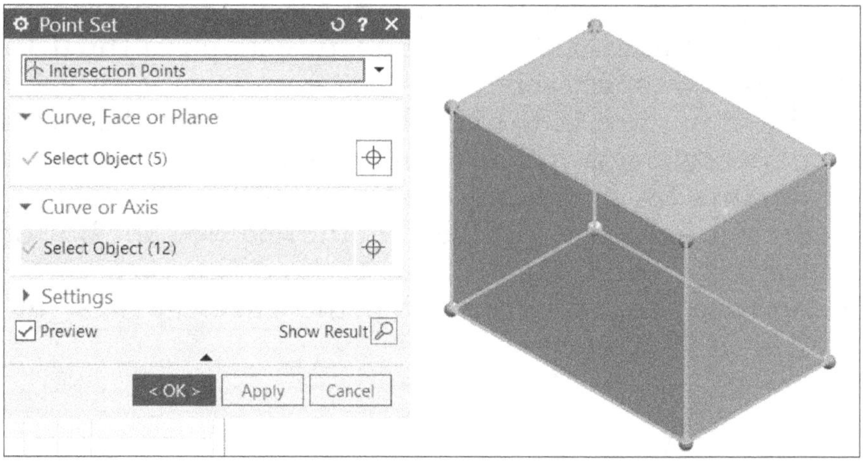

Figure-71. Preview of intersection points

- Click on the **OK** button from the dialog box to create the point set.

Creating Datum Plane Grid

The **Datum Plane Grid** tool is used to grid bounded by plane boundaries. The procedure to use this tool is given next.

- Click on the **Datum Plane Grid** tool from the **Datum Plane** drop-down in the **Construction** group of **Home** tab in the **Ribbon**. The **Datum Plane Grid** dialog box will be displayed; refer to Figure-72.

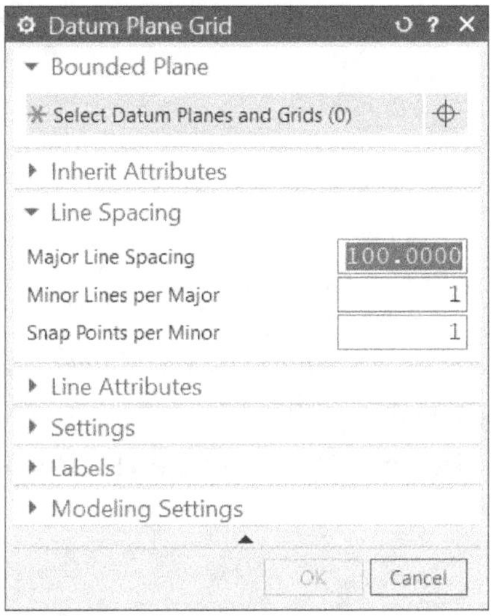

Figure-72. Datum Plane Grid dialog box

- Set the spacing parameters for grid in the edit boxes of **Line Spacing** rollout. Similarly, set the parameters in other rollouts like line style, line width, label style, and so on.
- After setting desired parameters, click on the plane on which you want to create the grid. Preview of grids will be displayed; refer to Figure-73.
- Click on the **OK** button from the dialog box to apply the grid lines.

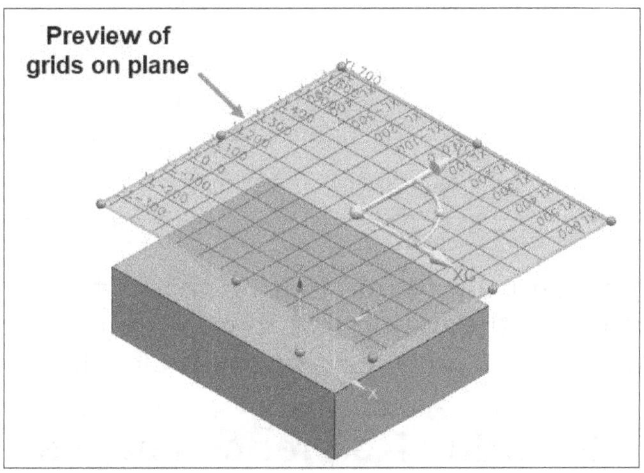

Figure-73. Preview of grids on plane

Creating Reference Point Cloud

The **Reference Point Cloud** tool is used to create points based on point cloud data file. This tool is not available in Student Edition of software. The procedure to use this tool is given next.

- Click on the **Reference Point Cloud** tool from the **Datum Plane** drop-down in the **Feature** panel of **Home** tab in the **Ribbon**. The **Reference Point Cloud** dialog box will be displayed; refer to Figure-74.

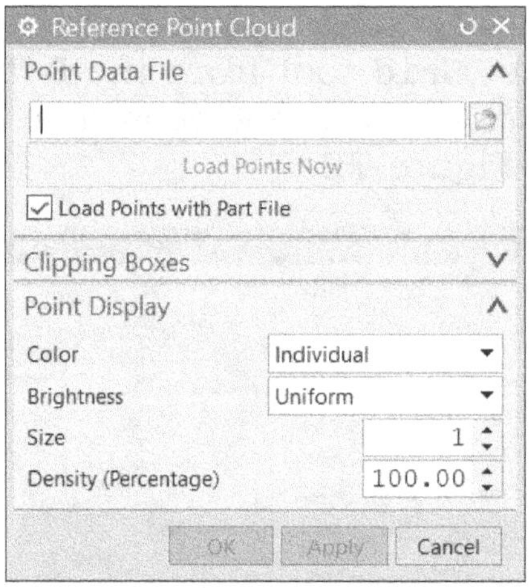

Figure-74. Reference Point Cloud dialog box

- Click on the **Browse** button for point cloud file in the **Point Data File** rollout of the dialog box. The **Define Point Data File** dialog box will be displayed; refer to Figure-75.

Figure-75. Define Point Data File dialog box

- Select desired file for point data and click on the **OK** button.
- Set desired parameters in the dialog box to clip the point cloud and define size.
- Click on the **OK** button to create reference point cloud.

Inserting Reference Images

The **Raster Image** tool is used to insert an image on selected plane. This image acts as reference for creating sketch and model. For example, you can insert top, front, and side view of a car in the form of images on respective planes and then use the images as reference for sketching and 3D operations. The procedure to insert image is given next.

- Click on the **Raster Image** tool from the **Utilities** group in the **Tools** tab of the **Ribbon**. The **Raster Image** dialog box will be displayed; refer to Figure-76.

- Select the plane/face on which you want to place the image. If you want to create image at an offset distance from selected face then specify desired offset distance in the **Distance** input box.
- Click on the **Choose Image File** button from the **Image Definition** rollout of the dialog box to select the image file. The **Raster Image File** dialog box will be displayed; refer to Figure-77.

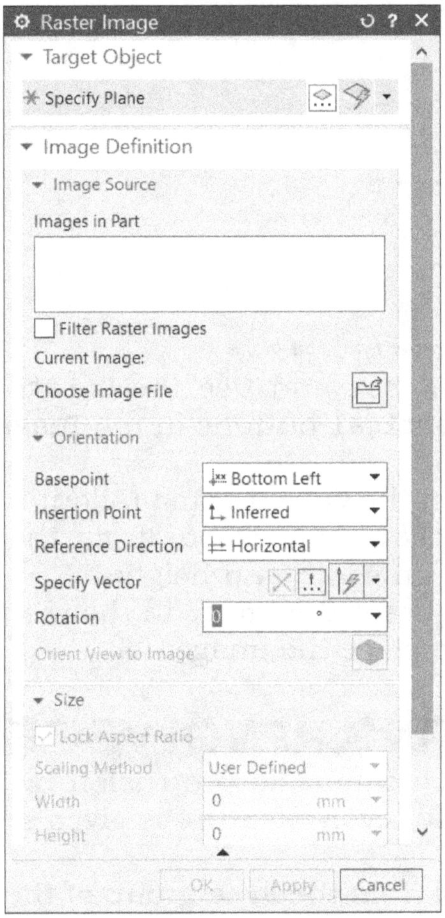

Figure-76. Raster Image dialog box

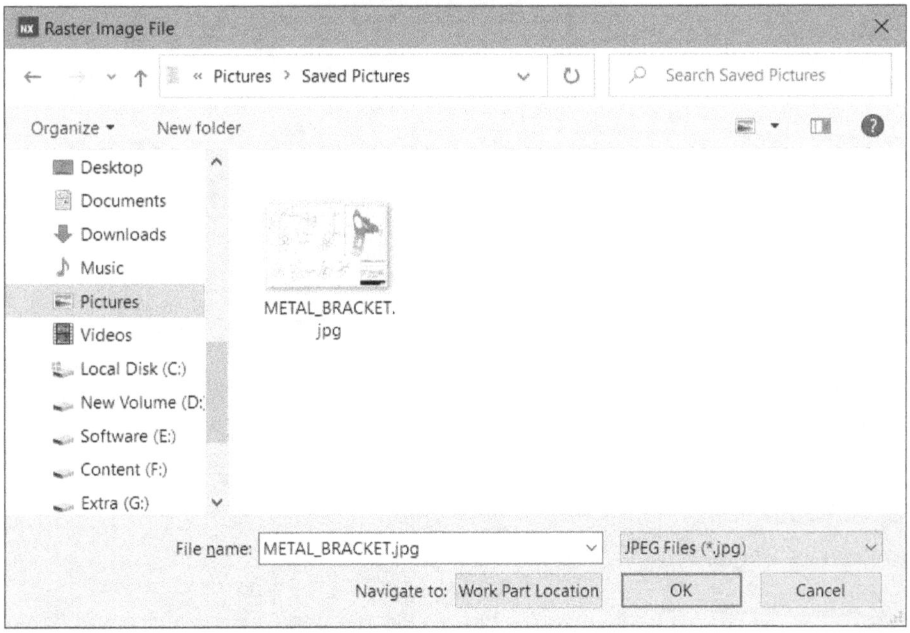

Figure-77. Raster Image File dialog box

- Select the image and click on the **OK** button. Preview of the image will be displayed; refer to Figure-78.

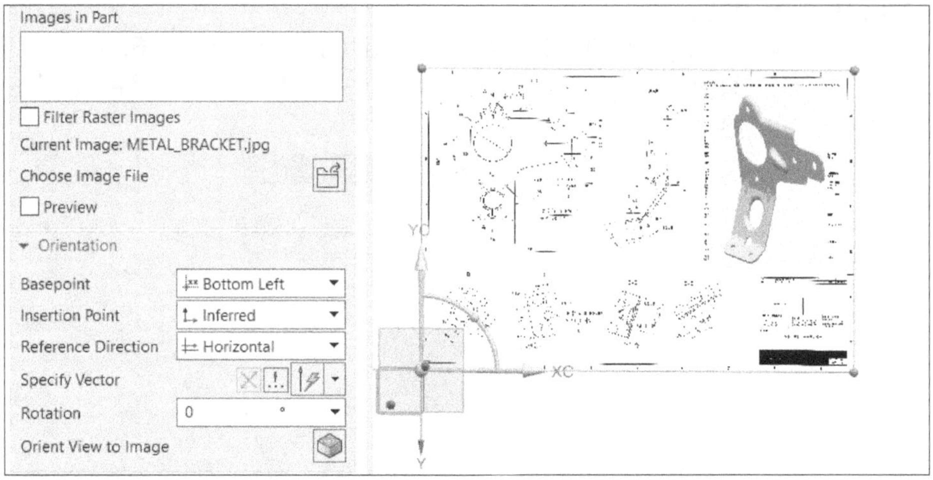

Figure-78. Preview of raster image on plane

- Select the **Preview** check box and use the **Rotate Left**, **Rotate Right**, **Flip Horizontal**, and **Flip Vertical** buttons in the **Image Definition** rollout of dialog box to orient the image.
- Set desired parameters in the **Orientation** rollout to further orient the image.
- Select the **Lock Aspect Ratio** check box from the **Size** rollout if you want to maintain size ratio between width and height.
- Specify the width or height for the image in the respective edit box.
- Click on the **OK** button to place the image.

CREATING REVOLVE FEATURE

The **Revolve** tool is used to create solid protrusion by revolving a sketch about an axis. The procedure to create revolve feature is given next.

- Click on the **Revolve** tool from the **Base** group of the **Home** tab in the **Ribbon**. The **Revolve** dialog box will be displayed; refer to Figure-79.

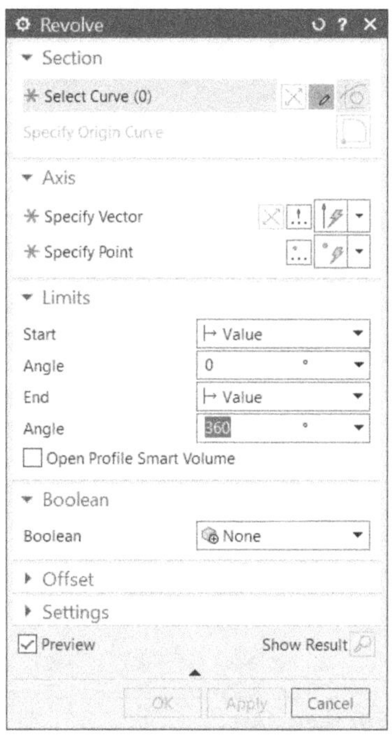

Figure-79. Revolve dialog box

- Select the curve (sketch) that you want to revolve to create protrusion. You will be asked to select axis.
- Select desired axis about which you want to revolve the sketch. Preview of revolve feature will be displayed; refer to Figure-80.

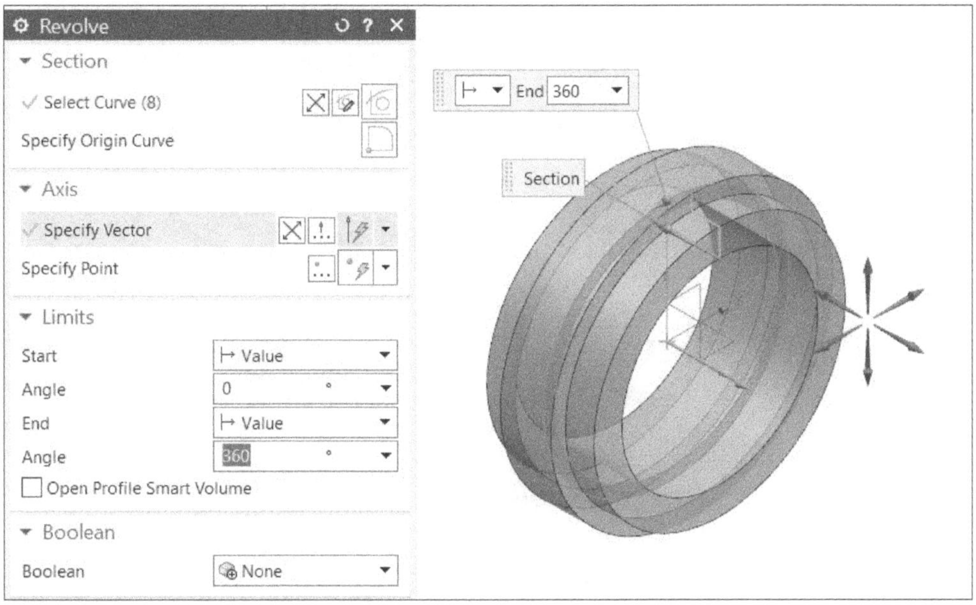

Figure-80. Preview of revolve feature

- Set the start angle and end angle values in respective **Angle** edit boxes of the **Limits** rollout.
- Select the **Until Selected** option from the **End** drop-down if you want to revolve the sketch up to selected face, body, or datum plane.
- Set the other parameters as discussed for extrude feature and click on the **OK** button.

CREATING SWEPT FEATURE

The **Swept** tool in **Base** group of **Surface** tab is used to create solid/surface protrusion by moving selected curves along selected path curve. The procedure to create swept feature is given next.

- Click on the **Swept** tool from the **Base** group of **Surface** tab in the **Ribbon**. The **Swept** dialog box will be displayed; refer to Figure-81.
- Select the curve that you want to be used as section for swept feature.
- If you want to add more curves as sections at different locations then click on the **Add New Set** button from the **Sections** rollout or press Middle Mouse Button (MMB) and select the next section; refer to Figure-82. Note that an arrow is displayed on selecting section. This arrow shows the orientation of section in sweep feature and starting point of this arrow shows origin of section to match with other sections when creating sweep feature. To get a smooth sweep feature, the origin on each section should be in same side otherwise you will get twisted sweep feature. When creating sweep feature, the software uses these points as matching reference on each section to create edges of sweep features. The arrow displayed on sections should also be pointing in same direction otherwise a twisted sweep feature will be created. But if you want to create a twisted feature then you can set the origin and direction of arrow as per the design.

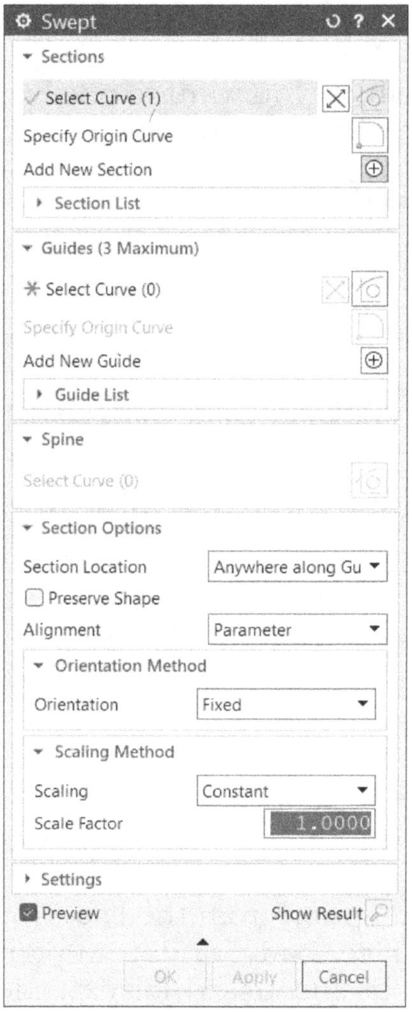

Figure-81. Swept dialog box

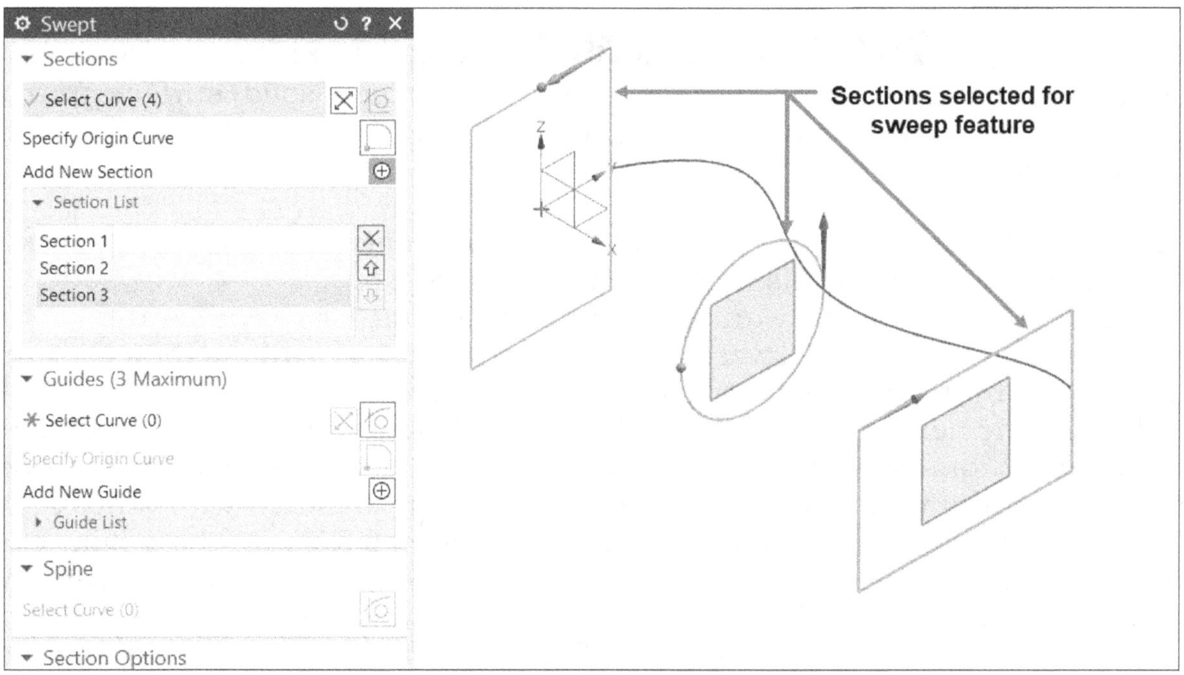

Figure-82. Sections selected for sweep

- To keep the origins on same side, you need to click on same side of each section but if you need to change the location of origin on section at later stage (as in our case) then expand the **Section List** rollout and click on the section whose origin is to be changed. The section will be highlighted in the graphics area. Now, click on the **Specify Origin Curve** selection button from the dialog box and select the curve on which origin should be located; refer to Figure-83. Note that although the origin location is now symmetric on each section but the arrow points in wrong direction (it should be pointing upward not downward!). Double-click on the arrow to flip its direction so that the sections have symmetry in origin direction; refer to Figure-84.

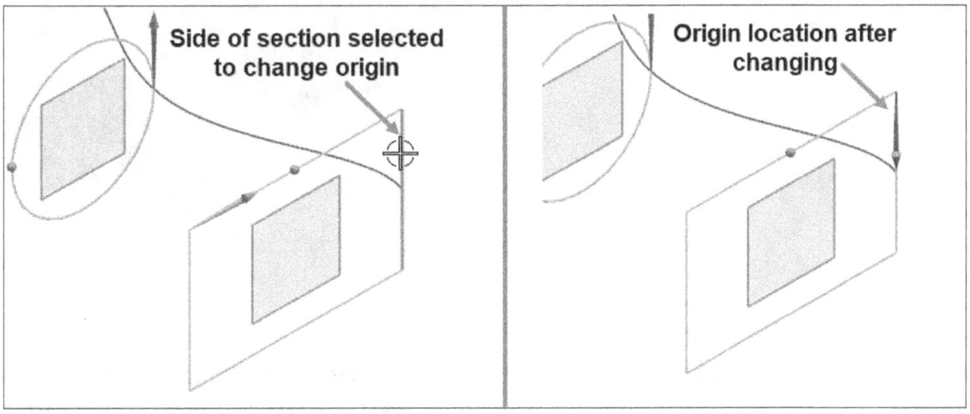

Figure-83. Changing origin location

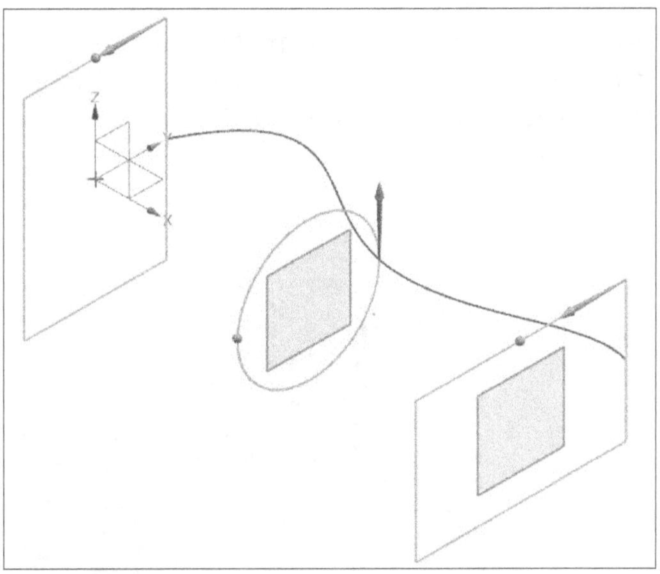

Figure-84. Sections after changing origin direction

- Click on the **Select Curve** selection button from **Guides** rollout to select the guide curve; refer to Figure-85.

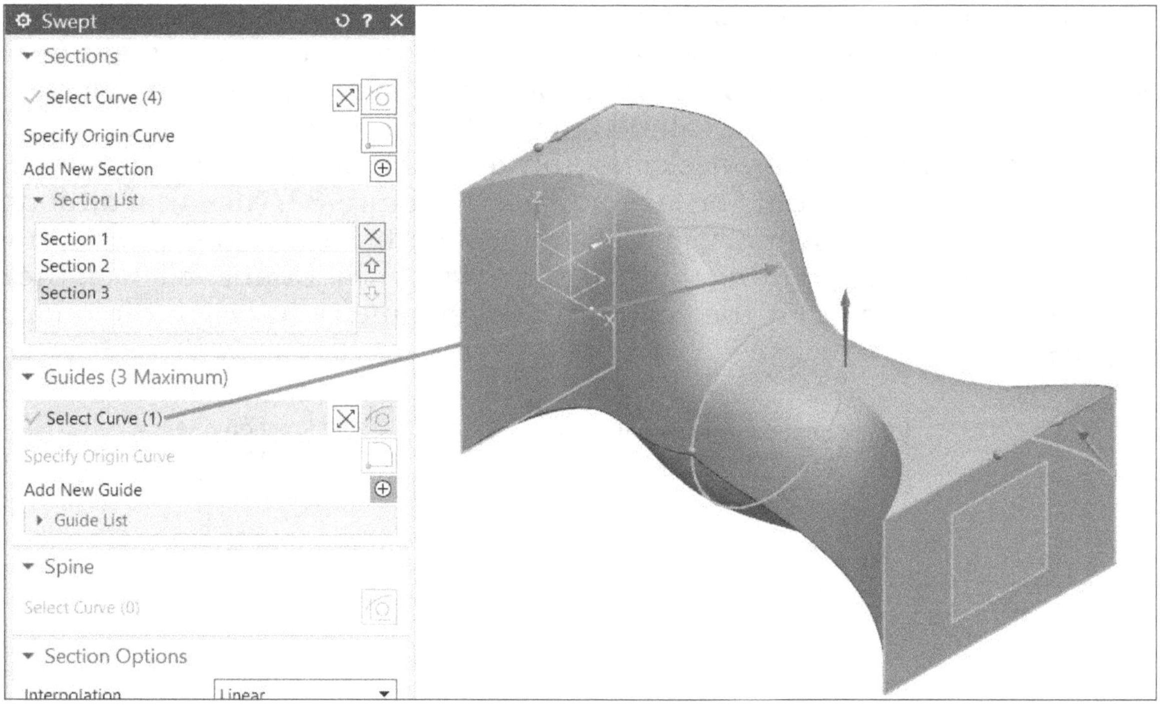

Figure-85. Preview of swept feature

- You can select up to 3 guide curves in the same way as discussed for sections. Note that it is not necessary for guide curves to touch or snap to section curves but they should be near to sections. Also, each guide curve should be created in separate sketch.
- After selecting section sketch and guide curves, the **Select Curve** selection button in the **Spine** rollout becomes active. Select desired curve from drawing area to be used as center of the sweep feature; refer to Figure-86.

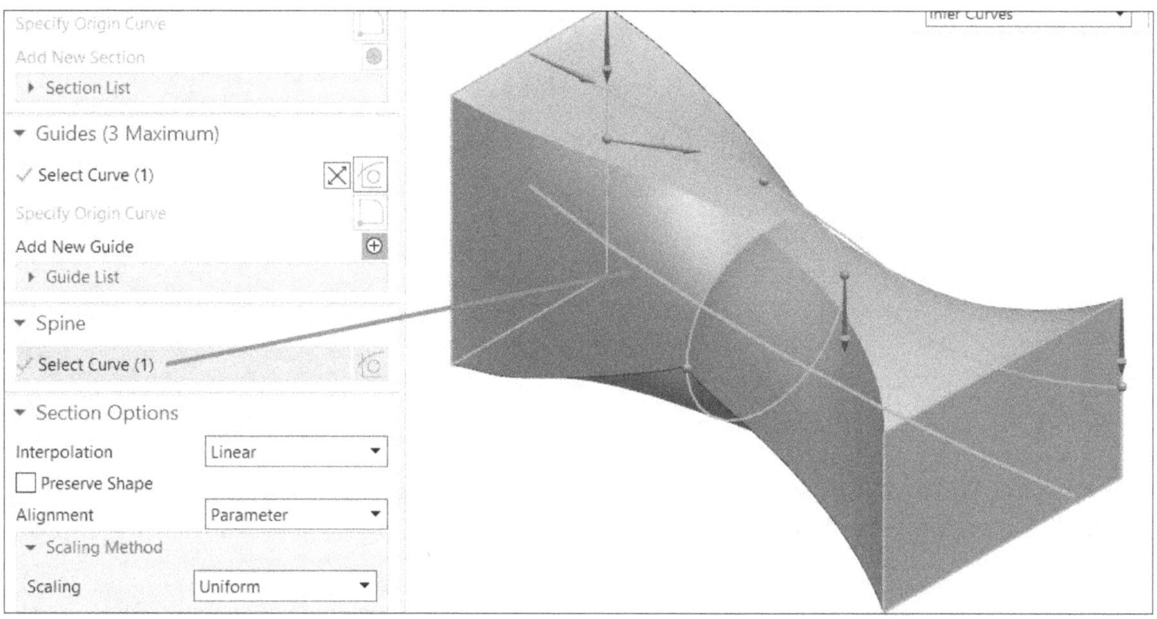

Figure-86. Spine curve selected

- Select desired option from the **Interpolation** drop-down to define how sections will blend with each other. Select the **Linear** option to make linear transition between selected sections making a smooth surface of feature. Select the **Cubic** option from the drop-down to make cubical transition between sections. On selecting this option, a tangent flow will be generated at sections giving more weightage to section orientation. Select the **Blend** option from the drop-down to G1 continuous surface transition between sections in the swept feature. Refer to Figure-87.

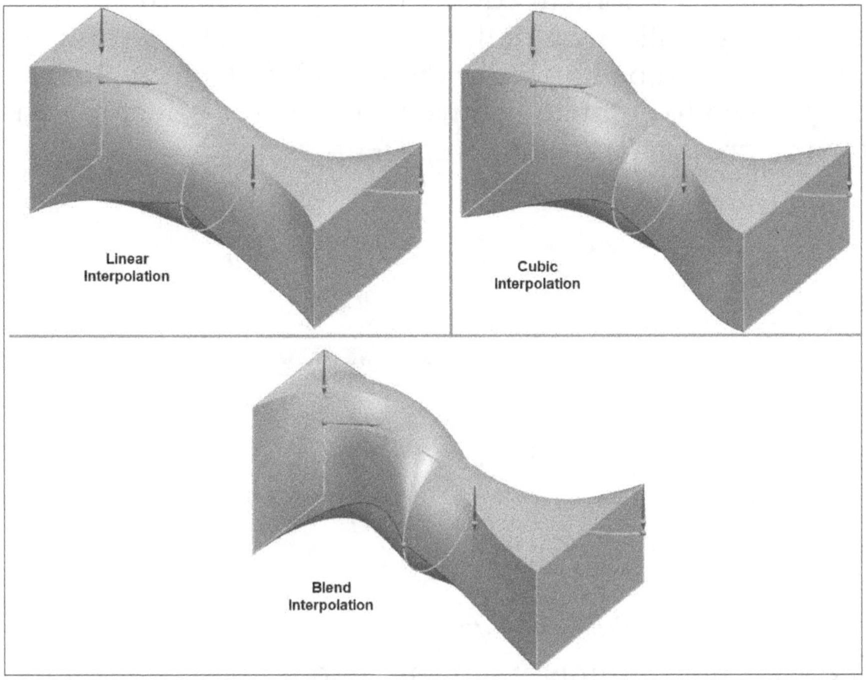

Figure-87. Interpolation options

- Select desired option from the **Alignment** drop-down to define how various sections will be matched to create swept feature. For example, if there are two triangles to be used as sections for swept then the options in this drop-down are used to define which vertex of first triangle will be matched with which vertex of second triangle. One of the easiest way to perform alignment of sections is by using points. To do so, select the **By Points** option from the **Alignment** drop-down. The key points on sections will be displayed for modifications; refer to Figure-88.

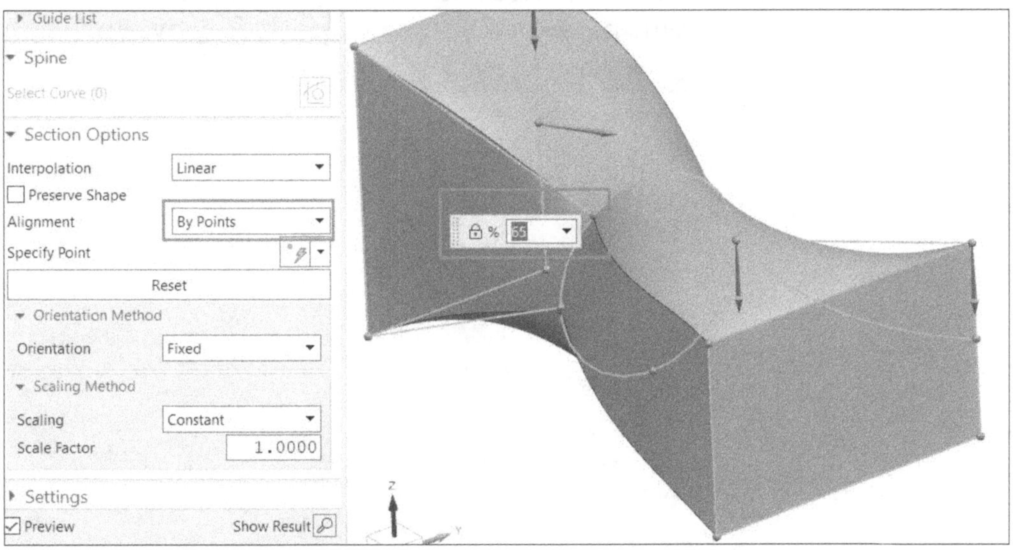

Figure-88. Modifying alignment of sections

- Drag desired points to modify alignment of sections or you can specify percentage value from starting location to place the alignment point.
- Select the **Preserve Shape** check box to preserve sharp corners in the sweep feature.

- If you want to adjust the alignment by using parameters then select the **Parameter** option from the **Alignment** drop-down and select desired option from the **Scaling** drop-down. Similarly, select the **Arc Length** option from the **Alignment** drop-down to adjust alignment of sections at equal arc length along the path of sweep feature.
- Expand the **Settings** rollout to define body type and tolerance parameters. The options will be displayed as shown in Figure-89. Select the **Solid** option from the **Body Type** drop-down to create a solid swept feature. Select the **Sheet** option from the drop-down to create a surface swept feature.

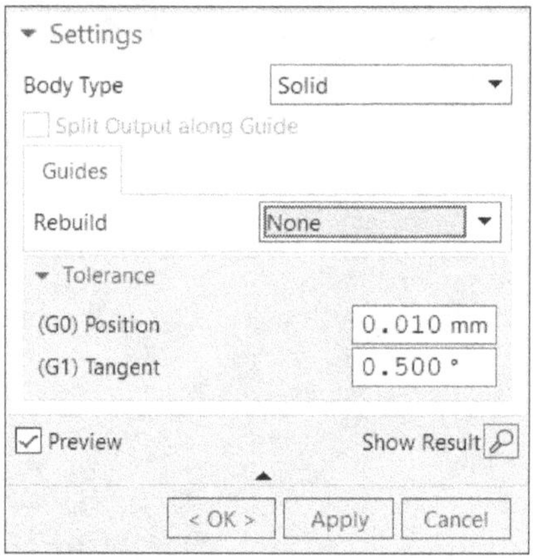

Figure-89. Settings rollout

- Similarly, specify other parameters in the rollout and click on the **OK** button from the dialog box to create the feature.

CREATING VARIATIONAL SWEEP

The **Variational Sweep** tool is used to create a swept feature with varying cross-section based on specified sketches. The procedure to use this tool is given next.

- Click on the **Variational Sweep** tool from the **More** drop-down in **Base** group of **Surface** tab in the **Ribbon**. The **Variational Sweep** dialog box will be displayed; refer to Figure-90 and you will be asked to select path for sweep.

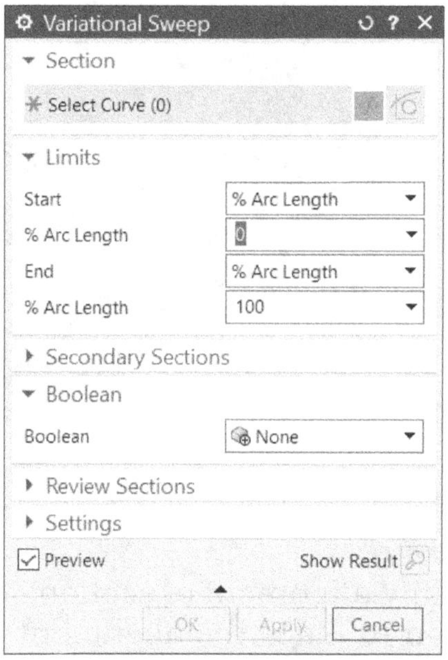

Figure-90. Variational Sweep dialog box

- Select the curve which you want to use as path for creating variational sweep. The **Create Sketch** dialog box will be displayed and you will be asked to specify the location on curve where sketch section is to be created; refer to Figure-91.

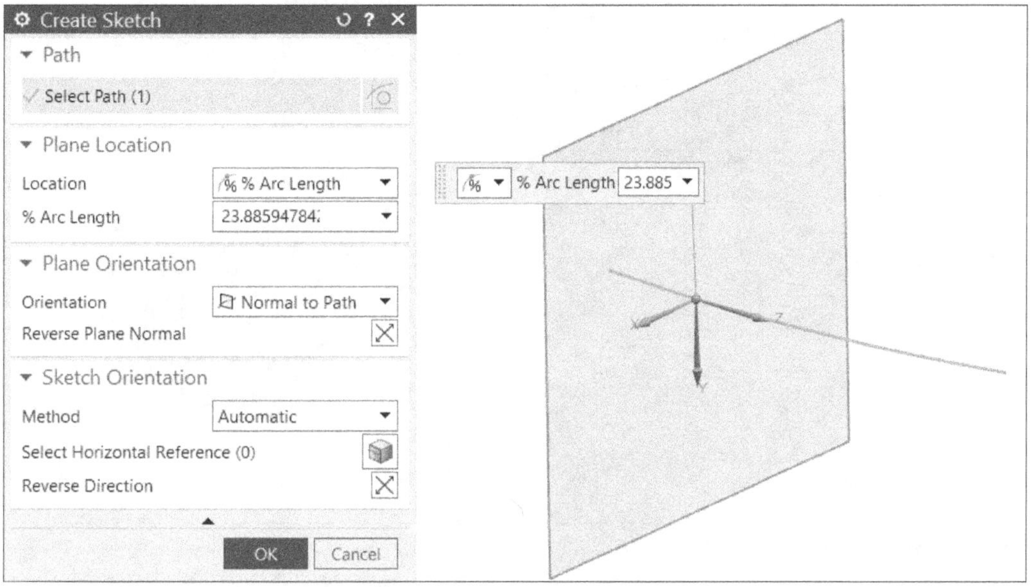

Figure-91. Preview of sketching plane

- Set desired percentage value in **% Arc Length** edit box to define the location of sketch plane on curve. Specify **0** in the edit box to create sketch at the start of path curve and specify **100** in the edit box to create sketch at the end of path curve.
- Click on the **OK** button from the dialog box to start sketching and create section for sweep. Create a closed loop section to create solid feature and create open section to create surface feature. After creating section, click on the **Finish** button from the **Ribbon**. Preview of variational sweep will be displayed; refer to Figure-92 and **Variational Sweep** dialog box will be displayed again.

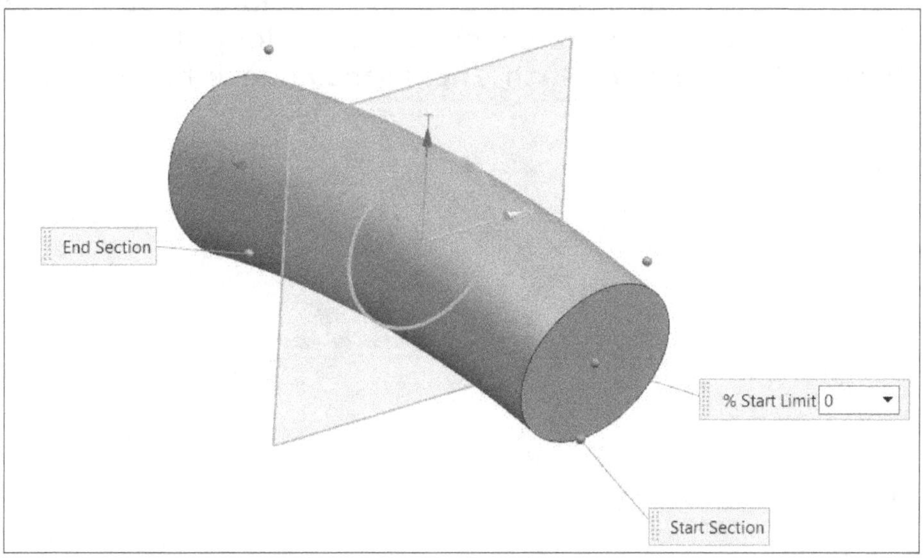

Figure-92. Preview of variational sweep

- Expand the **Secondary Sections** rollout if you want to add more sections for sweep feature and click on the **Add New Set** button. Preview of another section will be displayed; refer to Figure-93. If you are asked to convert dimensions to driving dimensions then click on the **Yes** button from dialog box displayed.

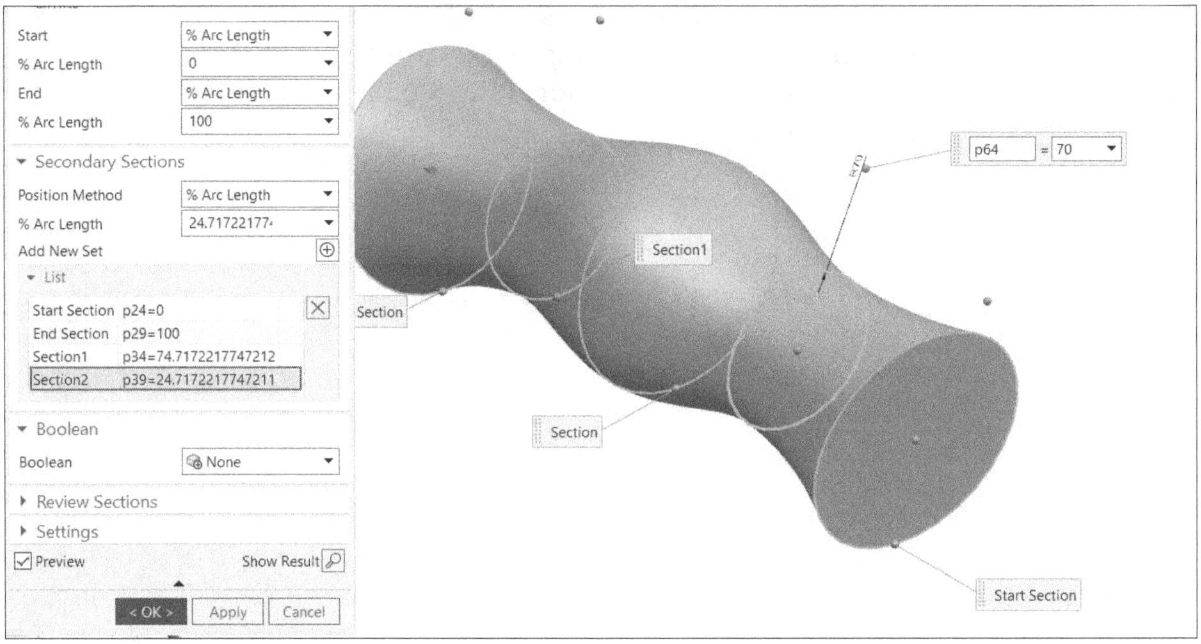

Figure-93. Preview of secondary section

- Specify desired percentage value in **% Arc Length** edit box to locate the new sketch section.
- Double-click on dimensions displayed for sketches to edit the sections. Expand the **List** sub-rollout in **Secondary Sections** rollout of dialog box to select desired section for editing.
- Select the **Review Sections at Path Increments** check box to analyze section of the sweep feature at various locations on the path. The options in dialog box will be displayed as shown in Figure-94.
- Specify desired value in the **% Path Increment** edit box to define the distance by which you want to move along the path while checking section when **Step** slider is moved. Move the **Step** slider to check sections along the path.
- Clear the **Review Sections at Path Increments** check box to exit the mode.

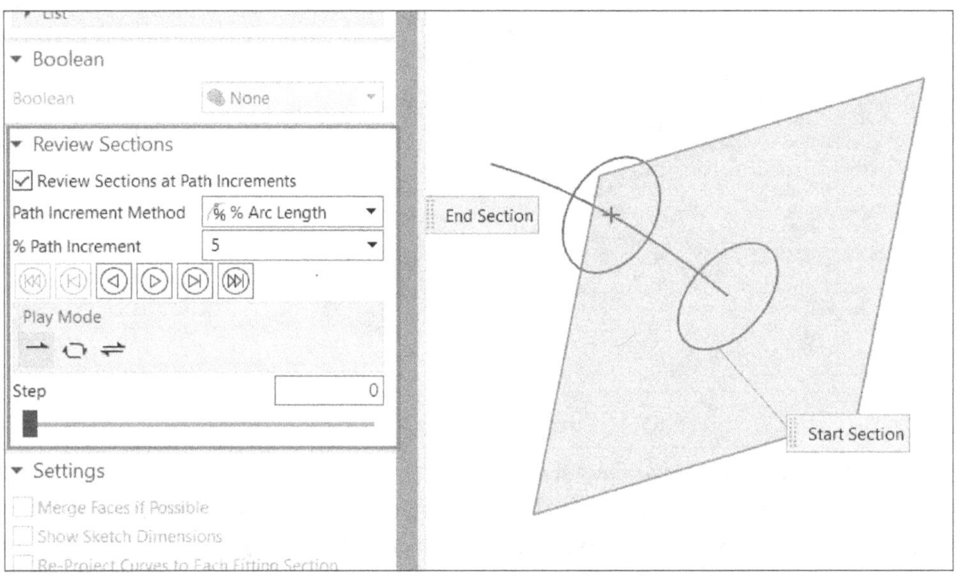

Figure-94. Review Sections rollout

- Expand the **Settings** rollout to define various settings related to feature. Select the **Merge Faces if Possible** check box to allow faces to be merged in the feature if they are in very close range.

- Select the **Show Sketch Dimensions** check box to display dimensions of sketches involved in creating the feature.
- Select the **User Specified** option from the **Fitting Section Method** drop-down if you want to manually define how many sections will be internally generated for sweep feature.
- Set the other options as discussed earlier and click on the **OK** button. The feature will be created.

CREATING SWEEP ALONG CURVE

The **Sweep along Guide** tool is used to create a sweep feature in which section follows the highs and lows of selected guide curve. Make sure you have section sketch and guide curve already created before using this tool. The procedure to use this tool is given next.

- Click on the **Sweep along Guide** tool from the **Sweep** section in the **More** drop-down of **Base** group in the **Surface** tab of **Ribbon**. The **Sweep Along Guide** dialog box will be displayed; refer to Figure-95.

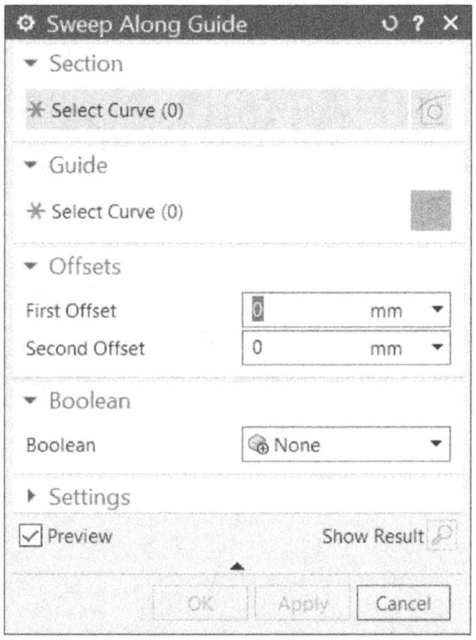

Figure-95. Sweep Along Guide dialog box

- Select the sketch section for sweep feature and then click on the **Select Curve** selection button in the **Guide** rollout of the dialog box. You will be asked to select the curve to be used as guide for sweep feature.
- Select desired curve. Preview of the sweep feature will be displayed; refer to Figure-96.

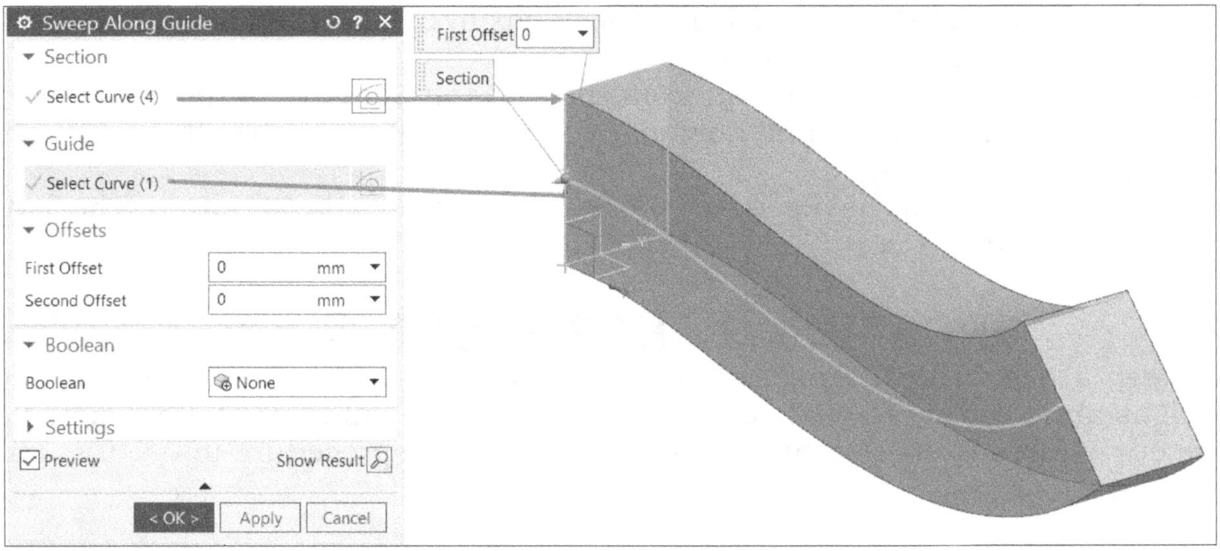

Figure-96. Preview of sweep along curve

- Specify desired offset value to create a sweep feature of respective thickness in **First Offset** or **Second Offset** edit box.
- Click on the **OK** button from the dialog box to create the feature.

CREATING TUBE

The **Tube** tool is used to create a circular tube of specified diameter along selected curve. The procedure to create tube is given next.

- Click on the **Tube** tool from the **Sweep** section of **More** drop-down in **Base** group of **Surface** tab in the **Ribbon**. The **Tube** dialog box will be displayed; refer to Figure-97.

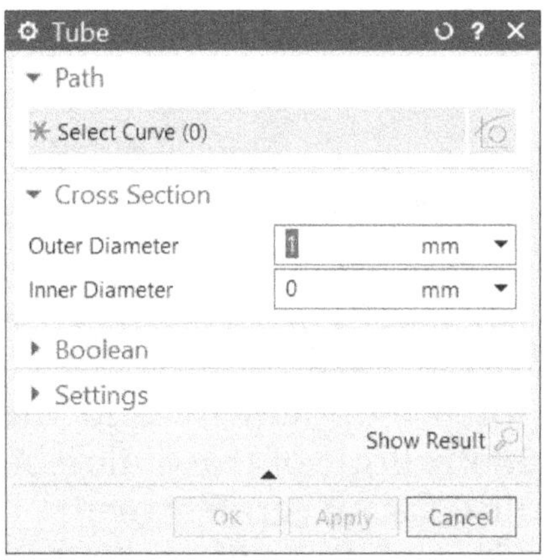

Figure-97. Tube dialog box

- Select the curve to be used as centerline of tube and specify the diameter values in **Outer Diameter** and **Inner Diameter** edit boxes.
- Expand the **Settings** rollout and select the **Single Segment** option from the **Output** drop-down to create single segment of tube otherwise tube will be in the form of multiple small sections. Click on the **Show Result** button at the bottom in the dialog box to check the preview; refer to Figure-98.

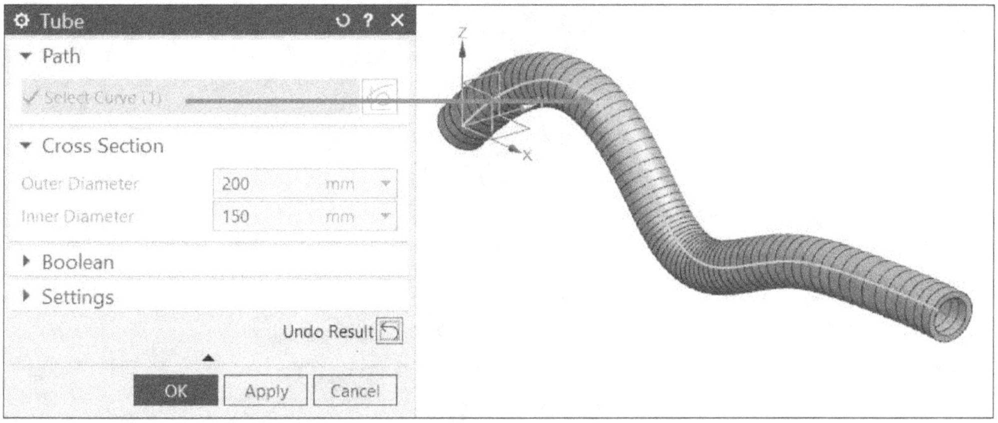

Figure-98. Preview of tube

- Set the other parameters as discussed earlier and click on the **OK** button.

CREATING SWEPT VOLUME

The **Swept Volume** tool is used to sweep a solid feature along the path to remove material from other features. Make sure you have a tool body, path, and another body from which swept volume will be removed. The procedure to use this tool is given next.

- Click on the **Swept Volume** tool from the **Sweep** section of **More** drop-down in the **Base** panel of **Surface** tab in the **Ribbon**. The **Swept Volume** dialog box will be displayed; refer to Figure-99.

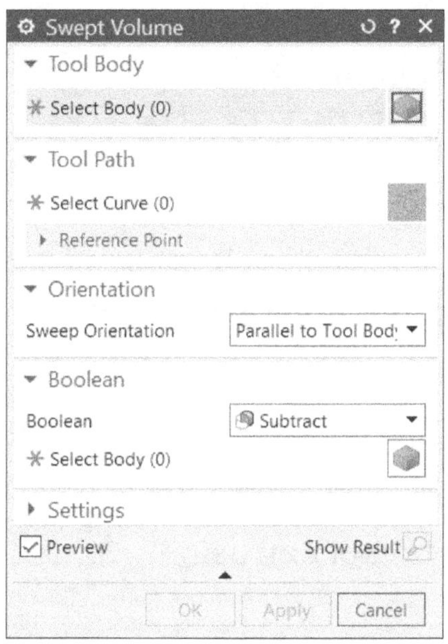

Figure-99. Swept Volume dialog box

- Select the tool body to be swept along the path. You will be asked to select the path curve.
- Select the path for body.
- Click on the **Select Body** button from the **Boolean** rollout and select the body from which you want to remove swept volume. Preview of swept volume will be displayed; refer to Figure-100.

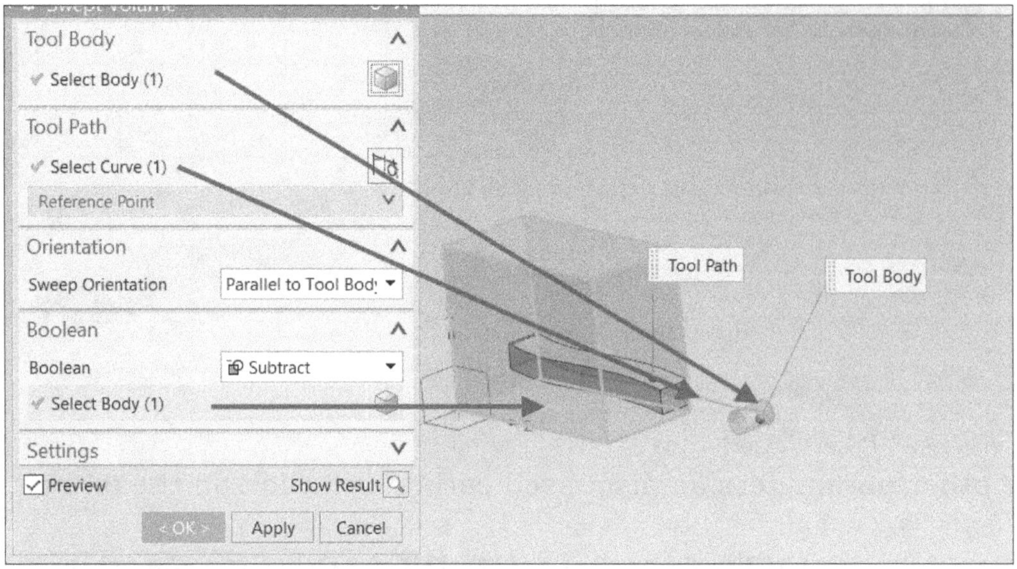

Figure-100. Preview of swept volume

- Click on the **OK** button from the dialog box to create the feature.

SELF-ASSESSMENT

Q1. What is the purpose of the Extrude feature in NX?
A. Remove material from sketch
B. Add material by moving sketch along a vector
C. Create 2D drawing
D. Apply color to model

Q2. Where is the Extrude tool located?
A. Insert menu
B. View tab
C. Feature panel of Home tab
D. Tools menu

Q3. What type of sketch is required for extrusion?
A. Open sketch only
B. Closed loop sketch
C. 3D sketch
D. Any random curve

Q4. What is the default direction of extrusion?
A. Parallel to X-axis
B. Parallel to Y-axis
C. Perpendicular to sketch plane
D. Along selected edge

Q5. Which option is used to reverse extrusion direction?
A. Flip Tool
B. Reverse Direction
C. Change Axis
D. Mirror

Q6. Which option allows defining extrusion distance manually?
A. Vector Dialog
B. Distance Tool
C. Length Command
D. Offset Tool

Q7. Which option is used to extrude equally on both sides of sketch plane?
A. Equal Distance
B. Symmetric Value
C. Mirror Extrude
D. Dual Direction

Q8. What does "Until Next" option do?
A. Stops extrusion randomly
B. Extrudes to next feature
C. Extrudes infinitely
D. Cancels operation

Q9. Which option allows selecting a face to define extrusion limit?
A. Until Selected
B. Until Next
C. Through All
D. Value

Q10. Which option extrudes feature up to the last face in direction?
A. Until Next
B. Through All
C. Value
D. Offset

Q11. What is required to use Open Profile Smart Volume?
A. Closed sketch
B. No nearby geometry
C. Solid boundaries near open profile
D. Only surfaces

Q12. Which Boolean option creates a separate body?
A. Unite
B. Subtract
C. None
D. Intersect

Q13. Which Boolean option removes material?
A. Unite
B. Subtract
C. Intersect
D. None

Q14. What does Intersect Boolean option do?
A. Adds material
B. Removes material
C. Keeps common portion
D. Duplicates feature

Q15. Draft in extrusion is used to:
A. Color faces
B. Apply taper angle
C. Create sketch
D. Move object

Q16. Which offset option creates thin feature?
A. Single-Sided
B. Two-Sided
C. Symmetric
D. None

Q17. Which Body Type option creates extruded surface?
A. Solid
B. Sheet
C. Mesh
D. Wireframe

Q18. Datum features are used as:
A. Final models
B. References
C. Colors
D. Layers

Q19. Which of the following is NOT a datum feature?
A. Plane
B. Axis
C. Coordinate system
D. Sketch

Q20. Which datum feature acts as direction reference?
A. Plane
B. Axis
C. Point
D. Face

Q21. Which option creates a plane at a specified distance?
A. At Angle
B. At Distance
C. Bisector
D. Curve

Q22. Which option creates a plane between two faces?
A. At Distance
B. Bisector
C. At Angle
D. Two Lines

Q23. Which option creates a plane tangent to a curved face?
A. Tangent
B. Bisector
C. At Distance
D. Curve

Q24. Which datum axis option uses two faces?
A. Curve Axis
B. Intersection
C. Two Points
D. Point Direction

Q25. Datum coordinate system is used for:
A. Coloring
B. Orientation and origin reference
C. Rendering
D. Printing only

Q26. Which tool is used to resize datum plane?
A. Scale Tool
B. Resize Datum Plane
C. Modify Tool
D. Stretch Tool

Q27. Print CSYS is used for:
A. Sketching
B. 3D printing orientation
C. Coloring
D. Measurement

Q28. What is the use of Point tool?
A. Create surfaces
B. Create reference points
C. Delete objects
D. Create solids

Q29. Point Set tool is used to:
A. Delete points
B. Create multiple points
C. Merge curves
D. Split bodies

Q30. Which option creates points equally spaced along a curve?
A. Equal Arc Length
B. Random Points
C. Offset Points
D. Manual Points

Q31. What is the use of Datum Plane Grid tool?
A. Create solid body
B. Create grid bounded by plane boundaries
C. Draw sketch
D. Apply texture

Q32. Where is the Datum Plane Grid tool located?
A. Insert tab
B. Tools tab
C. Construction group of Home tab
D. Surface tab

Q33. Which parameter is set to control spacing of grid lines?
A. Line Style
B. Line Width
C. Line Spacing
D. Label Style

Q34. What must be selected to display grid preview?
A. Curve
B. Axis
C. Plane
D. Point

Q35. What is the function of Reference Point Cloud tool?
A. Create sketch
B. Create points from data file
C. Delete points
D. Create surfaces

Q36. Reference Point Cloud tool is NOT available in:
A. Professional version
B. Student Edition
C. Commercial version
D. Enterprise version

Q37. Raster Image tool is used to:
A. Create solid
B. Insert image as reference
C. Delete image
D. Convert image

Q38. Where is Raster Image tool located?
A. Home tab
B. Surface tab
C. Tools tab
D. Insert tab

Q39. Which option maintains image proportion?
A. Lock Size
B. Lock Aspect Ratio
C. Fix Dimension
D. Scale Lock

Q40. Revolve tool is used to:
A. Move object
B. Rotate view
C. Create solid by revolving sketch
D. Create plane

Q41. What is required for revolve feature?
A. Only sketch
B. Only axis
C. Sketch and axis
D. Plane only

Q42. Which option defines revolve limits?
A. Distance
B. Angle
C. Offset
D. Radius

Q43. Swept tool is used to:
A. Delete curves
B. Move sketch
C. Create feature along path
D. Color model

Q44. What happens if section arrows are not aligned in sweep?
A. No effect
B. Error occurs
C. Twisted feature
D. Smooth feature

Q45. Which interpolation option creates smooth transition?
A. Linear
B. Cubic
C. Blend
D. Offset

Q46. Which alignment option uses key points?
A. Parameter
B. Arc Length
C. By Points
D. Manual

Q47. Variational Sweep is used to:
A. Create fixed section sweep
B. Create varying cross-section sweep
C. Delete sweep
D. Rotate sweep

Q48. Closed section in variational sweep creates:
A. Surface
B. Solid
C. Curve
D. Plane

Q49. Sweep Along Guide tool follows:
A. Straight line
B. Axis
C. Guide curve highs and lows
D. Grid

Q50. Tube tool creates:
A. Square pipe
B. Circular tube
C. Solid block
D. Plane

Chapter 5

3D Modeling-II

Topics Covered

The major topics covered in this chapter are:

- ***Creating Blocks, Cylinders, Cones, and Spheres***
- ***Creating Holes***
- ***Performing Boolean Operations***
- ***Creating Edge Blend and Chamfers***
- ***Performing Trim Body and Intersect Operations***
- ***Applying Draft and Shell Operations***
- ***Creating Pattern Features***
- ***Creating Mirror Copy Features***

INTRODUCTION

In this chapter, we will learn to insert various features like blocks, cylinders, cones, and so on. We will also learn to create grooves, ribs, and so on. These tools are discussed next.

CREATING BLOCKS

The **Block** tool is used to create rectangular blocks of specified length, width, and height. The procedure to use this tool is given next.

- Click on the **Block** tool from the **Design Feature** section of the **More** drop-down in **Base** group of **Home** tab in **Ribbon**. The **Block** dialog box will be displayed; refer to Figure-1.

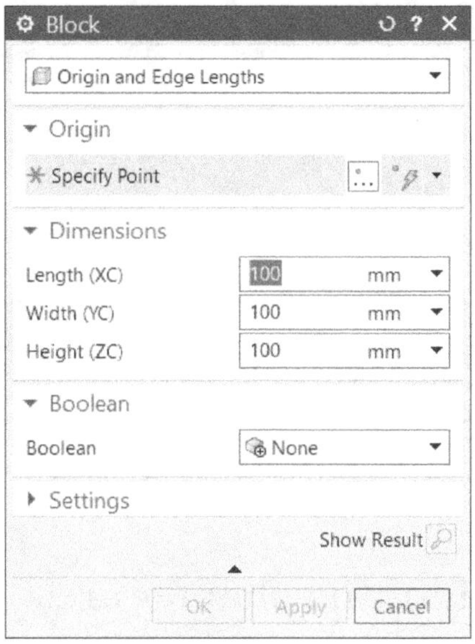

Figure-1. Block dialog box

- Select desired option from the drop-down at the top in the dialog box. Select the **Origin and Edge Lengths** option if you want to specify starting location of block and its dimensions. Select the **Two Points and Height** option from the drop-down if you want to create a block by specifying diagonal points of base and height value. Select the **Two Diagonal Points** option from the drop-down if you want to specify diagonal points of block to create it. The procedures to create blocks using different options are discussed next.

Block using Origin and Edge Lengths

- The **Origin and Edge Lengths** option is selected by default in the drop-down and hence the options in the dialog box are displayed as shown in Figure-1. If not selected in your case then select the option from the drop-down at the top in the dialog box.
- Click at desired location to specify the origin of block. You can select anywhere on the screen or you can select the snap points of various objects in the graphics window.
- Specify the length of block along different axes in the respective edit boxes of the dialog box.
- Select desired option from the **Boolean** drop-down if you want to perform any boolean operation.

- Click on the **Show Result** button at the bottom in the dialog box to check the result. Preview of block feature will be displayed; refer to Figure-2.

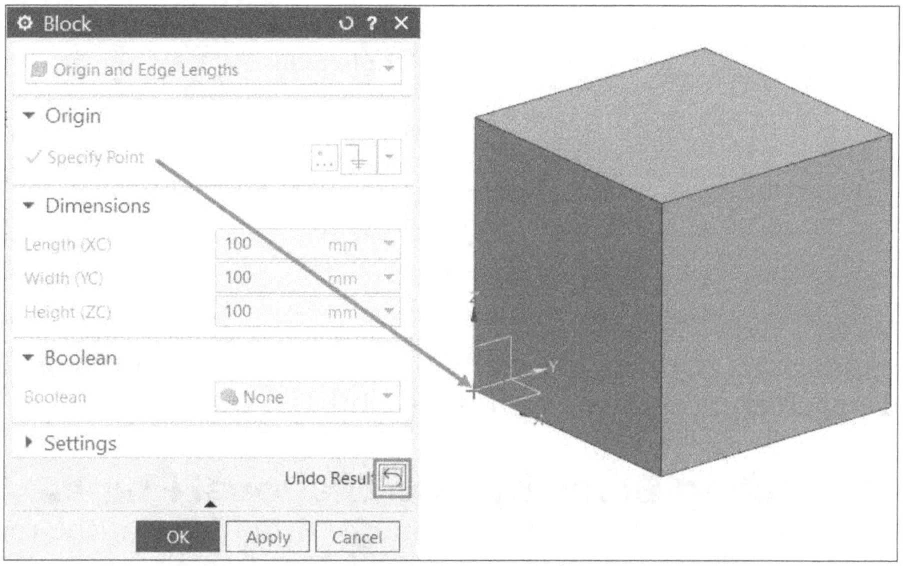

Figure-2. Preview of block by origin and edge lengths

- Click on the **OK** button from the dialog box to create the block and exit the dialog box.

Block Using Two Points and Height

- Select the **Two Points and Height** option from the drop-down at the top in the dialog box. The options in the dialog box will be displayed as shown in Figure-3.

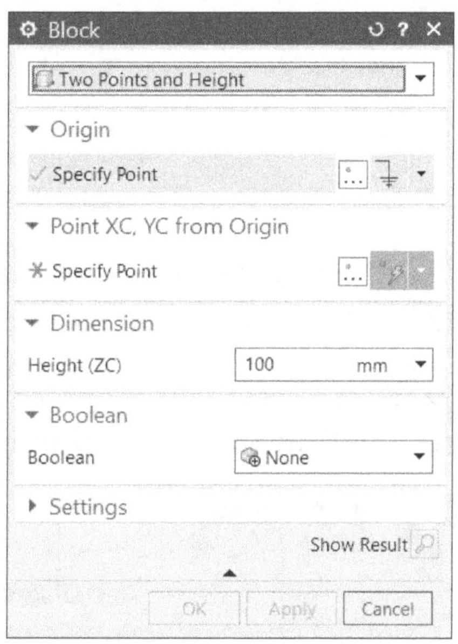

Figure-3. Block dialog box by Two Points and Height option

- Click at desired location to place starting point of base of block. You can also use the **Point** dialog box to define point. To do so, click on the **Point Dialog** button in **Origin** rollout. The **Point** dialog box will be displayed. Specify the point as discussed earlier.
- Click on the **Specify Point** selection option from the **Point XC, YC from Origin** rollout and click at desired location in XY plane; refer to Figure-4. You can also use the **Point** dialog box to define this point.

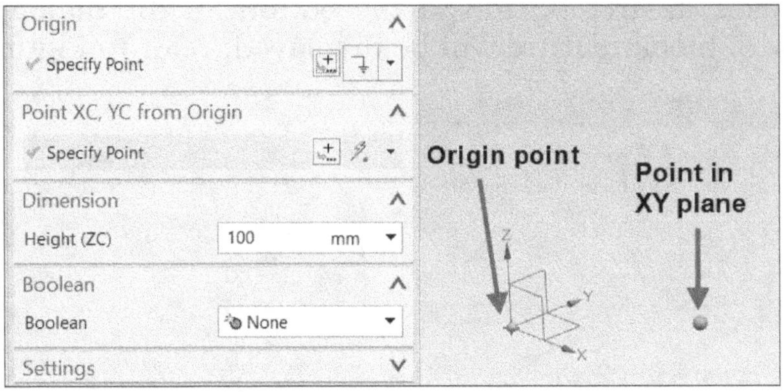

Figure-4. Defining points for block base

- Click in the **Height (ZC)** edit box and specify the height of block.
- Set desired parameters and click on the **OK** button from the dialog box.

Creating Block by Two Diagonal Points

- Select the **Two Diagonal Points** option from the drop-down at the top in the dialog box. The options in the dialog box will be displayed as shown in Figure-5.

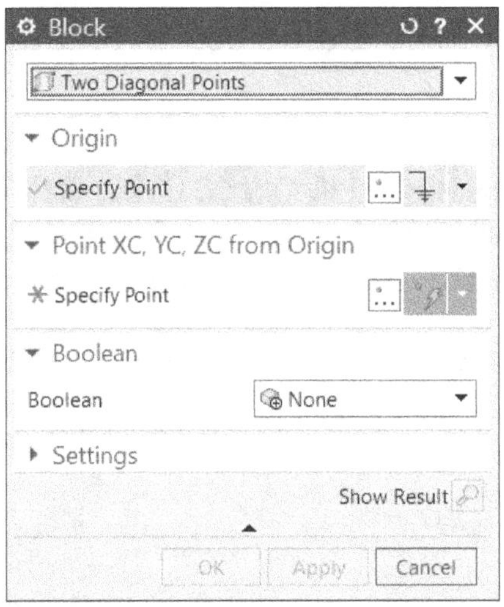

Figure-5. Block dialog box by Two Diagonal Points option

- Click on the **Specify Point** selection option in the **Origin** rollout and click at desired location to place origin.
- Click on the **Specify Point** selection option from the **Point XC, YC, ZC from Origin** rollout and click on desired location to define diagonal point; refer to Figure-6.

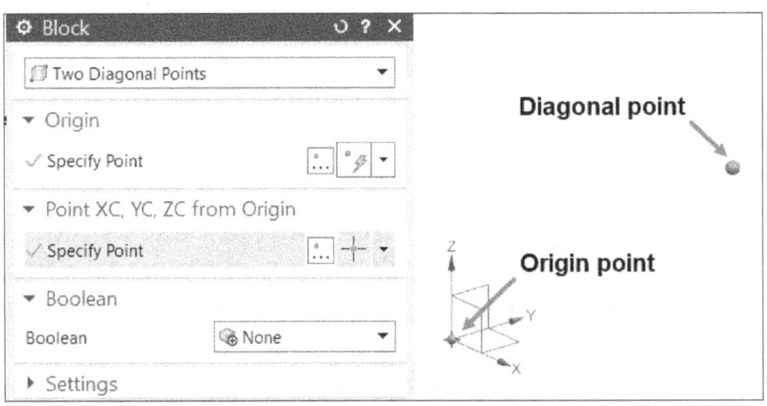

Figure-6. Diagonal points of block

- Click on the **Show Result** button at the bottom in the dialog box. Preview of block will be displayed.
- Click on the **OK** button to create the block.

CREATING CYLINDERS

The **Cylinder** tool is used to place cylinders of specified parameters at the specified locations. The procedure to insert cylinder is given next.

- Click on the **Cylinder** tool from the **Design Feature** section of **More** drop-down in the **Feature** panel of the **Home** tab in the **Ribbon**. The **Cylinder** dialog box will be displayed; refer to Figure-7.

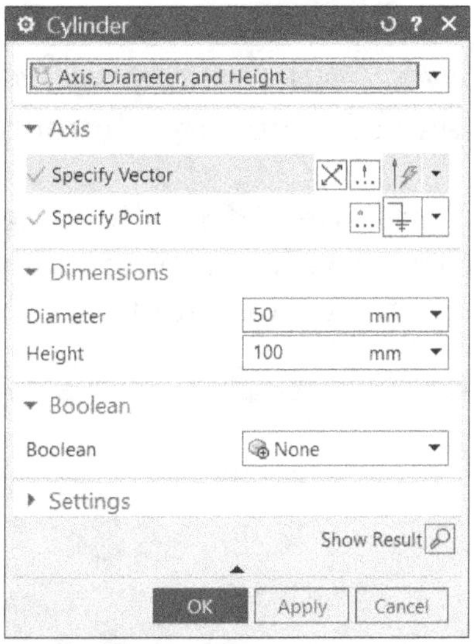

Figure-7. Cylinder dialog box

Creating Cylinder using Axis, Diameter, and Height

- Select the **Axis, Diameter, and Height** option from the drop-down at the top if you want to specify the axis, placement point, and parameters for the cylinder. The options of the dialog box will be displayed as shown in Figure-7.
- Select desired reference to define direction in which cylinder will be created. You can select the vectors displayed in blue color in graphics window or you can select edges/faces/planes/axis to define the direction of cylinder height.
- Click on the **Specify Point** selection option and specify the location of origin.
- Specify desired size parameters of cylinder in the **Dimensions** rollout and click on the **Show Result** button to check the preview of cylinder.
- Click on the **OK** button to create the cylinder.

Creating Cylinder using Arc and Height

- Select the **Arc and Height** option from the drop-down at the top in the dialog box. The options in the dialog box will be displayed as shown in Figure-8.

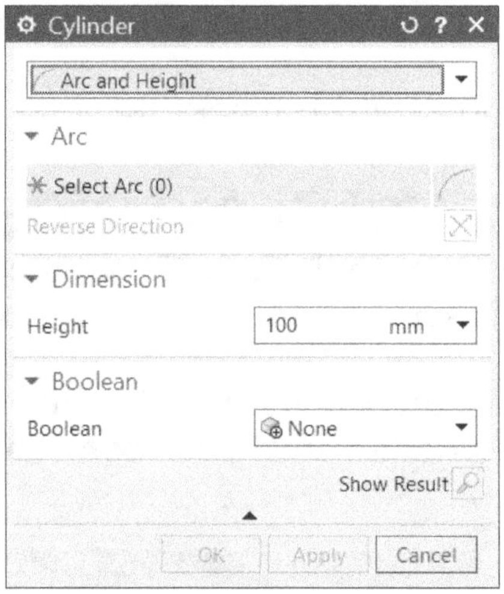

Figure-8. Cylinder dialog box using Arc and Height option

- Select the arc to be used as reference for diameter of cylinder and location of center point.
- Specify desired value of cylinder height in the **Height** edit box.
- Click on the **Show Result** button to check the preview of cylinder; refer to Figure-9. Click on the **OK** button to create the cylinder.

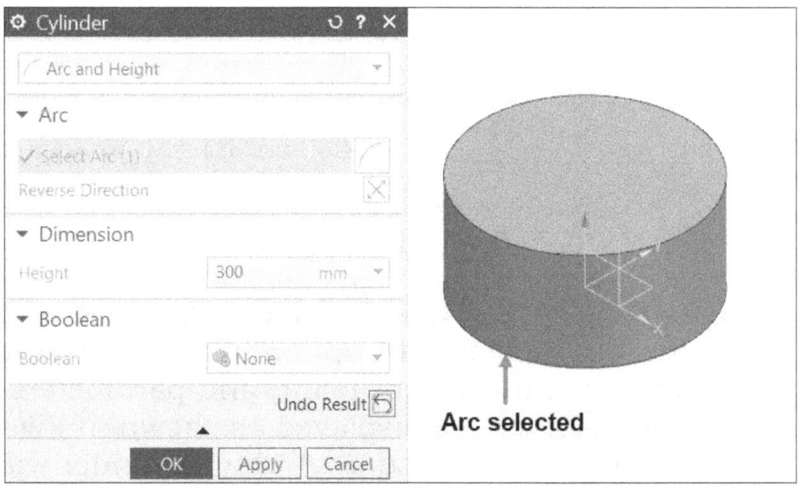

Figure-9. Preview of cylinder

CREATING CONES

The **Cone** tool is used to create cones based on specified parameters. The procedure to create cone is given next.

- Click on the **Cone** tool from the **Design Feature** section of **More** drop-down in the **Base** panel of the **Home** tab in the **Ribbon**. The **Cone** dialog box will be displayed; refer to Figure-10.

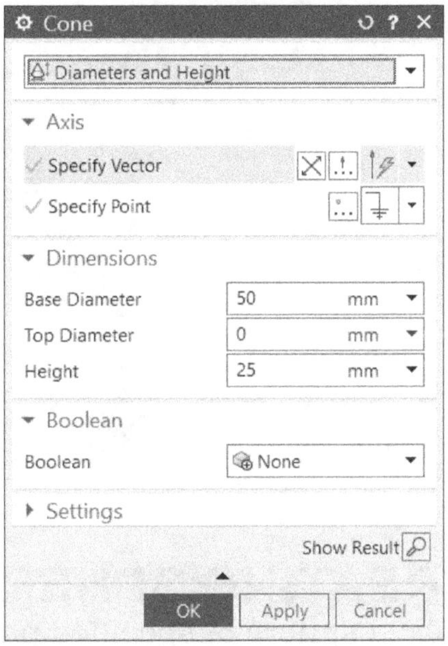

Figure-10. Cone dialog box

Creating Cone using Diameters and Height

- Select the **Diameters and Height** option from the drop-down at the top in the dialog box. The options in the dialog box will be displayed as shown in Figure-10.
- Click on the **Specify Vector** selection option and specify the vertical direction reference for cone.
- Click on the **Specify Point** selection option and specify the point where you want to place the cone.
- Specify the parameters in edit boxes of **Dimensions** rollout and click on the **Show Result** button to check the preview; refer to Figure-11.

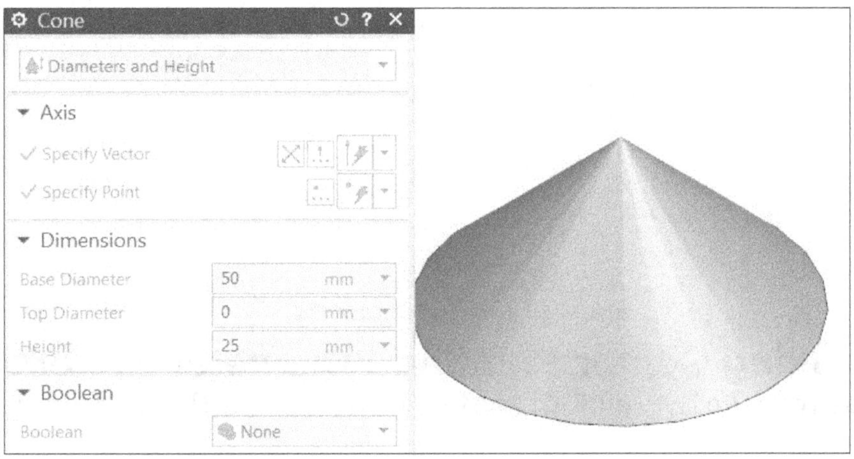

Figure-11. Preview of cone

- Click on the **OK** button to create cone.

You can use the other options of drop-down at the top in the dialog box in the same way.

Select the **Two Coaxial Arcs** option from the drop-down at the top in the **Cone** dialog box to create cone by selecting two coaxial arcs. Select the arcs and click on the **Show Result** button to check the preview; refer to Figure-12. Click on the **OK** button to create the cone.

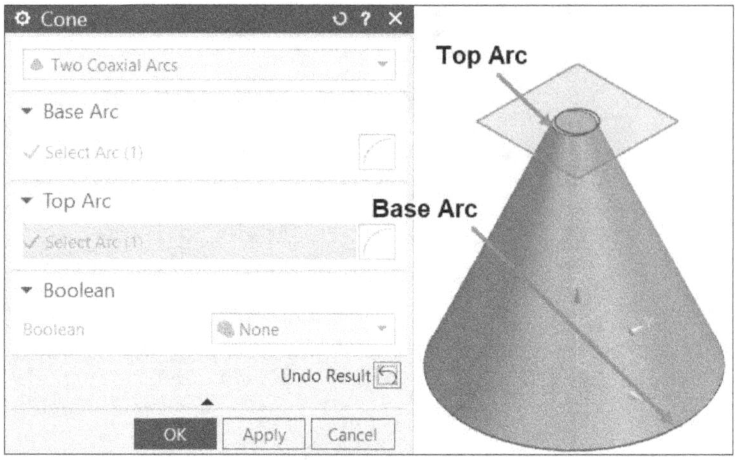

Figure-12. Preview of cone using arcs

CREATING SPHERE

The **Sphere** tool is used to place a sphere of specified parameters at desired location. The procedure to use this tool is given next.

- Click on the **Sphere** tool from the **Design Feature** section of **More** drop-down in the **Feature** panel of the **Ribbon**. The **Sphere** dialog box will be displayed; refer to Figure-13.

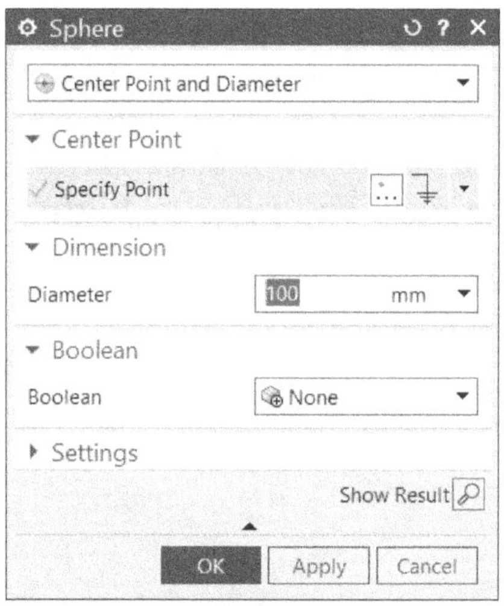

Figure-13. Sphere dialog box

Using Center Point and Diameter Sphere

- Select the **Center Point and Diameter** option from the drop-down at the top in the dialog box.
- Click at desired location to place the origin and specify the diameter of sphere in **Diameter** edit box of **Dimension** rollout.
- Click on the **Show Result** button at the bottom in the dialog box to check the preview of sphere.
- Click on the **OK** button to create the sphere.

Using Arc for Sphere

- Select the **Arc** option from the drop-down at the top in the dialog box. The options in the dialog box will be displayed as shown in Figure-14.

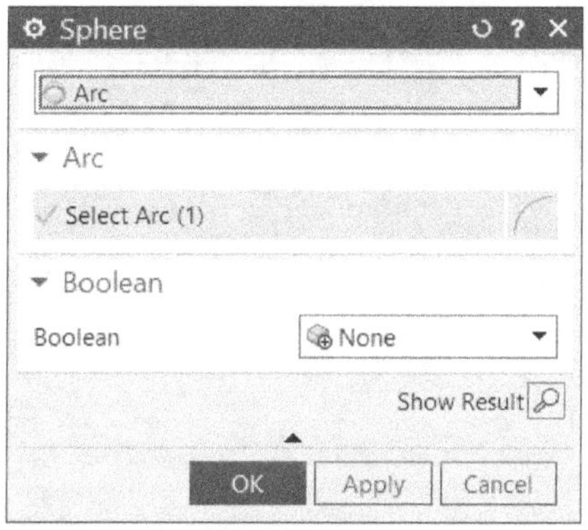

Figure-14. Sphere dialog box using Arc option

- Select the arc to be used as reference for diameter and center point for sphere. Click on the **Show Result** button to check the preview; refer to Figure-15.

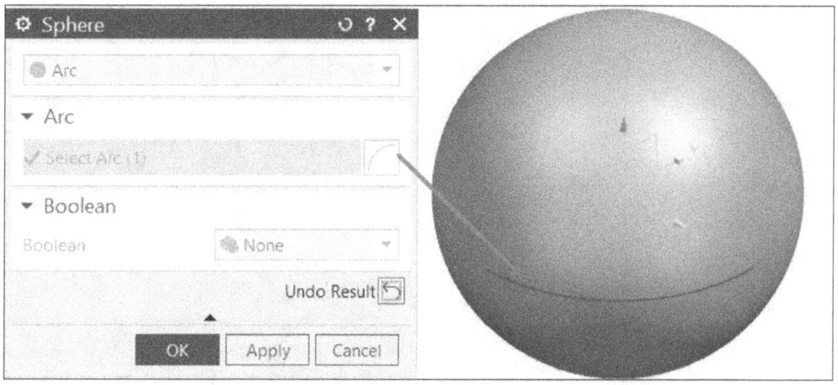

Figure-15. Preview of sphere using arc

- Click on the **OK** button to create the sphere.

CREATING HOLE FEATURE

The **Hole** tool is used to create standard and custom holes in the model. The procedure to use this tool is given next.

- Click on the **Hole** tool from the **Base** group in the **Home** tab of **Ribbon**. The **Hole** dialog box will be displayed; refer to Figure-16.

Creating Simple Hole

- Select the **Simple** option from the drop-down at the top in the dialog box to create simple holes with specified hole diameter and depth. The options will be displayed as shown in Figure-16.

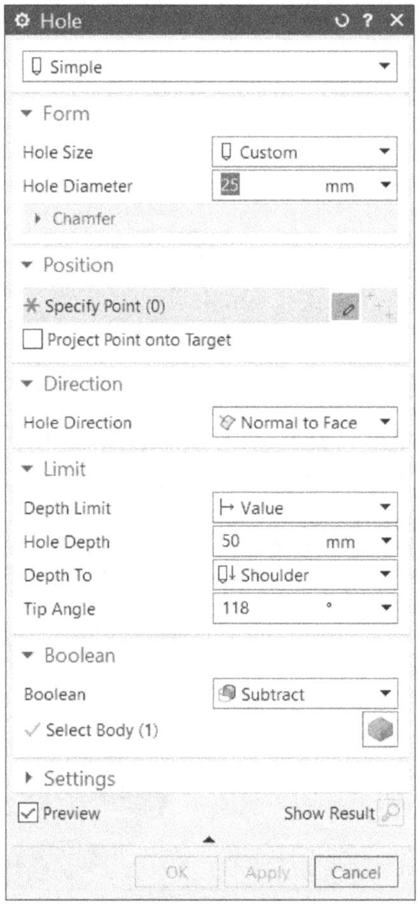

Figure-16. Hole dialog box

Custom Holes

- Select the **Custom** option from **Hole Size** drop-down to create holes of user-defined diameter. The **Hole Diameter** edit box will be displayed below the drop-down. Specify desired diameter value in the edit box.

Drill Size Holes

- Select the **Drill Size** option from the **Hole Size** drop-down to create standard holes. The options will be displayed as shown in Figure-17. Select desired option from the **Standard** drop-down to define standard to be used for defining hole size. There are two hole standards: **ISO** and **ANSI**. Select the **ISO** option if you want to specify size according to International Organization of Standardization. Select the **ANSI** option if you want to specify size according to American National Standards Institute.

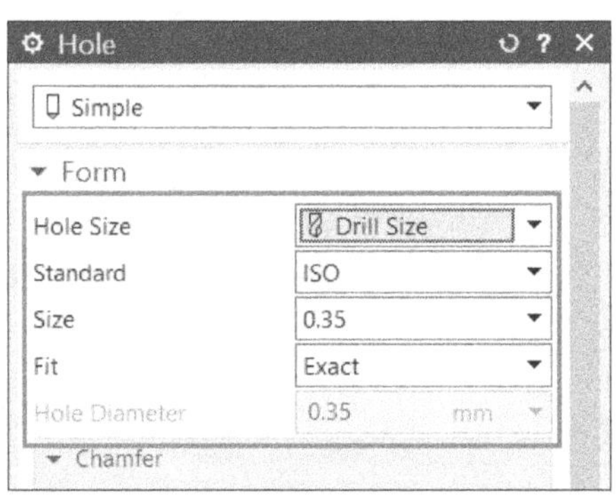

Figure-17. Drill size options

- Select desired option from the **Size** drop-down to define size of hole.
- By default, the **Exact** option is selected in the **Fit** drop-down to create hole of exact size. The hole diameter and chamfer parameters will be selected automatically based on selected drill size. Select the **Custom** option from the drop-down to define chamfer and hole diameter parameters, manually.

Screw Clearance Holes

- Select the **Screw Clearance** option from the **Hole Size** drop-down to create holes which allow creating holes with standard fits and tolerances. Select desired option from the **Standard** drop-down and specify hole parameters as discussed earlier in the **Form** rollout.
- After setting simple hole parameters, select the **Project Point onto Target** check box from the **Position** rollout to define hole depth using point projected on face of model. For example, if you are selecting point on a plane above solid feature and this check box is selected then distance between plane and face of solid feature will be ignored and specified hole depth will start from face of solid feature.
- Click at desired location on the plane/face to create the hole. Preview of hole will be displayed; refer to Figure-18.

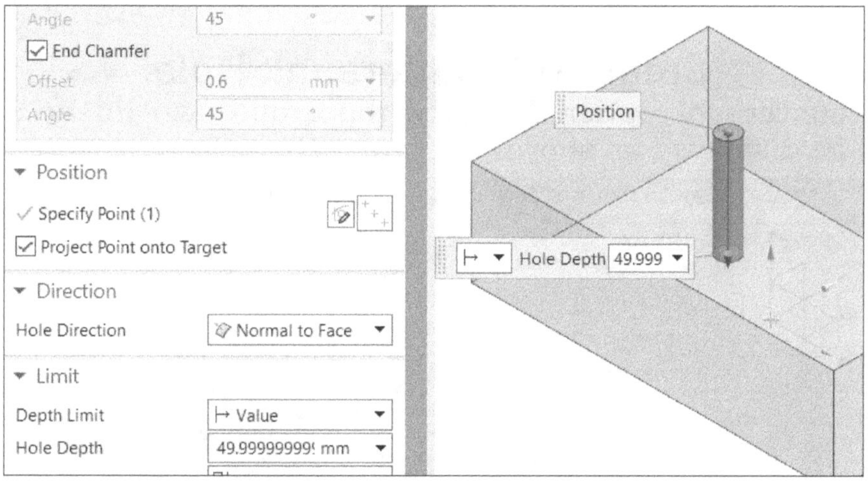

Figure-18. Preview of hole

- Select the **Normal to Face** option from the **Hole Direction** drop-down to create hole with axis perpendicular to selected face of model.
- Select the **Along Vector** option from the **Hole Direction** drop-down to create a hole along specified vector. You can use the **Vector Dialog** button from the **Direction** rollout to create direction vector as discussed earlier.
- Specify desired parameters in the **Limit** rollout to specify depth of hole.
- Set the other parameters as discussed earlier and click on the **Apply** button to create the hole.

Creating Counterbored Hole

- Select the **Counterbored** option from the drop-down at the top in the dialog box. The options will be displayed as shown in Figure-19.

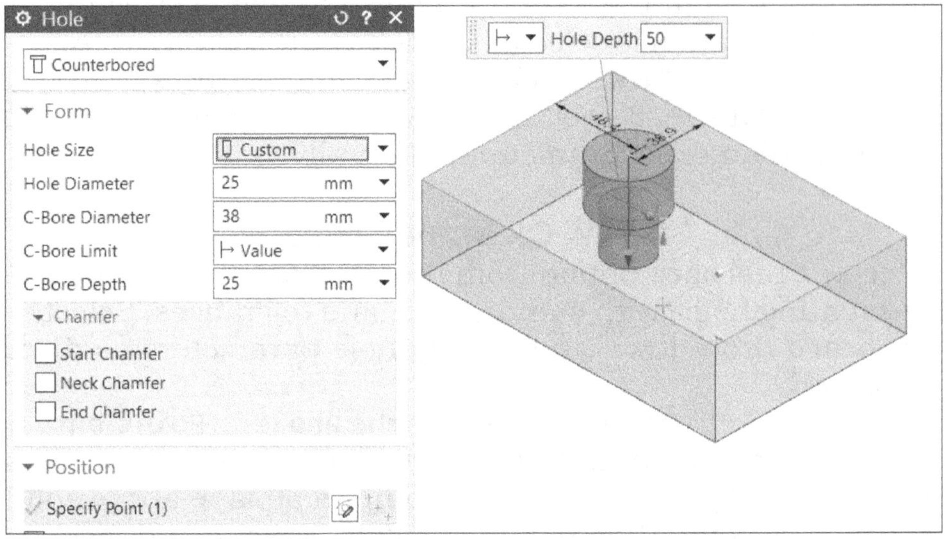

Figure-19. Counterbored hole options

- Specify the parameters for counter bore hole in the **Form** rollout like diameter of bigger hole, depth of bigger hole, and diameter of main drill hole.
- Click on the **Apply** button to create the hole.

Creating Countersunk Hole

- Select the **Countersunk** option from the top drop-down in the dialog box. The options will be displayed as shown in Figure-20.

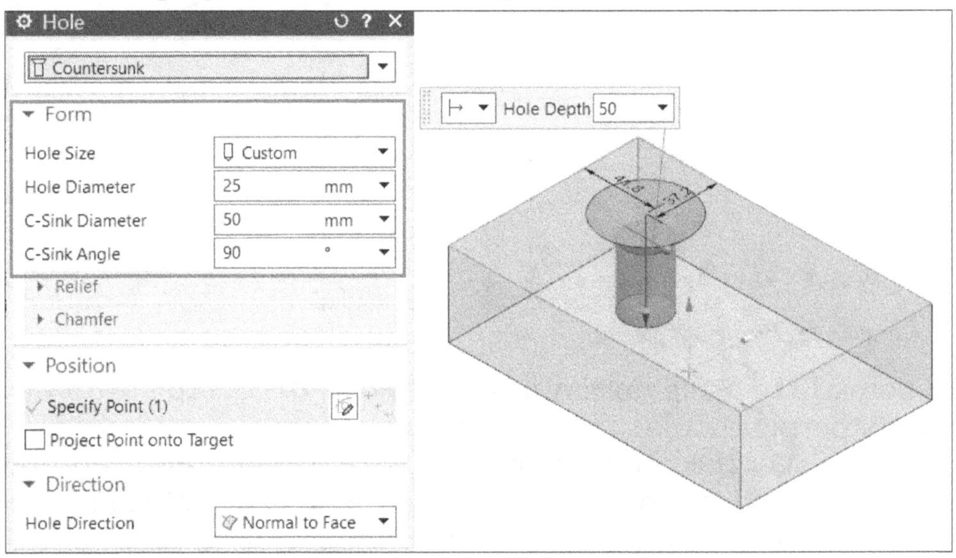

Figure-20. Countersunk hole options

- Set the parameters as discussed earlier and click on the **Apply** button to create the hole.

Creating Tapered Hole

- Select the **Tapered** option from the drop-down at the top in the dialog box. The options will be displayed as shown in Figure-21.

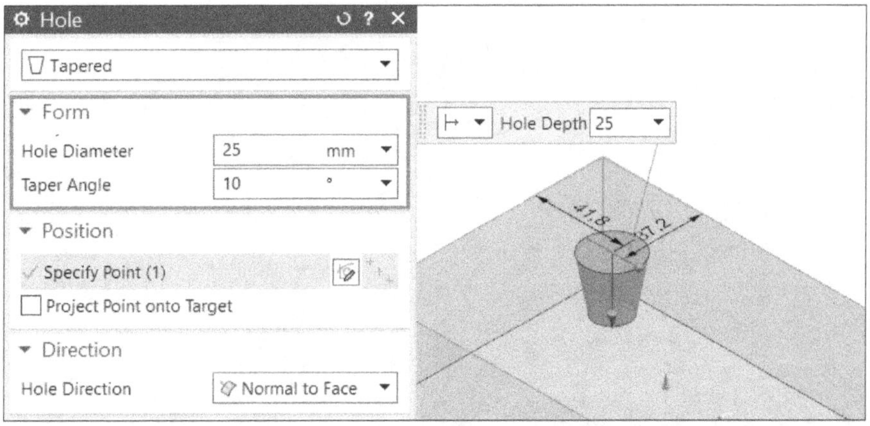

Figure-21. Tapered Hole options

- Specify the diameter of hole and taper angle in respective edit boxes. Set the other parameters as discussed earlier and click on the **Apply** button to create the hole.

Creating Threaded Hole

- Select the **Threaded** option from the drop-down at the top in the dialog box. The options will be displayed as shown in Figure-22.

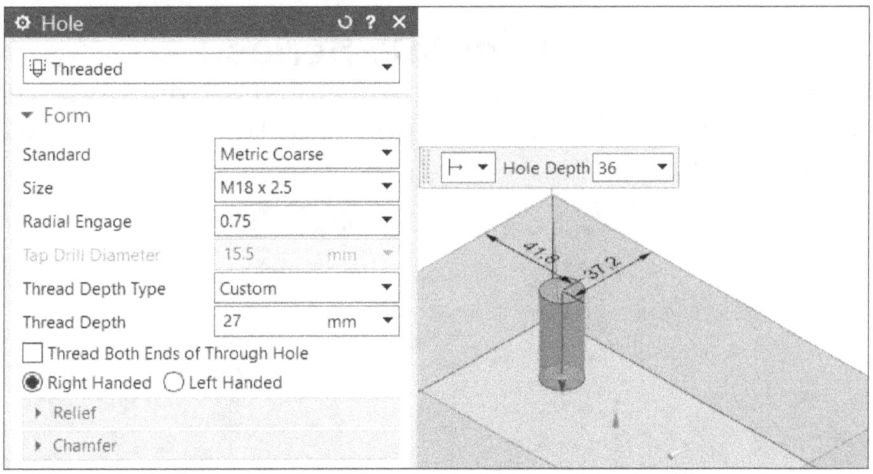

Figure-22. Threaded Hole options

- Specify desired value in **Size** drop-down to define the diameter and thread depth of the hole.
- Specify desired value in the **Radial Engage** drop-down to determine the tap drill diameter in percentage of thread depth of fastener. The higher the value specified in radial engage, the deeper will be the threads in solid. Select the **Custom** option from the drop-down to specify the value of tap drill diameter manually in the **Tap Drill Diameter** edit box.
- Specify desired value in the **Thread Depth** edit box to define depth of hole upto which threads will be created.
- Select the **Thread Both Ends of Through Hole** check box to create threads on both ends of through hole by specified thread depth value.
- Select the **Right Handed** or **Left Handed** radio button from the **Form** rollout to create respective type of thread.
- Expand the **Relief** sub-rollout and select the **Apply Relief** check box to create a small recess hole of specified diameter and depth.
- Select the **Relief Chamfer** check box to add extra relief chamfer in the hole; refer to Figure-23.

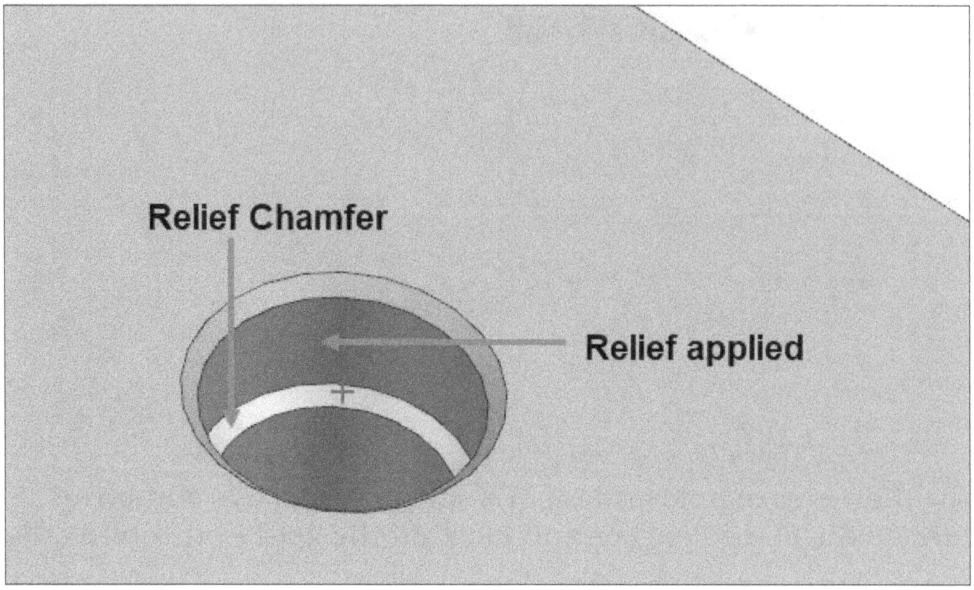

Figure-23. Relief applied to threaded hole

- Set the parameters as discussed earlier and click on the **Apply** button to create the hole.

Creating Hole Series

- Select the **Hole Series** option from the drop-down at the top in the dialog box to create a series of multiform holes. The options in the dialog box will be displayed as shown in Figure-24.

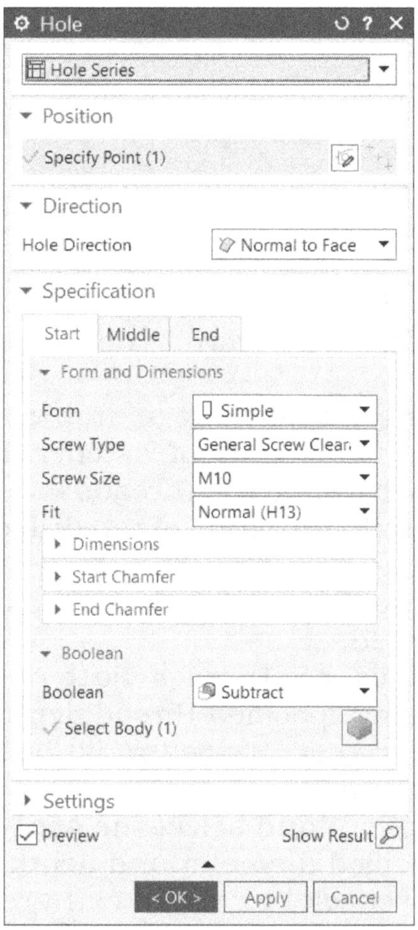

Figure-24. Hole Series options

- Specify the parameters of hole in **Start** tab of **Specification** rollout to define the shape and size of starting section of hole.
- Click on the **Middle** tab of **Specification** rollout to define fit parameter for middle section of hole.
- Click on the **End** tab to specify form and fit parameters for hole at the end section.
- Click at desired locations on the solid part to place holes; refer to Figure-25.
- After setting desired parameters, click on the **OK** button from the dialog box to create the holes and exit the dialog box.

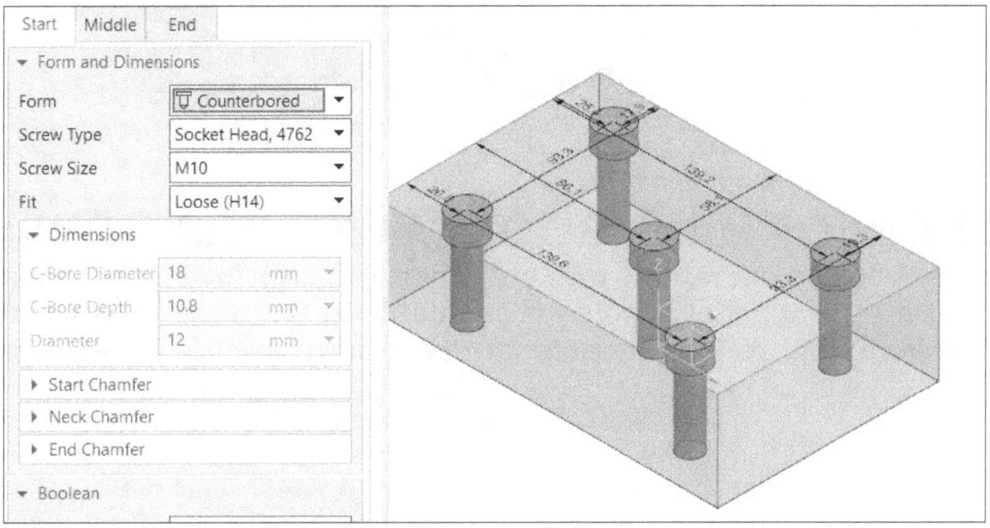

Figure-25. Preview of hole series

CREATING MULTI-BODY PART

Generally, a single body is generated after performing various modeling operations to get a single part. But sometimes, a multi-body part operation can significantly reduce the modeling time of a part. For example, when generating core and cavity of a part to be molded, it is much faster to generate the core and cavity by subtracting the part from rectangular blocks. The procedure to create a multi-body part is given next.

- Create an extrude/revolve base feature as discussed earlier.
- Create another solid feature and make sure the **None** option is selected from the **Boolean** drop-down of **Boolean** rollout in feature dialog box; refer to Figure-26. Similarly, you can create as many bodies as needed and then perform boolean operations.

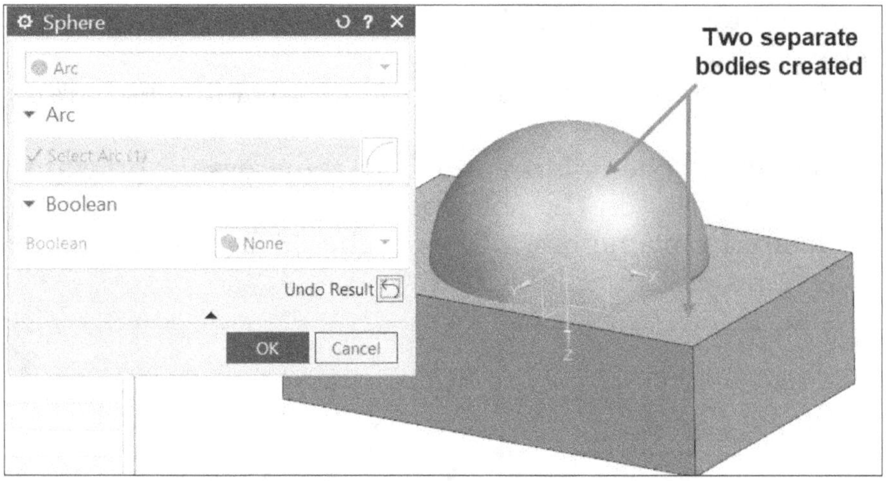

Figure-26. Creating multi-bodies

PERFORMING BOOLEAN OPERATIONS

There are three boolean operations that are generally performed on solid bodies: unite, subtract, and intersect. These tools are available in the **Base** group of **Home** tab in the **Ribbon**; refer to Figure-27. The procedures to use these tools are discussed next.

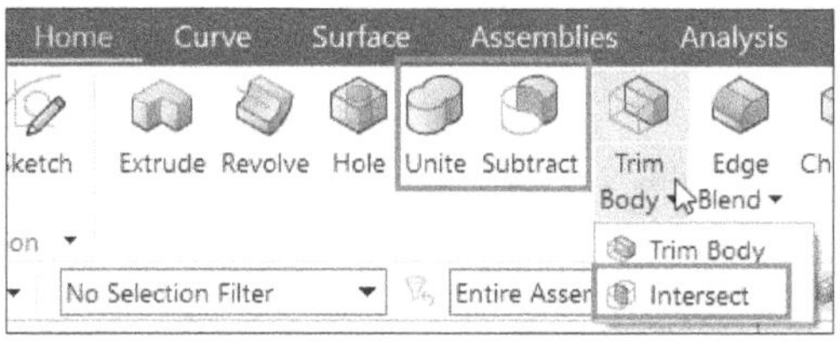

Figure-27. Boolean tools

Uniting Bodies

The **Unite** tool is used to combine two or more contacting bodies into a single body. The procedure to use this tool is given next.

- Click on the **Unite** tool from the **Base** group in the **Home** tab of the **Ribbon**. The **Unite** dialog box will be displayed; refer to Figure-28.

Figure-28. Unite dialog box

- Select the first body which is the main body from graphics area. You will be asked to select the tool body.
- Select the other body(s) which you want to combine with main body; refer to Figure-29.

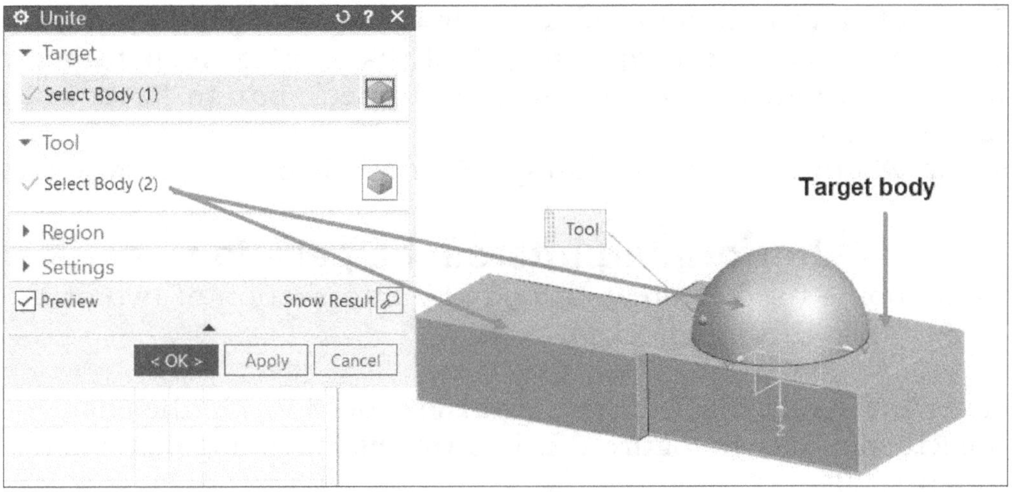

Figure-29. Selecting target and tool body

- Click on the **OK** button to create the combined body.

Subtracting One Body from Another

The **Subtract** tool is used to remove volume of one body from another body. The procedure to use this tool is given next.

- Click on the **Subtract** tool from the **Base** group in **Home** tab of the **Ribbon**. The **Subtract** dialog box will be displayed; refer to Figure-30.

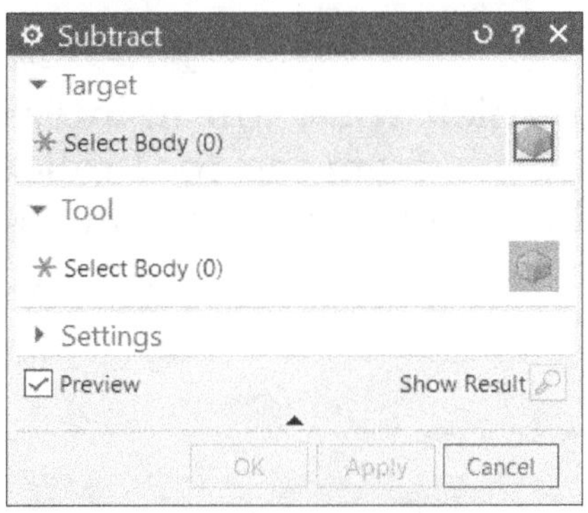

Figure-30. Subtract dialog box

- Select the target body from which other body will be subtracted.
- Click on the **Select Body** selection button from the **Tool** rollout in the dialog box and select the body to be used as tool. Preview of subtract operation will be displayed; refer to Figure-31.

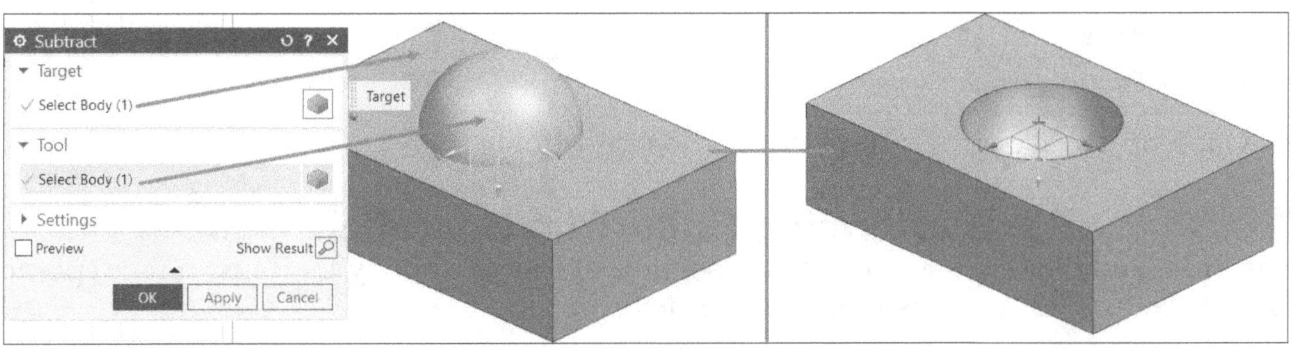

Figure-31. Subtract preview

- Expand the **Settings** rollout to define which bodies are to be kept after performing the operation. Select the **Keep Target** check box to keep target body after performing operation. Select the **Keep Tool** check box to keep tool body after performing operation.
- Click on the **OK** button from the dialog box to perform the operation.

Performing Intersect Operation

The **Intersect** tool is used to create a body by intersection of two or more bodies. The procedure to use this tool is given next.

- Click on the **Intersect** tool from the **Combine** drop-down in the **Base** group of **Home** tab in the **Ribbon**; refer to Figure-32. The **Intersect** dialog box will be displayed; refer to Figure-33.

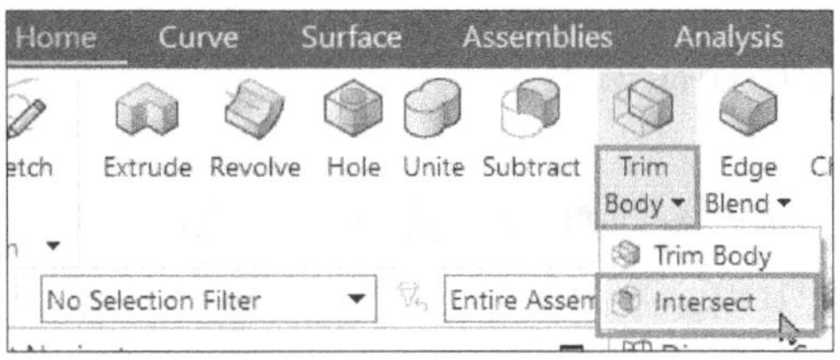

Figure-32. Intersect tool

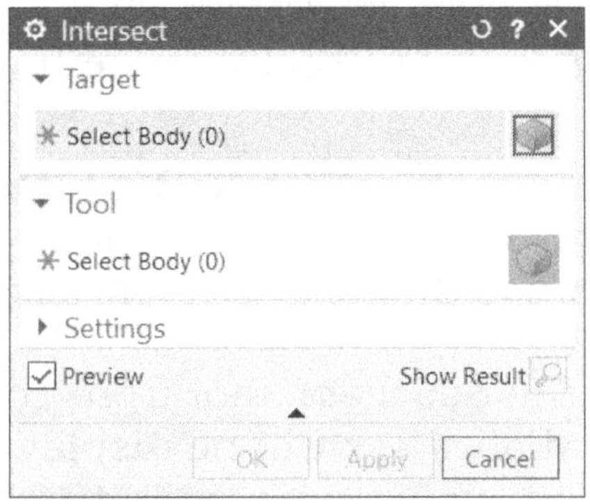

Figure-33. Intersect dialog box

- Select the main body with which you want to intersect other body(s).
- Click on the **Select Body** button from the **Tool** rollout and select the body(s) from graphics area. Preview of intersect operation will be displayed; refer to Figure-34.

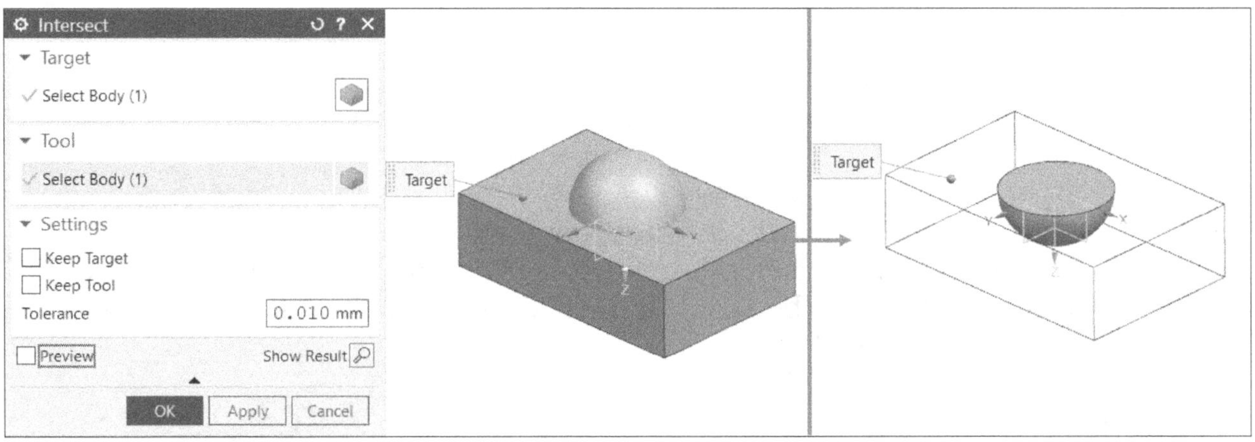

Figure-34. Preview of intersect feature

- Click on the **OK** button to perform the operation.

Performing Body Trim Operation

The **Trim Body** tool is used to remove section of the solid body by using a face/plane. The procedure to use this tool is given next.

- Click on the **Trim Body** tool from the **Combine** drop-down in the **Base** group of **Home** tab in the **Ribbon**. The **Trim Body** dialog box will be displayed; refer to Figure-35.

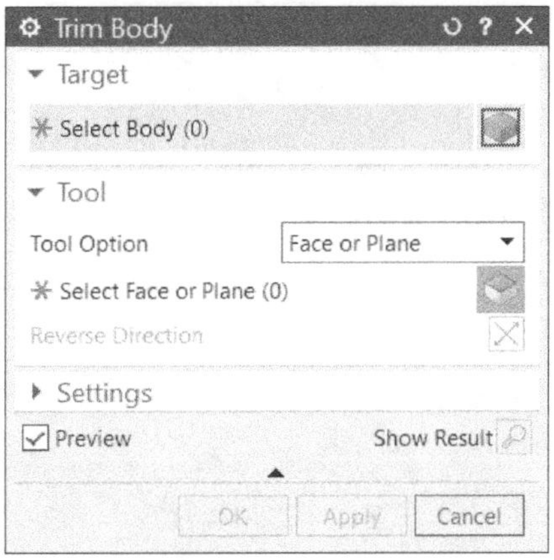

Figure-35. Trim Body dialog box

- Select the body which you want to trim from the graphics area.
- Click on the **Select Face or Plane** button from the **Tool** rollout and select the face or plane to be used as tool for trimming. Preview of the operation will be displayed; refer to Figure-36.

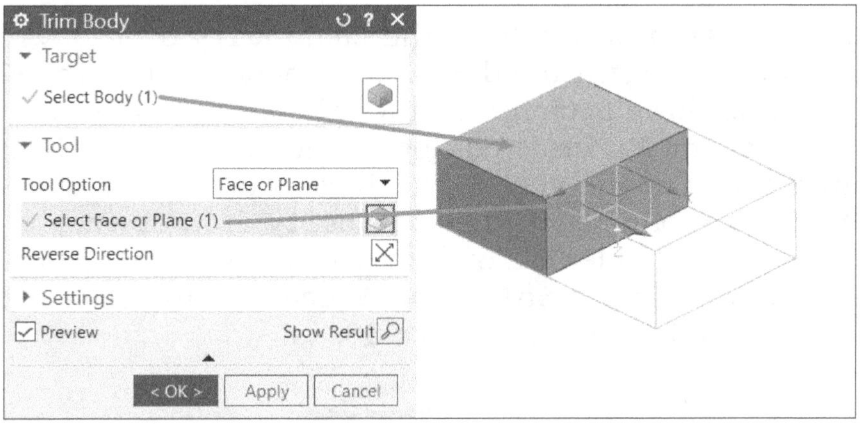

Figure-36. Preview of trimming body

- Set the other parameters as discussed earlier and click on the **OK** button. The trimmed body will be generated.

CREATING EDGE BLEND OPERATION

The **Edge Blend** tool is used to apply fillet at the sharp edges of the model. The procedure to use this tool is given next.

- Click on the **Edge Blend** tool from the **Blend** drop-down of **Base** group in the **Home** tab of the **Ribbon**. The **Edge Blend** dialog box will be displayed; refer to Figure-37.

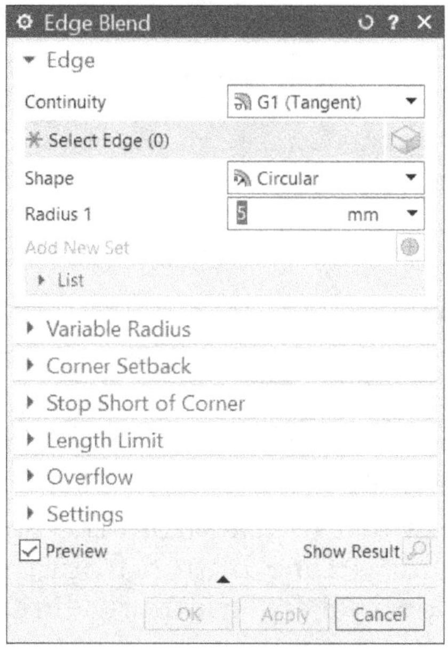

Figure-37. Edge Blend dialog box

- Select the **G1 (Tangent)** option from the **Continuity** drop-down to create fillet which has curvature tangent to edges of the model. Select the **G2 (Curvature)** option from the drop-down to create fillet which follows curvature of nearby edges.
- Set desired value in the **Radius 1** edit box to define radius of fillet.
- Specify desired value in the **Rho 1** edit box to determine shape of fillet if **G2 (Curvature)** option is selected in the **Continuity** drop-down.
- Select the edges to apply blend. You can select desired selection filter from the **Curve Rule** drop-down in the **Selection Scene Bar** to select respective type of geometry from the model; refer to Figure-38.

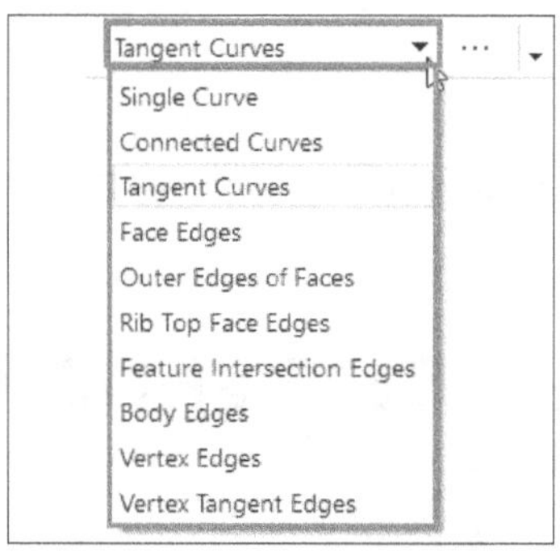

Figure-38. Curve Rule drop-down

- Expand the **Variable Radius** rollout if you want to define different radii of fillet at different points on the edge and click on the **Select Radius Point** selection button. You will be asked to select point on the edge to define variable radius point; refer to Figure-39.

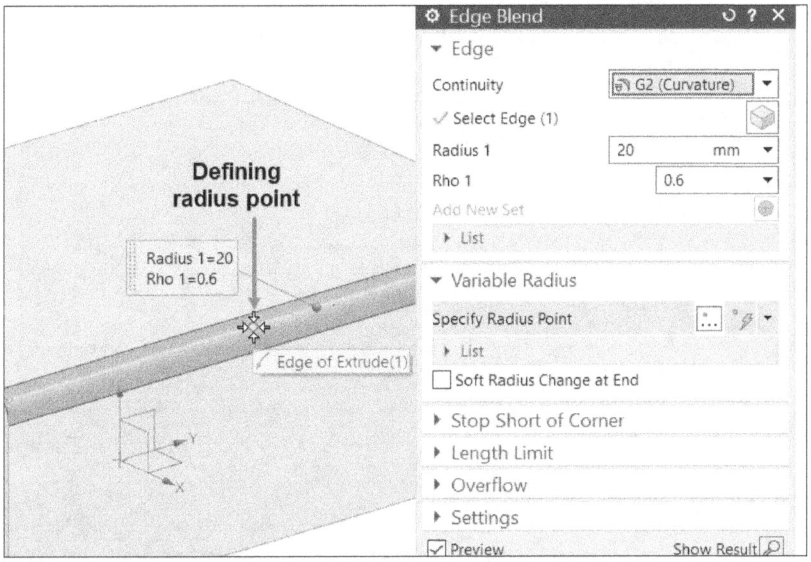

Figure-39. Defining radius point

- Click at desired location on the edge. Input boxes will be displayed to specify radius at the point; refer to Figure-40. Specify desired parameters in the input box and similarly create other radius points.

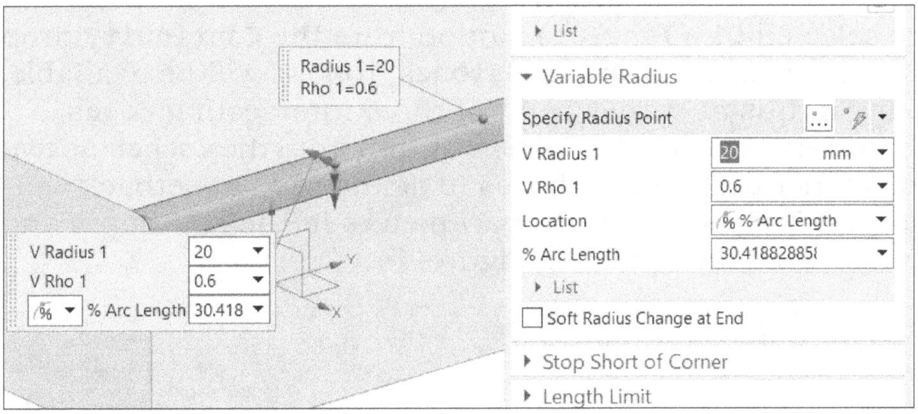

Figure-40. Input boxes for specifying radius

- Expand the **List** node in **Variable Radius** rollout and select desired radius point to modify the parameters, if needed.
- Select the **Soft Radius Change at End** check box to smoothly change the radius at end points of the edge.
- Expand the **Stop Short of Corner** rollout to define parameters for defining end point of radius if you do not want to create radius at full edge. Click on the **Select End Point** selection button from the rollout and click at desired corner point to be moved. An input box will be displayed for specifying arc length; refer to Figure-41.
- Specify desired parameters in the drop-downs of the rollout and press **TAB**. Preview of short corner will be displayed; refer to Figure-42.

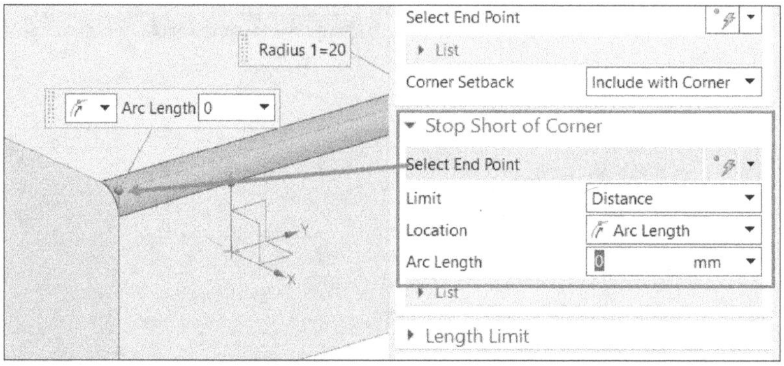

Figure-41. End point selected

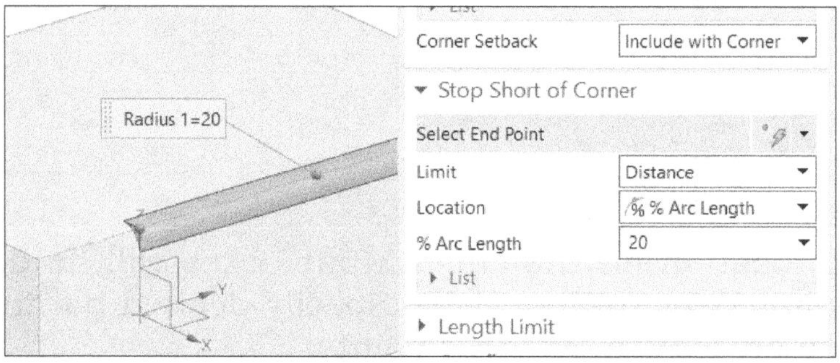

Figure-42. Short corner preview

- If you have selected **G1 (Tangent)** option from the **Continuity** drop-down at the top in the dialog box then **Corner Setback** rollout will be available in the dialog box to modify radius at corner point of three intersecting edges.
- Click on the **Select End Point** selection button from the **Corner Setback** rollout and click on the corner point. Input boxes to define radii at setback will be displayed; refer to Figure-43. Specify desired parameters in the edit boxes and press **TAB** to check preview of setback; refer to Figure-44.

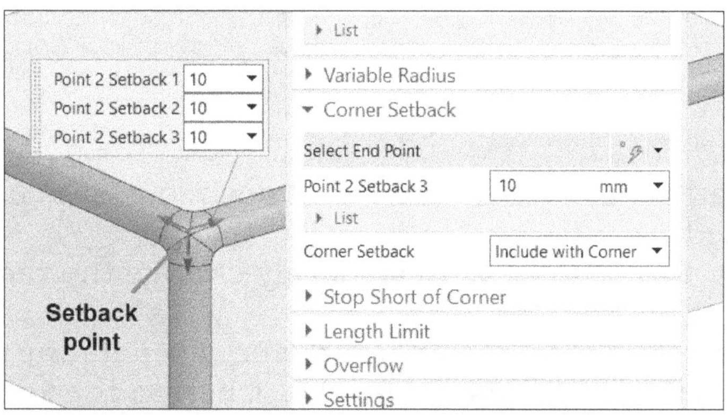

Figure-43. Defining setback point parameters

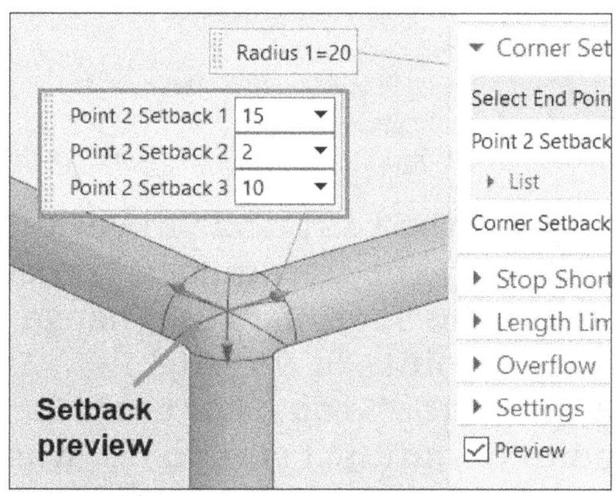

Figure-44. Preview of setback

- Expand the **Length Limit** rollout to define the plane for trimming edge blend and set the parameters as discussed earlier; refer to Figure-45.
- The options in **Overflow** rollout are used to define how edge blend overflow is controlled when selected tangent edge encounters other edge on the model.
- Expand the **Settings** rollout to define advanced parameters of edge blend; refer to Figure-46.

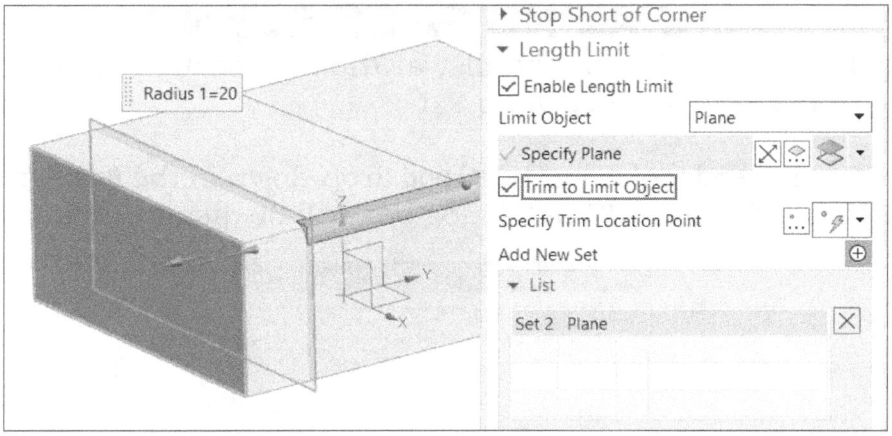

Figure-45. Setting length limit

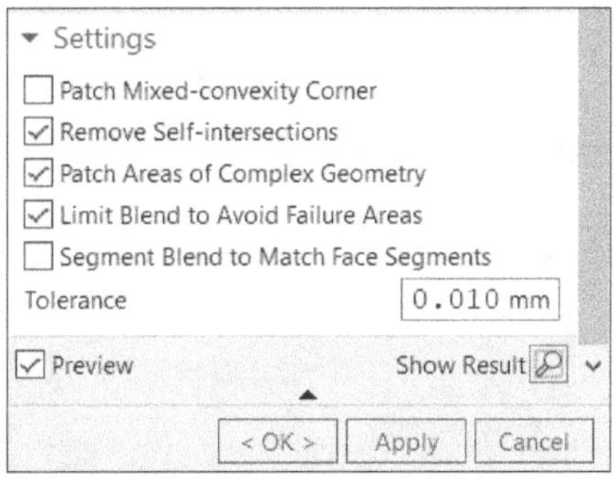

Figure-46. Settings rollout

- Select the **Patch Mixed-convexity Corner** check box to automatically patch edge blends at corners when convexity is applied; refer to Figure-47.

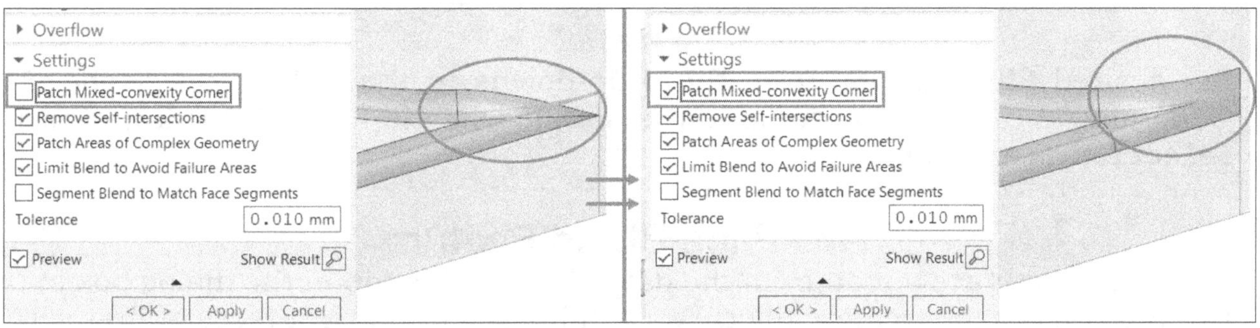

Figure-47. Patching mixed convexity

- Select the **Remove Self-intersections** check box to remove the self-intersection of feature after creating blend feature.
- Select the **Patch Areas of Complex Geometry** check box to automatically patch small segments of edges which may fail due to complex curvature.
- Select the **Limit Blend to Avoid Failure Areas** check box to stop the blend creation upto the point where it starts failing due to complex curvature even after using patches.
- Select the **Segment Blend to Match Face Segments** check box to create blend segments matching with number of face segments in the model.
- Set the other parameters as discussed earlier and click on the **OK** button.

CREATING FACE BLEND

The **Face Blend** tool is used to apply fillet at the intersection of two or more faces. The procedure to use this tool is given next.

- Click on the **Face Blend** tool from the **Blend** drop-down in the **Base** group of the **Home** tab in the **Ribbon**. The **Face Blend** dialog box will be displayed; refer to Figure-48.

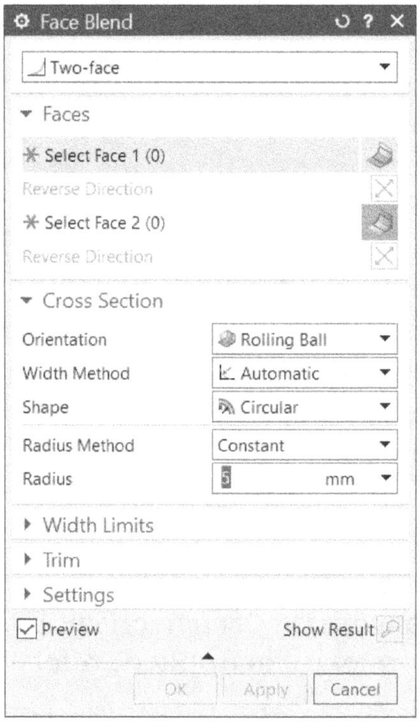

Figure-48. Face Blend dialog box

- Set desired filter options from the drop-downs in the **Selection Scene Bar**. Generally, the **Single Face** option is selected in the **Face Rule** drop-down of **Selection Scene Bar**.

Two-Face Blend Feature

- Select the **Two-face** option from the drop-down at the top in the dialog box to use two set of faces for creating fillet. You will be asked to select faces of first set.
- Click on the first set of faces and click on the **Select Face 2** selection button. You will be asked to select second set of faces.
- Select the faces of second set from the drawing area. Preview of blend will be displayed; refer to Figure-49.

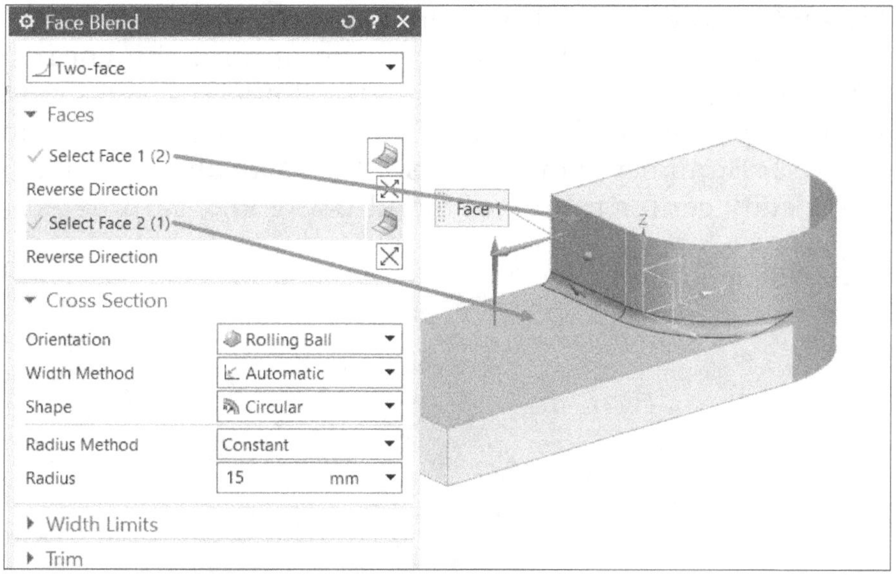

Figure-49. Preview of two face blend

- By default, the **Rolling Ball** option is selected in the **Orientation** drop-down to use an imaginary ball of specified radius as reference with center of ball lying at center place of selected edge. Select the **Swept Disc** option from the **Orientation** drop-down to define the curve to be used as reference center of blend; refer to Figure-50.

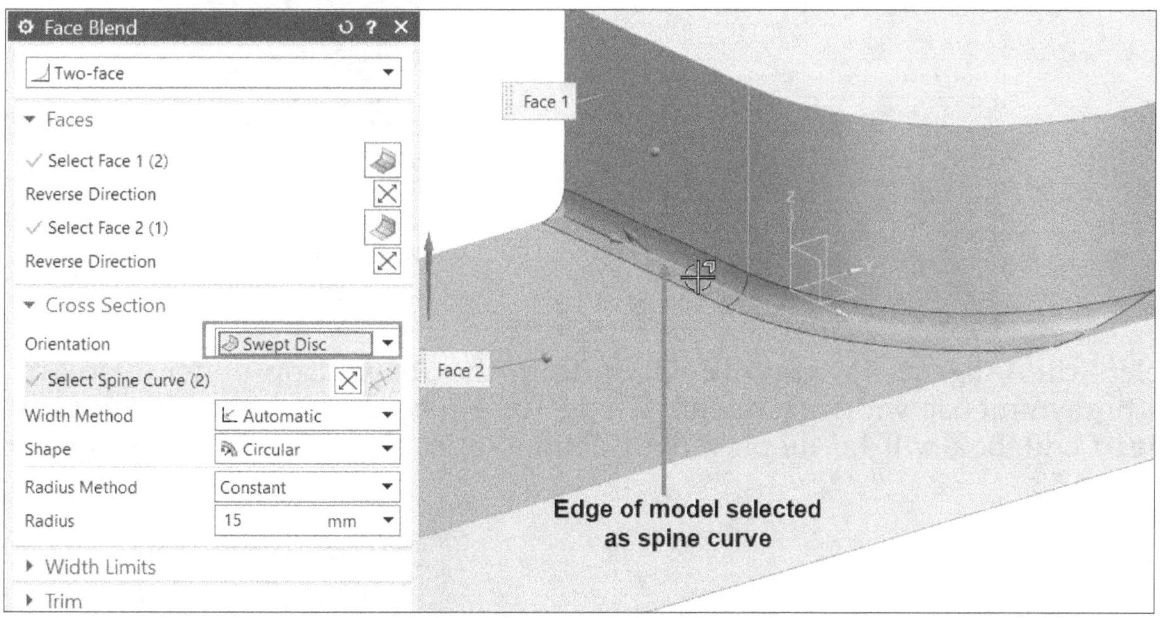

Figure-50. Spine curve selected for face blend

- Select the **Automatic** option from the **Width Method** drop-down to automatically select the method for deciding width of blend. Select the **Constant** option from the drop-down to set uniform width of blend along selected edges. Select the **Contact Curve** option from the drop-down to use two selected edges as reference for defining blend width.
- Select desired option from the **Shape** drop-down to define shape of blend. Select **Circular** option from the drop-down to create a symmetric circular blend with same width and shape along the edge.

- Select the **Tangent Symmetric** option from the drop-down to create blend with its edges tangent at end points. On selecting this option, the **Conic Method** drop-down is displayed; refer to Figure-51. Select the **Boundary and Center** option from the drop-down to specify the different values for center radius and blend width; refer to Figure-52. Similarly, you can use the **Boundary and Rho** option in this drop-down to specify center radius of blend using **Rho** parameter.

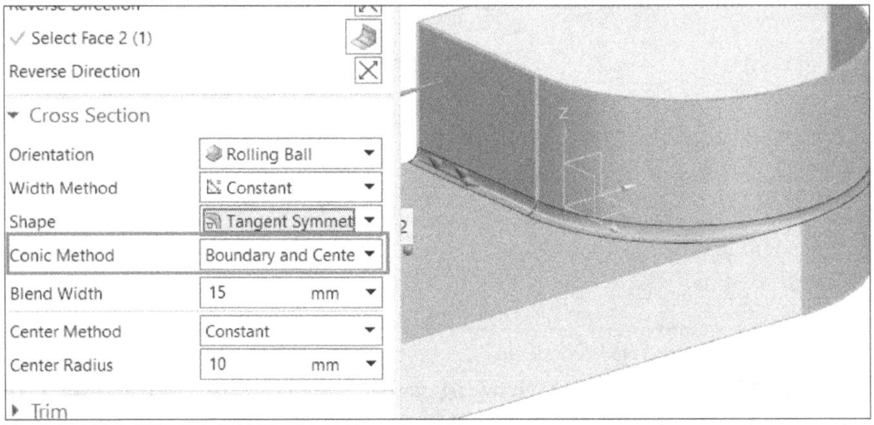

Figure-51. Conic Method drop-down

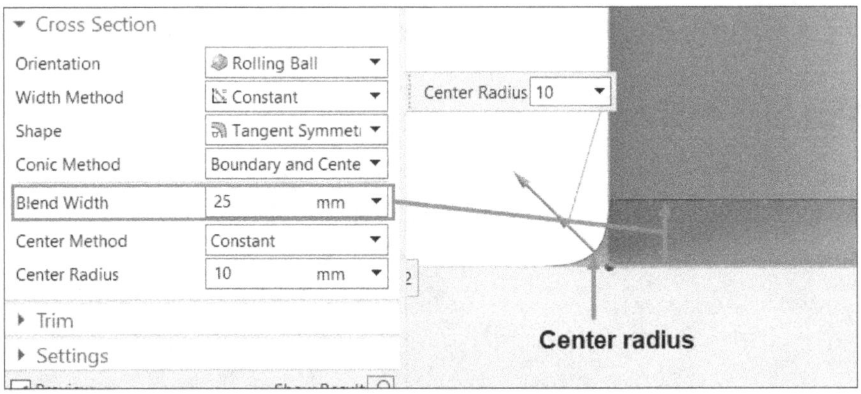

Figure-52. Specifying blend width and center radius

- Select the **Tangent Asymmetric** option from the **Shape** drop-down to create blend with asymmetric width from center edge of selected face sets. The **Offset Skew Ratio** edit box will be displayed to define ratio of widths from center; refer to Figure-53.

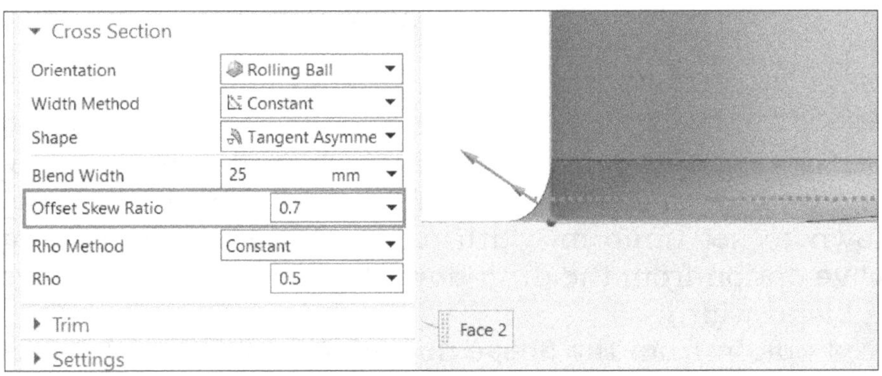

Figure-53. Specifying offset skew ratio

- Select the **Curvature Symmetric** option from the **Shape** drop-down to create blend which follows curvature of faces and is equal in width with respect to center edge of selected face sets. Select desired option from the **Depth Law Type** drop-down to define how depth will be defined and then specify depth values in related edit box(es) displayed below the drop-down.
- Similarly, you can use the **Curvature Asymmetric** option from the **Shape** drop-down to create curvature following blend with different width sides.
- Expand the **Trim** rollout to define limits of blend feature. The options will be displayed as shown in Figure-54. Select the **To All** option from the **Trim Blend** drop-down to trim the blends at start and end points of edge. Select the **To Short** option from the **Trim Blend** drop-down to stop the blend at the edge which is not extended by tangent or other progression. Select the **To Long** option from the drop-down to keep blend upto full selected edge. Select the **None** option from the drop-down to keep the blend untrimmed.
- Select the **Trim Body to Blend** check box to automatically trim the body as well based on requirement of blend.
- Select the **Trim Long Input Faces to Extended Rail** check box to automatically trim input faces for extending blend.
- Select the **Sew All Faces** check box to connect faces/surfaces after applying blend.

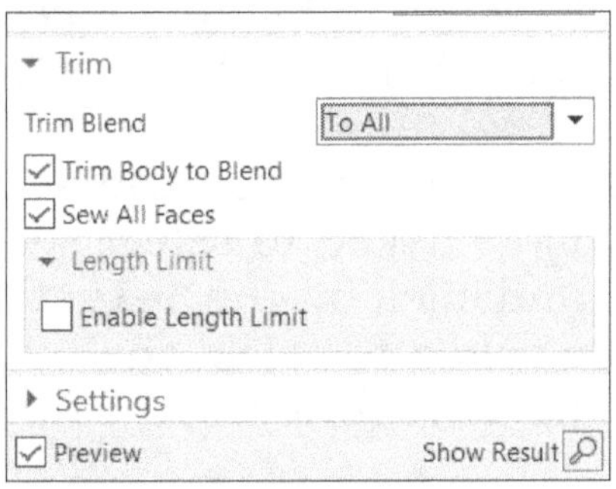

Figure-54. Trim rollout options

- Expand the **Settings** rollout to specify advanced settings of blend feature.
- Select the **Enable Length Limit** check box to use a plane/face/point as limit for creating blend.
- Select the **Blend across Tangent Edges** check box to extend blend across tangent edges.
- Select the **Blend across Sharp Edges** check box to extend blend across connected sharp edges.
- Select the **Terminate at Sharp Edge** check box to restrict blend upto next sharp edge in the path.
- Select the **Remove Self-intersections** check box to remove the portions of blend which self-intersect to avoid failure of feature.
- After setting desired parameters, click on the **Apply** button to create blend feature.

Creating Three-Face Blend

- Select the **Three-face** option from top drop-down in the **Face Blend** dialog box to create a round by using two wall faces and one floor face. The options in the dialog box will be displayed as shown in Figure-55.

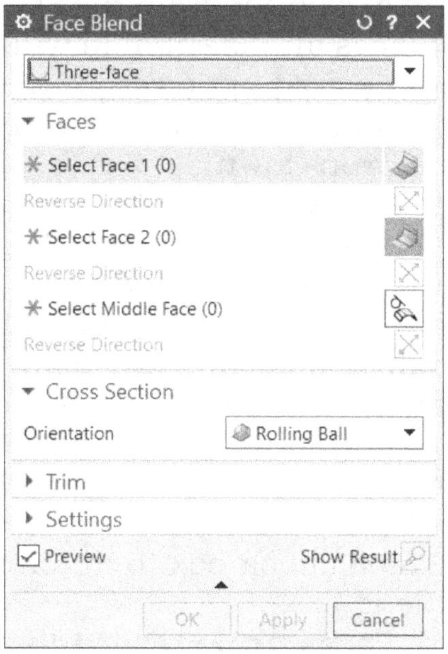

Figure-55. Three-face blend options

- Select the **Single Face** option from the **Face Rule** drop-down in the **Selection Scene Bar** of drawing area to select individual faces. By default, the **Select Face 1** selection button will be active in the dialog box and you will be asked to select first wall face.
- Select the first wall face and then click on the **Select Face 2** selection button from the dialog box. You will be asked to select second wall face.
- Select the face from model and click on the **Select Middle Face** selection button from dialog box. You will be asked to select the mid face joining two wall faces.
- Select desired face from the model. Preview of the three face blend will be displayed; refer to Figure-56.

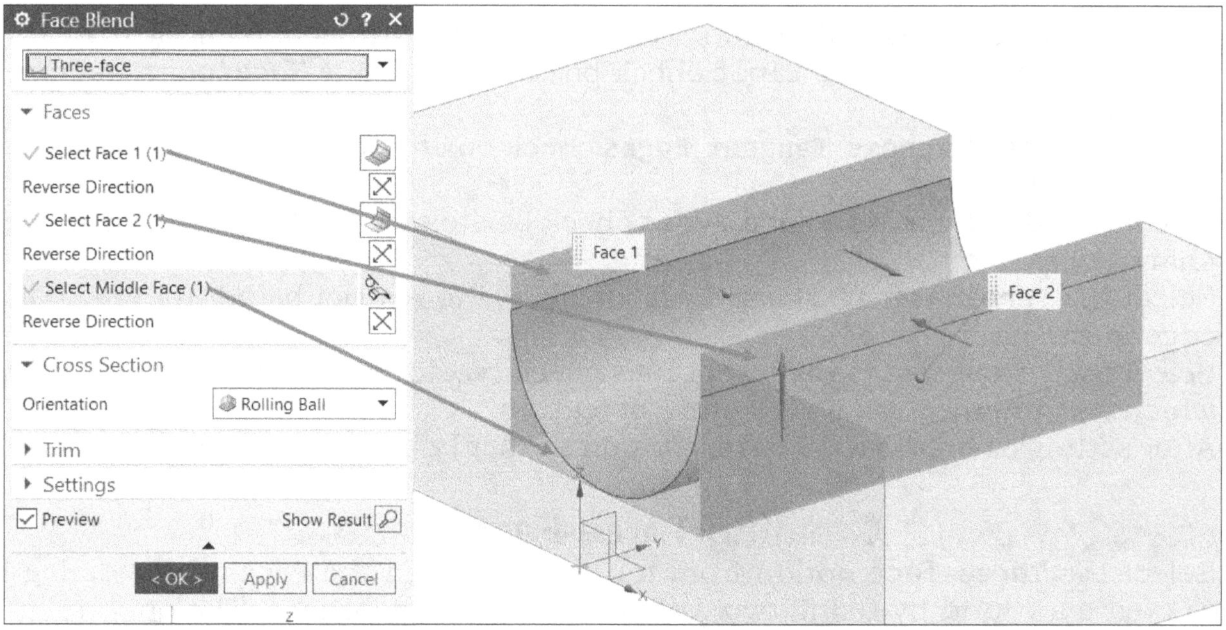

Figure-56. Preview of three face blend

- Set the other parameters as discussed earlier and click on the **Apply** button from the dialog box to create the feature.

Creating Blend at Feature Intersection

- Select the **Feature Intersection Edge** option from the drop-down at the top in the dialog box to create blend at edge on intersection of two features. The options will be displayed as shown in Figure-57.

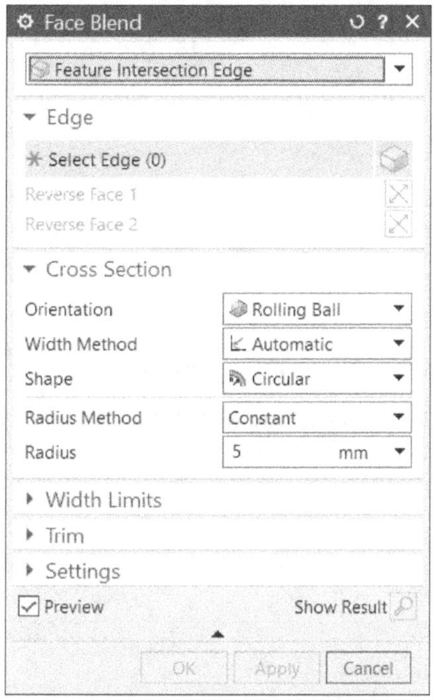

Figure-57. Feature intersection edge blend options

- By default, the **Feature Intersection Edges** option will be selected in the **Curve Rule** drop-down of **Selection Scene Bar** in graphics area and you will be asked to select the face of intersecting feature.
- Select desired feature face from graphics area. Preview of blend feature will be displayed; refer to Figure-58.
- Set the other parameters as discussed earlier and click on the **OK** button to create the feature.

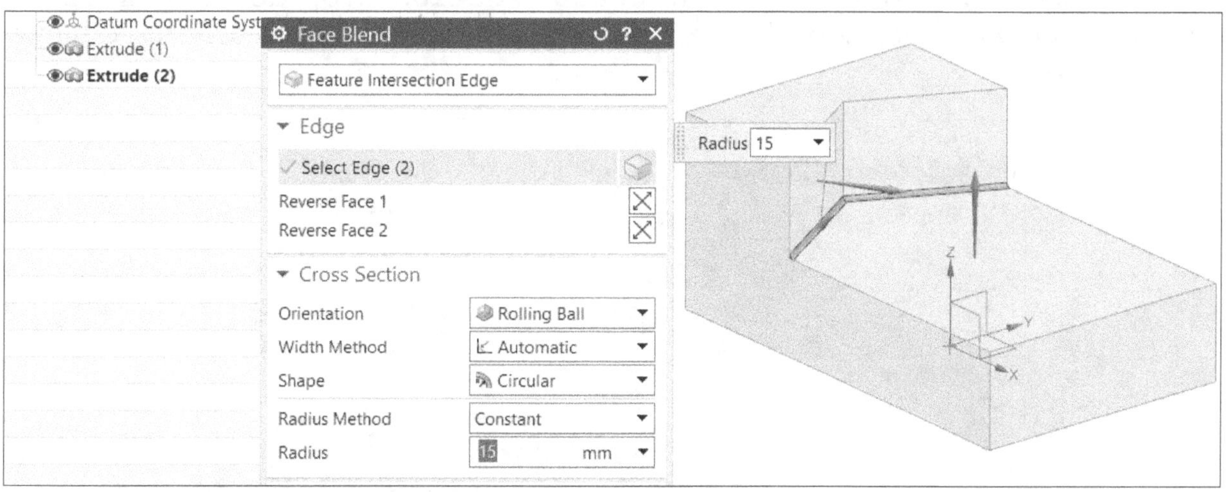

Figure-58. Preview of feature intersection edge blend

CREATING CHAMFER

The **Chamfer** tool is used to bevel sharp edges of the model. The procedure to use this tool is given next.

- Click on the **Chamfer** tool from the **Base** group in the **Home** tab of the **Ribbon**. The **Chamfer** dialog box will be displayed; refer to Figure-59.

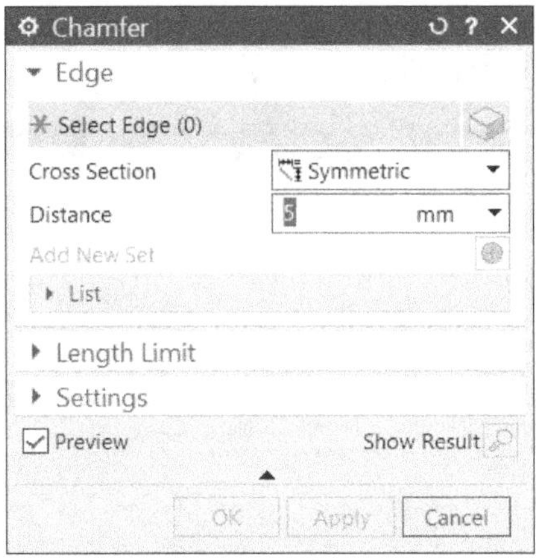

Figure-59. Chamfer dialog box

- Select the edges of the model to check preview of chamfer; refer to Figure-60.

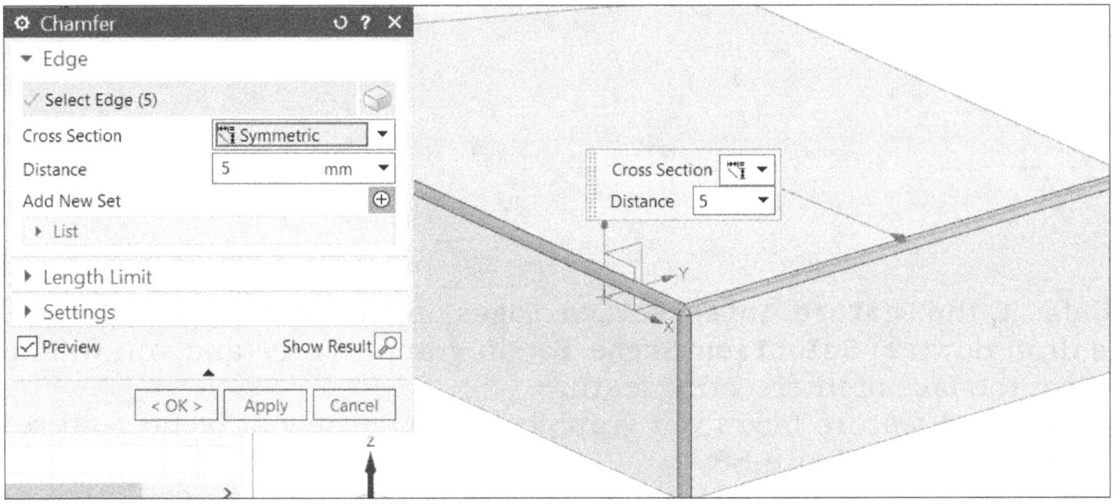

Figure-60. Preview of chamfer

- Select **Symmetric** option from the **Cross Section** drop-down to keep equal distances between horizontal & vertical edges of chamfer from original edge; refer to Figure-61.

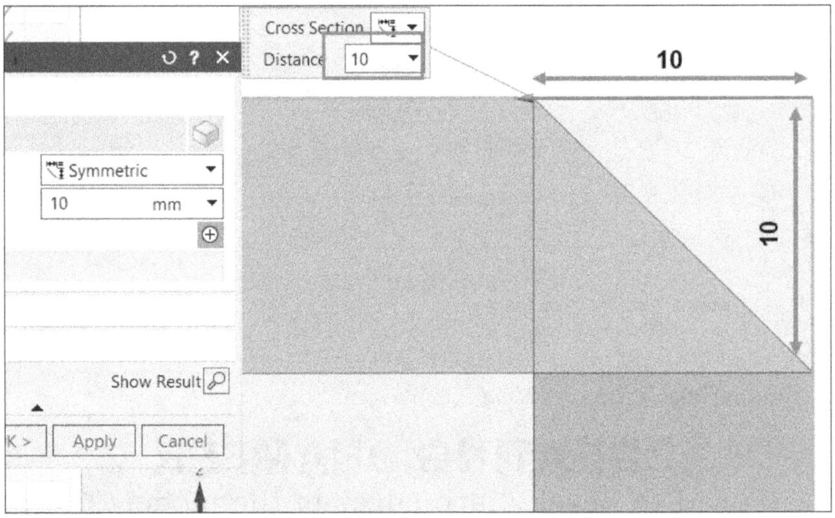

Figure-61. Symmetric chamfer

- Select the **Asymmetric** option from the **Cross Section** drop-down to specify different horizontal and vertical distances of the chamfer; refer to Figure-62.

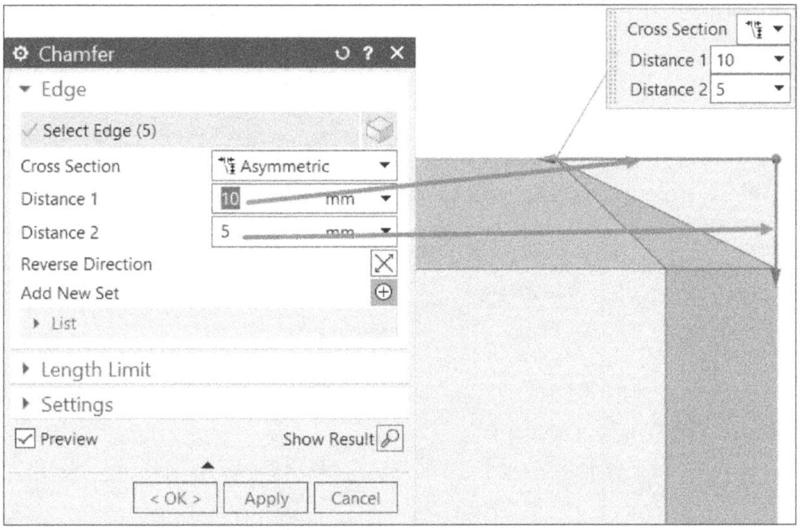

Figure-62. Asymmetric chamfer preview

- Select the **Offset and Angle** option from the **Cross Section** drop-down to specify horizontal distance of chamfer and angle of chamfer from horizontal line; refer to Figure-63.

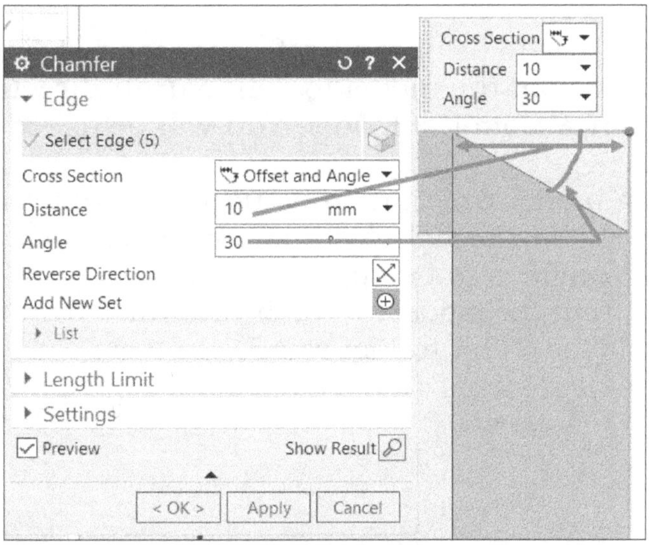

Figure-63. Chamfer with distance and angle

- Set the other parameters as discussed earlier and click on the **OK** button from the dialog box to create the chamfer(s).

APPLYING DRAFT

The **Draft** tool is used to apply taper angle to selected face(s) with respect to a fixed reference. Applying draft is useful in easy extraction of casting and forging components. You can apply draft to the model using various methods based on selection references like face, edge, parting edge, and so on. The procedure to use this tool is given next.

- Click on the **Draft** tool from the **Base** group in the **Home** tab of the **Ribbon**. The **Draft** dialog box will be displayed; refer to Figure-64.

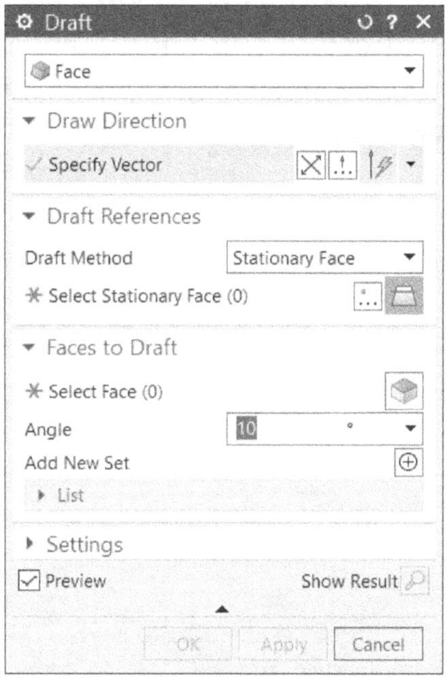

Figure-64. Draft dialog box

Applying Draft using Face Option

- Select the **Face** option from the drop-down at the top in the dialog box to apply drafts using faces.
- Select desired axis/plane to be used as reference for defining draft angle. You can select face/edge/axis from the model to define draft direction.
- Select desired reference from the model. You will be asked to select a stationary face.
- Select the face from model which is to be used as fixed reference. Note that the draw direction should be normal to stationary face. You will be asked to select faces to which draft angle is to be applied.
- Select desired faces from the model to which you want to apply draft angle. Preview of draft will be displayed; refer to Figure-65.

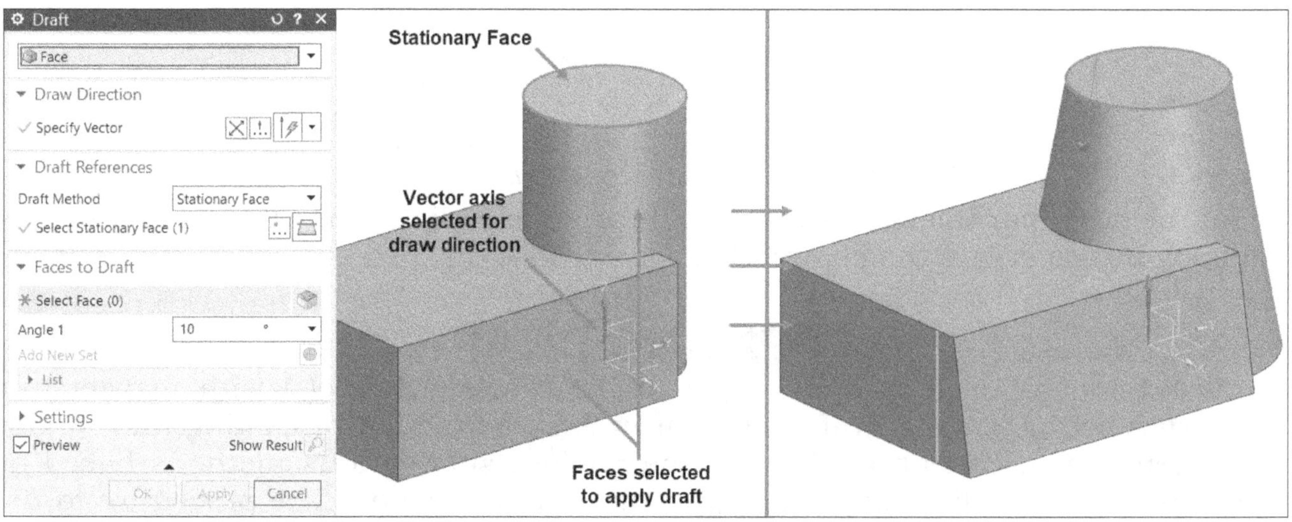

Figure-65. Preview of draft

- Specify desired value of draft angle in the **Angle 1** edit box and press **TAB**. Preview of draft will be updated accordingly. Click on the **Apply** button to create the draft.

Using Parting Face for Applying Draft

- Select the **Parting Face** option from the **Draft Method** drop-down in the **Draft References** rollout to apply draft with different angles against a face/plane dividing the face of model.
- Select the stationary face, vector, and draft faces as discussed earlier. Note that stationary face/plane should pass through the draft face(s). Preview of parting face draft will be displayed; refer to Figure-66.

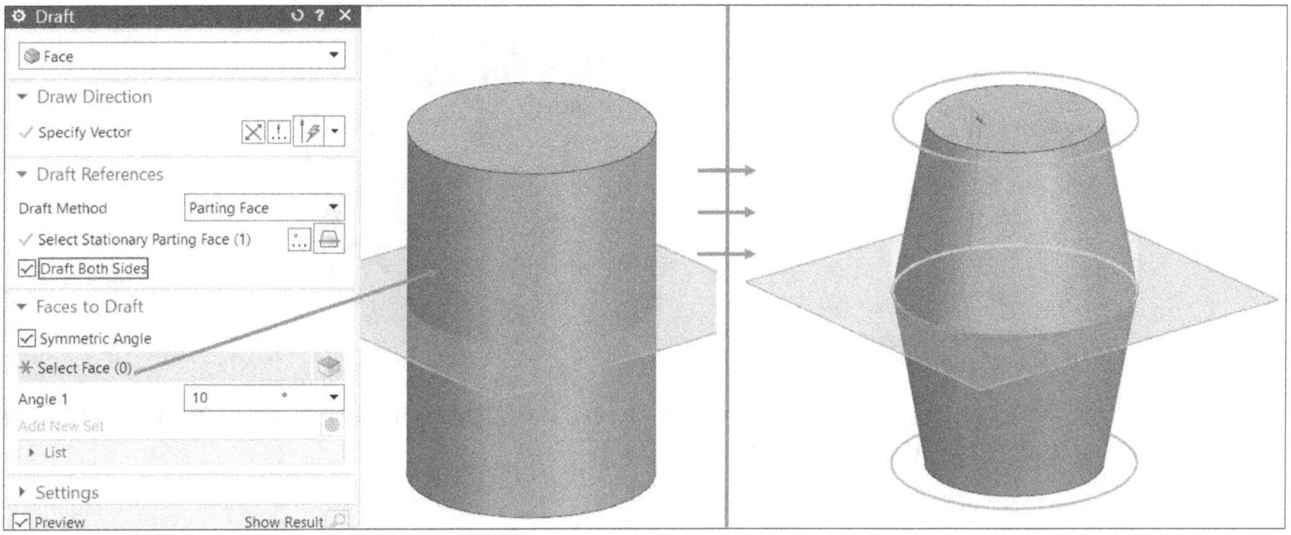

Figure-66. Preview of parting face draft

- Select the **Draft Both Sides** check box to apply draft on both sides of parting face/plane.
- Select the **Symmetric Angle** check box to apply same draft angle on both sides of parting face. Clear this check box if you want to specify different angle values for draft. The **Above Angle 1** and **Below Angle 1** edit boxes will be displayed in the **Faces to Draft** rollout.

Using Stationary and Parting Face for Applying Draft

- Select the **Stationary and Parting Face** option from the **Draft Method** drop-down to apply draft to the face upto parting face and select the faces as discussed earlier. Preview of draft will be displayed; refer to Figure-67.

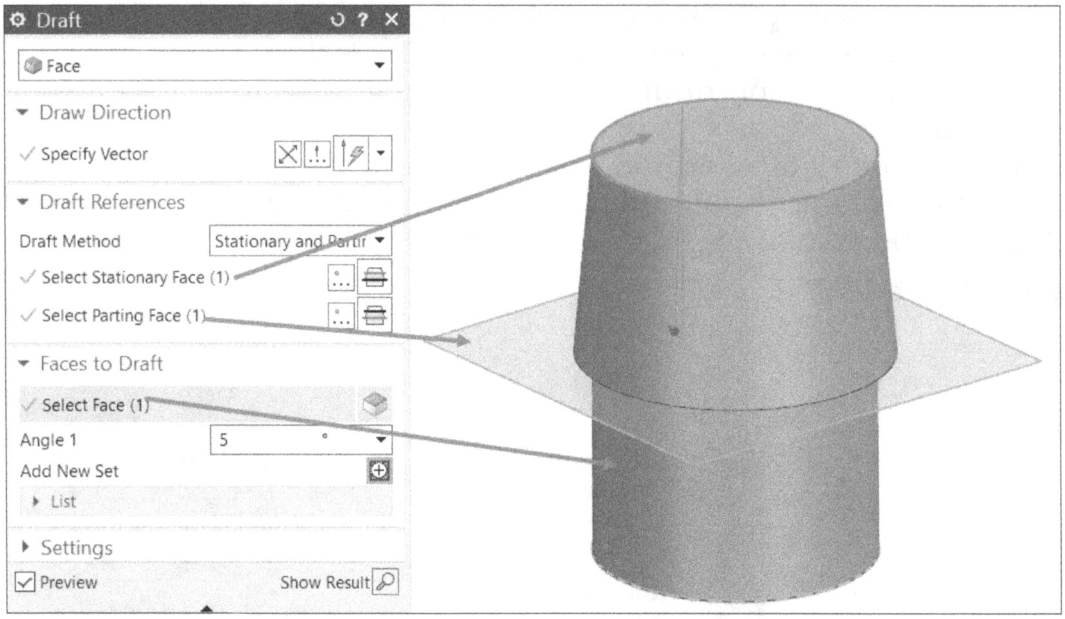

Figure-67. Preview of stationary and parting face draft

- Expand the **Settings** rollout to define advanced parameters. The options will be displayed as shown in Figure-68.

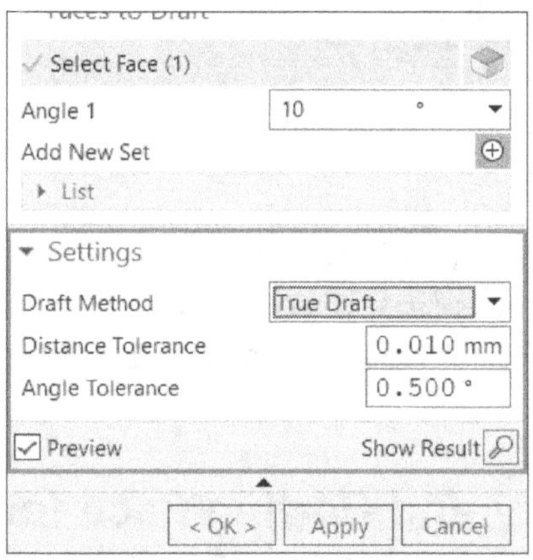

Figure-68. Settings rollout of Draft dialog box

- Select the **Isocline Draft** option from the drop-down to keep tangency angle equal to draft angle at the parting face. Select the **True Draft** option from the drop-down to keep fixed draft angle higher than the tangency angle.
- Set the other parameters as discussed earlier and click on the **Apply** button to create the draft.

Applying Draft using Edge Option

- Select the **Edge** option from the drop-down at the top in the dialog box to apply draft using edge as stationary reference. The options will be displayed as shown in Figure-69.

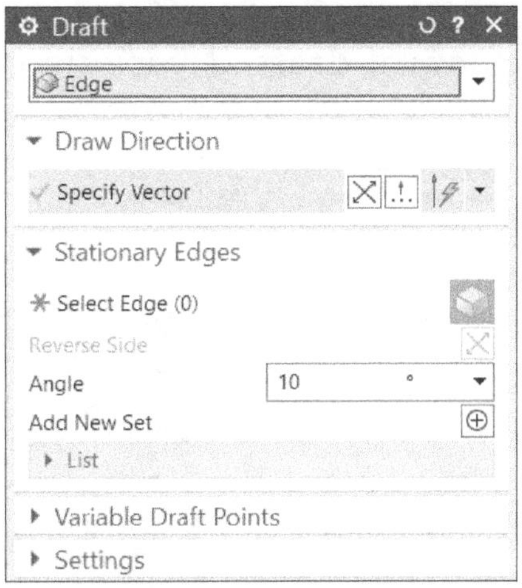

Figure-69. Edge options of Draft dialog box

- Click on the **Select Edge** selection button to select edge of model to be used as stationary reference and select the edge of model. Preview of draft will be displayed; refer to Figure-70.

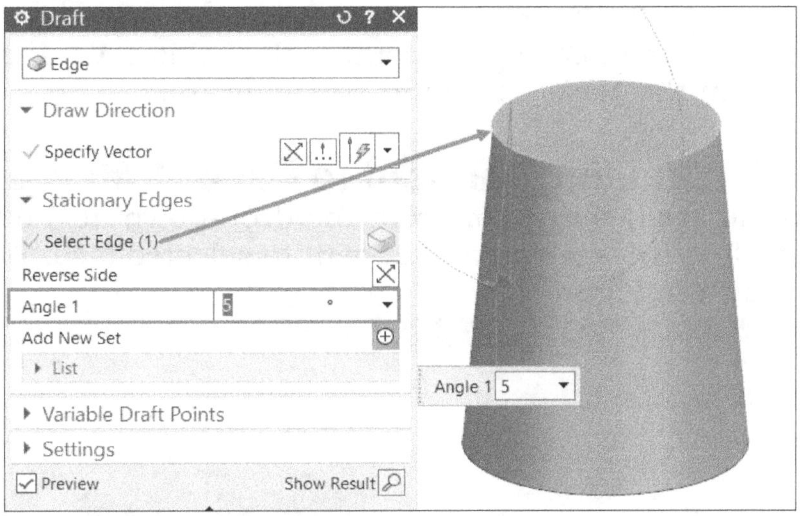

Figure-70. Preview of edge draft

- Expand the **Variable Draft Points** rollout to specify different draft values at desired points. The options will be displayed as shown in Figure-71.

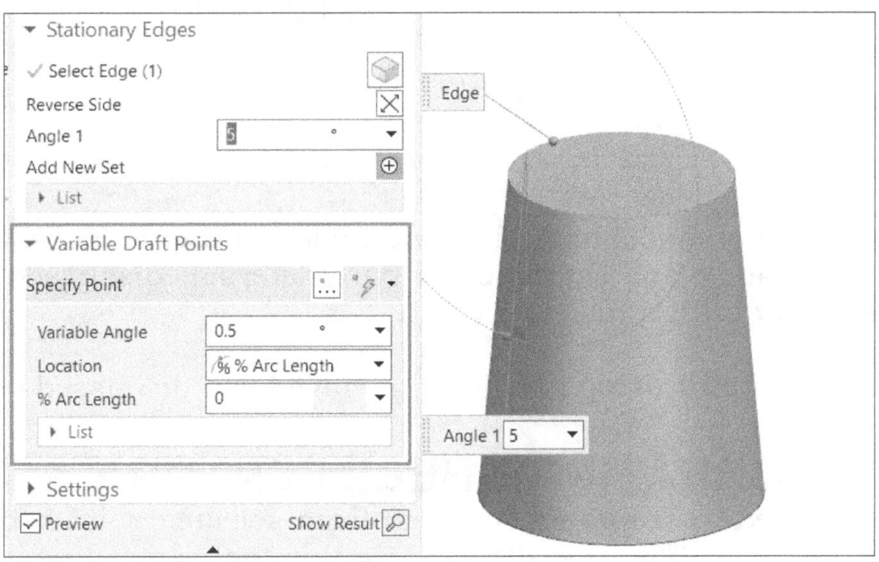

Figure-71. Variable Draft Points rollout

- Select the **Specify Point** selection button from the rollout and click at desired locations on the edge. Preview of draft at various points will be displayed; refer to Figure-72.

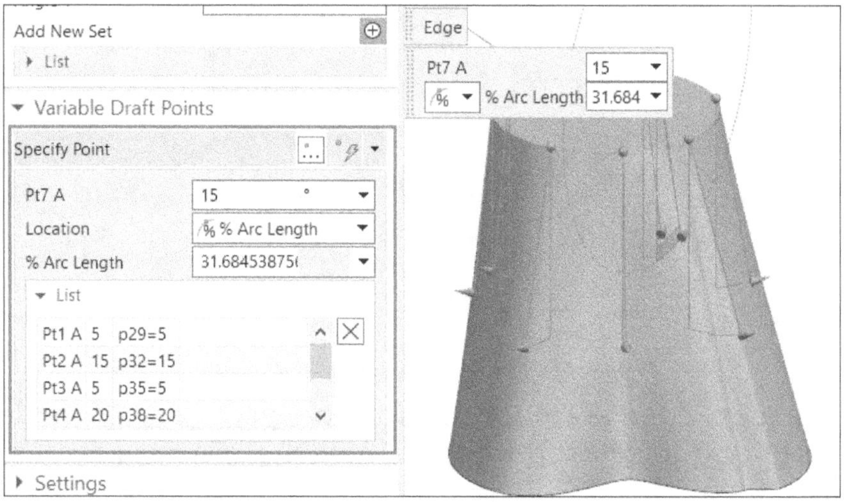

Figure-72. Preview of variable draft

- Set desired parameters for each draft point in the fields of **Variable Draft Points** rollout and click on the **Apply** button to create drafts.

Creating Tangent to Face Draft

- Select the **Tangent to Face** option from the drop-down at the top in the dialog box to create draft to faces which are tangent to selected face. The options will be displayed as shown in Figure-73.

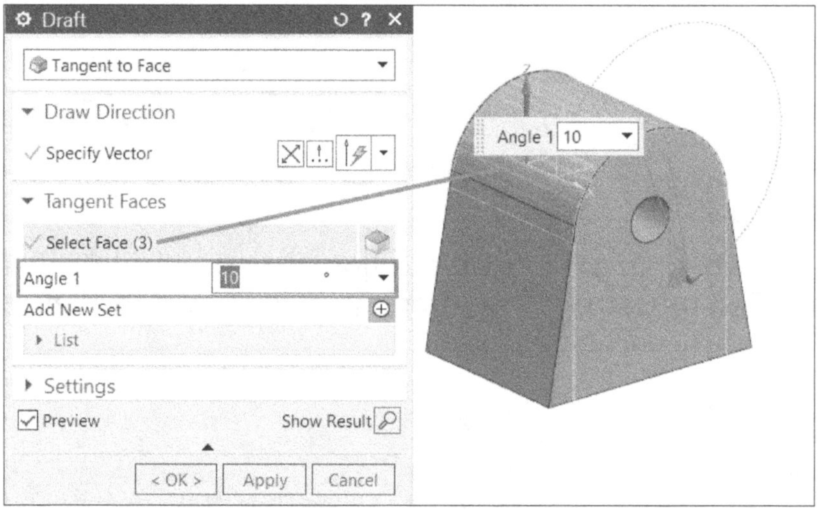

Figure-73. Applying tangent to face draft

- Select the top face of model to apply draft angle to tangent faces.
- Specify the draft angle and set the other parameters as discussed earlier.
- Click on the **Apply** button to create draft.

The options to create draft using parting edge have been discussed earlier.

CREATING SHELL FEATURE

The **Shell** tool is used to scoop out material from selected solid body and remove selected face of the body. The procedure to use this tool is given next.

- Click on the **Shell** tool from the **Base** group in the **Home** tab of the **Ribbon**. The **Shell** dialog box will be displayed; refer to Figure-74.

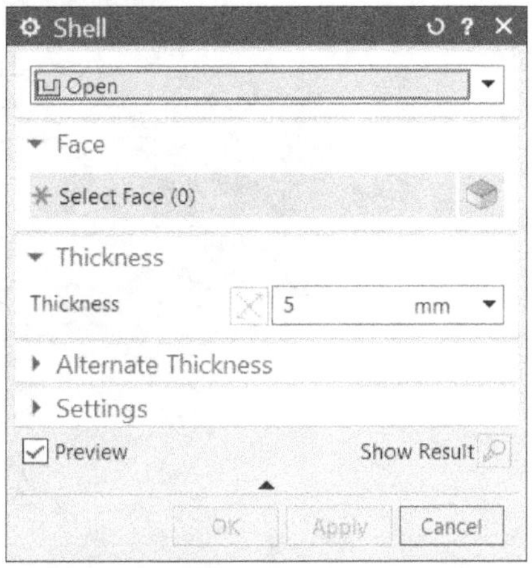

Figure-74. Shell dialog box

Creating Open Shell Feature

- Select the **Open** option from the drop-down at the top in the dialog box to create shell feature with selected face open.
- Click on the face of model to remove it and apply shell operation; refer to Figure-75.
- Specify desired value in the **Thickness** edit box to define thickness of shell walls.

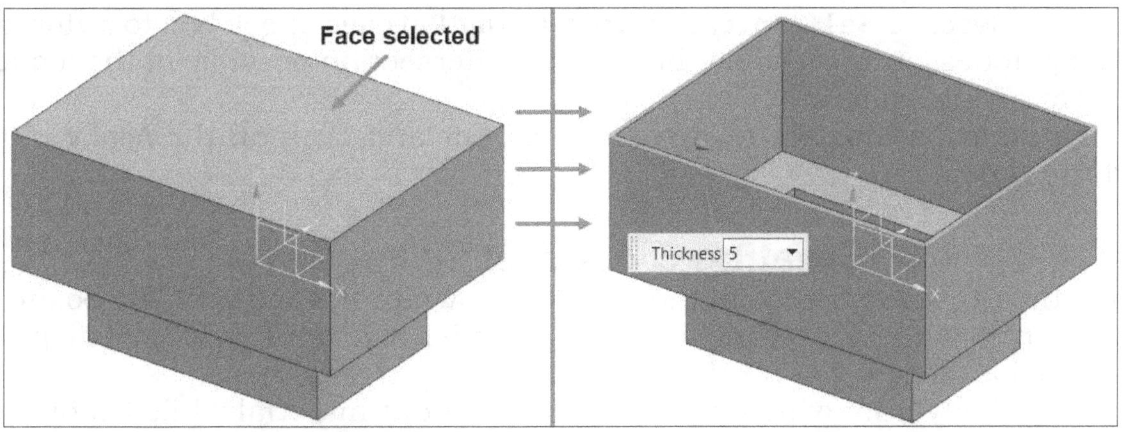

Figure-75. Preview of open shell feature

- Expand the **Alternative Thickness** rollout to specify different wall thickness to selected faces. The options similar to the **Thickness** rollout will be displayed.
- Select the faces to which you want to apply different thickness and specify desired thickness value; refer to Figure-76.

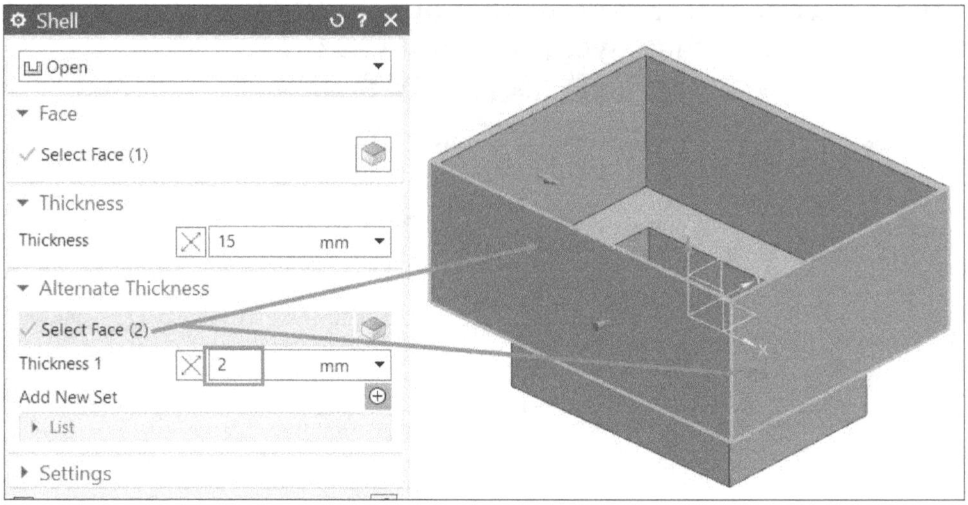

Figure-76. Faces selected for different thickness

- You can use the **Add New Set** button from the **Alternate Thickness** rollout to create new face set for defining different thickness.
- Select the **Add Shelf at Tangent Edges** option from the **Tangent Edges** drop-down to remove faces tangent to selected faces before creating offset of model walls. Select the **Extend Tangent Face** option from the drop-down to remove edges of tangent faces connected to nearby faces of faces to be removed.
- Select the **Resolve Self-intersections Using Patches** check box to automatically create patches (surface) when there is self-intersection possible in the model after performing shell operation.
- Set the other parameters as discussed earlier and click on the **Apply** button to perform operation.

Creating Closed Shell Feature

- Select the **Closed** option from the top drop-down in the **Shell** dialog box to create shell feature without opening any face of model. The options will be displayed as discussed earlier.
- Select the body from which you want to scoop-out material while keeping all the faces of model closed.
- Set the other parameters as discussed earlier and click on the **OK** button.

CREATING PATTERN FEATURE

The **Pattern Feature** tool is used to create multiple copies of selected feature/object in different patterns like linear, circular, spiral, polygonal, along path, and so on. The procedure to use this tool is given next.

- Click on the **Pattern Feature** tool from the **Base** group in **Home** tab of the **Ribbon**. The **Pattern Feature** dialog box will be displayed; refer to Figure-77.

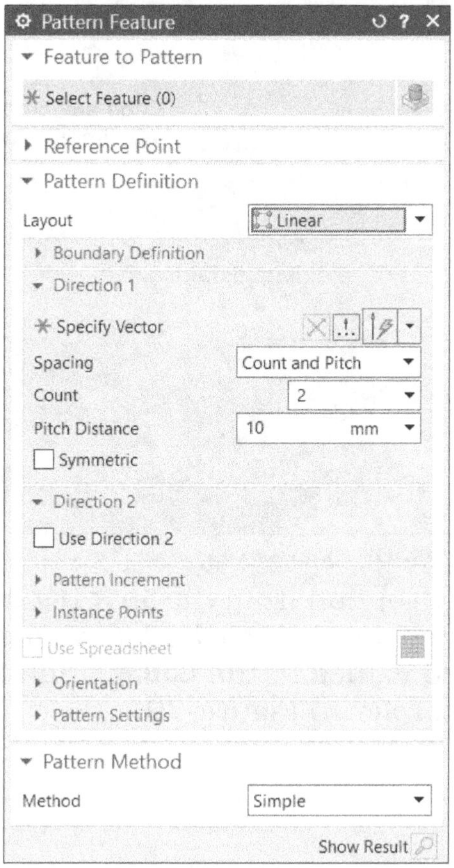

Figure-77. Pattern Feature dialog box

- Select the feature/object to be copied multiple times from the drawing area.
- Expand the **Reference Point** rollout to define the point on feature which will be used as reference for generating pattern. Note that this point will be used to define distance between various instances in the pattern.

Creating Linear Pattern

- Select the **Linear** option from the **Layout** drop-down to create pattern in one or two directions based on selected direction reference(s). The options in the dialog box will be displayed as shown in Figure-77.
- Select the **Specify Vector** selection button from the **Direction 1** rollout to define direction reference. You will be asked to select a face/plane/edge/axis to be used as direction reference.
- Select desired reference from the graphics area. Preview of linear pattern will be displayed with an arrow; refer to Figure-78.

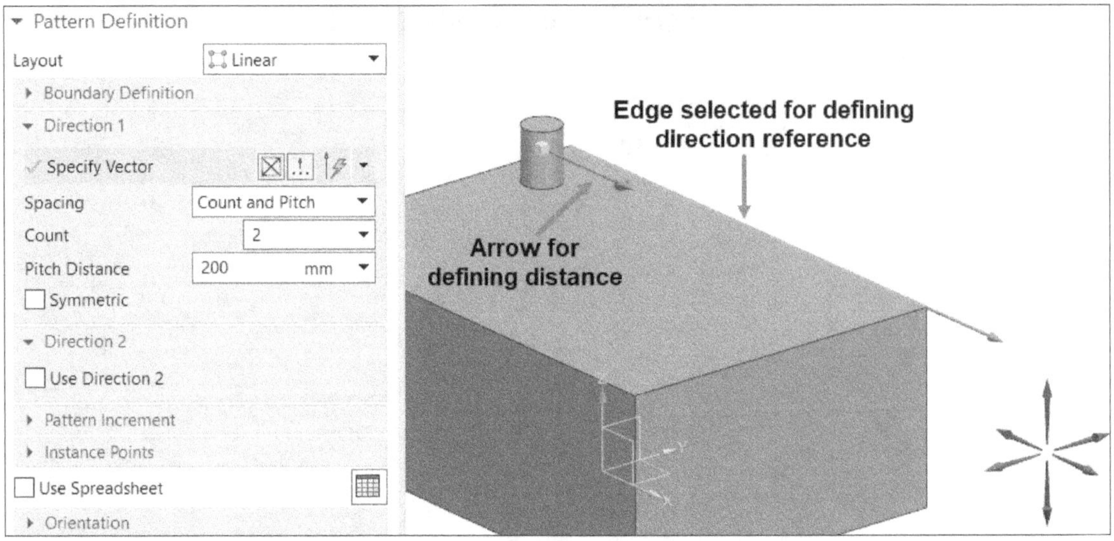

Figure-78. Direction reference selected for linear pattern

- Select the **Count and Pitch** option from the **Spacing** drop-down to specify number of instances to be created in pattern and distance between two consecutive instances. Specify desired values in the **Count** and **Pitch Distance** edit boxes to check preview of pattern; refer to Figure-79.

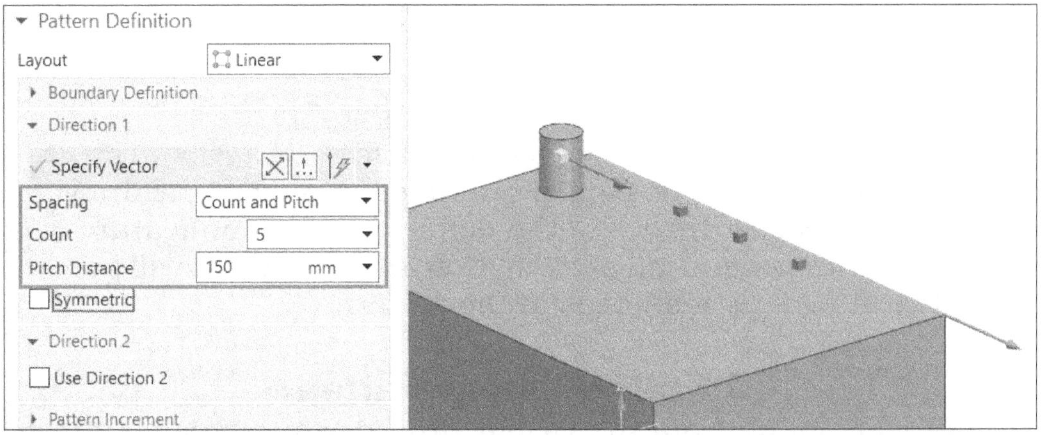

Figure-79. Preview of pattern with count and pitch

- Select the **Count and Span** option from the **Spacing** drop-down to specify number of instances to be created and total span within which pattern will be created; refer to Figure-80. Specify desired parameters in the **Count** and **Span Distance** edit boxes.

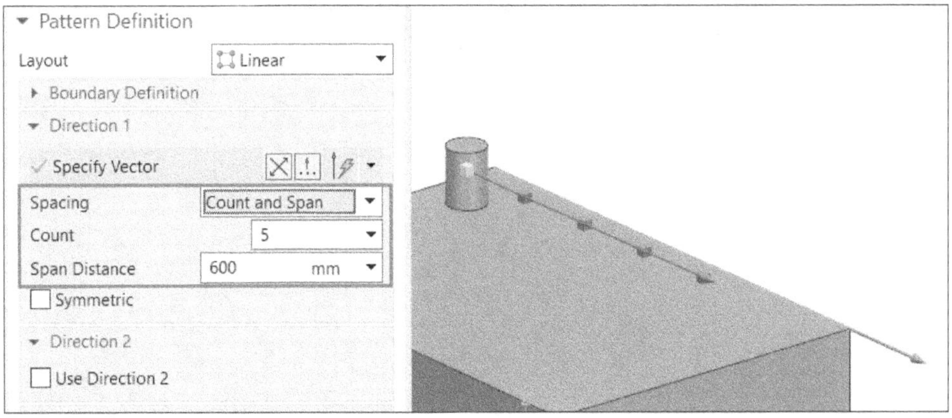

Figure-80. Using count and span option

- Select the **Pitch and Span** option from the **Spacing** drop-down to specify distance between two consecutive instances and total span within which pattern instances will be created.
- Select the **List** option from the **Spacing** drop-down to use a list where you can specify distance value for each instance individually; refer to Figure-81. To create a new instance, click on the **Add New Set** button from the right of list box.

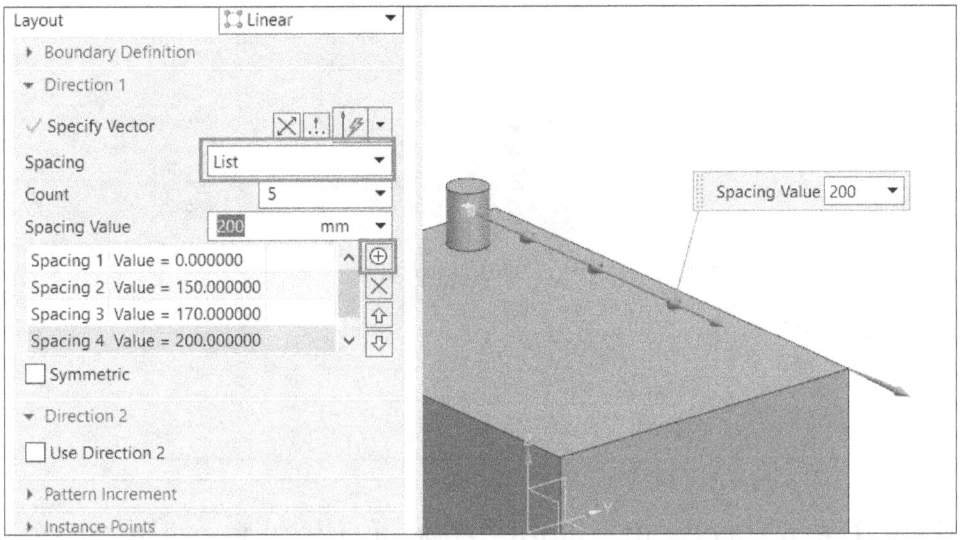

Figure-81. Using List option for pattern

- Select the **Points** option from the **Spacing** drop-down to select points from the drawing area to create instances of the pattern; refer to Figure-82.

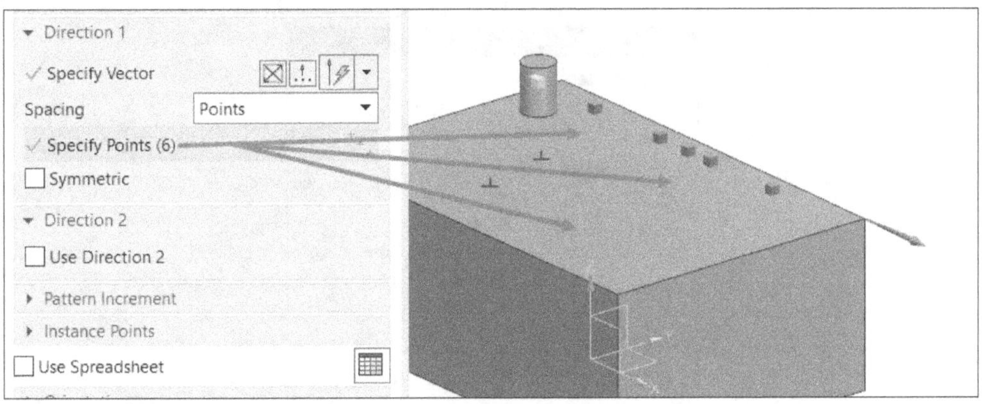

Figure-82. Points selected for pattern

- Select the **Symmetric** check box to create pattern in opposite direction of vector as well.
- Select the **Use Direction 2** check box to create pattern in second direction. The options similar to **Direction 1** rollout will be displayed. Set the parameters as discussed earlier; refer to Figure-83.

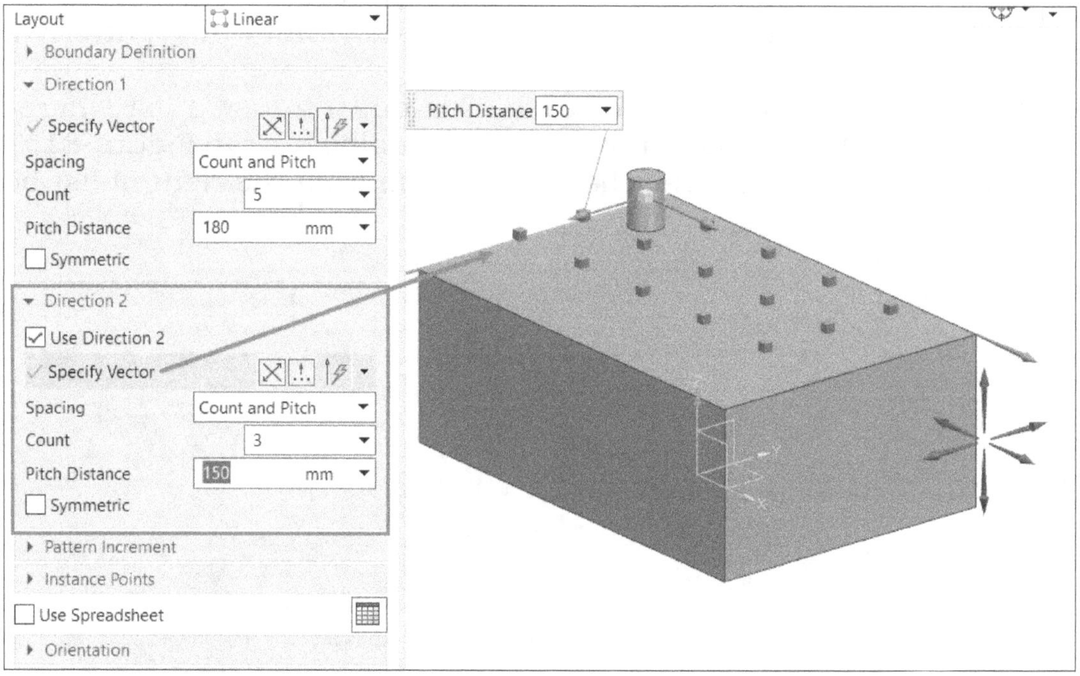

Figure-83. Creating pattern in Direction 2

- Expand the **Pattern Increment** rollout to specify the amount by which gap between instances will progress. The **Pattern Increment** button will be displayed. Click on the **Pattern Increment** button from the rollout. The **Pattern Increment** dialog box will be displayed; refer to Figure-84.

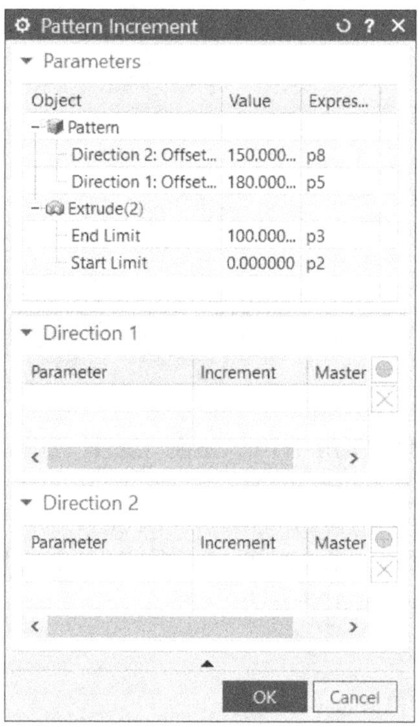

Figure-84. Pattern Increment dialog box

- Select the **Direction 1** option from **Pattern** node in table to define increment distance for the first direction. The **Add New Set** button in **Direction 1** rollout of the dialog box will become active.
- Click on the **Add New Set** button to create a new increment parameter; refer to Figure-85.

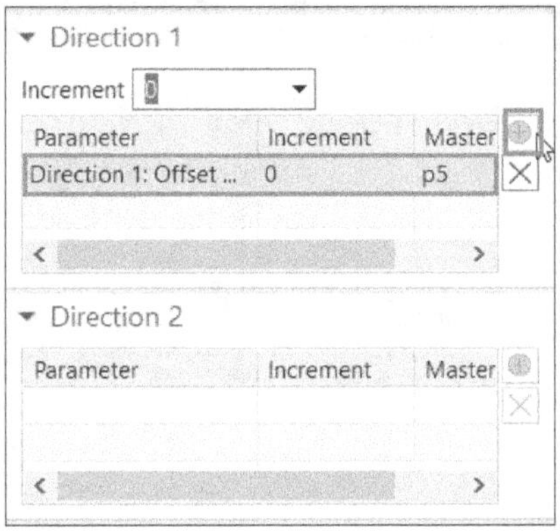

Figure-85. Increment parameter added

- Specify desired value in **Increment** edit box by which distance between instances in direction 1 will be changed. You can specify negative value in this edit box to reduce the distance; refer to Figure-86.

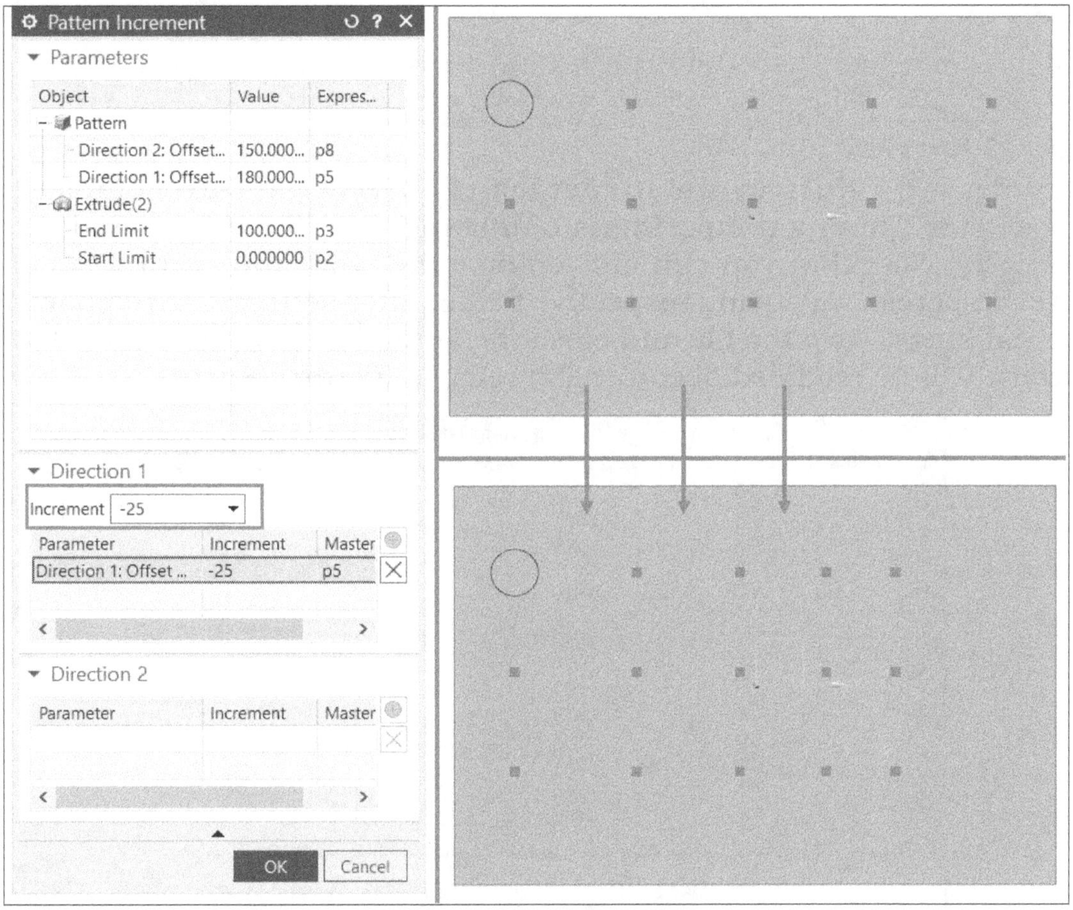

Figure-86. Reducing distance in pattern using Increment option

- Similarly, you can set increment value for Direction 2, start limit, and end limit in the dialog box. After setting desired parameter, click on the **OK** button from the dialog box to apply the changes.
- Select the **Use Spreadsheet** check box from **Instance Points** rollout to use a spreadsheet document for defining positions of pattern instances. The spreadsheet document will be displayed in default spreadsheet application; refer to Figure-87.

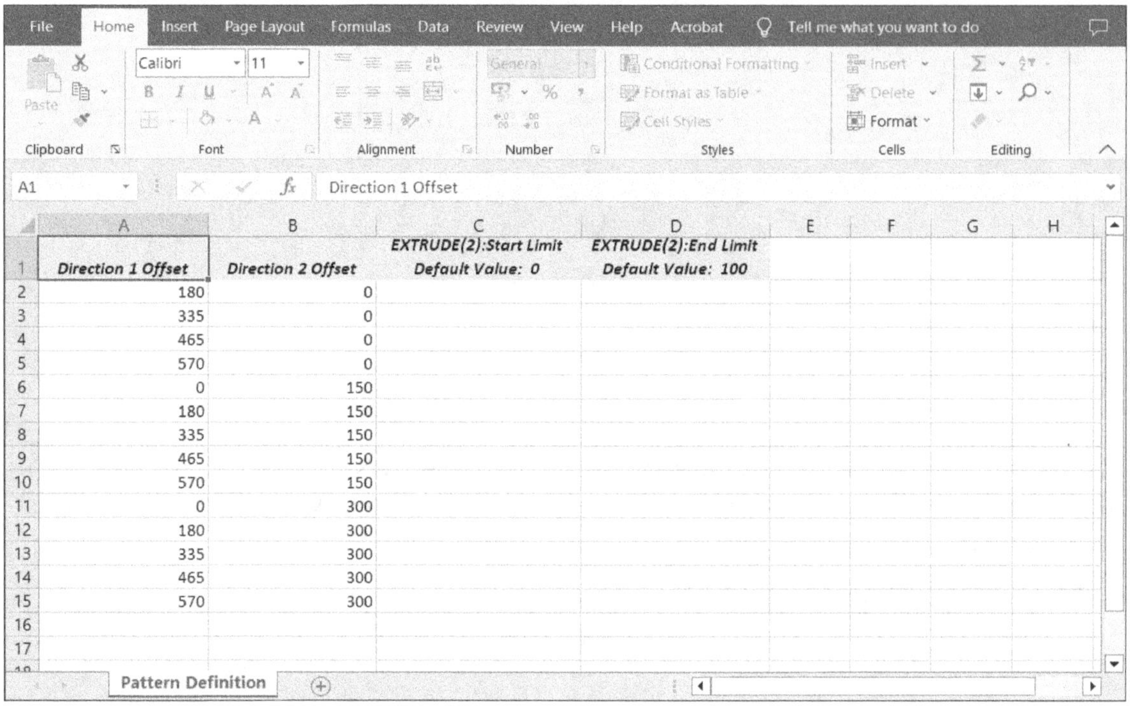

	A	B	C	D
1	Direction 1 Offset	Direction 2 Offset	EXTRUDE(2):Start Limit Default Value: 0	EXTRUDE(2):End Limit Default Value: 100
2	180	0		
3	335	0		
4	465	0		
5	570	0		
6	0	150		
7	180	150		
8	335	150		
9	465	150		
10	570	150		
11	0	300		
12	180	300		
13	335	300		
14	465	300		
15	570	300		

Figure-87. Pattern instance spreadsheet

- Specify desired values in the **Direction 1 Offset** and **Direction 2 Offset** edit boxes for defining the positions of instances in direction 1 and direction 2, respectively. Note that you can also change the start and end points of extrude features in percentage using respective fields. After setting desired parameters in the spreadsheet, save the file and close the spreadsheet application. The preview of pattern will be modified accordingly; refer to Figure-88.

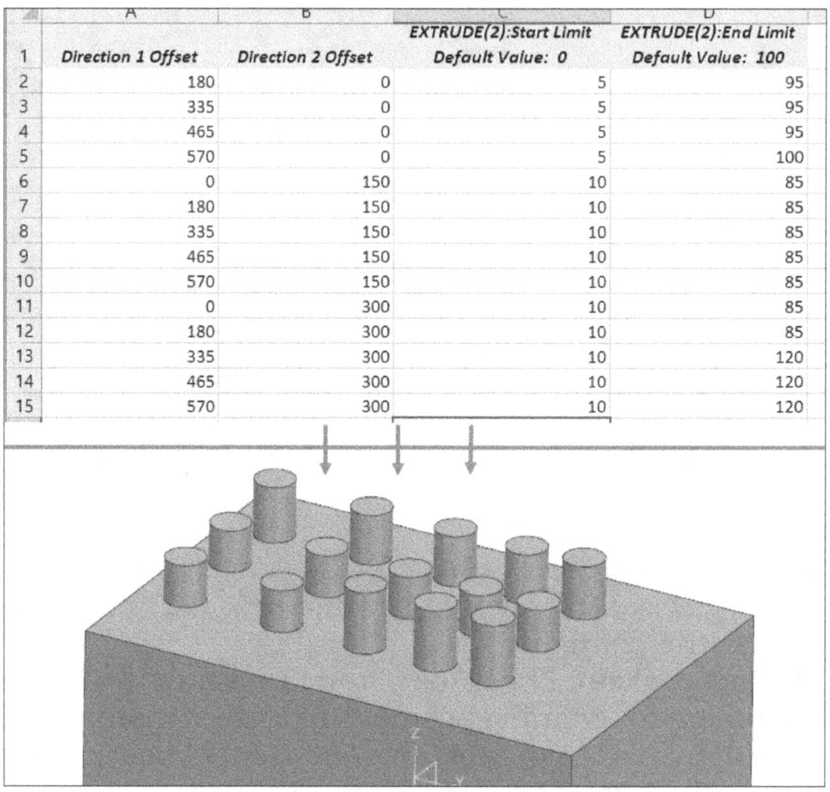

	A	B	C	D
1	Direction 1 Offset	Direction 2 Offset	EXTRUDE(2):Start Limit Default Value: 0	EXTRUDE(2):End Limit Default Value: 100
2	180	0	5	95
3	335	0	5	95
4	465	0	5	95
5	570	0	5	100
6	0	150	10	85
7	180	150	10	85
8	335	150	10	85
9	465	150	10	85
10	570	150	10	85
11	0	300	10	85
12	180	300	10	85
13	335	300	10	120
14	465	300	10	120
15	570	300	10	120

Figure-88. Preview of pattern using spreadsheet

- Expand the **Orientation** rollout and select desired option from the **Orientation** drop-down to define how coordinate systems will be used for orienting pattern.
- Select the **Follow Face** check box to define the face to which instances will maintain a perpendicular orientation. On selecting this check box, the **Select Face** selection button will be displayed. Click on the **Select Face** selection button and select the face to which instances will be normal.
- Select desired option from the **Method** drop-down in the **Pattern Method** rollout to define how pattern feature will be added in the **Part Navigator**. Select the **Single** option from the drop-down to create single feature in place of multiple individual instances of pattern. Select the **Simple** option from the drop-down to create pattern with list of instances but you cannot edit the instances individually. Select the **Variational** option from the drop-down to evaluate features like blend, chamfer, and so on when creating pattern.

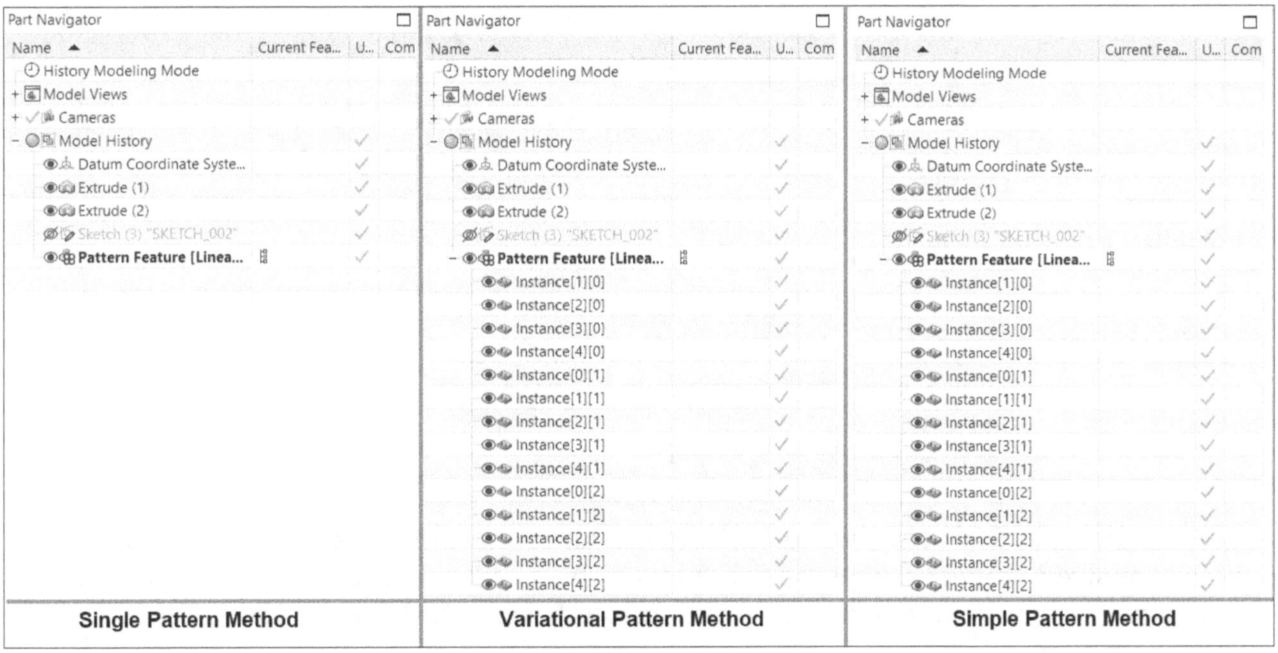

Figure-89. Pattern type added in Part Navigator

- You can suppress individual instances of the pattern from preview by right-clicking on instance node and selecting the **Suppress** option from shortcut menu; refer to Figure-90. Similarly, you can use **Unsuppress** option from same shortcut menu if you want to unsuppress a suppressed instance.

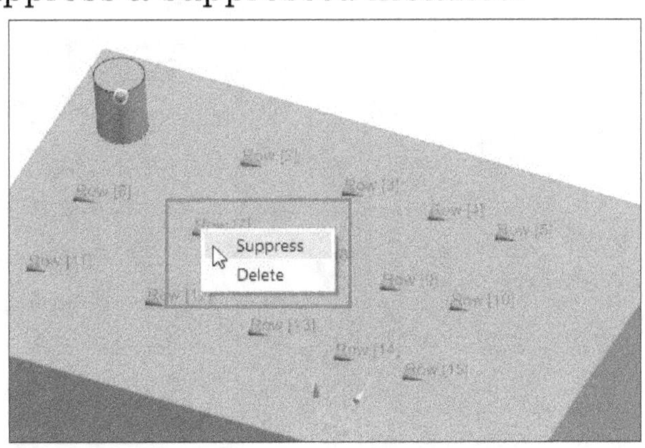

Figure-90. Shortcut menu for suppressing instance

- After setting desired parameters, click on the **Apply** button from dialog box to create the pattern.

Creating Circular Pattern

- Select the **Circular** option from the **Layout** drop-down in the **Pattern Definition** rollout after selecting the object to be patterned for creating a circular pattern. The options in the dialog box will be displayed as shown in Figure-91.

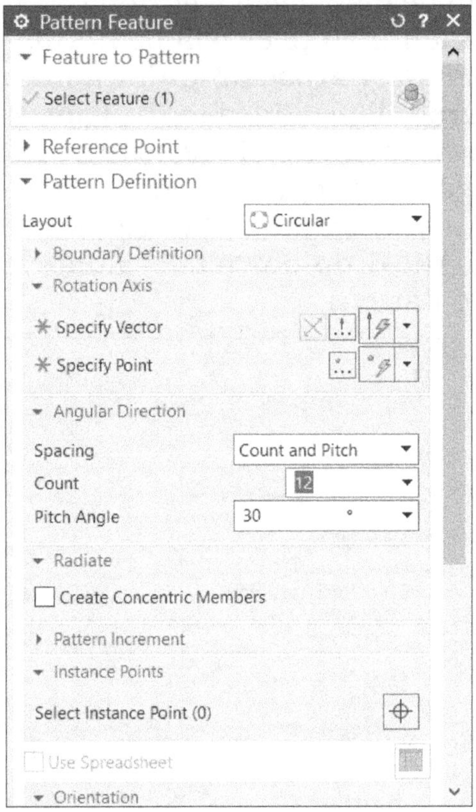

Figure-91. Circular pattern options

- Select the **Specify Vector** selection button from the **Rotation Axis** rollout and select desired axis from the model about which you want to create circular pattern. Preview of circular pattern will be displayed; refer to Figure-92.

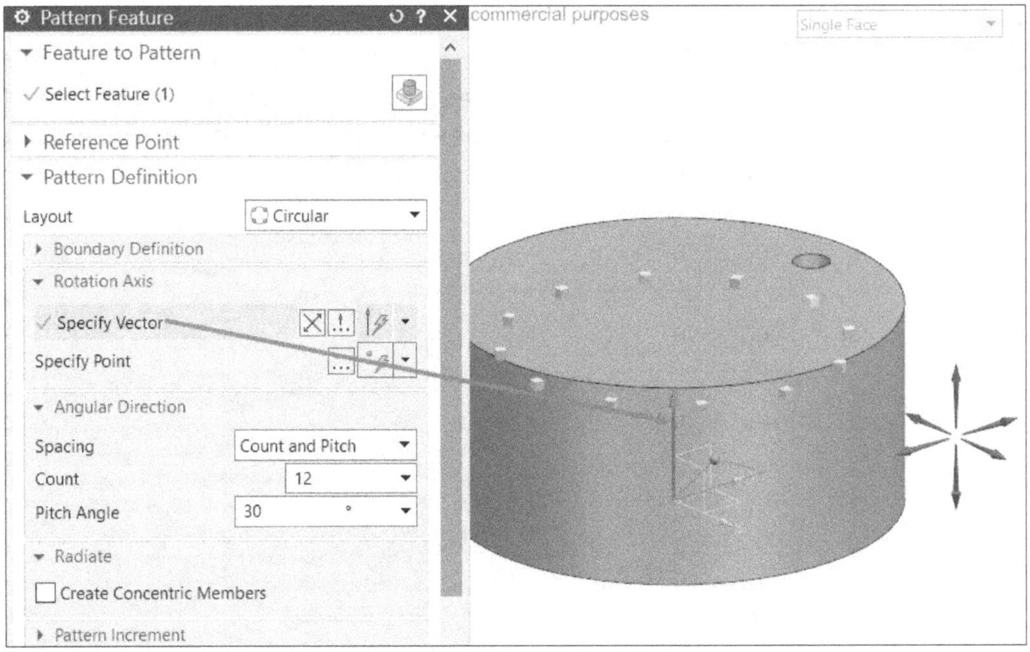

Figure-92. Preview of circular pattern feature

- Set desired parameters in the **Angular Direction** rollout to define the number of instances and the distance between two instances as discussed earlier.
- Select the **Create Concentric Members** check box to create pattern instances in direction pointing from center to circumference; refer to Figure-93.

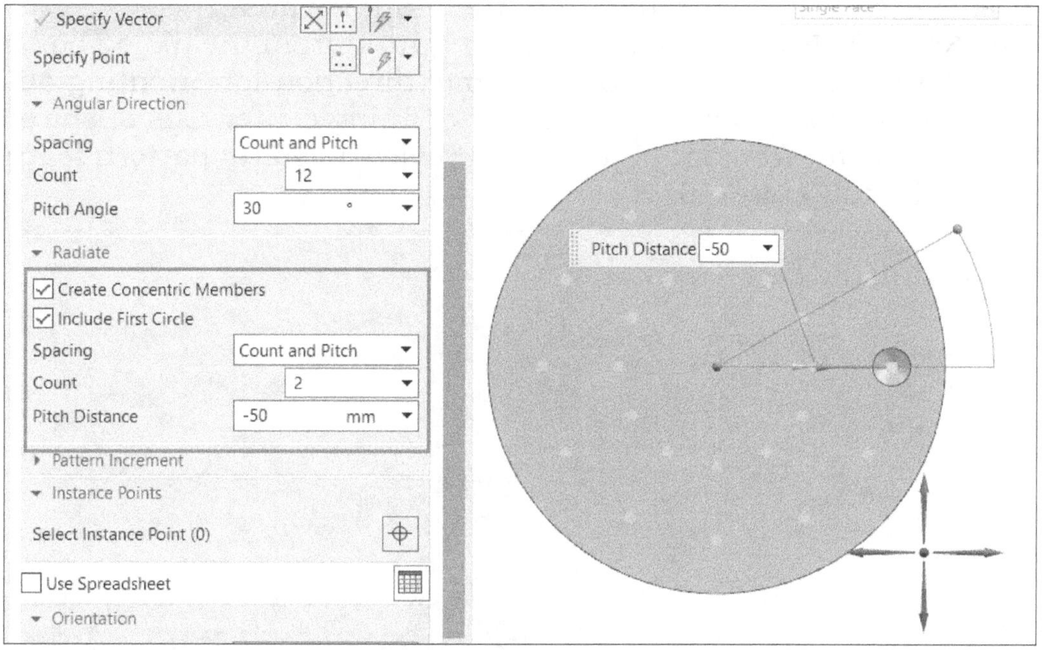

Figure-93. Preview of circular pattern with concentric members

- Set the other parameters as discussed earlier and click on the **Apply** button to create the pattern.

Creating Polygon Pattern

- Select the **Polygon** option from the **Layout** drop-down in the **Pattern Definition** rollout of the **Pattern Feature** dialog box to create pattern of selected object in the shape of a polygon; refer to Figure-94.

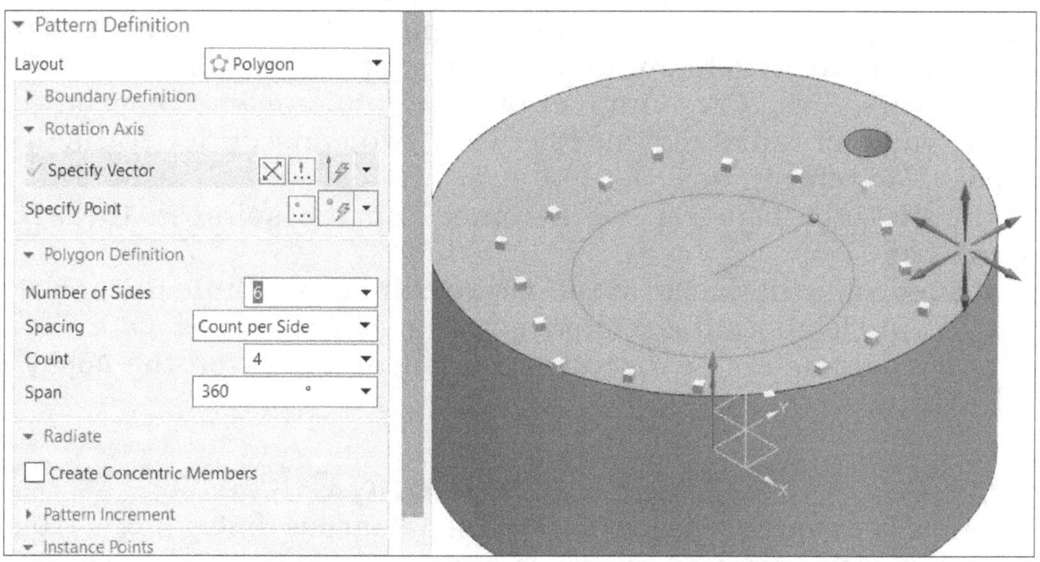

Figure-94. Preview of polygon pattern

- Set the parameters as discussed earlier.

Creating Spiral Pattern

- Select the **Spiral** option from the **Layout** drop-down in the **Pattern Definition** rollout in the dialog box to create instances of the pattern in spiral shape. The options will be displayed.
- Select the feature to be patterned from the graphics area.
- Select the **Specify Plane Normal** selection button from the dialog box and select face of model to be used for defining normal direction for orienting objects. You will be asked to select reference vector for defining center axis of spiral.
- Select desired vector from graphics area. Preview of spiral pattern feature will be displayed; refer to Figure-95.

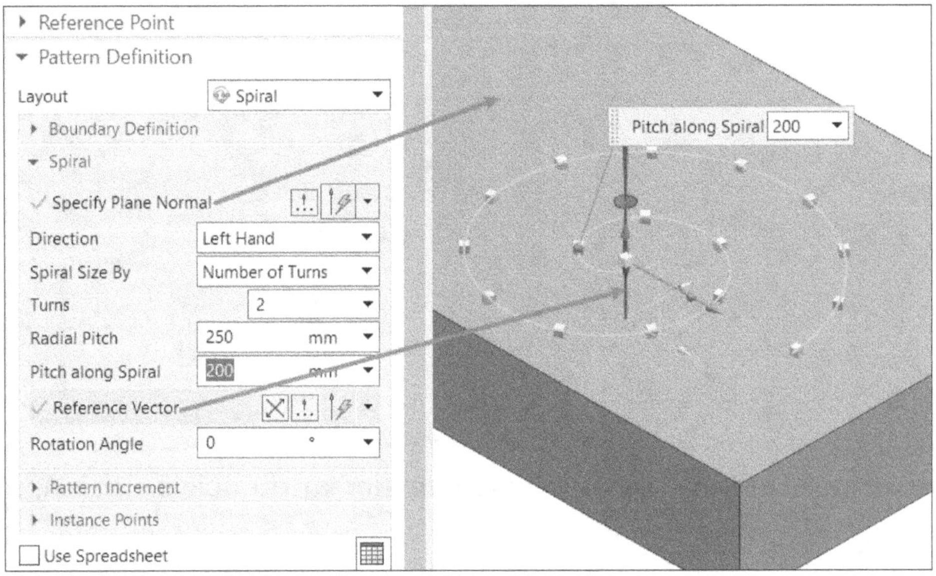

Figure-95. Preview of spiral pattern

- Select desired option from the **Direction** drop-down to define direction of spiral. Select the **Left Hand** option from the drop-down to create clockwise spiral. Select the **Right Hand** option from the drop-down to create counter-clockwise spiral.
- Select the **Number of Turns** option from the **Spiral Size By** drop-down to define the number of turns to be created in the spiral. Select the **Total Angle** option from the drop-down to define total angular span of spiral in place of specifying number of turns. Specify the number of turn/total angle in respective edit box.
- Specify the value of radial distance between two consecutive turns of the spiral in the **Radial Pitch** edit box.
- Specify the distance between two instances on the spiral in the **Pitch along Spiral** edit box.
- Specify desired value in the **Rotation Angle** edit box to rotate the spiral end point by respective angle about the reference vector.
- Set the other parameters as discussed earlier and click on the **Apply** button to create the feature.

Creating Pattern Along Curve

The **Along** option in **Layout** drop-down of **Pattern Feature** dialog box is used to create pattern of feature along selected reference curve. The procedure to create a pattern along curve is given next.

- Select the **Along** option from the **Layout** drop-down in the **Pattern Feature** dialog box. The options will be displayed as shown in Figure-96.

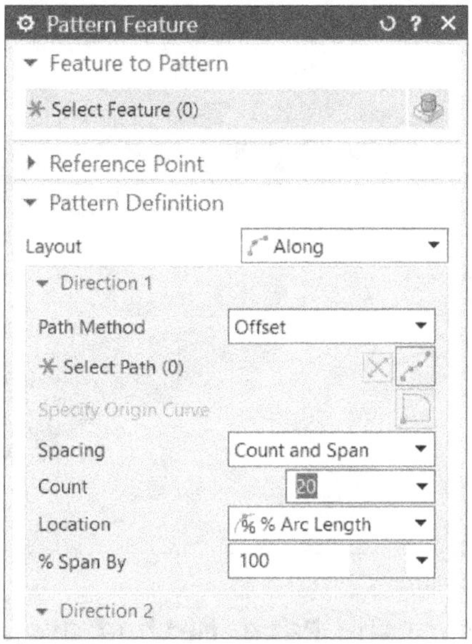

Figure-96. Options for pattern along curve

- Select the feature to be patterned from the graphics area; refer to Figure-97. **Note that it is less complex to create pattern of features which have no boolean operation applied to them and are separate bodies as in our case. After performing pattern, you can later perform boolean on the feature.**

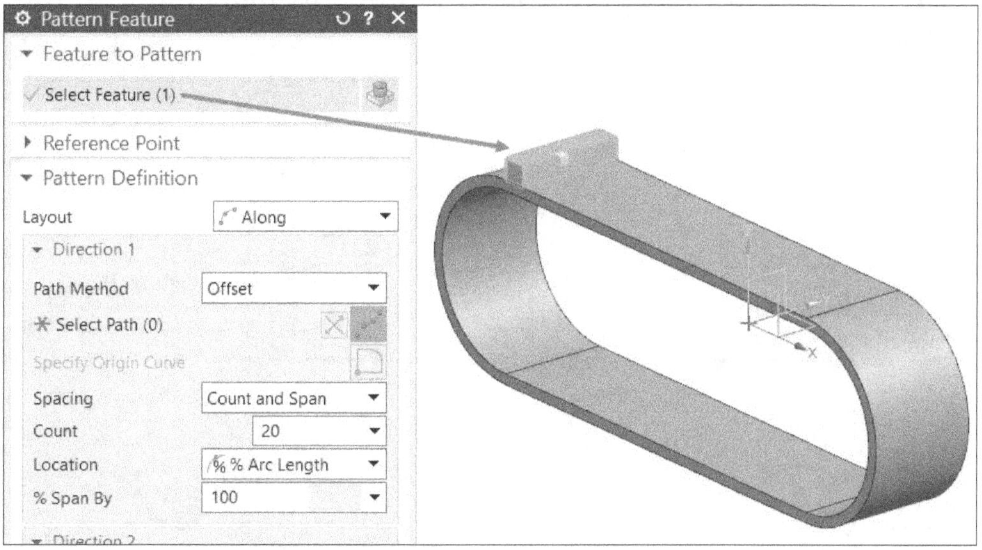

Figure-97. Feature selected for path pattern

- Click on the **Select Path** selection button and select the curve to be used as path along which pattern will be created. Preview of pattern will be displayed; refer to Figure-98.

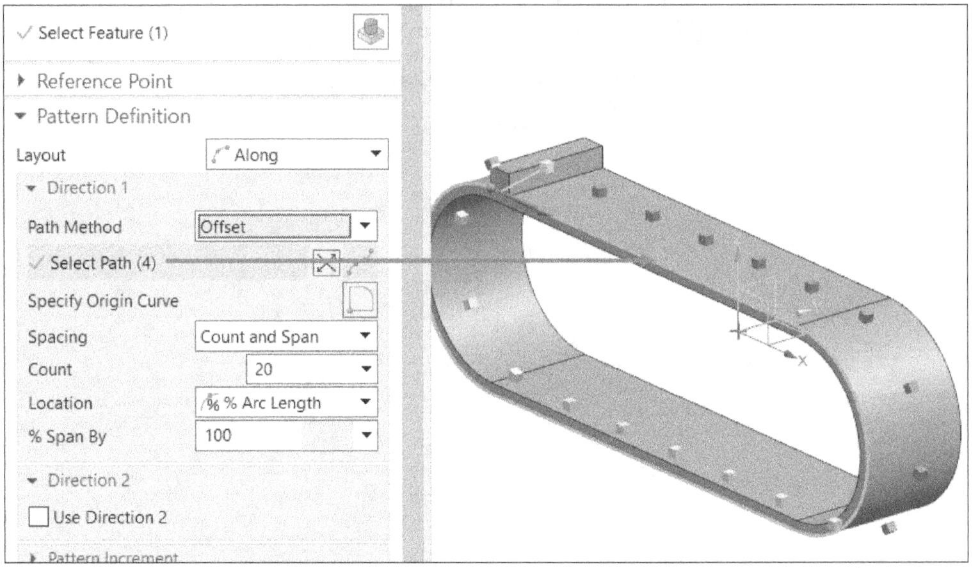

Figure-98. Preview of path pattern

- Select the **Rigid** option from the **Path Method** drop-down to calculate positions of instances along the path using rigid motion strictly following the contour path curve. Select the **Offset** option from the **Path Method** drop-down to calculate positions of instances using an imaginary curve offsetted from the path curve. Select the **Translate** option from the drop-down to calculate positions of instances by using imaginary curve created by moving path curve start point at the reference point. Refer to Figure-99 to check the difference in placement of instances with different options.

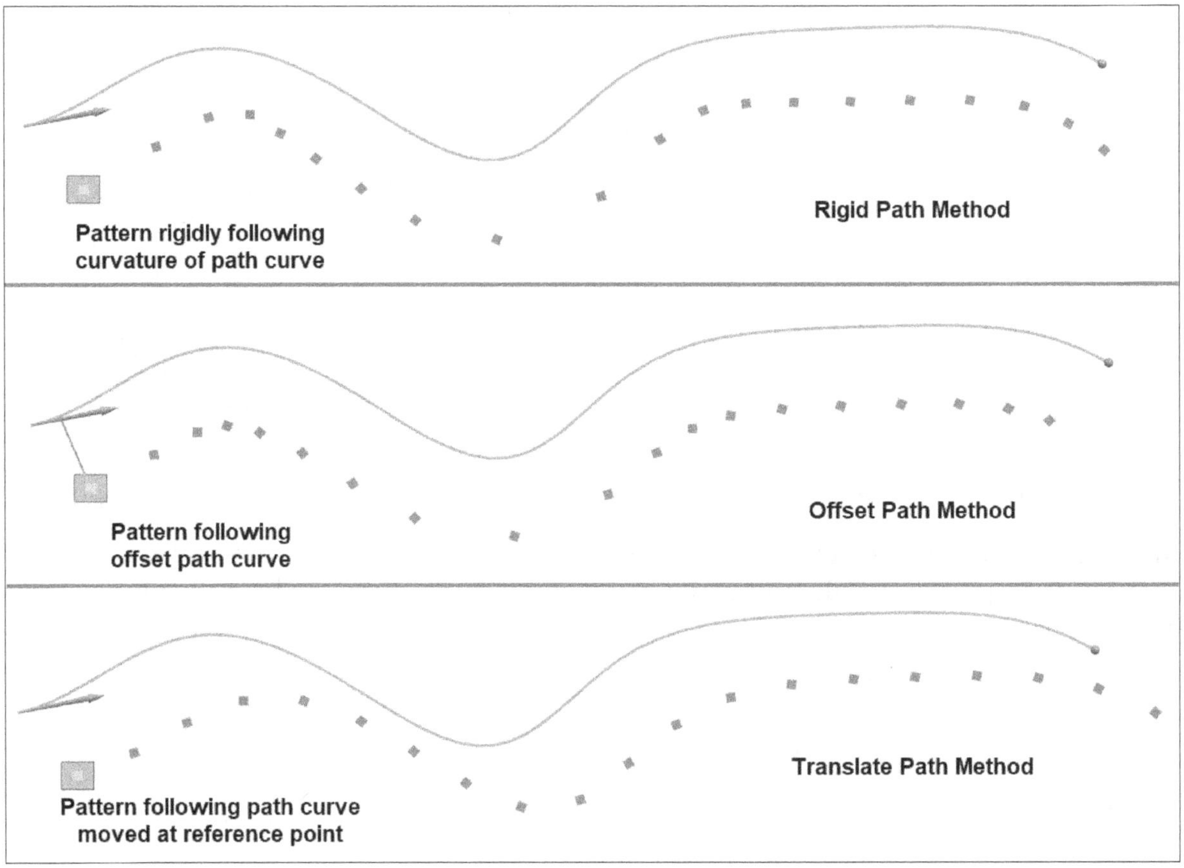

Figure-99. Preview of pattern with different path methods

- Set the other parameters as discussed earlier and click on the **Apply** button to create the pattern. Make sure to unite the path pattern feature with main body.

Creating General Pattern

- Select the **General** option from the **Layout** drop-down to use points or coordinate system for generating pattern instances. The options will be displayed as shown in Figure-100.

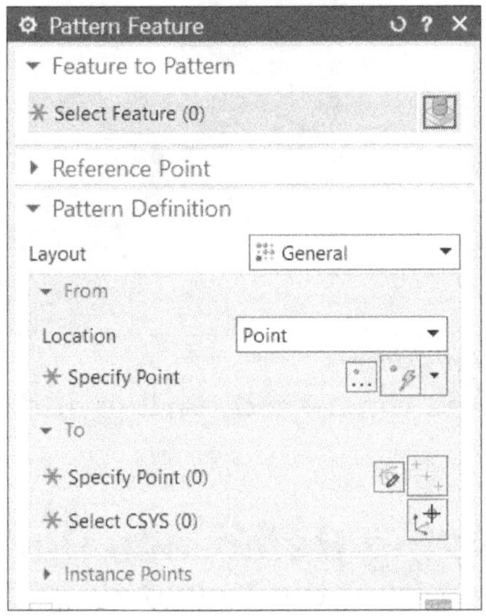

Figure-100. General pattern options

- Select the feature which you want to be patterned from the model.
- Select the **Point** option from the **Location** drop-down to specify a point as start position for creating pattern. Select the **Coordinate System** option from the **Location** drop-down to use selected coordinate system as starting position for pattern. We are selecting **Point** in our case, you can apply the same procedure for the **Coordinate System** option.
- Click on the **Specify Point** selection button from the **From** rollout in the dialog box and select desired point from the model to be used as starting point for pattern.
- Click on the **Specify Point** selection button from the **To** rollout in the dialog box and select desired point from the model to be used as end point for pattern. Preview of pattern will be displayed; refer to Figure-101.

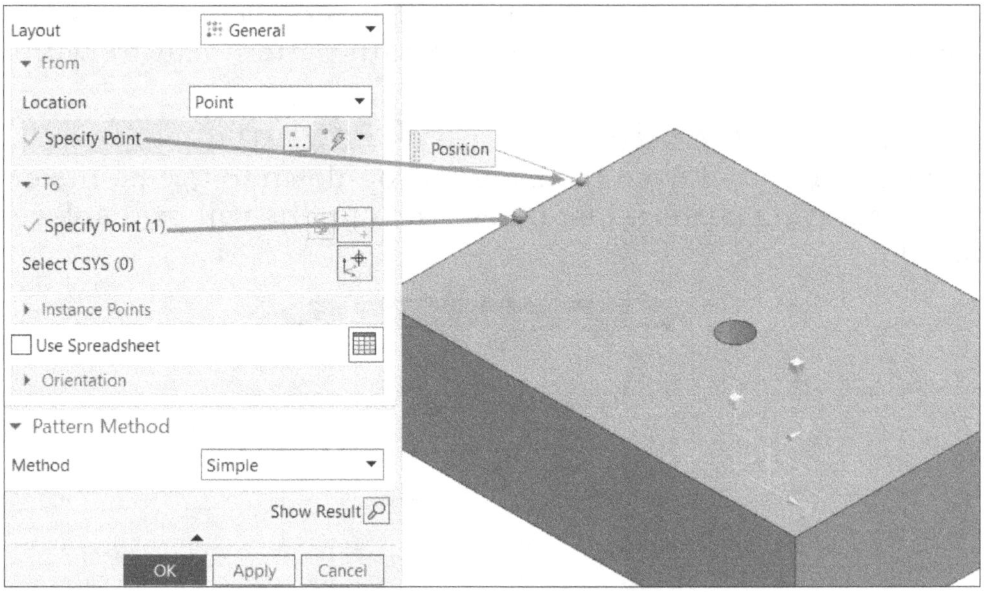

Figure-101. Preview of general pattern

- Set the other parameters as discussed earlier and click on the **Apply** button to create the pattern.

Creating Reference Pattern

- Select the **Reference** option from the **Layout** drop-down in the **Pattern Feature** dialog box to use previous patterns as reference template for creating new pattern. The options will be displayed as shown in Figure-102.

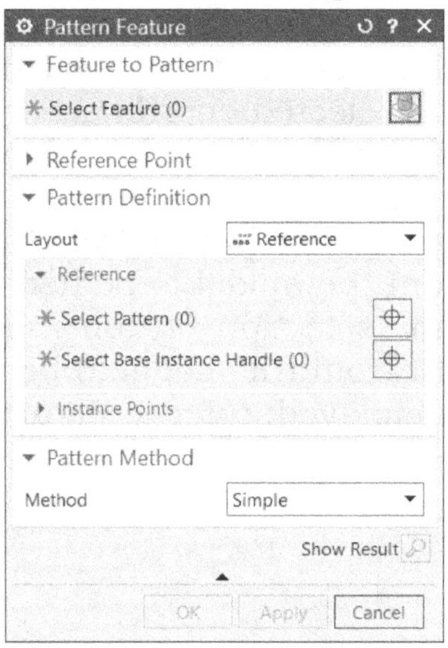

Figure-102. Pattern Feature dialog box with Reference option

- Select the feature that you want to pattern from the model.
- Click on the **Select Pattern** selection button from the **Reference** rollout in the dialog box and click on the desired pattern feature to be used as reference from the model or **Part Navigator**; refer to Figure-103. You will be asked to select base instance handle from the reference pattern.
- Select the instance handle from reference pattern which you want to use as starting instance in new pattern; refer to Figure-103. Note that selected feature will be placed at selected instance handle position in new pattern.

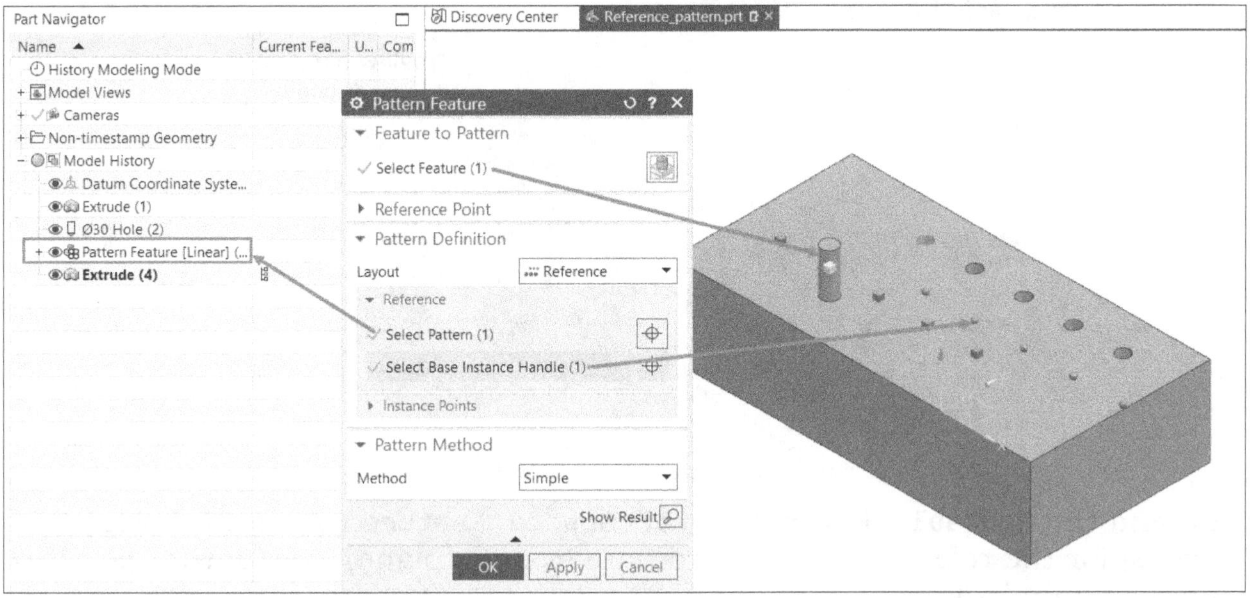

Figure-103. Preview of reference pattern

- Set the other parameters as discussed earlier and click on the **Apply** button. The pattern will be created.

CREATING MIRROR FEATURE

The **Mirror Feature** tool is used to create mirror copy of selected features with respect to selected plane/face. The procedure to use this tool is given next.

- Click on the **Mirror Feature** tool from the **Base** group in the **Home** tab of the **Ribbon**. The **Mirror Feature** dialog box will be displayed; refer to Figure-104.

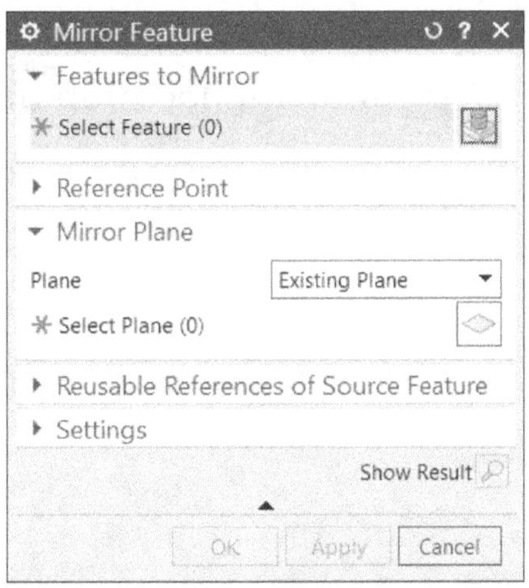

Figure-104. Mirror Feature dialog box

- Select the feature(s) whose mirror copy is to be created from the model.
- Select the **Select Plane** selection button from the **Mirror Plane** rollout to select desired plane as mirror plane reference. Preview of mirror feature will be displayed; refer to Figure-105.

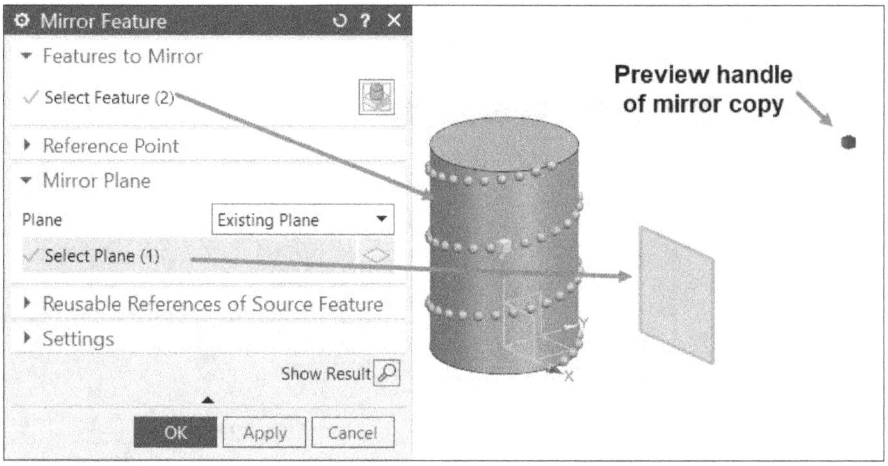

Figure-105. Preview of mirror feature

- Expand the **Reusable References of Source Feature** rollout and select check box(es) for the references like coordinate system/plane/axis/datum point to be included in mirror copy.
- Expand the **Settings** rollout and select check boxes to include threads and helix curves with their left handed or right handed orientation intact in mirror copy.
- Set the other parameters as discussed earlier and click on the **OK** button. The mirror copy will be created.

SELF-ASSESSMENT

Q1. Which tool is used to create rectangular blocks in NX?
A. Cylinder Tool
B. Block Tool
C. Cone Tool
D. Sphere Tool

Q2. Which option allows specifying starting location and dimensions of a block?
A. Two Points and Height
B. Two Diagonal Points
C. Origin and Edge Lengths
D. Axis and Height

Q3. Which button is used to preview the block before creation?
A. Apply
B. Show Result
C. Preview
D. Display

Q4. Which option is used to create a block using diagonal points and height?
A. Origin and Edge Lengths
B. Two Points and Height
C. Two Diagonal Points
D. Axis and Diameter

Q5. Which reference can be used to define cylinder direction?
A. Colors
B. Edges/Faces/Planes/Axis
C. Layers
D. Views

Q6. Which option is used to create cone using diameters and height?
A. Two Points
B. Diameters and Height
C. Arc and Height
D. Center and Radius

Q7. Which option is used to create sphere using center and diameter?
A. Arc
B. Center Point and Diameter
C. Two Points
D. Axis and Height

Q8. Which option is used to create simple holes?
A. Custom
B. Drill Size
C. Simple
D. Threaded

Q9. Which standard options are available for drill size holes?
A. ISO and ANSI
B. DIN and JIS
C. API and ASTM
D. BS and IS

Q10. Which option creates holes with standard fits and tolerances?
A. Simple
B. Custom
C. Screw Clearance
D. Drill Size

Q11. Which operation combines two or more bodies into one?
A. Subtract
B. Intersect
C. Unite
D. Trim

Q12. Which operation removes volume of one body from another?
A. Unite
B. Intersect
C. Subtract
D. Trim

Q13. Which operation creates a body from common volume of bodies?
A. Unite
B. Subtract
C. Intersect
D. Trim

Q14. Which tool is used to trim a solid body using a plane or face?
A. Edge Blend
B. Trim Body
C. Chamfer
D. Face Blend

Q15. Which tool is used to apply fillet on sharp edges?
A. Chamfer
B. Edge Blend
C. Trim
D. Hole

Q16. Which continuity option creates tangent fillet?
A. G0
B. G1
C. G2
D. G3

Q17. Which tool is used to apply fillet between faces?
A. Edge Blend
B. Face Blend
C. Chamfer
D. Trim

Q18. Which chamfer option keeps equal distances from edge?
A. Asymmetric
B. Offset and Angle
C. Symmetric
D. Variable

Q19. Which chamfer option allows different distances on both sides?
A. Symmetric
B. Offset
C. Asymmetric
D. Equal

Q20. Which tool is used to apply taper angle to selected faces?
A. Shell Tool
B. Draft Tool
C. Pattern Tool
D. Mirror Tool

Q21. Applying draft is useful for:
A. Coloring model
B. Easy extraction of casting components
C. Increasing weight
D. Rendering

Q22. Which option is used to apply draft using faces?
A. Edge
B. Face
C. Curve
D. Plane

Q23. In draft using face option, the draw direction should be:
A. Parallel to face
B. Perpendicular to edge
C. Normal to stationary face
D. Random

Q24. Which option allows applying draft on both sides of parting face?
A. Symmetric Angle
B. Draft Both Sides
C. True Draft
D. Isocline Draft

Q25. Which option applies same draft angle on both sides?
A. Draft Both Sides
B. Symmetric Angle
C. True Draft
D. Equal Draft

Q26. Which draft method uses both stationary and parting face?
A. Face
B. Edge
C. Stationary and Parting Face
D. Tangent

Q27. Which option keeps tangency angle equal to draft angle?
A. True Draft
B. Isocline Draft
C. Symmetric Draft
D. Equal Draft

Q28. Which option keeps fixed draft angle higher than tangency angle?
A. Isocline Draft
B. True Draft
C. Symmetric Draft
D. Variable Draft

Q29. Which option is used to apply draft using edge as reference?
A. Face
B. Edge
C. Plane
D. Axis

Q30. Which rollout is used to define different draft values at points?
A. Settings
B. Variable Draft Points
C. Direction
D. Dimensions

Q31. Which option applies draft to tangent faces?
A. Face
B. Edge
C. Tangent to Face
D. Parting Face

Q32. Which tool is used to remove material from a solid body?
A. Draft Tool
B. Shell Tool
C. Pattern Tool
D. Mirror Tool

Q33. Which option creates shell with an open face?
A. Closed
B. Open
C. Hollow
D. Remove

Q34. Which option allows different thickness on selected faces?
A. Thickness
B. Alternative Thickness
C. Variable Thickness
D. Custom Thickness

Q35. Which option creates shell without removing any face?
A. Open
B. Closed
C. Full
D. Solid

Q36. Which tool is used to create multiple copies of a feature?
A. Draft Tool
B. Pattern Feature Tool
C. Shell Tool
D. Blend Tool

Q37. Which pattern type creates copies in straight directions?
A. Circular
B. Spiral
C. Linear
D. Polygon

Q38. Which spacing option defines number and distance between instances?
A. Count and Pitch
B. Count and Span
C. Pitch and Span
D. List

Q39. Which option creates pattern in opposite direction also?
A. Reverse
B. Mirror
C. Symmetric
D. Duplicate

Q40. Which pattern type creates copies around an axis?
A. Linear
B. Circular
C. Spiral
D. General

For Student Notes

Chapter 6

3D Modeling - III

Topics Covered

The major topics covered in this chapter are:

- ***Creating Blocks, Cylinders, Cones, and Spheres***
- ***Creating Emboss, Groove, and Rib features***
- ***Creating Threads and Lattice***
- ***Creating and Managing User Defined Features***

INTRODUCTION

In previous chapters, you have learned to use tools for creating various base features like extrude, revolve, sweep, and so on. You have also learned to apply edge blend, chamfer, shell, draft, and so on. In this chapter, you will learn to create various features like draft body, rib, groove, and so on. These tools are discussed next.

APPLYING DRAFT BODY OPERATION

The **Draft Body** tool is used to apply matching draft symmetric draft to selected model face by using a parting plane as mid reference. The procedure to use this tool is given next.

- Click on the **Draft Body** tool from the **Detail Feature** section in the **More** drop-down of **Base** group in **Home** tab of **Ribbon**. The **Draft Body** dialog box will be displayed; refer to Figure-1.

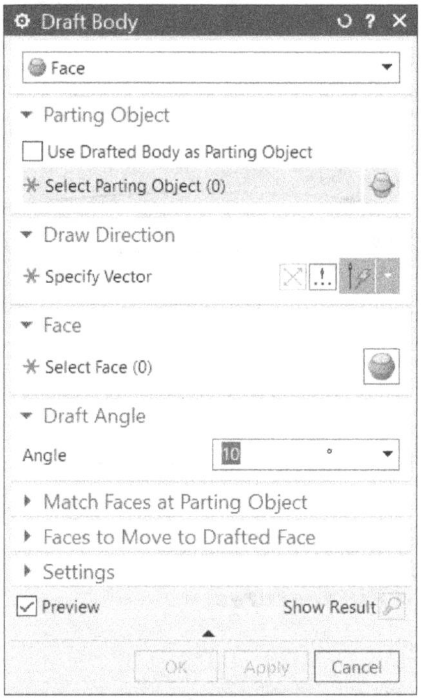

Figure-1. Draft Body dialog box

- Select the **Face** option from the drop-down at the top in the dialog box to use selected face for applying draft feature. Select the **Edge** option from the drop-down at the top in the dialog box to define start edge and end edge of face to which draft will be applied. Click on the **Select Face** selection button if **Face** option is selected in the drop-down and select the face. If **Edge** option is selected in the drop-down then click on the **Select Edges above Parting** selection button and select edge above the parting face/plane. Similarly, select the edge below the parting plane by using respective selection button. Refer to Figure-2 for different selections based on selected options.

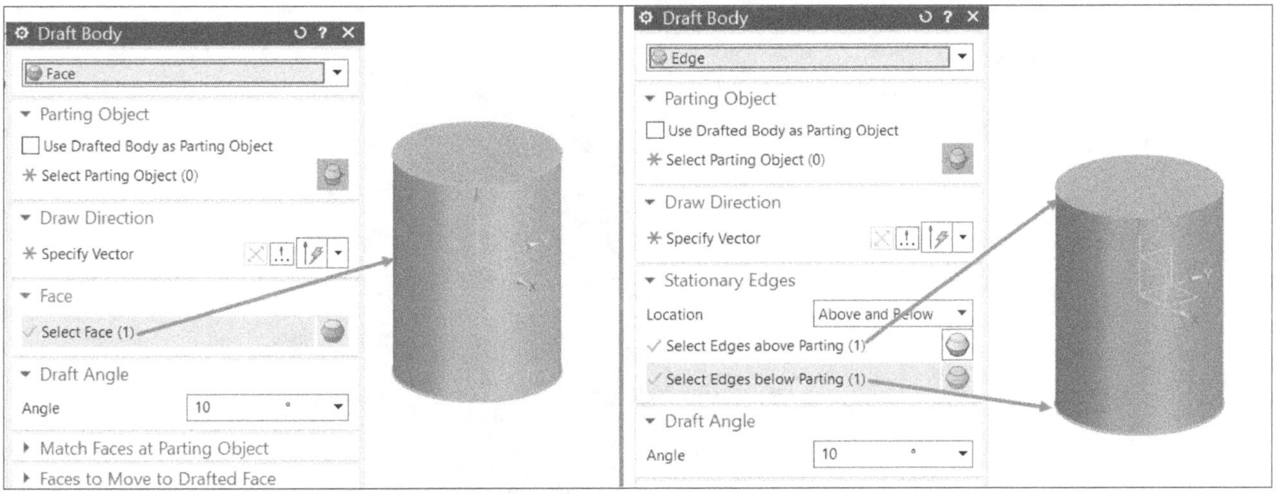

Figure-2. Selection for draft body

- After selecting desired face/edges, click on the **Select Parting Object** selection button from the dialog box and select the plane/face to be used as dividing plane for draft body; refer to Figure-3.

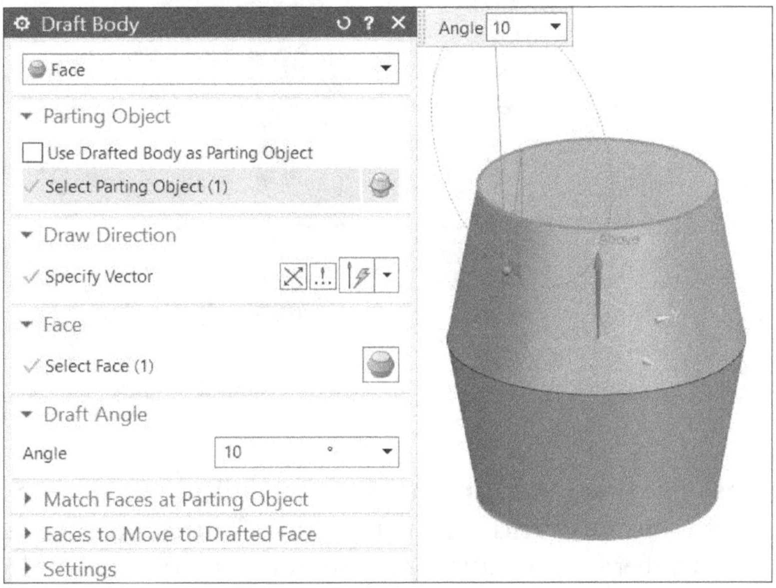

Figure-3. Preview of draft body

- Specify desired draft angle value in the **Angle** edit box of the **Draft Angle** rollout.
- If you are using a parting plane which is not dividing draft face symmetrically then there will be a step formed on draft face; refer to Figure-4. Expand the **Match Faces at Parting Object** rollout to define parameters for smooth transition of faces at parting plane. The options will be displayed as shown in Figure-4.
- Select the **To Isocline** option from the **Match Type** drop-down to connect edge of shorter face in straight path to edge of larger draft face making equal taper angle gradient. Select the **All** option from the **Match Scope** drop-down to include all faces of the model for matching two sides of parting plane. Using the options in the **Repair Parting Edges** drop-down, you can make the sharp edges connecting to parting plane model smooth by adding fillets or fillets with fade-in lines.
- Select the **Tangent to Face** option from the **Match Type** drop-down to make shorter face taper angle tangent to rounds applied on shorter face; refer to Figure-5.

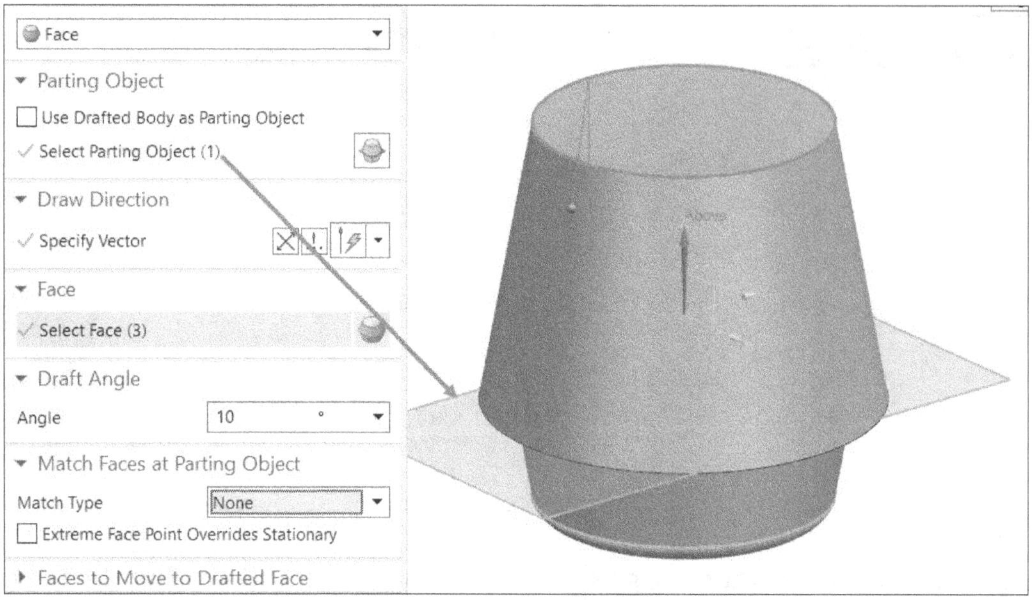

Figure-4. Unsymmetric draft face

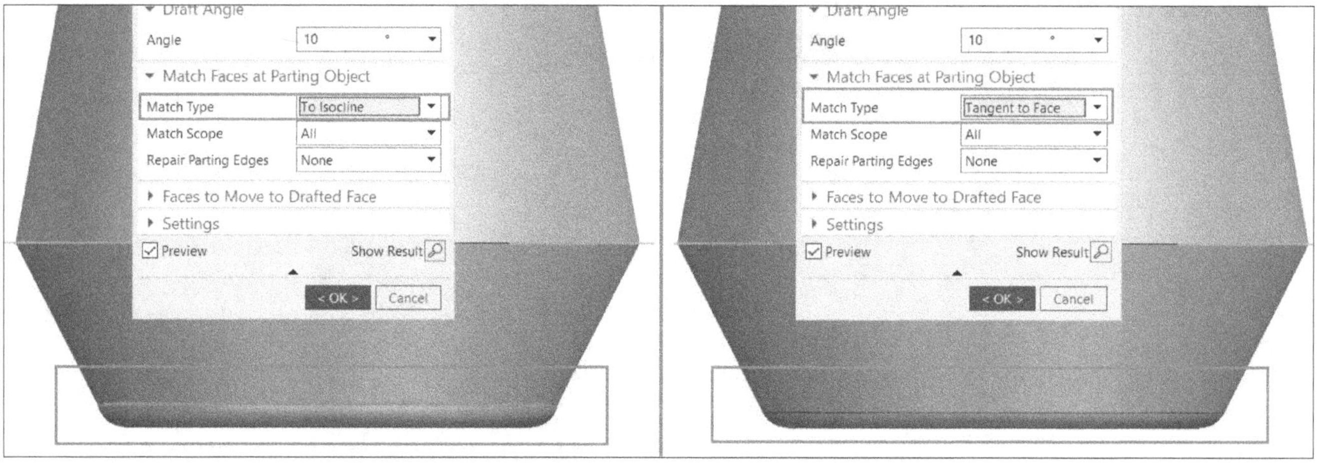

Figure-5. Preview of match type options

- Expand the **Faces to Move to Drafted Face** rollout and select desired faces to be included in draft feature and extended upto limits of main draft feature.
- Set the other parameters as discussed earlier and click on the **Apply** button to create the feature.

Creating Draft Body using Drafting Body as Parting Object

- Select the **Use Drafted Body as Parting Object** check box to create draft and fill the material with intersecting body. On selecting this check box, the options of the dialog box will be displayed; refer to Figure-6.
- Select the vector pointing in direction along which draft will be created. You will be asked to select faces to which draft will be applied.
- Select the faces to which you want to apply draft; refer to Figure-7. Preview of draft will be displayed; refer to Figure-8.
- Set the other parameters as discussed earlier and click on the **OK** button to create the feature.

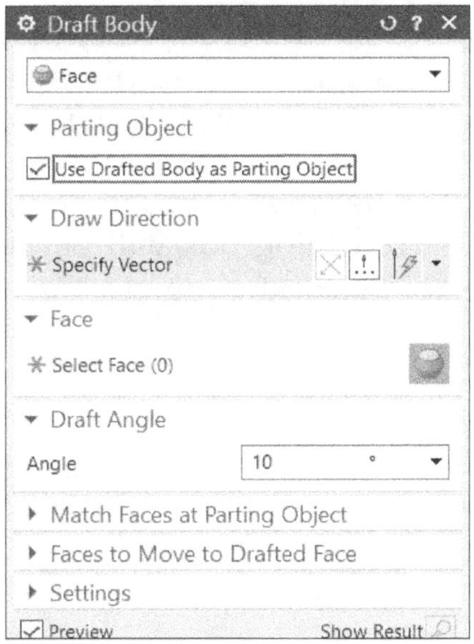

Figure-6. Using Drafted Body as Parting Object

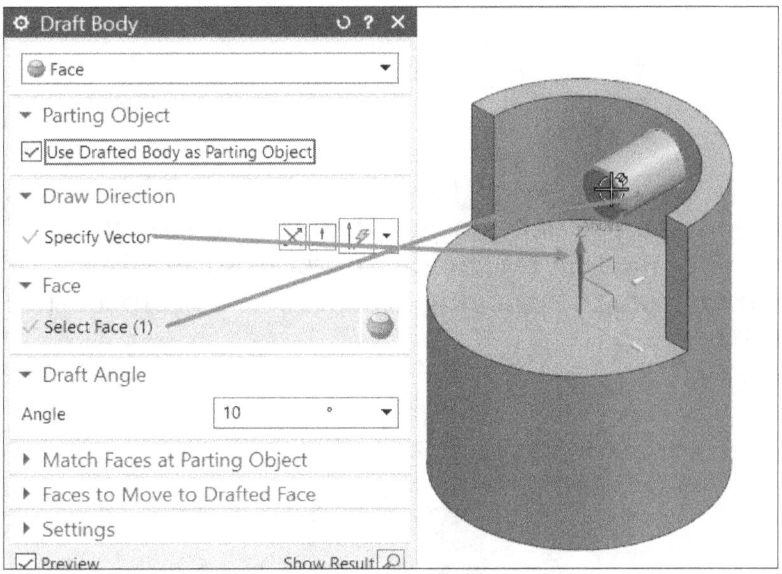

Figure-7. Selection for draft body used as parting object

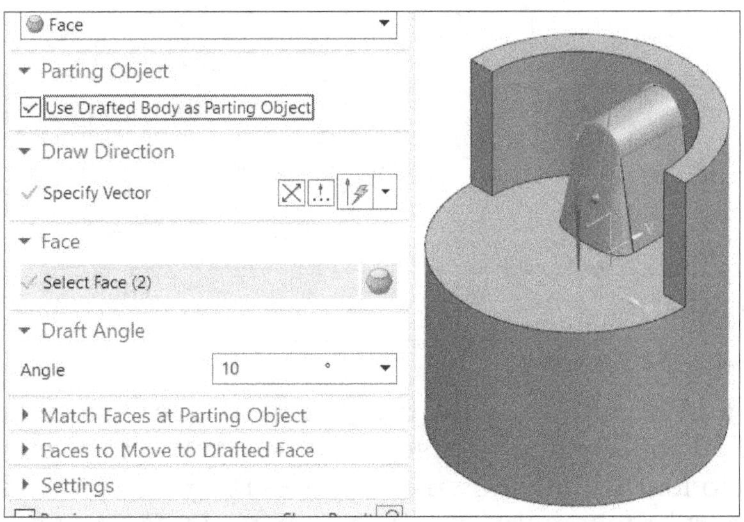

Figure-8. Preview of drafted body used as parting object

CREATING RIB FEATURE

Rib feature is used to provide strength to structure against tensile and compressive forces. The procedure to create a rib feature is given next.

- Click on the **Rib** tool from the **Detail Feature** section of **More** drop-down in the **Home** tab of the **Ribbon**. The **Rib** dialog box will be displayed; refer to Figure-9.

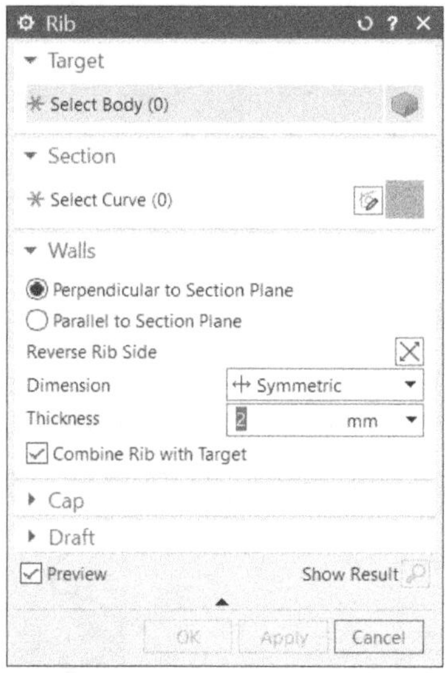

Figure-9. Rib dialog box

- Select the body (part) on which you want to create rib feature. You will be asked to select curve to be used as reference for generating rib feature.
- Select desired curve from the drawing area. Preview of rib feature will be displayed; refer to Figure-10.

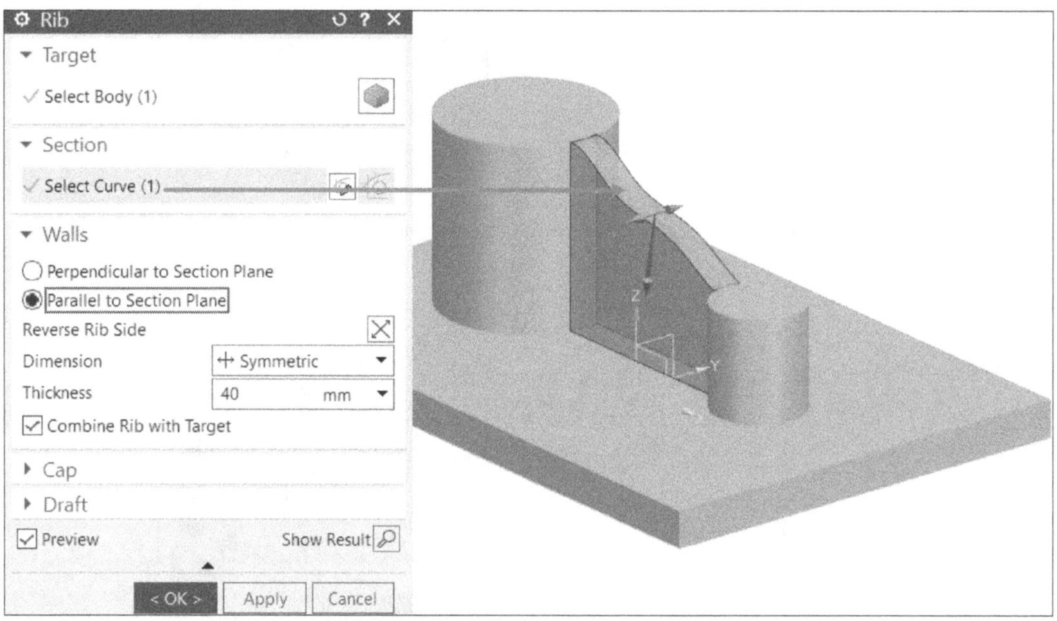

Figure-10. Preview of Rib feature

There are two types of ribs that can be created in 3D CAD software: **Profile Rib** and **Trajectory Rib**. In Profile rib, you use a single open chain curve connecting two walls for creating rib feature as shown in Figure-10. You can find this rib feature in wall mounted support brackets. In Trajectory rib, you use a net of intersecting curves to give tensile and compressive strength to box like thin structures. Procedures to create these features are discussed next.

Creating Rib Parallel to Plane (Profile Rib)

- After activating the **Rib** dialog box, select the **Parallel to Section Plane** radio button from the **Walls** rollout in the dialog box. You will be asked to select a curve to be used for creating rib feature.
- Select desired curve from the model. Preview of rib feature will be displayed; refer to Figure-11.

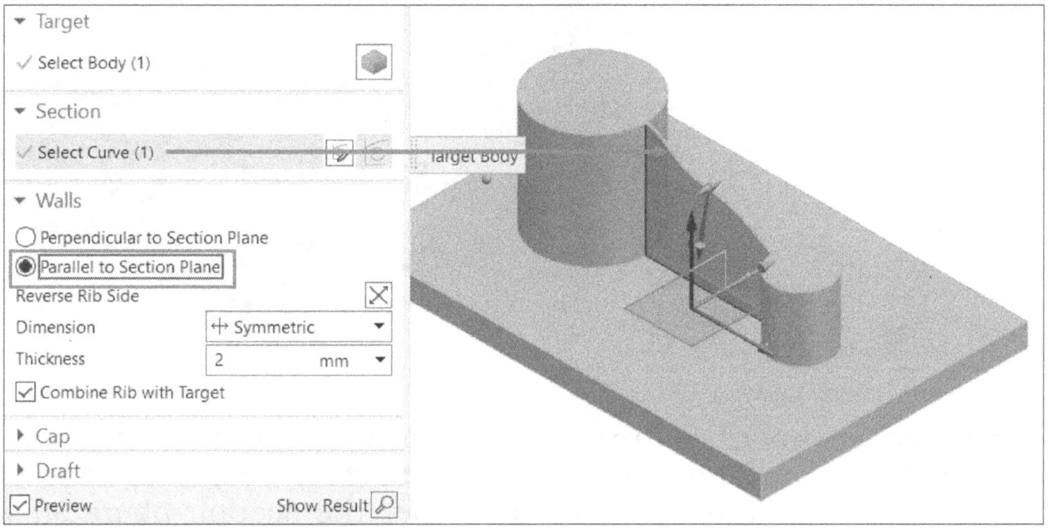

Figure-11. Preview of rib feature

- Select the **Symmetric** option from **Dimension** drop-down to keep rib symmetric about section plane of curve. Specify desired value in the **Thickness** edit box for defining rib width.
- Select the **Asymmetric** option from the **Dimension** drop-down to create rib on one side of the section plane; refer to Figure-12.

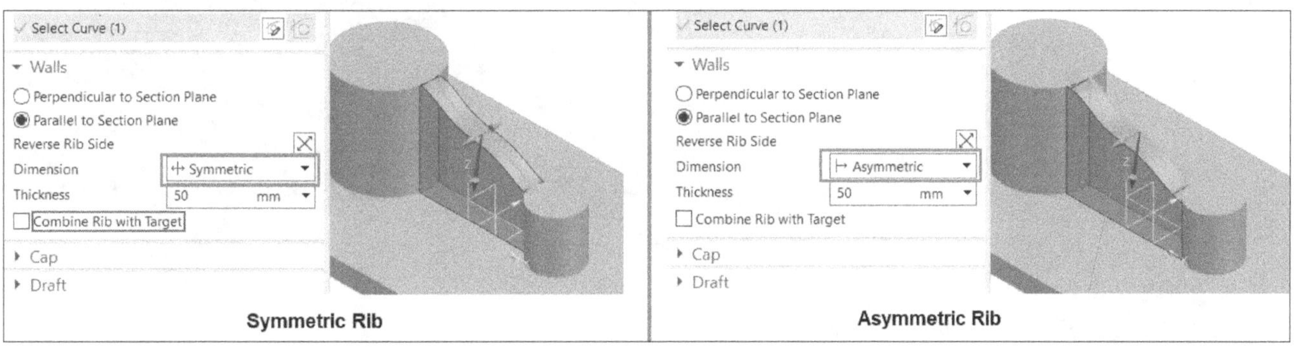

Figure-12. Symmetric and Asymmetric rib

- Select the **Combine Rib with Target** check box to unite the rib feature with base feature.
- Set the other parameters as discussed earlier and click on the **Apply** button to create the rib feature.

Creating Rib Perpendicular to Section Plane (Trajectory Rib)

- After activating the **Rib** dialog box, select the **Perpendicular to Section Plane** radio button from the **Walls** rollout to create net of rib feature. You will be asked to select curve(s).
- Select the curves to be used as reference for generating rib feature. Preview of rib feature will be displayed; refer to Figure-13.

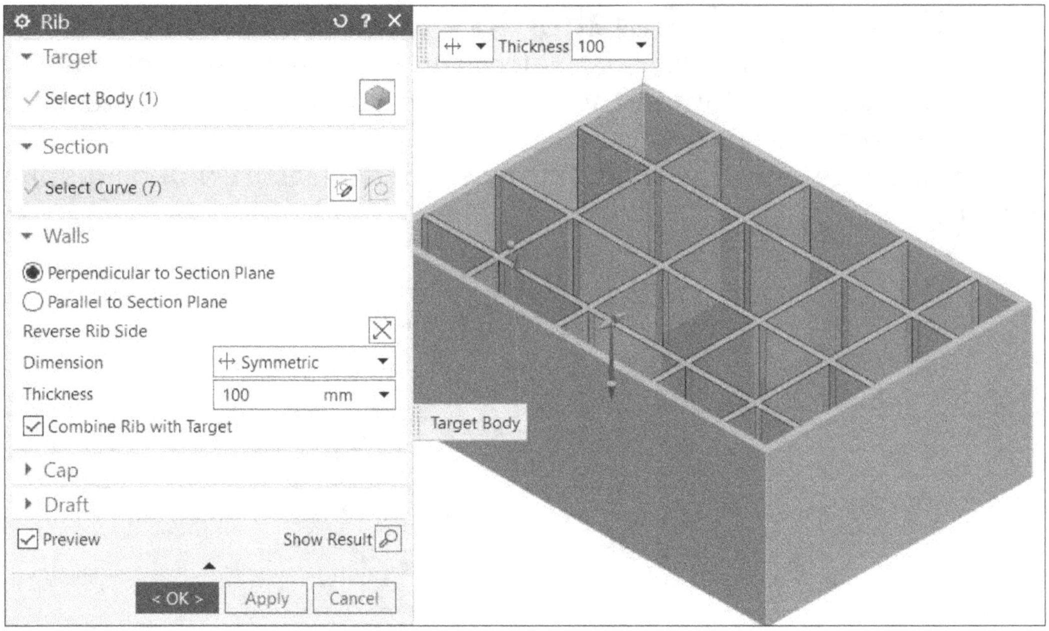

Figure-13. Preview of trajectory rib

- Set desired thickness of rib feature as discussed earlier in the **Thickness** edit box.
- Expand the **Cap** rollout and select the **From Section** option from the **Geometry** drop-down to define the top cap shape as per the section plane on which rib sketch was created as shown in Figure-13. Select the **From Selected** option from the **Geometry** drop-down to select a face/surface for defining shape of rib cap; refer to Figure-14.

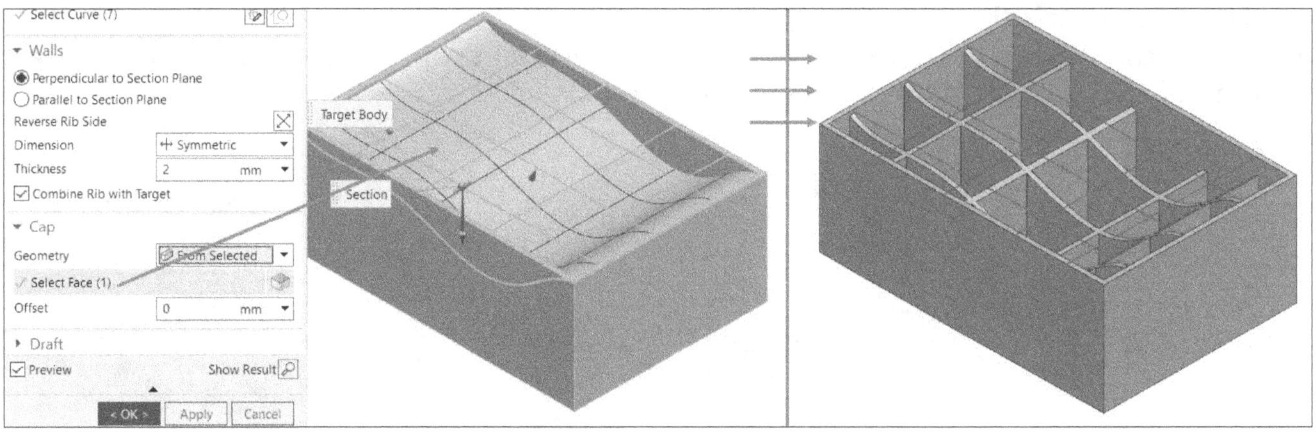

Figure-14. Preview of trajectory rib with selected cap surface

- Expand the **Draft** rollout and set desired taper angle for ribs as discussed earlier.
- Click on the **OK** button from the dialog box to create the ribs.

CREATING CONTOUR RIBS

The **Contour Rib** tool is used to create open rib feature perpendicular to selected face/surface. The procedure to use this tool is given next.

- Click on the **Contour Rib** tool from the **Detail Feature** section of **More** drop-down in the **Base** group of **Home** tab in the **Ribbon**. The **Contour Rib** dialog box will be displayed; refer to Figure-15 and you will be asked to select a face.

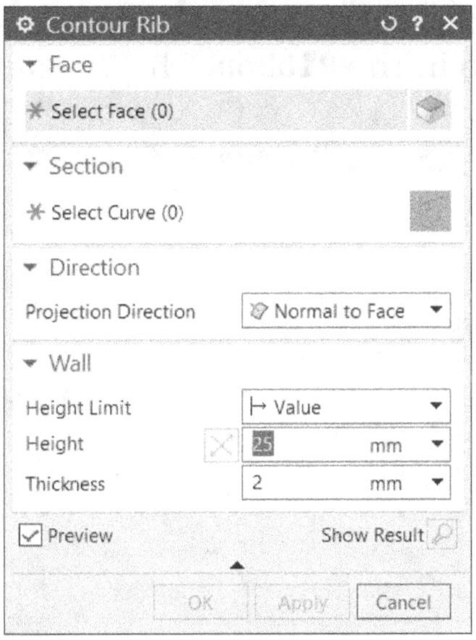

Figure-15. Contour Rib dialog box

- Select the face of model to be used as base of contour rib.
- Click on the **Select Curve** selection button from the **Section** rollout in the dialog box. You will be asked to select curve for creating contour rib.
- Select desired curve from the model. Preview of contour rib feature will be displayed; refer to Figure-16.

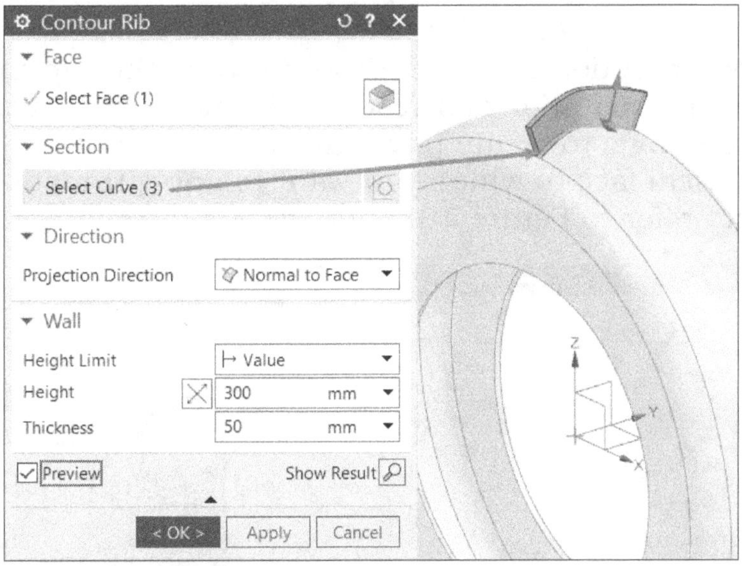

Figure-16. Preview of contour rib

- Specify desired values in the **Wall** rollout to define size of rib.
- Select the **Normal to Face** option from the **Projection Direction** drop-down in the **Direction** rollout of the dialog box to make rib feature perpendicular to selected face. Select the **Normal to Curve Plane** option from the drop-down to make rib feature perpendicular to plane of selected curve. Select the **Along Vector** option from the drop-down to use selected vector for defining direction of rib feature.
- Set the other parameters as discussed earlier and click on the **OK** button.

APPLYING THREADS TO CYLINDRICAL FACES

The **Thread** tool is used to apply internal and external threads to selected cylindrical faces. The procedure to use this tool is given next.

- Click on the **Thread** tool from the **Detail Feature** section of **More** drop-down in the **Base** group of **Home** tab in the **Ribbon**. The **Thread** dialog box will be displayed; refer to Figure-17.

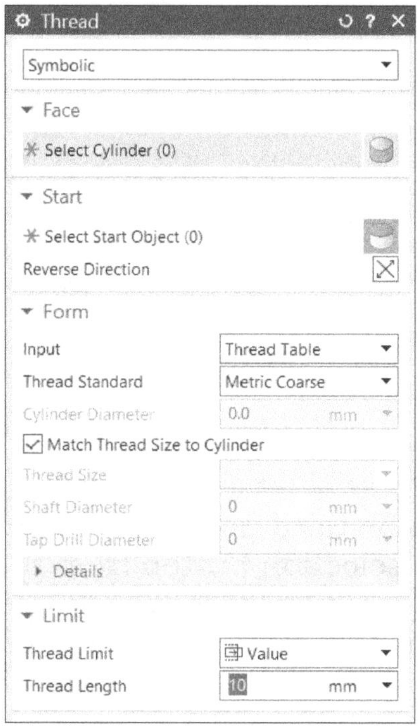

Figure-17. Thread dialog box

- Select the **Symbolic** option from the drop-down at the top in the dialog box to create symbolic representation of threads in the model. Select the **Detailed** option from the top drop-down to create physical thread form in the model.
- Select the cylindrical face to which you want to apply threads. Preview of thread will be displayed; refer to Figure-18.

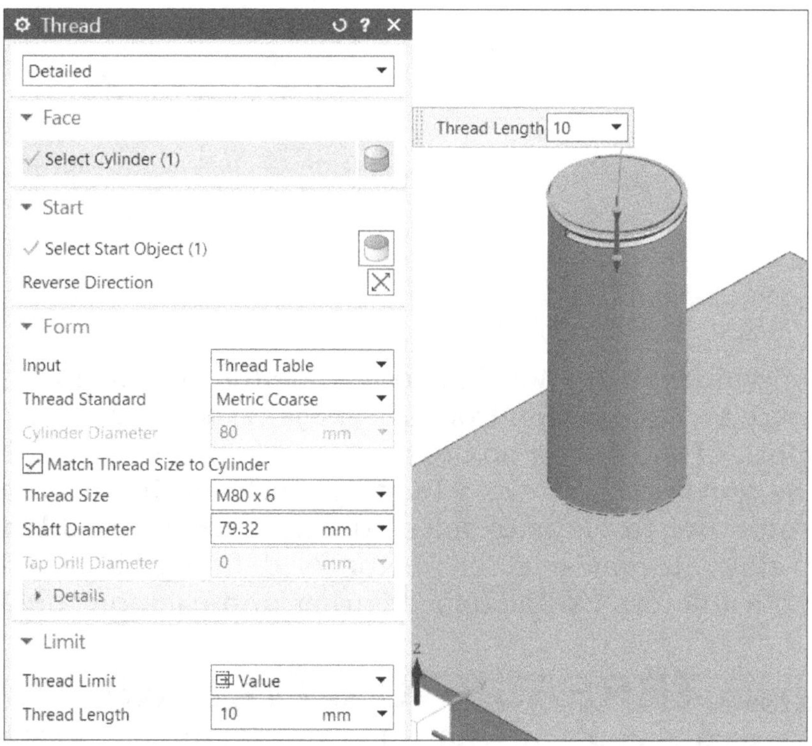

Figure-18. Preview of thread

Standard Thread Form

- Select the **Thread Table** option from the **Input** drop-down to use standard thread form using the thread form table. Note that you can easily find threading taps and cutting tools for standard thread form in the market.
- Select desired option from the **Thread Standard** drop-down to define the thread type to be used. You can find most of the standard thread forms in this drop-down like metric coarse, metric fine, Inch UNC, and so on.
- Select the **Match Thread Size to Cylinder** check box to automatically find thread sizes matching the diameter of cylinder. If you want to select different thread size then clear this check box and select desired option from the **Thread Size** drop-down.
- The value of shaft diameter is automatically defined in the **Shaft Diameter** edit box based on option selected in the **Thread Size** drop-down. You can also specify custom value in this edit box.
- Set desired parameters in the **Limit** rollout to define the length upto which threads will be created; refer to Figure-19.

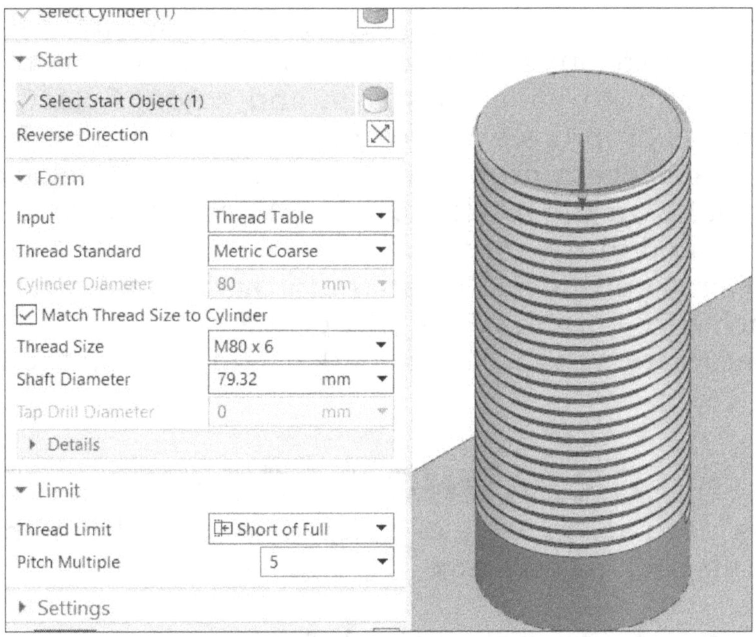

Figure-19. Preview of threads

- Expand the **Settings** rollout to define which diameter value will be used for deciding thread diameter. Select the **Tap Drill Diameter** option from the **Hole Size Preference** drop-down in the rollout to create thread based on diameter of tap drill cutting tool. Select the **Major Diameter** option from the drop-down to use diameter of shaft/hole as major diameter of thread.
- Set the other parameters as discussed earlier and click on the **Apply** button to create threads.

Manual Thread Form

- Select the **Manual** option from the **Input** drop-down to manually define thread size parameters which are not standard. The options in the dialog box will be displayed as shown in Figure-20.

Figure-20. Form rollout options

- Specify desired value in the **Shaft Diameter**, **Major Diameter**, **Minor Diameter**, **Pitch**, and **Angle** edit boxes to define shape & size of threads, manually.
- Expand the **Details** rollout to define the advanced parameters for thread form like thread orientation, number of starts, and so on. Select **Right Hand** option from the **Handedness** drop-down to create clockwise threads. Select the **Left Hand** option from the **Handedness** drop-down to create counter-clockwise threads.
- Specify desired value in the **Number of Starts** edit box to define the number of starts to be generated in the threads.
- Similarly, set desired cutting method in the **Method** drop-down to define machining process by which threads will be cut in workpiece.
- Set the other parameters as discussed earlier and click on the **OK** button to create the thread.

CREATING GROOVES

The **Groove** tool is used to cut slot of different shapes from the solid body. The procedure to use this tool is given next.

- Click on the **Groove** tool from the **Detail Feature** section of **More** drop-down in the **Base** group of **Home** tab in the **Ribbon**. The **Groove** dialog box will be displayed; refer to Figure-21.

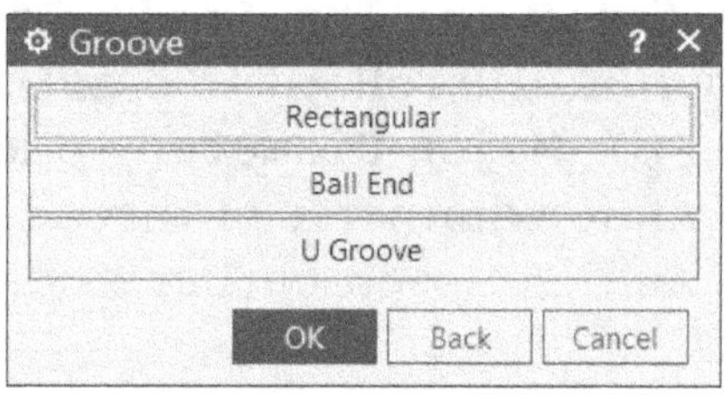

Figure-21. Groove dialog box

- Select desired button from the dialog box to define the shape of groove. Select the **Rectangular** button from the dialog box to create rectangular slot. Select the **Ball End** button from the dialog box. Select the **U Groove** button from the dialog box to create groove of U shape in the selected body. On selecting the button, respective dialog box will be displayed with edit box to specify name of the groove; refer to Figure-22.

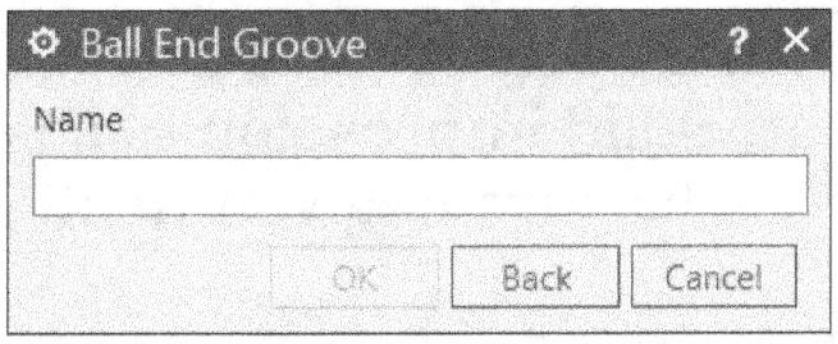

Figure-22. Ball End Groove dialog box

- Specify desired name of the feature and click on the face of model on which you want to create groove. The dialog box to specify size of groove will be displayed; refer to Figure-23.

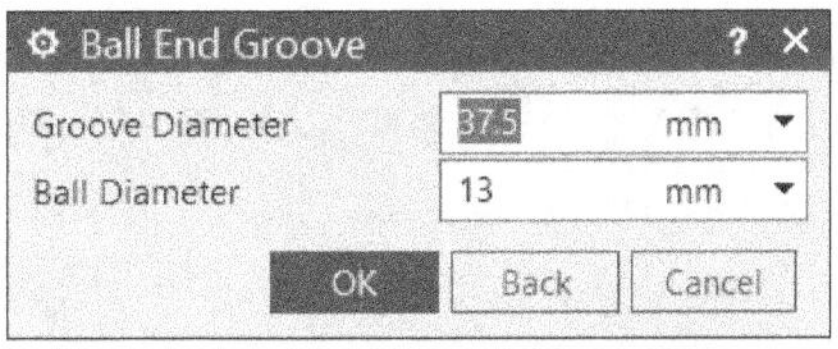

Figure-23. Ball End Groove dialog box

- Specify desired parameters in the dialog box and click on the **OK** button. Preview of groove position will be displayed with **Position Groove** dialog box; refer to Figure-24.

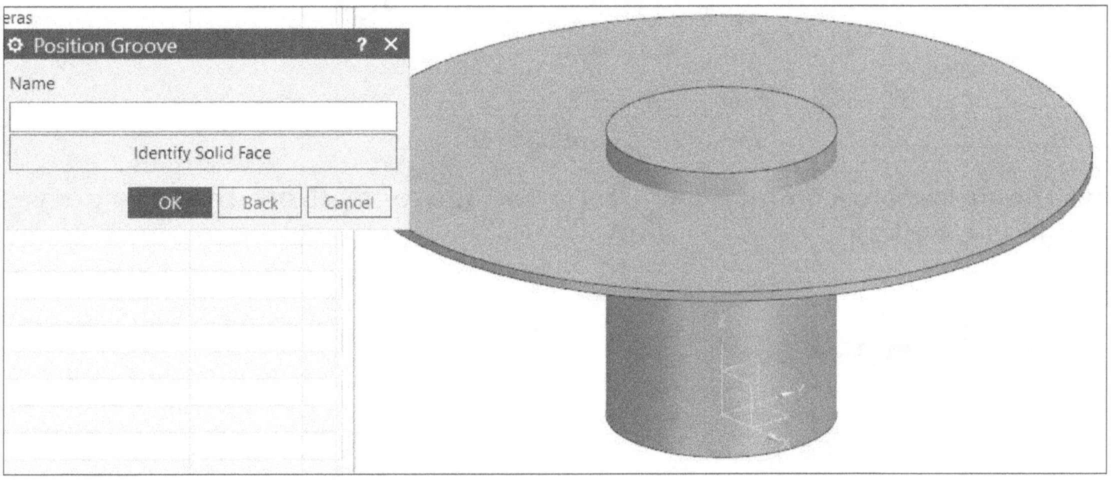

Figure-24. Preview of groove cut

- Click on the **OK** button from the dialog box. The groove will be created; refer to Figure-25. Press **ESC** to exit the tool.

Figure-25. Groove created

CREATING EMBOSS FEATURE

The **Emboss** tool is used to create solid impression of selected sketch on selected face. The procedure to create emboss feature is given next.

- Click on the **Emboss** tool from the **Design Feature** section of **More** drop-down in the **Feature** panel of **Ribbon**. The **Emboss** dialog box will be displayed; refer to Figure-26.

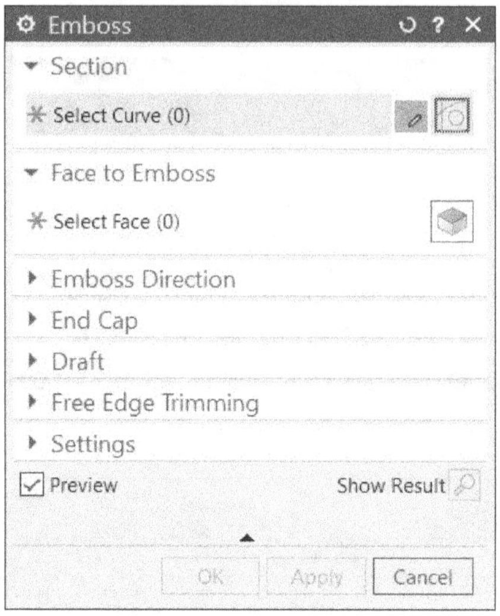

Figure-26. Emboss dialog box

- Select the curves to be embossed; refer to Figure-27. Note that the curve should be single closed loop.

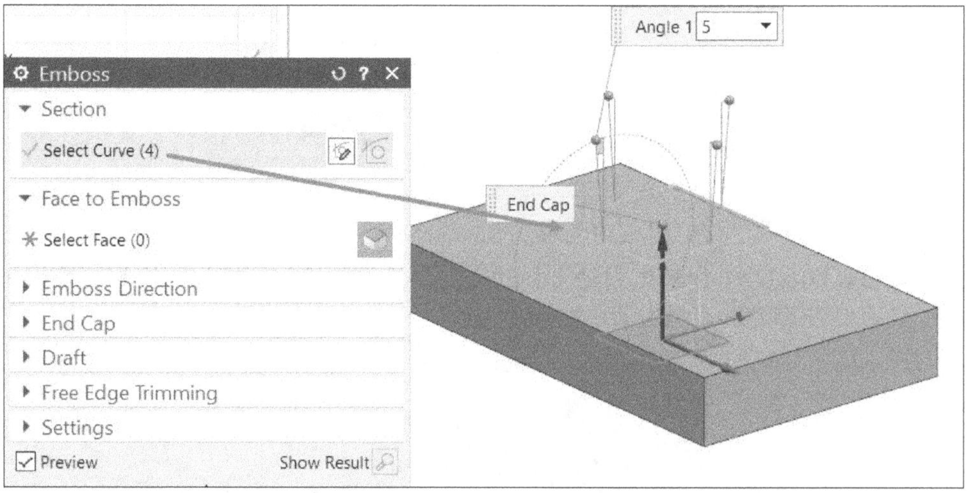

Figure-27. Curves selected for emboss

- Click on the **Select Face** selection option from the **Face to Emboss** rollout in the dialog box and select the face on which you want to emboss the sketch curves. Preview of the emboss feature will be displayed; refer to Figure-28.
- Expand the **Emboss Direction** rollout and click on the **Specify Direction** selection option from the dialog box and select desired vector for defining embossing direction.

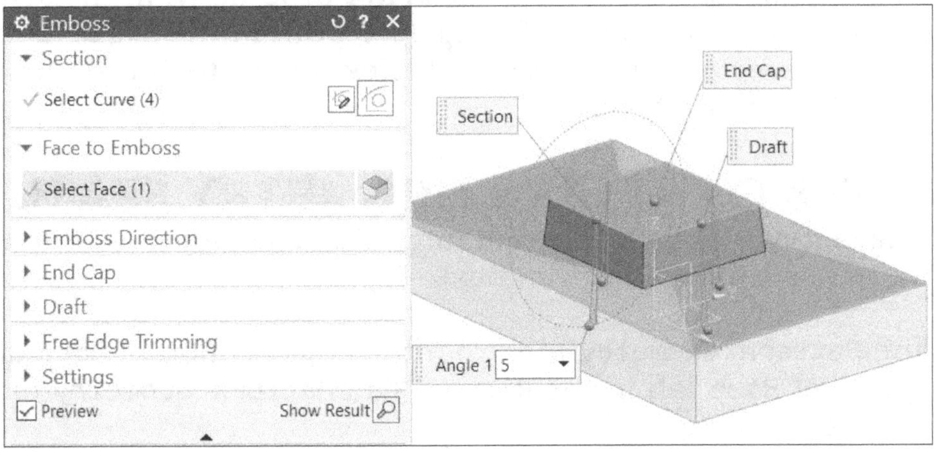

Figure-28. Preview of emboss feature

- Select the **Plane of Section** option from the **Geometry** drop-down in the **End Cap** rollout if you want the emboss feature to start from plane of sketch. Select the **Embossed Faces** option from the **Geometry** drop-down if you want to specify the thickness of emboss feature from the face on which it is being created; refer to Figure-29. Specify desired value of thickness in the **Distance** edit box below the drop-down. Select the **Datum Plane** option from the **Geometry** drop-down if you want the emboss feature to start from selected datum plane; refer to Figure-30. Select the **Selected Face** option from the **Geometry** drop-down if you want to specify the location from where emboss feature will start by selecting face.

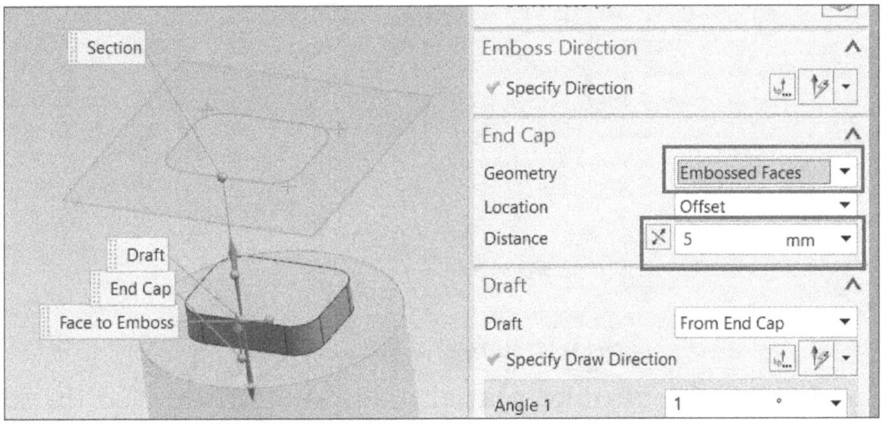

Figure-29. Using Embossed Faces option

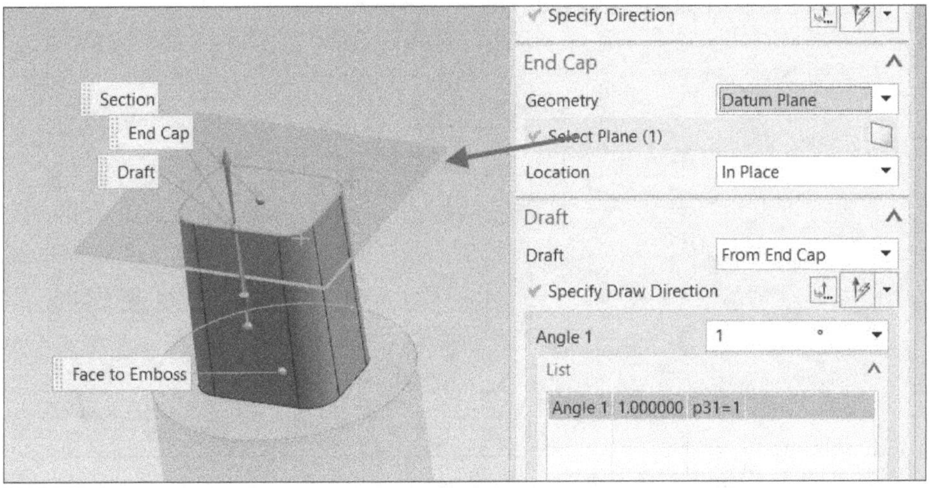

Figure-30. Preview of emboss feature using datum plane

- Select the **From End Cap** option from the **Draft** drop-down in the **Draft** rollout of the dialog box if you want to specify angle for draft in the **Angle 1** edit box.
- Set the other parameters as desired and click on the **OK** button from the dialog box to create the emboss feature.

CREATING PATTERN GEOMETRY FEATURE

The **Pattern Geometry** tool is used to create multiple copies of selected geometries. The procedure to use this tool is given next.

- Click on the **Pattern Geometry** tool from the **Copy** section of **More** drop-down in the **Base** group of **Home** tab in the **Ribbon**. The **Pattern Geometry** dialog box will be displayed; refer to Figure-31.

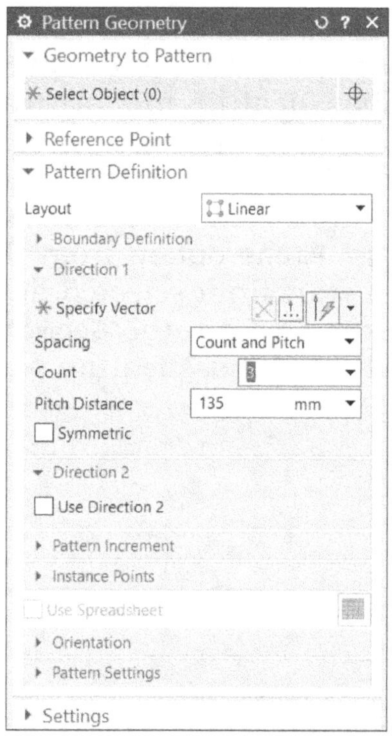

Figure-31. Pattern Geometry dialog box

- Select the geometry objects like plane, axis, sketch, and so on to be patterned from the model; refer to Figure-32.

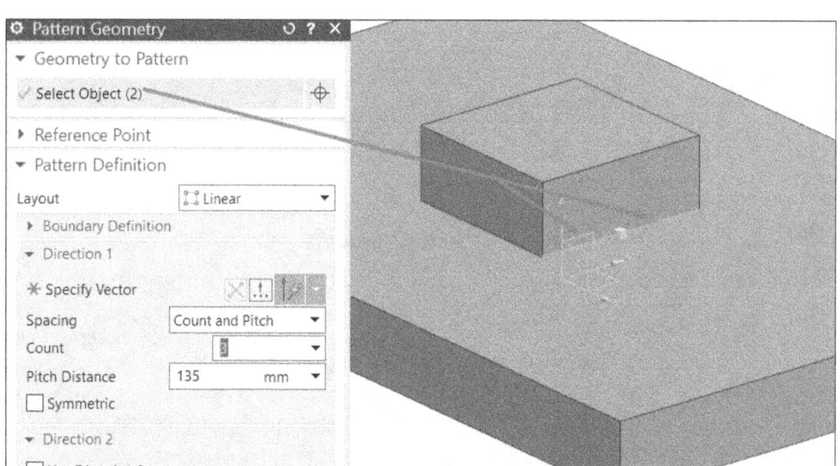

Figure-32. Object selected for pattern geometry

- Click on the **Specify Vector** selection option from the dialog box and select desired vector reference to be used as direction reference. Preview of pattern will be displayed; refer to Figure-33.

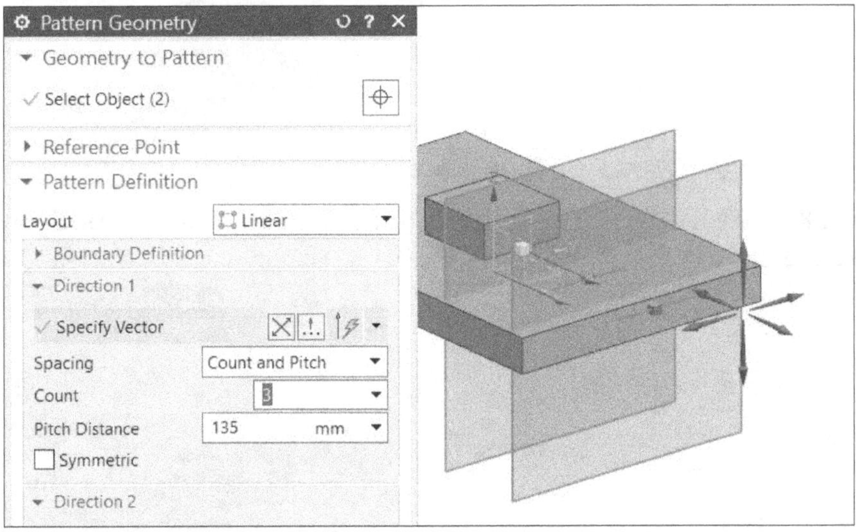

Figure-33. Preview of pattern geometry

- Set the other parameters as discussed earlier and click on the **OK** button to create the pattern.

Similarly, you can use the **Pattern Face**, **Pattern Body**, **Mirror Geometry**, and **Mirror Face** tools available in the **Copy** section of **More** drop-down in the **Base** group of **Home** tab in the **Ribbon**.

PROMOTING BODY

The **Promote Body** tool is used to bring loaded assembly component to the level of current assembly. The procedure to use this tool is given next.

- Click on the **Promote Body** tool from the **Copy** section of **More** drop-down in the **Base** group of **Home** tab in the **Ribbon**. The **Promote Body** dialog box will be displayed; refer to Figure-34.

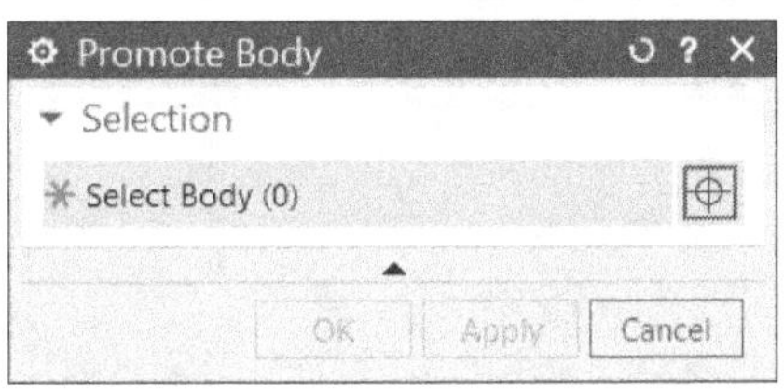

Figure-34. Promote Body dialog box

- Select the part of loaded assembly to make it a new body in the model; refer to Figure-35.

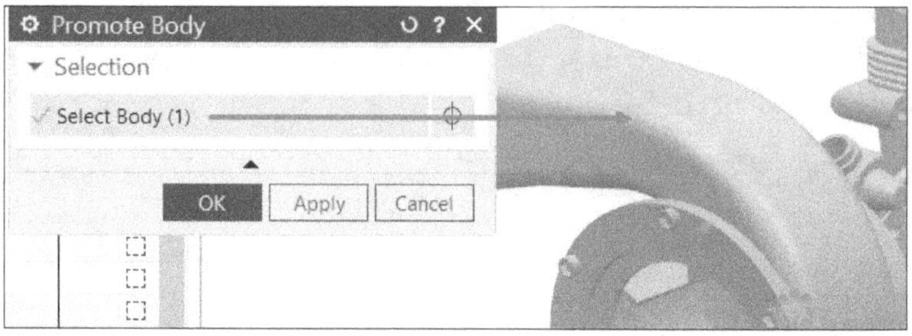

Figure-35. Selecting part for promote body

- Click on the **OK** button from the dialog box. The promoted body will be added in the **Part Navigator**; refer to Figure-36.

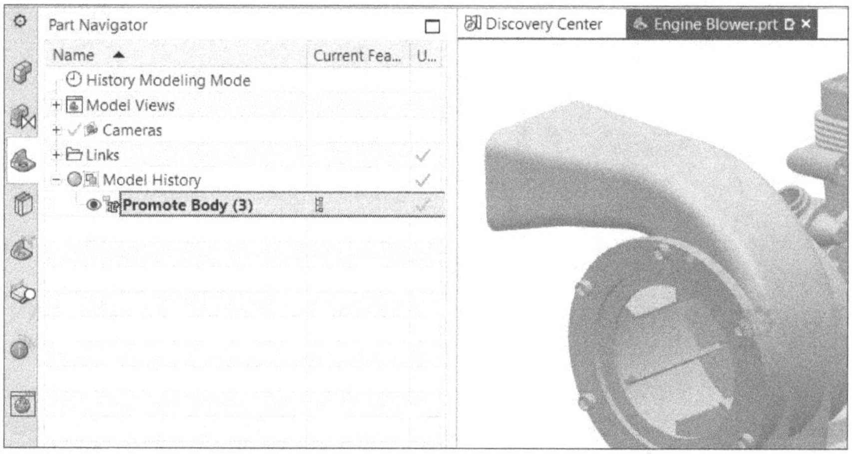

Figure-36. Promoted body in Part Navigator

ISOLATING OBJECTS OF FEATURE

The **Isolate Object of Feature** tool is used to isolate an object from selected feature which is nearest to a proximity object. In simple terms, you can extract a part (object) of selected feature which is nearest to specified datum reference for performing further operations on that object only. The procedure to use this tool is given next.

- Click on the **Isolate Object of Feature** tool from the **Copy** section of **More** drop-down in the **Base** group of **Home** tab in the **Ribbon**. The **Isolate Object of Feature** dialog box will be displayed; refer to Figure-37.

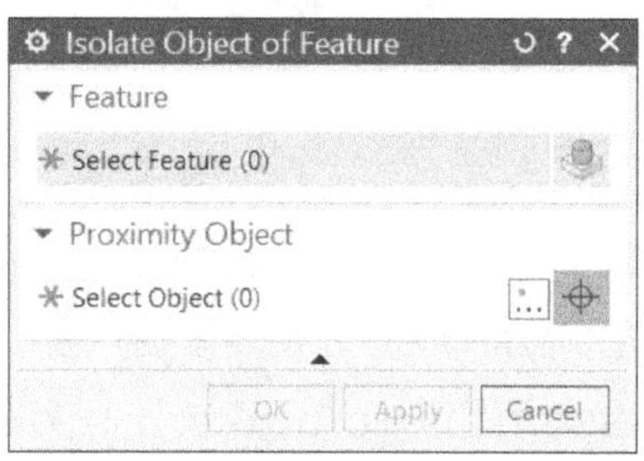

Figure-37. Isolate Object of Feature dialog box

- Select the feature from which you want to isolate the object. You will be asked to select proximity object.
- Select the object to be used as proximity reference; refer to Figure-38.

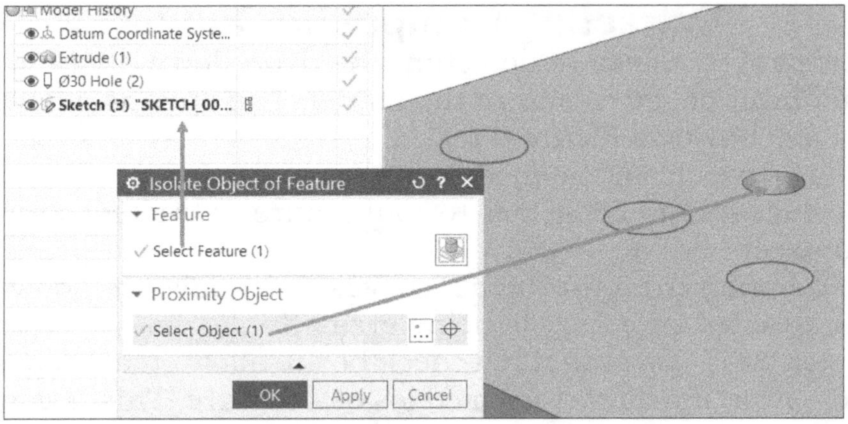

Figure-38. Selecting objects for isolation

- Click on the **OK** button from the dialog box after selecting desired objects. The isolated object will be added in the **Part Navigator**; refer to Figure-39.

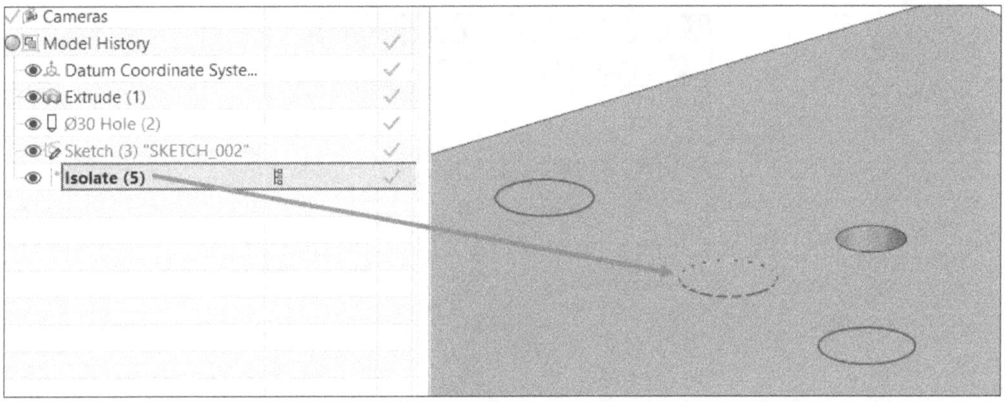

Figure-39. Isolated object nearest to proximity object

EXTRACTED GEOMETRY

The **Extract Geometry** tool is used to create associative copy of selected objects. The procedure to use this tool is given next.

- Click on the **Extract Geometry** tool from the **Copy** section of **More** drop-down in the **Base** group of **Home** tab in the **Ribbon**. The **Extract Geometry** dialog box will be displayed; refer to Figure-40.

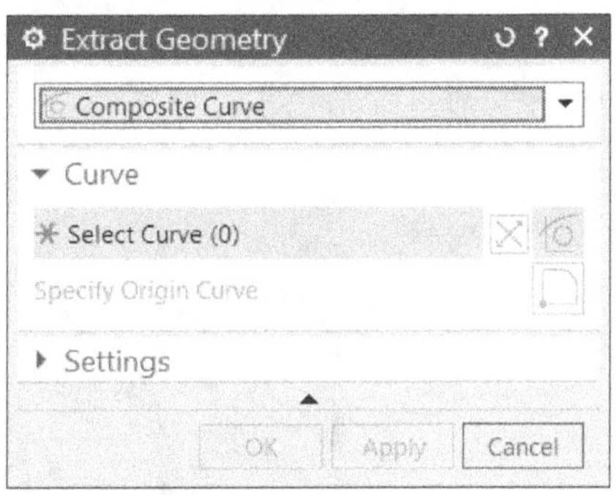

Figure-40. Extract Geometry dialog box

- Select desired option from the drop-down at the top in the dialog box to define the type of object to be extracted from the model. The procedures to use these options are discussed next.

Extracting Composite Curves

- Select the **Composite Curve** option from the drop-down at the top in the dialog box to extract multiple curves from the model. The options in the dialog box will be displayed as shown in Figure-41.
- Select desired curves from the model to be extracted.
- Select the **Associative** check box to make sure extracted curve gets changed according to parent curve.
- Select desired option from the **Input Curves** drop-down to show or hide objects from which extracted geometry is being created.
- Select the **Allow Self-intersection** check box to allow creation of self intersecting curves when extracting curves from edges of a feature. This is generally useful in extracting curves generated by selecting 3D edges.
- Select the **Advanced Curve Fit** check box to spline parameters like degree, number of segments, and so on.

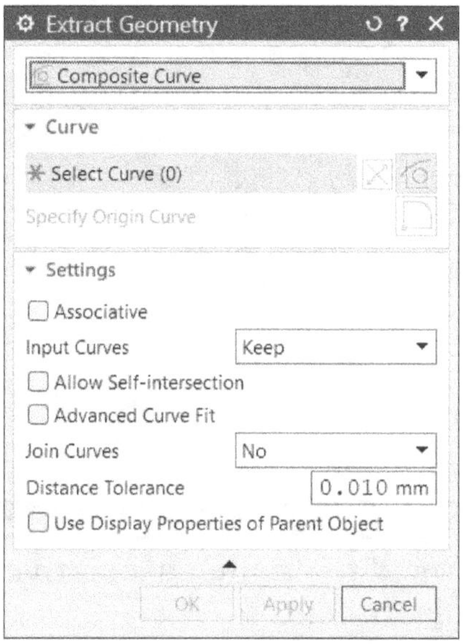

Figure-41. Extract Geometry dialog box for Composite Curve option

- Select the **Use Display Properties of Parent Object** check box to keep same properties in extracted geometry as in original geometry.
- Set the other parameters as discussed earlier and click on the **Apply** button to create extracted geometry.

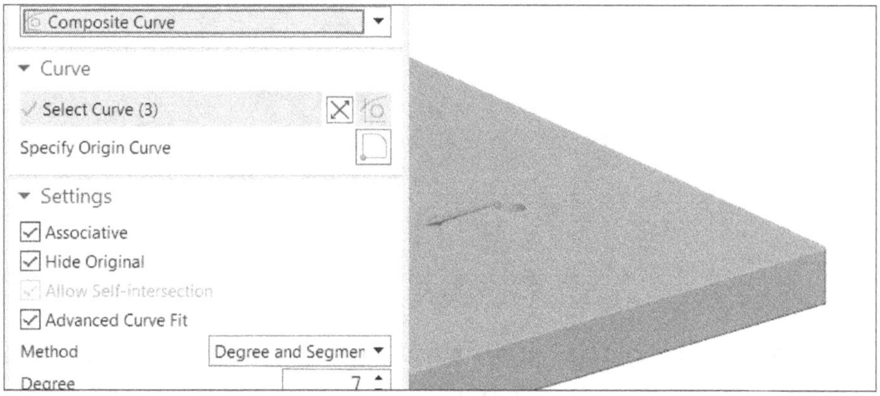

Figure-42. Preview of extracted composite curves

Extracting Point

- Select the **Point** option from the drop-down to extract selected points. The options in the dialog box will be displayed as shown in Figure-43.

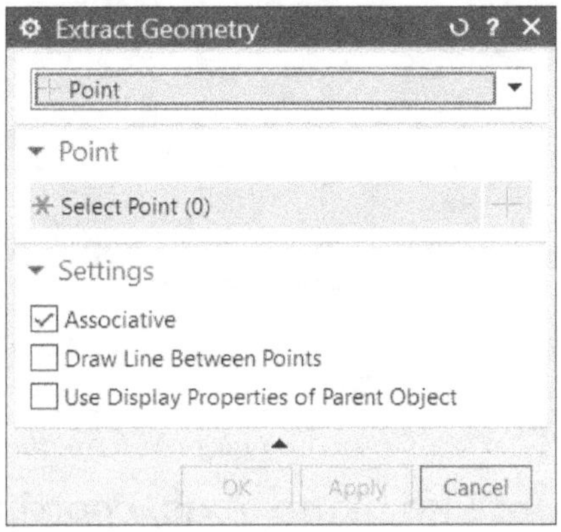

Figure-43. Extract Geometry dialog box for Point option

- Select desired snap toggle buttons from the **Snap Point** drop-down in the **Scene Bar** to activate respective point selection filters; refer to Figure-44.

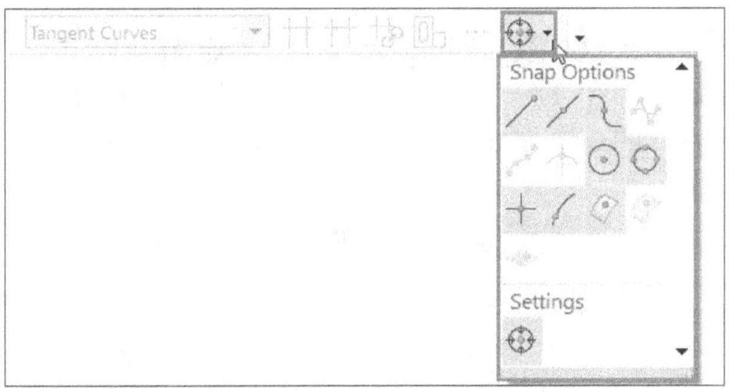

Figure-44. Snap Options

- Select desired points from the model to be extracted; refer to Figure-45 and click on the **Apply** button to perform the operation.

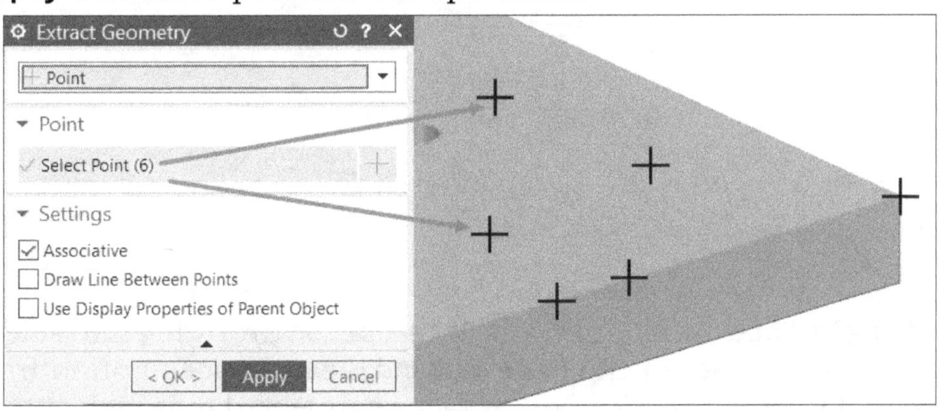

Figure-45. Preview of extracted points

Extracting Datum Feature

- Select the **Datum** option from the drop-down to extract selected datum reference like plane, axis, point, coordinate system, and so on. The options in the dialog box will be displayed as shown in Figure-46.

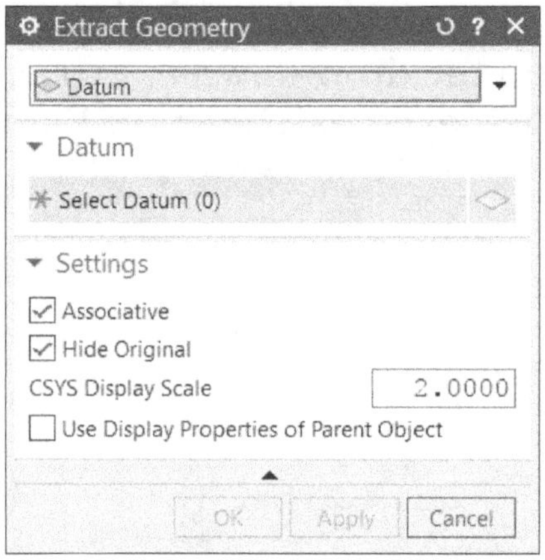

Figure-46. Extract Geometry dialog box for Datum option

- Select desired datum feature like plane, axis, coordinate system, and so on from the model and click on the **Apply** button to extract the feature.
- Similarly, you can select the **Sketch** option from the drop-down to extract selected sketch from the model.

Extracting Face Feature

- Select the **Face** option from the drop-down at the top in the dialog box to extract selected face(s) as separate feature. The options in the dialog box will be displayed as shown in Figure-47.

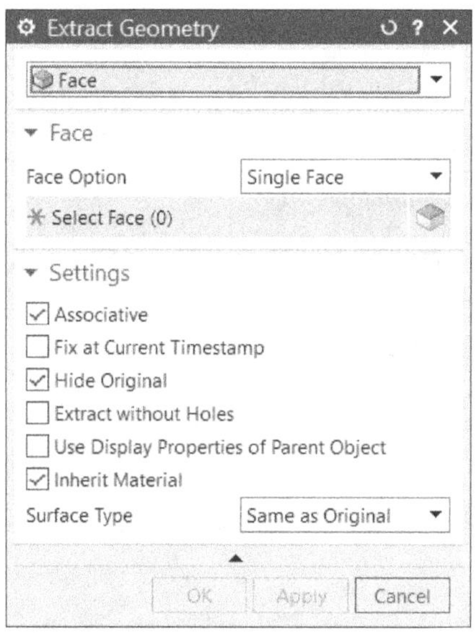

Figure-47. Extract Geometry dialog box for Face option

- Select the **Single Face** option from the **Face Option** drop-down to select individual faces to be extracted. Select the **Face and Adjacent Faces** option from the drop-down to extract selected face and other faces connected to it. Select the **Body Faces** option from the drop-down to extract all the faces of selected body. Select the **Face Chain** option from the drop-down to select chain of multiple faces.
- After selecting desired option from the drop-down, select respective face(s) from the model. Preview of extracted faces will be displayed.
- Select the **Fix at Current Timestamp** check box from **Settings** rollout to maintain order of extracted feature in **Part Navigator** after extraction.
- Select the **Extract without Holes** check box to ignore holes of selected faces when creating extracted faces.

- Select the **Inherit Material** check box to include material properties applied to the material properties applied to selected faces when created extracted faces.
- Set the other parameters as discussed earlier and click on the **Apply** button to create the feature.

Creating Extracted Region of Faces

- Select the **Region of Faces** option from the drop-down at the top in the **Extract Geometry** dialog box to extract a chain of faces starting from seed face and bound by boundary faces. Generally, this option is useful for extracting faces to later perform various analyses like CFD, stress analysis, and so on. On selecting this option, the options in the dialog box will be displayed as shown in Figure-48.

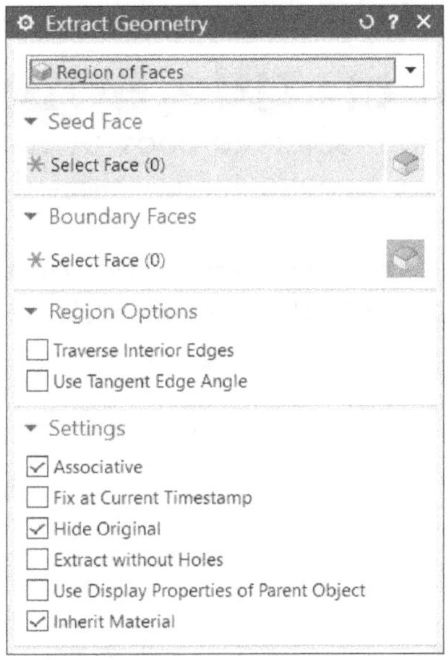

Figure-48. Extract Geometry dialog box for Region of Faces option

- By default, selection button for **Seed Face** is active. Select the face of model to be used as starting face for extracting connected faces. You will be asked to select boundary faces.

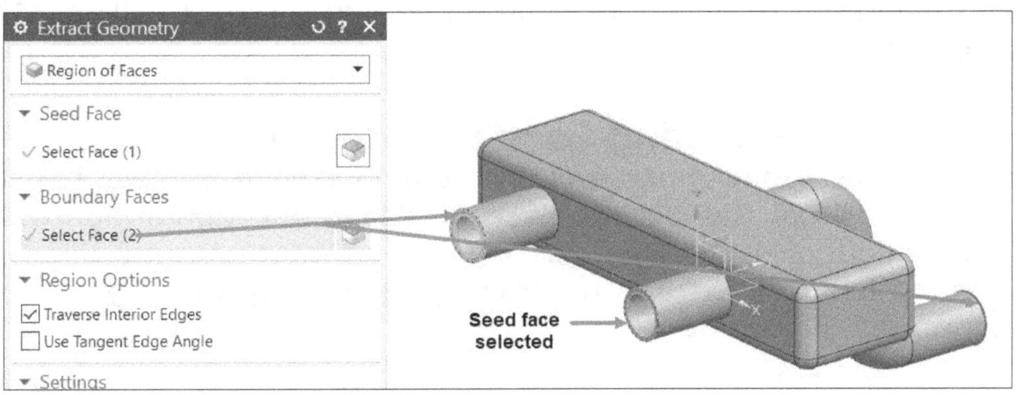

Figure-49. Selection for extracting region of faces

- Select the **Traverse Interior Edges** check box to select all the faces within specified boundaries excluding selected boundary faces.
- Select the **Use Tangent Edge Angle** check box to specify angle value above which tangent edges will not be considered for traverse.
- Set the other parameters as discussed earlier and click on the **Apply** button. The extracted region will be created; refer to Figure-50.

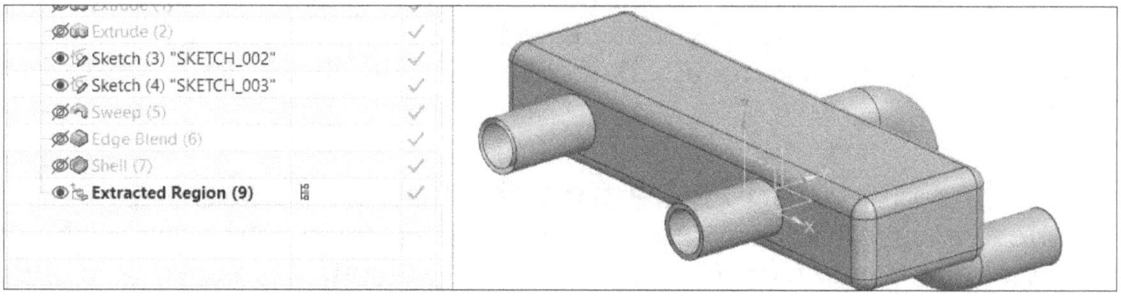

Figure-50. Extracted region created

Similarly, you can use the **Body** and **Mirror Body** options of the **Extract Geometry** dialog box.

SPLITTING BODY

The **Split Body** tool is used to split selected body by using a face, a plane, an extrude feature, or a revolve feature. The procedure to use this tool is given next.

- Click on the **Split Body** tool from the **Trim** section of **More** drop-down in the **Home** tab of the **Ribbon**. The **Split Body** dialog box will be displayed; refer to Figure-51.

Figure-51. Split Body dialog box

- Click on the **Select Body** selection option from the **Target** rollout of the dialog box and select the body to be split.

Selecting Face or Plane Tool

- Select the **Face or Plane** option from the **Tool Option** drop-down to use a face or plane as splitting tool. The **Select Face or Plane** selection option will be active in the **Tool** rollout of the dialog box.
- Select desired face/plane from the drawing area using which you want to split the body; refer to Figure-52.

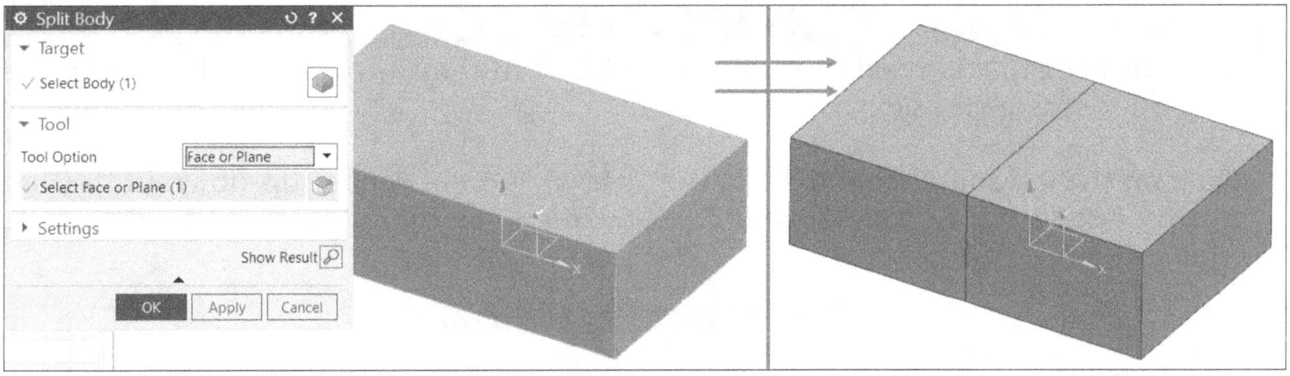

Figure-52. Preview of split body using face plane

Using New Plane as Tool

- Select the **New Plane** option from the drop-down to create a plane to be used as splitting tool. The options in the dialog box will be displayed as shown in Figure-53.

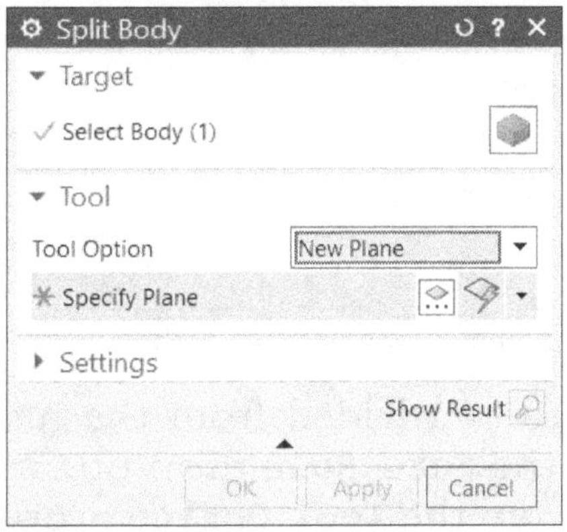

Figure-53. Plane option for Split Body dialog box

- Click on the **Plane Dialog** button from the **Specify Plane** selection options to use **Plane** dialog box for creating desired splitting plane. The options of this dialog box have been discussed earlier. The created plane will be selected automatically as splitting tool; refer to Figure-54.

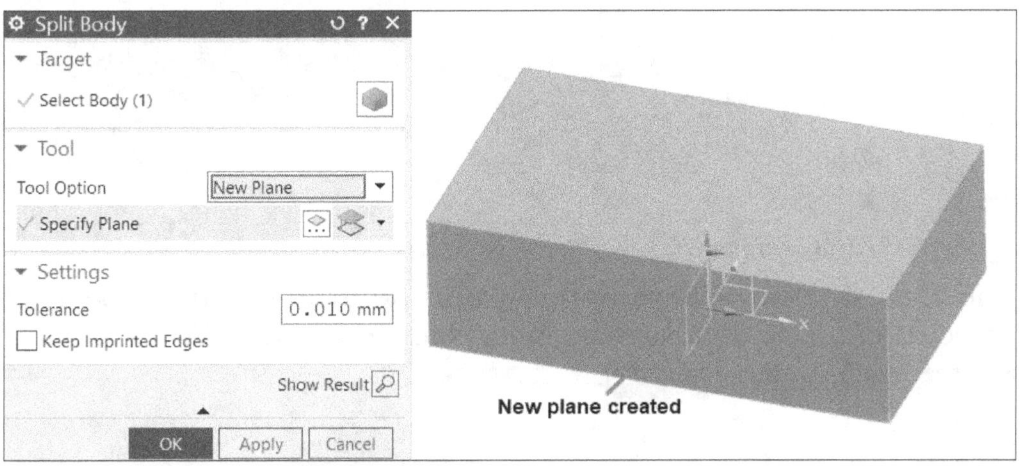

Figure-54. Using new plane for splitting body

- Select the **Keep Imprinted Edges** check box from the **Settings** rollout
- Set the other parameters as discussed earlier and click on the **Apply** button to perform splitting.

Similarly, you can use the **Extrude** and **Revolve** options from the **Tool Option** drop-down to create respective type of features as splitting tools.

DIVIDING FACE

The **Divide Face** tool is used to split selected face into multiple faces. The procedure to use this tool is given next.

- Click on the **Divide Face** tool from the **Trim** section of **More** drop-down in the **Base** group of **Home** tab in the **Ribbon**. The **Divide Face** dialog box will be displayed; refer to Figure-55.

Figure-55. Divide Face dialog box

- Select the face of model to be divided from the model. Make sure to select the **Single Face** option from the **Face Rule** drop-down of **Scene Bar**.
- Select the **Object** option from the **Tool Option** drop-down to select desired object like sketch, curve, face, plane, and so on; refer to Figure-56.

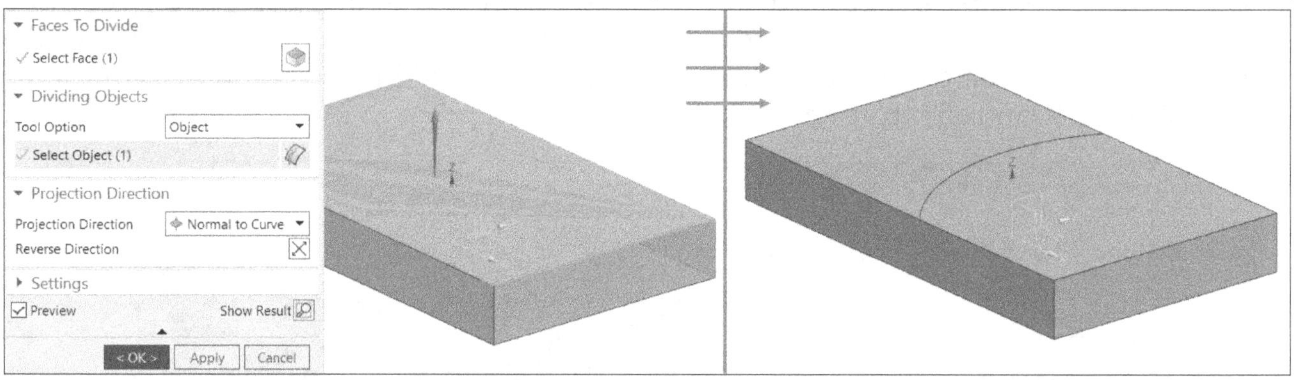

Figure-56. Selecting object for dividing face

- Select the **Line by Two Points** option from the drop-down to specify start point and end point of a line dividing the face; refer to Figure-57.

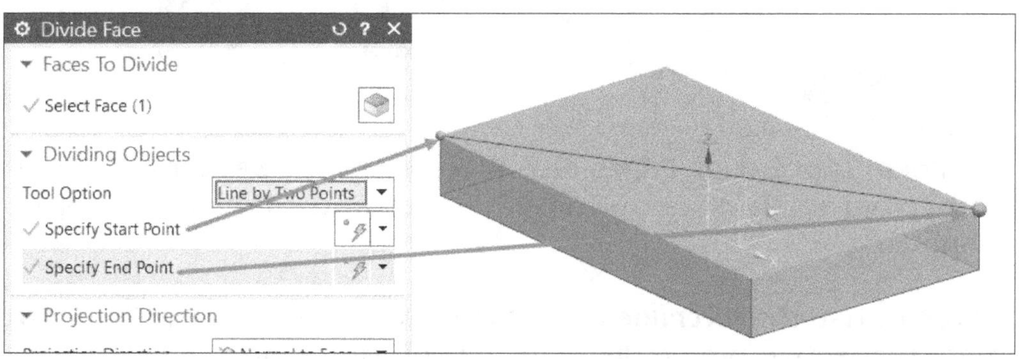

Figure-57. Using Line by Two Points for dividing face

- Select the **Offset Curve in Face** option from the **Tool Option** drop-down to select an edge/curve and offset it at specified distance to define face dividing tool; refer to Figure-58.

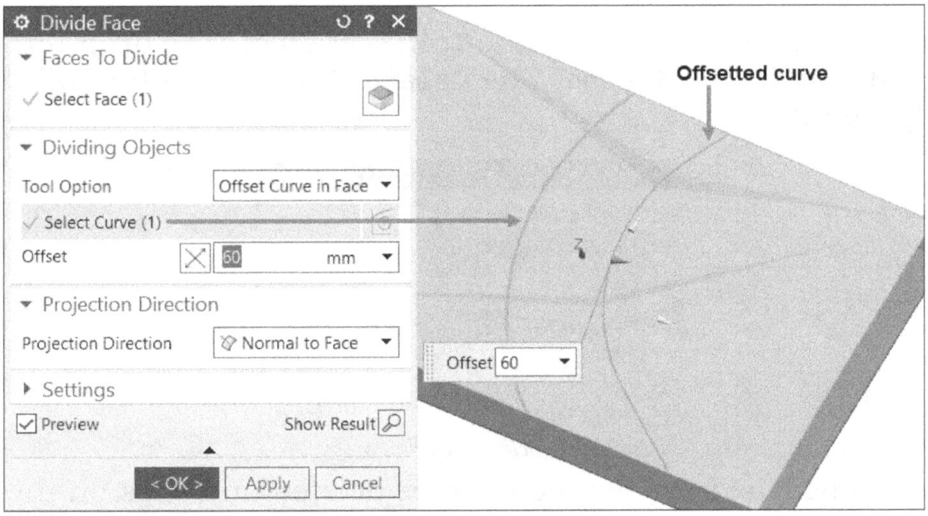

Figure-58. Preview of offsetted curve

- Select the **Iso-parametric Curve** option from the **Tool Option** drop-down to specify the location point at which selected face will be split; refer to Figure-59.

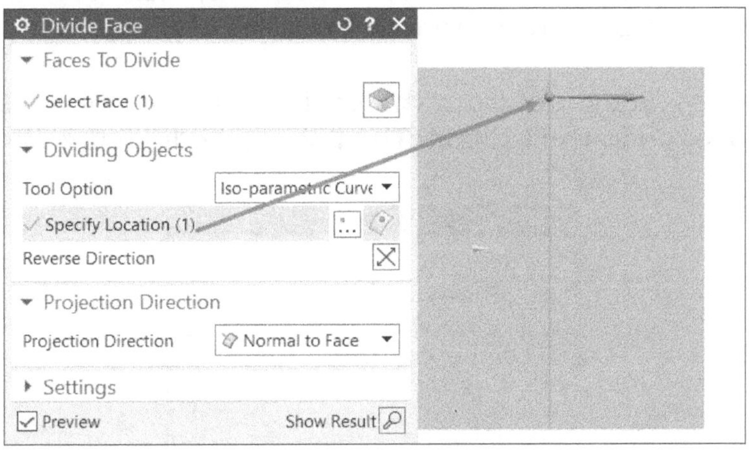

Figure-59. Location selected

- Select the **Normal to Face** option from the **Projection Direction** drop-down to define the direction in which selected tool object will be projected. Select the **Along Vector** option from the drop-down to specify direction of projection.
- Select the **Hide Dividing Objects** check box to hide tools being used for dividing the object.
- Select the **Do Not Project Curves That Lie in Faces** check box to ignore curves that lie on the selected face from being projected.
- Select the **Extend Dividing Object to Meet Face Edge** check box to automatically extend selected dividing object upto the edges of the selected face to perform divide operation.
- Set the other parameters as discussed earlier and click on the **OK** button. The divided faces will be created.

DELETE BODY

The **Delete Body** tool is used to delete selected body(s) from the model. The procedure to use this tool is given next.

- Click on the **Delete Body** tool from the **Trim** section of **More** drop-down in the **Base** group of **Home** tab in the **Ribbon**. The **Delete Body** dialog box will be displayed; refer to Figure-60.

Figure-60. Delete Body dialog box

- Select desired body(s) from the model to be deleted and click on the **OK** button to delete selected body(s).

EMBOSSING BODY

The **Emboss Body** tool is used to combine target body with tool body at intersecting section of tool body. The procedure to use this tool is given next.

- Click on the **Emboss Body** tool from the **Combine** section of **More** drop-down in the **Base** group of **Home** tab in the **Ribbon**. The **Emboss Body** dialog box will be displayed; refer to Figure-61.

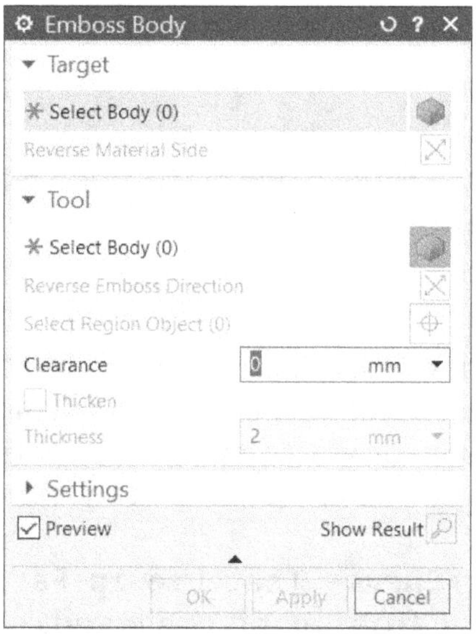

Figure-61. Emboss Body dialog box

- Select the main body to be modified by using the embossing operation from the drawing area. You will be asked to select the tool body.
- Select desired surface or solid body to be used as embossing tool. Preview of the operation will be displayed; refer to Figure-62.

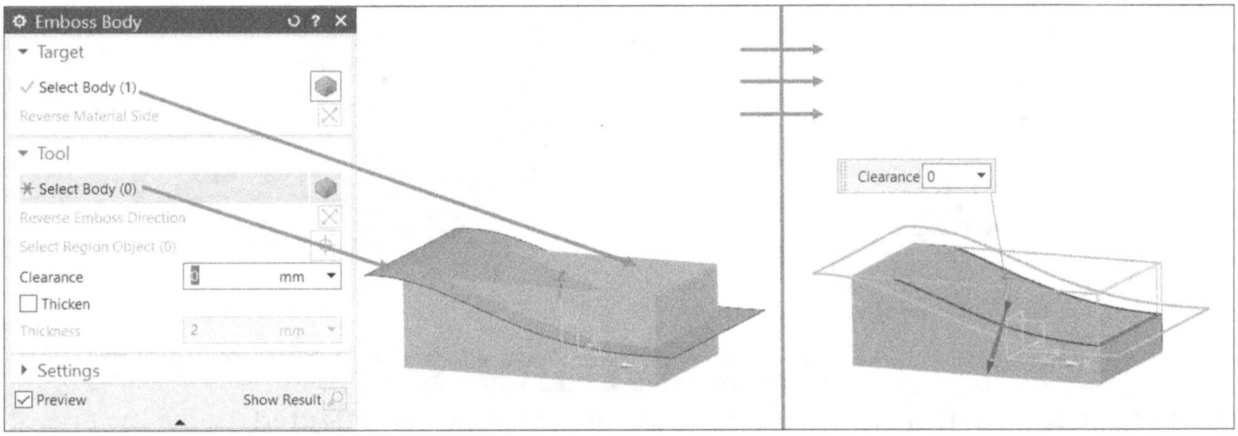

Figure-62. Preview of emboss body

- Specify desired value in the **Clearance** edit box to offset the emboss section by specified value.
- Select the **Thicken** check box to apply specified amount of thickness to the tool body before performing the embossing operation.
- Expand the **Settings** rollout and select the **Keep Target** and **Keep Tool** check boxes to keep respective bodies as well after performing the operation.
- After setting desired parameters, click on the **OK** button to perform the operation.

OFFSETTING FACES

The **Offset Face** tool is used to move selected faces of the model by specified distance value in direction normal to selected faces. The procedure to use this tool is given next.

- Click on the **Offset Face** tool from the **Offset** section of **More** drop-down in the **Base** group of **Home** tab in the **Ribbon**. The **Offset Face** dialog box will be displayed; refer to Figure-63.

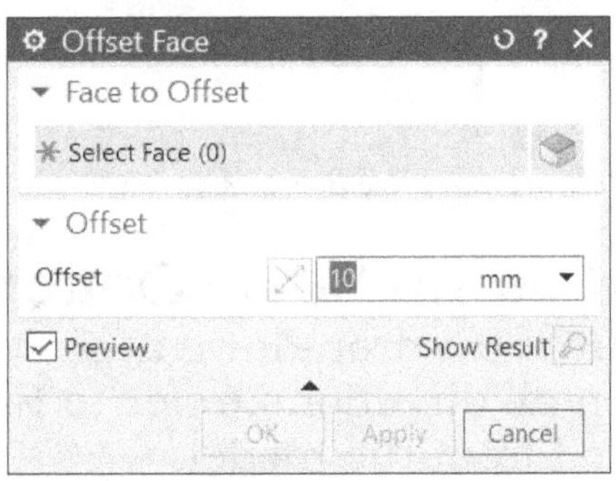

Figure-63. Offset Face dialog box

- Select desired face(s) of model to which you want to apply offset operation. Preview of the offset will be displayed; refer to Figure-64.
- Specify desired offset distance value in the **Offset** edit box and click on the **OK** button to perform the operation.

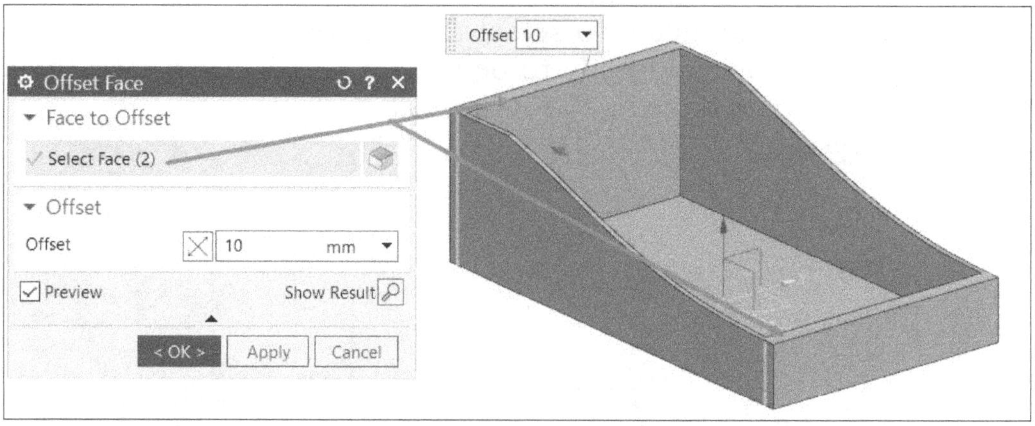

Figure-64. Preview of offset face operation

SCALING BODY

The **Scale Body** tool is used to scale up or scale down selected body by specified scaling factor. The procedure to use this tool is given next.

- Click on the **Scale Body** tool from the **Offset** section of **More** drop-down in the **Base** group of **Home** tab in the **Ribbon**. The **Scale Body** dialog box will be displayed; refer to Figure-65.

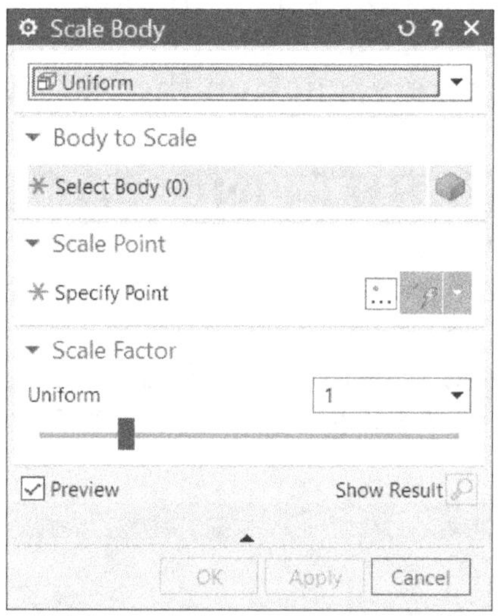

Figure-65. Scale Body dialog box

Uniform Scale Option

- Select the **Uniform** option from the drop-down at the top in the dialog box to equally scale up/down the body in all directions; refer to Figure-65.
- Select the body to be scaled from the model.
- Click on the **Specify Point** selection option from the **Scale Point** rollout and select desired point from the model to be used as reference point for scaling body. You will be asked to specify scale factor.
- Specify desired value of scale factor in the **Uniform** edit box of the **Scale Factor** rollout. Preview of the scale feature will be displayed; refer to Figure-66.
- After setting desired parameters, click on the **Apply** button to perform operation.

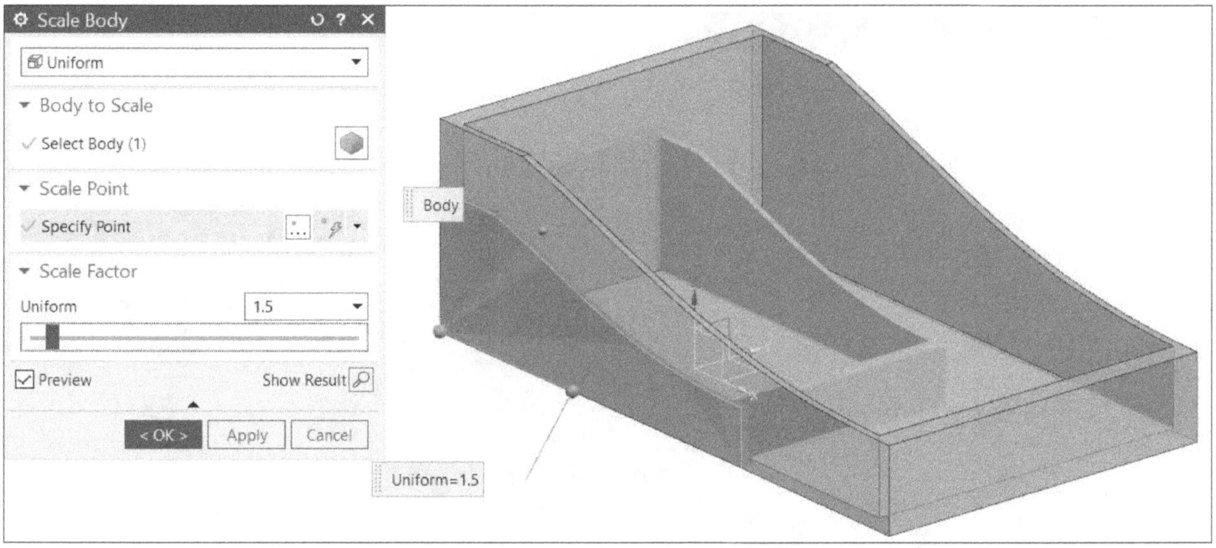

Figure-66. Preview of uniform scale body

Axisymmetric Scale Options

- Select the **Axisymmetric** option from the drop-down to scale cylindrical bodies about their axis by specified scale factor. The options in the dialog box will be displayed as shown in Figure-67.

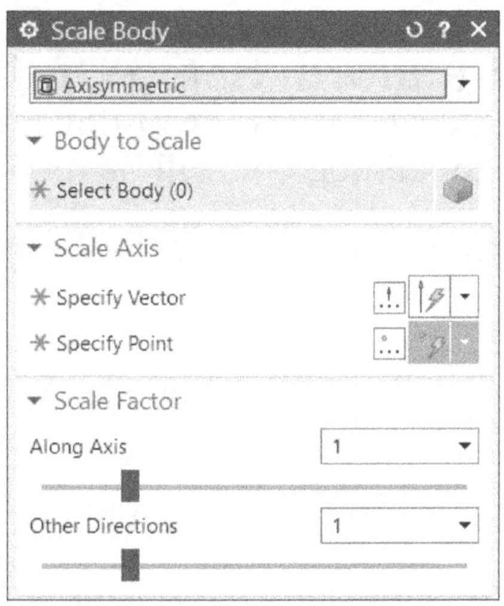

Figure-67. Axisymmetric options in Scale Body dialog box

- Select the body to be scaled from the model. The scale axis direction vector and point will be selected automatically based on the body.
- If you want to specify a different scale axis then click on the **Specify Vector** selection option and select desired axis/edge/plane/face from the model.
- Similarly, click on the **Specify Point** selection option from the **Scale Axis** rollout and select desired point to be used as reference point for scaling; refer to Figure-68.
- Set desired scale factor values in the **Along Axis** and **Other Directions** edit boxes or sliders to scale up/down the body.
- After setting desired parameters, click on the **Apply** button to perform the operation.

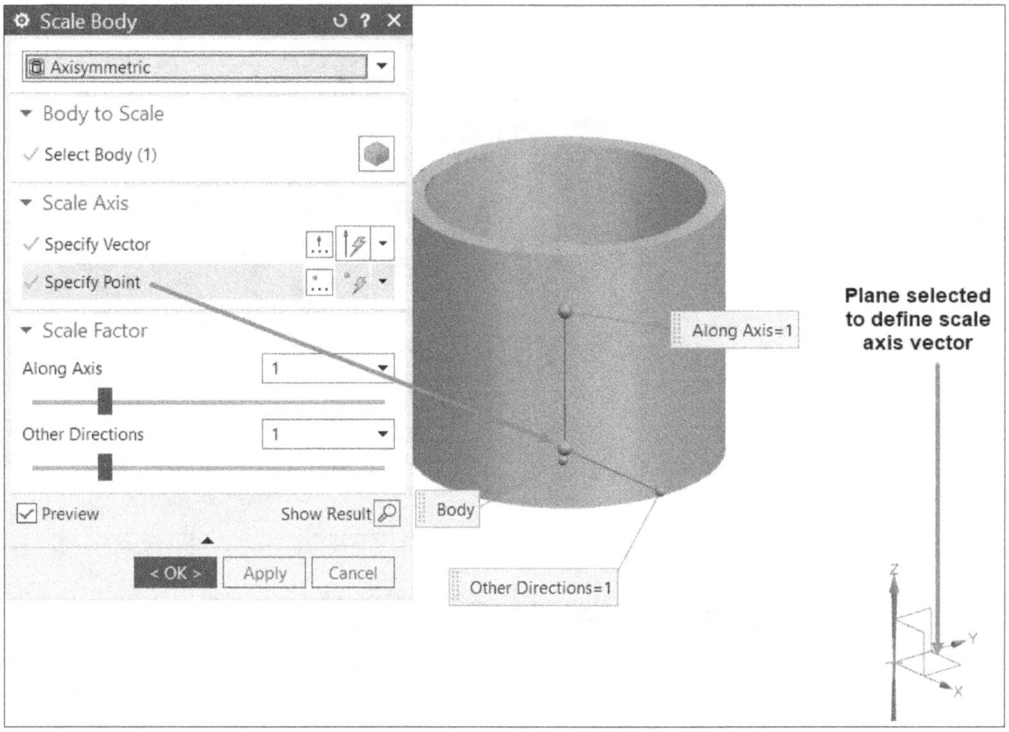

Figure-68. Axis vector and point selected

Non-uniform Scale Options

- Select the **Non-uniform** option from the drop-down at the top in the **Scale Body** dialog box. The options in the dialog box will be displayed as shown in Figure-69.

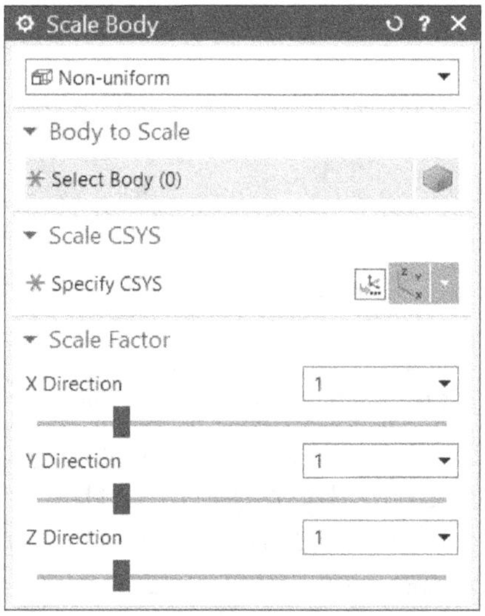

Figure-69. Non-uniform options

- Select desired body to which you want to apply scale operation. The scale coordinate system will be selected automatically. Click on the **Specify CSYS** selection option from the **Scale CSYS** rollout if you want to manually select the coordinate system.
- Set desired values in the **X Direction**, **Y Direction**, and **Z Direction** edit boxes/ sliders to define scale factors in respective directions. Preview of scale body will be displayed.
- Click on the **OK** button from the dialog box to perform the operation and exit the tool.

USER DEFINED FEATURES

User defined features are the combination of various objects and operations performed by user on other parts that can be brought as they are in the current model. Generally, you will be required to specify the placement references for user defined features. The procedure to insert a user defined feature in model is given next.

- Click on the **User Defined** tool from the **Feature Tools** section of the **More** drop-down in the **Base** group of **Home** tab in the **Ribbon**. The **User Defined Feature Library Browser** will be displayed; refer to Figure-70.

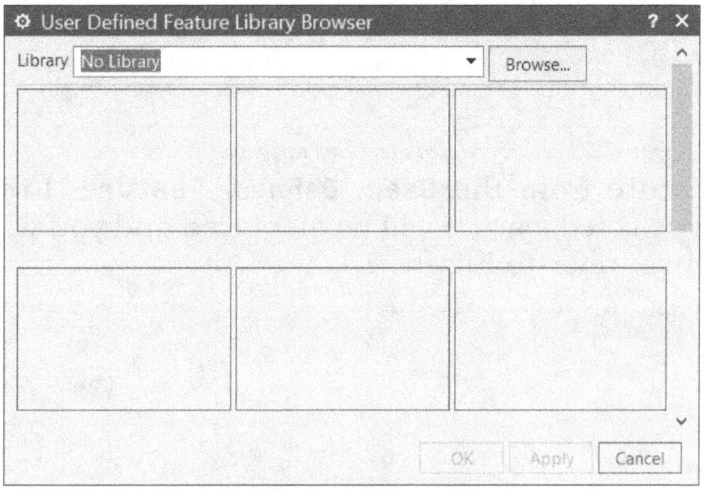

Figure-70. User Defined Feature Library Browser

- Click on the **Browse** button next to **Library** drop-down at the top in the window to select desired library. The **Library Class Selection** window will be displayed; refer to Figure-71.

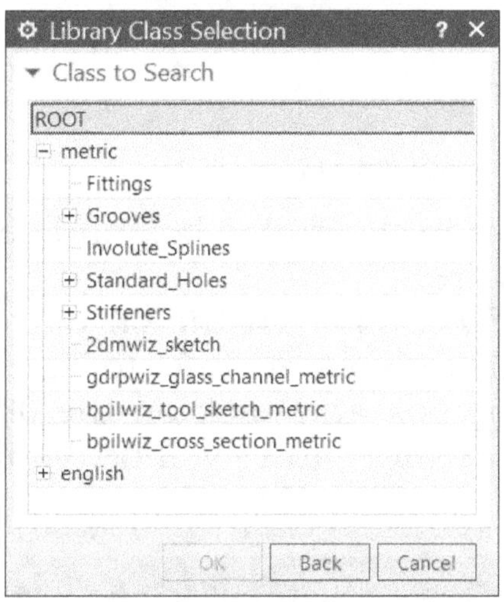

Figure-71. Library Class Selection window

- Expand desired categories from the **Library Class Selection** window and select desired library. The features related to selected category will be displayed in the window; refer to Figure-72.

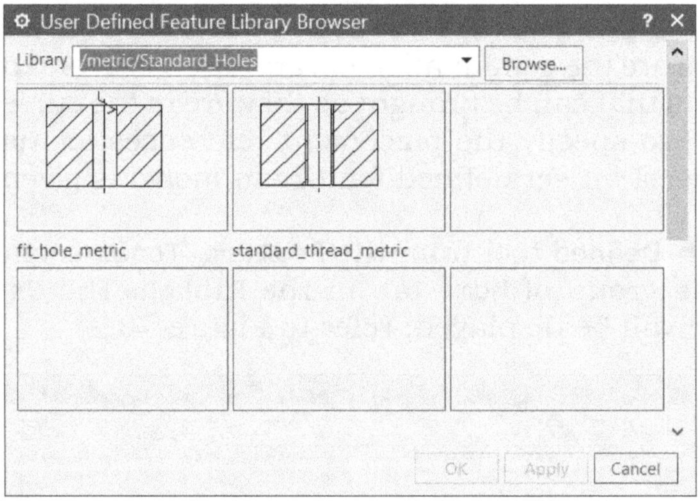

Figure-72. Features related to selected category

- Select desired feature from the **User Defined Feature Library Browser**. The options related to selected feature will be displayed and you will be asked to specify placement reference; refer to Figure-73.

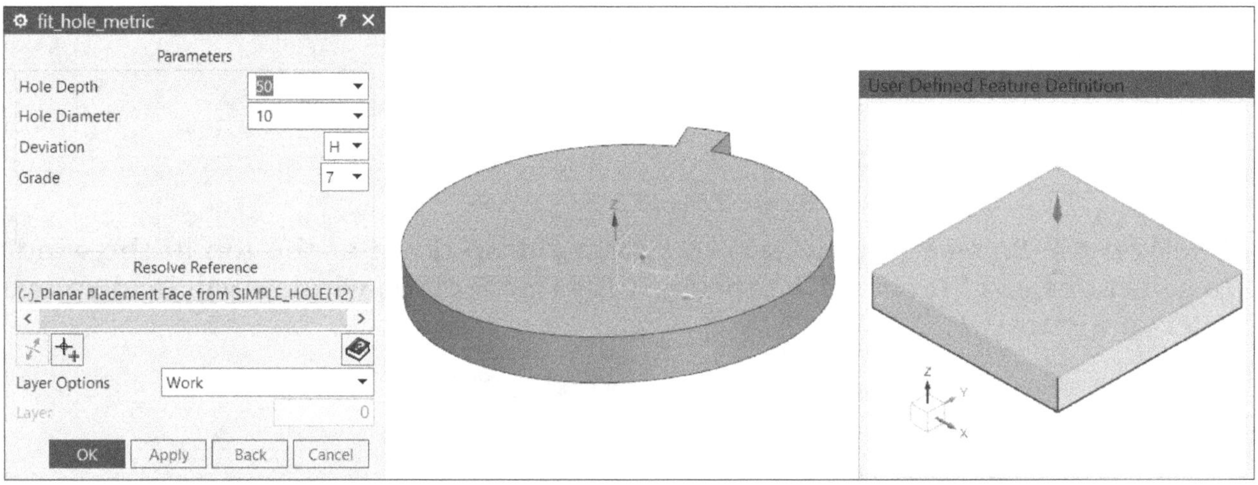

Figure-73. Dialog box for defining parameters to create feature

- Specify desired parameters in the dialog box and select the face of model where you want to place the feature.
- After selecting reference face, click on the **OK** button from the dialog box. The **Positioning** dialog box will be displayed; refer to Figure-74. Set desired parameters using options in the dialog box and click on the **OK** button. The feature will be created and dialog box to create feature will be displayed again. Close the dialog box to exit the tool.

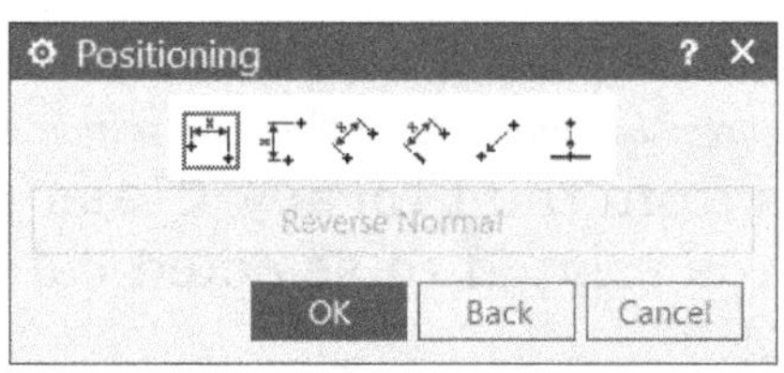

Figure-74. Positioning dialog box

WRAPPING GEOMETRY

The **Wrap Geometry** tool is used to create a simplified solid geometry for enveloping selected object. The procedure to use this tool is given next.

- Click on the **Wrap Geometry** tool from the **Feature Tools** section of the **More** drop-down in the **Base** group of **Home** tab in the **Ribbon**. The **Wrap Geometry** dialog box will be displayed; refer to Figure-75.

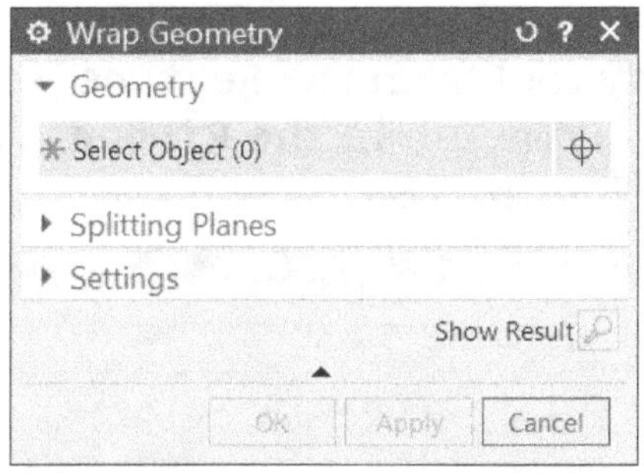

Figure-75. Wrap Geometry dialog box

- Select desired body to be wrapped up in solid feature from the model.
- If you want to split wrap geometry at selected face/plane, expand the **Splitting Planes** rollout, click on the **Specify Plane** selection option and select desired face/plane from the model. Preview of the wrap geometry should display as shown in Figure-76 on clicking the **Show Result** button in the dialog box. If you are not using the split plane option then whole model will be wrapped as shown in the preview; refer to Figure-77.

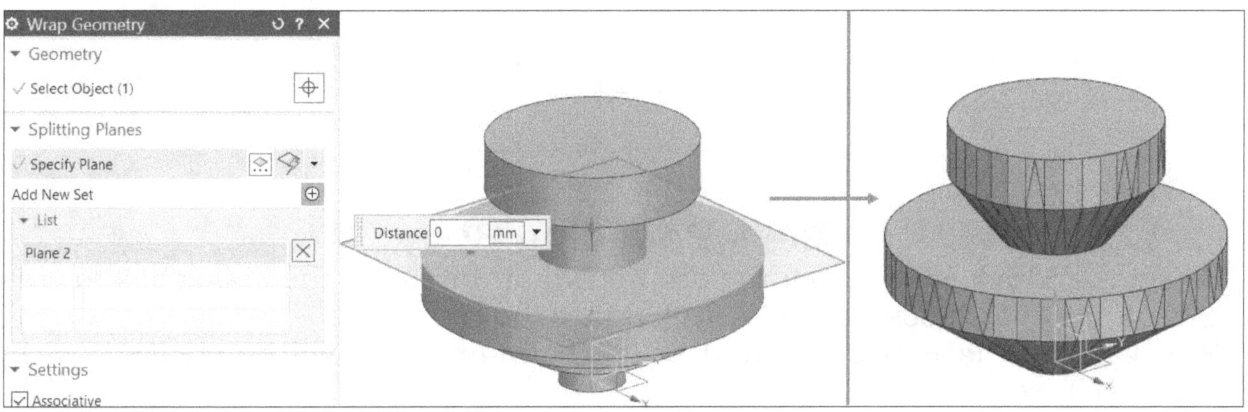

Figure-76. Preview of wrap geometry with split plane

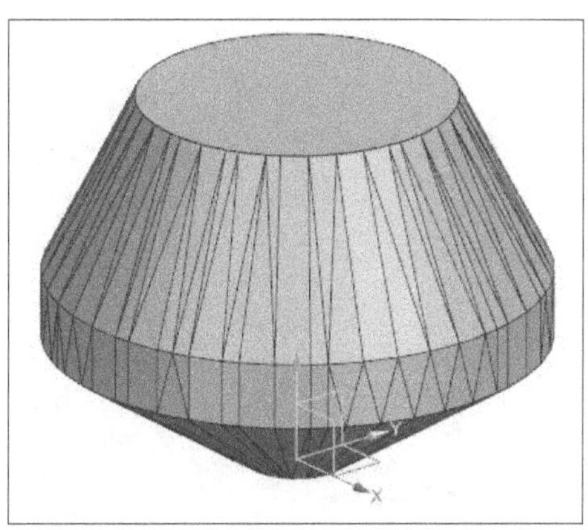

Figure-77. Preview of wrapped model

- Set the other parameters as discussed earlier and click on the **OK** button. The wrap geometry will be created.

CREATING BOUNDING BODY

The **Bounding Body** tool is used to create a bounding box/cylinder based on selected geometry. The procedure to use this tool is given next.

- Click on the **Bounding Body** tool from the **Feature Tools** section of the **More** drop-down in the **Base** group of **Home** tab in the **Ribbon**. The **Bounding Body** dialog box will be displayed; refer to Figure-78.

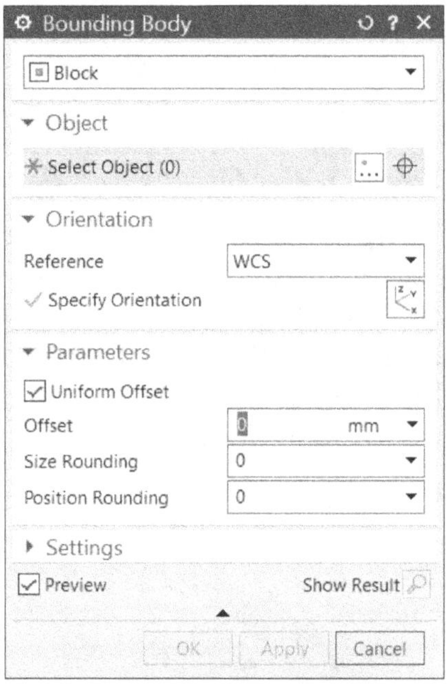

Figure-78. Bounding Body dialog box

Block Bounding Body

- Select the **Block** option from the drop-down at the top in the dialog box to create a bounding box block around selected face/body.
- Select desired face/body around which bounding box will be created; refer to Figure-79.

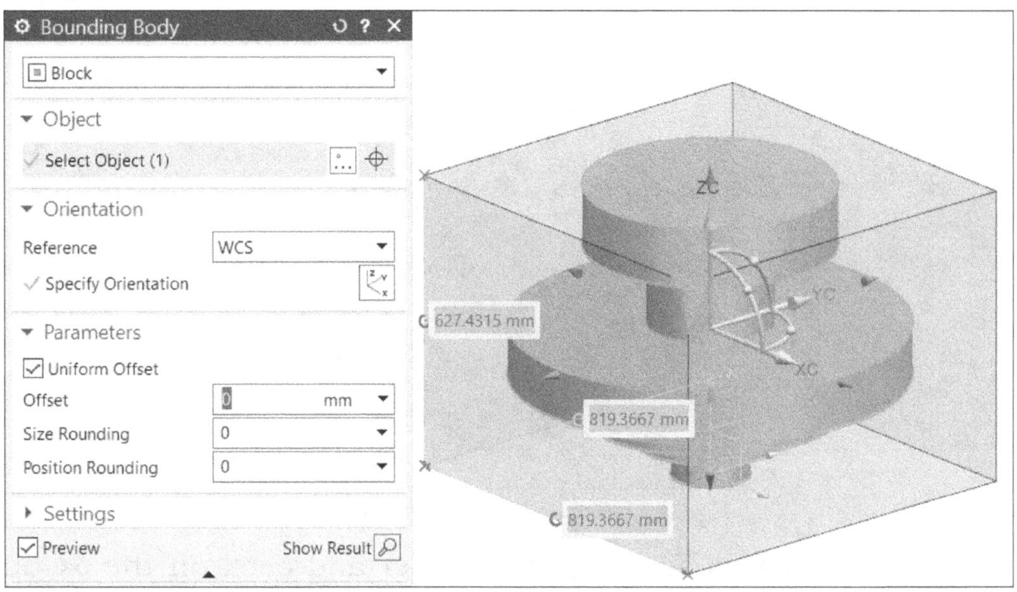

Figure-79. Block bounding box

Bounding Body using Center and Lengths

- Select the **Center and Lengths** option from the drop-down at the top in the dialog box to create a bounding box of specified dimensions at defined center point. The options in the dialog box will be displayed as shown in Figure-80.

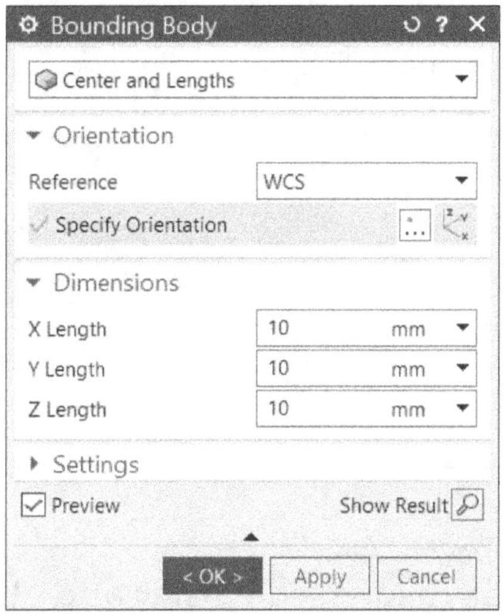

Figure-80. Center and Lengths options for bounding body

- Use the arrow handles of coordinate system to reposition the center of bounding body at desired location.
- Specify desired values in the **X Length**, **Y Length**, and **Z Length** edit boxes to define size of the bounding box; refer to Figure-81.

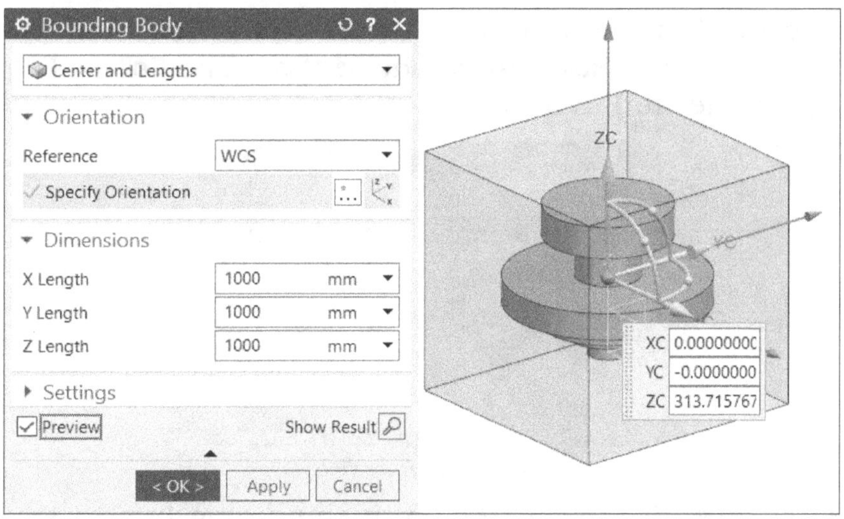

Figure-81. Preview of bounding box

Creating Cylinder Bounding Body

- Select the **Cylinder** option from the top drop-down in the dialog box. The options to create cylindrical bounding body will be displayed.
- Select the body around which cylindrical bounding body will be created and select desired axis to be used as centerline for cylinder; refer to Figure-82.

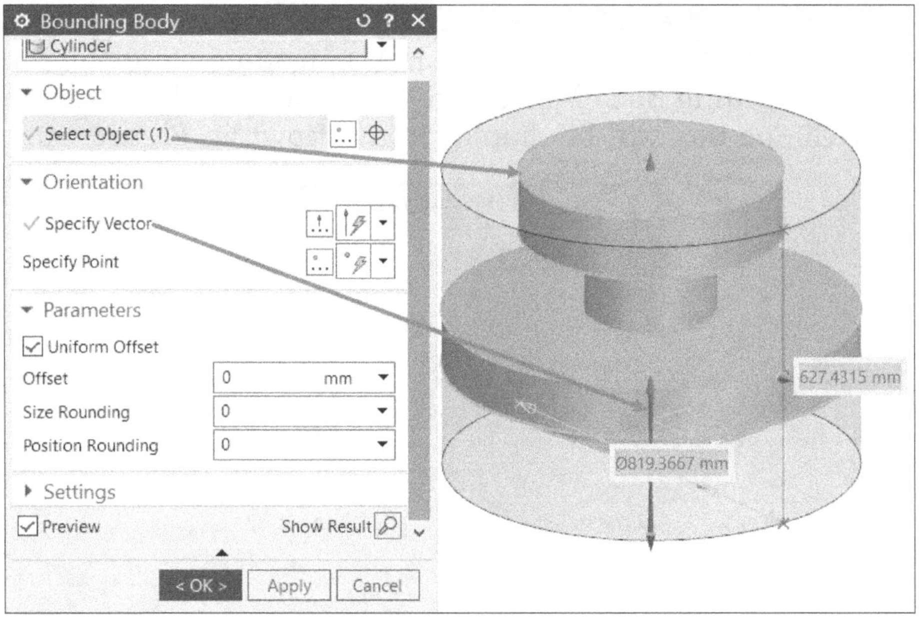

Figure-82. Preview of cylindrical bounding body

- Set the other parameters as discussed earlier and click on the **OK** button to create the bounding body.

Applying Colors to Features

The **Color Feature** tool is used to apply desired color to selected features of the model. The procedure to use this tool is given next.

- Click on the **Color Feature** tool from the **Feature Tools** section of **More** drop-down in the **Base** group of **Home** tab in the **Ribbon**. The **Color Feature** dialog box will be displayed; refer to Figure-83.

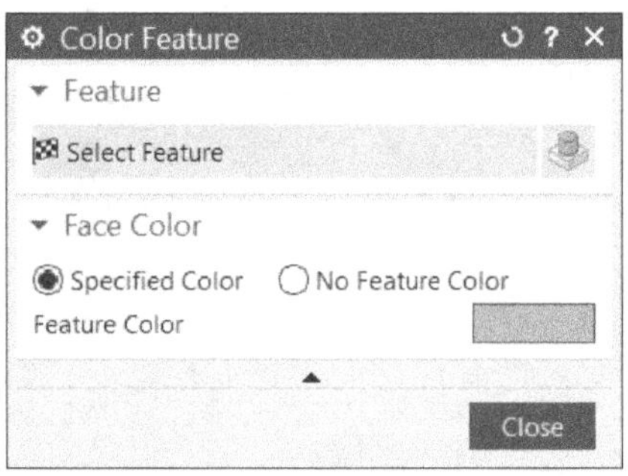

Figure-83. Color Feature dialog box

- Click on the **Feature Color** button from the dialog box to set the color to be applied to selected features. The **Object Color** dialog box will be displayed; refer to Figure-84.

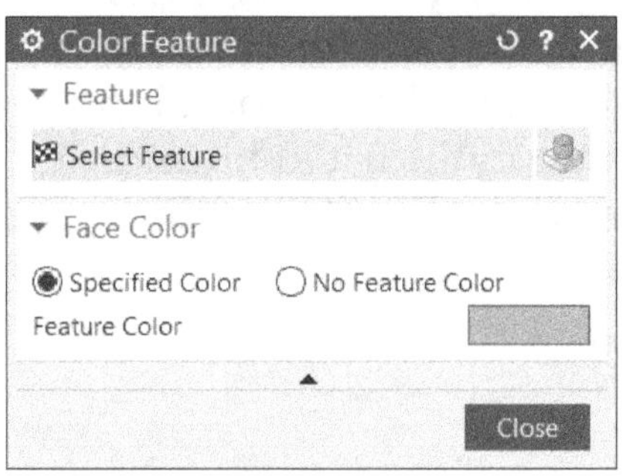

Figure-84. Color Feature dialog box

- Select desired color from the dialog box and click on the **OK** button. The selected color will be set for applying to features.
- Select desired features to which you want to apply color from the model; refer to Figure-85.

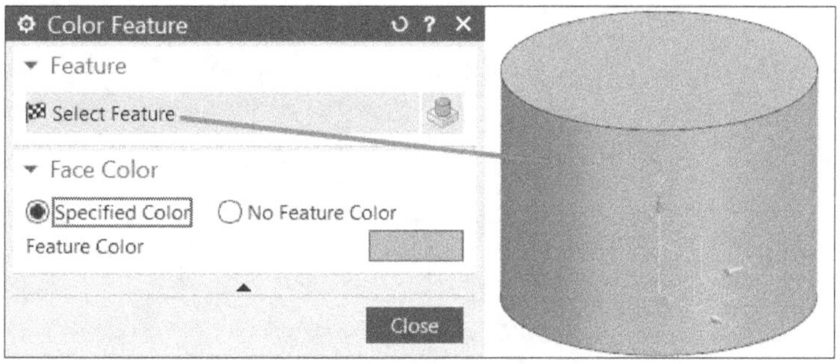

Figure-85. Feature selected for applying color

- To remove color of the feature, select the **No Feature Color** radio button and select the features to remove their colors.
- Click on the **Close** button to exit the tool.

Similarly, you can use the **Assign Feature Color** tool from the **Feature Tools** section of **More** drop-down in the **Base** group of **Ribbon** to apply colors to different feature.

SYNCHRONOUS MODELING

The Synchronous modeling tools are used to perform freeform operations on the model without creating modeling history. These tools are specially useful for modifying models imported from other CAD software. The tools to perform synchronous modeling are available in the **Synchronous Modeling** group of the **Home** tab in **Ribbon**; refer to Figure-86. Various tools of this group are discussed next.

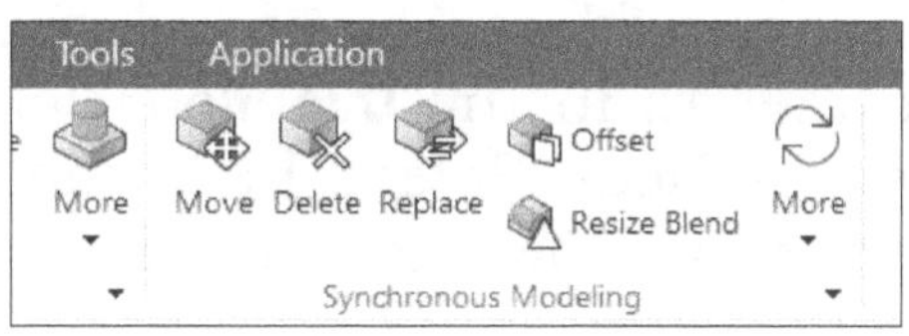

Figure-86. Synchronous Modeling group

Moving Faces

The **Move** tool is used to move selected face(s) in desired direction at specified distance. The procedure to use this tool is given next.

- Click on the **Move** tool from the **Synchronous Modeling** group in the **Home** tab of the **Ribbon**. The **Move Face** dialog box will be displayed; refer to Figure-87.
- Select desired face(s) from the model. The drag handle will be displayed with input boxes to specify move distance and angle; refer to Figure-88.

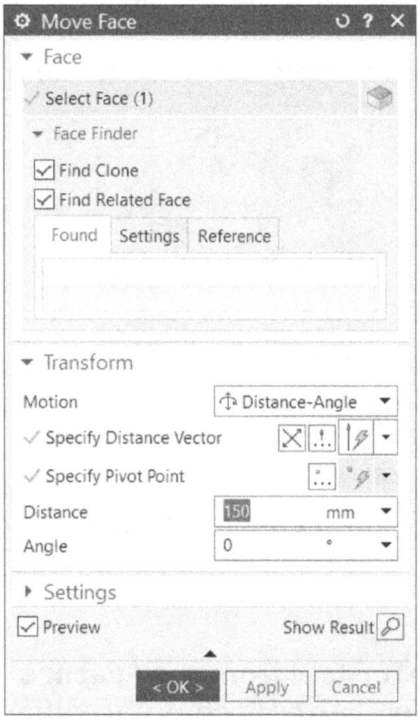

Figure-87. Move Face dialog box

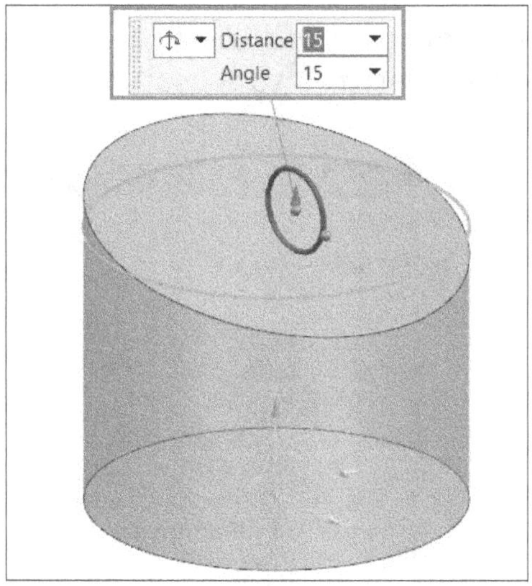

Figure-88. Input boxes for moving faces

- Set desired parameters in the input boxes or use the drag handle to define move distance with angle. You can change the motion type for moving faces using the options in the **Motion** drop-down of **Transform** rollout in the dialog box. Set the related parameters as discussed earlier.
- Expand the **Settings** rollout to modify advanced parameters related to moving faces. The options will be displayed as shown in Figure-89. By default, the **Move and Adapt** option is selected in the **Move Behavior** drop-down so selected face is moved to specified distance and nearby connected faces automatically adapt. You can set desired parameters in the **Overflow Behavior** drop-down to define adaptation method for nearby faces. Select the **Extend Neighbors at Smooth Edge** option from the **Step Face** drop-down to extend connected faces for generating smooth edges.

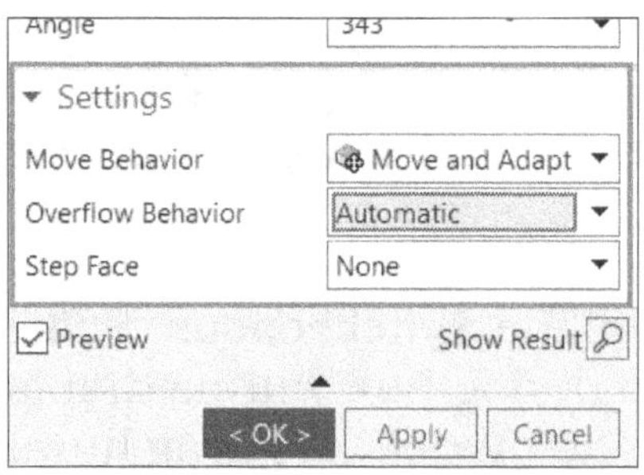

Figure-89. Settings rollout

- Select the **Cut and Paste** option from the **Move Behavior** drop-down to copy selected face(s) and delete the original faces. Select the **Heal** check box to close the open ends of model after moving selected faces. Select the **Paste** check box to create copy of connected faces as well when apply move operation.
- Set the other parameters as discussed earlier and click on the **OK** button.

Deleting Faces

The **Delete** tool is used to delete selected faces of the model while automatically extending connected faces to fill the open gap. The procedure to use this tool is given next.

- Click on the **Delete** tool from the **Synchronous Modeling** group of **Home** tab in the **Ribbon**. The **Delete Face** dialog box will be displayed; refer to Figure-90 and you will be asked to select face(s) to be deleted.

Figure-90. Delete Face dialog box

Deleting Faces

- Select the **Face** option from the drop-down at the top in the dialog box to delete selected faces and select the face to be deleted. You can select desired filter from the **Face Rule** drop-down in the **Scene Bar** of drawing area to perform related selections. Preview of delete operation will be displayed; refer to Figure-91.

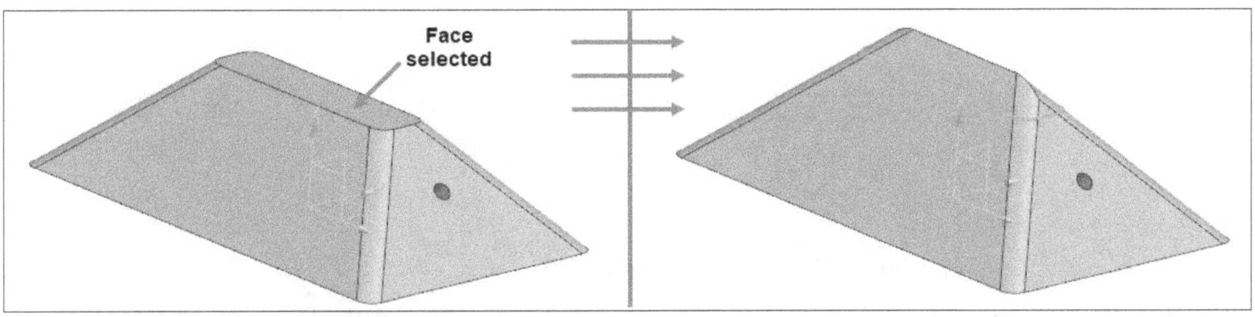

Figure-91. Preview after deleting face

- Select the **Find Clone** check box from the **Face Finder** rollout to automatically find faces related to currently selected faces like copies of faces.
- Clear the **Heal** check box from the **Settings** rollout in the dialog box if you do not want to cap the model after deleting the face(s). This will generate a hollow surface at the deleted face; refer to Figure-92.

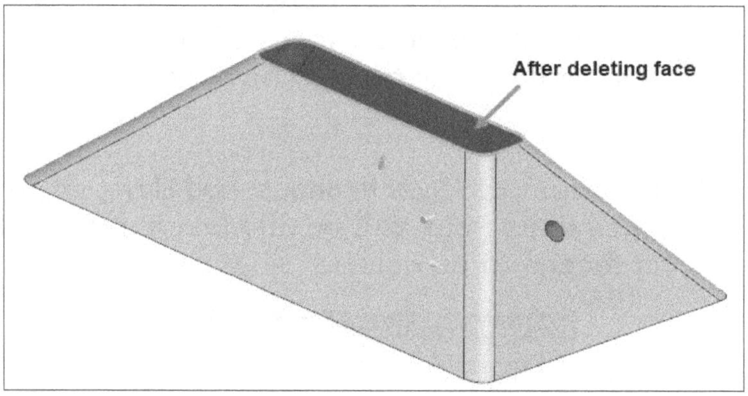

Figure-92. Preview of deletion without heal

Deleting Blend Faces

- Select the **Blend** option from the drop-down to delete fillets and other curved faces joining two planar faces. The options in the dialog box will be displayed as shown in Figure-93.

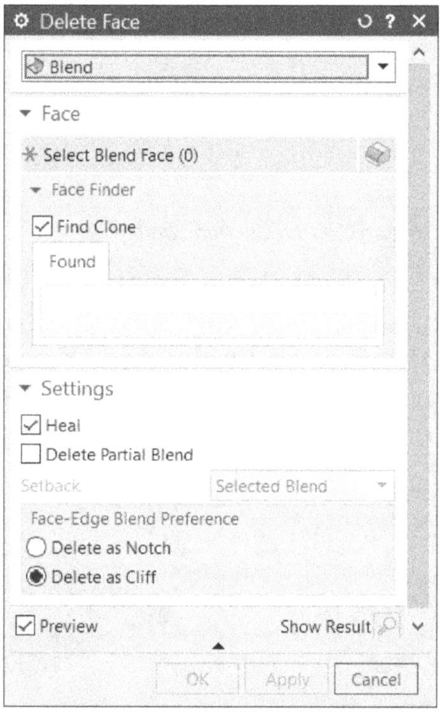

Figure-93. Blend option in Delete Face dialog box

- Select the blend face(s) to be removed from the model. Preview of delete face operation will be displayed; refer to Figure-94. Note that if there are similar blend faces in the model and you want to include them in deletion as well then you can select the **Exact Match** check box from the **Found** section displayed on selecting the **Find Clone** check box.

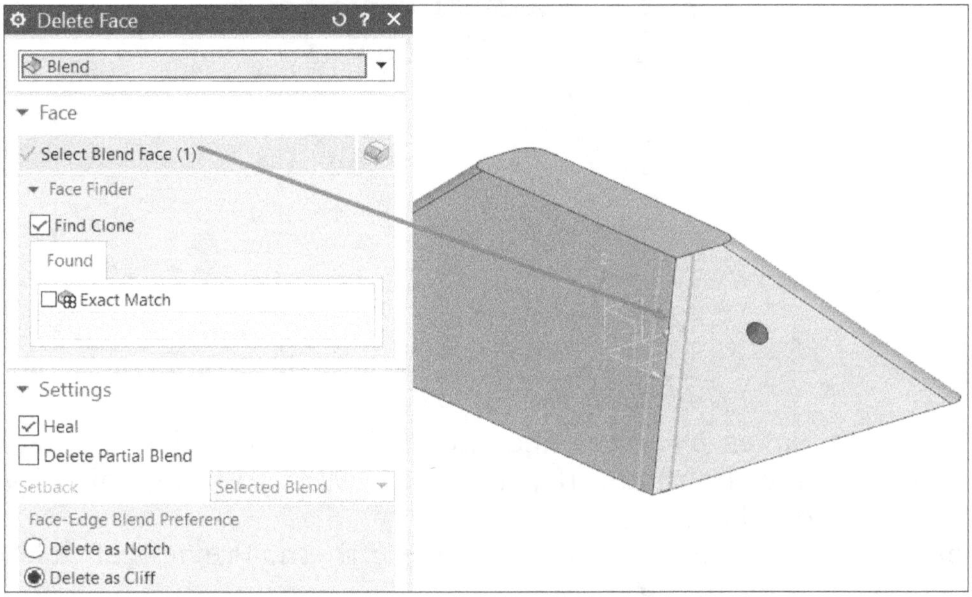

Figure-94. Preview of blend face delete operation

- Select the **Delete Partial Blend** check box from the **Settings** rollout to keep small section of blend near setback point intact; refer to Figure-95.

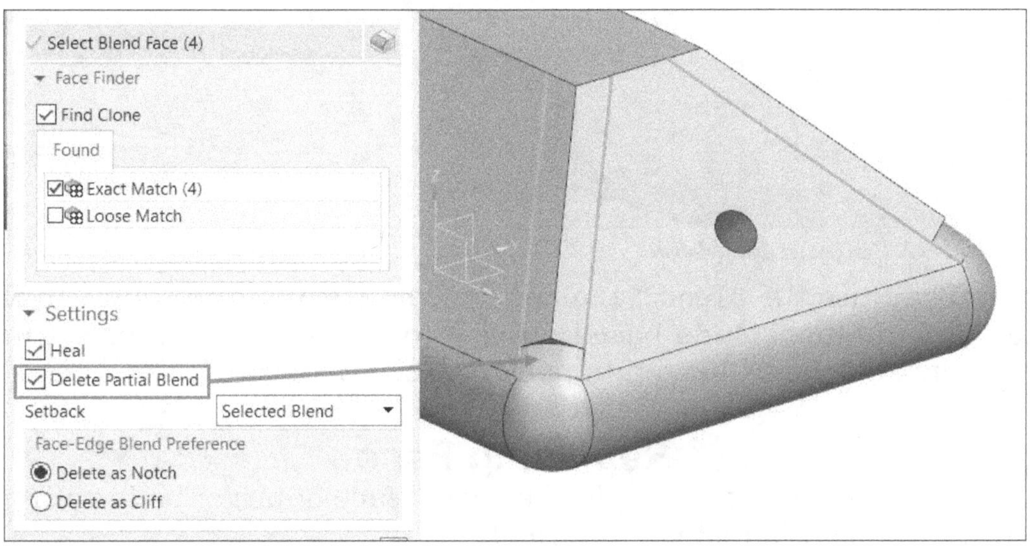

Figure-95. Deleting partial blend

Deleting Holes

- Select the **Hole** option from the drop-down to delete holes from the model and fill the gap. The options will be displayed as shown in Figure-96.

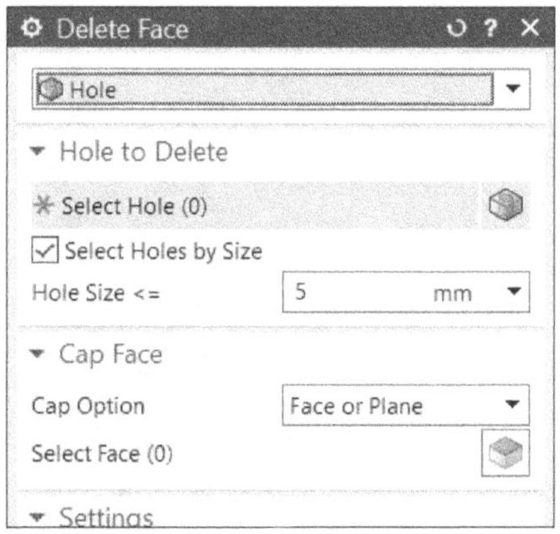

Figure-96. Delete Face dialog box for Hole option

- Select the **Select Holes by Size** check box to specify the size of holes upto which selection of holes can be made. If you do not want to filter holes based on size then clear this check box.
- Select desired holes from the model to delete them. Preview of delete operation will be displayed; refer to Figure-97.

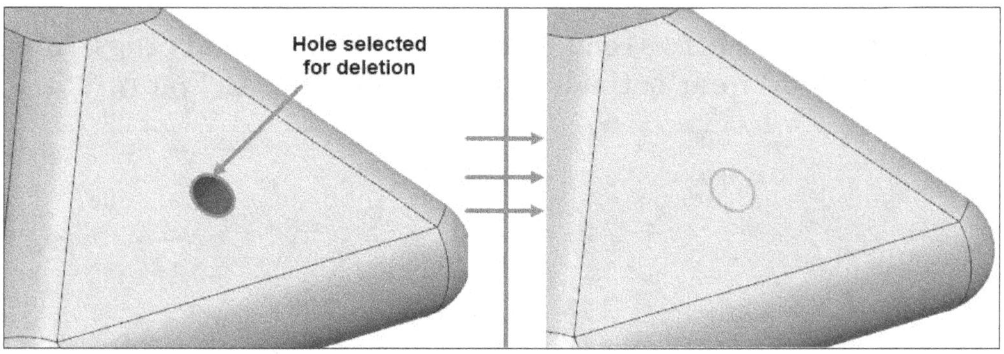

Figure-97. Preview of hole deletion

Similarly, you can use the **Blend Size** option from the top drop-down in the **Delete Face** dialog box to filter blends based on size to delete them. After setting desired parameters, click on the **OK** button to perform the operation.

Replacing Face

The **Replace Face** tool is used to replace selected face of target body with other face. The procedure to use this tool is given next.

- Click on the **Replace Face** tool from the **Synchronous Modeling** group of the **Home** tab in the **Ribbon**. The **Replace Face** dialog box will be displayed; refer to Figure-98.

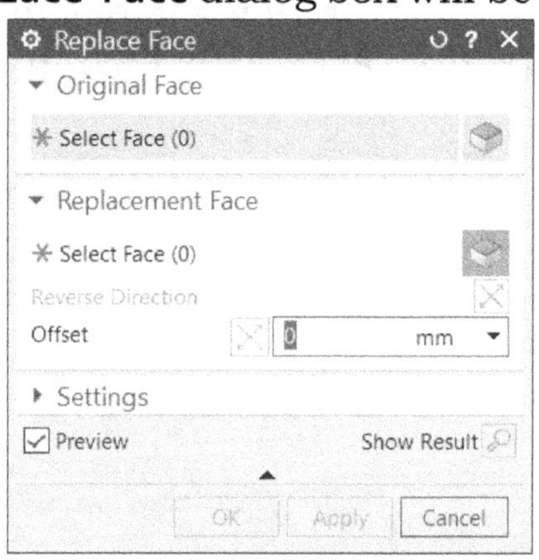

Figure-98. Replace Face dialog box

- Select desired face to be replaced from target body and then click on the **Select Face** selection option from the **Replacement Face** rollout in the dialog box. You will be asked to select the replacement face.
- Select desired face intersecting with the model and creating cap of the model. Preview of face replacement will be displayed; refer to Figure-99.
- Specify desired value in the **Offset** edit box to move replacement face by specified distance.

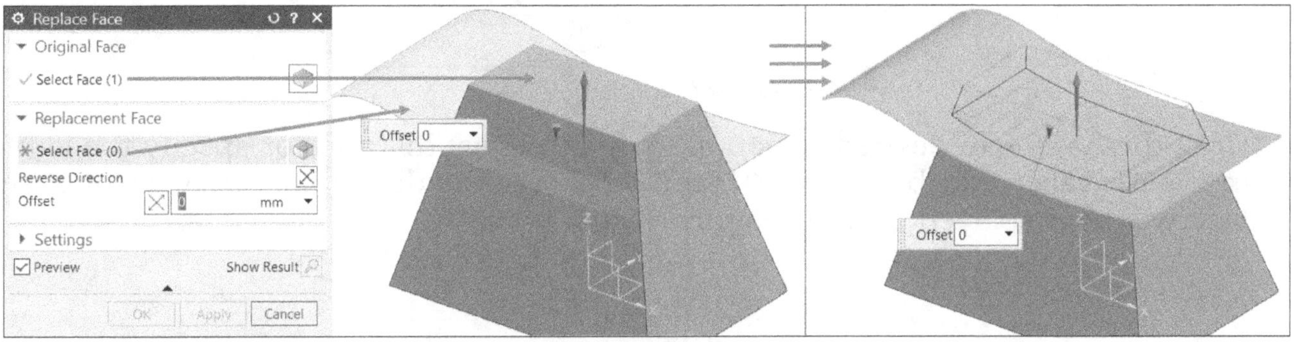

Figure-99. Preview of replace face operation

- Set the other parameters as discussed earlier and click on the **OK** button to apply the operation.

Offsetting Faces

The **Offset** tool is used to extend selected faces at specified distance. The procedure to use this tool is given next.

- Click on the **Offset** tool from the **Synchronous Modeling** group of **Home** tab in the **Ribbon**. The **Offset Region** dialog box will be displayed; refer to Figure-100.

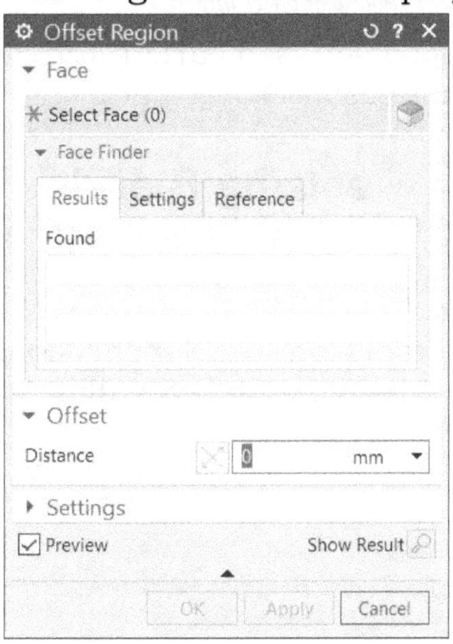

Figure-100. Offset Region dialog box

- Select the face(s) from the model to be offset. The handle to specify offset distance will be displayed on selected face; refer to Figure-101.

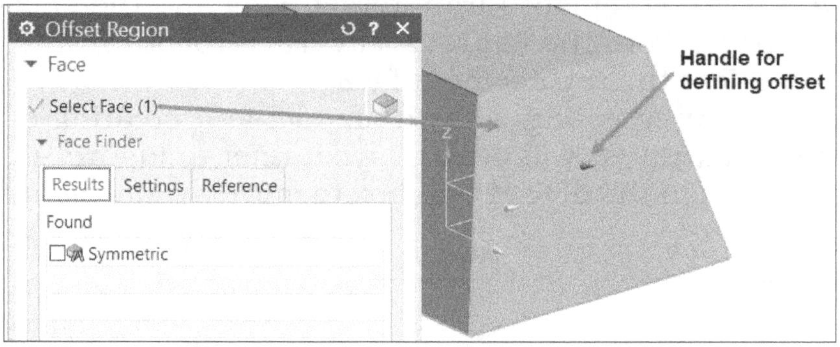

Figure-101. Offset handle displayed

- Drag the handle in desired direction to define offset distance or specify the value in the **Distance** edit box of the **Offset** rollout in the dialog box. Preview of offset face will be displayed; refer to Figure-102.

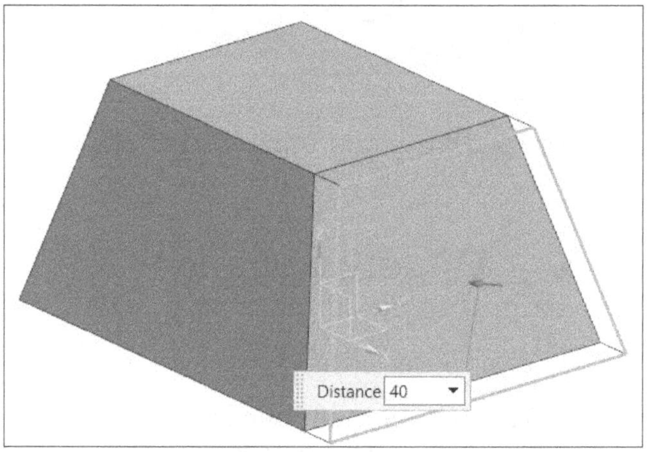

Figure-102. Preview of offset face

- Set the other parameters as discussed earlier and click on the **OK** button from the dialog box to apply the changes.

Resizing Blends

The **Resize Blend** tool is used to change the size of blend using dynamic handle. The procedure to use this tool is given next.

- Click on the **Resize Blend** tool from the **Synchronous Modeling** group of **Home** tab in the **Ribbon**. The **Resize Blend** dialog box will be displayed; refer to Figure-103.

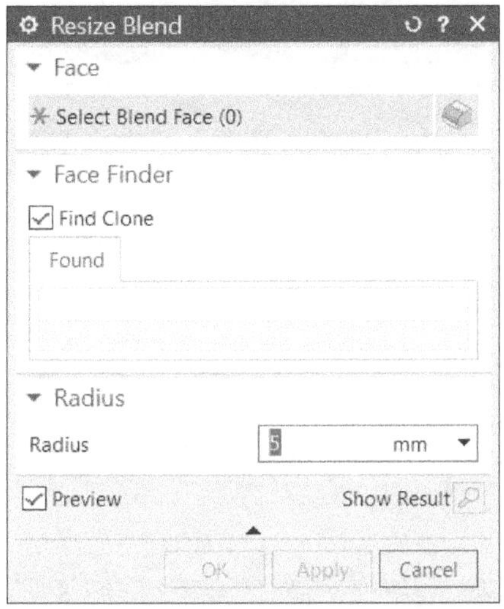

Figure-103. Resize Blend dialog box

- Select desired option from the **Selection Scene Bar** in drawing area to filter selection of objects and then select the blend face to be re-sized. Handle to change size will be displayed on selected blend face; refer to Figure-104.
- Set the other parameters as discussed earlier and click on the **OK** button from the dialog box to apply changes.

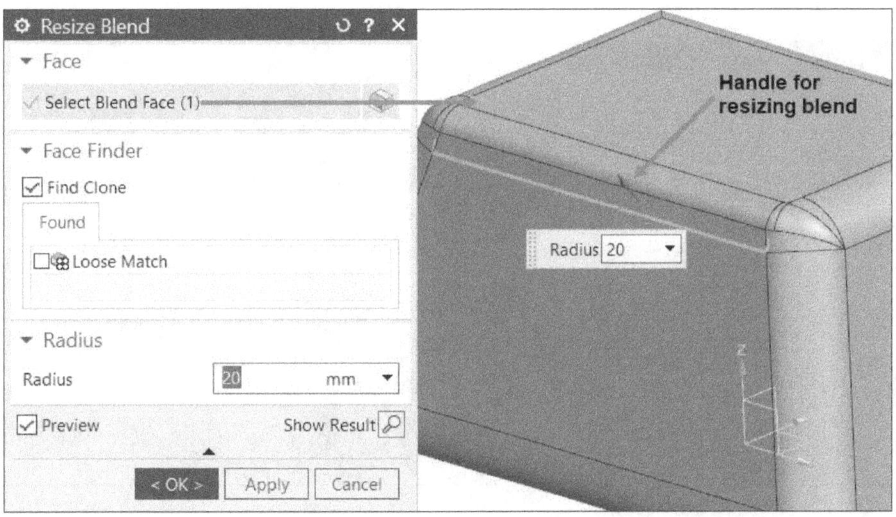

Figure-104. Preview of resizing blend

Edit Cross Section of Body

The **Edit Cross Section** tool is used to modify the model (body) using modification of cross section at selected section plane. The procedure to use this tool is given next.

- Click on the **Edit Cross Section** tool from the **Move** section in **More** drop-down of **Synchronous Modeling** group in the **Home** tab of **Ribbon**. The **Edit Cross Section** dialog box will be displayed; refer to Figure-105.

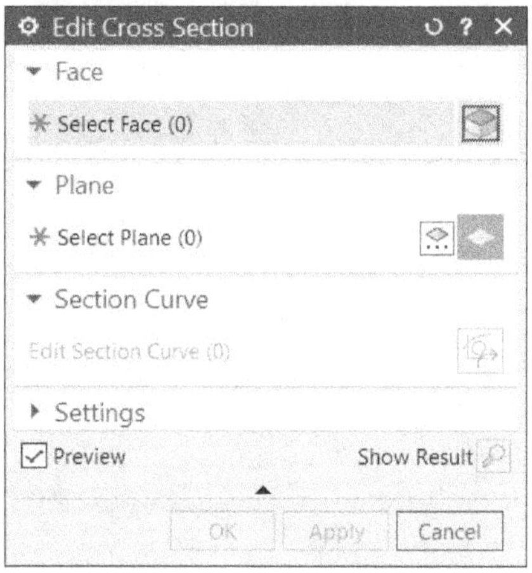

Figure-105. Edit Cross Section dialog box

- Select the faces to be used for generating cross-section.
- Click on the **Select Plane** selection option from the **Plane** rollout in the dialog box and select the plane intersecting with the faces. Preview of section curve will be displayed; refer to Figure-106.
- Click on the **Section** button from the **Section Curve** rollout in the dialog box. The sketching environment will be displayed with section curves; refer to Figure-107.

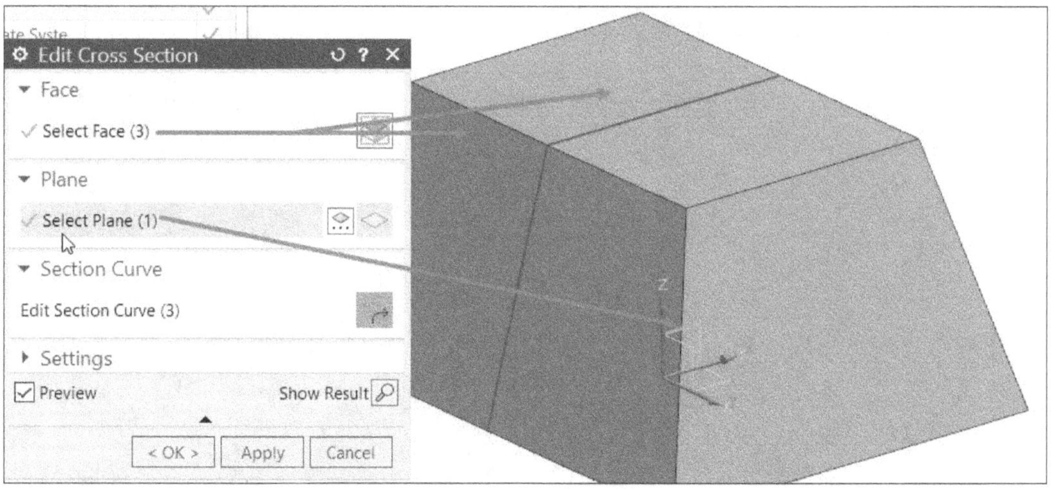

Figure-106. Preview of cross section

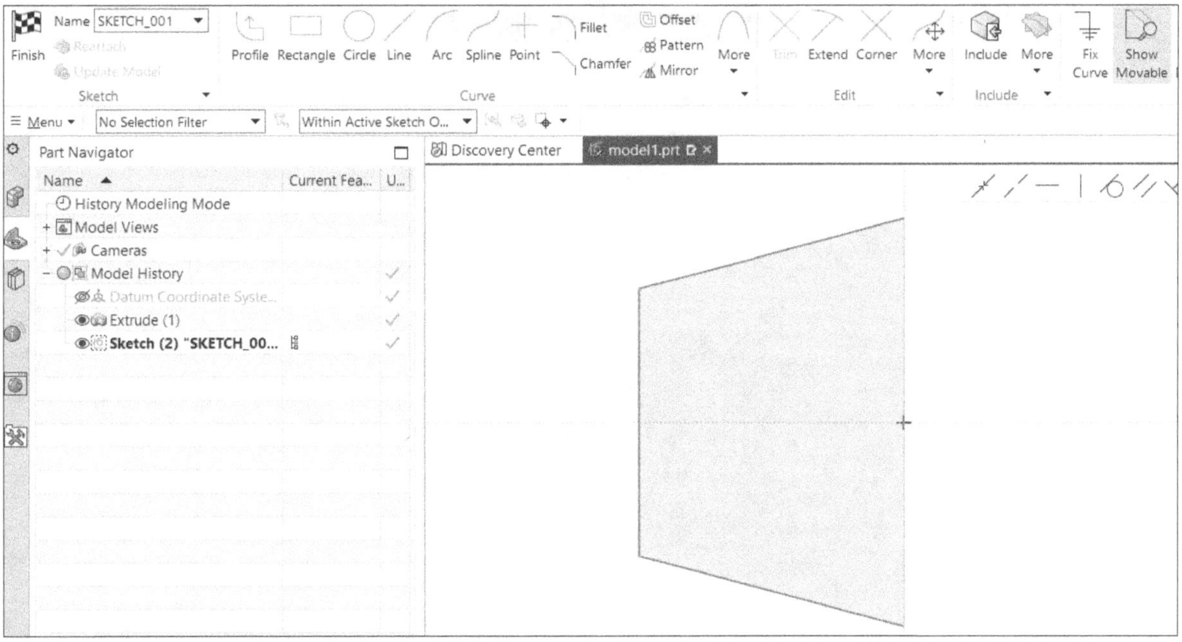

Figure-107. Cross-section curves

- Modify the cross-section sketch as desired; refer to Figure-108 and click on the **Finish** button from the **Ribbon**. Preview of modified body will be displayed; refer to Figure-109.

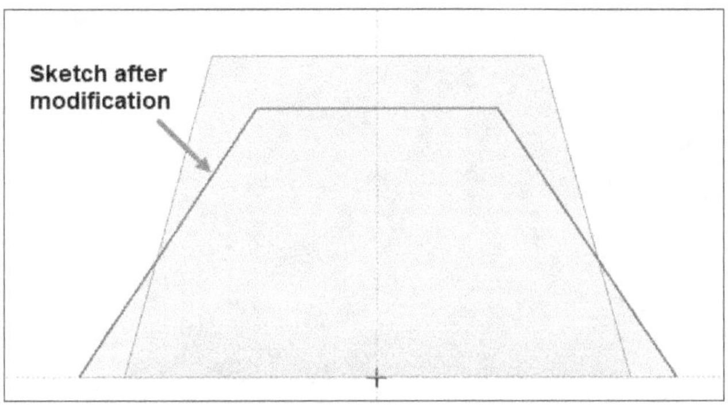

Figure-108. Sketch curve after modification

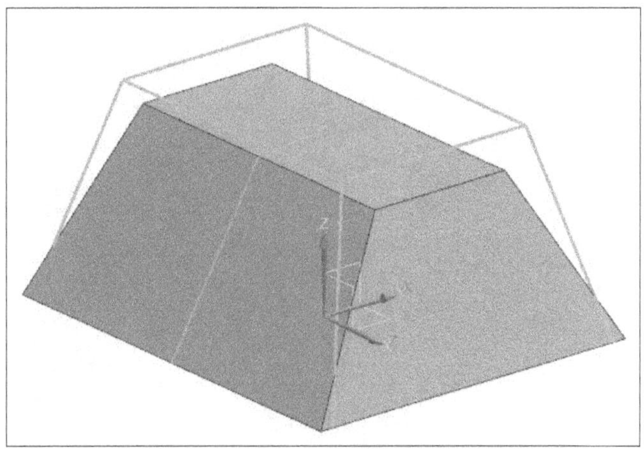

Figure-109. Body modified by cross-section

- Set the other parameters as discussed earlier and click on the **OK** button from the dialog box. The body will be modified.

Radiating Faces

The **Radiate Face** tool is used to apply scaling/shrinkage to selected faces about an axis. Note that this tool is applicable for cylindrical bodies. The procedure to use this tool is given next.

- Click on **Radiate Face** tool from the **Move** section in the **More** drop-down of **Synchronous Modeling** group in the **Home** tab of **Ribbon**. The **Radiate Face** dialog box will be displayed; refer to Figure-110.

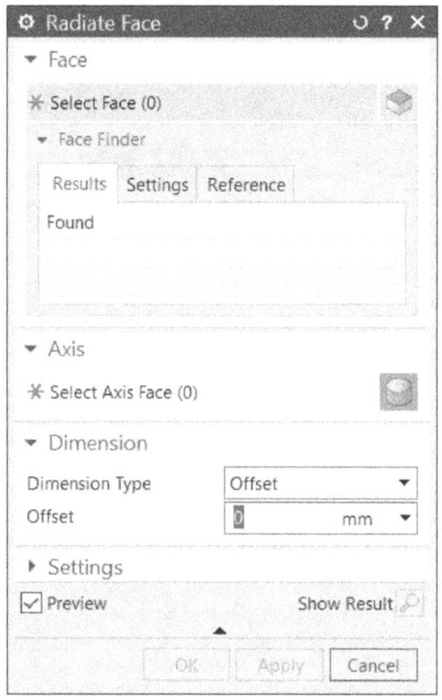

Figure-110. Radiate Face dialog box

- Select the faces to be modified. The axis of model will be selected automatically; refer to Figure-111.

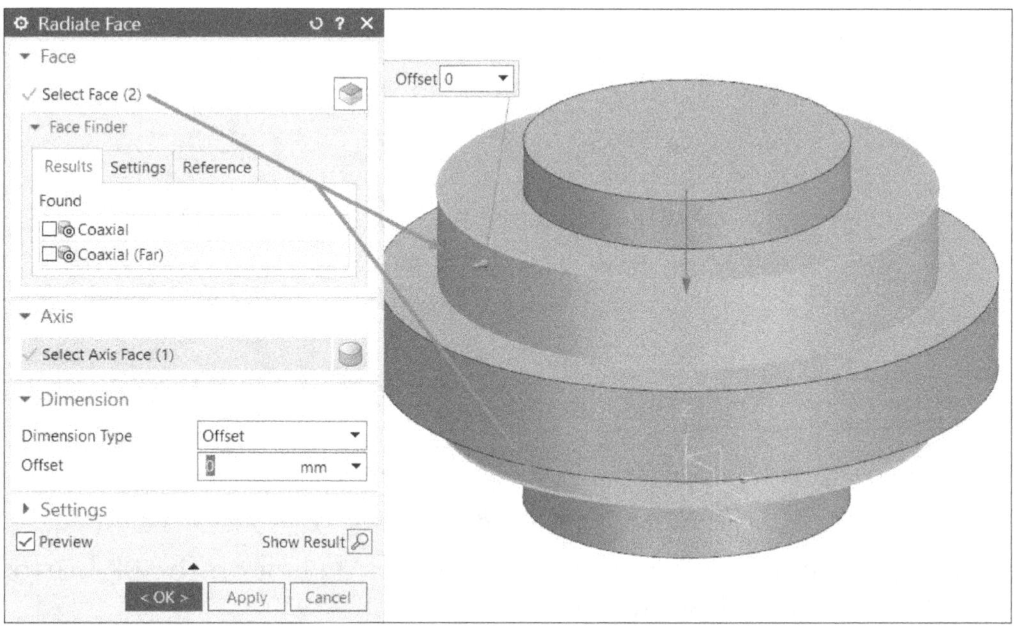

Figure-111. Faces selected

- Select desired option from the **Dimension Type** drop-down to define the dimensioning method for modifying selected faces. Select the **Offset** option from the drop-down to define distance by which selected faces will expand/shrink in direction normal to selected faces. Select the **Diameter** option from the drop-down to specify the value of diameter for selected cylindrical faces. Select the **Radius** option from the drop-down to specify radius value for selected cylindrical faces.
- Select desired option from the **Overflow Behavior** drop-down to define how radiating faces will expand to nearby connected faces.
- Set the other parameters as discussed earlier and click on the **OK** button to apply the operation.

Pulling Faces

The **Pull Face** tool is used to add or remove material from the model by pulling up or down selected face, respectively. The procedure to use this tool is given next.

- Click on the **Pull Face** tool from the **Move** section in the **More** drop-down of **Synchronous Modeling** group in **Home** tab of **Ribbon**. The **Pull Face** dialog box will be displayed; refer to Figure-112.

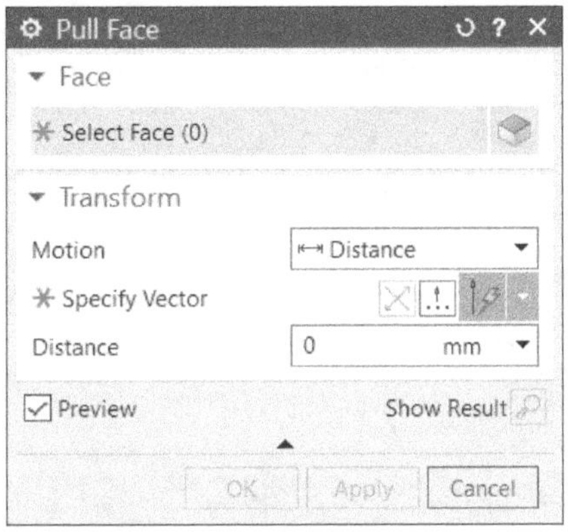

Figure-112. Pull Face dialog box

- Select the face to which you want to apply pull face operation. Handles to define pull direction will be displayed on the face.
- Select desired pull direction handle and specify desired distance value in the **Distance** edit box of the dialog box (a negative value in edit box to remove material from body).
- After setting desired parameters, click on the **OK** button from the dialog box to apply the operation.

Moving Faces using Linear Dimension

The **Linear Dimension** tool is used to move/expand selected face using linear dimension. The procedure to use this tool is given next.

- Click on the **Linear Dimension** tool from the **Dimension** section of the **More** drop-down in the **Synchronous Modeling** group of **Ribbon**. The **Linear Dimension** dialog box will be displayed; refer to Figure-113.

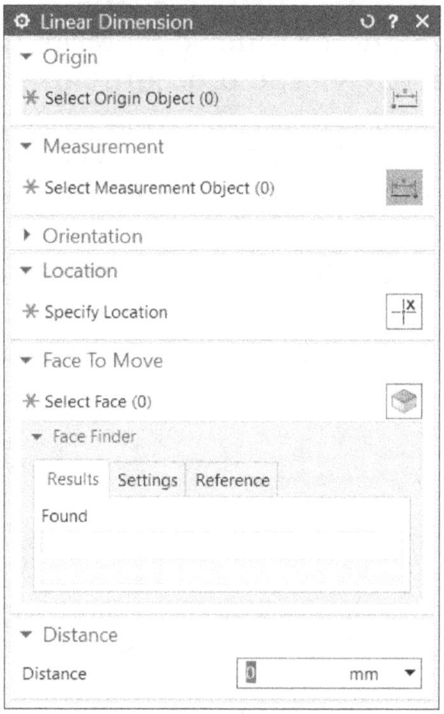

Figure-113. Linear Dimension dialog box

- Select desired edge of face to be used as starting point and then select next edge to be used for measuring the dimension. You will be asked to specify location to place dimension; refer to Figure-114.

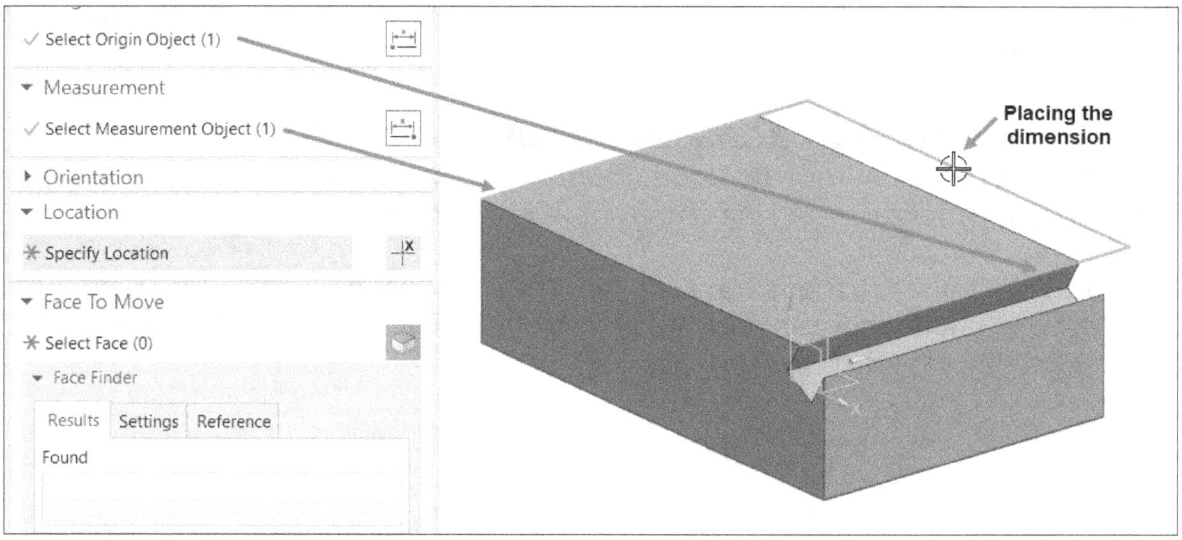

Figure-114. Selecting edges for defining dimension

- Click at desired location to place the dimension and specify distance value in the **Distance** edit box by which selected face will be moved. Preview of operation will be displayed; refer to Figure-115.
- Set the other parameters as discussed earlier and click on the **OK** button.

Similarly, you can use **Angular Dimension** and **Radial Dimension** tools of **Dimension** section in the **More** drop-down of **Synchronous Modeling** group in the **Ribbon** to perform respective face modification operations.

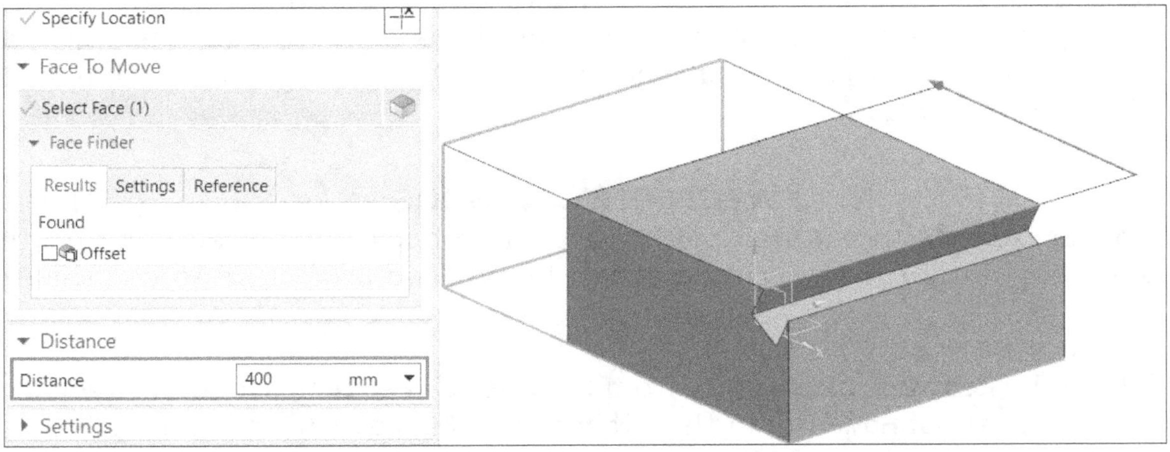

Figure-115. Preview of Linear dimension modification

Label Notch Blend

The **Label Notch Blend** tool is used to mark selected face(s) as notch blend for direction manipulation. This tool is generally used with imported bodies to identify their specific faces as blend faces. Note that blends marked as notch blends will maintain tangency with adjacent face. The procedure to use this tool is given next.

- Click on the **Label Notch Blend** tool from the **Detail Feature** section of **More** drop-down in the **Synchronous Modeling** group of **Home** tab in **Ribbon**. The **Label Notch Blend** dialog box will be displayed; refer to Figure-116 and you will be asked to select faces to be marked as notch blends.

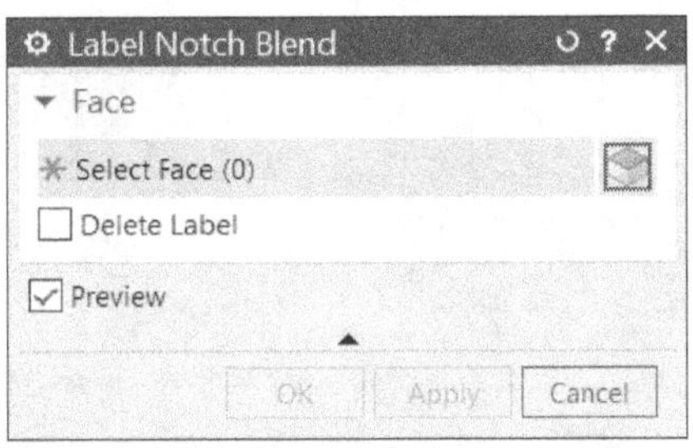

Figure-116. Label Notch Blend dialog box

- Select the blend faces of the model to be marked as notch blend; refer to Figure-117 and click on the **OK** button.

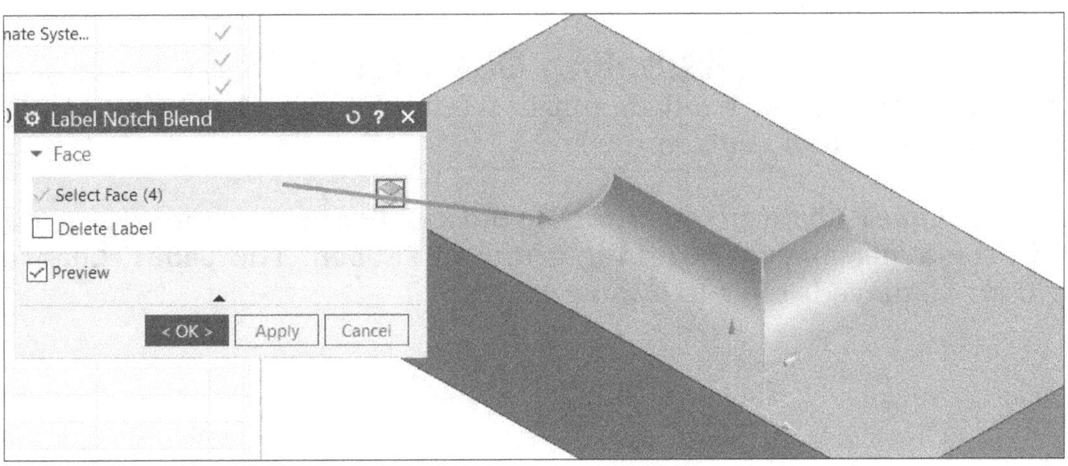

Figure-117. Faces selected to label notch blend

- Select the **Delete Label** check box to delete label of selected blends if earlier you have applied notch label on them. Clear this check box if you want to apply labels.
- After setting desired parameters, click on the **OK** button from the dialog box to perform the operation.

Reordering Blends

The **Reorder Blends** tool is used to change the order of blend faces connecting at the common point forming an intersection blend. The procedure to use this tool is given next.

- Click on the **Reorder Blends** tool from the **Detail Feature** section of **Synchronous Modeling** group of **Home** tab in the **Ribbon**. The **Reorder Blends** dialog box will be displayed; refer to Figure-118.

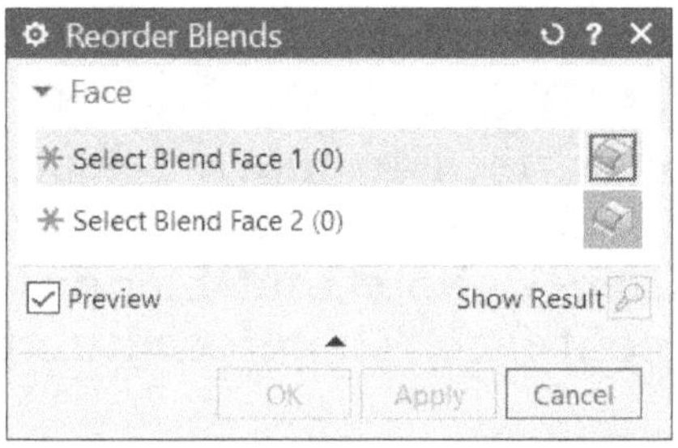

Figure-118. Reorder Blends dialog box

- Select the intersection blend for which blend faces are to be reordered. Preview of the reordered blend will be displayed; refer to Figure-119. Click on the **OK** button from the dialog box to apply operation.

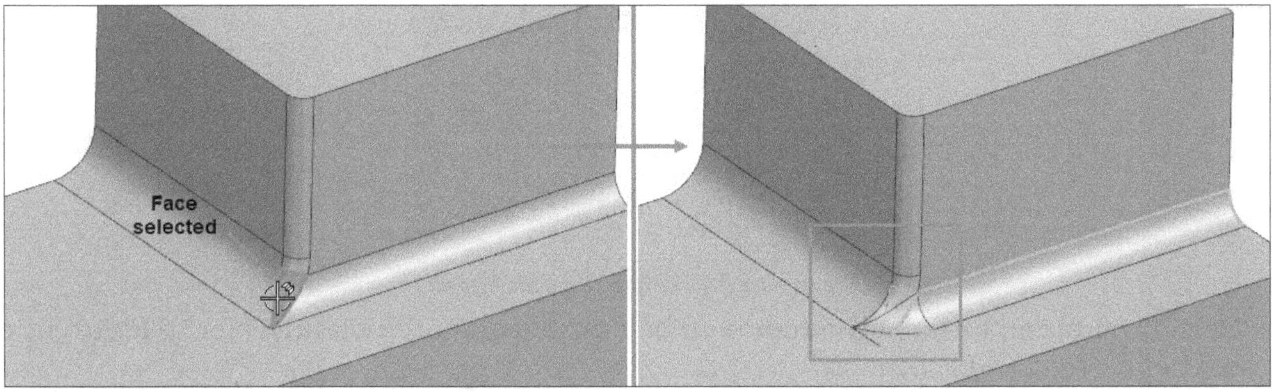

Figure-119. Reordered blend preview

Labeling Chamfer

The **Label Chamfer** tool is used to mark selected tapered face as chamfer. The procedure to use this tool is given next.

- Click on the **Label Chamfer** tool from the **Detail Feature** section of the **More** drop-down in the **Synchronous Modeling** group of **Ribbon**. The **Label Chamfer** dialog box will be displayed; refer to Figure-120.

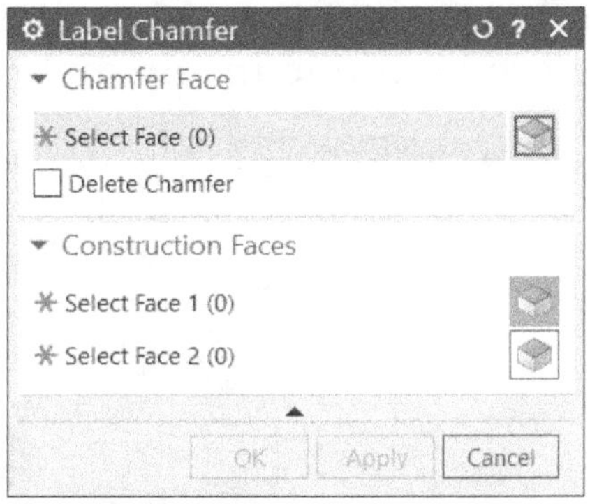

Figure-120. Label Chamfer dialog box

- Select desired face to be identified as chamfer; refer to Figure-121.

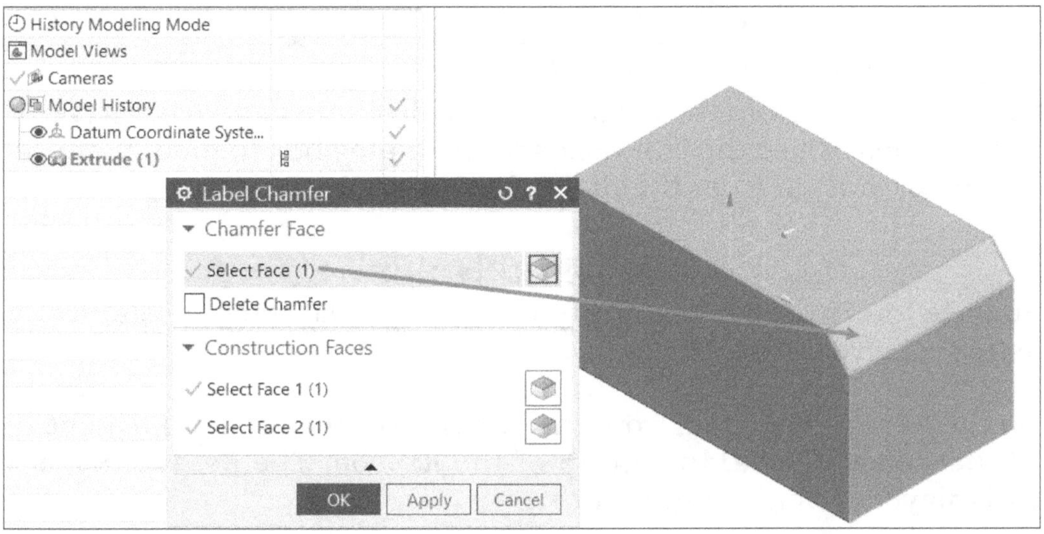

Figure-121. Face identified as chamfer

- Click on the **OK** button from the dialog box to make selected face identified as chamfer.

Resizing Chamfer

The **Resize Chamfer** tool is used to change the size of identified chamfer. The procedure to use this tool is given next.

- Click on the **Resize Chamfer** tool from the **Detail Feature** section of **Synchronous Modeling** group in **Home** tab of **Ribbon**. The **Resize Chamfer** dialog box will be displayed; refer to Figure-122.

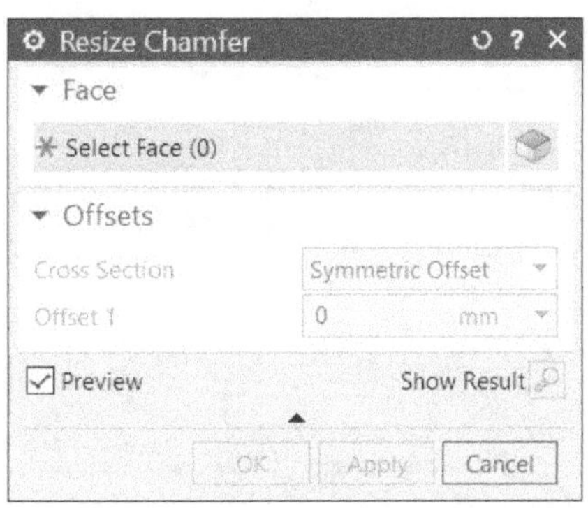

Figure-122. Resize Chamfer dialog box

- Select the chamfer face to be modified. The handles to modify chamfer size will be displayed along with related options in the dialog box; refer to Figure-123.

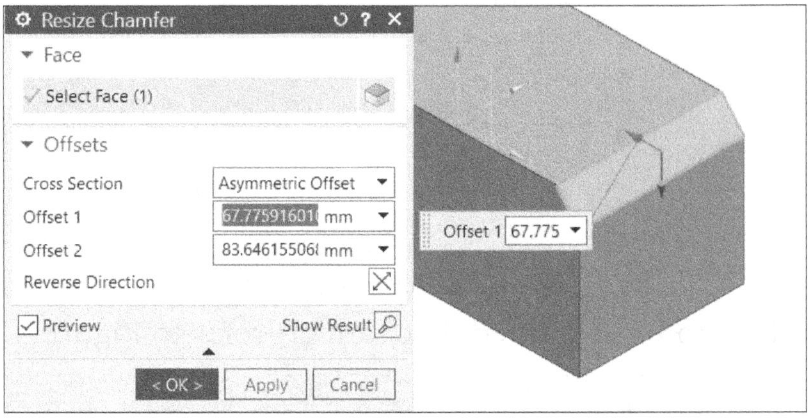

Figure-123. Handles to resize chamfer

- Select desired option from the **Cross Section** drop-down to define type of chamfer.
- Drag the handles or use the edit boxes in the dialog box to modify size of chamfer.
- Click on the **OK** button from the dialog box to apply the changes.

Resizing Holes

The **Resize Hole** tool is used to change type and size of selected hole(s). The procedure to use this tool is given next.

- Click on the **Resize Hole** tool from the **Detail Feature** section of **More** drop-down in the **Synchronous Modeling** group of the **Ribbon**. The **Resize Hole** dialog box will be displayed; refer to Figure-124.

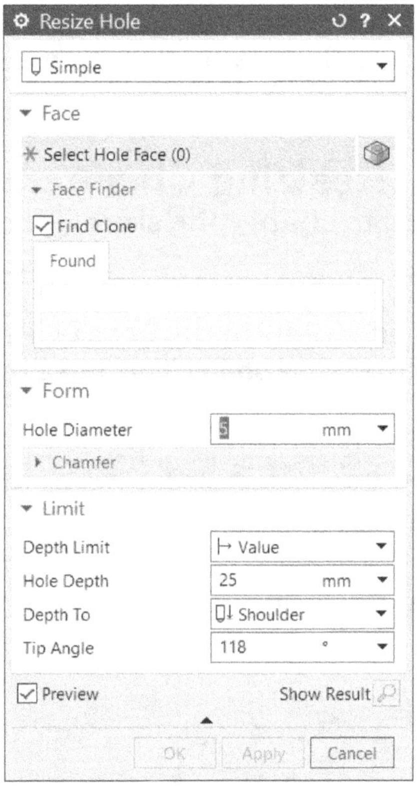

Figure-124. Resize Hole dialog box

- Select desired hole from the model to be re-sized. The hole will be selected; refer to Figure-125.

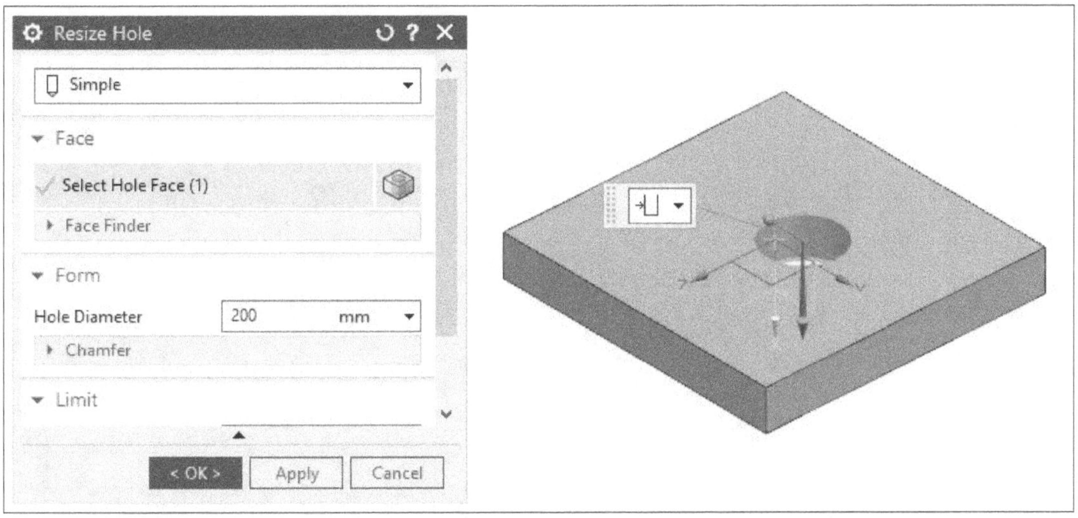

Figure-125. Hole selected

- Specify new diameter of hole as desired in the **Hole Diameter** edit box from **Form** rollout.
- Optionally, specify chamfer parameters by selecting **Entry Chamfer** and **Exit Chamfer** check boxes from **Chamfer** rollout.
- Select desired option from **Depth Limit** drop-down of **Limit** rollout to define depth limit for hole.
- Select the **Preview** check box to show the preview of hole resizing.
- After specifying desired parameters, click on the **Apply** or **OK** button. The hole will be resized; refer to Figure-126.

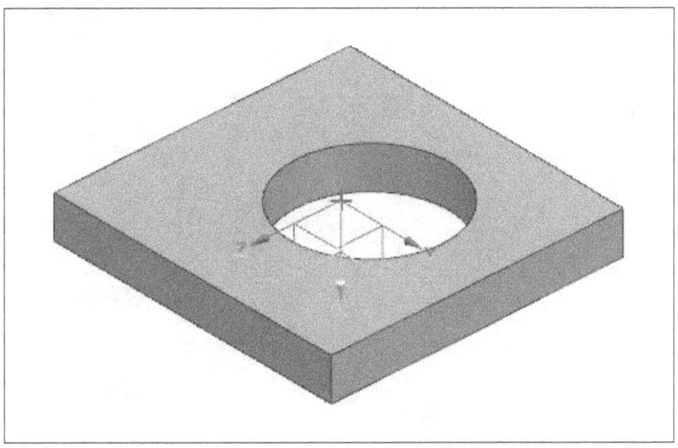

Figure-126. Hole resized

Resizing Pattern

The **Resize Pattern** tool is used to change the count and spacing of members in a recognized linear or circular pattern feature. The procedure to use this tool is discussed next.

- Click on the **Resize Pattern** tool from the **Detail Feature** section of **More** drop-down in the **Synchronous Modeling** group of the **Ribbon**. The **Resize Pattern** dialog box will be displayed; refer to Figure-127.

Figure-127. Resize Pattern dialog box

- Select desired pattern feature from the model to be re-sized. The pattern feature will be selected; refer to Figure-128.

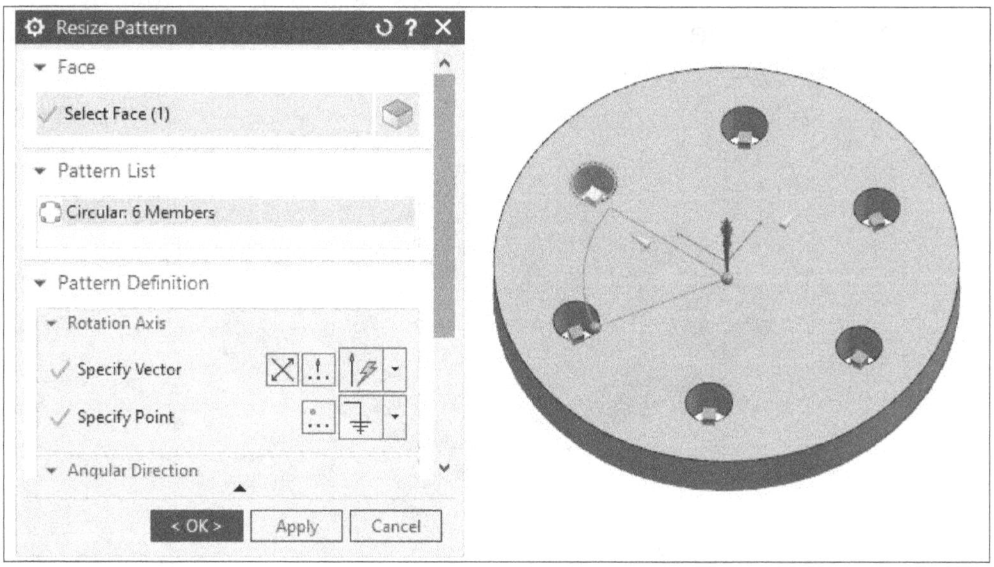

Figure-128. Pattern feature selected

- Modify the parameters as desired in the dialog box as discussed in the **Pattern Feature** tool. The pattern feature will be resized; refer to Figure-129.

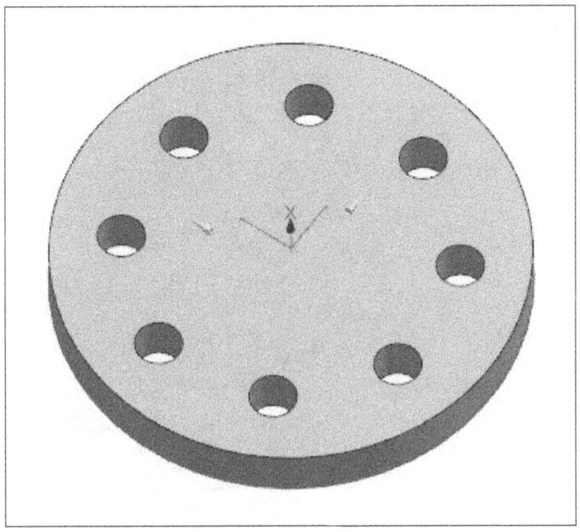

Figure-129. Pattern feature resized

Copy Face

The **Copy Face** tool is used to copy a set of faces from a body. The procedure to use this tool is discussed next.

- Click on the **Copy Face** tool from the **Reuse** section of **More** drop-down in the **Synchronous Modeling** group of the **Ribbon**. The **Copy Face** dialog box will be displayed; refer to Figure-130.

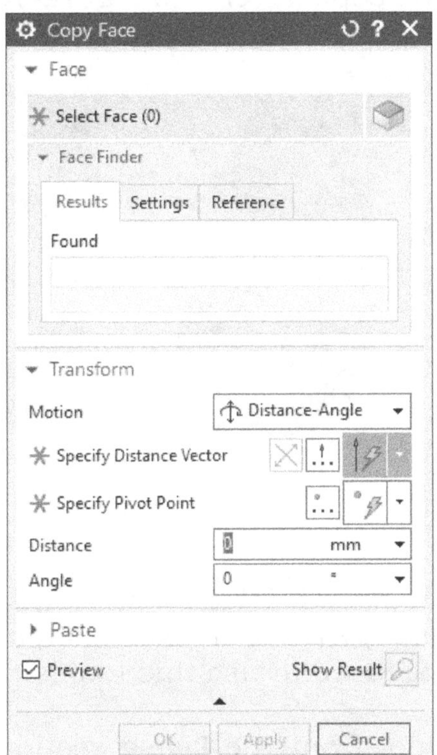

Figure-130. Copy Face dialog box

- Select desired face of body to be copied. The face will be selected in the **Results** tab of **Face** rollout; refer to Figure-131.

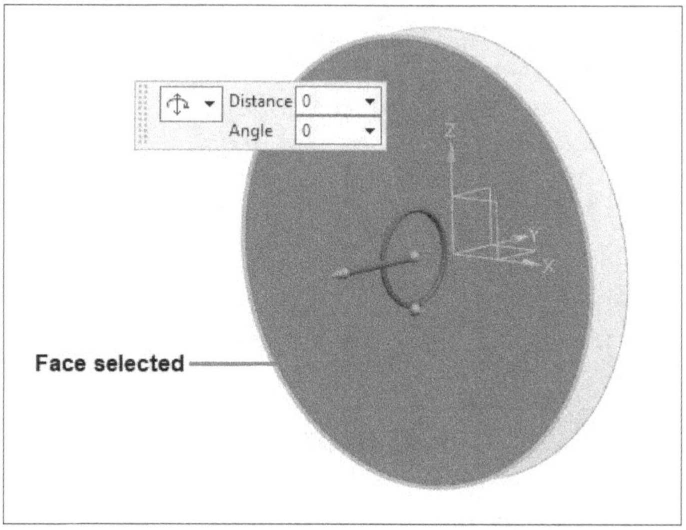

Figure-131. Face selected

- Select desired option from **Motion** drop-down in the **Transform** rollout for linear or angular motion and specify desired parameters as per the selected option.
- Specify desired distance and/or angle value at which the face to be copied in the **Distance** and/or **Angle** edit boxes.
- Select **Paste Copied Faces** check box from **Paste** rollout to paste the copied faces using the specified **Motion** option in the **Transform** rollout.
- After specifying desired parameters, click on the **Apply** or **OK** button from the dialog box. The face will be copied; refer to Figure-132.

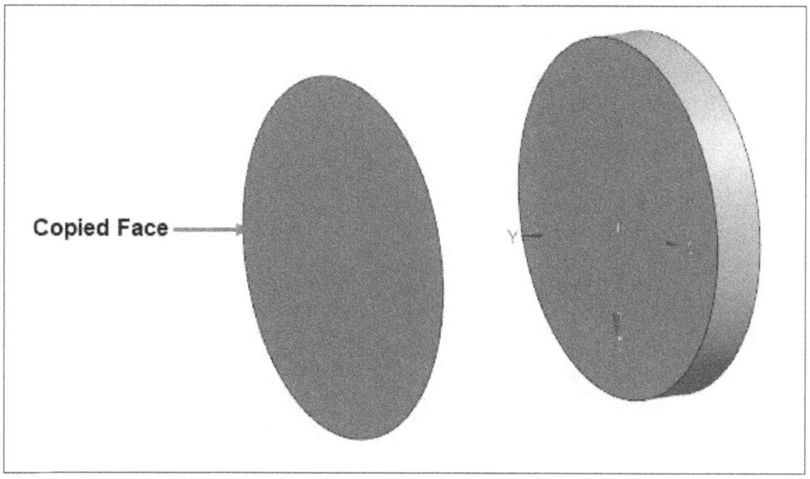

Figure-132. Face copied

Cut Face

The **Cut Face** tool is used to copy a set of faces from a body and then delete those faces from the body. The procedure to use this tool is discussed next.

- Click on the **Cut Face** tool from the **Reuse** section of **More** drop-down in the **Synchronous Modeling** group of the **Ribbon**. The **Cut Face** dialog box will be displayed; refer to Figure-133.

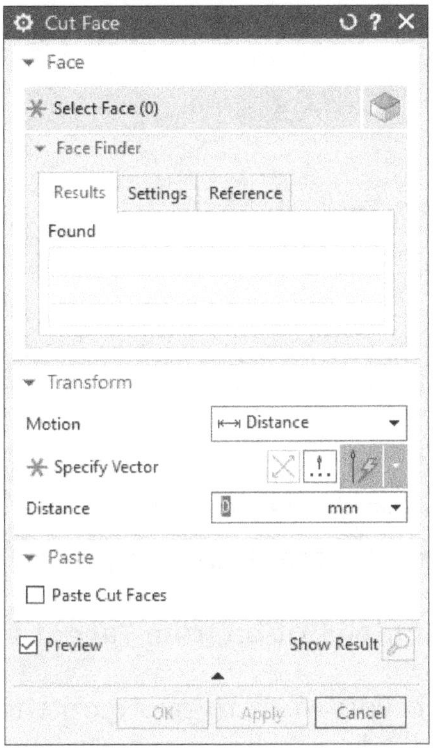

Figure-133. Cut Face dialog box

- The parameters in the dialog box is same as discussed for **Copy Face** tool.
- After specifying desired parameters, click on the **Apply** or **OK** button from the dialog box. The face will be cut; refer to Figure-134.

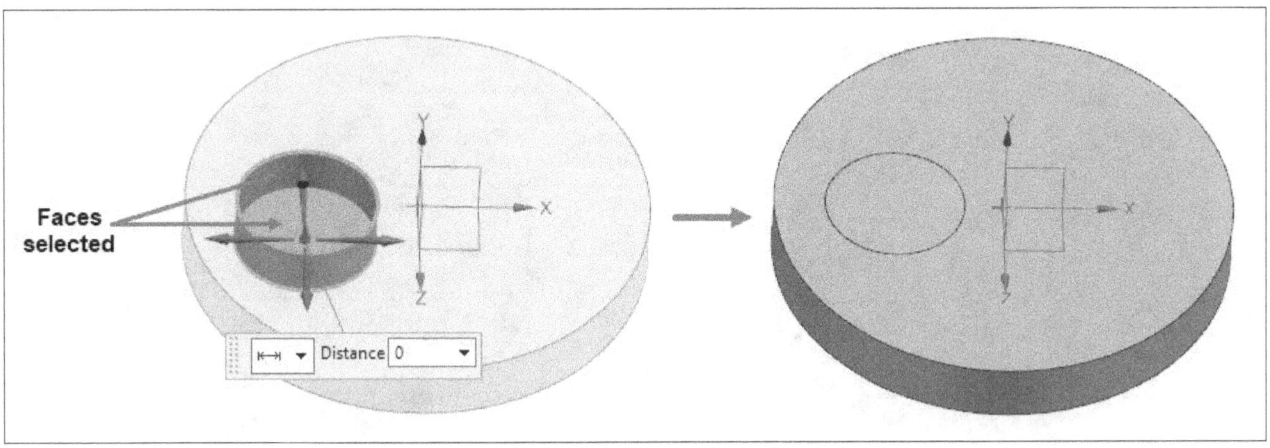

Figure-134. Face cut

Paste Face

The **Paste Face** tool is used to paste a sheet body into a solid body. The procedure to use this tool is discussed next.

- Click on the **Paste Face** tool from the **Reuse** section of **More** drop-down in the **Synchronous Modeling** group of the **Ribbon**. The **Paste Face** dialog box will be displayed; refer to Figure-135.

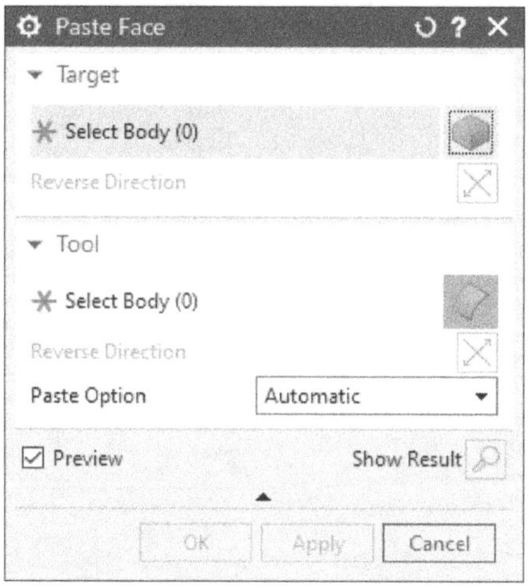

Figure-135. Paste Face dialog box

- Select the target body from the graphics window on which you want to paste the face.
- Click on the **Reverse Direction** button from **Target** rollout to reverse the direction of paste faces.
- Select the tool body which you want to paste on the target body. The preview of pasted body will be displayed.
- Select desired option from **Paste Option** drop-down to add or subtract the face.
- After specifying desired parameters, click on the **Apply** or **OK** button from the dialog box. The body will be pasted; refer to Figure-136.

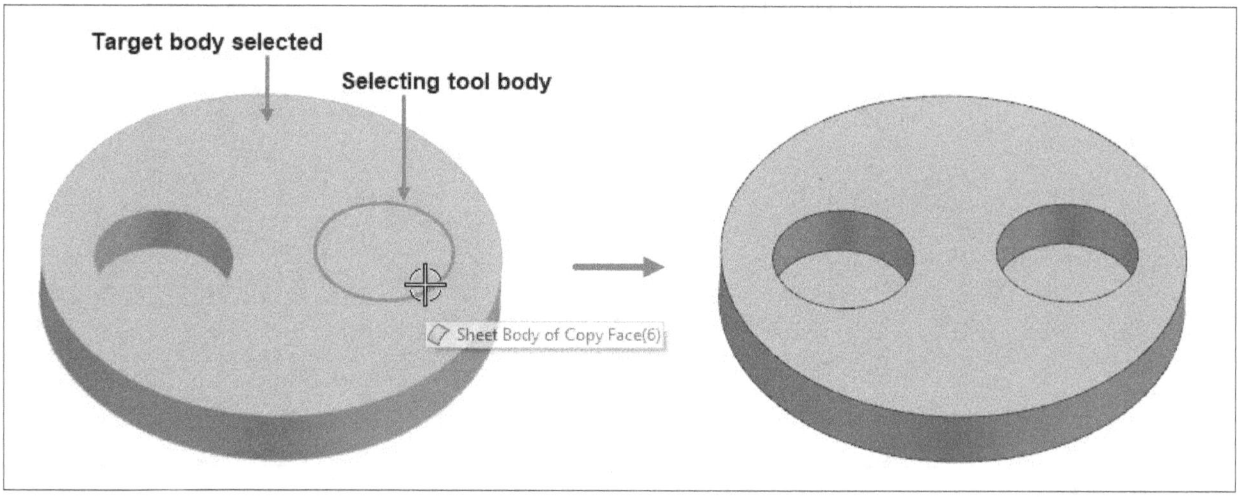

Figure-136. Body pasted

Mirror Face

The **Mirror Face** tool is used to copy a face set, mirror it about a plane, and paste it into the same solid or sheet body. The procedure to use this tool is discussed next.

- Click on the **Mirror Face** tool from the **Reuse** section of **More** drop-down in the **Synchronous Modeling** group of the **Ribbon**. The **Mirror Face** dialog box will be displayed; refer to Figure-137.

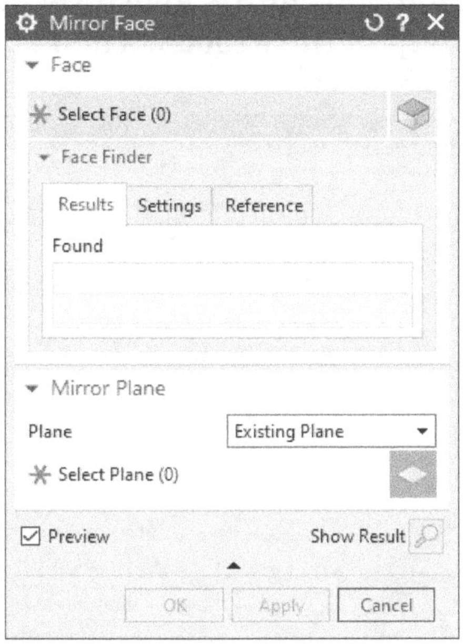

Figure-137. Mirror Face dialog box

- Select desired face/faces from the graphics window to be mirrored.
- The **Results** tab of **Face Finder** rollout lists the suggested faces you can select. The **Settings** tab lists the geometric conditions that you can use to select related faces. The **Reference** tab lists the coordinate systems for specifying symmetry planes and the initial orientation of the Dynamic manipulator handles.
- Select desired option from **Plane** drop-down in the **Mirror Plane** rollout. Select **Existing Plane** option to specify an existing datum plane or planar surface for the symmetry plane. Select **New Plane** option to create a new plane for the mirror plane.
- Click on the **Select Plane** button and select desired plane from graphics window.
- After specifying desired parameters, click on the **Apply** or **OK** button. The face will be mirrored; refer to Figure-138.

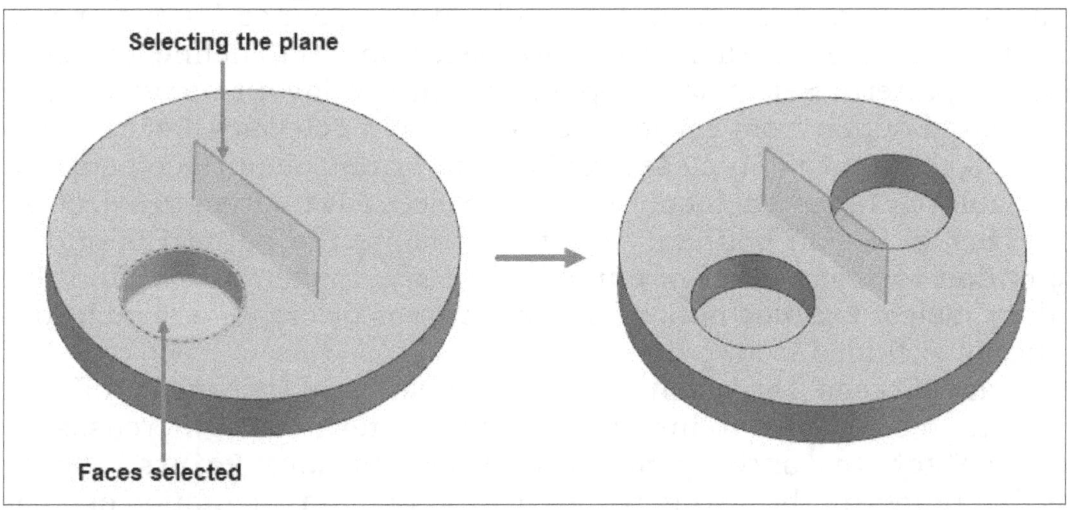

Figure-138. Face mirrored

Pattern Face

The **Pattern Face** tool is used to create patterns of faces in various pattern layouts and define pattern boundaries, reference points, orientation, and clocking. The procedure to use this tool is discussed next.

- Click on the **Pattern Face** tool from the **Reuse** section of **More** drop-down in the **Synchronous Modeling** group of the **Ribbon**. The **Pattern Face** dialog box will be displayed; refer to Figure-139.

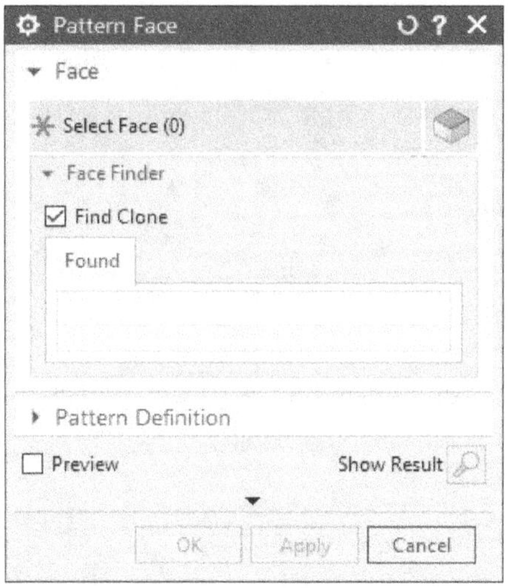

Figure-139. Pattern Face dialog box

- Select desired face/faces from graphics window to be patterned.
- Select **Find Clone** check box from **Face Finder** rollout to find faces that are geometrically the same as the selected face.
- Click on the **Specify Point** button from **Reference Point** rollout to specify the location on the input face to be used to define the pattern instance locations.
- Select desired pattern layout from **Layout** drop-down in the **Pattern Definition** rollout. Select **Linear** option to define a layout using one or two directions. Select **Circular** option to define a layout using a rotation axis and optional radial spacing parameters. Select **Polygon** option to define a layout using an equilateral polygon and optional radial spacing parameters. Select **Spiral** option to define a layout using a spiral path. Select **Along** option to define a layout that follows a continuous curve chain and optionally a second curve chain or a vector. Select **General** option to define a layout using locations defined by one or more target points or coordinate systems. Select **Reference** option to define a layout by using an existing pattern. Select **Helix** option to define a layout using a helical path.
- Select desired option from **Boundary** drop-down in **Boundary Definition** rollout to address objects that lie in close proximity to or on the surface being patterned, such as holes or repeated detail geometry. Select **Face** option to select face edges, sheet edges, or region boundary curves to define the pattern boundary. Select **Curve** option to select a set of curves, or create a sketch to define the pattern boundary. Select **Exclude** option to select curves or create a sketch to define an area that is excluded from patterning.
- Click on the **Pattern Increment** button from **Pattern Increment** rollout to define increments to be applied to instances as the pattern count increases.
- Click on **Select Instance Point** button from **Instance Points** rollout to select points that represent the layout, pattern definition, and orientation of the instances that are to be created.
- Select **Use Spreadsheet** check box or click **Display Spreadsheet** for **Pattern** button to edit pattern definition parameters, including any pattern-variance settings, only in a spreadsheet.

- Select desired option from **Orientation** drop-down in the **Orientation** rollout to determine if the pattern faces in the layout will maintain a constant orientation or follow an orientation derived from some defining geometry. Select **Follow Face** check box to maintain an orientation for the pattern faces that is normal to the specified face at the location of the instance. Select desired option from **Project Direction** drop-down to specify location of the instances.
- Select **Copy Chamfer Labels** check box from **Settings** rollout to copy the chamfer labels on unparameterized angled faces and have them applied in the resulting pattern. Select **Copy Threads** check box to copy symbolic threads so that you do not need to recreate additional symbolic threads that look the same as the source body.
- After specifying desired parameters, click on the **Apply** or **OK** button from the dialog box. The pattern of the face will be created; refer to Figure-140.

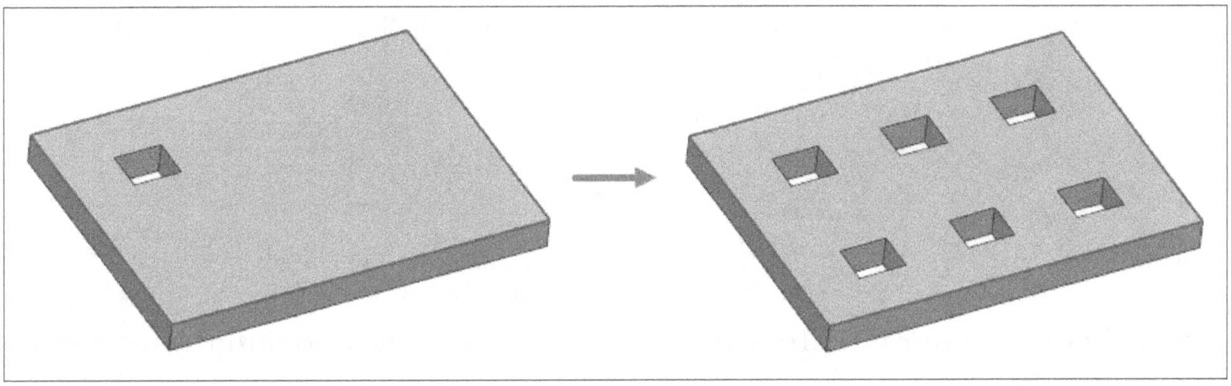

Figure-140. Face patterned

Make Coplanar

The **Make Coplanar** tool is used to move faces so they are coplanar to another face or datum plane. The procedure to use this tool is discussed next.

- Click on the **Make Coplanar** tool from the **Reuse** section of **More** drop-down in the **Synchronous Modeling** group of the **Ribbon**. The **Make Coplanar** dialog box will be displayed; refer to Figure-141.

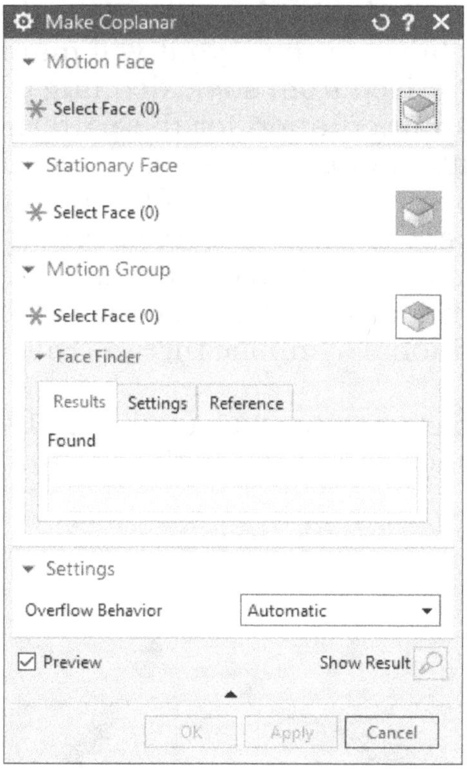

Figure-141. Make Coplanar dialog box

- Select desired planar face from graphics window to create coplanar with a selected stationary face.
- Click on the **Select Face** button from **Stationary Face** rollout to select a planar face that remains stationary.
- Click on the **Select Face** button from **Motion Group** rollout to select additional planar faces to create coplanar face. The preview of coplanar face will be displayed.
- Select desired option from **Overflow Behavior** drop-down in the **Settings** rollout to control the overflow characteristics of faces you relate. Select the **Automatic** option to extend either the modified faces or the stationary faces depending on what gives the smallest change of volume or area. Select **Extend Change Face** option to extend the faces being modified to form a complete intersection with the model. Select **Extend Incident Face** option to extend the stationary faces when they intersect the faces being modified. Select **Extend Cap Face** option to extend the caps when the modified faces overflow an edge.
- After specifying desired parameters, click on the **Apply** or **OK** button from the dialog box. The coplanar face will be created; refer to Figure-142.

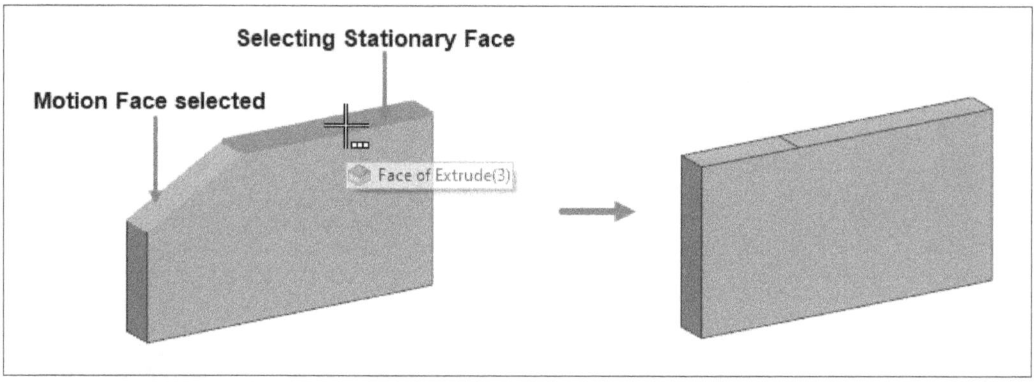

Figure-142. Coplanar Face created

Make Coaxial

The **Make Coaxial** tool is used to modify a cylinder or cone to be coaxial with another cylinder or cone. The procedure to use this tool is discussed next.

- Click on the **Make Coaxial** tool from the **Reuse** section of **More** drop-down in the **Synchronous Modeling** group of the **Ribbon**. The **Make Coaxial** dialog box will be displayed; refer to Figure-143.

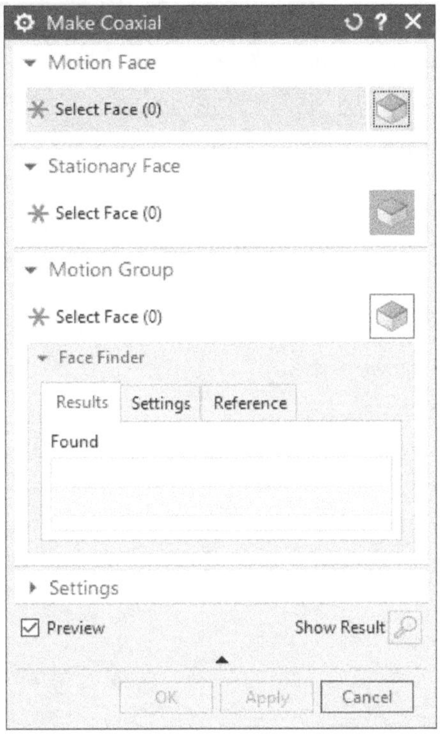

Figure-143. Make Coaxial dialog box

- Select desired cylinder, cone, or torus face (an axial face) to be coaxial with a selected stationary face.
- Click on the **Select Face** button from **Stationary Face** rollout and select a full or partial cylinder, cone, or torus face, or a datum axis as the stationary face. The preview of coaxial face will be displayed.
- After specifying desired parameters, click on the **Apply** or **OK** button from the dialog box. The coaxial face will be created; refer to Figure-144.

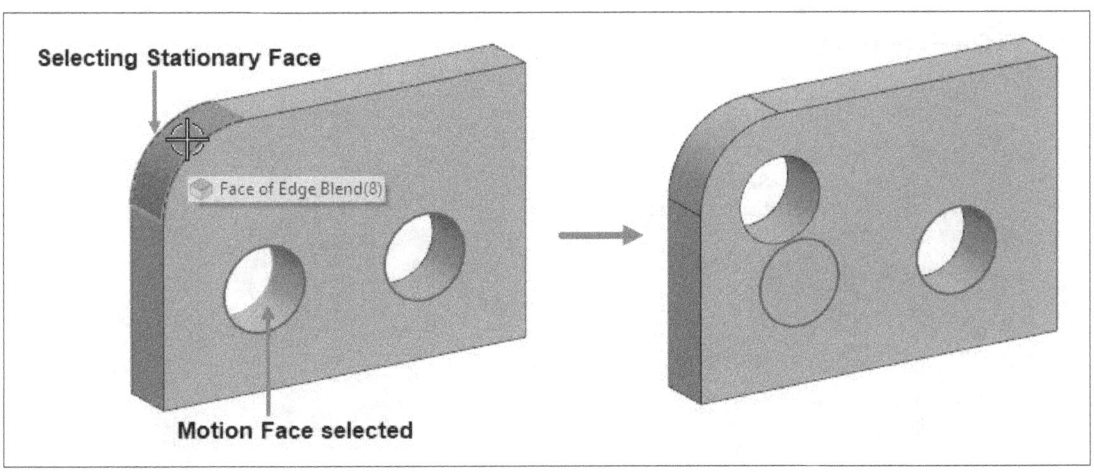

Figure-144. Coaxial Face created

Make Tangent

The **Make Tangent** tool is used to make one face tangent to another face or datum plane. The procedure to use this tool is discussed next.

- Click on the **Make Tangent** tool from the **Reuse** section of **More** drop-down in the **Synchronous Modeling** group of the **Ribbon**. The **Make Tangent** dialog box will be displayed; refer to Figure-145.

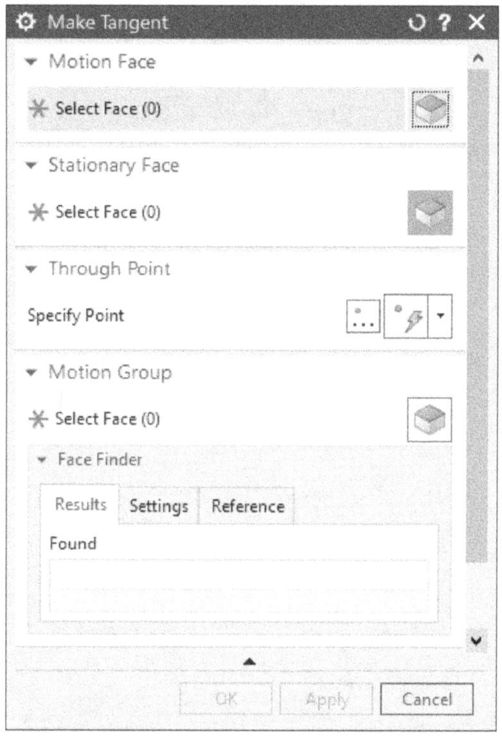

Figure-145. Make Tangent dialog box

- Select desired face to create it tangent with a selected stationary face.
- Click on the **Select Face** button from **Stationary Face** rollout to select a face or datum plane to be stationary. The preview of tangent face will be displayed.
- Click on the **Specify Point** button from **Through Point** rollout to select a point through which the motion face must pass when the transform is applied.
- After specifying desired parameters, click on the **Apply** or **OK** button from the dialog box. The tangent face will be created; refer to Figure-146.

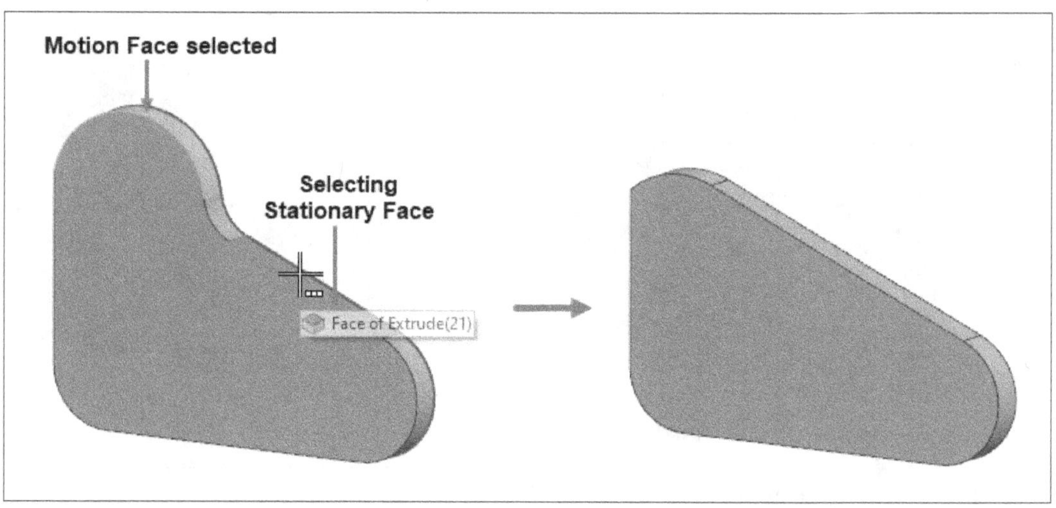

Figure-146. Tangent face created

Make Symmetric

The **Make Symmetric** tool is used to make one face symmetric to another face about a plane of symmetry. The procedure to use this tool is discussed next.

- Click on the **Make Symmetric** tool from the **Reuse** section of **More** drop-down in the **Synchronous Modeling** group of the **Ribbon**. The **Make Symmetry** dialog box will be displayed; refer to Figure-147.

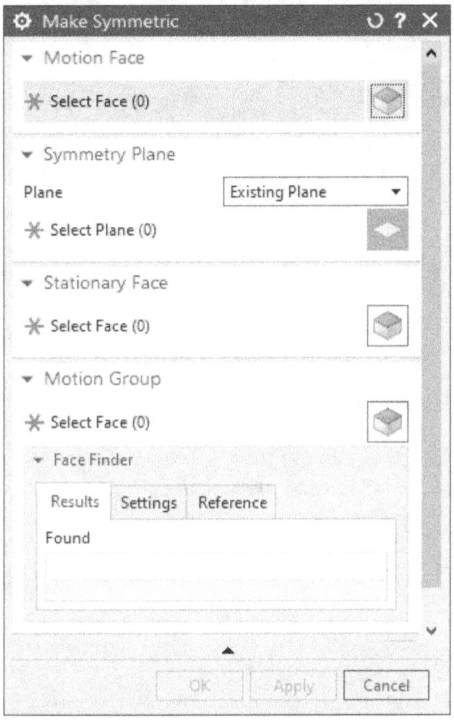

Figure-147. Make Symmetric dialog box

- Select desired face of the model to be symmetric to a selected stationary face.
- Click on the **Select Plane** button from **Symmetry Plane** drop-down and select the plane of symmetry about which a face to be symmetry.
- Click on the **Select Face** button from **Stationary Face** rollout and select a face from the model to be stationary. The preview of symmetric face will be displayed.
- After specifying desired parameters, click on the **Apply** or **OK** button from the dialog box. The symmetric face will be displayed; refer to Figure-148.

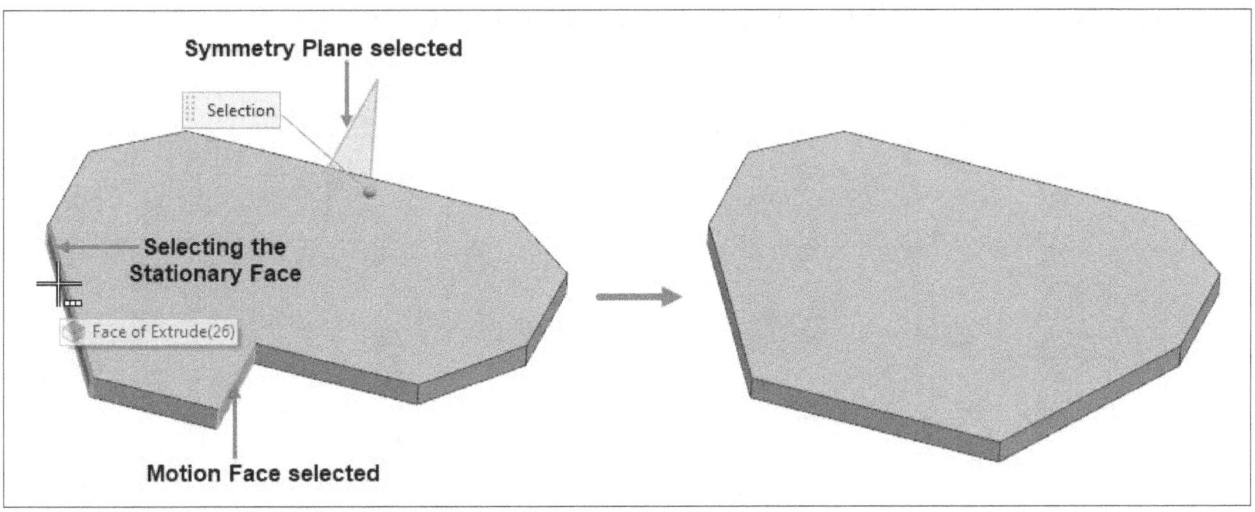

Figure-148. Symmetric face created

Make Parallel

The **Make Parallel** tool is used to make one planar face parallel to another planar face or datum plane. The procedure to use this tool is discussed next.

- Click on the **Make Parallel** tool from the **Reuse** section of **More** drop-down in the **Synchronous Modeling** group of the **Ribbon**. The **Make Parallel** dialog box will be displayed; refer to Figure-149.

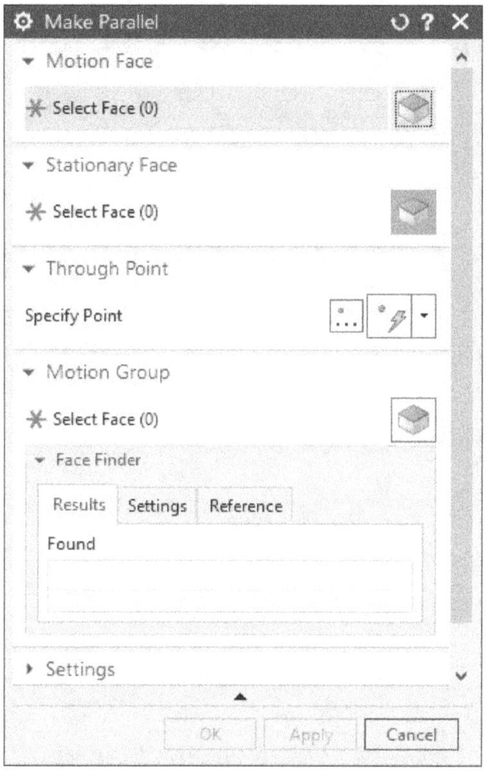

Figure-149. Make Parallel dialog box

- Select desired planar face to be parallel with selected stationary face.
- Click on the **Select Face** button from **Stationary Face** rollout to select a planar face or datum plane to be stationary. The preview of parallel face will be displayed.
- Click on the **Specify Point** button from **Through Point** rollout and select a point through which the motion face must pass through when the transform is applied.
- After specifying desired parameters, click on the **Apply** or **OK** button from the dialog box. The parallel face will be created; refer to Figure-150.

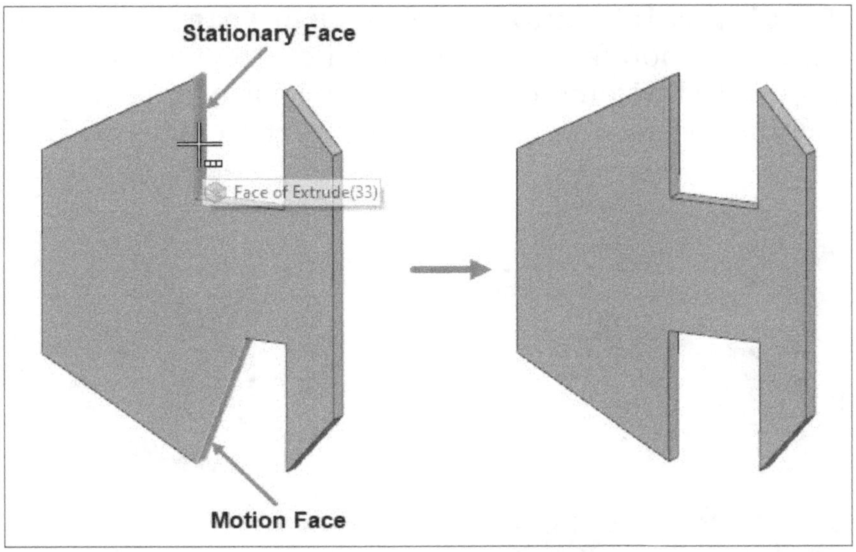

Figure-150. Parallel Face created

Make Perpendicular

The **Make Perpendicular** tool is used to make one planar face perpendicular to another planar face or datum plane. The procedure to use this tool is discussed next.

- Click on the **Make Perpendicular** tool from the **Reuse** section of **More** drop-down in the **Synchronous Modeling** group of the **Ribbon**. The **Make Perpendicular** dialog box will be displayed; refer to Figure-151.

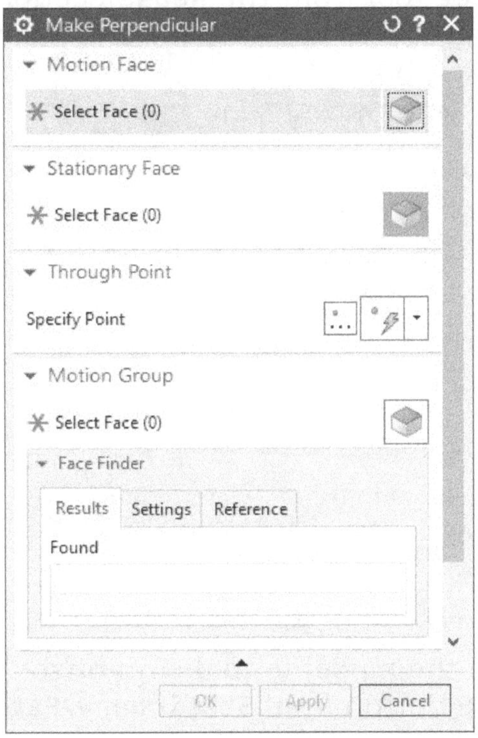

Figure-151. Make Perpendicular dialog box

- Select desired planar face from the model to be perpendicular with a selected stationary face.
- Click on the **Select Face** button from **Stationary Face** rollout and select a planar face or datum plane to be stationary. The preview of perpendicular face will be displayed.

- Click on the **Specify Point** button from **Through Point** rollout and select a point through which the motion face must pass when the transform is applied.
- After specifying desired parameters, click on the **Apply** or **OK** button from the dialog box. The perpendicular face will be created; refer to Figure-152.

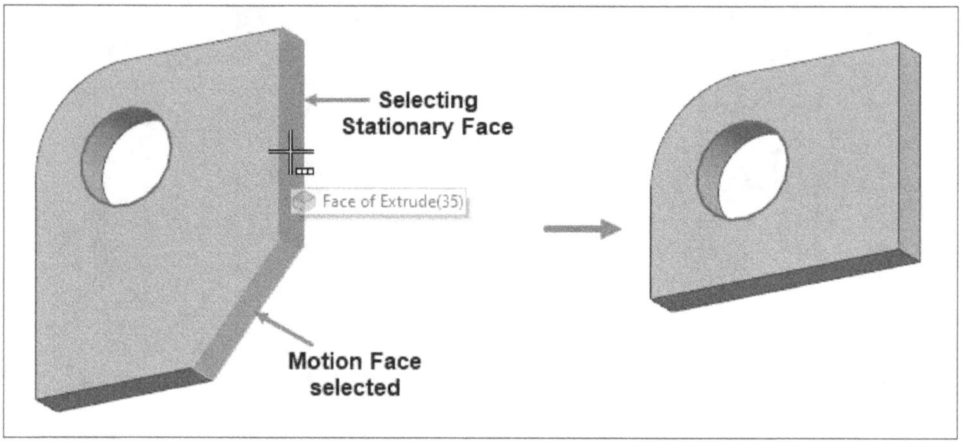

Figure-152. Perpendicular Face selected

Make Offset

The **Make Offset** tool is used to establish and save an offset (for example, wall thickness) relationship with another similar face. The procedure to use this tool is discussed next.

- Click on the **Make Offset** tool from the **Reuse** section of **More** drop-down in the **Synchronous Modeling** group of the **Ribbon**. The **Make Offset** dialog box will be displayed; refer to Figure-153.

Figure-153. Make Offset dialog box

- Select desired face from the model to make an offset of another face.
- Click on the **Select Face** button from **Stationary Face** rollout and select the face from which you want to measure the offset distance.
- Specify desired offset distance in the **Distance** edit box of **Offset** rollout. The preview of offset face will be displayed.
- After specifying desired parameters, click on the **Apply** or **OK** button from the dialog box. The offset face will be created; refer to Figure-154.

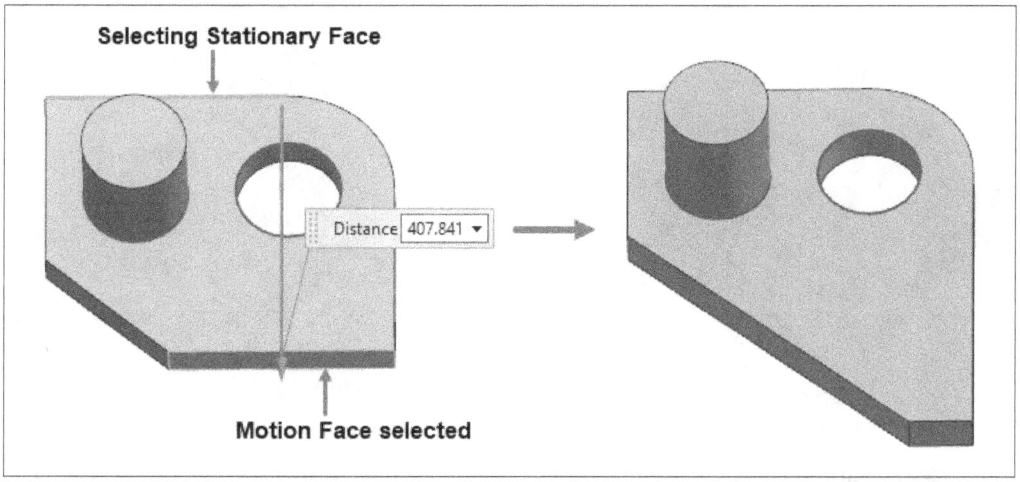

Figure-154. Offset Face created

Group Face

The **Group Face** tool is used to group sets of faces to select the faces easily. The procedure to use this tool is discussed next.

- Click on the **Group Face** tool from the **Reuse** section of **More** drop-down in the **Synchronous Modeling** group of the **Ribbon**. The **Group Face** dialog box will be displayed; refer to Figure-155.

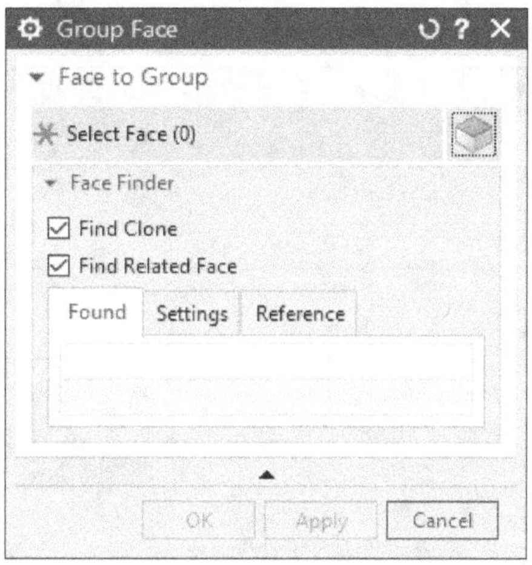

Figure-155. Group Face dialog box

- Select desired faces from the model to collect into a **Group Face** feature.
- After specifying desired parameters, click on the **Apply** or **OK** button. The faces will be grouped; refer to Figure-156.

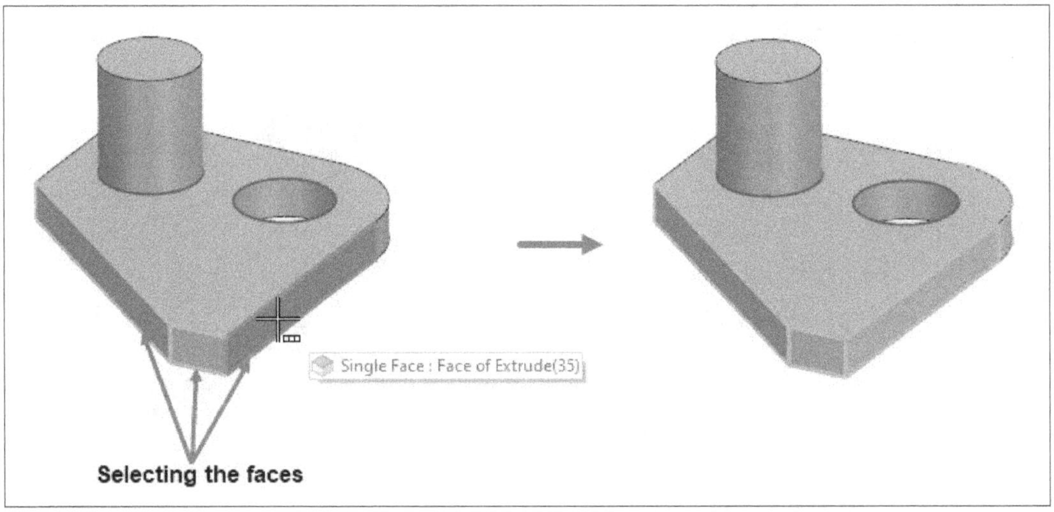

Figure-156. Faces grouped

Optimize Face

The **Optimize Face** tool is used to simplify surface types, merge faces, improve edge accuracy, and recognize blends. The procedure to use this tool is discussed next.

- Click on the **Optimize Face** tool from the **Reuse** section of **More** drop-down in the **Synchronous Modeling** group of the **Ribbon**. The **Optimize Face** dialog box will be displayed; refer to Figure-157.

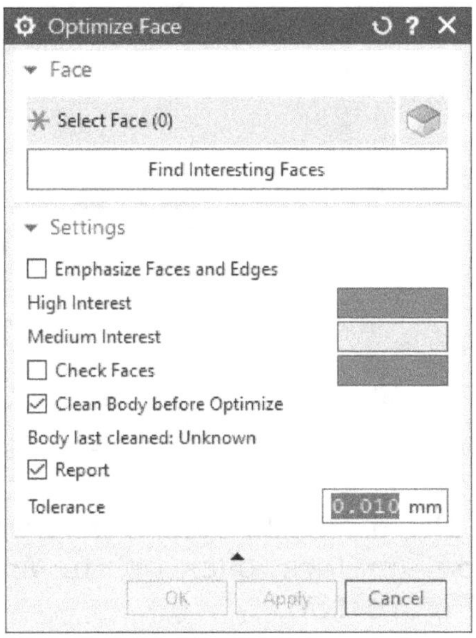

Figure-157. Optimize Face dialog box

- Click on the **Find Interesting Faces** button to find and select desired faces of the model to be optimized, including non-analytic faces and faces that are adjacent to tolerant edges.
- Select **Emphasize Faces and Edges** check box from **Settings** rollout to highlight faces and edges that are not analytic on which it may be difficult to perform synchronous modeling operations.
- Click on the **High Interest** button, the **Object Color** dialog box will be displayed to select desired color for the highligted faces or edges. The **High Interest** option highlights the B-surfaces and faces neighbouring tolerant edges to improve such selected edges to accurate edges.

- Click on the **Medium Interest** button, the **Object Color** dialog box will be displayed to select desired color. The **Medium Interest** option highlights the B-surface, extruded, or revolved faces to replace such selected faces with analytic types or blends.
- Select **Check Faces** check box to highlight invalid faces before doing an optimize face operation. The invalid faces may be removed or merged. Click on the button next to the **Check Faces** check box, the **Object Color** dialog box will be displayed to specify desired color for the faces or edges.
- Select **Clean Body before Optimize** check box to create a valid body by removing invalid geometry and bad topology.
- Select **Report** check box to display a report of all the faces and edges that are optimized.
- Specify desired distance tolerance value in the **Tolerance** edit box.
- After specifying desired parameters, click on the **Apply** or **OK** button from the dialog box. The faces will be optimized and the **Information** window will be displayed; refer to Figure-158.

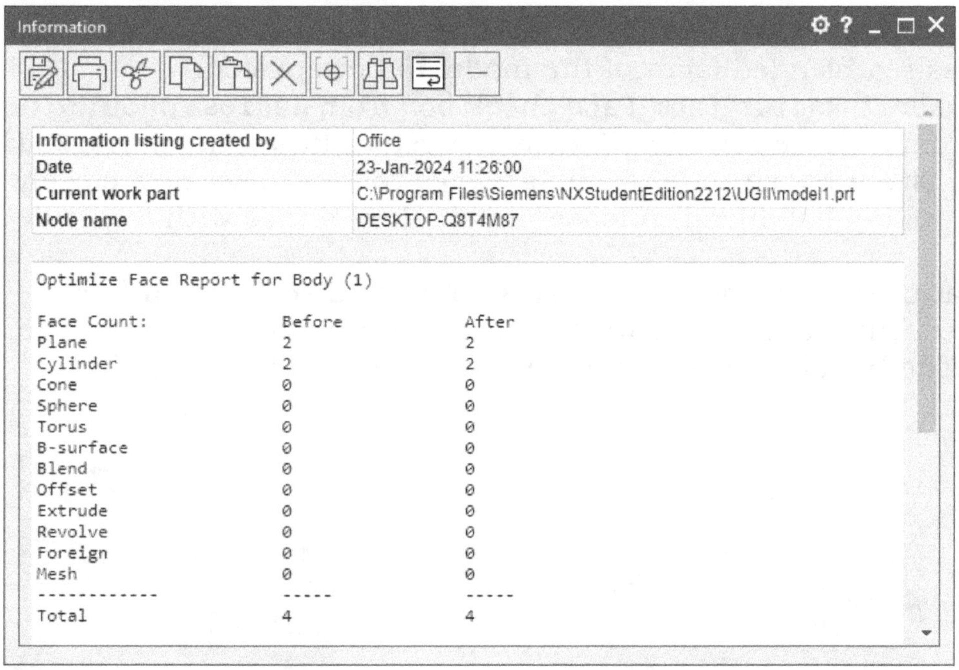

Figure-158. Information window

Replace Blend

The **Replace Blend** tool is used to convert B-surface faces that appear like blends to a replace blend feature. The procedure to use this tool is discussed next.

- Click on the **Replace Blend** tool from the **Reuse** section of **More** drop-down in the **Synchronous Modeling** group of the **Ribbon**. The **Replace Blend** dialog box will be displayed; refer to Figure-159.

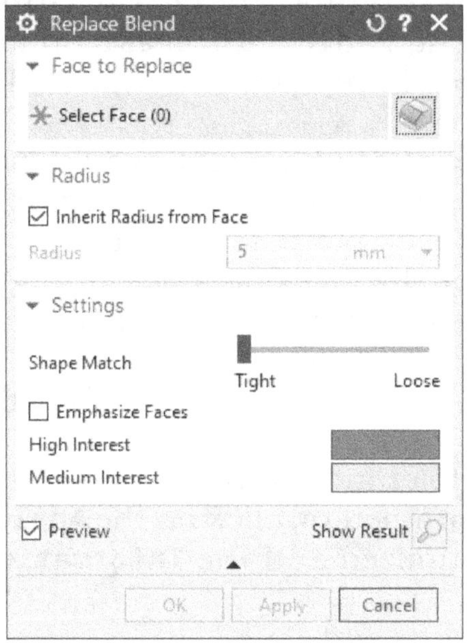

Figure-159. Replace Blend dialog box

- Select desired blended faces of the model to be replaced.
- Select **Inherit Radius from Face** check box from **Radius** rollout to determine the radius from the face selected. Specify desired radius value in the **Radius** edit box.
- Drag the **Shape Match** slider from **Settings** rollout to set how closely a face must match a rolling ball blend. A loose match allow a face with larger deviation to be replaced.
- Other parameters in the dialog box is same as discussed earlier.
- After specifying desired parameters in the dialog box, click on the **Apply** or **OK** button. The blend feature will be replaced; refer to Figure-160.

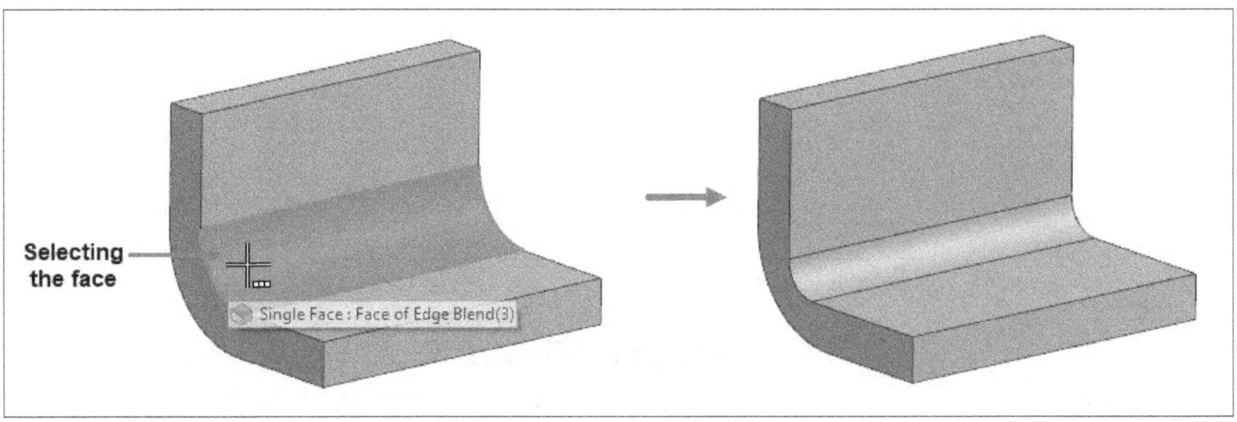

Figure-160. Blend feature replaced

Move Edge

The **Move Edge** tool is used to edit a shape by directly manipulating its edges. Faces adjacent to the edges you edit adapt to follow the motion you apply. The procedure to use this tool is discussed next.

- Click on the **Move Edge** tool from the **Reuse** section of **More** drop-down in the **Synchronous Modeling** group of the **Ribbon**. The **Move Edge** dialog box will be displayed; refer to Figure-161.

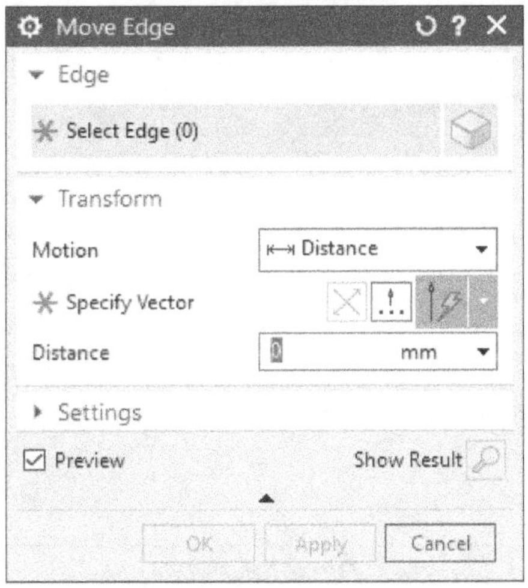

Figure-161. Move Edge dialog box

- Select a single, end-connected chain of edges to be moved from the model.
- Select desired transform method from **Motion** drop-down in the **Transform** rollout for the edges to be moved and specify desired parameters.
- Select **Extend** option from **End Face Behavior** drop-down from **Settings** rollout to extend the faces along the existing topography. Select **Morph** option from the drop-down to reconstruct the adjacent faces to accommodate the motion faces.
- After specifying desired parameters in the dialog box, click on the **Apply** or **OK** button. The edge will be moved; refer to Figure-162.

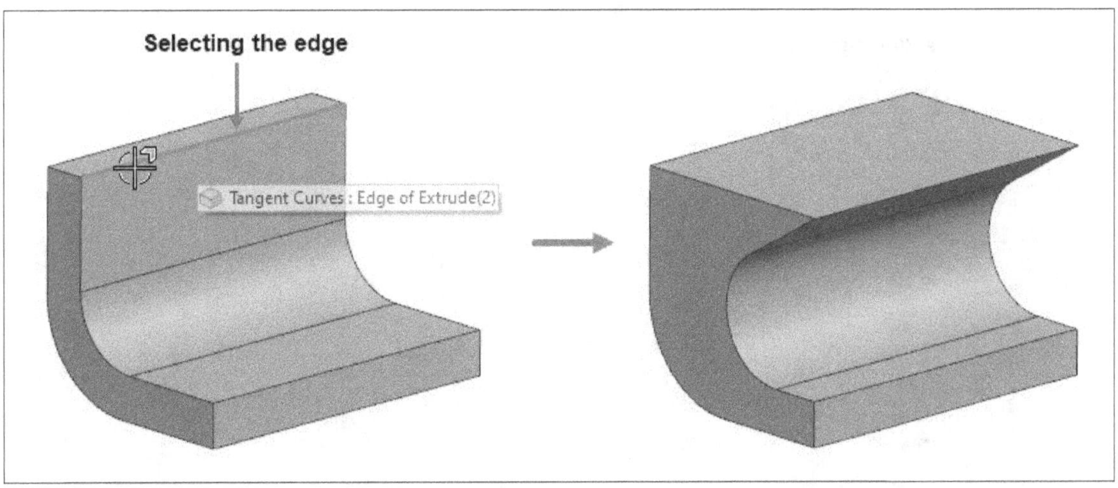

Figure-162. Edge moved

Offset Edge

The **Offset Edge** tool is used to offset an edge or a set of contiguous edges. The procedure to use this tool is discussed next.

- Click on the **Offset Edge** tool from the **Reuse** section of **More** drop-down in the **Synchronous Modeling** group of the **Ribbon**. The **Offset Edge** dialog box will be displayed; refer to Figure-163.

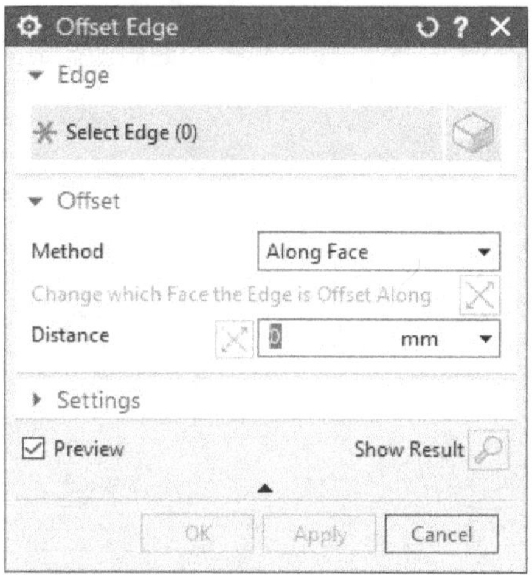

Figure-163. Offset Edge dialog box

- Select a single, end-connected chain of edges to be offset from the model.
- Select desired offset method from **Method** drop-down of **Offset** rollout. Select **Along Face** option to offset an edge along a face adjacent to the edge. Select **Along Plane of Edge** option to offset a planar edge along the plane of a set of edges.
- Click on the **Change which Face the Edge is Offset Along** button to switch between the faces along which the edge to be offset.
- Specify desired value for the distance to offset the edges in the **Distance** edit box.
- After specifying desired parameters in the dialog box, click on the **Apply** or **OK** button. The edge will be offset; refer to Figure-164.

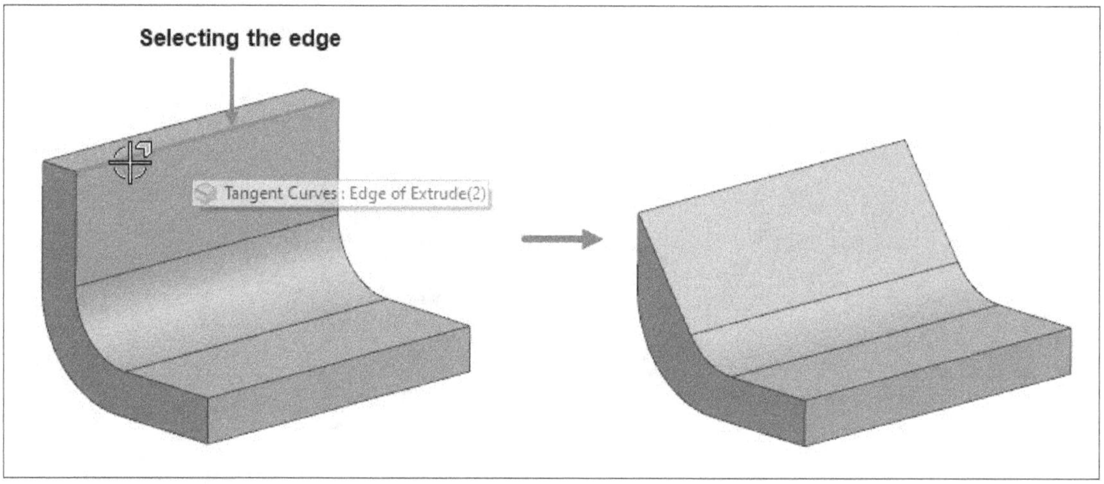

Figure-164. Edge offset

SELF-ASSESSMENT

Q1. What is the Draft Body tool used for?
A. Creating holes
B. Applying symmetric draft to faces
C. Adding color to model
D. Creating patterns

Q2. In Draft Body, which option is used to select a face for draft?
A. Edge
B. Face
C. Curve
D. Axis

Q3. Which option is used to define start and end edges in Draft Body?
A. Face
B. Edge
C. Plane
D. Vector

Q4. What is selected as a dividing reference in Draft Body?
A. Axis
B. Curve
C. Parting object
D. Sketch

Q5. Where is the draft angle specified?
A. Settings
B. Angle edit box
C. Direction rollout
D. Feature tree

Q6. Which option ensures smooth transition at parting plane?
A. Match Faces at Parting Object
B. Draft Both Sides
C. Symmetric Draft
D. Extend Faces

Q7. Which Match Type creates equal taper angle gradient?
A. Tangent to Face
B. To Isocline
C. Symmetric
D. Linear

Q8. Which option includes all faces for matching?
A. Partial
B. Selected
C. All
D. Limited

Q9. Which option smoothens sharp edges at parting plane?
A. Extend Edges
B. Repair Parting Edges
C. Draft Fix
D. Blend Faces

Q10. What does "Use Drafted Body as Parting Object" do?
A. Deletes body
B. Creates draft using intersecting body
C. Rotates body
D. Mirrors body

Q11. Rib feature is mainly used for:
A. Decoration
B. Strength
C. Coloring
D. Rendering

Q12. Which rib type uses a single open curve?
A. Trajectory Rib
B. Profile Rib
C. Contour Rib
D. Surface Rib

Q13. Which rib type uses intersecting curves?
A. Profile Rib
B. Contour Rib
C. Trajectory Rib
D. Linear Rib

Q14. Which option keeps rib symmetric?
A. Asymmetric
B. Symmetric
C. Equal
D. Balanced

Q15. Which option creates rib on one side?
A. Symmetric
B. Parallel
C. Asymmetric
D. Centered

Q16. Which option unites rib with base feature?
A. Merge
B. Combine Rib with Target
C. Join
D. Unite All

Q17. Contour Rib is created:
A. Along axis
B. Parallel to edge
C. Perpendicular to face
D. Randomly

Q18. Which direction makes rib perpendicular to face?
A. Along Vector
B. Normal to Face
C. Normal to Curve
D. Tangent

Q19. Thread tool is used for:
A. Cutting slots
B. Creating ribs
C. Applying threads
D. Splitting body

Q20. Which option creates actual threads?
A. Symbolic
B. Detailed
C. Manual
D. Standard

Q21. Which input uses standard thread table?
A. Manual
B. Thread Table
C. Custom
D. Default

Q22. Which checkbox auto selects thread size?
A. Match Thread Size to Cylinder
B. Auto Fit
C. Standard Match
D. Size Lock

Q23. Which diameter option uses cutting tool size?
A. Major Diameter
B. Minor Diameter
C. Tap Drill Diameter
D. Shaft Diameter

Q24. Groove tool is used to:
A. Add material
B. Remove material
C. Color model
D. Rotate part

Q25. Which groove type creates U-shaped slot?
A. Rectangular
B. Ball End
C. U Groove
D. Circular

Q26. Emboss tool creates:
A. Hole
B. Pattern
C. Solid impression
D. Cut

Q27. Which curve is required for emboss?
A. Open curve
B. Multiple curves
C. Closed loop
D. Line only

Q28. Pattern Geometry tool is used to:
A. Delete objects
B. Create copies
C. Split faces
D. Add ribs

Q29. Promote Body tool is used to:
A. Delete body
B. Move assembly component
C. Create sketch
D. Apply draft

Q30. Extract Geometry tool creates:
A. New model
B. Associative copy
C. Draft
D. Thread

Q31. Split Body tool is used to:
A. Combine bodies
B. Split body
C. Offset faces
D. Pattern body

Q32. Divide Face tool is used to:
A. Delete face
B. Split face
C. Color face
D. Offset face

Q33. Delete Body tool is used to:
A. Copy body
B. Remove body
C. Mirror body
D. Offset body

Q34. Offset Face tool is used to:
A. Rotate face
B. Move face by distance
C. Split face
D. Delete face

Q35. Scale Body tool is used to:
A. Rotate body
B. Scale body size
C. Delete body
D. Split body

Q36. Which option scales body equally in all directions?
A. Axisymmetric
B. Uniform
C. Non-uniform
D. Linear

Q37. What is required as reference point in scaling?
A. Axis
B. Edge
C. Scale point
D. Face

Q38. Axisymmetric scaling is mainly used for:
A. Flat surfaces
B. Cylindrical bodies
C. Sketches
D. Curves

Q39. Which option allows scaling in different directions?
A. Uniform
B. Axisymmetric
C. Non-uniform
D. Symmetric

Q40. In Non-uniform scaling, scaling is defined along:
A. Axis only
B. Edges only
C. X, Y, Z directions
D. Curve

Q41. User Defined Features are:
A. Pre-installed tools
B. Combination of user operations
C. Only sketches
D. Only solids

Q42. Which tool is used to insert user defined features?
A. Pattern Tool
B. User Defined Tool
C. Copy Tool
D. Mirror Tool

Q43. Wrap Geometry tool is used to:
A. Cut body
B. Create simplified solid
C. Apply color
D. Add holes

Q44. Bounding Body tool creates:
A. Pattern
B. Draft
C. Bounding box or cylinder
D. Thread

Q45. Which option creates box around body?
A. Cylinder
B. Block
C. Sphere
D. Curve

Q46. Which option allows defining box using dimensions?
A. Block
B. Center and Lengths
C. Axis
D. Curve

Q47. Color Feature tool is used to:
A. Delete features
B. Apply color
C. Offset faces
D. Split body

Q48. Which option removes applied color?
A. Reset Color
B. No Feature Color
C. Remove Style
D. Clear

Q49. Synchronous modeling is used for:
A. History-based modeling
B. Freeform modification
C. Rendering
D. Drafting

Q50. Move tool is used to:
A. Delete face
B. Move faces
C. Split body
D. Copy feature

Q51. Which option copies and deletes original face?
A. Move and Adapt
B. Cut and Paste
C. Extend
D. Heal

Q52. Delete Face tool fills gap by:
A. Adding material
B. Extending nearby faces
C. Splitting faces
D. Coloring

Q53. Which option deletes curved faces like fillets?
A. Face
B. Hole
C. Blend
D. Edge

Q54. Replace Face tool is used to:
A. Copy face
B. Replace face
C. Delete face
D. Offset face

Q55. Offset tool in synchronous modeling is used to:
A. Rotate face
B. Extend face
C. Delete face
D. Color face

Q56. Resize Blend tool is used to:
A. Delete blends
B. Change blend size
C. Create blends
D. Move blends

Q57. Edit Cross Section tool modifies:
A. Sketch only
B. Whole body via section
C. Edges only
D. Faces only

Q58. Radiate Face tool is applicable to:
A. Flat bodies
B. Cylindrical bodies
C. Curves
D. Sketches

Q59. Pull Face tool is used to:
A. Copy face
B. Add/remove material
C. Split face
D. Color face

Q60. Linear Dimension tool is used to:
A. Measure only
B. Move faces using dimension
C. Delete faces
D. Create sketch

Q61. Label Notch Blend tool is used to:
A. Delete blends
B. Identify blends
C. Resize blends
D. Copy blends

Q62. Reorder Blends tool changes:
A. Size
B. Color
C. Order of blends
D. Shape

Chapter 7

Rendering and 3D Modeling Practice

Topics Covered

The major topics covered in this chapter are:

- ***Display and Rendering Tools***
- ***Practical 1***
- ***Practical 2***
- ***Practical 3***
- ***Practice 1 to 7***

INTRODUCTION

In this chapter, we will work on creating models using the tools discussed earlier. We will use some basic engineering models as target for our practical and practice here. Later, we will work on various tools related to model coloring, display, and rendering for presentation of the model.

PRACTICAL 1

Create the model (isometric view) as shown in Figure-1. The views of the model with dimensions are given in Figure-2.

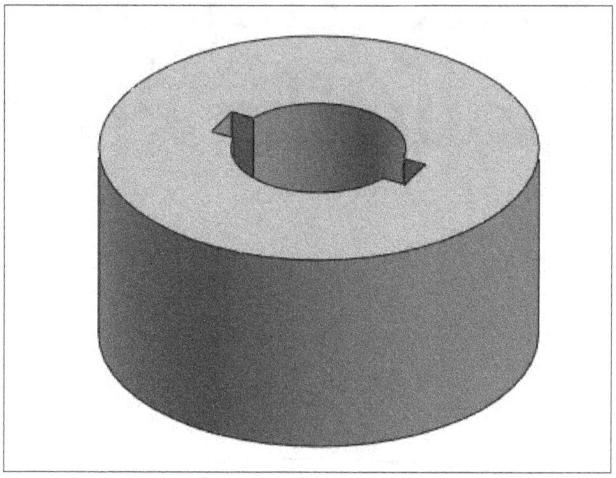

Figure-1. Practical 1 model

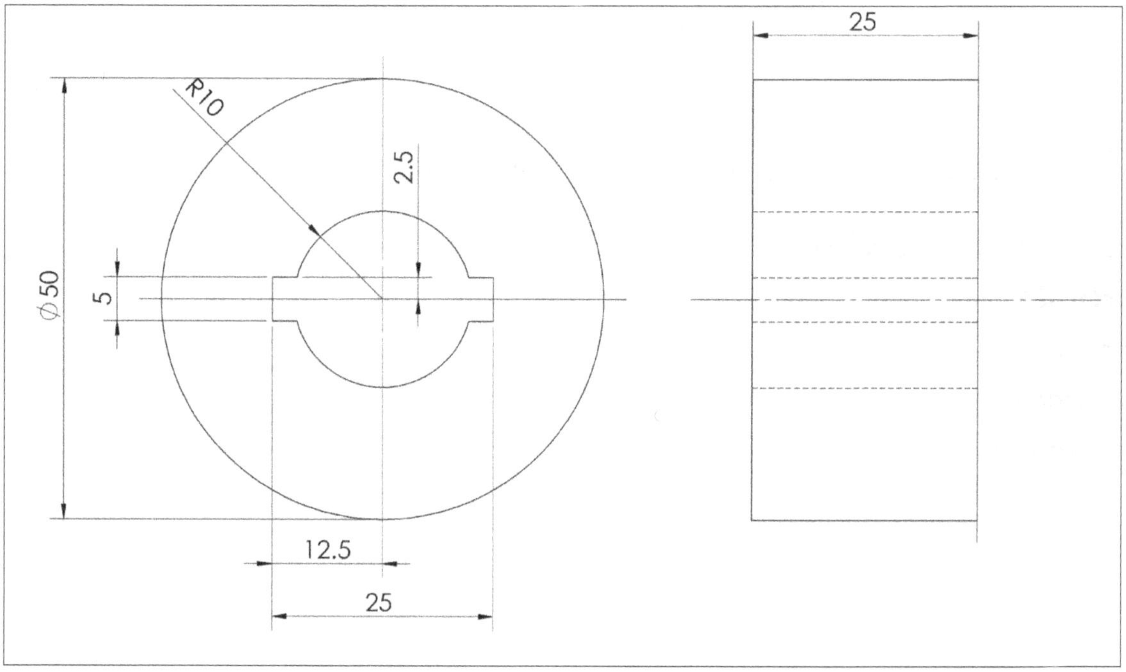

Figure-2. Views for Practical 1

Before we start working on the Practical, it is important to understand two terms; first angle projection and third angle projection. These are the standards of placing views in the engineering drawing. The views placed in the above figure are using third angle projection. In first angle projection, the top view of model is placed below the front view and

right side view is placed at left of the front view. You will learn more about projection in chapter related to drafting.

Starting Modeling environment and creating Extrude feature

- Start NX by double-clicking on the icon from the desktop.
- Click on the **New** button from the **Quick Access Toolbar**. The **New** dialog box will be displayed.
- Select the **Model** option from **Templates** rollout of the dialog box and select the **Inches** option from the **Units** drop-down in the rollout.
- Specify desired name in the **Name** edit box and set desired location in **Folder** edit box of the dialog box.
- Click on the **OK** button from the **New** dialog box. The Modeling environment will be displayed.
- Click on the **Sketch** button from the **Construction** group of **Home** tab in the **Ribbon**. The **Create Sketch** dialog box will be displayed and you will be asked to select the sketching plane.
- Select the **TOP Plane** from the graphics area to select the plane; refer to Figure-3. After selecting the plane, click on **OK** button from the dialog box. The sketching environment will be activated.

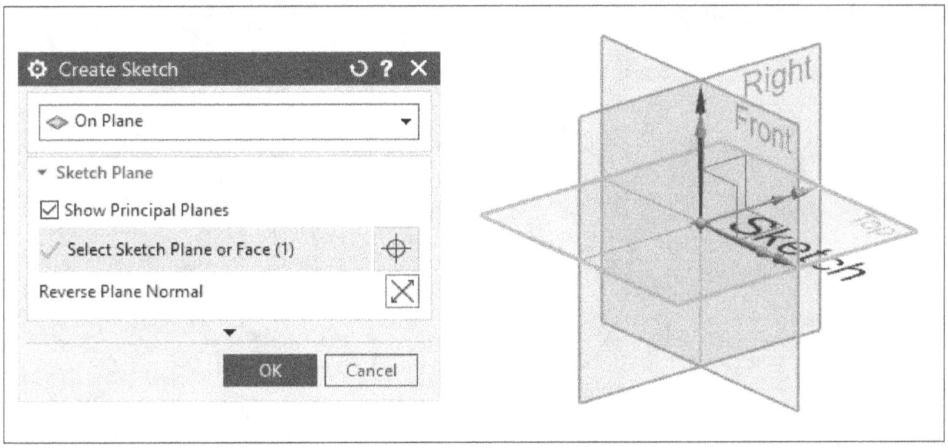

Figure-3. Selecting the top plane

From the isometric view as well as from the other views, we can judge that this model can be easily created by extruding the sketch.

Creating the Sketch

- Click on the **Circle** tool and create a circle of diameter **50** mm and **20** mm at the same center as shown in Figure-4.

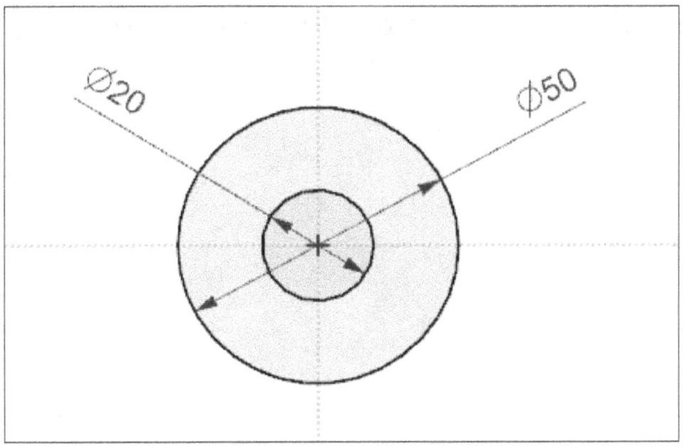

Figure-4. Circles created

- Click on the **Rectangle from Center** tool and create a center rectangle of height **5** mm and width **25** mm at the same centers of circle as shown in Figure-5.

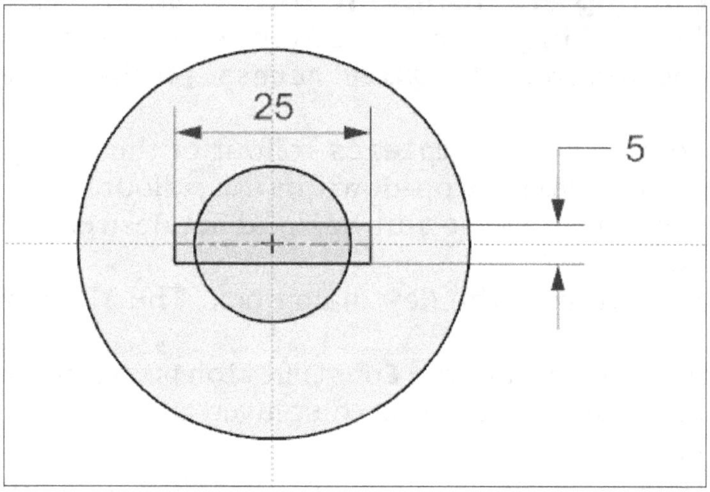

Figure-5. Rectangle created

- Click on the **Trim** tool and trim the entities in such a way that the sketch is displayed as shown in Figure-6.

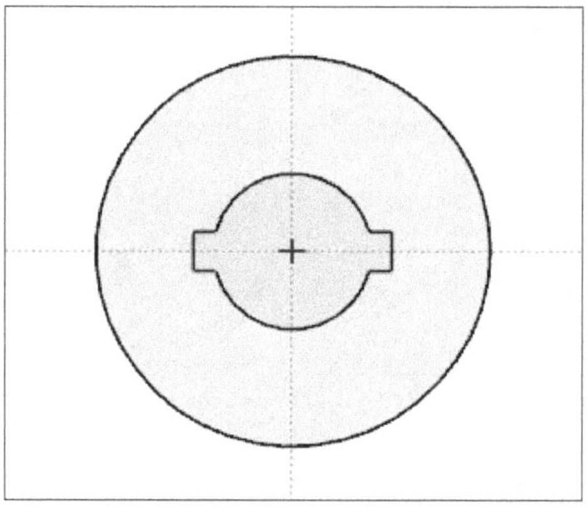

Figure-6. Sketch after trimming

- After creating the sketch, click on the **Finish** button from **Sketch** group of **Home** tab in the **Ribbon**. Now, click on the **Extrude** tool from **Base** group in the **Home** tab of the **Ribbon**. The **Extrude** dialog box will be displayed.
- Select the recently created sketch to be extruded. The preview of extrusion will be displayed.
- Specify the distance of extrusion as **25** mm in the **Distance** edit box and click on **OK** button from the dialog box. The model will be created; refer to Figure-7.

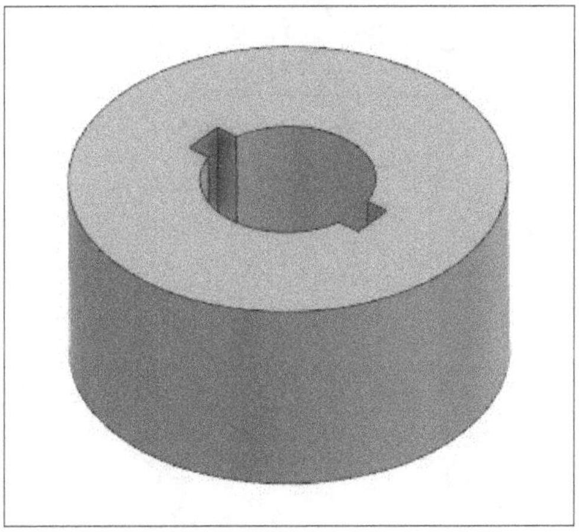

Figure-7. Practical 1 created

PRACTICAL 2

Create the model (isometric view) as shown in Figure-8. The dimensions and view is given in Figure-9.

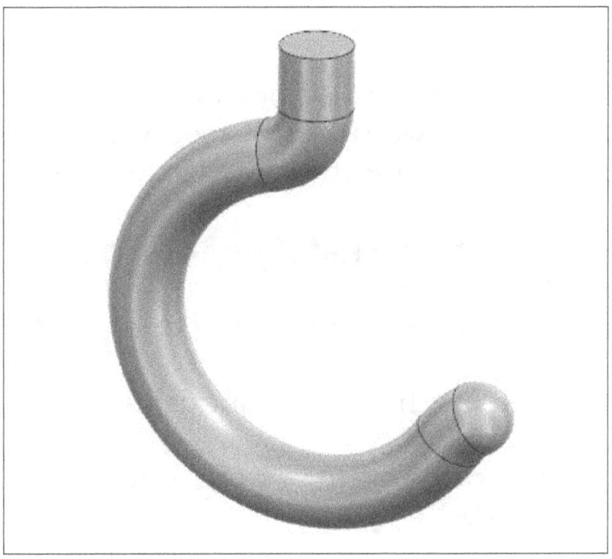

Figure-8. Model for Practical 2

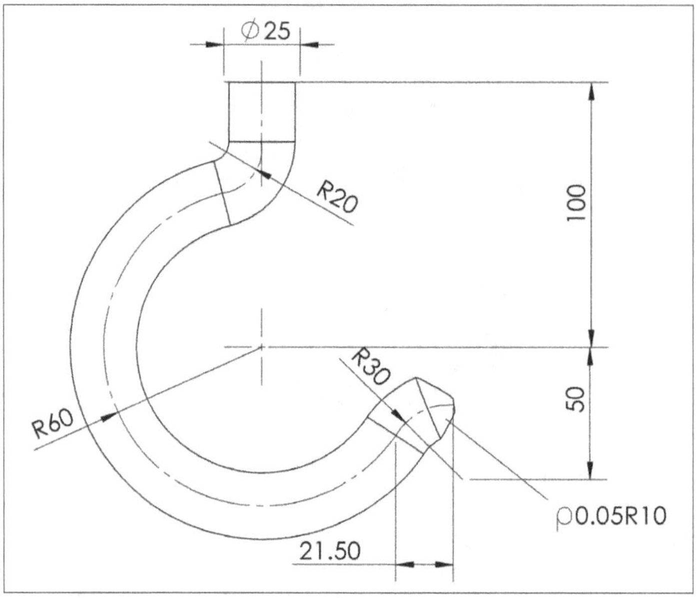

Figure-9. Practical 2 drawing view

Start the NX if not started and open the modeling environment as explained in previous practical.

You can find out from the model that this hook can be easily created with the help of **Swept Boss/Base** tool. But before we use that tool, we must have sketches for path as well as section. The steps to create them are as follows:

Creating Sketches for Hook

- Start a new sketch on Front Plane.
- Click on the **Circle** tool and create the circle of diameter **120** taking coordinate system as center.
- Draw a straight line starting from top quadrant point and having length of approximately **40**.
- Click on the **Arc** tool and draw an arc of radius **30** mm in the bottom area of the circle as shown in Figure-10.

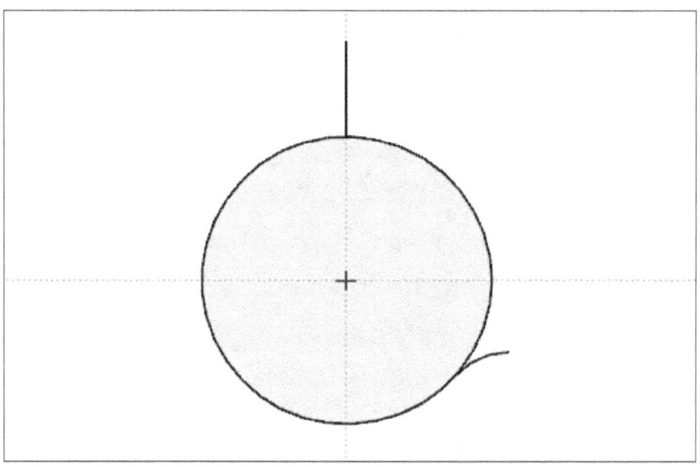

Figure-10. Sketch after creating the arc

- Click on the **Trim** tool and trim the portion between the straight line and the arc; refer to Figure-11.

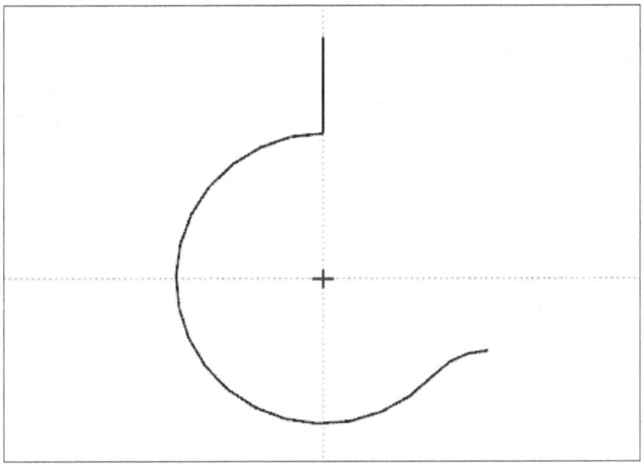

Figure-11. Sketch after trimming the circle

- Click on the **Fillet** tool and apply fillet between the straight line and circle. Specify the fillet radius as **20**.
- Now, dimension the sketch as shown in Figure-12.

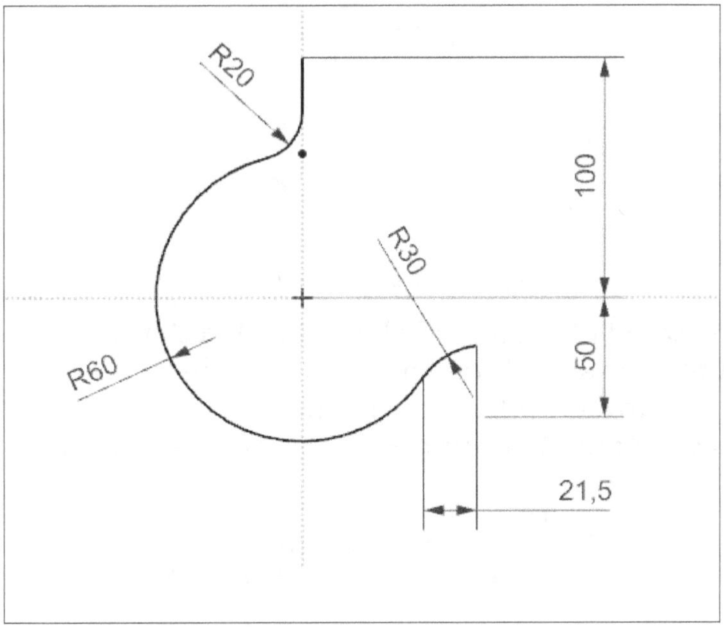

Figure-12. Dimension sketch of hook

- Exit the sketch by clicking **Finish** button from the **Ribbon**.

In previous steps, we have created the sketch of the path. Now, we will create the section sketch.

- Click on the **Datum Plane** tool from **Datum** drop-down in the **Construction** group of the **Ribbon**. The **Datum Plane** dialog box will be displayed.
- Click on the top point of the line and click on **OK** button from the dialog box; refer to Figure-13. The datum plane will be created; refer to Figure-14.

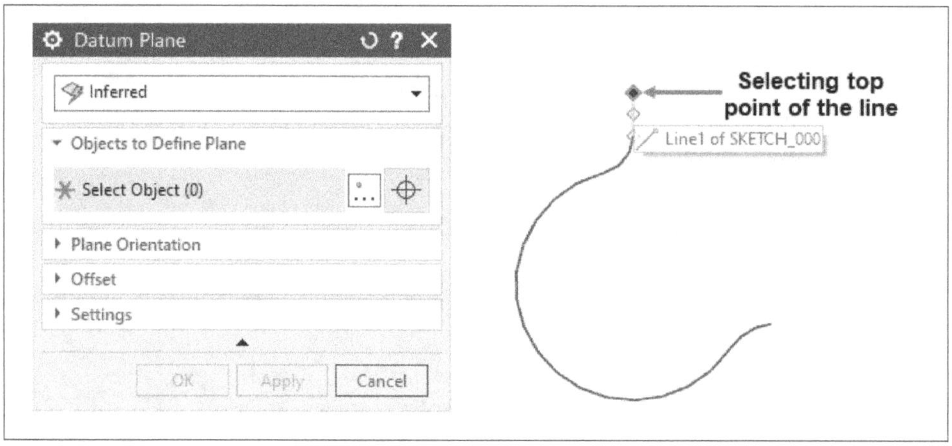

Figure-13. Selecting top point of the line

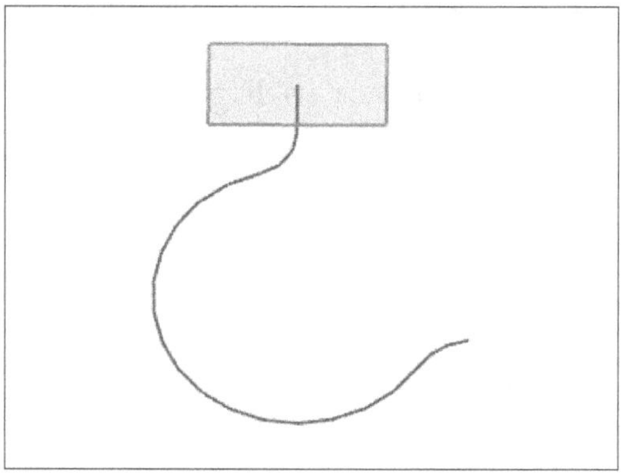

Figure-14. Datum plane created

- Select the newly created plane and click on the **Sketch** button from the **Construction** group of the **Ribbon**. The sketching environment will be displayed and the sketching plane will become parallel to the viewport.
- Create a circle of diameter **25** taking end point of line as center; refer to Figure-15.

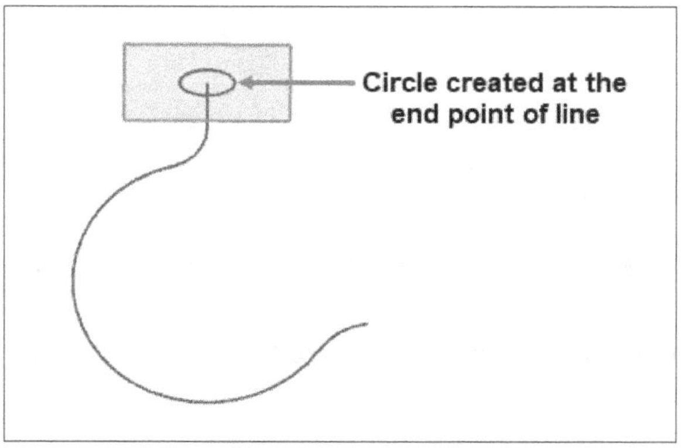

Figure-15. Circle created at the end point of line

Creating the sweep feature

Now, we have all the sketches to create the hook. The steps to create the sweep feature using these sketches is given next.

- Click on the **Sweep along Guide** tool from **More** drop-down in the **Base** group of **Surface** tab in the **Ribbon**. The **Sweep Along Guide** dialog box will be displayed.

- Select the circle created for section. Click on the **Select Curve** selection button from the **Curve** section and then select the sketch created for the guide profile. The preview of sweep feature will be displayed.
- Click on **OK** button from the dialog box. The sweep feature will be created; refer to Figure-16.

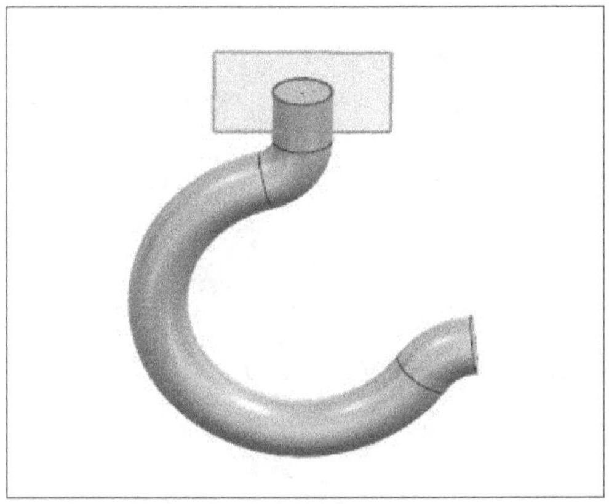

Figure-16. Sweep feature created

Applying tangent blend face at the end

As we all know, hooks doesn't end with sharp edges. So, we need to apply tangent blend face at the end. Steps to do so are given next.

- Click on the **Edge Blend** tool from **Base** group in the **Surface** tab of the **Ribbon**. The **Edge Blend** dialog box will be displayed.
- Select the edge of the end and specify the parameters in the dialog box as shown in Figure-17.

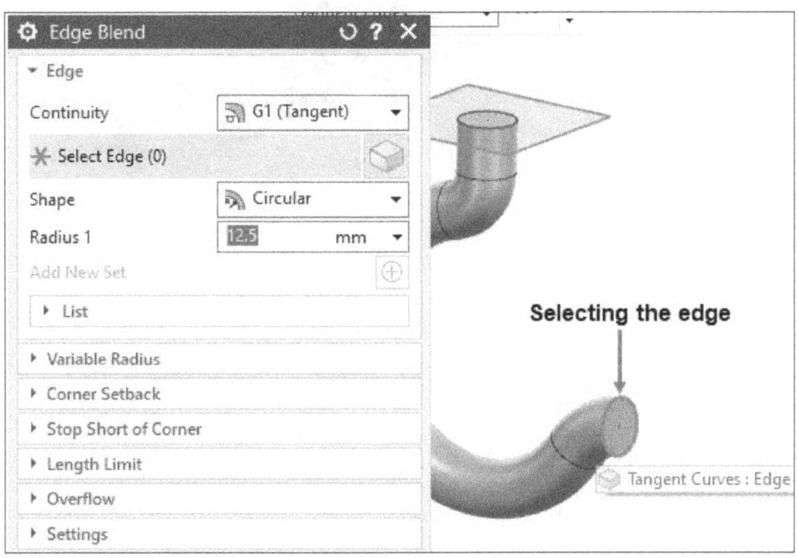

Figure-17. Selecting the edge to be blend

- Click on **OK** button from the dialog box to create the feature. The final model will be displayed as shown in Figure-18.

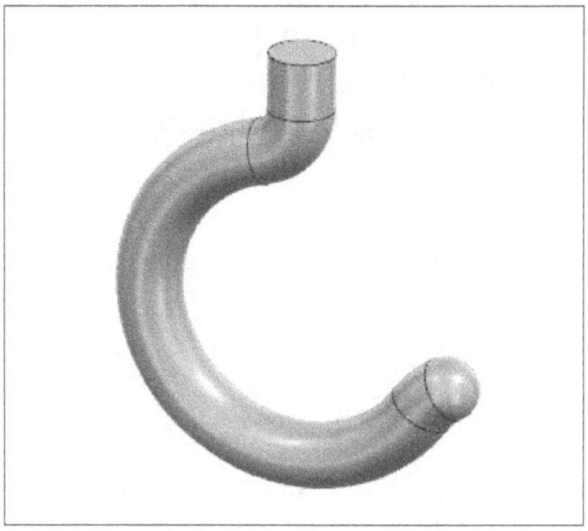

Figure-18. Practical 2 created

PRACTICAL 3

Create the model (isometric view) as shown in Figure-19. The dimensions of the model are given in Figure-20.

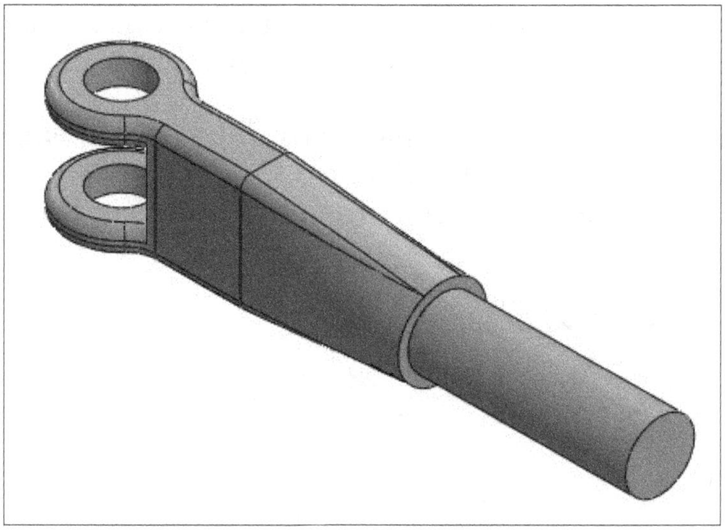

Figure-19. Model for Practical 3

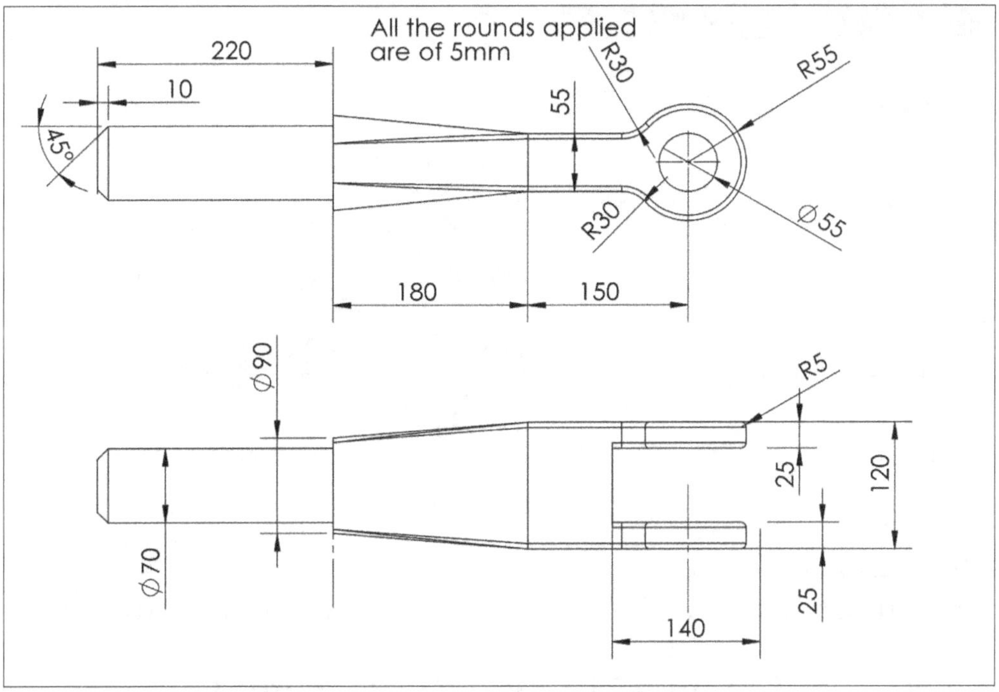

Figure-20. Practical 3 drawing views

Start the NX if not started and open the modeling environment as explained in previous practical.

Creating first extrude feature

- Start a new sketch on **Top** plane and create the sketch as shown in Figure-21.

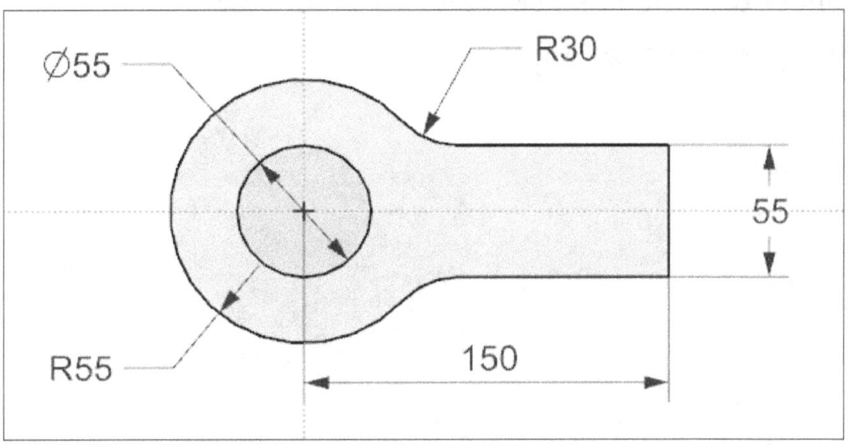

Figure-21. Sketch created on top plane

- Click on **Finish** button from the **Ribbon** to exit the sketch.
- Click on the **Extrude** tool from **Base** group in the **Ribbon** and extrude symmetrically up to the distance of **120**; refer to Figure-22.

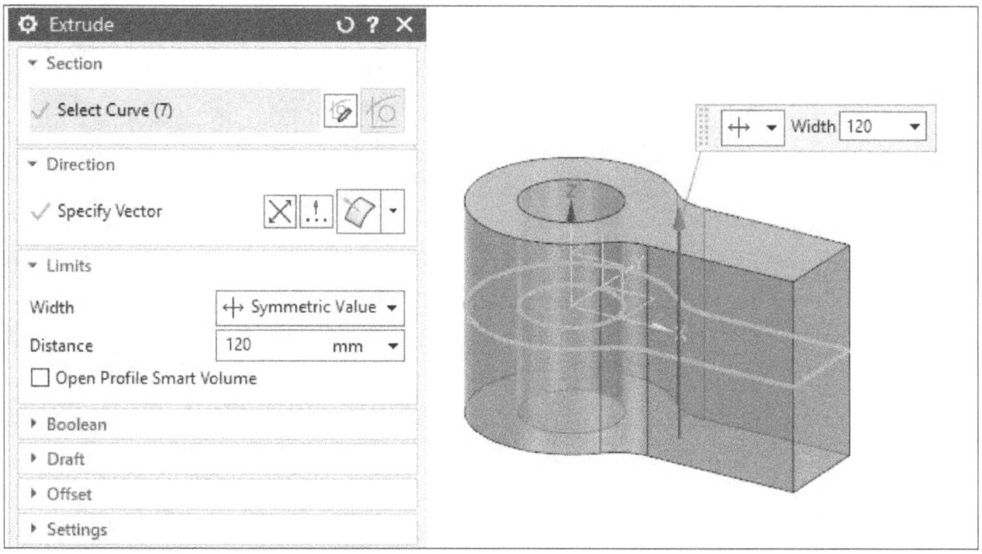

Figure-22. Extruding the sketch

- Click on **OK** button from the dialog box. The first extrude feature created.

Creating Through Curve feature

Before creating through curve feature, we must have at least two sketch sections. First, we will create a plane at a distance of **180** from the vertical flat face of the model and then, we will create sketches and through curve feature, successively.

- Click on the **Datum Plane** tool from **Construction** group in the **Ribbon** and select the vertical flat face of the model.
- Specify the offset distance as **180**; refer to Figure-23.

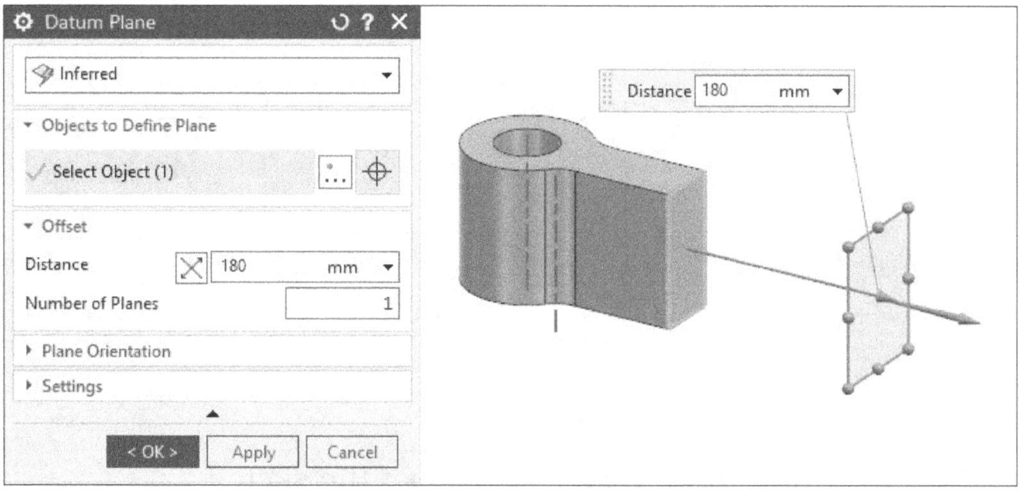

Figure-23. Plane to be created

- Click on **OK** button from the dialog box to create the plane.
- Select this plane and create the sketch as shown in Figure-24.

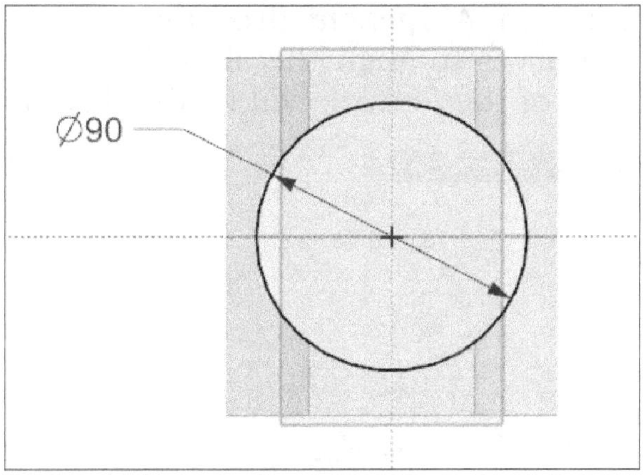

Figure-24. Sketch to be created

- Exit the sketch by clicking **Finish** button from **Sketch** group in the **Ribbon**.

Now, we are ready to create the **Through Curve** feature.

- Click on the **Through Curves** tool from **Base** group in the **Surface** tab of the **Ribbon**. The **Through Curves** dialog box will be displayed.
- Select the two section curves to create the through curve feature as shown in Figure-25. The preview of the through curve feature will be displayed; refer to Figure-26.

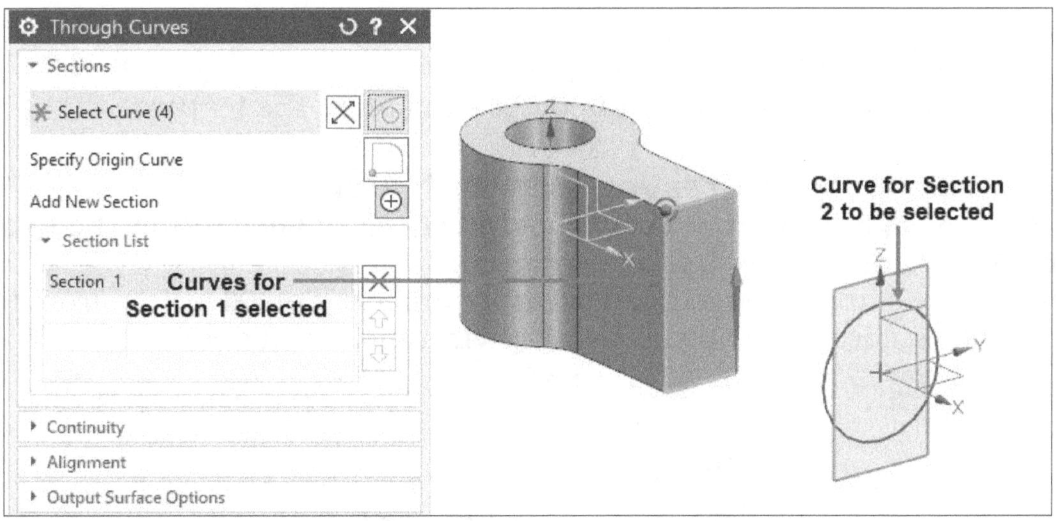

Figure-25. Selecting the curves for sections

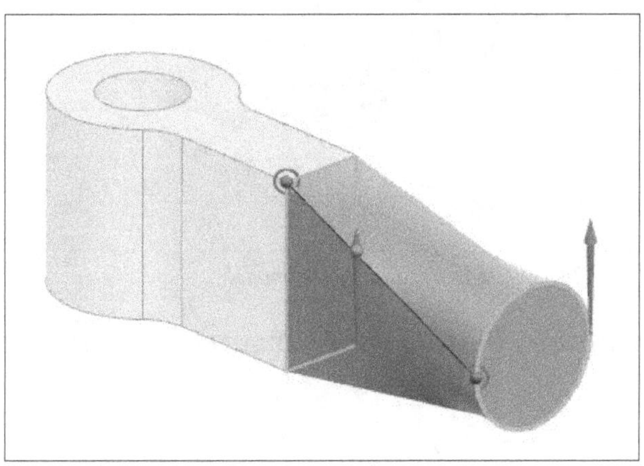

Figure-26. Preview of through curve feature

- Select **By Points** option from **Alignment** drop-down in the **Alignment** rollout and drag the nodes on the curves to align the shape of through curve feature if you get it twisted. The shape of the feature will be displayed as shown in Figure-27.

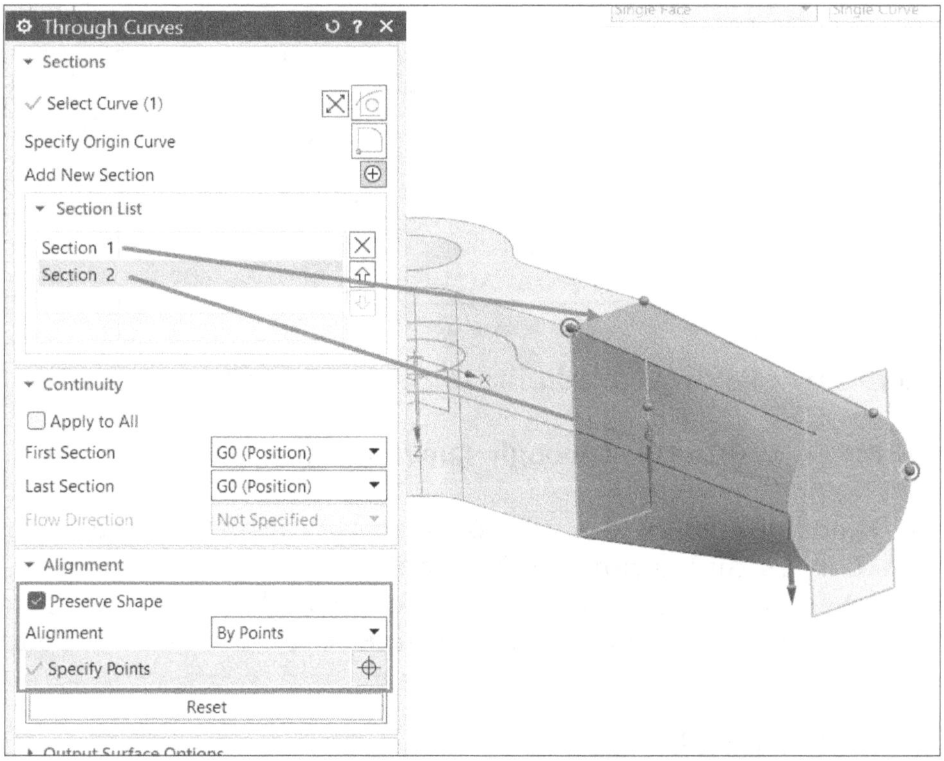

Figure-27. Shape of the feature aligned

- Click on the **OK** button from the dialog box to create the feature.

Creating extrude feature

- Click on **Sketch** button from **Construction** group of **Home** tab in the **Ribbon**. The **Create Sketch** dialog box will be displayed.
- Select flat face of the through curves feature and click on **OK** button from the dialog box; refer to Figure-28. The sketching environment will open.

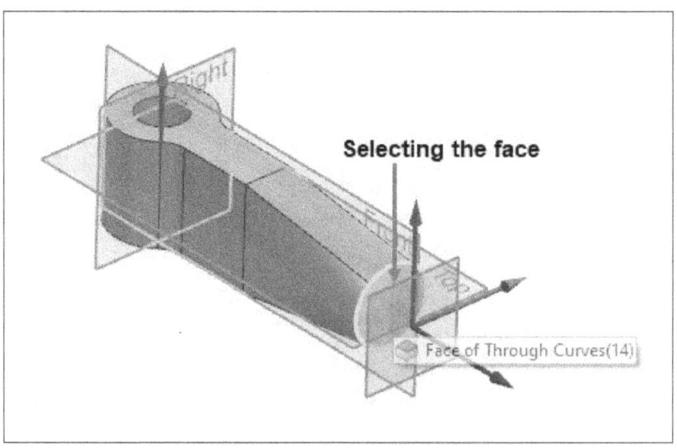

Figure-28. Selecting flat face of the model

- Create a circle of diameter **70** at the center and exit the sketch; refer to Figure-29.

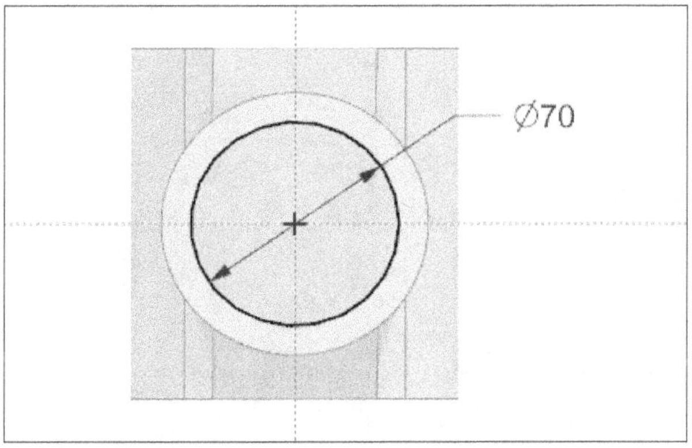

Figure-29. Circle created for second extruding feature

- Click on the **Extrude** tool from **Base** group in the **Ribbon** and extrude the sketch up to the distance of **220**. The preview of the extrude feature will be displayed; refer to Figure-30.

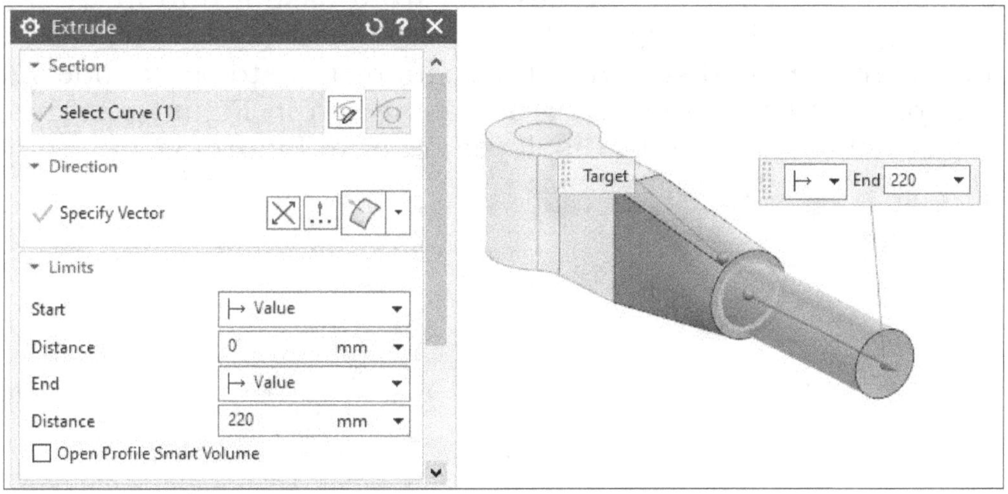

Figure-30. Preview of second extrusion

- Click on **OK** button from the dialog box to create the feature.

Now, we need to create the cut feature to give front shape to model.

Creating extrude cut feature

After looking at the model, we can find that the front cut can be easily created by using the **Extrude** tool.

- Click on **Sketch** button from **Construction** group of **Home** tab in the **Ribbon**. The **Create Sketch** dialog box will be displayed.
- Select **Front** plane from the graphics window and click on **OK** button from the dialog box. The sketching environment will be displayed.
- Create the sketch for the extrude cut feature as shown in Figure-31.

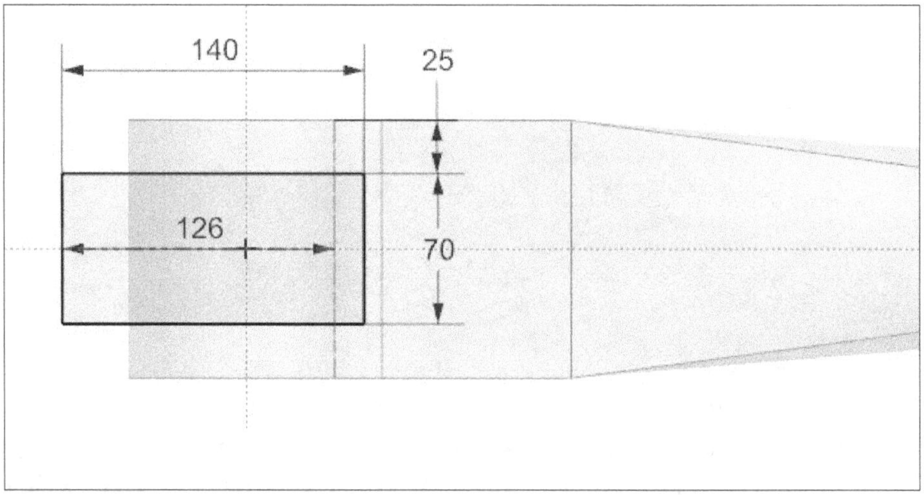

Figure-31. Sketch for extrude cut feature

- Exit the sketch and click on **Extrude** tool from **Base** group in the **Ribbon**. The **Extrude** dialog box will be displayed.
- Select the recently created sketch as the section curve to be extrude subtract and specify the parameters in the dialog box as shown in Figure-32. The preview of extrude subtract feature will be displayed; refer to Figure-32.

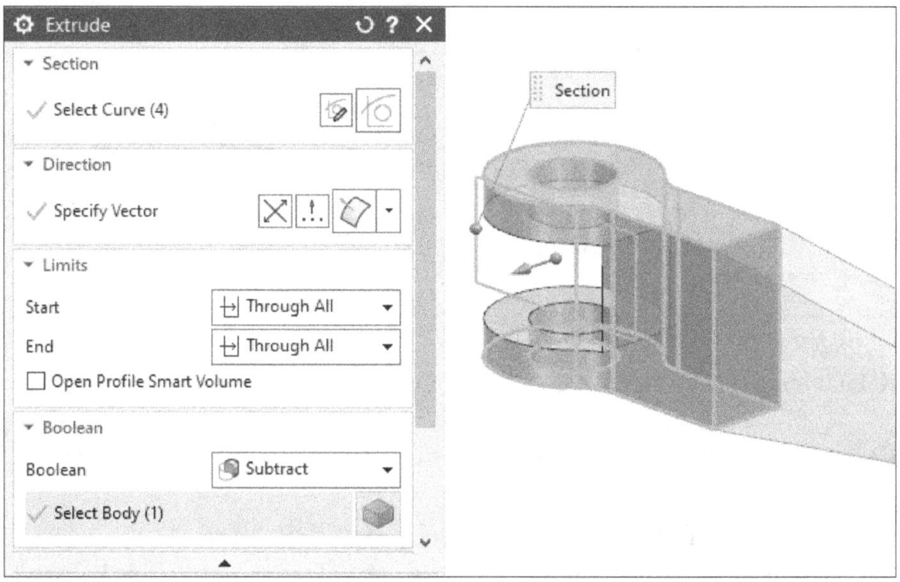

Figure-32. Preview of extrude subtract feature

- Click on **OK** button from the dialog box. The model will be displayed as shown in Figure-33.

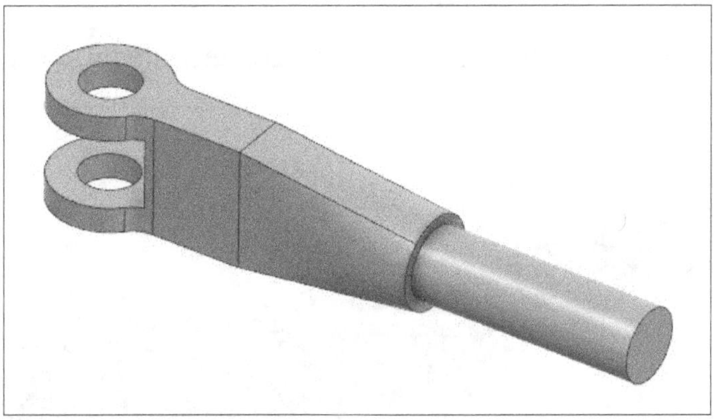

Figure-33. Model after extrude subtract feature

Creating Edge blends and Chamfer

Click on the **Edge Blend** tool from **Base** group in the **Home** tab of **Ribbon**. The **Edge Blend** dialog box will be displayed. Specify the radius as **5** and select all the edges to be blended. Click on **OK** button from the dialog box. All the selected edges will be blended.

Similarly, click on the **Chamfer** tool from **Base** group in the **Home** tab of **Ribbon**. The **Chamfer** dialog box will be displayed. Specify the chamfer distance as **10** and select desired edge to be chamfer as per the drawing. The final model after applying the edge blend and chamfer will be displayed as shown in Figure-34.

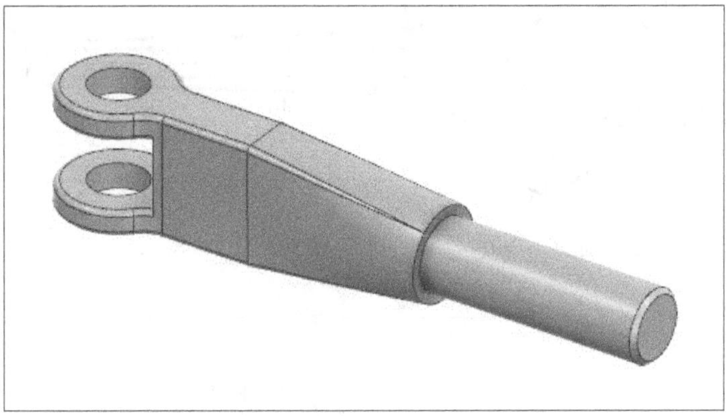

Figure-34. Practical 3 created

Practice 1

Create the model as shown in Figure-35. The dimensions are given in Figure-36.

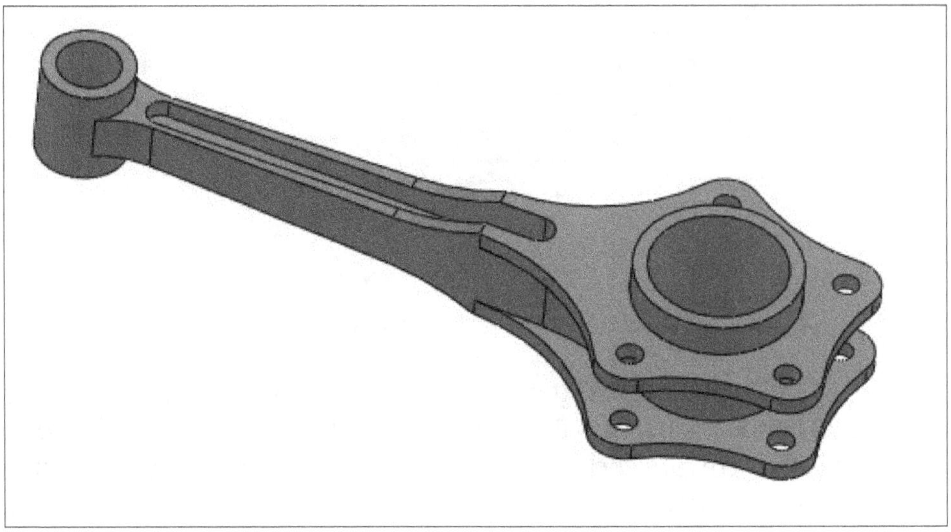

Figure-35. Practice 1

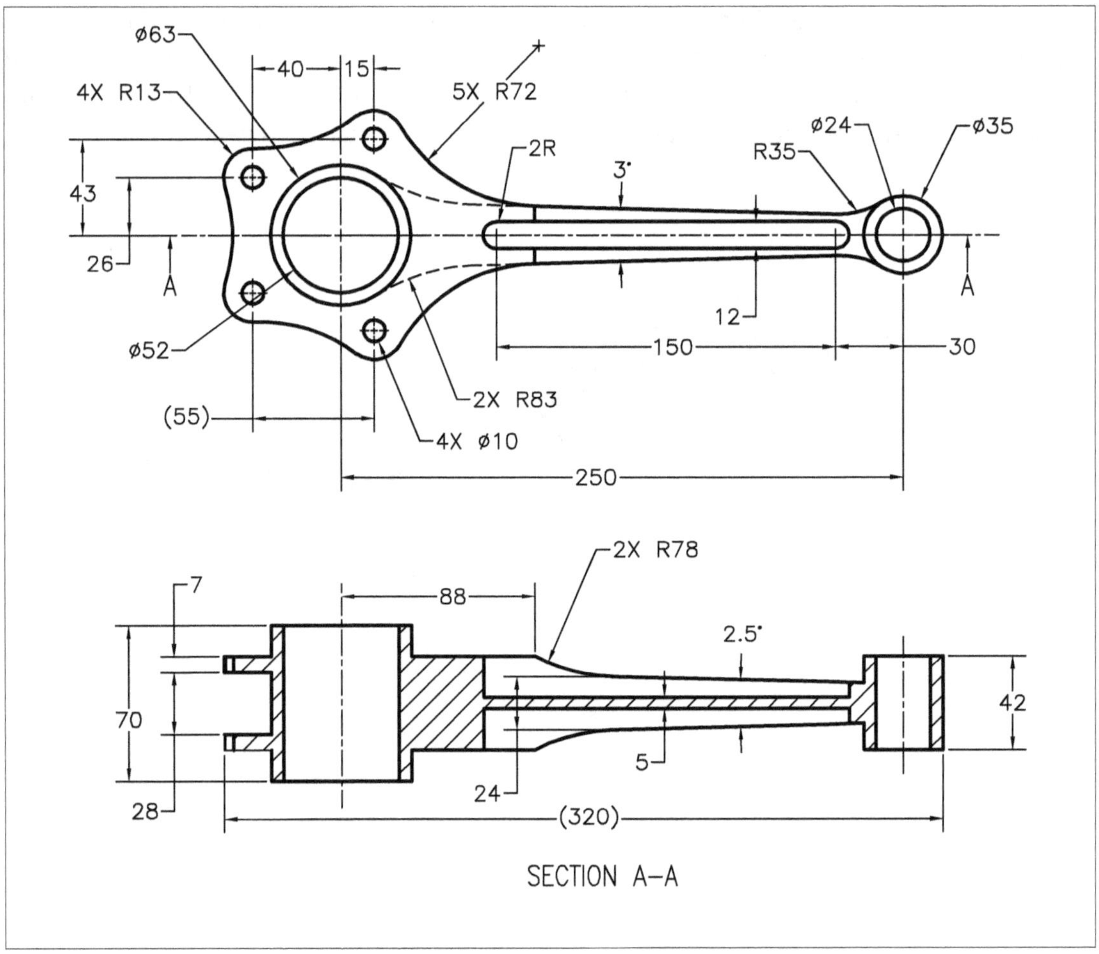

Figure-36. Dimensions of the Practice 1 model

PRACTICE 2

Create the model using the drawings shown in Figure-37.

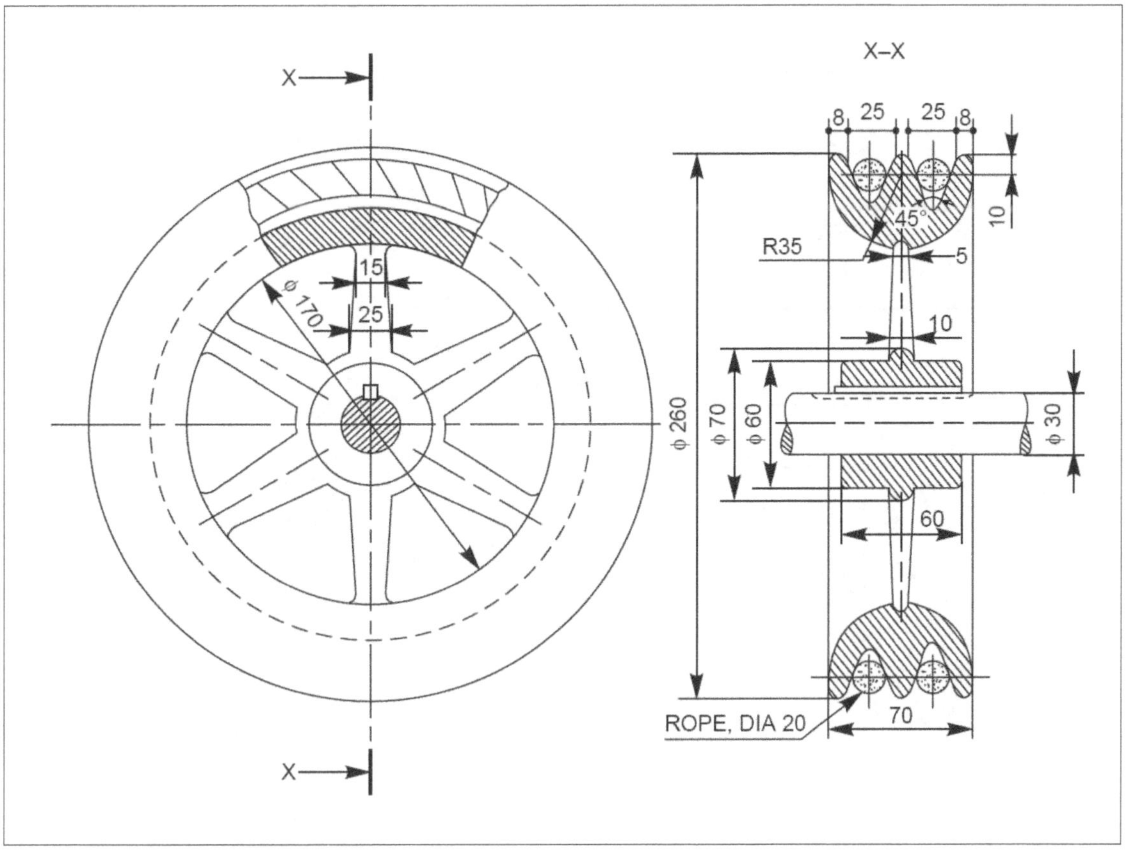

Figure-37. Rope Pulley

PRACTICE 3

Create the model as shown in Figure-38. Dimensions are given in Figure-39. Assume the missing dimensions.

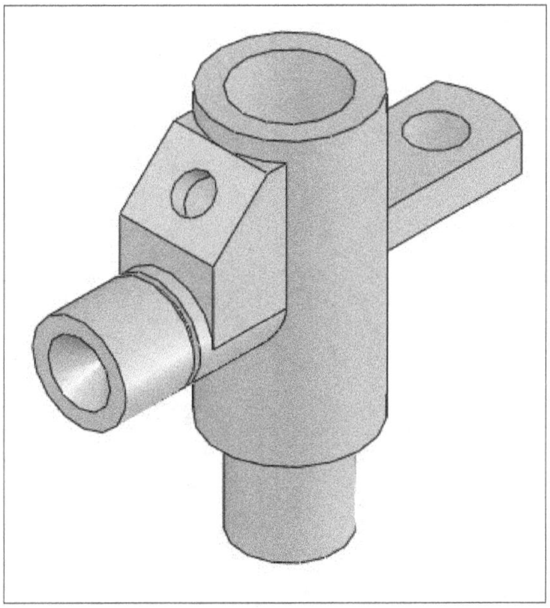

Figure-38. Practice 3 model

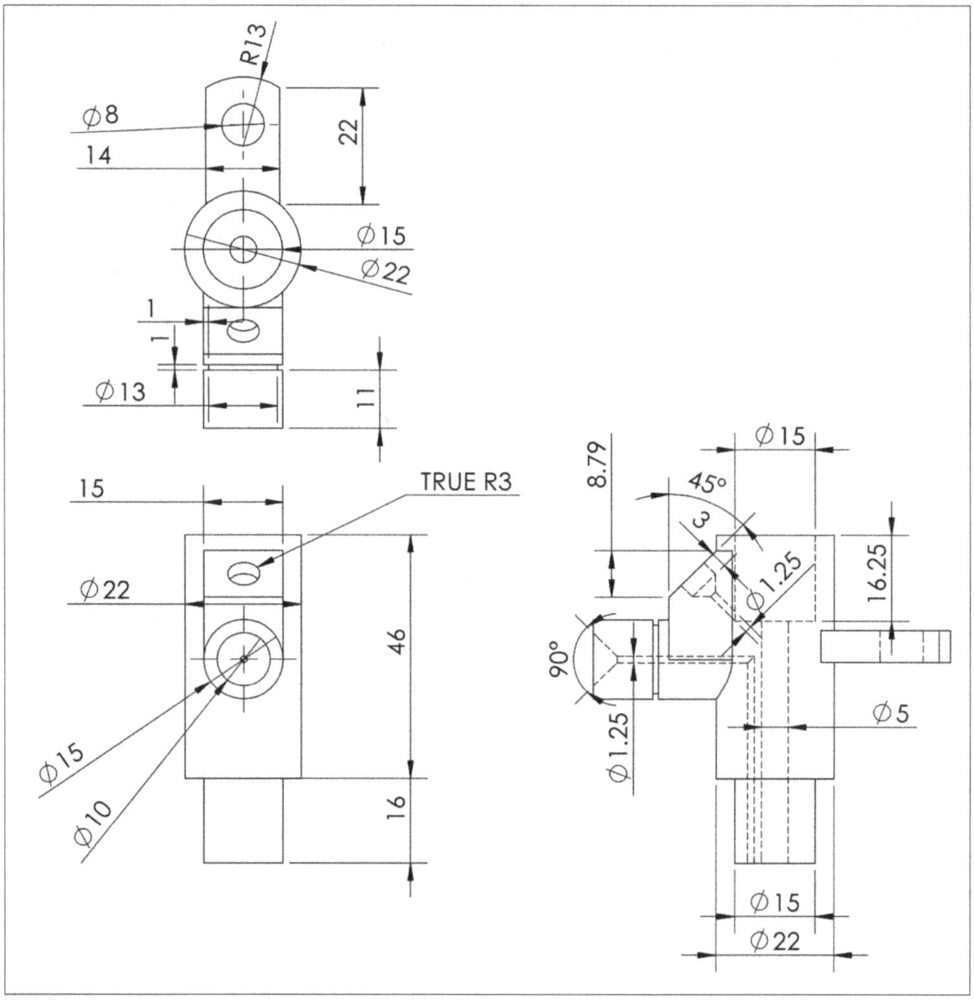

Figure-39. Practice 3 Drawing

PRACTICE 4

Create the model by using the dimensions given in Figure-40.

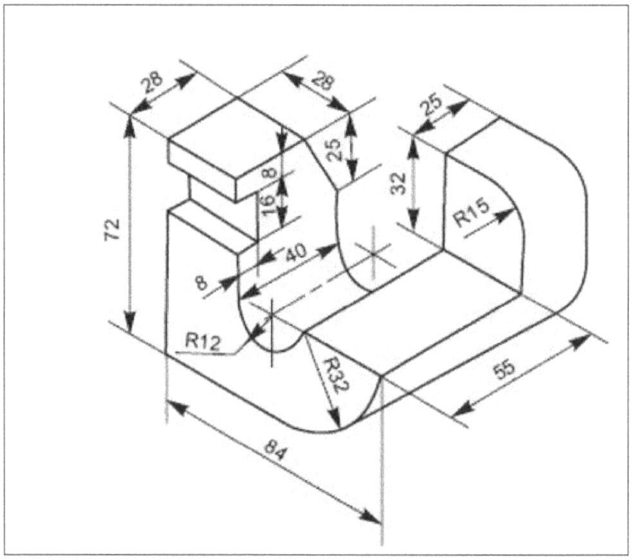

Figure-40. Practice 4

PRACTICE 5

Create the model by using the dimensions given in Figure-41.

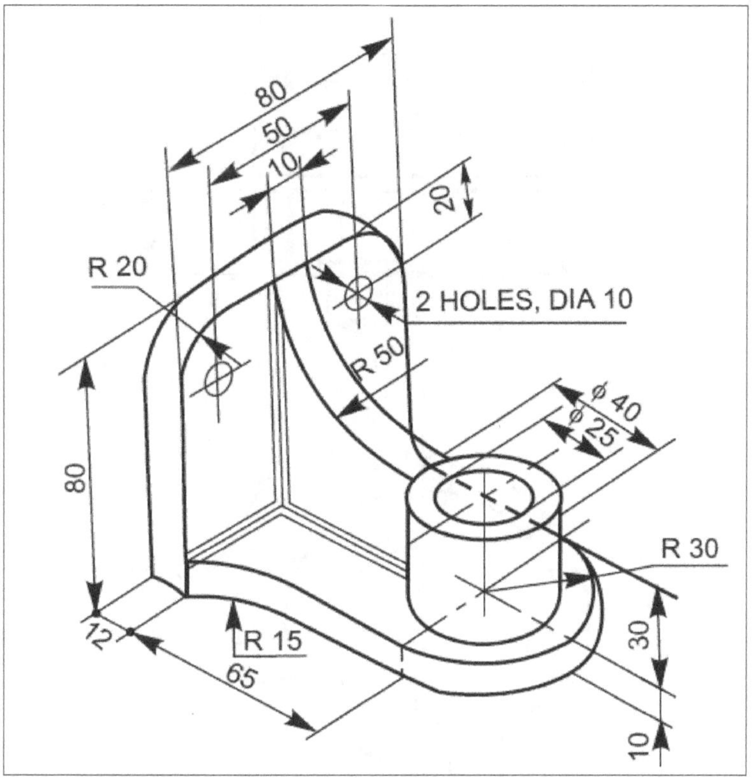

Figure-41. Practice 5

PRACTICE 6

Create the model by using the dimensions given in Figure-42.

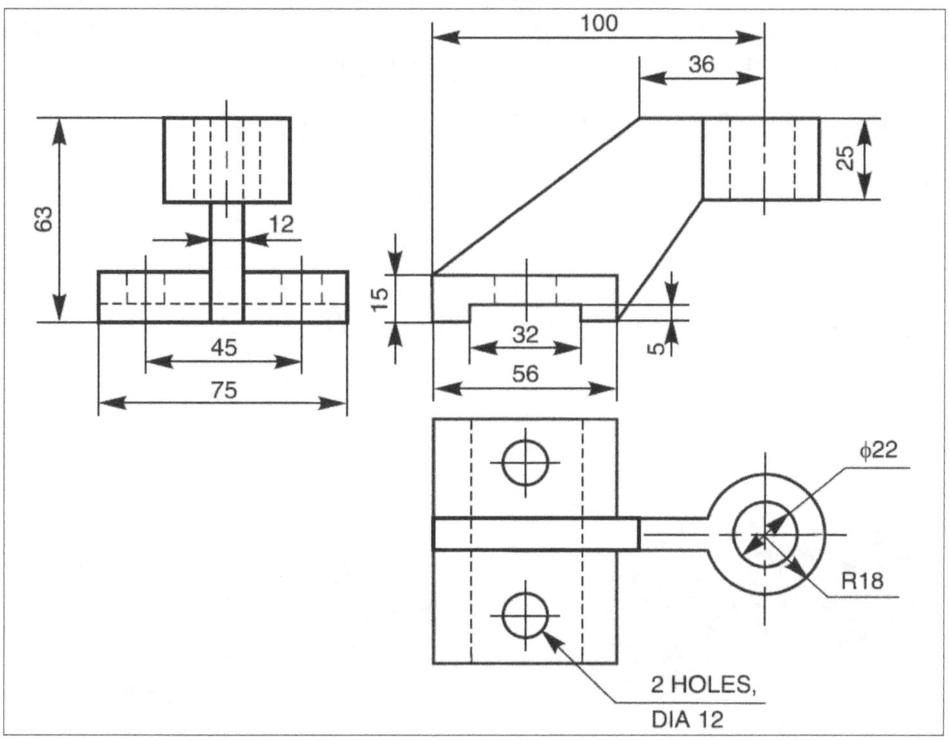

Figure-42. Practice 6

PRACTICE 7

Create a ring nut with value of **D** as **5**,**6**,**8**, and **10** using equation and design table. Dimensions are given in Figure-43.

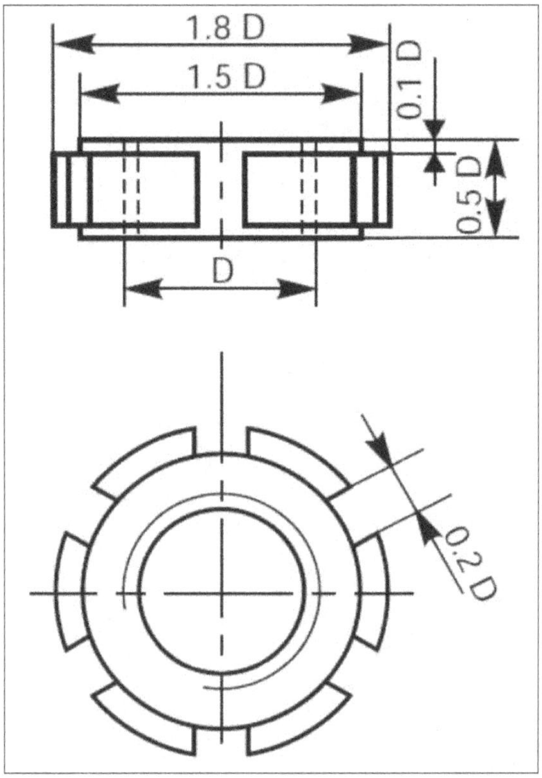

Figure-43. Ring Nut

MODEL DISPLAY PREFERENCES

The options in **Preferences** group of **Display** tab in the **Ribbon** of Modeling environment are used to tweak display of various objects in the model like face edges, hidden edges, effects, and so on; refer to Figure-44. Some of the options have been discussed earlier. Various rest of the options of this group are discussed next.

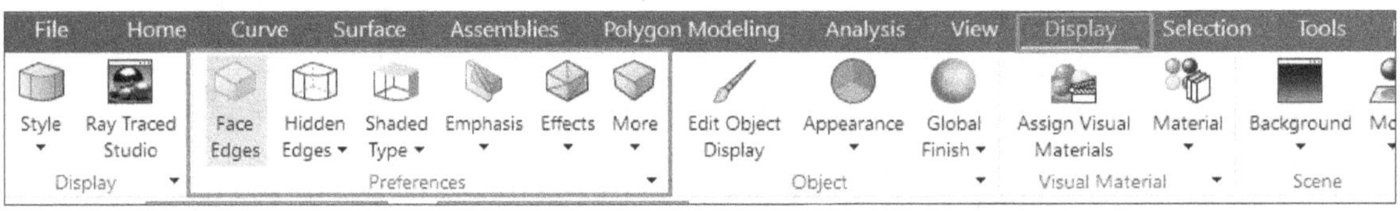

Figure-44. Preferences group

- Select the **Face Edges** toggle button to display/hide edges of faces in the model; refer to Figure-45.

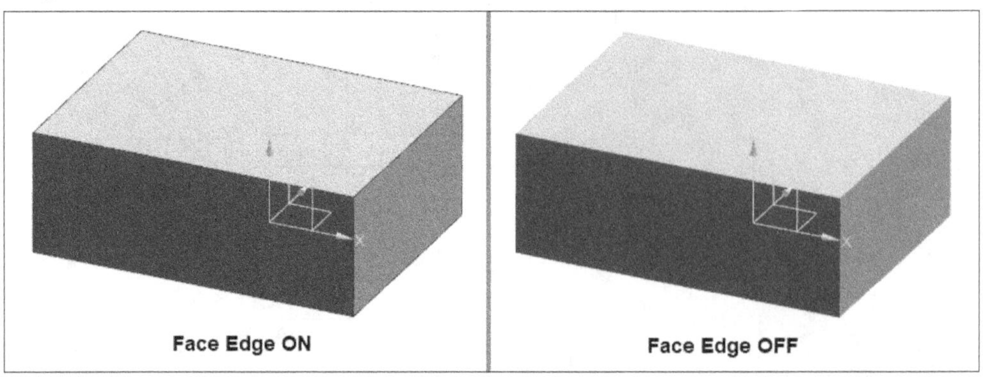

Figure-45. Face Edge toggle

- When **Face Edges** toggle button is set to ON, select desired option from the **Hidden Edges** drop-down to define whether hidden edges will be displayed solid, dashed, or they will be invisible; refer to Figure-46.

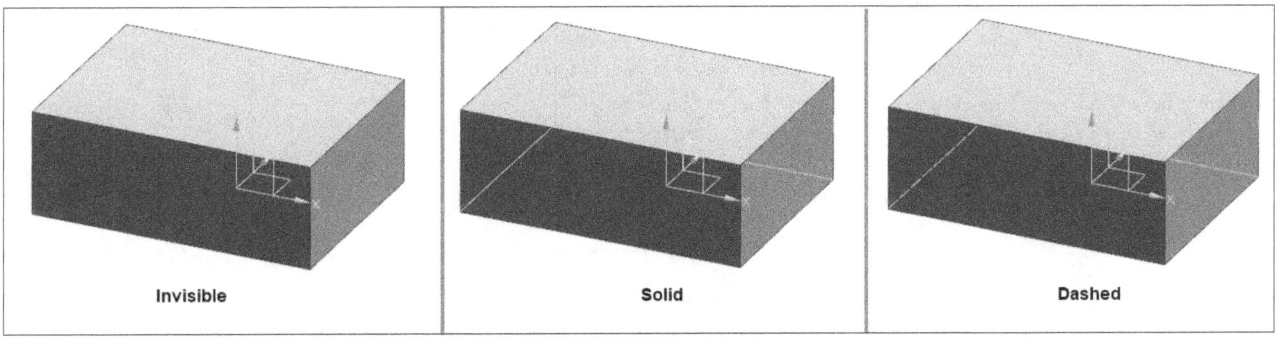

Figure-46. Hidden Edges options

- The options in the **Emphasis** drop-down are used to define how objects that are not in current display focus will be displayed; refer to Figure-47. These options are specially useful when working on assemblies. Select the **See-Thru All** check box from the drop-down if you want to make selected object visible through all the other objects/components in model/assembly; refer to Figure-48. Select the **See-Thru Preview** check box to make objects see through during preview. Select the **See-Thru De-emphasized Objects** check box to make higher priority objects see through from de-emphasized objects (objects which have been made translucent, or non-selection). Select the **See-Thru Shell** check box to make selected object see through with selection color while rest of the objects are grayed out. Select the **See-Thru Original Color Shell** check box to allow retention of colors of other objects while selected object can be see through other objects. Select the **See-Thru Layers** check box to make all objects transparent in grayed out color.

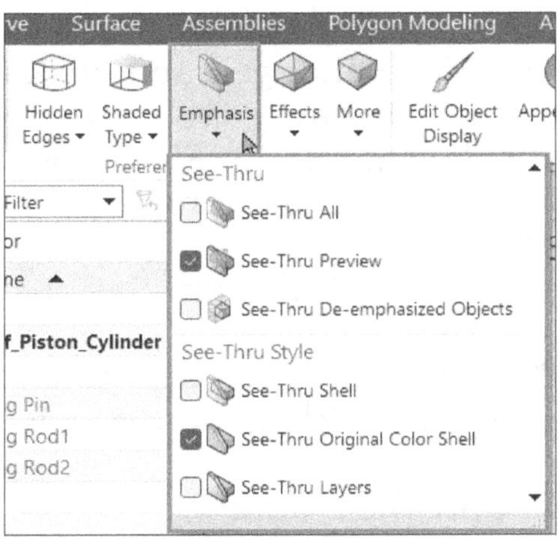

Figure-47. Emphasis drop-down

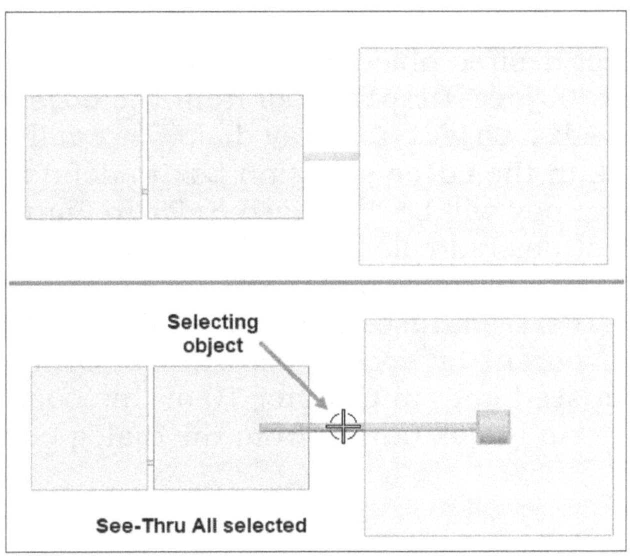

Figure-48. See Thru All check box selected

- Select desired check boxes from the **Effects** drop-down to apply related display effects to the model; refer to Figure-49. Select the **Facet Edges** check box to display model with tessellated mesh edges. Select the **Smooth Edges** check box to show smooth edges generated at shared regions of tangent surfaces. Select the **Reduce Edge Bleed-through** check box to smoothen display of edges near complex areas where thin sheets overlap. Select the **Wireframe Contrast** check box to display edges and other parameters in contrast with background. Select the **Flat Shading** check box to replace smooth shading with flat shading in patches at curves.

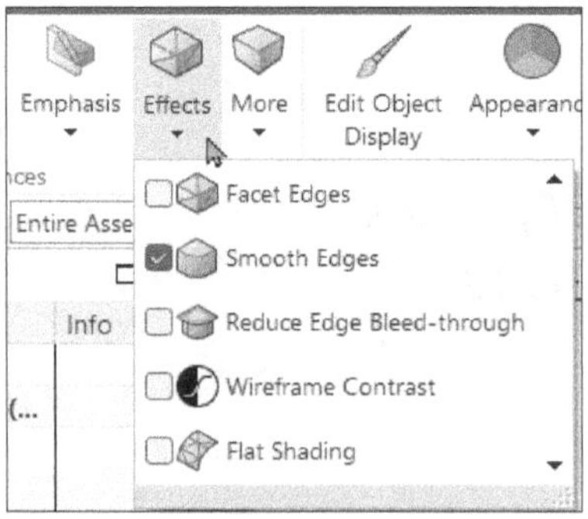

Figure-49. Effects drop-down

- Select the **Perspective** option from **More** drop-down to display model in perspective projection (objects near the views are shown larger). De-select this option to display model in parallel projection. When **Perspective** option is selected, click on the **Perspective Options** tool from the **More** drop-down to define distance of viewer camera from target.
- Select the **Translucency** option to display objects transparent to which translucency was applied when defining color/visual materials.
- Similarly, you can use other options in the More drop-down to apply display preferences.

APPLYING COLORS TO MODEL

The **Edit Object Display** tool is used to apply desired color and display properties to selected object. The procedure to use this tool is given next.

- Select desired object whose color properties are to be changed and click on the **Edit Object Display** tool from the **Object** group of **Display** tab in the **Ribbon.** The **Edit Object Display** dialog box will be displayed; refer to Figure-50.
- Click in the **Color** selection box to define color for the model. The **Object Color** dialog box will be displayed; refer to Figure-51.
- Select desired color from the palette and click on the **OK** button. Selected color will be applied to the model.
- Use the **Translucency** slider in **Shaded Display** rollout to make selected object transparent by specify percentage. Other options of this dialog box have been discussed later in Chapter 10 of this book.
- Click on the **OK** button from the dialog box to apply the changes.

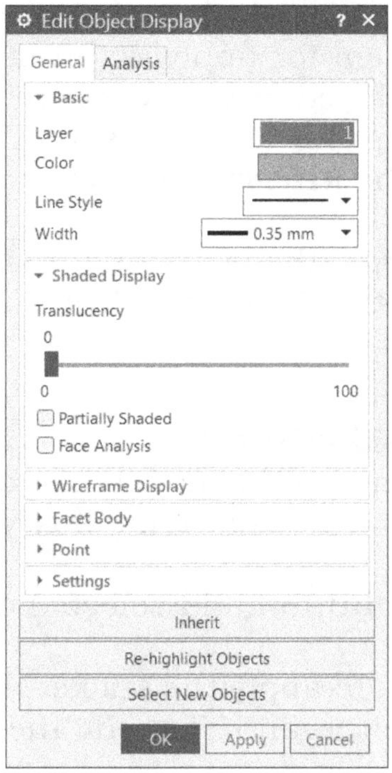

Figure-50. Edit Object Display dialog box

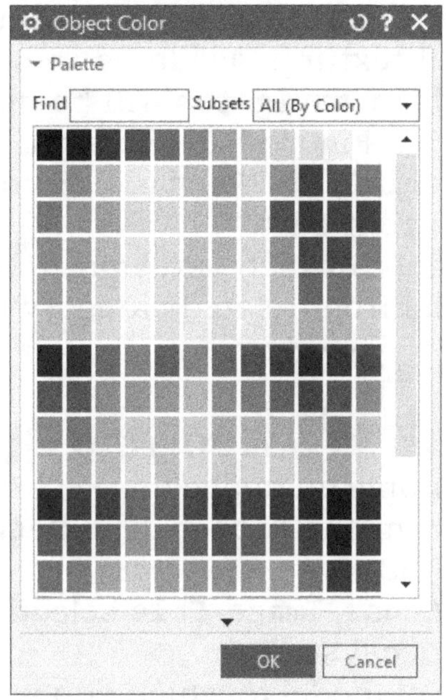

Figure-51. Object Color dialog box

APPLYING VISUAL MATERIALS

The **Assign Visual Materials** tool is used to apply physical material textures like glass, wood, metal, stone, and so on. The procedure to use this tool is given next.

- Click on the **Assign Visual Materials** tool from the **Visual Material** group in the **Display** tab of the **Ribbon**. The tools to apply visual material will be displayed in the **Ribbon** and **Resource Bar**; refer to Figure-52.

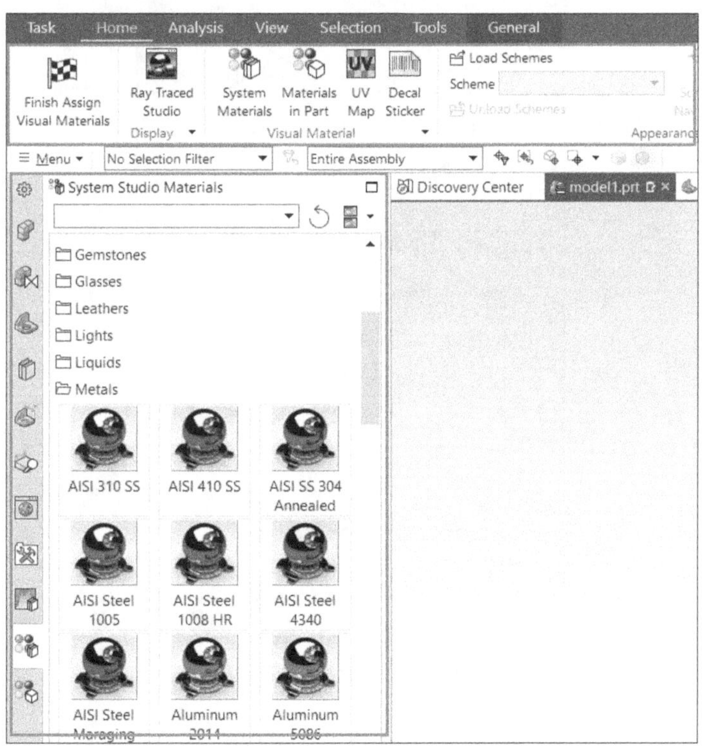

Figure-52. Interface to apply Visual Materials

- Select the **System Materials** tool from the **Visual Material** group in the **Ribbon** to use material textures available in system for applying on model. The **System Studio Materials Navigator** will be displayed in the **Resource Bar** at the left in interface; refer to Figure-52. (We are using this in our case).
- Select the **Materials in Part** tool from the **Ribbon** to use only material textures available in current part.
- Select the model to which you want to apply the visual material and then select desired material from related category in the **Navigator**. The visual material will be applied.

Applying Decal Sticker

- If you want to apply an image to selected face of the model then click on the **Decal Sticker** tool from the **Ribbon**. The **Decal Sticker** dialog box will be displayed; refer to Figure-53.
- Click on the **Choose Image File** selection button and selected desired image file to be used as decal sticker.
- Select the face of model to which you want to apply the sticker. Preview of sticker will be displayed. Use the handles to resize and reorient the sticker; refer to Figure-54.
- Specify the other parameters as discussed earlier and click on the **OK** button to apply the decal.

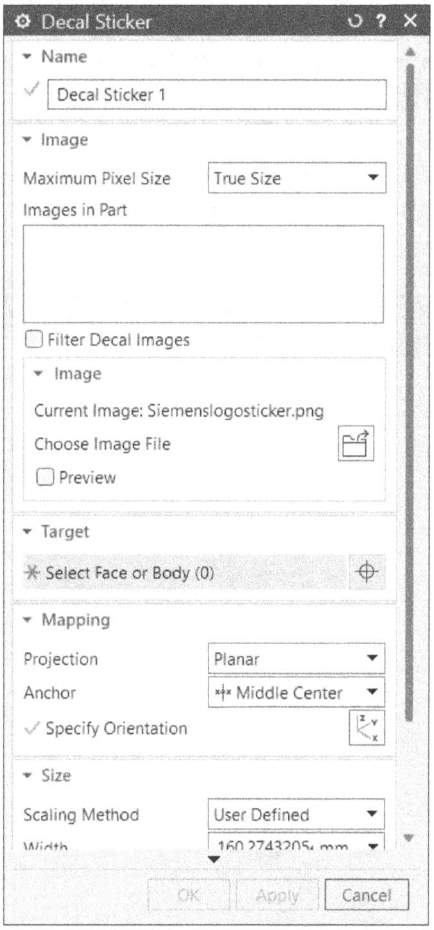

Figure-53. Decal Sticker dialog box

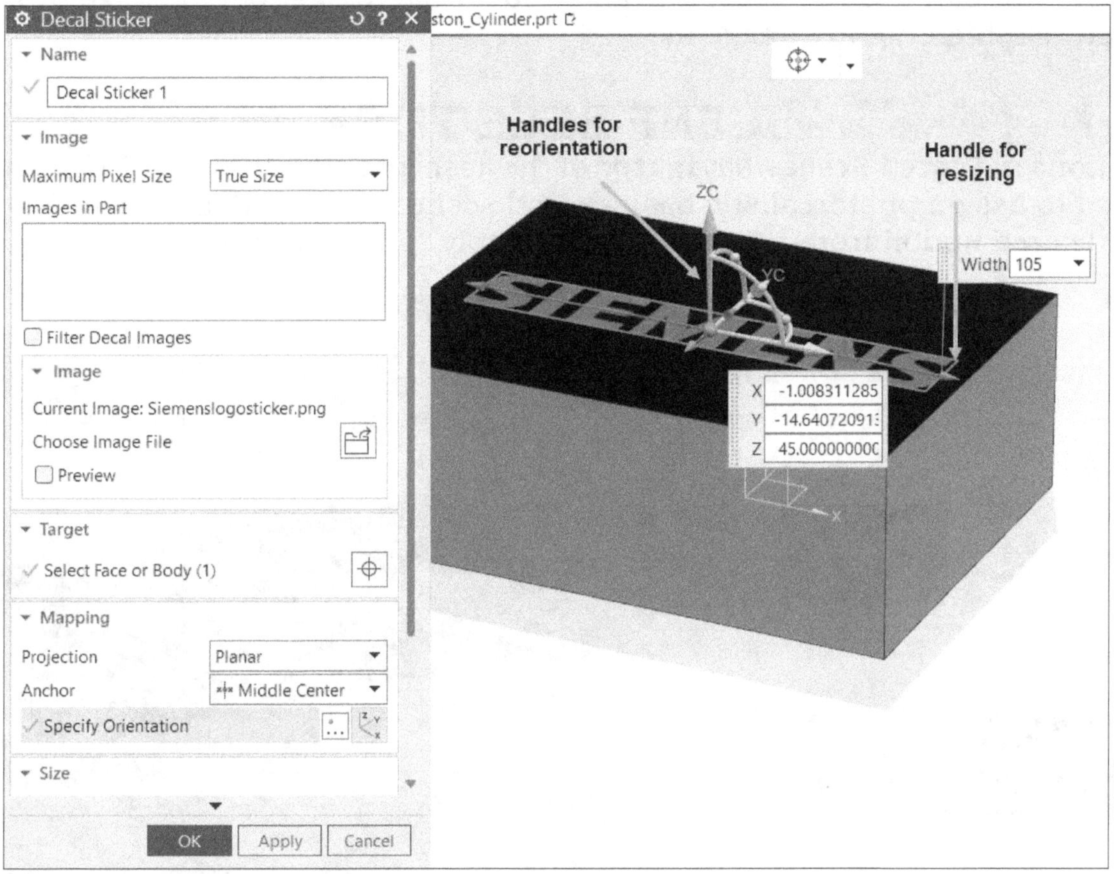

Figure-54. Applying decal sticker

- Click on the **Finish Assign Visual Materials** tool from the **Ribbon** to exit the mode and apply visual materials. The model will be automatically displayed in Studio display style in graphics area.

EXPORTING THE MODEL DISPLAY AS IMAGE

The **Export Image** tool is used to export current displayed model view as image file. The procedure to use this tool is given next.

- Click on the **Export Image** tool from the **Image** drop-down of **Image Gallery** group in the **Display** tab of the **Ribbon**. The Export Image dialog box will be displayed; refer to Figure-55.

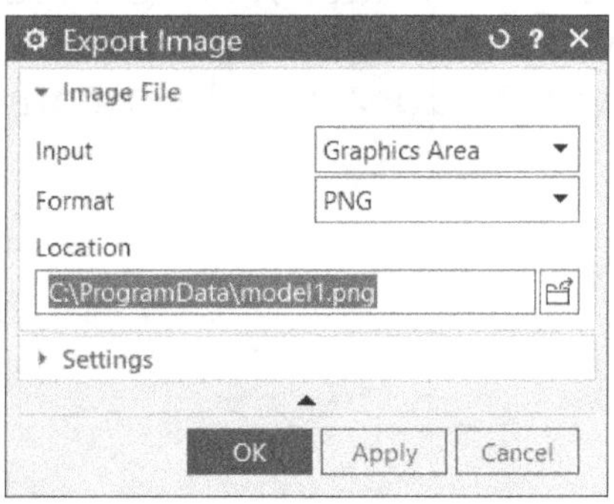

Figure-55. Export Image dialog box

- Set desired parameters as discussed earlier in Chapter 1 and click on the **OK** button to export image of model.

Similarly, you can use the **Export High Resolution Image** tool in **Image** drop-down to generate a high quality image file.

SCENE SELECTION

The options in **System Scenes Navigator** of the **Resource Bar** at the left in the interface are used to assign photorealistic background scene to the model; refer to Figure-56. Select desired option from the Navigator to apply respective scene.

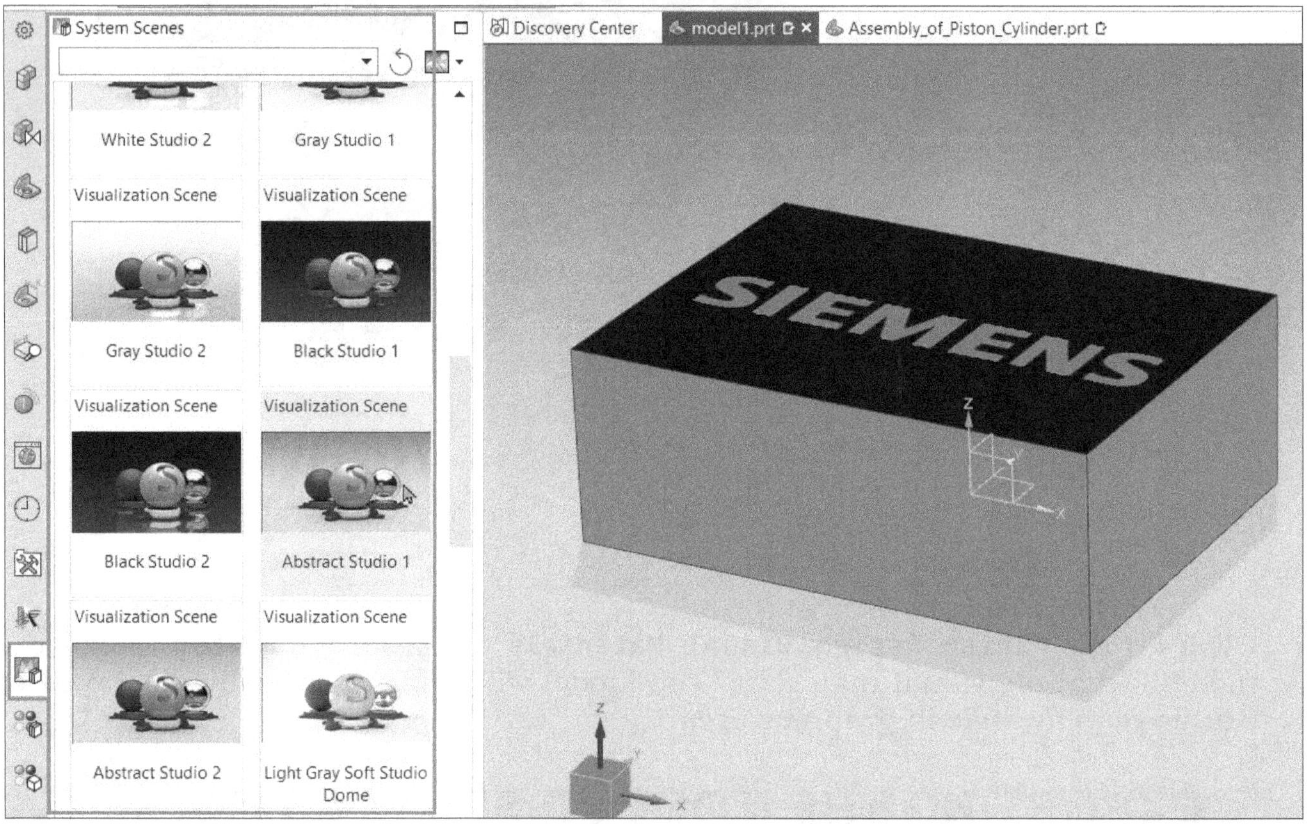

Figure-56. System Scenes Navigator

RAY TRACED STUDIO

The **Ray Traced Studio** tool is used to generate photorealistic rendering of the model with apply materials and scenes. On clicking this tool from the **Display** group in the **Display** tab of **Ribbon**, the **Ray Traced Studio** window will be displayed; refer to Figure-57. Select desired quality of rendering and then save the image as discussed earlier. Click on the **Close** button to exit the window. Note that **Save** tool is not active in **Ray Traced Studio** window for educational version of the software.

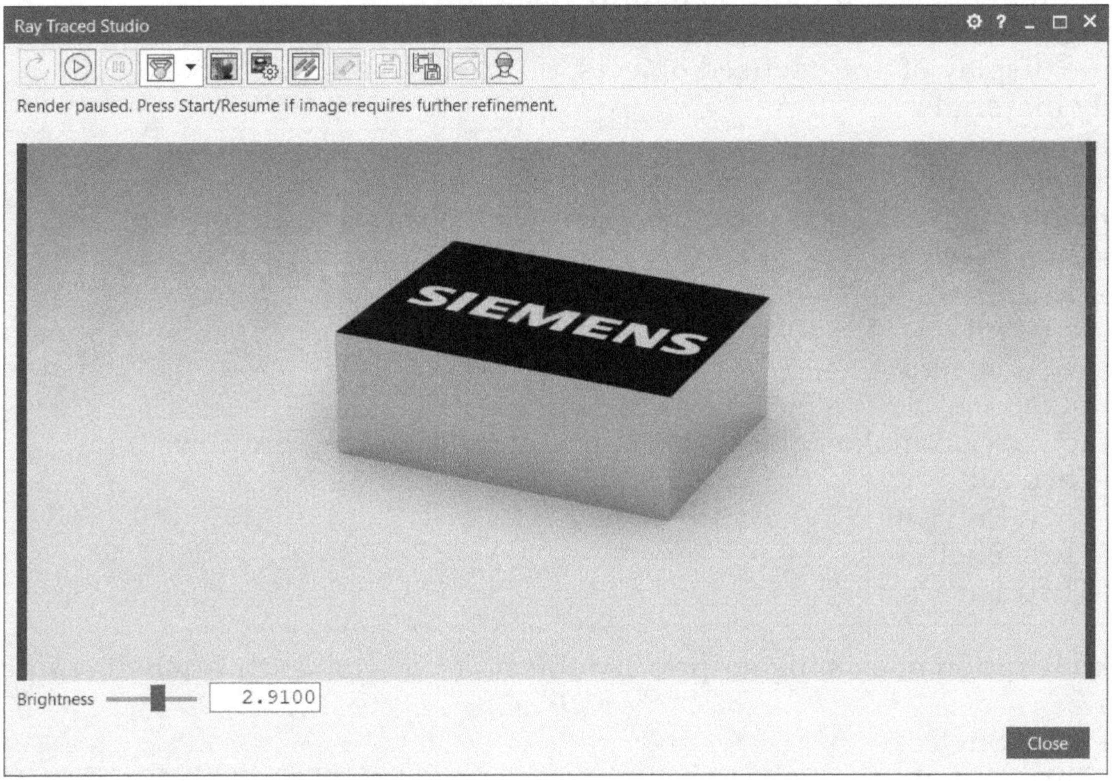

Figure-57. Ray Traced Studio window

SELF-ASSESSMENT

Q1. Which group in the Display tab is used to tweak the display of objects like face edges and hidden edges?
A. Object group
B. Preferences group
C. Visual Material group
D. Image Gallery group

Q2. What is the function of the Face Edges toggle button?
A. Apply color to faces
B. Display/hide edges of faces
C. Show materials on faces
D. Export face images

Q3. When Face Edges is ON, what does the Hidden Edges drop-down control?
A. Color of edges
B. Thickness of edges
C. Display style of hidden edges
D. Visibility of faces

Q4. Which of the following is NOT a Hidden Edges display option?
A. Solid
B. Dashed
C. Invisible
D. Transparent

Q5. The Emphasis drop-down is mainly used to:
A. Change object color
B. Define display of non-focused objects
C. Apply materials
D. Export models

Q6. Which option makes a selected object visible through all other objects?
A. See-Thru Preview
B. See-Thru Shell
C. See-Thru All
D. See-Thru Layers

Q7. Which option makes objects see-through only during preview?
A. See-Thru All
B. See-Thru Preview
C. See-Thru Shell
D. See-Thru Layers

Q8. Which option allows higher priority objects to be visible through de-emphasized objects?
A. See-Thru Shell
B. See-Thru Layers
C. See-Thru De-emphasized Objects
D. See-Thru Preview

Q9. Which option makes the selected object see-through with selection color while others are grayed out?
A. See-Thru Shell
B. See-Thru Layers
C. See-Thru All
D. See-Thru Preview

Q10. Which option retains original colors of other objects while selected object is see-through?
A. See-Thru Shell
B. See-Thru Original Color Shell
C. See-Thru Layers
D. See-Thru All

Q11. Which option makes all objects transparent in gray color?
A. See-Thru Preview
B. See-Thru Layers
C. See-Thru All
D. See-Thru Shell

Q12. Which Effects option displays tessellated mesh edges?
A. Smooth Edges
B. Facet Edges
C. Flat Shading
D. Wireframe Contrast

Q13. Which Effects option shows smooth edges at tangent surfaces?
A. Smooth Edges
B. Facet Edges
C. Flat Shading
D. Reduce Edge Bleed-through

Q14. Which option smoothens edges in complex overlapping areas?
A. Smooth Edges
B. Facet Edges
C. Reduce Edge Bleed-through
D. Flat Shading

Q15. Which option enhances contrast of edges with the background?
A. Wireframe Contrast
B. Flat Shading
C. Smooth Edges
D. Facet Edges

Q16. Which option replaces smooth shading with flat shading?
A. Smooth Edges
B. Flat Shading
C. Facet Edges
D. Wireframe Contrast

Q17. What does enabling Perspective option do?
A. Shows objects equally sized
B. Shows near objects larger
C. Hides distant objects
D. Applies transparency

Q18. What happens when Perspective is disabled?
A. Parallel projection is used
B. Objects become transparent
C. Colors are removed
D. Edges are hidden

Q19. Which tool is used to apply color to a model?
A. Assign Visual Materials
B. Edit Object Display
C. Export Image
D. Decal Sticker

Q20. What does the Translucency slider control?
A. Edge thickness
B. Transparency level
C. Color intensity
D. Material type

Q21. Which tool is used to apply textures like glass or wood?
A. Edit Object Display
B. Assign Visual Materials
C. Export Image
D. Scene Selection

Q22. Which tool allows using system-available material textures?
A. Materials in Part
B. System Materials
C. Edit Object Display
D. Decal Sticker

Q23. Which tool applies an image onto a model face?
A. Assign Visual Materials
B. Edit Object Display
C. Decal Sticker
D. Export Image

Q24. What is the function of Export Image tool?
A. Apply materials
B. Export model as image
C. Change color
D. Apply scene

Q25. Which tool generates high-quality image output?
A. Export Image
B. Export High Resolution Image
C. Ray Traced Studio
D. Scene Navigator

Q26. What is the purpose of System Scenes Navigator?
A. Apply textures
B. Apply background scenes
C. Change edge style
D. Export images

Q27. Which tool is used for photorealistic rendering?
A. Export Image
B. Ray Traced Studio
C. Edit Object Display
D. Decal Sticker

Chapter 8

Curve Sketching

Topics Covered

The major topics covered in this chapter are:

- ***Creating Points, Lines, Arcs/Circles, Studio Splines***
- ***Creating Text, Curve on surface, Helix, Conic, Law Curve, Spline***
- ***Creating Project Curve, Fit Curve, Intersection Curve, Shadow Curve,***
- ***Creating Offset Curve, Offset in Face, Bridge, Composite, Circular Blend Curve***
- ***Creating Combined Projection, Wrap Curve, Isoparametric Curve, Isocline Curve***
- ***Creating Section Curve, Extract Virtual Curve, Revolve outline, Mirror Curve***
- ***Creating Offset 3D Curve, Scale Curve, Trim Curve, Curve Length, X-Form***
- ***Editing Curve Parameters***
- ***Creating Smooth Curve String***

INTRODUCTION

In previous chapters, you have learned to use tools for creating various base features like extrude, revolve, sweep, and so on. You have also learned to apply edge blend, chamfer, shell, draft, and so on. In this chapter, you will learn to create various features like draft body, rib, groove, and so on. These tools are discussed next.

POINT

The **Point** tool in **Base** group of the **Curve** tab in the **Ribbon** is used to specify temporary point locations when creating or editing objects. The procedure to use this tool has been discussed earlier.

POINT SET

The **Point Set** tool in **Base** group of the **Curve** tab in the **Ribbon** is used to create a set of points that correspond to existing geometry. The procedure to use this tool has been discussed earlier.

LINE

The **Line** tool is used to create straight line segments. The procedure to use this tool is discussed next.

- Click on the **Line** tool from **Base** group in the **Curve** tab of the **Ribbon**. The **Line** dialog box will be displayed; refer to Figure-1.

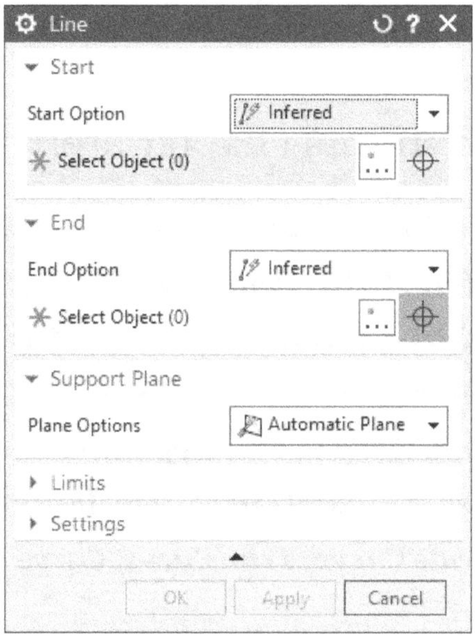

Figure-1. Line dialog box

- Select desired option from **Start Option** drop-down in the **Start** rollout to specify starting point of the line and specify the parameters. Select **Inferred** option to determine the best start and end option to be selected on the object. Select **Point** option from the drop-down to create a line using one or more points. Select **Tangent** option to create a line that is tangent to a curved object.

- Select desired option from **End Option** drop-down in the **End** rollout to specify end point of the line and specify the parameters. Select **At Angle** option to create a line at an angle to a selected reference object. Select **Along XC** option to create a line parallel to the XC-axis. Select **Along YC** option to create a line parallel to the YC-axis. Select **Along ZC** option to create a line parallel to the ZC-axis.
- Select desired option from **Plane Options** drop-down in the **Support Plane** rollout to specify the plane on which the line to be created. Select **Automatic Plane** option to select a temporary automatic plane based on the specified start and end points of line. Select the **Locked Plane** option to make the automatic plane immovable if you change the start or end points. Select the **Select Plane** option to specify a plane on which the line to be constructed.
- Select desired option from **Start Limit** and **End Limit** drop-down in the **Limits** rollout to specify points, objects, or distance values that limit where the line starts and ends.
- After specifying desired parameters in the dialog box, click on the **Apply** or **OK** button. The line will be created; refer to Figure-2.

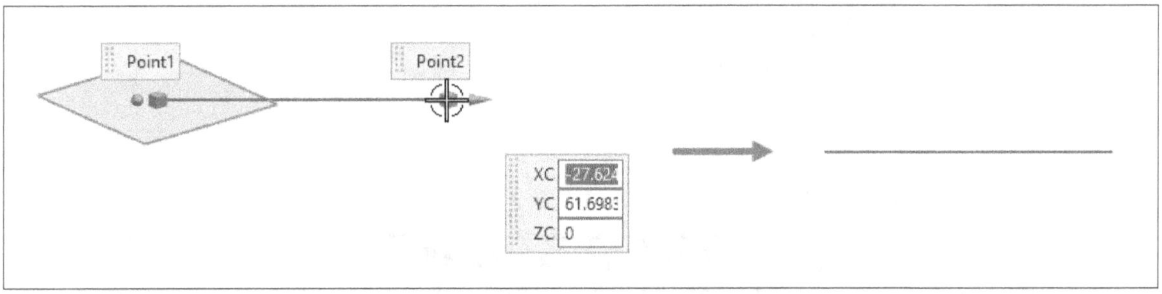

Figure-2. Line created

ARC/CIRCLE

The **Arc/Circle** tool is used to create associative arcs and circle features. The procedure to use this tool is discussed next.

- Click on the **Arc/Circle** tool from **Base** group in the **Curve** tab of the **Ribbon**. The **Arc/Circle** dialog box will be displayed; refer to Figure-3.

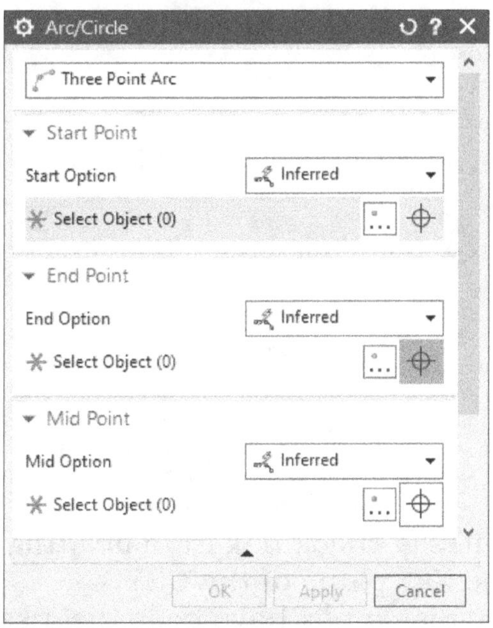

Figure-3. Arc Circle dialog box

- Select desired type of creation method from the drop-down to create the arc or circle. Select **Three Point Arc** option to create an arc by specifying three points that the arc must pass through or two points and a radius. Select **Arc/Circle from Center** option to create an arc by specifying an arc center and a second point or radius.
- Specify desired radius of arc or circle in the **Radius** edit box of **Size** rollout.
- Other parameters in the dialog box have been discussed earlier.
- After specifying desired parameters in the dialog box, click on the **Apply** or **OK** button. The arc will be created; refer to Figure-4.

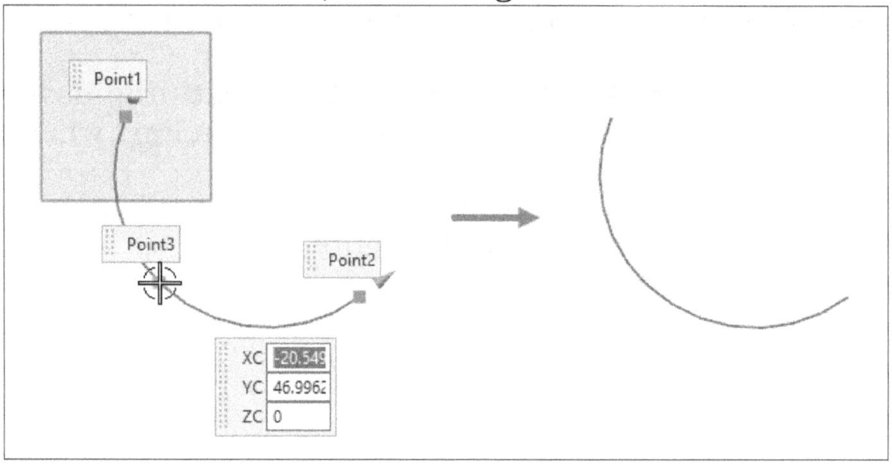

Figure-4. Arc created

STUDIO SPLINE

The **Studio Spline** tool is used to interactively create an associative or non-associative spline in two or three dimensions. The procedure to use this tool is discussed next.

- Click on the **Studio Spline** tool from **Base** group in the **Curve** tab of the **Ribbon**. The **Studio Spline** dialog box will be displayed; refer to Figure-5.

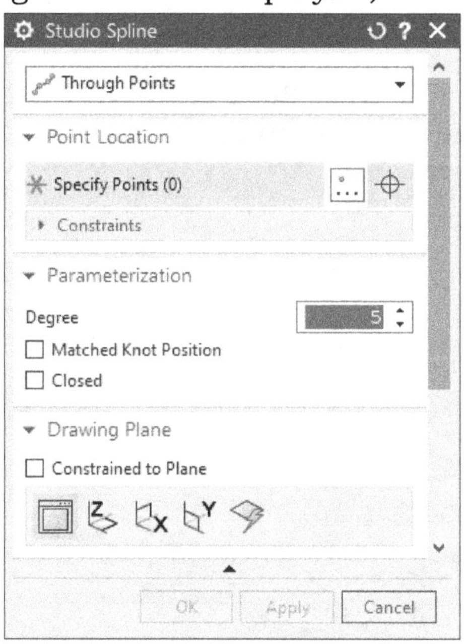

Figure-5. Studio Spline dialog box

- Select **Constrained to Plane** check box from **Drawing Plane** rollout to constrain the drawing plane to the X-Y plane of the CSYS.
- Other parameters in the dialog box have been discussed earlier in this book.

- After specifying desired parameters in the dialog box, click on the **Apply** or **OK** button. The spline will be created.

TEXT

The **Text** tool is used to generate NX curves from the True Type fonts in your native windows font library. The procedure to use this tool is discussed next.

- Click on the **Text** tool from **Base** group in the **Curve** tab of the **Ribbon**. The **Text** dialog box will be displayed along with the preview of text; refer to Figure-6.

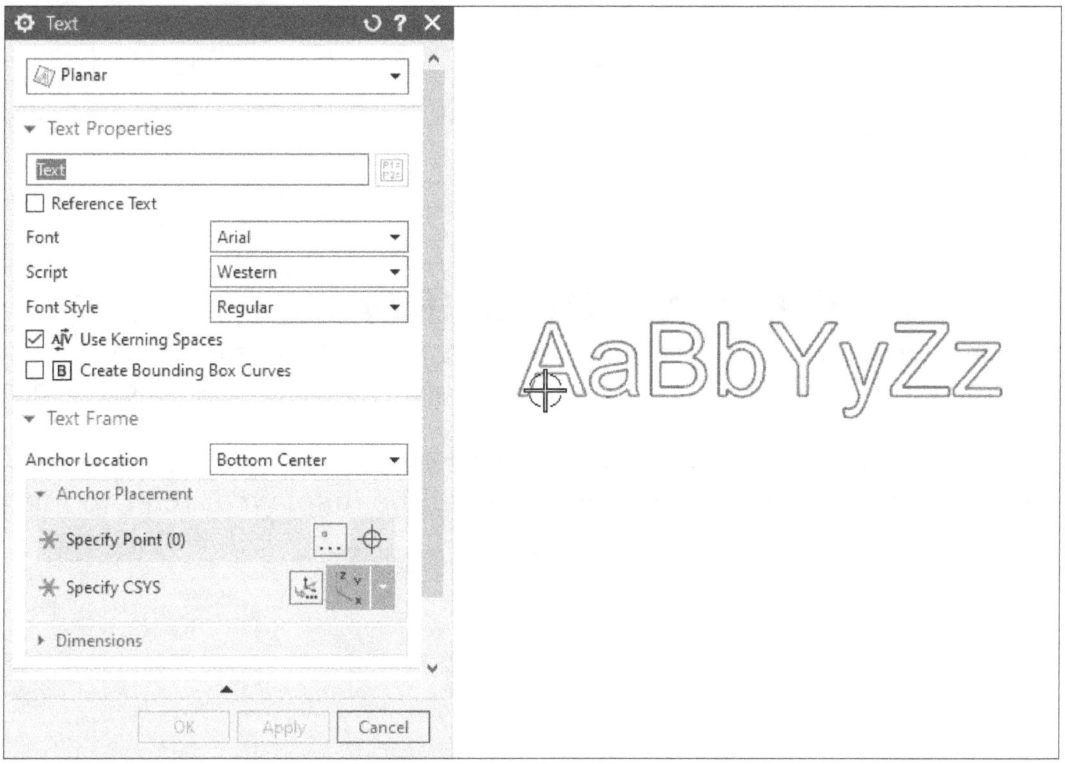

Figure-6. Text dialog box with preview of text

- Select desired type of text from drop-down in the dialog box. Select **Planar** option to create text on a plane. Select **On Curve** option to create text along a connected curve string. Select **On Face** option to create text on one or more connected faces.
- Specify desired single line of text in the box of **Text Properties** rollout.
- Click on the **Select Expression** button, the **Relationship** dialog box will be displayed to select an existing expression to associate with the text string or define an expression for a text string.
- Select **Reference Text** check box to create any generated text as a text string expression.
- Select desired font, script, and font style from **Font**, **Script**, and **Font Style** drop-downs, respectively.
- Select **Use Kerning Spaces** check box to increase or decrease the kerning between characters.
- Select **Create Bounding Box Curves** check box to create a frame around the geometry when it is generated.
- Specify desired anchor location of the text from **Anchor Location** drop-down of **Text Frame** rollout. Specify desired parameters in the **Anchor Placement** and **Dimensions** rollout.

- Select **Create Print Mark** check box from **Print Mark Settings** rollout to define areas as print marks, which determine where textual markings, such as serial numbers or date codes, will be applied in the downstream 3D printing process. Specify desired thickening offset value for the print mark in the **Thickness** edit box. Specify desired name of each print mark in the **Usage Label** edit box.
- Select **Associative** check box from **Settings** rollout to create an associative text feature. Select **Join Curves** check box to join all the curves forming one loop into a single spline.
- After specifying desired parameters in the dialog box, click on the **Apply** or **OK** button. The text will be created; refer to Figure-7.

Figure-7. Text created

CURVE ON SURFACE

The **Curve on Surface** tool is used to create a surface spline directly on a face or faces of one or more surfaces. The procedure to use this tool is discussed next.

- Click on the **Curve on Surface** tool from **Advanced** group in the **Curve** tab of the **Ribbon**. The **Curve on Surface** dialog box will be displayed; refer to Figure-8.

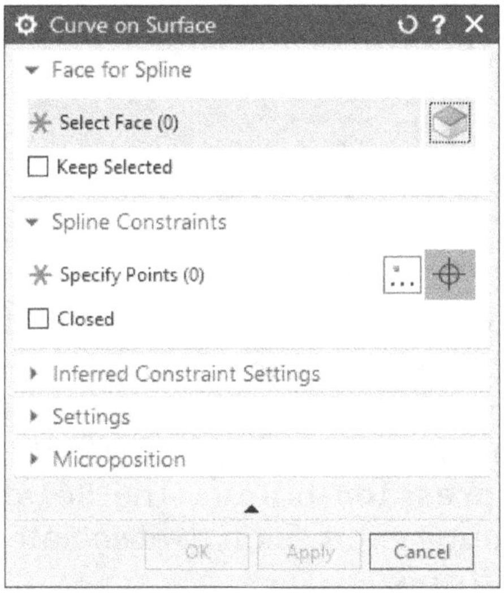

Figure-8. Curve on Surface dialog box

- Select desired target face or faces from the graphics window on which the curve to be created.
- Select **Keep Selected** check box to keep the current target face or faces selected.
- Click on the **Specify Points** button from **Spline Constraints** rollout to create and constrain curve points on the target face or faces. Select **Closed** check box to create a curve that starts and ends at the same point.

- Select **Isoparametric** radio button from **Surface Constraint Direction** of **Inferred Constraint Settings** rollout to drag the curve point in either the U or V parametric direction. Select **Sectional** radio button to rotate or align the curve direction. Select **Fix Tangent Direction** check box to keep the G1 or G2 direction of the current end point fixed when you edit other points on the curve.
- Select **Advanced Curve Fit** check box from **Settings** rollout to specify method, degree, and segments. Select desired option from **Method** drop-down to control the parameterization of output curves. Specify desired degree of the curve in the **Degree** edit box. Specify desired number of segments of the curve in the **Segments** edit box. Specify a minimum and maximum degree of the curve in the **Minimum Degree** and **Maximum degree** edit boxes, respectively. Specify maximum number of segments for the curve in the **Maximum Segments** edit box. Specify positional distance tolerance for G0 continuity in the **Distance Tolerance** edit box. Specify tangency angle tolerane for G1 continuity in the **Angle Tolerance** edit box.
- Select **Rate** check box from **Microposition** rollout to specify the relative amount of movement required to drag a handle in order to move the corresponding constraint point.
- After specifying desired parameters in the dialog box, click on the **Apply** or **OK** button. The curve will be created on the surface; refer to Figure-9.

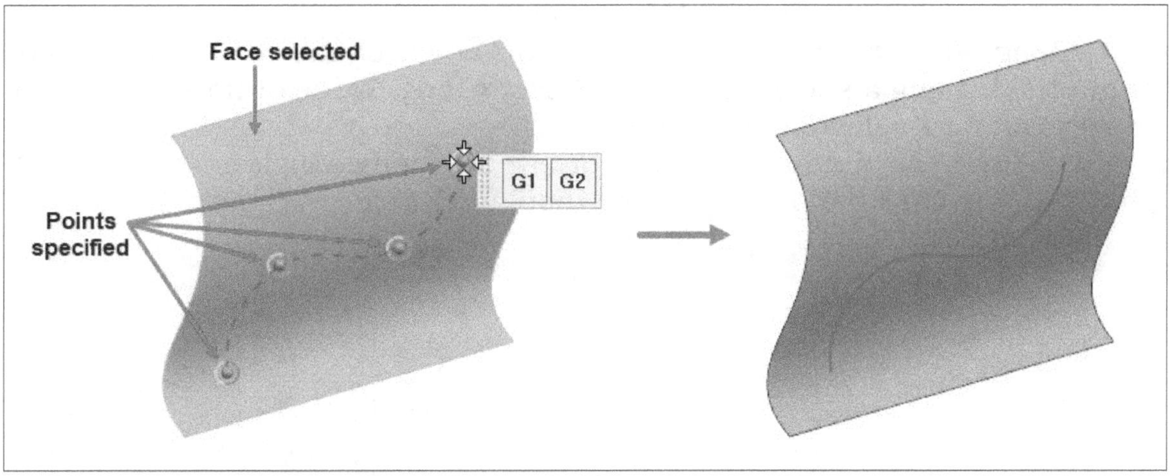

Figure-9. Curve created on the surface

HELIX

The **Helix** tool is used to create a helix with a specified number of turns, pitch, radius or diameter, turn direction, and orientation. The procedure to use this tool is discussed next.

- Click on the **Helix** tool from **Advanced** group in the **Curve** tab of the **Ribbon**. The **Helix** dialog box will be displayed; refer to Figure-10.

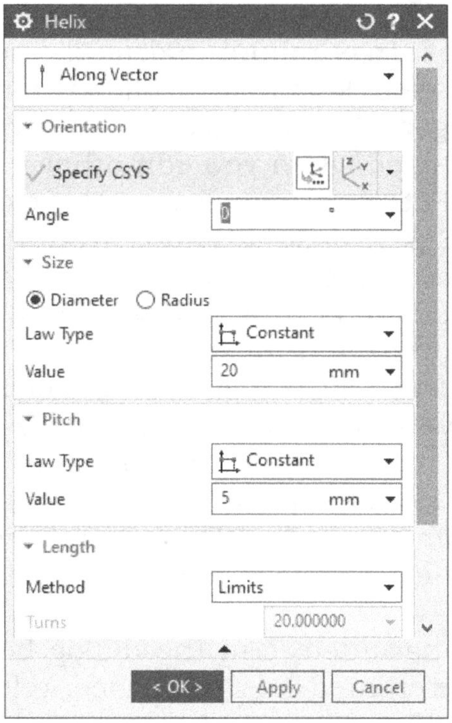

Figure-10. Helix dialog box

- Select **Along Vector** option from **Type** drop-down of the dialog box to create a straight helix along a specified vector. Select **Along Spine** option to create a helix that runs along a selected spine curve.
- Specify desired coordinate system to orient the helix. Click on the **CSYS Dialog** button. The **CSYS** dialog box will be displayed; refer to Figure-11.

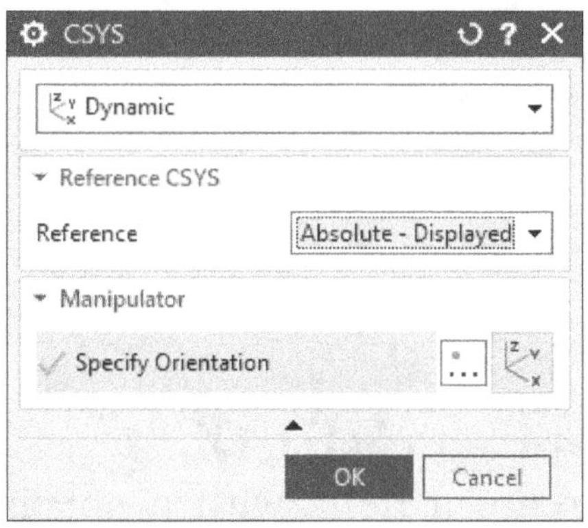

Figure-11. CSYS dialog box

- Specify desired parameters in the dialog box and click on the **OK** button. The coordinate system will be defined.
- Specify desired start angle of the helix in the **Angle** edit box.
- Select **Diameter** or **Radius** radio button from **Size** rollout to specify desired diameter or radius value of the helix, respectively in the **Value** edit box. Select desired type of law from **Law Type** drop-down to specify the size of helix.
- Select desired type of law from **Law Type** drop-down of **Pitch** rollout to specify the pitch of helix. Specify desired distance between turns of the helix along the helical axis or spine curve in the **Value** edit box.
- Select **Limits** option from **Method** drop-down of **Length** rollout and enter desired value in the **Start Limit** and **End Limit** edit boxes which is based on arc length or percentage of arc length. Select **Turns** option from the drop-down and specify desired number of turns in the **Turns** edit box.

- Select desired option from **Turn Direction** drop-down of **Settings** rollout to specify the direction of the turns around the helical axis. Specify desired value in the **Distance Tolerance** edit box to control the deviation of the helix from a theoretical helix. Specify desired value in the **Angle Tolerance** edit box to control the maximum allowable angle between normals at corresponding points along the helix.
- After specifying desired parameters, click on **OK** button from the dialog box. The helix will be created; refer to Figure-12.

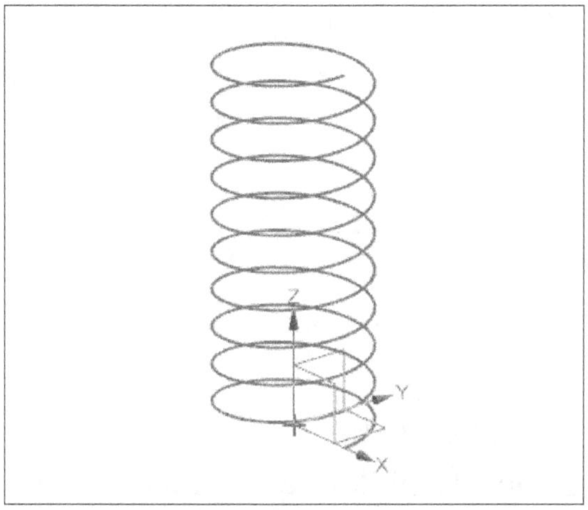

Figure-12. Helix created

GENERAL CONIC

The **General Conic** tool is used to create a conic section curves. Conic sections are derived by intersecting internal cones with a user-defined plane. The procedure to use this tool is discussed next.

- Click on the **General Conic** tool from **More** drop-down in the **Advanced** group of **Curve** tab in the **Ribbon**. The **General Conic** dialog box will be displayed; refer to Figure-13.

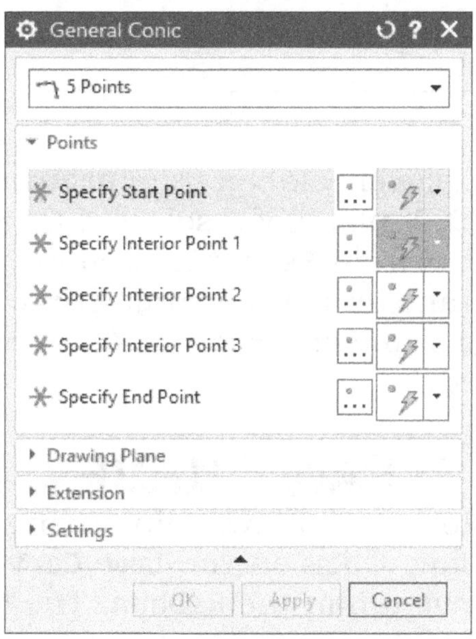

Figure-13. General Conic dialog box

- Select desired option from drop-down in the top of the dialog box to create a conic curve defined by the coplanar points, slopes, anchor point, value of rho, and conic quadratic equations.
- Click on the workplane and specify start point of the curve; refer to Figure-14.

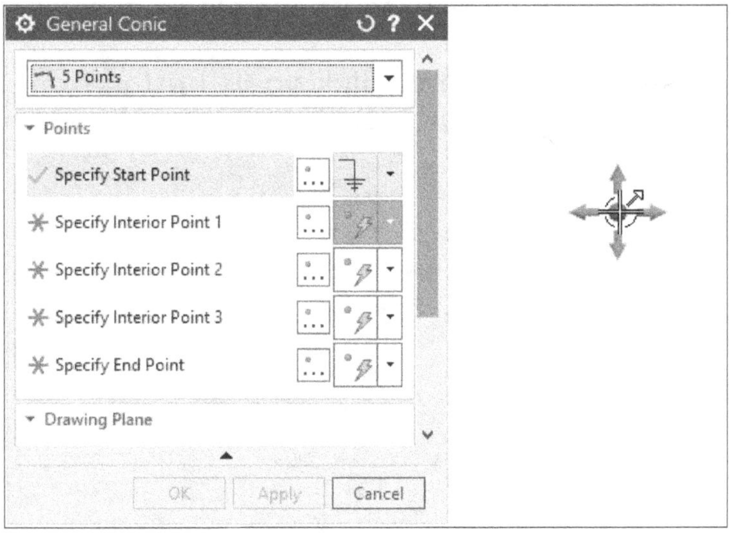

Figure-14. Specifying starting point of the curve

- After specifying the first point, click **MMB** to place the point. Move the cursor away and click at desired location(s) to specify the next points.
- As you specify the end point, the preview of conic curve will be displayed; refer to Figure-15.

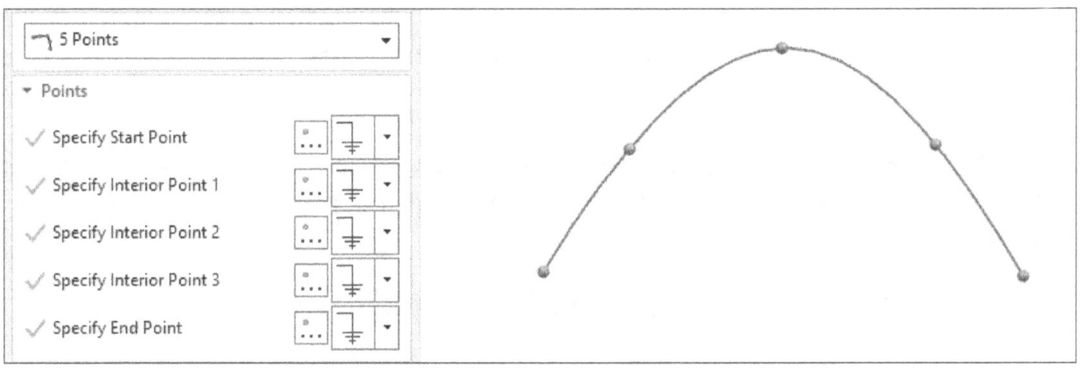

Figure-15. Preview of conic curve

- Select **Constrained to Plane** check box from **Drawing Plane** rollout to constrain the drawing plane to the X-Y plane of a selected CSYS.
- Select **Symmetric** check box from **Extension** rollout to apply the same extension to both start and end parameters of the conic curve.
- After specifying desired parameters, click on **OK** button from the dialog box. The conic curve will be created.

LAW CURVE

The **Law Curve** tool is used to create a law spline using the law subfunctions, such as a linear law, or a cubic law. Click on the **Law Curve** tool from **More** drop-down in the **Advanced** group of **Curve** tab in the **Ribbon**. The **Law Curve** dialog box will be displayed; refer to Figure-16.

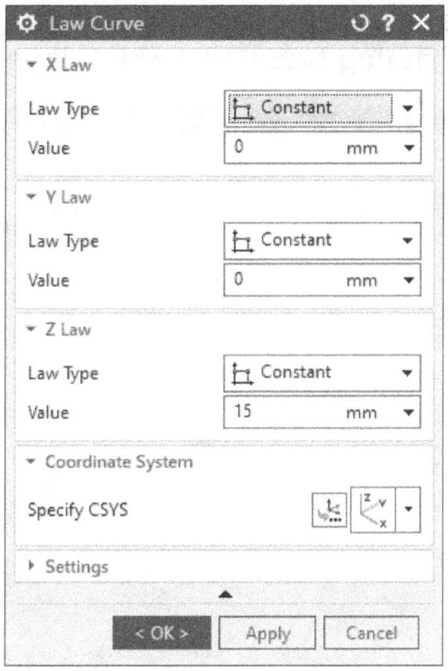

Figure-16. Law Curve dialog box

Law Curve using Constant option

- Select **Constant** option from **Law Type** drop-down in the dialog box to define a constant value. The options will be displayed as shown in Figure-16.
- Specify desired value in the **Value** edit box of **X Law**, **Y Law**, and **Z Law** rollouts.
- Click on the **Specify CSYS** button from **Coordinate System** rollout to select desired coordinate system.
- Specify desired value in the **Distance Tolerance** edit box of **Settings** rollout.
- After specifying desired parameters, click on **OK** button from the dialog box. The curve will be created; refer to Figure-17.

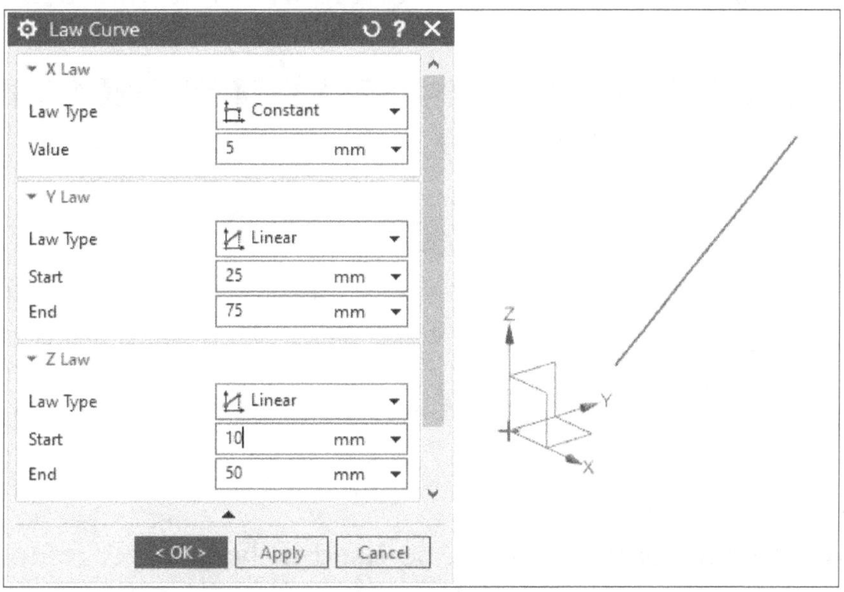

Figure-17. Law spline curve created

Creating Law Curve Using Equation

You can use parameters created by Expressions tool to generate equations for law curve. The procedure is given next.

- Click on the **Expressions** tool from the **Utilities** group in the **Tools** tab of the **Ribbon**. The **Expressions** dialog box will be displayed; refer to Figure-18.

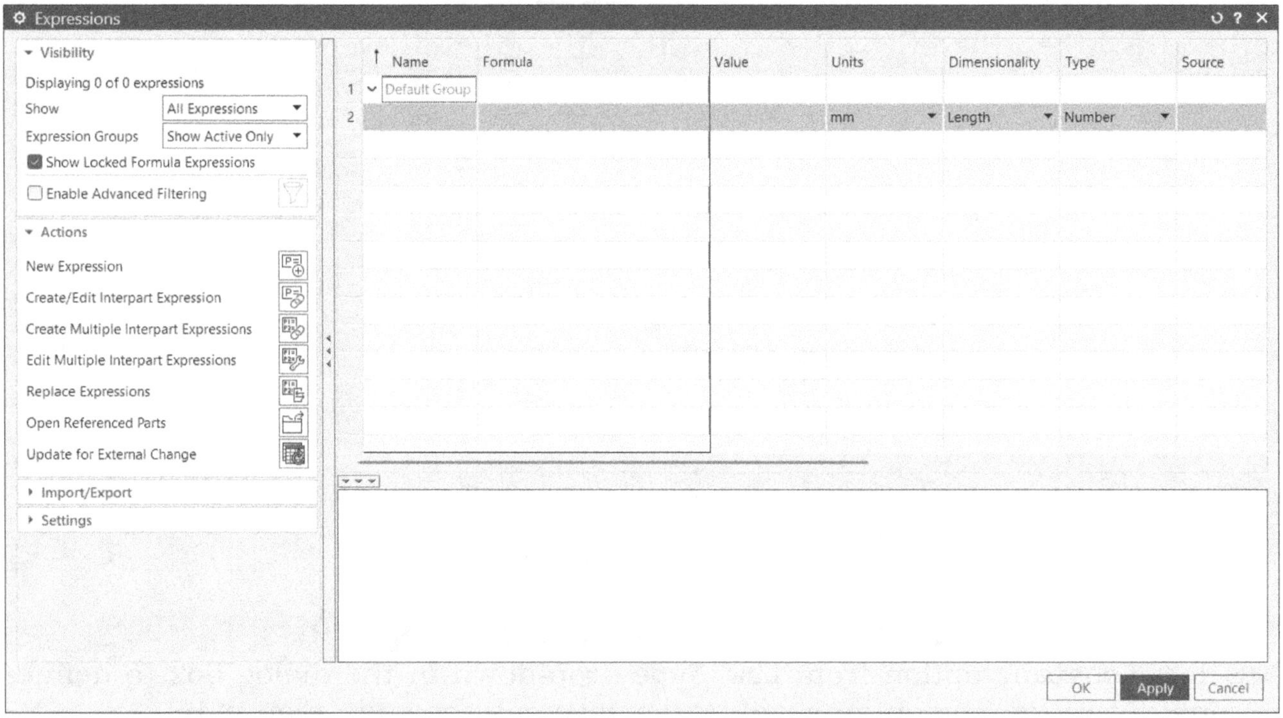

Figure-18. Expressions dialog box

- Double-click in the **Name** field and specify desired name for parameter to be used in the equation of law curve. For example, type **t** as name of the parameter.
- Double-click in the **Formula** field and specify desired value of the parameter like **50** in the field. Set the dimension to **Unitless** option from the **Dimensionality** field.
- Right-click in empty area of table in the dialog box and select the **New Expression** option from the shortcut menu; refer to Figure-19 to add a new row for next parameter.

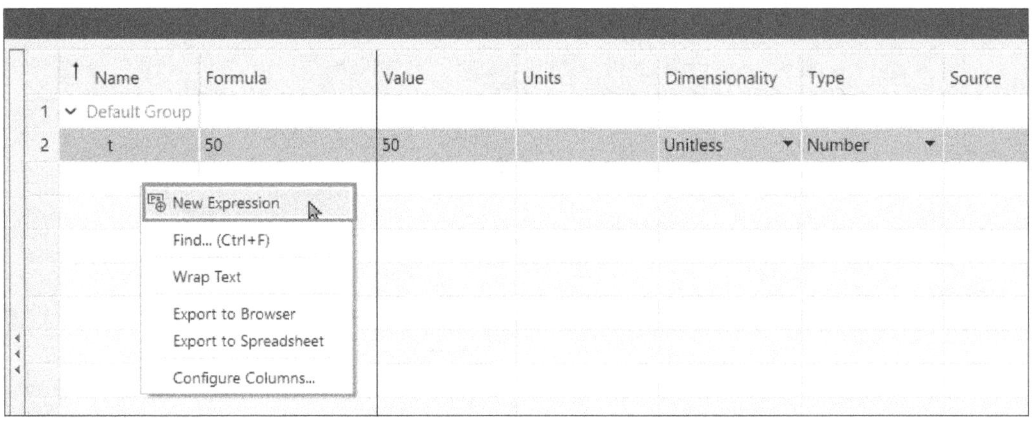

Figure-19. New Expression option

- Similarly, create other parameters to be used in law curve; refer to Figure-20.

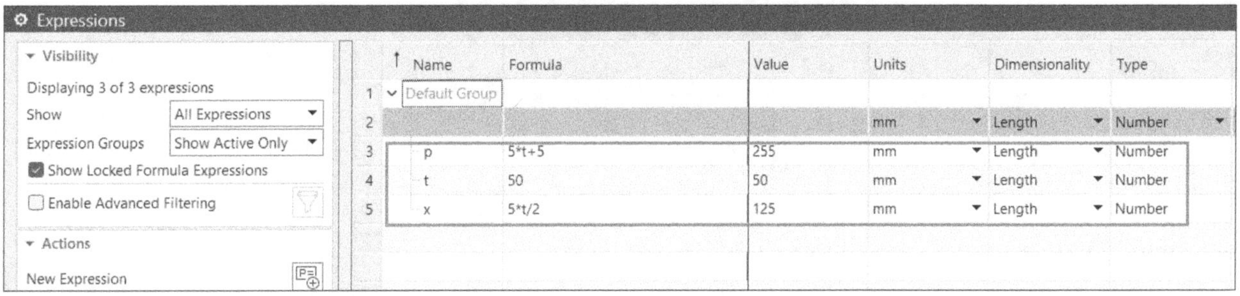

Figure-20. Parameter expressions created

- After applying changes, click on the **OK** button from the dialog box. The parameters will be created.
- Click on the **Law Curve** tool from **More** drop-down in **Advanced** group of **Curve** tab in **Ribbon** and select the **By Equation** option from the **Law Type** drop-down in **X Law** rollout of the dialog box to define equation for X coordinate of curve.
- Set desired parameters earlier created by **Expressions** tool to define coordinate values; refer to Figure-21.

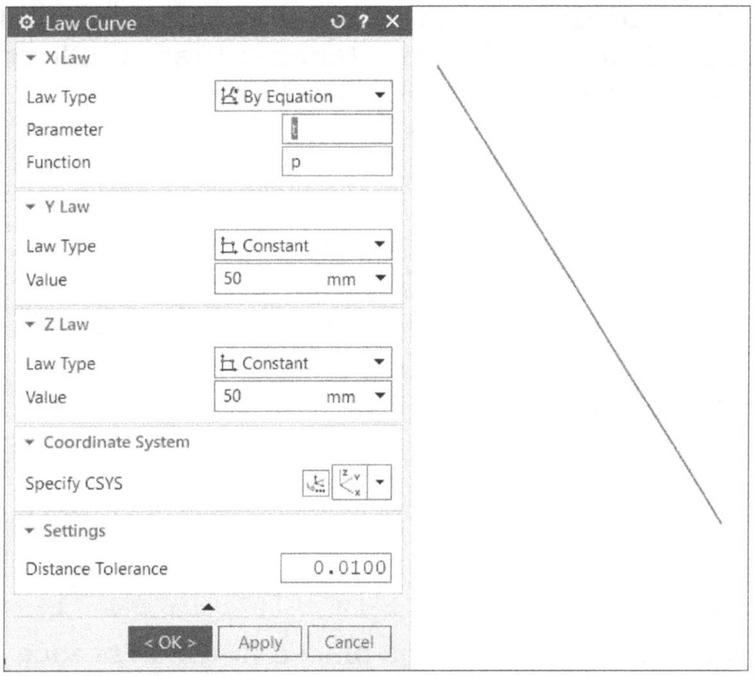

Figure-21. Creating law curve using equation

- Set the other parameters as discussed earlier and click on the **OK** button to create the curve.

Similarly, you can create curve by using other parameters.

SPINE

The **Spine** tool is used to create spine curves that are perpendicular to selected planes. The procedure to use this tool is discussed next.

- Click on the **Spine** tool from **More** drop-down in the **Advanced** group of **Curve** tab in the **Ribbon**. The **Spine Curve** dialog box will be displayed; refer to Figure-22.

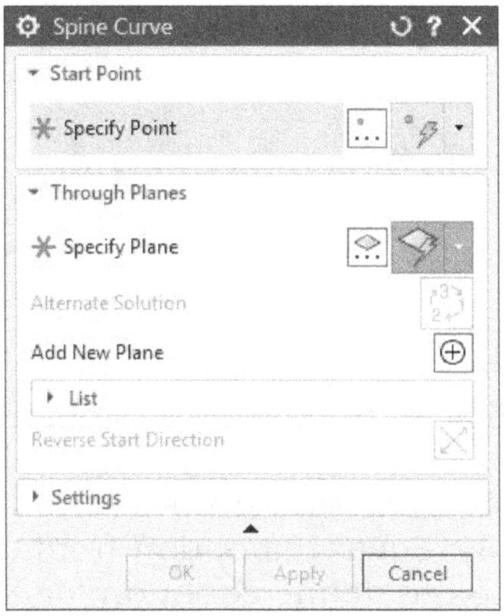

Figure-22. Spine Curve dialog box

- Click on the existing point in the workplane to select starting point of the spine or click on the **Point Dialog** button to create the point using **Point** dialog box.
- Click on the **Specify Plane** button from **Through Planes** rollout and select desired plane of coordinate system; refer to Figure-23.

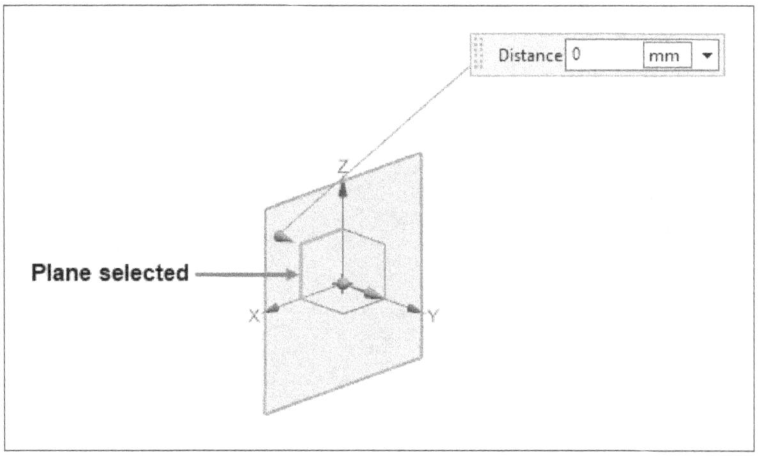

Figure-23. Plane selected

- Specify desired distance of plane to be placed in the **Distance** edit box and press **Enter**. The plane will be placed.
- Click on the **Add New Plane** button and create desired number of planes as discussed earlier. The preview of spine curve will be displayed; refer to Figure-24.
- Click on the **Alternate Solution** button to create the longer arc segment which is more than 180 degrees instead of the shorter arc segment.
- Click on the **Reverse Start Direction** button to reverse the direction of spine.
- Select the **Associative** check box from **Settings** rollout to associate the spine to its inputs. Select **Closed** check box to create the closed spine.
- Select **Simple** option from **Arc Segments** drop-down to use arc segments for the spine to not be curvature continuous to their neighboring segments. Select **Smooth** option from the drop-down to use arc segments for the spine to be curvature continuous to their neighboring segments.
- After specifying desired parameters, click on **OK** button from the dialog box. The spine curve will be created.

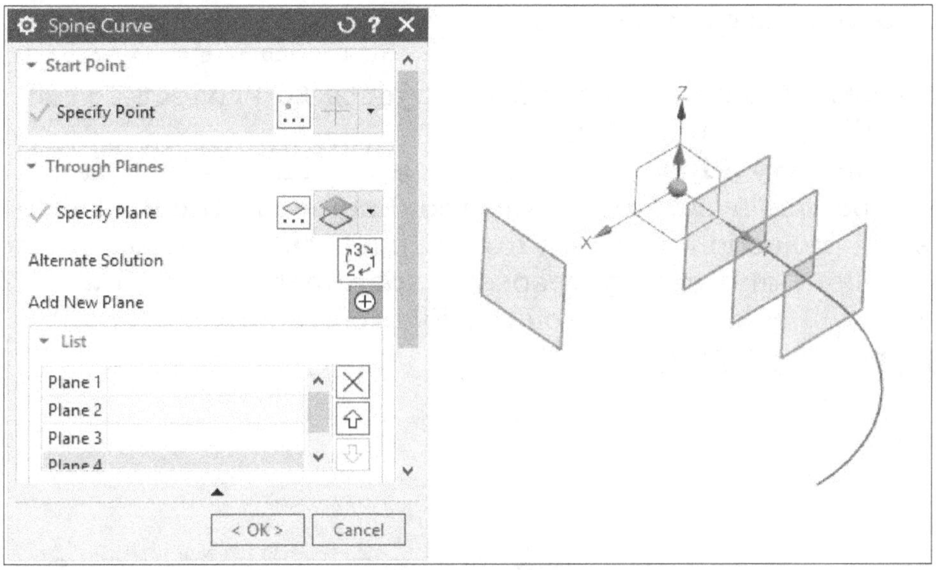

Figure-24. Preview of spine curve

FIT CURVE

The **Fit Curve** tool is used to create various curves like spline, line, circle, and ellipse using selected points/vertices. The procedure to use this tool has been discussed earlier.

PROJECT CURVE

The **Project Curve** tool is used to project edges, curves, and points of other external features/sketches on the current sketching plane. In simple words, if you want to use edges, curves, or points of other sketches of solid/surface features then you can use this tool. The procedure to use this tool is discussed next.

- Click on the **Project Curve** tool from **Derived** group of **Curve** tab in the **Ribbon**. The **Project Curve** dialog box will be displayed; refer to Figure-25.

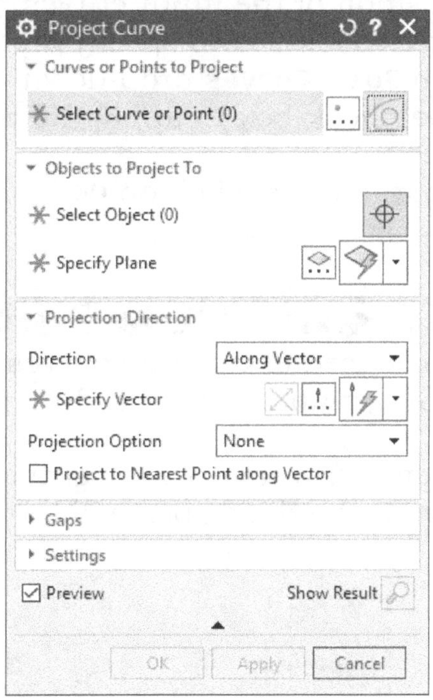

Figure-25. Project Curve dialog box

- Select the curves, edges, faces, points, or vertices to be projected on the sketching plane.
- Click on the **Select Object** button from **Objects to Project To** rollout and select the faces, bodies, or datum planes.
- Click on the **Specify Plane** button and select desired target plane, the **Distance** edit box will be displayed. Specify desired distance in the **Distance** edit box.
- Select desired projection direction from **Direction** drop-down in the **Projection Direction** rollout and specify respective parameters. Preview of the projected edges/points will be displayed; refer to Figure-26.

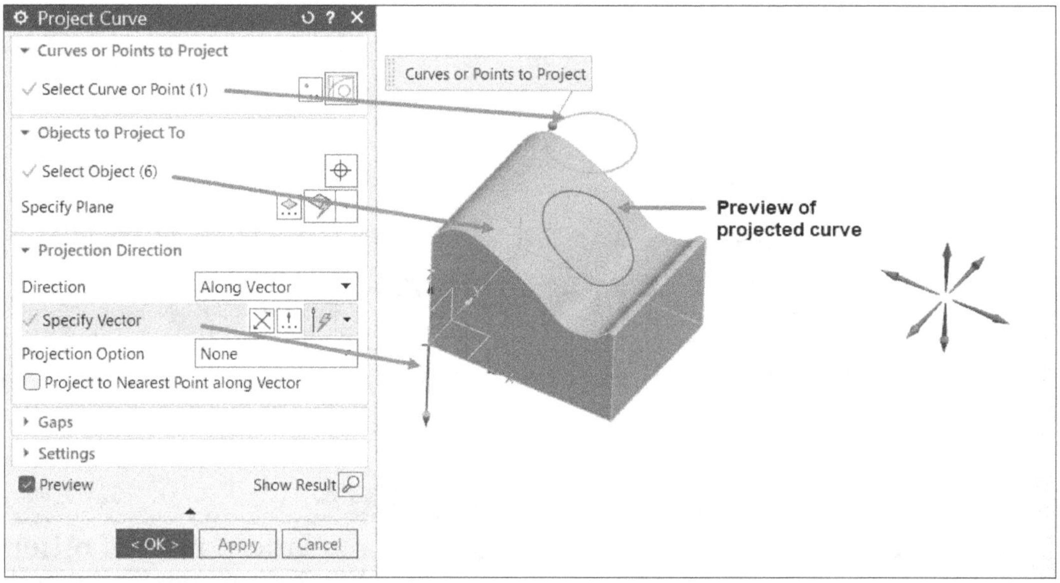

Figure-26. Preview of projected edges

- Select **Create Curves to Bridge Gaps** check box from **Gaps** rollout to join any two segments in projection curves as a single curve.
- Select **Associative** check box from **Settings** rollout to associate created curves of points to the original objects. Select desired option from **Input Curves** drop-down to specify the disposition of the input curves.
- Select **Advanced Curve Fit** check box to specify Method, Degree, and Segments. Select desired option from **Join Curves** drop-down to join the projected curves.
- Select **Align Curve Shape** check box to apply the pole distribution of the input curve to the projected curve.
- After specifying desired parameters, click on **OK** button from the dialog box. The edges will be projected.

INTERSECTION CURVE

The **Intersection Curve** tool is used to generate curves at the intersection of solids/surfaces with current sketching plane. The procedure to use this tool is given next.

- Click on the **Intersection Curve** tool from **Derived** group of **Curve** tab in the **Ribbon**. The **Intersection Curve** dialog box will be displayed; refer to Figure-27.

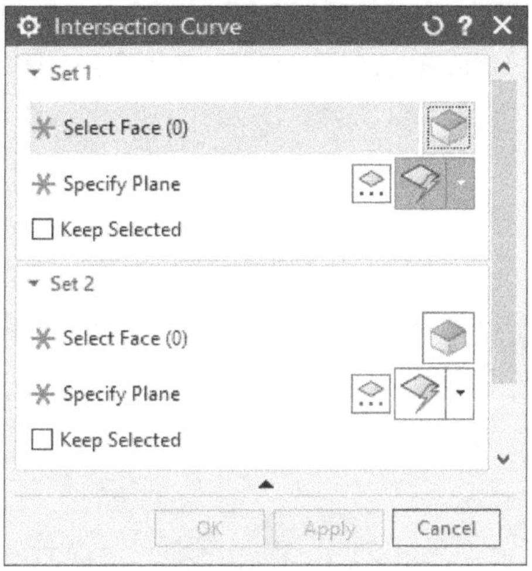

Figure-27. Intersection Curve dialog box

- Select the faces that are to be projected at intersection with sketching plane. Preview of the intersection curves will be displayed; refer to Figure-28.

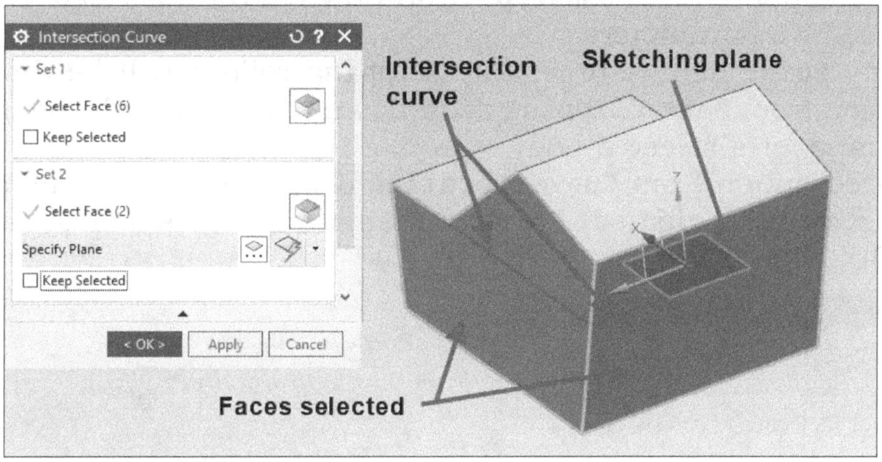

Figure-28. Creating intersection curve

- Click on the **Specify Plane** button from **Set 2** rollout and select a datum plane to include in the set of objects to intersect.
- Select **Keep Selected** check box from **Set 1** or **Set 2** rollout to reuse the selected objects for the sebsequent intersection curve feature.
- Set the other parameters as discussed earlier and click on the **OK** button from the dialog box to create the intersection curves.

SHADOW CURVE

The **Shadow Curve** tool is used to extract silhouette curves from bodies, or to project shadow curves of bodies to other geometry. The procedure to use this tool is discussed next.

- Click on the **Shadow Curve** tool from **Derived** group of **Curve** tab in the **Ribbon**. The **Shadow Curve** dialog box will be displayed; refer to Figure-29.

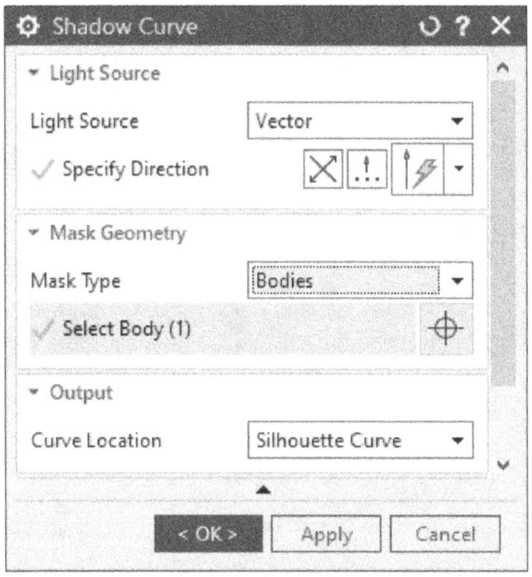

Figure-29. Shadow Curve dialog box

- Select desired option from **Light Source** drop-down in the **Light Source** rollout to define the light source for bodies by specifying a point or a vector.
- Select desired option from **Mask Type** drop-down in the **Mask Geometry** rollout and specify respective parameters.
- On selecting **Point** light source, the **Clipping** rollout will be displayed. Select desired option from **Beam Clipping** drop-down to clip the light beam with a cone, pyramid shape, or a selected body.
- Select desired option from **Curve Location** drop-down to specify the location of shadow curves to be created. Preview of shadow curves will be displayed; refer to Figure-30.

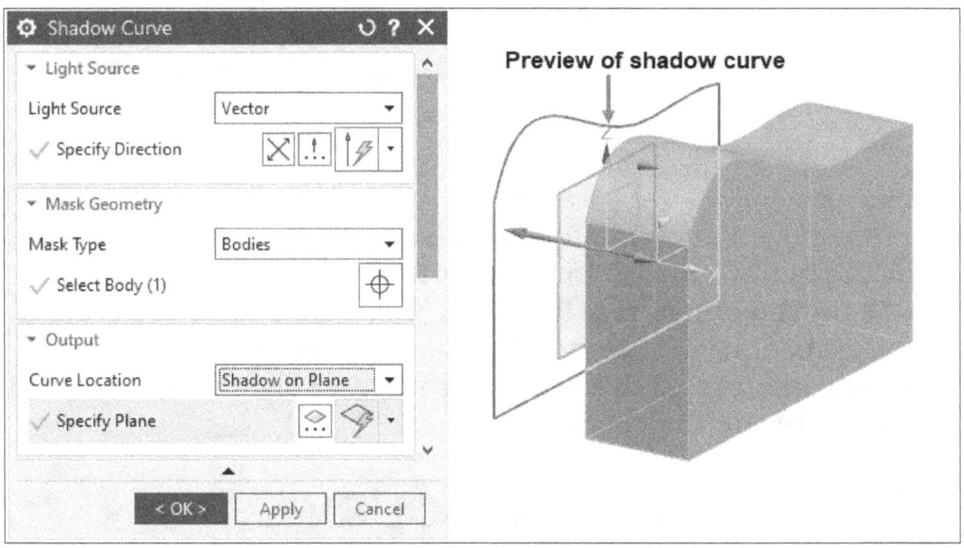

Figure-30. Preview of shadow curve

- Select **Optimize Curve** check box from **Settings** rollout to close gap in the shadow curves. Enter desired value in the **Distance Threshold** edit box to specify the maximum size of the gaps to close. Enter desired value in the **Distance Tolerance** edit box to specify the distance tolerance value different from that of the default value.
- Select **Faster Result** radio button from **Mask Body Processing** area of the **Settings** rollout to generate shadow curves by processing only the bodies that can be seen through the beam. Select **More Precise Result** radio button to generate shadow curves by processing all the selected bodies.

- Set the other parameters as discussed earlier and click on the **OK** button from the dialog box to create the shadow curves.

OFFSET CURVE

The **Offset Curve** tool is used to create curves at a specified distance from existing lines, arcs, conics, splines, and edges. The procedure to use this tool is discussed next.

- Click on the **Offset Curve** tool from **Derived** group in the **Curve** tab of the **Ribbon**. The **Offset Curve** dialog box will be displayed; refer to Figure-31.

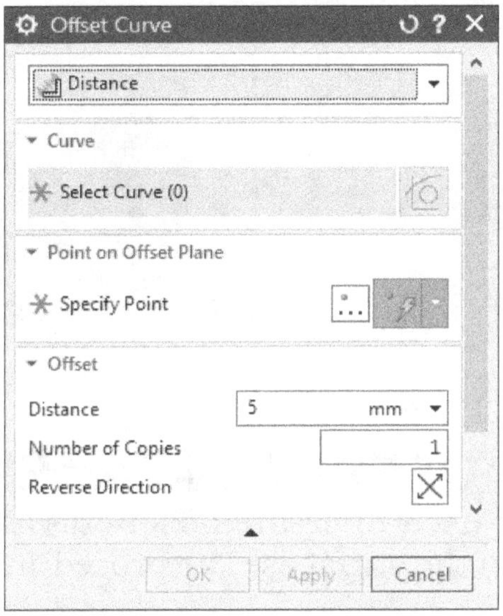

Figure-31. Offset Curve dialog box

- Select desired type of offset curve from drop-down in the top of the dialog box and specify respective parameters. Select **Distance** option from the drop-down to offset the curve in the plane of the selected curve at a desired constant distance. Select **Draft** option from the drop-down to offset the curve at a desired angle to the plane of the selected curve at a desired constant distance. Select **Law Control** option from the drop-down to offset the curve using law (expressions and equation) as discussed earlier. Select **3D Axial** option to offset the curve in selected vector direction at desired constant distance.
- Set the other parameters in the dialog box as discussed earlier. The preview of offset curve will be displayed; refer to Figure-32.
- Click on **OK** button from the dialog box to create the curve.

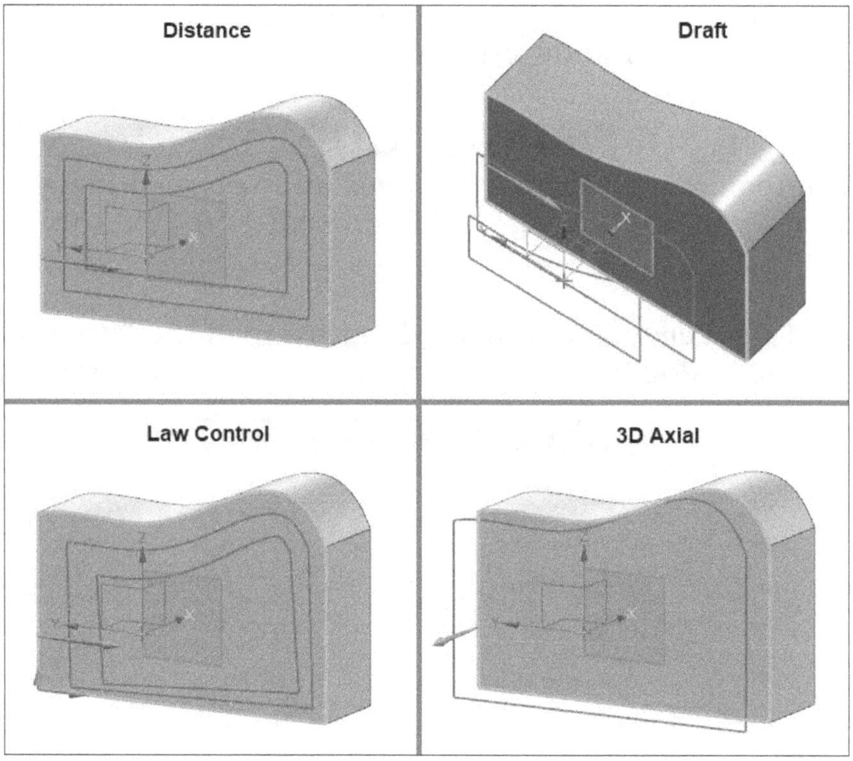

Figure-32. Preview of offset curves

OFFSET IN FACE

The **Offset in Face** tool is used to create offset curves on one or more faces from connected edges or curves on the surfaces. The procedure to use this tool is discussed next.

- Click on the **Offset in Face** tool from **Derived** group in the **Curve** tab of the **Ribbon**. The **Offset Curve in Face** dialog box will be displayed; refer to Figure-33.

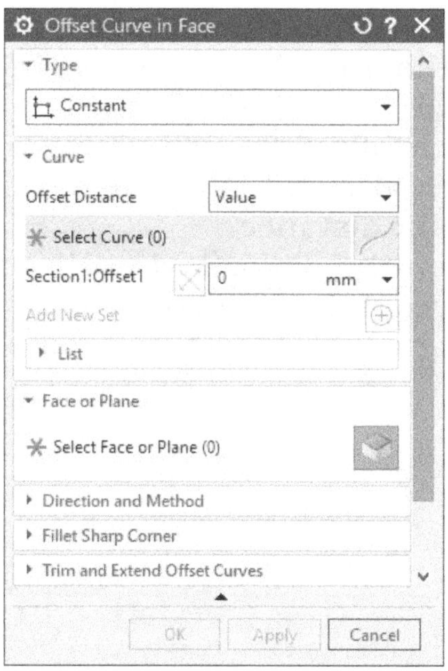

Figure-33. Offset Curve in Face dialog box

- Select desired type of offset curve from **Type** drop-down. Select **Constant** option to create a curve with a constant offset from the selected in-face curve. Select

Variable option to create a variable curve by specifying different distances from point locations on the selected curve.

- Select **Value** option from **Offset Distance** drop-down of **Curve** rollout and specify desired value for the offset distance. Select **Through Point** option from the drop-down and select a point on the surface to specify the offset distance.
- Select desired curve or edge to be offset on the specified face; refer to Figure-34.

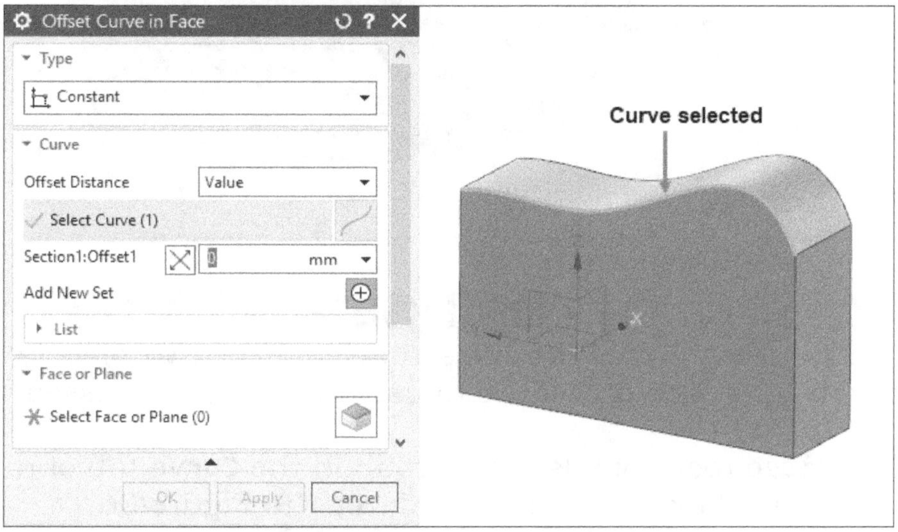

Figure-34. Curve selected to be offset

- Specify desired offset value in the **Offset** edit box.
- Click on the **Add New Set** button to add new offset section.
- Click on the **Select Face or Plane** button from **Face or Plane** rollout and select faces and planes on which the offset curve to be created.
- Select **Normal to Curve** option from the **Offset Direction** drop-down of **Direction and Method** rollout to create the offset curve along the direction which is perpendicular to the selected curve. Select **Normal to Vector** option from the drop-down and specify a vector that determine the perpendicular direction of the offset.
- Select desired option from **Offset Method** drop-down to define the measurement method to measure the offset distance.
- Select desired option from **Fillet** drop-down of **Fillet Sharp Corner** rollout to smoothen the offset curve sharp corners.
- Select **Trim to Each Other within Section** check box from **Trim and Extend Offset Curves** rollout to trim the corners between two curves within the same section. Select **Extend to Each Other within Section** check box to extend the corners between two curves within the same section. Select **Trim to Face Edges** check box to trim the offset curves to the face edges. Select **Extend to Face Edges** check box to extend the offset curves to the face edges. Select **Remove Self-Intersections within Offset Curve** check box to trim the intersection areas of the offset curve.
- On selecting the **Infer Body Faces from Curve** check box from **Settings** rollout, the offset body faces are determined by the curves selected to be offset. Select **Split Curve at Face Boundary** check box to split the output offset curve into separate curve segments. Specify desired value in the **Tolerance** edit box to define the accuracy of the offset curve.
- Set the other parameters in the dialog box as discussed earlier and click on **OK** button from the dialog box. The offset curve in face will be created; refer to Figure-35.

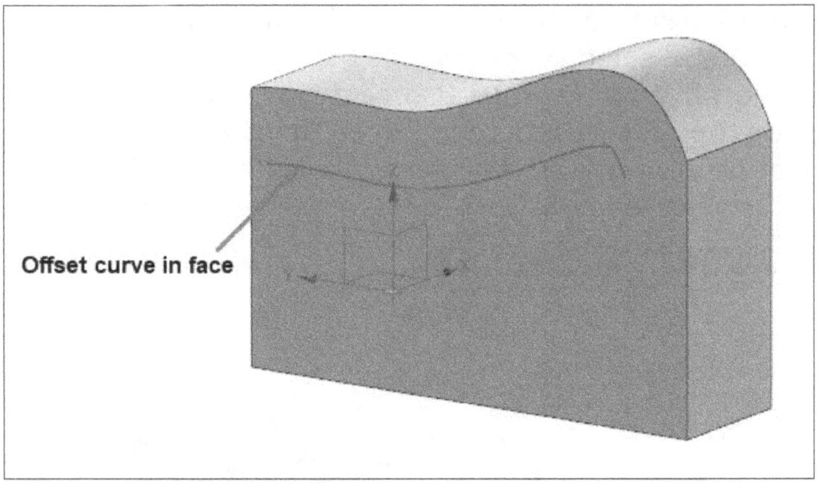

Figure-35. Offset curve in face created

BRIDGE

The **Bridge** tool is used to create curves that connect two objects with optional smoothness constraints. The procedure to use this tool is discussed next.

- Click on the **Bridge** tool from **Derived** group in the **Curve** tab of the **Ribbon**. The **Bridge Curve** dialog box will be displayed; refer to Figure-36.

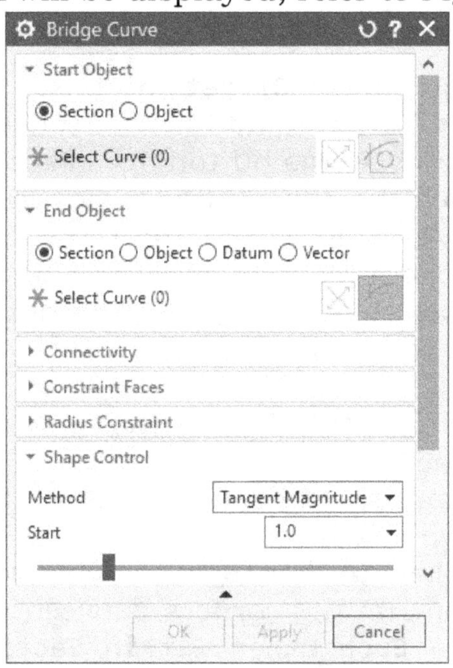

Figure-36. Bridge Curve dialog box

- Select **Section** radio button from **Start Object** rollout and select desired curve or edge to define the start of the curve. Select **Object** radio button and select desired face or point to define the start of the curve.
- Select **Datum** radio button from **End Object** rollout and select a datum for the end of the curve. Select **Vector** radio button and select a vector to define the end of the curve. Figure-37 shows edge selected for start and end curves (**Section** radio button selected for both).
- Click on the **Reverse Direction** button to reverse the direction of the selected end section.

- Click on the **Start** and **End** tab from **Connectivity** rollout and specify desired parameters for **Continuity**, **Position**, and **Direction** options for the start and end points of a bridge curve.
- Click on the **Select Face** option from **Constraint Faces** rollout and select constraint faces for the bridge curve.
- Select desired option from **Method** drop-down of **Radius Constraint** rollout and specify the minimum or peak constraint values for complex transitions.
- Specify desired option from **Method** drop-down of **Shape Control** rollout to reshape the bridge curve. Select **Tangent Magnitude** option and specify desired value in the **Start** and **End** edit boxes to specify the tangency of bridge curve. Select **Depth and Skew** option and specify desired values in the **Depth** and **Skew** edit boxes to control the curvature of curve and location of the maximum curvature, respectively.
- Select **Use Nearest Point on Section** check box from **Settings** rollout to specify the start and end object position points of the bridge curve on the nearest points on the paths.
- Select **Rate** check box from **Microposition** rollout and specify desired value by dragging the slider for the fine curve point editing. Lower value produces finer point movement.
- Set the other parameters in the dialog box as discussed earlier and click on **OK** button from the dialog box. The bridge curve will be created; refer to Figure-37.

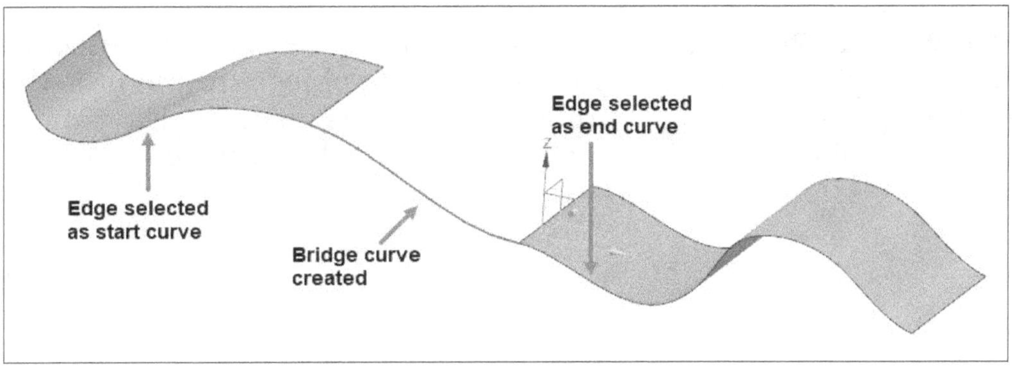

Figure-37. Bridge curve created

COMPOSITE

The **Composite Curve** tool is used to extract curves and edges from the work part. The procedure to use this tool is discussed next.

- Click on the **Composite tool** from **Derived** group in the **Curve** tab of the **Ribbon**. The **Composite Curve** dialog box will be displayed; refer to Figure-38.

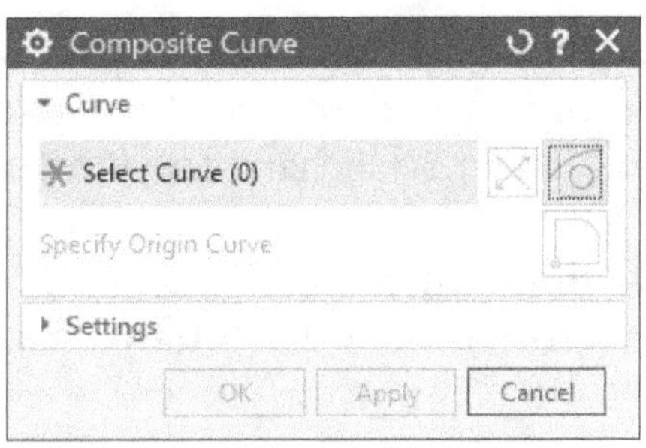

Figure-38. Composite Curve dialog box

- Select desired curves or edges to be copied; refer to Figure-39.

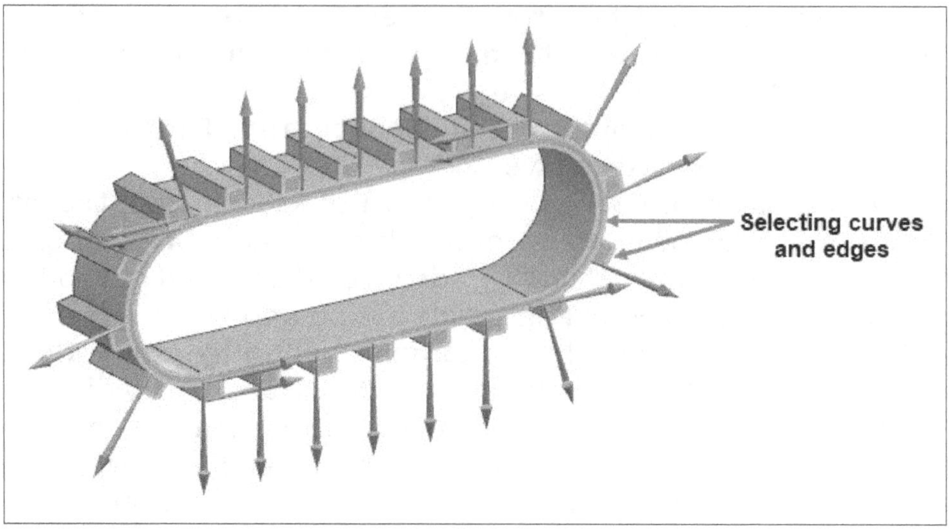

Figure-39. Curves and edges selected

- Click on the **Specify Origin Curve** button from **Curve** rollout to specify the origin curve from the set of curves.
- Select **Hide Original** check box from **Settings** rollout to hide the original curve when the composite feature is created.
- Select **Allow Self-intersection** check box to allow the selection of self-intersecting curves.
- Select **Use Display Properties of Parent Object** check box to reflect the changes made to the display properties of the composite objects to the linked objects.
- Set the other parameters in the dialog box as discussed earlier and click on **OK** button from the dialog box. The composite curve will be created; refer to Figure-40.

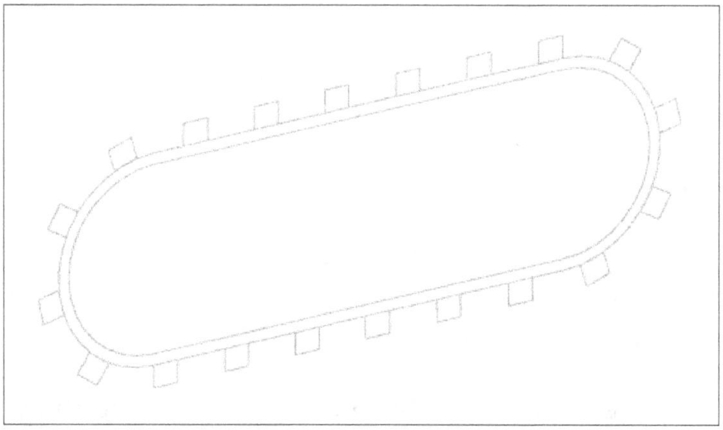

Figure-40. Composite curve created

CIRCULAR BLEND CURVE

The **Circular Blend Curve** tool is used to create a smooth blended curve between two 3D curves or edge chains. The procedure to use this tool is discussed next.

- Click on the **Circular Blend Curve** tool from **More** drop-down in the **Derived** group of **Curve** tab in the **Ribbon**. The **Circular Blend Curve** dialog box will be displayed; refer to Figure-41.

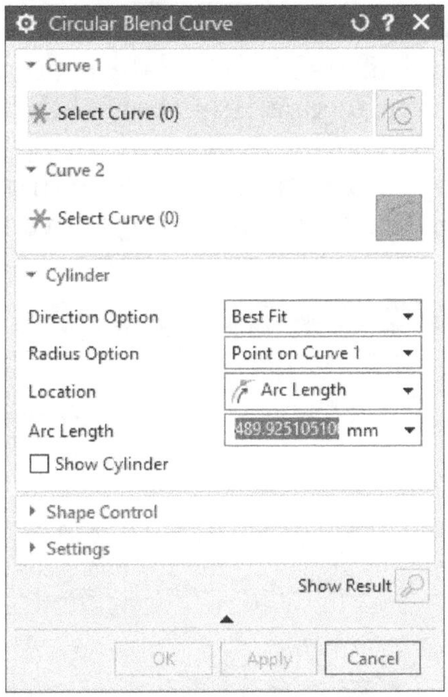

Figure-41. Circular Blend Curve dialog box

- Select the first and second chain of curves of which the circular blend curve to be created.
- Select desired option from **Direction Option** drop-down of **Cylinder** rollout to specify the direction of the cylinder axis. Select desired option from **Radius Option** drop-down to specify the value for the cylinder radius. Select desired option from **Location** drop-down to specify the location of the point of contact. Enter desired value in the **Arc Length** edit box to specify a distance along the arc length as the point of contact. Select **Show Cylinder** check box to show the cylinder that is used to create the circular blend curve.
- Specify desired value in the **Curve 1** and **Curve 2** edit boxes of **Shape Control** rollout to control the curvature of the circular blend curve and its deviation.
- Click on the **Complement Arc** button from **Settings** rollout to create a circular blend curve that is the complement of the existing arc.
- Set the other parameters in the dialog box as discussed earlier and click on the **OK** button. The circular blend curve will be created; refer to Figure-42.

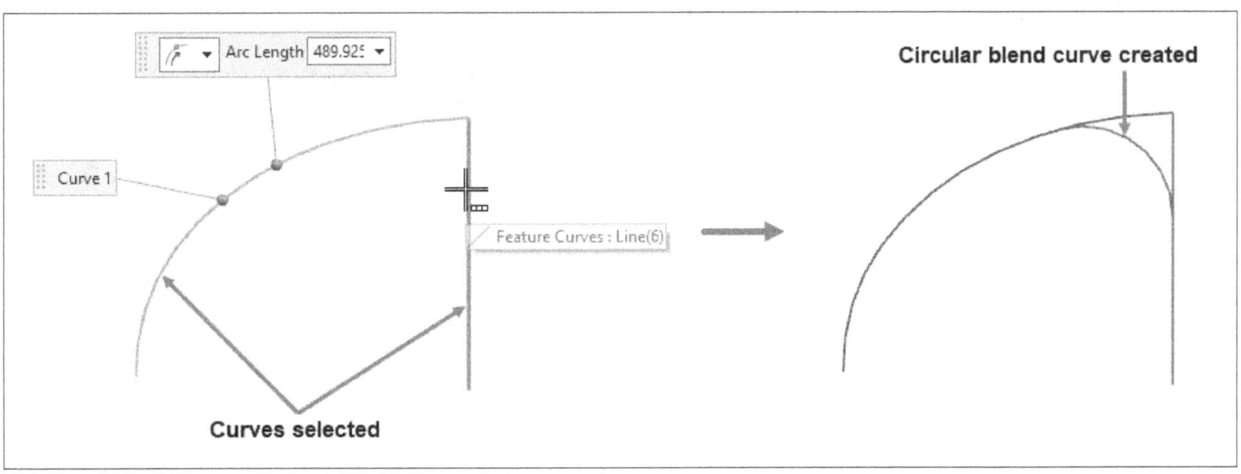

Figure-42. Circular blend curve created

COMBINED PROJECTION

The **Combined Projection** tool is used to create a curve at the intersection of two projected curves. The procedure to use this tool is discussed next.

- Click on the **Combined Projection** tool from **More** drop-down in the **Derived** group of **Curve** tab in the **Ribbon**. The **Combined Projection** dialog box will be displayed; refer to Figure-43.

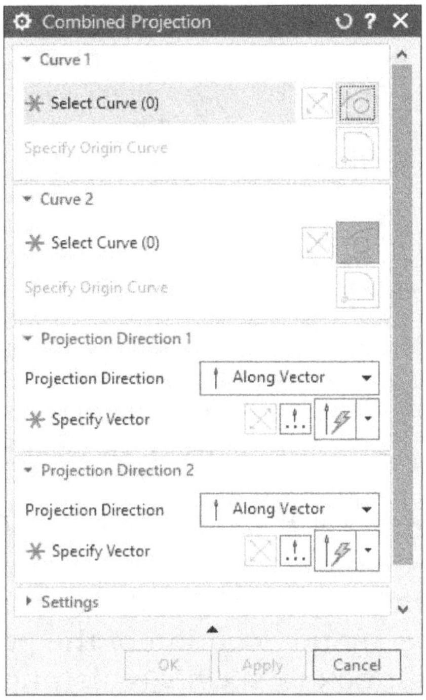

Figure-43. Combined Projection dialog box

- Select the first and second chain of curves of which the curve to be projected.
- Click on the **Specify Origin Curve** button to specify the origin curve from the set of curves.
- Select desired option from **Projection Direction** drop-downs and specify the respective parameters to specify the direction for the first and second chain of selected curves.
- Set the other parameters in the dialog box as discussed earlier and click on the **OK** button. The combined projection curve will be created; refer to Figure-44.

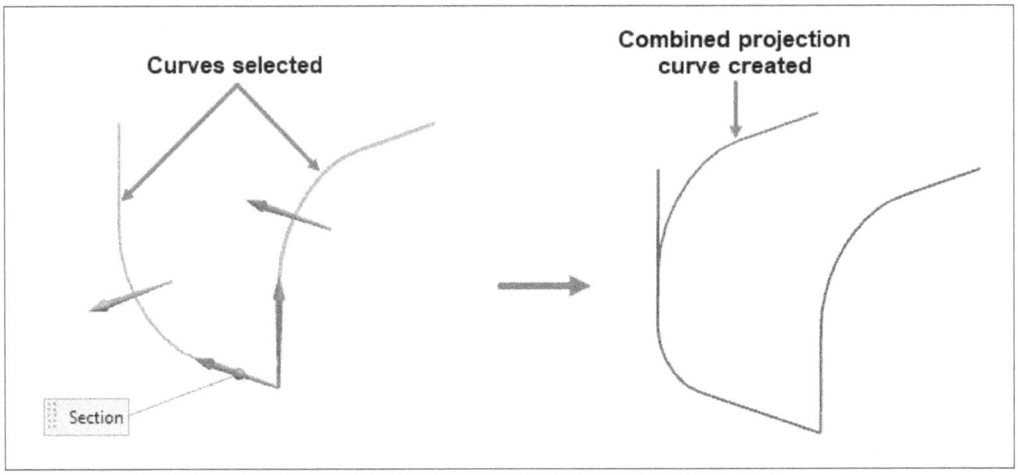

Figure-44. Combined projection curve created

WRAP/UNWRAP CURVE

The **Wrap or Unwrap Curve** tool is used to wrap any set of curves or points from a plane on to the faces, such as a cylinders, cones, or ruled surfaces and vice-versa. The procedure to use this tool is discussed next.

- Click on the **Wrap/Unwrap Curve** tool from **More** drop-down in the **Derived** group of **Curve** tab in the **Ribbon**. The **Wrap/Unwrap Curve** dialog box will be displayed; refer to Figure-45.

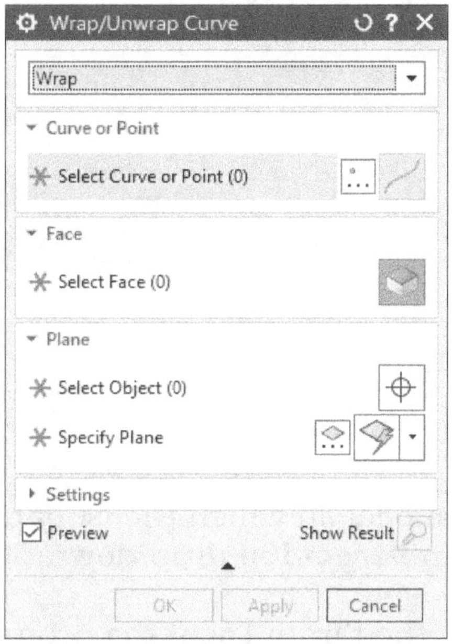

Figure-45. Wrap Unwrap Curve dialog box

- Select the **Wrap** or **Unwrap** option from drop-down in the dialog box. In our case, we selected the **Wrap** option.
- Select desired curves or points from the workplane to be wrapped.
- Click on the **Select Face** button from **Face** rollout and select desired conical, cylindrical, or developable face on which curves or points to be wrapped.
- Click on the **Select Object** button from **Plane** rollout and select a datum plane or face tangent to the conical, cylindrical, or developable face.
- Click on the **Specify Plane** button and select a plane as the wrap or unwrap plane.
- Set the other parameters in the dialog box as discussed earlier and click on the **OK** button. The curve will be wrapped; refer to Figure-46.

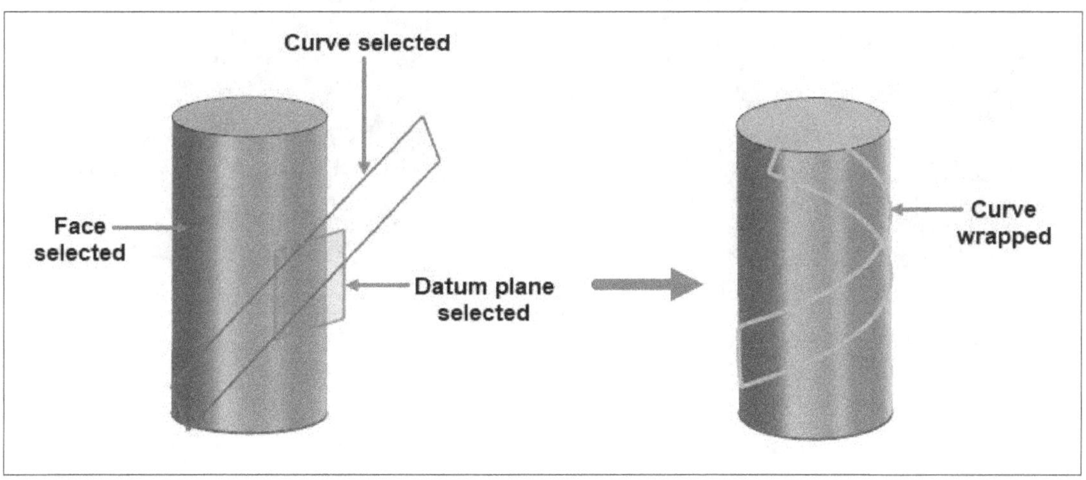

Figure-46. Curve wrapped on the face

ISOPARAMETRIC CURVE

The **Isoparametric Curve** tool is used to generate curves on a face along given U/V lines of direction. The procedure to use this tool is discussed next.

- Click on the **Isoparametric Curve** tool from **More** drop-down in the **Derived** group of **Curve** tab in the **Ribbon**. The **Isoparametric Curve** dialog box will be displayed; refer to Figure-47.

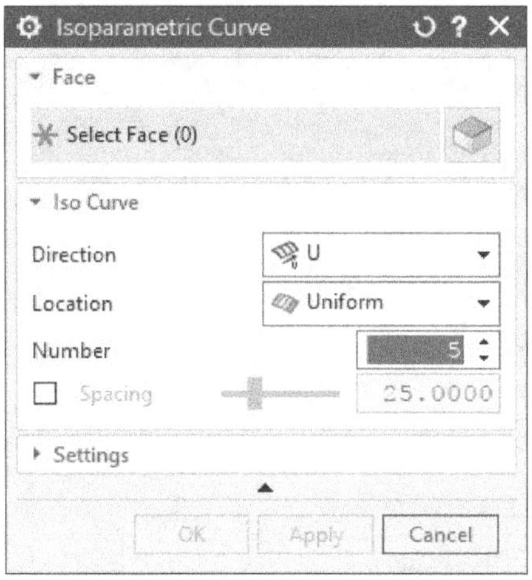

Figure-47. Isoparametric Curve dialog box

- Select desired face of the model on which the isoparametric curves to be created.
- Select desired option from **Direction** drop-down of **Iso Curve** rollout to create isoparametric curves.
- Select desired location method from **Location** drop-down to place isoparametric curves on the selected face.
- Specify desired number of isoparametric curves in the **Number** edit box to create.
- Select **Spacing** check box and specify desired constant distance value between each isoparametric curve.
- Set the other parameters in the dialog box as discussed earlier and click on the **OK** button. The isoparametric curve will be created; refer to Figure-48.

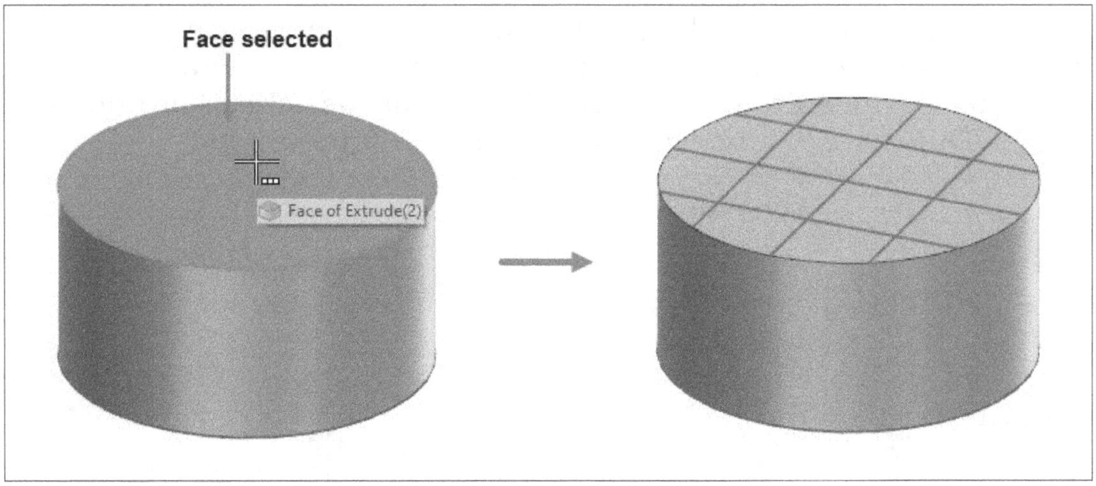

Figure-48. Isoparametric curve created

ISOCLINE CURVE

The **Isocline Curve** is used to create curves at an angle that is constant to surface relative to a reference direction. The procedure to use this tool is discussed next.

- Click on the **Isocline Curve** tool from **More** drop-down in the **Derived** group of **Curve** tab in the **Ribbon**. The **Isocline Curve** dialog box will be displayed; refer to Figure-49.

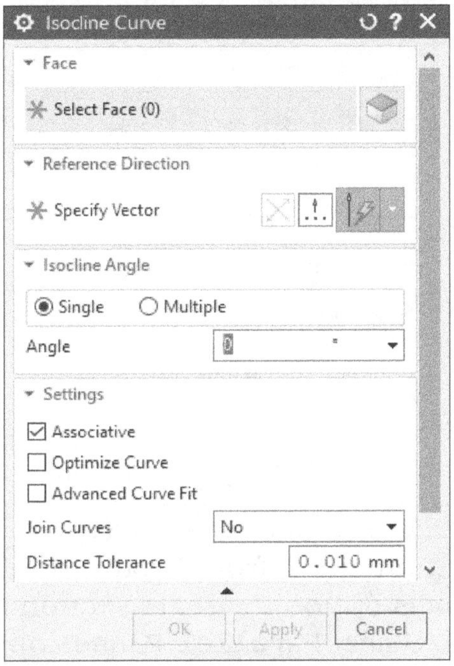

Figure-49. Isocline Curve dialog box

- Select desired face on which the isocline curve is to be created.
- Click on the **Specify Vector** button from **Reference Direction** rollout and select the vector from which the angle is measured to calculate the isocline curves.
- Select **Single** or **Multiple** radio button from **Isocline Angle** rollout and specify the respective parameters to create single or multiple curves, respectively.
- Select **Optimize Curve** check box from **Settings** rollout to optimize the curve by closing gaps within the specified distance.
- Set the other parameters in the dialog box as discussed earlier and click on the **OK** button. The isocline curve will be created; refer to Figure-50.

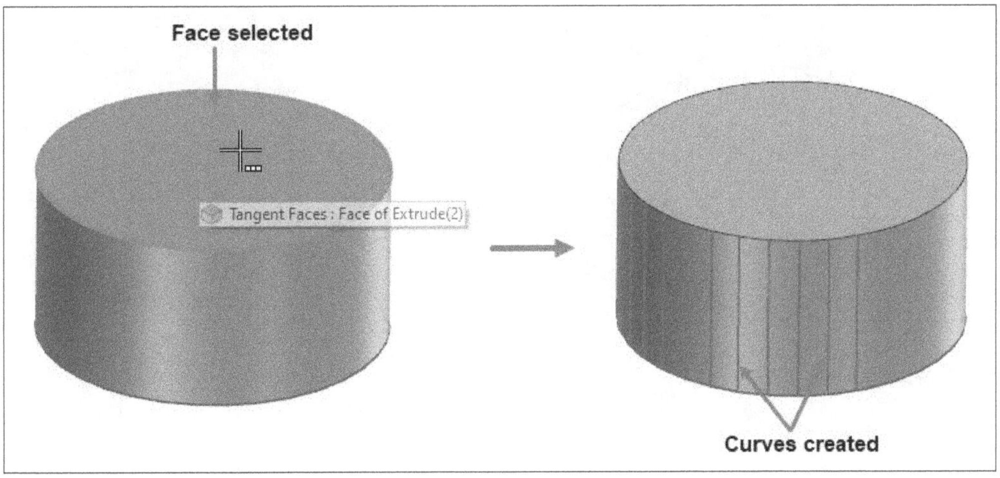

Figure-50. Isocline curve created

SECTION CURVE

The **Section Curve** tool is used to create intersection geometry between specified planes and bodies, faces, or curves. The procedure to use this tool is discussed next.

- Click on the **Section Curve** tool from **More** drop-down in the **Derived** group of **Curve** tab in the **Ribbon**. The **Section Curve** dialog box will be displayed; refer to Figure-51.

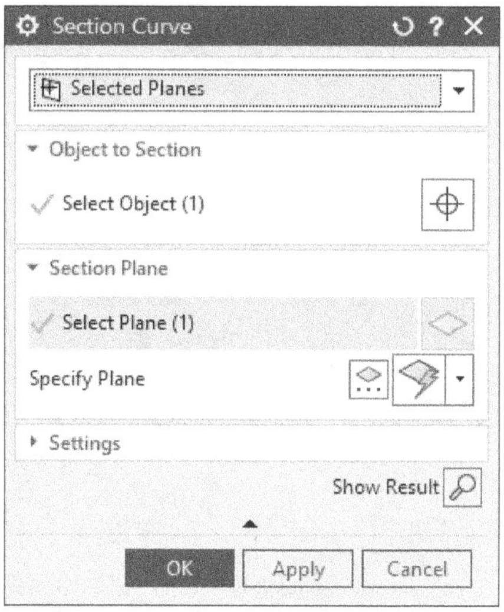

Figure-51. Section Curve dialog box

- Select desired type of section curve from **Type** drop-down in the top of the dialog box. Select **Selected Planes** option to create section curves using existing planes or by defining the planes. Select **Parallel Planes** option to create section curves using series of parallel planes. Select **Radial Planes** option to create section curves using specified planes that extend from a specified axis.
- Select desired object to be sectioned like solid, sheet, curves, faces, or planes.
- Click on the **Select Plane** button from **Section Plane** rollout and select an existing or defined plane(s).
- Set the other parameters in the dialog box as discussed earlier and click on the **OK** button. The section curve will be created; refer to Figure-52.

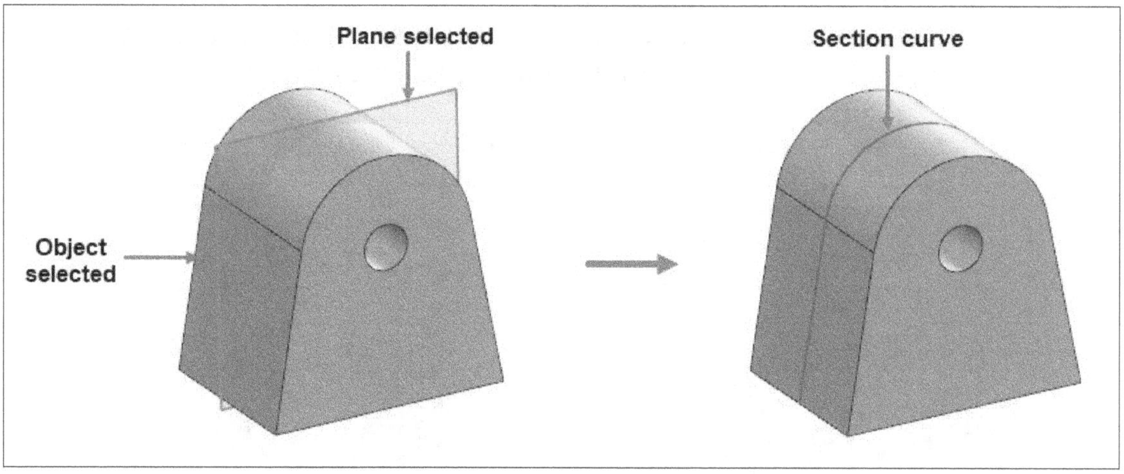

Figure-52. Section curve created

EXTRACT VIRTUAL CURVE

The **Extract Virtual Curve** tool is used to create curves from face rotation axes, blend centerlines, and virtual intersections of blend faces. The procedure to use this tool is discussed next.

- Click on the **Extract Virtual Curve** tool from **More** drop-down in the **Derived** group of **Curve** tab in the **Ribbon**. The **Extract Virtual Curve** dialog box will be displayed; refer to Figure-53.

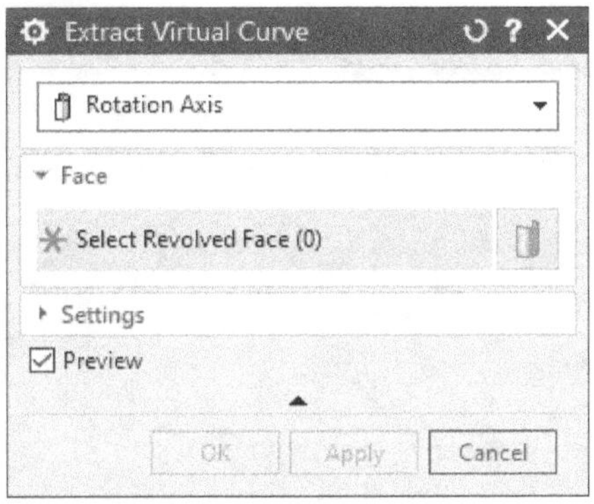

Figure-53. Extract Virtual Curve dialog box

- Select desired type of virtual curve to be created from **Type** drop-down in the top of the dialog box. Select **Rotation Axis** option to extract the axis of a cylindrical, conical, toroidal, or revolved face to construct a rotation axis virtual curve. Select **Blend Centerline** option to extract the centerline of a blend face to construct a virtual centerline curve. Select **Virtual Intersection** option to extract the virtual intersection of the surfaces of the two construction faces of the input blend face to create a virtual intersection curve. Select **Tube Centerline** option to extract a new centerline curve feature or reconstruct a missing centerline curve feature using a circular body, or a sheet shaped body like a tube or a hose.
- Select desired face(s) to extract the virtual face.
- Set the other parameters in the dialog box as discussed earlier and click on **OK** button. The virtual curve will be created; refer to Figure-54.

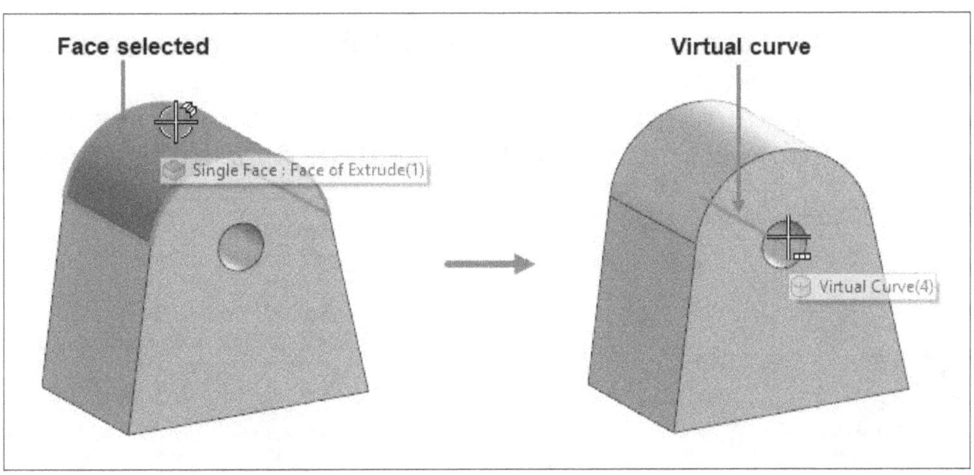

Figure-54. Virtual curve created

REVOLVE OUTLINE

The **Revolve Outline** tool is used to create outlines of one or more bodies. The outlines are created for specified spin axis and you can save them as curve feature. The procedure to use this tool is discussed next.

- Click on the **Revolve Outline** tool from **More** drop-down in the **Derived** group of **Curve** tab in the **Ribbon**. The **Revolve Outline** dialog box will be displayed; refer to Figure-55.

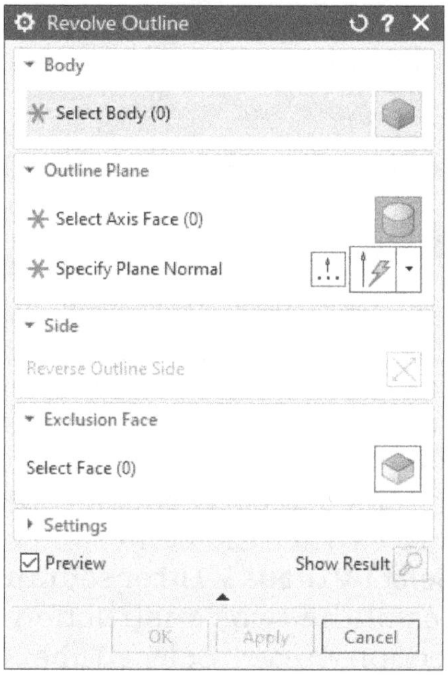

Figure-55. Revolve Outline dialog box

- Select desired body of which the revolve outline to be created. On selecting the body, the face and plane will be automatically selected and the preview of outline will be displayed.
- Click on the **Reverse Outline Side** button from **Side** rollout to create outline on the other side.
- Click on the **Select Face** button from **Exclusion Face** rollout and select the face to be excluded from the outline.
- Set the other parameters in the dialog box as discussed earlier and click on the **OK** button. The outline of the body will be created; refer to Figure-56.

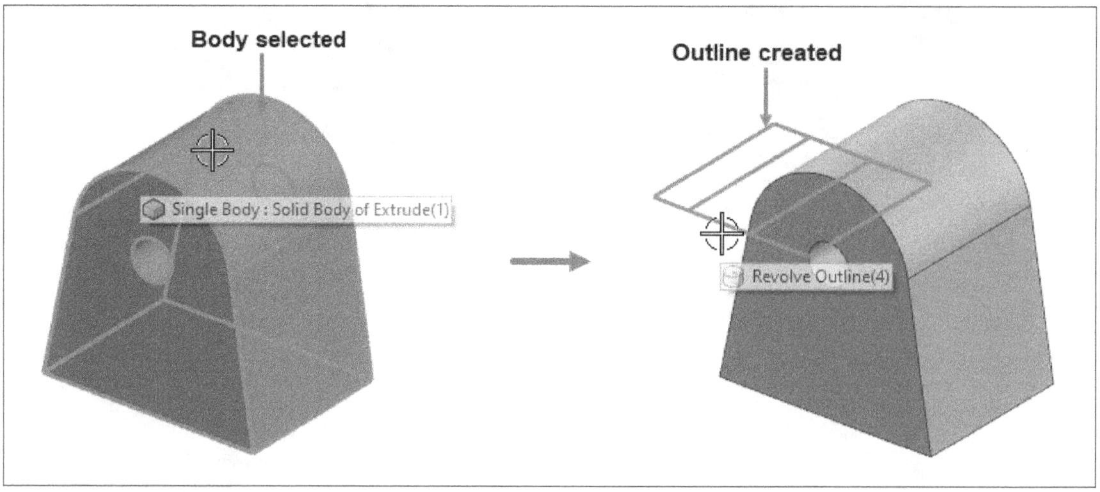

Figure-56. Revolve outline created

MIRROR CURVE

The **Mirror Curve** tool is used to create mirror curve features across a datum plane or planar surface. The procedure to use this tool is discussed next.

- Click on the **Mirror Curve** tool from **More** drop-down in the **Derived** group of **Curve** tab in the **Ribbon**. The **Mirror Curve** dialog box will be displayed; refer to Figure-57.

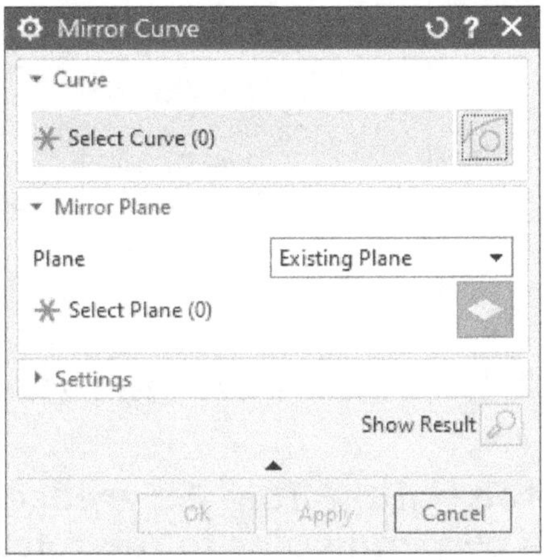

Figure-57. Mirror Curve dialog box

- Select desired curve, edges, or curve features of sketches to be mirrored.
- Select desired option from **Plane** drop-down of **Mirror Plane** rollout and select desired planar face or datum plane across which the selected curves or edges to be mirrored.
- Set the other parameters in the dialog box as discussed earlier and click on the **OK** button. The mirror curve will be created; refer to Figure-58.

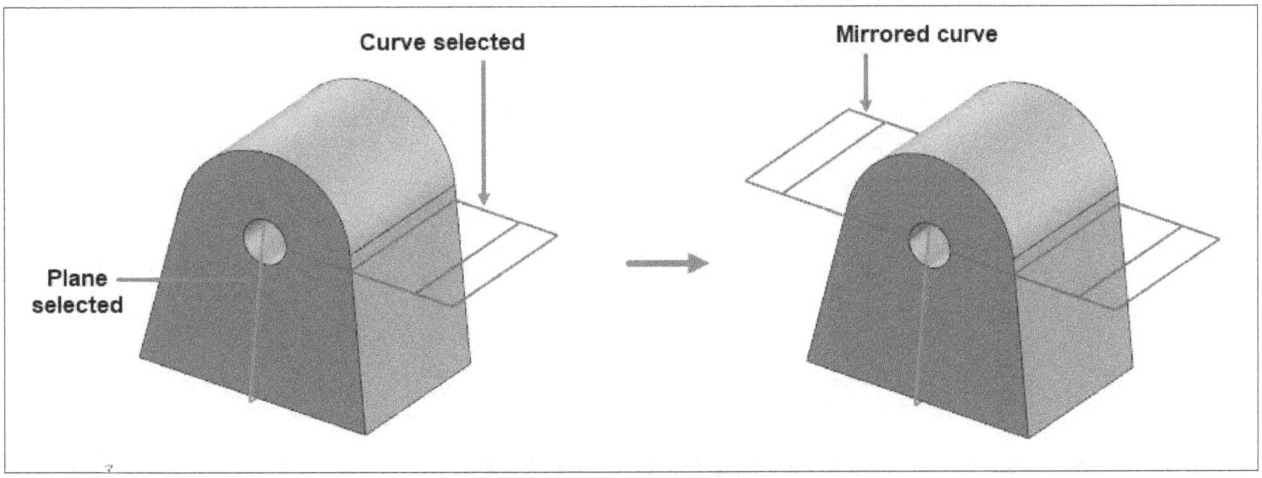

Figure-58. Mirror curve created

OFFSET 3D CURVE

The **Offset 3D Curve** tool is used to offset three dimensional curves or edges by a specified distance in the direction perpendicular to the specified direction. The procedure to use this tool is discussed next.

- Click on the **Offset 3D Curve** tool from **More** drop-down in the **Derived** group of **Curve** tab in the **Ribbon**. The **Offset 3D Curve** dialog box will be displayed; refer to Figure-59.

- Select desired 3D curves or edges to be offset; refer to Figure-60.

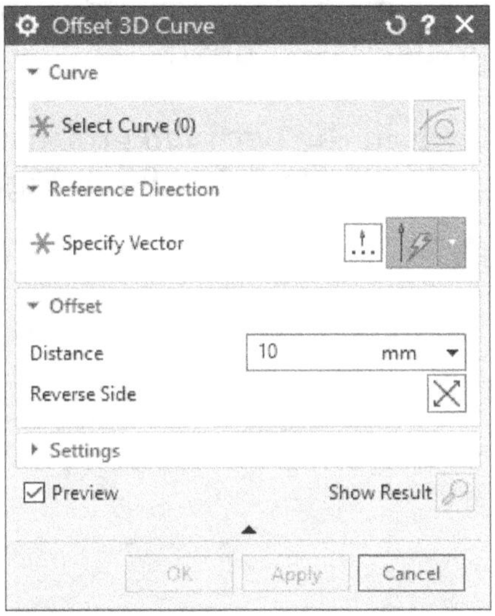

Figure-59. Offset 3D Curve dialog box

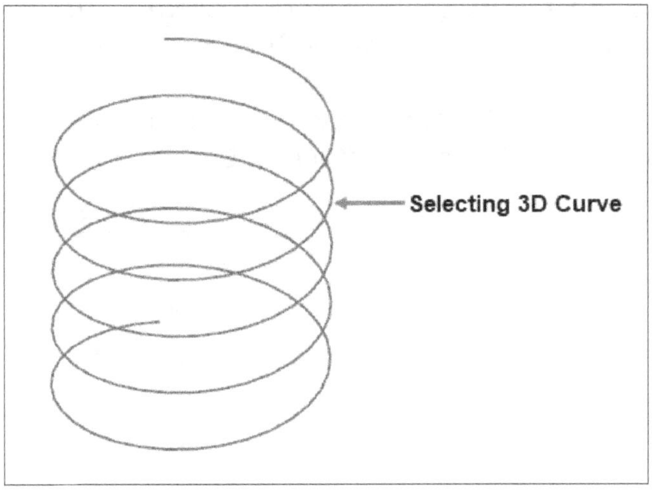

Figure-60. Selecting 3D Curve

- Click on the **Specify Vector** button from **Reference Direction** rollout to specify the offset direction that is perpendicular to the reference direction.
- Specify desired value in the **Distance** edit box of **Offset** rollout to specify the distance to offset the selected curves in the specified direction.
- Click on the **Reverse Side** button to reverse the direction of the 3D offset curve.
- Set the other parameters in the dialog box as discussed earlier and click on the **OK** button. The offset of 3D curve will be created; refer to Figure-61.

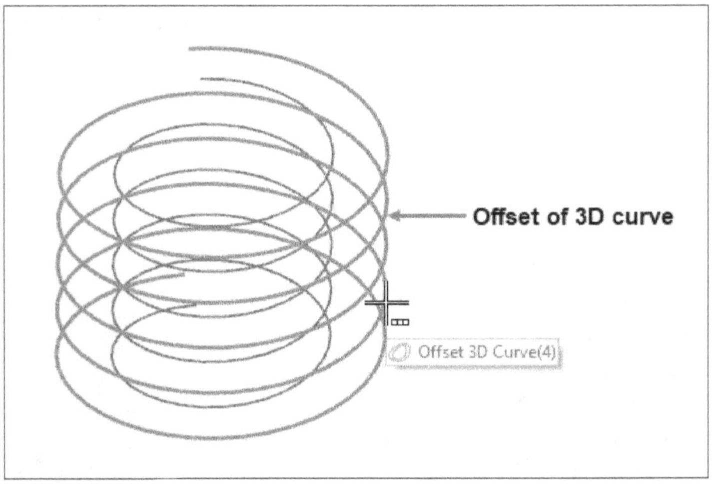

Figure-61. Offset of 3D curve created

SCALE CURVE

The **Scale Curve** tool is used to scale curves, edges, points, or sketches to scale uniformly or non-uniformly. The procedure to use this tool is discussed next.

- Click on the **Scale Curve** tool from **More** drop-down in the **Derived** group of **Curve** tab in the **Ribbon**. The **Scale Curve** dialog box will be displayed; refer to Figure-62.

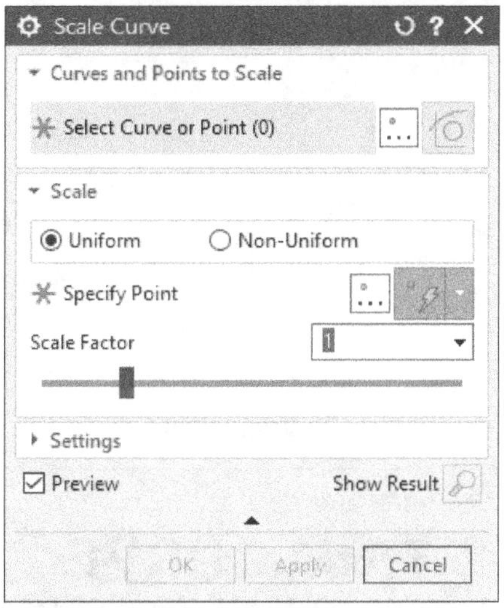

Figure-62. Scale Curve dialog box

- Select desired curve or point to be scaled.
- Select the **Uniform** radio button from **Scale** rollout to scale the curve in all directions. Click on the **Specify Point** button and select desired point to specify origin point of the scale. Specify desired scaling size of the curve in the **Scale Factor** edit box or by using the slider. The preview of scaled curve will be displayed; refer to Figure-63.

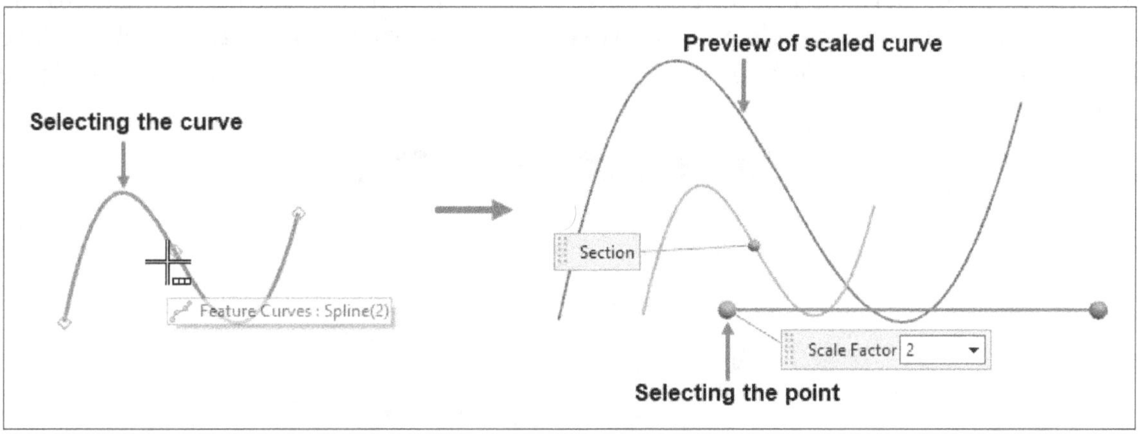

Figure-63. Preview of scaled curve

- Select the **Non-Uniform** radio button from **Scale** rollout to scale the curve in x, y, and z directions, separately. Click on the **Specify CSYS** button and select the reference coordinate system to scale the curve. Specify desired value in the **X Scale**, **Y Scale**, or **Z Scale** edit boxes to scale the curve in x, y, or z directions, respectively.
- Set the other parameters in the dialog box as discussed earlier and click on the **OK** button. The curve will be scaled; refer to Figure-64.

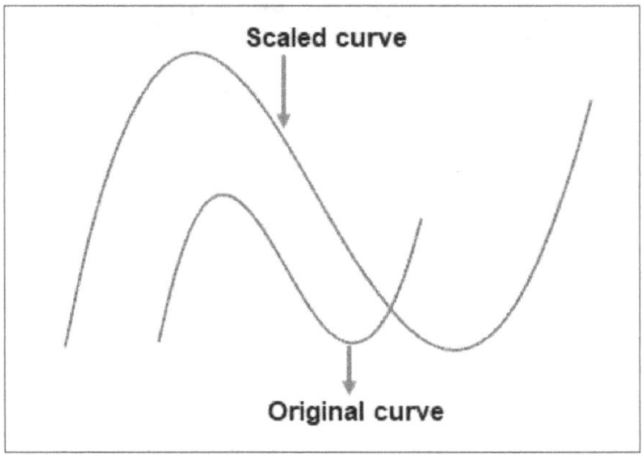

Figure-64. Curve scaled

TRIM CURVE

The **Trim Curve** tool is used to trim, extend, or divide curves. The procedure to use this tool is discussed next.

- Click on the **Trim Curve** tool from **Edit** group of **Curve** tab in the **Ribbon**. The **Trim Curve** dialog box will be displayed; refer to Figure-65.
- Select desired curve to be trimmed, extended, or divided.
- Select **Selected Object** option from **Object Type** drop-down and select curves, edges, bodies, faces, and points to be used as bounding object. Select **Plane** option from the drop-down and select datum plane to be used as bounding object. The bounding objects will be displayed in the **List** rollout of **Bounding Object** rollout. Click on the **Add New Set** button to add a new set of bounding object; refer to Figure-66.

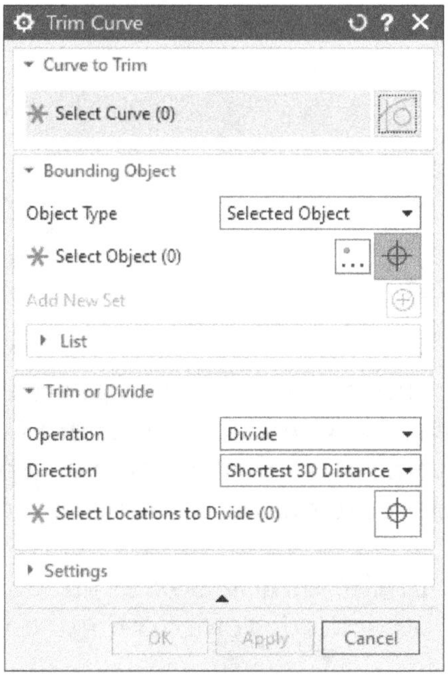

Figure-65. Trim Curve dialog box

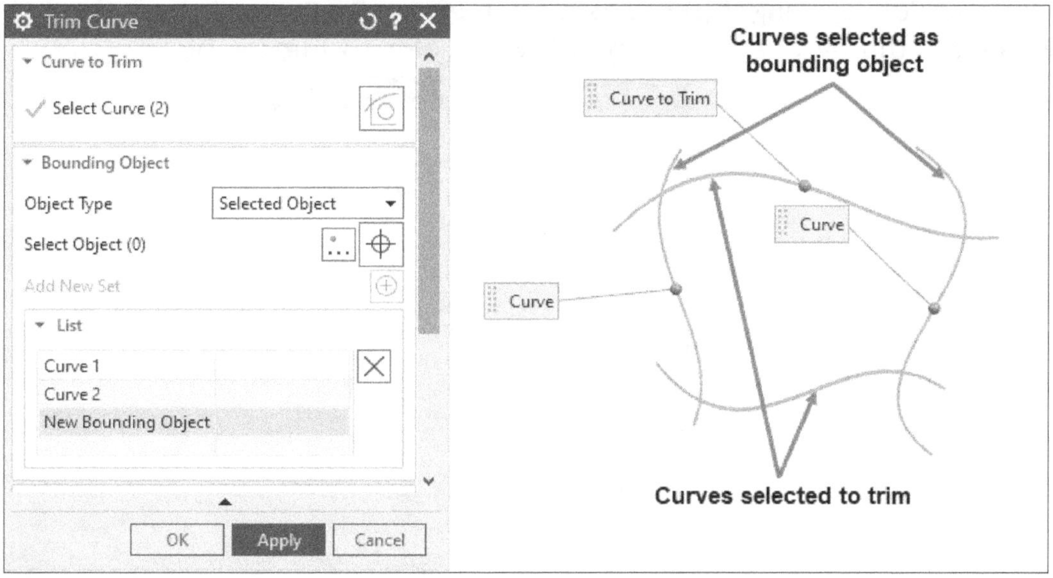

Figure-66. Curves selected to trim

- Select **Trim** or **Divide** option from **Operation** drop-down of **Trim** or **Divide** rollout to trim or divide the selected curve, respectively. Select desired option from **Direction** drop-down to specify the vector direction for trimming the curve. Select **Keep** or **Discard** radio button to keep or discard the selected curve for trimming after the trimming operation.
- Select the **Associative** check box from **Settings** rollout to create a trim curve feature as a trimmed copy of the original curve. Select desired option from **Input Curves** drop-down to keep, hide, delete, or replace the input curves. Select **Make Input Curves Dashed** check box to create the input curves dashed after the trim operation. Select desired extension method of selected curve from **Curve Extension** drop-down. Select **Trim Bounding Curves** check box to trim and divide the bounding curves. Select **Extended Intersection Calculation** check box to allow intersection calculation that exceed the default distance tolerance. Select **Single Selection** check box to enable automatic selection of curves.
- After specifying desired parameters in the dialog box, click on **OK** button from the dialog box. The curve will be trimmed; refer to Figure-67.

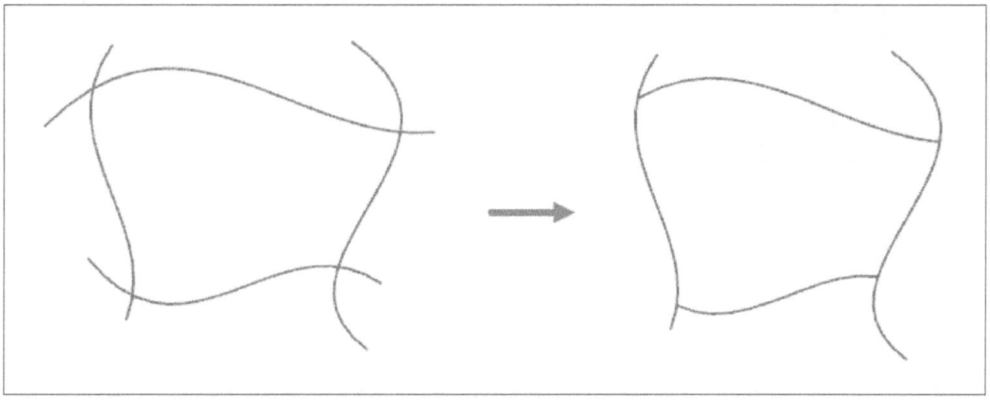

Figure-67. Curves trimmed

CURVE LENGTH

The **Curve Length** tool is used to extend or trim a curve by specified curve length increment. The procedure to use this tool is discussed next.

- Click on the **Curve Length** tool from **Edit** group of **Curve** tab in the **Ribbon**. The **Curve Length** dialog box will be displayed; refer to Figure-68.

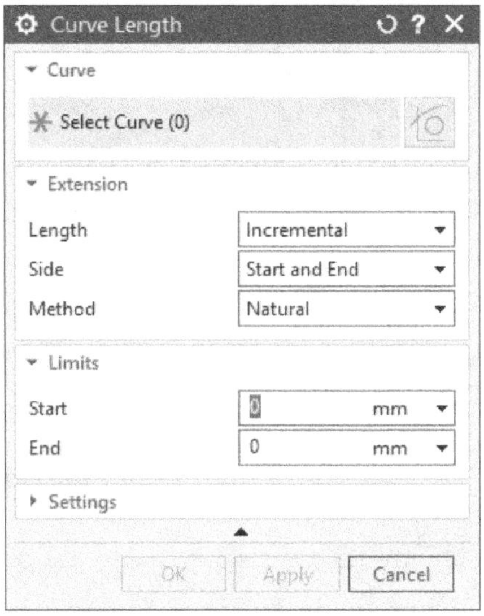

Figure-68. Curve Length dialog box

- Select desired curve from the drawing area of which the length to be extended or trimmed.
- Select **Incremental** option from **Length** drop-down of **Extension** rollout to extend or trim a curve by specified curve length increment. Select **Total** option from **Length** drop-down of **Extension** rollout to extend or trim a curve by specified total curve length. Select desired option from **Side** drop-down to extend or trim the curve from start, end, or both directions of the curve. Select **Natural**, **Linear**, or **Circular** option from **Method** drop-down to extend or trim the end point of the curve along natural path, linear path, or circular path of the curve, respectively.
- Specify desired length value of extended or trimmed curve at the starting and end points in the **Start** and **End** edit boxes of **Limits** rollout, respectively. Specify desired total length value in the **Total** edit box by which the curve to be extended or trimmed.
- Set the other parameters in the dialog box as discussed earlier and click on the **OK** button. The length of the curve will be extended; refer to Figure-69.

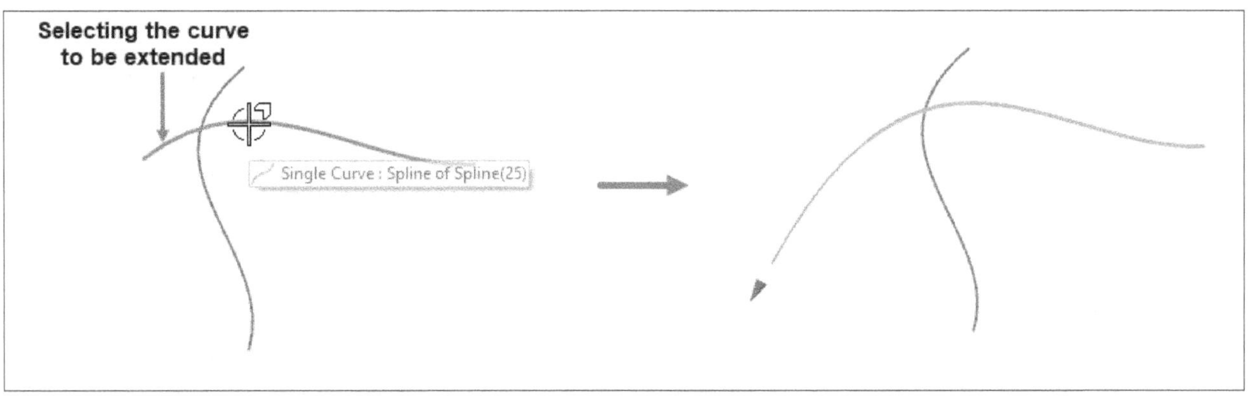

Figure-69. Curve extended

X-FORM

The **X-Form** tool is used to edit surfaces or spline curves by dynamically manipulating the pole locations. The procedure to use this tool is discussed next.

- Click on the **X-Form** tool from **Edit** group of **Curve** tab in the **Ribbon**. The **X-Form** dialog box will be displayed; refer to Figure-70.

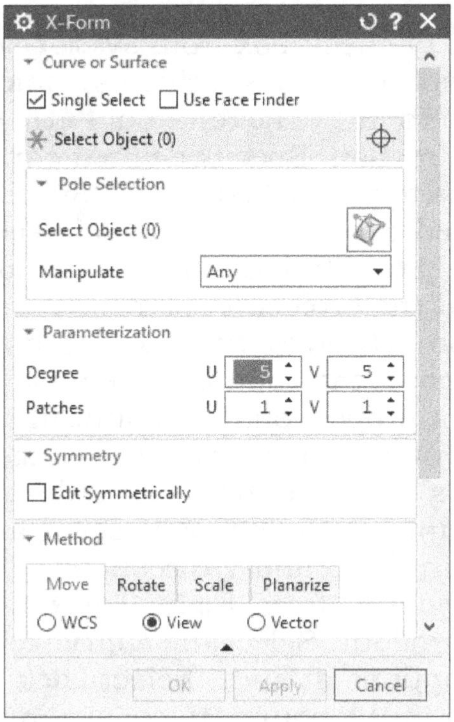

Figure-70. X-Form dialog box

- Select **Single Select** check box from **Curve or Surface** rollout to select single or multiple curves or surfaces to be edited. Select **Use Face Finder** check box to display the face finder group to identify faces based on geometric conditions. Select desired curve or surface to be edited from the drawing area.
- Select **Any** option from **Manipulate** drop-down of **Pole Selection** rollout to select individual poles or rows of poles. Select **Poles** option from the drop-down to select only individual poles and select **Rows** option from the drop-down to select only rows of poles; refer to Figure-71.

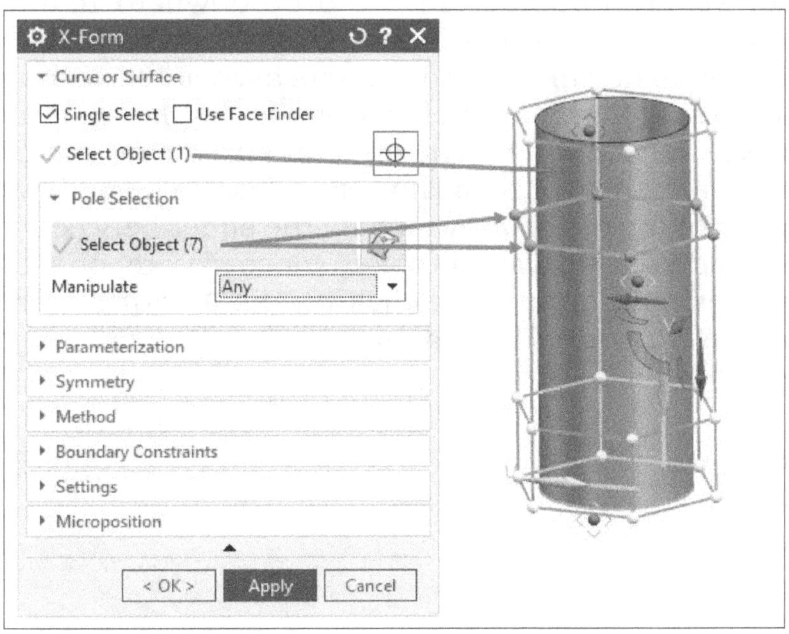

Figure-71. Surface and poles selected

- Specify desired number of degrees and patches in both u and v directions in the **U** and **V** edit boxes of **Degree** and **Patches** section in the **Parameterization** rollout, respectively.
- Select **Edit Symmetrically** check box from **Symmetry** rollout to edit the curve or surface to become symmetric to the specified symmetry plane.
- Specify desired parameters in the **Move** tab of **Method** rollout to move poles and polylines in a specified direction. Specify desired parameters in the **Rotate** tab to rotate poles and polylines to a specified vector. Specify desired parameters in the **Scale** tab to scale selected poles using principal axes and planes. Select desired parameters in the **Planarize** tab to define a plane location and direction by the manipulator displayed at the projection plane.
- Select desired option from **Advanced Method** drop-down to get additional control while editing. Select **Proportional** option to define a region of non-selected poles or points that will move a proportionate amount in relation to the selected poles and points using a percentage of isoparametric range. Select **Lock Region** option to define a region of poles or points that is locked from edits. Select **Insert Knot** option to insert knot points in the defined region and to a surface or curve by dragging location slider in the U and V directions.
- Select desired continuity option from **U-min**, **U-max**, **V-min**, and **V-max** drop-downs of **Boundary Conditions** rollout. Select the **Apply to All** check box to apply the settings to all U and V options at once. Select **Lock Poles** check box to lock all the poles that are within in the boundary constraints.
- Select **Original** option from **Extraction Method** drop-down of **Settings** rollout to extract the face based on the original parametric, rectangular surface. Select **Minimum Boundary** option from the drop-down to extract the face based on a rectangular border enclosing the trimmed surface. Select **Fit to Boundary** option from the drop-down to extract the face by fitting a quadrilateral surface using the trimmed boundary of the trimmed surface. Specify desired tolerance value in the **Extract Tolerance** edit box to be used when extracting a surface from a selected face. Select **Relation** option from **Feature Save Method** drop-down to maintain the location of the poles relative to the parent features when you edit the parent features. Select **Static** option from the drop-down to maintain the absolute location of the poles when you edit the parent features. Click on the **Restore Parent Face** button to delete pole movements associated with the current X-form feature. Select **Display Deviation** check box to display the maximum deviation that exist between the edited and the original surface or curve.
- Select **Rate** check box from **Microposition** rollout to slow down or speed up the rate of micro-positioning of curve by moving the slider between 0 and 100. Specify desired value in the **Step Value** edit box to move, rotate, or scale a selected pole.
- After specifying desired parameters, click on the **OK** button from the dialog box. The surface will be edited; refer to Figure-72.

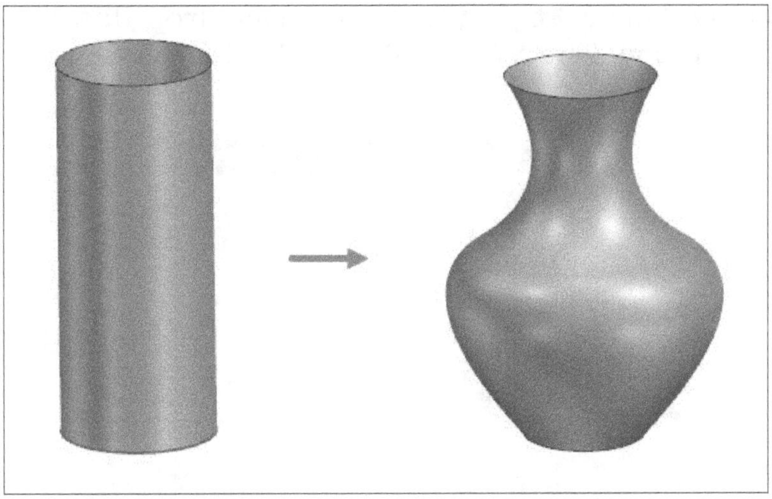

Figure-72. Surface edited

EDIT CURVE PARAMETERS

The **Edit Curve Parameters** tool is used to edit a curve using the creation dialog box for the type of curve selected. The procedure to use this tool is discussed next.

- Click on the **Edit Curve Parameters** tool from **More** drop-down in the **Edit** group of **Curve** tab in the **Ribbon**. The **Edit Curve Parameters** dialog box will be displayed; refer to Figure-73.

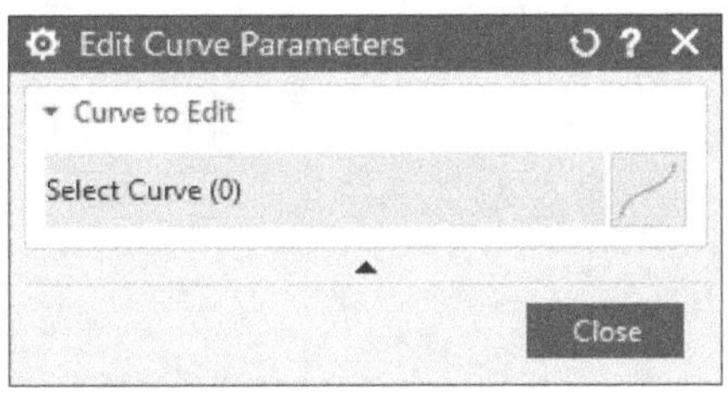

Figure-73. Edit Curve Parameters dialog box

- Select desired curve to be edited from drawing area; refer to Figure-74.
- On selecting the curve, the **Arc/Circle** dialog box will be displayed as discussed earlier to edit the curve.

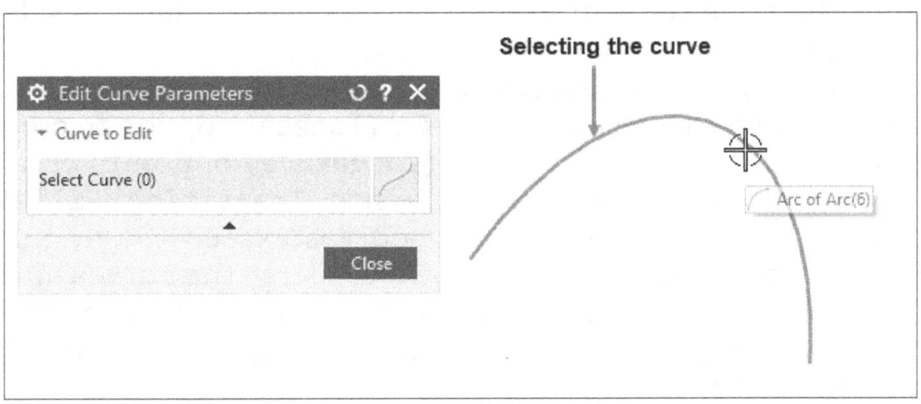

Figure-74. Selecting the curve

SMOOTH CURVE STRING

The **Smooth Curve String** tool is used to create a single feature from a set of input curves. The procedure to use this tool is discussed next.

- Click on the **Smooth Curve String** tool from **More** drop-down in the **Edit** group of **Curve** tab in the **Ribbon**. The **Smooth Curve String** dialog box will be displayed; refer to Figure-75.

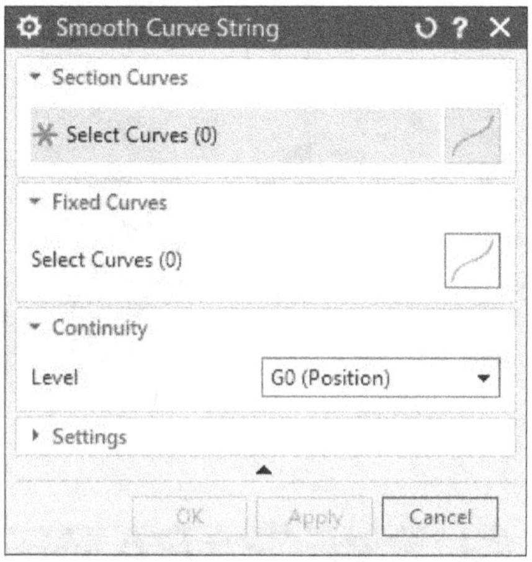

Figure-75. Smooth Curve String dialog box

- Select desired curves from the drawing area to create the smooth curve feature; refer to Figure-76.

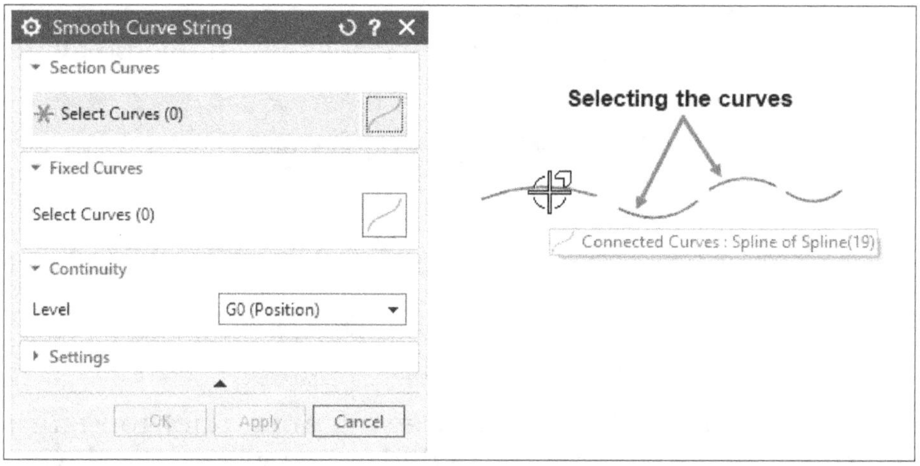

Figure-76. Selecting the curves

- Click on the **Select Curves** button from **Fixed Curves** rollout to select the curves not to be modified in the smoothing process.
- Select **G0 (Position)** option from **Level** drop-down of **Continuity** rollout to create the output curve of sharp corners. Select **G1 (Tangent)** option to create the output curve of tangent continuous. Select **G2 (Curvature)** option to create the output curve of curvature continuous. Select the **Add Transition Fillets** check box to create fillets where selected adjacent curves exceed the angular threshold. Select desired option from **Merge** drop-down to merge the curves after being made continuous. Select **None** option to not to merge any curves. Select **Same Types** option to merge the adjacent curves of the same type. Select **All Curves** option to merge all the curves.
- Specify desired value in the **Distance Threshold** and **Angular Threshold** edit boxes of **Settings** rollout to specify maximum distance and maximum angle between adjacent selected curves, respectively. Specify desired value in the **Maximum Deviation** edit box to specify maximum distance the output curve can deviate from the input curves.

- Other parameters in the dialog box is same as discussed earlier. After specifying desired parameters, click on the **OK** button from the dialog box. The smooth curve string will be created; refer to Figure-77.

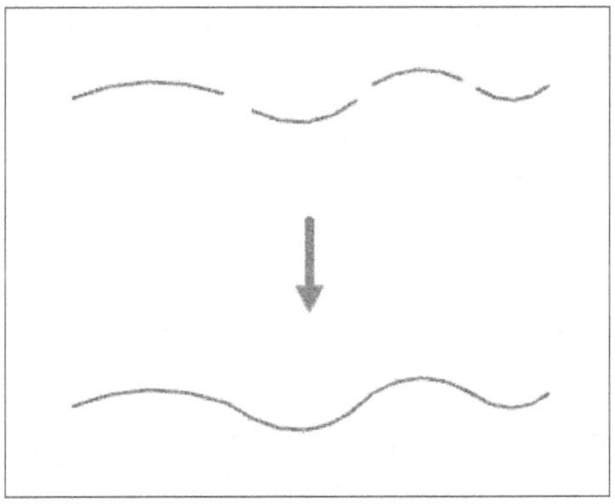

Figure-77. Smooth curve string created

SELF-ASSESSMENT

Q1. Which tool is used to specify temporary point locations while creating or editing objects?
A. Line
B. Point
C. Arc/Circle
D. Fit Curve

Q2. The Point Set tool is primarily used to:
A. Create lines between points
B. Create a set of points corresponding to existing geometry
C. Edit spline curves
D. Project curves onto surfaces

Q3. Which tool is used to create straight line segments?
A. Line
B. Arc/Circle
C. Spine
D. Bridge

Q4. In the Line tool, which Start Option helps determine the best start and end automatically?
A. Point
B. Tangent
C. Inferred
D. At Angle

Q5. Which End Option creates a line parallel to the XC-axis?
A. At Angle
B. Along XC
C. Along YC
D. Along ZC

Q6. Which option in Plane Options makes the plane immovable?
A. Automatic Plane
B. Locked Plane
C. Select Plane
D. Fixed Plane

Q7. The Arc/Circle tool is used to create:
A. Only circles
B. Only arcs
C. Associative arcs and circles
D. Non-associative curves only

Q8. Which option allows creating an arc using three points?
A. Center Option
B. Radius Option
C. Three Point Arc
D. Tangent Option

Q9. The Studio Spline tool is used to create:
A. Only 2D splines
B. Only 3D splines
C. Associative or non-associative splines in 2D or 3D
D. Only constrained splines

Q10. Which checkbox constrains the spline to the X-Y plane?
A. Associative
B. Closed
C. Constrained to Plane
D. Smooth

Q11. The Text tool generates curves using:
A. Bitmap fonts
B. Vector fonts only
C. TrueType fonts
D. CAD fonts only

Q12. Which text option creates text along a curve?
A. Planar
B. On Curve
C. On Face
D. Reference

Q13. What does the Create Bounding Box Curves option do?
A. Deletes text boundaries
B. Creates a frame around text geometry
C. Aligns text
D. Changes font size

Q14. Curve on Surface tool is used to:
A. Create curves in air
B. Create surface splines on faces
C. Project curves
D. Offset curves

Q15. Which option keeps selected faces active in Curve on Surface?
A. Keep Selected
B. Lock Faces
C. Fix Faces
D. Hold Faces

Q16. The Helix tool can create a helix based on:
A. Only radius
B. Only pitch
C. Vector or spine
D. Only diameter

Q17. Which parameter defines the distance between turns in a helix?
A. Radius
B. Pitch
C. Angle
D. Diameter

Q18. General Conic tool is used to create:
A. Straight lines
B. Splines
C. Conic section curves
D. Helical curves

Q19. The Law Curve tool creates curves using:
A. Only points
B. Only edges
C. Mathematical laws or equations
D. Only planes

Q20. Which option in Law Curve defines a constant value?
A. Equation
B. Linear
C. Constant
D. Cubic

Q21. The Spine tool creates curves that are:
A. Parallel to planes
B. Perpendicular to planes
C. Circular
D. Random

Q22. Project Curve tool is used to:
A. Delete curves
B. Offset curves
C. Project curves/edges/points onto a plane
D. Join curves

Q23. Intersection Curve tool creates curves at:
A. Offset positions
B. Curve intersections only
C. Intersection of surfaces/solids with a plane
D. Random positions

Q24. Shadow Curve tool is used to:
A. Create reflections
B. Extract silhouette or shadow curves
C. Offset curves
D. Join curves

Q25. Offset Curve tool creates:
A. Duplicate curves
B. Curves at a specified distance
C. Projected curves
D. Intersection curves

Q26. Which option offsets a curve using equations?
A. Distance
B. Draft
C. Law Control
D. 3D Axial

Q27. Offset in Face tool creates:
A. 3D curves
B. Curves on planes
C. Offset curves on surfaces
D. Helix curves

Q28. Bridge tool is used to:
A. Split curves
B. Connect two objects with curves
C. Delete curves
D. Offset curves

Q29. Composite Curve tool is used to:
A. Create new splines
B. Extract and combine curves/edges
C. Project curves
D. Offset curves

Q30. Circular Blend Curve tool creates:
A. Straight lines
B. Offset curves
C. Smooth blended curves between two curves
D. Helix curves

Q31. Combined Projection tool creates:
A. Offset curves
B. Intersection of two projected curves
C. Shadow curves
D. Helix curves

Q32. Wrap/Unwrap Curve tool is used to:
A. Project curves
B. Wrap curves onto surfaces or unwrap them
C. Offset curves
D. Blend curves

Q33. Isoparametric Curve tool generates curves along:
A. Random directions
B. U/V directions on a surface
C. Circular paths
D. Helix paths

Q34. Isocline Curve tool creates curves with:
A. Variable angle
B. Constant angle to surface
C. Random angle
D. Zero angle

Q35. Section Curve tool creates:
A. Offset curves
B. Intersection geometry between planes and objects
C. Helix curves
D. Spline curves

Q36. The Section Curve tool is used to create:
A. Offset curves
B. Intersection geometry between planes and objects
C. Helix curves
D. Projection curves

Q37. Which option creates section curves using existing or defined planes?
A. Parallel Planes
B. Radial Planes
C. Selected Planes
D. Axis Planes

Q38. The Parallel Planes option is used to create section curves using:
A. Random planes
B. Series of parallel planes
C. Single plane
D. Curved surfaces

Q39. Radial Planes option creates section curves using planes that:
A. Are parallel
B. Intersect randomly
C. Extend from a specified axis
D. Are perpendicular to curves

Q40. Extract Virtual Curve tool is used to:
A. Offset curves
B. Create virtual curves from specific features
C. Trim curves
D. Scale curves

Q41. Which option extracts the axis of cylindrical or conical faces?
A. Blend Centerline
B. Virtual Intersection
C. Rotation Axis
D. Tube Centerline

Q42. Which option extracts the centerline of a blend face?
A. Rotation Axis
B. Blend Centerline
C. Virtual Intersection
D. Tube Centerline

Q43. Tube Centerline option is used to:
A. Create helix
B. Extract centerline from tube-like bodies
C. Trim curves
D. Scale curves

Q44. Revolve Outline tool is used to:
A. Create helix
B. Create outlines of bodies
C. Offset curves
D. Trim curves

Q45. Which button is used to reverse the outline side?
A. Reverse Side
B. Reverse Outline Side
C. Flip Direction
D. Invert Side

Q46. Mirror Curve tool creates curves:
A. Offset from original
B. Rotated
C. Mirrored across a plane
D. Scaled

Q47. Mirror Curve requires selection of:
A. Axis
B. Plane or planar face
C. Curve length
D. Radius

Q48. Offset 3D Curve tool offsets curves:
A. In 2D plane only
B. Along curve direction
C. In 3D space perpendicular to direction
D. Only along axis

Q49. Which option specifies direction in Offset 3D Curve?
A. Specify Axis
B. Specify Vector
C. Specify Plane
D. Specify Curve

Q50. Scale Curve tool is used to:
A. Trim curves
B. Extend curves
C. Scale curves, edges, or points
D. Mirror curves

Q51. Uniform scaling scales curve:
A. In one direction
B. In two directions
C. In all directions equally
D. Randomly

Q52. Non-uniform scaling scales curve:
A. Equally in all directions
B. Separately in X, Y, Z directions
C. Only in Z direction
D. Only along curve

Q53. Trim Curve tool is used to:
A. Scale curves
B. Offset curves
C. Trim, extend, or divide curves
D. Mirror curves

Q54. Which option is used as bounding object in Trim Curve?
A. Only curves
B. Only planes
C. Curves, edges, bodies, faces, points, or planes
D. Only solids

Q55. Curve Length tool is used to:
A. Measure curve only
B. Extend or trim curve by length
C. Offset curves
D. Project curves

Chapter 9

Surfacing

Topics Covered

The major topics covered in this chapter are:

- ***Creating Base Surface using Extrude, Swept, Through Curve, Edge Blend, Offset Surface etc.***
- ***Creating Mesh surfaces***
- ***Performing Blend operation***
- ***Creating Fill surfaces***
- ***Performing Fit, Offset, and Flange operations***
- ***Creating mid surfaces***

SURFACE

Surface is a separate world in the field of CAD. The complicated shapes which are difficult for solid modeling are most of the time easy for surface. Basic tools of surface are very similar to the solid creation tools discussed earlier like extrude, revolve, swept and so on. But, there are some other tools that allow to modify the part shape freely in 3D. In **NX**, the tools to create surface models available in the **Surface** tab of the **Ribbon** in the part environment; refer to Figure-1. By default most of the surfacing tools are not active. These tools will be active automatically when related objects are available in the drawing area.

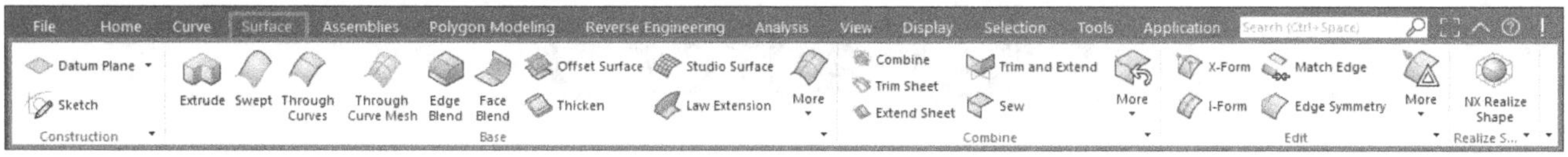

Figure-1. Surface tab

Extrude

The **Extrude** feature is used to add material to the sketch while moving it along any vector. The procedure to use this tool is same as discussed in chapter 4.

Swept

The **Swept** tool in **Base** group of **Surface** tab is used to create solid/surface protrusion by moving selected curves along selected path curve. The procedure to use this tool has been discussed earlier in Chapter 4.

Through Curves

The **Through Curves** tool is used to create a body that transitions through multiple sections, with the shape adapting to pass through each section. The procedure to use this tool is discussed next.

- Click on the **Through Curves** tool from the **Base** group in **Surface** tab of the **Ribbon**. The **Through Curves** dialog box will be displayed; refer to Figure-2.

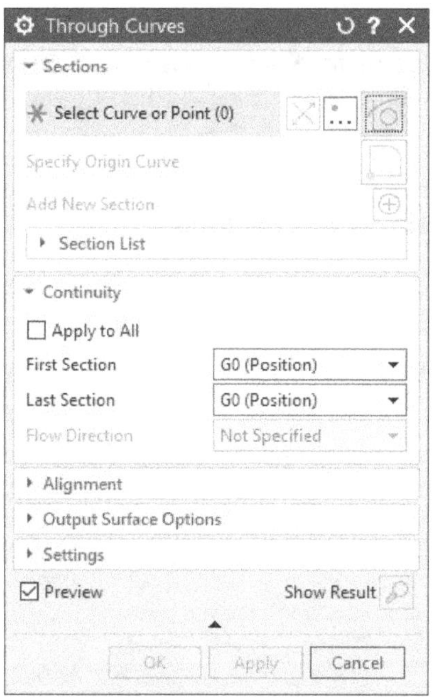

Figure-2. Through Curves dialog box

- Select desired curve or point that you want to be used as section for through curve feature.
- If you want to add more curves as sections at different locations then click on the **Add New Set** button from the **Sections** rollout or press Middle Mouse Button (MMB) and select the next section; refer to Figure-3.

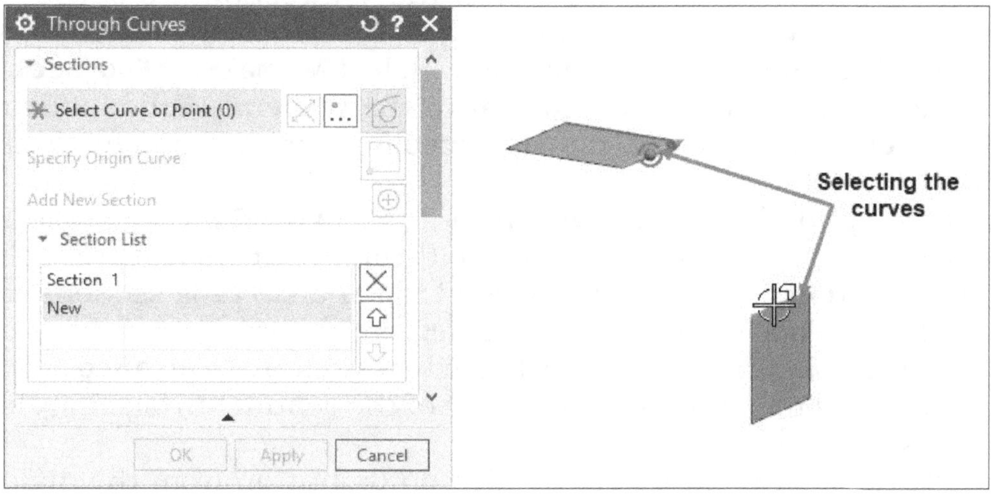

Figure-3. Selecting the curves as sections

- Select **Apply to All** check box from the **Continuity** rollout to apply the continuity constraint selected for one section to both the first and last sections.
- Select desired option from **First Section** and **Last Section** drop-downs to select constraining faces and specify continuity for the selected section; refer to Figure-4.

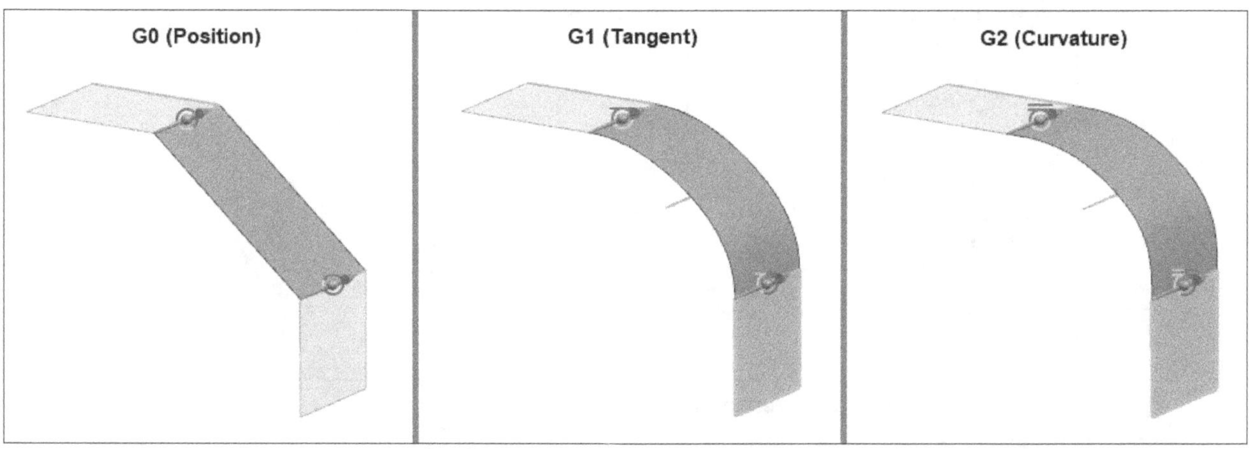

Figure-4. Continuity options

- Select desired option from **Flow Direction** drop-down that applies only to models that use a constraint surface. On selecting the **Not Specified** option from the drop-down, the isoparameter flow direction flows directly through to the opposite side and is not restricted to any specific direction. On selecting the **Isoparametric** option, the isoparametric direction (U or V) of the constraint input surface is followed by the isoparameter direction of the surface. On selecting the **Perpendicular** option, the isoparameter direction of the surface is perpendicular to the base input curve or edge. On selecting the **Adjacent Edges** option, the V directional isoparametric lines of the surface follow the side edges of the constraining faces.

- Select **Preserve Shape** check box from **Alignment** rollout to preserve sharp corners by forcing a tolerance value of 0,0. Select desired option from **Alignment** drop-down to control the shape of the feature by defining how NX places the isoparametric curves of the new surface along the sections.
- Select desired option from **Patch Type** drop-down in the **Output Surface Options** rollout to specify whether the patches in the V direction are single or multiple. Select **Closed in V** check box to close the feature between the first and last sections along columns in the V direction. Select **Normal to End Sections** check box to make the output surface normal to the two end sections. Select desired option from **Construction** drop-down to specify a construction method to be used to create the surface.
- Select desired option from **Body Type** drop-down in the **Settings** rollout to specify either a sheet body or a solid body for the through curves feature. Select desired option from **Rebuild** drop-down in the **Section** and **Lofting** sections to construct a high-quality surface by redefining the degree or segments of the sections.
- Specify desired tolerance values in the edit boxes of **Tolerance** rollout for the continuity options to control the accuracy of the rebuilt surface in relation to the input curves.
- After specifying desired parameters, click on **OK** button from the dialog box. The through curves feature will be created; refer to Figure-5.

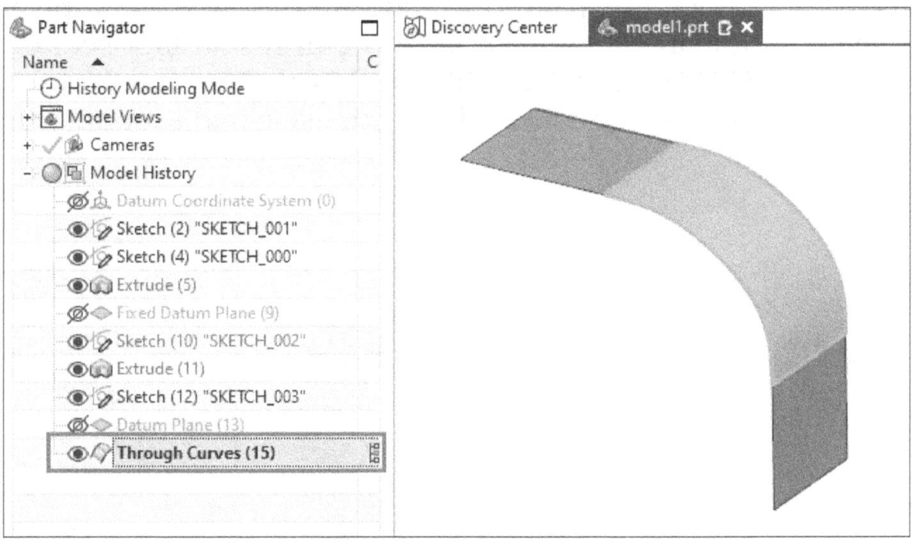

Figure-5. Through curves feature created

Through Curve Mesh

The **Through Curve Mesh** tool is used to create a body through a mesh of sections in one direction, and guides in another direction, where the shape fits through the mesh of curves.. The procedure to use this tool is discussed next.

- Click on the **Through Curve Mesh** tool from **Base** group in the **Surface** tab of the **Ribbon**. The **Through Curve Mesh** dialog box will be displayed; refer to Figure-6.

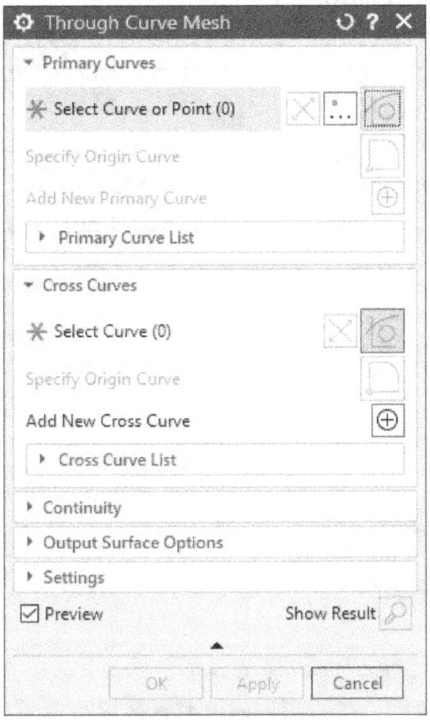

Figure-6. Through Curve Mesh dialog box

- Select desired curve or point that you want to be used as a primary curve for through curve mesh feature.
- If you want to add more curves as primary curve then click on the **Add New Primary Curve** button from the **Primary Curves** rollout or press Middle Mouse Button (MMB).
- Click on the **Select Curve** button from the **Cross Curves** rollout and select curves that you want to be used as a cross curves; refer to Figure-7.

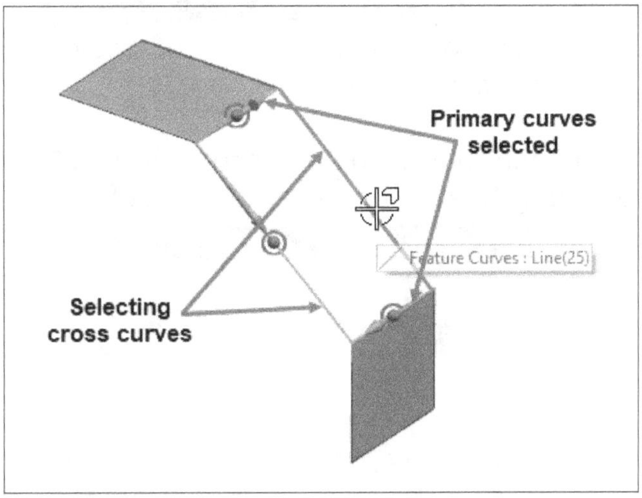

Figure-7. Selecting primary and cross curves

- Select **Apply to All** check box from **Continuity** rollout to apply the same continuity setting to the first and last sections.
- Select desired continuity constraints from the **First Primary**, **Last Primary**, **First Cross**, and **Last Cross** drop-downs to control the accuracy of the surface in relation to the input curves.
- Click on the **Select Curve** button from **Spine** rollout and select desired spline to control the parameterization of the cross sections.

- Select desired option from **Emphasis** drop-down in the **Output Surface Options** rollout to specify whether the surface cross the primary curves, the cross curves, or a combination of the two. Select desired construction method from **Construction** drop-down to create the surface.
- Other parameters in the dialog box are same as discussed earlier.
- After specifying desired parameters, click on **OK** button from the dialog box. The through curve mesh feature will be created; refer to Figure-8.

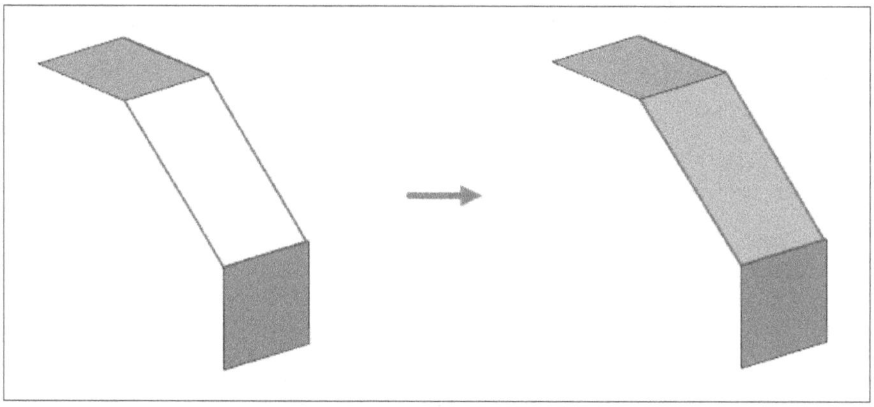

Figure-8. Through curve mesh feature created

Edge Blend

The **Edge Blend** tool is used to apply fillet at the sharp edges of the model. The procedure to use this tool has been discussed earlier in chapter 5.

Face Blend

The **Face Blend** tool is used to apply fillet at the intersection of two or more faces. The procedure to use this tool has been discussed earlier in chapter 5.

Offset Surface

The **Offset Surface** tool is used to create an offset of one or more existing faces. The procedure to use this tool is discussed next.

- Click on the **Offset Surface** tool from **Base** group in the **Surface** tab of the **Ribbon**. The **Offset Surface** dialog box will be displayed; refer to Figure-9.

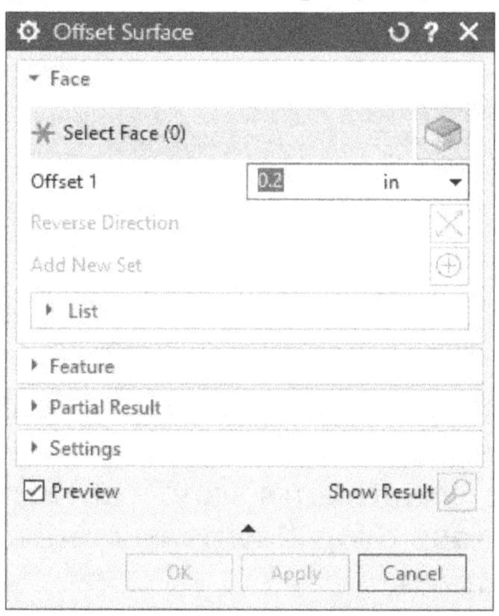

Figure-9. Offset Surface dialog box

- Select desired face(s) of the model to be offset, the preview of offset feature will be displayed; refer to Figure-10.

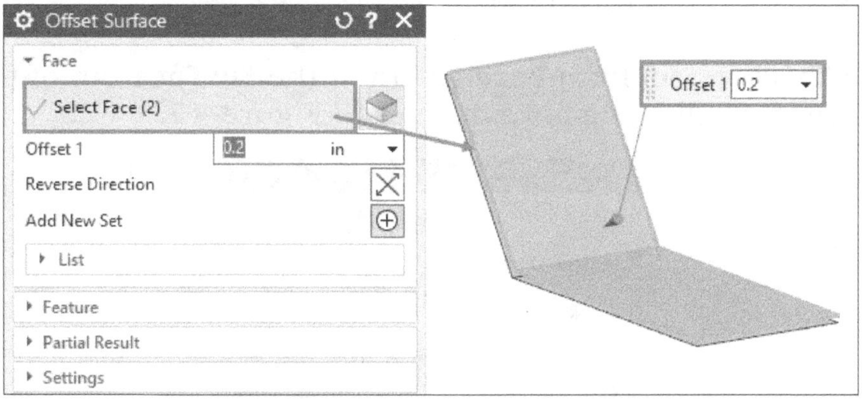

Figure-10. Preview of offset feature

- Specify desired offset value in the **Offset** edit box.
- Select **One Feature for Each Face** option from **Output** drop-down in the **Feature** rollout to create an offset surface feature for each selected face. Select desired option from **Face Normals** drop-down to determine the vector direction for each surface to be offset.
- Select **One Feature for All Faces** option from **Output** drop-down to create a single offset surface feature for all selected faces. Select **Enable Partial Offset** check box from **Partial Result** rollout to provide a partial offset result. Select **Dynamically Update Exclusion List** check box to find faces to be excluded as faces are selected. Specify desired number of faces to be excluded in the **Maximum Objects to Exclude** edit box. Select **Remove Problem Vertices Locally** check box to trim the faces around an error vertex using a sphere tool. Specify desired size of the sphere to be used to trim an error vertex in the **Sphere Tool Radius** edit box.
- On selecting the **Do Not Add Shelf Face** option from **Tangent Edges** drop-down in the **Settings** rollout, no shelf face will be formed at tangent edges. Select **Add Shelf Face at Tangent Edge** option from the drop-down to add a shelf face at a tangent edge between the faces with an offset distance of zero and greater than zero. Specify desired distance tolerance for the offset surface feature in the **Tolerance** edit box.
- Other parameters in the dialog box are same as discussed earlier.
- After specifying desired parameters, click on **OK** button from the dialog box. The offset surface feature will created; refer to Figure-11.

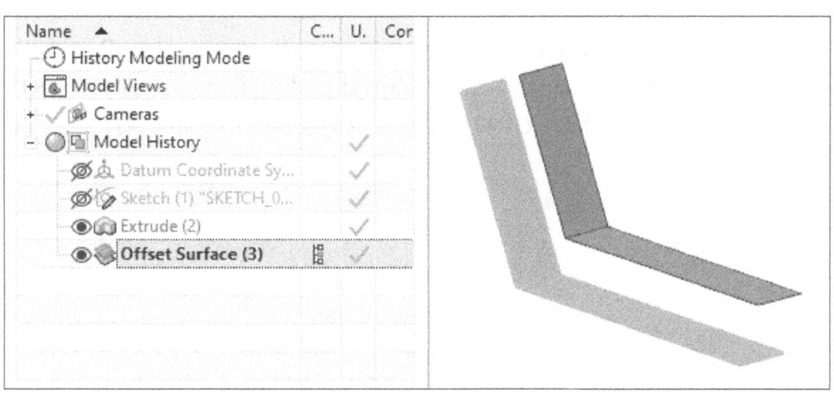

Figure-11. Offset surface feature created

Thicken

The **Thicken** tool is used to offset one or more faces or sheets into a solid body. The procedure to use this tool is discussed next.

- Click on the **Thicken** tool from **Base** group in the **Surface** tab of the **Ribbon**. The **Thicken** dialog box will be displayed; refer to Figure-12.

Figure-12. Thicken dialog box

- Select desired face(s) of the model to be thicken, the preview of thicken feature will be displayed; refer to Figure-13.

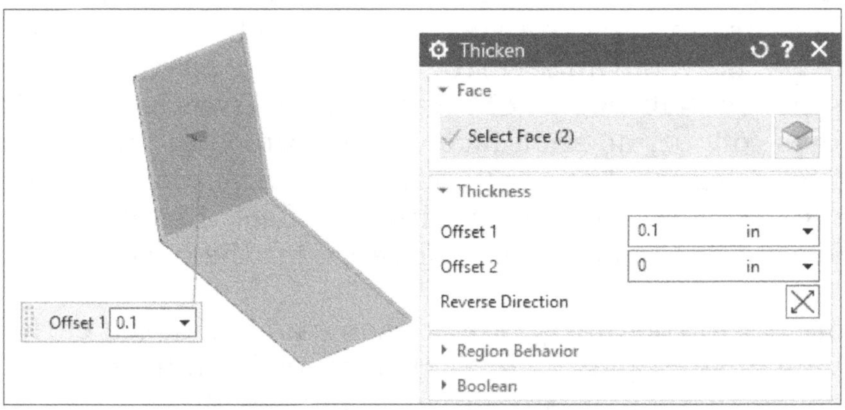

Figure-13. Preview of thicken feature

- Specify desired offset values for the thicken feature in the **Offset 1** and **Offset 2** edit boxes of **Thickness** rollout; refer to Figure-14. Click on the **Reverse Direction** button to reverse the direction of thicken feature creation.

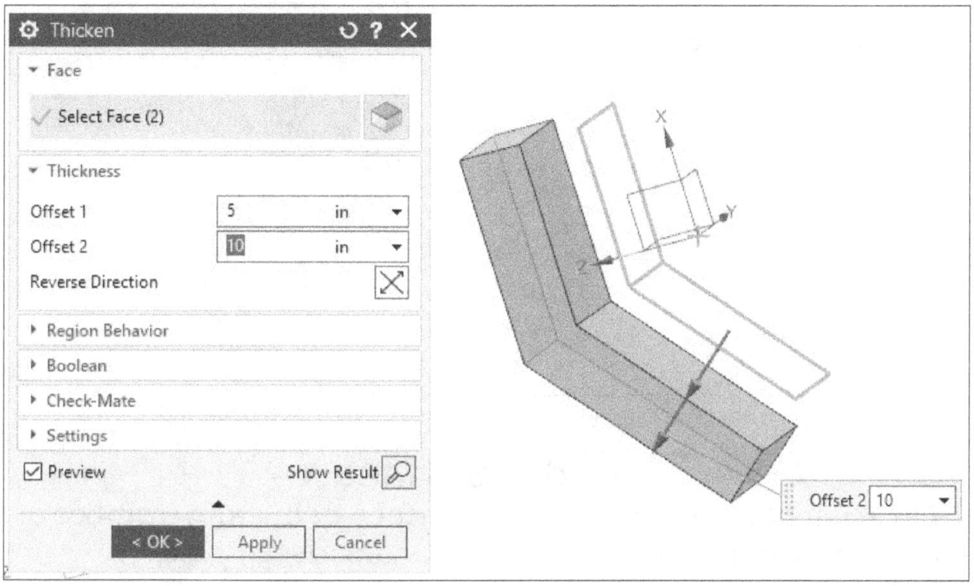

Figure-14. Specifying offset values

- Click on the **Select Boundary Curve** button from **Region to Pierce** area of **Region Behavior** rollout to select a region defined by a set of closed curves or edges. Click on the **Select Boundary Curve** button from **Region of Different Thickness** area to select regions defined by a set of closed curves or edges.
- Select **None** option from **Boolean** drop-down in the **Boolean** rollout to create a thicken feature body. Select **Unite** option from the drop-down to combine the volume of the thicken feature with one other body into a single body. Select **Subtract** option from the drop-down to remove the volume of thicken feature from a target body. Select **Intersect** option from the drop-down to generate a body that represents the volume common to both the thicken feature and any existing bodies it intersects.
- Click on the **Execute Check-Mate** button from the **Check-Mate** rollout, the **Check-Mate** dialog will be displayed to check the quality of parts, assemblies, and drawings; refer to Figure-15.

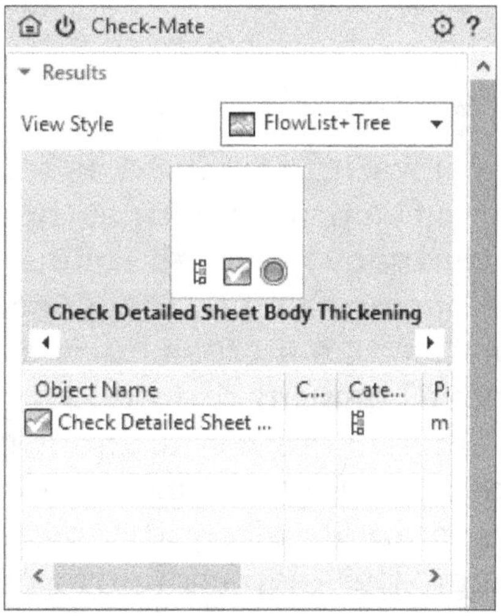

Figure-15. Check Mate dialog

- Select **Improve Gash Topology to Enable Thickening** check box from **Settings** rollout to heal gashes during a thicken operation.
- After specifying desired parameters, click on **OK** button from the dialog box. The thicken feature will be created; refer to Figure-16.

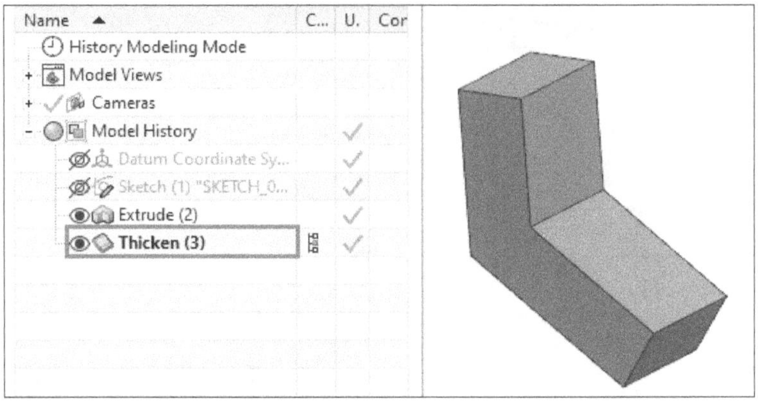

Figure-16. Thicken feature created

Studio Surface

The **Studio Surface** tool is used to create a surface using any number of section and guide strings. The procedure to use this tool is discussed next.

- Click on the **Studio Surface** tool from **Base** group in the **Surface** tab of the **Ribbon**. The **Studio Surface** dialog box will be displayed; refer to Figure-17.

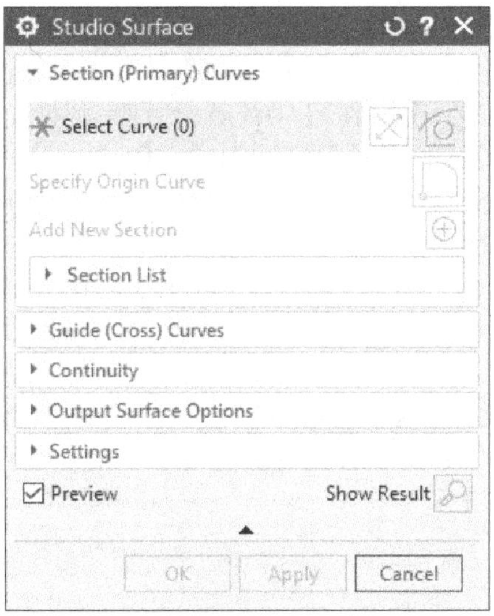

Figure-17. Studio Surface dialog box

- Select desired curve that you want to be used as a primary curve for the surface.
- If you want to add more curves as primary curve then click on the **Add New Section** button from the **Section (Primary) Curves** rollout.
- Click on the **Select Curve** button from **Guide (Cross) Curves** rollout and select curves that you want to be used as a cross curves; refer to Figure-18.
- Select **Parameter** option from **Alignment** drop-down in the **Output Surface Options** rollout to align the isoparametric curves at equal parameter intervals along the sections. Select **Arc Length** option from the drop-down to align the isoparametric curves at equal arc length intervals along the sections. Select **By Points** option from the drop-down to align the isoparametric curves at the specified points between the sections.

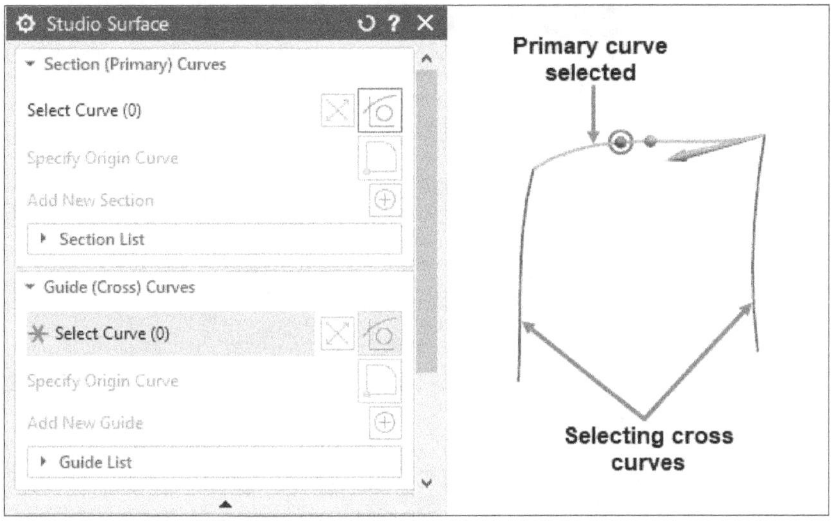

Figure-18. Selecting primary and cross curves

- Click on the **Reset** button to undo all the changes and restore the original handles to their original positions.
- Select desired option from **Transition Control** drop-down to specify the section to section transition type that matches the surface shape to be needed.
- Click on the **Switch Strings** button to swap guide and section strings that changes the shape of the surface.
- Other parameters in the dialog box are same as discussed earlier.
- After specifying desired parameters, click on **OK** button from the dialog box. The studio surface feature will be created; refer to Figure-19.

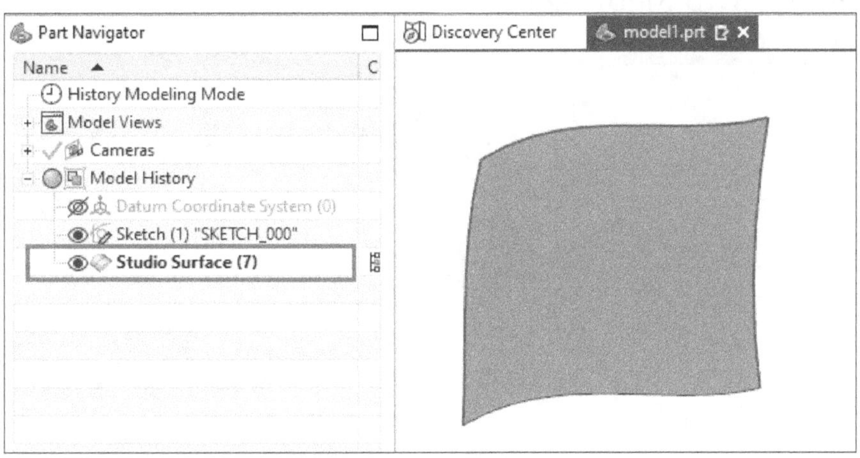

Figure-19. Studio surface feature created

Law Extension

The **Law Extension** tool is used to create an extension from a base sheet, using a defined law or rule to control the distance and angle. The procedure to use this tool is discussed next.

- Click on the **Law Extension** tool from **Base** group in the **Surface** tab of the **Ribbon**. The **Law Extension** dialog box will be displayed; refer to Figure-20.

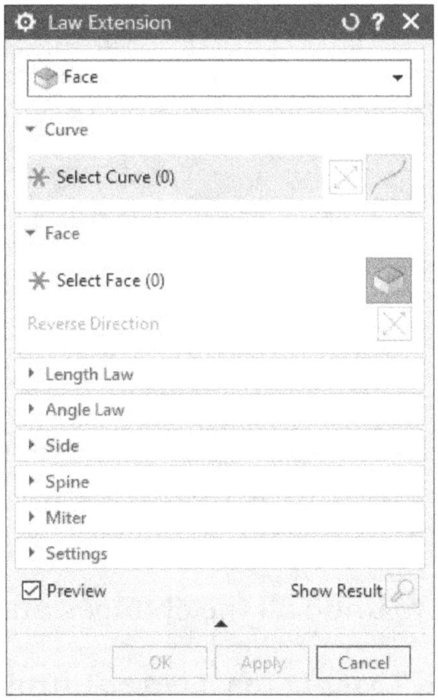

Figure-20. Law Extension dialog box

- Select desired method of extension from drop-down in the top area of the dialog box to specify the reference direction for extension.
- Select desired curve or an edge from the graphics window through which the surface extension is to be created and then click on the **Select Face** button from the **Face** rollout to select one or more faces to define the reference direction for the extension; refer to Figure-21.

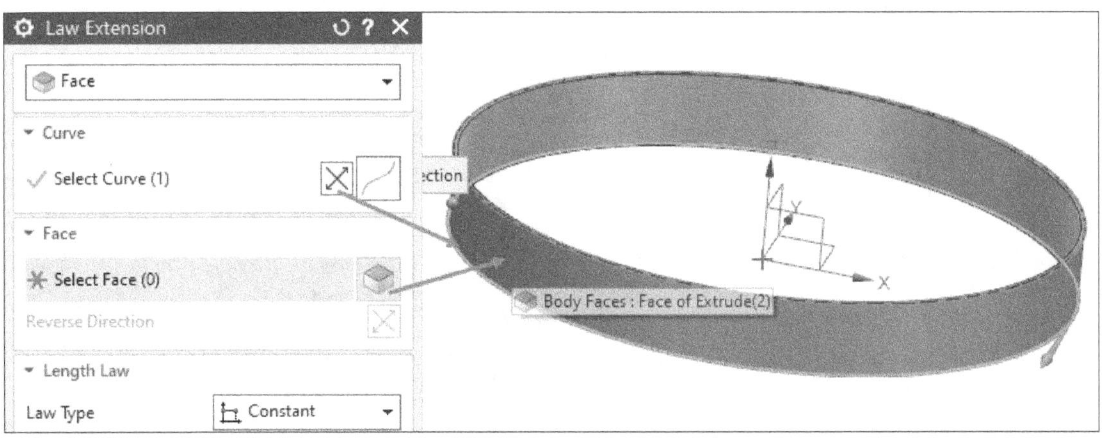

Figure-21. Selecting the curve and face for extension

- Select desired type of length method to be used for the surface extension from **Law Type** drop-down and specify respective parameters in the **Length Law** rollout.
- Similarly, specify desired parameters in the **Angle Law** rollout. Select **Angular Correction** check box and specify desired angle value that will help surface variation to create a smoother surface.
- Select desired option from **Extension Side** drop-down in the **Side** rollout to specify the side of the base curve on which the law extension will be created.
- Select desired option from **Method** drop-down in the **Spine** rollout to specify a spine based on a curve or vector. Select **Curve** or **Vector** option from the drop-downs to specify the orientation of the angle law normal to a curve or angle law aligned to a vector, respectively.

- Select **None** option from **Method** drop-down in the **Miter** rollout to not create a miter between the law extensions. Select **Sharp** option to create sharp miters between the law extensions. Select **Blend** option to create blend between the law extensions.
- Select **Project Curve onto Face** check box from **Settings** rollout to project the curve onto the surface to make it fit. Select **Merge Faces if Possible** check box to create the law extension feature as a single sheet body. Select **Lock End Length/Angle Handles** check box to lock the end length handles and angle handles together. Select **Advanced Curve Fit** check box and specify method, degree, and segments parameters.
- Other parameters in the dialog box are same as discussed earlier.
- After specifying desired parameters, click on **OK** button from the dialog box. The law extension feature will be created; refer to Figure-22.

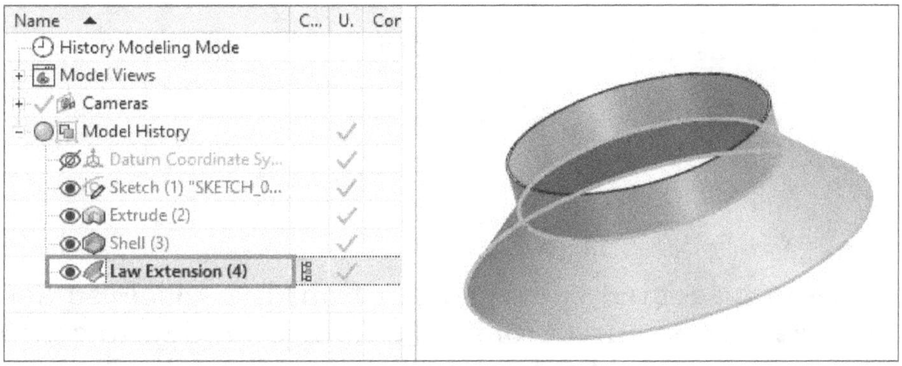

Figure-22. Law extension feature created

Styled Sweep

The **Styled Sweep** tool is used to create a smooth and high-quality surface from a set of curves. The procedure to use this tool is discussed next.

- Click on the **Styled Sweep** tool from **Sweep** area in the **More** drop-down of **Base** group in the **Surface** tab of the **Ribbon**. The **Styled Sweep** dialog box will be displayed; refer to Figure-23.

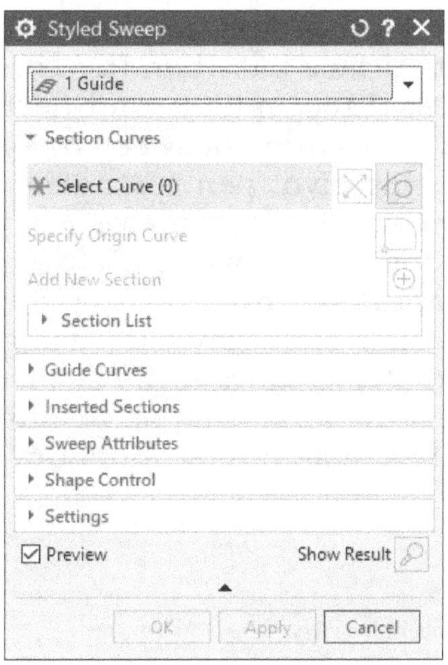

Figure-23. Styled Sweep dialog box

- Select desired sweep type from drop-down in the top area of the dialog box.
- Select desired curves from the graphics window as a section strings, a set of section strings will be added in the **Section List** rollout.
- Click on the **Select Guide Curve** button from the **Guide Curves** rollout and select desired curves from the graphics window as guide curves; refer to Figure-24.

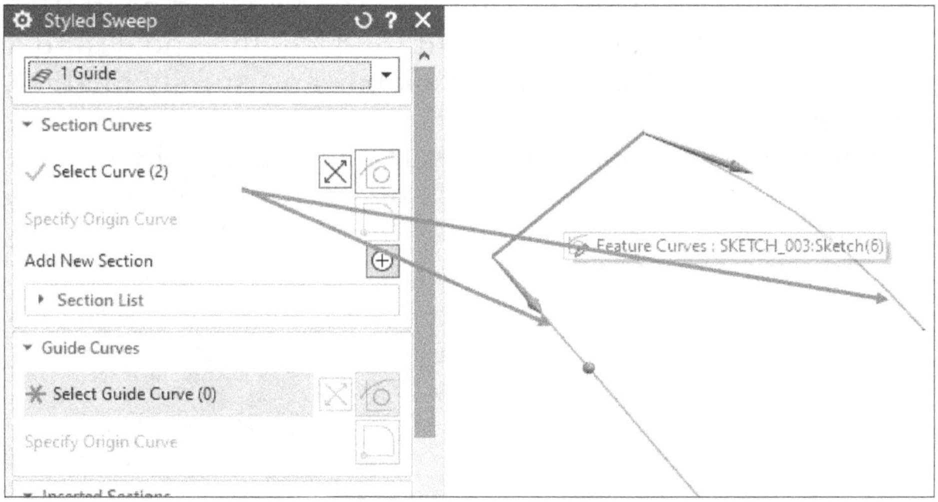

Figure-24. Selecting the curves as guide curves

- Click on the **Insert Section Curve** button from the **Inserted Sections** rollout and select desired section curve from the graphics window to control the surface shape, the section curve will be displayed in the **List** rollout.
- Select desired option from **Fixed String** drop-down in the **Sweep Attributes** rollout to specify that the sweep remain in contact with the section string, guide string, or both. Select **Translate** option from the **Section Orientation** drop-down to create a sweep by translating the section along the guide while maintaining its original orientation. Select **Keep Angle** option from the drop-down to maintain the sections to their initial angle to the reference while they swept along the guide. Select **Make Normal** option from the drop-down to keep the sections perpendicular to the reference at each point along the guide curve. Select **User Defined** option from the drop-down to automatically position the sweep so that the section will be aligned perpendicular to the guide. Select **Arc Length** option from the drop-down to extend the swept surface based on the arc lengths of the guide curves.
- Select the **Pivot Point Position** option from **Method** drop-down in the **Shape Control** rollout to change the location of sweep by specifying two points along the section or guide curves using pivot point handles. Select **Rotation** option from the drop-down to rotate the surface from a specified point using rotation handles. Select **Scale** option from the drop-down to change the depth of the curve using scaling handles. Select **Partial Sweep** option from the drop-down to trim the sweep along the U and/or V direction from any edge using the partial sweep handles.
- Other parameters in the dialog box are same as discussed earlier.
- After specifying desired parameters, click on **OK** button from the dialog box. The styled sweep feature will be created; refer to Figure-25.

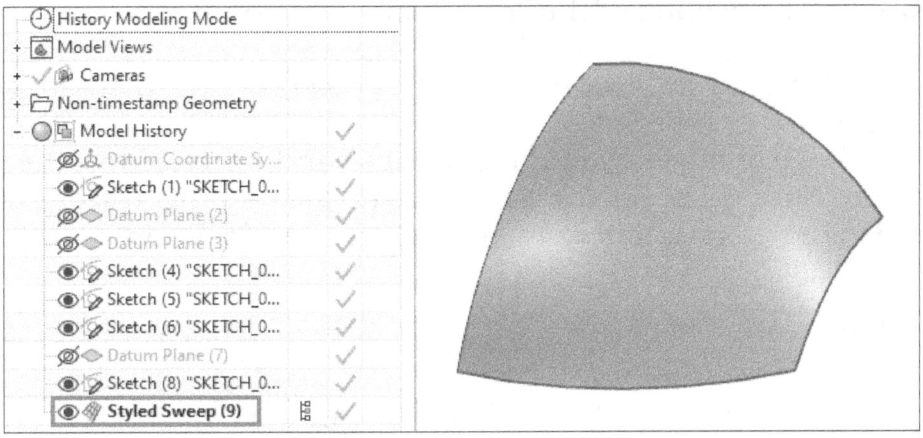

Figure-25. Styled sweep feature created

Sweep along Guide

The **Sweep along Guide** tool is used to create a sweep feature in which section follows the highs and lows of selected guide curve. The procedure to use this tool is same as discussed earlier in chapter 4.

Variational Sweep

The **Variational Sweep** tool is used to create a swept feature with varying cross section based on specified sketches. The procedure to use this tool is same as discussed earlier in chapter 4.

Section Surface

The **Section Surface** tool is used to create a surface through curve or edge sections using conic shapes. The procedure to use this tool is discussed next.

- Click on the **Section Surface** tool from **Sweep** area in the **More** drop-down of **Base** group in the **Surface** tab of the **Ribbon**. The **Section Surface** dialog box will be displayed; refer to Figure-26.

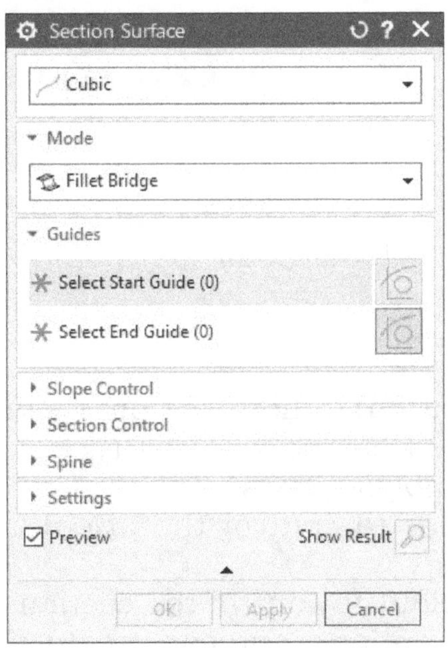

Figure-26. Section Surface dialog box

- Select desired cross-section of the section surface from drop-down in the top area of the dialog box.
- Select desired option from drop-down in the **Mode** rollout to create the respective section surface.
- Select desired edge or curve from the graphics window to control the start location of the surface. Now, click on the **Select End Guide** button from **Guides** rollout and select desired edge or curve to control the end location of the surface; refer to Figure-27.

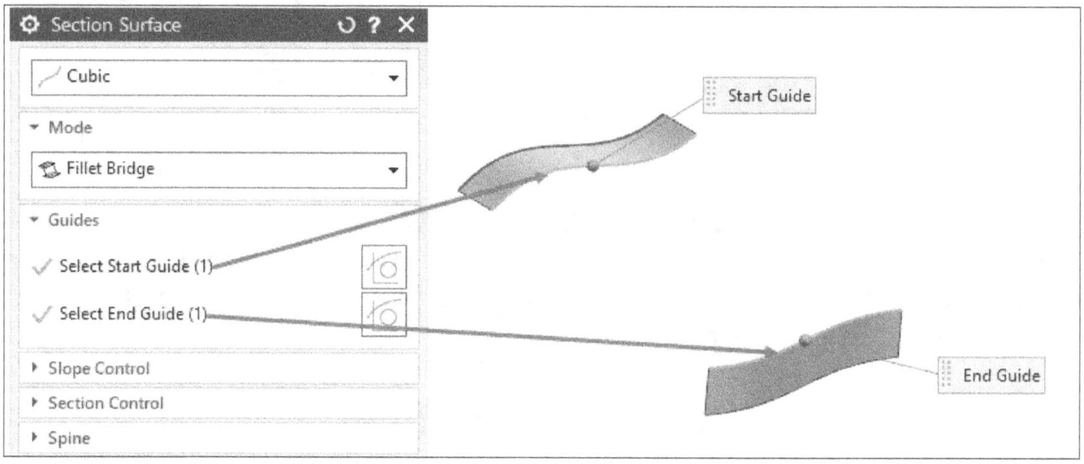

Figure-27. Curves selected as start and end guides

- Select the start face from the graphics window to control the section surface slope from the selected start guide. Now, click on the **Select End Face** button from **Slope Control** rollout and select the end face to control the section surface slope from the selected end guide. On selecting the end face, the preview of section surface will be displayed; refer to Figure-28.

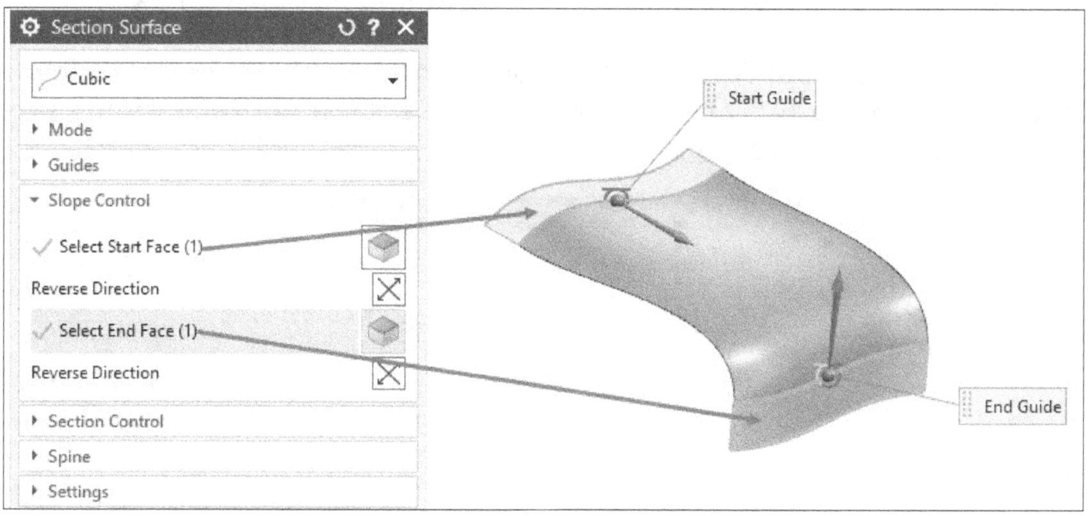

Figure-28. Preview of section surface

- Click on the **Section Control** rollout to control how the sections in a section surface are defined. Based on the selected type, you can define them using a curve, edge, face, or by applying laws.
- Click on the **Spine** rollout to control the orientation of sectioning planes by specifying vector or curve.
- Click on the **Settings** rollout to control the section shape along the U direction, set tolerance and rebuild options, and can create an apex curve.
- Other parameters in the dialog box are same as discussed earlier.

- After specifying desired parameters, click on **OK** button from the dialog box. The section surface feature will be created; refer to Figure-29.

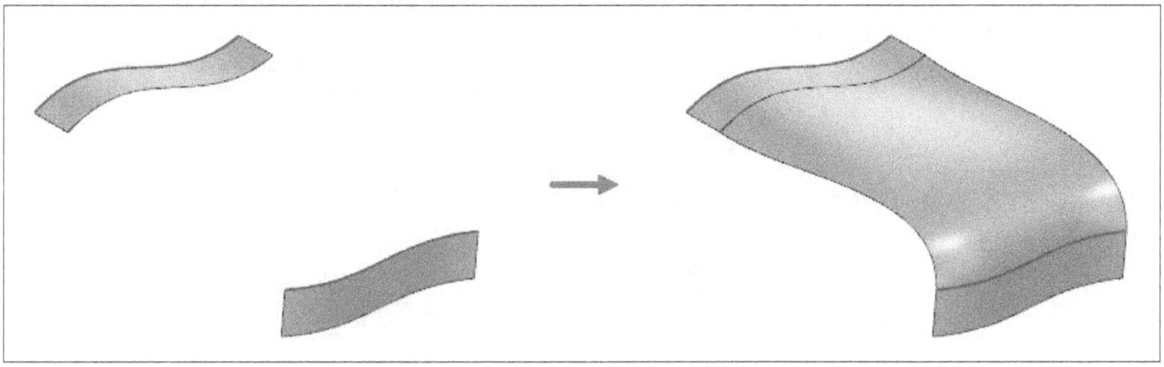

Figure-29. Section surface feature created

Tube

The **Tube** tool is used to create a circular tube of specified diameter along selected curve. The procedure to use this tool is same as discussed earlier in chapter 4.

Swept Volume

The **Swept Volume** tool is used to sweep a solid feature along the path to remove material from other features. The procedure to use this tool is same as discussed earlier in chapter 4.

Ruled

The **Ruled** tool is used to create a body between two sections, where the ruled shape forms a linear transition between the sections. The procedure to use this tool is discussed next.

- Click on the **Ruled** tool from **Mesh** area in the **More** drop-down of **Base** group in **Surface** tab of the **Ribbon**. The **Ruled** dialog box will be displayed; refer to Figure-30.

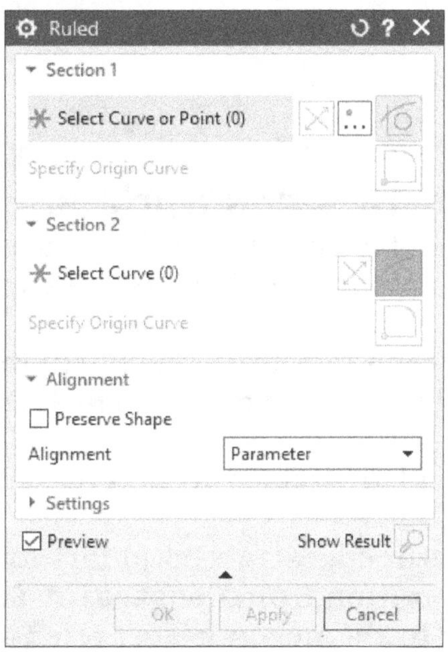

Figure-30. Ruled dialog box

- Select desired curve or point from the graphics window as the section string and then click on the **Select Curve** button from the **Section 2** rollout to select desired curve or point as the second section string. The preview of ruled surface will be displayed; refer to Figure-31.

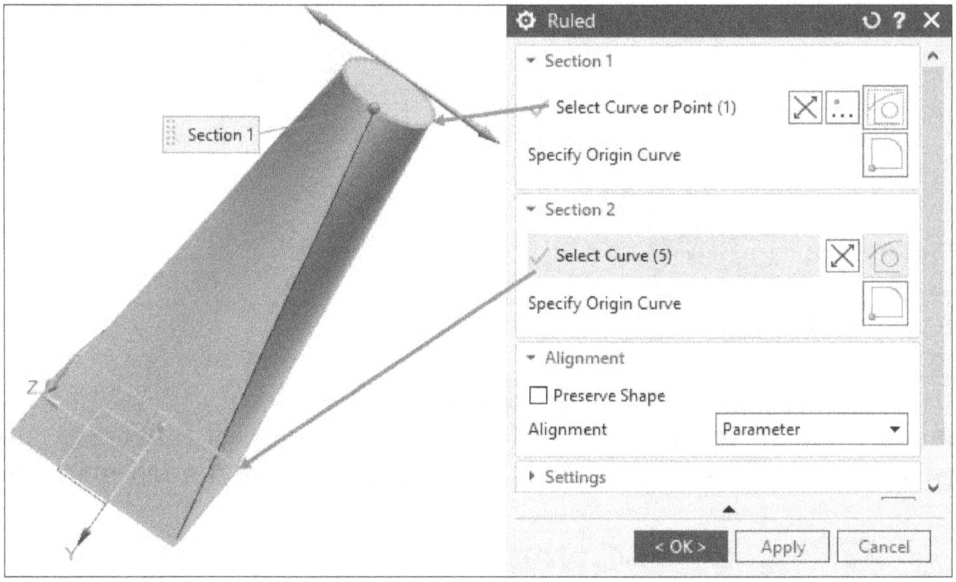

Figure-31. Preview of ruled surface

- Other parameters in the dialog box are same as discussed earlier.
- After specifying desired parameters, click on **OK** button from the dialog box. The ruled surface will be created; refer to Figure-32.

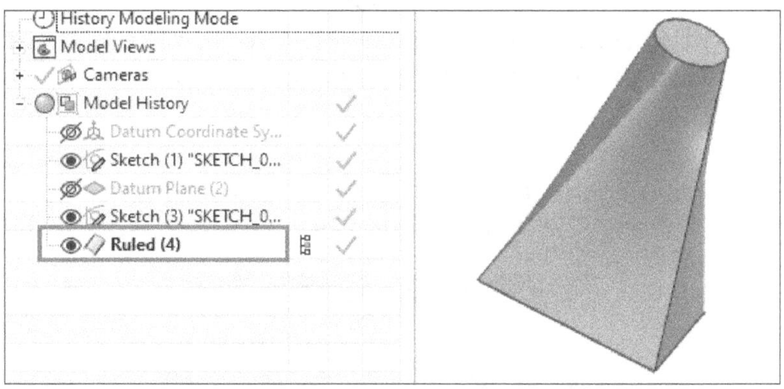

Figure-32. Ruled surface created

N- sided Surface

The **N-sided Surface** tool is used to create a surface enclosed by a set of end connected curve. The procedure to use this tool is discussed next.

- Click on the **N-sided Surface** tool from the **Mesh** area in the **More** drop-down of **Base** group in **Surface** tab of the **Ribbon**. The **N-Sided Surface** dialog box will be displayed; refer to Figure-33.
- Select desired type of N-sided surface to be created from drop-down in the top area of the dialog box.
- Select closed loop of curves or edges as a boundary for creating an N-sided surface.
- Click on the **Select Face** button from **Constraint Faces** rollout to add tangency and curvature continuity to the new surface; refer to Figure-34.

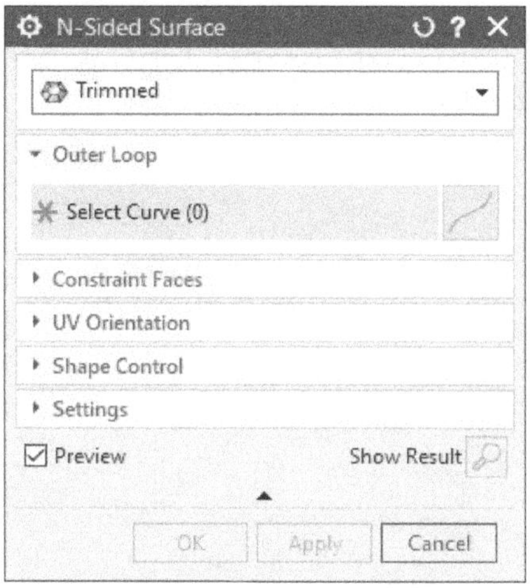

Figure-33. N-Sided Surface dialog box

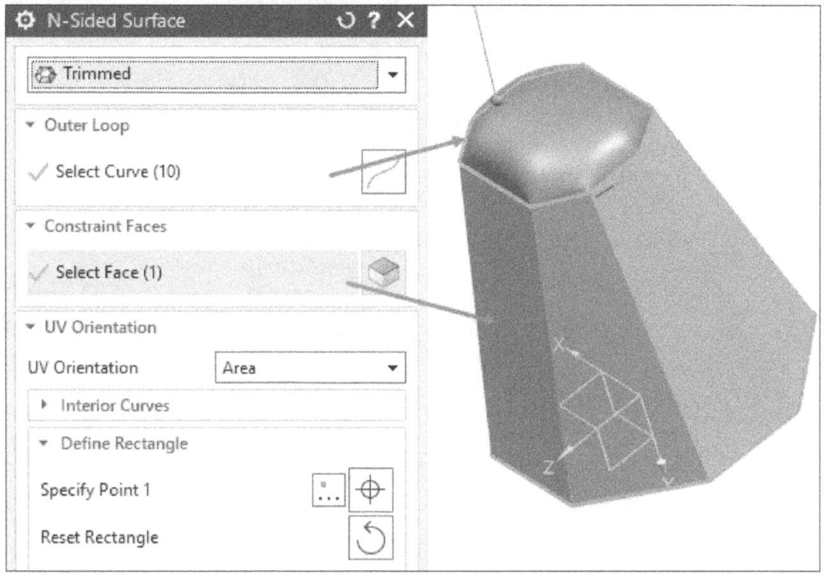

Figure-34. Selecting the face to add tangency and continuity

- Select desired option from **UV Orientation** drop-down of **UV Orientation** rollout to specify the direction of the new surface. Select **Spine** or **Vector** option from the drop-down and specify respective parameters to define the V orientation of the new surface using a spine curve or using a vector, respectively. Select **Area** option from the drop-down and specify respective parameters to create a new surface connecting the boundary curves.
- Specify desired position of the center point in the **Center Control** section of the **Shape Control** rollout and specify desired continuity of the N-sided surface with the selected constraint face in the **Constraint** section of the rollout.
- Other parameters in the dialog box are same as discussed earlier.
- After specifying desired parameters, click on **OK** button from the dialog box. The n-sided surface will be created; refer to Figure-35.

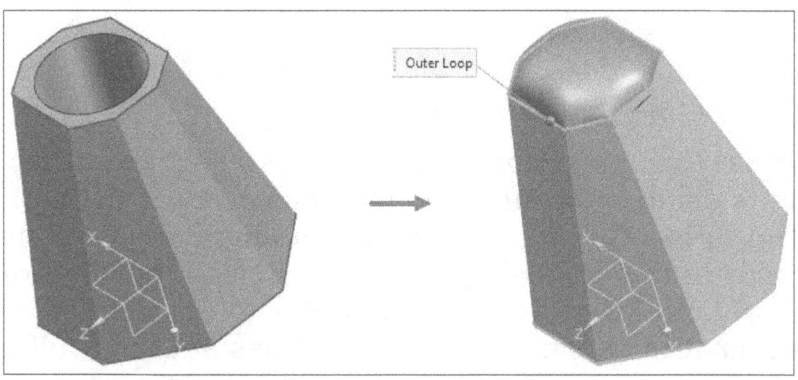

Figure-35. N sided surface created

Aesthetic Face Blend

The **Aesthetic Face Blend** tool is used to create blend surface while applying curvature or tangent constraint. The blend shape can be of circular, conic, or lead-in type. The procedure to use this tool is discussed next.

- Click on the **Aesthetic Face Blend** tool from **Blend** area in the **More** drop-down of **Base** group in the **Surface** tab of the **Ribbon**. The **Aesthetic Face Blend** dialog box will be displayed; refer to Figure-36.

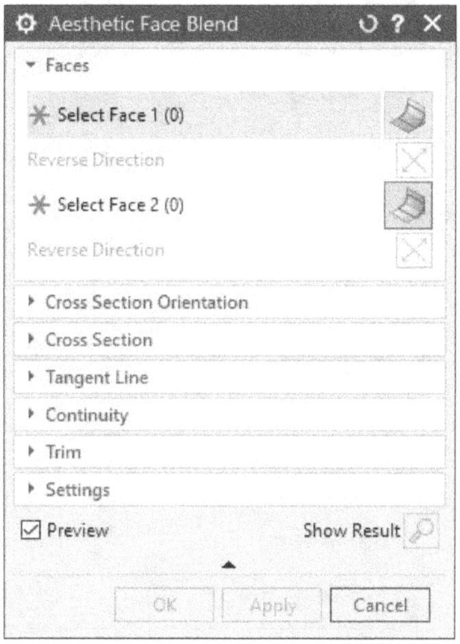

Figure-36. Aesthetic Face Blend dialog box

- Select first set of faces from the graphics window and then click on the **Select Face 2** button from **Faces** rollout to select second set of faces to be blend; refer to Figure-37.

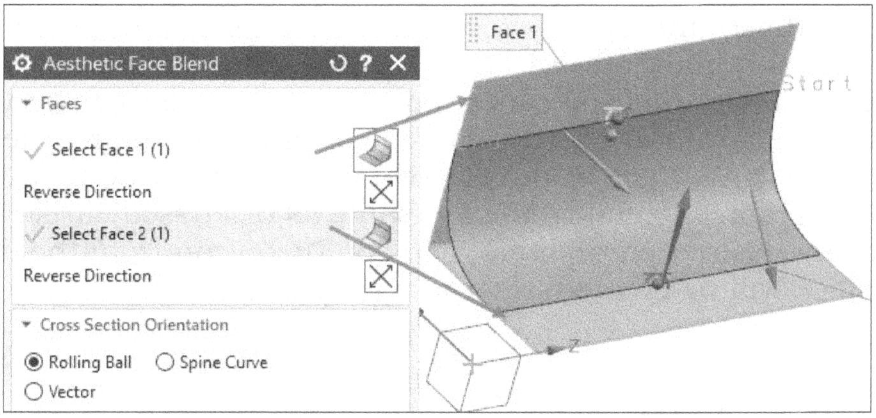

Figure-37. Selecting the faces to be blend

- Select **Rolling Ball** radio button from the **Cross Section Orientation** rollout to align the sections using two contact points and center of the ball as it moves along the faces. Select **Spine Curve** radio button to align the sections using radii that are perpendicular to the defined spine curve. Select **Vector** radio button to align the sections using radii that are perpendicular to the defined direction.
- Select the **Accelerated** check box from the **Cross Section** rollout to control how the blend starts from the first set of faces and connects to the second set of faces. Select **Center Radius** radio button and specify respective parameters to define the depth of the blend. Select **Rho** radio button and specify desired rho value between 0.001 and 1 to create a conic cross-section.
- Select **By Radius** radio button from **Tangent Line** rollout and specify respective parameters to define the rolling ball radius at different points along the blend. Select **By Chord Length** radio button and specify respective parameters to define one or more chord lengths to create the blend tangent curves.

- Select desired continuity constraint for each face of the face chain from **Face 1** and **Face 2** drop-downs in the **Continuity** rollout. On selecting the **Minimum Radius Check** check box, the blend radius will be checked for points that are smaller than the specified threshold value.
- Select desired method from **Trim Blend** drop-down in the **Trim** rollout to trim the blend faces. Select **Trim Body to Blend** check box to trim all the selected faces to be blend. Select **Sew All Faces** check box to sew all trimmed faces of the blend together.
- Select **Enable Length Limit** check box from **Length Limit** rollout and specify the respective parameters to manually start and stop the blend surface based on the selection of objects.
- Select **Specify Minimum Subtended Angle** check box from **Partial Blend** rollout and specify the respective parameters to create partial blends as creating a full blend may create errors.
- Select **Create Washout Surface** check box from **Blend Start** or **Blend End** tab of the **Washout Surface Creation** rollout and specify the respective parameters to scale the start or end section of the washout surface.
- Specify desired degree value for the blend in the U and V directions in the **U** and **V** edit boxes of **Degree** area in the **Settings** rollout.
- Select **Rational Output** check box from **Output** rollout to create the output blend as a rational B-surface. Select **Bezier** check box to create the output blend as bezier surface. Select **Non-associative Centerline Curve** check box to create a non-associative centerline curve of the blend. Select desired option from **Segmentation** drop-down to define the segmentation of blends at different locations or under different conditions.
- Specify desired parameters in the **Tolerance** rollout to define the degree of smoothness needed to transition from one face to another.
- After specifying desired parameters, click on **OK** button from the dialog box. The aesthetic face blend will be created; refer to Figure-38.

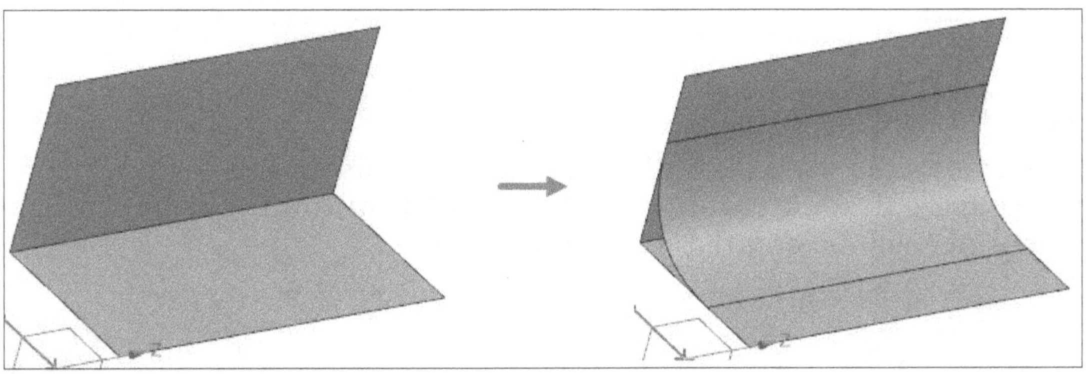

Figure-38. Aesthetic face blend created

Bridge Surface

The **Bridge Surface** tool is used to join two faces with a sheet body. The procedure to use this tool is discussed next.

- Click on the **Bridge Surface** tool from **Blend** area in the **More** drop-down of **Base** group in the **Surface** tab of the **Ribbon**. The **Bridge Surface** dialog box will be displayed; refer to Figure-39.

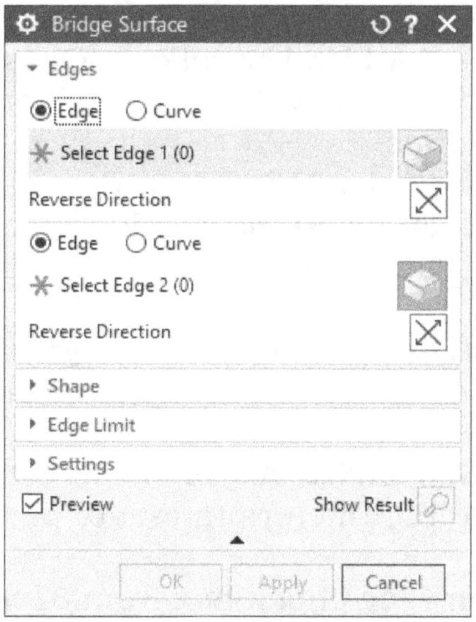

Figure-39. Bridge Surface dialog box

- Select **Edge** or **Curve** radio button from **Edges** rollout to select face edges or face curves for **Edge 1** selection, respectively and then click on the **Select Edge 2** button to select face edges or face curves for **Edge 2** selection; refer to Figure-40.

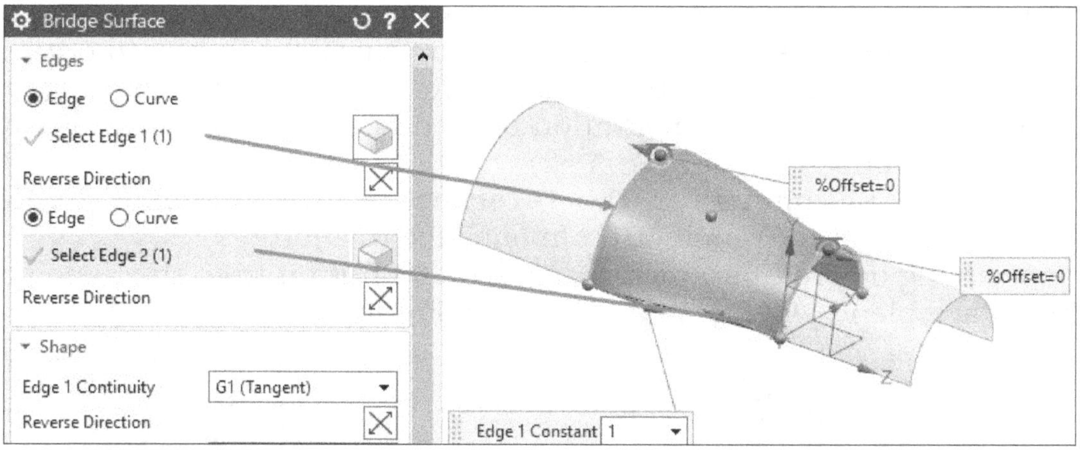

Figure-40. Selecting the edge of faces

- Other parameters in the dialog box are same as discussed earlier.
- After specifying desired parameters, click on **OK** button from the dialog box. The bridge surface will be created; refer to Figure-41.

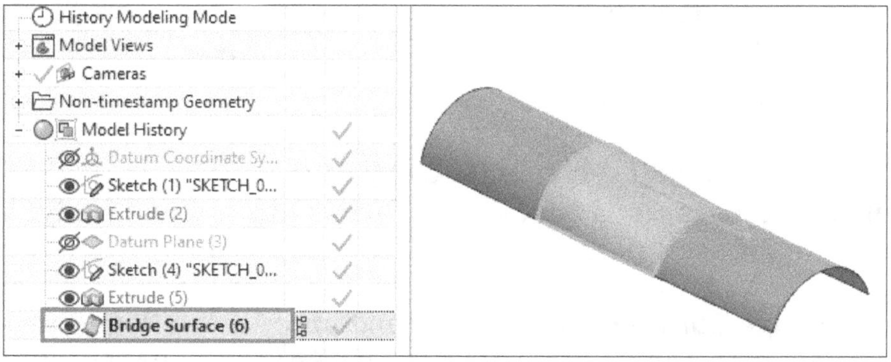

Figure-41. Bridge surface created

Blend Corner

The **Blend Corner** tool is used to create a patch to replace blended corners or interacting blends of existing faces. The procedure to use this tool is discussed next.

- Click on the **Blend Corner** tool from **Blend** area in the **More** drop-down of **Base** group in the **Surface** tab of the **Ribbon**. The **Blend Corner** dialog box will be displayed; refer to Figure-42.

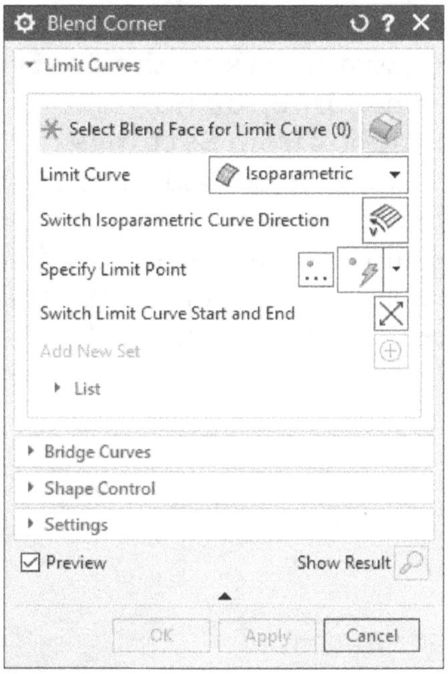

Figure-42. Blend Corner dialog box

- Select desired blend faces from the graphics window for limit curves; refer to Figure-43.

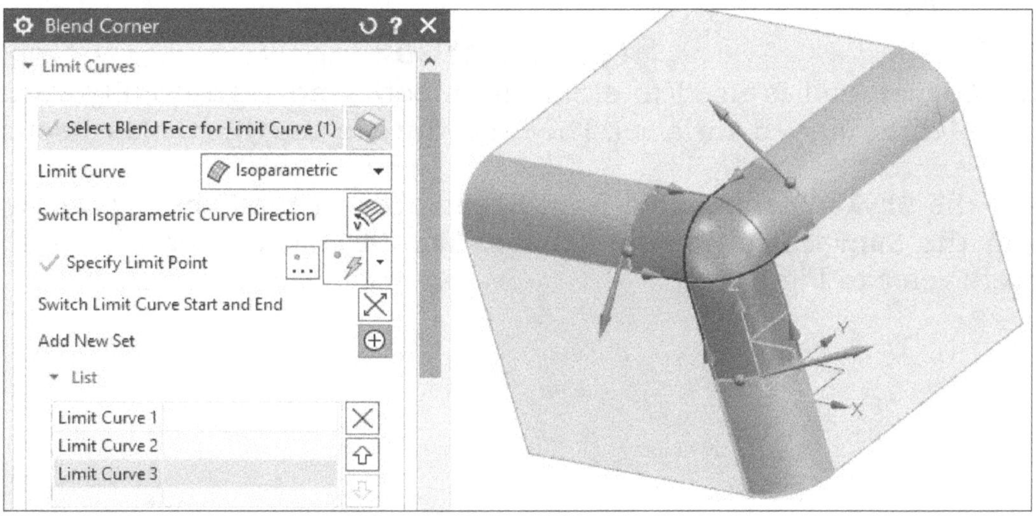

Figure-43. Selecting the blend faces

- Select **Isoparametric** option from the **Limit Curve** drop-down of **Limit Curves** rollout to insert the isoparametric limit curves on the face at the selection point. Select **Planar Intersection** option from the drop-down to insert the planar intersection limit curves on the face at the intersection of specified plane.
- Toggle the **Switch Isoparametric Curve Direction** button to switch the isoparametric curve direction between U and V. Click on the **Specify Limit Point** button to define the location of the limit curve along the blend surface.

- Toggle the **Switch Limit Curve Start and End** button to switch the start and end values and handles of the selected limit curve.
- Select **Blend Face Rail** or **Limit Curve** option from the **Start Tangency Object** and **End Tangency Object** drop-downs to tangent the start and/or end of the selected transition curve to the edge rail of the blend face or to the limit curve of the blend face, respectively. Specify desired tangency value at the start and end of the selected transition curve to the boundaries of the bordering limit curves in the **Start Tangent Magnitude** and **End Tangent Magnitude** edit boxes, respectively.
- Select **Enable Patch Fullness Control** check box from the **Shape Control** rollout and specify the respective parameters in the **Control Point Offset** edit box to inflate or deflate the shape of corner blend.
- Select **Patch into Body** check box from **Settings** rollout to create a separate sheet body from the blend corner face. Select **Allow Bridge Curve on Blend Face** check box to extend bridge curve over a blend surface.
- Other parameters in the dialog box are same as discussed earlier.
- After specifying desired parameters, click on **OK** button from the dialog box. The blend corner will be created; refer to Figure-44.

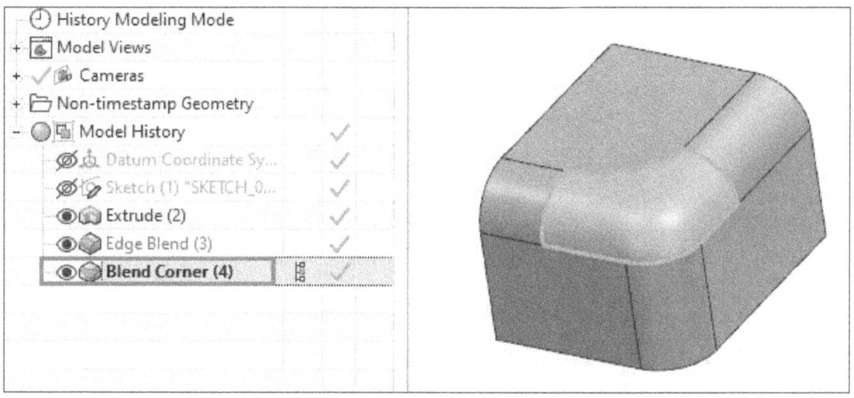

Figure-44. Blend corner created

Styled Corner

The **Styled Corner** tool is used to create a smooth and high-quality corner at the intersection of three curved surfaces. The procedure to use this tool is discussed next.

- Click on the **Styled Corner** tool from **Blend** area in the **More** drop-down of **Base** group in the **Surface** tab of the **Ribbon**. The **Styled Corner** dialog box will be displayed; refer to Figure-45.

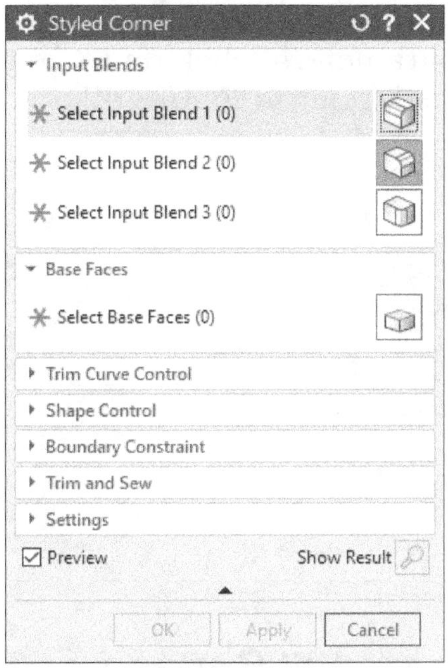

Figure-45. Styled Corner dialog box

- Select three intersecting surfaces one by one from the graphics window to create the corner; refer to Figure-46.

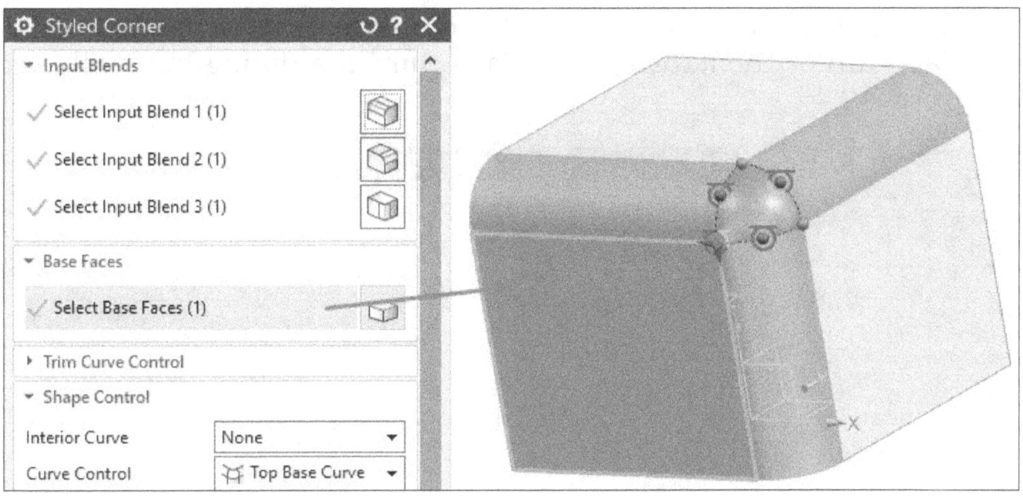

Figure-46. Selecting the intersecting surfaces

- After selecting the intersecting surfaces, select desired base surface(s) that should be opposite to the selected blend surfaces.
- Select **Tangent Continuous** option from **Trim Curve 1** drop-down of **Trim Curve Control** rollout to create a curve tangent to the surface selected for **Input Blend 3** selection button and projects that curve onto the surface selected for either **Input Blend 1** or **Input Blend 2** selection button. Select **Line Projection** option from the drop-down to create a linear curve between the vertex points and projects it onto the blend surface to create the trim curve. Select **Isoparametric** option from the drop-down to create a trim curve along the Iso-U or Iso-V direction, starting from the intersection point of tangent lines of the blend. Similarly, select desired option from the **Trim Curve 2** drop-down.
- Select desired option from **Interior Curve** drop-down of **Shape Control** rollout to define the shape of the styled corner at points inside the curve. Select desired option from **Curve Control** drop-down to specify the start and end point of the base curve or the bottom bridge curve by the position handles.

- Other parameters in the dialog box are same as discussed earlier.
- After specifying desired parameters, click on **OK** button from the dialog box. The styled corner will be created; refer to Figure-47.

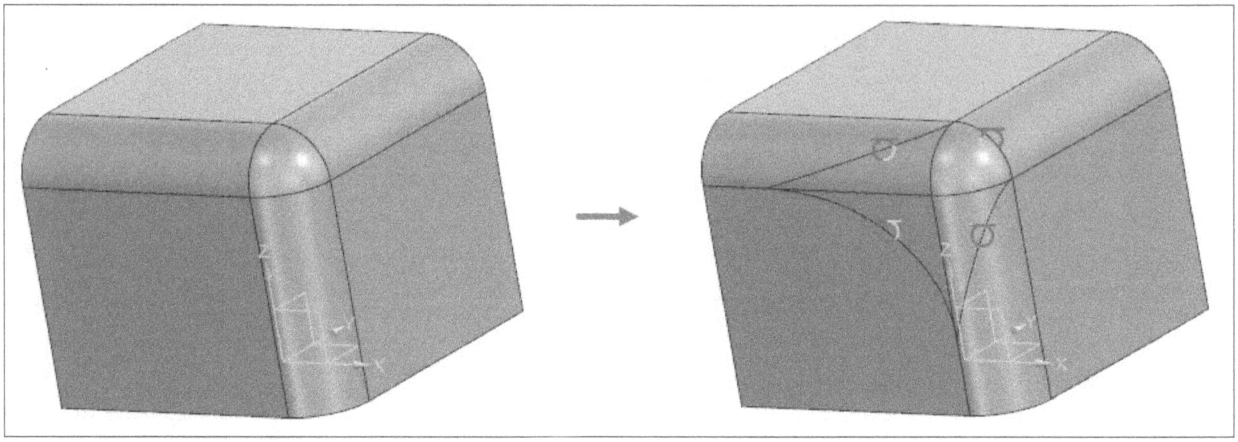

Figure-47. Styled corner created

Fill Surface

The **Fill Surface** tool is used to create a surface using boundary curves or edges. The procedure to use this tool is discussed next.

- Click on the **Fill Surface** tool from **Fill** area in the **More** drop-down of **Base** group in the **Surface** tab of the **Ribbon**. The **Fill Surface** dialog box will be displayed; refer to Figure-48.

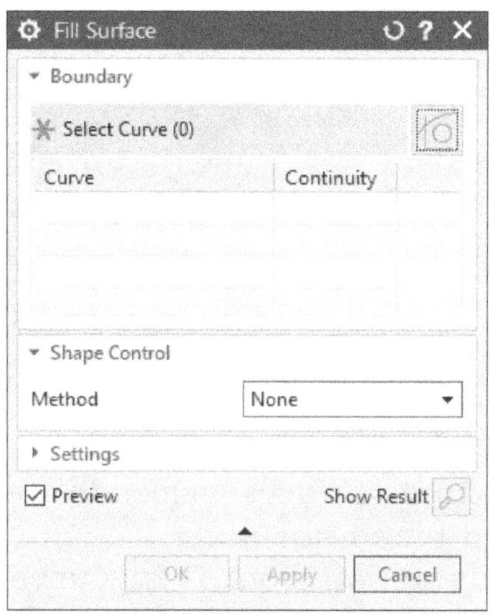

Figure-48. Fill Surface dialog box

- Select desired set of connected edges and curves from the graphics window to create the boundary of a fill surface, the selected curve will be displayed in the list box of **Boundary** rollout; refer to Figure-49.

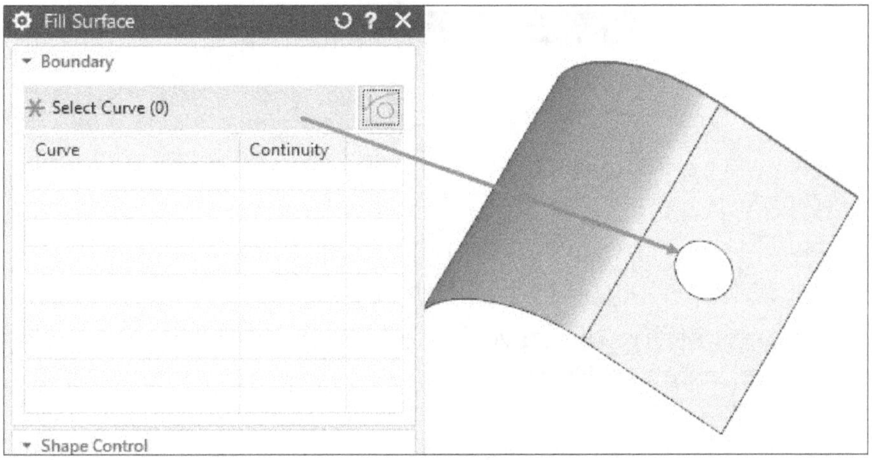

Figure-49. Selecting the set of connected edges or curves

- Select **None** option from **Method** drop-down of **Shape Control** rollout to apply no more constraints on the surface. Select **Fullness** option from the drop-down and specify the respective parameters to modify the surface by dragging it along its normal direction at specified point. Select **Fit to Curves** option from the drop-down and select desired curves to fit the surface to the selected curves. Select **Fit to Facet Body** option from the drop-down and select desired facet body to fit the surface to a selected facet body.
- Other parameters in the dialog box are same as discussed earlier.
- After specifying desired parameters, click on **OK** button from the dialog box. The fill surface will be created; refer to Figure-50.

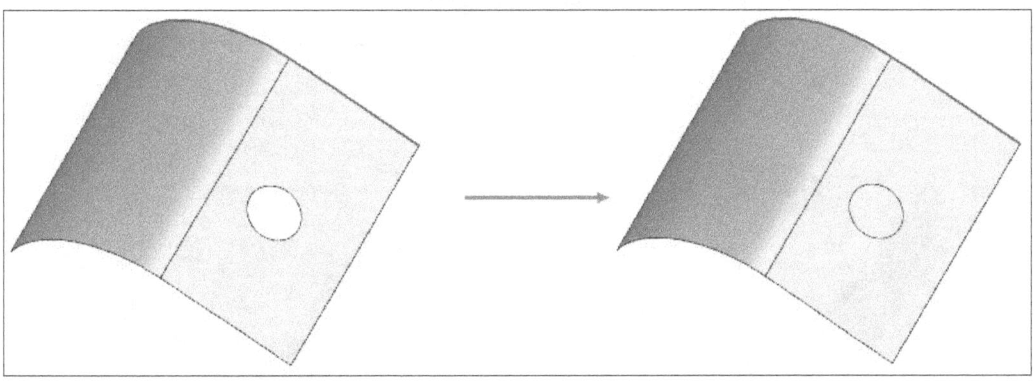
Figure-50. Fill surface created

Bounded Plane

The **Bounded Plane** tool is used to create a planar sheet body enclosed by a set of closed planar curves. The procedure to use this tool is discussed next.

- Click on the **Bounded Plane** tool from **Fill** area in the **More** drop-down of **Base** group in the **Surface** tab of the **Ribbon**. The **Bounded Plane** dialog box will be displayed; refer to Figure-51.

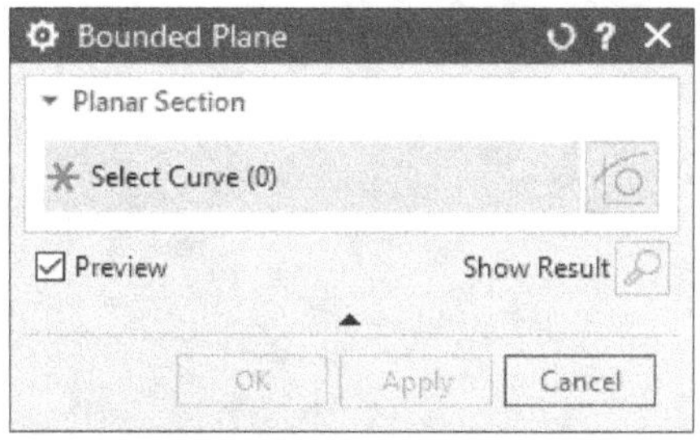

Figure-51. Bounded Plane dialog box

- Select desired closed string of curves or edges from the graphics window to create the bounded plane; refer to Figure-52.

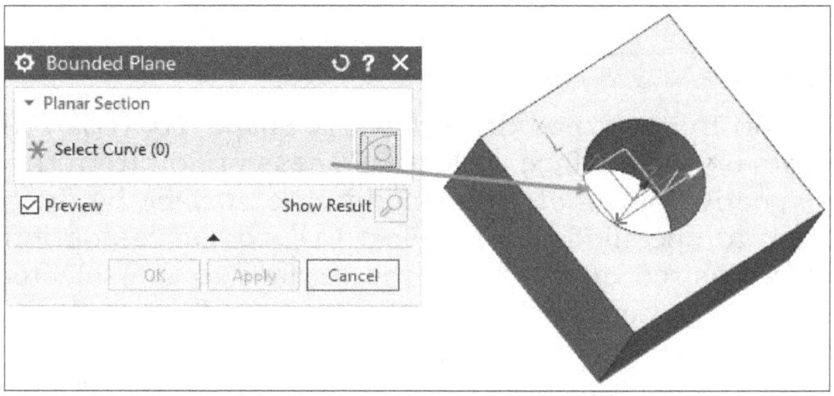

Figure-52. Selecting the string of curves

- After specifying desired parameters, click on **OK** button from the dialog box. The bounded plane will be created; refer to Figure-53.

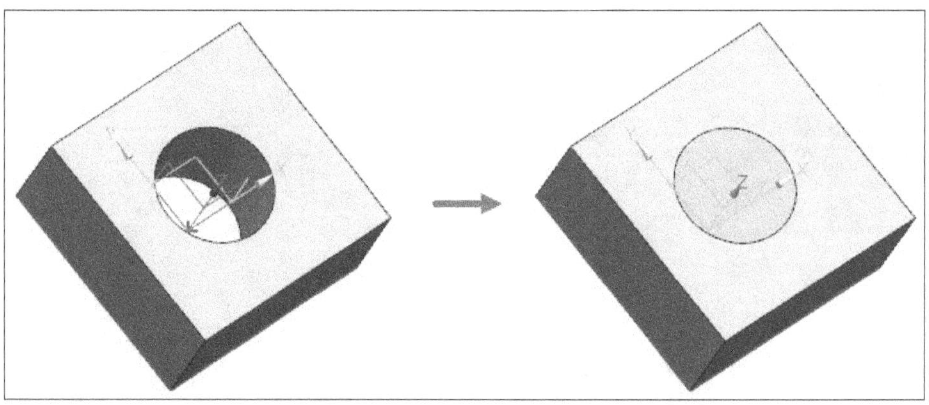

Figure-53. Bounded plane created

Patch Openings

The **Patch Openings** tool is used to create a sheet body to fill gaps between the faces. The procedure to use this tool is discussed next.

- Click on the **Patch Openings** tool from **Fill** area in the **More** drop-down of **Base** group in the **Surface** tab of the **Ribbon**. The **Patch Openings** dialog box will be displayed; refer to Figure-54.

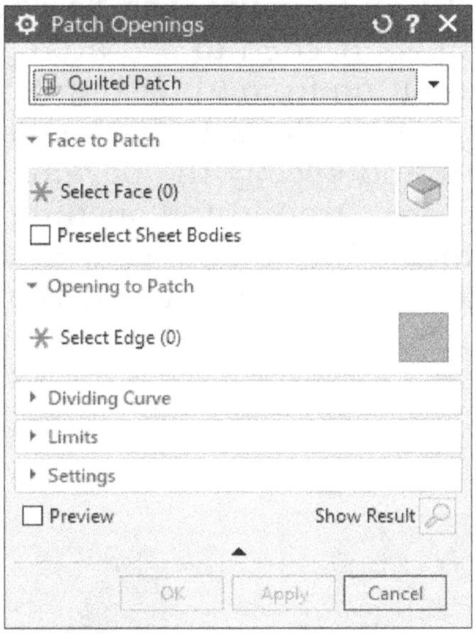

Figure-54. Patch Openings dialog box

- Select desired method from drop-down in the top area of the dialog box to create the patch openings feature. Select **Quilted Patch** option to fill the opening with a series of patches that closely match its shape. Select **N-sided Area Patch** option to create an N-sided patch surface using curves or edges that form a simple, open, or closed loop. Select **Mesh** option to create a mesh sheet body to fill the gaps. Select **By Removing Edges** option to remove the edges around the opening and joins the surrounding faces. Select **Extension Only** option to extend the edges of the opening in a direction that is tangential to the surrounding faces. Select **Notch** option to fill a notch or a cutout of a larger opening. Select **Joggle** option to fill an area of a larger opening where the edges of opening are on multiple planes. Select **Mold Wizard Face Patch** option to create a feature using the Edge Patch method in the Mold Wizard application. Select **By Suppression** option to identify features linked to the edges and suppresses them to fill the hole.
- Select desired faces with openings that need to be filled; refer to Figure-55.

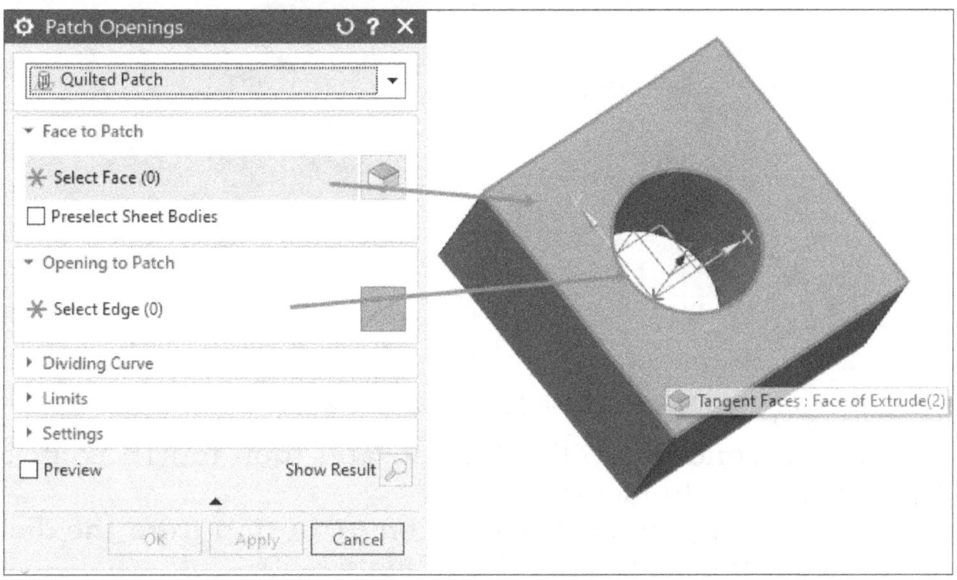

Figure-55. Selecting the face with opening

- Select **Preselect Sheet Bodies** check box from **Face to Patch** rollout to automatically select all the sheet bodies.

- Click on the **Select Edge** button from **Opening to Patch** rollout and select desired edges that define the openings needed to be patch.
- Click on the **Select Curve** button from **Dividing Curve** rollout and select desired curve between two points on the selected edge to split the opening into two parts.
- Click on the **Limits** rollout and specify the parameters to create a partial patch sheet body by limiting the area around the opening.
- Other parameters in the dialog box are same as discussed earlier.
- After specifying desired parameters, click on **OK** button from the dialog box. The opening will be patched; refer to Figure-56.

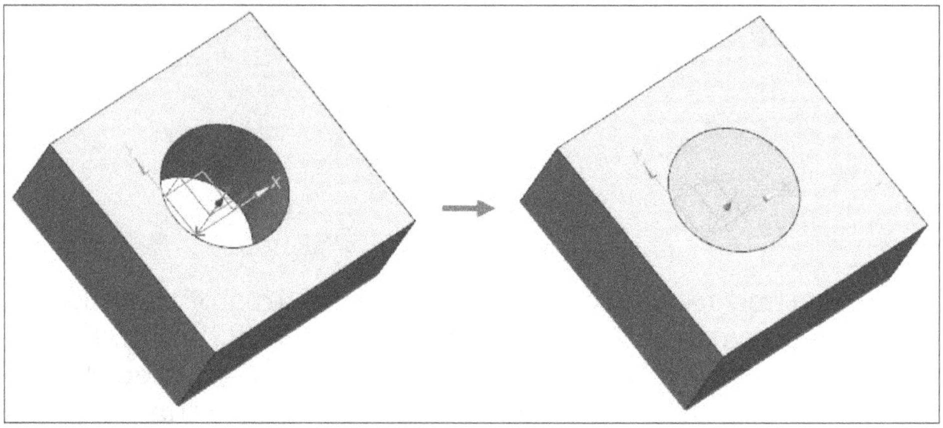

Figure-56. Opening patched

Four Point Surface

The **Four Point Surface** tool is used to create a surface by defining four corner points. The procedure to use this tool is discussed next.

- Click on the **Four Point Surface** tool from **Fill** area in the **More** drop-down of **Base** group in the **Surface** tab of the **Ribbon**. The **Four Point Surface** dialog box will be displayed; refer to Figure-57.

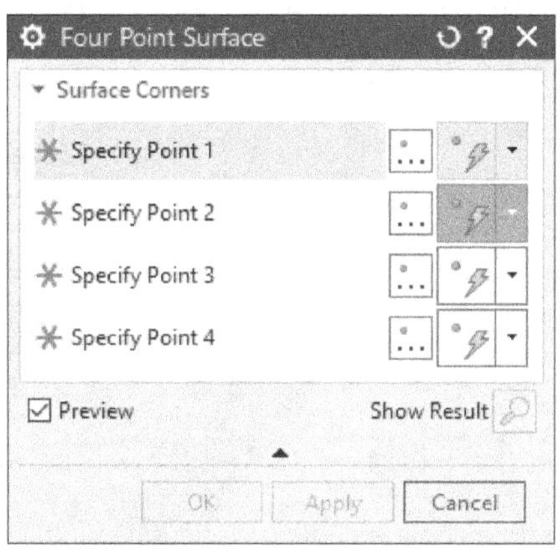

Figure-57. Four Point Surface dialog box

- Select first point, second point, third point, and then fourth point to create the four point surface; refer to Figure-58.
- After specifying desired parameters, click on **OK** button from the dialog box. The four point surface will be created; refer to Figure-59.

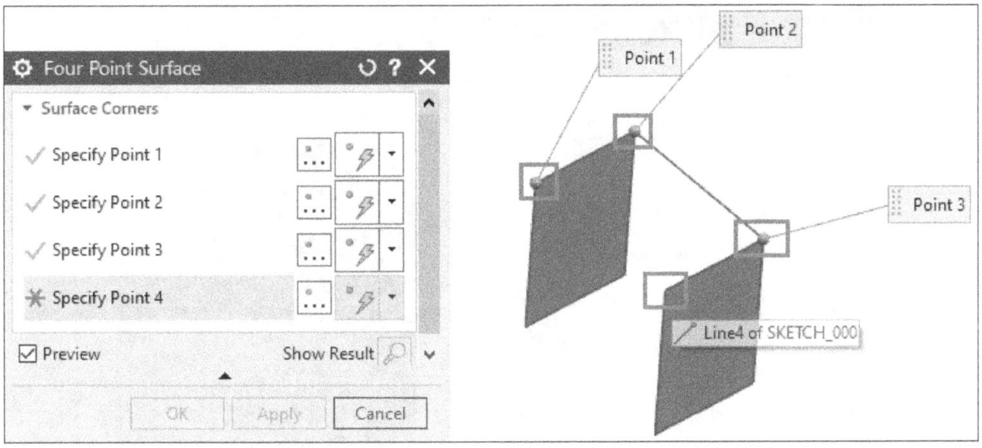

Figure-58. Selecting the four points

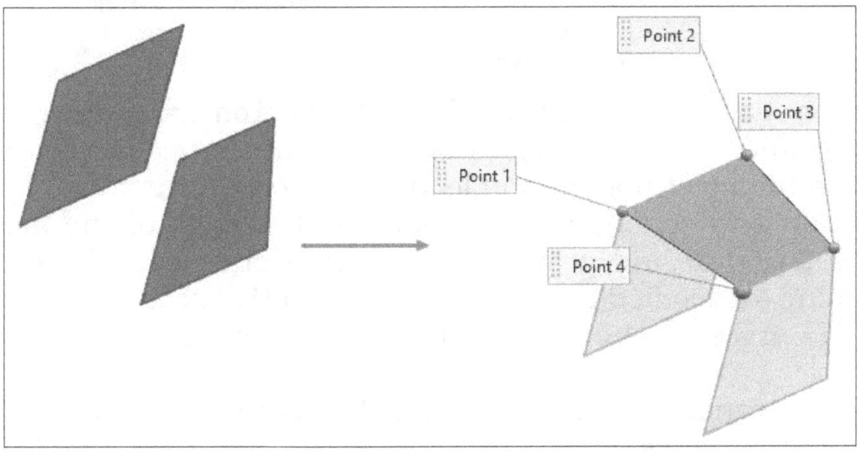

Figure-59. Four points surface created

Rapid Surfacing

The **Rapid Surfacing** tool is used to create a surface model from a facet body (The procedures to create and manage facet bodies are discussed in Chapter 11). The procedure to use this tool is discussed next.

- Click on the **Rapid Surfacing** tool from **Fit** area in the **More** drop-down of **Base** group in the **Surface** tab of the **Ribbon**. The **Rapid Surfacing** dialog box will be displayed; refer to Figure-60.

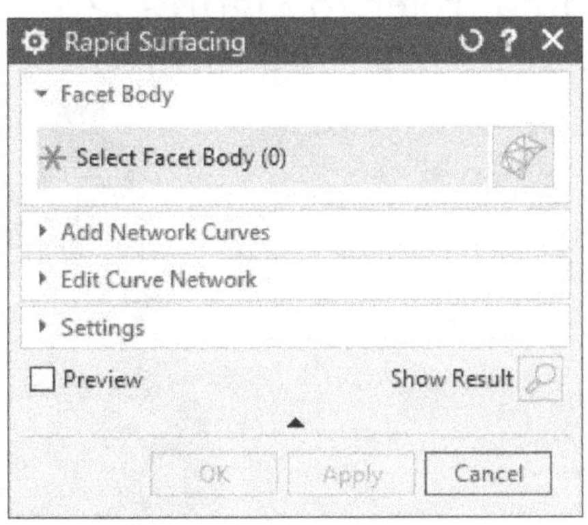

Figure-60. Rapid Surfacing dialog box

- Select desired facet body from the graphics window to create surface; refer to Figure-61.

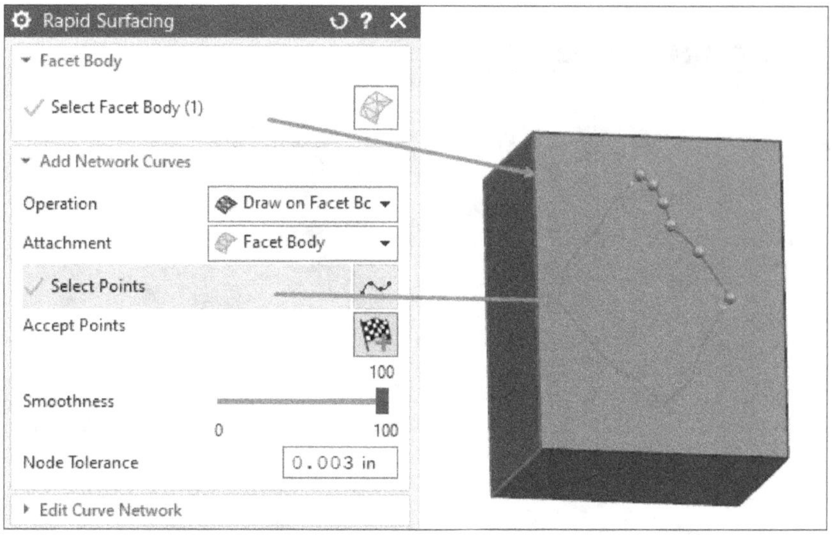

Figure-61. Selecting the facet body and points

- Select **Draw on Facet Body** option from **Operation** drop-down of **Add Network Curves** rollout and select desired points to create a temporary spline, which is projected onto the facet body along local direction of the surface. Select **Draw on Boundary** option and specify the points along the edge of the facet body. Select **Import Curves** option and project the selected curves to the curve network of facet body using a specified direction. Select **Subdivide Loop** option to divide one closed loop of curves on the facet body into multiple loops by selecting U and V loop curves.
- Enter desired tolerance value in the **Node Tolerance** edit box to specify the selection tolerance on patch nodes.
- Click on the **Delete Curves** or **Delete Nodes** button from **Edit Curve Network** rollout to delete curves or delete mesh nodes from the network, respectively. Click on the **Drag Curve Point** button to modify a mesh curve by dragging handles along the surface of facet body. Click on the **Drag Mesh Node** button to modify the mesh node position by dragging the node handle along the surface of facet body.
- Specify degree and number of segments for all feature surfaces in the U and V direction in the **Degree** and **Segments** edit boxes of **Settings** rollout, respectively.
- Other options in the dialog box is same as discussed earlier.
- After specifying desired parameters, click on **OK** button from the dialog box. The surface model will be created; refer to Figure-62.

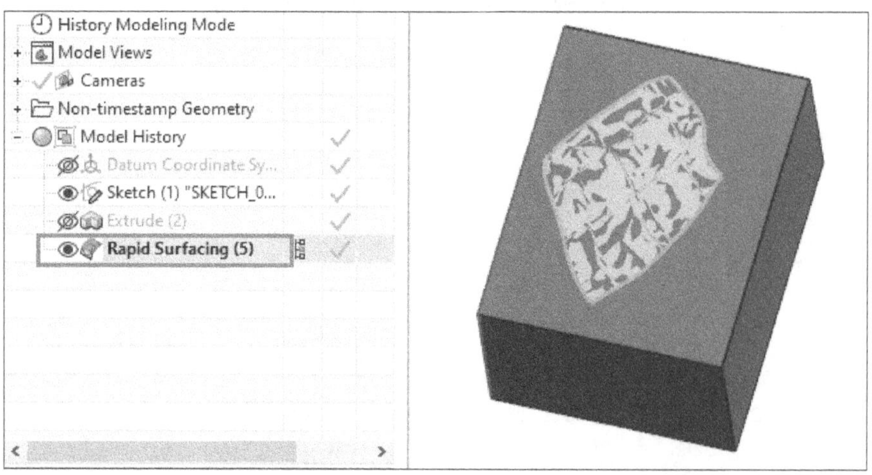

Figure-62. Surface model created

Fit Surface

The **Fit Surface** tool is used to create a freeform surface, sphere, plane, cone, or cylinder by fitting it to specified data points or facet bodies. The procedure to use this tool is discussed next.

- Click on the **Fit Surface** tool from **Fit** area in the **More** drop-down of **Base** group in the **Surface** tab of the **Ribbon**. The **Fit Surface** dialog box will be displayed; refer to Figure-63.

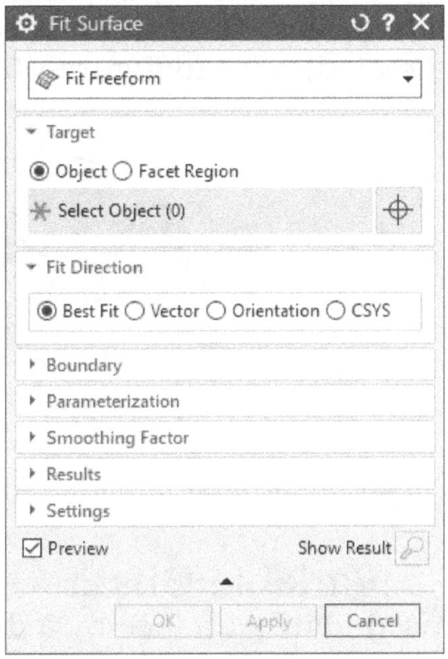

Figure-63. Fit Surface dialog box

- Select desired type of geometry to be fitted to specified data points from drop-down in the top area of the dialog box and specify respective parameters.
- Select **Object** radio button from **Target** rollout to select facet body, curve feature, or point groups as a target for a fit surface. Select **Facet Region** radio button to select one or more regions on facet bodies; refer to Figure-64.

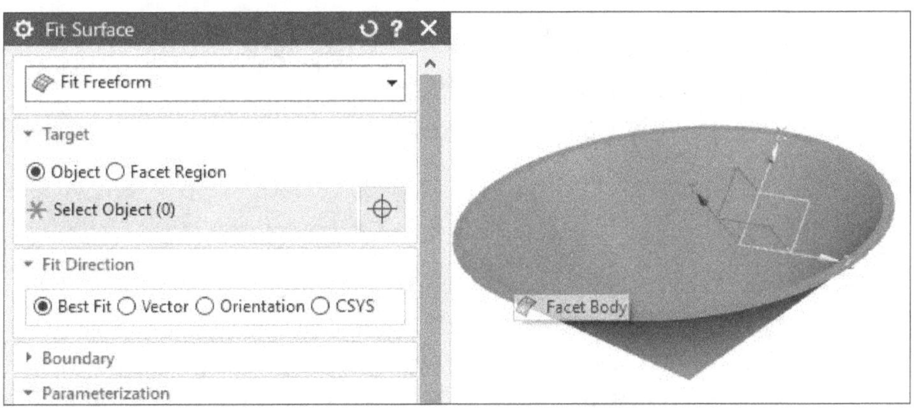

Figure-64. Selecting the object as target for fit surface

- The **Radius** area in the **Results** rollout displays the radius value of the sphere or cylinder. The **Half Angle** area displays the half angle value of a fitted cone. The **Maximum Error** area displays the maximum deviation distance from target to the fitted surface. The **Average Error** area displays the average deviation distance from target to the fitted surface.

- Select **Single Surface** check box from **Settings** rollout to fit one object to all the selected objects or facet regions. Select **Create Multiple Features** check box to create a separate fit surface feature for facet region or the selected object. Select **Automatic Point Rejection** check box and specify rejection threshold distance in the respective edit box to remove all points beyond the defined threshold to reduce the influence of spikes.
- Select **Sheet** or **Solid** option from the **Body Type** drop-down to fit a sheet body or solid body to the target, respectively.
- Other options in the dialog box is same as discussed earlier.
- After specifying desired parameters, click on **OK** button from the dialog box. The fit surface feature will be created; refer to Figure-65.

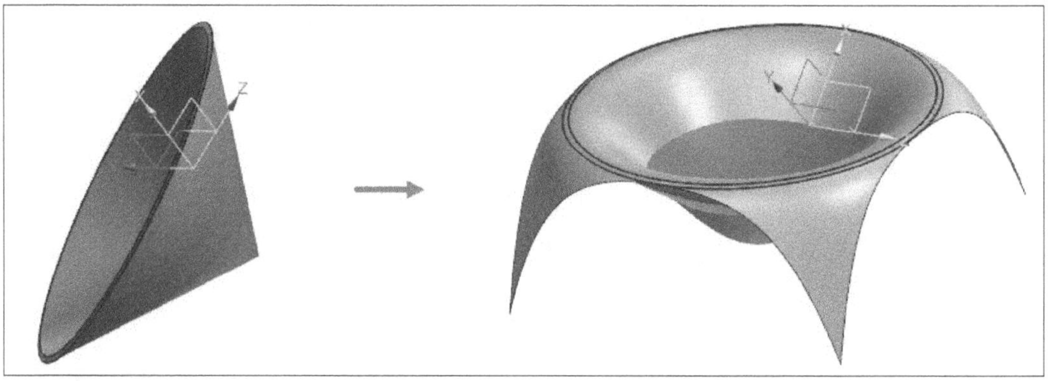

Figure-65. Fit surface created

Variable Offset

The **Variable Offset** tool is used to offset a face by a distance that can vary at four different points. The procedure to use this tool is discussed next.

- Click on the **Variable Offset** tool from **Offset** area in the **More** drop-down of **Base** group in the **Surface** tab of the **Ribbon**. The **Variable Offset** dialog box will be displayed; refer to Figure-66.

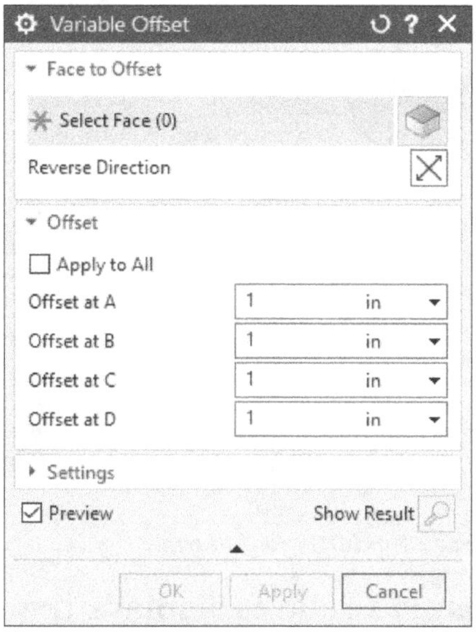

Figure-66. Variable Offset dialog box

- Select desired face from the graphics window to be offset; refer to Figure-67.

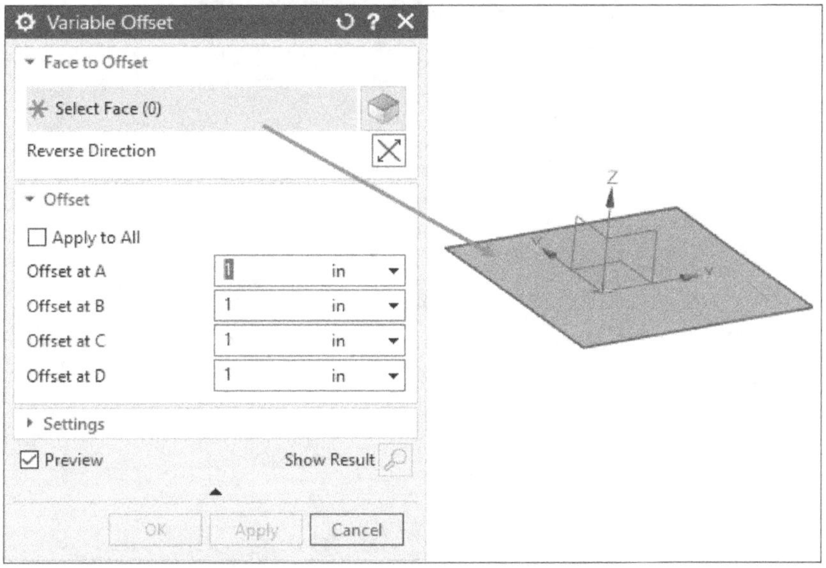

Figure-67. Selecting the face to be offset

- Select **Apply to All** check box from **Offset** rollout to link all offsets to a single value. Specify desired value for the A, B, C and D offset points on the surface in the respective edit boxes.
- Select **Keep Parameterization** check box from **Settings** rollout to match the b-surface parameters to the output variable offset surface. Select **Linear** or **Cubic** interpolation method from **Method** drop-down.
- Other parameters in the dialog box are same as discussed earlier.
- After specifying desired parameters, click on **OK** button from the dialog box. The variable offset feature will be created; refer to Figure-68.

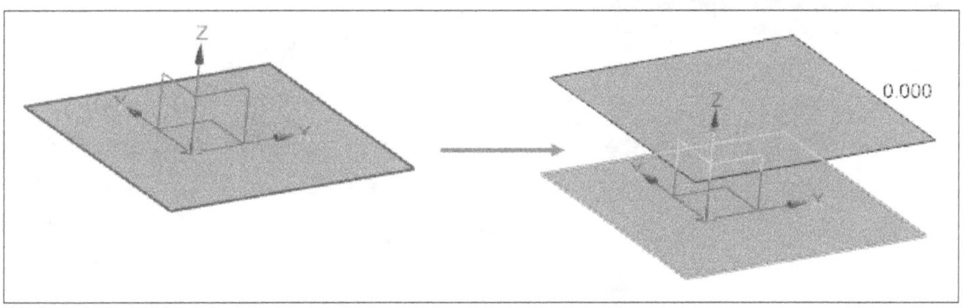

Figure-68. Variable offset feature created

Variable Offset Face

The **Variable Offset Face** tool is used to offset multiple regions of a body, using constant offset in some regions and variable offset at another regions to create a bridge between constant-offset regions. The procedure to use this tool is discussed next.

- Click on the **Variable Offset Face** tool from **Offset** area in the **More** drop-down of **Base** group in the **Surface** tab of the **Ribbon**. The **Variable Offset Face** dialog box will be displayed; refer to Figure-69.

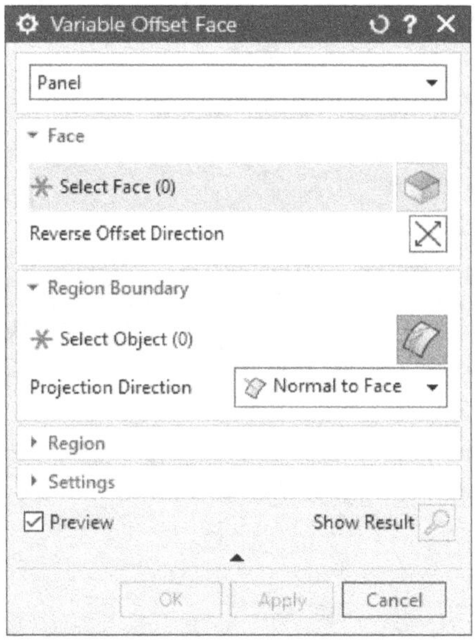

Figure-69. Variable Offset Face dialog box

- Select desired option from drop-down in the top area of the dialog box to be used to offset.
- Select one or more faces from the graphics window to be offset or bridge; refer to Figure-70.
- Click on the **Select Object** button from **Region Boundary** rollout to select desired plane, curve, or surface that define the offset area of selected face; refer to Figure-70. Select desired option from **Projection Direction** drop-down to define the direction of the pad thickness.

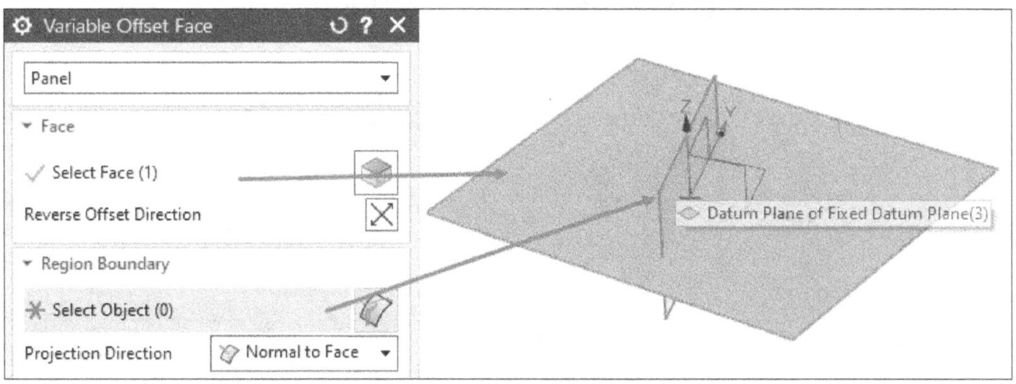

Figure-70. Selecting the face to be offset

- Click on the **Select Region** button from the **Region** rollout and select desired region of face to be defined as offset or bridge. Select **Offset** radio button to specify desired offset value of a region. Select **Bridge** radio button to defined the selected region as a bridge between offset thickness.
- Other parameters in the dialog box are same as discussed earlier.
- After specifying desired parameters, click on **OK** button from the dialog box. The variable offset face will be created; refer to Figure-71.

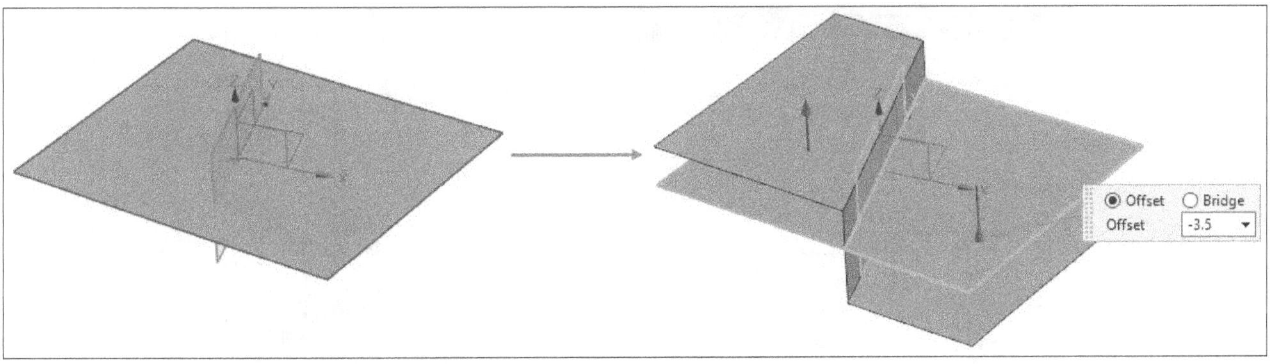

Figure-71. Variable offset face created

Extension Surface

The **Extension Surface** tool is used to create an extension surface sheet from an existing base sheet. The procedure to use this tool is discussed next.

- Click on the **Extension Surface** tool from **Flange** area in the **More** drop-down of **Base** group in the **Surface** tab of the **Ribbon**. The **Extension Surface** dialog box will be displayed; refer to Figure-72.

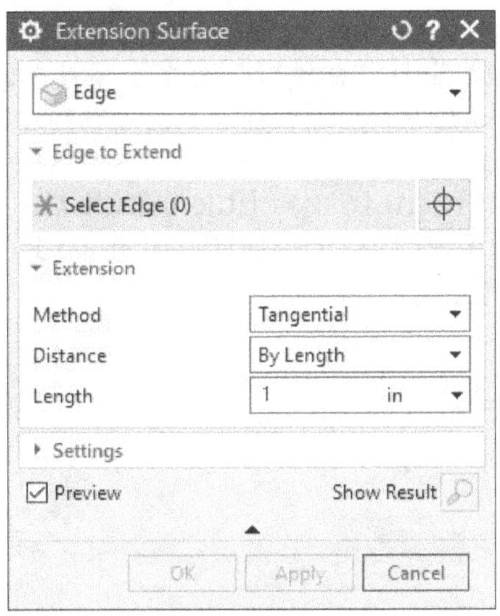

Figure-72. Extension Surface dialog box

- Select desired option from drop-down in the top area of the dialog box to specify the location of creating the new extension surface sheet body.
- Click on the **Select Edge** button from **Edge to Extend** rollout and select desired edge or corner of the face from the graphics window to create an extension surface feature; refer to Figure-73.

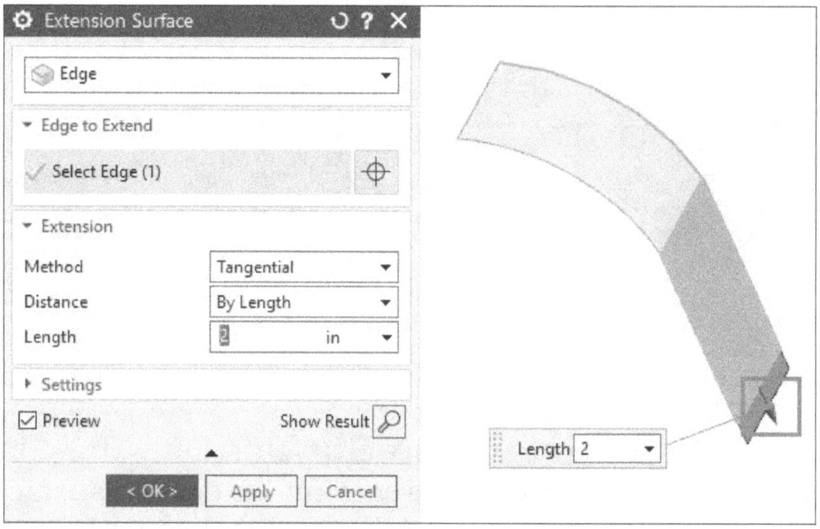

Figure-73. Selecting the edge to create an extension surface

- Select **Tangential** option from **Method** drop-down in the **Extension** rollout to create an extension surface feature that is tangent to a specified edge. Select **Circular** option from the drop-down to create an extension surface feature that is circular along the selected edge. Select desired option from **Distance** drop-down to specify desired distance of the extension surface by length or by percentage. Specify desired length value in the **% U Length** and **% V Length** edit boxes for the corner extension surface in the U and V directions, respectively.
- Other options in the dialog box is same as discussed earlier.
- After specifying desired parameters, click on **OK** button from the dialog box. The extension surface feature will be created; refer to Figure-74.

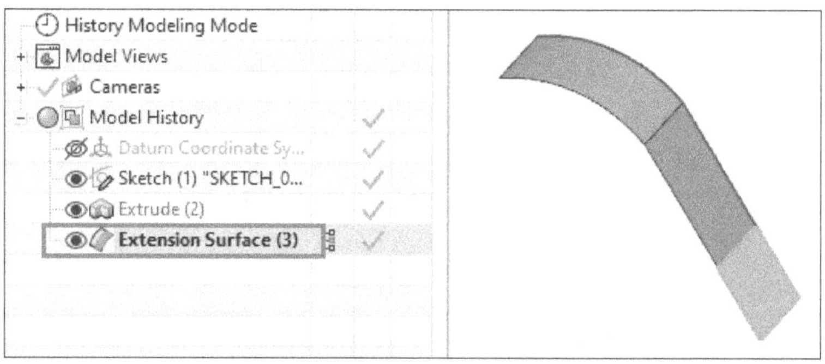

Figure-74. Extension surface feature created

Silhouette Flange

The **Silhouette Flange** tool is used to create a smooth, high-quality surface with smooth edge details, optimized shape, and continuous slope transitions. The procedure to use this tool is discussed next.

- Click on the **Silhouette Flange** tool from **Flange** area in the **More** drop-down of **Base** group in the **Surface** tab of the **Ribbon**. The **Silhouette Flange** dialog box will be displayed; refer to Figure-75.

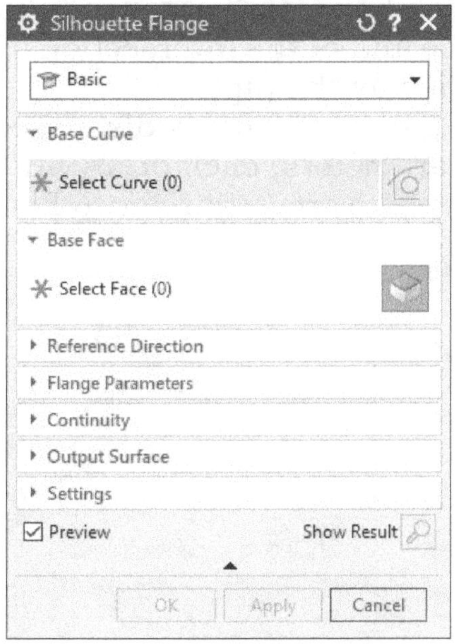

Figure-75. Silhouette Flange dialog box

- Select desired type of silhoutte flange to be created from drop-down in the top area of the dialog box.
- Select desired curve or edge on a surface to specify the attach point for the pipe.
- Click on the **Select Face** button from **Base Face** rollout and select desired face on which the pipe surface is to be placed; refer to Figure-76.

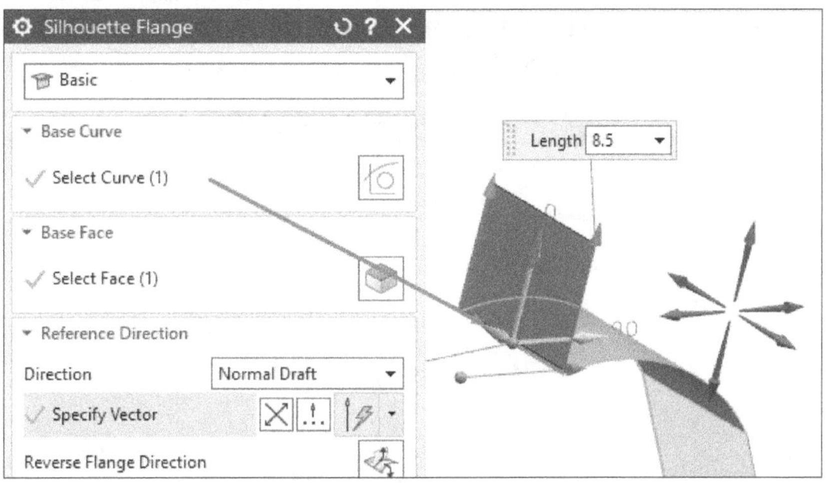

Figure-76. Selecting the curve on a surface

- Select desired option from **Direction** drop-down in the **Reference Direction** rollout and specify the respective parameters to define the flange direction in relation to the base face.
- Click on the **Reverse Flange Direction** button to reverse the flange extension to the opposite side of the defined curve and click on the **Reverse Flange Side** button to reverse the flange extension to the opposite side of the base curve.
- Click on the **Flange Parameters** rollout and specify desired radius, length, and angle of a flange in the **Radius**, **Length**, and **Angle** rollouts, respectively.
- Select desired output to be created from **Output Options** drop-down in the **Output Surface** rollout. Select **Trim Base Faces** rollout to trim the base face. Select **Merge Faces if Possible** check box to merge the tangent faces into a single face. Select **Extend Flange** check box to extend the flange across the whole area of the base surface.

- Select **Create Curves** check box from **Settings** rollout to create b-spline curves along the center of the tube and at the intersection of the blend and flange. Select **Show Pipe** check box to display the pipe.
- Other options in the dialog box is same as discussed earlier.
- After specifying desired parameters, click on **OK** button from the dialog box. The silhouette flange feature will be created; refer to Figure-77.

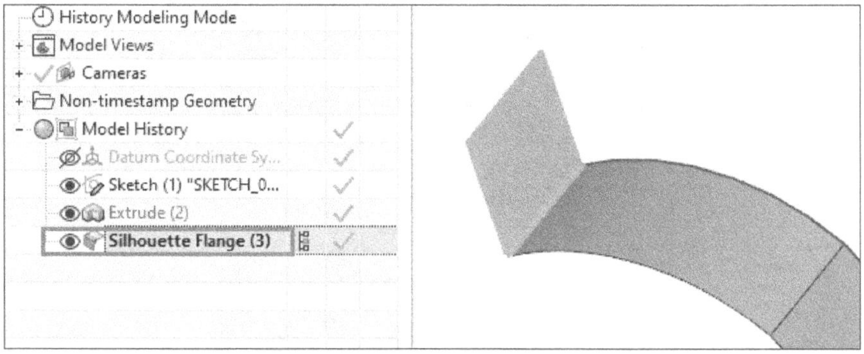

Figure-77. Silhouette flange feature created

Face Pairs

The **Face Pairs** tool is used to create a continuous surface feature between opposite faces of a thin-walled solid body. The procedure to use this tool is discussed next.

- Click on the **Face Pairs** tool from **Midsurface** area in the **More** drop-down of **Base** group in the **Surface** tab of the **Ribbon**. The **Midsurface by Face Pairs** dialog box will be displayed; refer to Figure-78.

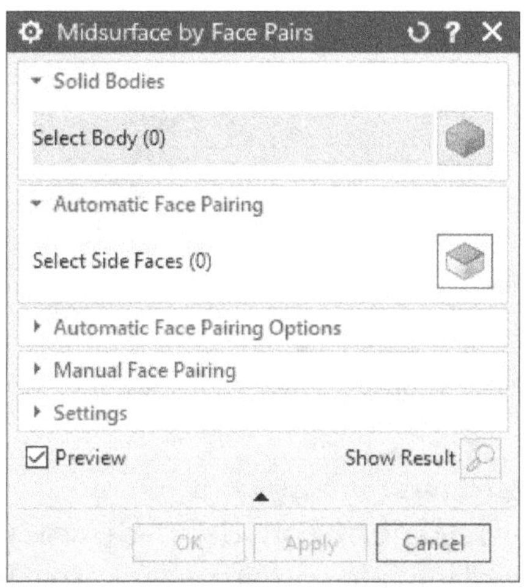

Figure-78. Midsurface by Face Pairs dialog box

- Select desired solid body from the graphics window on which the midsurface is to be created; refer to Figure-79.

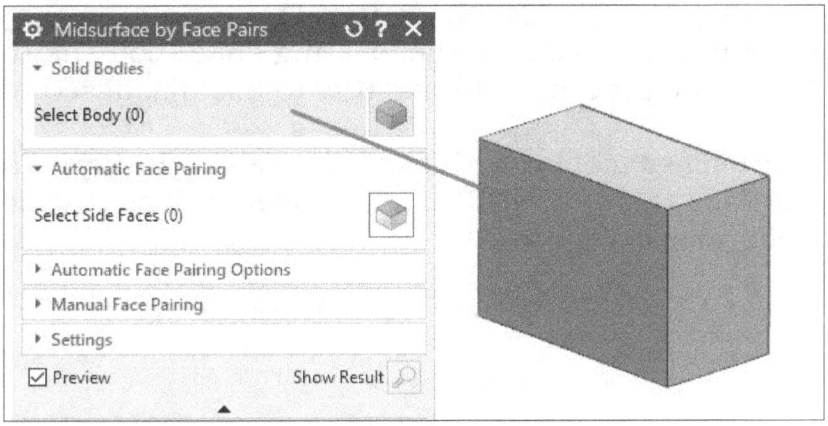

Figure-79. Selecting the body to create midsurface

- On selecting the solid body, the side faces of the body will be automatically selected for the **Automatic Face Pairing** rollout and the preview of midsurface feature will be displayed; refer to Figure-80.

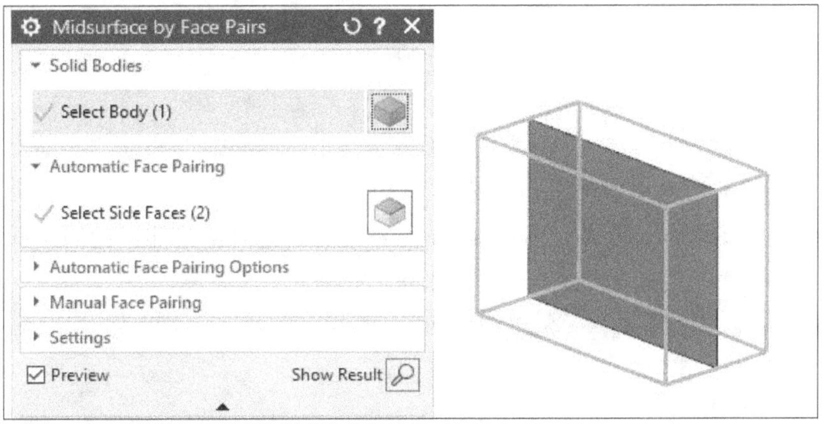

Figure-80. Preview of midsurface feature

- Select desired strategy from **Strategy** drop-down in the **Automatic Face Pairing Options** rollout to be used to define the pairs of opposite faces. Specify desired value in the **Thickness Ratio** edit box to create face pairs relative to the size of faces with their thickness. Specify desired value in the **Merge Angle Tolerance** edit box to merge the face pairs if the angle between the individual pair is less than the specified value. Select **Offset Only** check box to create a mid-sheet by offsetting the face from Side 1 of the selected pair. Select **Trim** check box to automatically trim the midsurface.
- Select desired primary and secondary faces to define the midsurface pair. Specify desired distance in the **Search Distance** edit box of **Side 2 Search** rollout to find the faces for side 2 from the specified faces for side 1. Select **Dynamic Search** check box to find the faces for side 2 of the pair, automatically by the software.
- Click on the **Select Object** button from **Replacement Mid-Sheet** rollout to select desired face, plane, or sheet body to be used as the mid-sheet for the selected face pair.
- Other options in the dialog box is same as discussed earlier.
- After specifying desired parameters, click on **OK** button from the dialog box. The face pairs feature will be created.

User Defined

The **User Defined** tool is used to define the existing sheet body as the midsurface of a selected solid body. The procedure to use this tool is discussed next.

- Click on the **User Defined** tool from **Midsurface** area in the **More** drop-down of **Base** group in the **Surface** tab of the **Ribbon**. The **User Defined Midsurface** dialog box will be displayed; refer to Figure-81.

Figure-81. User Defined Midsurface dialog box

- Select desired solid body for which the midsurface is to be created; refer to Figure-82.

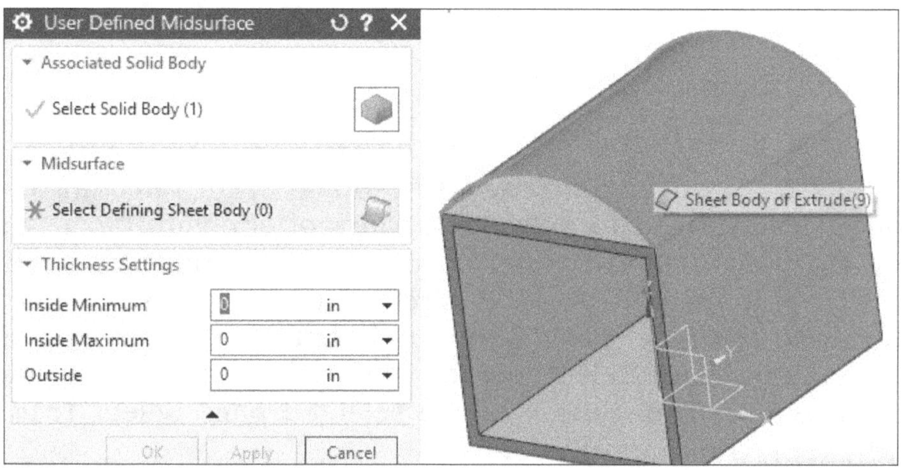

Figure-82. Solid body selected to create midsurface

- Select desired sheet body to be used as the midsurface for the solid body.
- Specify desired minimum and maximum thickness value that can be assigned to any node inside the solid body in the **Inside Minimum** and **Inside Maximum** edit boxes of **Thickness Settings** rollout, respectively. Specify desired value in the **Outside** edit box to be assigned for nodes that are located outside the solid body.
- After specifying desired parameters, click on **OK** button from the dialog box. The user defined midsurface will be created; refer to Figure-83.

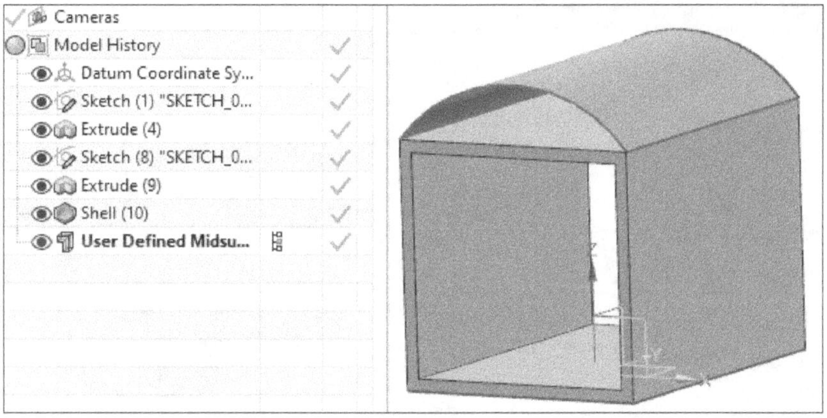

Figure-83. User defined midsurface created

Offset

The **Offset** tool is used to create a midsurface sheet body using an offset from the solid geometry. The procedure to use this tool is discussed next.

- Click on the **Offset** tool from **Midsurface** area in the **More** drop-down of **Base** group in the **Surface** tab of the **Ribbon**. The **Offset Midsurface** dialog box will be displayed; refer to Figure-84.

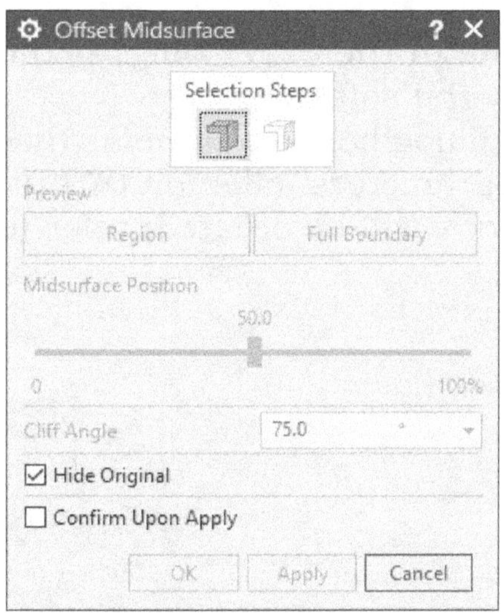

Figure-84. Offset Midsurface dialog box

- Select desired target solid body from which the midsurface is to be created and then click on the **Seed Face** button from **Selection Steps** area to select desired seed face of the target body from which the midsurface extraction is to be started using the offset method; refer to Figure-85.

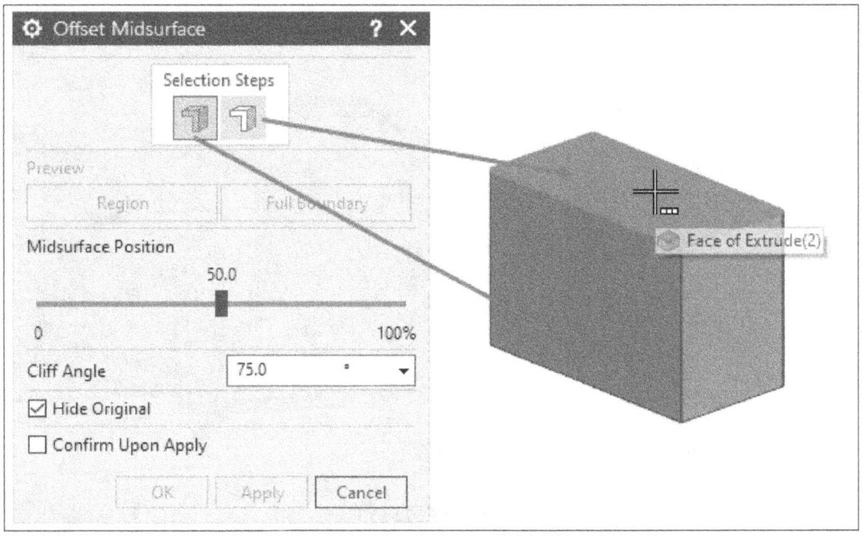

Figure-85. Selecting the target body and its face

- Click on the **Region** button from **Preview** area to display faces in the region generated by extending the seed faces upto the edges of the boundary faces. Click on the **Full Boundary** button to display the boundary faces generated from the boundary calculation.
- Move the **Midsurface Position** slider to define the midsurface depth relative to the seed face.
- Specify desired angle value in the **Cliff Angle** edit box at which the boundary faces is to be identified by the software.
- Other parameters in the dialog box are same as discussed earlier.
- After specifying desired parameters, click on **OK** button from the dialog box. The offset midsurface sheet body will be created; refer to Figure-86.

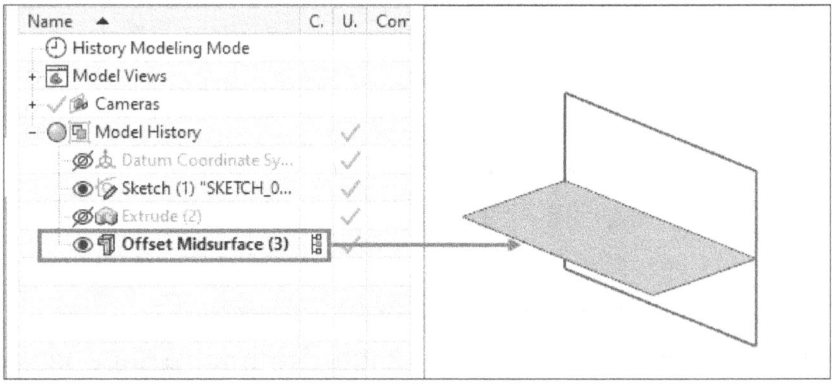

Figure-86. Offset midsurface sheet body created

Bisector

The **Bisector** tool is used to create a surface between two sheets bodies. The procedure to use this tool is discussed next.

- Click on the **Bisector** tool from **Midsurface** area in the **More** drop-down of **Base** group in the **Surface** tab of the **Ribbon**. The **Bisector Surface** dialog box will be displayed; refer to Figure-87.

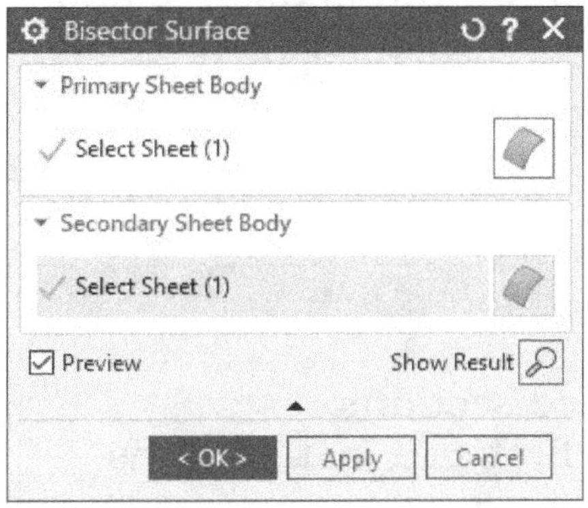

Figure-87. Bisector Surface dialog box

- Select primary and secondary sheet bodies from the graphics window using which a new sheet body is to be created; refer to Figure-88. The preview of new sheet body will be displayed.

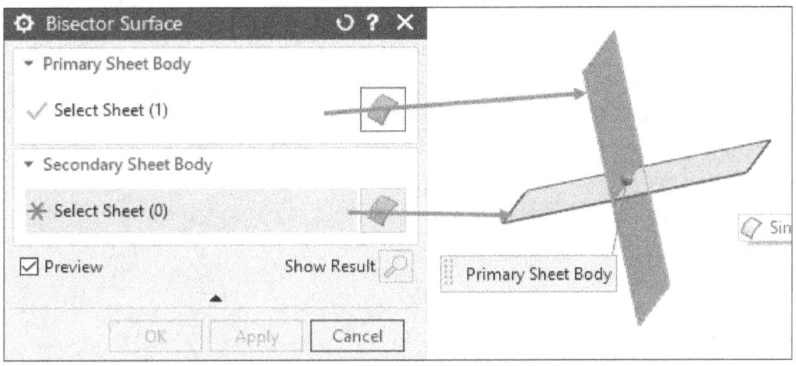

Figure-88. Selecting the primary and secondary sheet bodies

- After specifying desired parameters, click on **OK** button from the dialog box. A surface between sheet bodies will be created; refer to Figure-89.

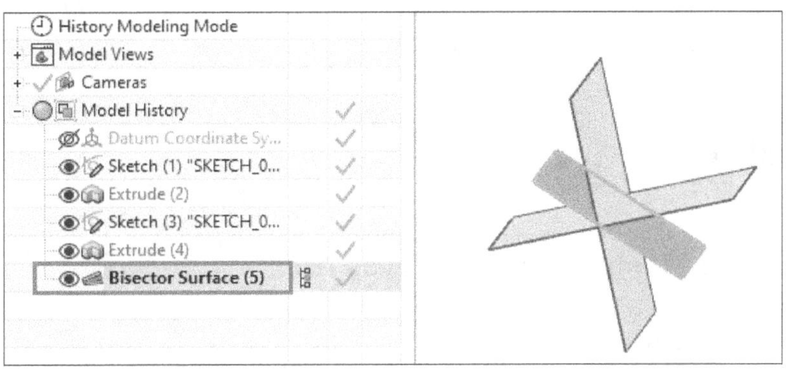

Figure-89. Bisector surface created

SELF-ASSESSMENT

Q1. What is Through Curves tool is used to:

A. Create a solid cube

B. Create a body passing through multiple sections

C. Create a sketch only

D. Delete curves

Q2. In Through Curves, which button is used to add more sections?
A. Add Curve
B. Add New Set
C. Insert Section
D. New Curve

Q3. Apply to All option is used to:
A. Delete all sections
B. Apply continuity to selected sections
C. Apply same continuity to first and last sections
D. Create new surfaces

Q4. Which Flow Direction option allows free flow without restriction?
A. Isoparametric
B. Perpendicular
C. Adjacent Edges
D. Not Specified

Q5. What is Preserve Shape option is used to:
A. Smooth surfaces
B. Delete corners
C. Preserve sharp corners
D. Change color

Q6. What is Patch Type option defines:
A. Surface color
B. Number of patches in V direction
C. Curve thickness
D. Edge length

Q7. What is Through Curve Mesh uses:
A. Only sections
B. Only guides
C. Sections and guides
D. Only points

Q8. In Through Curve Mesh, primary curves are:
A. Secondary curves
B. Main curves defining shape
C. Hidden curves
D. Temporary curves

Q9. What is Edge Blend tool is used to:
A. Create surfaces
B. Apply fillet on edges
C. Delete edges
D. Extend surfaces

Q10. What is Face Blend tool is used at:
A. Single edge
B. Multiple faces intersection
C. Sketch level
D. Solid body center

Q11. What is Offset Surface tool is used to:
A. Delete faces
B. Create offset of faces
C. Create curves
D. Join edges

Q12. Which One Feature for Each Face option creates:
A. One body
B. One feature per face
C. No feature
D. Multiple solids

Q13. What is Thicken tool converts:
A. Curve to point
B. Surface to solid
C. Solid to sketch
D. Face to edge

Q14. What is Boolean Unite option in Thicken is used to:
A. Subtract bodies
B. Combine bodies
C. Intersect bodies
D. Delete bodies

Q15. What is Studio Surface tool uses:
A. Only one curve
B. Sections and guide curves
C. Only points
D. Only edges

Q16. What is Arc Length option aligns curves based on:
A. Equal angles
B. Equal length
C. Equal arc length
D. Equal height

Q17. What is Law Extension tool uses:
A. Fixed rule
B. Law/rule to control distance and angle
C. Only distance
D. Only angle

Q18. What is Styled Sweep tool creates:
A. Rough surfaces
B. High-quality smooth surfaces
C. Only solids
D. Only sketches

Q19. What is Sweep along Guide tool follows:
A. Straight path
B. Guide curve highs and lows
C. Random path
D. Fixed line

Q20. What is Variational Sweep creates:
A. Constant section
B. Varying cross-section
C. No section
D. Circular section only

Q21. What is Section Surface tool creates surface using:
A. Lines
B. Conic shapes
C. Points
D. Solids

Q22. What is Tube tool creates:
A. Square pipe
B. Circular tube
C. Triangle tube
D. Solid cube

Q23. What is Ruled tool creates:
A. Curved transition
B. Linear transition between sections
C. Random surface
D. Closed body

Q24. What is N-sided Surface tool requires:
A. Open curves
B. Closed loop curves
C. Single point
D. Only edges

Q25. Aesthetic Face Blend creates:
A. Rough blend
B. Smooth blend with constraints
C. Only edges
D. Only curves

Q26. Bridge Surface tool is used to:
A. Delete surfaces
B. Join two faces
C. Split faces
D. Offset faces

Q27. Blend Corner tool is used to:
A. Remove corners
B. Create patch at blended corners
C. Extend edges
D. Create curves

Q28. Styled Corner tool creates:
A. Sharp corner
B. Smooth corner between three surfaces
C. Flat surface
D. Only edge

Q29. Fill Surface tool is used to:
A. Create solid bodies
B. Create surface using boundary curves or edges
C. Delete surfaces
D. Offset curves

Q30. In Fill Surface, selected curves are displayed in:
A. Output box
B. Boundary rollout list
C. Settings panel
D. Preview window

Q31. Which option applies no constraints in Fill Surface?
A. Fullness
B. Fit to Curves
C. None
D. Fit to Facet Body

Q32. Fullness option is used to:
A. Delete surface
B. Modify surface along normal direction
C. Create curves
D. Offset edges

Q33. Fit to Curves option is used to:
A. Fit surface to selected curves
B. Delete curves
C. Extend surface
D. Smooth edges

Q34. Bounded Plane tool creates:
A. Curved surface
B. Planar sheet body
C. Solid body
D. Mesh surface

Q35. Bounded Plane requires:
A. Open curves
B. Closed planar curves
C. Single edge
D. Points only

Q36. Patch Openings tool is used to:
A. Create holes
B. Fill gaps between faces
C. Delete edges
D. Offset faces

Q37. Quilted Patch option creates:
A. Single surface
B. Series of patches
C. Solid body
D. Mesh only

Q38. N-sided Area Patch option creates:
A. 3-sided surface
B. Multi-sided patch surface
C. Line
D. Plane

Q39. Mesh option in Patch Openings creates:
A. Solid
B. Mesh sheet body
C. Curve
D. Plane

Q40. Four Point Surface tool requires:
A. Two points
B. Three points
C. Four points
D. Five points

Q41. Rapid Surfacing tool is used to:
A. Create sketch
B. Create surface from facet body
C. Delete mesh
D. Offset surface

Q42. Node Tolerance defines:
A. Surface color
B. Selection tolerance on patch nodes
C. Curve length
D. Thickness

Q43. Fit Surface tool creates:
A. Only planes
B. Only spheres
C. Freeform and analytical surfaces
D. Only curves

Q44. Maximum Error shows:
A. Minimum deviation
B. Maximum deviation distance
C. Curve error
D. Thickness error

Q45. Automatic Point Rejection is used to:
A. Add points
B. Remove unwanted points
C. Smooth curves
D. Extend surface

Q46. Variable Offset tool allows:
A. Constant offset
B. Variable offset at different points
C. No offset
D. Only edge offset

Q48. Variable Offset Face tool is used to:
A. Offset single face
B. Offset multiple regions with variation
C. Delete regions
D. Create sketch

Q49. Extension Surface tool creates:
A. Solid extension
B. Surface extension from base sheet
C. Curve extension
D. Mesh extension

Q50. Tangential method creates extension that is:
A. Perpendicular
B. Tangent to edge
C. Random
D. Parallel

Q51. Silhouette Flange tool creates:
A. Rough surface
B. Smooth high-quality surface
C. Only curves
D. Only solids

Q53. Face Pairs tool creates:
A. Surface between curves
B. Midsurface between opposite faces
C. Solid body
D. Edge

Q54. Thickness Ratio is used to:
A. Define color
B. Define face pairing size relation
C. Delete faces
D. Offset curves

Q55. User Defined tool is used to:
A. Create sketch
B. Define existing sheet as midsurface
C. Delete surface
D. Offset face

Q56. Offset (Midsurface) tool creates:
A. Solid body
B. Midsurface using offset
C. Curve
D. Plane

Q57. Bisector tool creates:
A. Curve
B. Surface between two sheet bodies
C. Solid
D. Edge

Q58. Midsurface Position slider is used to:
A. Change color
B. Define midsurface depth
C. Delete faces
D. Extend curves

Chapter 10

Surface Editing

Topics Covered

The major topics covered in this chapter are:

- ***Performing Surface Combination operations***
- ***Performing Trimming Operations***
- ***Performing Emboss, Patch, and Unsew Operations***
- ***Performing Surface Editing Operations***
- ***NX Realize Shape environment***

SURFACE EDITING

In previous chapter, you have learned about creating surfaces using various standard 3D modeling and surface specific modeling tools. Most of the time, you will need further editing of these surfaces to achieve desired shape and dimensions. In this chapter, you will learn about various surface editing tools available in the **Surface** tab of **Ribbon**.

Combine

The **Combine** tool is used to combine the regions of multiple intersecting sheet bodies. The procedure to use this tool is discussed next.

- Click on the **Combine** tool from **Combine** group in the **Surface** tab of the **Ribbon**. The **Combine** dialog box will be displayed; refer to Figure-1.

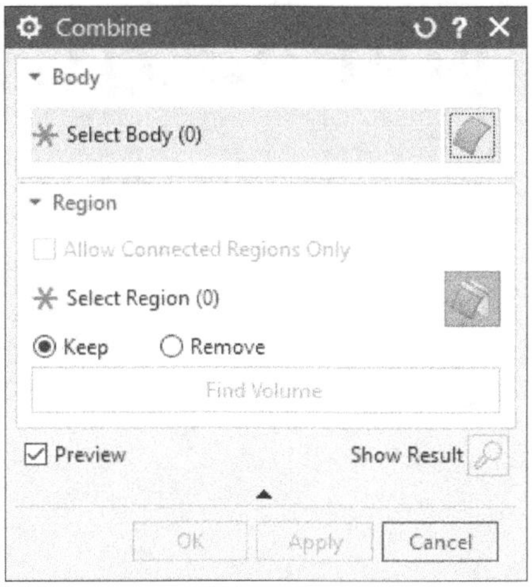

Figure-1. Combine dialog box

- Select desired sheet body from the graphics window to be combined; refer to Figure-2.

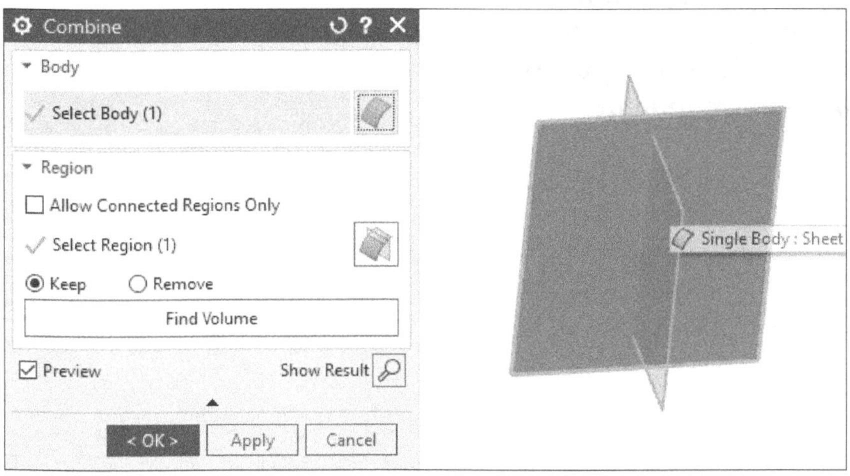

Figure-2. Selecting the sheet body to be combined

- Select **Allow Connected Regions Only** check box from **Region** rollout to select only those regions edge that are connected to a previously selected region. Select **Keep** or **Remove** radio button to keep or remove the selected regions, respectively.
- Select desired region of a body from the graphics window to be kept or removed.
- Click on the **Find Volume** button to find and select regions that enclosed a solid volume.

- After specifying desired parameters, click on **OK** button from the dialog box. The sheet bodies will be combined; refer to Figure-3.

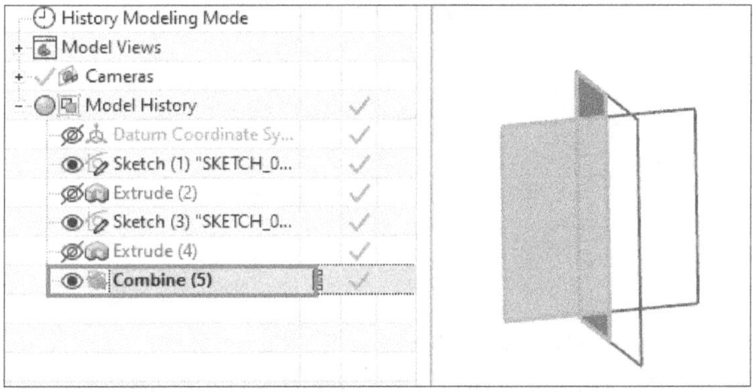

Figure-3. Sheet bodies combined

Trim Sheet

The **Trim Sheet** tool is used to trim a portion of a sheet body. The procedure to use this tool is discussed next.

- Click on the **Trim Sheet** tool from **Combine** group in the **Surface** tab of the **Ribbon**. The **Trim Sheet** dialog box will be displayed; refer to Figure-4.

Figure-4. Trim Sheet dialog box

- Select desired target sheet body from the graphics window to be trimmed.
- Click on the **Select Object** button from **Boundary** rollout to select the object to be used for trimming; refer to Figure-5.

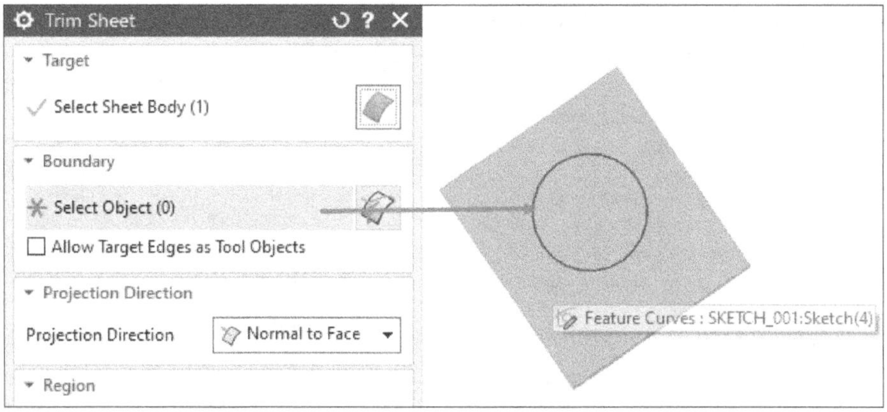

Figure-5. Selecting the object to be trimmed

- Select **Allow Target Edges as Tool Objects** check box to select target edges as trimming objects.
- Select desired option to be used for projection direction from **Projection Direction** drop-down of **Projection Direction** rollout.
- Click on the **Select Region** button from **Region** rollout and select desired regions to be kept or discarded while trimming.
- Select **Keep Target** check box from **Settings** rollout to keep the selection of trimming boundary objects. Select **Output Exact Geometry** check box to output intersection curves. Select **Extend Boundary Object to Target Edges** check box to extend boundary objects to other boundary objects.
- Other parameters in the dialog box are same as discussed earlier.
- After specifying desired parameters, click on **OK** button from the dialog box. The sheet body will be trimmed; refer to Figure-6.

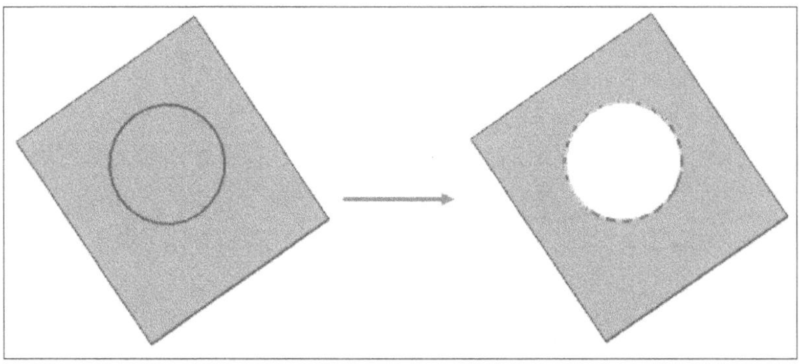

Figure-6. Sheet body trimmed

Extend Sheet

The **Extend Sheet** tool is used to extend a sheet body by a specified distance or to the intersection with another body. The procedure to use this tool is discussed next.

- Click on the **Extend Sheet** tool from **Combine** group in the **Surface** tab of the **Ribbon**. The **Extend Sheet** dialog box will be displayed; refer to Figure-7.

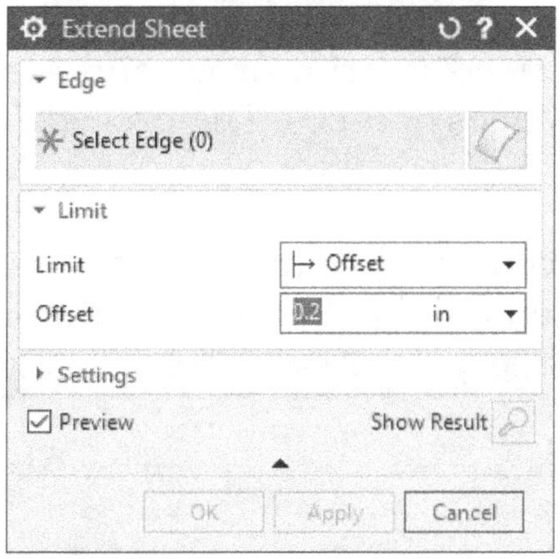

Figure-7. Extend Sheet dialog box

- Select desired edge(s) from the graphics window to be offset; refer to Figure-8.

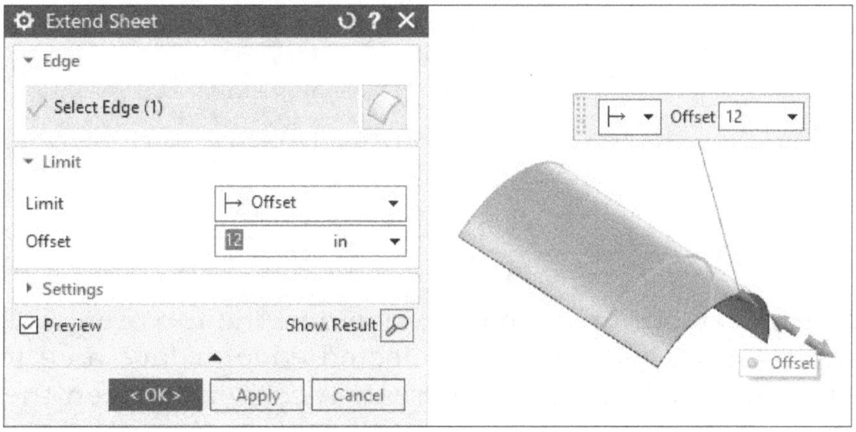

Figure-8. Selecting the edge to be offset

- Select **Offset** option from **Limit** drop-down in the **Limit** rollout to define desired distance in the **Offset** edit box as an offset of the edge. Select **Until Selected** option from the drop-down to extend to intersect a selected body or plane.
- On selecting **Natural Curvature** option from **Surface Extension Shape** rollout, a B-surface will be extended with a small area that is curvature continuous at the boundary. On selecting **Tangent** option, a B-surface will be extended tangent from the boundary. On selecting **Mirrored** option, a B-surface will be extended by mirroring the curvature continuous shape.
- Select desired option from **Edge Extension Shape** drop-down to extend adjacent boundaries of the surface.
- Other parameters in the dialog box are same as discussed earlier.
- After specifying desired parameters, click on **OK** button from the dialog box. The sheet will be extended; refer to Figure-9.

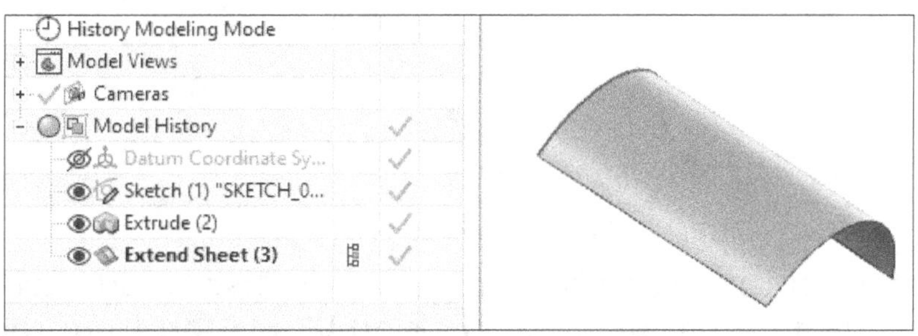

Figure-9. Sheet extended

Trim and Extend

The **Trim and Extend** tool is used to trim or extend a set of edges and faces at the intersection of another set of edges or faces. The procedure to use this tool is discussed next.

- Click on the **Trim and Extend** tool from the **Combine** group in **Surface** tab of the **Ribbon**. The **Trim and Extend** dialog box will be displayed; refer to Figure-10.

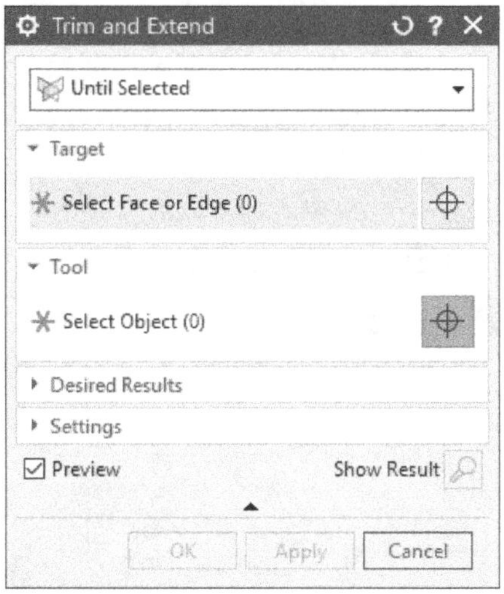

Figure-10. Trim and Extend dialog box

- Select **Until Selected** option from drop-down in the top area of the dialog box to trim or extend a target body using a selected edge or face as a tool. Select **Make Corner** option from the drop-down to create a corner between the target and the tool.
- Select desired face or edge from the graphics window as a target object to be trimmed or extended.
- Click on the **Select Object** button from **Tool** rollout and select desired face or edge of a sheet as a tool to trim or extend the target object; refer to Figure-11.

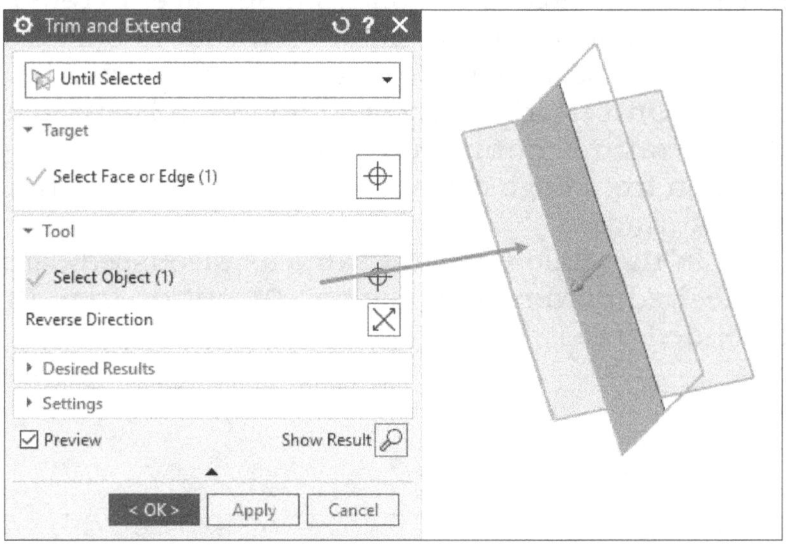

Figure-11. Selecting the face as a tool to trim

- Other parameters in the dialog box are same as discussed earlier.
- After specifying desired parameters, click on **OK** button from the dialog box. The trim and extend feature will be created; refer to Figure-12.

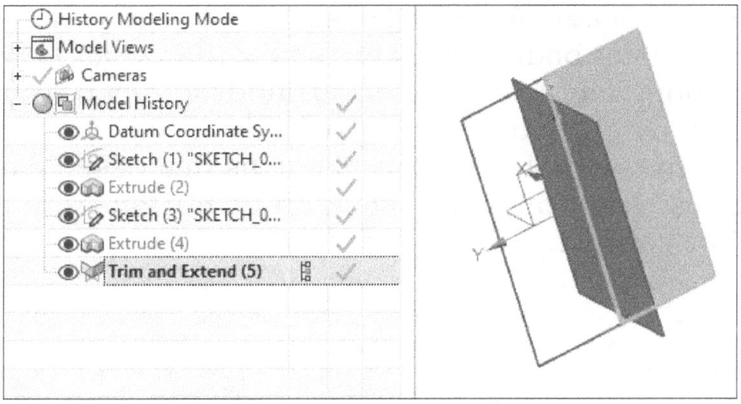

Figure-12. Trim and extend feature created

Sew

The **Sew** tool is used to combine sheet bodies by sewing shared edges or combine solid bodies by sewing common faces. The procedure to use this tool is discussed next.

- Click on the **Sew** tool from **Combine** group in the **Surface** tab of the **Ribbon**. The **Sew** dialog box will be displayed; refer to Figure-13.

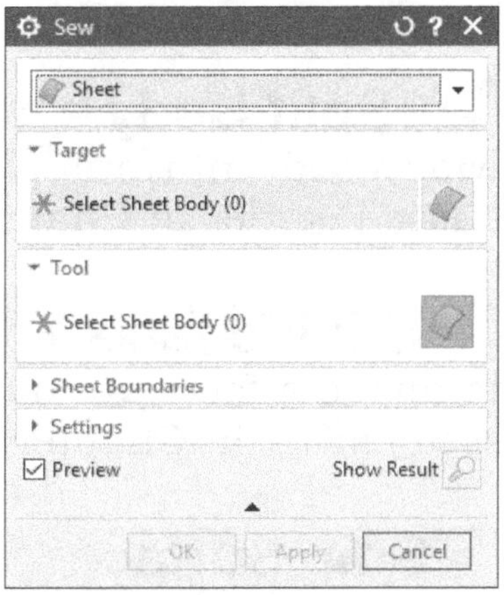

Figure-13. Sew dialog box

- Select **Sheet** or **Solid** option from drop-down in the top area of the dialog box to sew sheet bodies or solid bodies together, respectively.
- Select desired target sheet body or face of solid body to be sew; refer to Figure-14.

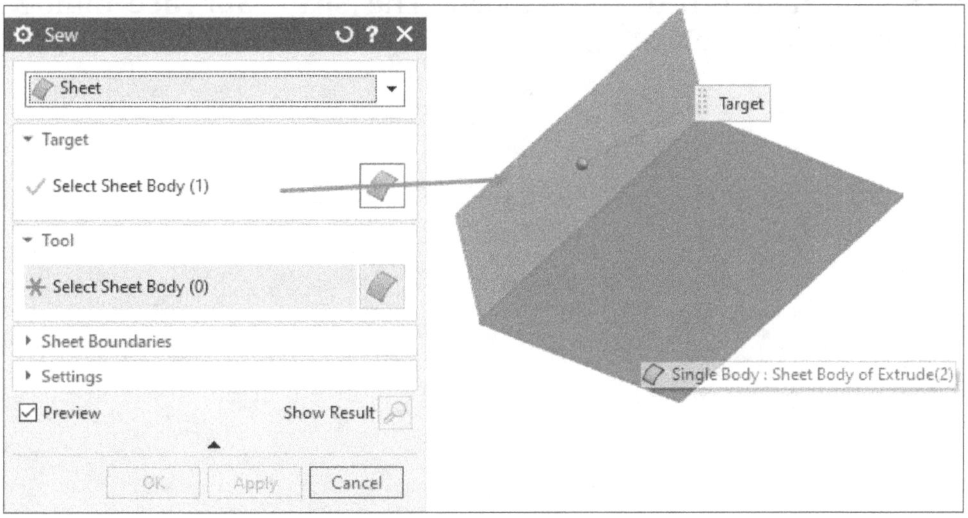

Figure-14. Selecting the target sheet body to be sew

- Click on the **Select Sheet Body** or **Select Face** button from **Tool** rollout and select one or more sheet bodies or faces to sew the target body, respectively.
- Select desired option from **Boundary Display** drop-down and specify respective parameters to display or hide the sheet boundaries on selecting the sheets.
- Other parameters in the dialog box are same as discussed earlier.
- After specifying desired parameters, click on **OK** button from the dialog box. The sew feature will be created; refer to Figure-15.

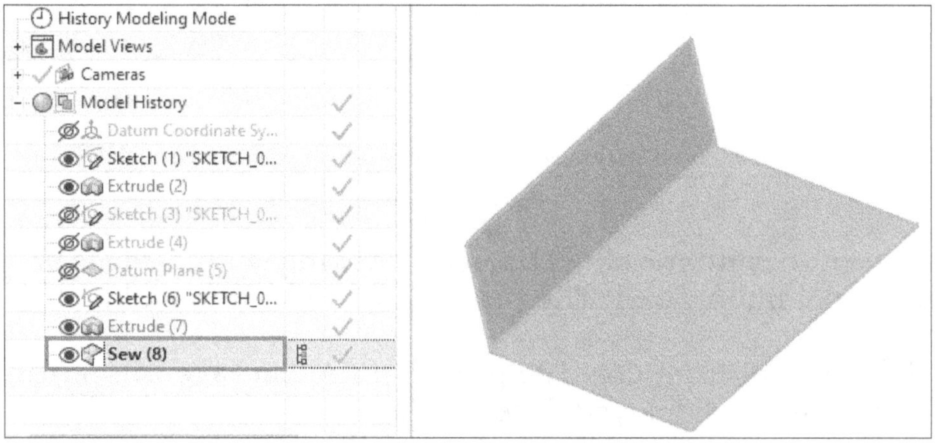

Figure-15. Sew feature created

Split Body

The **Split Body** tool is used to divide a body into multiple separate body. The procedure to use this tool is same as discussed earlier in Chapter 6.

Divide face

The **Divide Face** tool is used to divide a face into multiple faces. The procedure to use this tool is same as discussed earlier in Chapter 6.

Snip Surface

The **Snip Surface** tool is used to divide a surface at a specific point or remove unwanted portions of a surface. The procedure to use this tool is discussed next.

- Click on the **Snip Surface** tool from **Trim** area in the **More** drop-down of **Combine** group in the **Surface** tab of the **Ribbon**. The **Snip Surface** dialog box will be displayed; refer to Figure-16.

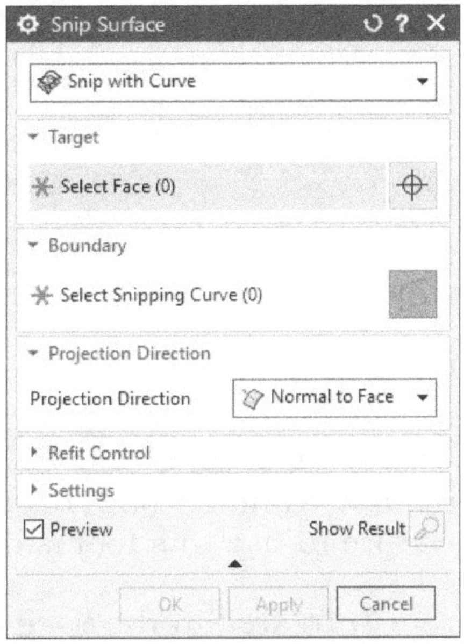

Figure-16. Snip Surface dialog box

- Select desired method from drop-down in the top area of the dialog box to be used to snip the selected surface.
- Select desired face from the graphics window to be snipped.
- Click on the **Select Snipping Curve** button from **Boundary** rollout and select desired curve to define the snip boundary; refer to Figure-17.

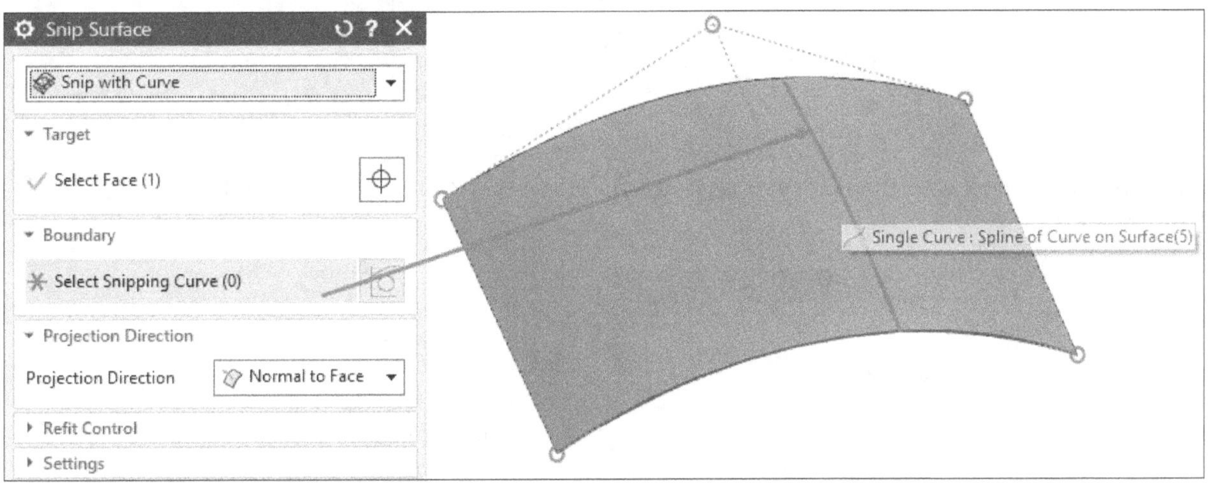

Figure-17. Selecting the snipping curve

- Select desired option from **Projection Direction** drop-down of **Projection Direction** rollout to specify the vector direction in which boundary curves or edges are projected onto the target face.
- Select desired option from **Refit Method** drop-down in the **Refit Control** rollout and specify the respective parameters to repair an inappropriate surface by modifying its control points along the snipping curve direction.
- Select **Divide** check box from **Settings** rollout to keep both regions of the target surface and create a separate snip surface feature for each region. Select **Edit a Copy** check box to create a copy of the selected face and modify the copied feature instead of changing the original feature. Click on the **Switch Region** button to select the surface region to be retained.
- After specifying desired parameters, click on **OK** button from the dialog box. The snip surface feature will be created; refer to Figure-18.

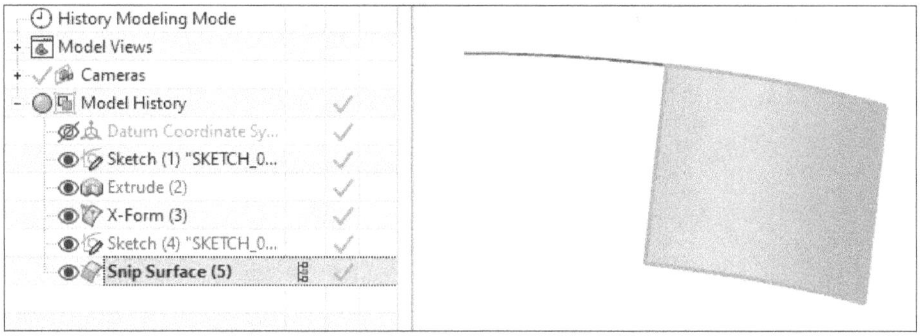

Figure-18. Snip surface feature created

Untrim

The **Untrim** tool is used to remove trimmed boundaries to restore the faces with natural boundaries. The procedure to use this tool is discussed next.

- Click on the **Untrim** tool from **Trim** area in the **More** drop-down of **Combine** group in the **Surface** tab of the **Ribbon**. The **Untrim** dialog box will be displayed; refer to Figure-19.

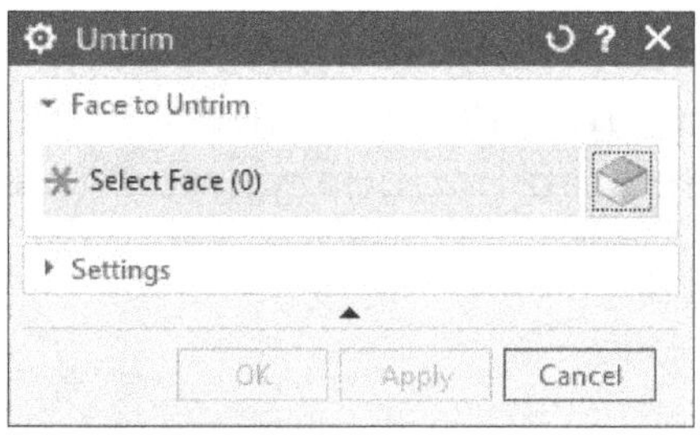

Figure-19. Untrim dialog box

- Specify desired face(s) from the graphics window to be untrimmed; refer to Figure-20.

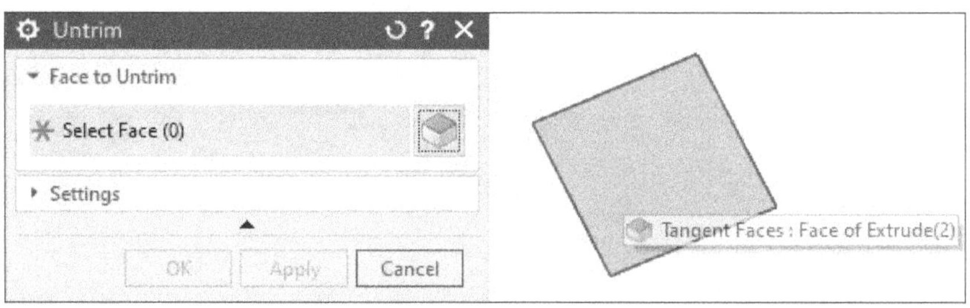

Figure-20. Selecting the face to be untrimmed

- Select **Hide Original** check box from **Settings** rollout to hide the original body after creating the untrim feature. Select **Associative** check box to create an untrim feature otherwise non-associative body will be created.
- After specifying desired parameters, click on **OK** button from the dialog box. The untrim feature will be created; refer to Figure-21.

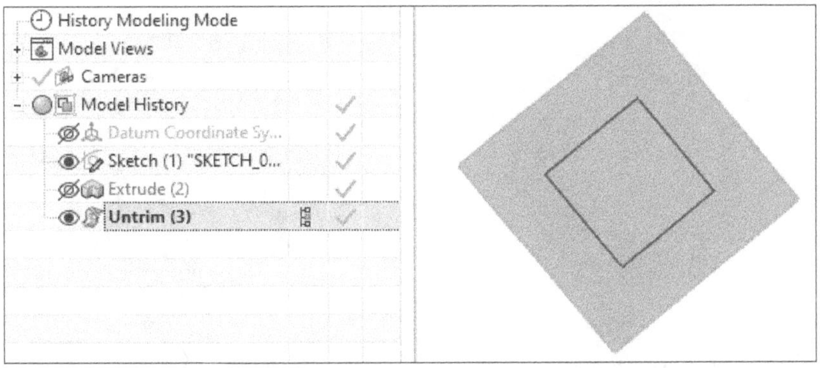

Figure-21. Untrim feature created

Delete Edge

The **Delete Edge** tool is used to delete one or more edges from a sheet body to remove an inner or outer boundary. The procedure to use this tool is discussed next.

- Click on the **Delete Edge** tool from **Trim** area in the **More** drop-down of **Combine** group in the **Surface** tab of the **Ribbon**. The **Delete Edge** dialog box will be displayed; refer to Figure-22.

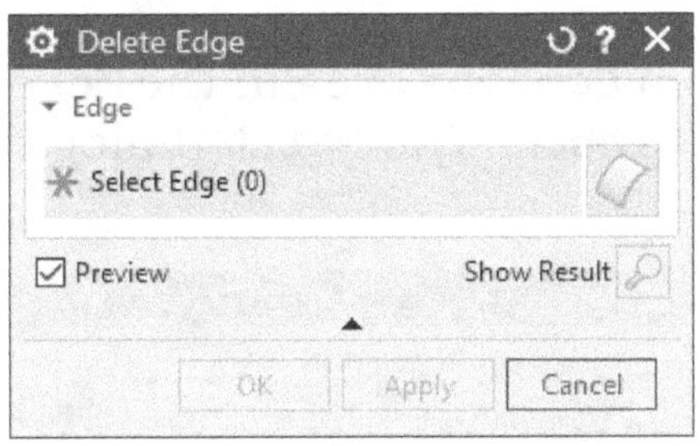

Figure-22. Delete Edge dialog box

- Select desired edge(s) from the graphics window to be deleted; refer to Figure-23.

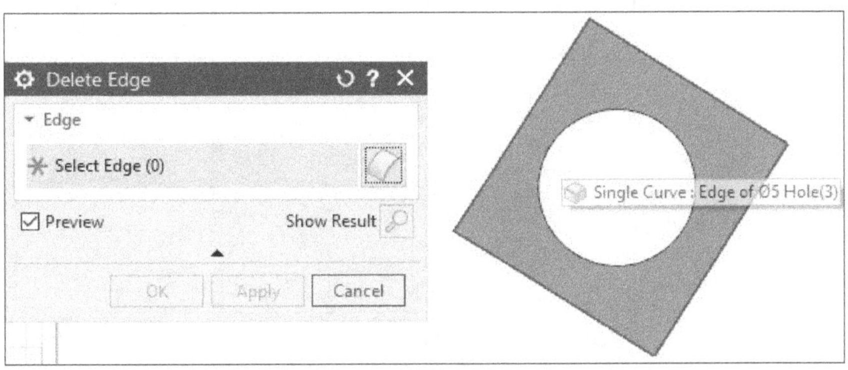

Figure-23. Selecting the edge to be deleted

- After specifying desired parameters, click on **OK** button from the dialog box. The edge will be deleted; refer to Figure-24.

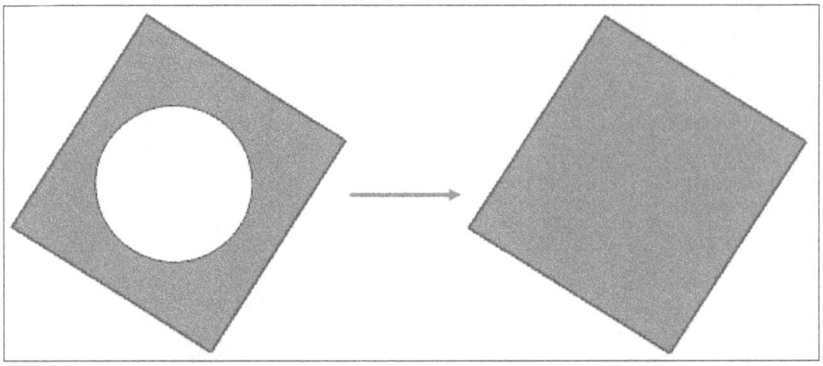

Figure-24. Edge deleted

Emboss Body

The **Emboss Body** tool is used to modify a target body by combining a region of faces from a tool body that intersects the target. The procedure to use this tool is same as discussed earlier in chapter 6.

Patch

The **Patch** tool is used to modify a sheet or solid body by replacing its faces with those from another sheet. The procedure to use this tool is discussed next.

- Click on the **Patch** tool from **Combine** area in the **More** drop-down of **Combine** group in the **Surface** tab of the **Ribbon**. The **Patch** dialog box will be displayed; refer to Figure-25.

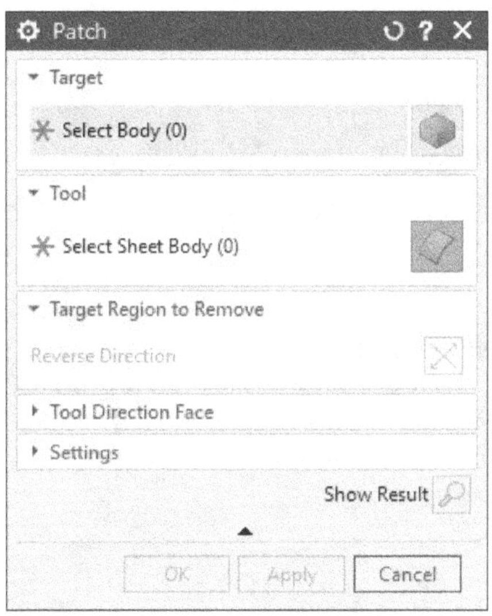

Figure-25. Patch dialog box

- Select desired sheet or solid body from the graphics window as a target body to be patched.
- Click on the **Select Sheet Body** button from **Tool** rollout and select desired sheet body to patch to the target; refer to Figure-26.

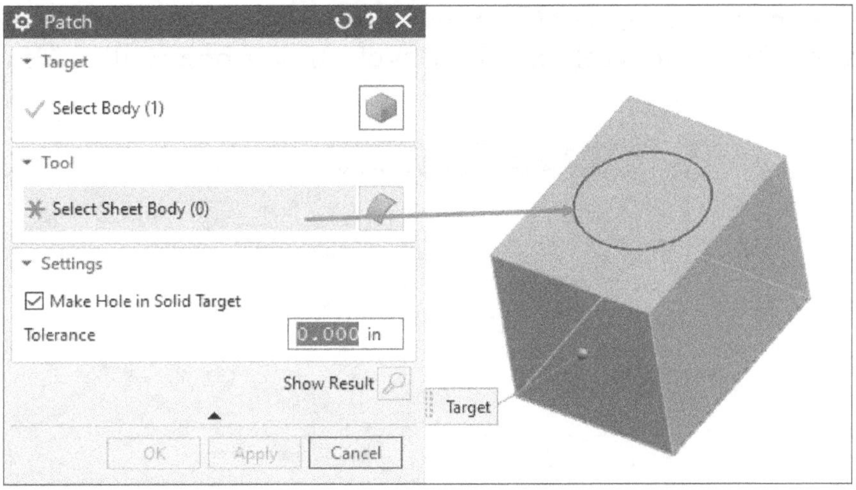

Figure-26. Selecting the sheet body as a tool to patch to the target

- Select **Make Hole in Solid Target** check box from **Settings** rollout to attach a closed sheet to the target body to create a hole; refer to Figure-27.

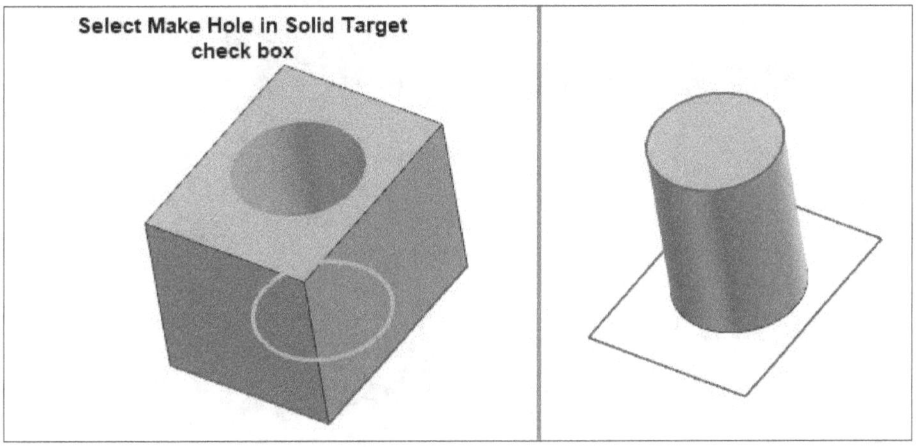

Figure-27. Selecting the hole using check box

- Other parameters in the dialog box are same as discussed earlier.
- After specifying desired parameters, click on **OK** button from the dialog box. The patch feature will be created; refer to Figure-28.

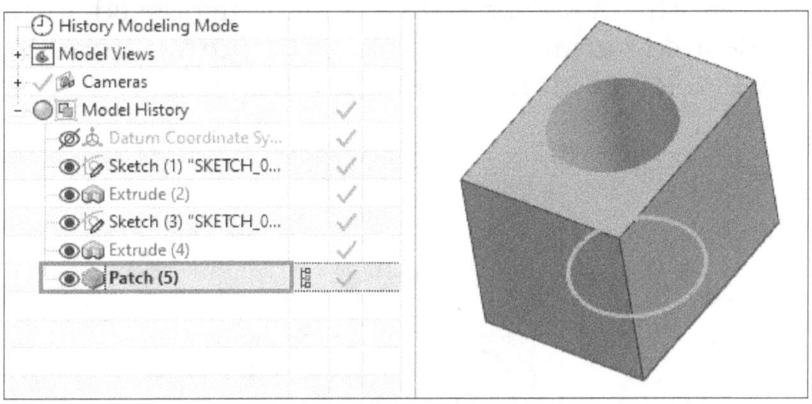

Figure-28. Patch feature created

Unsew

The **Unsew** tool is used to unsew faces from a body. The procedure to use this tool is discussed next.

- Click on the **Unsew** tool from **Combine** area in the **More** drop-down of **Combine** group in the **Surface** tab of the **Ribbon**. The **Unsew** dialog box will be displayed; refer to Figure-29.

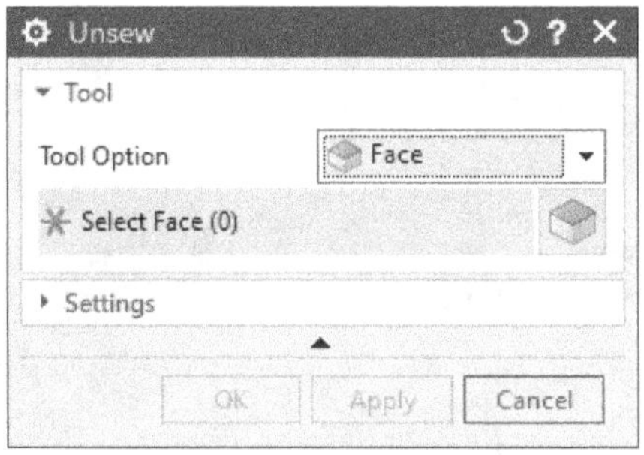

Figure-29. Unsew dialog box

- Select **Face** option from **Tool Option** drop-down in the **Tool** rollout and select desired faces to unsew along the edges of the selected face; refer to Figure-30. Select **Edge** option from the drop-down and select desired edges to unsew.

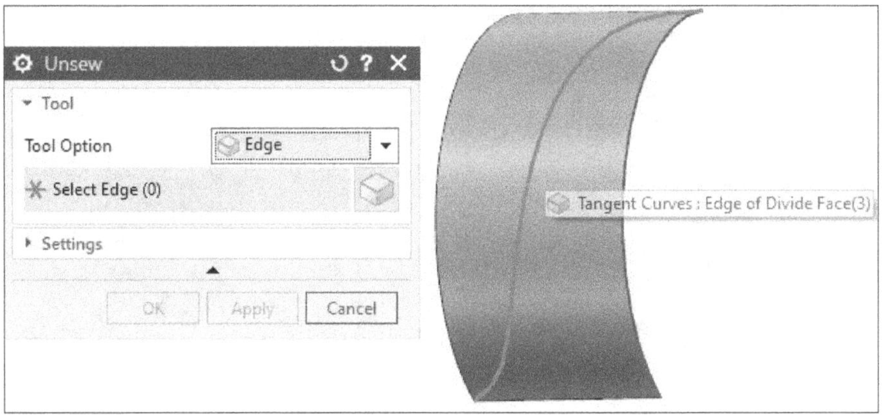

Figure-30. Selecting the edge to unsew

- Select **Keep Original** check box from **Settings** rollout to create the unsew feature as a copy of the selected body. Select desired option from **Output** drop-down to specify the number of bodies to be created for the selected faces.
- Other parameters in the dialog box are same as discussed earlier.
- After specifying desired parameters, click on **OK** button from the dialog box. The unsew feature will be created; refer to Figure-31.

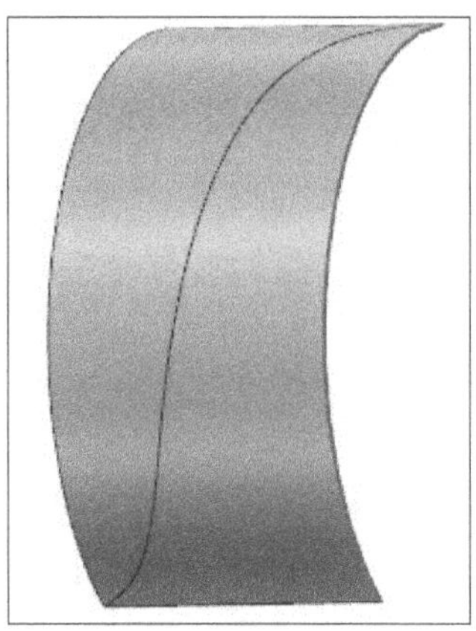

Figure-31. Unsew feature created

X-Form

The **X-Form** tool is used to modify poles and points of splines and surfaces. The procedure to use this tool is discussed next.

- Click on the **X-Form** tool from **Edit** group in the **Surface** tab of the **Ribbon**. The **X-Form** dialog box will be displayed; refer to Figure-32.

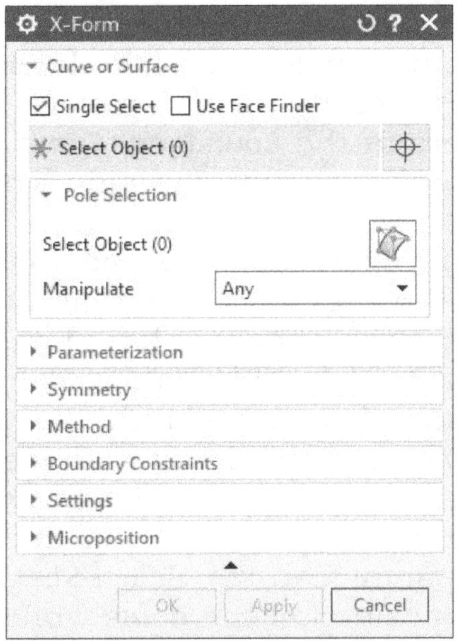

Figure-32. X Form dialog box

- Select **Single Select** check box from **Curve or Surface** rollout and select one or more surfaces or curves to be edited. Select **Use Face Finder** check box to display the face finder group to identify faces using specific geometric conditions.
- Select desired surface, curve, or face from the graphics window to be edited.
- Select desired poles and polylines to be manipulated; refer to Figure-33.

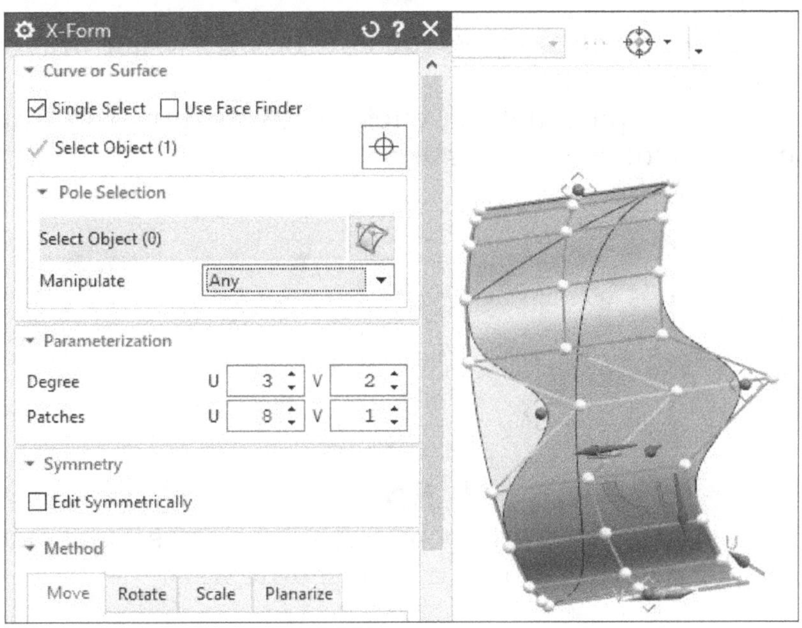

Figure-33. Selecting the poles to be manipulated

- Select desired type of objects to be selected from **Manipulate** drop-down.

- Increase or decrease desired number of degree and patches of the selected surface in the u and v directions in the **U** and **V** edit boxes of **Degree** and **Patches** areas of **Parameterization** rollout, respectively.
- Select the **Edit Symmetrically** check box from **Symmetry** rollout to make a curve or surface symmetric about a selected symmetry plane.
- Click on the **Move** tab from **Method** rollout and specify the parameters to move poles and polylines in a specified direction. Click on the **Rotate** tab and specify the parameters to rotate poles and polylines to a specified vector. Click on the **Scale** tab and specify the parameters to scale the selected poles using principal axes and planes. Similarly, specify the parameters of **Planarize** tab.
- Specify desired parameters in the **Boundary Constraints** rollout to move rows or columns of poles along the tangent direction while keeping the curvature or tangency at the edges.
- Select **Original** option from **Extraction Method** drop-down of **Settings** rollout to extract the face based on the original rectangular surface and parameters. Select **Minimum Bounded** option to extract the face based on a rectangular boundary that encloses the trimmed surface. Select **Fit to Boundary** option to extract the face by creating a quadrilateral surface using boundary of the trimmed surface. Specify desired tolerance value to be used while extracting a surface from a selected face in the **Extract Tolerance** edit box. Select **Relative** option from **Feature Save Method** drop-down to maintain the position of the poles relative to the parent features while editing the parent features. Select **Static** option from the drop-down to maintain the absolute position of the poles while editing the parent features. Click on the **Restore Parent Face** button to remove the pole movements that are associated with the current X-form feaure. Select **Display Deviation** check box to display the maximum deviation that exists between the modified and the original surface or curve.
- Select **Rate** check box from **Microposition** rollout to move the pole using micro-movements to control the shape of the curve. You can modify the rate percentage by moving the slider.
- Specify desired value in the **Step Value** edit box by which the selected pole is to be moved, rotated, or scaled.
- After specifying desired parameters, click on **OK** button from the dialog box. The surface will be modified; refer to Figure-34.

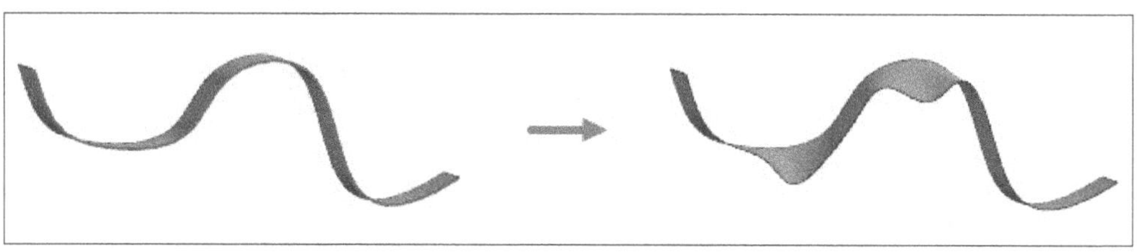

Figure-34. Surface modified

I- Form

The **I-Form** tool is used to modify a face by adjusting its isoparameter curves in real time. The procedure to use this tool is discussed next.

- Click on the **I-Form** tool from **Edit** group in the **Surface** tab of the **Ribbon**. The **I-Form** dialog box will be displayed; refer to Figure-35.

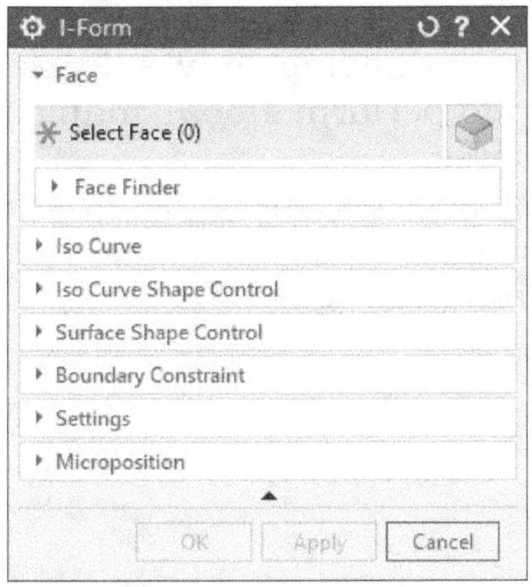

Figure-35. I-Form dialog box

- Select desired face from the graphics window to be edited; refer to Figure-36. Click on the **Face Finder** rollout in the **Face** rollout and specify the parameters to select additional faces based on geometric conditions how their geometry compares with the selected face.

Figure-36. Selecting the face to be edited

- Select desired direction for the isoparametric curves from the **Direction** drop-down in the **Iso Curve** rollout. Select desired method from **Location** drop-down to align the isoparametric curves on the selected face. Specify desired number of isoparametric curves in the **Number** edit box to be inserted on the selected face.
- Select desired method from **Insert Handle** drop-down in the **Iso Curve Shape Control** rollout to place the constraint point handles on the isoparametric curves. Specify desired number of constraint point handles to be available on the selected isoparametric curves. Click on the **Select Iso Curves** button and select desired isoparametric curves on which the points are to be inserted. Click on the **Edit Iso Curves** button and select desired isoparametric curves to be edited. Select **Linear Transition** check box to move the isoparametric curves and the face together in a linear progression while dragging a constraint point handle. Select **Move Handle along Curve** check box to move any constraint point handles along their isoparametric curves. Click on the **Direction** rollout and select desired radio button to specify a direction to move the isoparametric curve constraint point handles which result into the change of their shape and that of the selected face.

- Select **Local** radio button from **Surface Shape Control** rollout to perform local changes to the surface by modifying only selected isoparametric curves. And select **Global** radio button to perform global changes to the surface by modifying multiple isoparametric curves.
- Other parameters in the dialog box are same as discussed earlier.
- After specifying desired parameters, click on **OK** button from the dialog box. The surface will be modified; refer to Figure-37.

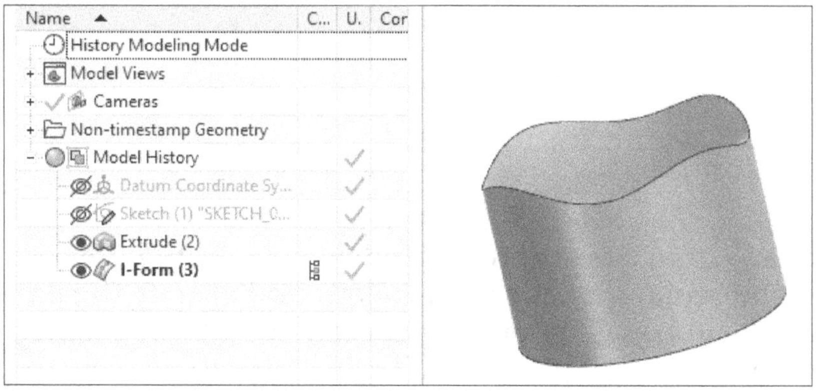

Figure-37. Surface modified

Match Edge

The **Match Edge** tool is used to modify a face so that it is geometrically continuous with the shared boundary of a reference object. The procedure to use this tool is discussed next.

- Click on the **Match Edge** tool from **Edit** group in the **Surface** tab of the **Ribbon**. The **Match Edge** dialog box will be displayed; refer to Figure-38.

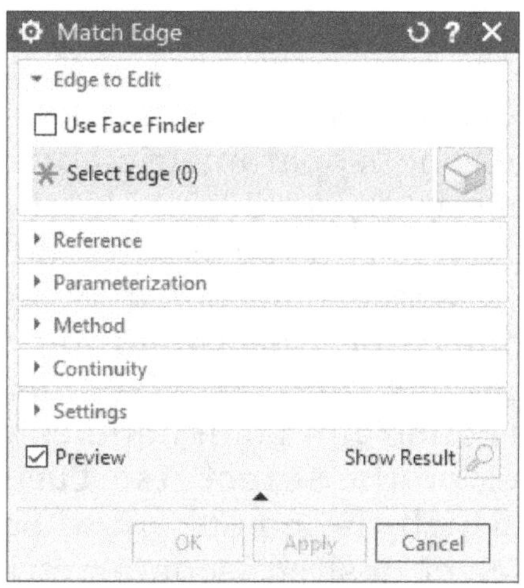

Figure-38. Match Edge dialog box

- Select desired edge of a face from the graphics window to be matched; refer to Figure-39.

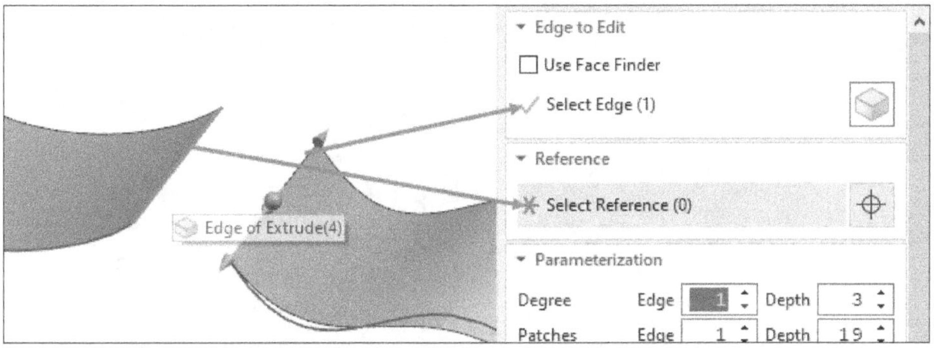

Figure-39. Selecting the edge to be matched

- Select one or more desired edges, curves, or faces as reference objects from the graphics window.
- Other parameters in the dialog box are same as discussed earlier.
- After specifying desired parameters, click on **OK** button from the dialog box. The edge will be matched; refer to Figure-40.

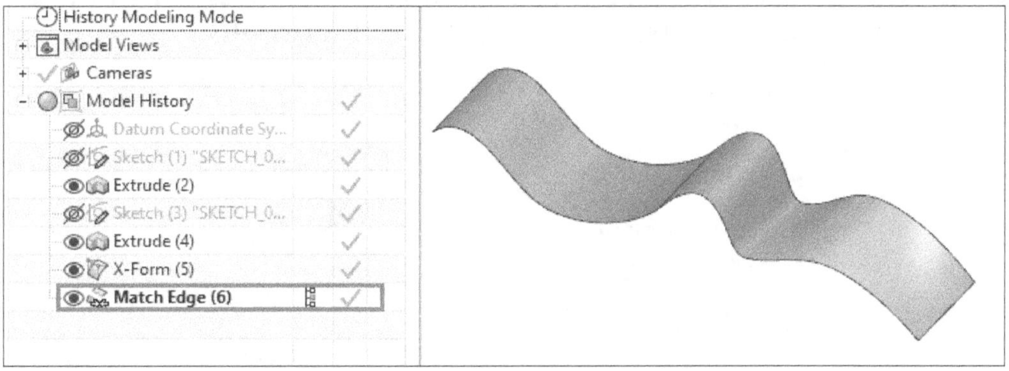

Figure-40. Edge matched

Edge Symmetry

The **Edge Symmetry** tool is used to modify a surface to ensure its geometric continuity with its mirrored image about a plane. The procedure to use this tool is discussed next.

- Click on the **Edge Symmetry** tool from **Edit** group in the **Surface** tab of the **Ribbon**. The **Edge Symmetry** dialog box will be displayed; refer to Figure-41.
- Select desired surface edge from the graphics window to be symmetrical; refer to Figure-42.

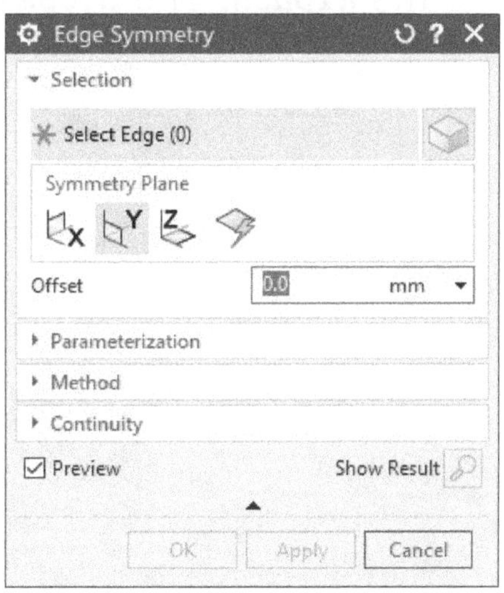

Figure-41. Edge Symmetry dialog box

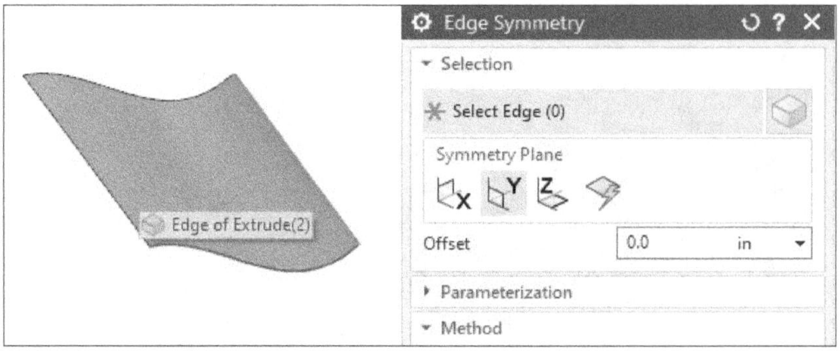

Figure-42. Selecting the edge to be symmetrical

- Select desired option from **Symmetry Plane** area in the **Selection** rollout to define the plane of symmetry.
- Specify desired value in the **Offset** edit box to offset the edge from the symmetry plane.
- Other parameters in the dialog box are same as discussed earlier.
- After specifying desired parameters, click on **OK** button from the dialog box. The edge symmetry feature will be created; refer to Figure-43.

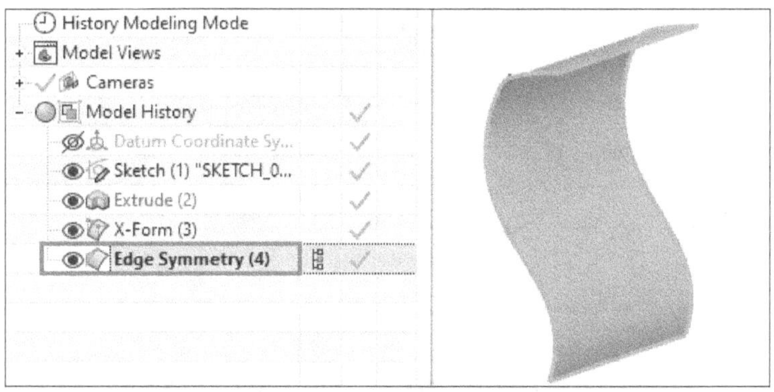

Figure-43. Edge symmetry feature created

Global Shaping

The **Global Shaping** tool is used to deform a surface region by using geometry and values, or by defining relationships between two curves or two surfaces. The procedure to use this tool is discussed next.

- Click on the **Global Shaping** tool from **Shape** area in the **More** drop-down of **Edit** group in the **Surface** tab of the **Ribbon**. The **Global Shaping** dialog box will be displayed; refer to Figure-44.

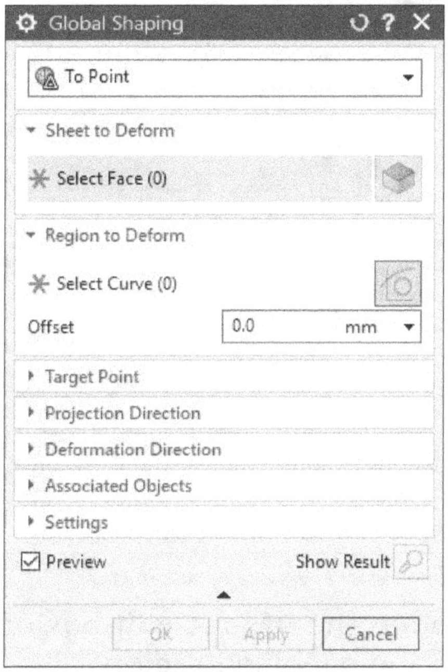

Figure-44. Global Shaping dialog box

- Select desired shaping method to be used from drop-down in the top area of the dialog box. Select **To Point** option to extend selected faces or a sheet body, with maximum height at the specified point. Select **To Curves** option to extend selected faces or a sheet body to selected open or closed curves. Select **Open Region** option to extend the selected faces or sheet body to the selected open height curve. Select **Wall Deformation** option to deform the wall in a set direction while keeping the tangency with adjacent blend faces. Select **Overbend** option to deform a body by rotating it around a selected bend line using specified rotation angle or distance along a curve. Select **Match to Sheet** option to deform the sheet edge to match the target curve on a target sheet. Select **Stretch to Point** option to extend and stretch the selected faces or sheet body, with maximum height at the specified point. Select **Stretch to Curve** option to extend and stretch the selected faces or sheet body to the selected open height curve. Select **Radius Reduction** option to decrease the radius of a freeform blend in a sheet metal body to allow clearance and material flow during cutting. Select **By Surface** or **By Curve** option to deform a sheet or facet body by editing a reference surface or reference curve, respectively.
- Select desired sheet body or faces from the graphics window to be modified. Now, click on the **Select Curve** button from **Region to Deform** rollout and select desired closed curve for the region to be modified; refer to Figure-45.

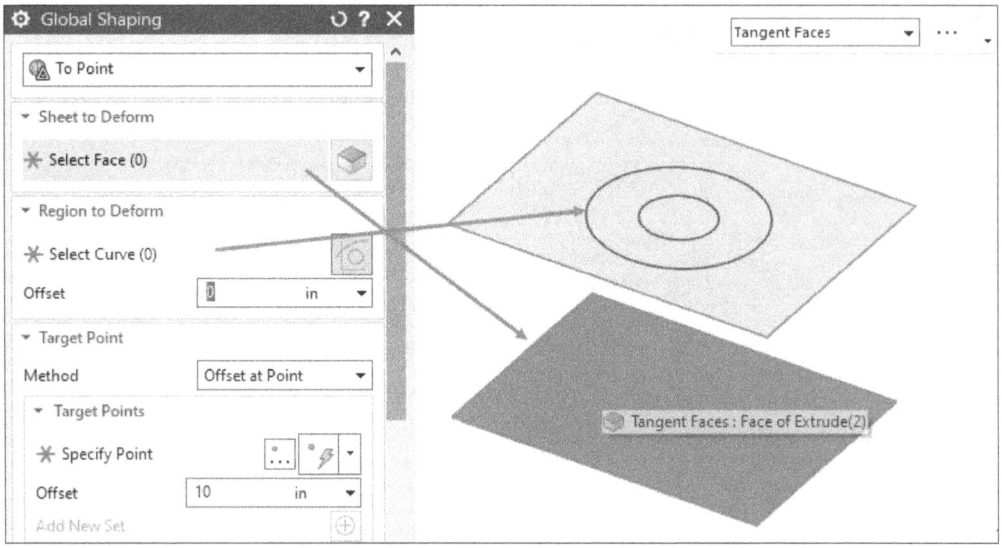

Figure-45. Selecting the face and closed curve to be modified

- Specify desired offset value in the **Offset** edit box of **Region to Deform** rollout to deform the region outside the specified region.
- Select **Offset at Point** option from **Method** drop-down in the **Target Point** rollout to specify a point at desired location inside the region boundary and an offset value in the **Offset** edit box; refer to Figure-46. Select **Through Point** option from the drop-down to specify a 3D point as the maximum height point within the region boundary.

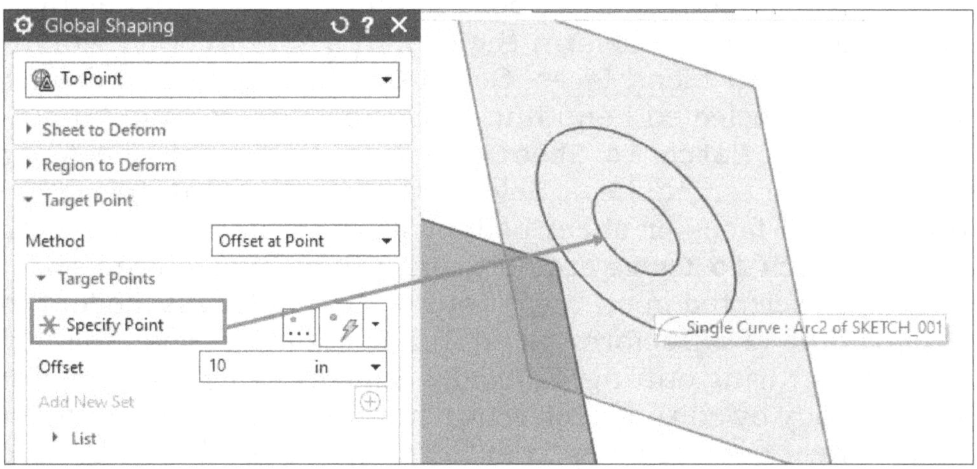

Figure-46. Specifying the point inside the region

- Click on the **Projection Direction** rollout to specify desired vector for the deformation direction.
- Select **Projection Direction** or **Normal to Sheet** option from **Direction** drop-down in the **Deformation Direction** rollout to specify the deformation direction along the projection direction or normal to the sheet, respectively.
- Click on the **Associated Objects** rollout and select desired curves, points, datum planes, and datum axes as additional objects to be deformed.
- Select desired option from **Transition** drop-down in the **Settings** rollout to define the modification to be made to the sheet body.
- Other parameters in the dialog box are same as discussed earlier.
- After specifying desired parameters, click on **OK** button from the dialog box. The surface region will be deformed; refer to Figure-47.

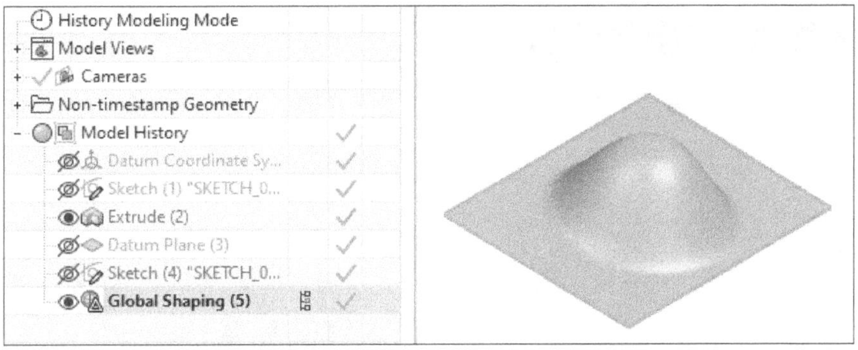

Figure-47. Surface region deformed

Global Deformation

The **Global Deformation** tool is used to create a sheet body in its deformed position while keeping its topology and continuity. The procedure to use this tool is discussed next.

- Click on the **Global Deformation** tool from **Shape** area in the **More** drop-down of **Edit** group in the **Surface** tab of the **Ribbon**. The **Global Deformation** dialog box will be displayed; refer to Figure-48.

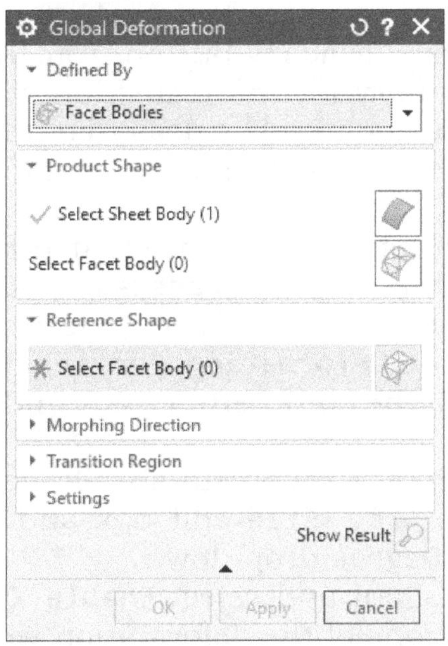

Figure-48. Global Deformation dialog box

- Select desired method to be used for global deformation from drop-down in the **Defined By** rollout. Select **One-step Feature** option to select an analyze formability one-step feature from the **Part Navigator** to define the geometric input. Select **Facet Bodies** option to select desired facets on the sprung body and, if needed, on the facet sheet body in the graphics window. Select **Points from File** option to select a data file with XYZ coordinates for points that define the sprung sheet.
- Select desired sheet body as a product shape body from the graphics window and then select desired facet body as a reference shape body; refer to Figure-49.

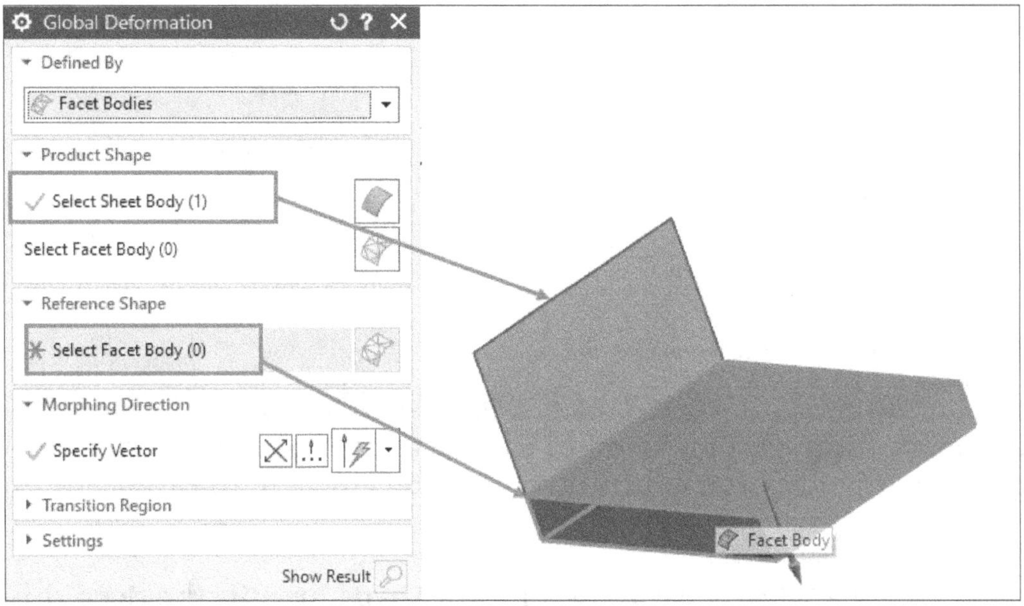

Figure-49. Selecting the sheet and facet body

- Click on the **Specify Vector** button from **Morphing Direction** rollout and specify desired direction to be used to create the product sheet.
- Click on the **Select Inner Boundary** button from **Transition Region** rollout to select desired inner boundary for the transition region. Similarly, click on the **Select Outer Boundary** button to select desired outer boundary for the transition region. Define the steepness of the transition surface by specifying desired value in the **Parameter** edit box.
- Select desired type of resultant body to be created from **Result Body** drop-down in the **Settings** rollout. Select **Create Facets** check box to create a faceted body along with the resulting sheet body. Specify desired value for the deformation between **0.6** and **2.5** in the **Deformation Factor** edit box. Specify desired value for the smoothing shape of the body between **0.0** and **0.2** in the **Smoothing Factor** edit box.
- Click on the **Deformation Box** rollout to specify desired value for the grid size between **3** and **10** in the **Grid Size** edit box and select desired value for the deformation degree from **Degree** drop-down.
- Click on the **Convexity** rollout and select **Enable Convexity Constraint** check box to constraint the sections of the deformation within a convex shape.
- Select **Calculate Maximum Deviation** check box to calculate the maximum and average deviations displaying a line which indicates the maximum deviation between the deformed surface and the original.
- Other parameters in the dialog box are same as discussed earlier.
- After specifying desired parameters, click on **OK** button from the dialog box. The sheet body will be deformed; refer to Figure-50.

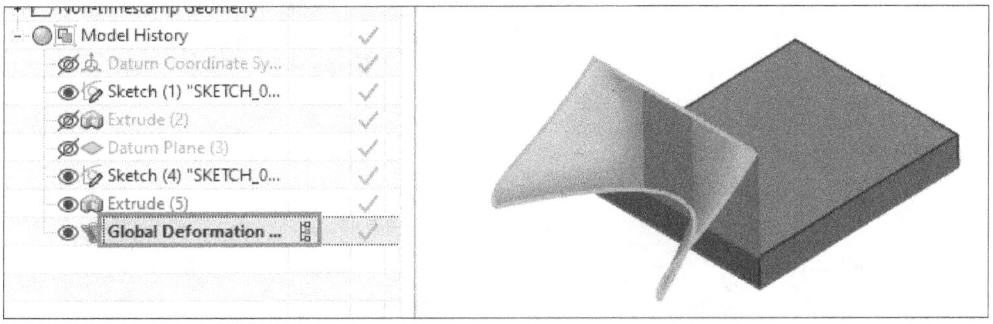

Figure-50. Sheet body deformed

Flattening and Forming

The **Flattening and Forming** tool is used to flatten 3D faces, curves, and points from one or more bodies into a 2D plane to make it easier to design new curves and points. The procedure to use this tool is discussed next.

- Click on the **Flattening and Forming** tool from **Shape** area in the **More** drop-down of **Edit** group in the **Surface** tab of the **Ribbon**. The **Flattening and Forming** dialog box will be displayed; refer to Figure-51.

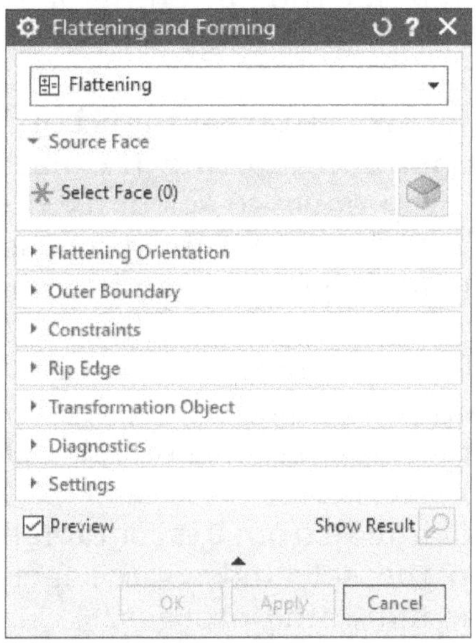

Figure-51. Flattening and Forming dialog box

- Select **Flattening** option from drop-down in the top area of the dialog box to flatten the selected faces, curves, and points into a flattened 2D copy as a flattening and forming feature. Select **Forming and Reuse** option from the drop-down to reuse an existing flattening and forming feature to unwrap selected objects to the existing flattened feature and rewrap them back onto the original surfaces.
- Select desired connected 3D faces from the graphics window to be flattened; refer to Figure-52.

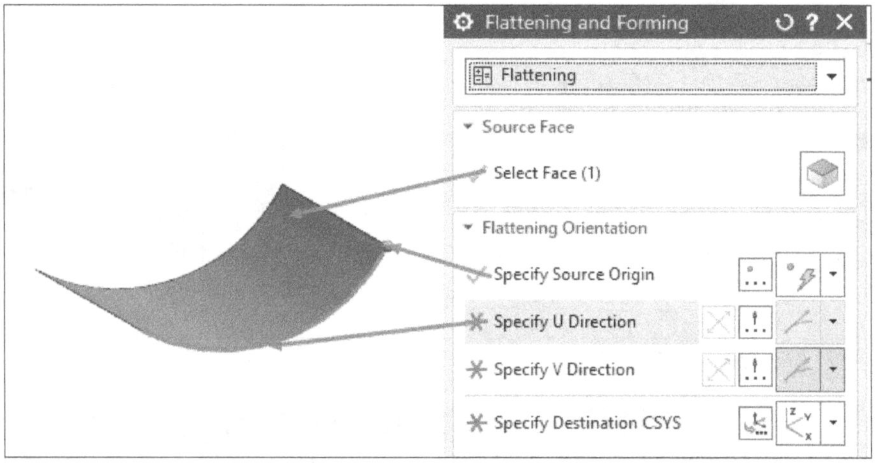

Figure-52. Selecting the source face and flattening orientation

- Click on the **Specify Source Origin** button from **Flattening Orientation** rollout and select desired point on a source faces as the origin of the flattened surface plane. Click on the **Specify U Direction** and **Specify V Direction** button to specify desired U and V direction for the flatten surface plane, respectively. Click on the **Specify Destination CSYS** button and specify desired point to define the location of coordinate system for the flattening plane.
- Click on the **Outer Boundary** rollout and select desired curve or edge as an outer boundary for the flatten faces.
- Select **No Constraints** option from **Flattening with** drop-down in the **Constraints** rollout to not use any constraints during the flattening process. Select **Fixed Elements** option from the drop-down to select fixed elements on the source faces to control distortion during the flattening process. Select **Fixed Arc Length** option to select a series of face edges and maintain their original arc length while flattening the body.
- Click on the **Rip Edge** rollout to control distortion by selecting curves or edges on the original faces to split them along the edges during the flattening process.
- Click on the **Transformation Object** rollout to select desired point and curve objects that lie on the selected faces.
- Select desired distortion color map from **Distortion Map** drop-down of **Diagnostics** rollout to be displayed on the selected source faces to show the magnitude of distorted object during the flattening process.
- Select desired amount of distortion in the flattened object from **Accuracy** drop-down in the **Settings** rollout.
- After specifying desired parameters, click on **OK** button from the dialog box. The 3D face will be flattened; refer to Figure-53.

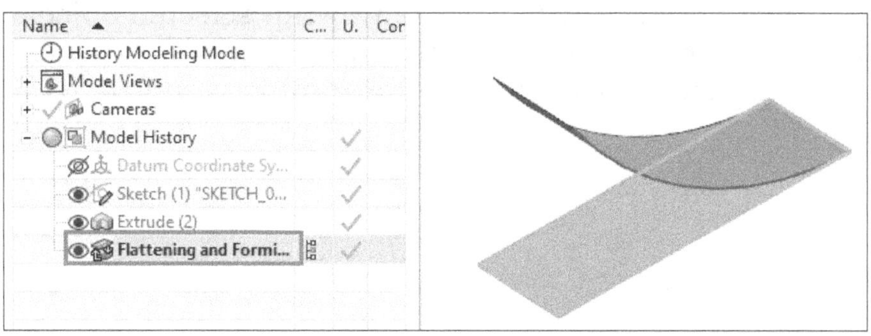

Figure-53. 3D face flattened

Heal Surface

The **Heat Surface** tool is used to heal geometry faults commonly found in imported or exported sheet and solid bodies. The procedure to use this tool is discussed next.

- Click on the **Heat Surface** tool from **Shape** area in the **More** drop-down of **Edit** group in the **Surface** tab of the **Ribbon**. The **Heal Surface** dialog box will be displayed; refer to Figure-54.

Figure-54. Heal Surface dialog box

- On selecting the **Remove Gashes** option from drop-down in the top area of the dialog box, all the gashes in the selected sheet bodies will be closed and the geometric discontinuities will be healed. Select **Heal Internal Edges** option to select non-laminar edges of a body and heal them to a defined level of continuity.
- Select desired sheet bodies from the graphics window to be healed.
- Click on the **Select Face** button from **Fixed Faces** rollout and select desired faces to be fixed while healing the surface.
- Select **Tolerance Markup** check box from **Result Analysis** rollout to display the continuous edges in green, and the edges with discontinuities exceeding the specified tolerance in red. Select desired option from **Maximum Discontinuity** drop-down to not to create the labels or create the labels for maximum discontinuity for the edge or body.
- Specify desired maximum distance of the laminar edge pairs to be converted into internal edges in the **Max Gash Distance** edit box of **Settings** rollout.
- Other parameters in the dialog box are same as discussed earlier.
- After specifying desired parameters, click on **OK** button from the dialog box. The heal surface feature will be created.

Reverse Normal

The **Reverse Normal** tool is used to reverse the normal direction of one or more sheet bodies. The procedure to use this tool is discussed next.

- Click on the **Reverse Normal** tool from the **Direction** area in the **More** drop-down of **Edit** group in the **Surface** tab of the **Ribbon**. The **Reverse Normal** dialog box will be displayed; refer to Figure-55.

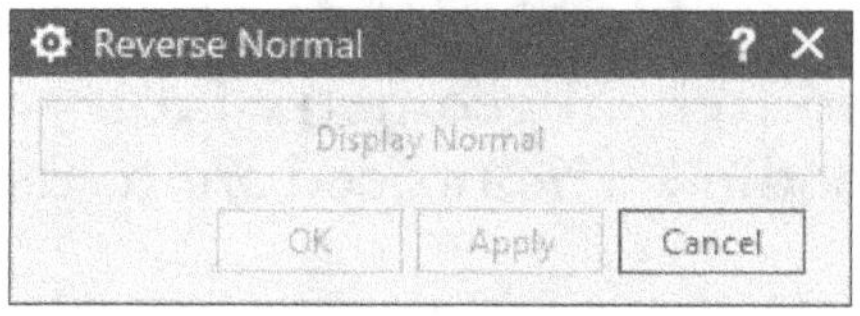

Figure-55. Reverse Normal dialog box

- Select desired one or more sheet bodies from the graphics window to be reversed; refer to Figure-56.

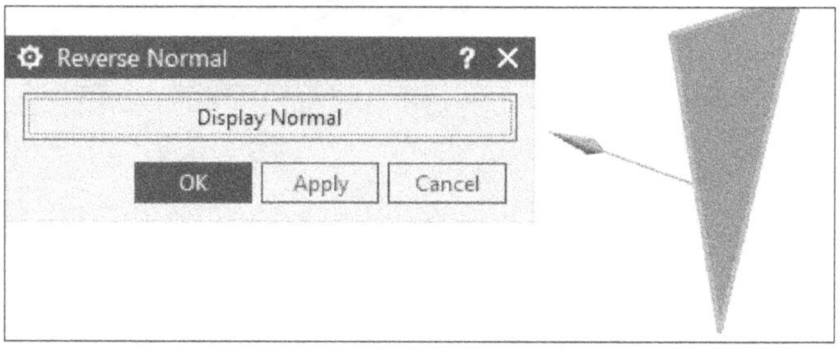

Figure-56. Selecting the sheet body to be reversed

- Click on the **Display Normal** button to re-display the normal direction of sheet body.
- After specifying desired parameters, click on **OK** button from the dialog box. The direction of sheet body will be reversed; refer to Figure-57.

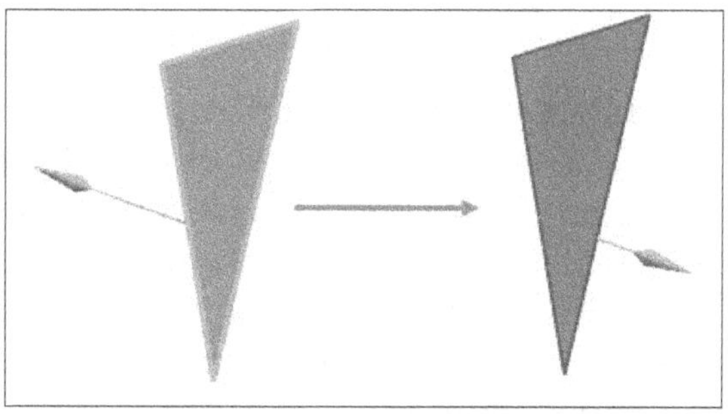

Figure-57. Direction of sheet body reversed

Edit U/V Direction

The **Edit U/V Direction** tool is used to modify the U and V directions of B-surface geometry. The procedure to use this tool is discussed next.

- Click on the **Edit U/V Direction** tool from **Direction** area in the **More** drop-down of **Edit** group in the **Surface** tab of the **Ribbon**. The **Edit U/V Direction** dialog box will be displayed; refer to Figure-58.

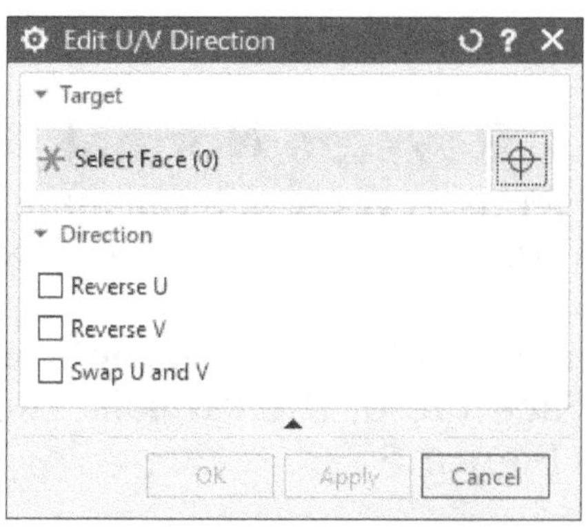

Figure-58. Edit U/V Direction dialog box

- Select desired face of B-surface geometry from the graphics window whose direction is to be changed. Note that you must have modified the surface in **History-Free Modeling Mode** to use this tool. To activate history free modeling mode, right-click on the **History Modeling Mode** option in the **Part Navigator** and select the **History-Free Modeling Mode** option from the shortcut menu; refer to Figure-59.

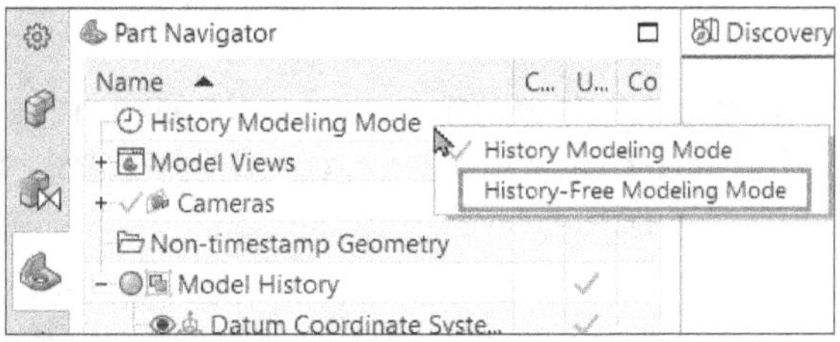

Figure-59. History-Free Modeling Mode option

- Select **Reverse U** check box from the **Direction** rollout to reverse only the U direction. Select **Reverse V** check box to reverse only the V direction. Select **Swap U and V** check box to swap the U and V direction.
- After specifying desired parameters, click on **OK** button from the dialog box. The u and v directions will be modified.

Enlarge

The **Enlarge** tool is used to modify the size of an untrimmed face or sheet. The procedure to use this tool is discussed next.

- Click on the **Enlarge** tool from **Boundary** area in the **More** drop-down of **Edit** group in the **Surface** tab of the **Ribbon**. The **Enlarge** dialog box will be displayed; refer to Figure-60.

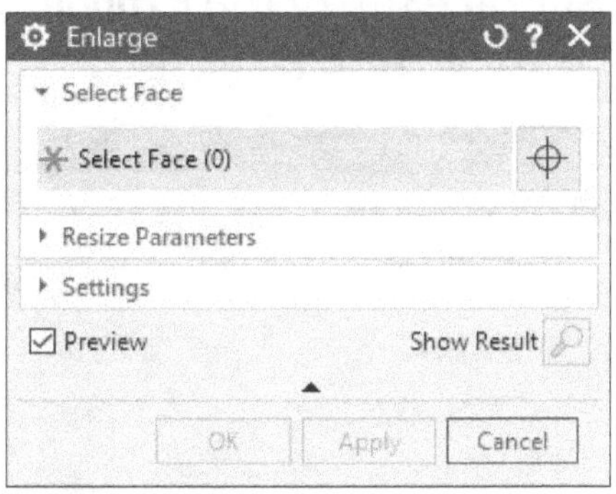

Figure-60. Enlarge dialog box

- Select desired face from the graphics window to be enlarged; refer to Figure-61.

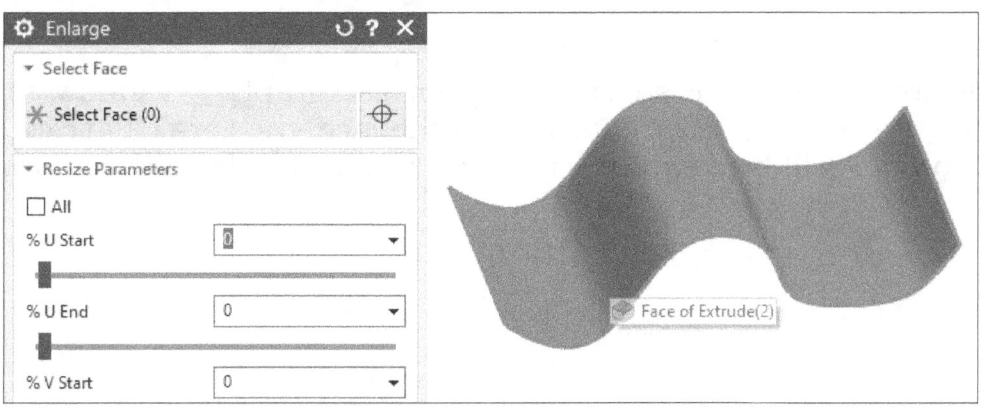

Figure-61. Selecting the face to be enlarged

- Specify desired percentage value in the **% U Start**, **% U End**, **% V Start**, and **% V End** edit boxes to define the modification for each edge of the sheet.
- Select **All** check box from **Resize Parameters** rollout to apply the same modification to all edges of the sheet.
- Select **Linear** or **Natural** radio button from **Mode** area of the **Settings** rollout to extend the edges of the sheet linearly or by following the natural curvature of the surface.
- Other parameters in the dialog box are same as discussed earlier.
- After specifying desired parameters, click on **OK** button from the dialog box. The sheet body will be enlarged; refer to Figure-62.

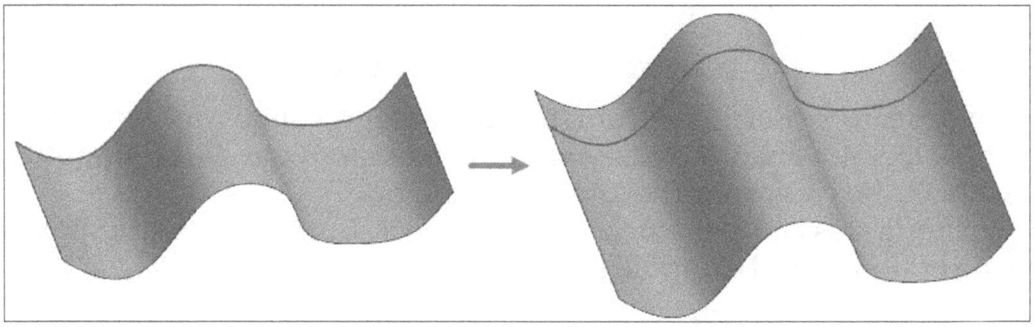

Figure-62. Sheet body enlarged

Local Untrim and Extend

The **Local Untrim and Extend** tool is used to trim, untrim, or extend a single surface of a sheet body. The procedure to use this tool is discussed next.

- Click on the **Local Untrim and Extend** tool from **Boundary** area in the **More** drop-down of **Edit** group in the **Surface** tab of the **Ribbon**. The **Local Untrim and Extend** dialog box will be displayed; refer to Figure-63.

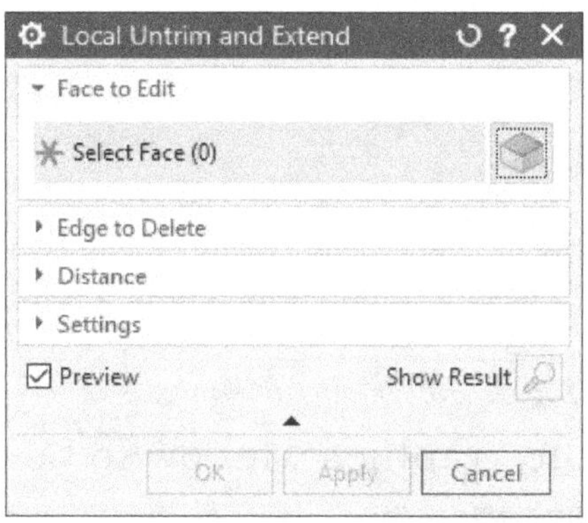

Figure-63. Local Untrim and Extend dialog box

- Select desired face of the sheet body from the graphics window to be edited; refer to Figure-64. Note that, on selecting the face, the **Local Untrim and Extend** information box will be displayed. Click on **Yes** button from the information box.

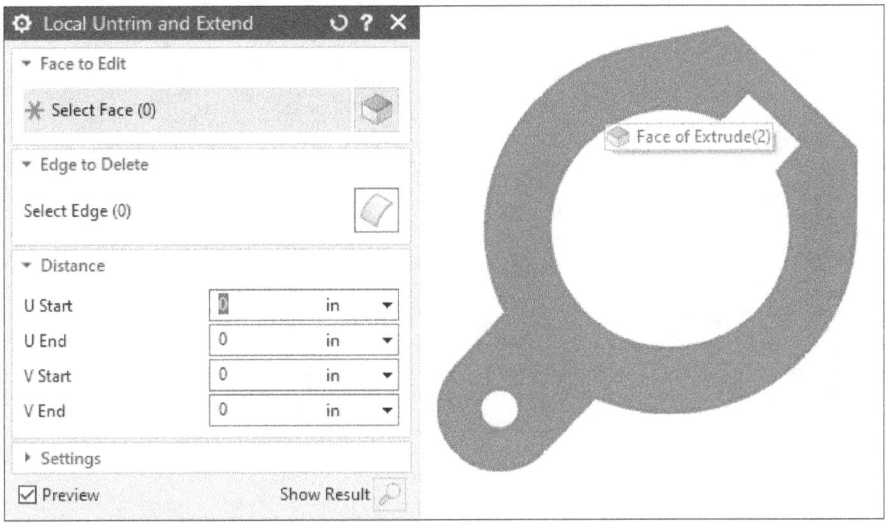

Figure-64. Selecting the sheet body to be edited

- Select desired edges of the sheet body to be extended; refer to Figure-65.

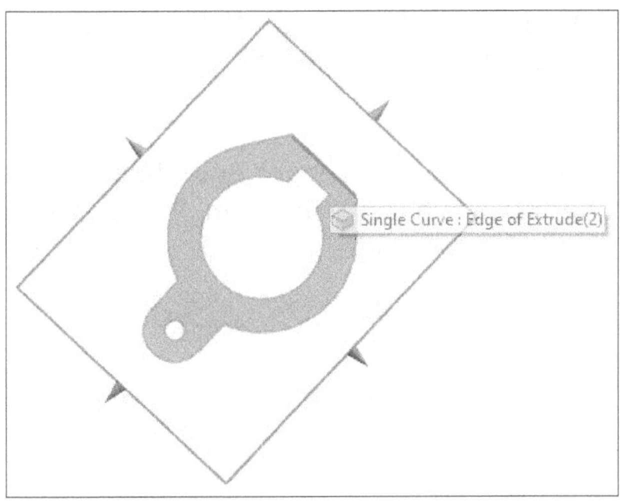

Figure-65. Selecting the edge of sheet body

- Specify desired length of the U start, U end, V start, and V end boundaries in the **U Start**, **U End**, **V Start**, and **V End** edit boxes of the **Distance** rollout, respectively.
- Other parameters in the dialog box are same as discussed earlier.
- After specifying desired parameters, click on **OK** button from the dialog box. The sheet body will be extended; refer to Figure-66.

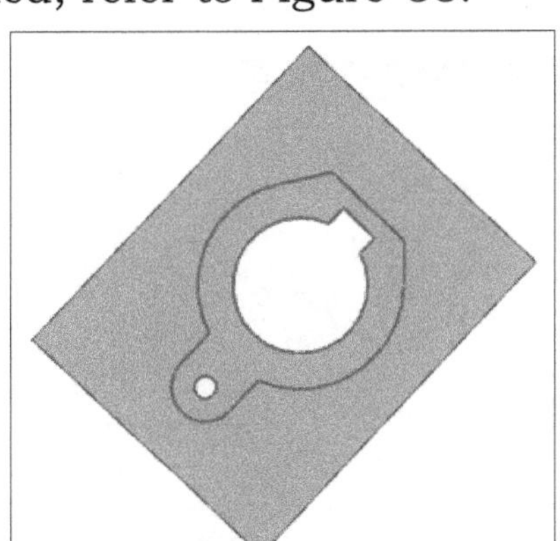

Figure-66. Sheet body extended

- You can also extend the edges using arrow buttons displayed in the graphics window; refer to Figure-67.

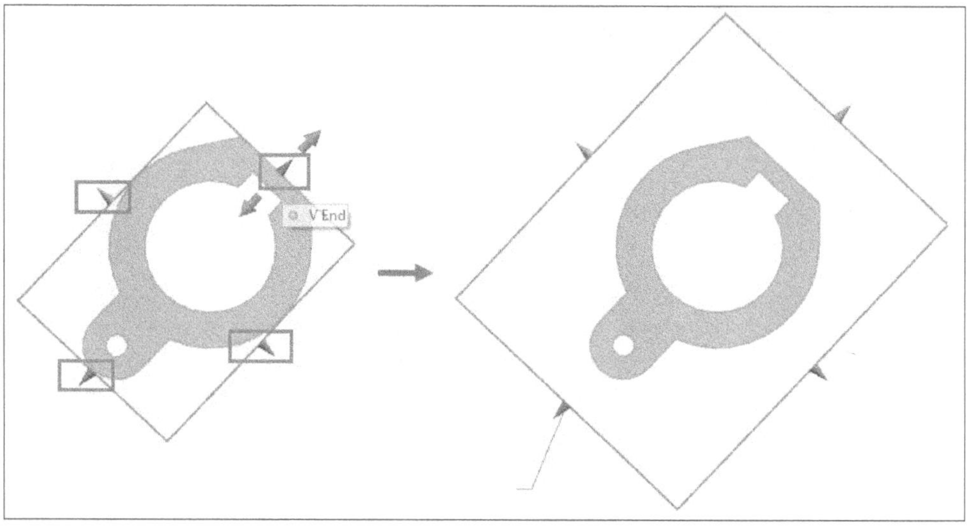

Figure-67. Extending the edges using arrow buttons

Snip into Patches

The **Snip into Patches** tool is used to divide the face into separate sheet bodies or delete desired number of patches from the original sheet. The procedure to use this tool is discussed next.

- Click on the **Snip into Patches** tool from **Boundary** area in the **More** drop-down of **Edit** group in the **Surface** tab of the **Ribbon**. The **Snip into Patches** dialog box will be displayed; refer to Figure-68.

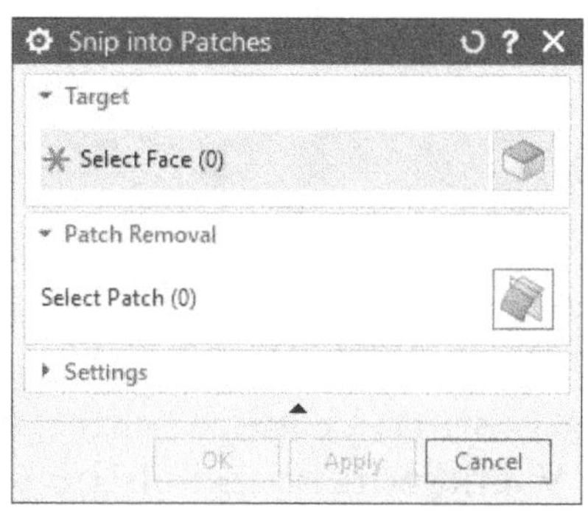

Figure-68. Snip into Patches dialog box

- Select desired face from the graphics window that contains the region to be replaced; refer to Figure-69.

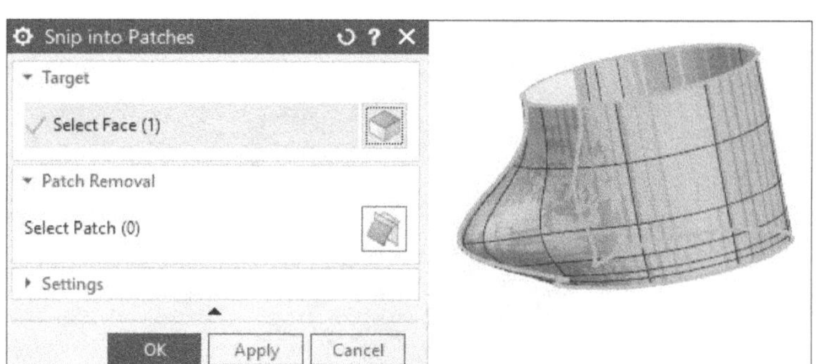

Figure-69. Selecting the target face to be replaced

- Click on the **Select Patch** button from **Patch Removal** rollout and select desired patches on the regions to be removed; refer to Figure-70.

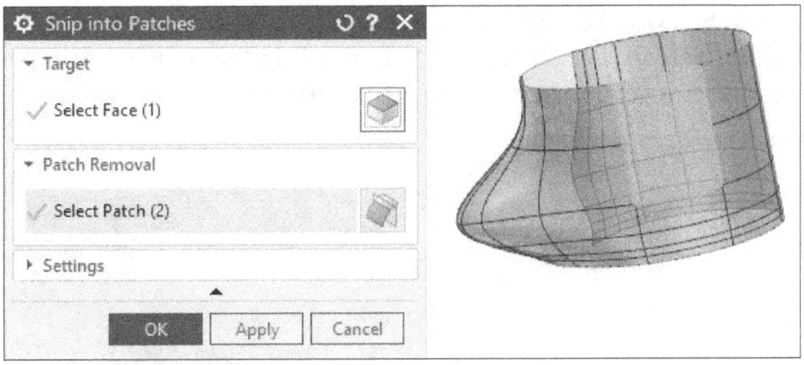

Figure-70. Selecting the patches to be removed

- Select **Hide Original Sheet Body** check box from **Settings** rollout to display the sheet body with patches either visible or hidden.
- After specifying desired parameters, click on **OK** button from the dialog box. The patches will be deleted; refer to Figure-71.

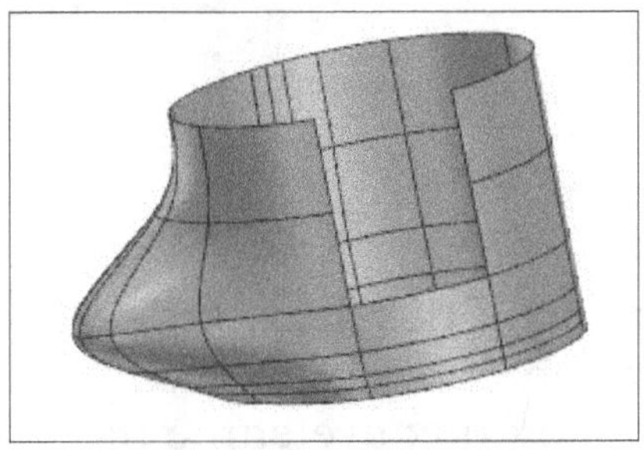

Figure-71. Patches deleted

Smooth Poles

The **Smooth Poles** tool is used to modify the distribution of selected pole by determining the location of selected poles in relation to the surrounding surfaces. The procedure to use this tool is discussed next.

- Click on the **Smooth Poles** tool from **Smooth** area in the **More** drop-down of **Edit** group in the **Surface** tab of the **Ribbon**. The **Smooth Poles** dialog box will be displayed; refer to Figure-72.

Figure-72. Smooth Poles dialog box

- Select desired faces from the graphics window to be smoothen.
- Select **Move Selected Only** check box from **Poles** rollout to display and specify the poles for surface smoothing; refer to Figure-73.

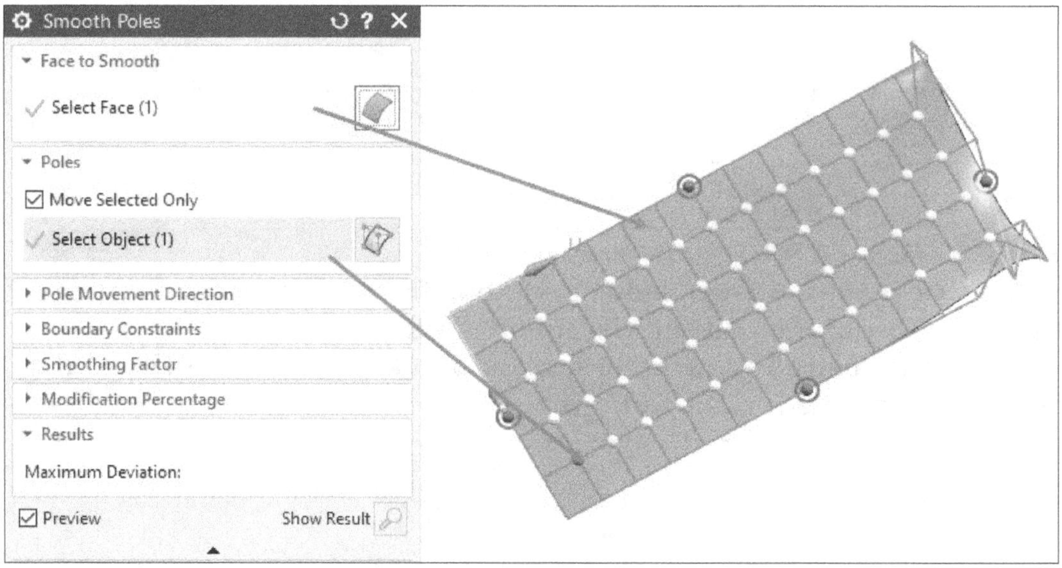

Figure-73. Face and poles selected for surface smoothing

- Select **Specify Direction** check box from **Pole Movement Direction** rollout and specify desired direction for the pole movement.
- Other parameters in the dialog box are same as discussed earlier.
- After specifying desired parameters, click on **OK** button from the dialog box. The poles will be smoothen; refer to Figure-74.

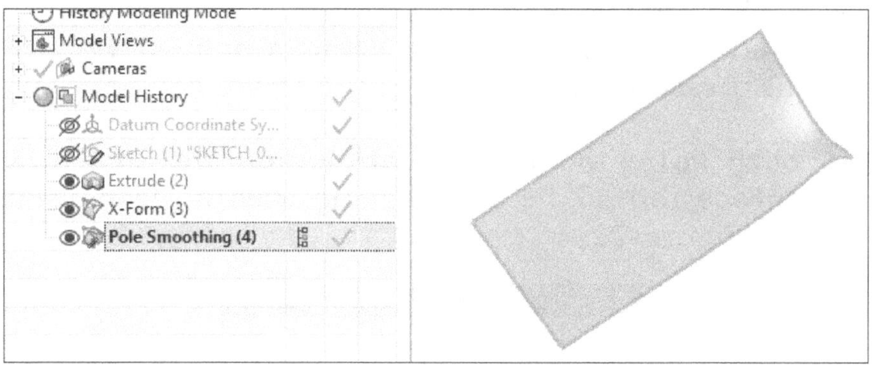

Figure-74. Poles smoothen

Refit Face

The **Refit Face** tool is used to modify an existing surface by modifying its degree, tolerance, or patch count. You can also fit the surface to target geometry. The procedure to use this tool is discussed next.

- Click on the **Refit Face** tool from **Smooth** area in the **More** drop-down of **Edit** group in the **Surface** tab of the **Ribbon**. The **Refit Face** dialog box will be displayed; refer to Figure-75.

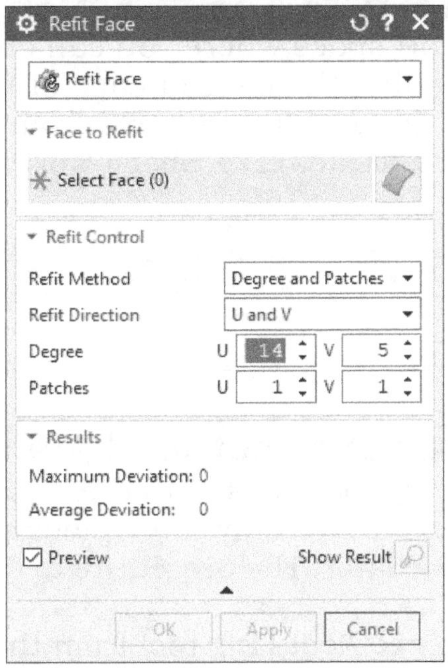

Figure-75. Refit Face dialog box

- Select **Refit Face** option from drop-down in the top area of the dialog box to modify a surface by modifying its degree, tolerance, or patch count. Select **Fit to Target** option to modify a surface so that it fits a target shape.
- Select desired untrimmed surface from the graphics window to be modified; refer to Figure-76.

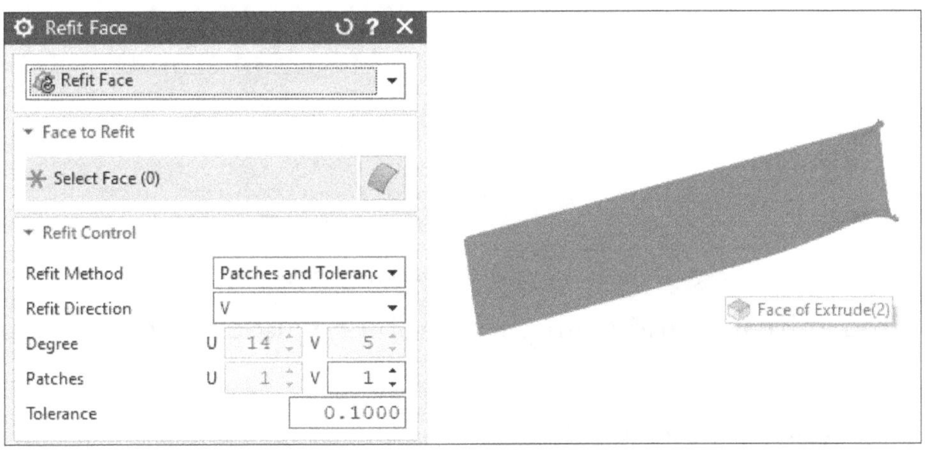

Figure-76. Selecting the untrimmed surface to be modified

- Other parameters in the dialog box are same as discussed earlier.
- After specifying desired parameters, click on **OK** button from the dialog box. The surface will be modified; refer to Figure-77.

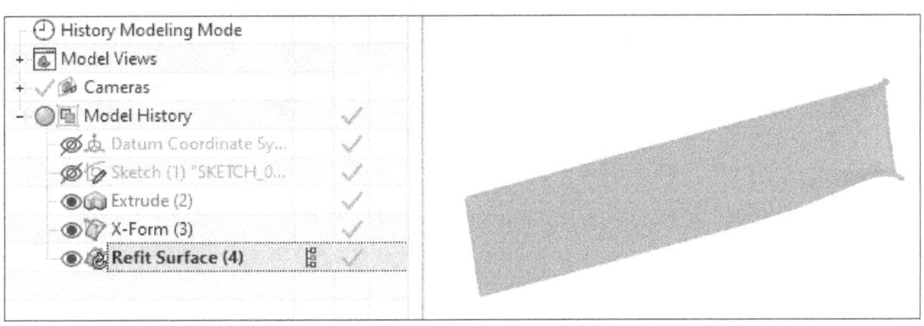

Figure-77. Surface modified

NX REALIZE SHAPE

The **NX Realize Shape** is a workspace where you can create B-surface solid or sheet bodies by modifying and dividing the control cage of the primitive shape such as, a block, cylinder, or sphere. On clicking this tool from **Realize Shape** group in the **Surface** tab of the **Ribbon**, the **NX Realize Shape** workspace will be displayed; refer to Figure-78.

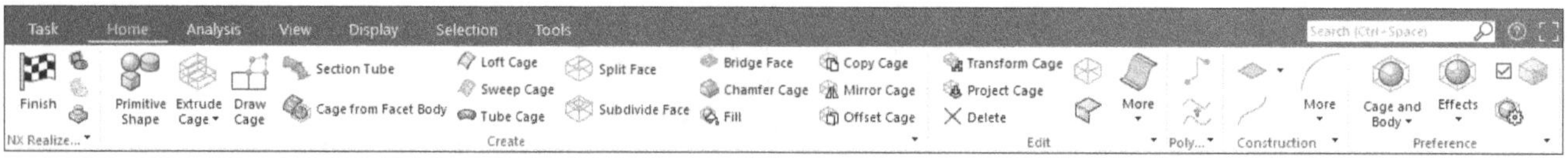

Figure-78. NX Realize Shape workspace

Start Symmetric Modeling

The **Start Symmetric Modeling** tool is used to create geometry that is symmetrical in the model. This tool will be active only after placing first primitive shape using **Primitive Shape** tool discussed later. The procedure to use this tool is discussed next.

- Click on the **Start Symmetric Modeling** tool from the **NX Realize Shape** group in **Home** tab of the **Ribbon**. The **Start Symmetric Modeling** dialog box will be displayed; refer to Figure-79.

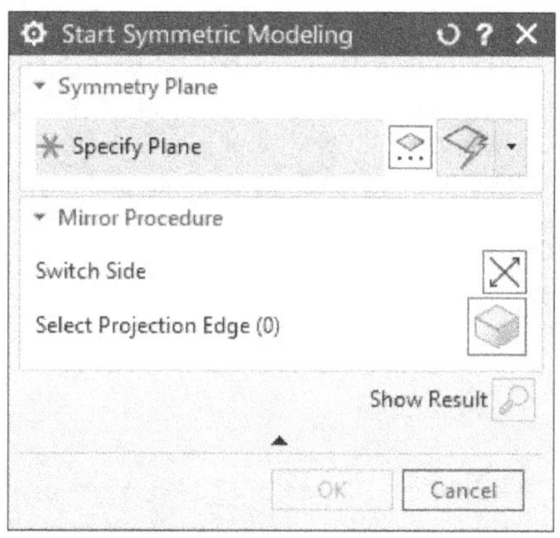

Figure-79. Start Symmetric Modeling dialog box

- Select desired mirror plane from the graphics window for symmetric modeling; refer to Figure-80.

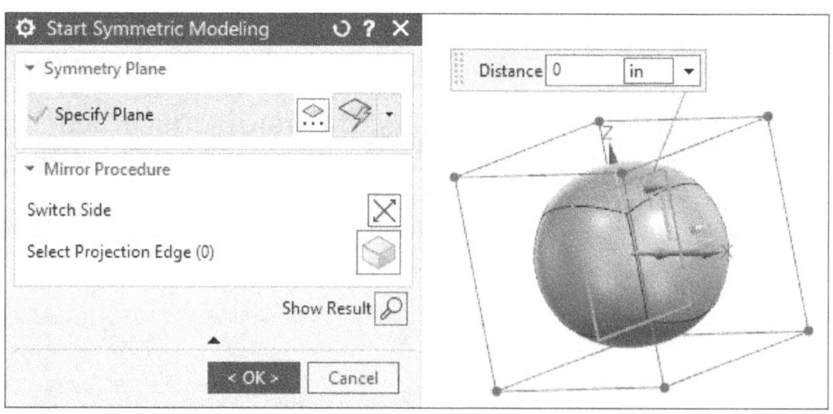

Figure-80. Selecting the mirror plane for symmetric modeling

- Click on the **Switch Side** button from **Mirror Procedure** rollout to switch the side of the control cage to be created. Click on the **Select Projection Edge** button and select desired control edges to be projected to the symmetry plane with C2 continuity.
- After specifying desired parameters, click on **OK** button from the dialog box. The symmetric modeling will be started; refer to Figure-81.

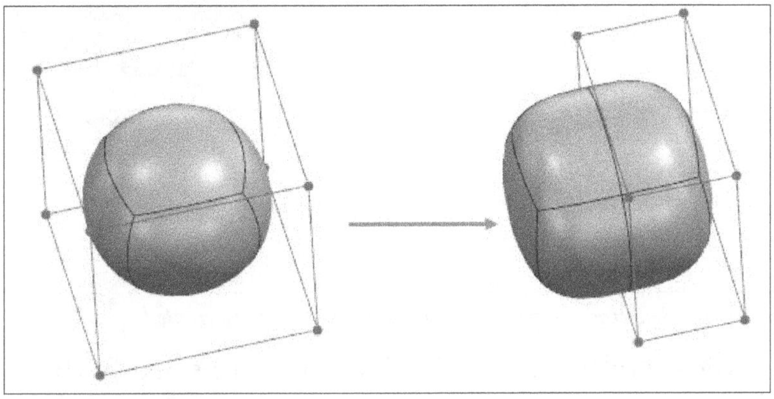

Figure-81. Symmetric modeling started

Primitive Shape

The **Primitive Shape** tool is used to create a base body for starting NX Realize Shape modeling. The procedure to use this tool is discussed next.

- Click on the **Primitive Shape** tool from **Create** group in the **Home** tab of the **Ribbon**. The **Primitive Shape** dialog box will be displayed; refer to Figure-82.

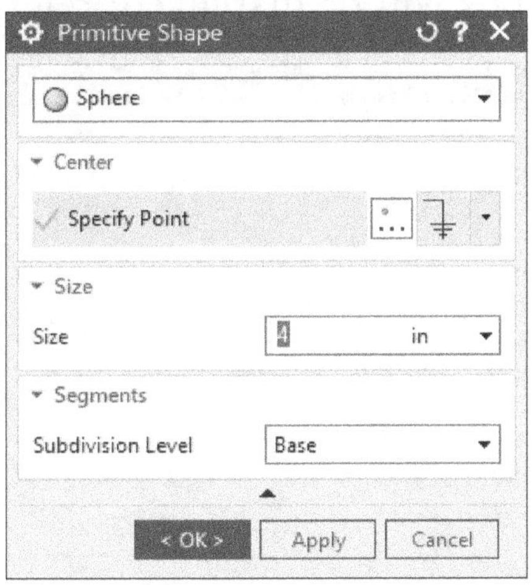

Figure-82. Primitive Shape dialog box

- Select desired primitive shape to be created from drop-down in the top area of the dialog box. The selected shape will be inserted in the graphics window; refer to Figure-83.

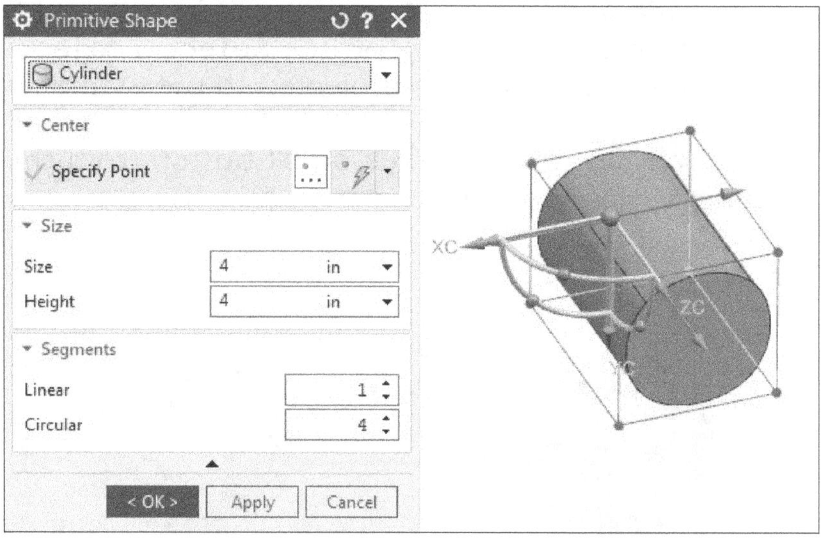

Figure-83. Selecting the cylinder as primitive shape to be created

- Click in the graphics window at desired location to specify the origin of the shape.
- Specify desired parameters in the dialog box related to the shape and click on the **OK** button. The primitive shape will be created.

Extrude Cage

The **Extrude Cage** tool is used to create new cage faces by extruding existing cage edges, cage faces, or cage polylines. The procedure to use this tool is discussed next.

- Click on the **Extrude Cage** tool from **Create** group in the **Home** tab of the **Ribbon**. The **Extrude Cage** dialog box will be displayed; refer to Figure-84.

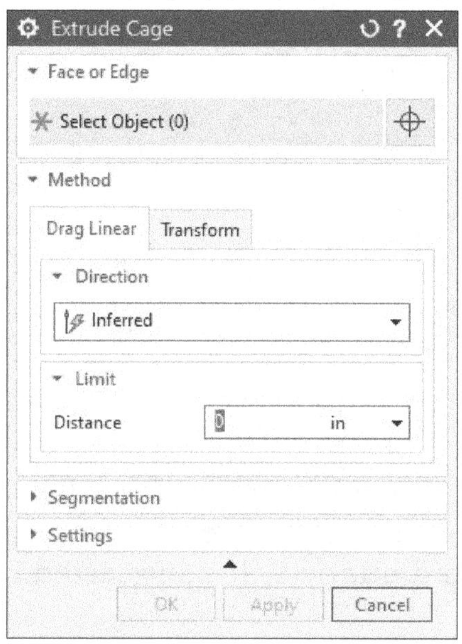

Figure-84. Extrude Cage dialog box

- Select desired cage faces, cage edges, or cage polylines from the graphics window to be extruded; refer to Figure-85.
- Select desired option from **Direction** drop-down in the **Drag Linear** tab of **Method** rollout to move cage objects directly in the graphics window without using the transform tool. Specify desired extrusion distance of the selected edges or faces in the **Distance** edit box of **Limit** rollout.

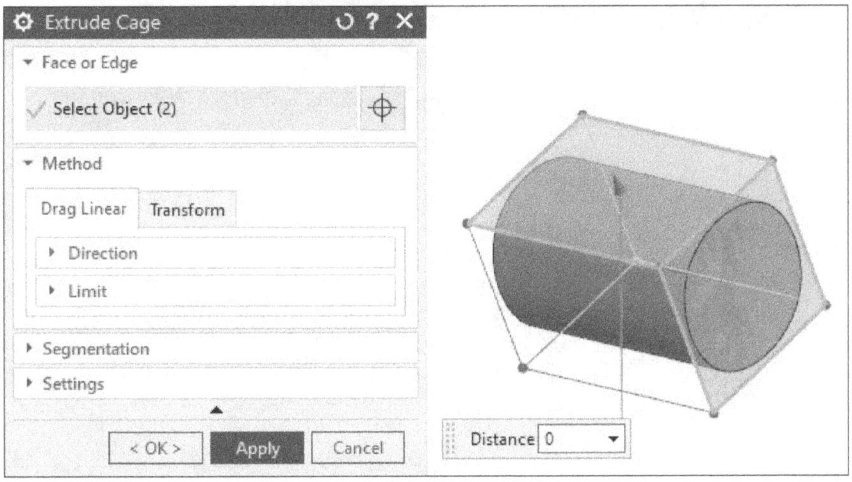

Figure-85. Selecting the cage faces to be extruded

- Select **Move Tool Only** check box from **Transform** tab of **Method** rollout to move the tool only without moving the cage objects. Select **Relocate Tool to Selection** or **Reorient Tool to Selection** check box to relocate or reorient the transform tool to the newly selected objects. Select **Linear**, **Planar**, or **Uniform** radio button from **Scaling** area of the tab to control the direction of scaling the selected cage objects.
- Specify desired number of cage segments to be created in the **Number of Segments** edit box of **Segmentation** rollout.
- Specify desired continuity at the outer edges of selected cage faces from **Continuity** area in the **Settings** rollout.
- After specifying desired parameters, click on **OK** button from the dialog box. The cage faces will be extruded; refer to Figure-86.

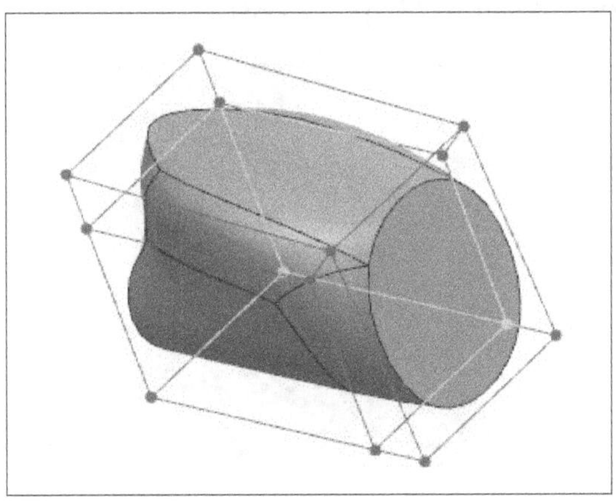

Figure-86. Cage faces extruded

Revolve Cage

The **Revolve Cage** tool is used to revolve selected polylines or cage edges around an axis to create a control cage. The procedure to use this tool is discussed next.

- Click on the **Revolve Cage** tool from **Create** group in the **Home** tab of the **Ribbon**. The **Revolve Cage** dialog box will be displayed; refer to Figure-87.
- Select desired edges or polyline from the graphics window to be revolved; refer to Figure-88.

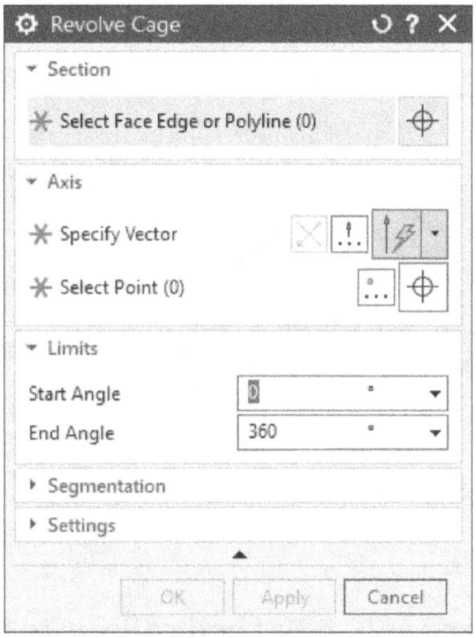

Figure-87. Revolve Cage dialog box

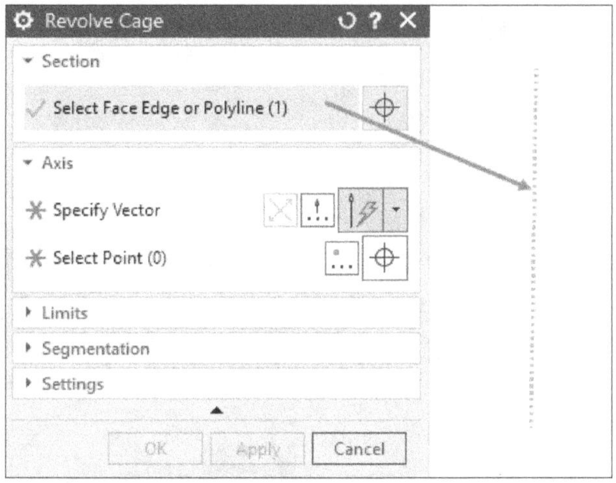

Figure-88. Selecting the polyline to be revolved

- Click in the **Specify Vector** button from **Axis** rollout to define the orientation of the axis of rotation.
- Specify desired point on the axis about which the polyline is to be rotated.
- Specify desired start and end angle of the revolution in the **Start Angle** and **End Angle** edit boxes of **Limits** rollout, respectively.
- Select **Sew Selected Open Edges** check box from **Settings** rollout to close any open edges of the new cage by connecting them to nearby faces.
- Other parameters in the dialog box are same as discussed earlier.
- After specifying desired parameters, click on **OK** button from the dialog box. The polyline will be revolved; refer to Figure-89.

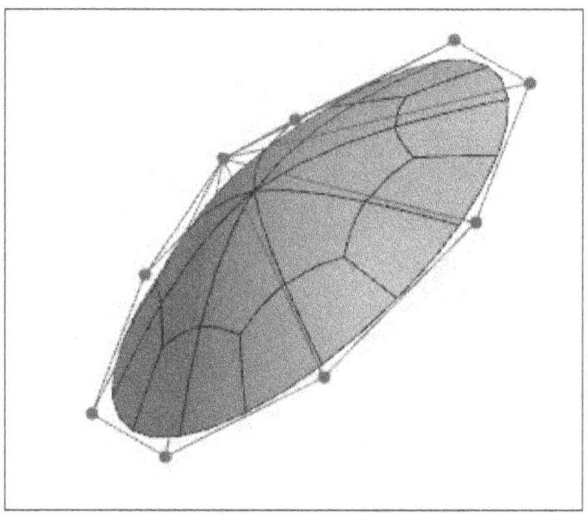

Figure-89. Polyline revolved

Draw Cage

The **Draw Cage** tool is used to create faces of the control cage by specifying their corner points. Note that you need add this tool in **Ribbon** by selecting it from **Group Options** menu; refer to Figure-90. The procedure to use this tool is discussed next.

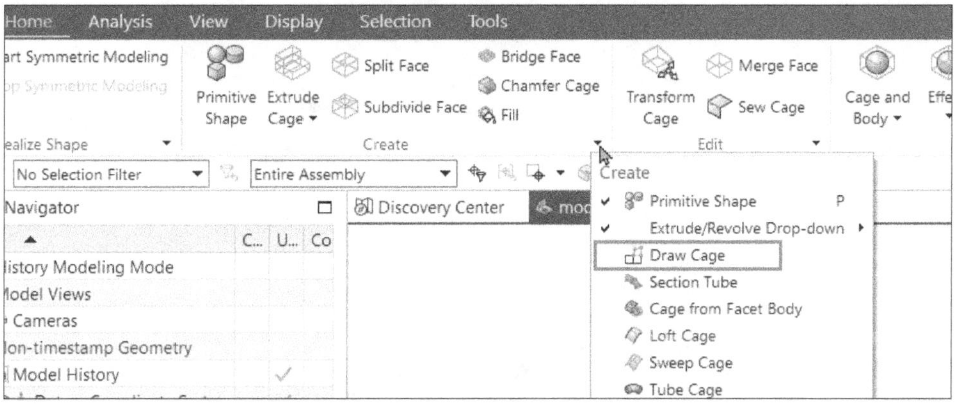

Figure-90. Draw Cage tool

- Click on the **Draw Cage** tool from **Create** group in the **Home** tab of the **Ribbon**. The **Draw Cage** dialog box will be displayed; refer to Figure-91.

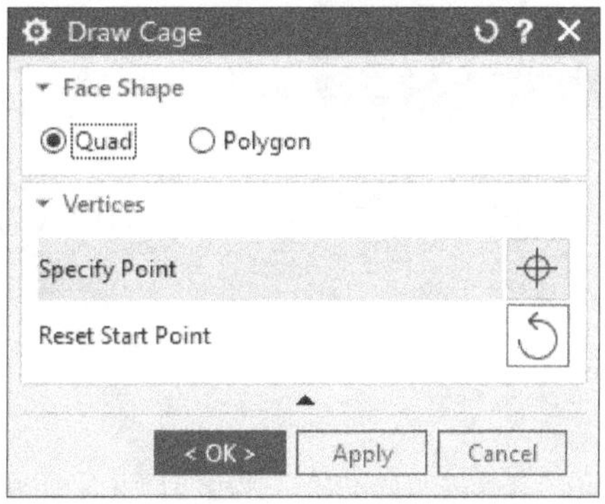

Figure-91. Draw Cage dialog box

- Select **Quad** or **Polygon** radio button from **Face Shape** rollout to create four sided or n-sided control cage faces, respectively.
- Specify desired corner points as cage vertices for the new face in the graphics window. Click on the **Reset Start Point** button from **Vertices** rollout to delete all the previously specified points.
- After specifying desired parameters, click on **OK** button from the dialog box. The faces of the control cage will be created; refer to Figure-92.

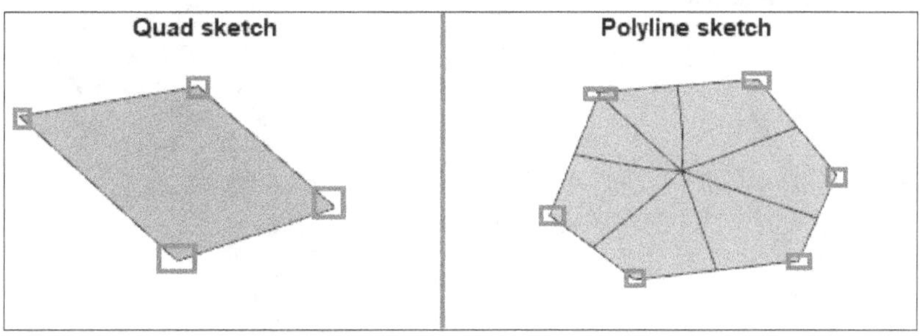

Figure-92. Faces of the control cage created

Section Tube

The **Section Tube** tool is used to create a tube-like control cage using cross-sections through a facet body. The procedure to use this tool is discussed next.

- Click on the **Section Tube** tool from **Create** group in the **Home** tab of the **Ribbon**. The **Section Tube** dialog box will be displayed; refer to Figure-93.

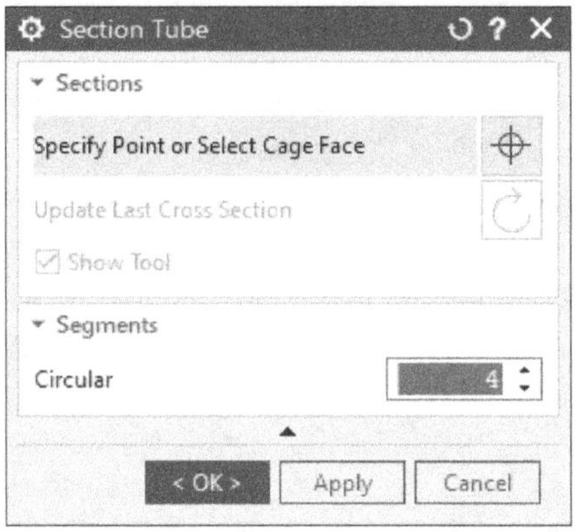

Figure-93. Section Tube dialog box

- Select desired point or cage faces from the graphics window to create a section tube; refer to Figure-94.

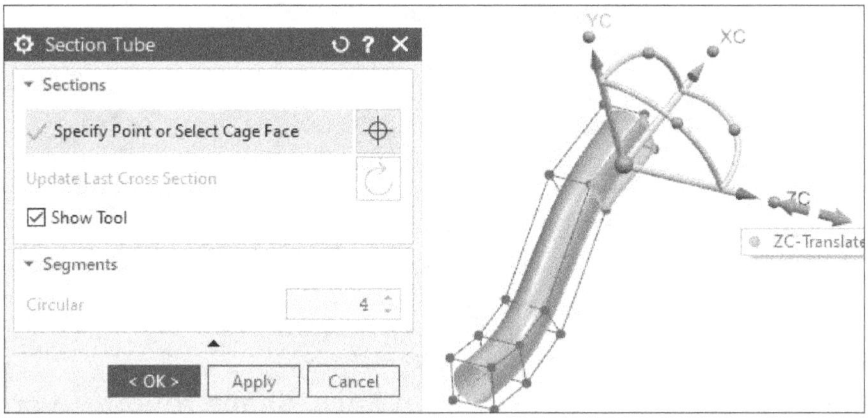

Figure-94. Cage faces selected to create section tube

- Click on the **Update Last Cross Section** button from **Sections** rollout to realign the control cage after reorienting the section plane using the manipulator tool. Select **Show Tool** check box to display the manipulator tool to reorient the section plane; refer to Figure-95.

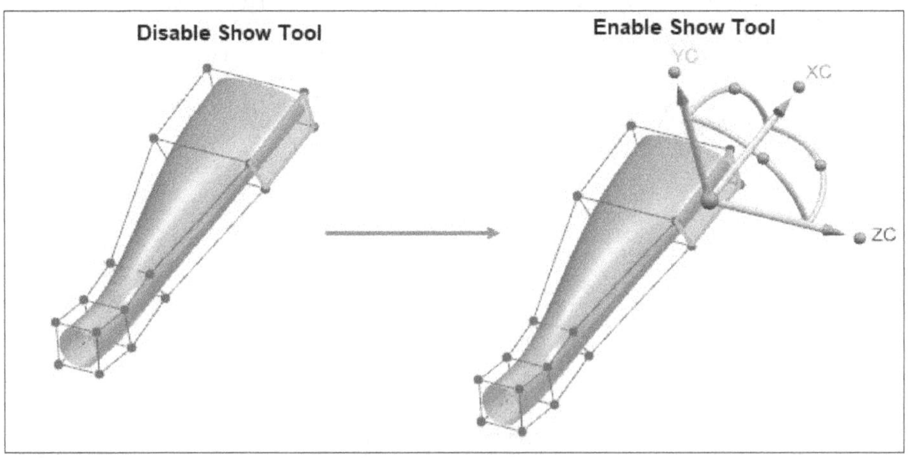

Figure-95. Manipulator tool displayed

- Specify desired number of segments to be created per cross section in the **Circular** edit box of **Segments** rollout. You can specify the segments between **3** and **36**.
- After specifying desired parameters, click on the **OK** button from the dialog box. The section tube will be created; refer to Figure-96.

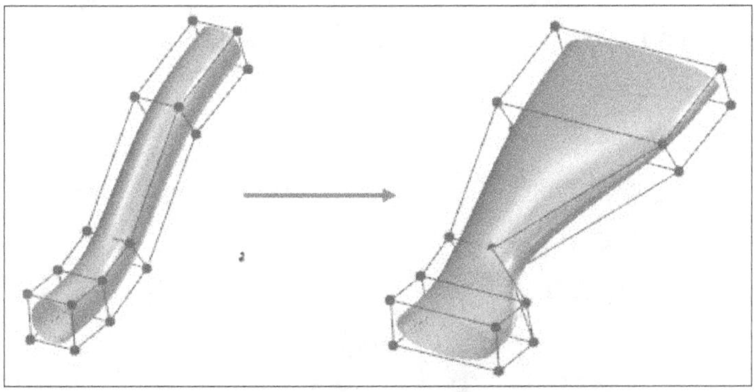

Figure-96. Section tube created

Cage from Facet Body

The **Cage from Facet Body** tool is used to create a new control cage from the regions of a facet body. The procedure to use this tool is discussed next.

- Click on the **Cage from Facet Body** tool from **Create** group in the **Home** tab of the **Ribbon**. The **Cage from Facet Body** dialog box will be displayed; refer to Figure-97.

Figure-97. Cage from Facet Body dialog box

- Select desired facet body or regions of a facet body from which the new cage is to be created; refer to Figure-98.

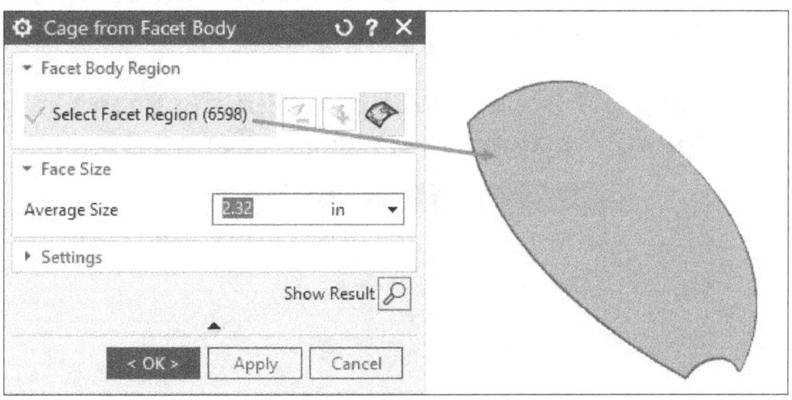

Figure-98. Facet body regions selected

- Specify desired average size of face in the **Average Size** edit box of **Face Size** rollout.

- Select **Show Deviation Plot** check box from **Settings** rollout to display the deviation between the input region and the subdivision faces of the output cage; refer to Figure-99.

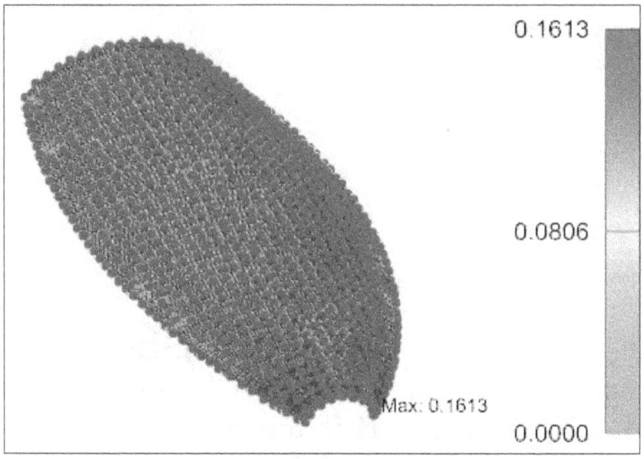

Figure-99. Displaying the deviation

- After specifying desired parameters, click on **OK** button from the dialog box. The cage from facet body will be created; refer to Figure-100.

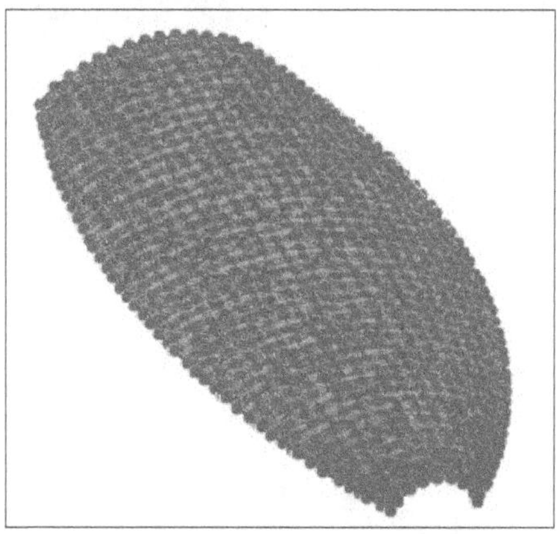

Figure-100. Cage from facet body created

Loft Cage

The **Loft Cage** tool is used to create a lofted shape by connecting control cages using the face edges and polylines. The procedure to use this tool is discussed next.

- Click on the **Loft Cage** tool from **Create** group in the **Home** tab of the **Ribbon**. The **Loft Cage** dialog box will be displayed; refer to Figure-101.

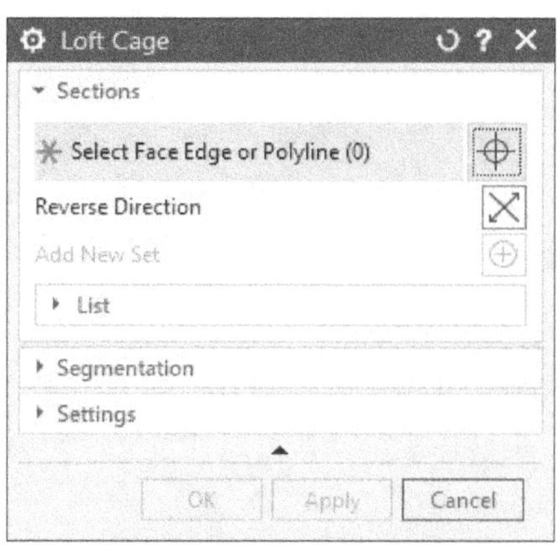

Figure-101. Loft Cage dialog box

- Select desired cage edges or polyline from the graphics window to be lofted; refer to Figure-102. The selected sections will be displayed in the **List** area of the **Sections** rollout.

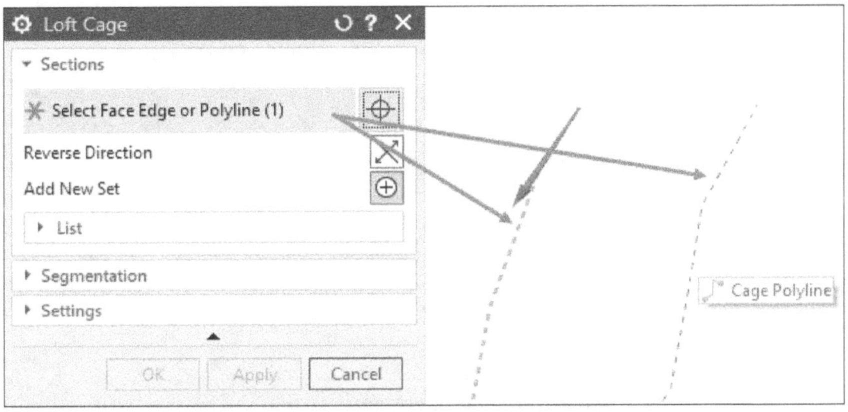

Figure-102. Selecting the polylines to be lofted

- Select **Closed** check box from **Settings** rollout to close the cage between last and first section.
- Other parameters in the dialog box are same as discussed earlier.
- After specifying desired parameters, click on **OK** button from the dialog box. The loft cage will be created; refer to Figure-103.

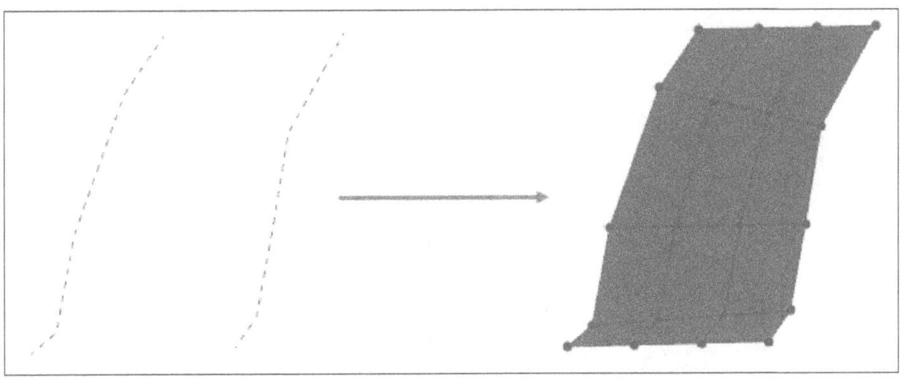

Figure-103. Loft cage created

Sweep Cage

The **Sweep Cage** tool is used to create a sweep structure of control cage faces by using the face edges and polylines as sections and guides. The procedure to use this tool is same as discussed in **Curve Through Mesh** tool.

Tube Cage

The **Tube Cage** tool is used to create a tubular structure of control cage faces using polyline path. The procedure to use this tool is discussed next.

- Click on the **Tube Cage** tool from **Create** group in the **Home** tab of the **Ribbon**. The **Tube Cage** dialog box will be displayed; refer to Figure-104.

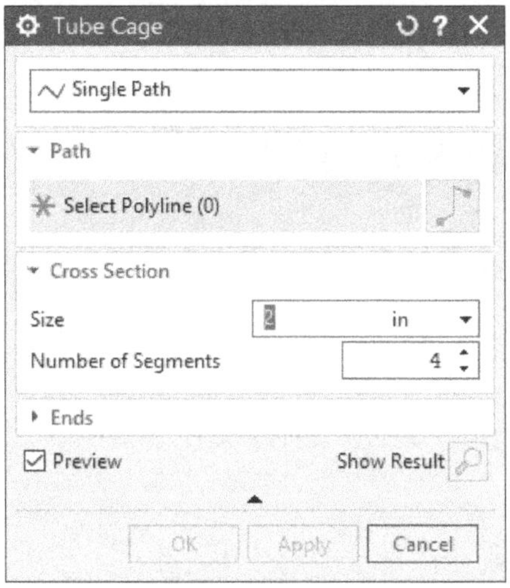

Figure-104. Tube Cage dialog box

- Select desired type of path to be used to create the tube from drop-down in the top area of the dialog box. Select **Single Path** option to create a tube from connected polylines. Select **Branched Path** tool to create a tube from a network of polylines.
- Select desired polyline from the graphics window as a centerline of the tube to be created; refer to Figure-105.

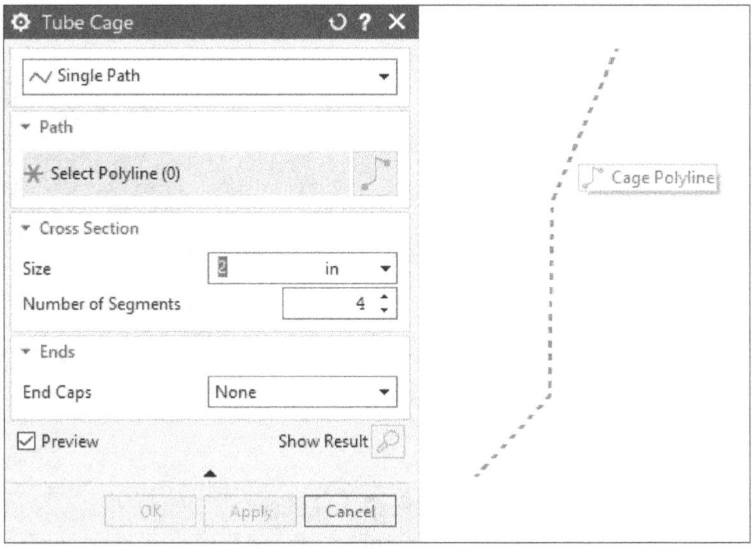

Figure-105. Selecting the polyline as a centerline

- Specify desired size of the cage cross-section in the **Size** edit box of **Cross Section** rollout.
- Specify desired size of the nodes at the path intersection in the **Node Size** edit box and specify desired size of the rods in the **Rod Size** edit box of **Size** rollout. Specify desired transition distance between nodes and rods in the **Falloff Distance** edit box.
- Specify desired number of segments to be used for the cross-section of the tube and along the rods in the **Cross Section** and **Rods** edit box of **Segments** rollout, respectively.
- Select desired shape of the ends of open rods from **End Caps** drop-down in the **Ends** rollout.
- After specifying desired parameters, click on **OK** button from the dialog box. The tube cage will be created; refer to Figure-106.

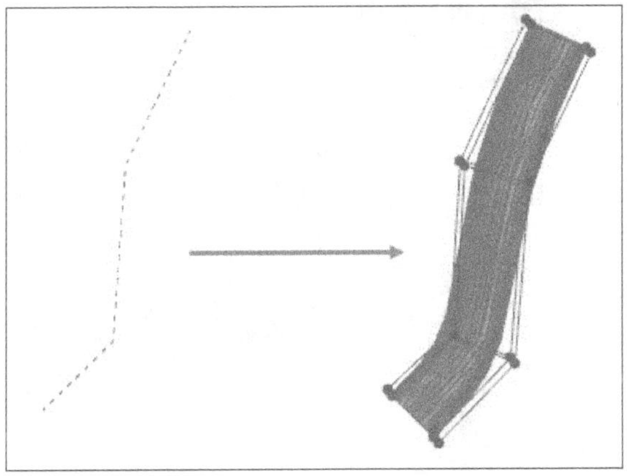

Figure-106. Tube cage created

Split Face

The **Split Face** tool is used to divide selected faces into multiple smaller faces for detailed and local shape editing. The procedure to use this tool is discussed next.

- Click on the **Split Face** tool from **Create** group in the **Home** tab of the **Ribbon**. The **Split Face** dialog box will be displayed; refer to Figure-107.

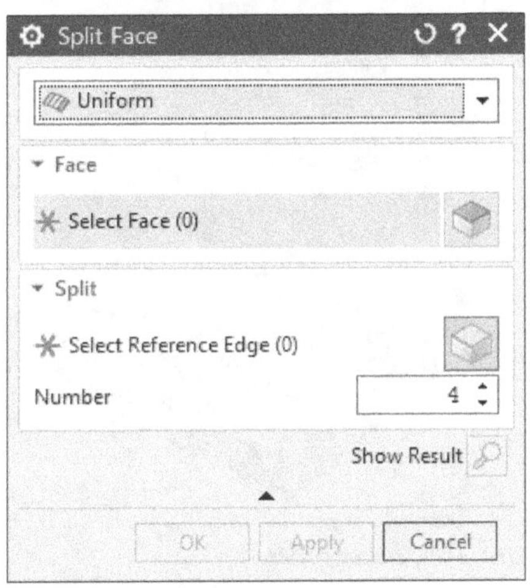

Figure-107. Split Face dialog box

- Select **Uniform** option from drop-down in the top area of the dialog box to split a face into several uniformly spaced smaller faces. Select **Along Polyline** option to split faces along lines specified between points on the face edges.
- Select desired faces from the graphics window to be split.
- Click on the **Select Reference Edge** button from **Split** rollout and select desired edge along which the uniform division is to be created; refer to Figure-108.

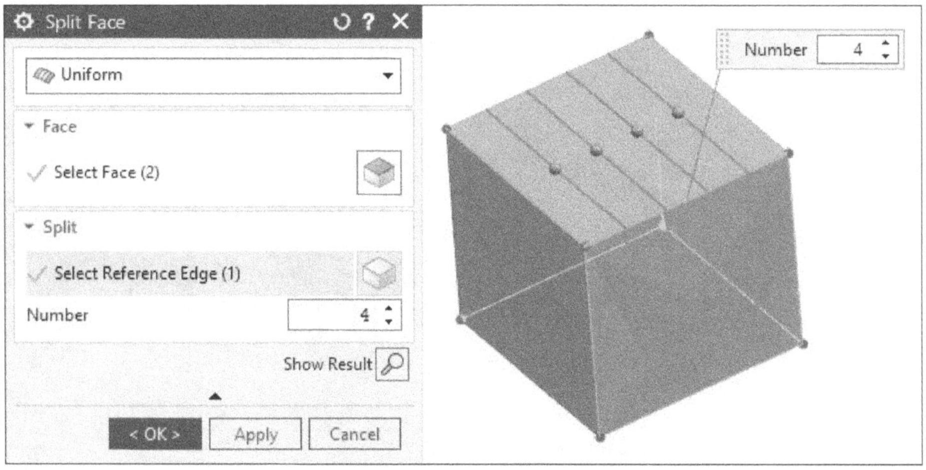

Figure-108. Faces and edge selected for uniform division

- Specify desired number of subdivisions to be created in the **Number** edit box of **Split** rollout.
- After specifying desired parameters, click on **OK** button from the dialog box. The faces will be splitted; refer to Figure-109.

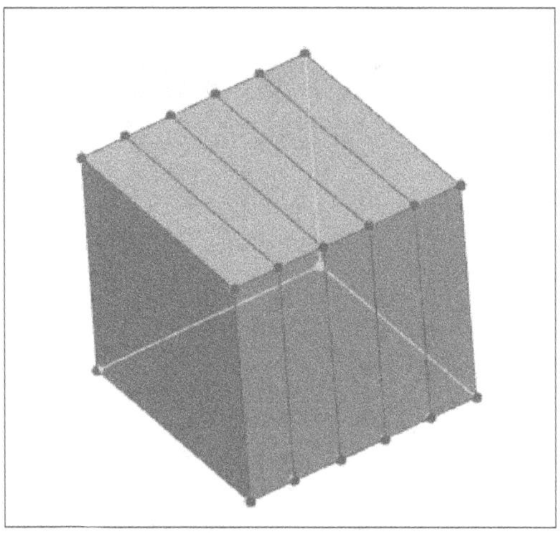

Figure-109. Faces splitted

Subdivide Face

The **Subdivide Face** tool is used to offset the outer edges of selected control cage faces inward to subdivide the faces. The procedure to use this tool is discussed next.

- Click on the **Subdivide Face** tool from **Create** group in the **Home** tab of the **Ribbon**. The **Subdivide Face** dialog box will be displayed; refer to Figure-110.

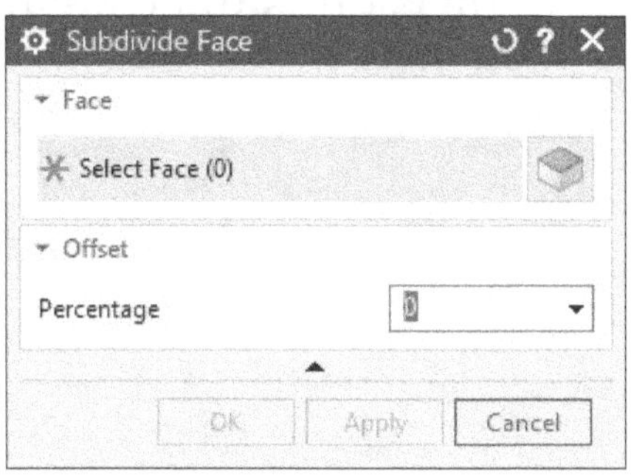

Figure-110. Subdivide Face dialog box

- Select desired face from the graphics window to be subdivided; refer to Figure-111.

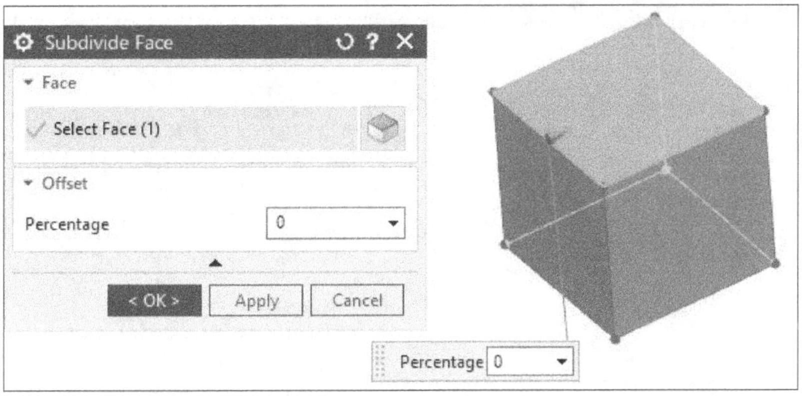

Figure-111. Face selected to subdivide

- Specify desired scale value to create the offset in the **Percentage** edit box of **Offset** rollout.
- After specifying desired parameters, click on **OK** button from the dialog box. The face will be subdivided; refer to Figure-112.

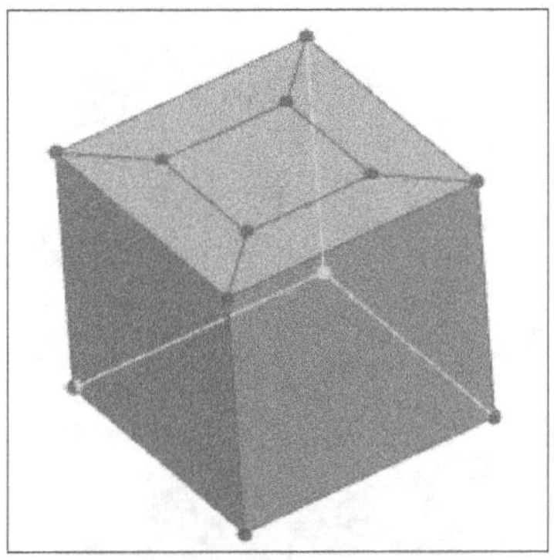

Figure-112. Face subdivided

Bridge Face

The **Bridge Face** tool is used to create a bridge or a tunnel by connecting selected sets of faces. The procedure to use this tool is discussed next.

- Click on the **Bridge Face** tool from **Create** group in the **Home** tab of the **Ribbon**. The **Bridge Face** dialog box will be created; refer to Figure-113.

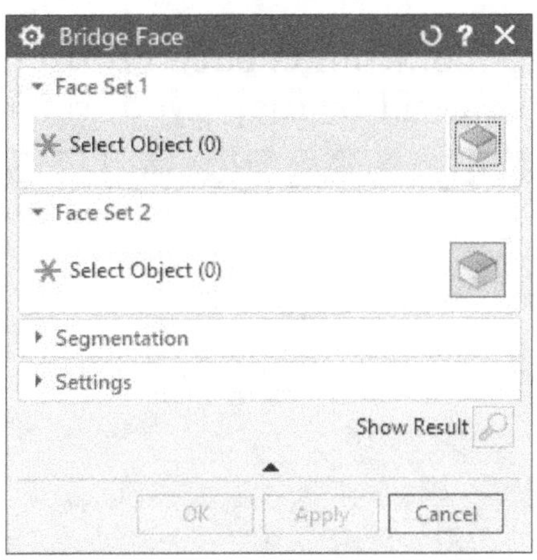

Figure-113. Bridge Face dialog box

- Select first set of objects from the graphics window to be bridged and then click on the **Select Object** button from **Face Set 2** rollout to select second set of objects to be bridged; refer to Figure-114.

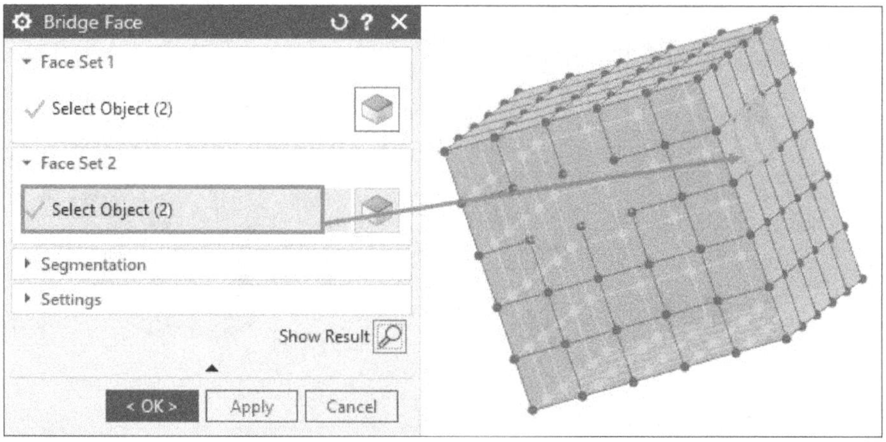

Figure-114. First and second set of objects selected

- Other parameters in the dialog box are same as discussed earlier.
- After specifying desired parameters, click on **OK** button from the dialog box. The bridge will be created; refer to Figure-115.

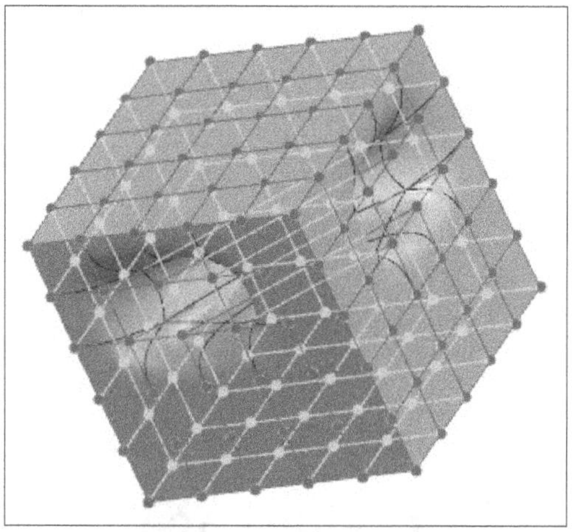

Figure-115. Bridge created

Chamfer Cage

The **Chamfer Cage** tool is used to create a chamfer on selected edges of the control cage. The procedure to use this tool is discussed next.

- Click on the **Chamfer Cage** tool from **Create** group in the **Home** tab of the **Ribbon**. The **Chamfer Cage** dialog box will be displayed; refer to Figure-116.

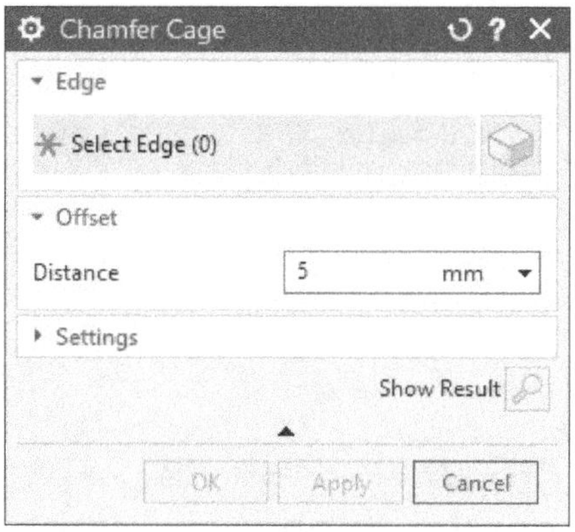

Figure-116. Chamfer Cage dialog box

- Select desired edges of the cage from the graphics window to be chamfer; refer to Figure-117.
- Specify desired distance of the chamfer offset in the **Distance** edit box of the **Offset** rollout.
- Other parameters in the dialog box are same as discussed earlier.
- After specifying desired parameters, click on **OK** button from the dialog box. The chamfer cage feature will be created; refer to Figure-117.

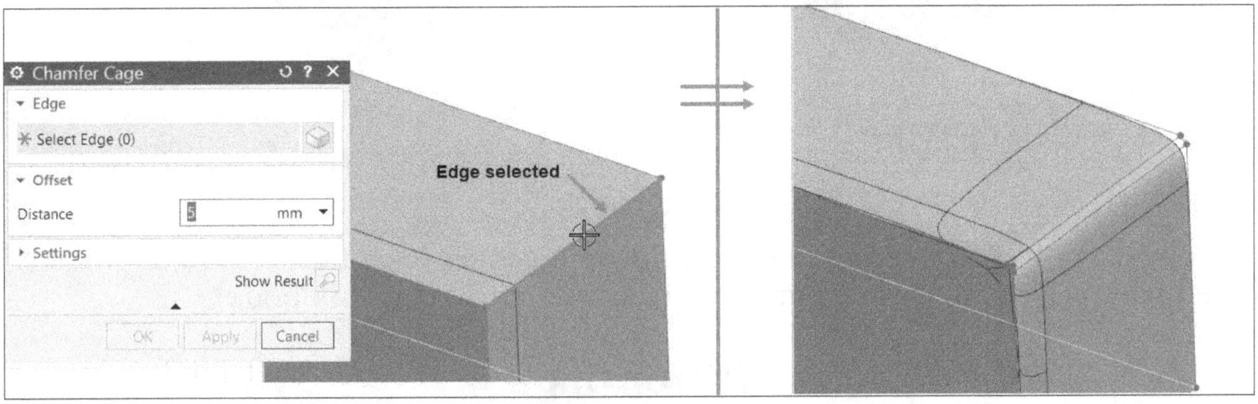

Figure-117. Chamfer cage generated

Fill

The **Fill** tool is used to create a new face on the control cage by selecting two to four open edges. The procedure to use this tool is discussed next.

- Click on the **Fill** tool from **Create** group in the **Home** tab of the **Ribbon**. The **Fill** dialog box will be displayed; refer to Figure-118.

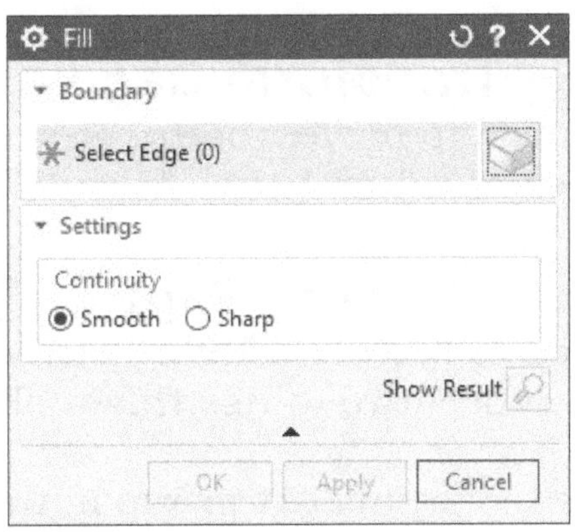

Figure-118. Fill dialog box

- Select desired edges from the graphics window to close the area; refer to Figure-119.

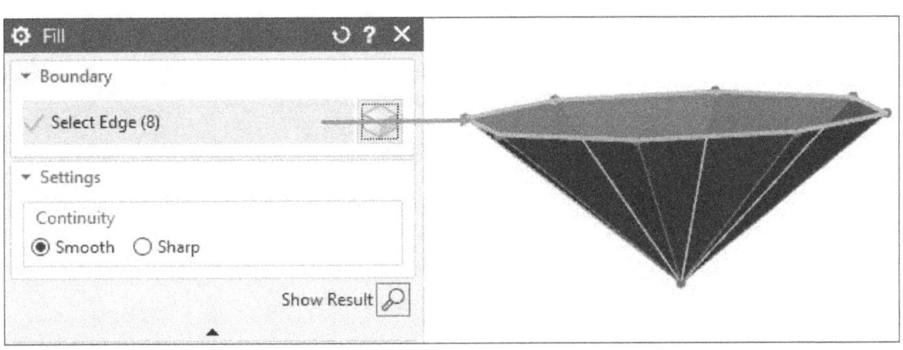

Figure-119. Selecting the edge to be filled

- Other parameters in the dialog box are same as discussed earlier.
- After specifying desired parameters, click on **OK** button from the dialog box. The edges will be filled with face; refer to Figure-120.

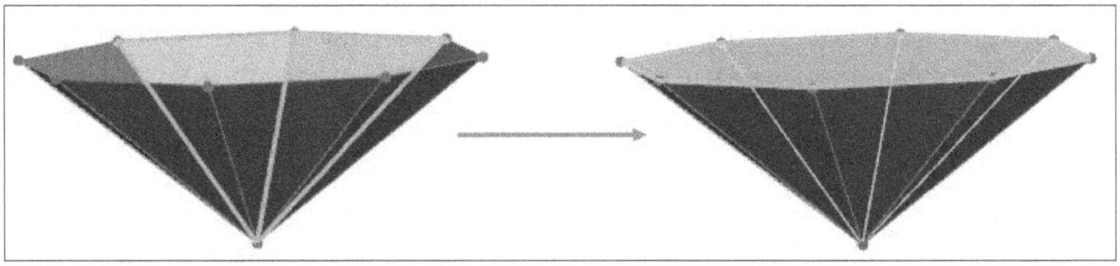

Figure-120. Edges filled with face

Copy Cage

The **Copy Cage** tool is used to copy and move selected cage faces and polylines. The procedure to use this tool is same as discussed earlier in this book.

Mirror Cage

The **Mirror Cage** tool is used to create a mirrored copy of the selected cage geometry across a specified plane. The procedure to use this tool is same as discussed earlier in this book.

Offset Cage

The **Offset Cage** tool is used to create one or more copies of selected cage faces at a specified distance. The procedure to use this tool is same as discussed earlier in this book.

Transform Cage

The **Transform Cage** tool is used to move, rotate, or scale the faces, edges, vertices, or the entire control cage. The procedure to use this tool is same as discussed earlier.

Project Cage

The **Project Cage** tool is used to project selected elements of the control cage onto planar or linear targets. The procedure to use this tool is discussed next.

- Click on the **Project Cage** tool from **Edit** group in the **Home** tab of the **Ribbon**. The **Project Cage** dialog box will be displayed; refer to Figure-121.

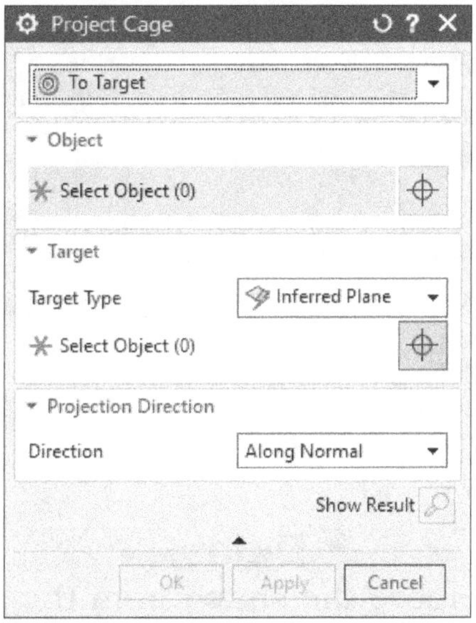

Figure-121. Project Cage dialog box

- Select desired type of projection operation to be processed to project the cage from drop-down in the top area of the dialog box.
- Select desired vertices, edges, and faces of the control cage from the graphics window to be projected.
- Select desired option from **Target Type** drop-down in the **Target** rollout and select respective object in the graphics widow to target the projection through selected control cage elements; refer to Figure-122.

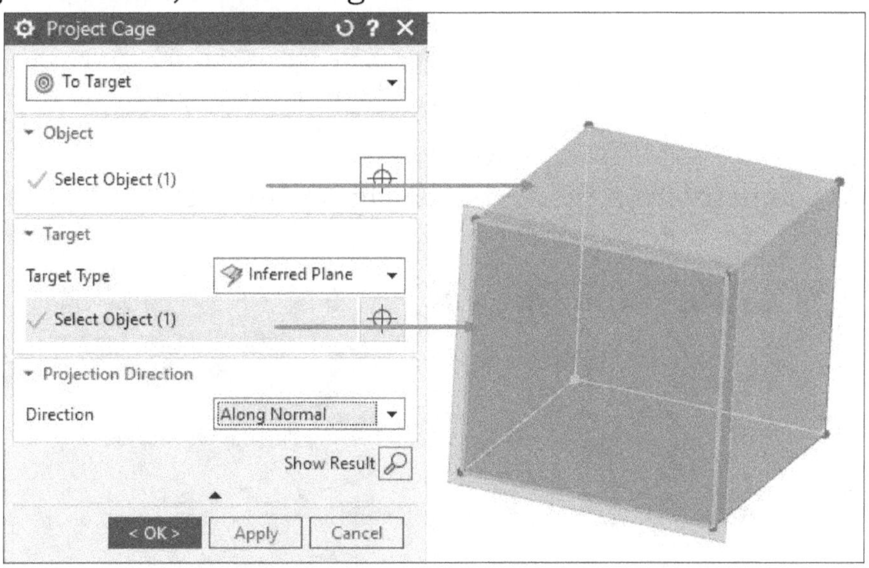

Figure-122. Face and plane selected for projection

- Select **Linear** or **Planar** radio button from **Mode** rollout to fit a temporary line or plane through all the control cage vertices of the selected object, respectively.
- Other parameters in the dialog box are same as discussed earlier.
- After specifying desired parameters, click on **OK** button from the dialog box. The cage element will be projected; refer to Figure-123.

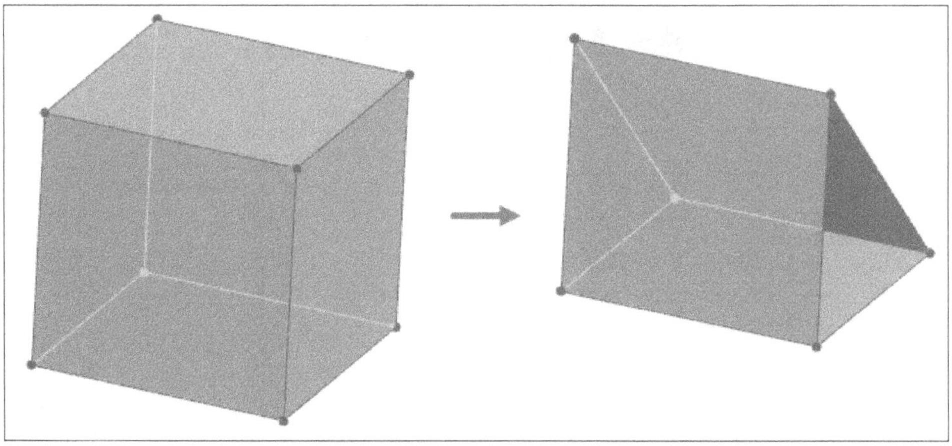

Figure-123. Cage element projected

Delete

The **Delete** tool is used to remove the shape from the model. The procedure to use this tool is discussed next.

- Click on the **Delete** tool from the **Edit** group in **Home** tab of the **Ribbon**. The **Delete** dialog box will be displayed; refer to Figure-124.

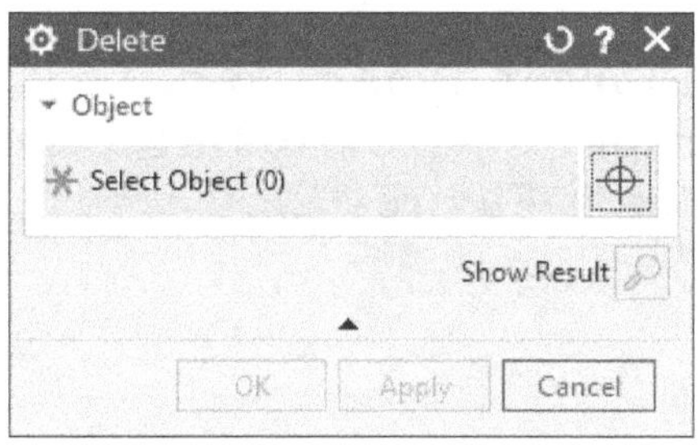

Figure-124. Delete dialog box

- Select desired geometry from the graphics window to be deleted; refer to Figure-125.

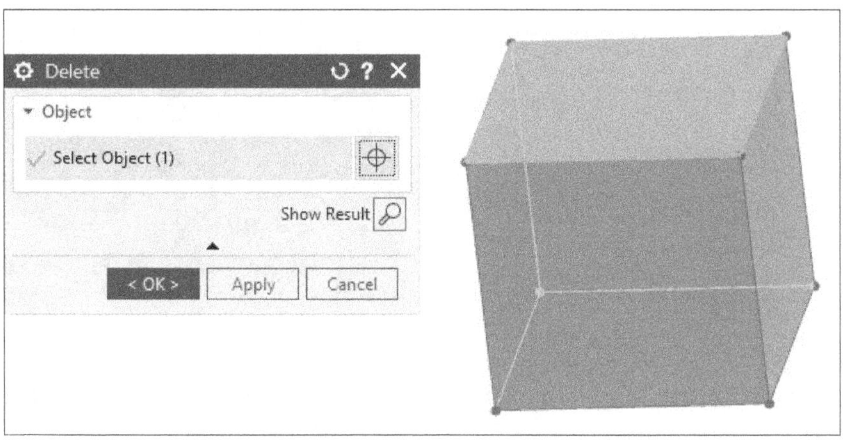

Figure-125. Geometry selected to delete

- After specifying desired parameters, click on **OK** button from the dialog box. The geometry will be deleted; refer to Figure-126.

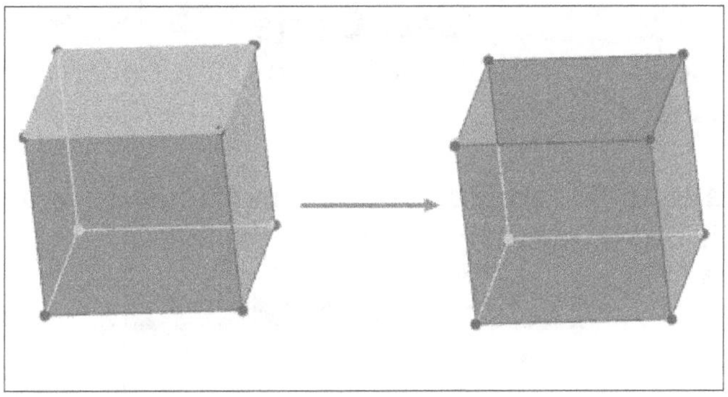

Figure-126. Geometry deleted

Merge Face

The **Merge Face** tool is used to combine selected cage faces into a single cage face. The procedure to use this tool is discussed next.

- Click on the **Merge Face** tool from **Edit** group in the **Home** tab of the **Ribbon**. The **Merge face** dialog box will be displayed; refer to Figure-127.

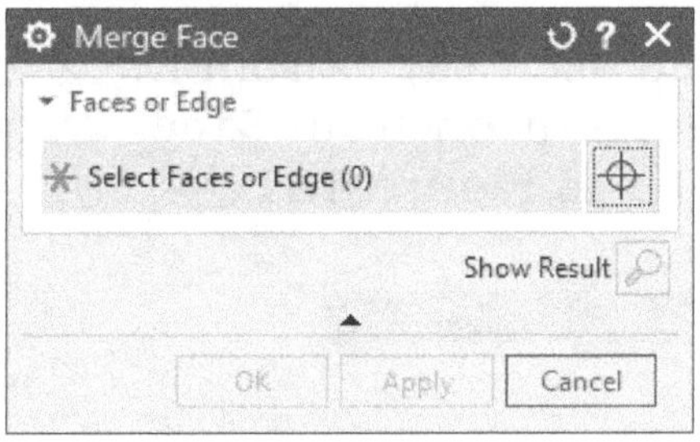

Figure-127. Merge Face dialog box

- Select desired connected cage faces from the graphics window to be merged into one face; refer to Figure-128.

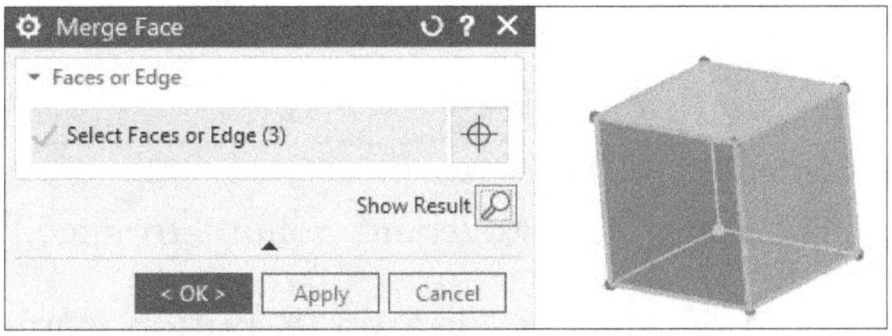

Figure-128. Selecting the faces to be merged

- After specifying desired parameters, click on **OK** button from the dialog box. The connected faces will be merged; refer to Figure-129.

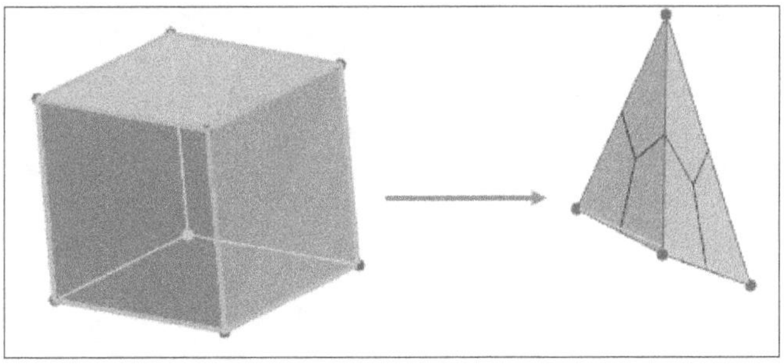

Figure-129. Faces merged

Sew Cage

The **Sew Cage** tool is used to connect open edges of a control cage. The procedure to use this tool is discussed next.

- Click on the **Sew Cage** tool from **Edit** group in the **Home** tab of the **Ribbon**. The **Sew Cage** dialog box will be displayed; refer to Figure-130.

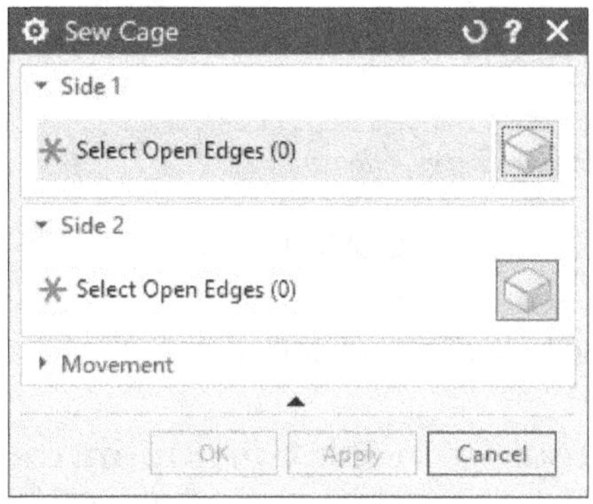

Figure-130. Sew Cage dialog box

- Select first set of connected open edges from the graphics window and then click on the **Select Open Edges** button from **Side 2** rollout to select second set of connected open edges; refer to Figure-131.

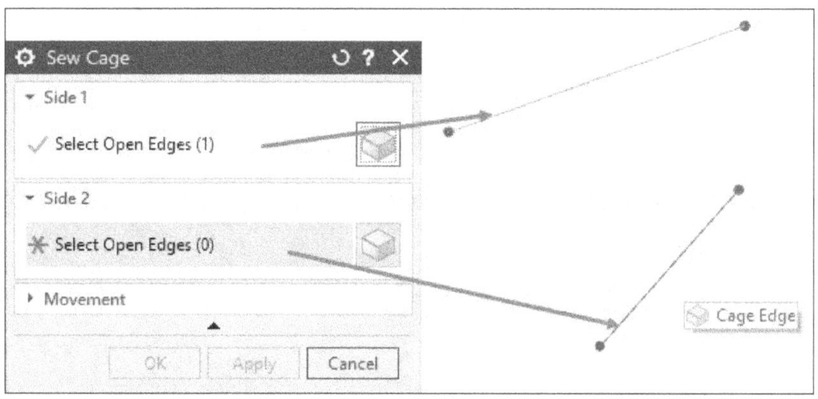

Figure-131. Selecting the set of open edges

- Select desired radio button from **Movement** rollout to specify which side of the sewn object is moved.
- After specifying desired parametes, click on **OK** button from the dialog box. The edges of control cage will be connected; refer to Figure-132.

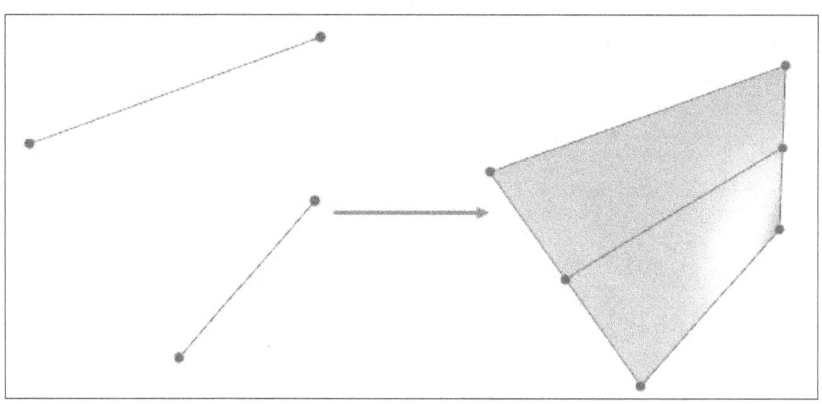

Figure-132. Control cage edges connected

Connect Cage

The **Connect Cage** tool is used to create a constant connection between the subdivision feature and an external sheet bodies. The procedure to use this tool is discussed next.

- Click on the **Connect Cage** tool from **More** drop-down in the **Edit** group of **Home** tab in the **Ribbon**. The **Connect Cage** dialog box will be displayed; refer to Figure-133.

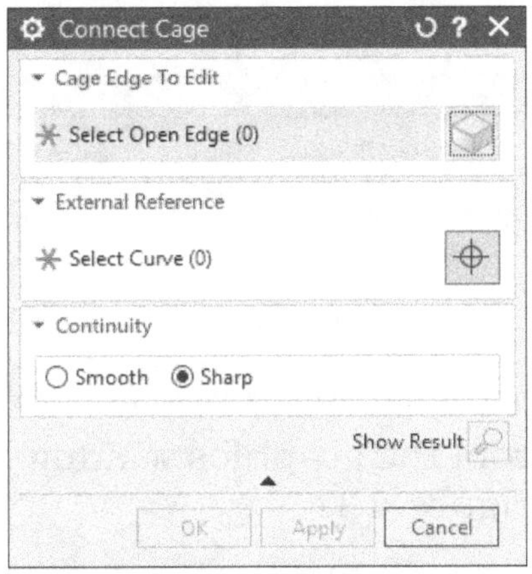

Figure-133. Connect Cage dialog box

- Select desired continuous string of open cage edges from the graphics window to be connected.
- Click on the **Select Curve** button from **External Reference** rollout and select desired continuous string of open cage edges or curve; refer to Figure-134.

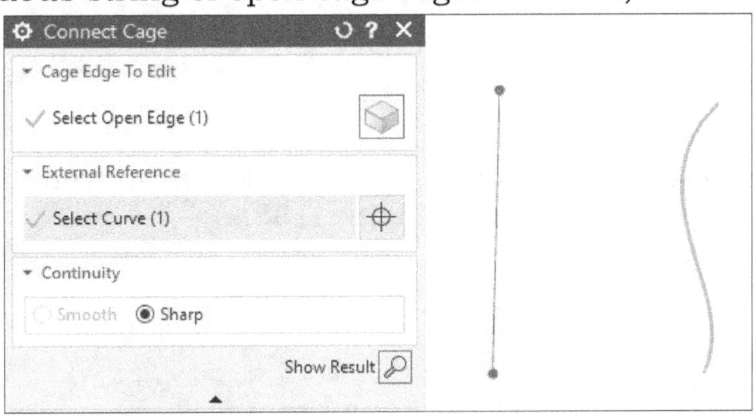

Figure-134. Selecting the open edge and curve

- Other parameters in the dialog box are same as discussed earlier.
- After specifying desired parameters, click on **OK** button from the dialog box. The cage edges will be connected; refer to Figure-135.

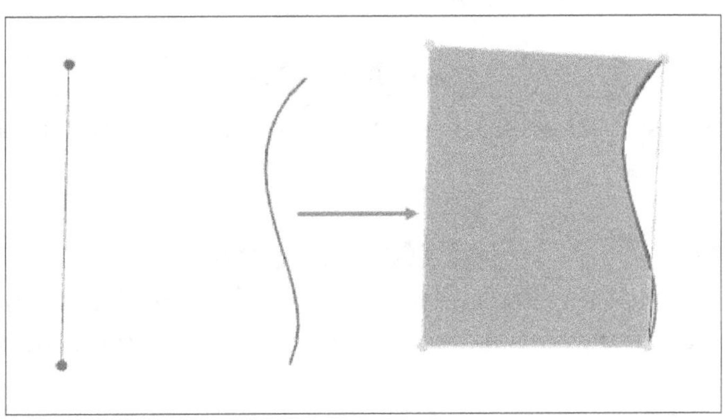

Figure-135. Cage edges connected

Delete Constraint

The **Delete Constraint** tool is used to remove associative constraint of cage objects to external geometry. The procedure to use this tool is discussed next.

- Click on the **Delete Constraint** tool from **More** drop-down in the **Edit** group of **Home** tab in the **Ribbon**. The **Delete Constraint** dialog box will be displayed; refer to Figure-136.

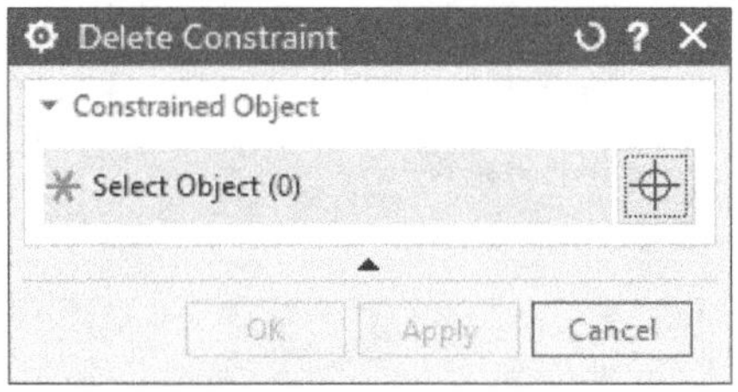

Figure-136. Delete Constraint dialog box

- Select desired cage object from the graphics window whose associative constraints is to be removed; refer to Figure-137.

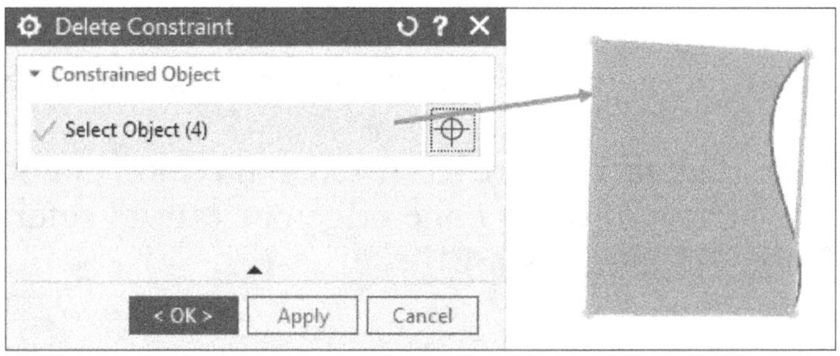

Figure-137. Cage object selected to delete the constraints

- After specifying desired parameters, click on **OK** button from the dialog box. The constraints will be deleted; refer to Figure-138.

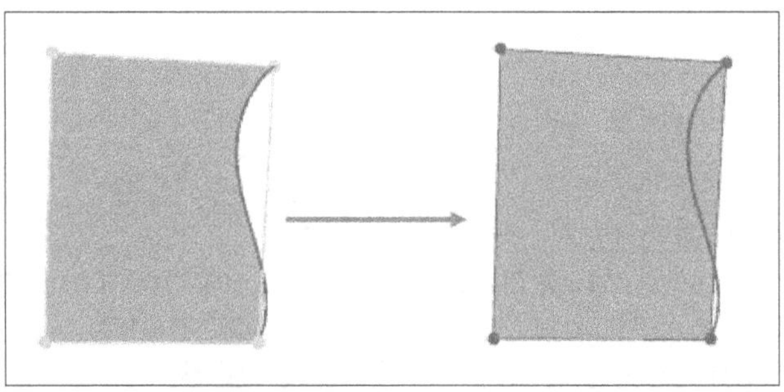

Figure-138. Constraints deleted

Set Weight

The **Set Weight** tool is used to assign a weight to the selected faces, edges, or vertices of the control cage.

Set Continuity

The **Set Continuity** tool is used to define continuity for the selected faces or edges of the control cage. You can switch between smooth and sharp continuity using this tool.

Cage Polyline

The **Cage Polyline** tool is used to add a polyline to the control cage that can be used to extrude the cage faces. The procedure to use this tool is discussed next.

- Click on the **Cage Polyline** tool from **Polyline** group in the **Home** tab of the **Ribbon**. The **Cage Polyline** dialog box will be displayed; refer to Figure-139.

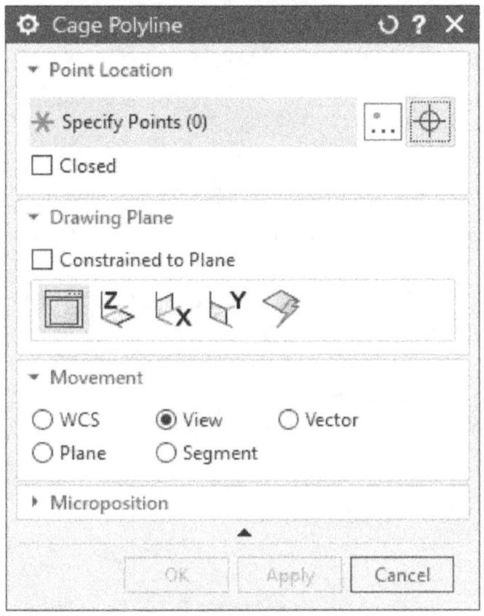

Figure-139. Cage Polyline dialog box

- Specify desired point location in the graphics window to define the endpoints of polyline segments.
- Select **Closed** check box to specify that the polyline starts and ends at the same point, creating a closed shape.
- Select **Constrained to Plane** check box from **Drawing Plane** rollout and select desired plane on which the polyline is to be constrained.
- Other parameters in the dialog box are same as discussed earlier.
- After specifying desired parameters, click on **OK** button from the dialog box. The cage polyline will be created; refer to Figure-140.

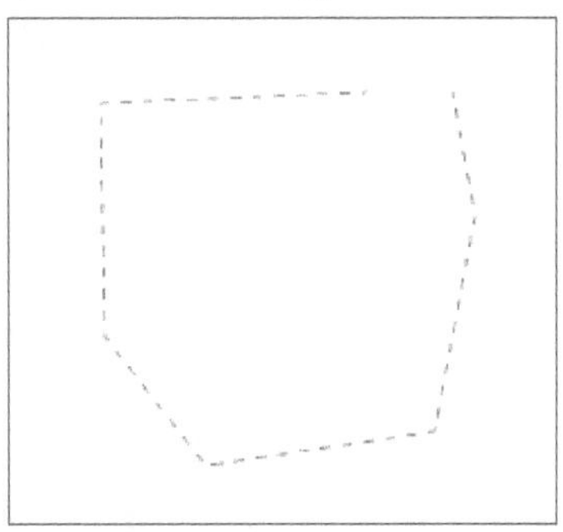

Figure-140. Cage polyline created

Extract Cage Polyline

The **Extract Cage Polyline** tool is used to extract a cage polylines using the selected curve or face edges. The procedure to use this tool is discussed next.

- Click on the **Extract Cage Polyline** tool from **Polyline** group in the **Home** tab of the **Ribbon**. The **Extract Cage Polyline** dialog box will be displayed; refer to Figure-141.

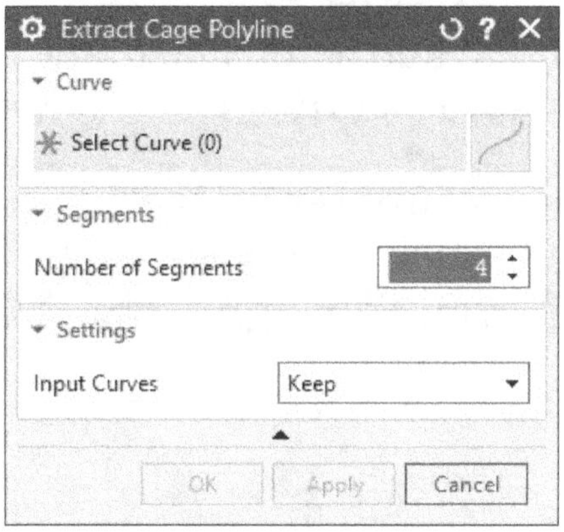

Figure-141. Extract Cage Polyline dialog box

- Select desired curves or edges of non-cage geometry from which the cage polyline is to be extracted; refer to Figure-142.

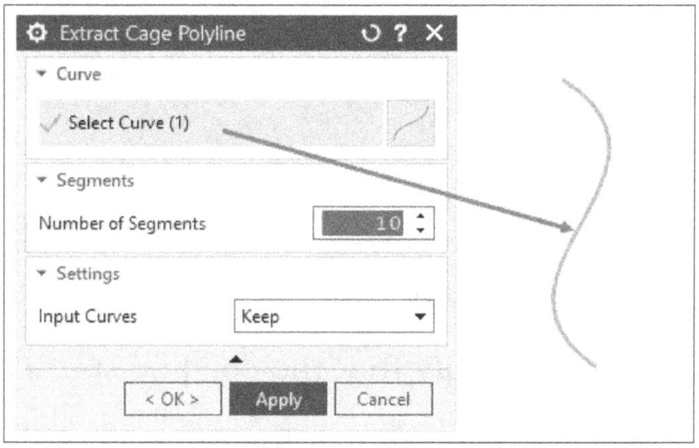

Figure-142. Curve selected to extract cage polyline

- Other parameters in the dialog box are same as discussed earlier.
- After specifying desired parameters, click on **OK** button from the dialog box. The cage polyline will be extracted; refer to Figure-143.

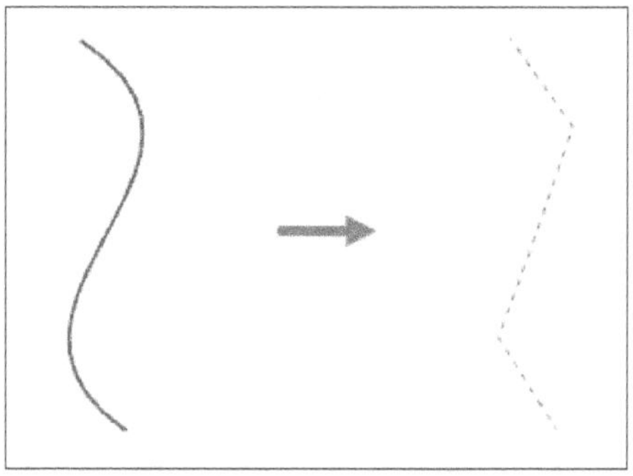

Figure-143. Cage polyline extracted

Cage and Body

The **Cage and Body** tool is used to display the control cage as well as the resulting subdivision body; refer to Figure-144.

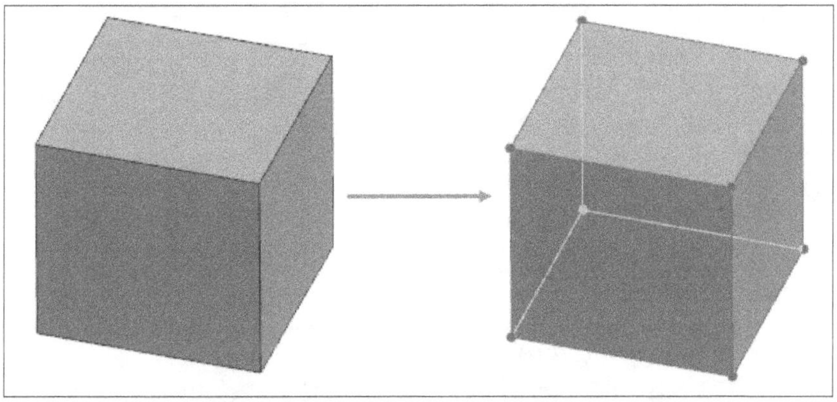

Figure-144. Cage and Body displayed

Cage Only

The **Cage Only** tool is used to display the control cage only and hide the resulting subdivision body; refer to Figure-145.

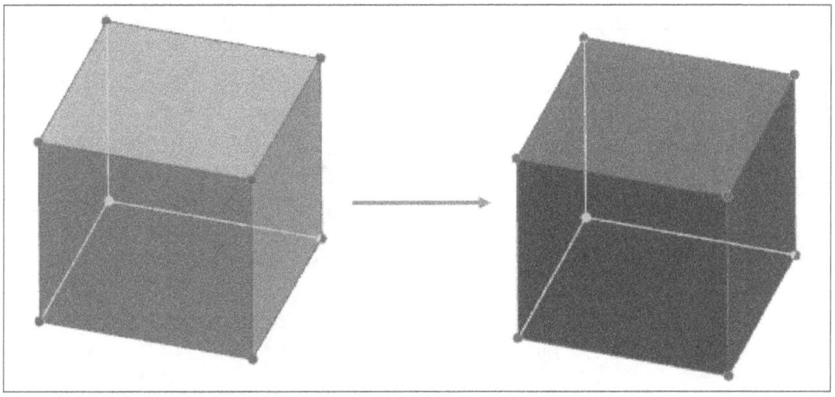

Figure-145. Displaying only control cage

Body Only

The **Body Only** tool is used to display the resulting subdivision body only and hide the control cage; refer to Figure-146.

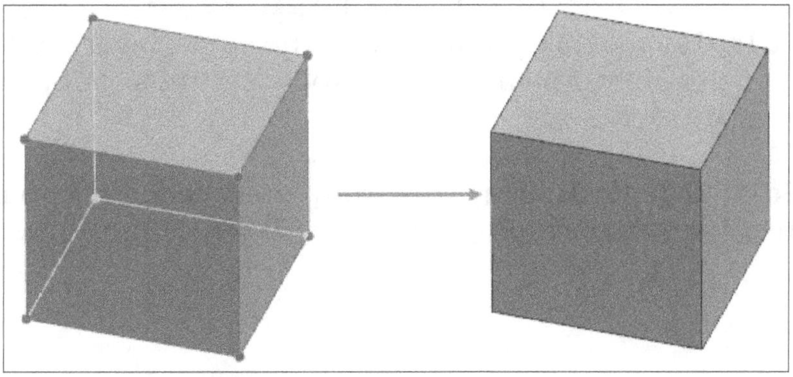

Figure-146. Displaying only subdivision body

X-ray Cage

The **X-ray Cage** tool is used to display hidden control cage objects; refer to Figure-147.

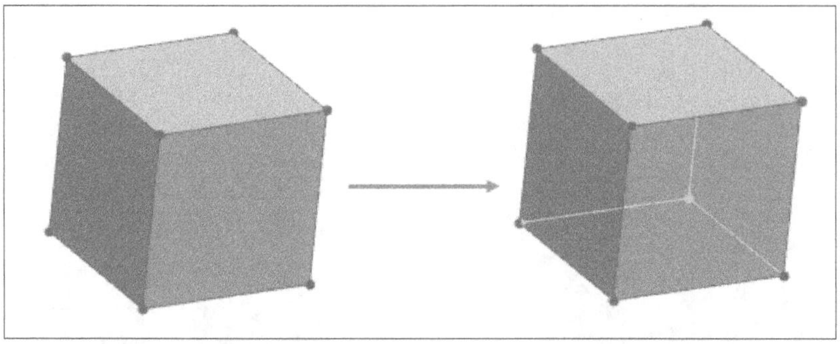

Figure-147. Displaying the X ray cage objects

Show Weight

The **Show Weight** tool is used to display the current weight factors set on cage elements.

Show Grid

The **Show Grid** tool is used to display grid on the workplane; refer to Figure-148.

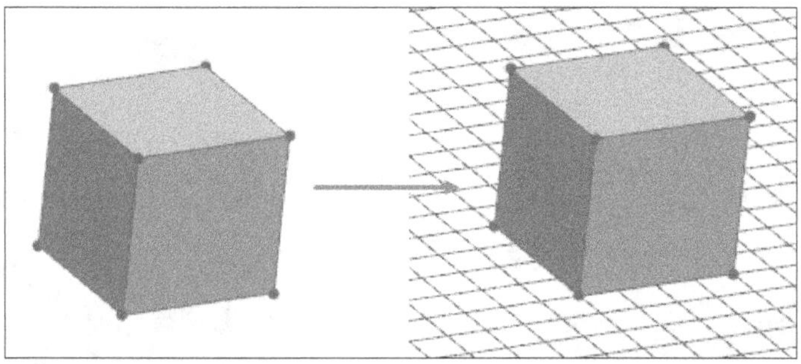

Figure-148. Displaying the grid

Allow Backside Selection

The **Allow Backside Selection** tool is used to enable the selection of control cage elements that are hidden behind other elements.

Edit Object Display

The **Edit Object Display** tool is used to modify the color, layer, style, grid count, line width, shading, translucency, and analysis display settings of objects. The procedure to use this tool is discussed next.

- Click on the **Edit Object Display** tool from **Preference** group in the **Home** tab of the **Ribbon**. The **Class Selection** dialog box will be displayed; refer to Figure-149.

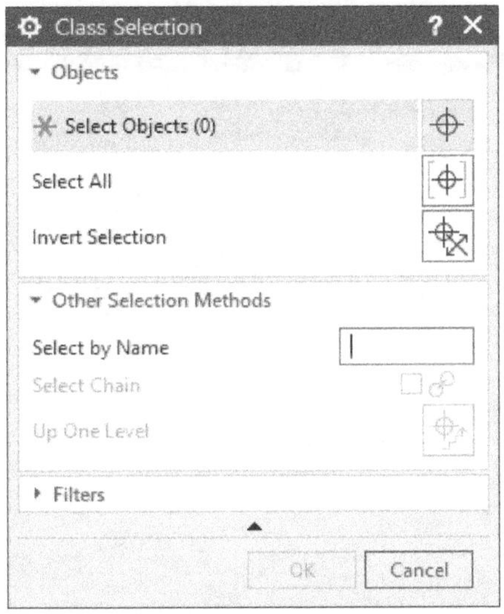

Figure-149. Class Selection dialog box

- Select desired objects from the graphics window based on the currently specified filter; refer to Figure-150.

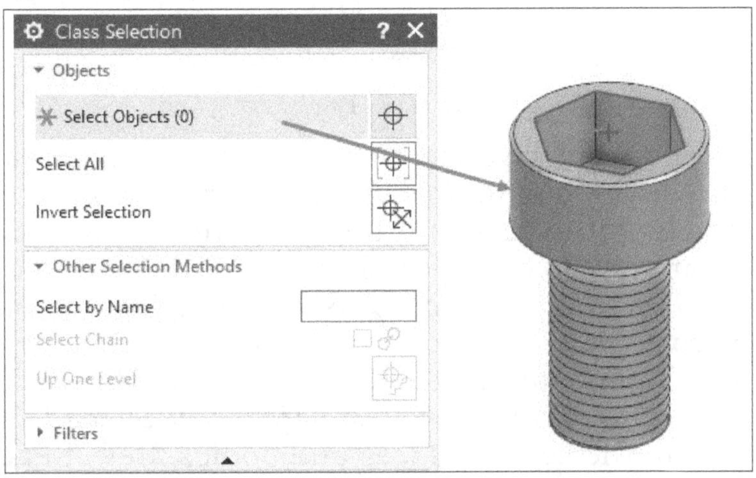

Figure-150. Selecting the object

- Click on the **Select All** button from **Objects** rollout to select all the visible objects in the graphics window. Click on the **Invert Selection** button to deselect all the currently selected objects and select the previously not selected objects.
- Specify desired object name assigned earlier in the **Select by Name** edit box of **Other Selection Methods** rollout. Select the **Select Chain** check box to select connected objects, solid edges, or wireframe geometry. Click on the **Up One Level** button to select the next level component in the selection hierarchy.
- Click on the **Type Filter** button from **Filters** rollout to select one or more object types to be included or excluded. Click on the **Layer Filter** button to specify a single layer, a range of layers, or an existing layer category. Click on the **Color Filter** button to select or deselect colors from the palette. Click on the **Attribute Filter** button to filter the objects by line, width, font, and user-defined attributes. Click on the **Reset Filter** button to reset all the filters to their default state.
- After specifying desired parameters, click on **OK** button from the dialog box. The **Edit Object Display** dialog box will be displayed; refer to Figure-151.

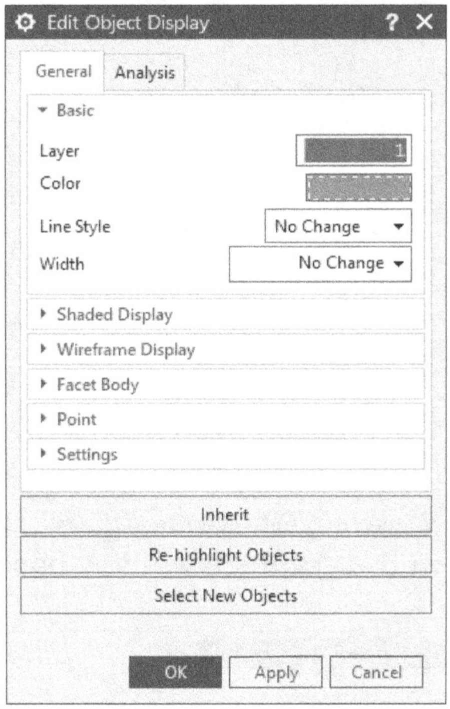

Figure-151. Edit Object Display dialog box

- Specify desired number of layer in the **Layer** edit box of **Basic** rollout in the **General** tab of the dialog box to specify the layer on which the selected objects is to be placed. Click on the **Color** button to change desired color of the selected objects. Select desired style of line such as solid, dashed, etc. from **Line Style** drop-down. Select desired width to be used to display the curve for the object type from **Width** drop-down.
- Specify the amount of light passing through selected objects using the **Transluceny** slider from **Shaded Display** rollout. Select **Partially Shaded** check box to apply a partial shade effect to the selected faces and bodies. Select **Face Analysis** check box to set the face analysis attribute on or off.
- Select **Show Poles**, **Show Knots**, or **Show End Points** check box from **Wireframe Display** rollout to display the control polygon, knot points, or end points for selected splines or surfaces, respectively. Select desired display style and color for end point from **End Point Color** and **End Point Style** drop-downs, respectively. Modify the surface grid count by specifying the number of grid curves along U and V directions in the **U** and **V** edit boxes, respectively.
- Select desired display style of the selected facet body from **Display** drop-down in the **Facet Body** rollout. Specify desired number of samples to be displayed in the **Display Sample** edit box.
- Select desired symbol for the point from **Point Symbol** drop-down in the **Point** rollout. Select **Show Through** check box to display the point and datum point through solid and opaque models.
- Select **Apply to All Faces of Selected Body** check box from **Settings** rollout to apply the faces of solid bodies with the display attributes of color, grid count, translucency, etc. Select **Apply Changes to Owning Part** check box to update the display property to the part file that contains the geometry.

- Click on the **Inherit** button to apply the properties of object to those of an existing object.
- Click on the **Re-highlight Objects** button to test different option combinations on the selected objects.
- Click on the **Select New Objects** button to modify the additional objects.
- Click on the **Analysis** tab of the dialog box, the options will be displayed as shown in Figure-152.

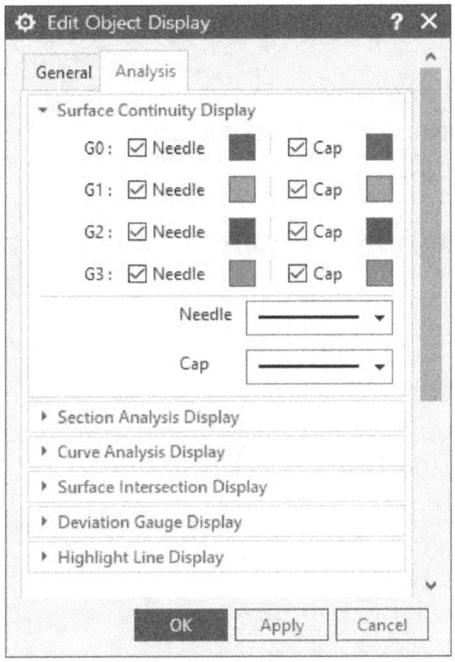

Figure-152. Analysis tab of the dialog box

- Click on desired rollout in the tab and specify the color, visibility, and line styles for the selected objects of the respective rollout.
- After specifying desired parameters, click on **OK** button from the dialog box. The display of the object will be modified; refer to Figure-153.

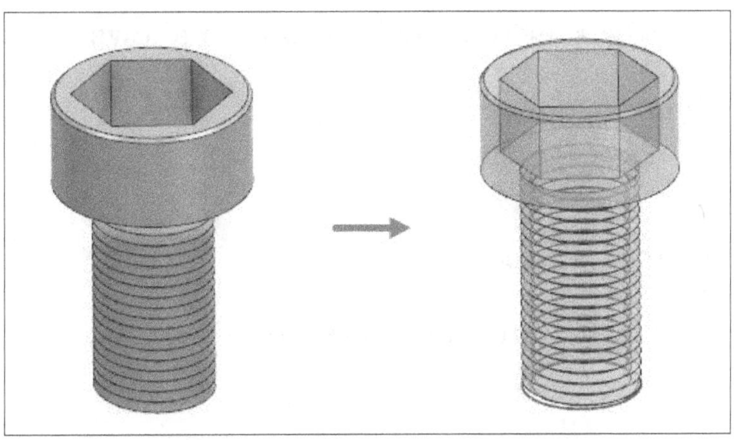

Figure-153. Object display modified

NX Realize Shape

The **NX Realize Shape** tool is used to control the settings of NX Realize Shape Task environment and the display of its control cage. The parameters of this tool have been discussed earlier in this chapter.

SELF-ASSESSMENT

Q1. The Combine tool is used to:
A. Trim a sheet body
B. Combine regions of multiple intersecting sheet bodies
C. Extend edges of a surface
D. Delete unwanted edges

Q2. In the Combine dialog box, the "Allow Connected Regions Only" option is used to:
A. Select all regions
B. Select only disconnected regions
C. Select only regions connected to a previously selected region
D. Delete regions automatically

Q3. The "Find Volume" button in Combine tool is used to:
A. Delete volumes
B. Measure volume
C. Find regions enclosing a solid volume
D. Extend volume boundaries

Q4. The Trim Sheet tool is used to:
A. Extend a sheet body
B. Combine sheet bodies
C. Trim a portion of a sheet body
D. Split a sheet body

Q5. In Trim Sheet, the "Select Object" button is used to:
A. Select target body
B. Select trimming boundary object
C. Select projection direction
D. Delete regions

Q6. The "Allow Target Edges as Tool Objects" option allows:
A. Ignoring edges
B. Using edges as trimming objects
C. Deleting edges
D. Extending edges

Q7. The Extend Sheet tool is used to:
A. Trim sheet bodies
B. Extend a sheet body by distance or intersection
C. Delete edges
D. Sew surfaces

Q8. In Extend Sheet, "Offset" option is used to:
A. Trim edges
B. Define distance for extension
C. Delete regions
D. Rotate surface

Q9. The "Natural Curvature" option extends a surface by:
A. Linear extension
B. Random shape
C. Curvature continuous extension
D. Mirroring

Q10. The Trim and Extend tool is used to:
A. Delete surfaces
B. Trim or extend edges and faces at intersection
C. Combine solids
D. Modify curves only

Q11. The Sew tool is used to:
A. Delete faces
B. Combine sheet or solid bodies by sewing edges or faces
C. Trim surfaces
D. Extend edges

Q12. In Sew tool, "Sheet or Solid" option specifies:
A. Type of projection
B. Type of body to sew
C. Type of edge
D. Type of trimming

Q13. The Split Body tool is used to:
A. Combine bodies
B. Divide a body into multiple bodies
C. Extend surfaces
D. Heal surfaces

Q14. The Snip Surface tool is used to:
A. Extend surfaces
B. Divide or remove portions of a surface
C. Combine surfaces
D. Match edges

Q15. In Snip Surface, "Divide" check box is used to:
A. Delete region
B. Keep both regions and create separate features
C. Merge regions
D. Extend region

Q16. The Untrim tool is used to:
A. Trim faces
B. Restore faces to natural boundaries
C. Extend edges
D. Delete edges

Q17. The Delete Edge tool is used to:
A. Extend edges
B. Delete one or more edges from a sheet body
C. Combine edges
D. Match edges

Q18. The Patch tool is used to:
A. Delete faces
B. Replace faces with those from another sheet
C. Extend surfaces
D. Sew bodies

Q19. The Unsew tool is used to:
A. Combine bodies
B. Separate faces from a body
C. Extend surfaces
D. Trim edges

Q20. The X-Form tool is used to:
A. Trim surfaces
B. Modify poles and points of splines and surfaces
C. Delete edges
D. Combine bodies

Q21. The I-Form tool modifies:
A. Edges only
B. Faces using isoparametric curves
C. Volumes
D. Regions

Q22. The Match Edge tool ensures:
A. Edge deletion
B. Geometric continuity with reference object
C. Edge extension
D. Surface trimming

Q23. The Edge Symmetry tool is used to:
A. Trim edges
B. Ensure symmetry of surface about a plane
C. Delete surfaces
D. Combine bodies

Q24. The Global Shaping tool is used to:
A. Delete regions
B. Deform surface region using geometry or relationships
C. Trim surfaces
D. Split bodies

Q25. The Global Deformation tool creates:
A. Flat surface
B. Deformed sheet body maintaining topology
C. Trimmed surface
D. Combined body

Q26. The Flattening and Forming tool is used to:
A. Combine bodies
B. Flatten 3D faces into 2D plane
C. Extend surfaces
D. Delete edges

Q27. The Heal Surface tool is used to:
A. Trim surfaces
B. Fix geometry faults in bodies
C. Extend surfaces
D. Combine edges

Q28. The Reverse Normal tool is used to:
A. Delete normals
B. Reverse normal direction of sheet bodies
C. Extend surfaces
D. Match edges

Q29. The Edit U/V Direction tool modifies:
A. Edge length
B. Surface directions U and V
C. Face color
D. Volume

Q30. The Enlarge tool is used to:
A. Trim surfaces
B. Modify size of an untrimmed face or sheet
C. Delete edges
D. Combine surfaces

Q31. The Local Untrim and Extend tool is used to:
A. Modify entire body
B. Trim, untrim, or extend a single surface
C. Delete regions
D. Match edges

Q32. The Snip into Patches tool is used to:
A. Extend surfaces
B. Divide a face into separate sheet bodies or remove patches
C. Combine faces
D. Smooth surfaces

Q33. In Snip into Patches, the "Select Patch" button is used to:
A. Select target face
B. Select patches to be removed
C. Select projection direction
D. Merge patches

Q34. The Smooth Poles tool is used to:
A. Delete poles
B. Modify distribution of selected poles
C. Extend poles
D. Combine poles

Q35. In Smooth Poles, "Move Selected Only" option is used to:
A. Move all poles
B. Move only selected poles
C. Delete poles
D. Lock poles

Q36. The Refit Face tool is used to:
A. Trim surface
B. Modify surface degree, tolerance, or patch count
C. Combine surfaces
D. Delete faces

Q37. The "Fit to Target" option in Refit Face is used to:
A. Delete surface
B. Fit surface to a target shape
C. Extend surface
D. Merge surfaces

Q38. NX Realize Shape workspace is used to:
A. Delete geometry
B. Create B-surface solid or sheet bodies
C. Trim surfaces
D. Match edges

Q39. The Start Symmetric Modeling tool is used to:
A. Delete symmetry
B. Create symmetrical geometry
C. Trim geometry
D. Extend geometry

Q40. The Primitive Shape tool is used to:
A. Modify surfaces
B. Create base body for modeling
C. Delete shapes
D. Combine bodies

Q41. The Extrude Cage tool is used to:
A. Delete cage faces
B. Create new cage faces by extrusion
C. Trim cage edges
D. Combine cages

Q42. In Extrude Cage, "Number of Segments" defines:
A. Number of edges
B. Number of cage divisions
C. Number of faces
D. Number of bodies

Q43. The Revolve Cage tool is used to:
A. Rotate surface
B. Revolve edges or polylines to create cage
C. Delete cage
D. Trim cage

Q44. In Revolve Cage, "Sew Selected Open Edges" is used to:
A. Delete edges
B. Close open edges
C. Extend edges
D. Mirror edges

Q45. The Draw Cage tool is used to:
A. Delete cage
B. Create cage faces using corner points
C. Trim cage
D. Extend cage

Q46. The Section Tube tool is used to:
A. Delete sections
B. Create tube-like control cage
C. Combine faces
D. Trim sections

Q47. The Cage from Facet Body tool is used to:
A. Delete facet body
B. Create control cage from facet body
C. Trim facets
D. Merge facets

Q48. The Loft Cage tool is used to:
A. Delete cage
B. Create lofted cage shape
C. Trim cage
D. Extend cage

Q49. The Tube Cage tool creates:
A. Flat surfaces
B. Tubular cage structures
C. Solid blocks
D. Trimmed surfaces

Q50. The Split Face tool is used to:
A. Combine faces
B. Divide faces into smaller faces
C. Delete faces
D. Extend faces

Chapter 11

Assembly

Topics Covered

The major topics covered in this chapter are:

- ***Inserting Components in Assembly***
- ***Creating Components in Assembly***
- ***Applying Positional Constraints***
- ***Managing Components in Assembly***
- ***Assembly Context tools***
- ***Interpart Linking***
- ***Simplifying Assembly***
- ***Performing Clearance Analysis***
- ***Creating Exploded Views***
- ***Generating Sequence of Assembly***

INTRODUCTION

Assembly modeling in Siemens NX involves combining multiple components into a single assembly to create complex systems. This allows you to visualize how parts fit and interact, check for interferences, and analyze assembly relationships. Assembly modeling in NX is a powerful way to bring together various parts into a coherent system, enabling thorough design evaluation and validation. Familiarizing yourself with the tools and techniques available will help you streamline your design process and improve your overall productivity.

Assemble

The file extension for part model and assembly model of NX is same **.prt**. You can work on assemblies by accessing the tools from Assembly tab. You can also work on new assembly designs by clicking on the **OK** button from **New** dialog box of **New** option in the **File** tab; refer to Figure-1 and Figure-2. The **Assembly** environment will be displayed along with the **Assemble** dialog box; refer to Figure-3.

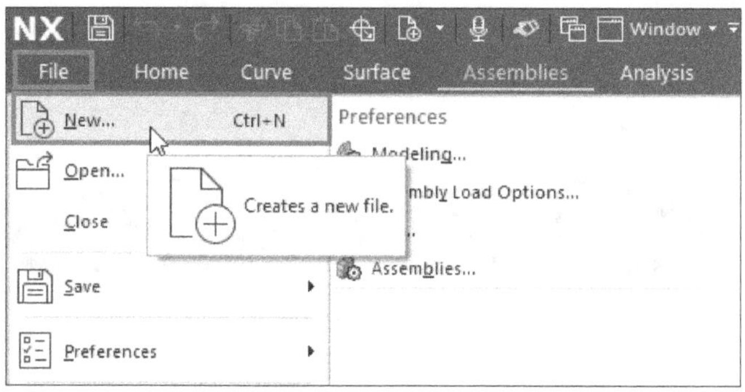

Figure-1. New option

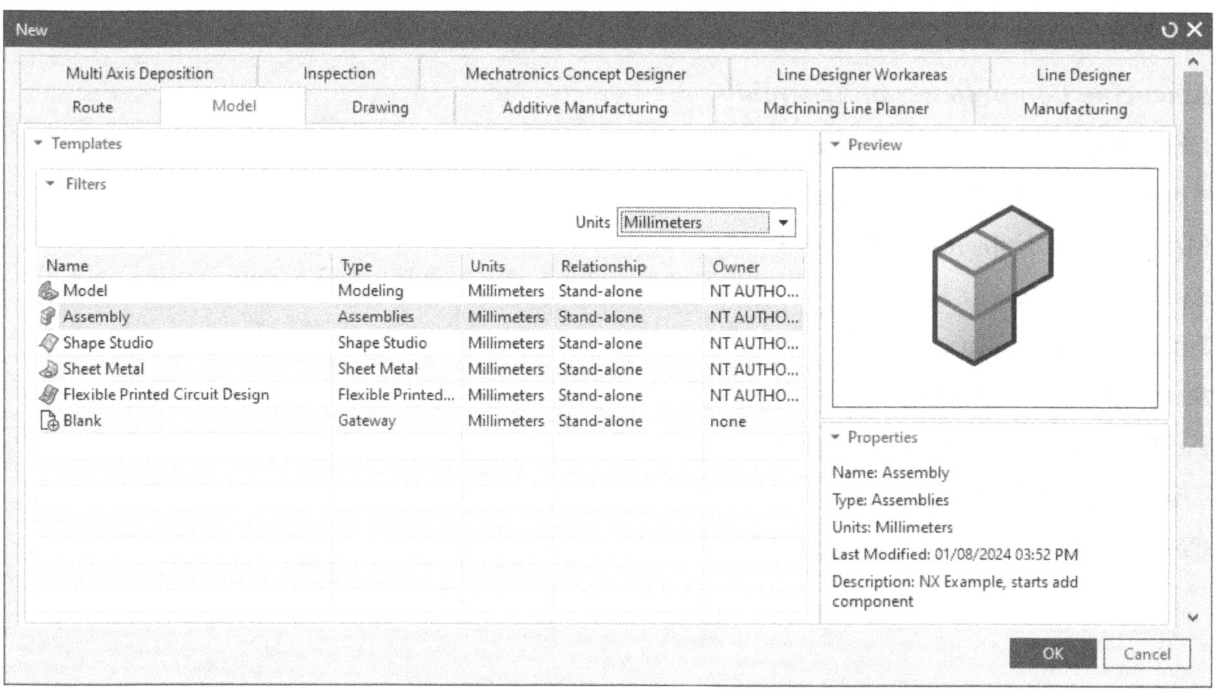

Figure-2. New dialog box

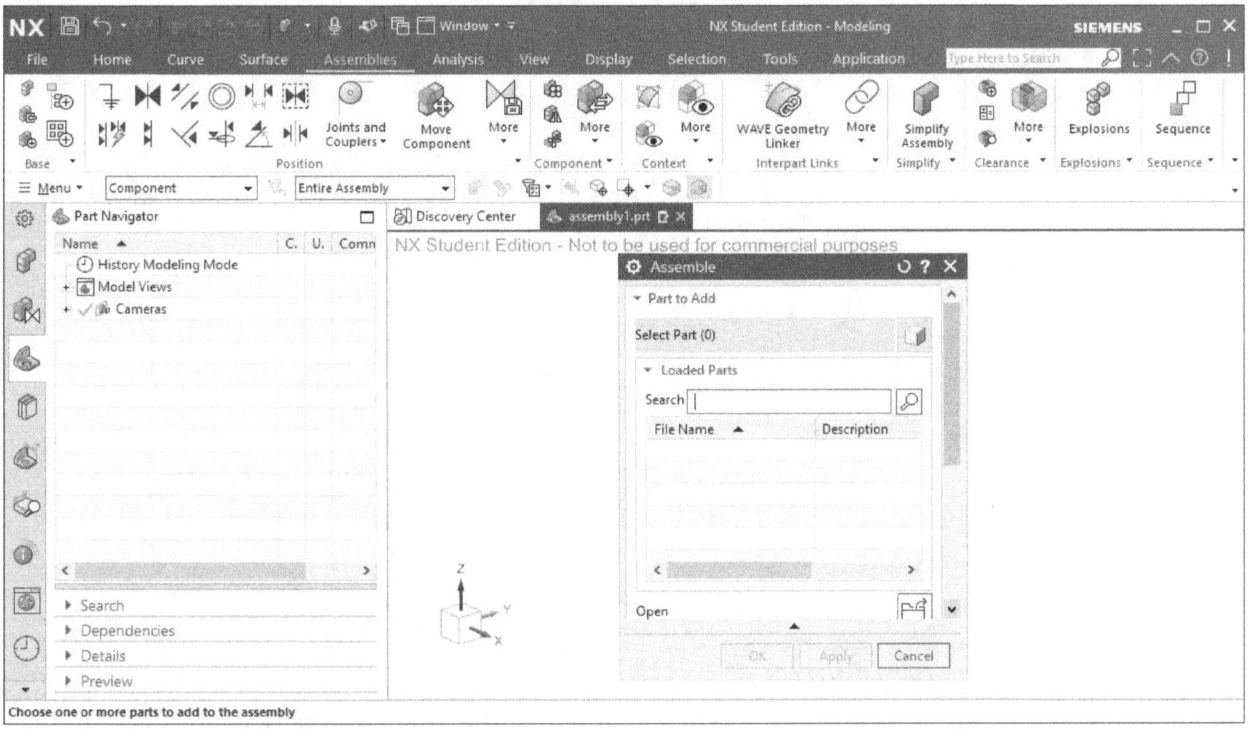

Figure-3. Assembly environment

Assemble

The **Assemble** tool is used to quickly and efficiently create or edit an assembly. You can add new components or duplicate existing components, position the components by dragging them into place, and constrain a component by simply dragging it over relevant geometry. The procedure to use this tool is discussed next.

- Click on the **Assemble** tool from **Base** group in the **Assemblies** tab of the **Ribbon**. The **Assemble** dialog box will be displayed; refer to Figure-4.

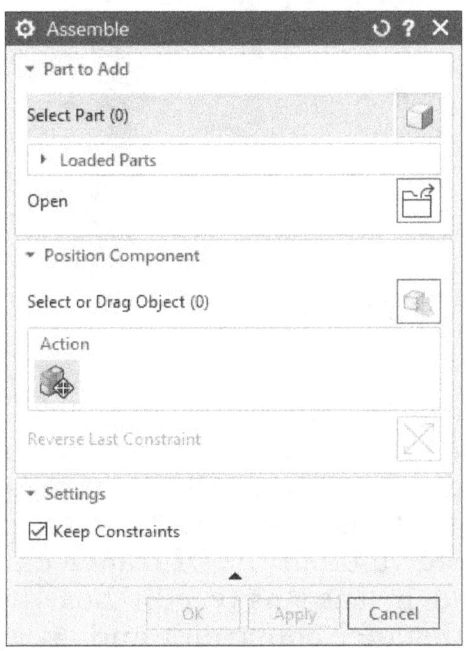

Figure-4. Assemble dialog box

- Click on the **Open** button from **Parts to Add** rollout of the dialog box. The **Part Name** dialog box will be displayed; refer to Figure-5.

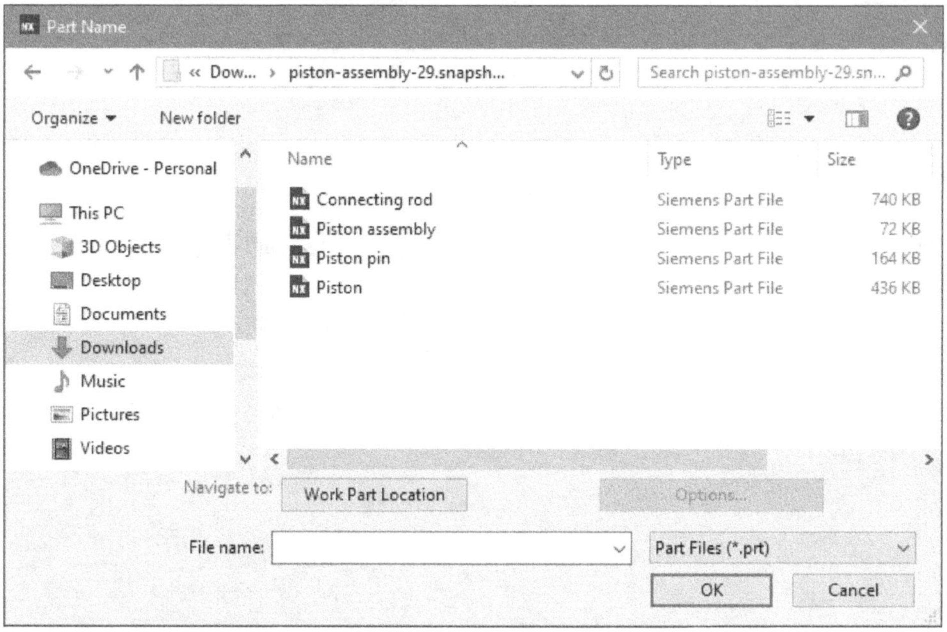

Figure-5. Part Name dialog box

- Select desired part(s) from the dialog box and click on the **OK** button. The selected parts will be opened in the graphics area and displayed in the **Loaded Parts** rollout of the dialog box; refer to Figure-6.

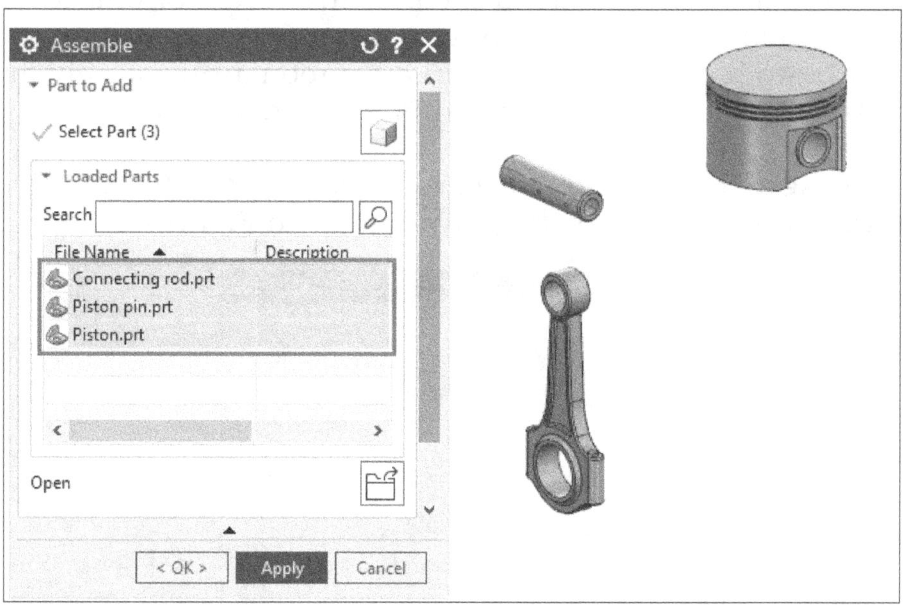

Figure-6. Parts opened

- Click on the **Select** or **Drag Object** button from **Position Component** rollout and select desired parts to constrain, or to reposition by dragging. Select desired option from **Action** section and select the positioning action for the selected objects. Click on the **Reverse Last Constraint** button to apply the other solution to the constraint. Specify desired value in the **Distance** edit box available on selecting **Distance** constraint and in the **Angle** edit box available on selecting **Angle** constraint to create the distance constraint and an angle constraint between the selected objects, respectively.

- Select **Keep Constraints** check box from **Settings** rollout to create the constraints used to place the component.
- After specifying desired parameters, click on **OK** button from the dialog box. The parts will be assembled.

Add Component

The **Add Component** tool is used to add one or more component parts to the assembly. The procedure to use this tool is discussed next.

- Click on the **Add Component** tool from **Base** group of **Assemblies** tab of the **Ribbon**. The **Add Component** dialog box will be displayed; refer to Figure-7.

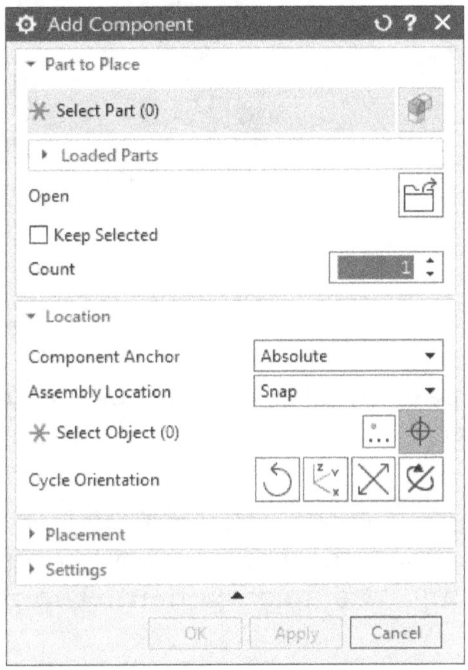

Figure-7. Add Component dialog box

- Select **Keep Selected** check box from **Part to Place** rollout to maintain the parts selection after clicking **Apply** button. Specify desired number of instances in the **Count** edit box to create for the added parts. Other parameters in the **Part to Place** rollout is same as discussed earlier. Select desired component to be inserted as discussed earlier.
- The **Component Anchor** section of **Location** rollout display the absolute origin of the component. Select desired option from **Assembly Location** drop-down to select the location of Component Anchor to be initially placed in the assembly. Select desired option from **Cycle Orientation** section to specify different component orientations based on the assembly location setting.
- Click on the **Specify Orientation** button from **Placement** rollout and select the placement point of the component. Select **Move Handles Only** check box to reposition the CSYS manipulator without repositioning the selected objects.

- Select **Scatter Components** check box from **Interaction Options** rollout of **Settings** rollout to automatically place components in multiple positions to not be overlapped. Select **Preview** check box to display the preview of component in the graphics window. Select **Preview Window** check box to display the preview of component in a separate **Component Preview** window; refer to Figure-8. Select desired reference set for the added components from **Reference Set** drop-down of **Settings** rollout. Select desired layer to which components and geometry are added from **Layer Option** drop-down.

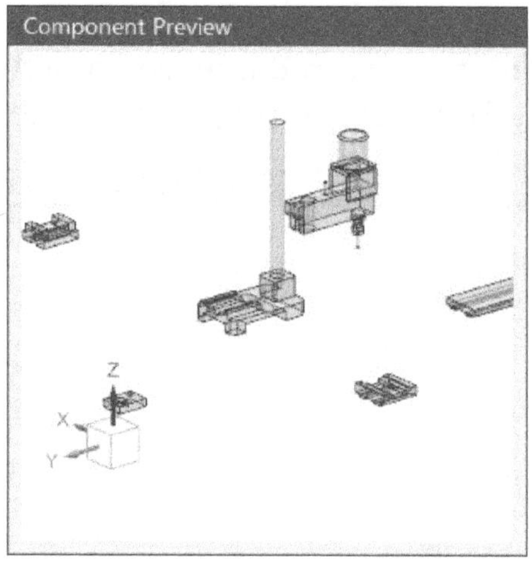

Figure-8. Component Preview window

- After specifying desired parameters, click on **OK** button from the dialog box. The components will be added.

New Component

The **New Component** tool is used to create a new component in the assembly by selecting geometry and saving it as a component. The procedure to use this tool is discussed next.

- Click on the **New Component** tool from **Base** group in the **Assemblies** tab of the **Ribbon**. The **New Component** dialog box will be displayed; refer to Figure-9.

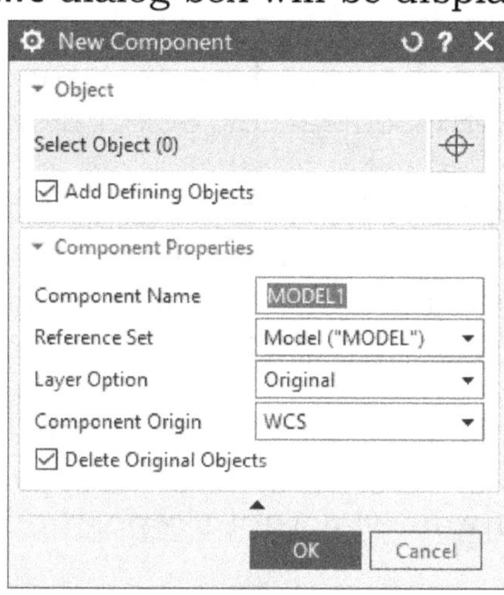

Figure-9. New Component dialog box

- Select desired object from the graphics window to create the new component with geometry. Select the **Add Defining Objects** check box from **Object** rollout to include all reference objects in the new component part file.

- Specify desired name of component in the **Component Name** edit box of **Component Properties** rollout. Select desired option from **Component Origin** drop-down to specify the location of absolute coordinate system (CSYS) within the component part. Select **Delete Original Objects** check box to delete the original objects.
- Other parameters in the dialog box are same as discussed earlier.
- After specifying desired parameters, click on **OK** button from the dialog box. A new component will be created; refer to Figure-10.

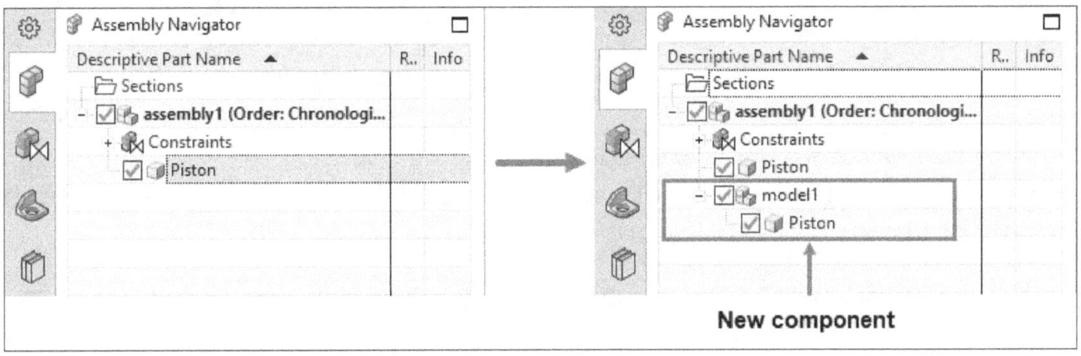

Figure-10. New component created

New Parent Assembly

The **New Parent Assembly** tool is used to create a new parent assembly file for the current active part.

Fix

The **Fix** tool is used to fix objects in their current position. The procedure to use this tool is discussed next.

- Click on the **Fix** tool from **Position** group of **Assemblies** tab in the **Ribbon**. The **Fix** dialog box will be displayed; refer to Figure-11.

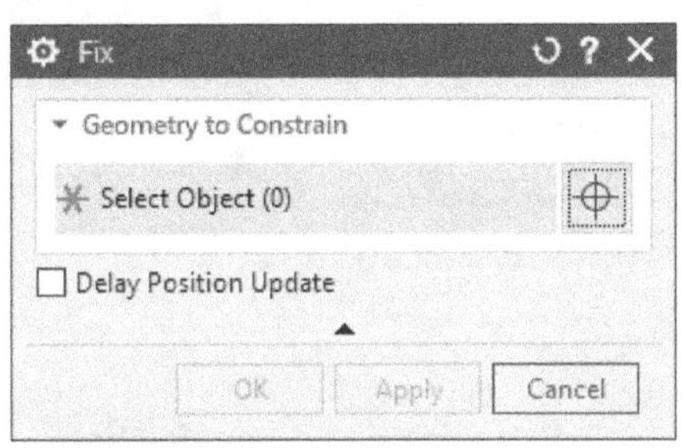

Figure-11. Fix dialog box

- Select desired object in the graphics window to be fixed in place; refer to Figure-12. Select **Delay Position Update** check box to move the components after clicking **OK** or **Apply** button.

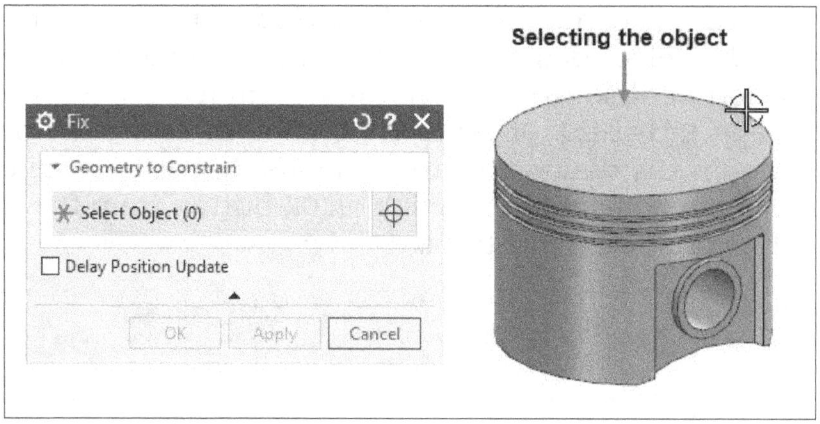

Figure-12. Selecting the object to be fixed

- After specifying desired parameters, click on **OK** button from the dialog box. The object will be fixed; refer to Figure-13.

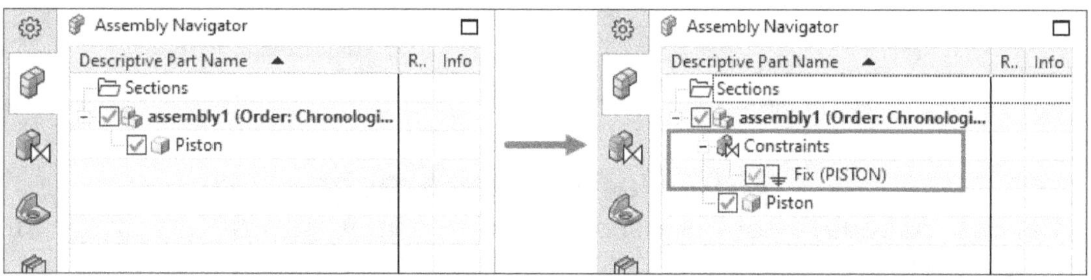

Figure-13. Fix constraint applied

Auto Align

The **Auto Align** tool constrain selected objects to become touching or aligned with each other. The procedure to use this tool is discussed next.

- Click on the **Auto Align** tool from **Position** group of **Assemblies** tab in the **Ribbon**. The **Auto Align** dialog box will be displayed; refer to Figure-14.

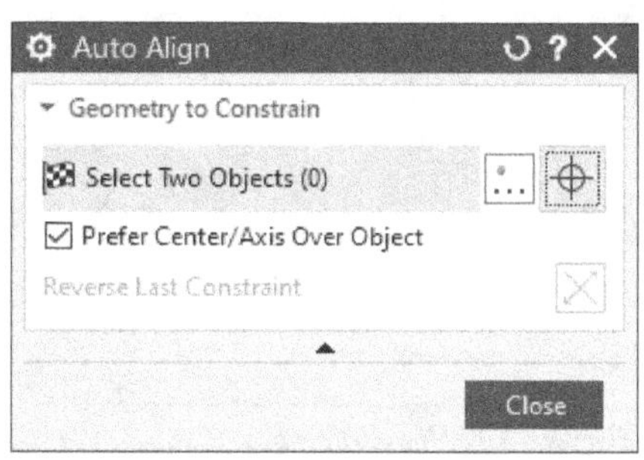

Figure-14. Auto Align dialog box

- Select desired face or axis of first component from the graphics window to which the constraint is to be applied. Note that this component will move to fulfill applied constraint.
- Select face or axis of the second component. The constraint will be applied; refer to Figure-15.

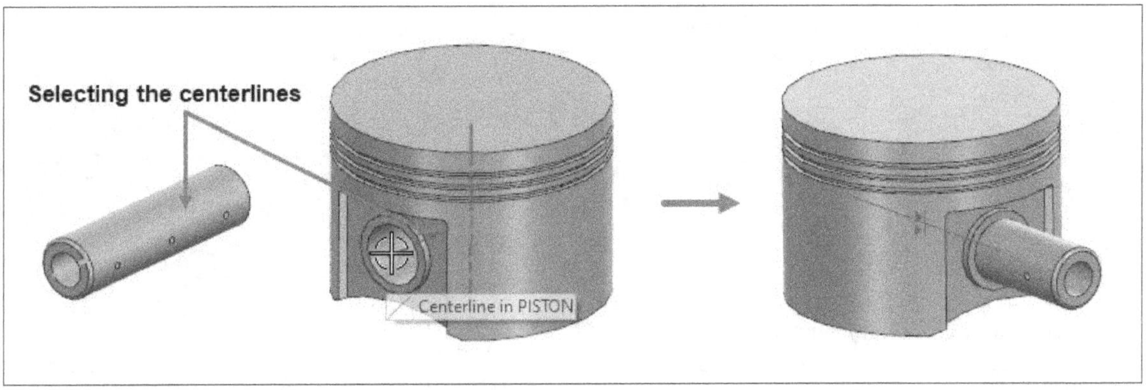

Figure-15. Auto Align constraint applied

- Select **Prefer Center/Axis Over Object** check box from **Geometry to Constrain** rollout to use center of object or axis itself for the constraint on selecting a cylindrical, conical, or spherical face or a circular edge. Click on the **Reverse Last Constraint** button to switch between touch and align mode for the last constraint.
- After specifying desired parameters, click on **Close** button to close the dialog box.

Touch

The **Touch** tool is used to constrain selected objects to touch each other at selected reference geometry (face, edge, curve, and so on). The procedure to use this tool is discussed next.

- Click on the **Touch** tool from **Position** group of **Assemblies** tab in the **Ribbon**. The **Touch** dialog box will be displayed; refer to Figure-16.

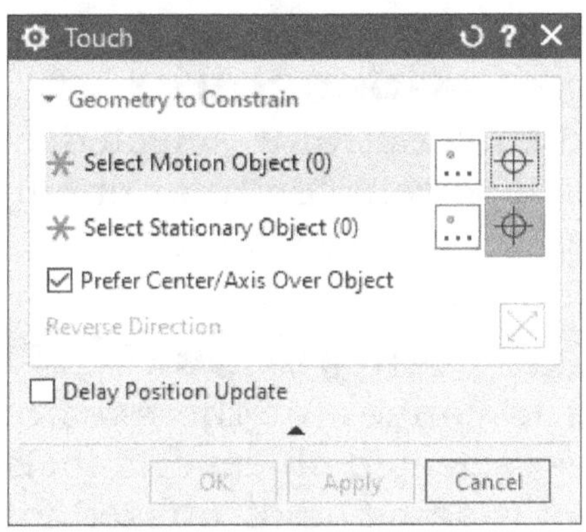

Figure-16. Touch dialog box

- Select desired object from graphics window to be moved and then select desired object to be stationary for applying constraint.
- Other parameters in the dialog box are same as discussed earlier.
- After specifying desired parameters, click on **OK** button from the dialog box. The touch constraint will be applied; refer to Figure-17.

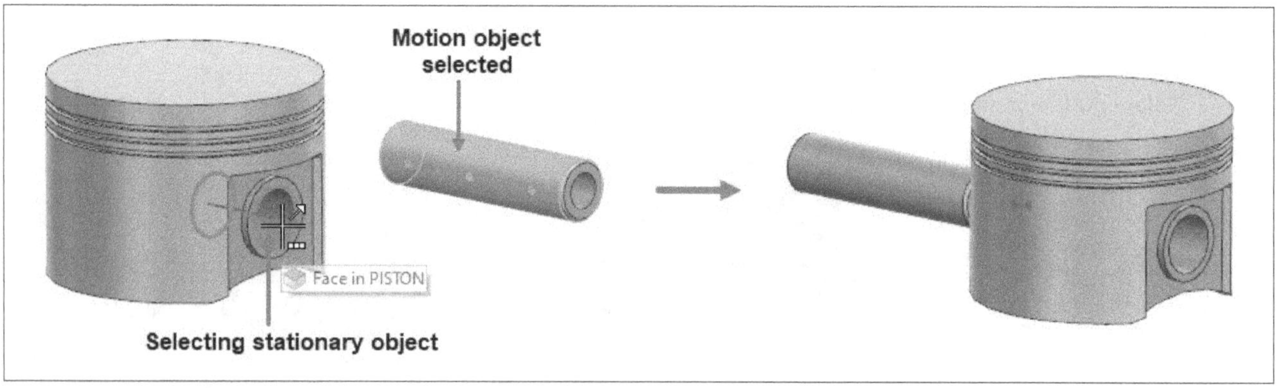

Figure-17. Touch constraint applied

Align

The **Align** tool is used to constraint selected objects to become aligned with the last selected object. The procedure to use this tool is same as discussed for **Touch** tool.

Parallel

The **Parallel** tool is used to constraint the direction vectors of selected objects to become parallel with the direction vector of the last selected object. The procedure to use this tool is same as discussed for **Touch** tool.

Perpendicular

The **Perpendicular** tool is used to constraint the direction vector of selected object to become perpendicular with the direction vector of the last selected object. The procedure to use this tool is same as discussed for **Touch** tool.

Concentric

The **Concentric** tool is used to constraint selected circular or elliptical edges to become concentric with the last selected circular or elliptical edge. The procedure to use this tool is same as discussed for **Touch** tool.

Align/Lock

The **Align/Lock** tool is used to constraint the axes of selected objects to become aligned with the axis of the last selected object and locks the rotation about the axis. The procedure to use this tool is same as discussed for **Touch** tool.

Distance

The **Distance** tool is used to define a 3D distance constraint between two objects. The procedure to use this tool is discussed next.

- Click on the **Distance** tool from **Position** group of **Assemblies** tab in the **Ribbon**. The **Distance** dialog box will be displayed; refer to Figure-18.

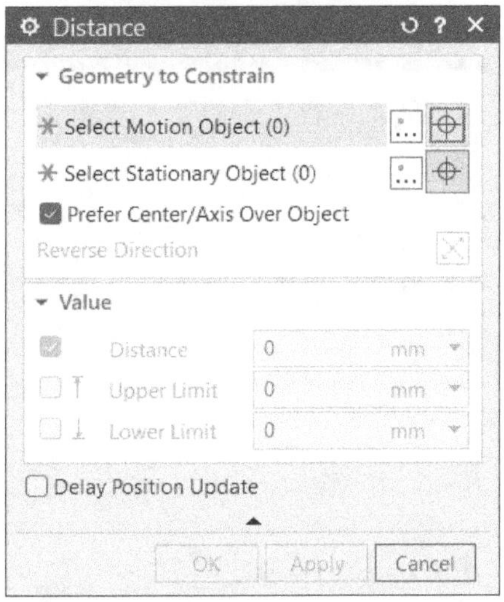

Figure-18. Distance dialog box

- Select desired object from graphics window to be moved and then select desired object to be stationary for applying constraint. On selecting the stationary object, the options in the **Value** rollout will be activated.
- The **Distance** area of **Value** rollout displays the distance value between the selected objects. The **Upper Limit** and **Lower Limit** areas display the range of motion for the components. You can modify the value of distance, upper limit, and lower limit by selecting the respective check boxes.
- Other parameters in the dialog box have been discussed earlier.
- After specifying desired parameters, click on **OK** button from the dialog box. The distance constraint will be applied; refer to Figure-19.

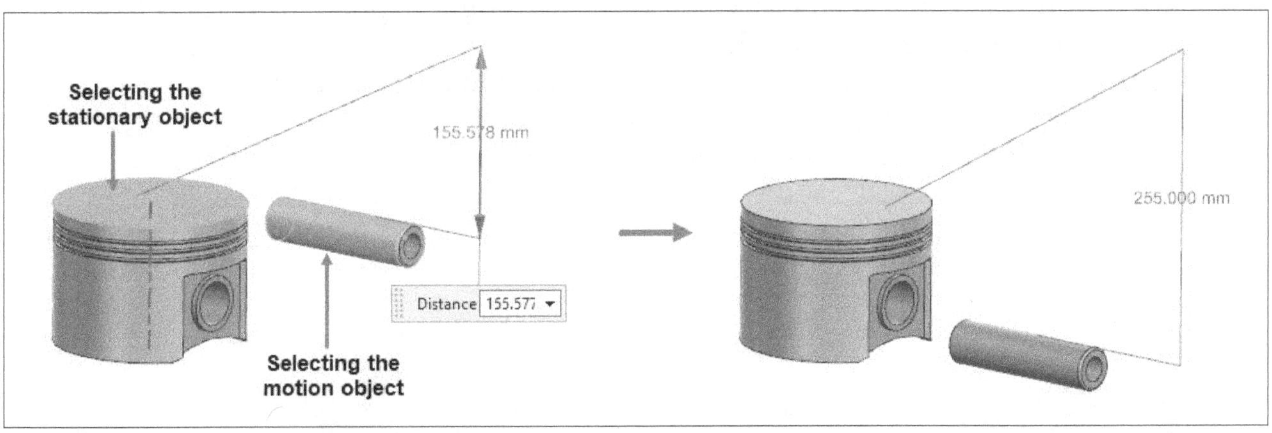

Figure-19. Distance constraint applied

Angle

The **Angle** tool is used to define an angle constraint between two objects, optionally through an axis. The procedure to use this tool is discussed next.

- Click on the **Angle** tool from **Position** group of **Assemblies** tab in the **Ribbon**. The **Angle** dialog box will be displayed; refer to Figure-20.

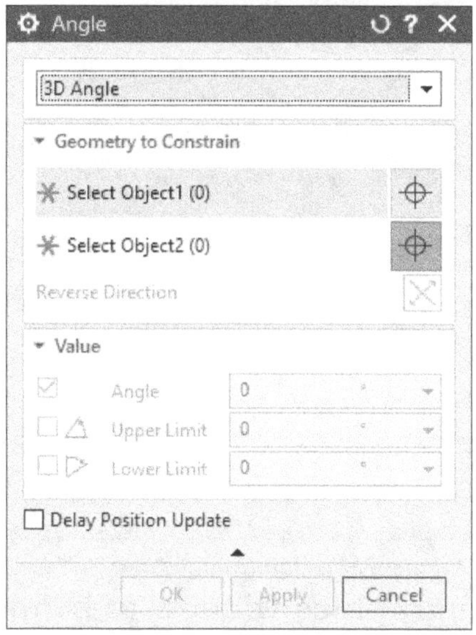

Figure-20. Angle dialog box

- Select the **3D Angle** option from drop-down in the dialog box to measure the angle constraint between objects without requiring a defined axis of rotation. Select **Orient Angle** option from the drop-down to measure the angle constraint between two objects, using selected axis of rotation.
- Select desired two objects between which the constraint to be applied. On selecting the second object, the options in the **Value** rollout will be activated.
- The **Angle** area of **Value** rollout displays the angle value between the selected objects. The **Upper Limit** and **Lower Limit** areas display the range of motion for the components. You can modify the value of angle, upper limit, and lower limit by selecting the respective check boxes.
- Other parameters in the dialog box have been discussed earlier.
- After specifying desired parameters, click on **OK** button from the dialog box. The angle constraint will be applied; refer to Figure-21.

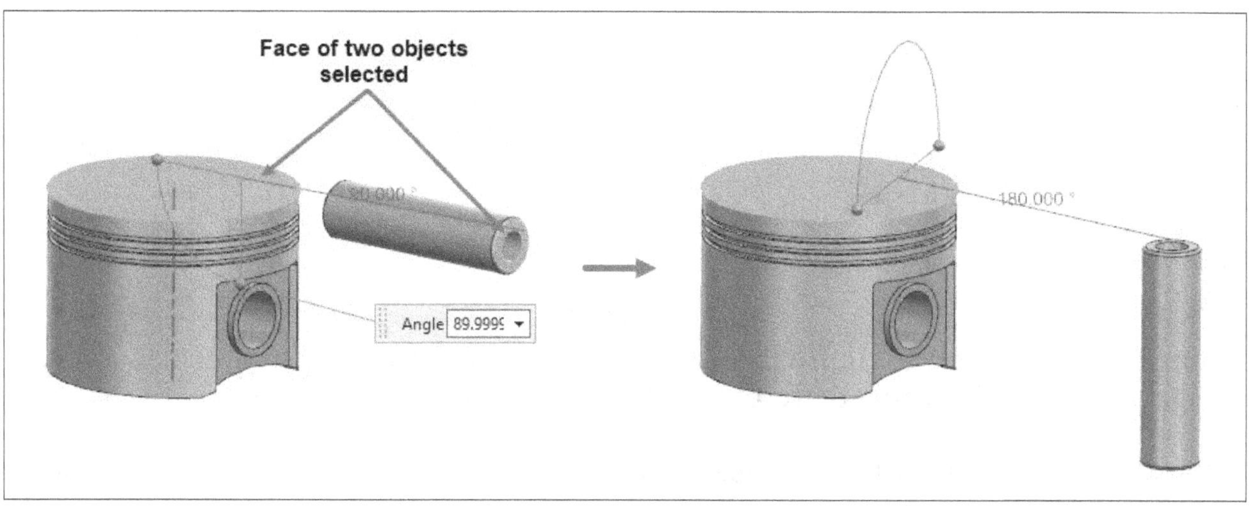

Figure-21. Angle constraint applied

Bond

The **Bond** tool is used to constraint objects together so they move as a rigid set. The procedure to use this tool is discussed next.

- Click on the **Bond** tool from **Position** group of **Assemblies** tab in the **Ribbon**. The **Bond** dialog box will be displayed; refer to Figure-22.

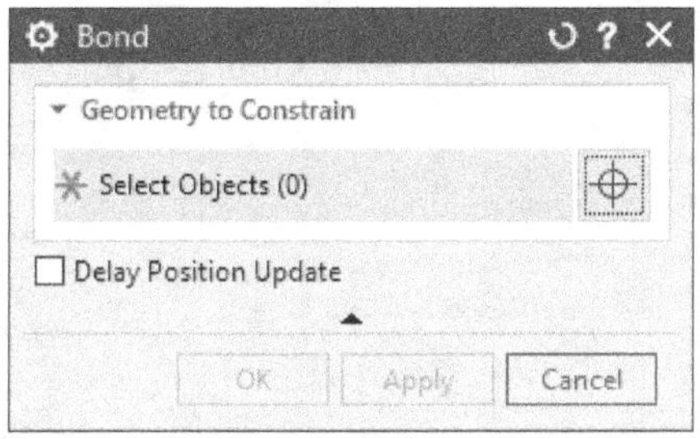

Figure-22. Bond dialog box

- Select two or more objects from the graphics window to define bond constraint.
- Other parameters in the dialog box have been discussed earlier.
- After specifying desired parameters, click on **OK** button from the diaog box. The bond constraint will be applied; refer to Figure-23.

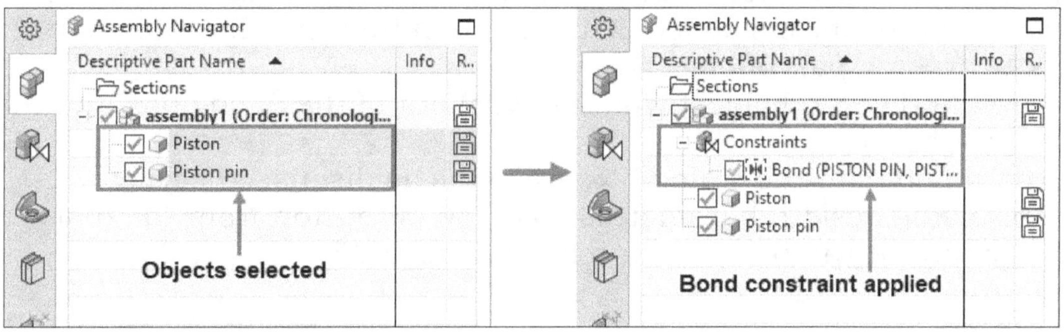

Figure-23. Bond constraint applied

Center

The **Center** tool is used to center one or two objects between a pair of objects, or center a pair of objects along another object. The procedure to use this tool is discussed next.

- Click on the **Center** tool from **Position** group of **Assemblies** tab in the **Ribbon**. The **Center** dialog box will be displayed; refer to Figure-24.

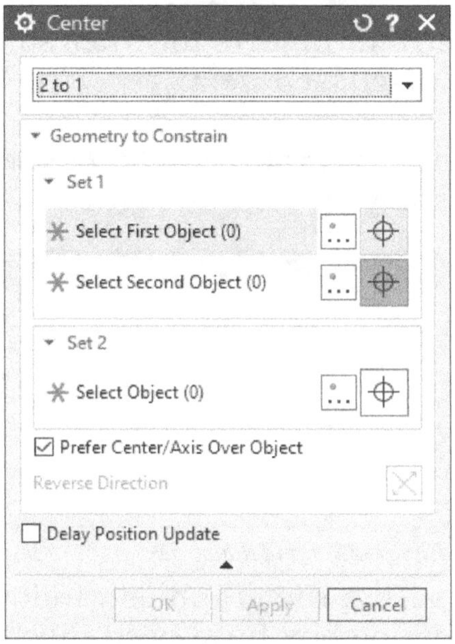

Figure-24. Center dialog box

- Select **2 to 1** option from drop-down in the dialog box to center a pair of objects along another object. Select **1 to 2** option from the drop-down to center one object between a pair of objects. Select **2 to 2** option from the drop-down to center two objects between a pair of objects.
- Select first and second objects for **Set 1** rollout of the dialog box and then select object for **Set 2**.
- Other parameters in the dialog box are same as discussed earlier.
- After specifying desired parameters, click on **OK** button from the dialog box. The center constraint will be applied; refer to Figure-25.

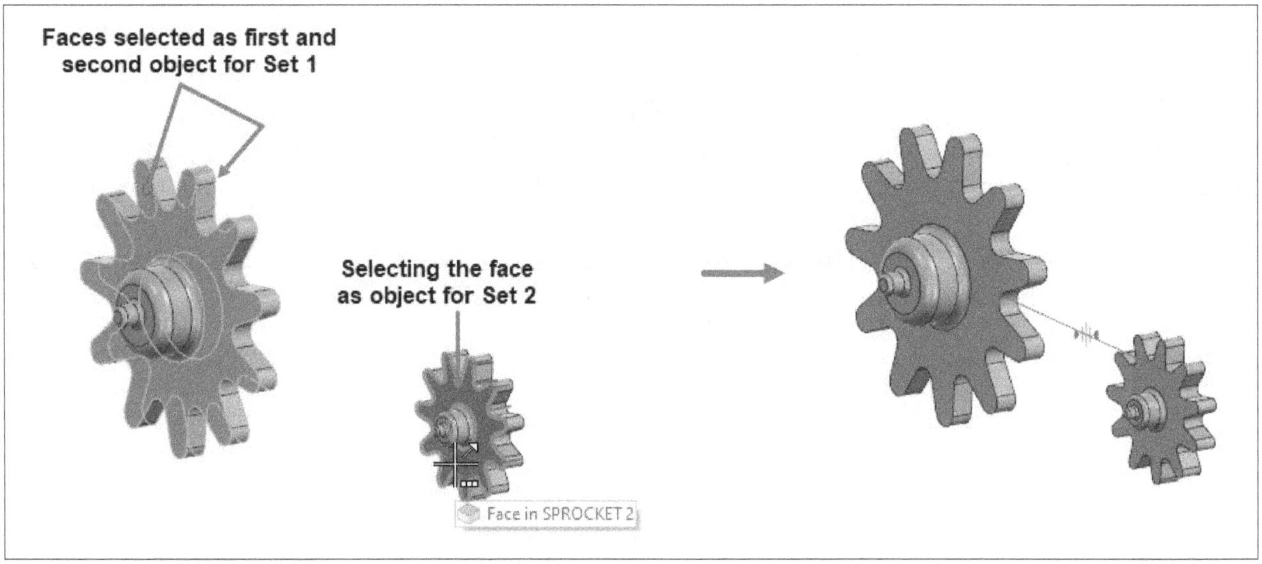

Figure-25. Center constraint applied

Hinge

The **Hinge** tool is used to constraint two objects along an axis of rotation. The procedure to use this tool is discussed next.

- Click on the **Hinge** tool from **Joints and Couplers** drop-down in the **Position** group of **Assemblies** tab in the **Ribbon**. The **Hinge** dialog box will be displayed; refer to Figure-26.

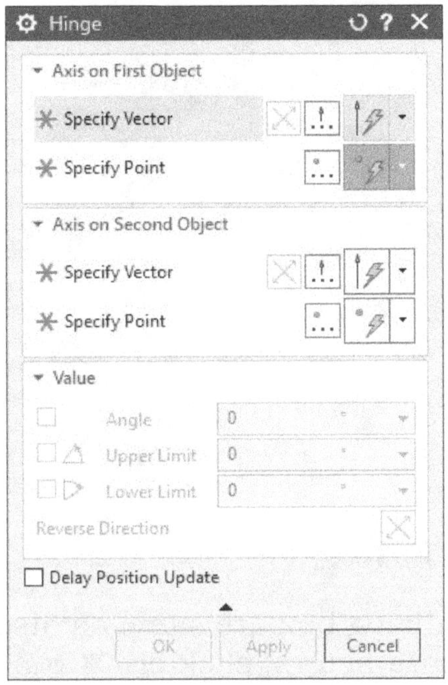

Figure-26. Hinge dialog box

- Specify desired vector and point for the first object and then specify desired vector and point for the second object; refer to Figure-27.

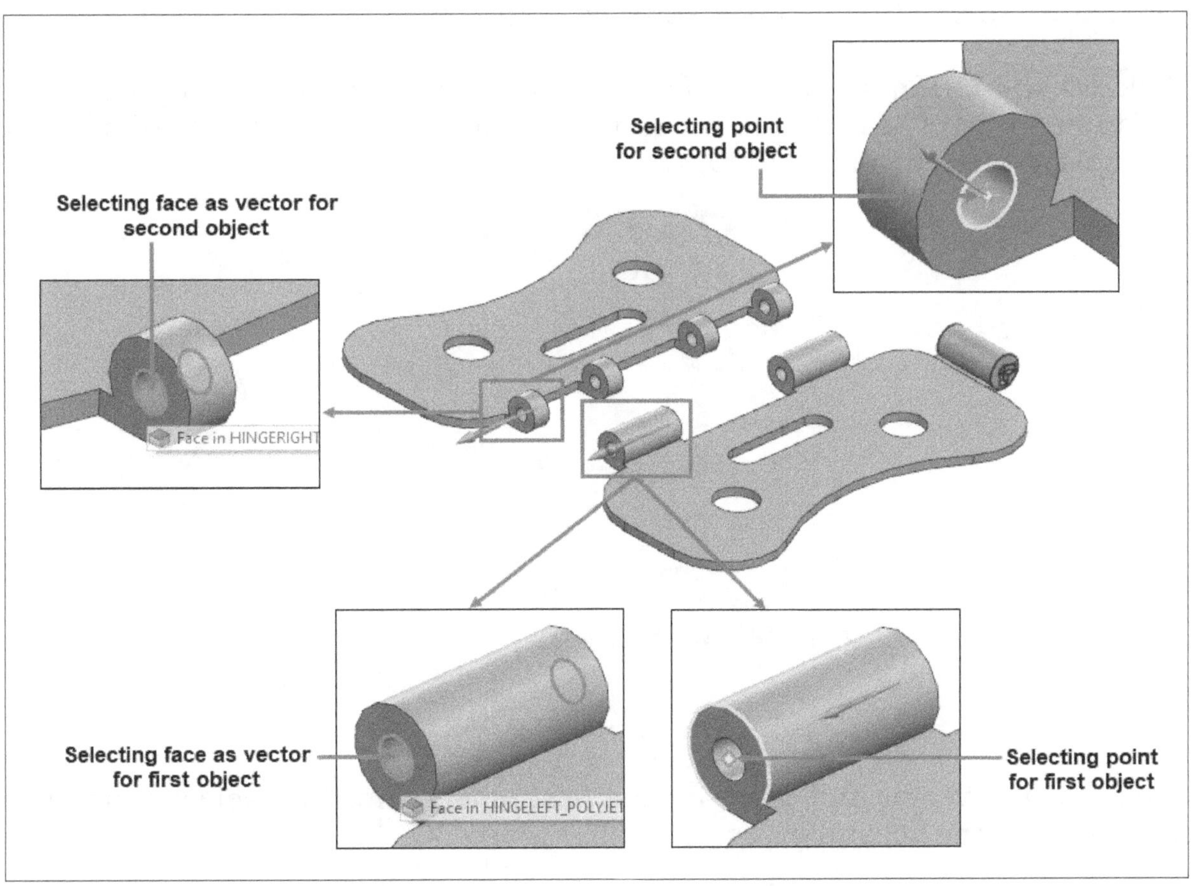

Figure-27. Selecting vectors and points

- On selecting the vector and point for second object, the hinge constraint will be applied; refer to Figure-28.

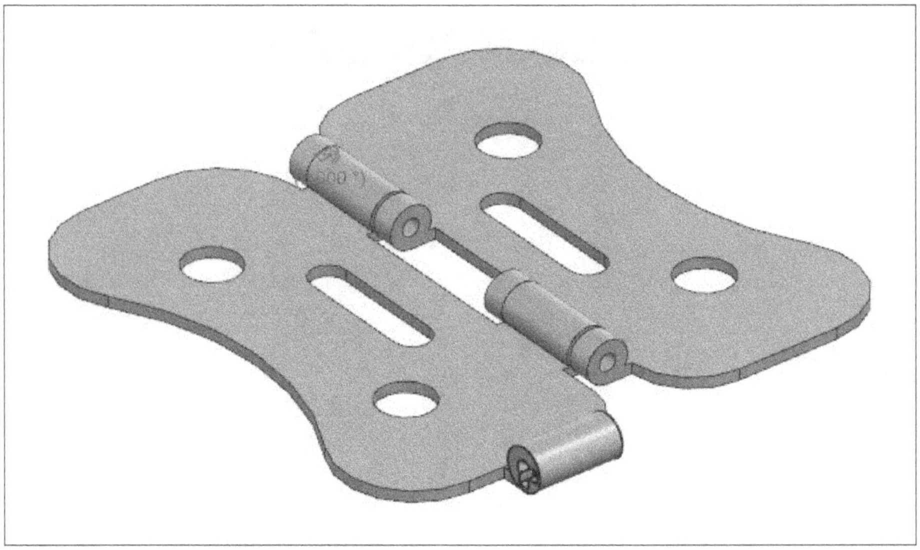

Figure-28. Hinge constraint applied

- Other parameters in the dialog box are same as discussed earlier.
- After specifying desired parameters, click on **OK** button to close the dialog box.

Cylindrical

The **Cylindrical** tool is used to constraint two objects along a rotatable linear axis. The procedure to use this tool is discussed next.

- Click on the **Cylindrical** tool from **Joints and Couplers** drop-down in the **Position** group of **Assemblies** tab in the **Ribbon**. The **Cylindrical** dialog box will be displayed; refer to Figure-29.

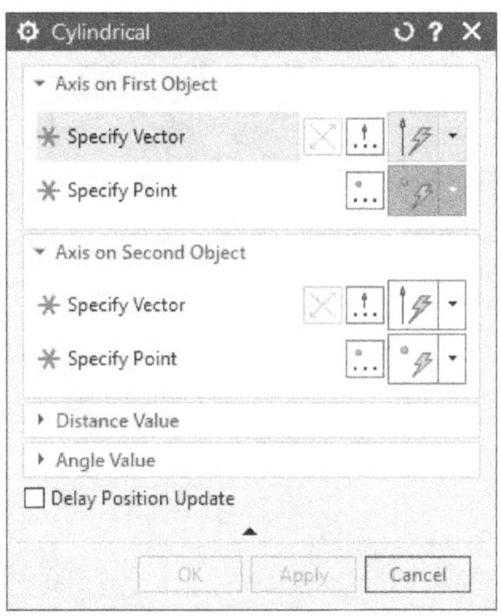

Figure-29. Cylindrical dialog box

- Select desired vector and point for the first object and then select desired vector and point for the second object; refer to Figure-30.

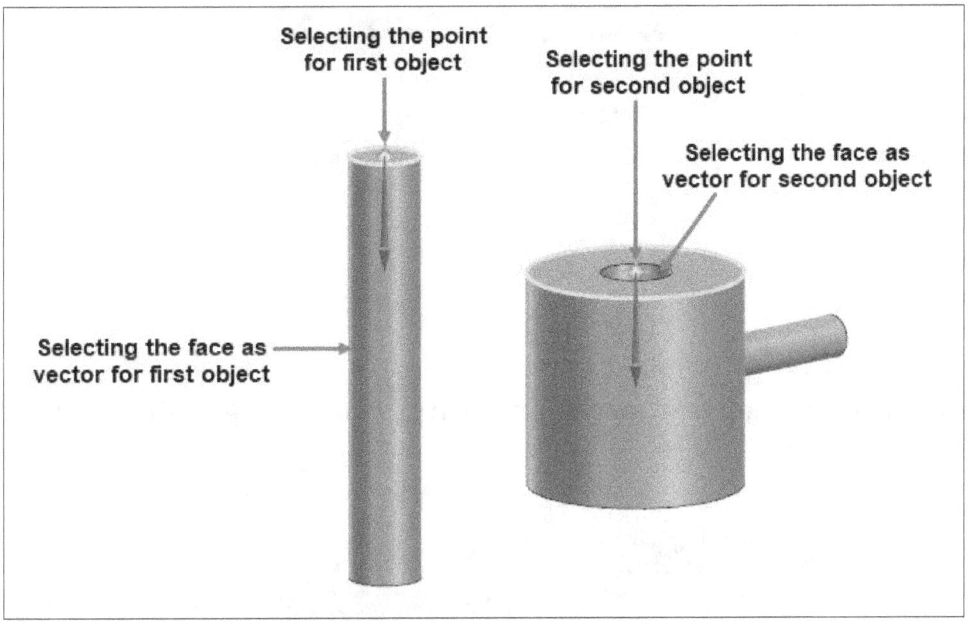

Figure-30. Selecting vectors and points

- On selecting the vector and point for second object, the cylindrical constraint will be applied; refer to Figure-31.

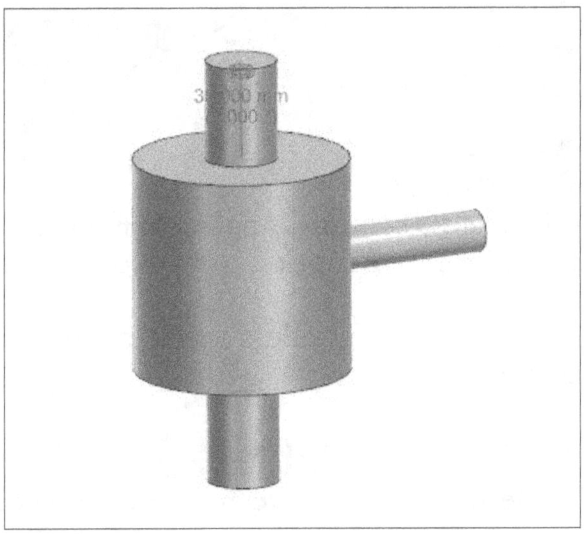

Figure-31. Cylindrical constraint applied

- Other parameters in the dialog box are same as discussed earlier.
- After specifying desired parameters, click on **OK** button to close the dialog box.

Gear

The **Gear** tool is used to define the relative motion between two joints with angular values. The procedure to use this tool is discussed next.

- Click on the **Gear** tool from **Joints and Couplers** drop-down in the **Position** group of **Assemblies** tab in the **Ribbon**. The **Gear** dialog box will be displayed; refer to Figure-32.

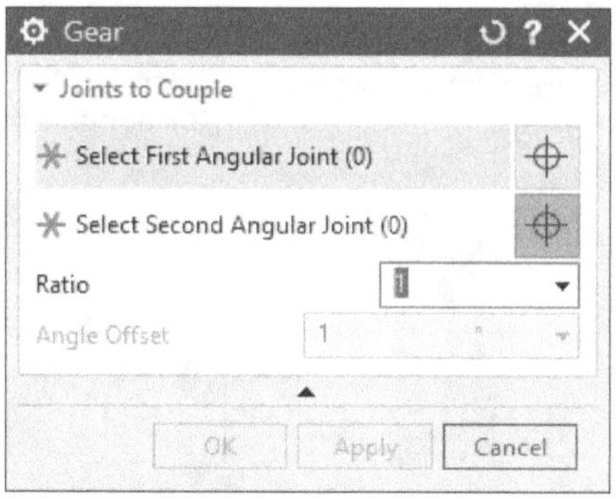

Figure-32. Gear dialog box

- Select the first and second angular joints from the graphics window; refer to Figure-33.

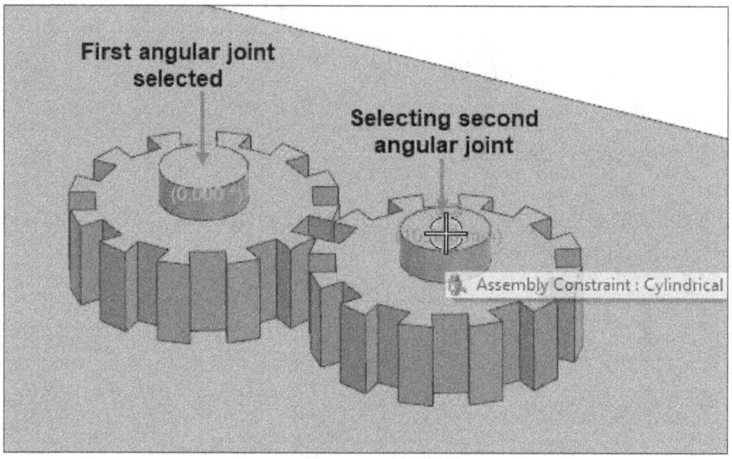

Figure-33. Selecting angular joints

- Specify desired value in the **Ratio** and **Angle Offset** edit boxes from **Joints to Couple** rollout to define the relative motion of two joints that have linear or angular expressions.
- After specifying desired parameters, click on **OK** button from the dialog box. The gear constraint will be defined.

Cable

The **Cable** tool is used to define the relative motion between two joints with linear values. The procedure to use this tool is discussed next.

- First, apply slider constraint (discussed in next topic) or any linear constraint on the objects; refer to Figure-34.

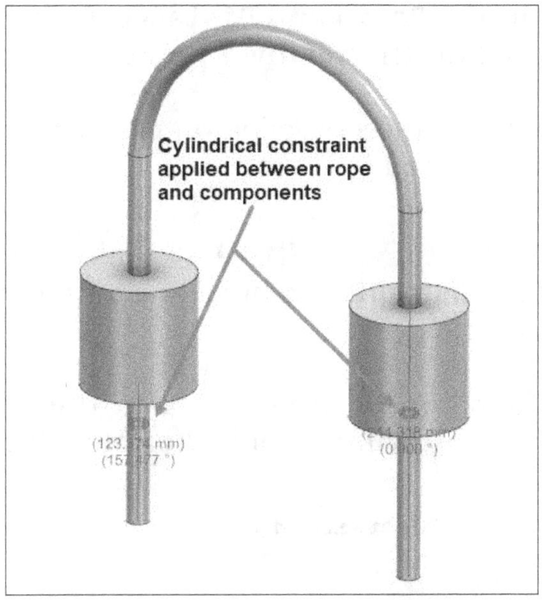

Figure-34. Cylindrical constraint applied

- Now, click on the **Cable** tool from **Joints and Couplers** drop-down in the **Position** group of **Assemblies** tab in the **Ribbon**. The **Cable** dialog box will be displayed; refer to Figure-35.

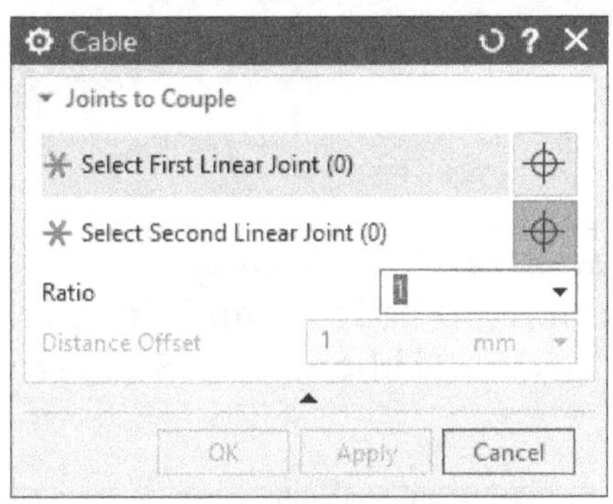

Figure-35. Cable dialog box

- Select the first and second linear joints from the graphics window; refer to Figure-36.

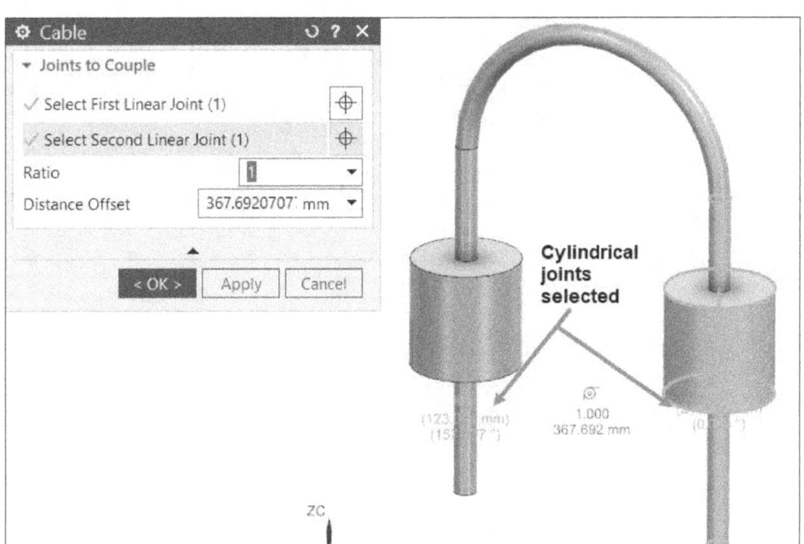

Figure-36. Selecting the linear joints

- Specify desired value in the **Ratio** and **Distance Offset** edit boxes from **Joints to Couple** rollout to define the relative motion of two joints that have linear expressions.
- After specifying desired parameters, click on **OK** button from the dialog box. The cable constraint will be defined.

Slider

The **Slider** tool is used to constraint two objects along a linear axis. The procedure to use this tool is discussed next.

- First, apply fix constraint on desired object in the graphics window; refer to Figure-37. The fix constraint will be applied on the object.

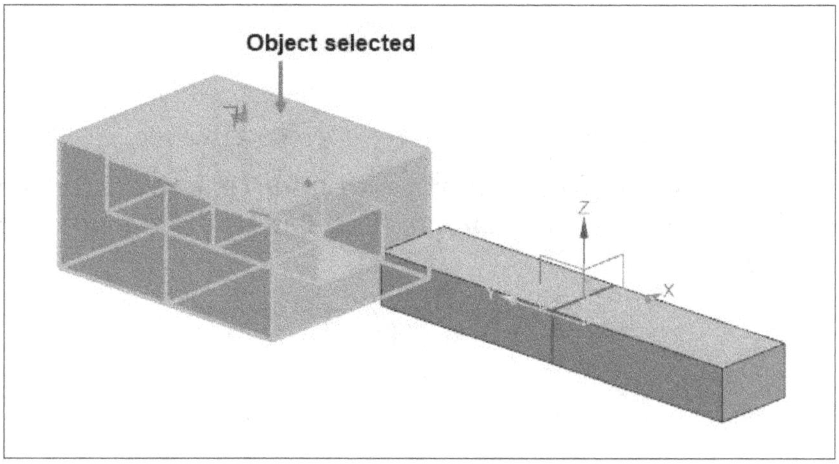

Figure-37. Object selected to apply fix constraint

- Now, click on the **Slider** tool from **Joints and Couplers** drop-down in the **Position** group of **Assemblies** tab in the **Ribbon**. The **Slider** dialog box will be displayed; refer to Figure-38.

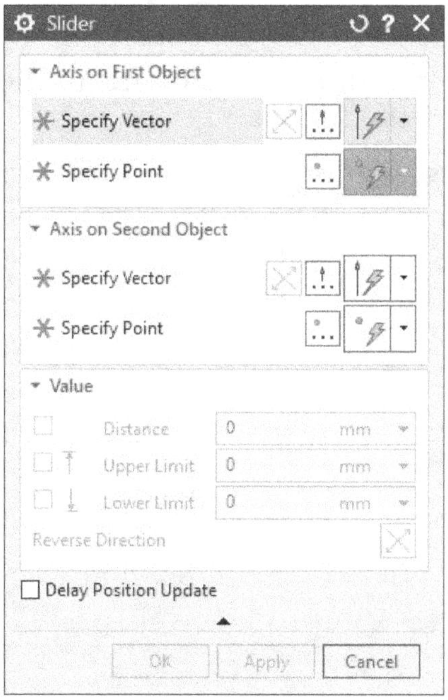

Figure-38. Slider dialog box

- Specify desired vector and point for the first object and then specify desired vector and point for the second object; refer to Figure-39.

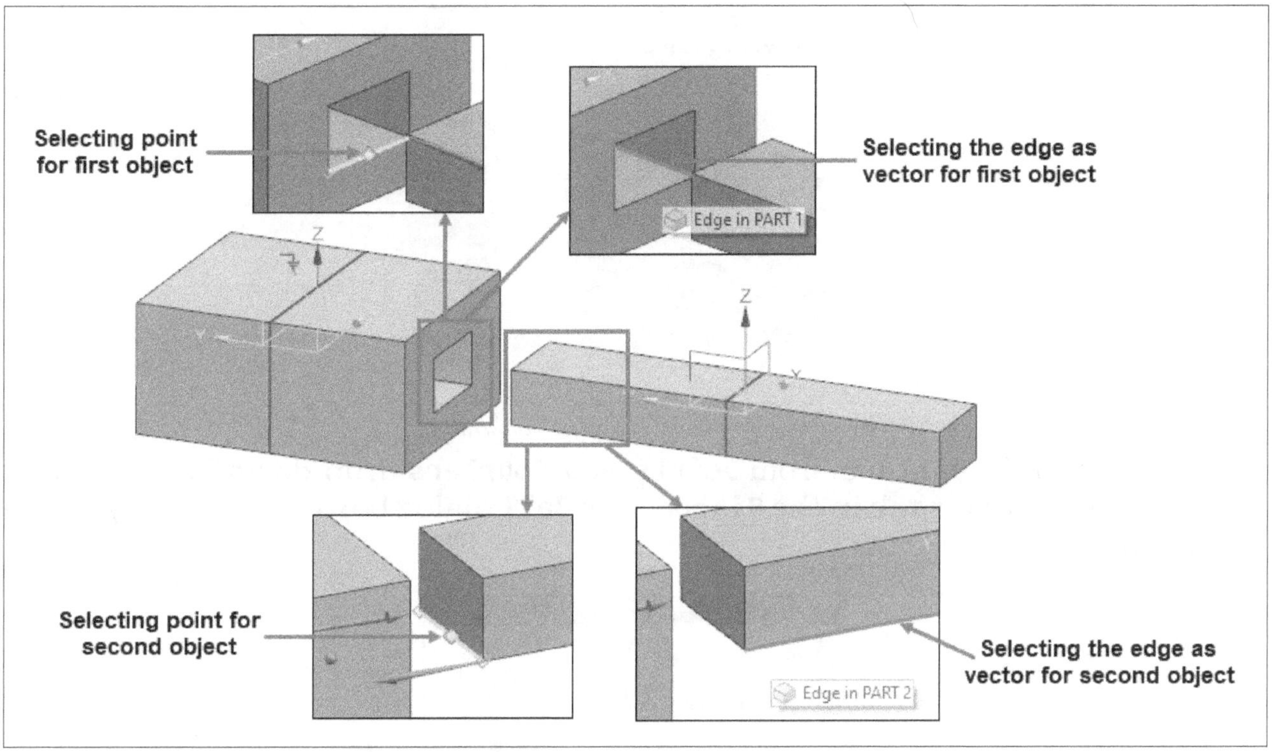

Figure-39. Selecting vectors and points

- On selecting the vector and point for second object, the slider joint will be applied; refer to Figure-40.

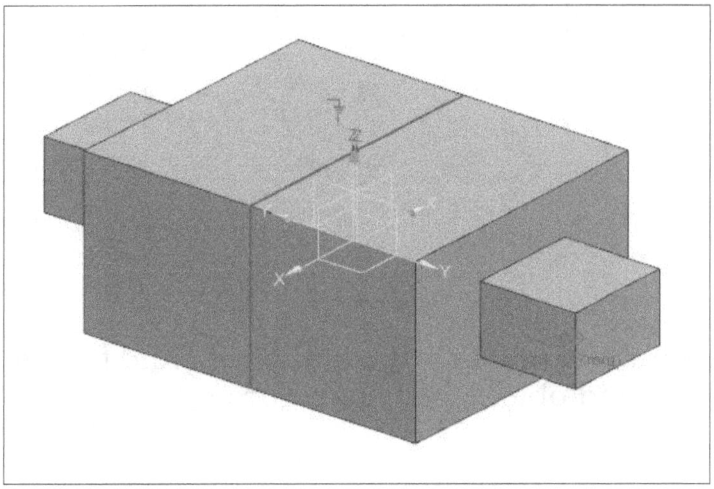

Figure-40. Slider joint applied

- Other parameters in the dialog box are same as discussed earlier.
- After specifying desired parameters, click on **OK** button to close the dialog box.

Ball

The **Ball** tool is used to constraint two objects at a shared point. The procedure to use this tool is discussed next.

- First, apply fix constraint on desired object in the graphics window; refer to Figure-41. The fix constraint will be applied on the object.

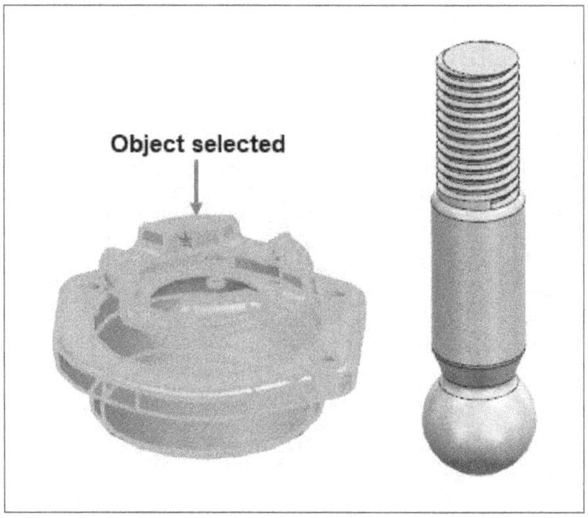

Figure-41. Object selected to apply fix constraint

- Now, click on the **Ball** tool from **Joints and Couplers** drop-down in the **Position** group of **Assemblies** tab in the **Ribbon**. The **Ball** dialog box will be displayed; refer to Figure-42.

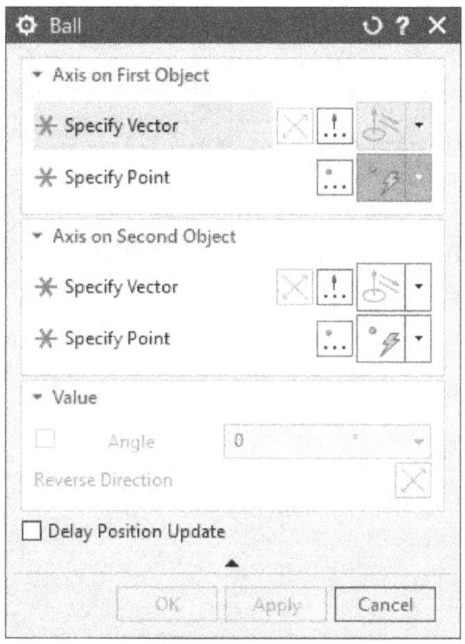

Figure-42. Ball dialog box

- Specify desired vector and point for the first object and then specify desired vector and point for the second object; refer to Figure-43.

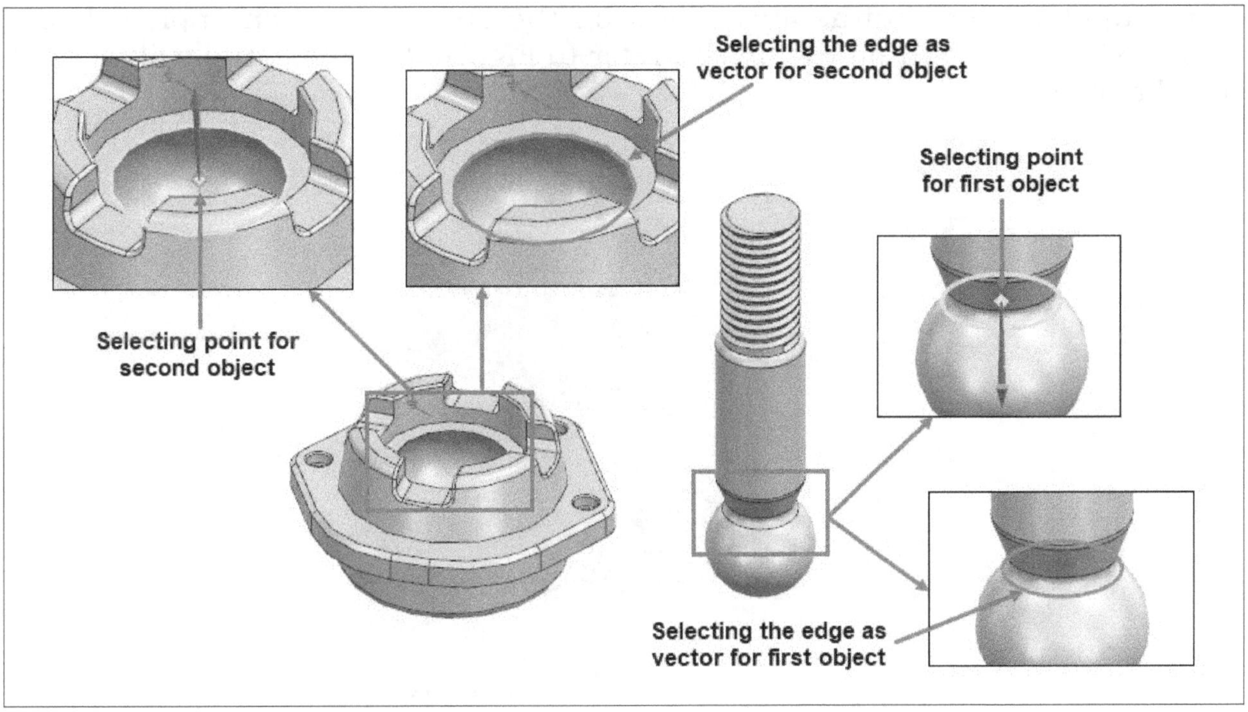

Figure-43. Selecting vectors and points

- On selecting the vector and point for second object, the slider joint will be applied; refer to Figure-44.

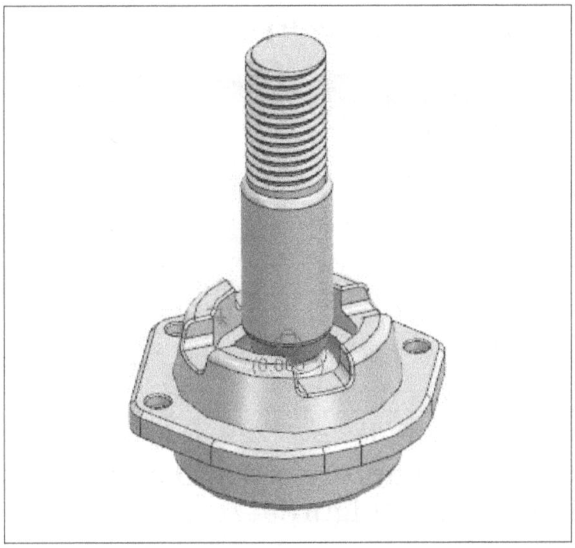

Figure-44. Ball joint applied

- Other parameters in the dialog box are same as discussed earlier.
- After specifying desired parameters, click on **OK** button to close the dialog box.

Rack and Pinion

The **Rack and Pinion** tool is used to define the relative motion between a joint with a linear value and a joint with an angular value. The procedure to use this tool is discussed next.

- First, apply slider joint as linear joint on the object and then apply cylindrical joint as angular joint on the object; refer to Figure-45. The joints will be applied on the object.

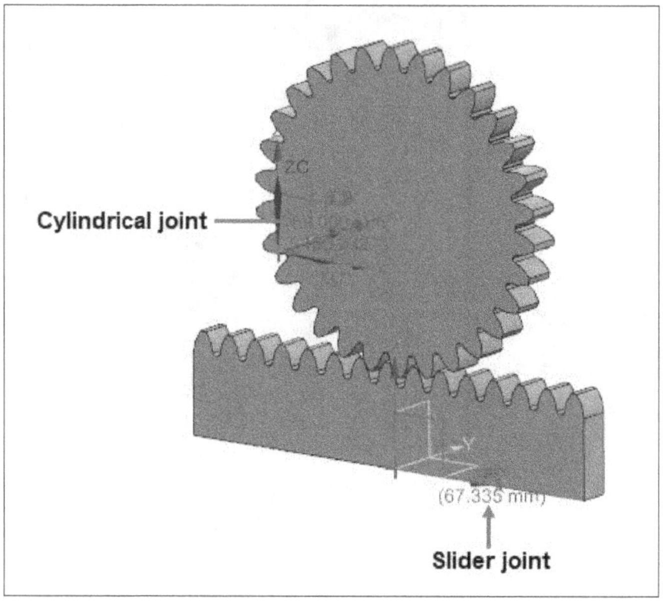

Figure-45. Slider and cylindrical joints applied

- Now, click on the **Rack and Pinion** tool from **Joints and Couplers** drop-down in the **Position** group of **Assemblies** tab in the **Ribbon**. The **Rack and Pinion** dialog box will be displayed; refer to Figure-46.

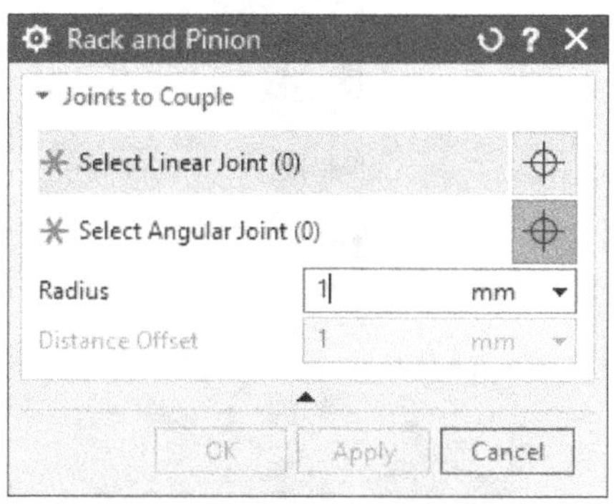

Figure-46. Rack and Pinion dialog box

- Select slider joint as linear joint and cylinder joint as angular joint from the objects in the graphics window; refer to Figure-47.

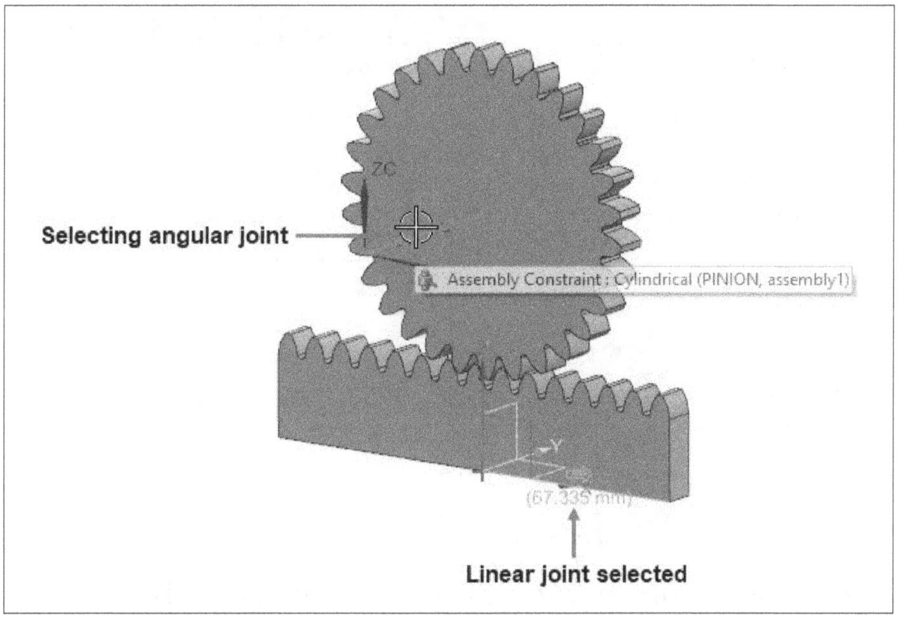

Figure-47. Selecting the joints

- Other parameters in the dialog box are same as discussed earlier.
- After specifying desired parameters, click on **OK** button from the dialog box. The rock and pinion joint will be applied.

Move Component

The **Move Component** tool is used to move a component in the assembly. The procedure to use this tool is discussed next.

- Click on the **Move Component** tool from **Position** group of **Assemblies** tab in the **Ribbon**. The **Move Component** dialog box will be displayed; refer to Figure-48.

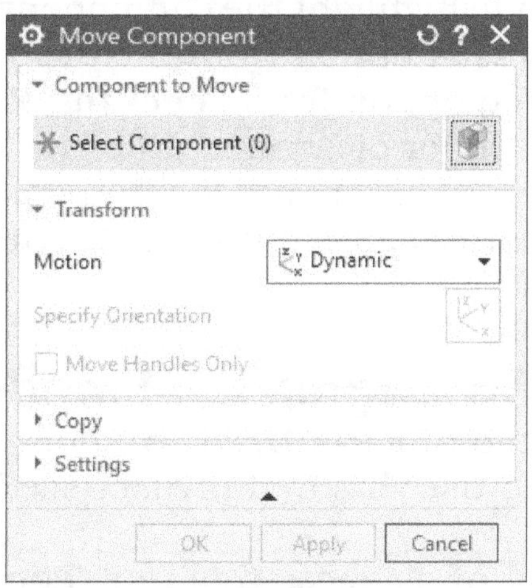

Figure-48. Move Component dialog box

- Select desired component from the graphics window to be moved; refer to Figure-49.

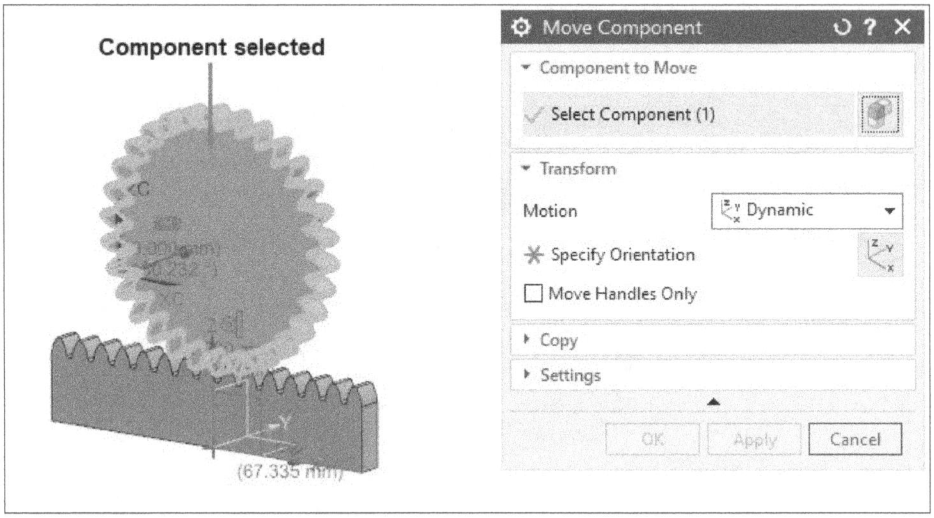

Figure-49. Component selected to be moved

- Select desired option from **Motion** drop-down of **Transform** rollout and specify respective parameters to define how the selected components move. These options have been discussed earlier.
- Select **No Copy** option from **Mode** drop-down of **Copy** rollout to not copy the components during the move. Select **Copy** option from the drop-down to automatically copy the components during the move. Select **Manual Copy** option from the drop-down to copy the components whenever you needed during the move.
- Select **Move Selected Components Only** check box from **Settings** rollout to move the components you selected. Set desired number of steps in the **Animation Steps** edit box for the component movement in the graphics window.
- When **No Copy** mode is selected in the **Copy** rollout, the **Collision Detection** rollout is available. Select **None** option from **Collision Action** drop-down to ignore all collisions during the movement of components. Select **Highlight Collision** option from the drop-down to highlight the component where the collision occurred. Select **Stop Before Collision** option from the drop-down to stop the movement at a collision. Select desired option from **Checking Mode** drop-down to specify the type of objects to be checked for clearance. Click on the **Acknowledge Collisions** button to continue to move components when a collision occurs.
- After specifying desired parameters, click on **OK** button from the dialog box. The component will be moved.

Show Degrees of Freedom

The **Show Degrees of Freedom** tool is used to show the degrees of freedom of a component. The procedure to use this tool is discussed next.

- Click on the **Show Degrees of Freedom** tool from **More** drop-down in the **Position** group of **Assemblies** tab in the **Ribbon**. The **Component Selection** dialog box will be displayed; refer to Figure-50.

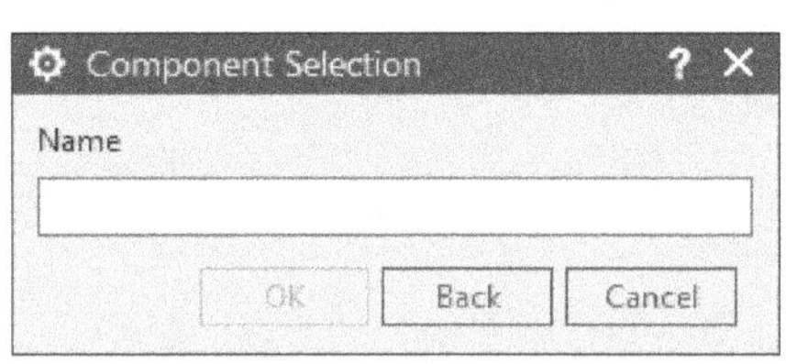

Figure-50. Component Selection dialog box

- Specify desired name of component in the **Name** edit box or select that component from the graphics window of which the degrees of freedom to be shown. The degrees of freedom will be displayed and the dialog box will be closed; refer to Figure-51.

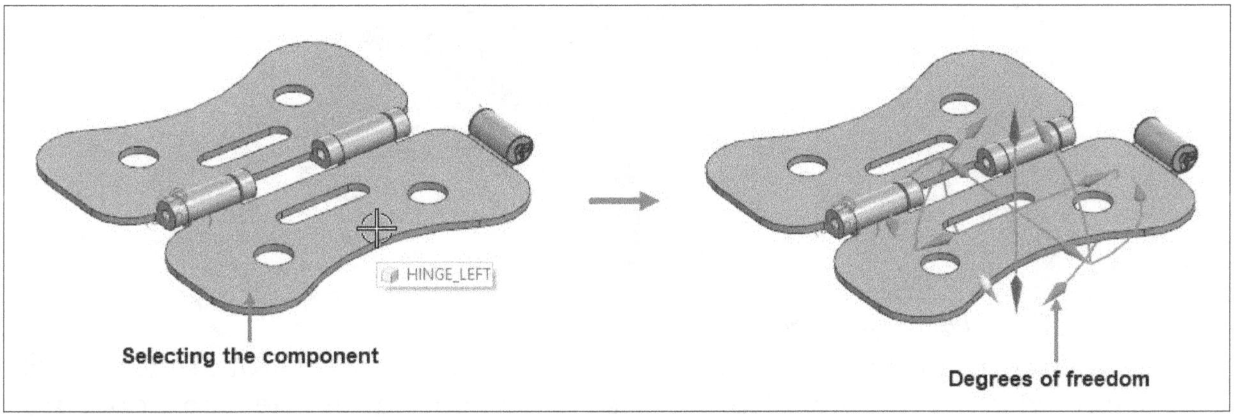

Figure-51. Degrees of freedom displayed

Show and Hide Constraints

The **Show and Hide Constraints** tool is used to show or hide constraints and components using their relationships. The procedure to use this tool is discussed next.

- Click on the **Show and Hide Constraints** tool from **More** drop-down in the **Position** group of **Assemblies** tab in the **Ribbon**. The **Show and Hide Constraints** dialog box will be displayed; refer to Figure-52.

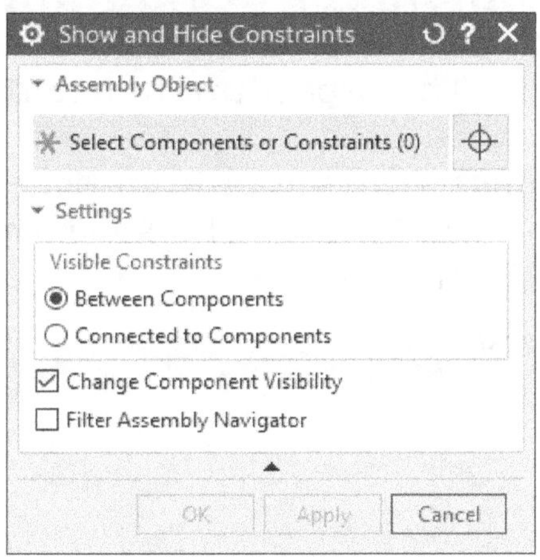

Figure-52. Show and Hide Constraints dialog box

- Select desired components or constraints to be shown or hidden from the graphics window; refer to Figure-53.

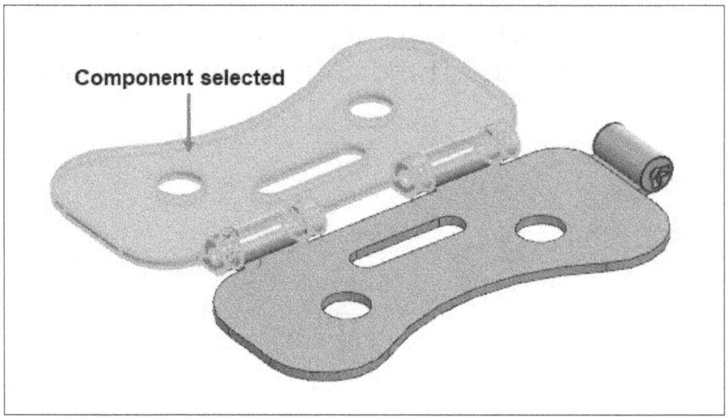

Figure-53. Component selected

- Select desired radio button from **Visible Constraints** area of **Settings** rollout to specify whether the constraints that are visible after the operation are the constraints only between the selected components, or all constraints connected to any of the selected components. Select **Change Component Visibility** check box to specify whether the components involved in the results of the operation are visible or not. Select **Filter Assembly Navigator** check box to specify whether components that are not involved in the results of the operation are filtered in the Assembly Navigator or not.
- After specifying desired parameters, click on **OK** button from the dialog box. The components or constraint will be hidden.

Remember Constraints

The **Remember Constraints** tool is used to remember assembly constraints in parts for reuse in other components. The procedure to use this tool is discussed next.

- Click on the **Remember Constraints** tool from **More** drop-down in the **Position** group of **Assemblies** tab in the **Ribbon**. The **Remembered Constraints** dialog box will be displayed; refer to Figure-54.

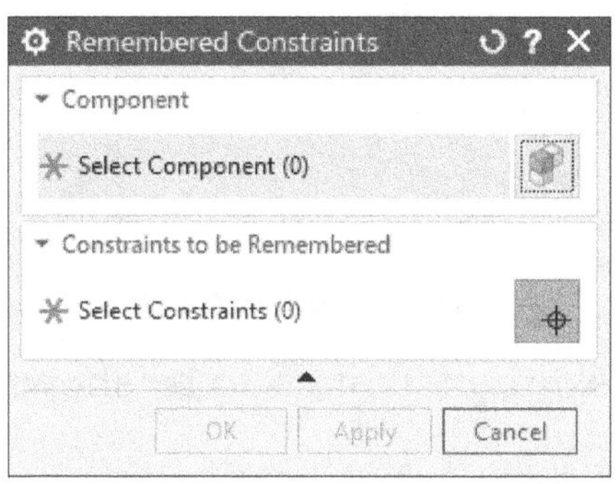

Figure-54. Remembered Constraints dialog box

- Select desired component from the graphics window where the selected positioning constraints to be saved and then select one or more assembly constraints to be remembered; refer to Figure-55.

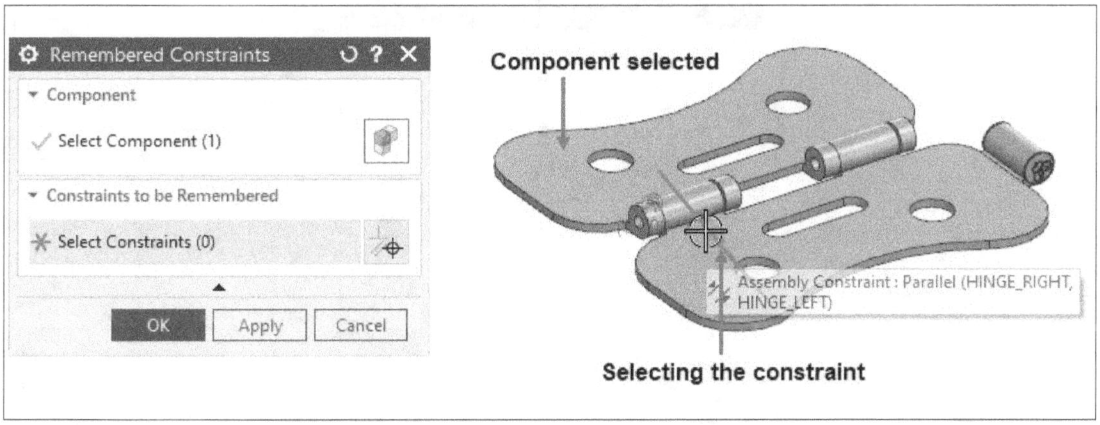

Figure-55. Selecting component and constraint

- After specifying the parameters, click on **OK** button from the dialog box. The constraints will be remembered. Note that the list of remembered constraints for the selected component will be displayed in the **Part File** tab of **Component Properties** dialog box; refer to Figure-56.

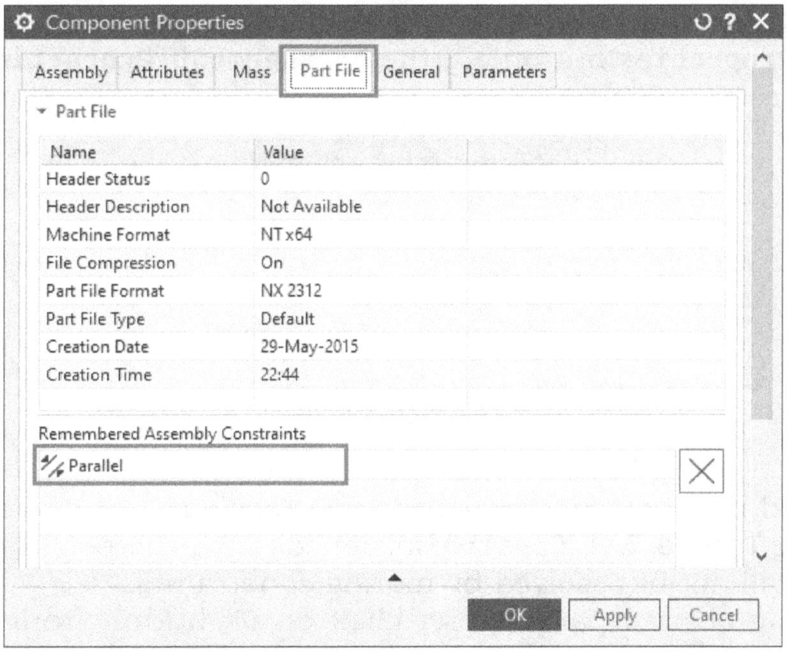

Figure-56. Remembered constraint

Create Persistent Constraints

The **Create Persistent Constraints** toggle button is used to enable the creation of persistent constraints for the assembly constraint commands.

Arrangements

The **Arrangements** tool is used to create and edit assembly arrangements, which define alternative component positions. The procedure to use this tool is discussed next.

- Click on the **Arrangements** tool from **More** drop-down in the **Position** group of **Assemblies** tab in the **Ribbon**. The **Assembly Arrangements** dialog box will be displayed; refer to Figure-57.

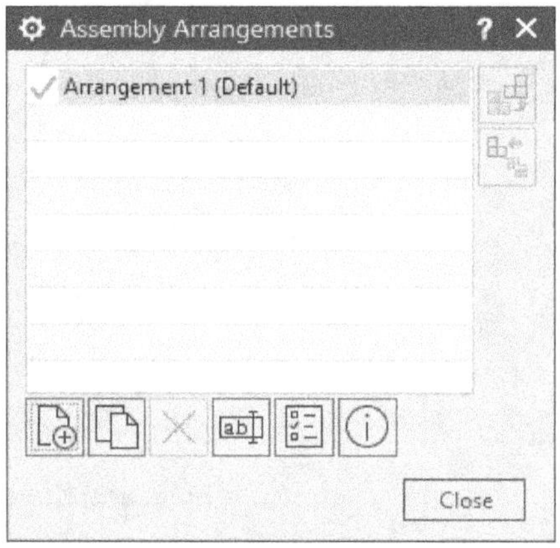

Figure-57. Assembly Arrangements dialog box

- The **Arrangement List** displays the existing assembly arrangements list.
- Click on the **New Arrangement** button to create a new arrangement.
- Click on the **Copy** button to copy an existing arrangement which can modified and renamed to create a new arrangement.
- Click on the **Delete** button to delete the selected arrangement.
- Click on the **Rename** button to rename the selected arrangement.
- Click on the **Properties** button , the **Arrangement Properties** dialog box will be displayed; refer to Figure-58.

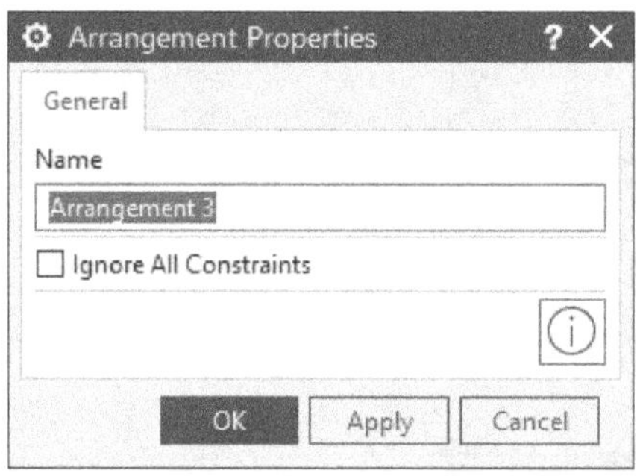

Figure-58. Arrangement Properties dialog box

- Specify desired name of arrangement in the **Name** edit box of dialog box.
- After selecting **Ignore All Constraints** check box, the position of the arranged components will not be resolved by mating constraints.
- After specifying desired parameters, click on **OK** button from the **Arrangement Properties** dialog box.
- Click on the **Information** button , the **Information** dialog box will be displayed displaying the information on assembly arrangement; refer to Figure-59.

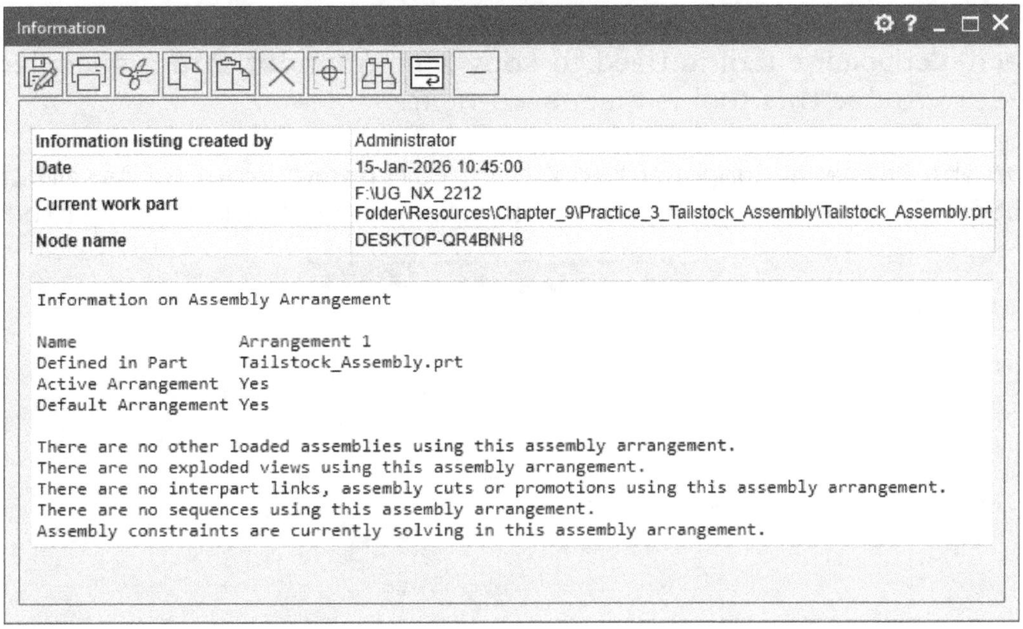

Figure-59. Information dialog box

- Click on **Close** button from **Information** dialog box to close the dialog box.
- Select desired arrangement from the list and click on the **Use** button to set the selected arrangement as the current arrangement to be used.
- Select desired arrangement from the list and click on the **Set as Default** button to set the selected arrangement as the default.
- Select desired arrangement from the list to be used and click on the **Close** button. Now, modify assembly arrangement as desired.
- You can see the modified arrangements by right-clicking on **Assembly** component in the **Assembly Navigator**; refer to Figure-60 and Figure-61.

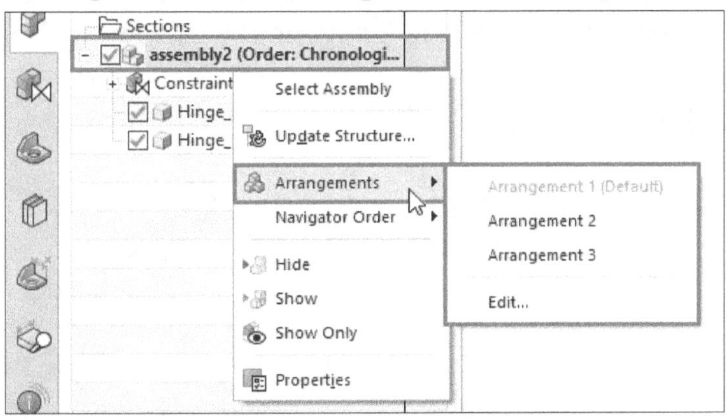

Figure-60. Arrangements displayed in Assembly Navigator

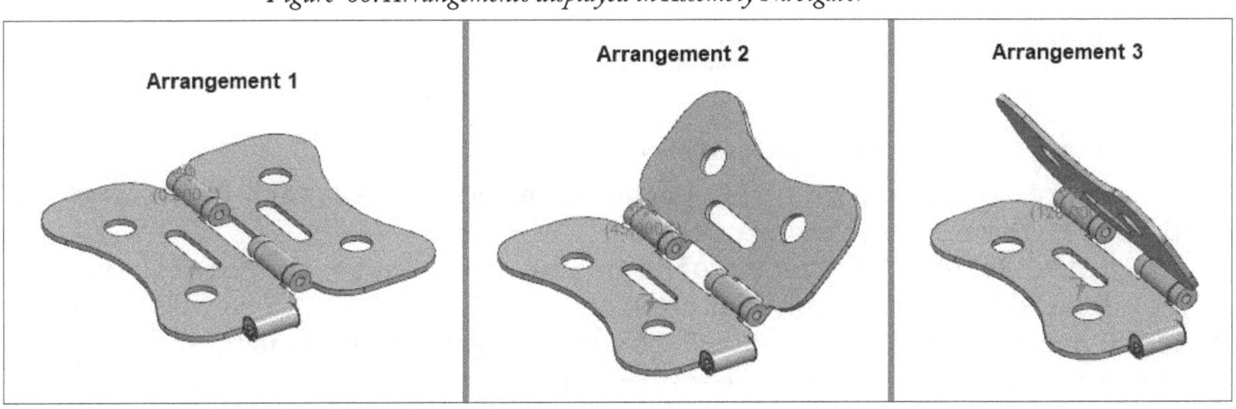

Figure-61. Modified arrangements

Pattern Component

The **Pattern Component** tool is used to copy a component into a specified pattern. The procedure to use this tool is discussed next.

- Click on the **Pattern Component** tool from **Component** group of **Assemblies** tab in the **Ribbon**. The **Pattern Component** dialog box will be displayed; refer to Figure-62.

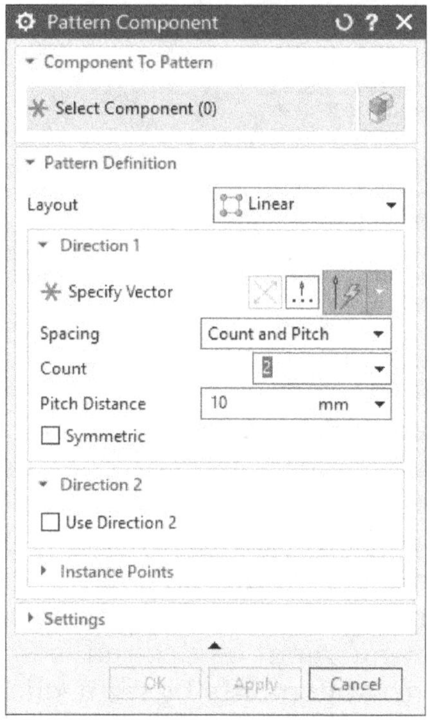

Figure-62. Pattern Component dialog box

- Select desired component from the graphics window to be patterned; refer to Figure-63.

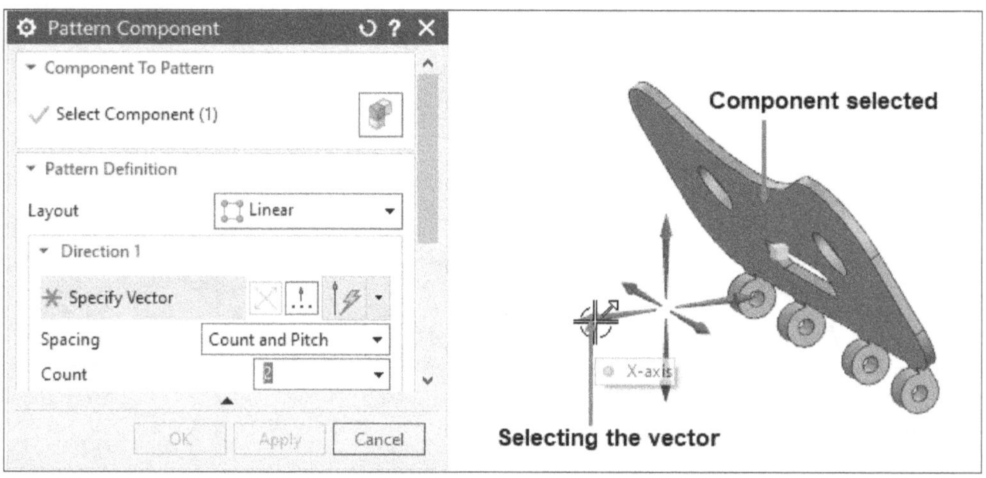

Figure-63. Component selected to be patterned

- Select desired pattern layout from **Layout** drop-down of **Pattern Definition** rollout and specify the respective parameters.
- Click on the **Select Instance Point** button from **Instance Points** rollout and select desired pattern instance points.
- Select **Dynamic Positioning** check box from **Settings** rollout to show a preview of the component geometry for each member of the pattern.

- Select **Associative** check box to create a patterned component in the **Component Patterns** folder that can be edited.
- After specifying desired parameters, click on **OK** button from the dialog box. The pattern of component will be created; refer to Figure-64.

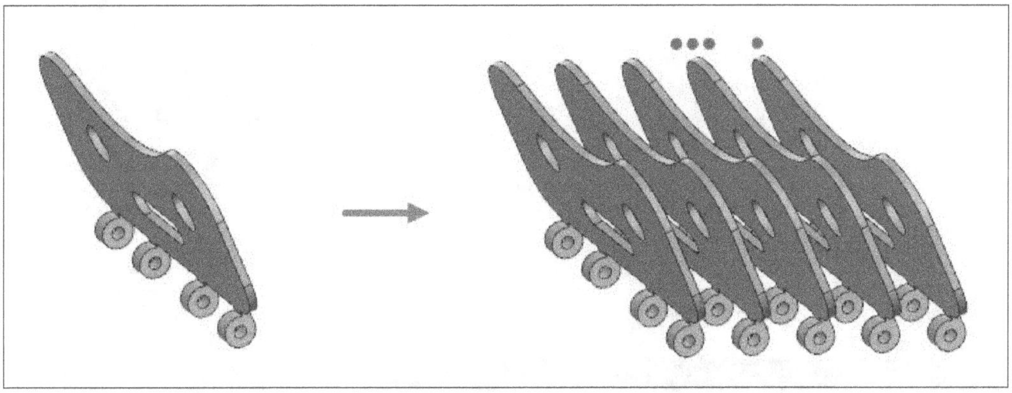

Figure-64. Pattern of component created

Mirror Assembly

The **Mirror Assembly** tool is used to create a mirrored version of the entire assembly or of selected components. The procedure to use this tool is discussed next.

- Click on the **Mirror Assembly** tool from **Component** group of **Assemblies** tab in the **Ribbon**. The **Mirror Assemblies Wizard** dialog box will be displayed; refer to Figure-65.

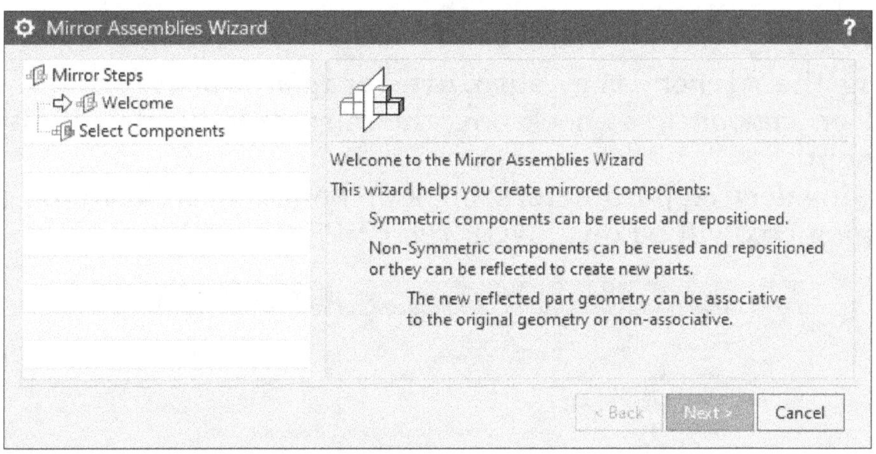

Figure-65. Mirror Assemblies Wizard dialog box

- Click on **Next** button from the dialog box, the updated dialog box will be displayed and you will be asked to select the component.
- Select desired component to be mirrored from the graphics window; refer to Figure-66.
- After selecting the component from the graphics window to be mirrored, click on **Next** button from the dialog box. The updated dialog box will be displayed and you will be asked to select the plane.
- Select desired plane from the graphics window along which the component to be mirrored; refer to Figure-67.

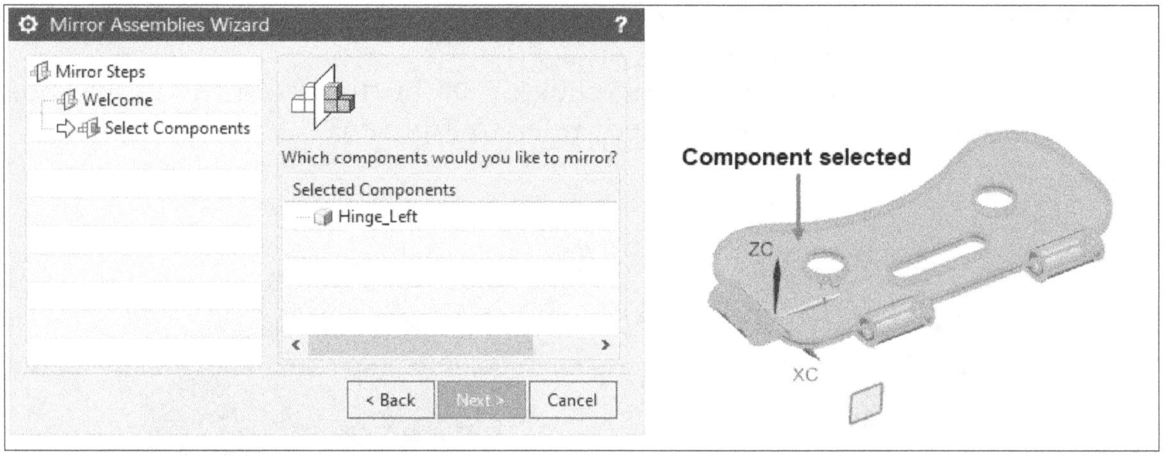

Figure-66. Component selected for mirroring

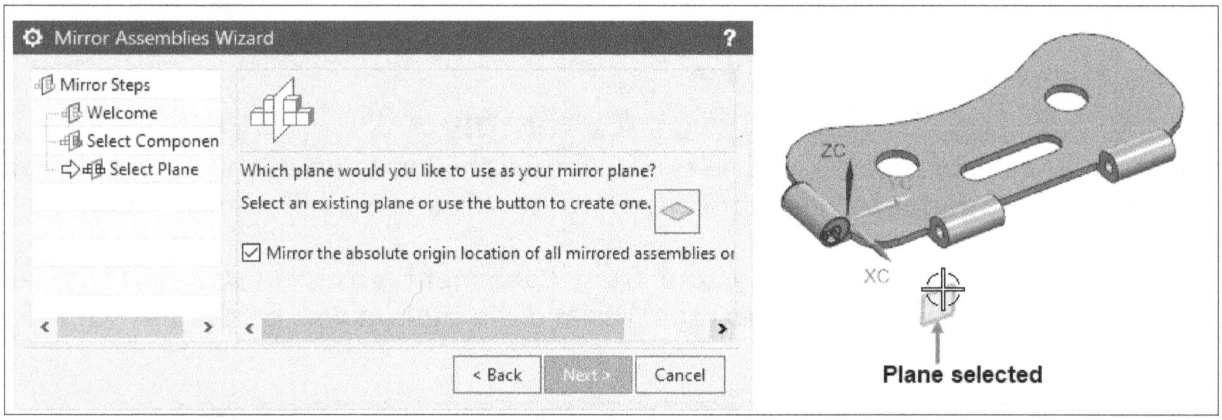

Figure-67. Plane selected

- On selecting the **Mirror the absolute origin location of all mirrored assemblies or components** check box, the mirrored objects will use the mirrored absolute origin.
- After specifying desired parameters, click on **Next** button from the dialog box. The updated dialog box will be displayed; refer to Figure-68.

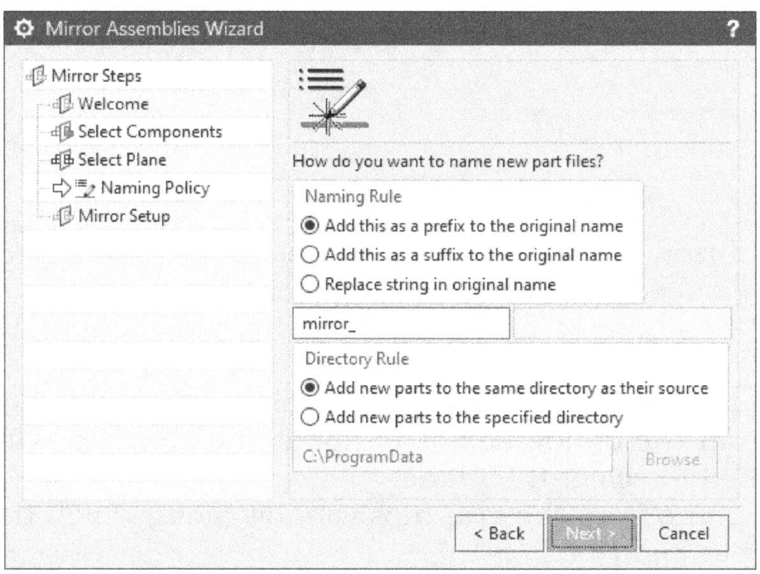

Figure-68. Updated Mirror Assemblies Wizard dialog box

- Specify desired naming policy for new parts from the **Naming Rule** area and specify desired directory for new parts from the **Directory Rule** area.

- After specifying desired parameters, click on **Next** button from the dialog box. The updated dialog box will be displayed asking you to select the type of mirror to be used; refer to Figure-69.

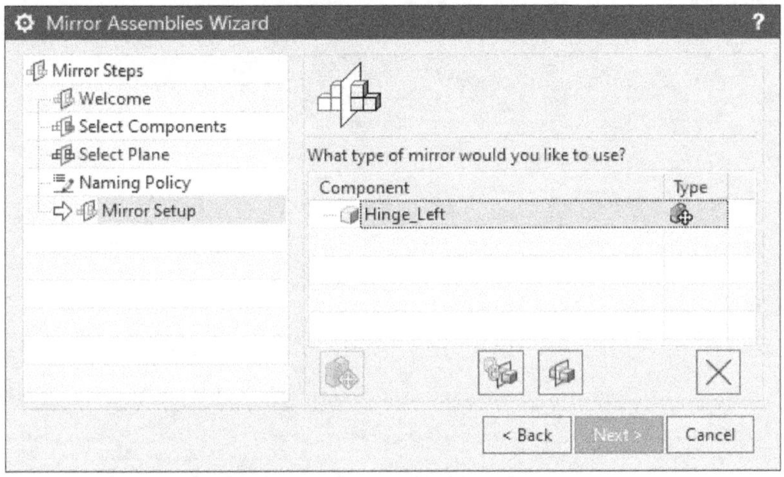

Figure-69. Updated Mirror Assemblies Wizard dialog box

- Select **Reuse and Reposition** button to create a new instance of the selected component.
- Select **Associative Mirror** button to create new part files that contain associative mirrored geometry.
- Select **Non-Associative Mirror** button to create new part files that contain non-associative mirrored geometry.
- Select **Exclude** button to exclude selected components from the mirrored assembly.
- After specifying desired parameters, click on **Next** button from the dialog box. A **Mirror Components** information box will be displayed informing about the creation of new part files; refer to Figure-70.

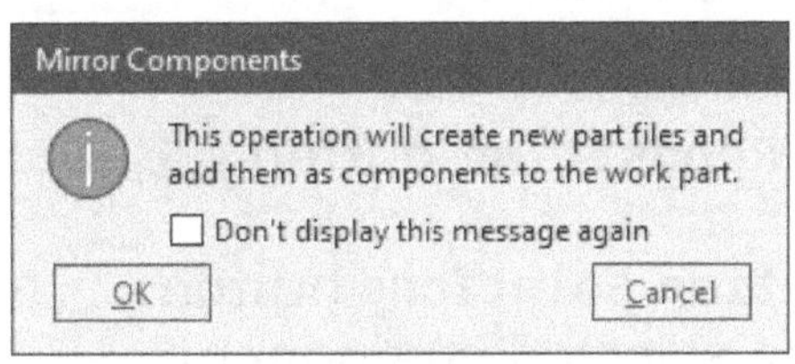

Figure-70. Mirror Components information box

- Click on **OK** button from the **Information** box. The **Information** dialog box will be displayed; refer to Figure-71.
- Click on **Close** button to close the dialog box. The updated **Mirror Assemblies Wizard** dialog box will be displayed; refer to Figure-72.

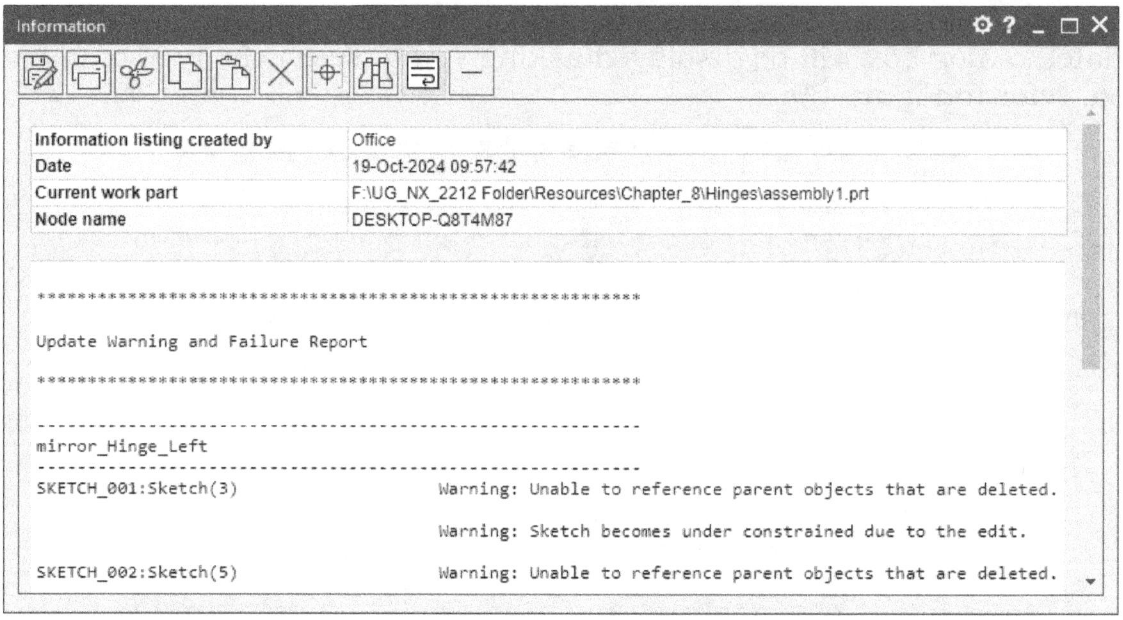

Figure-71. Information dialog box

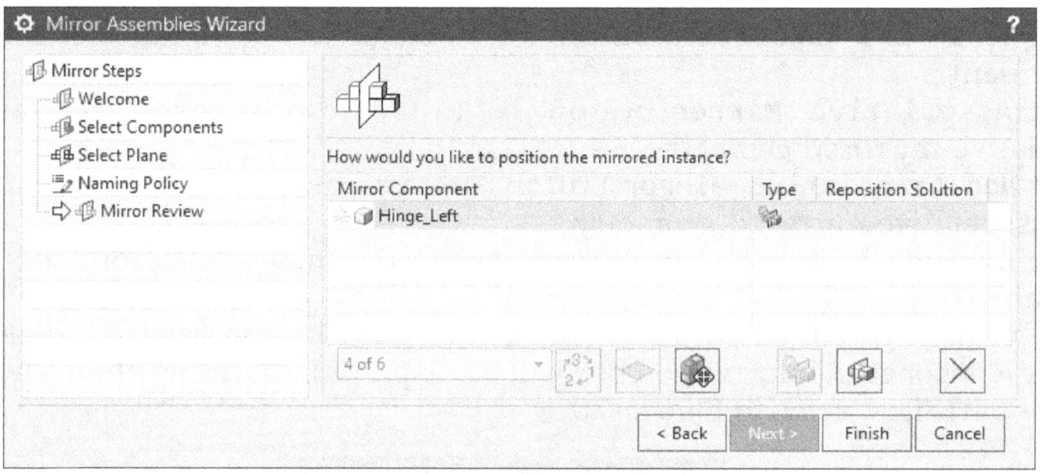

Figure-72. Updated Mirror Assemblies Wizard dialog box

- Click on the **Reuse and Reposition** button, the other options in the dialog box will be activated.
- Click on the **Cycle Reposition Solutions** button to cycle through each possible reposition solution for the selected component.
- After specifying desired parameters, click on **Finish** button from the dialog box. The mirror of assembly component will be created; refer to Figure-73.

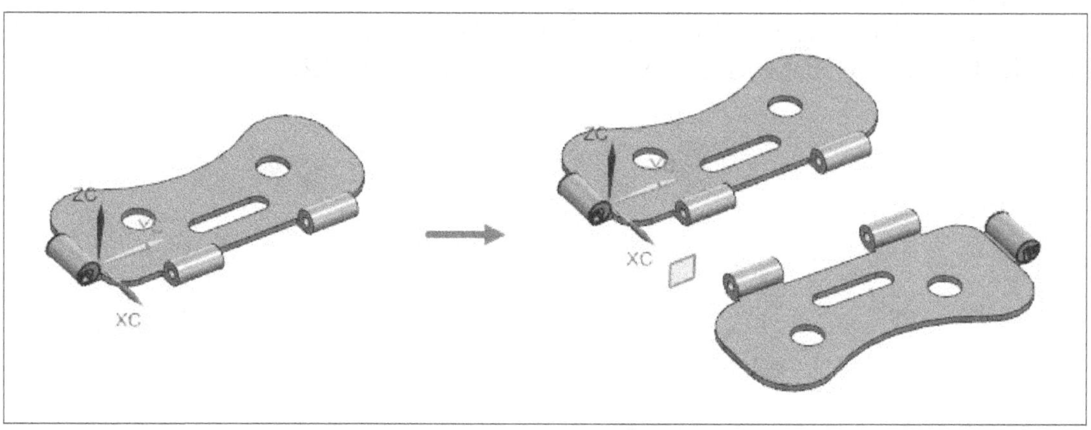

Figure-73. Component mirrored

Make Unique

The **Make Unique** tool is used to create a new part file for the selected occurrences. This tool is specially useful when there are multiple copies of same component in assembly and you want to make slight modification in one of those copies. The procedure to use this tool is discussed next.

- Click on the **Make Unique** tool from **Component** group of **Assemblies** tab in the **Ribbon**. The **Make Unique** dialog box will be displayed; refer to Figure-74.

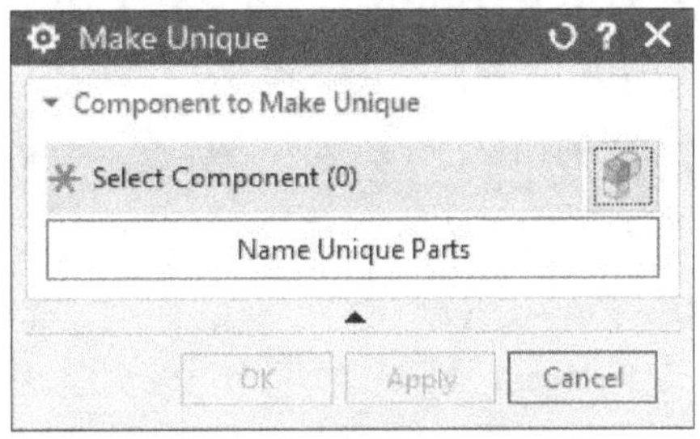

Figure-74. Make Unique dialog box

- Select desired component from the graphics window to be created unique; refer to Figure-75.

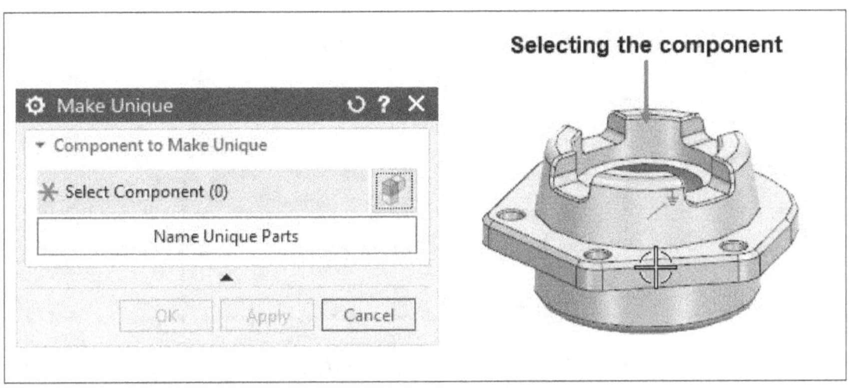

Figure-75. Selecting the component

- Click on the **Name Unique Parts** button from the dialog box, the **Name Unique Parts** dialog box will be displayed; refer to Figure-76.

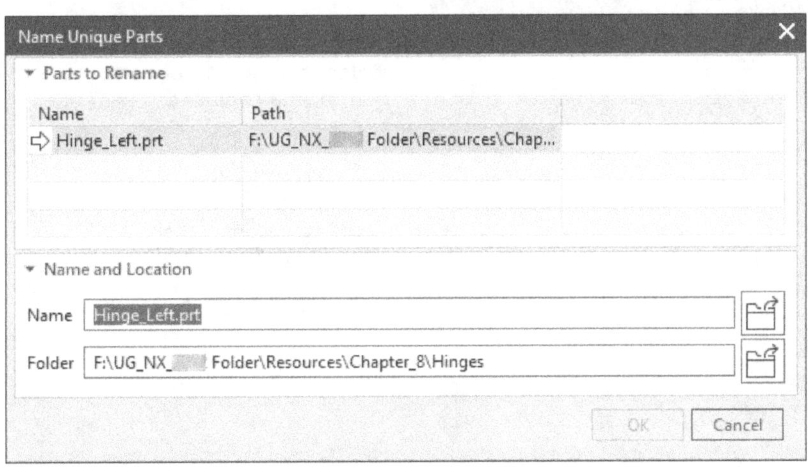

Figure-76. Name Unique Parts dialog box

- Select desired part to be renamed from **Part to Rename** rollout.
- Now, specify desired name and location of component in the **Name** and **Folder** area of **Name** and **Location** rollout, respectively.

- After specifying desired parameters, click on **OK** button from the dialog box. The component will be renamed.

Replace Component

The **Replace Component** tool is used to replace one component with another component. The procedure to use this tool is discussed next.

- Click on the **Replace Component** tool from **More** drop-down in the **Component** group of **Assemblies** tab in the **Ribbon**. The **Replace Component** dialog box will be displayed; refer to Figure-77.

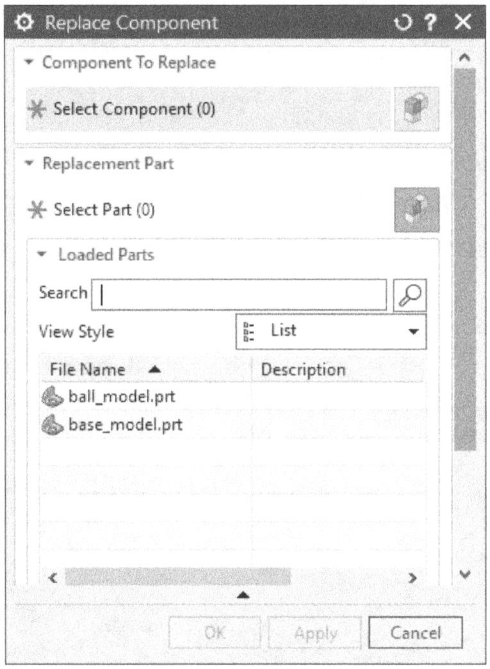

Figure-77. Replace Component dialog box

- Select desired component from the graphics window to be replaced; refer to Figure-78.

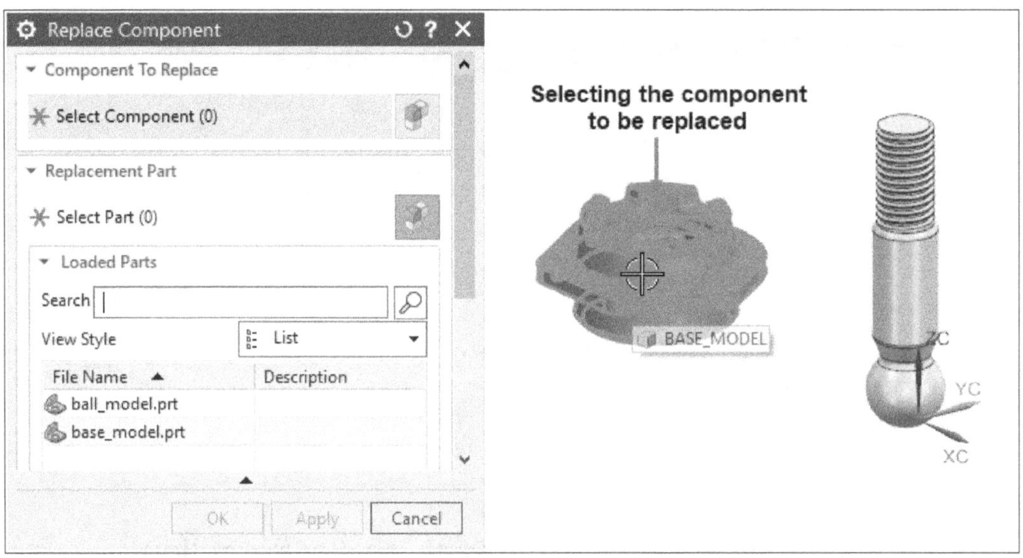

Figure-78. Selecting the component to be replaced

- Click on the **Select Part** button from **Replacement Part** rollout and select desired component from the graphics window as a replacement part; refer to Figure-79.

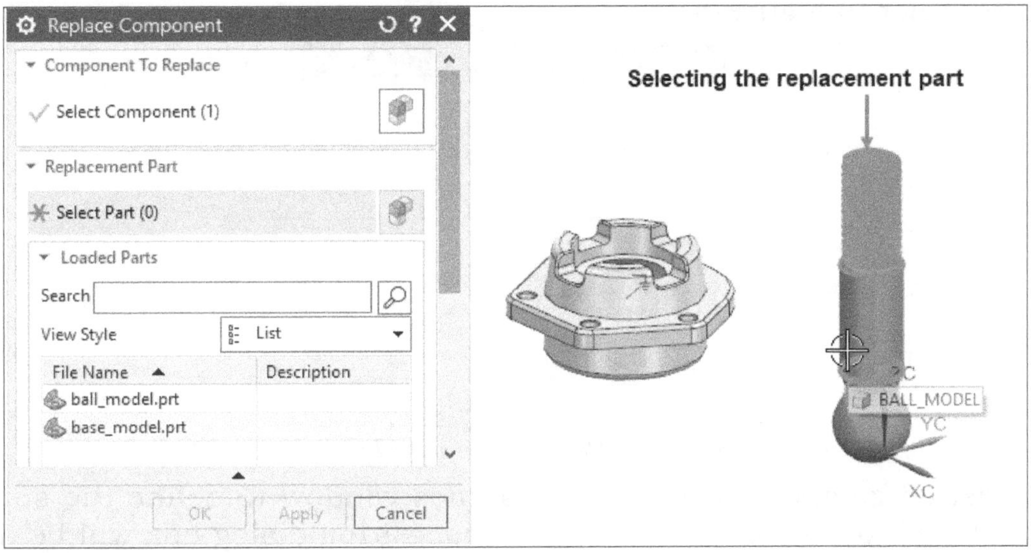

Figure-79. Selecting the replacement part

- Enter full or partial name of desired part to be searched in the **Search** box of **Loaded Parts** rollout. Select desired option from **View Style** drop-down to specify whether the loaded parts are displayed as name, tiles, or icons.
- Click on the **Open** button from **Browse** area of **Unloaded Parts** rollout to open the part to be used as replacement component.
- Select **Maintain Relationships** check box from **Settings** rollout to maintain relationships such as assembly constraints and attributes. Select **Replace All Occurrences in Assembly** check box to replace all occurrences when the component is replaced.
- Specify desired component name, reference set, and layer properties for the replacement component from **Component Properties** rollout.
- After specifying desired parameters, click on **OK** button from the dialog box. The component will be replaced; refer to Figure-80.

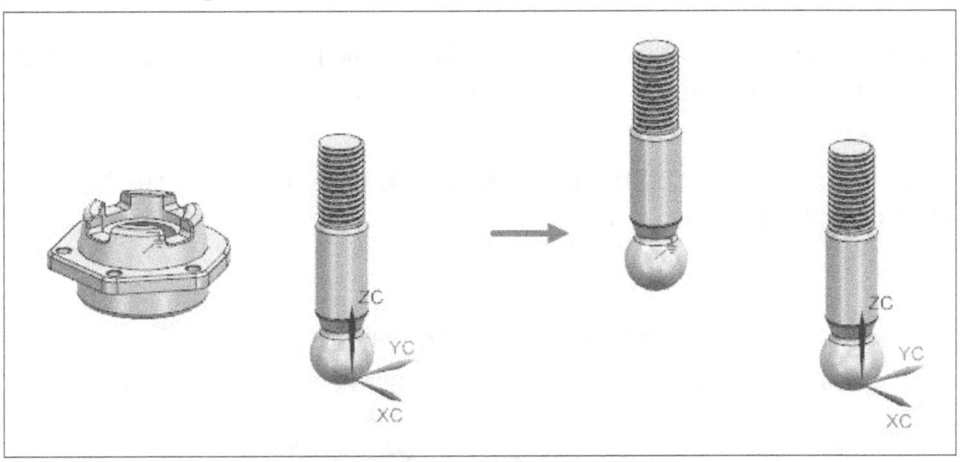

Figure-80. Component replaced

Edit Suppression State

The **Edit Suppression State** is used to define the suppression state of components in the assembly arrangement. The procedure to use this tool is discussed next.

- Click on the **Edit Suppression State** tool from **More** drop-down in the **Component** group of **Assemblies** tab in the **Ribbon**. The **Class Selection** dialog box will be displayed; refer to Figure-81.

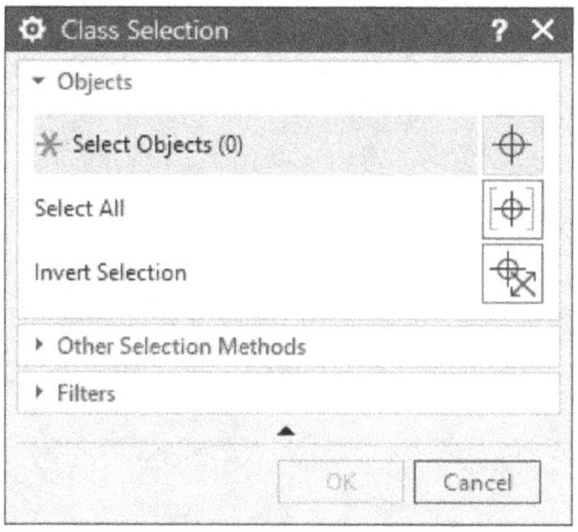

Figure-81. Class Selection dialog box

- Select desired component from the graphics window to define the suppression state and click on the **OK** button. The **Suppression** dialog box will be displayed; refer to Figure-82.

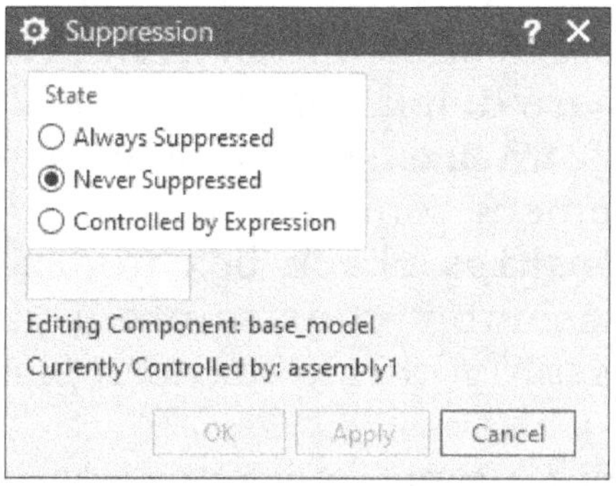

Figure-82. Suppression dialog box

- Select desired radio button from **State** area of the dialog box to define the suppression state of the selected components in the arrangements that you selected.
- After specifying desired parameters, click on **OK** button from the dialog box. The suppression state of components will be defined.

Suppress Component

The **Suppress Component** tool is used to remove a component and its children from the display.

Unsuppress Component

The **Unsuppress** tool is used to display a previously suppressed component.

Reference Sets

The **Reference Sets** tool is used to create or edit reference sets which control the amount of data that is loaded from each component and viewed in the context of an assembly. The procedure to use this tool is discussed next.

- Click on the **Reference Sets** tool from **Context** group of **Assemblies** tab in the **Ribbon**. The **Reference Sets** dialog box will be displayed; refer to Figure-83.

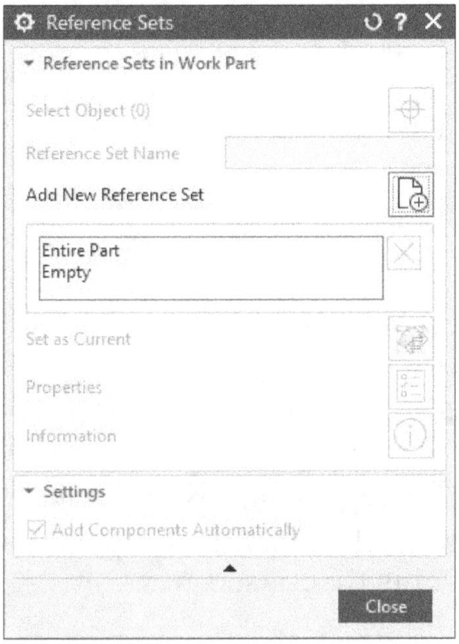

Figure-83. Reference Sets dialog box

- Select desired reference set from the list in the dialog box or click on the **Add New Reference Set** button from **Reference Sets in Work Part** rollout, a new reference set will be added in the list and the object will be selected in the graphics window. Specify desired name of reference set in the **Reference Set Name** edit box.
- Click on the **Set as Current** button to set the selected reference set as the current reference set. Click on the **Properties** button, the **Reference Set Properties** dialog box will be displayed to set desired properties of reference set. Click on the **Information** button, the **Information** window will be displayed displaying information about the selected reference set including reference set name, number of member components, and object types.
- Select **Add Components Automatically** check box from **Settings** rollout to specify whether newly-created components are automatically added to the highlighted reference set.
- After specifying desired parameters, click on **Close** button from the dialog box. The reference set will be created.

Replace Reference Set

The **Replace Reference Set** tool is used to choose a reference set to display for selected components. The procedure to use this tool is discussed next.

- Click on the **Replace Reference Set** tool from **More** drop-down in the **Context** group of **Assemblies** tab in the **Ribbon**. The **Class Selection** dialog box will be displayed as discussed earlier asking you to select the object.
- Select desired component from the graphics window, the **Replace Reference Set** dialog box will be displayed; refer to Figure-84.

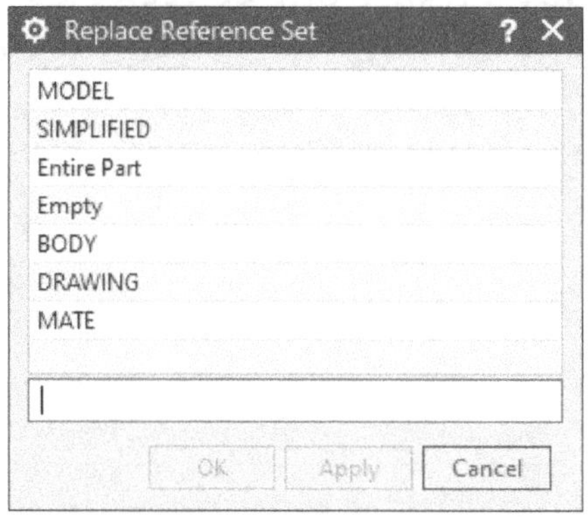

Figure-84. Replace Reference Set dialog box

- Select desired component from the list in the dialog box to be replaced and click on the **OK** button. The reference set will be replaced.

Find Components

The **Find Components** tool is used to locate components using any global property. The procedure to use this tool is discussed next.

- Click on the **Find Components** tool from **More** drop-down in the **Context** group of **Assemblies** tab in the **Ribbon**. The **Find Components** dialog box will be displayed; refer to Figure-85.

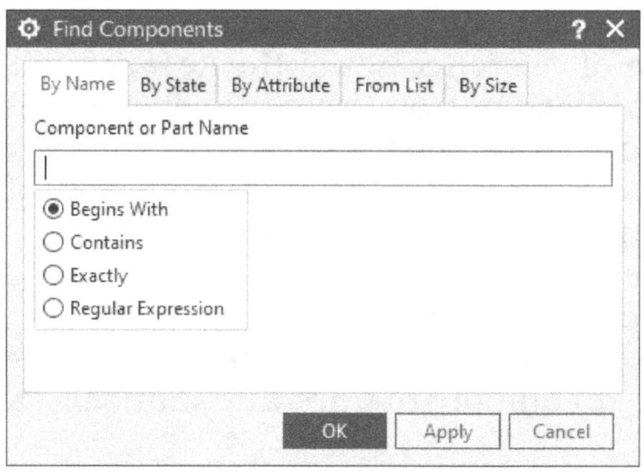

Figure-85. Find Components dialog box

- Search desired component by all or part of their names, by specified state of component like loaded, visible, or work part, by specified attribute, by the size of the component, or from the list of loaded or unloaded components.
- After specifying desired parameters, click on **OK** button from the dialog box. The model will be located.

Hide Components in View

The **Hide Components in View** tool is used to hide selected components in the view. The procedure to use this tool is discussed next.

- Click on the **Hide Components in View** tool from **More** drop-down in the **Context** group of **Assemblies** tab in the **Ribbon**. The **Hide Components in View** dialog box will be displayed; refer to Figure-86.

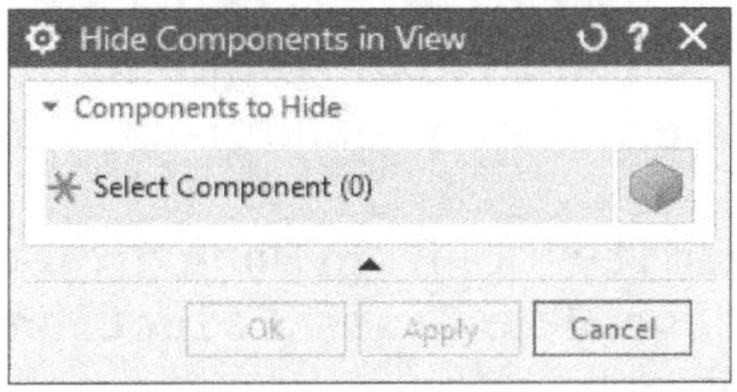

Figure-86. Hide Components in View dialog box

- Select desired component from the graphics window to be hidden; refer to Figure-87 and click on the **OK** button. The component will be hidden.

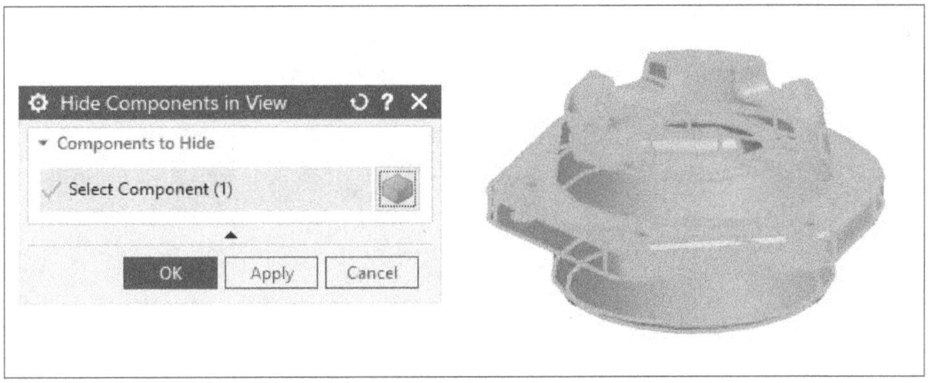

Figure-87. Component selected to be hidden

Show Components in View

The **Show Components in View** tool is used to show hidden components in the view. The procedure to use this tool is discussed next.

- Click on the **Show Components in View** tool from **More** drop-down in the **Context** group of **Assemblies** tab in the **Ribbon**. The **Show Components in View** dialog box will be displayed; refer to Figure-88.

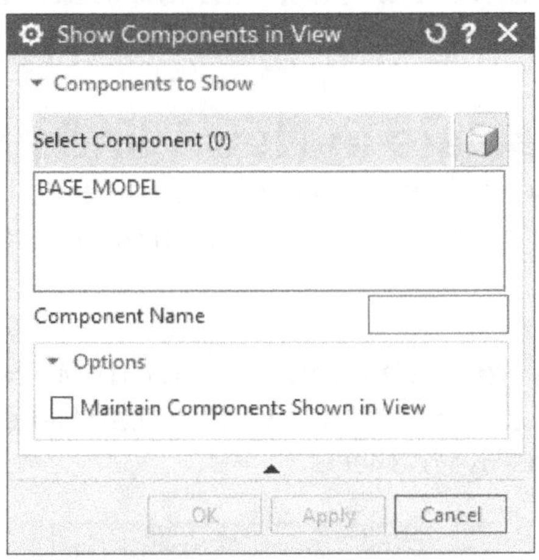

Figure-88. Show Components in View dialog box

- Select desired hidden component from the list in the dialog box to be shown.
- Specify desired name of component in the **Component Name** edit box.
- Select **Maintain Components Shown in View** check box from **Options** rollout to maintain the list of visible components shown in a view when new components are added to an assembly.
- After specifying desired parameters, click on **OK** button from the dialog box. The hidden components will be shown.

Open by Proximity

The **Open by Proximity** tool is used to load components which are within a specified distance of a selected component. The procedure to use this tool is discussed next.

- Click on the **Open by Proximity** tool from **More** drop-down in the **Context** group of **Assemblies** tab in the **Ribbon**. The **Class Selection** dialog box will be displayed asking you to select the object.
- Select desired component from the graphics window to be loaded and click on the **OK** button. The **Open by Proximity** dialog box will be displayed; refer to Figure-89.

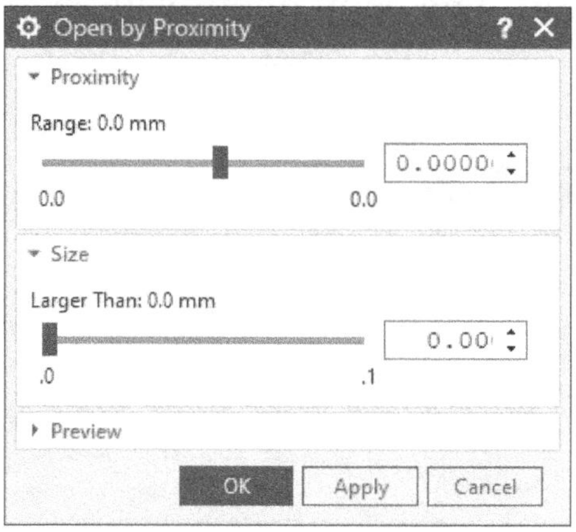

Figure-89. Open by Proximity dialog box

- Specify desired range of component by sliding the **Range** slider from **Proximity** rollout or specify desired value in the edit box.
- Specify desired size of component to be opened by sliding the **Larger Than** slider from **Size** rollout or specify desired value in the edit box. Only components that are larger than this value will be opened.
- Select **Preview** check box from **Preview** rollout to draw bounding boxes to represent the components that are loaded after clicking **OK** button.
- After specifying the parameters, click on **OK** button from the dialog box. The components will be loaded.

Isolate in New Window

The **Isolate in New Window** tool is used to show just the selected components in a new window, hiding all other components. The procedure to use this tool is discussed next.

- Click on the **Isolate in New Window** tool from **More** drop-down in the **Context** group of **Assemblies** tab in the **Ribbon**. The **Isolate in New Window** dialog box will be displayed; refer to Figure-90.

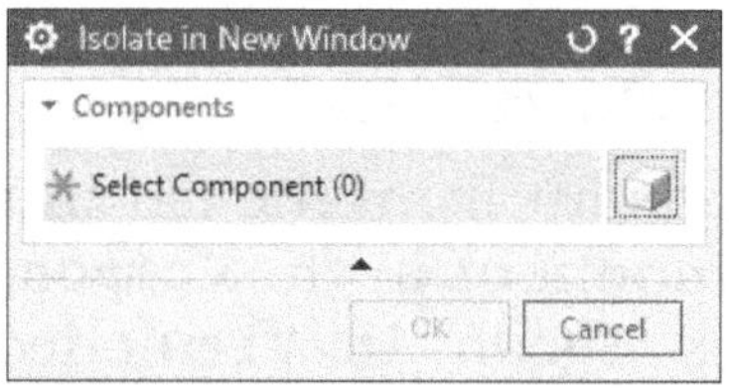

Figure-90. Isolate in New Window dialog box

- Select desired component from the graphics window to be loaded in a new window and click on the **OK** button. The selected component will be displayed in a new window; refer to Figure-91.

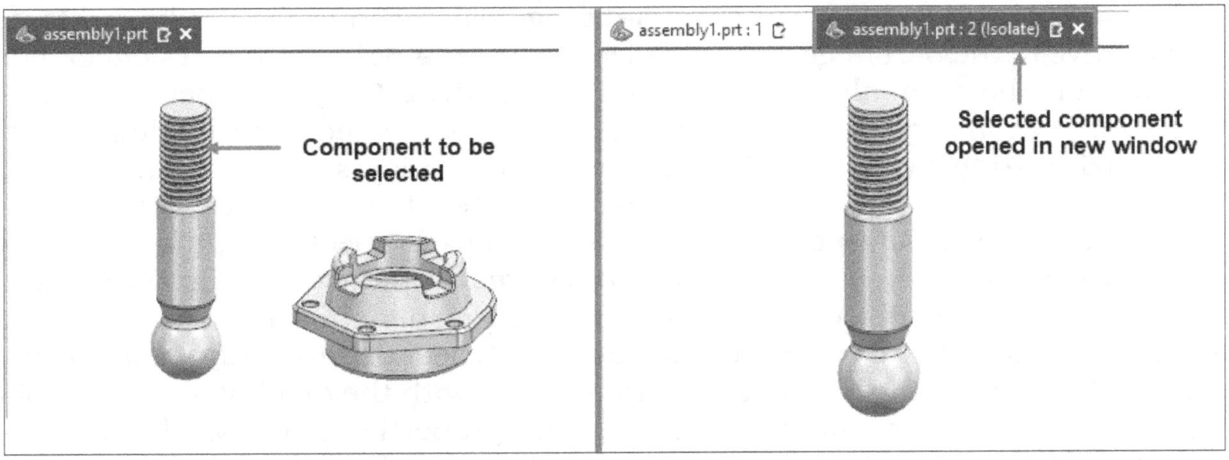

Figure-91. Selected component opened in new window

Show Product Outline

The **Show Product Outline** tool is used to show an outline of the overall assembly.

Save Context

The **Save Context** tool is used to store the context, i.e. the work part and component visibility.

Restore Context

The **Restore Context** tool is used to restore the previously stored context, i.e. work part and component visibility.

Define Product Outline

The **Define Product Outline** tool is used to define which objects appear in a product outline, which is a set of geometry that gives a hint of the overall size and shape of an assembly.

WAVE Geometry Linker

The **WAVE Geometry Linker** tool is used to copy geometry from other parts in the assembly into the work part. The procedure to use this tool is discussed next.

- Click on the **WAVE Geometry Linker** tool from **Interpart Links** group of **Assemblies** tab in the **Ribbon**. The **WAVE Geometry Linker** dialog box will be displayed; refer to Figure-92.

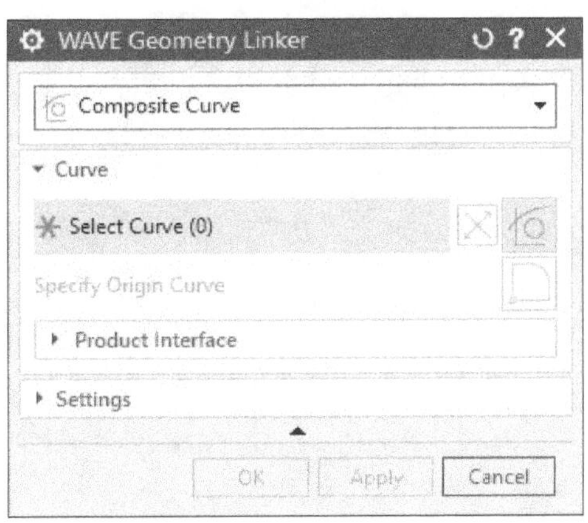

Figure-92. WAVE Geometry Linker dialog box

- Select **Associative** check box from **Settings** rollout to make the linked feature associative to the parent geometry. Select **Draw Line Between Points** check box to create a line between all selected points. Select **Hide Original** check box to hide the source geometry after the linked geometry is created. Specify desired value in the **CSYS Display Scale** edit box to set the display scale for a linked Datum CSYS. Select **Allow Self-intersection** check box to select curves that are self-intersecting. Select **Advanced Curve Fit** check box to specify method, degree, and segments. Select desired option from **Join Curves** drop-down to specify whether the curves in the linked object are joined into a single spline. Specify desired distance tolerance in the **Distance Tolerance** edit box. Select **Use Display Properties of Parent Part** check box to create the linked data with the display properties of the parent part instead of inheriting the display properties of the work part. Select **Fix at Current Timestamp** check box to set the location of the linked feature in the **Part Navigator** feature creation list. Select **Make Context-independent** check box to create the content independent links from a source part to a work part.
- Select desired type of geometry from drop-down in the dialog box and select desired respective geometry to be linked from the graphics window; refer to Figure-93.

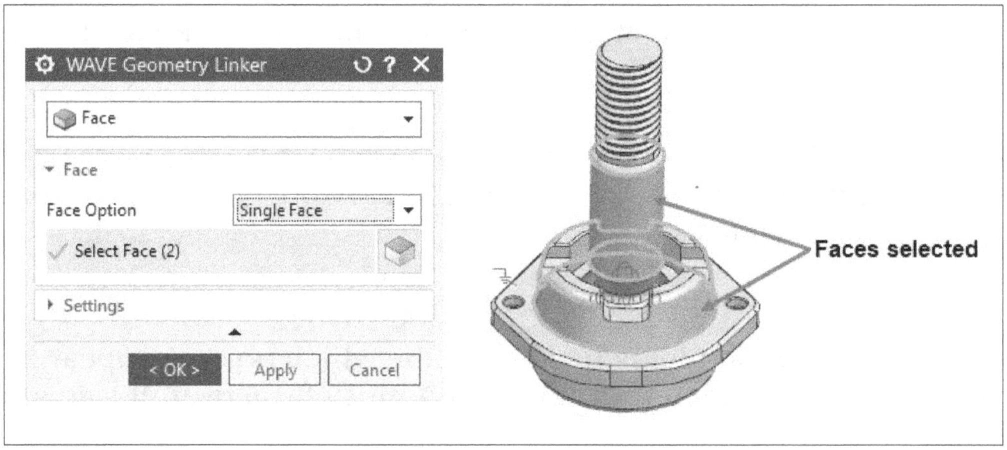

Figure-93. Faces selected to be linked

- After specifying desired parameters, click on **OK** button from the dialog box. The geometry will be linked to current work part; refer to Figure-94.

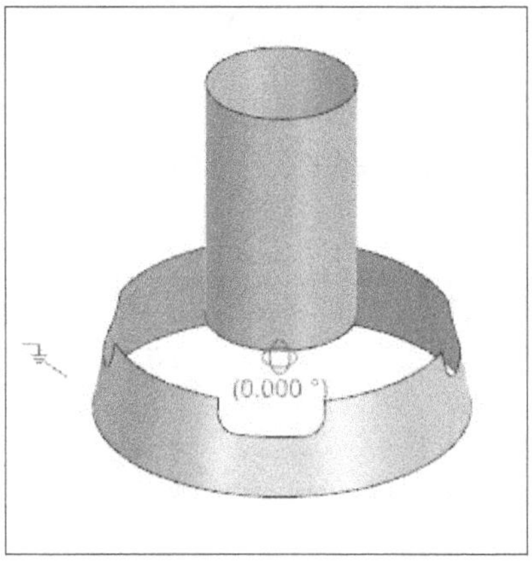

Figure-94. Linked geometry displayed

- Consider an assembly as shown in Figure-95 in which you want to create hole in hexagonal part with diameter linked to shaft diameter. In this case, you will open the assembly of models and make the part to be modified by wave link geometry (to be cut for hole creation) as work part using right-click shortcut menu; refer to Figure-96. Then, you can use **WAVE Geometry Linker** tool to reference part for creating hole feature like subtracting other part from current one.

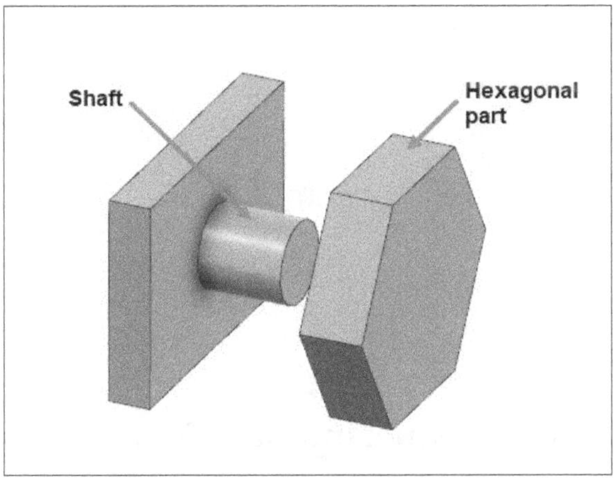

Figure-95. Assembly example

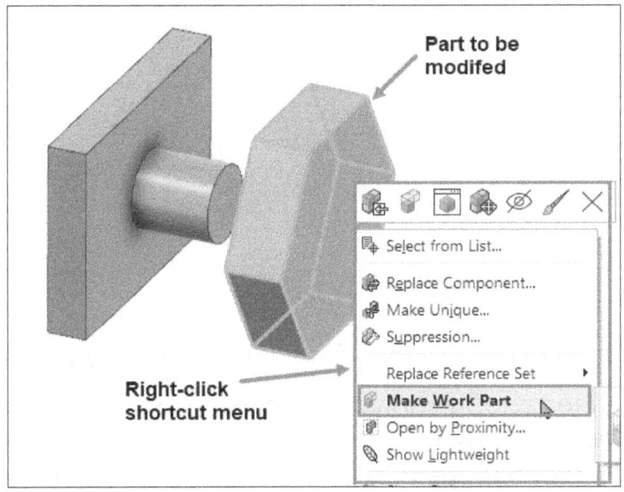

Figure-96. Make Work Part option

Video QR Code:

https://www.youtube.com/watch?v=U6c3hd1D pk

Associativity Manager

The **Associativity Manager** tool allows updating of individual parts, displays outdated parts, and controls updated inter-part linkages. This tool is not available in educational version of software.

Product Interface

The **Product Interface** tool is used to define geometry and expressions that other parts can reference/sets referencing rules, and lists parts that reference the work part. The procedure to use this tool is discussed next.

- Click on the **Product Interface** tool from **More** drop-down in the **Interpart Links** group of **Assemblies** tab in the **Ribbon**. The **Product Interface** dialog box will be displayed; refer to Figure-97.

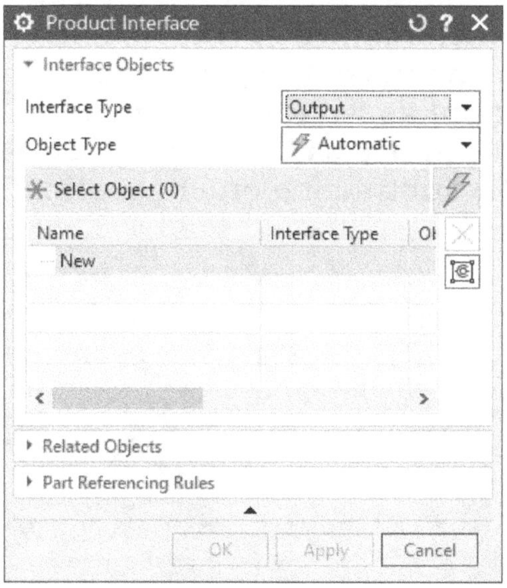

Figure-97. Product Interface dialog box

- Select desired type of interface to be selected as a product interface from **Interface Type** drop-down.
- Select desired type of object to be selected as a product interface from **Object Type** drop-down.
- Click on the **Select Object** button from **Interface Objects** rollout and select desired geometry to be created as product interface for the part file. The selected geometry will be displayed in the list box of **Interface Objects** rollout; refer to Figure-98.

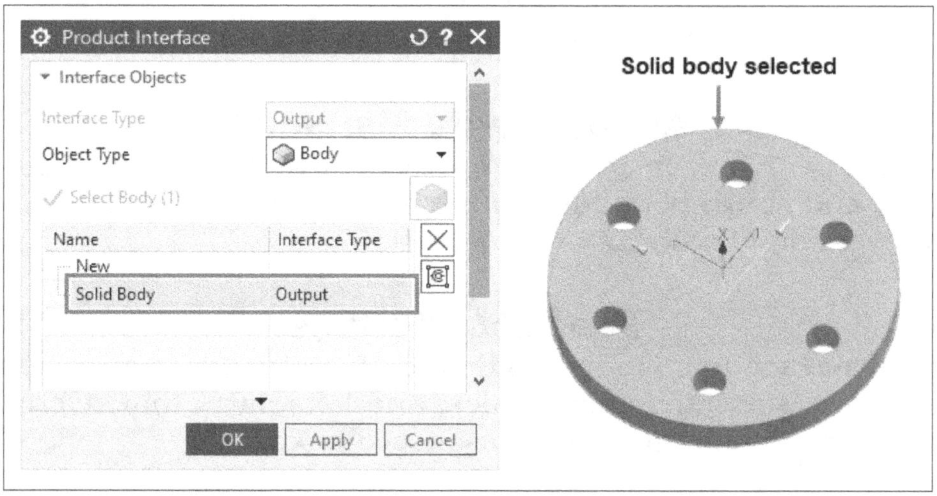

Figure-98. Solid body selected as product interface

- The **Related Objects** rollout displays the list of PMI objects and expressions related to the product interface.
- Select desired option from **Interpart Linking** drop-down of **Part Referencing Rules** rollout to allow linking to any geometry or expression, encourage linking to interface objects, or restrict linking to interface objects only.
- Similarly, select desired option from **Assembly Constraints** drop-down to allow constraints to any geometry or expression, encourage linking to interface objects, or restrict constraining to interface objects only.

- After specifying desired parameters, click on **OK** button from the dialog box. The selected object will be created as product interface; refer to Figure-99.

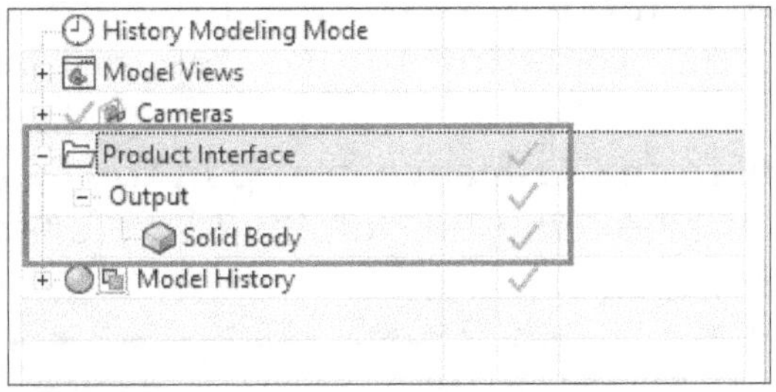

Figure-99. Product interface created

WAVE Interface Linker

The **WAVE Interface Linker** tool is used to copy geometry from another part into current work part when working with assemblies. The procedure to use this tool is same as discussed for **Wave Geometry Linker** tool. The only difference is that in this case, you can select only geometries are already defined using **Product Interface** tool.

WAVE PMI Linker

The **WAVE PMI Linker** tool is used to create an associative copy of a PMI object in one part based on a PMI object in another part, so that other applications, such as Manufacturing, can reference the PMI. The procedure to use this tool is same as discussed earlier for **Wave Geometry Linker** tool but the other part in assembly must have PMI annotations applied so that it can be linked in current work part.

Synchronize Links

The **Synchronize Links** tool is used to update linked features, features that are dependent on the linked features, and linked expressions to match in their parent features. The procedure to use this tool is discussed next.

- Click on the **Synchronize Links** tool from **More** drop-down in the **Interpart Links** group of **Assemblies** tab in the **Ribbon**. The **Synchronize Links** dialog box will be displayed; refer to Figure-100.

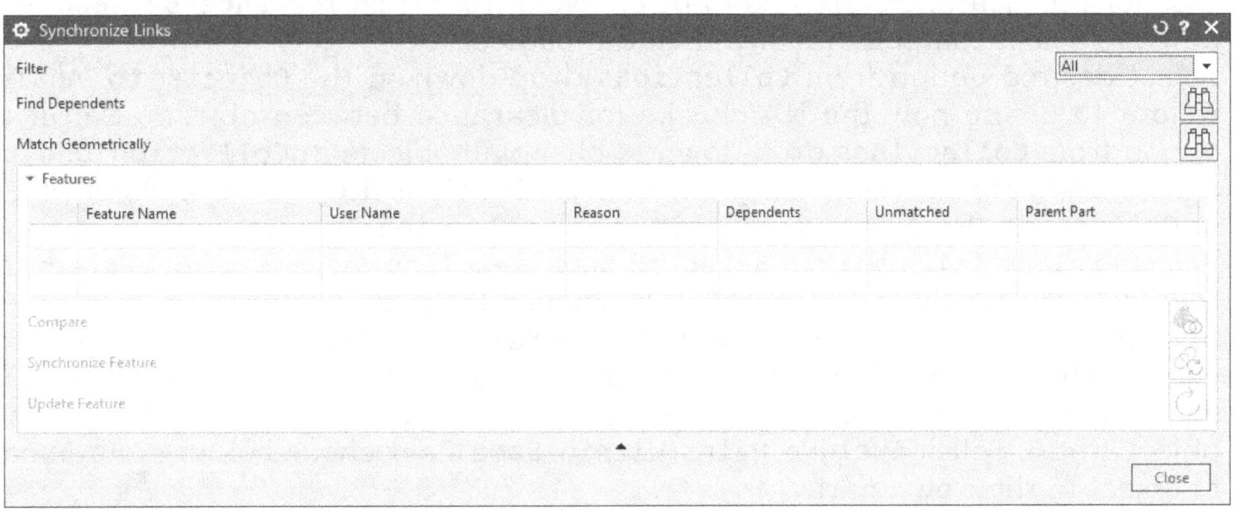

Figure-100. Synchronize Links dialog box

New Set

The **New Set** tool is used to create a new clearance set. The clearance set is a set of rules to check whether two components in assembly are interfering or have enough clearance between them. The procedure to use this tool is discussed next.

- Click on the **New Set** tool from **Clearance** group in the **Assemblies** tab of the **Ribbon**. The **Clearance Set** dialog box will be displayed; refer to Figure-101.

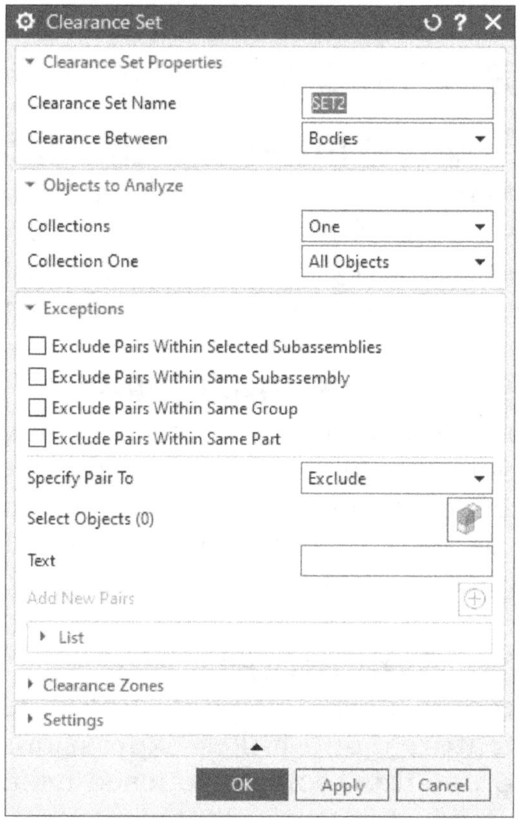

Figure-101. Clearance Set dialog box

- Specify desired name to the clearance analysis set to be created in the **Clearance Set Name** edit box of **Clearance Set Properties** rollout. Select desired selection type for the clearance analysis to be checked from the **Clearance Between** drop-down to select components or individual bodies.
- Select desired option from **Collections** drop-down in the **Objects to Analyze** rollout to define how the NX checks for clearance between objects. Select **One** option from **Collections** drop-down to check all objects in **Collection One** area against each other. Select **Two** option from **Collections** drop-down to check objects in **Collection One** area against objects in **Collection Two** area.
- Select **Exclude Pairs Within Selected Subassemblies** check box from **Exceptions** rollout to select a unit subassembly from which the pairs of object can be excluded from the analysis. Select **Exclude Pairs Within Same Subassembly** check box to exclude the pairs of object within the same first level subassembly. Select **Exclude Pairs Within Same Group** check box to exclude pairs of object within the own object group. Select **Exclude Pairs Within Same Part** check box to exclude pairs of object in their own part.
- Select desired option from **Specify Pair To** drop-down to exclude or include a pair of objects from the clearance analysis.

- Click on the **Select Objects** button to select components or bodies for the pair.
- Specify desired description for the pair of objects in the **Text** edit box.
- Click on the **Add New Pairs** button to add pair of objects for the analysis.
- The **List** area displays the exceptions to be created for the clearance analysis.
- Specify desired clearance distance in the **Default Clearance Zone** edit box to be applied to every object in the analysis.
- Select desired option from **Specify Zone** drop-down to specify whether the clearance zone is between selected pairs of objects or around selected objects.
- Specify desired description for the clearance zone in the **Name** edit box.
- Specify desired clearance distance for the analysis in the **Distance** edit box.
- Click on the **Select Objects** button to select bodies or components to define the zone.
- Click on the **Add New Clearance Zone** button to add new zones in the clearance analysis.
- The **List** area displays the clearance zones in the clearance set.
- Click on the **Report Effective Zones Between Pairs** button or **Report Zones Around Objects** button, the **Class Selection** dialog box will be displayed to select the objects used to create a report displaying the clearance analysis zone defined for a specific pair of objects or specific object, respectively.
- Select **Save Interference Geometry** check box from **Interference Geometry** rollout in the **Settings** rollout to save the interference geometry generated by the clearance analysis.
- Specify desired number of layer(s) and interference color to save the interference geometry in the **Layer** edit box and **Interference** area, respectively.
- Select desired option from **Calculate Using** drop-down to calculate the clearance analysis using either exact or lightweight geometry.
- Select **Calculate Penetration Depth** check box to add a linear measurement of the amount of interference between bodies or components to the clearance analysis.
- Select **Perform Analysis on OK** check box to perform the clearance analysis on clicking the **OK** button.
- After specifying desired parameters, click on **OK** button from the dialog box. The clearance analysis will be performed.

Perform Analysis

The **Perform Analysis** tool is used to generate a summary of the current clearance set. The procedure to use this tool is discussed next.

- Click on the **Perform Analysis** tool from **Clearance** group in the **Assemblies** tab of the **Ribbon**. The **Set Clearance Set** dialog box will be displayed; refer to Figure-102.

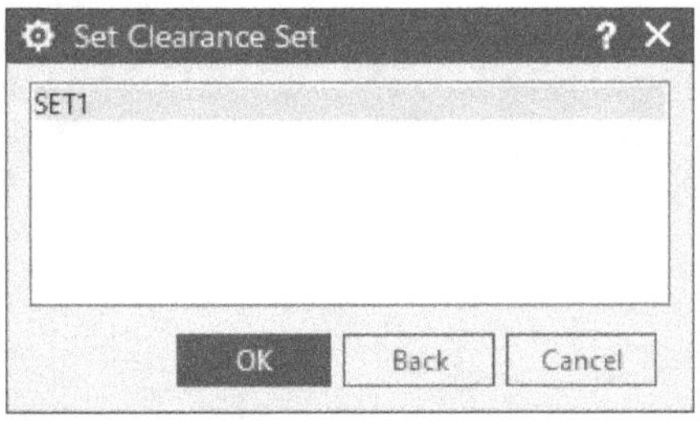

Figure-102. Set Clearance Set dialog box

- Select desired set created from the dialog box and click on the **OK** button. The **Clearance Browser** window will be displayed; refer to Figure-103.

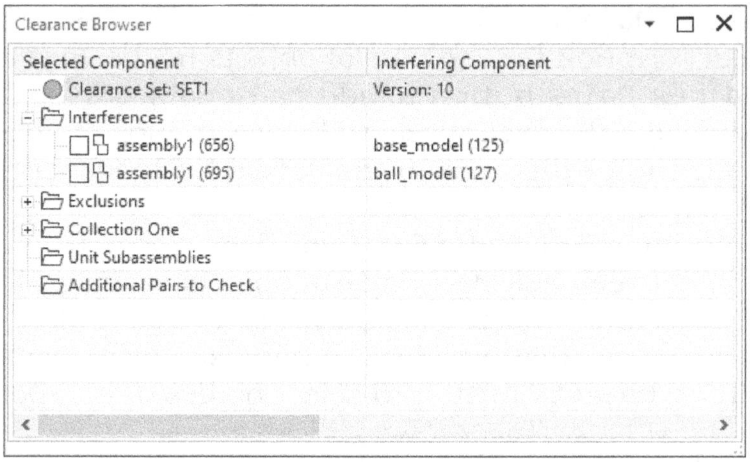

Figure-103. Clearance Browser dialog box

- The **Clearance Browser** window displays the results of a clearance analysis such as active clearance set, interfering components, type of new or existing interference, list of ignored interfering pairs, the list of unit subassemblies, etc.

Set

The **Set** tool is used to create a new set and activate an existing set to analyze, modify, copy, or delete. The procedure to use this tool is same as discussed for **New Set** tool.

Edit Set

The **Edit Set** tool is used to edit the existing set. On clicking this tool, the **Clearance Set** dialog box will be displayed which have been discussed earlier in this chapter.

Batch Analysis

The **Batch Analysis** tool is used to perform clearance analysis on a large assembly and save the results in one or more report files. The procedure to use this tool is discussed next.

- Click on the **Batch Analysis** tool from **More** drop-down in the **Clearance** group of **Assemblies** tab in the **Ribbon**. The **Batch Clearance Analysis** dialog box will be displayed; refer to Figure-104.

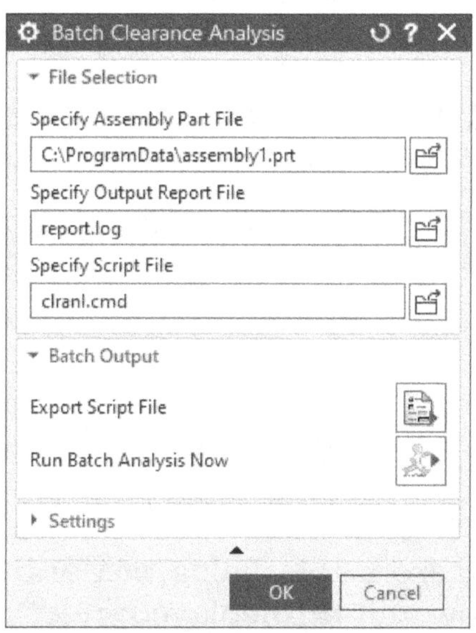

Figure-104. Batch Clearance Analysis dialog box

- Click on the button from **Specify Assembly Part File** area in the **File Selection** rollout, the **Assembly Part FileName** dialog box will be displayed to select the part file on which the analysis to be run.
- Click on the button from **Specify Output Report File** area, the **Output Filename** dialog box will be displayed to specify the name and the directory location for the report file.
- Click on the button from **Specify Script File** area, the **Script Filename** dialog box will be displayed to specify the name and the directory location for the report file.
- Click on the **Export Script File** button from **Batch Output** rollout to create a script to run the batch job.
- Click on the **Run Batch Analysis Now** button to run the batch job when selected. The **Batch Clearance Analysis** box will be displayed asking you to submit the clearance analysis batch job; refer to Figure-105.

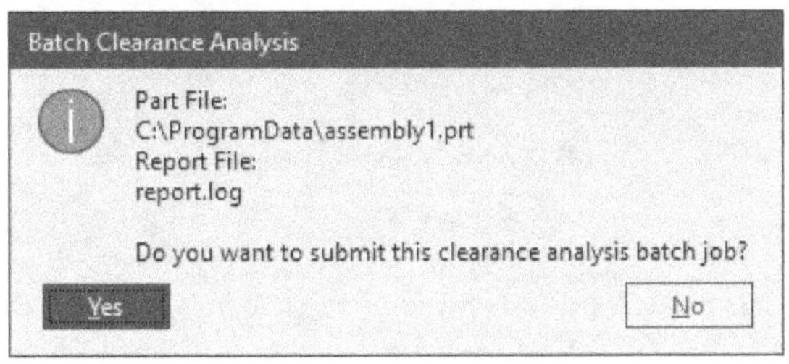

Figure-105. Batch Clearance Analysis box

- Click on the **Yes** button from the box displayed, the updated box will be displayed asking you to save the part or not.
- Click on the **Yes** button from the dialog box, a message will be displayed in the box showing that the clearance analysis batch job has been submitted.
- Select **Send Mail When Complete** check box from **Settings** rollout to send an email notification when the analysis is completed.
- Select the **Divide Assembly into Zones** check box to divide the assembly into smaller zones.
- After specifying desired parameters, click on **OK** button from the dialog box. The clearance analysis will be performed.

Delete

On clicking **Delete** tool from **More** drop-down in the **Clearance** group of **Assemblies** tab in the **Ribbon**. The **Delete Clearance Sets** dialog box will be displayed; refer to Figure-106. Select desired set to be deleted from **Sets** rollout of the dialog box and click on the **OK** button. The set will be deleted.

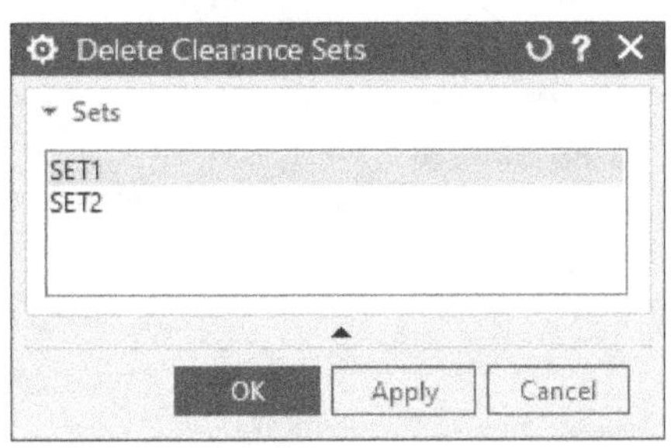

Figure-106. Delete Clearance Sets dialog box

Copy

On clicking **Copy** tool from **More** drop-down in the **Clearance** group of **Assemblies** tab in the **Ribbon**. The **Clearance Set** dialog box will be displayed which have been discussed earlier in this chapter.

Report

On clicking **Report** tool from **More** drop-down in the **Clearance** group of **Assemblies** tab in the **Ribbon**. The **Information** window will be displayed to view the general or specific information for the selected objects, expressions, parts, layers, and so on; refer to Figure-107.

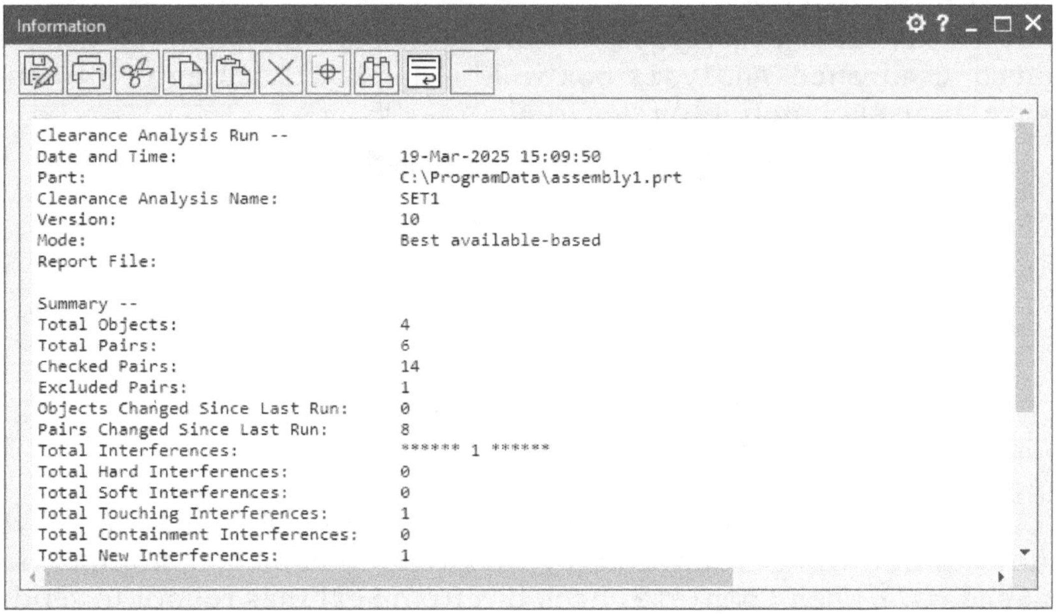

Figure-107. Information window

Study Clearance Violations

The **Study Clearance Violations** tool is used to illustrate clearance violations for soft interferences. It displays soft interferences in lines or pair points format. The procedure to use this tool is discussed next.

- Click on the **Study Clearance Violations** tool from **More** drop-down in the **Clearance** group of **Assemblies** tab in the **Ribbon**. The **Study Clearance Violations** dialog box will be displayed; refer to Figure-108.

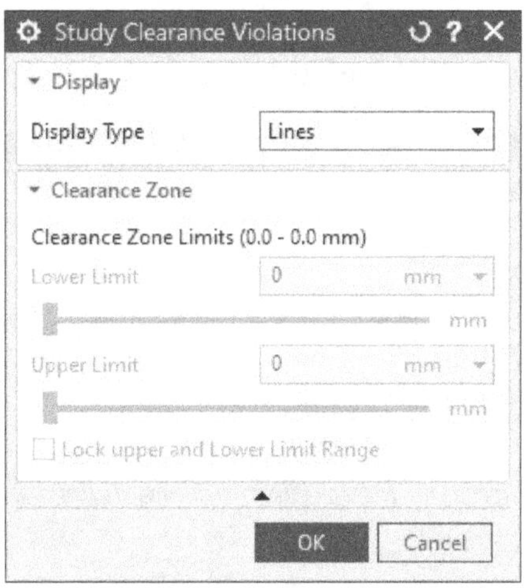

Figure-108. Study Clearance Violations dialog box

- Select desired type of display from **Display Type** drop-down in the **Display** rollout to display the soft interferences in the lines or points format.
- Specify desired parameters in the **Clearance Zone** rollout to modify the components to resolve a clearance issue.
- After specifying desired parameters, click on **OK** button from the dialog box.

Store Component Visibility

The **Store Component Visibility** tool is used to restore the component visibility to the settings saved earlier. Similarly, you can use **Restore Component Visibility** tool.

Save Report

The **Save Report** tool is used to save the clearance analysis report to a file. On clicking this tool from **More** drop-down in the **Clearance** group of **Assemblies** tab in the **Ribbon**, the **Report File** dialog box will be displayed; refer to Figure-109. Specify desired name of report file in **File name** edit box and click on the **OK** button. The report file will be saved.

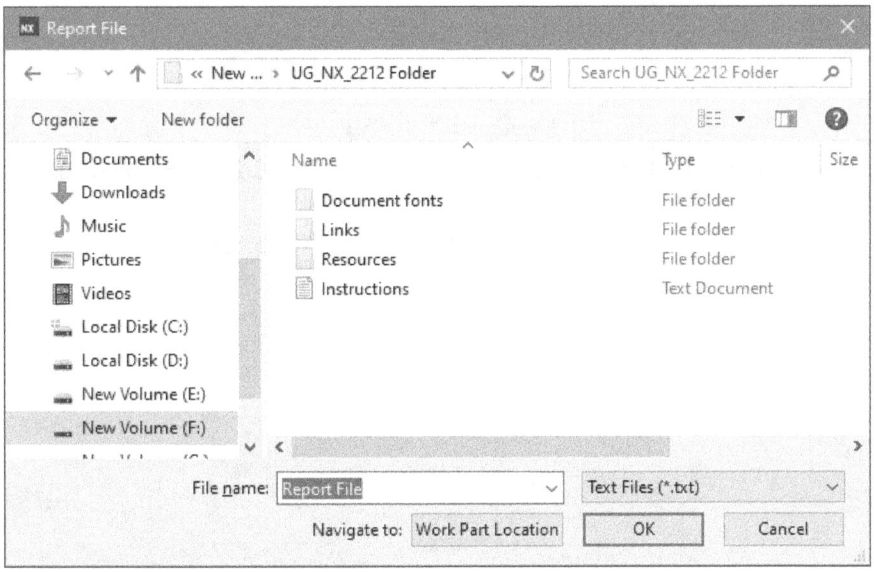

Figure-109. Report File dialog box

Similarly, the procedure to use **Save Bookmark** tool is same as discussed for **Save Report** tool.

Summary

On clicking **Summary** tool from **More** drop-down in the **Clearance** group of **Assemblies** tab in the **Ribbon**. The **Information** window will be displayed as discussed earlier with the summary of the current clearance set.

Redraw Studied Nodes

The **Redraw Studied Nodes** tool is used to draw an interference geometry in the selected interference and then redraws all of the underlying objects.

Reset All Nodes

The **Reset All Nodes** tool is used to restore the model to state prior to running interference node study.

Explosions

The **Explosions** tool is used to create explosions in which selected parts or subassemblies are moved apart visually. The procedure to use this tool is discussed next.

- Click on the **Explosions** tool from **Explosions** group of **Assemblies** tab in the **Ribbon**. The **Explosions** dialog box will be displayed; refer to Figure-110.

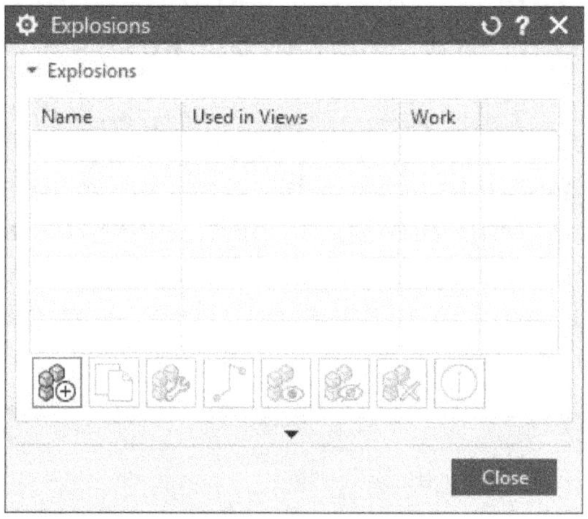

Figure-110. Explosions dialog box

- Click on the button from the dialog box, the **Edit Explosion** dialog box will be displayed; refer to Figure-111.

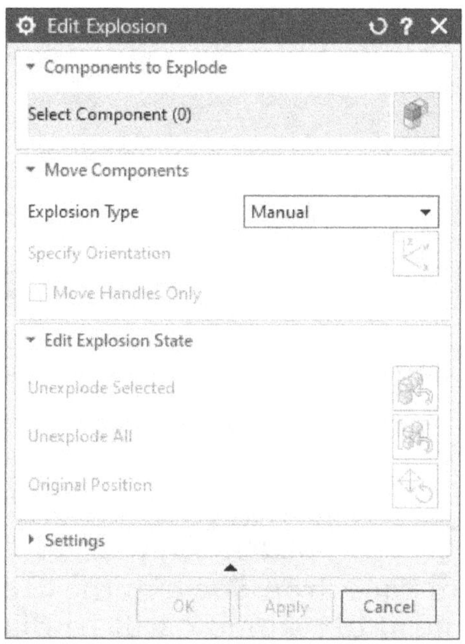

Figure-111. Edit Explosion dialog box

- Select desired components from the graphics window to be exploded; refer to Figure-112.
- Select desired type of explosion to be performed from **Explosion Type** drop-down in the **Move Components** rollout. Select **Manual** option to translate or rotate selected components about the specified vector, manually. And select **Automatic** option to explode the selected components through software derived directions.
- Click on the **Specify Orientation** button to display the positioning tool.
- Select **Move Handles Only** check box to move only the tool on moving the handle of the positioning tool.

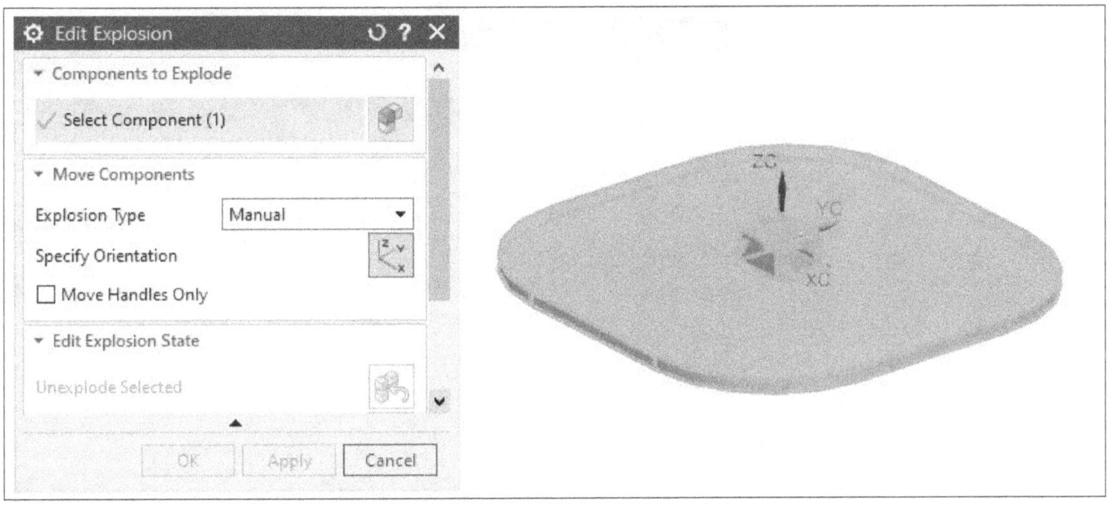

Figure-112. Component selected for explosion

- Click on the **Unexplode Selected** button from **Edit Explosion State** rollout to move selected components back to their unexploded positions.
- Click on the **Unexplode All** button to move all exploded components back to their unexploded positions.
- Click on the **Original Position** button to move the selected component back to its original position in the assembly.
- Specify desired name of explosion in the **Explosion Name** edit box of **Settings** rollout.
- On selecting **Use Additional Directions** check box from **Auto-explode** rollout in the **Settings** rollout, when NX autoexplode components, it consider component coordinate systems and constraints in addition to the assembly's coordinate system.
- After specifying desired parameters, click on **OK** button from dialog box. The explosion will be created and displayed in the **Explosions** dialog box; refer to Figure-113.

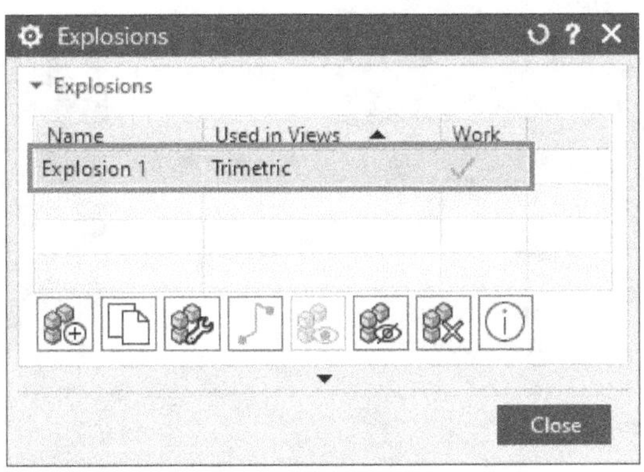

Figure-113. Explosion created

- Click on the button from the dialog box, the **Edit Explosion** dialog box will be displayed to create a new explosion based on the existing explosion, the options of which have been discussed earlier.
- Click on the button from the dialog box, the **Edit Explosion** dialog box will be displayed again to reposition one or more selected components in the work explosion, the options of which have been discussed earlier.
- Click on the button to create a line that traces possible paths that an exploded component can follow during assembly or disassembly. The **Tracelines** dialog box will be displayed; refer to Figure-114.

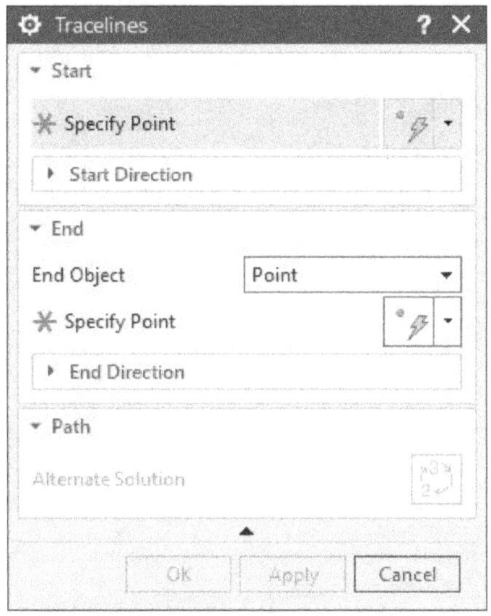

Figure-114. Tracelines dialog box

- Click on the component at desired location to specify the point as starting point for traceline.
- Click on the **Start Direction** rollout and specify desired vector to define the starting direction of the traceline.
- Select desired type of object to be used to define the end point for the traceline from **End Object** drop-down in the **End** rollout and specify desired parameters.
- Click on the **End Direction** rollout and specify desired vector to define the end direction of the traceline.
- Click on the **Alternate Solution** button from **Path** rollout to display alternate solution to create a traceline between the specified start and end points.
- After specifying desired parameters, click on **OK** button from the dialog box. The traceline will be created; refer to Figure-115.

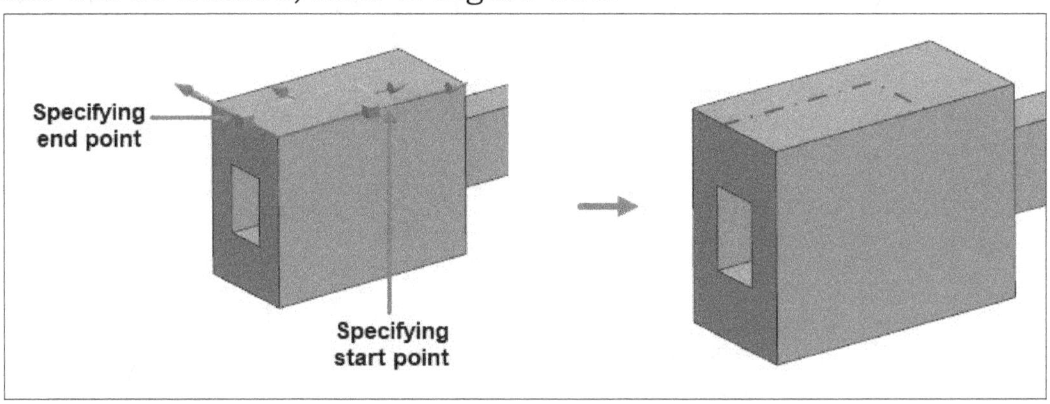

Figure-115. Traceline created

- Click on the button from **Explosions** dialog box to display the selected explosion in the graphics window.
- Click on the button to hide selected explosion(s) in all the views.
- Click on the button to delete one or more selected explosion(s).
- Click on the button to display report for explosion(s) in the **Information** window.
- After specifying desired parameters, click on **Close** button to close the dialog box.

Sequence

The **Sequence** tools are useful in sequencing how the various components will be assembled in real-world based on assembly model. On clicking the **Sequence** tool from **Sequence** group of **Assemblies** tab in the **Ribbon**. The **Sequence** environment will be displayed with the sequencing tools; refer to Figure-116. The general process of creating a sequence is discussed next.

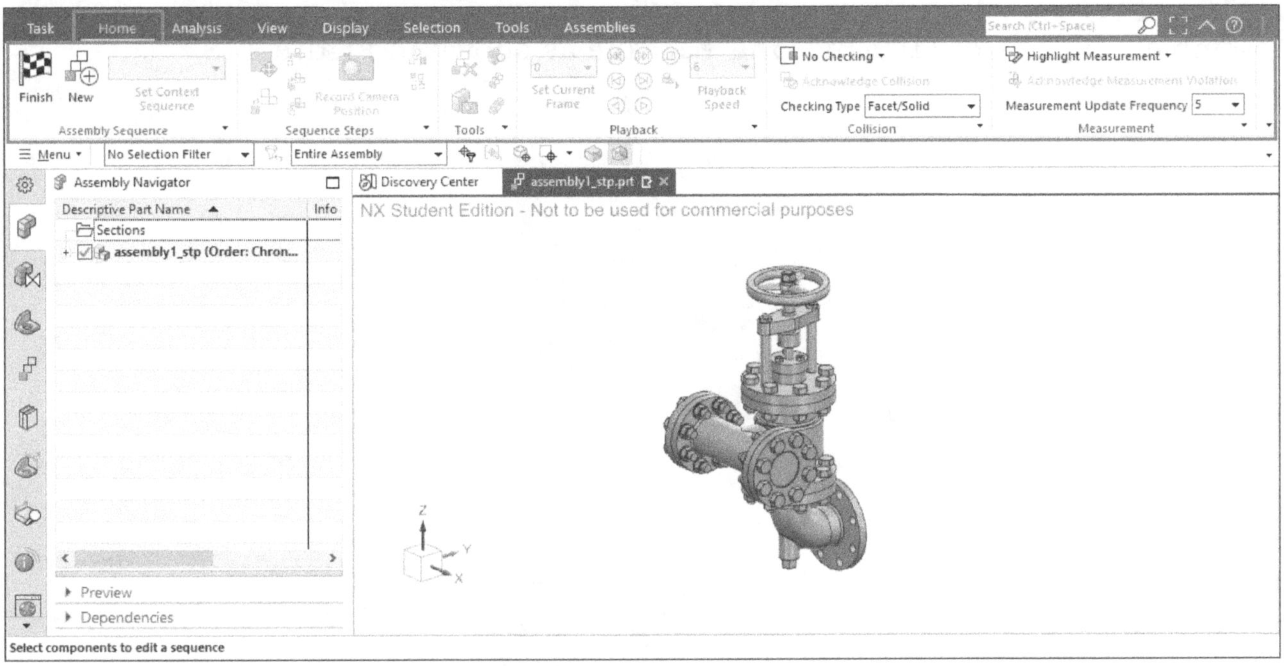

Figure-116. Sequence environment

- Click on the **New** tool from the **Assembly Sequence** group of the **Ribbon** to create a new sequence setup.
- Select desired components to be assembled (added) or disassembled (removed) from the **Assembly Navigator** and select the **Assemble** or **Disassemble** tool, respectively from the **Sequence Steps** group in the **Ribbon**.
- Click on the **Insert Motion** tool from the **Ribbon** and select component to which you want to apply motion in assembly sequence. The options in the **Record Component Motion** toolbar will become active; refer to Figure-117.

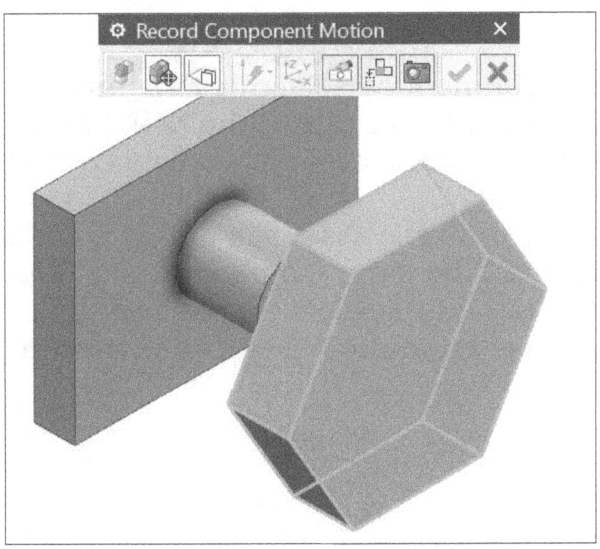

Figure-117. Record Component Motion toolbar

- Use **Move Objects** and other tools of toolbar to record motion of objects in assembling operation. After adding motion, click on the **OK** button from the toolbar. Click on the **Cancel** tool to exit the toolbar.
- Use the tools of **Playback** group in the **Ribbon** to place sequence of assembly.
- Click on the **Finish** tool from the **Ribbon** to exit the mode.

PRACTICAL 1

Assemble the parts of **Tiny Milling Machine** as shown in Figure-118.

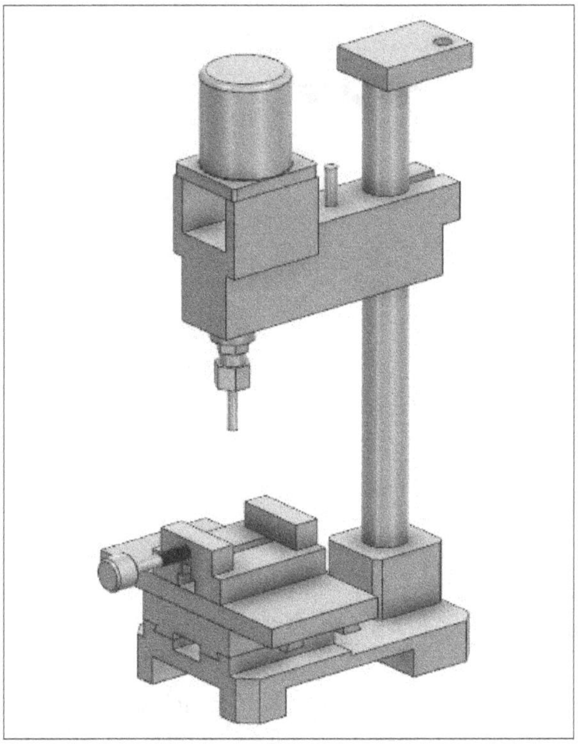

Figure-118. Assemble view of tiny milling machine

All the part files can be downloaded from the link provided on e-mail. In this practical, we will use parts of **Tiny Milling Machine** folder from downloaded files/folders in resource kit. The steps to assemble these parts are given next.

Inserting Body

- Start the assembly environment by selecting **New** button from **Home** tab and select **Assembly** template from the **Model** tab in the **New** dialog box and click on the **OK** button. The Assembly environment will be displayed along with the **Assemble** dialog box.
- Click on the **Open** button from the **Assemble** dialog box. The **Part Name** dialog box will be displayed. Select all the parts (components) of **Practical 1 Tiny Milling Machine Assembly** folder and click on the **OK** button; refer to Figure-119. The selected parts will be inserted in the Assembly environment; refer to Figure-120.

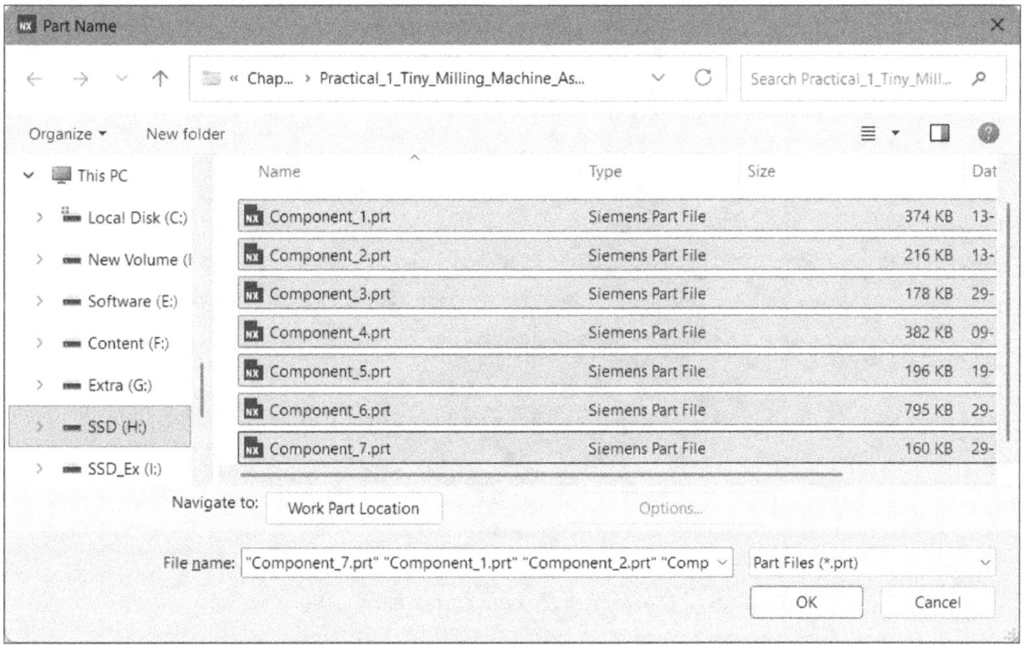

Figure-119. Selecting the parts of tiny milling machine

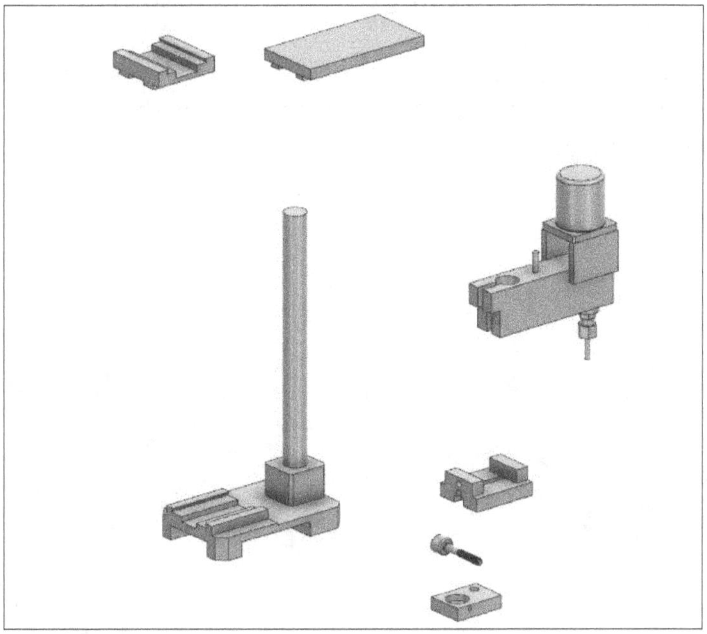

Figure-120. Parts opened in the Assembly environment

- After inserting the parts, click on **OK** button from the dialog box.

Constraining the first component

- Click on the **Fix** tool from **Position** group of **Assemblies** tab in the **Ribbon**. The **Fix** dialog box will be displayed.
- Select the object from the graphics window to be fixed as shown in Figure-121.
- After selecting the object, click on **OK** button from the dialog box. The fix constraint will be applied to the object.

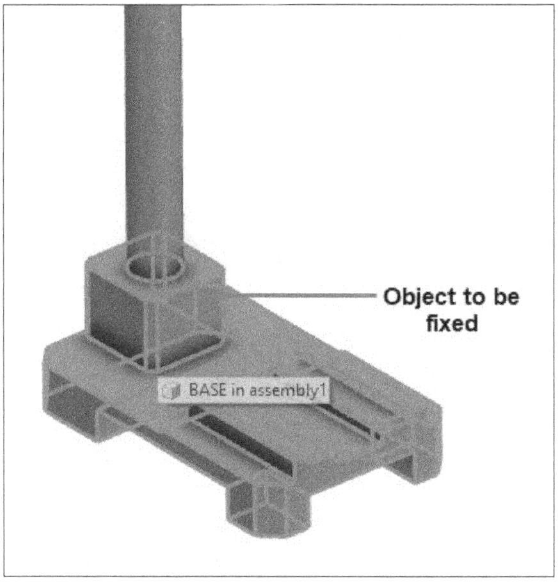

Figure-121. Selecting the object to be fixed

Constraining the second component

- Click on **Touch** tool from **Position** group of **Assemblies** tab in the **Ribbon**. The **Touch** dialog box will be displayed.
- Select face of motion object to be constrained and then select face of stationary object from the graphics window as shown in Figure-122. The preview of touch constraint will be displayed.

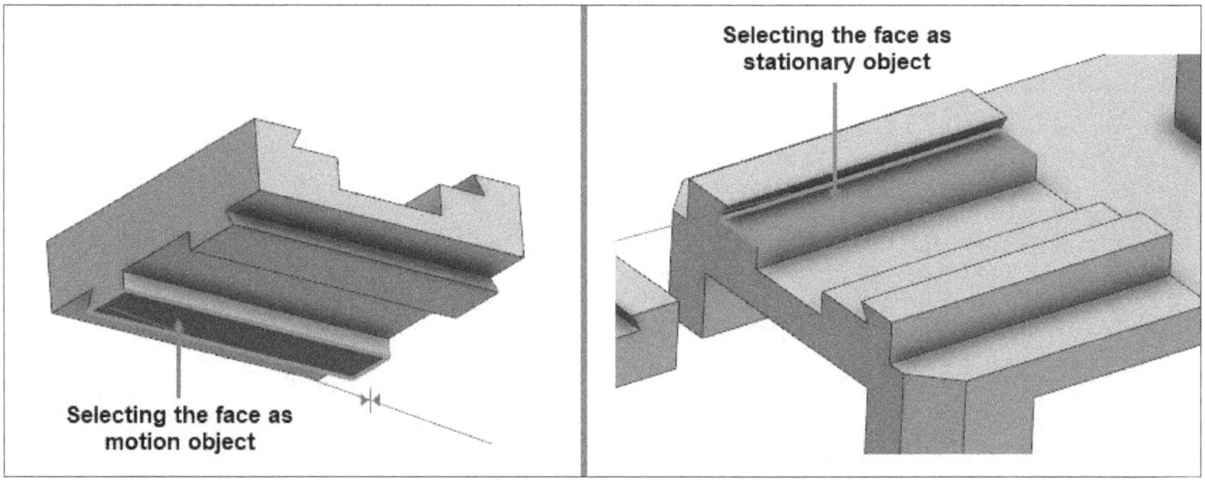

Figure-122. Selecting the geometries to be touch constrained

- Click on **OK** button from the dialog box. The touch constraint will be applied.
- Click on the **Align** tool from **Position** group of **Assemblies** tab in the **Ribbon**. The **Align** dialog box will be displayed.
- Select face of motion object to be constrained and then select face of stationary object from the graphics window as shown in Figure-123. The preview of align constraint will be displayed.

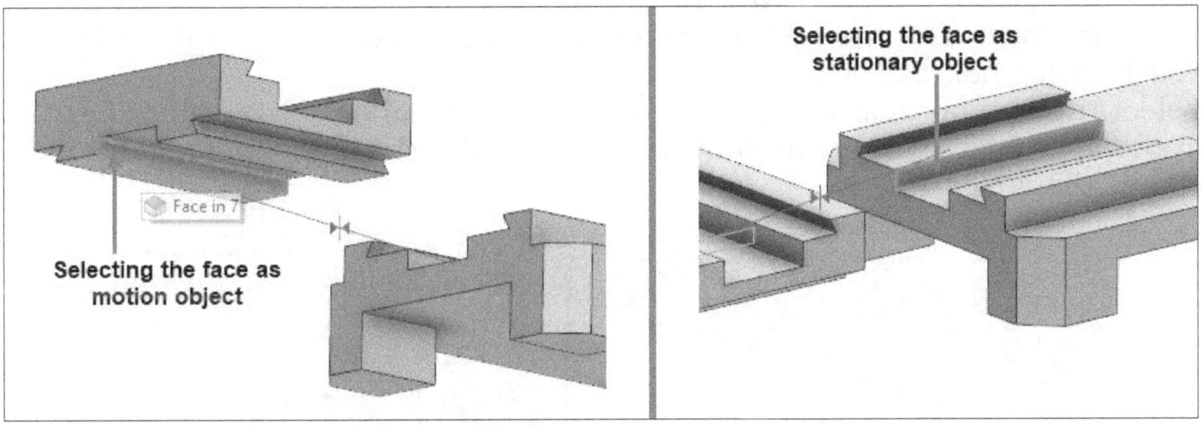

Figure-123. Selecting the geometries to be align constrained

- After selecting the geometries, click on **Apply** button from the dialog box to apply the align constraint.
- Now, select the geometries as shown in Figure-124 and click on the **OK** button from the dialog box to apply the constraint. The second component will be constrained; refer to Figure-125.

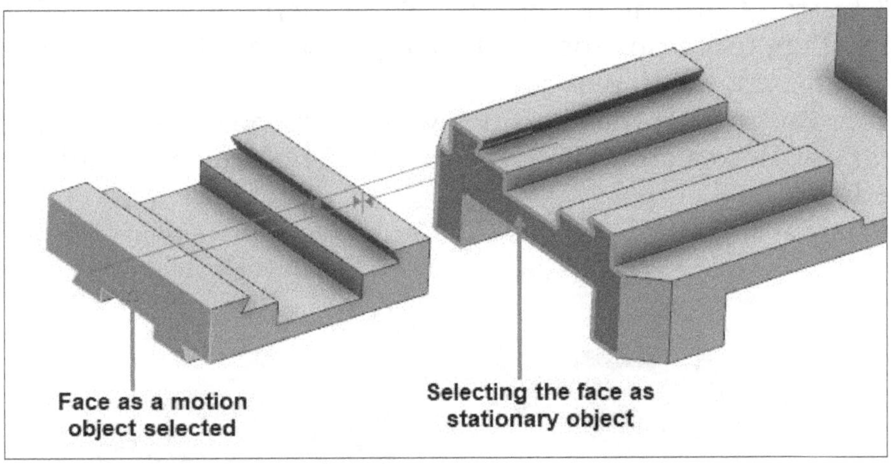

Figure-124. Selecting the geometries to be distance constrained

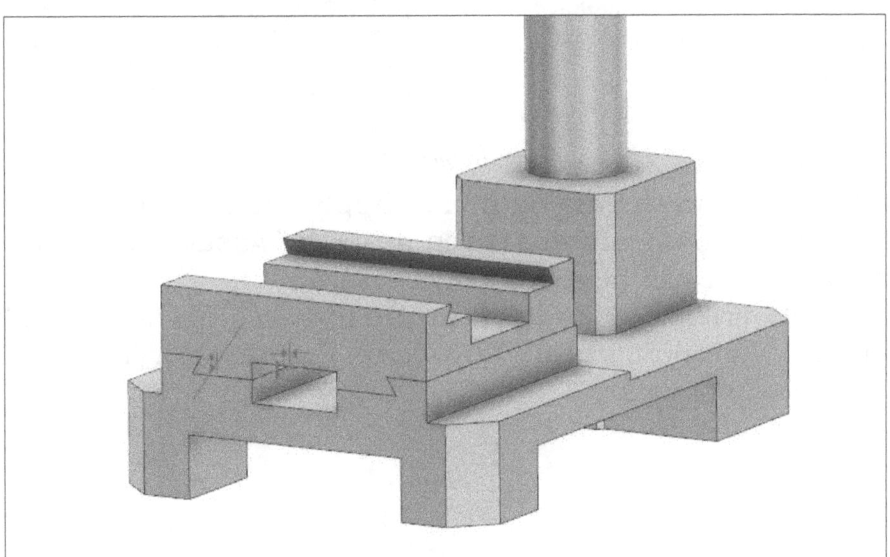

Figure-125. Second component constrained

Constraining the third component

- Click on **Touch** tool from **Position** group of **Assemblies** tab in the **Ribbon**. The **Touch** dialog box will be displayed.
- Select the motion object to be constrained and then select the stationary object from the graphics window as shown in Figure-126. The preview of touch constraint will be displayed.

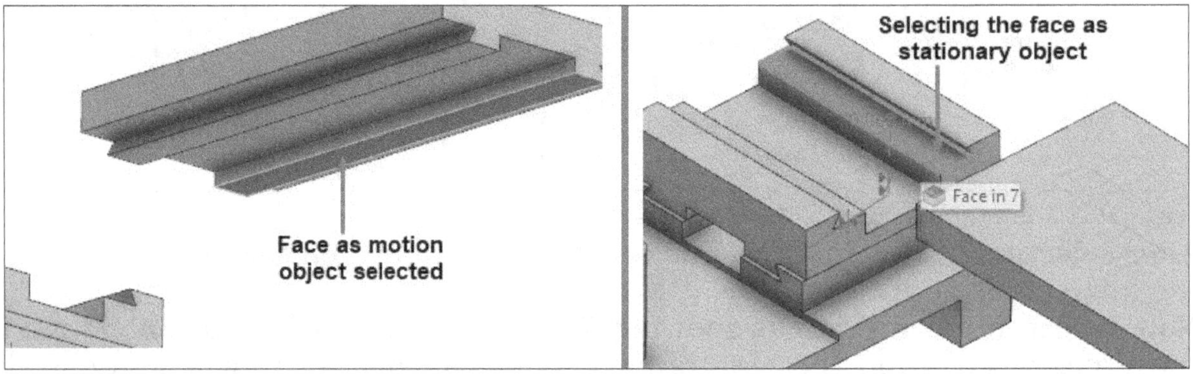

Figure-126. Selecting the geometries to be touch constrained

- Click on **OK** button from the dialog box. The touch constraint will be applied.
- Click on the **Align** tool from **Position** group of **Assemblies** tab in the **Ribbon**. The **Align** dialog box will be displayed.
- Select motion object from the graphics window to be constrained and then select the stationary object as shown in Figure-127. The preview of align constraint will be displayed.

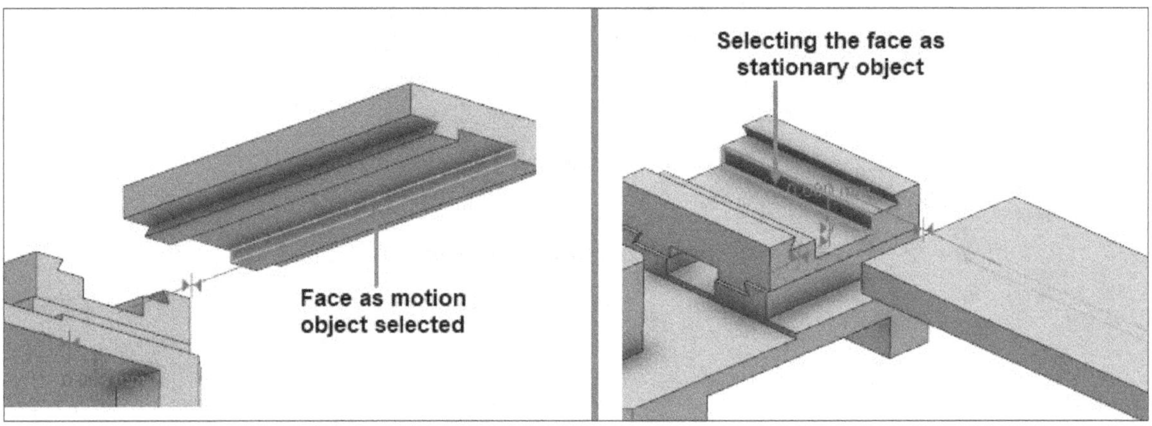

Figure-127. Selecting the geometries to be align constrained

- Click on **OK** button from the dialog box to apply the align constraint.
- Click on the **Center** tool from **Position** group of **Assemblies** tab in the **Ribbon**. The **Center** dialog box will be displayed.
- Select **2 to 2** option from drop-down in the top area of the dialog box and select the geometries of components as shown in Figure-128. The preview of center constraint will be displayed.

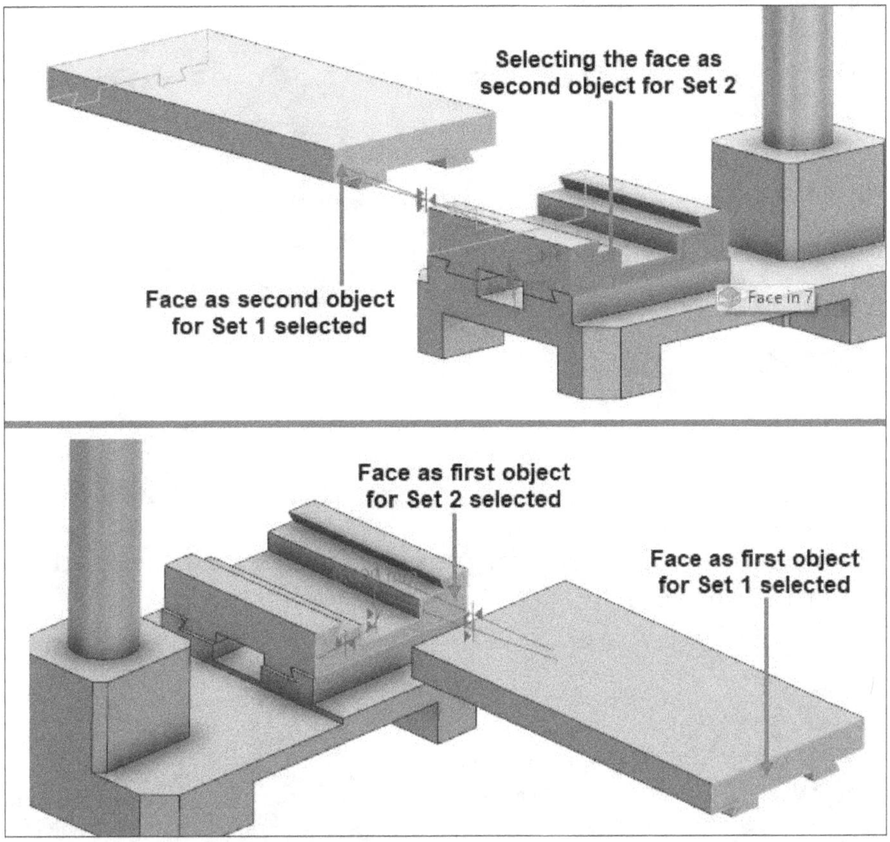

Figure-128. Selecting the geometries to be center constrained

- Click on **OK** button from the dialog box to apply the constraint. The third component will be constrained; refer to Figure-129.

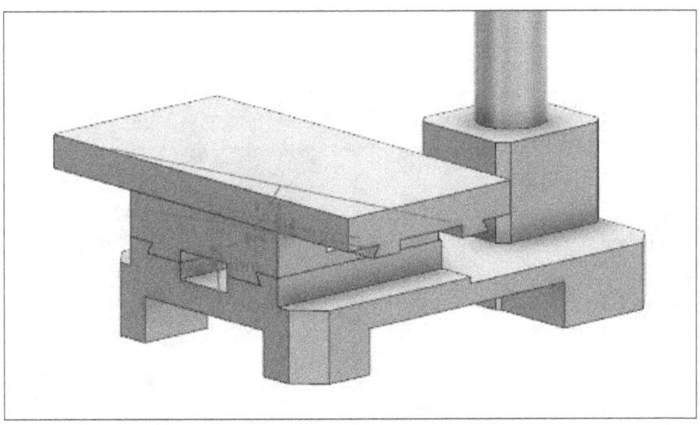

Figure-129. Third component constrained

Constraining the fourth component

- Use the **Move Component** tool and make sure the Component 4 is aligned to size face of model as shown in Figure-130. Click on the **Slider** tool from **Joints and Couplers** drop-down in the **Position** group of **Assemblies** tab in the **Ribbon**. The **Slider** dialog box will be displayed.

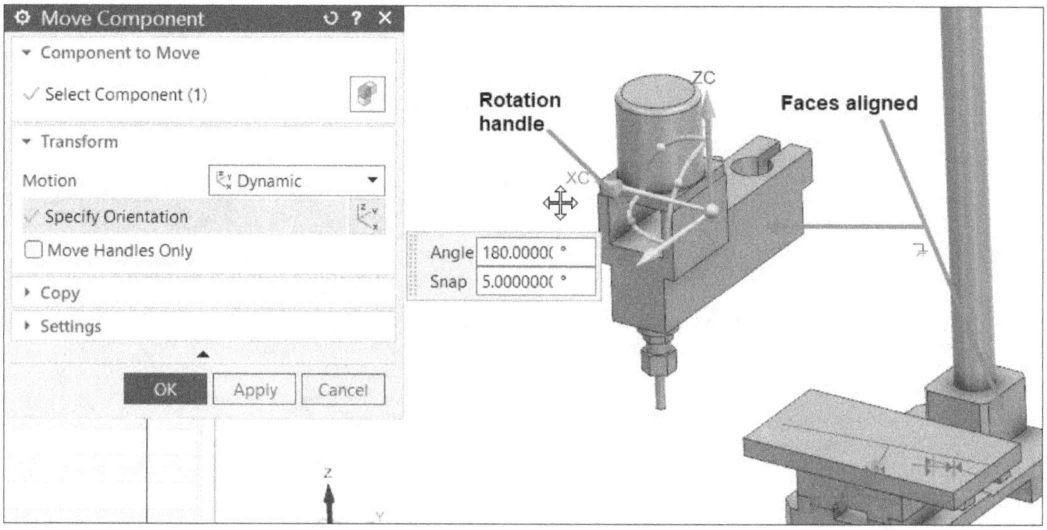

Figure-130. Moving component

- Specify the vector and point on first object and then on second object as shown in Figure-131 and Figure-132.

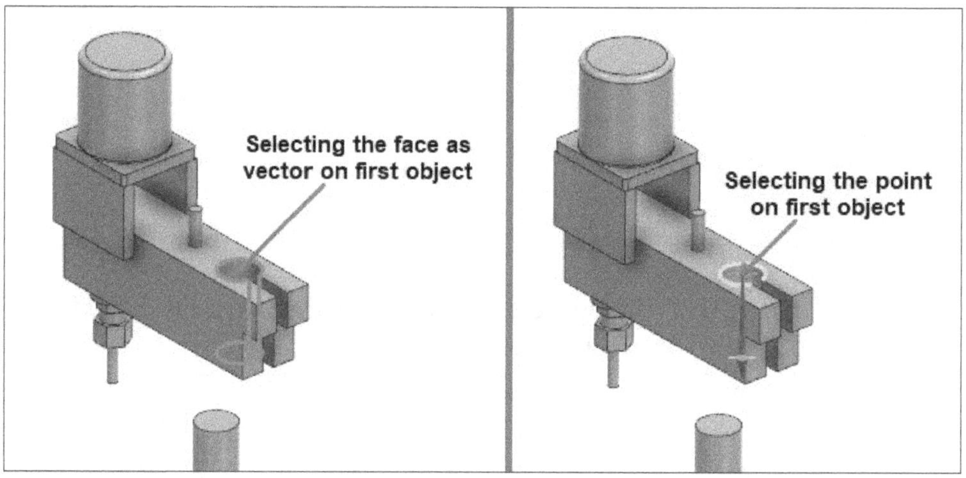

Figure-131. Specifying the axis on first object

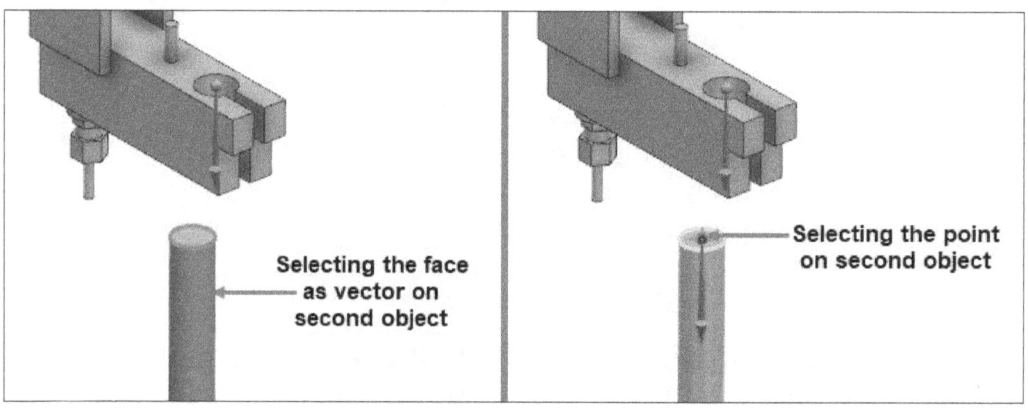

Figure-132. Specifying the axis on second object

- After specifying axis on both the objects, select **Distance** check box from **Value** rollout and specify desired distance in the respective edit box to set it in middle of shaft. You may need to use **Reverse Direction** button from dialog box.
- After specifying the parameters, click on **OK** button from the dialog box. The slider constraint will be applied and the fourth component will be constrained; refer to Figure-133.

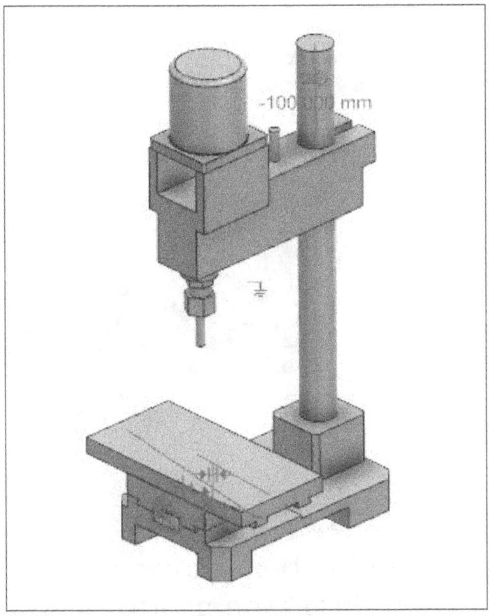

Figure-133. Fourth component constrained

Constraining the fifth component

- Click on the **Align** tool from **Position** group of **Assemblies** tab in the **Ribbon**. The **Align** dialog box will be displayed.
- Select motion object from the graphics window to be constrained and then select the stationary object as shown in Figure-134. The preview of align constraint will be displayed.

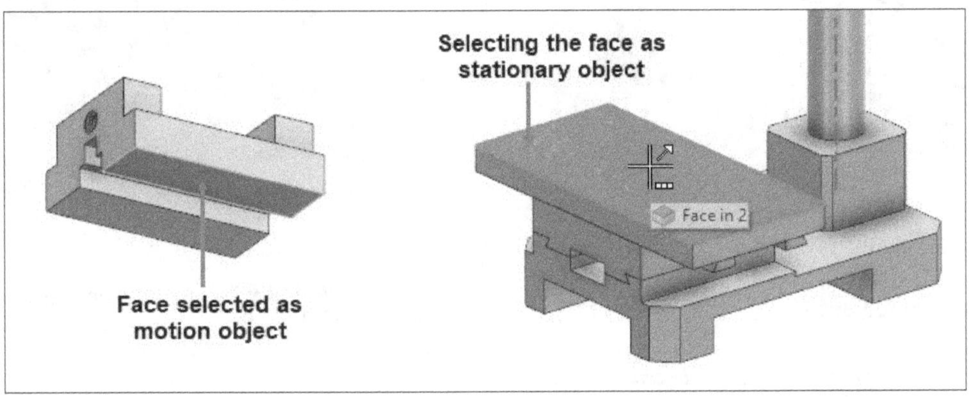

Figure-134. Selecting the geometries to be align constrained

- Click on **Apply** button from the dialog box to apply the align constraint.
- Again, select the motion and stationary object for align constraint from the graphics window as shown in Figure-135.

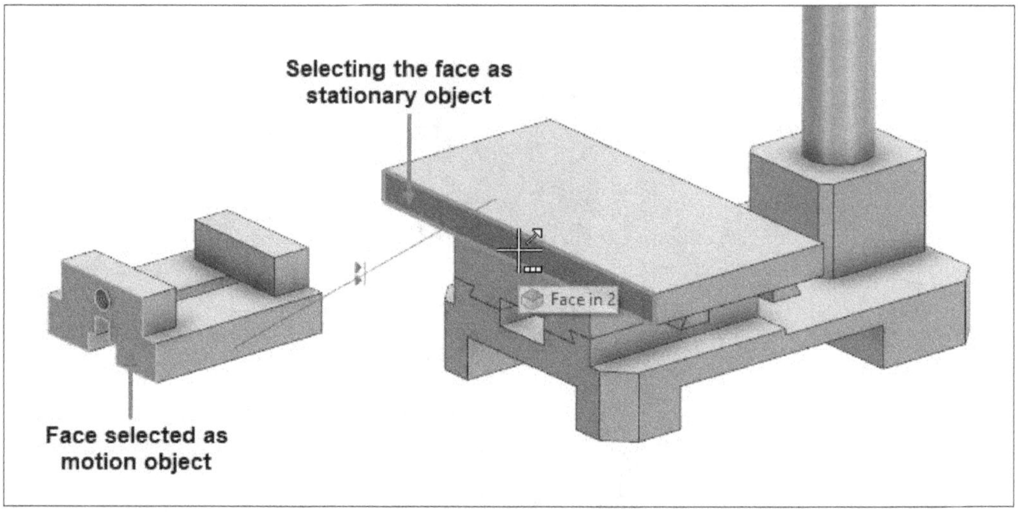

Figure-135. Selecting the geometries to be align constrained

- Click on **OK** button from the dialog box to apply the align constraint.
- Click on the **Center** tool from **Position** group of **Assemblies** tab in the **Ribbon**. The **Center** dialog box will be displayed.
- Select **2 to 2** option from drop-down in the top area of the dialog box and select the geometries of components as shown in Figure-136. The preview of center constraint will be displayed.

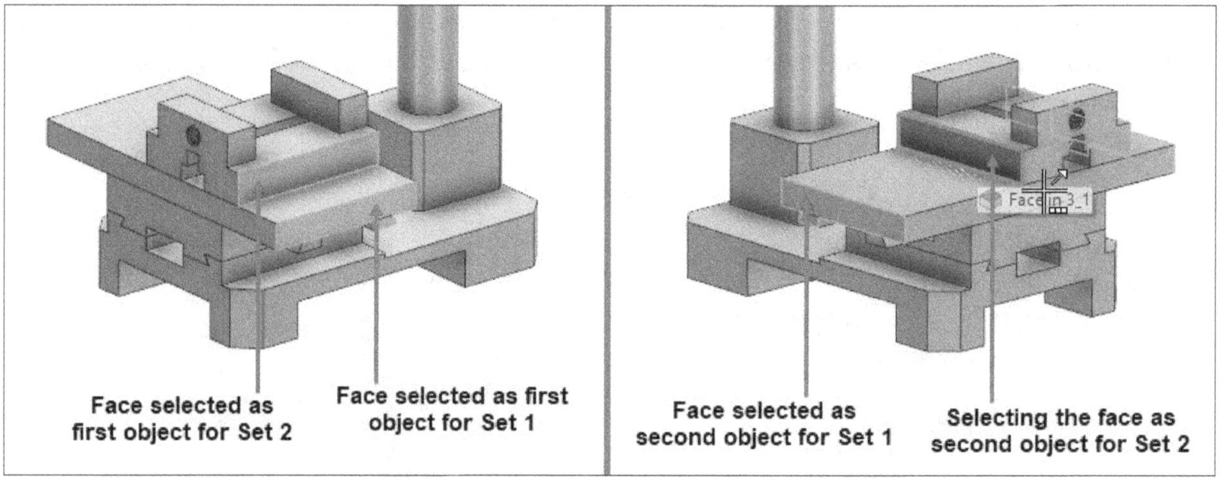

Figure-136. Selecting the geometries to be center constrained

- Click on **OK** button from the dialog box to apply the constraint. The fifth component will be constrained; refer to Figure-137.

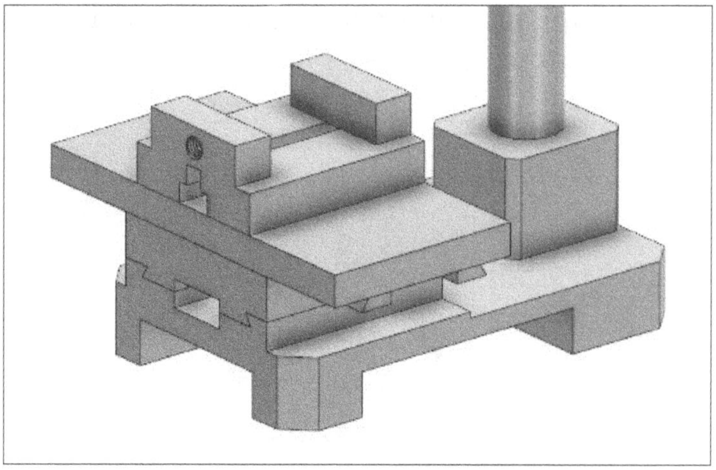

Figure-137. Fifth component constrained

Constraining the sixth component

- Click on the **Auto Align** tool from **Position** group of **Assemblies** tab in the **Ribbon**. The **Auto Align** dialog box will be displayed.
- Select the centerline of both the components as the geometries to be constrained as shown in Figure-138. On selecting the centerline of second component, the auto align constraint will be applied.

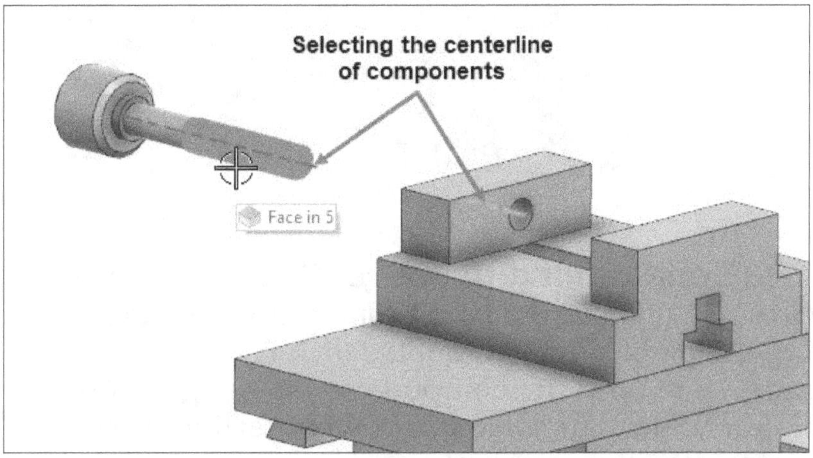

Figure-138. Selecting the geometries to be auto align constrained

- Click on **Close** button to close the **Auto Align** dialog box.
- Click on **Touch** tool from **Position** group of **Assemblies** tab in the **Ribbon**. The **Touch** dialog box will be displayed.
- Select the motion object to be constrained and then select the stationary object from the graphics window as shown in Figure-139.

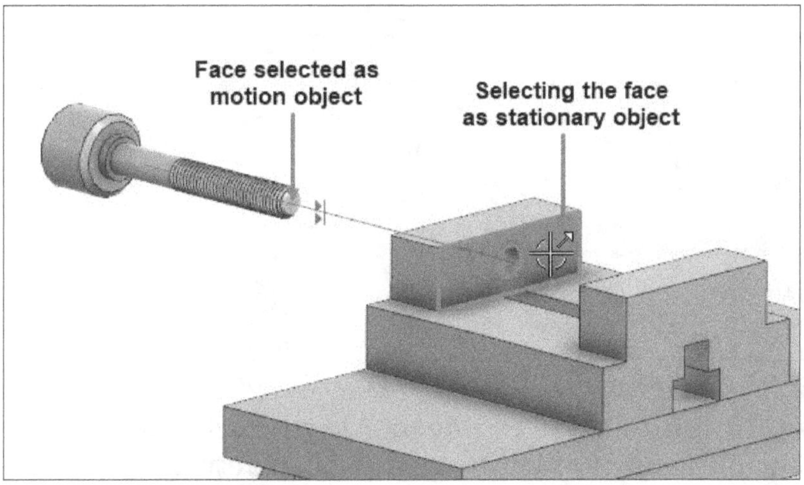

Figure-139. Selecting the geometries to be touch constrained

- Click on the **Reverse Direction** button from the dialog box. The preview of touch constraint will be displayed.
- Click on **OK** button from the dialog box. The touch constraint will be applied and the sixth component will be constrained; refer to Figure-140.

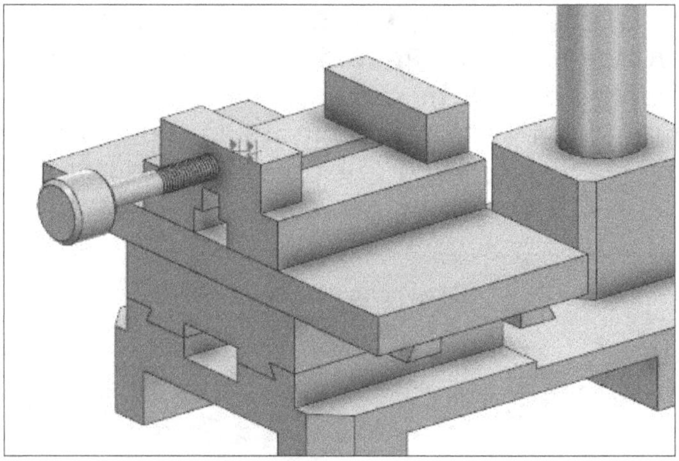

Figure-140. Sixth component constrained

Constraining the seventh component

- Click on the **Auto Align** tool from **Position** group of **Assemblies** tab in the **Ribbon**. The **Auto Align** dialog box will be displayed.
- Select the centerline of both the components as the geometries to be constrained as shown in Figure-141. On selecting the centerline of second component, the auto align constraint will be applied.

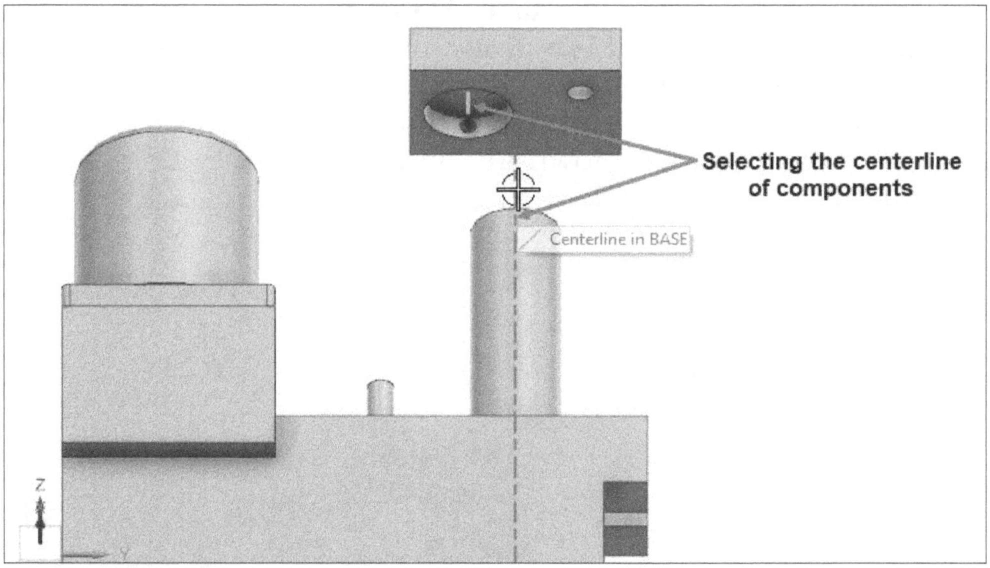

Figure-141. Selecting the geometries to be auto align constrained

- Click on **Close** button to close the **Auto Align** dialog box.
- Click on **Touch** tool from **Position** group of **Assemblies** tab in the **Ribbon**. The **Touch** dialog box will be displayed.
- Select the motion object to be constrained and then select the stationary object from the graphics window as shown in Figure-142. The preview of touch constraint will be displayed.
- Click on **OK** button from the dialog box. The touch constraint will be applied. Use the **Parallel** tool from the **Ribbon** and align side face of Component 7 to side face of Component 1. The seventh component will be constrained; refer to Figure-143.

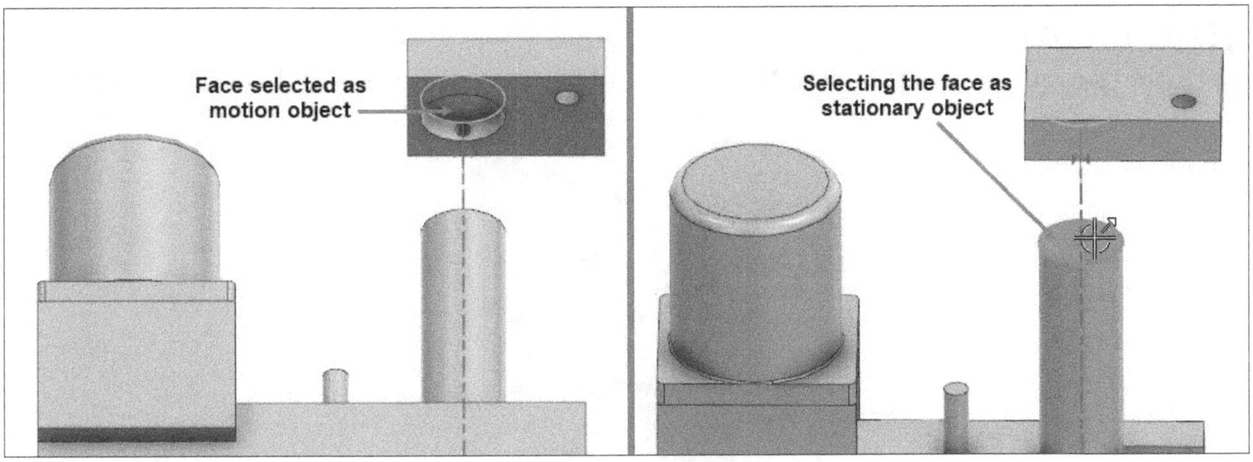

Figure-142. Selecting the geometries to be touch constrained

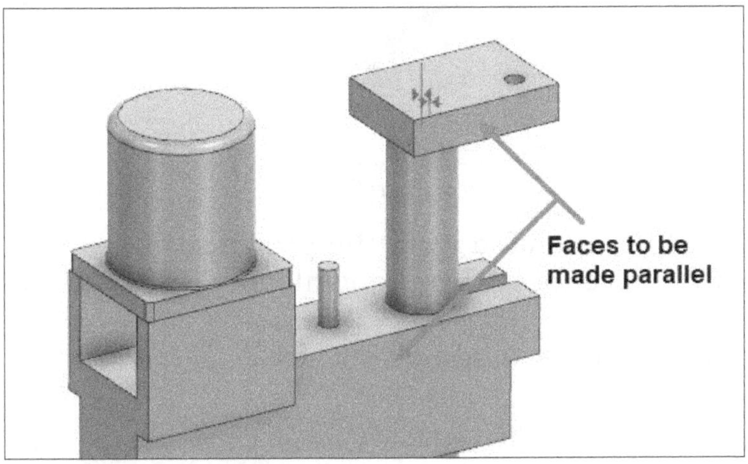

Figure-143. Seventh component constrained

After constraining all the components, the assembly of tiny milling machine will be displayed as shown in Figure-144.

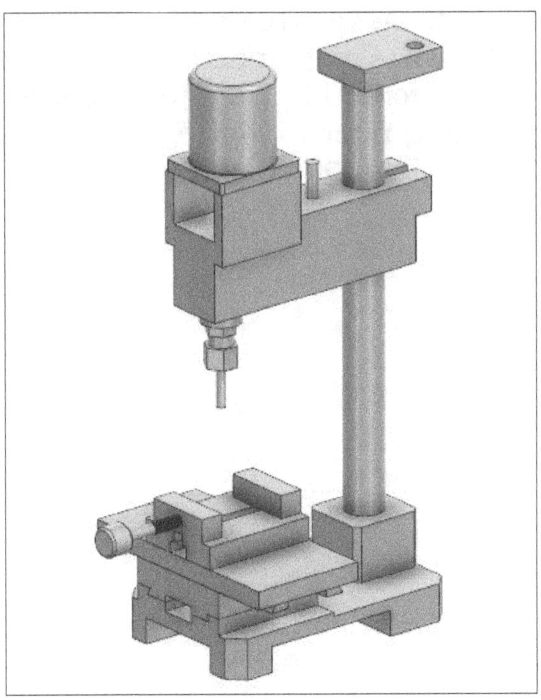

Figure-144. Assembly of tiny milling machine

PRACTICAL 2

Assemble the parts of **Butterfly Valve and its components** as shown in Figure-145.

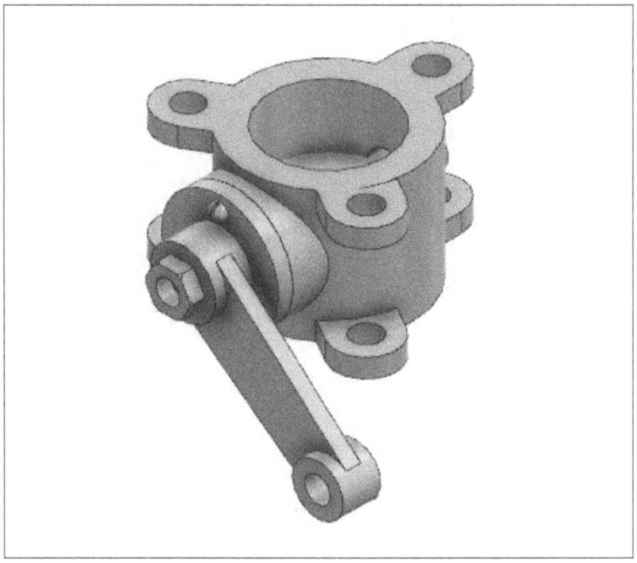

Figure-145. Assembly of Butterfly Valve

All the part files can be downloaded from the provided link. In this practical, we will use parts of **Butterfly Valve** folder from downloaded files/folders in resource kit.

The steps to assemble these parts are given next.

Inserting Body

- Start the assembly environment by selecting **New** button from **Home** tab and select **Assembly** template from the **Model** tab in the **New** dialog box and click on the **OK** button. The Assembly environment will be displayed along with the **Assemble** dialog box.
- Click on **Open** button from the **Assemble** dialog box. The **Part Name** dialog box will be displayed. Select all the parts of **Practical 2 Butterfly Valve Assembly** folder and click on the **OK** button; refer to Figure-146. The selected parts will be inserted in the Assembly environment; refer to Figure-147.
- After inserting the parts, click on **OK** button from the dialog box.

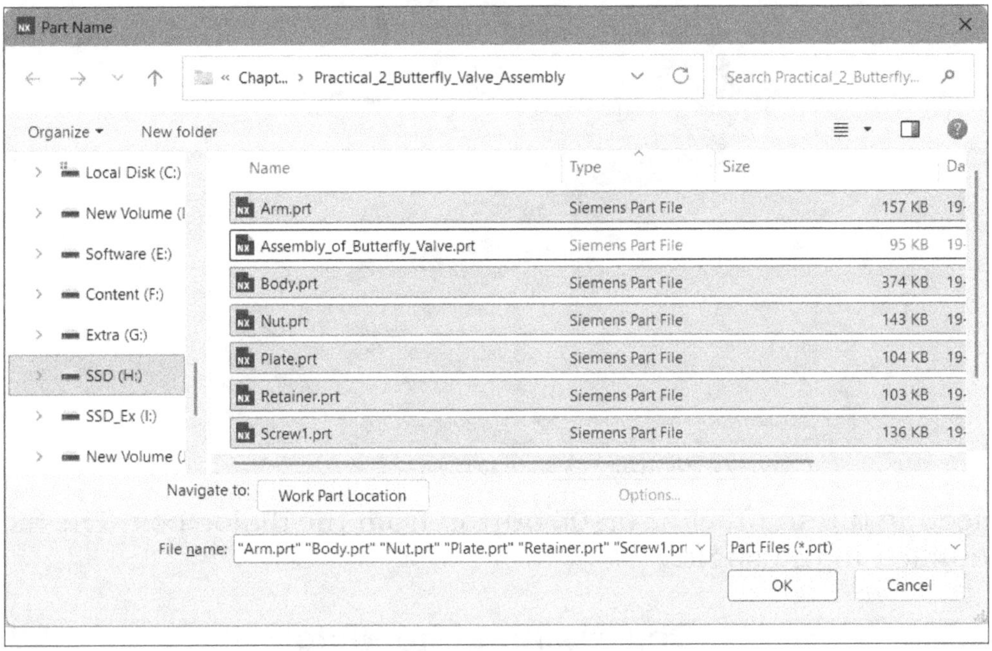

Figure-146. Selecting the parts of butterfly valve

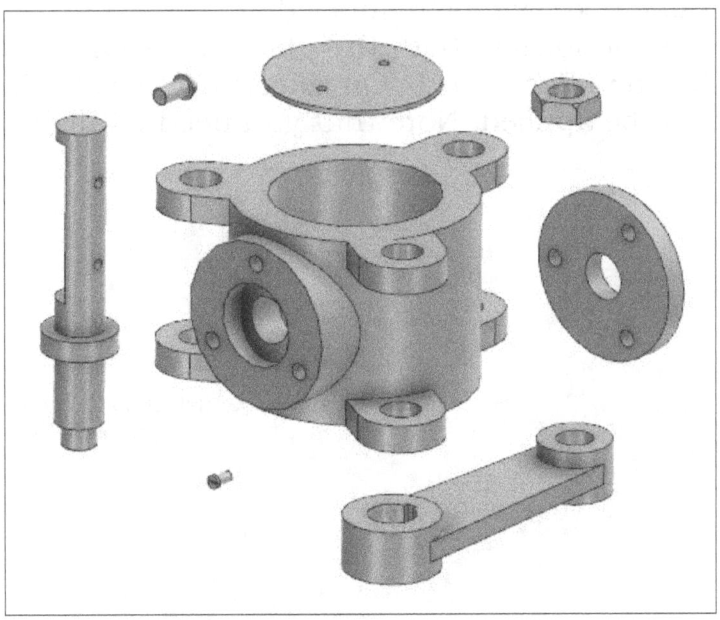

Figure-147. Parts opened in the Assembly environment

Constraining the Shaft

- Click on the **Fix** tool from **Position** group of **Assemblies** tab in the **Ribbon**. The **Fix** dialog box will be displayed.
- Select the shaft from the graphics window as shown in Figure-148.

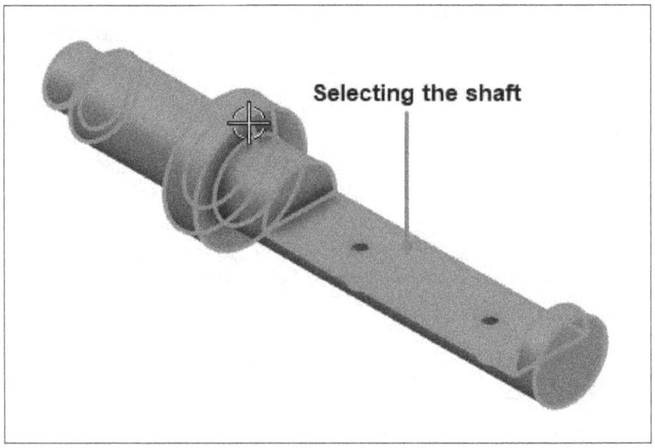

Figure-148. Selecting the shaft to be fixed

- After selecting the shaft, click on **OK** button from the dialog box. The fix constraint will be applied to the shaft.

Constraining the Plate

- Click on the **Auto Align** tool from **Position** group of **Assemblies** tab in the **Ribbon**. The **Auto Align** dialog box will be displayed.
- Select the centerline of holes in both the plate and shaft as the geometries to be constrained as shown in Figure-149. On selecting the centerline of shaft, the auto align constraint will be applied. Note that you need to align both holes.

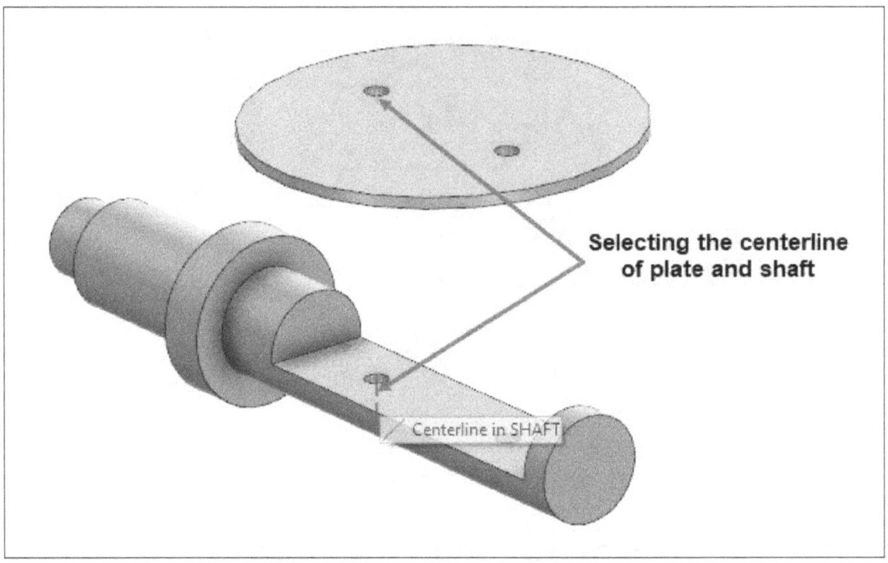

Figure-149. Selecting the geometries to be auto align constrained

- Click on **Close** button to close the **Auto Align** dialog box.
- Click on **Touch** tool from **Position** group of **Assemblies** tab in the **Ribbon**. The **Touch** dialog box will be displayed.
- Select face of motion object to be constrained and then select face of stationary object from the graphics window as shown in Figure-150. The preview of touch constraint will be displayed.

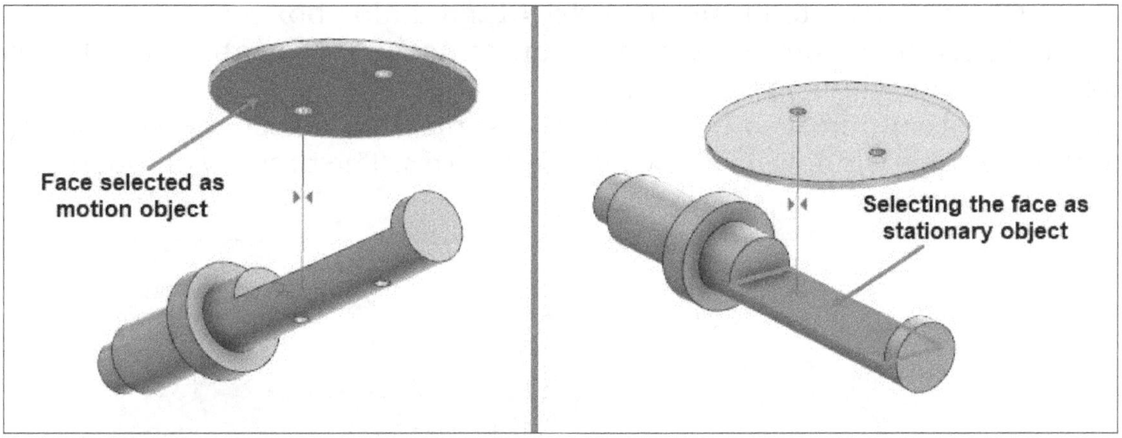

Figure-150. Selecting the geometries to be touch constrained

- Click on **OK** button from the dialog box. The touch constraint will be applied and the plate will be constrained; refer to Figure-151.

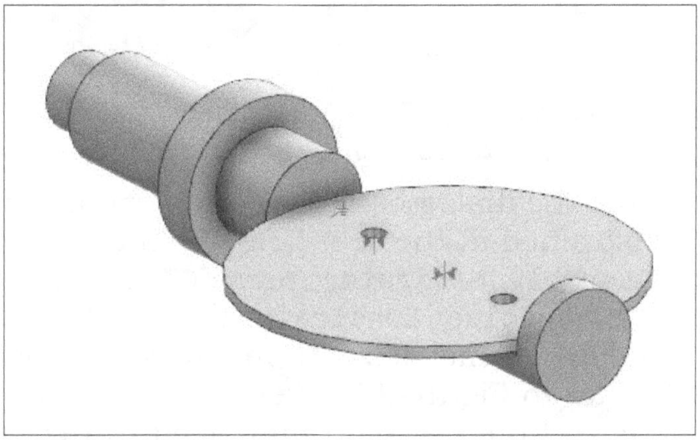

Figure-151. Plate constrained

Constraining the Screw1

- Click on the **Auto Align** tool from **Position** group of **Assemblies** tab in the **Ribbon**. The **Auto Align** dialog box will be displayed.
- Select the centerline of screw1 and the plate as the geometries to be constrained as shown in Figure-152. On selecting the centerline of the plate, the auto align constraint will be applied.

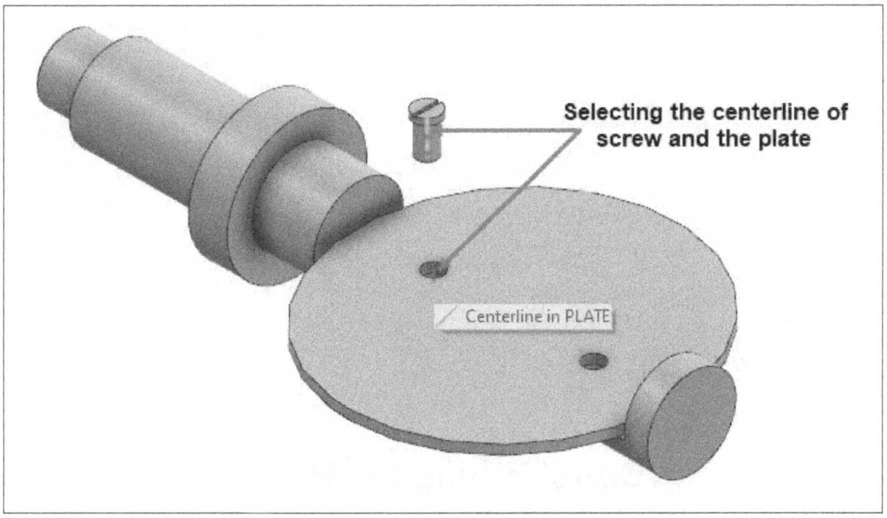

Figure-152. Selecting the geometries to be auto align constrained

- Click on **Close** button to close the **Auto Align** dialog box.
- Click on **Touch** tool from **Position** group of **Assemblies** tab in the **Ribbon**. The **Touch** dialog box will be displayed.
- Select the motion object to be constrained and then select the stationary object from the graphics window as shown in Figure-153. The preview of touch constraint will be displayed.

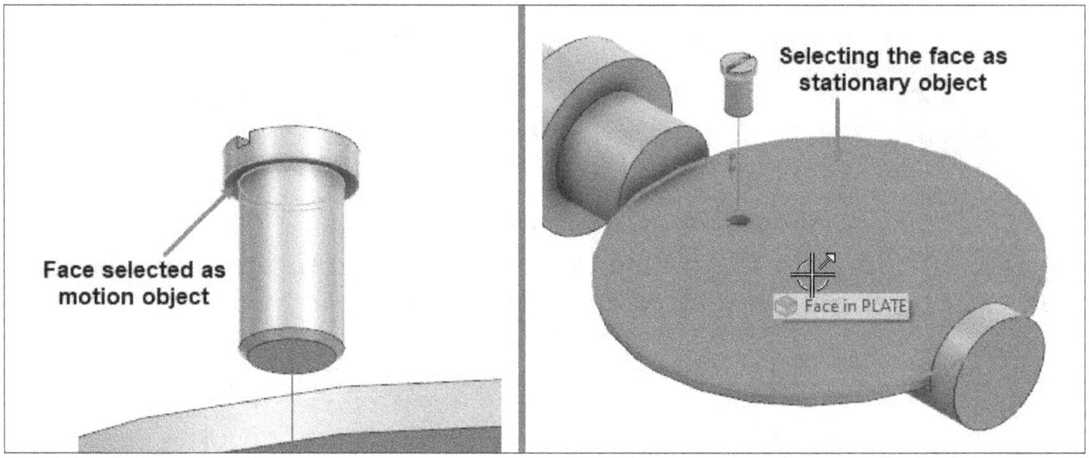

Figure-153. Selecting the geometries to be touch constrained

- Click on **OK** button from the dialog box. The touch constraint will be applied and the screw will be constrained in the first hole of plate.
- Select **Screw1** from **Assembly Navigator**, press **CTRL+C** key (copy) and the press **CTRL+V** key (paste). The **Resolve Constraints** dialog box will be displayed and you will be asked to define geometries for applying same constraints as define for earlier copy of part; refer to Figure-154. Select the axis of another hole in Plate and then select the face. Note that you may need to reverse direction of **Align** constraint; refer to Figure-155. Click on the **OK** button from dialog box to exit.

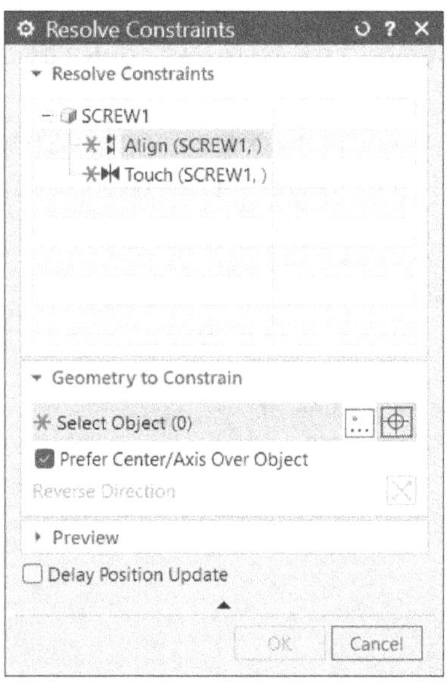

Figure-154. Resolve Constraints dialog box

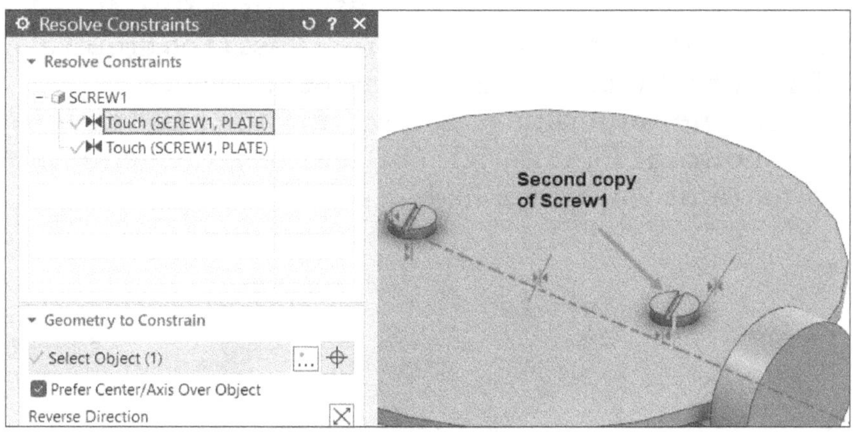

Figure-155. Applying constraints to copy

Constraining the Body

- Click on the **Align** tool from **Position** group of **Assemblies** tab in the **Ribbon**. The **Align** dialog box will be displayed.

- Select motion object from the graphics window to be constrained and then select the stationary object as shown in Figure-156. The preview of align constraint will be displayed.

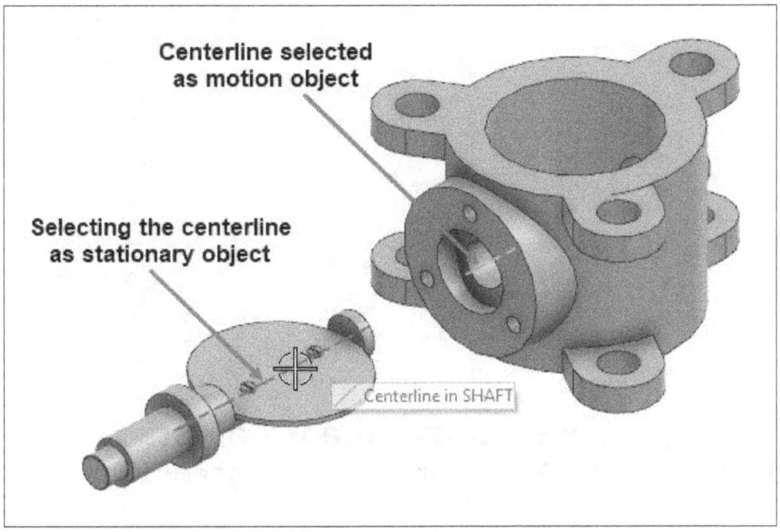

Figure-156. Selecting the geometries to be align constrained

- Click on **OK** button from the dialog box to apply the align constraint.
- Click on **Distance** tool from **Position** group of **Assemblies** tab in the **Ribbon**. The **Touch** dialog box will be displayed.
- Select the motion object to be constrained and then select the stationary object from the graphics window as shown in Figure-157. The preview of touch constraint will be displayed.

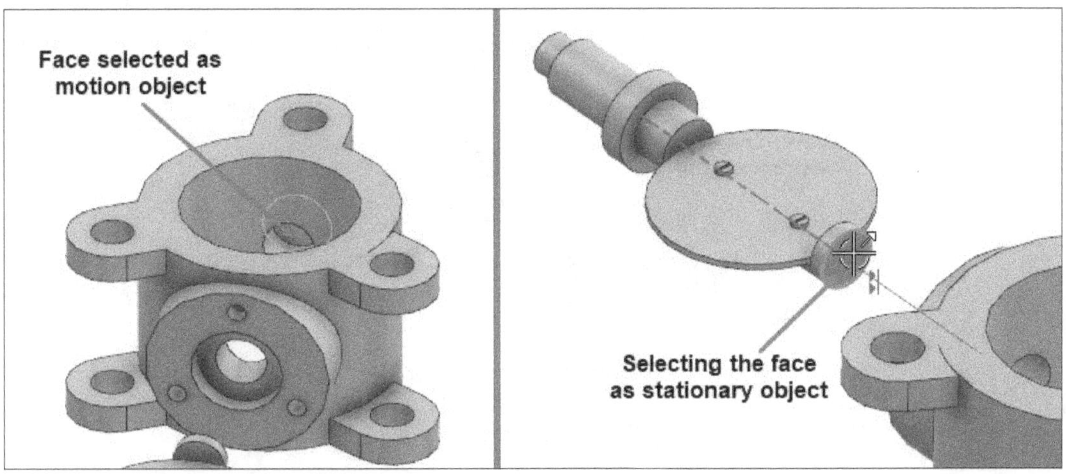

Figure-157. Selecting the geometries to be touch constrained

- Set the parameters as shown in Figure-158 and click on the **OK** button from the dialog box.

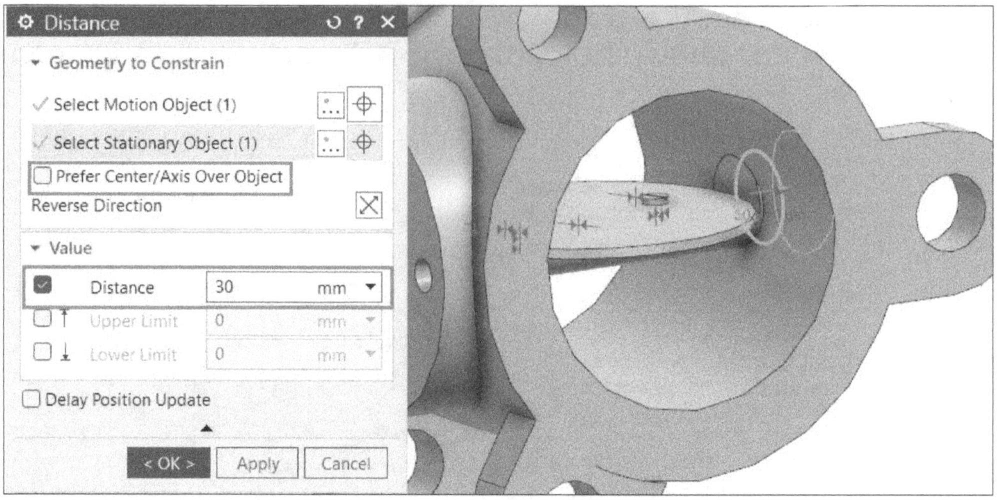

Figure-158. Body constrained

Constraining the Retainer

- Click on the **Align** tool from **Position** group of **Assemblies** tab in the **Ribbon**. The **Align** dialog box will be displayed.
- Select motion object from the graphics window to be constrained and then select the stationary object as shown in Figure-159. The preview of align constraint will be displayed. Click on the **Apply** button and similarly align small holes of RETAINER part to small holes of Body part.

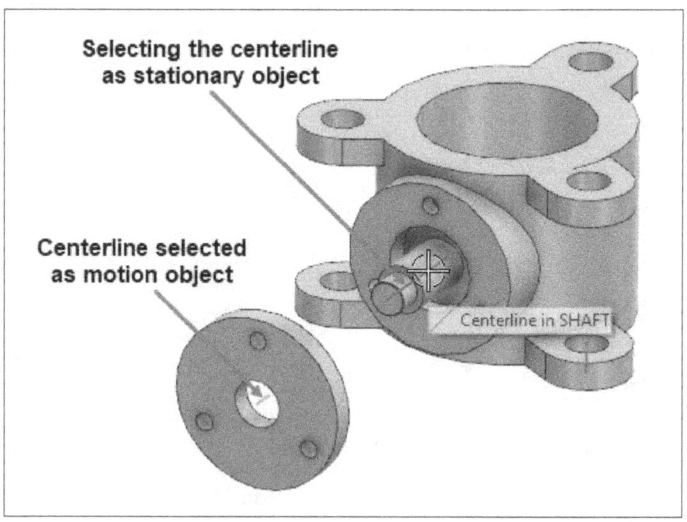

Figure-159. Selecting the geometries to be align constrained

- Click on **OK** button from the dialog box to apply the align constraint.
- Click on **Touch** tool from **Position** group of **Assemblies** tab in the **Ribbon**. The **Touch** dialog box will be displayed.
- Select the motion object to be constrained and then select the stationary object from the graphics window as shown in Figure-160. The preview of touch constraint will be displayed.
- Click on **OK** button from the dialog box. The touch constraint will be applied and the retainer will be constrained; refer to Figure-161.

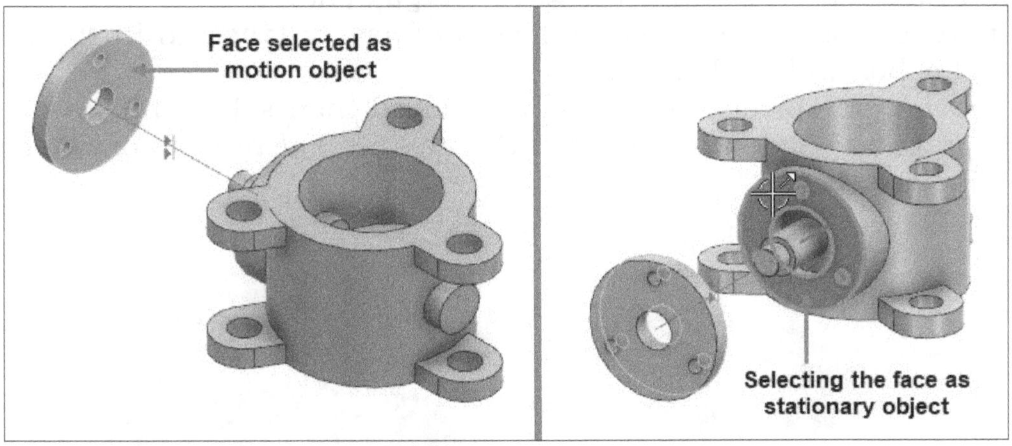

Figure-160. Selecting the geometries to be touch constrained

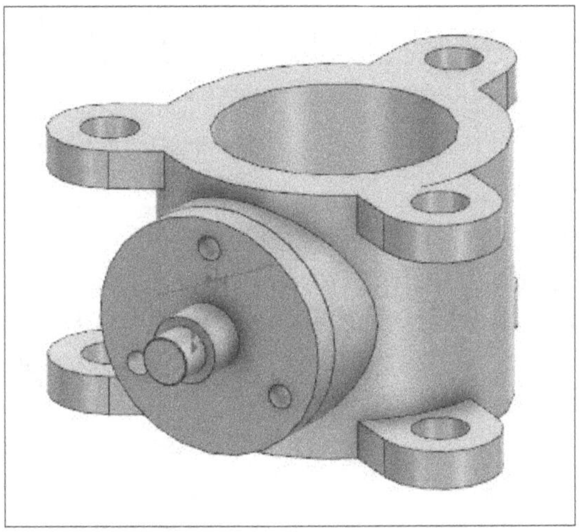

Figure-161. Retainer constrained

Constraining the Screw2

- Click on the **Auto Align** tool from **Position** group of **Assemblies** tab in the **Ribbon**. The **Auto Align** dialog box will be displayed.
- Select the centerline of both the screw and the retainer as the geometries to be constrained as shown in Figure-162. On selecting the centerline of retainer, the auto align constraint will be applied.

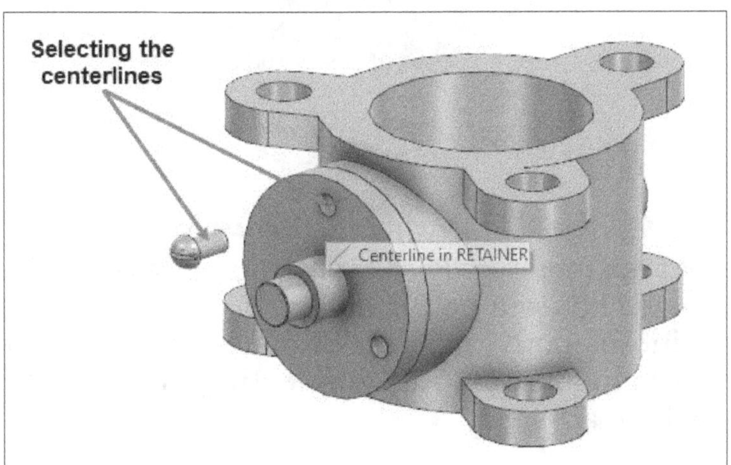

Figure-162. Selecting the geometries to be auto align constrained

- Click on **Close** button to close the **Auto Align** dialog box.
- Click on **Touch** tool from **Position** group of **Assemblies** tab in the **Ribbon**. The **Touch** dialog box will be displayed.
- Select the motion object to be constrained and then select the stationary object from the graphics window as shown in Figure-163. The preview of touch constraint will be displayed.

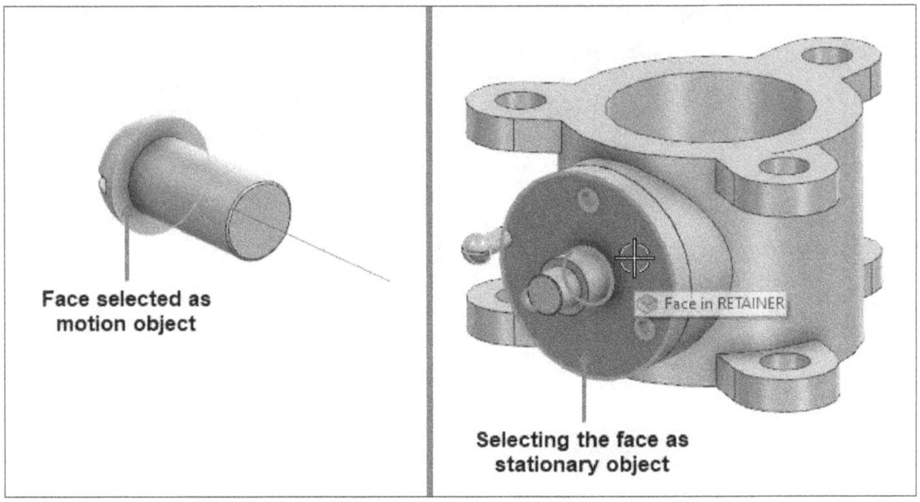

Figure-163. Selecting the geometries to be touch constrained

- Click on **OK** button from the dialog box. The touch constraint will be applied and the screw will be constrained in the first hole of retainer.
- Create copies of Screw2 and constraint them as discussed earlier. The components will be displayed as shown in Figure-164.

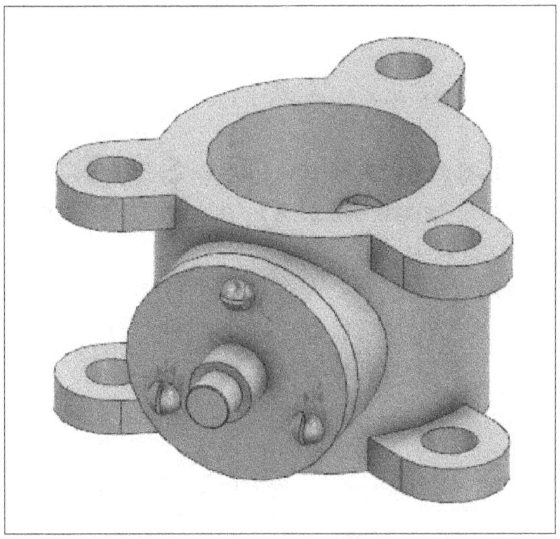

Figure-164. Screws constrained

Constraining the Arm

- Click on the **Auto Align** tool from **Position** group of **Assemblies** tab in the **Ribbon**. The **Auto Align** dialog box will be displayed.
- Select the centerline of both the arm and the shaft as the geometries to be constrained as shown in Figure-165. On selecting the centerline of shaft, the auto align constraint will be applied.

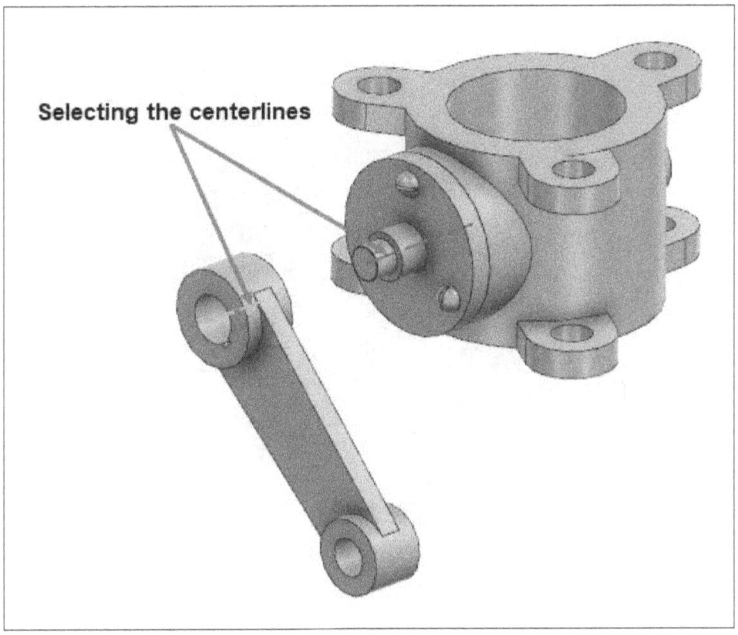

Figure-165. Selecting the geometries to be auto align constrained

- Click on **Close** button to close the **Auto Align** dialog box.
- Click on **Touch** tool from **Position** group of **Assemblies** tab in the **Ribbon**. The **Touch** dialog box will be displayed.
- Select the motion object to be constrained and then select the stationary object from the graphics window as shown in Figure-166. The preview of touch constraint will be displayed.

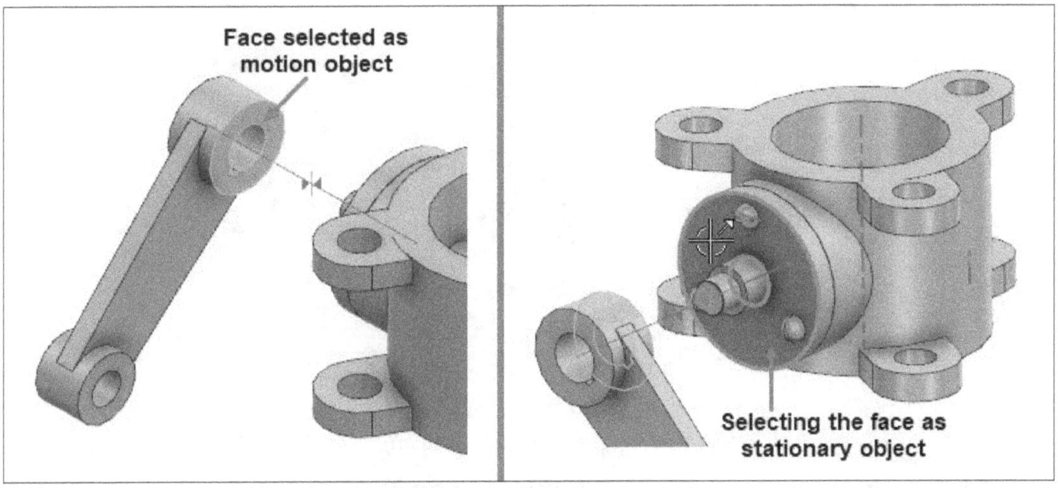

Figure-166. Selecting the geometries to be touch constrained

- Click on **OK** button from the dialog box. The touch constraint will be applied and the arm will be constrained; refer to Figure-167.

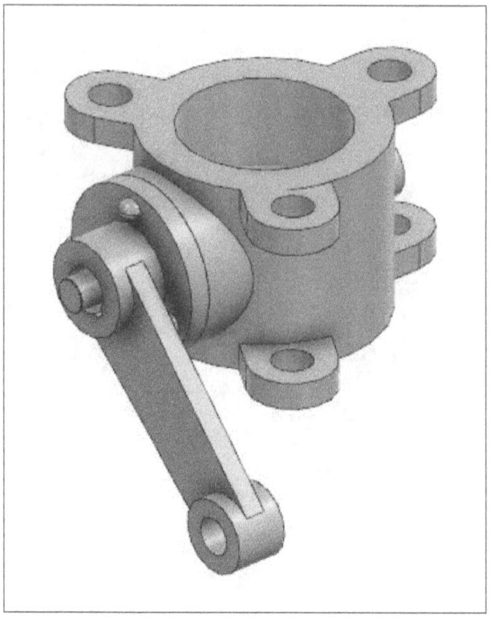

Figure-167. Arm constrained

Constraining the Nut

- Click on the **Auto Align** tool from **Position** group of **Assemblies** tab in the **Ribbon**. The **Auto Align** dialog box will be displayed.
- Select the centerline of both the nut and the shaft as the geometries to be constrained as shown in Figure-168. On selecting the centerline of shaft, the auto align constraint will be applied.

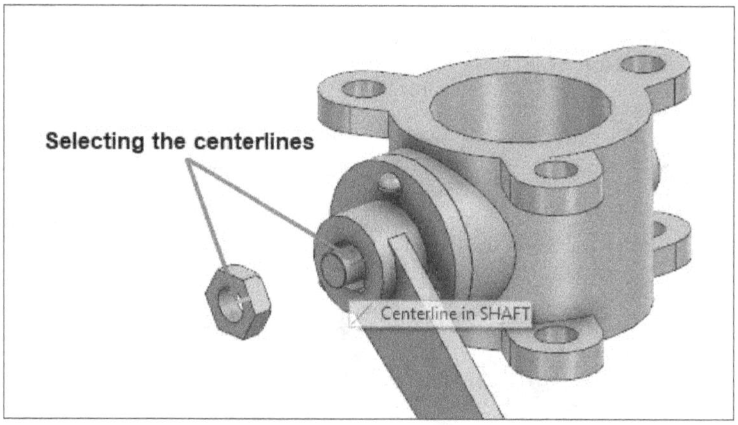

Figure-168. Selecting the geometries to be auto align constrained

- Click on **Close** button to close the **Auto Align** dialog box.
- Click on **Touch** tool from **Position** group of **Assemblies** tab in the **Ribbon**. The **Touch** dialog box will be displayed.
- Select the motion object to be constrained and then select the stationary object from the graphics window as shown in Figure-169. The preview of touch constraint will be displayed.

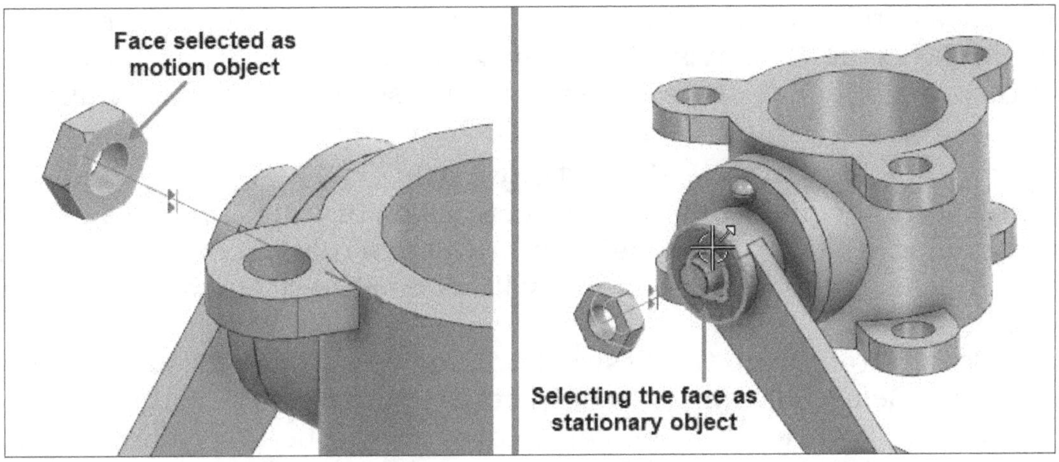

Figure-169. Selecting the geometries to be touch constrained

- Click on **OK** button from the dialog box. The touch constraint will be applied and the nut will be constrained.

After constraining all the components, the assembly of butterfly valve will be displayed as shown in Figure-170.

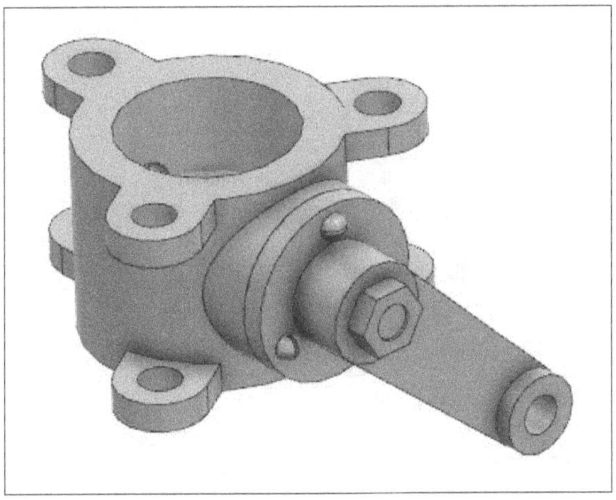

Figure-170. Butterfly valve assembled

PRACTICAL 3

Assemble the parts of **Piston Cylinder** as shown in Figure-171.

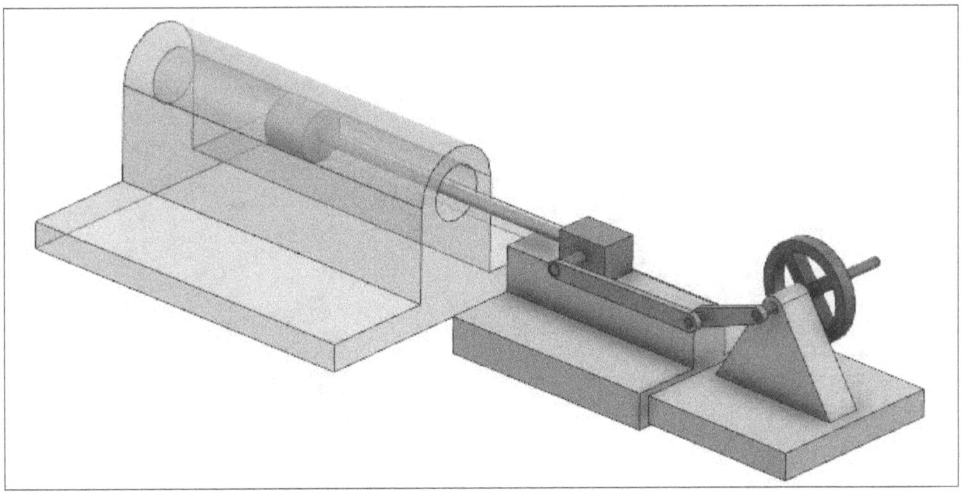

Figure-171. Assembly of Piston Cylinder

All the part files can be downloaded from the provided link. In this practical, we will use parts of **Practical 3 Piston Cylinder Assembly** folder from downloaded files/folders in resource kit. The steps to assemble these parts are given next.

Inserting Body

- Start the assembly environment by selecting **New** button from **Home** tab and select **Assembly** template from the **Model** tab in the **New** dialog box and click on the **OK** button. The Assembly environment will be displayed along with the **Assemble** dialog box.
- Click on **Open** button from the **Assemble** dialog box. The **Part Name** dialog box will be displayed. Select all the parts of **Piston Cylinder** folder and click on the **OK** button; refer to Figure-172. The selected parts will be inserted in the Assembly environment; refer to Figure-173.
- After inserting the parts, click on **OK** button from the dialog box.

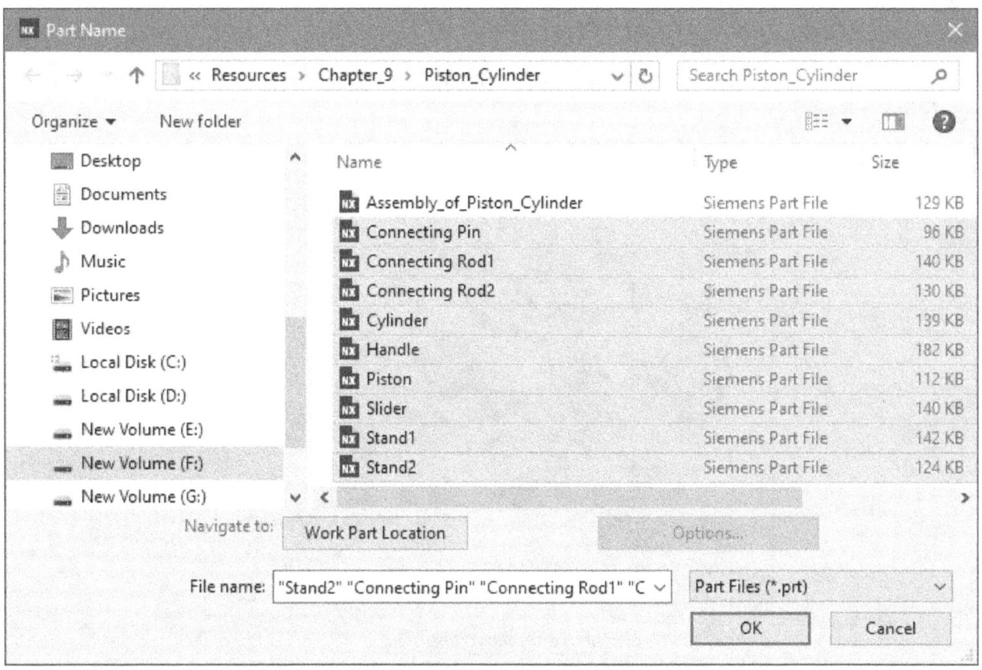

Figure-172. Selecting the parts of piston cylinder assembly

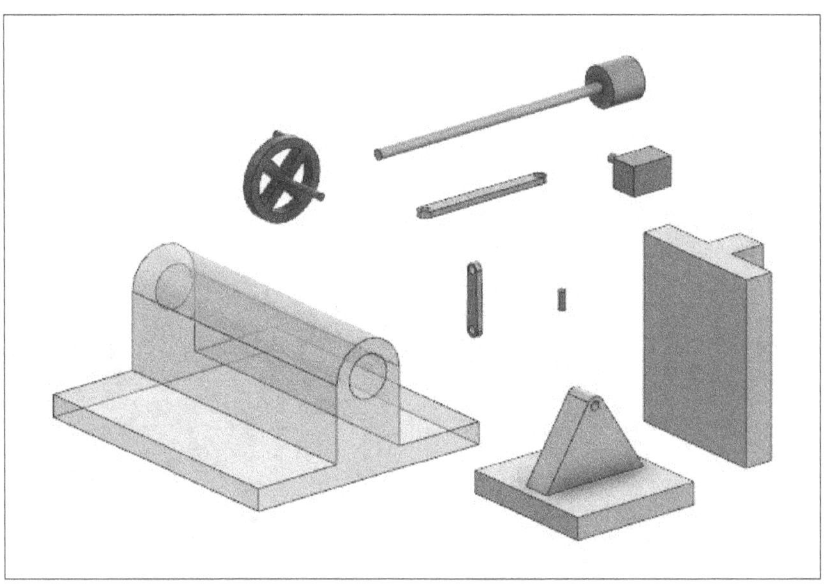

Figure-173. Parts opened in the Assembly environment

Constraining the Stand1

- Click on the **Fix** tool from **Position** group of **Assemblies** tab in the **Ribbon**. The **Fix** dialog box will be displayed.
- Select the Stand1 from the graphics window as shown in Figure-174.

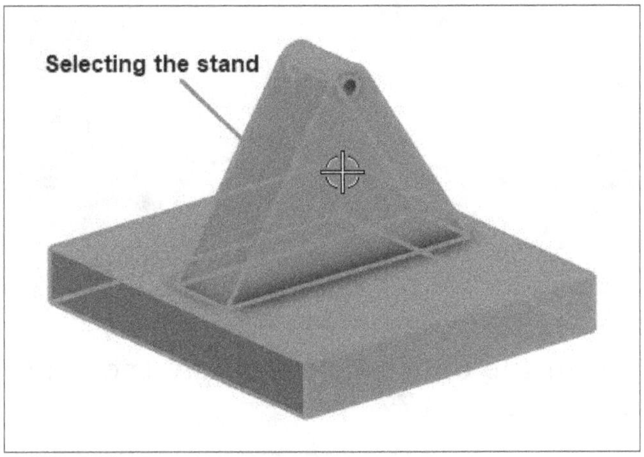

Figure-174. Selecting the Stand1 to be fixed

- After selecting the Stand1, click on **OK** button from the dialog box. The fix constraint will be applied to the Stand1.

Constraining the Handle

- Click on the **Auto Align** tool from **Position** group of **Assemblies** tab in the **Ribbon**. The **Auto Align** dialog box will be displayed.
- Select the centerline of handle and the stand as the geometries to be constrained as shown in Figure-175. On selecting the centerline of the stand, the auto align constraint will be applied.

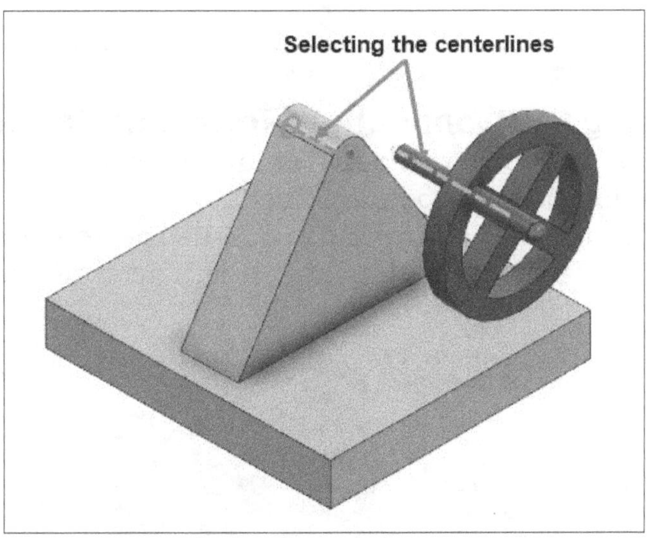

Figure-175. Selecting the geometries to be auto align constrained

- Click on **Close** button to close the **Auto Align** dialog box.
- Click on the **Distance** tool from **Position** group of **Assemblies** tab in the **Ribbon**. The **Distance** dialog box will be displayed.
- Select the geometries as shown in Figure-176 and specify the distance value as **7** in the **Distance** edit box of **Value** rollout. The preview of distance constrained will be displayed.

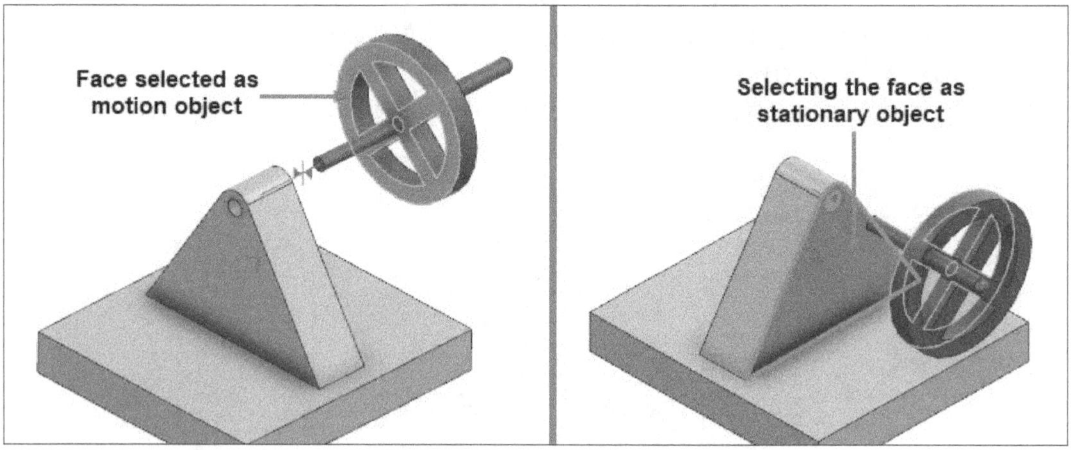

Figure-176. Selecting the geometries to be distance constrained

- Click on **OK** button from the dialog box to apply the constraint. The handle will be constrained; refer to Figure-177.

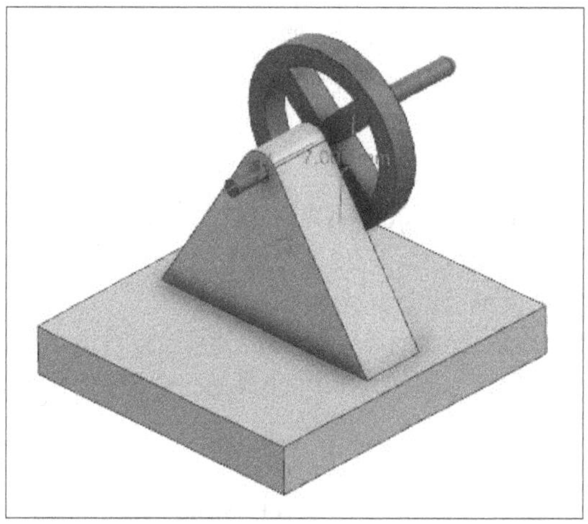

Figure-177. Handle constrained

Constraining the Connecting Rods and Connecting Pin

- Click on the **Concentric** tool from **Position** group of **Assemblies** tab in the **Ribbon**. The **Concentric** dialog box will be displayed.
- Select the edge of handle and connecting rod1 as the geometries to be constrained as shown in Figure-178. The preview of concentric constraint will be displayed.

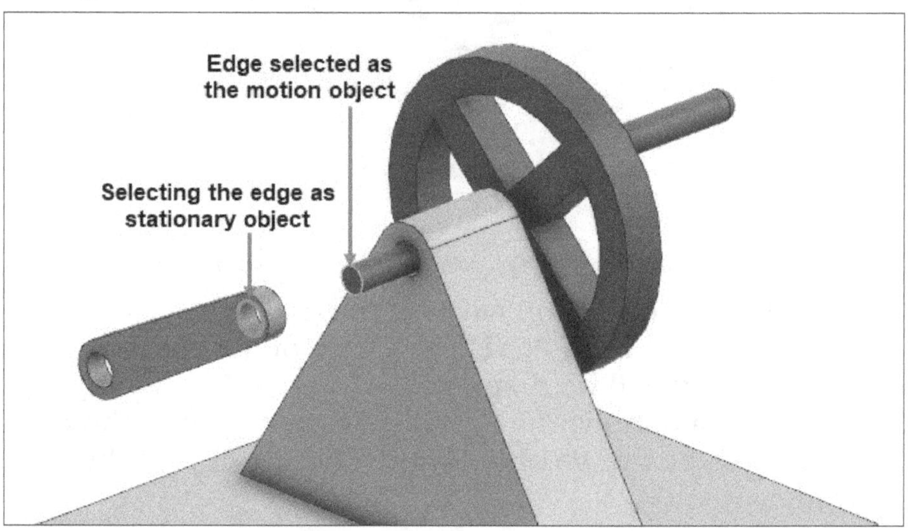

Figure-178. Selecting the geometries to be concentric constrained

- Click on **Apply** button from the dialog box. The connecting rod1 will be constrained.
- Similarly, constrain the connecting pin and then connecting rod2 using the **Concentric** tool as discussed earlier. The components will be displayed as shown in Figure-179.

Figure-179. Connecting rods and connecting pin constrained

Constraining the Stand2

- Click on the **Align** tool from **Position** group of **Assemblies** tab in the **Ribbon**. The **Align** dialog box will be displayed.
- Select motion object from the graphics window to be constrained and then select the stationary object as shown in Figure-180. The preview of align constraint will be displayed.

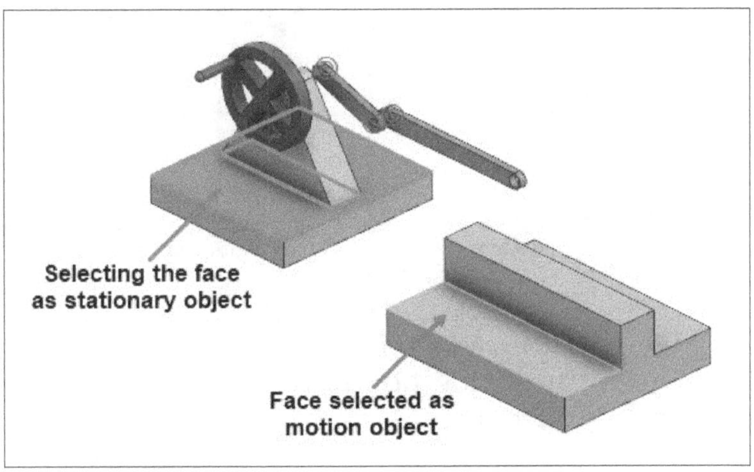

Figure-180. Selecting the geometries to be align constrained

- Click on **Apply** button from the dialog box to apply the align constraint.
- Again, select the motion and stationary object for align constraint from the graphics window as shown in Figure-181.

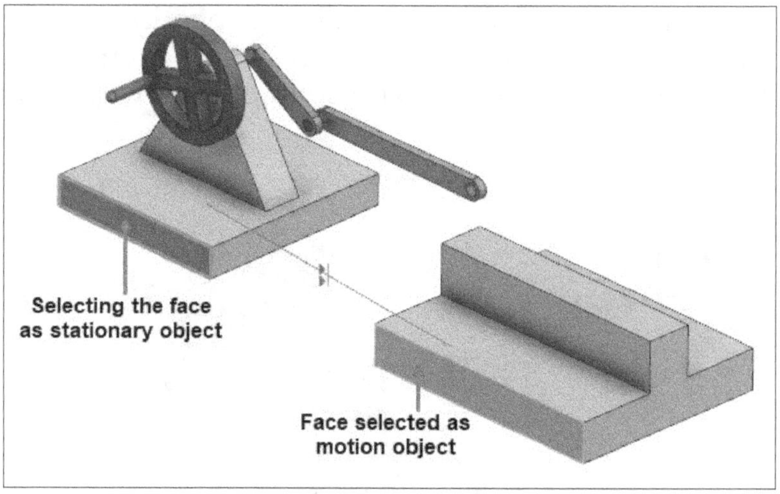

Figure-181. Selecting the geometries to be align constrained

- Click on **OK** button from the dialog box to apply the align constraint.
- Click on the **Distance** tool from **Position** group of **Assemblies** tab in the **Ribbon**. The **Distance** dialog box will be displayed.
- Select the geometries as shown in Figure-182 and specify the distance value as **10** in the **Distance** edit box of **Value** rollout. The preview of distance constraint will be displayed.

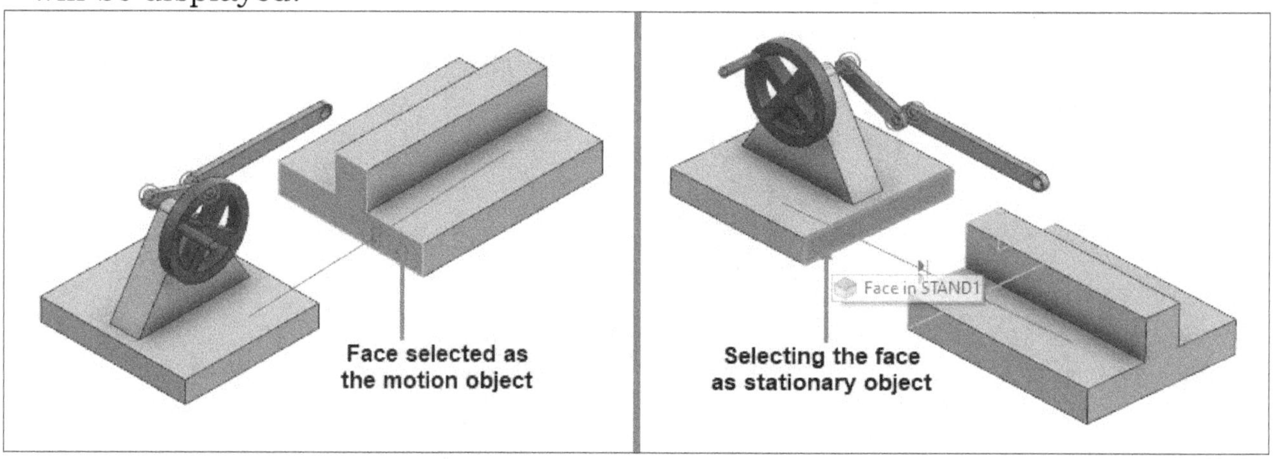

Figure-182. Selecting the geometries to be distance constrained

- Click on **OK** button from the dialog box to apply the constraint. The stand2 will be constrained; refer to Figure-183.

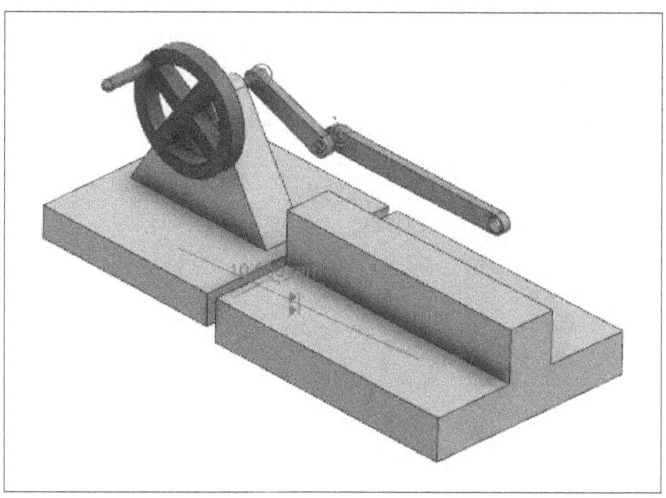

Figure-183. Stand2 constrained

Constraining the Slider

- Click on the **Touch** tool from **Position** group of **Assemblies** tab in the **Ribbon**. The **Touch** dialog box will be displayed.
- Select the motion object to be constrained and then select the stationary object from the graphics window as shown in Figure-184. The preview of touch constraint will be displayed.

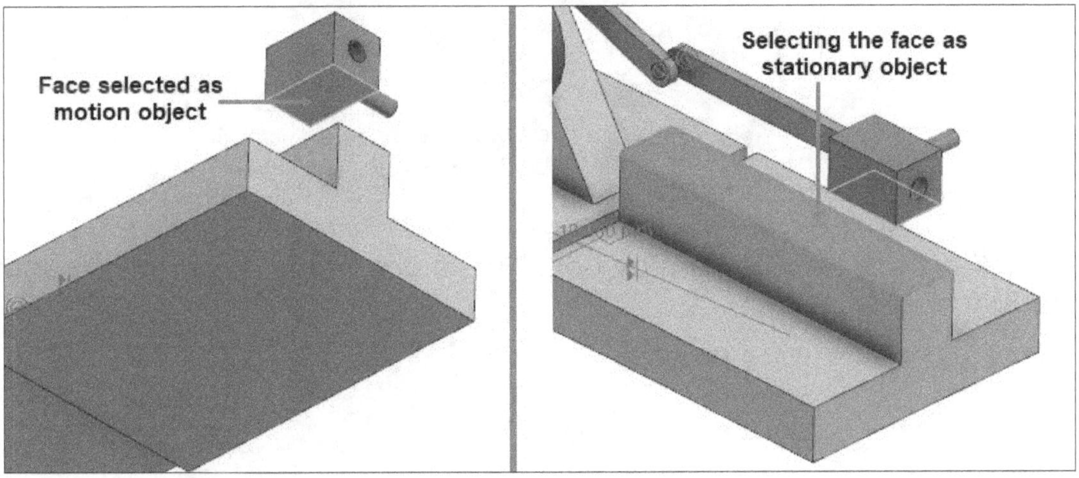

Figure-184. Selecting the geometries to be touch constrained

- Click on **OK** button from the dialog box to apply the touch constraint.
- Click on the **Center** tool from **Position** group of **Assemblies** tab in the **Ribbon**. The **Center** dialog box will be displayed.
- Select **2 to 2** option from drop-down in the top area of the dialog box and select the geometries of components as shown in Figure-185. The preview of center constraint will be displayed.

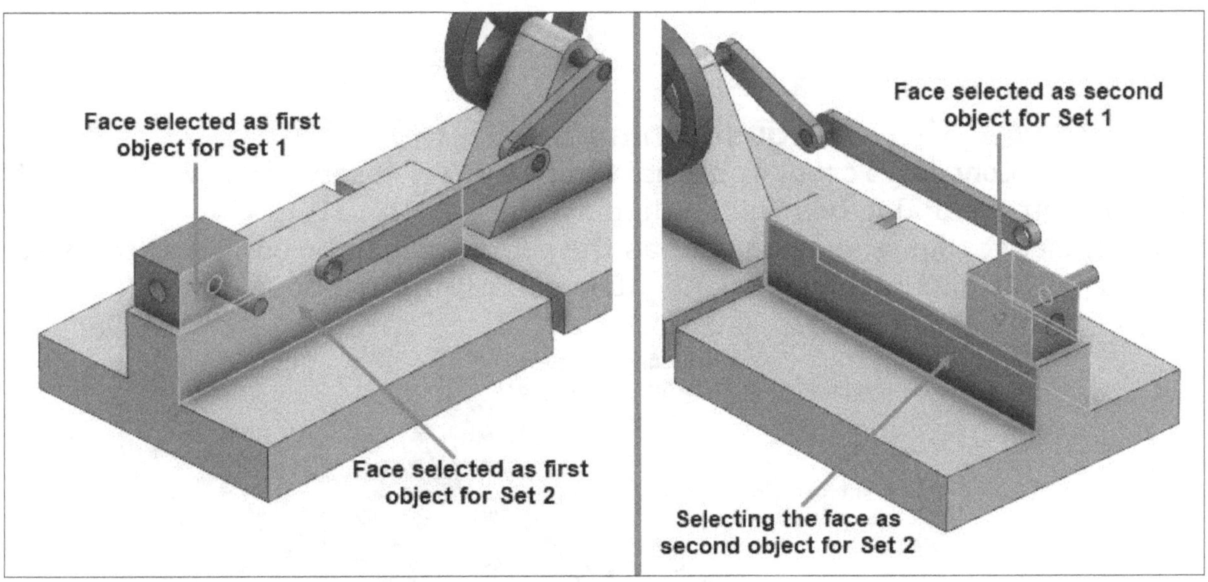

Figure-185. Selecting the geometries to be center constrained

- Click on **OK** button from the dialog box to apply the center constraint.
- Click on the **Concentric** tool from **Position** group of **Assemblies** tab in the **Ribbon**. The **Concentric** dialog box will be displayed.
- Select the edge of slider and connecting rod2 as the geometries to be constrained as shown in Figure-186. The preview of concentric constraint will be displayed.

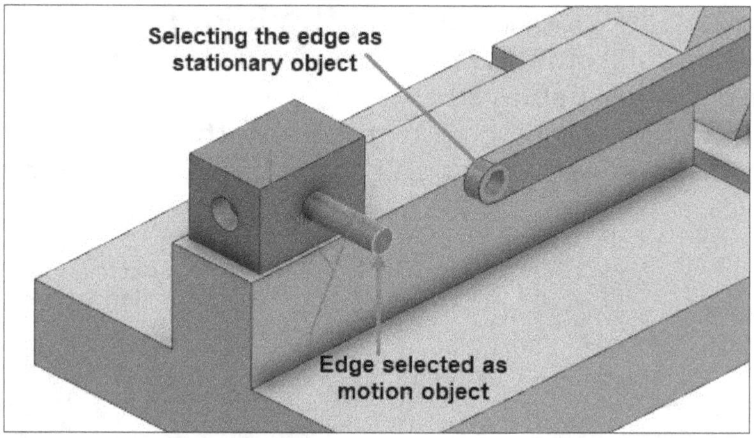

Figure-186. Selecting the geometries to be concentric constrained

- Click on **OK** button from the dialog box. The slider will be concentric constrained; refer to Figure-187.

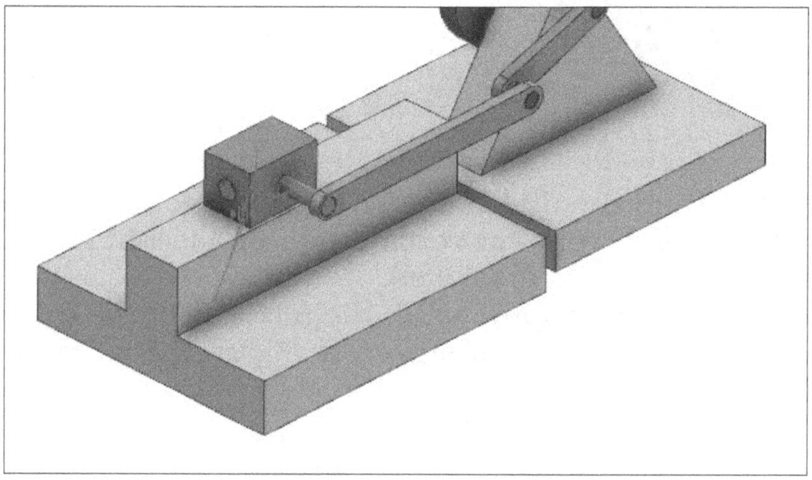

Figure-187. Slider constrained

Constraining the Piston

- Click on the **Concentric** tool from **Position** group of **Assemblies** tab in the **Ribbon**. The **Concentric** dialog box will be displayed.
- Select the edge of piston and slider as the geometries to be constrained as shown in Figure-188. The preview of concentric constraint will be displayed.

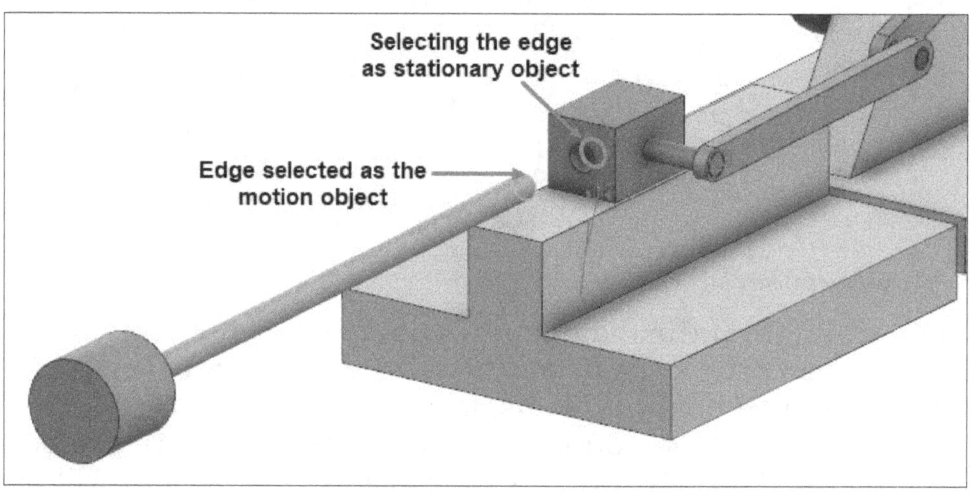

Figure-188. Selecting the geometries to be concentric constrained

- Click on **OK** button from the dialog box. The piston will be concentric constrained; refer to Figure-189.

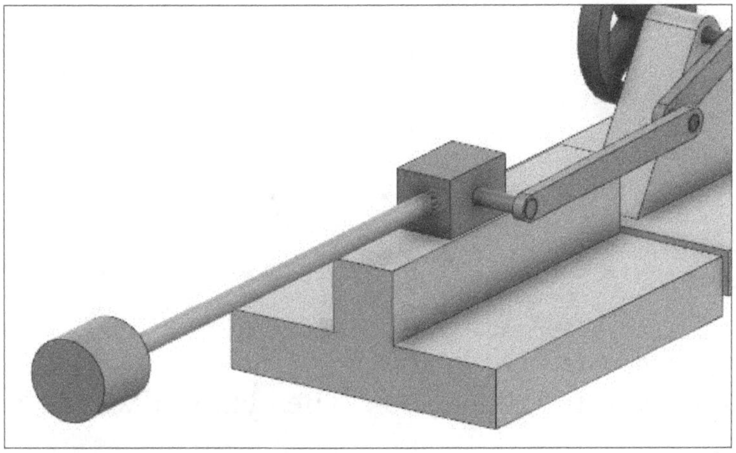

Figure-189. Piston constrained

Constraining the Cylinder

- Click on the **Auto Align** tool from **Position** group of **Assemblies** tab in the **Ribbon**. The **Auto Align** dialog box will be displayed.
- Select the centerline of cylinder and the piston as the geometries to be constrained as shown in Figure-190. On selecting the centerline of piston, the auto align constraint will be applied.

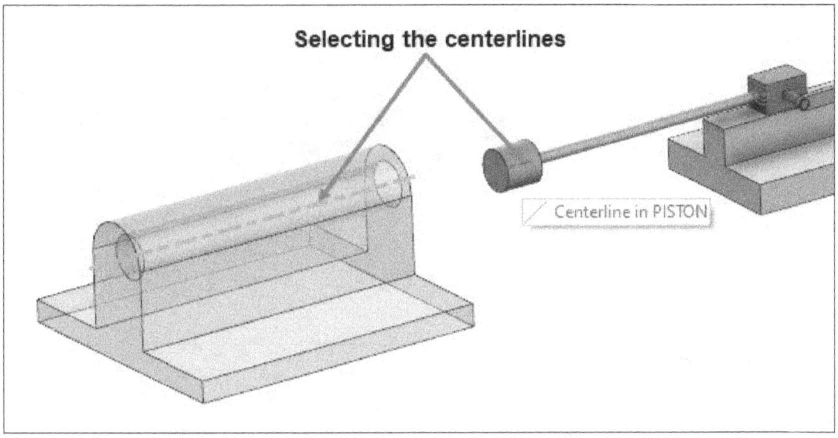

Figure-190. Selecting the geometries to be auto align constrained

- Click on **Close** button to close the **Auto Align** dialog box.
- Click on the **Distance** tool from **Position** group of **Assemblies** tab in the **Ribbon**. The **Distance** dialog box will be displayed.
- Select the geometries as shown in Figure-191 and specify the distance value as **90** in the **Distance** edit box of **Value** rollout. The preview of distance constraint will be displayed.

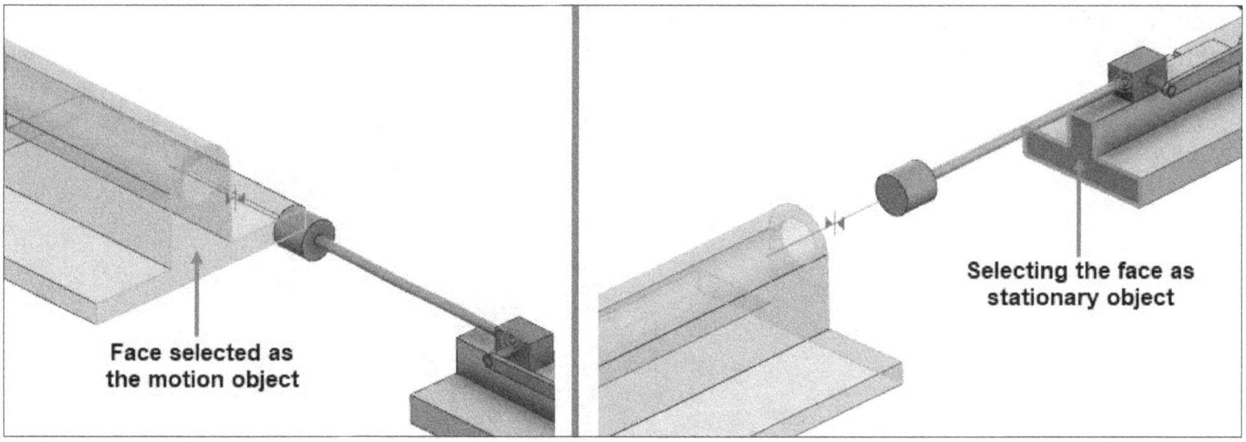

Figure-191. Selecting the geometries to be distance constrained

- Click on **OK** button from the dialog box. The cylinder will be constrained.

After constraining all the components, the assembly of **Piston Cylinder** will be displayed as shown in Figure-192.

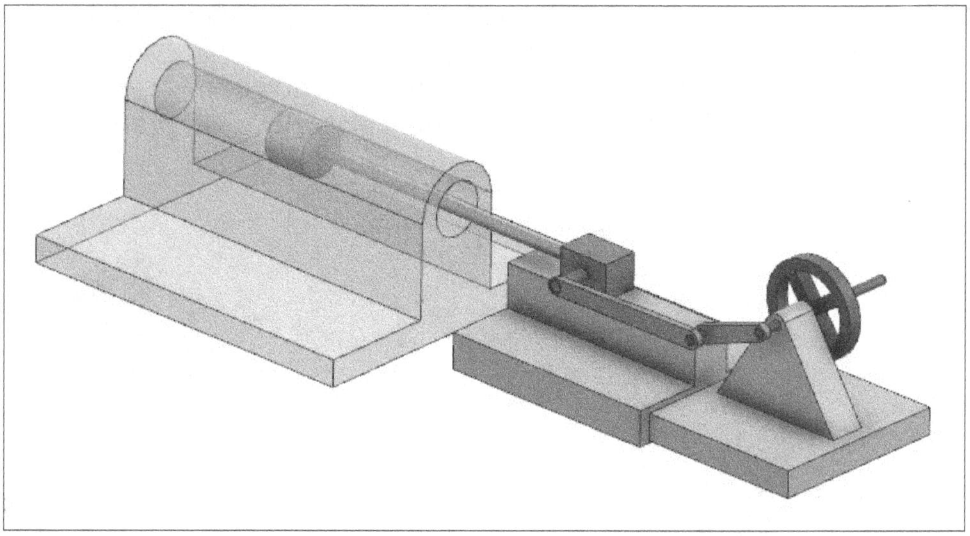

Figure-192. Piston Cylinder assembled

PRACTICE 1

Assemble the model as shown in Figure-193.

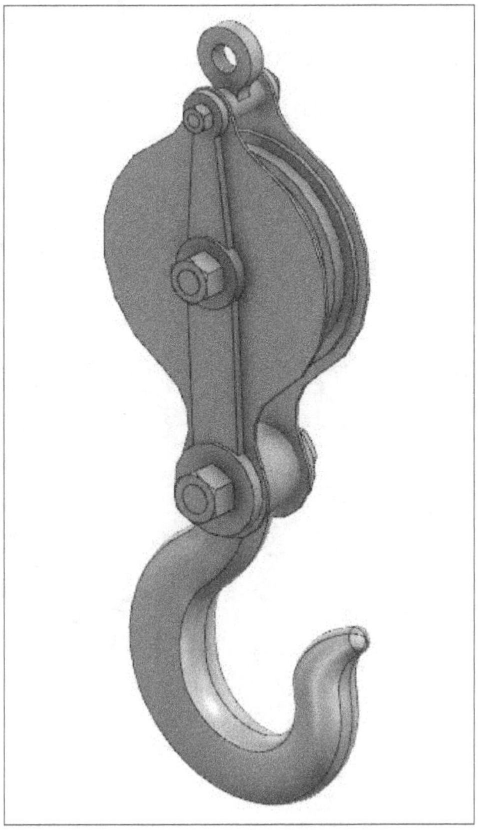

Figure-193. Crane Hook Assembly

PRACTICE 2

Assemble the model as shown in Figure-194.

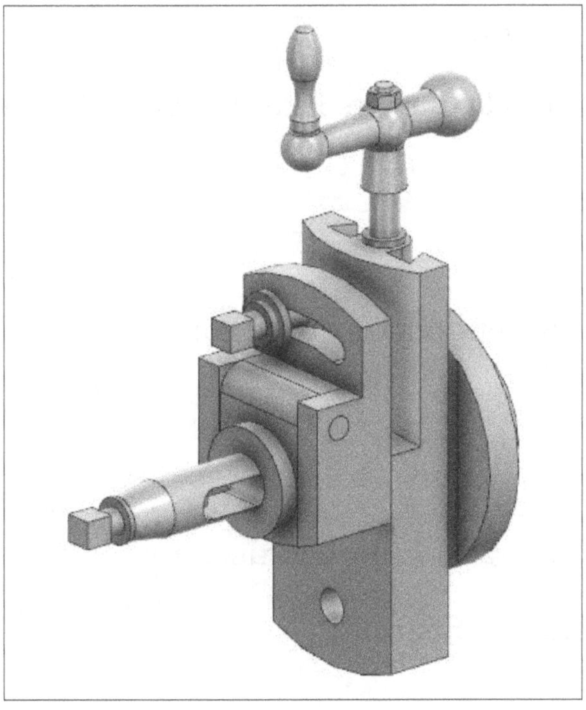

Figure-194. Shaper Tool Assembly

PRACTICE 3

Assemble the model as shown in Figure-195.

Figure-195. Tailstock Assembly

SELF-ASSESSMENT

Q1. The Assemble tool is used to:
A. Delete components from assembly
B. Create or edit an assembly
C. Only view components
D. Apply colors to components

Q2. Which option is used to load parts into the Assemble dialog box?
A. Save button
B. Open button
C. Apply button
D. Close button

Q3. The Select or Drag Object option is used to:
A. Delete parts
B. Rename parts
C. Position or constrain parts
D. Hide parts

Q4. The Reverse Last Constraint button is used to:
A. Delete constraints
B. Apply another solution to constraint
C. Lock constraint
D. Hide constraint

Q5. The Keep Constraints checkbox is used to:
A. Remove constraints
B. Save constraints for reuse
C. Create constraints while placing components
D. Ignore constraints

Q6. The Add Component tool is used to:
A. Remove components
B. Add one or more components
C. Fix components
D. Align components

Q7. The Count edit box in Add Component tool specifies:
A. Size of component
B. Number of instances
C. Color of component
D. Layer of component

Q8. The Scatter Components option is used to:
A. Delete components
B. Overlap components
C. Automatically place components without overlapping
D. Rotate components

Q9. The New Component tool is used to:
A. Delete component
B. Create new component from geometry
C. Align components
D. Move components

Q10. The Delete Original Objects checkbox is used to:
A. Hide objects
B. Lock objects
C. Delete original geometry after creating component
D. Rename objects

Q11. The New Parent Assembly tool is used to:
A. Delete assembly
B. Create new parent assembly file
C. Move assembly
D. Align assembly

Q12. The Fix tool is used to:
A. Move objects
B. Fix objects in position
C. Delete objects
D. Rotate objects

Q13. The Auto Align tool is used to:
A. Delete objects
B. Align or touch objects
C. Rename objects
D. Hide objects

Q14. The Touch tool is used to:
A. Rotate objects
B. Make objects touch each other
C. Delete objects
D. Scale objects

Q15. The Align tool is used to:
A. Delete objects
B. Align objects
C. Rotate objects
D. Hide objects

Q16. The Parallel tool makes objects:
A. Perpendicular
B. Parallel
C. Circular
D. Fixed

Q17. The Perpendicular tool makes objects:
A. Parallel
B. Circular
C. Perpendicular
D. Fixed

Q18. The Concentric tool is used for:
A. Lines
B. Circular or elliptical edges
C. Surfaces only
D. Points only

Q19. The Align/Lock tool also:
A. Deletes rotation
B. Locks rotation about axis
C. Hides objects
D. Changes color

Q20. The Distance tool is used to:
A. Measure only
B. Define 3D distance constraint
C. Rotate objects
D. Delete objects

Q21. The Angle tool defines:
A. Distance
B. Color
C. Angle constraint
D. Layer

Q22. The Bond tool makes objects:
A. Move freely
B. Fixed separately
C. Move as rigid set
D. Invisible

Q23. The Center tool is used to:
A. Delete objects
B. Center objects between others
C. Rotate objects
D. Scale objects

Q24. The Hinge tool constrains objects along:
A. Plane
B. Axis of rotation
C. Surface
D. Edge

Q25. The Cylindrical tool constrains objects along:
A. Fixed axis
B. Rotatable linear axis
C. Plane
D. Curve

Q26. The Gear tool defines:
A. Linear motion
B. Angular relation between joints
C. Distance constraint
D. Fix constraint

Q27. The Cable tool defines:
A. Angular motion
B. Linear relation between joints
C. Rotation lock
D. Alignment

Q28. The Slider tool is used to:
A. Rotate objects
B. Constrain along linear axis
C. Delete objects
D. Hide objects

Q29. The Ball tool constrains objects at:
A. Edge
B. Face
C. Shared point
D. Axis

Q30. The Rack and Pinion tool defines motion between:
A. Two linear joints
B. Two angular joints
C. Linear and angular joint
D. Fixed joints

Q31. The Move Component tool is used to:
A. Delete components
B. Move components
C. Align components
D. Hide components

Q32. The No Copy option in Move Component means:
A. Duplicate components
B. Do not copy components
C. Delete components
D. Hide components

Q33. Collision Detection option "Stop Before Collision" will:
A. Ignore collision
B. Highlight collision
C. Stop movement before collision
D. Delete object

Q34. The Show Degrees of Freedom tool shows:
A. Color of component
B. Movement freedom of component
C. Size of component
D. Layer of component

Q35. The Show and Hide Constraints tool is used to:
A. Delete constraints
B. Show or hide constraints and components
C. Move constraints
D. Rename constraints

Q36. The Remember Constraints tool is used to:
A. Delete constraints
B. Save constraints for reuse
C. Hide constraints
D. Lock constraints

Q37. The Create Persistent Constraints toggle is used to:
A. Delete constraints
B. Enable persistent constraints
C. Hide constraints
D. Rename constraints

Q38. The Arrangements tool is used to:
A. Delete assembly
B. Create and edit assembly arrangements
C. Move assembly
D. Fix assembly

Q39. The Copy button in Arrangements tool is used to:
A. Delete arrangement
B. Copy arrangement
C. Rename arrangement
D. Hide arrangement

Q40. The Ignore All Constraints option means:
A. Apply constraints
B. Do not resolve positions by constraints
C. Delete constraints
D. Lock constraints

Q41. The Pattern Component tool is used to:
A. Delete components
B. Copy a component into a specified pattern
C. Hide components
D. Rename components

Q42. Which tab contains the Pattern Component tool?
A. Home tab
B. View tab
C. Assemblies tab
D. Insert tab

Q43. In Pattern Component, which option is used to preview component geometry?
A. Associative
B. Dynamic Positioning
C. Instance Points
D. Layout

Q44. The Associative check box in Pattern Component creates:
A. Static components
B. Temporary components
C. Editable patterned components
D. Hidden components

Q45. The Mirror Assembly tool is used to:
A. Rotate assembly
B. Copy assembly randomly
C. Create mirrored version of assembly/components
D. Delete assembly

Q46. In Mirror Assembly, selecting a plane is required to:
A. Hide component
B. Rename component
C. Define mirror direction
D. Delete component

Q47. Which option creates associative mirrored geometry?
A. Reuse and Reposition
B. Non-Associative Mirror
C. Associative Mirror
D. Exclude

Q48. The Exclude option in Mirror Assembly is used to:
A. Add components
B. Remove selected components from mirroring
C. Rename components
D. Rotate components

Q49. The Make Unique tool is used to:
A. Delete parts
B. Create a new part file for selected occurrences
C. Copy assembly
D. Hide components

Q50. Replace Component tool is used to:
A. Add new part
B. Delete part
C. Replace one component with another
D. Hide part

Q51. Maintain Relationships option ensures:
A. Component deletion
B. Relationships like constraints are preserved
C. Faster processing
D. New geometry creation

Q52. Edit Suppression State tool is used to:
A. Rename components
B. Define suppression state of components
C. Delete components
D. Copy components

Q53. Suppress Component tool is used to:
A. Rename component
B. Hide component and its children
C. Duplicate component
D. Rotate component

Q54. Unsuppress Component tool is used to:
A. Delete hidden component
B. Show previously suppressed component
C. Rename component
D. Move component

Q55. Reference Sets tool controls:
A. Color of components
B. Data loaded and viewed in assembly
C. File size only
D. Component rotation

Q56. Replace Reference Set tool is used to:
A. Delete reference
B. Choose reference set to display
C. Rename reference
D. Hide reference

Q57. Find Components tool is used to:
A. Delete components
B. Locate components using properties
C. Rotate components
D. Mirror components

Q58. Hide Components in View tool is used to:
A. Show components
B. Hide selected components
C. Delete components
D. Copy components

Q59. Show Components in View tool is used to:
A. Hide components
B. Show hidden components
C. Delete components
D. Replace components

Q60. Open by Proximity tool loads components based on:
A. Name
B. Color
C. Distance from selected component
D. Size only

Q61. Isolate in New Window tool is used to:
A. Delete components
B. Show selected components in new window
C. Rename components
D. Hide all components

Q62. Show Product Outline tool displays:
A. Component names
B. Outline of overall assembly
C. Hidden parts
D. Errors

Q63. Save Context tool stores:
A. File name
B. Work part and visibility
C. Geometry
D. Constraints

Q64. Restore Context tool restores:
A. Deleted parts
B. Stored context
C. Hidden geometry only
D. Constraints

Q65. WAVE Geometry Linker is used to:
A. Delete geometry
B. Copy geometry from other parts
C. Hide geometry
D. Rename geometry

Chapter 12

Drawing and Practice

Topics Covered

The major topics covered in this chapter are:

- ***Drawing Introduction.***
- ***Drawing Sheet Selection.***
- ***Adding Views to sheet.***
- ***Annotating Views.***
- ***Exploded View and Bill of Material.***
- ***Balloons and Title Block***
- ***Practice.***

INTRODUCTION

Drawing is the engineering representation of a model on the paper. For manufacturing a model in real world, we need some means by which we can tell the manufacturer what to make. For this purpose, we create drawings from the models. These drawings have information like dimensions, material, tolerances, objective, precautions, and so on. In NX, we create drawings by using the Drawing environment. To activate this environment, click on the **New** button from **Standard** group of **Home** tab in the **Ribbon**. The **New** dialog box will be displayed. Click on the **Drawing** tab in the dialog box. The options will be displayed as shown in Figure-1.

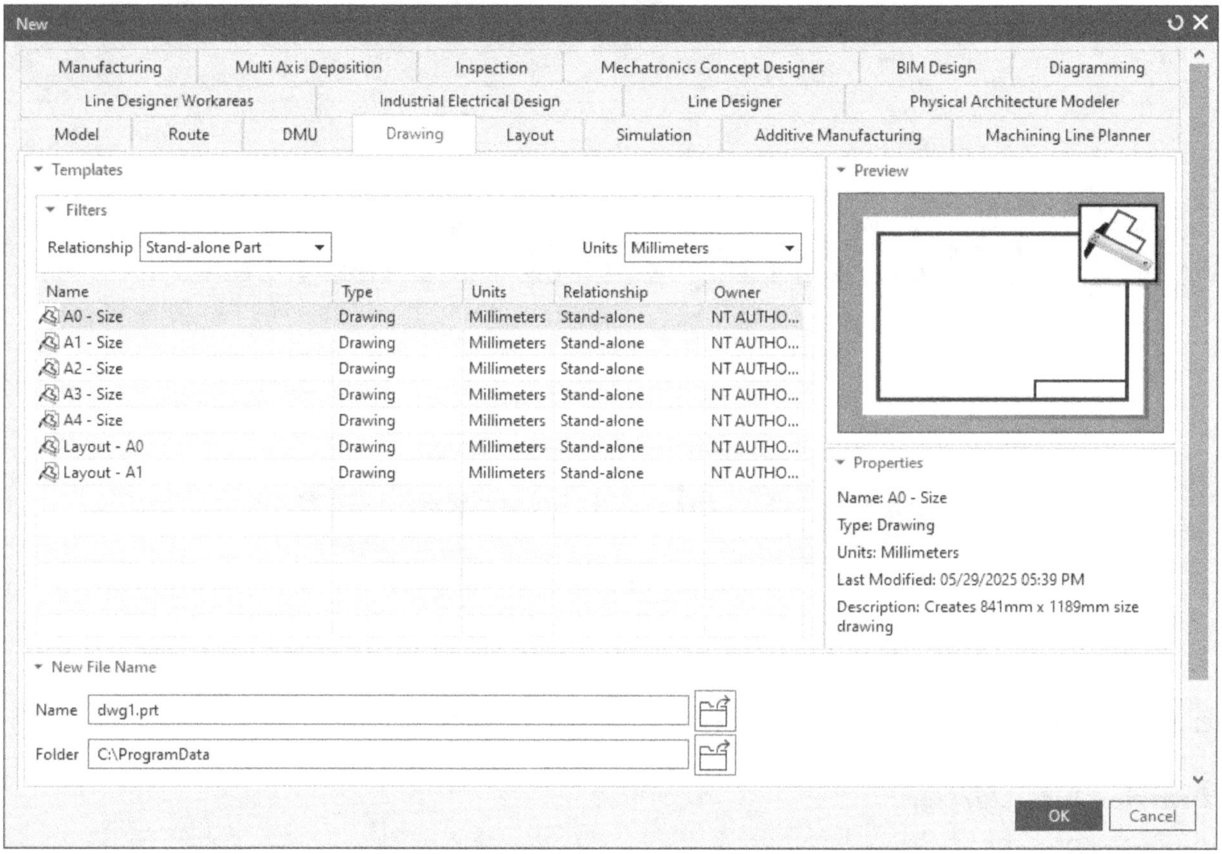

Figure-1. Drawing tab in New dialog box

- Select the **Stand-alone Part** option from the **Relationship** drop-down at the top in the dialog box if you want to create a new drawing without attaching any 3D model. List of related templates will be displayed in the dialog box.
- Select the **Reference Existing Part** option from the **Relationship** drop-down if you want to include a reference 3D model whose views will be generated in the drawing. The list of templates will be displayed accordingly. Select the **All** option from **Relationship** drop-down to display all the available templates.
- Select desired template file from the list in **Templates** rollout to create the drawing.
- Specify desired name of file in the **Name** edit box of **New File Name** rollout and specify desired directory to save the file in the **Folder** edit box.
- Select desired model file using the **Browse** button in the **Part to Create a Drawing of** rollout to use it for creating drawing. The **Select CAD Source Part** dialog box will be displayed; refer to Figure-2.

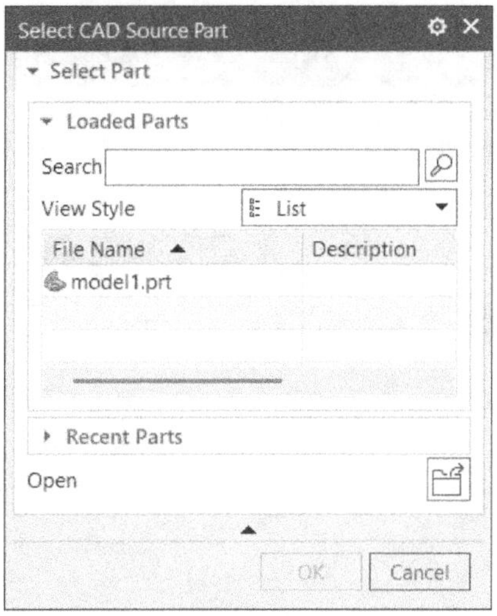

Figure-2. Select CAD Source Part dialog box

- Click on the **Open** button from the bottom in the dialog box and select desired model file from the **Part Name** dialog box; refer to Figure-3.

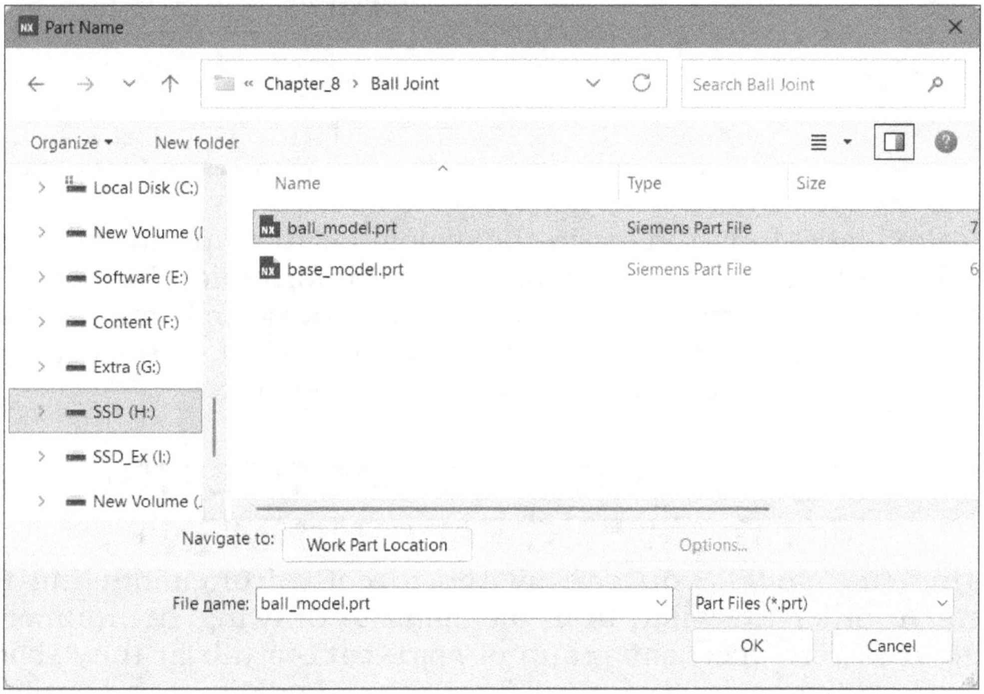

Figure-3. Part Name dialog box

- Click on the **OK** button from the dialog box to set current selected part as model for drawing and then click on the **OK** button from the **Select CAD Source Part** dialog box.
- After specifying desired parameters, click on **OK** button from the dialog box. The drawing environment will be displayed; refer to Figure-4.

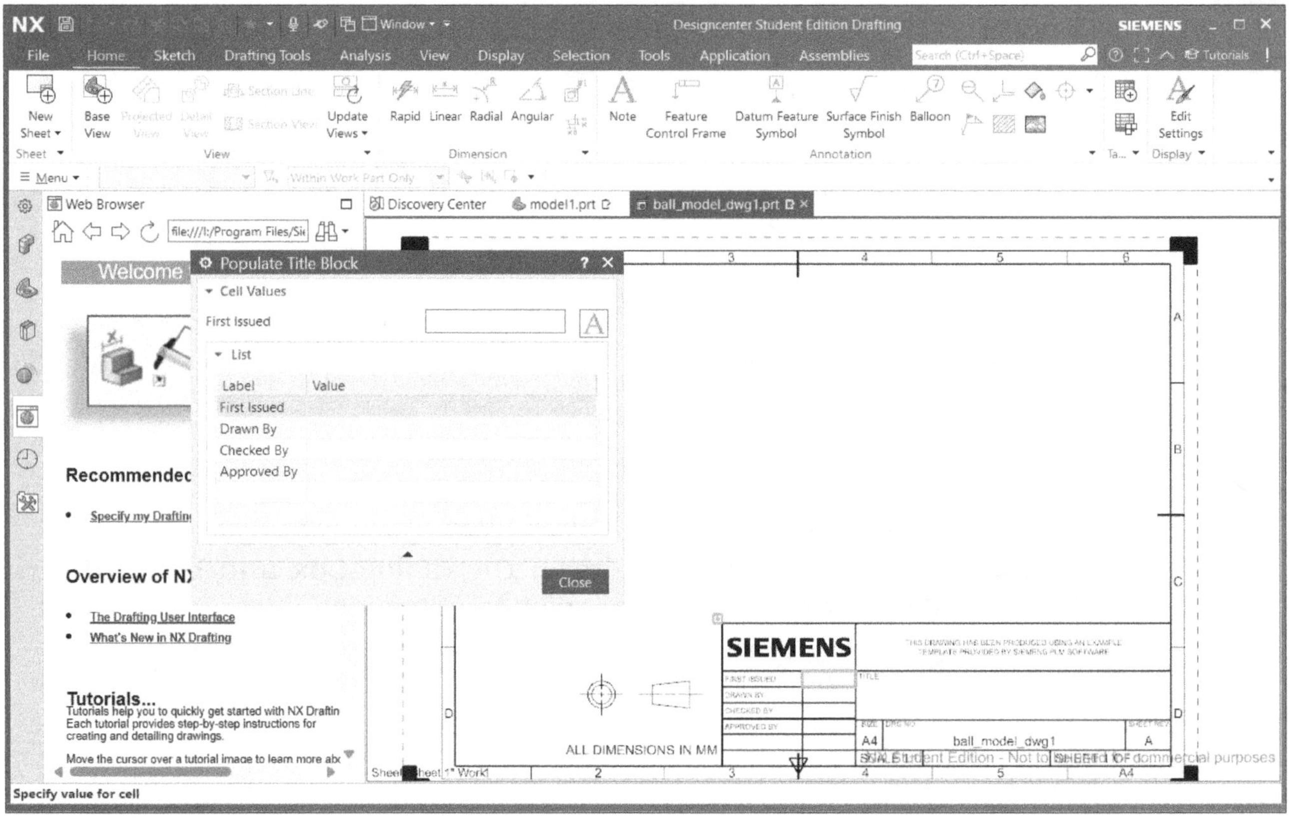

Figure-4. Drawing environment

- Select desired label from the list in the dialog box and specify value to be added in the Title block of drawing. Title block is an information box generally placed at the bottom right corner and it is used to provide information like name of designer, date of being drawn, checked by, approved by, and so on. Click on the **Close** button from the **Populate Title Block** dialog box.

SWITCHING FROM MODELING TO DRAWING ENVIRONMENT

After creating the model, you can switch directly from modeling to drawing environment. In order to switch from modeling to drawing environment, click on the **Drafting** tool from **Document** group of **Application** tab in the **Ribbon**; refer to Figure-5. The **Drawing** environment will be displayed as discussed earlier. Also, the **Sheet** dialog box will be displayed; refer to Figure-6. Using this dialog box, you can set the size of sheet for placing the drawing views.

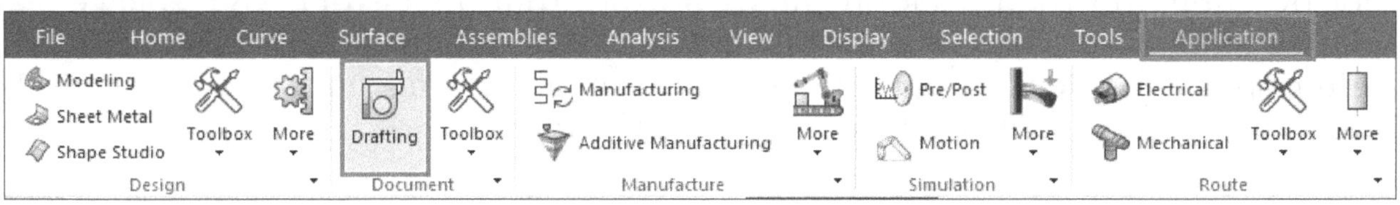

Figure-5. Drafting tool

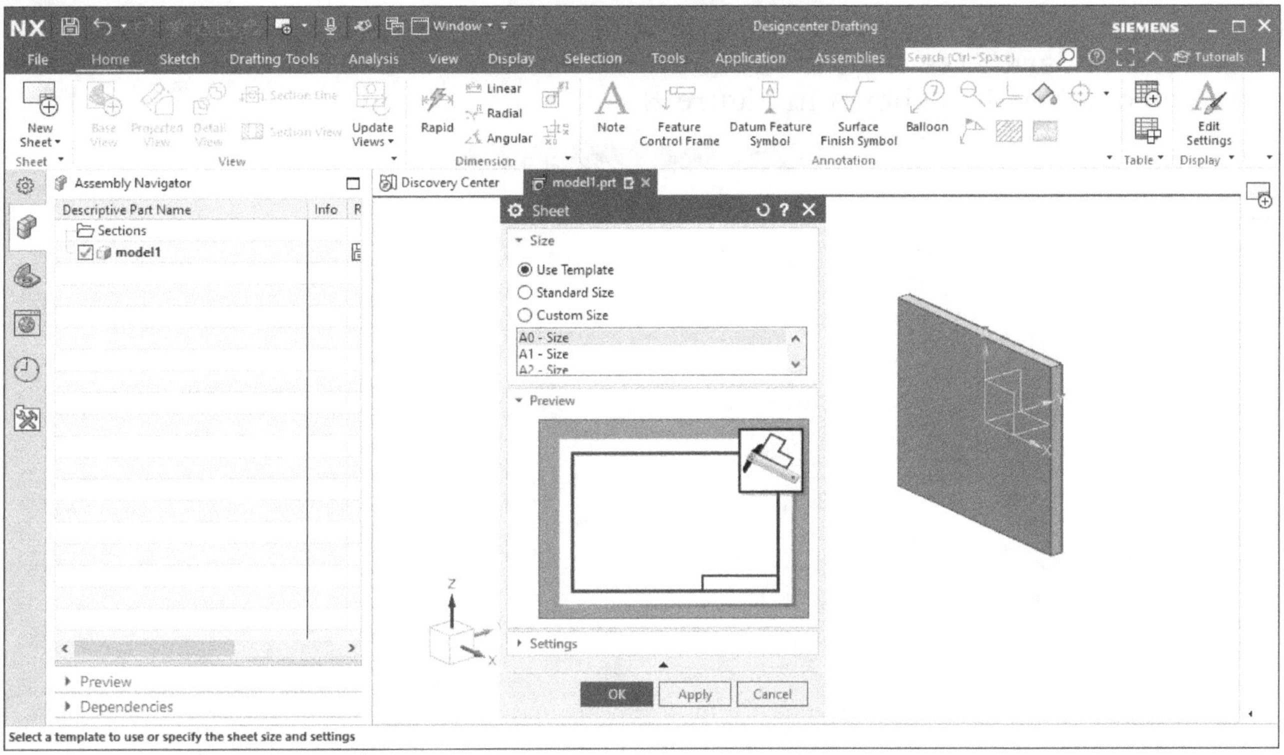

Figure-6. Drawing environment along with Sheet dialog box

Select sheet size using template

- Select **Use Template** radio button from **Size** rollout in the **Sheet** dialog box, the options will be displayed as shown in Figure-7.

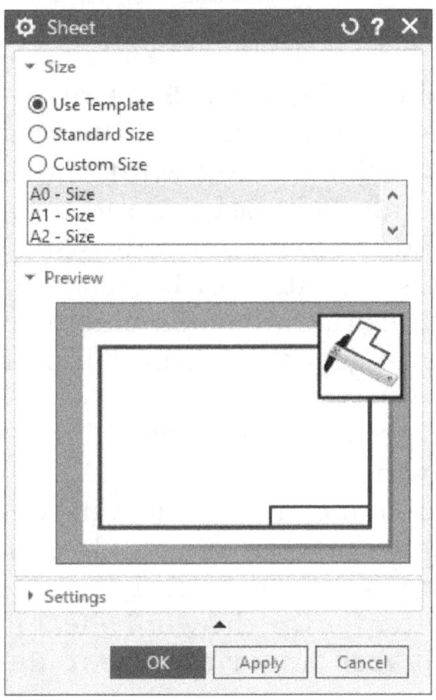

Figure-7. Use Template option

- Select desired sheet size from size template list available in the **Size** rollout. The preview of selected drawing sheet template will be displayed in the preview box of **Preview** rollout.

Select standard sheet size

- Select **Standard Size** radio button from **Size** rollout of the dialog box. The options will be displayed as shown in Figure-8.

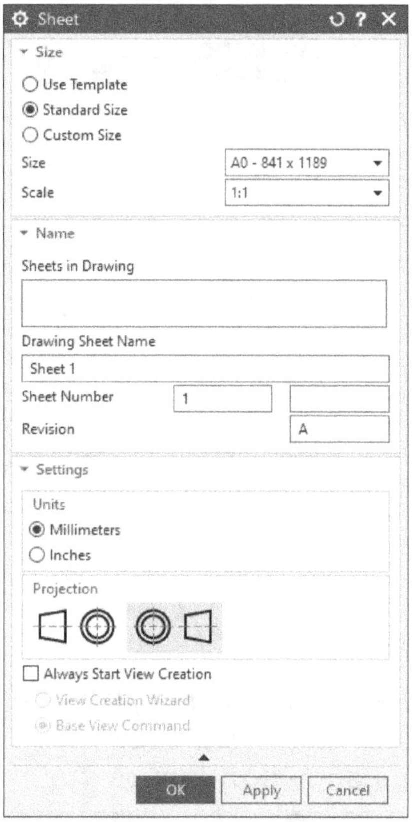

Figure-8. Standard Size option

- Select desired drawing sheet size from **Size** drop-down in the **Size** rollout to define the paper size on which drawing will be printed. Select the **Custom Size** radio button from the **Size** rollout if you want to use non-standard paper size for printing and then set the values in **Height** and **Length** edit boxes.
- Select desired scale to be added to model in drawing views from **Scale** drop-down. Selecting a scale which has first number bigger than second like 4:1 will increase the size of model (4 times the original) when placing drawing. Selecting scale value which has second number bigger than first will make the model smaller like 1:2 will half the size.
- The **Sheets in Drawing** area in the **Name** rollout displays all the sheets that currently exist in the drawing.
- Specify desired name of current drawing sheet in the **Drawing Sheet Name** edit box.
- Specify primary sheet number and secondary sheet number in the first and second edit boxes of **Sheet Number** area, respectively.
- Specify desired revision letter for the drawing sheet in the **Revision** edit box which displays in the **Part Navigator** under the **Sheet Revision** column.

(Note that the first sheet number must match the initial sheet number and secondary sheet number must match the initial secondary number specified in the **Drafting Preferences**.)

- Select desired unit for the sheet from **Units** area in the **Settings** rollout.

- Select **1st Angle Projection** or **3rd Angle Projection** option from **Projection** area of the rollout to display all the projected and section views. Select **Always Start View Creation** check box and select desired type of view to be started while creating a drawing sheet.
- After specifying desired parameters, click on **OK** button from the dialog box. A new sheet will be created.

First Angle Projection and Third Angle Projection

Figure-9 shows an object with different view directions say, a, b, c, d, e, and f.

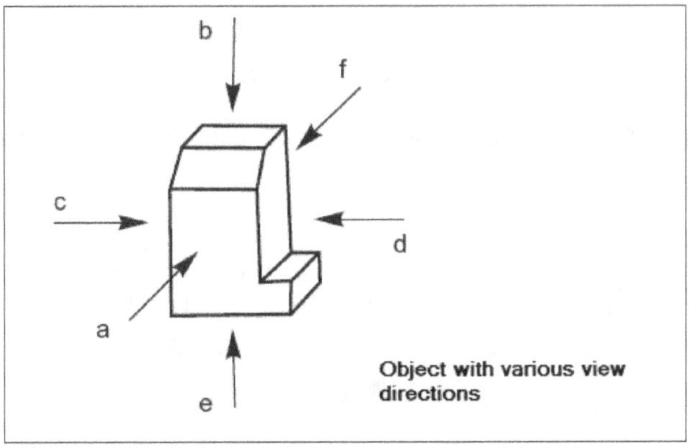

Figure-9. Object with view directions

Here,
1. View in the direction a = view from the front
2. View in the direction b = view from top
3. View in the direction c = view from the left
4. View in the direction d = view from the right
5. View in the direction e = view from bottom
6. View in the direction f = view from the back

In First Angle projection, these views are arranged as shown in Figure-10. In Third Angle projection, these views are arranged as shown in Figure-11.

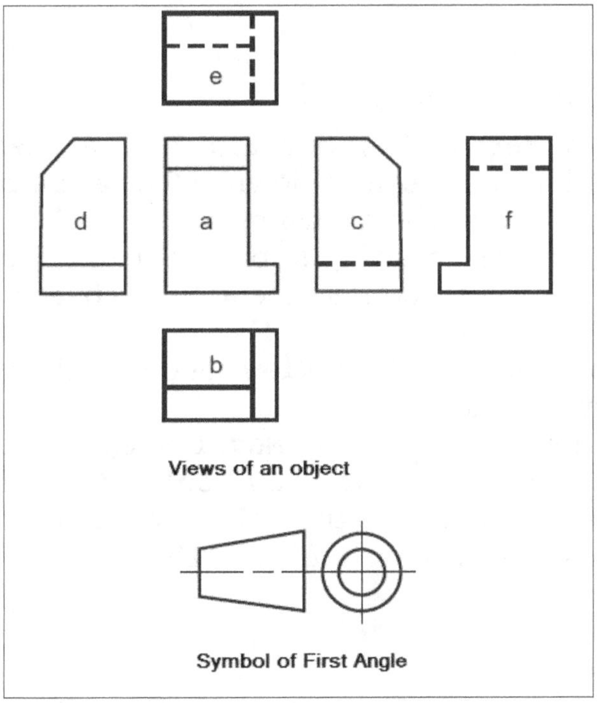

Figure-10. Views in First Angle projection

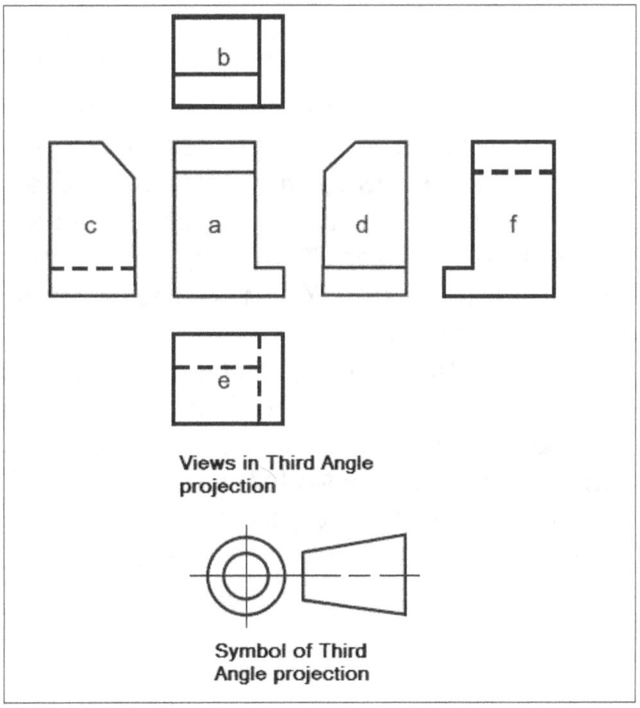

Figure-11. Views in Third Angle projection

- Click on the **OK** button from the **Sheet** dialog box. The base view of model will be attached to cursor and **Base View** dialog box will be displayed.

After setting the sheet size, the next step is to add various views of the model in the sheet.

ADDING VIEWS TO SHEET

The tools to add views are available in the **View** group of the **Ribbon**. These tools are discussed next.

Base View

The **Base View** tool is used to add base view to the sheet. To add these views, follow the steps given next.

- Click on the **Base View** tool from **View** group in the **Home** tab of the **Ribbon**. The **Base View** dialog box will be displayed along with the base view of model attached with the cursor; refer to Figure-12. You will be asked to specify the location.

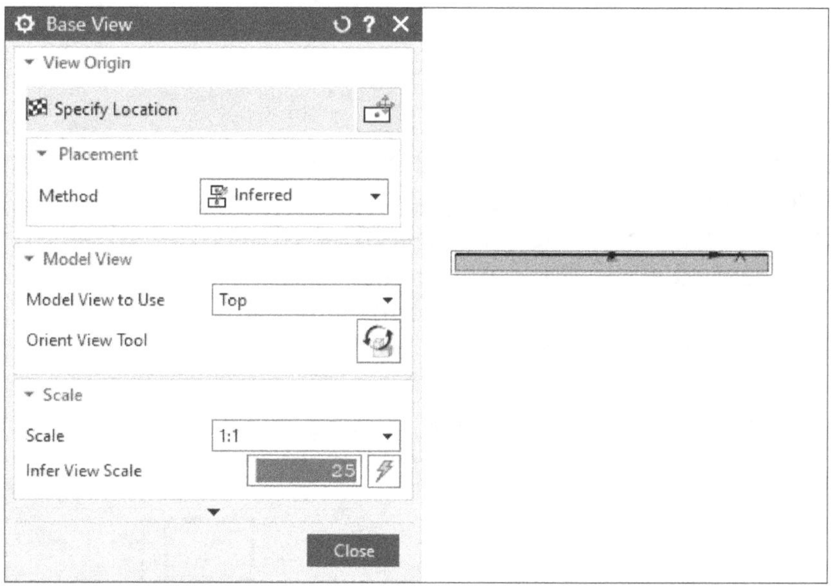

Figure-12. Base View dialog box along with base view attached with the cursor

- Select desired view alignment method from **Method** drop-down in the **Placement** rollout of **View Origin** rollout. Note that options in this drop-down will be available when you have already placed at least one view in the drawing.
- Select the **Cursor Tracking** check box from the **Tracking** sub-rollout to enable the offset XC and YC tracking. This will allow you change location of insertion point of views.
- Click on the **Specify Screen Position** button from **Move View** rollout and drag the current view of the drawing to the new location.
- Select desired model view to be used as the base view from **Model View to Use** drop-down in the **Model View** rollout. Click on the **Orient View Tool** button, the **Orient View Tool** dialog box will be displayed along with the **Orient View** display box to customize the orientation of the base view; refer to Figure-13.

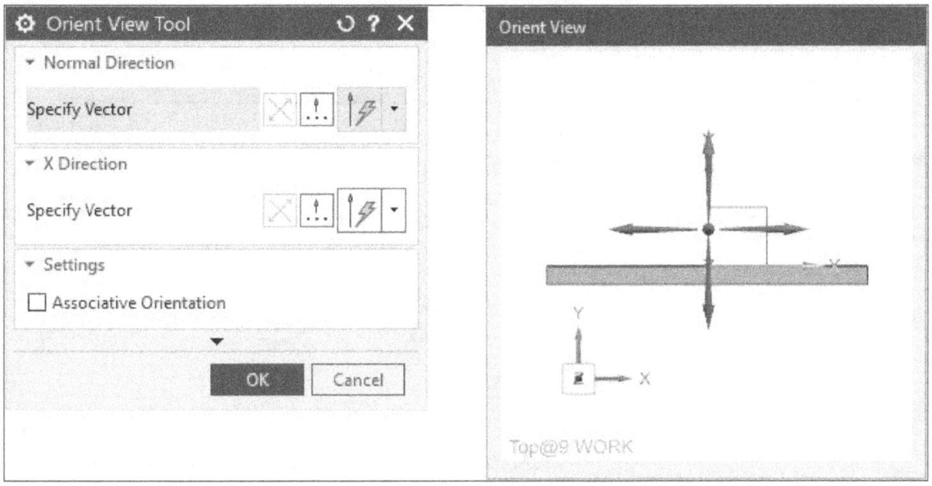

Figure-13. Orient View Tool dialog box along with Orient View display box

- After specifying desired parameters, click on **OK** button from **Orient View Tool** dialog box.
- Select desired view scale for the drawing view to be added to a drawing sheet from **Scale** drop-down of **Scale** rollout. Specify desired value in the **Infer View Scale** edit box to determine the appropriate scale for the base view with respect to the size of drawing sheet.
- Click on the **Settings** button from **Settings** rollout. The **Base View Settings** dialog box will be displayed which will be discussed later in this chapter.
- Click on the **Select Object** button in the **Non-Sectioned** rollout and select desired components or solid bodies to be non-sectioned in the view.
- After specifying desired parameters, click in the drawing window at desired location. The base view of the model will be placed; refer to Figure-14.

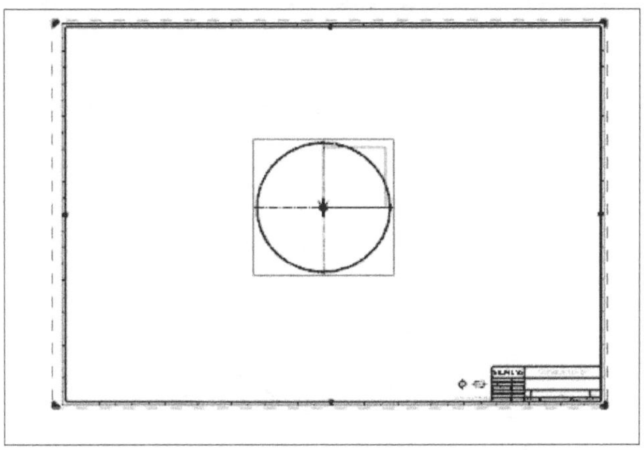

Figure-14. Base view of the model placed

Projected View

The **Projected View** tool is used to create projected view from the parent drawing view in the sheet. The procedure to use this tool is given next.

- Click on the **Projected View** tool from **View** group of **Home** tab in the **Ribbon**. The **Projected View** dialog box will be displayed with the projected view attached to the cursor in the drawing sheet; refer to Figure-15.

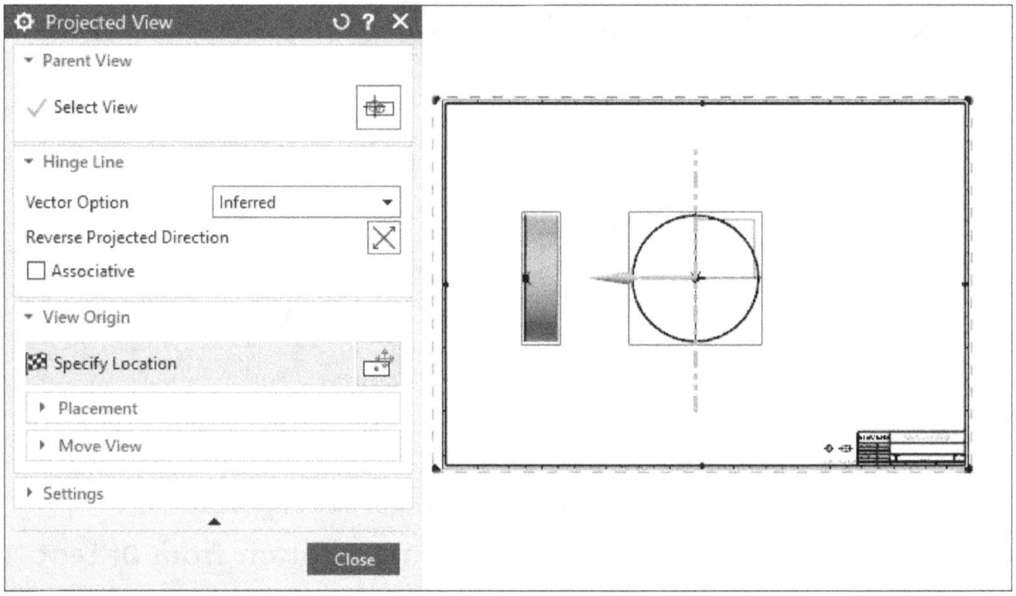

Figure-15. Projected View dialog box with the projected view attached with cursor

- Select **Inferred** option from **Vector Option** drop-down in the **Hinge Line** rollout to automatically find the hinge line and projection direction for the view. Select **Defined** option from the drop-down to define a hinge line and projection direction for the view.
- Click on the **Reverse Projected Direction** button from **Hinge Line** rollout to reverse the projected view through the hinge line. Select **Associative** check box to automatically associate a hinge line with a planar face.
- Other parameters in the dialog box are same as discussed earlier.
- After specifying desired parameters, click in the drawing sheet at desired location to place the projected view. The projected view will be placed in the sheet; refer to Figure-16.

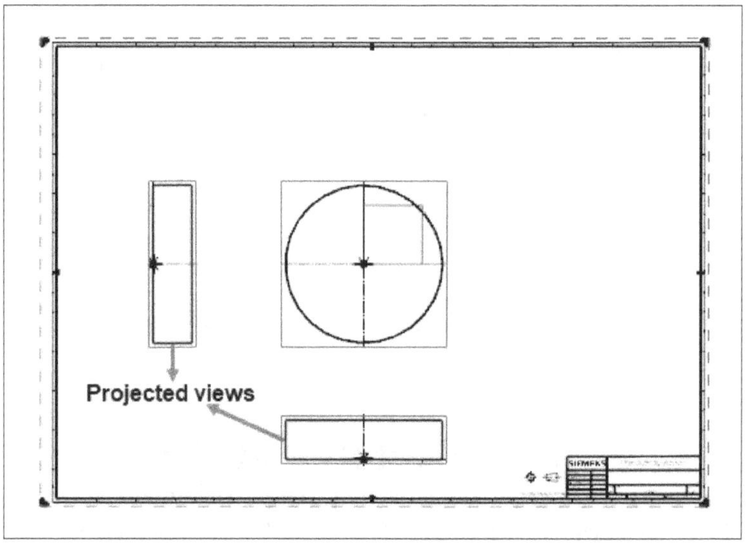

Figure-16. Projected views placed

- You can place as many projected views as you want. The orientation of view depends on direction of cursor with respect to center point of selected base view. After placing desired number of projected views, click on **Close** button to close the dialog box.

Detail View

The **Detail View** tool is used to create detailed view of a specific portion of the model. The procedure to create detail view is given next.

- Click on the **Detail View** tool from **View** group of **Home** tab in the **Ribbon**. The **Detail View** dialog box will be displayed; refer to Figure-17.

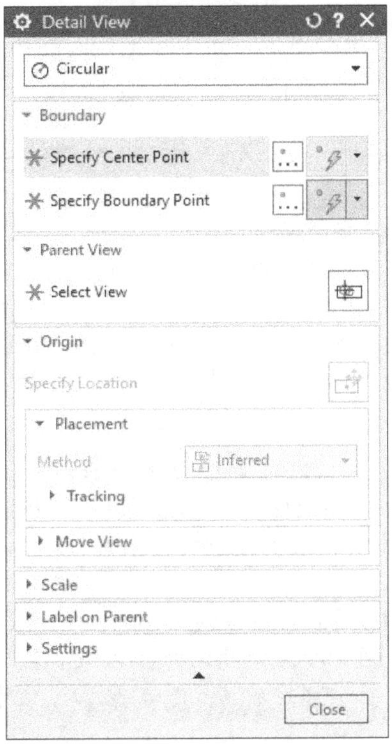

Figure-17. Detail View dialog box

- Select desired boundary type (circular or rectangular) for the detail view from drop-down in the top area of the dialog box. (In our case, we selected **Circular** boundary type). You will be asked to specify the center point.
- Click on desired view at desired location to specify the center point of the circular boundary. You will be asked to specify the radius.
- Move the cursor away and click at desired location to specify the radius of circular boundary; refer to Figure-18. The detail view will get attached to cursor and you will be asked to specify the location of detail view.

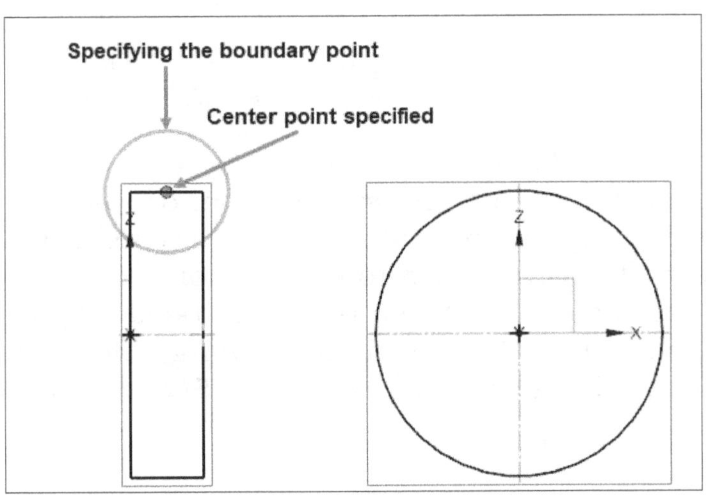

Figure-18. Specifying center and boundary point

- Move the cursor away and click at desired location to place the detail view. The detail view will be placed in the drawing sheet; refer to Figure-19.

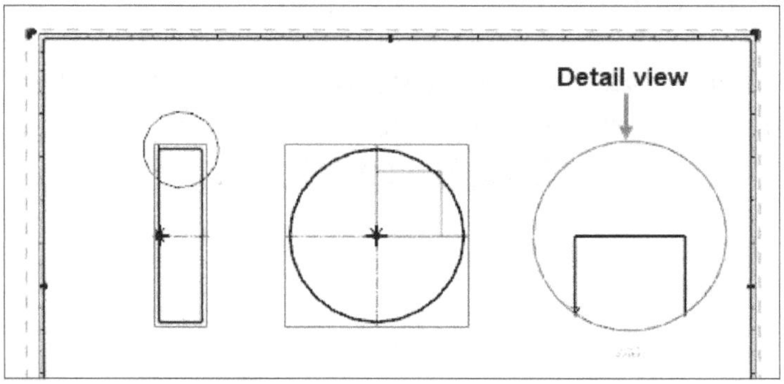

Figure-19. Detail view placed

- Select desired option from **Label** drop-down in the **Label on Parent** rollout to place a label on the parent view.
- Other parameters in the dialog box is same as discussed earlier.
- After specifying desired parameters, click on **Close** button to close the dialog box.

Section Line

The **Section Line** tool is used to create section lines that can be used with the **Section View** tool to create section views. The procedure to use this tool is discussed next.

- Click on the **Section Line** tool from **View** group in the **Home** tab of the **Ribbon**. The **Section Line** dialog box will be displayed; refer to Figure-20.

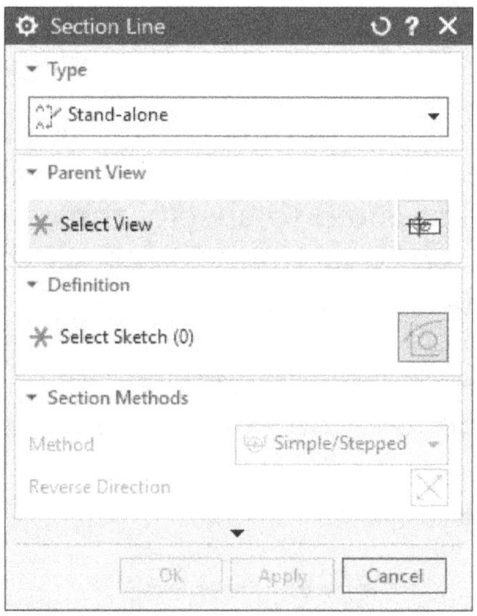

Figure-20. Section Line dialog box

- Select the type of section line to be created from drop-down in the **Type** rollout. Select the **Stand-alone** option to create a section line using sketch tools. Select the **Derived** option from the drop-down to use section line derived from PMI cutting plane symbol. Note that the **Derived** option is used when you have inserted a section view created using PMI tools in the drawing; refer to Figure-21. You will be asked to select the drafting view. (We are using **Stand-alone** option in this case).

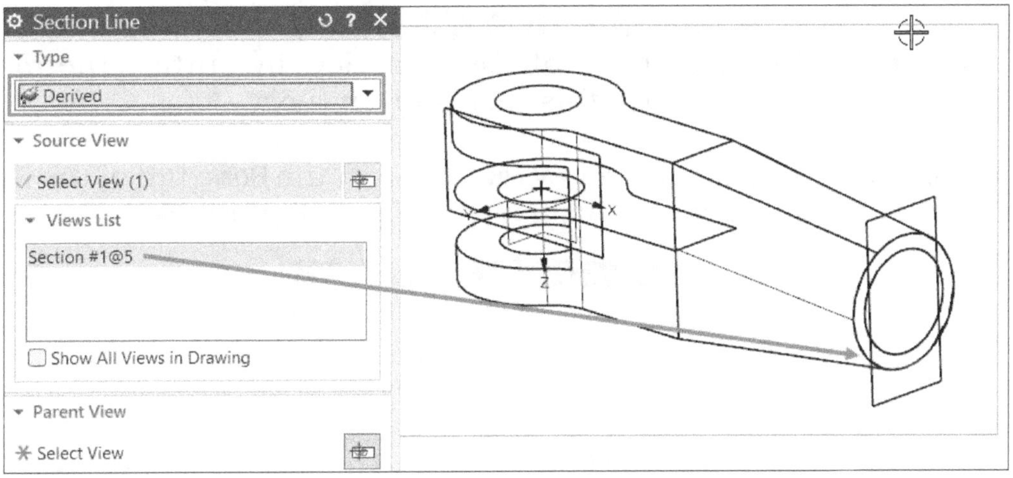

Figure-21. Derived section line

- Select desired drafting view from the drawing window in which the section line is to be created.
- On clicking desired drafting view, the **Section Line** contextual tab will be displayed; refer to Figure-22.

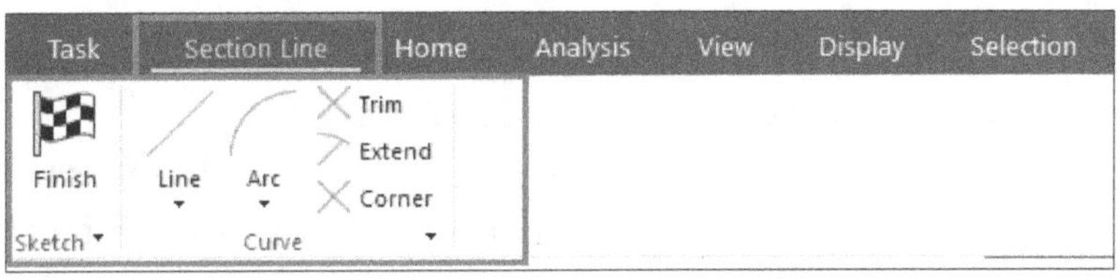

Figure-22. Section Line contextual tab

- Click on the **Line** tool from **Line** drop-down in the **Curve** group of **Section Line** tab and create section line on the selected view; refer to Figure-23.

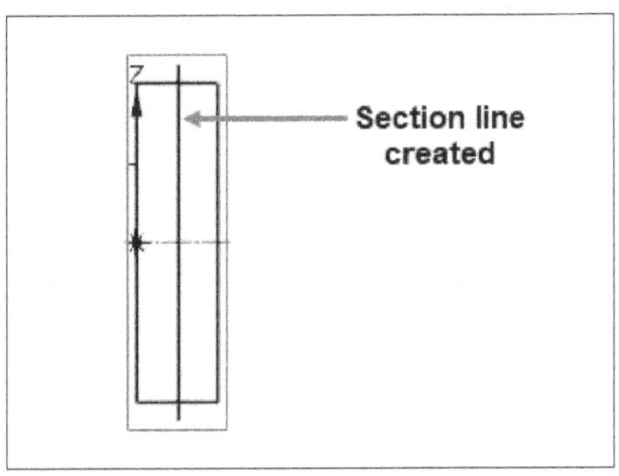

Figure-23. Section line created

- After creating the line, click on **Close** button to close the dialog box. Click on **Finish** button from **Section Line** contextual tab. The recently created sketch will be selected in the **Definition** rollout.
- Select desired type of section view to be created from **Method** drop-down in the **Section Methods** rollout. Click on the **Reverse Direction** button to reverse the cut direction and orientation of the section line.
- Other parameters in the dialog box are same as discussed earlier.
- After specifying desired parameters, click on **OK** button to close the dialog box. The section line will be created.

Section View

The **Section View** tool is used to create section view by cutting the model using section lines. The procedure to use this tool is given next.

- Click on the **Section View** tool from **View** group in the **Home** tab of the **Ribbon**. The **Section View** dialog box will be displayed; refer to Figure-24.

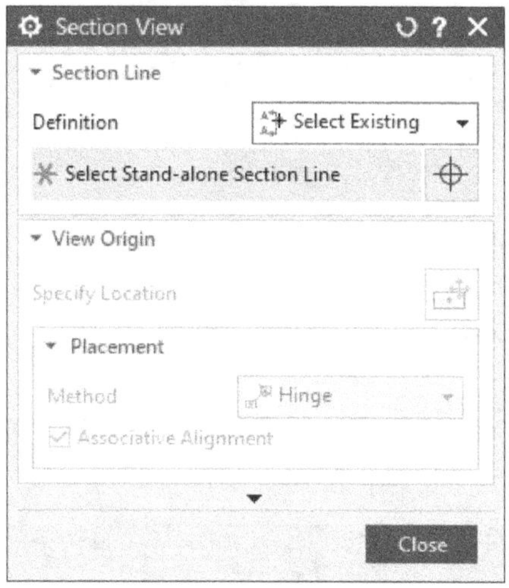

Figure-24. Section View dialog box

- Select **Dynamic** option from **Definition** drop-down in the **Section Line** rollout to create and select the dynamic section lines. Select the **Select Existing** option from the drop-down and select an existing section line from the drawing window; refer to Figure-25.

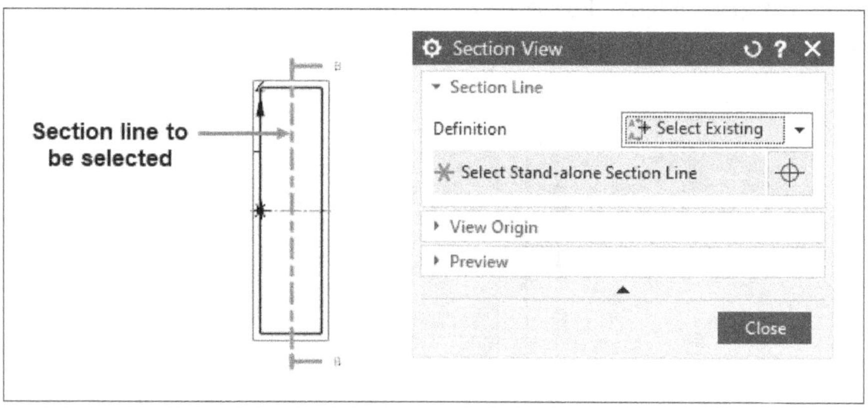

Figure-25. Selecting the section line

- On selecting the section line, a section view will be attached to cursor and you will be asked to specify the placement location.
- Move the cursor away and click at desired location to place the section view. The section view will be placed; refer to Figure-26.

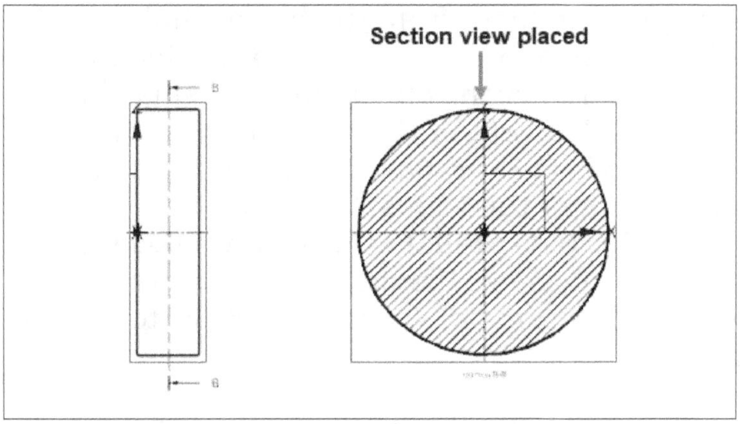

Figure-26. Section view placed

- Other parameters in the dialog box is same as discussed earlier.
- After specifying desired parameters, click on **Close** button to close the dialog box.

Update Views

The **Update Views** tool is used to manually update the drafting views to reflect the changes made to the model or other drafting objects since the last update. The procedure to use this tool is discussed next.

- Click on the **Update Views** tool from **Edit View** drop-down in the **View** group of **Home** tab in the **Ribbon**; refer to Figure-27. The **Update Views** dialog box will be displayed; refer to Figure-28.

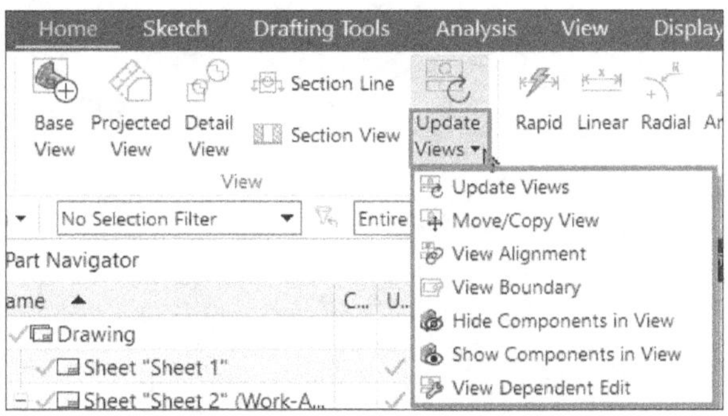

Figure-27. Update Views drop-down

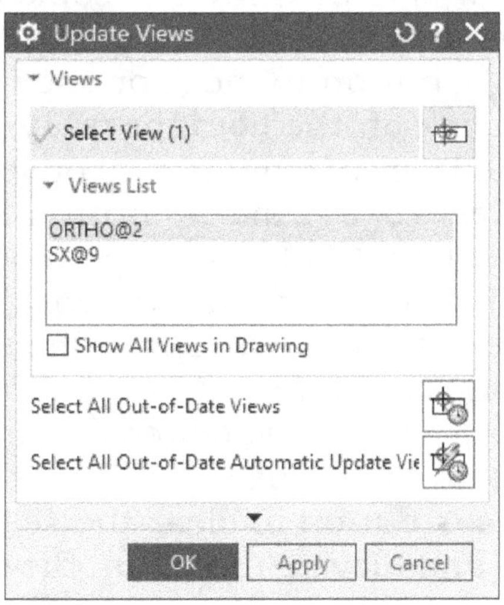

Figure-28. Update Views dialog box

- Select desired view to be updated from the box available in the **Views List** rollout which displays the names of outdated views available in the drawing window.
- Select **Show All Views in Drawing** check box to display all the outdated view that currently available on all sheets in the drawing window.
- Click on the **Select All Out-of-Date Views** button to select all the outdated drawing views displaying in the **Views List** box.
- Click on the **Select All Out-of-Date Automatic Update Views** button to select only the outdated drafting views displaying in the **Views List** box.
- After specifying desired parameters, click on **OK** button from the dialog box. The views will be updated.

Move/Copy View

The **Move/Copy View** tool is used to move or copy the selected views within or to the another drawing sheet. The procedure to use this tool is discussed next.

- Click on the **Move/Copy View** tool from **Update Views** drop-down in the **View** group of **Home** tab in the **Ribbon**. The **Move/Copy View** dialog box will be displayed; refer to Figure-29.

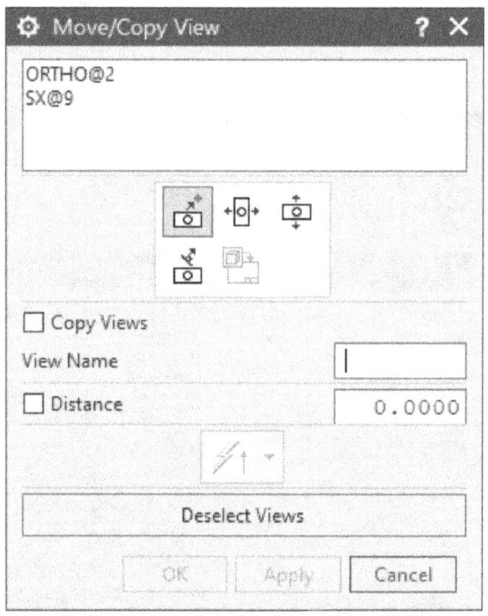

Figure-29. Move Copy View dialog box

- Select desired drawing view(s) to be moved or copied from the **Views List** box in the top area of the dialog box.
- Click on the **To a Point** button to move or copy the selected views to a point in the drawing window. Click on the **Horizontally** or **Vertically** button to move or copy the selected views in horizontal or vertical direction, respectively. Click on the **Perpendicular to a Line** button to move or copy the selected views perpendicularly to a line. Click on the **To Another Drawing** button to move or copy the selected views to another drawing sheet.
- Select **Copy Views** check box to create a copy of the selected view without moving the original view. Specify desired name of view in the **View Name** edit box.
- Select **Distance** check box and specify desired distance value to move or copy the selected view in the respective edit box.
- Click on the **Deselect Views** button to clear the selection of all the views.
- As you select desired view and moving direction, the selected view will be attached to the cursor.

- Move the cursor away and click at desired location to place the view. The view will be placed; refer to Figure-30.
- After placing desired number of views, press **ESC** button to exit the tool.

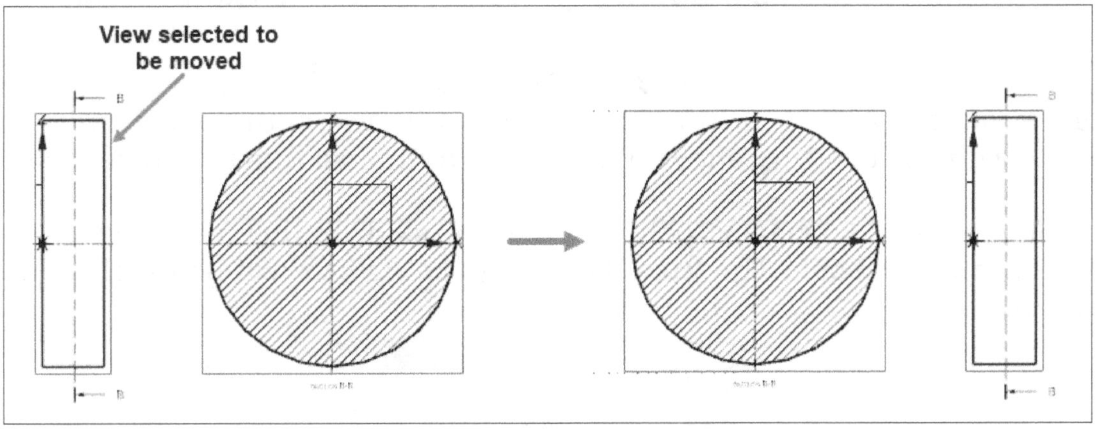

Figure-30. View moved

View Alignment

The **View Alignment** tool is used to add, edit, or remove the alignments between views. The procedure to use this tool is discussed next.

- Click on the **View Alignment** tool from **Edit View** drop-down in the **View** group of **Home** tab in the **Ribbon**. The **View Alignment** dialog box will be displayed; refer to Figure-31.

Figure-31. View Alignment dialog box

- Select desired view from the graphics window to be aligned. You will be asked to specify the location.
- Click in the drawing window at desired location to specify the location of alignment. The view will be aligned.
- Select desired view alignment method and specify respective parameters from **Method** drop-down in the **Placement** area of **Alignment** rollout.

- The **List** rollout displays all the view alignments along with the informations such as alignment ID number, alignment method, and alignment view. Click on the button to remove the selected view alignment.
- After specifying desired parameters, press **Esc** button to exit the tool.

View Boundary

The **View Boundary** tool is used to create or modify the boundary surrounding the drafting view on the drawing sheet. The procedure to use this tool is discussed next.

- Click on the **View Boundary** tool from **Edit View** drop-down in the **View** group of **Home** tab in the **Ribbon**. The **View Boundary** dialog box will be displayed; refer to Figure-32.

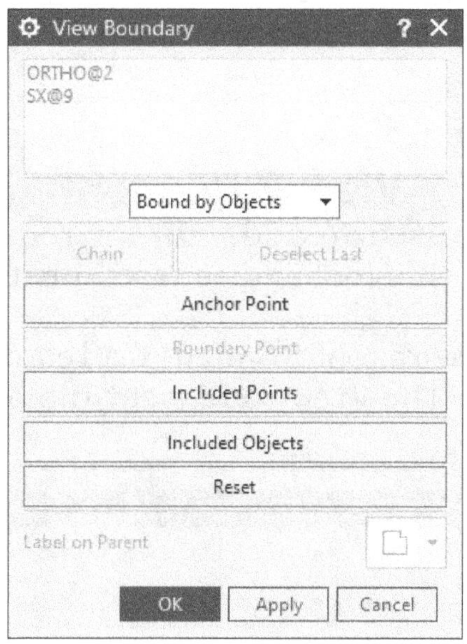

Figure-32. View Boundary dialog box

- Select desired view in the current sheet from the list in the dialog box whose boundary is to be checked or modified.
- Select desired boundary type to be applied to the selected view from drop-down in the dialog box. Select the **Break Line/Detail** option from the drop-down to define boundary of desired view using user-defined curves. Select the **Manual Rectangle** option to define the boundary of selected view by creating a rectangle manually (click and drag cursor to make rectange). Select the **Automatic Rectangle** option to define the boundary of selected view that automatically updates the size when the model updates. Select **Bound by Objects** option to define the boundary of selected view that automatically updates the size to include selected solid edges and points of the model geometry.
- Click on the **Chain** button to select an existing chain of curves to define the boundary of selected view.
- Click on the **Deselect Last** button to deselect the last selected curve while defining the boundary of selected view.
- Click on the **Anchor Point** button to lock the contents of a view to the drawing to not to update the view or its contents when the model updates.
- Click on the **Boundary Point** button to associate the boundary of selected view with model features so that the boundary automatically updates to keep the model features within the view when the model updates.

- Click on the **Included Points** or **Included Objects** button to specify the model points or model objects, respectively, that will remain inside the rectangular boundary of the view when the model updates.
- Click on the **Reset** buttton to revert the current update and reset the dialog box.
- Select desired option from **Label on Parent** drop-down to define the appearance of the boundary curves of the parent view for a detailed view.
- After specifying desired parameters, click on **OK** button from the dialog box. The boundary will be created for the view.

The **Hide Components in View** tool and **Show Components in View** tool have been discussed earlier in this book.

View Dependent Edit

The **View Dependent Edit** tool is used to modify the display of objects in a selected drafting view without changing their appearance in other views. The procedure to use this tool is discussed next.

- Click on the **View Dependent Edit** tool from **Edit View** drop-down in the **View** group of **Home** tab in the **Ribbon**. The **View Dependent Edit** dialog box will be displayed; refer to Figure-33.

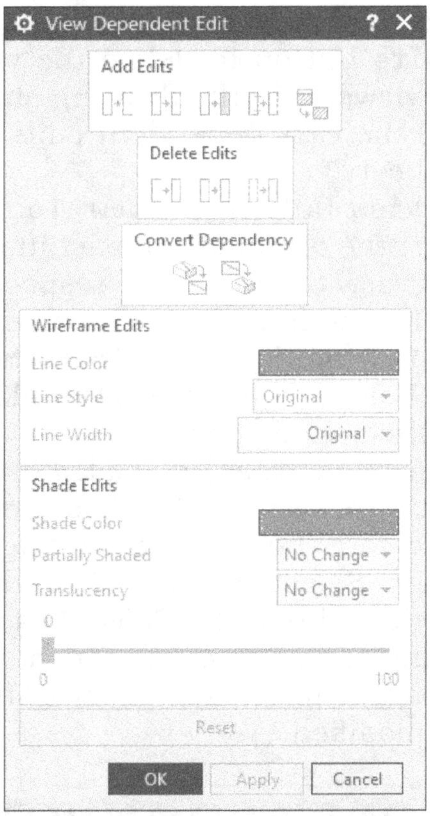

Figure-33. View Dependent Edit dialog box

- Select desired drafting view from the drawing window to be modified. As you select the drafting view, the options in the dialog box will be activated; refer to Figure-34.

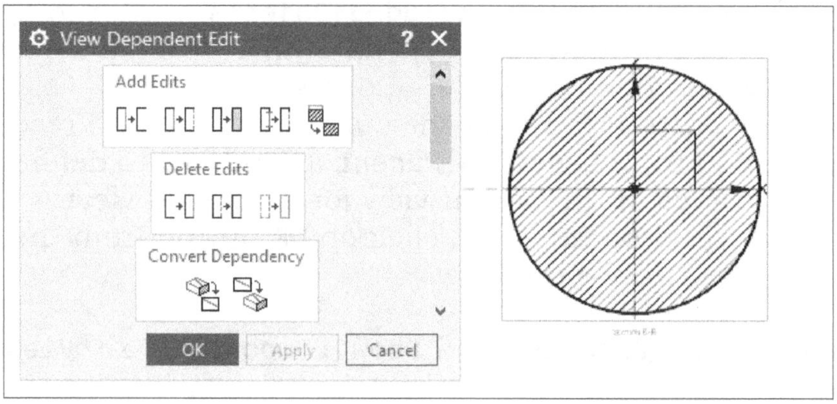

Figure-34. View selected to modify

- Click on the **Erase Objects** button from **Add Edits** area to erase geometric objects such as edges, curves, splines, and so on from a selected drawing view. Click on the **Edit Entire Objects** button to modify the style, color, and width of objects (such as edges, curves, and splines). Click on the **Edit Shaded Objects** button to control the shading and translucency of objects in the drafting views. Click on the **Edit Object Segments** button to modify the color, width, and style of object segments in the drafting views. Click on the **Edit Section View Background** button to control the visibility of bodies or faces in the background of a section view.
- Click on the **Delete Selected Erasures** button from **Delete Edits** area to delete the erasures that applied to objects earlier using **Erase Objects** tool. Click on the **Delete Selected Edits** button to delete the view dependent edits applied to objects in the drafting views or in the drawing sheet. Click on the **Delete All Edits** button to delete all the view dependent edits made earlier in the drafting views or in the drawing sheet.
- Click on the **Model To View** button or **View To Model** button from **Convert Dependency** area to convert the objects that exist in the model to the objects that exist in a specific drafting view or vice versa, respectively.
- Change the color, line style, and line width of geometric objects from **Line Color**, **Line Style**, and **Line Width** drop-downs of **Wireframe Edits** rollout, respectively.
- Click on the **Shade Color** box from **Shade Edits** rollout, the **Color** dialog box will be displayed to select desired shade color.
- Select **No Change** option from **Partially Shaded** or **Translucency** drop-down to keep unchanged any existing edits made for these options. Select **Original** option from the drop-downs to restore the object to its original settings by deleting any existing edits for this option. Select **No** option from the drop-downs to disable the editing option from the selected objects. Select **Yes** option from the drop-downs to apply the partial shading or translucency for the selected objects.
- After specifying desired parameters, click on **OK** button from the dialog box. The display of objects will be modified.

ADDING DIMENSIONS AND ANNOTATIONS TO VIEW

Till this point, we have learned to place views but without dimensions and annotations these views are of no use for manufacturers. So, we will now add dimensions and annotations to views. The tools to apply dimensions and annotations are available in the **Dimension** and **Annotation** group of **Home** tab in the **Ribbon**; refer to Figure-35. We have discussed Rapid, Linear, Radial, and Angular dimension tools earlier.

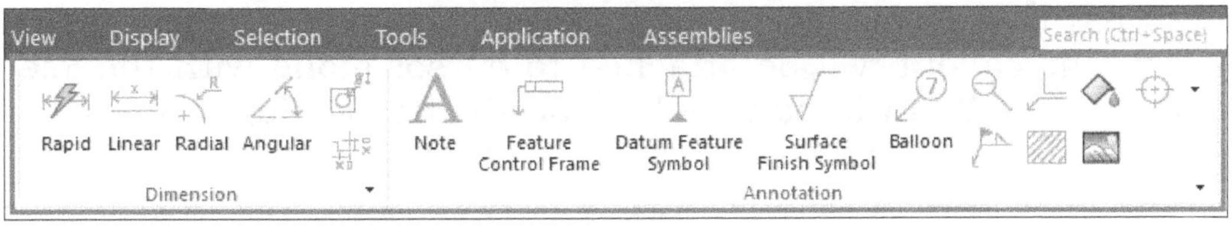

Figure-35. Dimension and Annotation tools

Hole and Thread Callout

The **Hole and Thread Callout** tool is used to create an associative cylindrical hole and thread callouts that display the feature parameters of a hole. The procedure to use this tool is discussed next.

- Click on the **Hole and Thread Callout** tool from **Dimension** group of **Home** tab in the **Ribbon**. The **Hole and Thread Callout** dialog box will be displayed; refer to Figure-36.

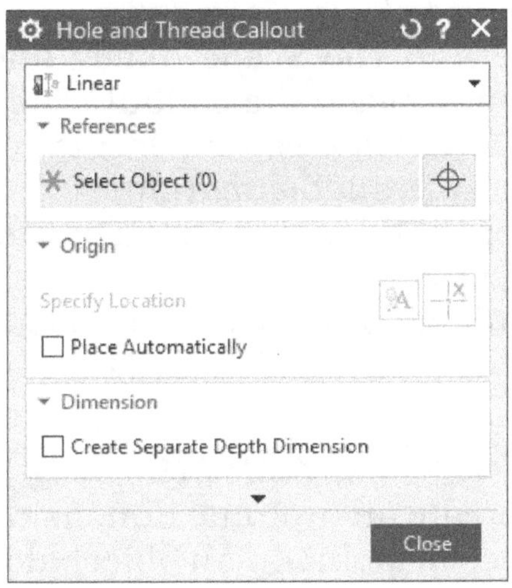

Figure-36. Hole and Thread Callout dialog box

- Select desired type of dimension to be created for the hole feature parameters from drop-down in the top area of the dialog box. Select the **Linear** option to place the callout with linear vertical lines showing hole and select the **Radial** option to place the callout with radial leader; refer to Figure-37.

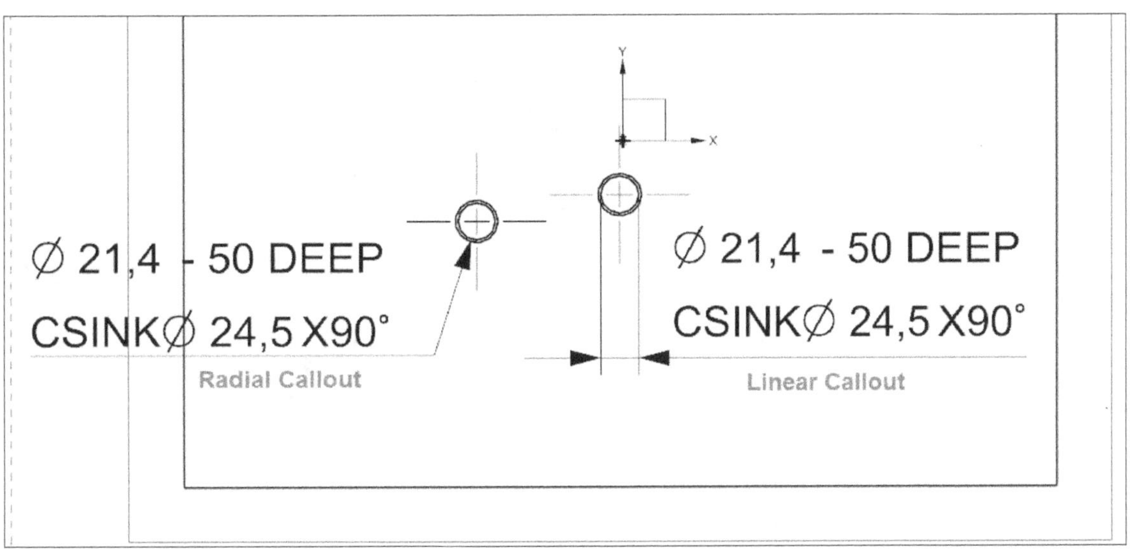

Figure-37. Callout types

- Select desired hole from the drawing window to which the dimension is to be associated. The callout will be attached to cursor along with the **Scene** dialog; refer to Figure-38. You will be asked to specify the location.

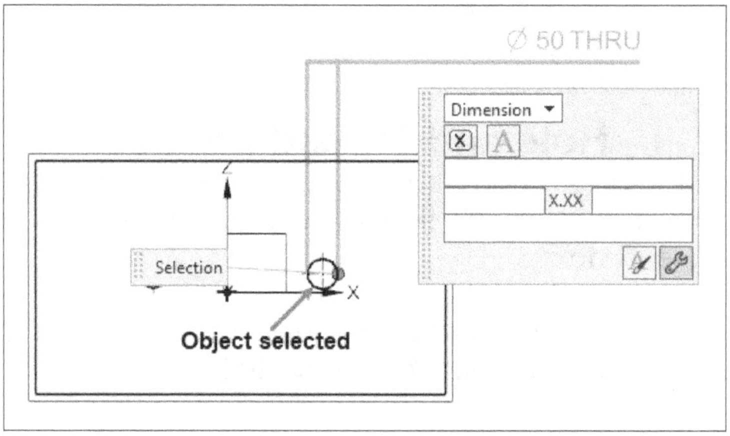

Figure-38. Callout displayed with Scene dialog

- Specify desired parameters in the **Scene** dialog and then click in the drawing window at desired location to place the callout. The callout will be placed.
- Select **Place Automatically** check box from **Origin** rollout to place the dimensions automatically at the nearest available margins.
- Select **Create Separate Depth Dimension** check box to create a separate dimension to define the depth of the selected feature.
- Other parameters in the dialog box have been discussed earlier.
- After specifying desired parameters, click on **Close** button to close the dialog box.

Ordinate

The **Ordinate** tool is used to create an ordinate dimension that measures the distance from a reference point to a specific point on an object along a baseline. The procedure to use this tool is discussed next.

- Click on the **Ordinate** tool from **Dimension** group in the **Home** tab in the **Ribbon**. The **Ordinate Dimension** dialog box will be displayed; refer to Figure-39.

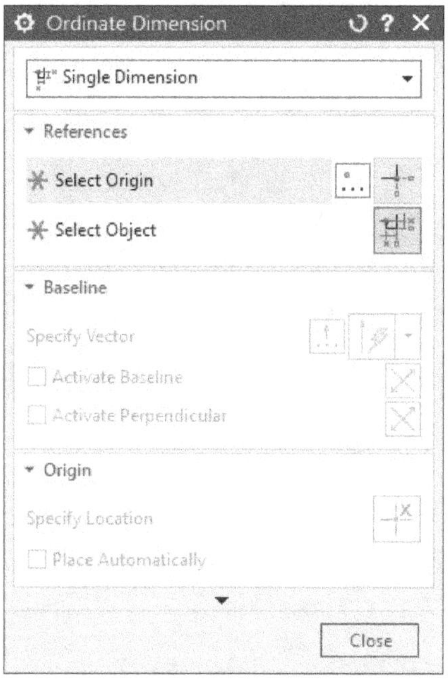

Figure-39. Ordinate Dimension dialog box

- Select **Single Dimension** option from drop-down in the top area of the dialog box to create ordinate dimensions at a single point. Select **Multiple Dimensions** option to select multiple dimension points simultaneously using a rectangular selection.
- Click in the view at desired location to specify the origin point for the ordinate dimension set. You will be asked to select the object.
- Select single or multiple objects in the drawing window to be dimensioned. The ordinate dimension will be attached to cursor along with the **Scene** dialog; refer to Figure-40.

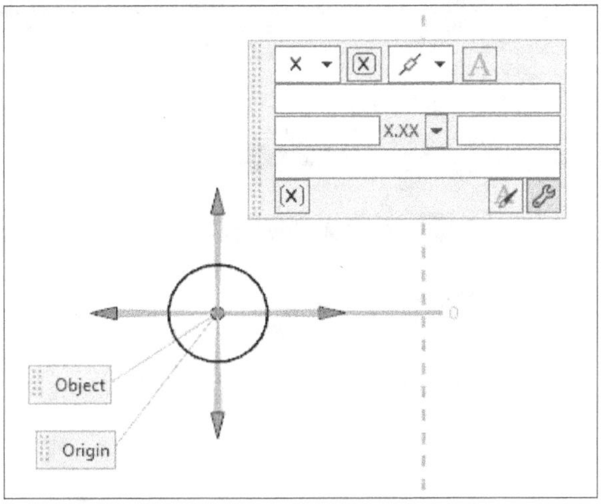

Figure-40. Ordinate dimension attached to cursor along with Scene dialog

- Click on the **Specify Vector** button from **Baseline** rollout to specify user-defined baseline dimension for the view. Select **Activate Baseline** check box to activate the primary baseline. This baseline define the x direction of measurement. Select **Activate Perpendicular** check box to activate the secondary baseline. This baseline define the y direction of measurement.
- Click on the **Specify Location** button from **Origin** rollout to move a new dimension and its margins to a desired location on the drawing sheet. The ordinate dimension will be placed.
- Other parameters in the dialog box have been discussed earlier.
- After specifying desired parameters, click on **Close** button to close the dialog box.

Thickness Dimension

The **Thickness Dimension** tool is used to create a dimension between two curves by measuring the distance from a point on the first curve to its intersection with the second curve.

Arc Length Dimension

The **Arc Length Dimension** tool is used to measure the distance along a circular arc.

Other tools in the **Dimension** group have been discussed earlier in **Chapter 2**.

Note

The **Note** tool is used to specify extra information in the drawing that are not mentioned in the dimensions. For example, if you want to say "All dimensions are in mm" then this is the tool to do so. The steps to use this tool are given next.

- Click on the **Note** tool from **Annotation** group in the **Home** tab of the **Ribbon**. The **General** contextual tab will be displayed along with **Note** dialog box and a note box will get attached to the cursor; refer to Figure-41.

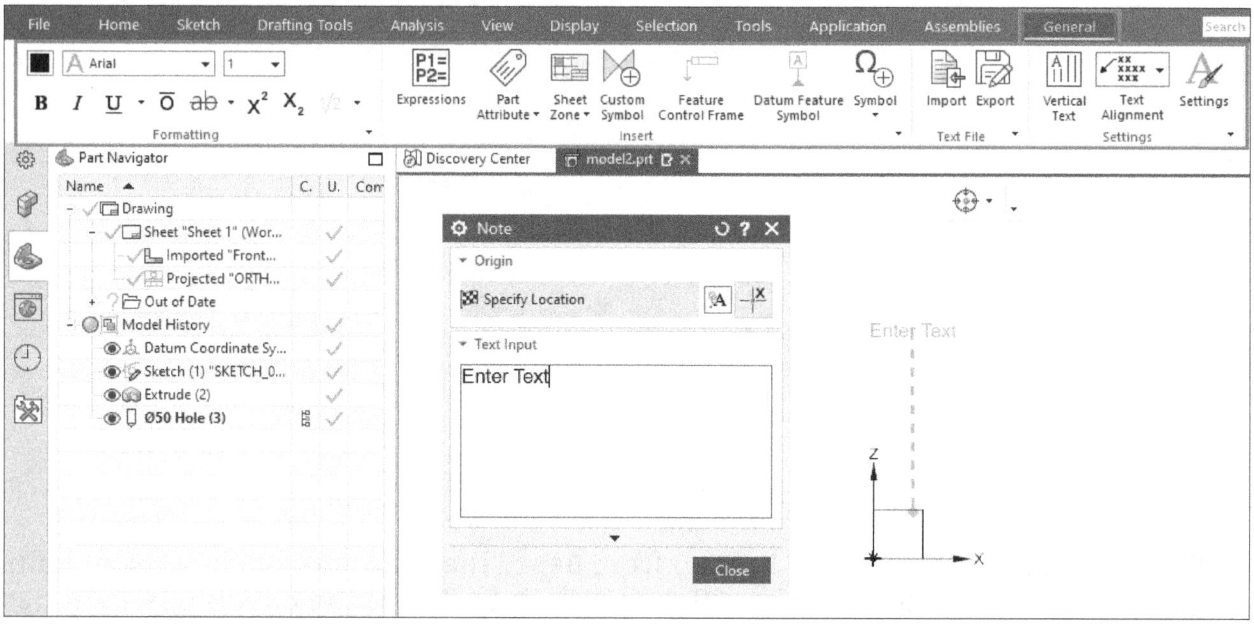

Figure-41. General contextual tab with Note dialog box

- Specify desired parameters of formatting the text from **Formatting** group of **General** tab in the **Ribbon**.
- After specifying the formatting of text, specify desired text in the box of **Text Input** rollout.
- Now, click in the drawing window at desired location to place the text. The text will be placed; refer to Figure-42.

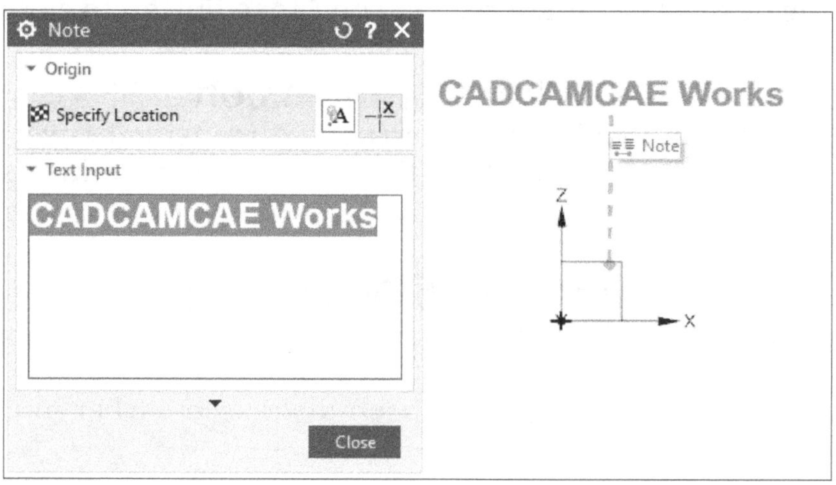

Figure-42. Placing the text

- After specifying desired parameters, click on **Close** button to close the dialog box.

Feature Control Frame

The feature control frame is also known as GD&T box in laymen's language. In GD&T, a feature control frame is required to describe the conditions and tolerances of a geometric control on a part's feature. The feature control frame consists of four pieces of information:

1. GD&T symbol or control symbol
2. Tolerance zone type and dimensions
3. Tolerance zone modifiers: features of size, projections, and so on
4. Datum references (if required by the GD&T symbol)

This information provides everything you need to know about geometry of part like what geometrical tolerance needs to be on the part and how to measure or determine if the part is in specification; refer to Figure-43. The common elements of feature control frame are discussed next.

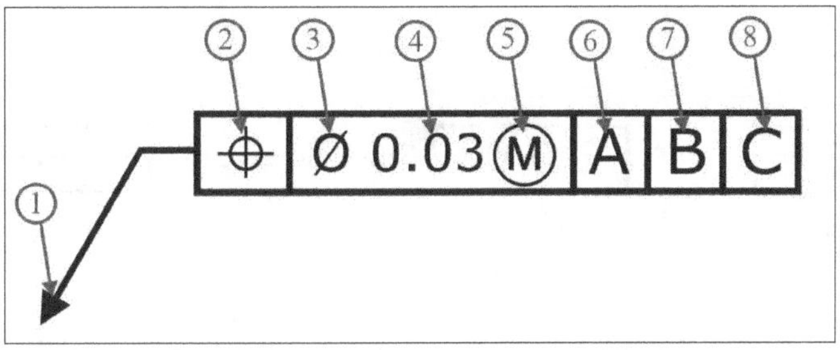

Figure-43. Feature control frame

1. **Leader Arrow** – This arrow points to the feature that the geometric control is placed on. If the arrow points to a surface than the surface is controlled by the GD&T. If it points to a diametric dimension, then the axis is controlled by GD&T. The arrow is optional but helps clarify the feature being controlled.

2. **Geometric Symbol** – This is where your geometric control is specified.

3. **Diameter Symbol (if required)** – If the geometric control is a diametrical tolerance then the diameter symbol (Ø) will be in front of the tolerance value.

4. **Tolerance Value** – If the tolerance is a diameter you will see the Ø symbol next to the dimension signifying a diametric tolerance zone. The tolerance of the GD&T is in same unit of measure that the drawing is written in.

5. **Feature of Size or Tolerance Modifiers (if required)** – This is where you call out max material condition or a projected tolerance in the feature control frame.

6. **Primary Datum (if required)** – If a datum is required, this is the main datum used for the GD&T control. The letter corresponds to a feature somewhere on the part which will be marked with the same letter. This is the datum that must be constrained first when measuring the part. Note: The order of the datum is important for measurement of the part. The primary datum is usually held in three places to fix 3 degrees of freedom

7. **Secondary Datum (if required)** – If a secondary datum is required, it will be to the right of the primary datum. This letter corresponds to a feature somewhere on the part which will be marked with the same letter. During measurement, this is the datum fixated after the primary datum.

8. **Tertiary Datum (if required)** – If a third datum is required, it will be to the right of the secondary datum. This letter corresponds to a feature somewhere on the part which will be marked with the same letter. During measurement, this is the datum fixated last.

Reading Feature Control Frame

The feature control frame forms a kind of sentence when you read it. Below is how you would read the frame in order to describe the feature.

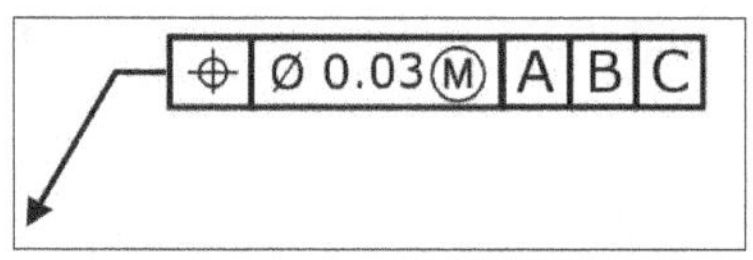

gives meaning of

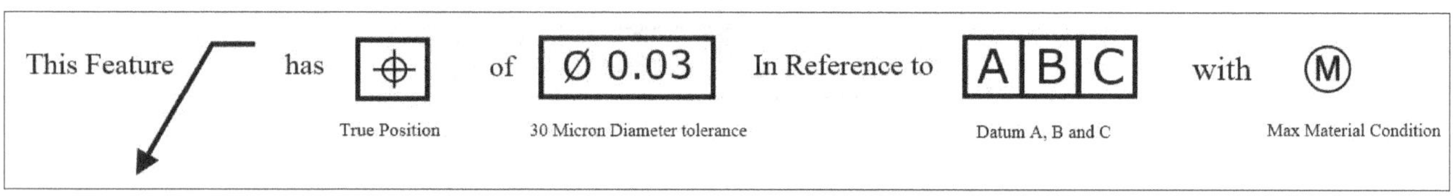

Meaning of various geometric symbols are given in Figure-44.

SYMBOL	CHARACTERISTICS	CATEGORY
—	Straightness	Form
⏥	Flatness	
○	Circulatity	
⌭	Cylindricity	
⌒	Profile of a Line	Profile
⌓	Profile of Surface	
∠	Angularity	Orientation
⊥	Perpendicularity	
//	Parallelism	
⌖	Position	Location
◎	Concentricity	
⌯	Symmetry	
↗	Circular Runout	Runout
⌰	Total Runout	

Figure-44. Geometric Symbols

Figure-45 and Figure-46 show the use of geometric tolerances in real-drawing.

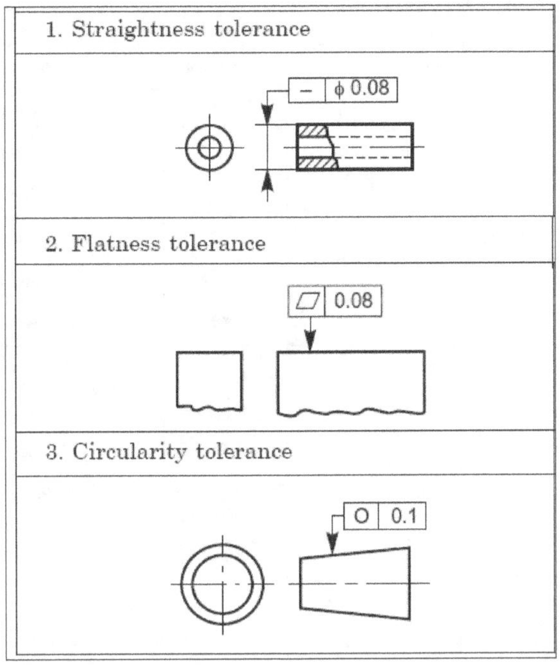

Figure-45. Use of geometric tolerance 1

Note that in applying most of the Geometrical tolerances, you need to define a datum plane like in Perpendicularity, Parallelism, and so on.

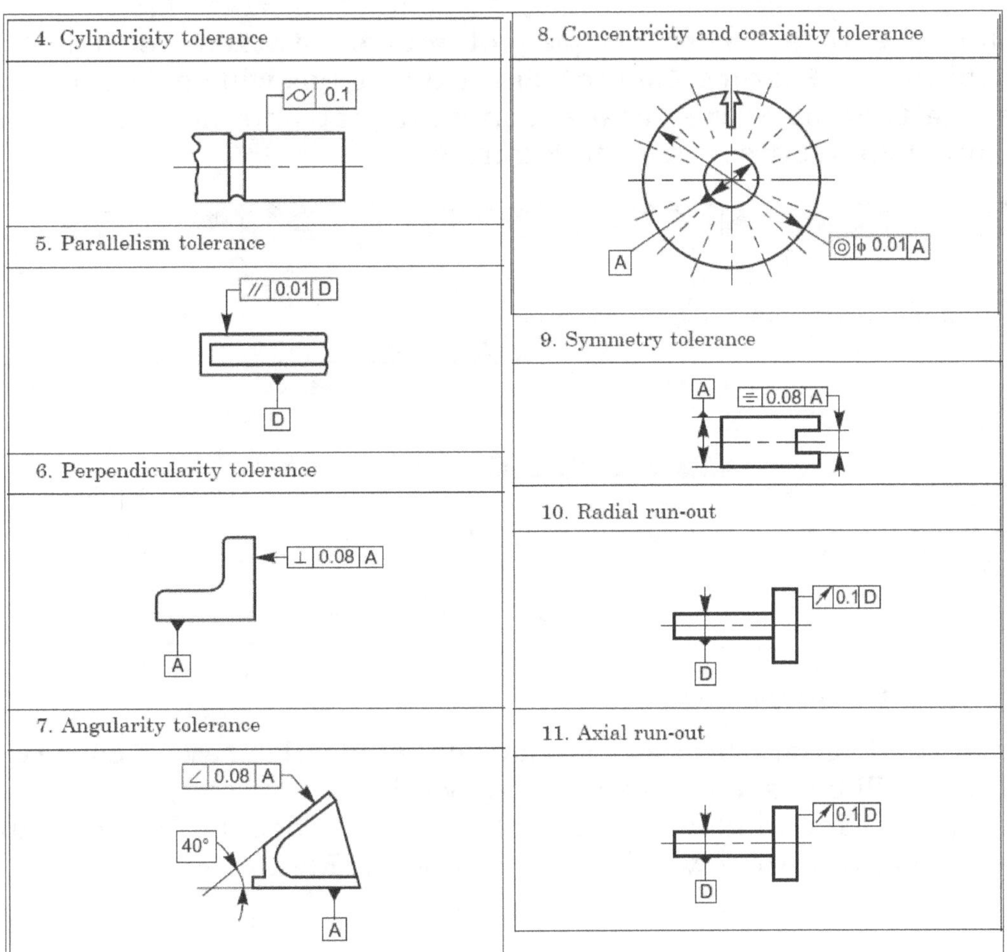

Figure-46. Use of geometric tolerance 2

There are a few dimensioning symbols also used in geometric dimensioning and tolerances, which are given in Figure-47.

Symbol	Meaning	Symbol	Meaning
Ⓛ	LMC – Least Material Condition	⌖	Dimension Origin
Ⓜ	MMC – Maximum Material Condition	⌴	Counterbore
Ⓣ	Tangent Plane	⌵	Countersink
Ⓟ	Projected Tolerance Zone	↧	Depth
Ⓕ	Free State	⌀	All Around
Ø	Diameter	↔	Between
R	Radius	✕	Target Point
SR	Spherical Radius	⌲	Conical Taper
SØ	Spherical Diameter	⌳	Slope
CR	Controlled Radius	□	Square
⟨ST⟩	Statistical Tolerance		
[77]	Basic Dimension		
(77)	Reference Dimension		
5X	Places		

Figure-47. Dimensioning symbols

The steps to create feature control frame are given next.

- Click on the **Feature Control Frame** tool from **Annotation** group in the **Home** tab of the **Ribbon**. The **Feature Control Frame** dialog box will be displayed along with the **Feature Control Frame General** contextual tab and the feature control frame will be attached to cursor; refer to Figure-48.

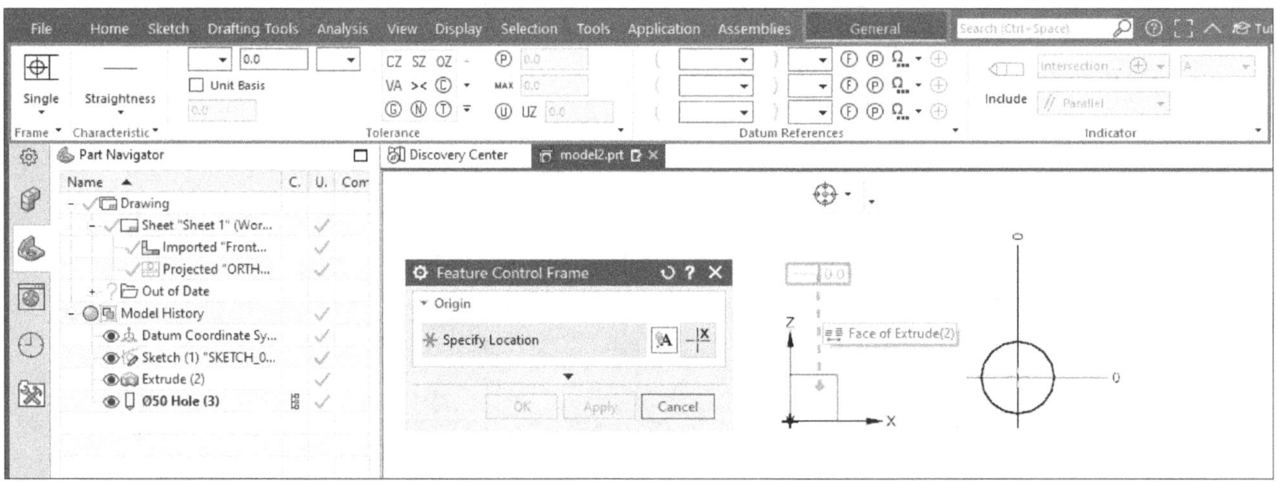

Figure-48. Feature Control Frame General tab

- Specify desired parameters in the **Feature Control Frame General** tab of the **Ribbon**. You will be asked to specify the location.
- Click in the drawing window at desired location to place the feature control frame. The feature control frame will be placed; refer to Figure-49.

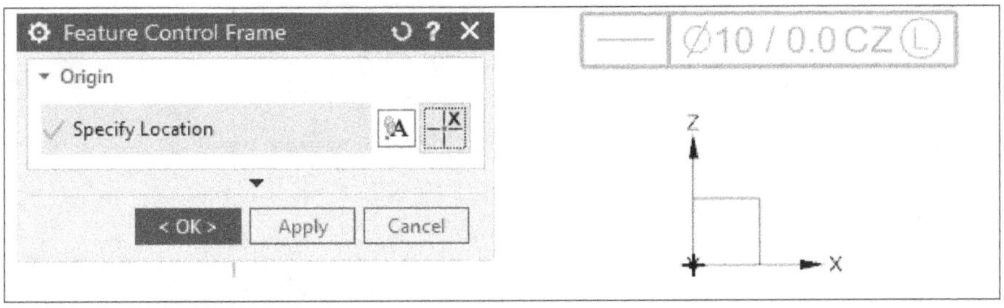

Figure-49. Feature control frame placed

- Expand the dialog box by clicking on **More** button. The options will be displayed as shown in Figure-50.

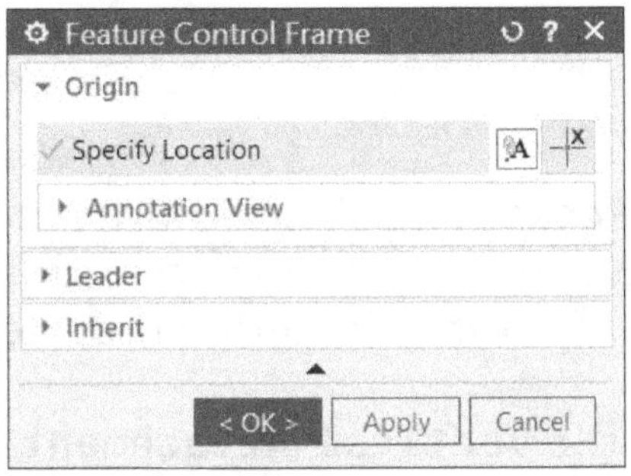

Figure-50. Feature Control Frame dialog box

- Expand the **Annotation View** sub-rollout and click on the **Select View** selection button. You will be asked to select the view to which you want to apply current feature control frame as annotation. Select desired view to annotate.
- Expand the **Leader** rollout to modify parameters related to leader attached to feature control frame. The options will be displayed as shown in Figure-51.

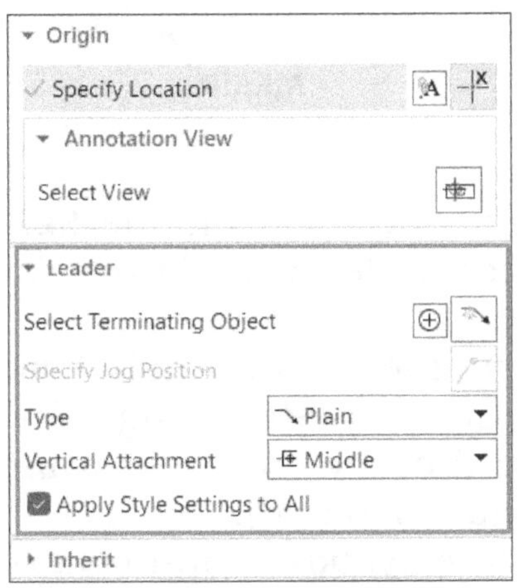

Figure-51. Leader options

- Click on the **Select Terminating Object** selection button and click at the location where you want to point the arrow of leader; refer to Figure-52.

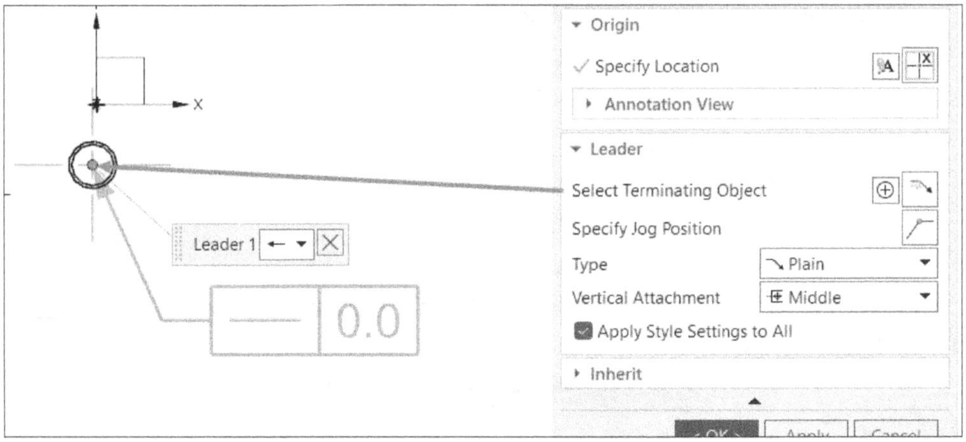

Figure-52. Terminating object selected for arrow

- Click on the **Specify Jog Position** selection button and click at desired location to define mid point of leader line where arrow and landing line join.
- Select desired option from the **Type** drop-down to define the type of leader arrow to be used for annotation.
- Select desired option from the **Vertical Attachment** drop-down to define location where end point of leader will be attached to feature control frame; refer to Figure-53.

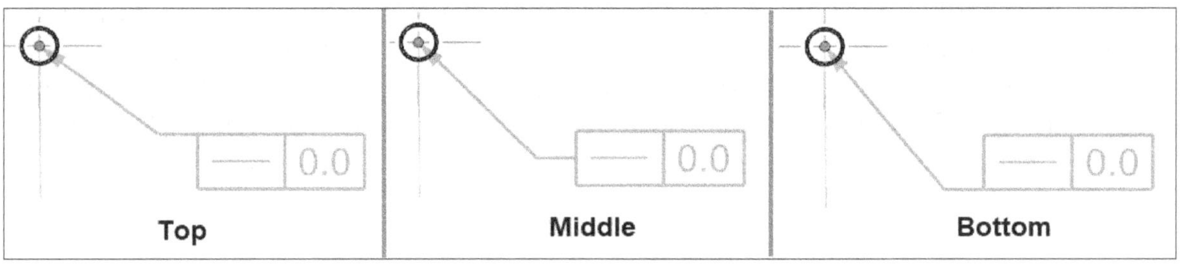

Figure-53. Vertical alignment options

- Expand the **Inherit** rollout and click on the **Select Feature Control Frame** selection button to use another feature control frame for setting parameters in the dialog box.
- Select the **Single** option from the drop-down in **Frame** panel of **General** contextual tab in the **Ribbon** if you want to create a single feature control frame. Select the **Composite** option from the drop-down if you want to create a composite frame (multiple feature control frames joined).
- Select desired option from the **Symbol** drop-down of **Characteristic** panel in the **Ribbon** to define the symbol being used for GD&T.
- Specify the value of tolerance, symbols, and modifiers using the options in the **Tolerance** panel of the **Ribbon**.
- Use the options in the **Data References** panel of the **Ribbon** to add Datum plane references.
- If you are working on composite feature control frame then click on node of frame to be modified; refer to Figure-54 and specify related parameters in the **Tolerance** panel of **General** contextual tab in the **Ribbon**.
- If you want to add more frames in the composite feature control frame then click on the **Add New Frame** button from the drawing area as shown in Figure-54.

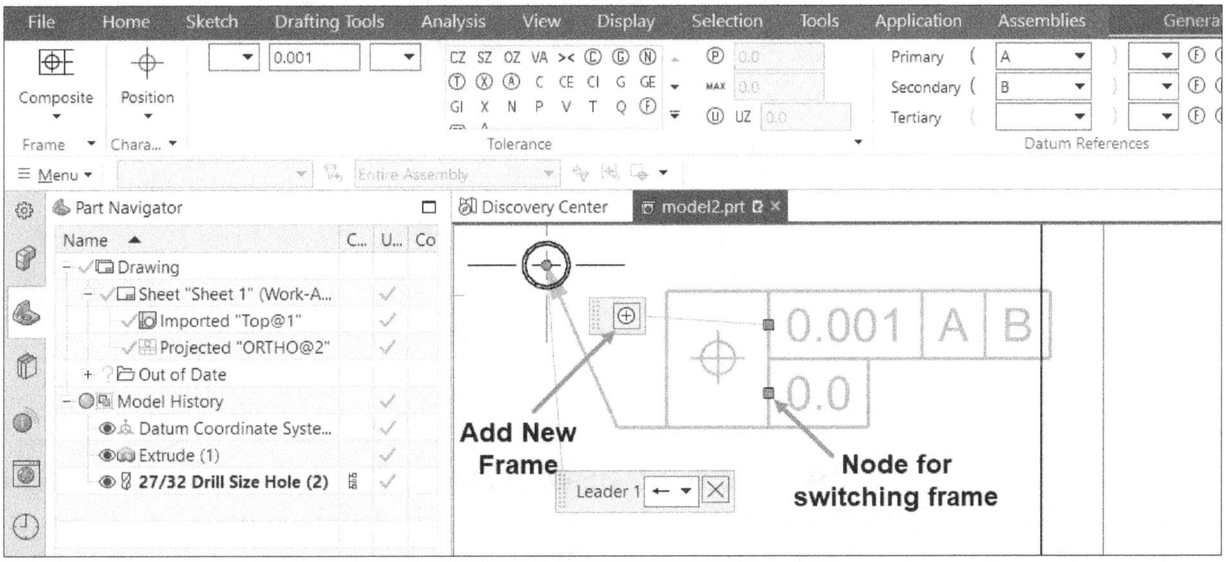

Figure-54. Composite frame nodes

- After placing the feature control frame and specifying desired parameters, click on **OK** button to close the dialog box.

Datum Feature Symbol

The **Datum Feature Symbol** tool is used to add reference for measuring all the geometric tolerances. For example, if you want to check perpendicularity of a face then you need to give a reference with respect to which the perpendicularity will be measured. The steps to create datum feature symbol are given next.

- Click on the **Datum Feature Symbol** tool from the **Annotation** group in the **Home** tab of the **Ribbon**. The **Datum Feature Symbol** dialog box will be displayed along with the datum symbol attached to the cursor; refer to Figure-55. You will be asked to specify the location.

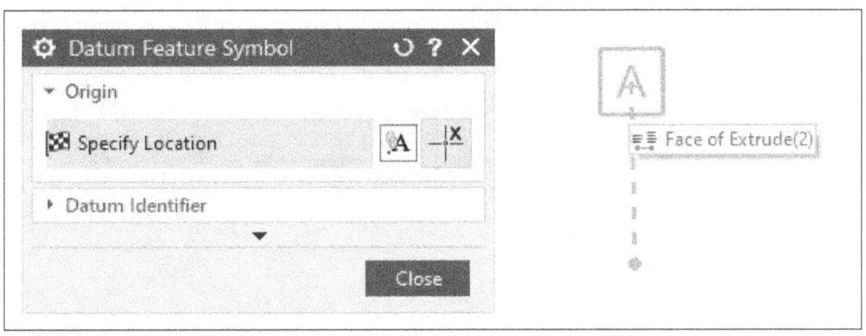

Figure-55. Datum Feature Symbol dialog box along with datum feature symbol

- Click in the drawing window at desired location to place the symbol. The datum feature symbol will be placed.
- Specify desired letter to be assigned to the datum feature symbol in the **Letter** edit box of **Datum Identifier** rollout.
- After specifying desired parameters, click on **Close** button to close the dialog box.

Figure-56 shows the break-up of a datum feature symbol.

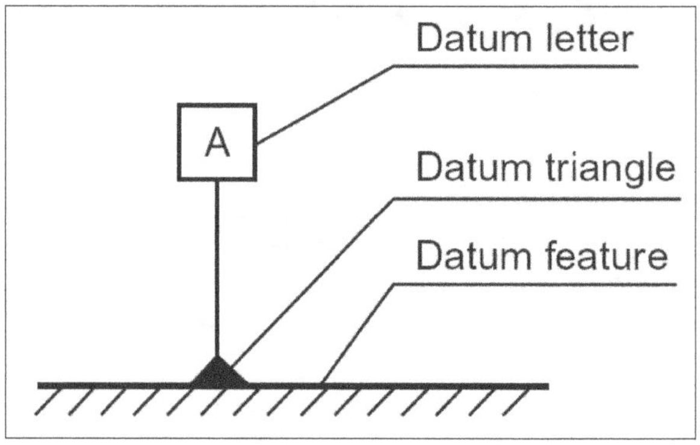

Figure-56. Datum feature symbol

Surface Finish Symbol

The **Surface Finish Symbol** tool is used to add surface finish symbol to the surface of a part. The procedure to use this tool is given next.

- Click on the **Surface Finish Symbol** tool from **Annotation** group of **Home** tab in the **Ribbon**. The surface finish symbol will get attached to cursor and the **Surface Finish** dialog box will be displayed; refer to Figure-57.

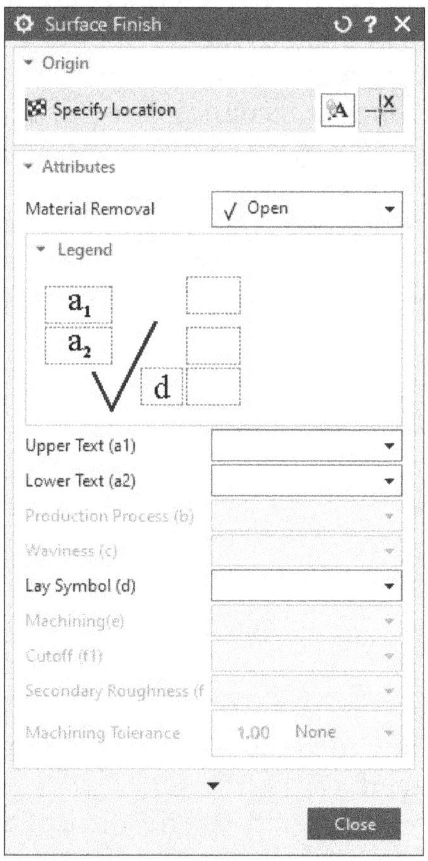

Figure-57. Surface Finish dialog box

- Select desired symbol type from **Material Removal** drop-down in the **Attributes** rollout. The **Legend** rollout displays a legend for the parameters of the surface finish symbol.
- Select desired value from **Upper Text** and **Lower Text** drop-down to specify the maximum and minimum limit of surface roughness, respectively.

- Select desired production method, coating, or treatment from **Production Process** drop-down.
- Select desired option from **Waviness** drop-down to define the waviness which is surface irregularities that are more widely spaced than roughness.
- Select desired option from **Lay Symbol** drop-down to specify the direction of lay.
- Select desired option from **Machining** drop-down to define the minimum amount of material that can be removed.
- Select desired option from **Cutoff** drop-down to specify the roughness cutoff.
- Select desired secondary roughness value and tertiary roughness from **Secondary Roughness** and **Tertiary Roughness** drop-downs, respectively.
- Select desired tolerance type for the machining tolerance from **Machining Tolerance** drop-down.
- Other parameters in the dialog box have been discussed earlier.
- After specifying desired parameters, click in the drawing window at desired location to place the surface finish symbol. The surface finish symbol will be placed; refer to Figure-58.
- Click on **Close** button to close the dialog box.

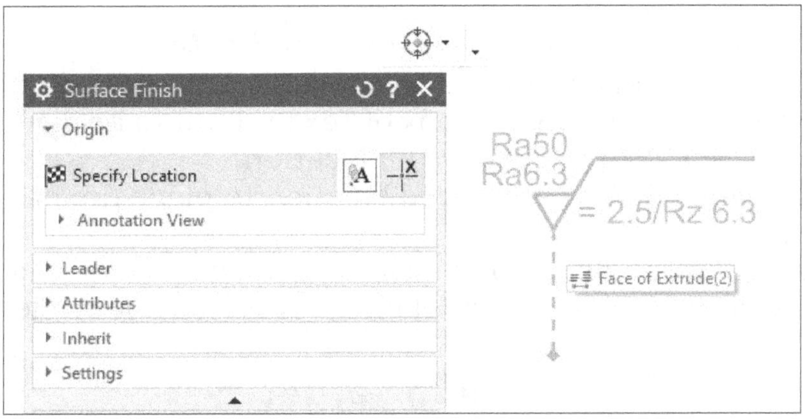

Figure-58. Placing the surface finish symbol

Surface Texture Symbols or Surface Roughness Symbols

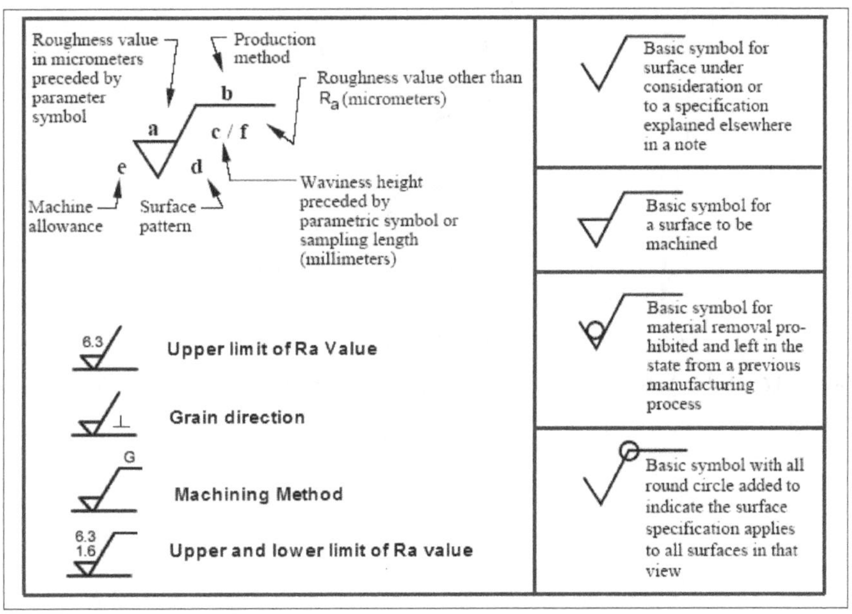

Balloon

The **Balloon** tool is used to create and edit balloon symbols in a drawing. The procedure to use this tool is discussed next.

- Click on the **Balloon** tool from **Annotation** group of **Home** tab in the **Ribbon**. The balloon will be attached to the cursor and the **Balloon** dialog box will be displayed; refer to Figure-59.

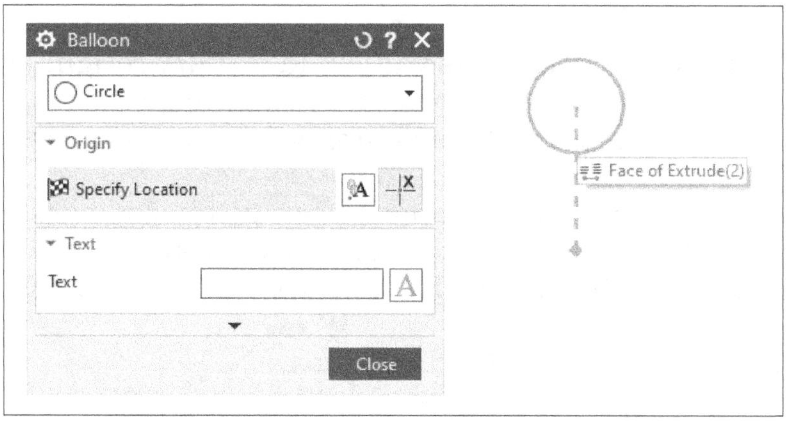

Figure-59. Balloon attached to cursor along with Balloon dialog box

- Select desired type of balloon from drop-down in the top area of the dialog box.
- Specify desired text in the **Text** edit box of **Text** rollout to be displayed in a balloon symbol. You will be asked to specify the location.
- Click in the drawing window at desired location to place the balloon. The balloon will be placed.
- Other parameters in the dialog box have been discussed earlier.
- After specifying desired parameters, click on **Close** button to close the dialog box.

Datum Target

Datum targets are circular frames divided in two parts by a horizontal line. The lower half represents the datum feature, and the upper half is for additional information, such as dimensions of the datum target area; refer to Figure-60.

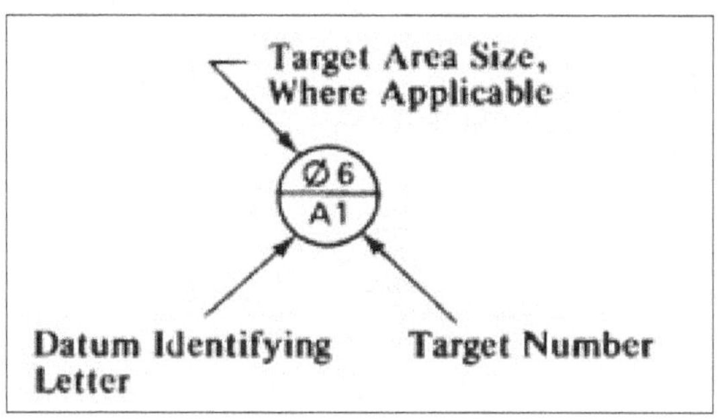

Figure-60. Datum target symbol

The **Datum Target** tool is used to add datum target to the drawing. The steps to do so are given next.

- Click on the **Datum Target** tool from **Annotation** group of **Home** tab in the **Ribbon**. The **Datum Target** dialog box will be displayed along with datum target symbol attached to cursor; refer to Figure-61.

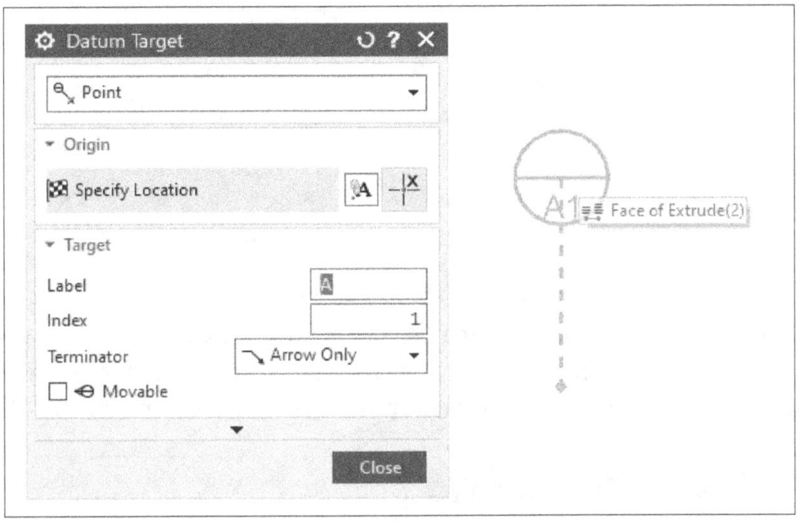

Figure-61. Datum Target dialog box along with datum target symbol

- Select desired shape of datum target area from drop-down in the top area of the dialog box.
- Specify desired datum identifier in the **Label** edit box of **Target** rollout. Specify desired number for the index in the **Index** edit box. Select desired type of marker from **Terminator** drop-down to be placed at the terminator of the leader. Select **Movable** check box to add a modifier to the circular datum target symbol.
- Other parameters in the dialog box have been discussed earlier.
- After specifying desired parameters, click in the drawing window at desired location to place the datum target symbol. The datum target symbol will be placed.
- Click on **Close** button to close the dialog box.

Weld Symbol and Edge Condition Symbol

The weld symbols and edge condition symbols are placed in the same way as you place geometric tolerances. Click on the tool, define the parameters and place the symbol by clicking.

In the same way, you can annotate center line and center mark by selecting the tools in the **Centerline** drop-down of **Annotation** group of **Home** tab in the **Ribbon**.

Crosshatch

The **Crosshatch** tool is used to fill a pattern within a specified boundary. The procedure to use this tool is discussed next.

- Click on the **Crosshatch** tool from the **Annotation** group of **Home** tab in the **Ribbon**. The **Crosshatch** dialog box will be displayed; refer to Figure-62.

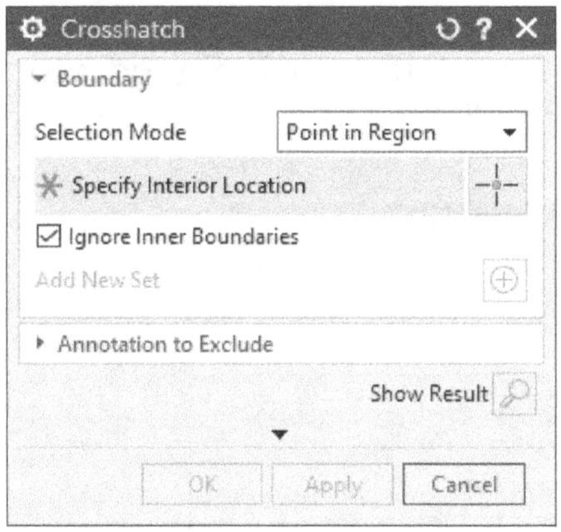

Figure-62. Crosshatch dialog box

- Select **Boundary Curves** option from **Selection Mode** drop-down in the **Boundary** rollout and select desired closed set of curves. Select **Point in Region** option from the drop-down and select desired point in the region; refer to Figure-63.

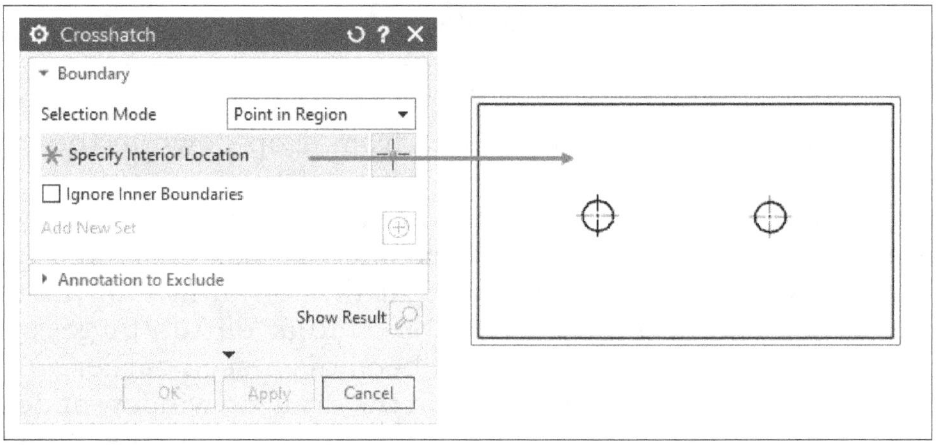

Figure-63. Specifying interior location

- Select **Ignore Inner Boundaries** check box to exclude the holes and isands for cross-hatching.
- Select **Automatically Exclude Annotation** check box from **Annotation to Exclude** rollout to create the annotation islands in the crosshatch, automatically. Select **Set Margin Individually** check box to specify the margin value around excluded annotations individually.
- After specifying desired parameters, click on **OK** button from the dialog box. The crosshatch will be created; refer to Figure-64.

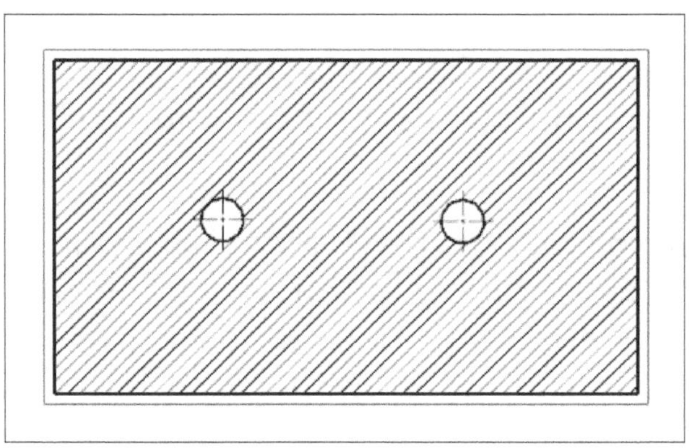

Figure-64. Crosshatch created

Area Fill

The **Area Fill** tool is used to create a pattern or solid fill within a specified boundary. The procedure to use this tool is same as discussed for **Crosshatch** tool.

Image

The **Image** tool is used to place a raster image on the drawing sheet. The procedure to use this tool is same as **Raster Image** tool discussed in **Chapter 4**.

Tabular Note

The **Tabular Note** tool is used to create and edit the tables of information in the drawing sheet. The procedure to use this tool is discussed next.

- Click on the **Tabular Note** tool from **Table** group of **Home** tab in the **Ribbon**. The **Tabular Note** dialog box will be displayed along with the table attached to cursor; refer to Figure-65.

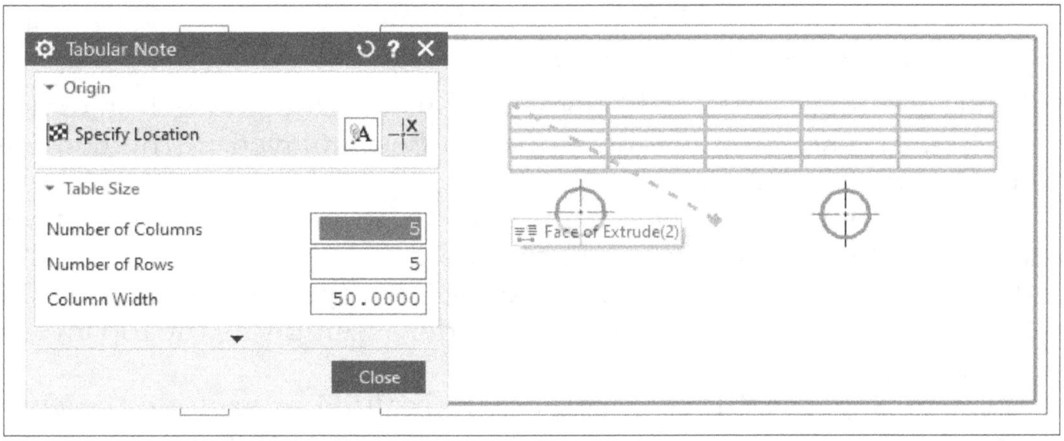

Figure-65. Tabular Note dialog box with the table attached to cursor

- Specify desired number of columns, number of rows, and column width in the **Number of Columns**, **Number of Rows**, and **Column Width** edit boxes of **Table Size** rollout, respectively.
- After specifying desired parameters, click in the drawing window at desired location to place the table. The tabular table will be placed.
- Click on **Close** button to close the dialog box.

Parts List

The **Parts List** tool is used to create a bill of materials for the assembly. The procedure to use this tool is discussed next.

- Click on the **Parts List** tool from **Table** group of **Home** tab in the **Ribbon**. The **Parts List** dialog box will be displayed along with parts list table attached to cursor; refer to Figure-66.

Figure-66. Parts List dialog box with parts list table

- Select desired components, solid bodies, or so on to be added or removed from the parts list. The selected components will be displayed in the component list area of **Contents** rollout.
- Select desired option from **Scope** drop-down to specify which components in the top assembly to be displayed in the parts list.
- Select desired option from **Top Level Assembly** drop-down to include the master model assembly or the children of master model assembly as the top level assembly in the parts list.
- Select **Include Subassemblies** check box to include or exclude the components of sub-assembly from the Assembly navigator or from the graphics window.
- Select **Show** check box from **Balloons** rollout to add callouts to one or more drawing views while creating the parts list.
- Other parameters in the dialog box have been discussed earlier.
- After specifying desired parameters, click in the drawing window at desired location to place the parts list. The parts list will be placed.
- Click on **Close** button to close the dialog box.

PRACTICAL 1

Create the drawing of the part using the model of **Practical 2** from the **Chapter 7** as shown in Figure-67 and Figure-68.

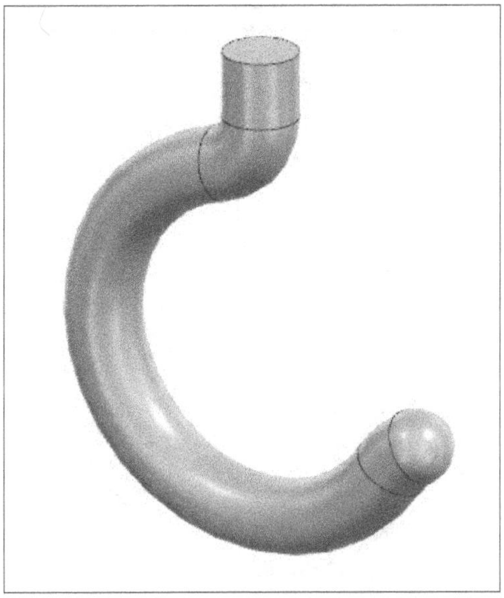

Figure-67. Practical 1 model

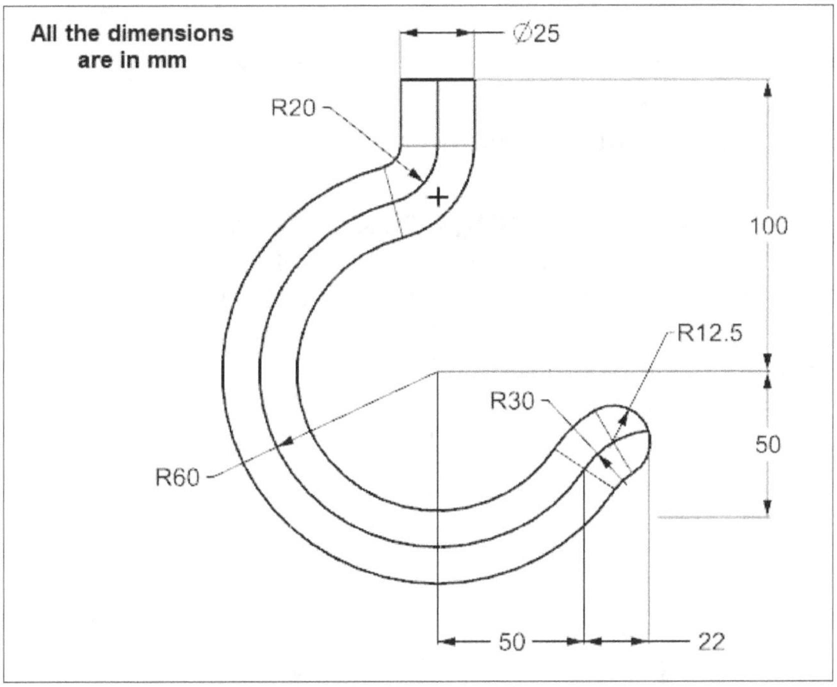

Figure-68. Practical 1 drawing

Starting A New Drawing

After opening the model, switch from modeling to drawing environment by clicking on the **Drafting** tool from **Document** group of **Application** tab in the **Ribbon**. The **Drawing** environment will be displayed along with the **Sheet** dialog box.

Placing Views

- Set desired size of sheet for placing the drawing views. After selecting the sheet size, click on **OK** button from the dialog box. The **Base View** dialog box will be displayed along with the base view attached to the cursor.
- Set the parameters as required and place the views in the drawing sheet of the drawing area; refer to Figure-69.

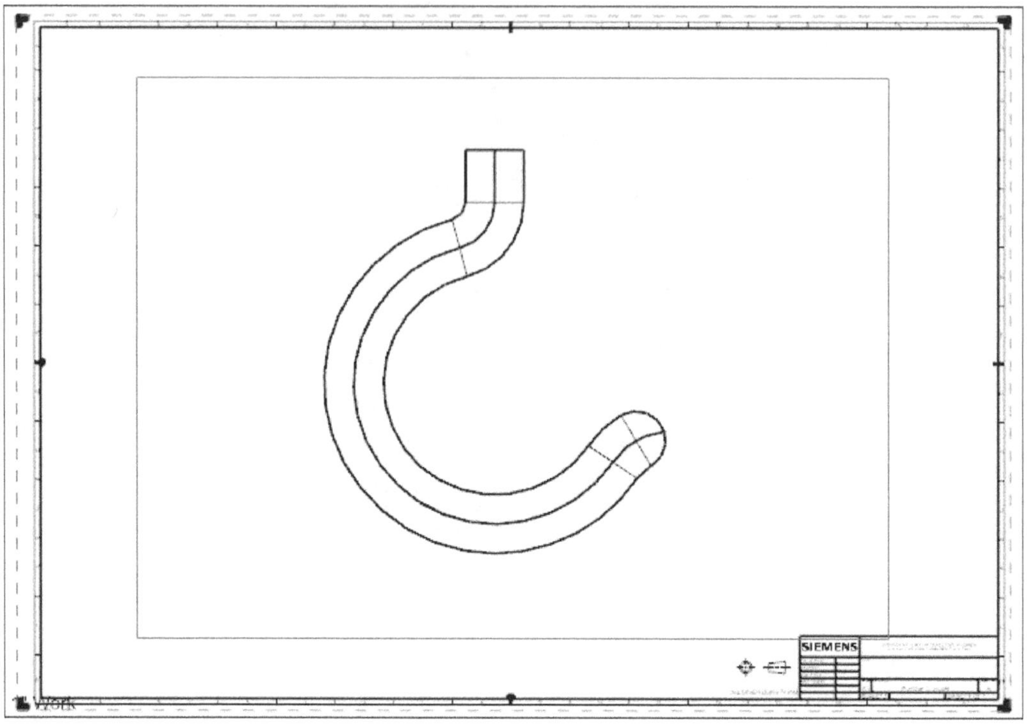

Figure-69. Placing drawing view

- Click on the **OK** button from the dialog box.

Applying Annotations

- Click on the **Linear** tool from **Dimension** group of **Home** tab in the **Ribbon** and apply the linear dimensions in the view as shown in Figure-70.

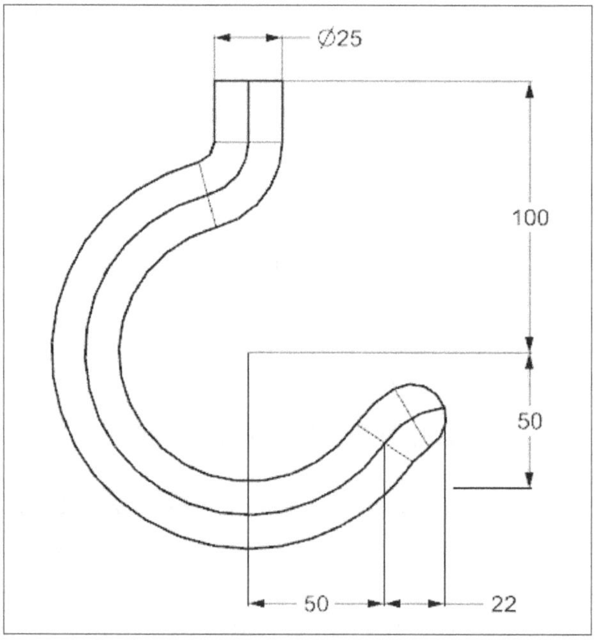

Figure-70. Applying linear dimensions

- Click on the **Radial** tool from **Dimension** group of the **Ribbon** and apply the radial dimensions as shown in Figure-71.

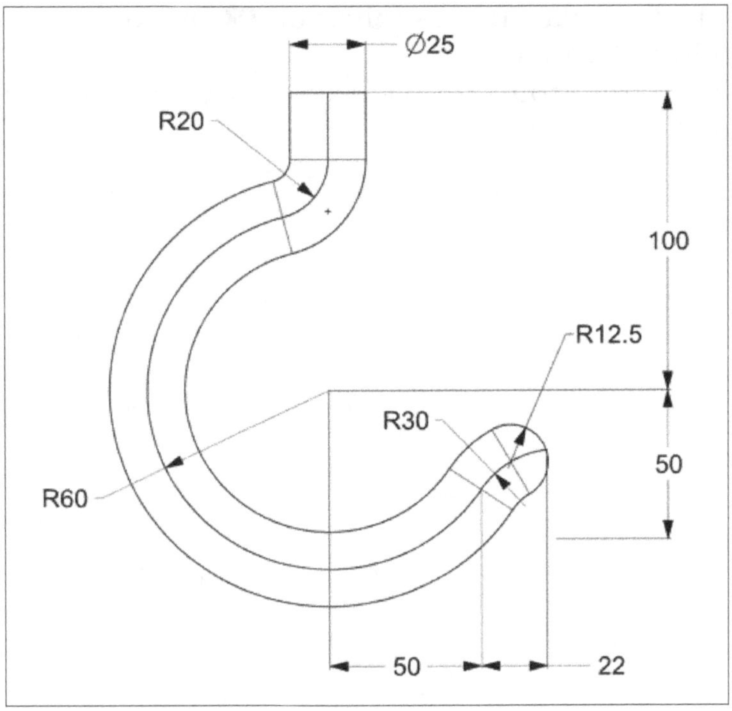

Figure-71. Applying radial dimensions

- After applying annotations to the drawing, save the drawing using **CTRL+S** at desired location. Yes! It is common sense in Computer world.

Printing Drawing

- Click on the **Plot** tool from the **File** menu. The **Plot** dialog box will be displayed.
- Specify desired parameters in the dialog box or as shown in Figure-72.

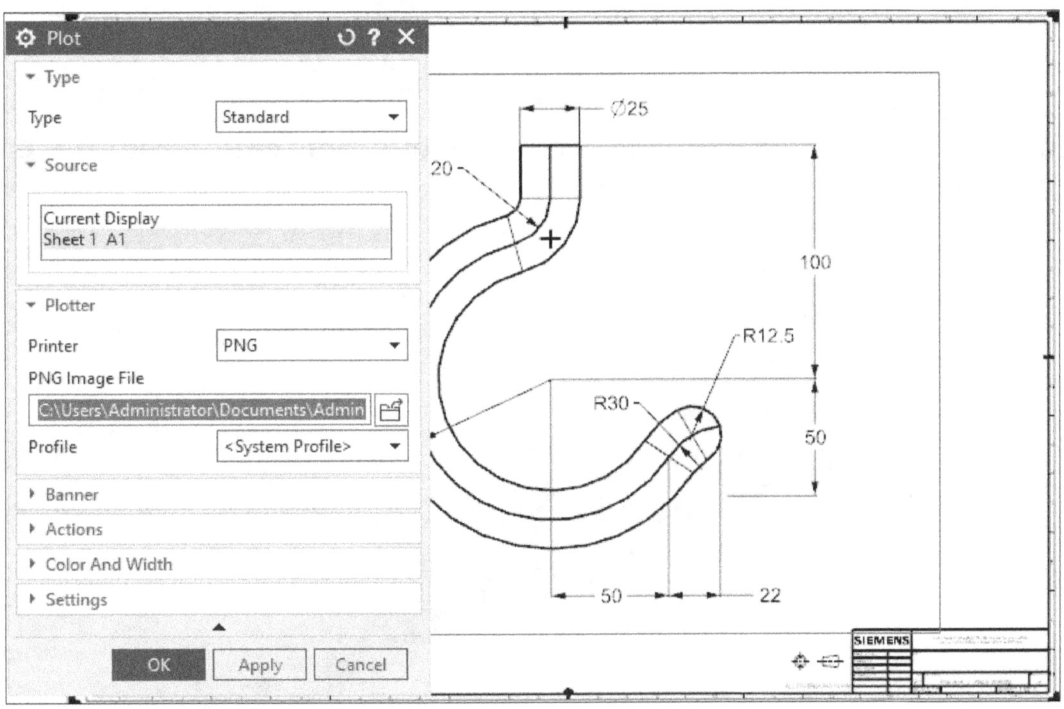

Figure-72. Specifying parameters in Plot dialog box

- After specifying desired parameters, click on **OK** button from the dialog box. The drawing will be plotted and saved.
- Open the saved drawing from the local directory, the drawing will be displayed as shown in Figure-73.

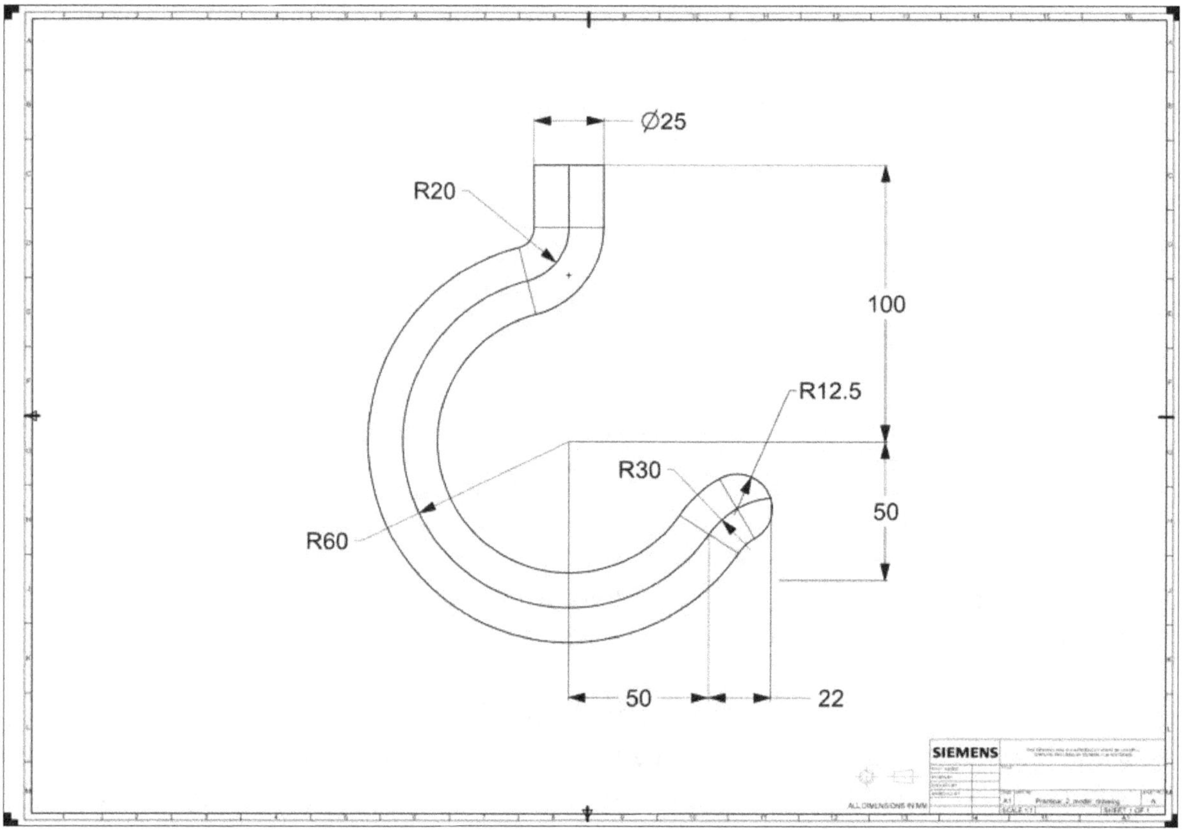

Figure-73. Drawing displayed

PRACTICAL 2

Create the drawing of the part using the model of **Practical 3** from the **Chapter 7** as shown in Figure-74 and Figure-75.

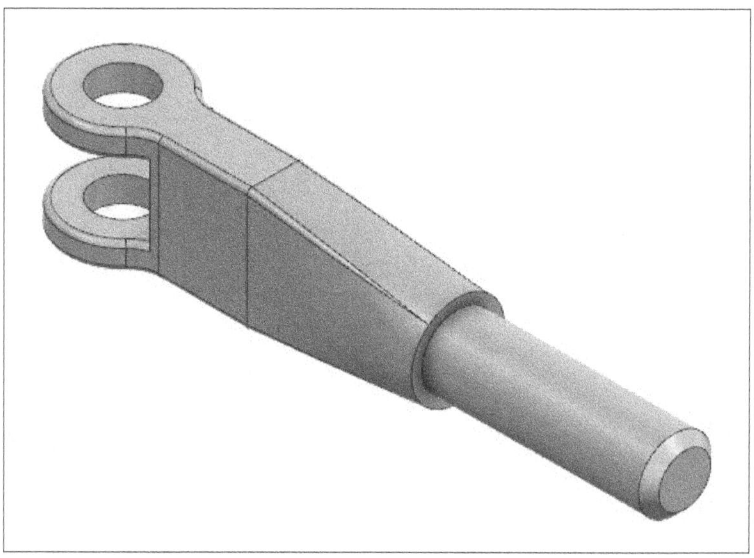

Figure-74. Practical 2 model

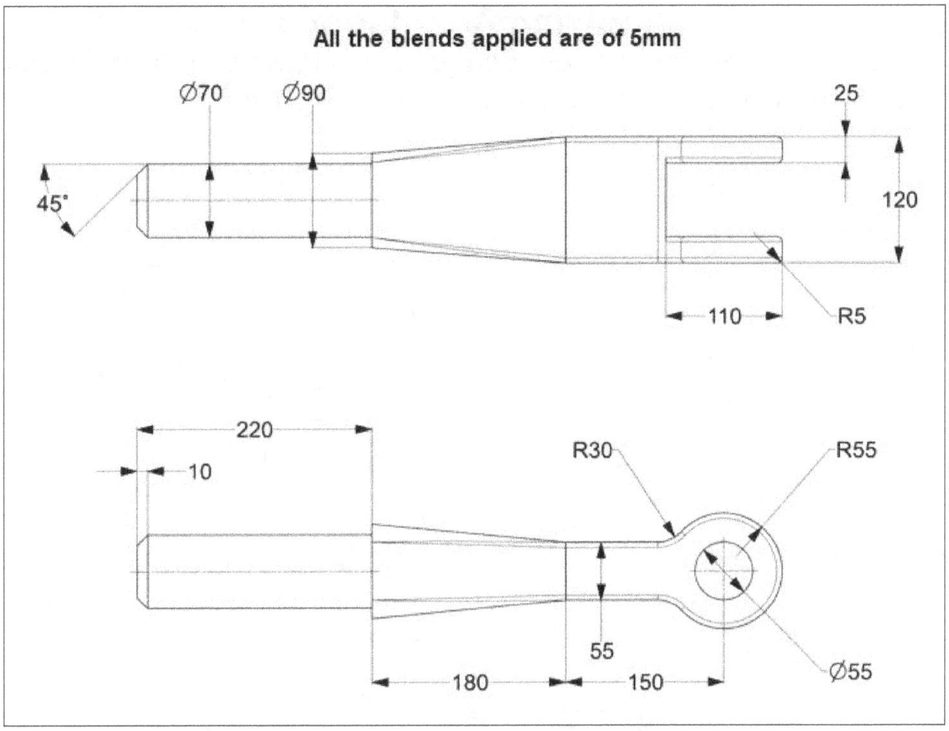

Figure-75. Practical 2 drawing

Starting A New Drawing

After opening the model, switch from modeling to drawing environment by clicking on the **Drafting** tool from **Document** group of **Application** tab in the **Ribbon**. The **Drawing** environment will be displayed along with the **Sheet** dialog box.

Placing Views

- Set desired size of sheet for placing the drawing views. After selecting the sheet size, click on **OK** button from the dialog box. The **Base View** dialog box will be displayed along with the base view attached to the cursor.
- Set the parameters as required and place the views in the drawing sheet of the drawing area; refer to Figure-76.

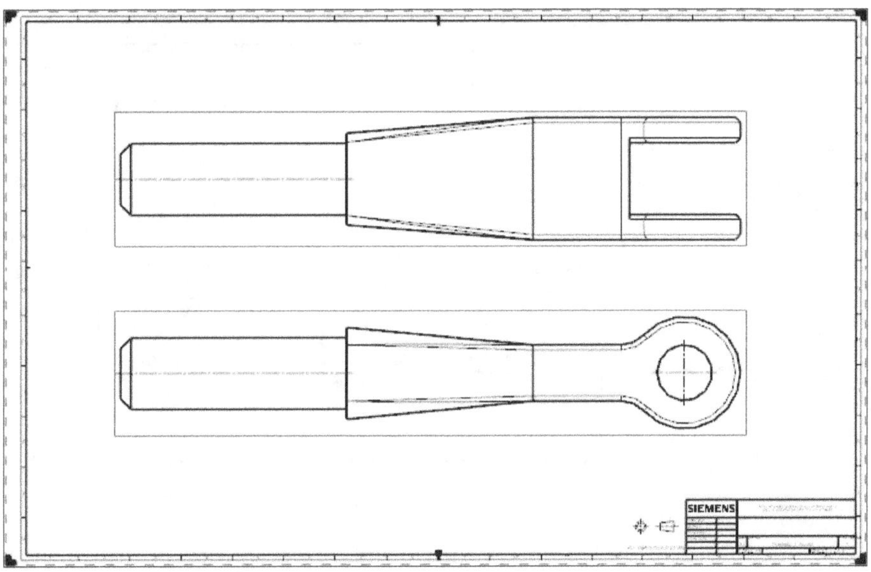

Figure-76. Placing drawing views

- Click on the **OK** button from the dialog box.

Applying Annotations

- Click on the **Linear** tool from **Dimension** group of **Home** tab in the **Ribbon** and apply the linear dimensions in the view as shown in Figure-77.

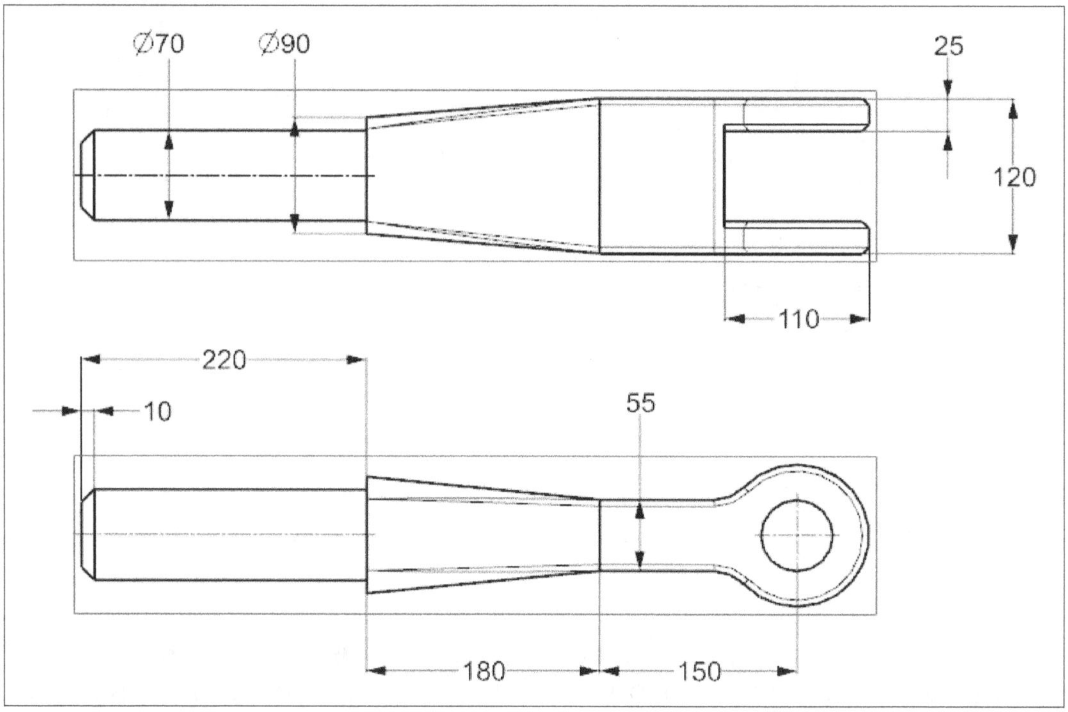

Figure-77. Applying linear dimensions

- Click on the **Radial** tool from **Dimension** group of the **Ribbon** and apply the radial dimensions as shown in Figure-78.

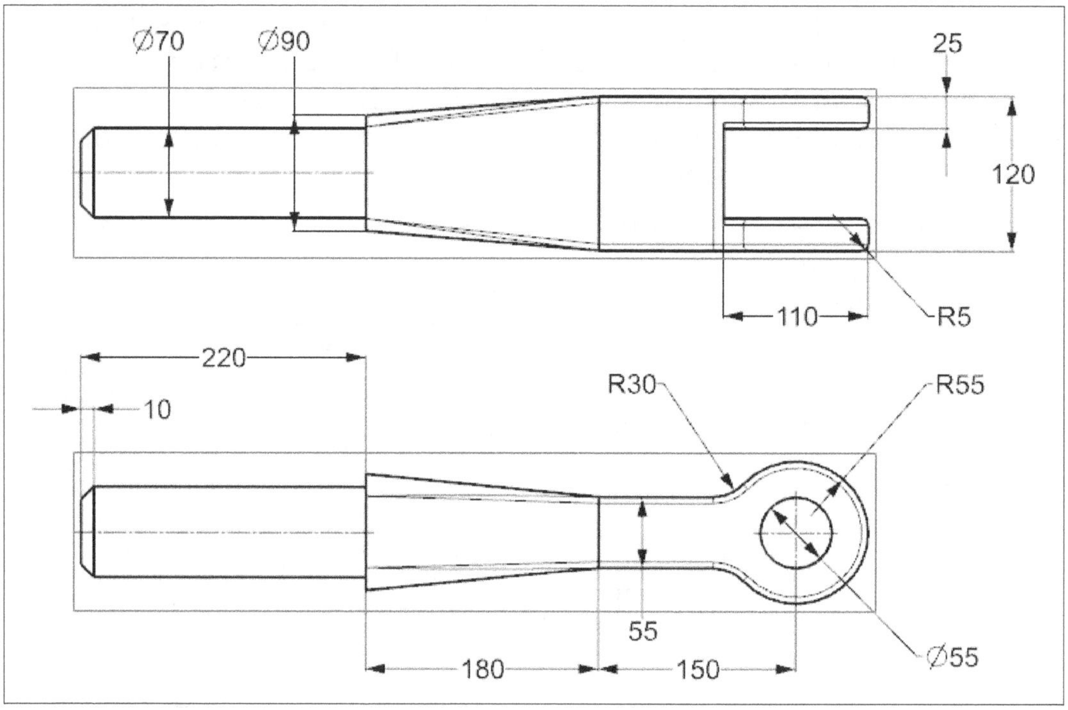

Figure-78. Applying radial dimensions

- Click on the **Angular** tool from **Dimension** group of the **Ribbon** and apply the angular dimension as shown in Figure-79.

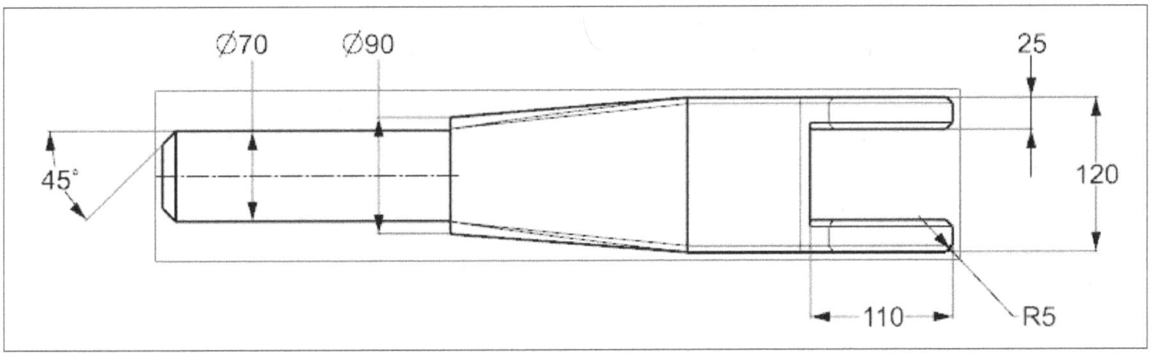

Figure-79. Applying angular dimension

Printing Drawing

- Click on the **Plot** tool from the **File** menu. The **Plot** dialog box will be displayed.
- Specify desired parameters in the dialog box or as shown in Figure-80.

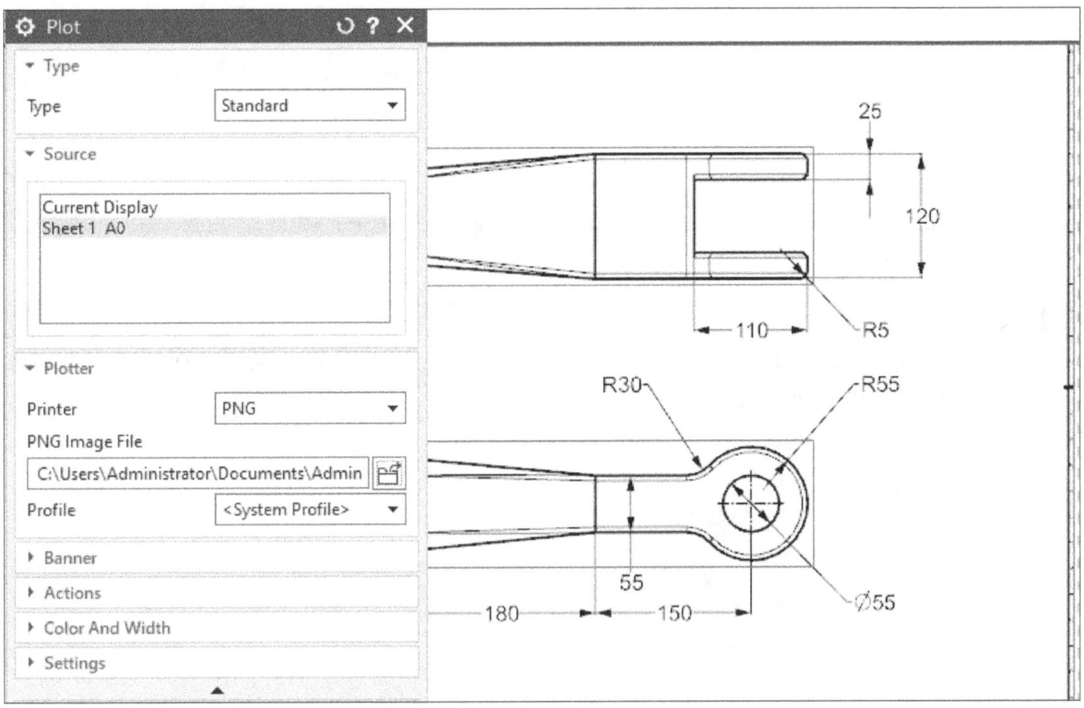

Figure-80. Specifying parameters in Plot dialog box

- After specifying desired parameters, click on **OK** button from the dialog box. The drawing will be plotted and saved.
- Open the saved drawing from the local directory, the drawing will be displayed as shown in Figure-81.

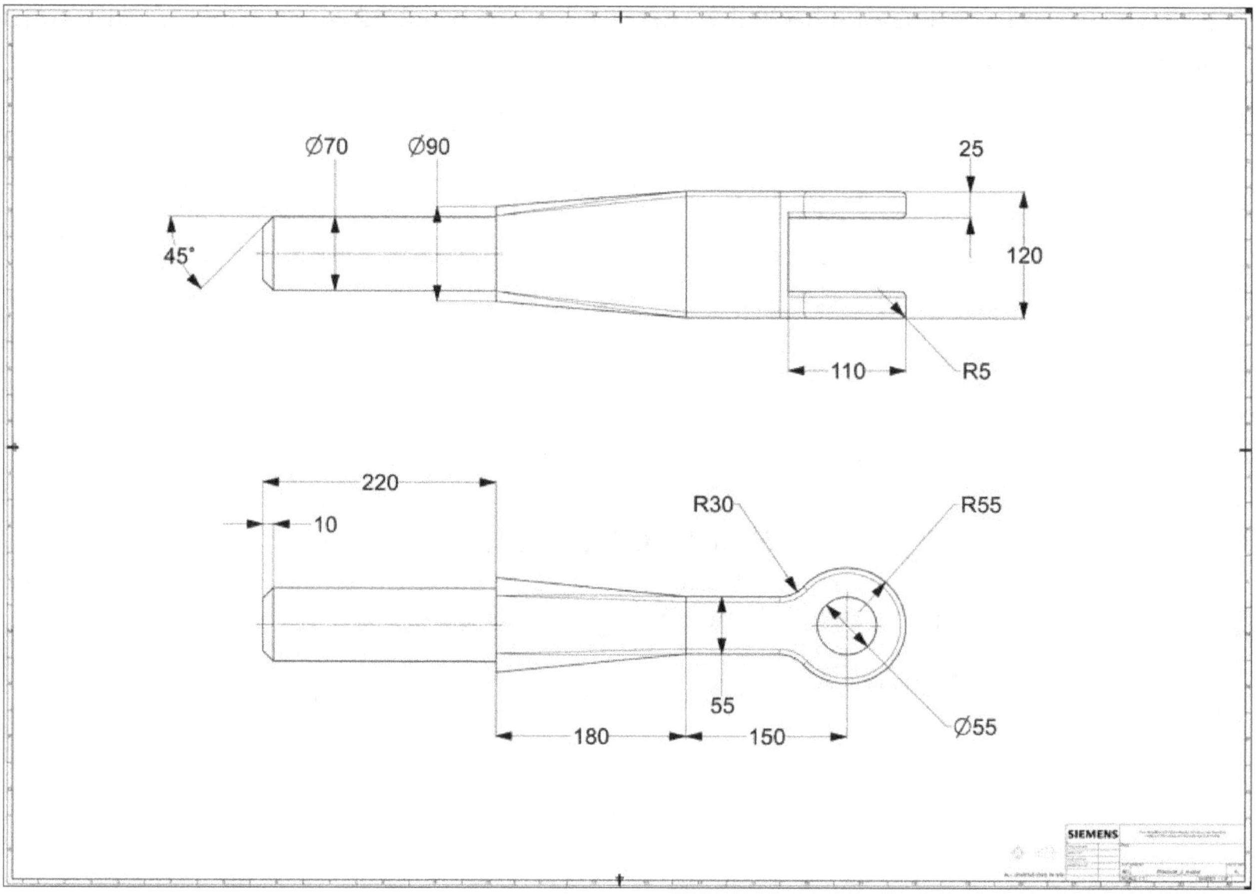

Figure-81. Drawing displayed

PRACTICAL 3

Create the drawing of the part using the model of **Practice 6** from the **Chapter 7** as shown in Figure-82 and Figure-83.

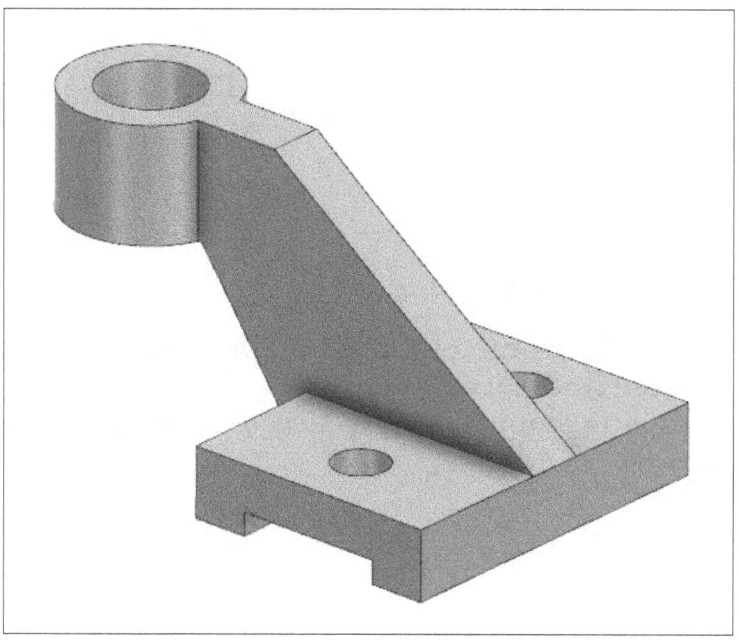

Figure-82. Practical 3 model

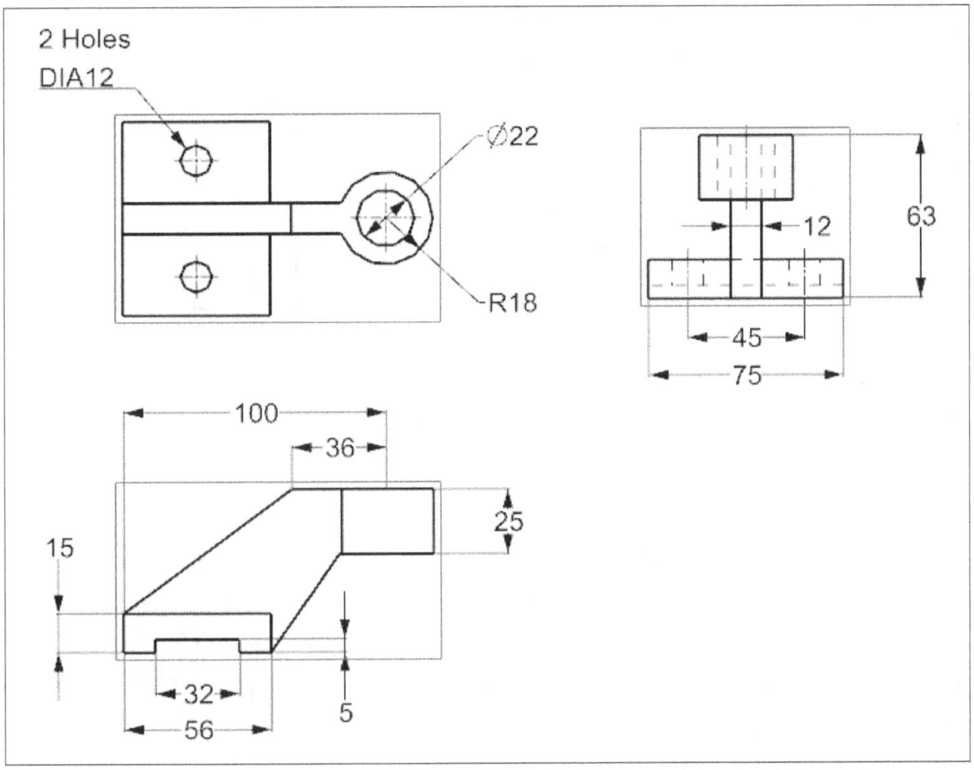

Figure-83. Practical 3 drawing

Starting A New Drawing

After opening the model, switch from modeling to drawing environment by clicking on the **Drafting** tool from **Document** group of **Application** tab in the **Ribbon**. The **Drawing** environment will be displayed along with the **Sheet** dialog box.

Placing Views

- Set desired size of sheet for placing the drawing views. After selecting the sheet size, click on **OK** button from the dialog box. The **Base View** dialog box will be displayed along with the base view attached to the cursor.
- Set the parameters as required and place the views in the drawing sheet of the drawing area; refer to Figure-84.

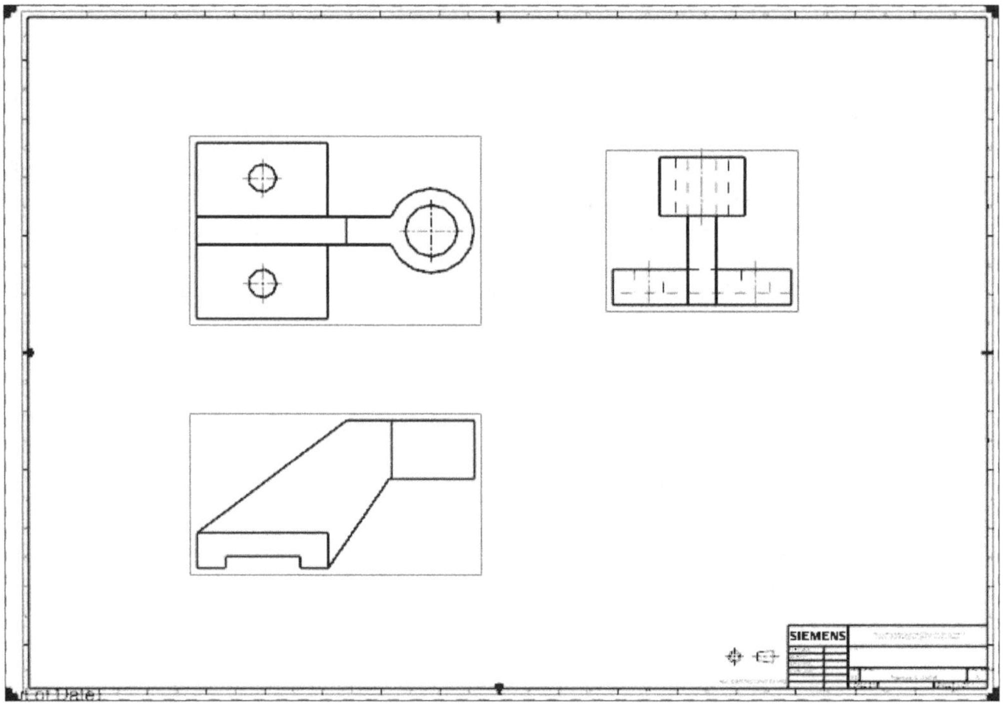

Figure-84. Placing drawing views

- Click on the **OK** button from the dialog box.

Applying Annotations

- Click on the **Linear** tool from **Dimension** group of **Home** tab in the **Ribbon** and apply the linear dimensions in the view as shown in Figure-85.

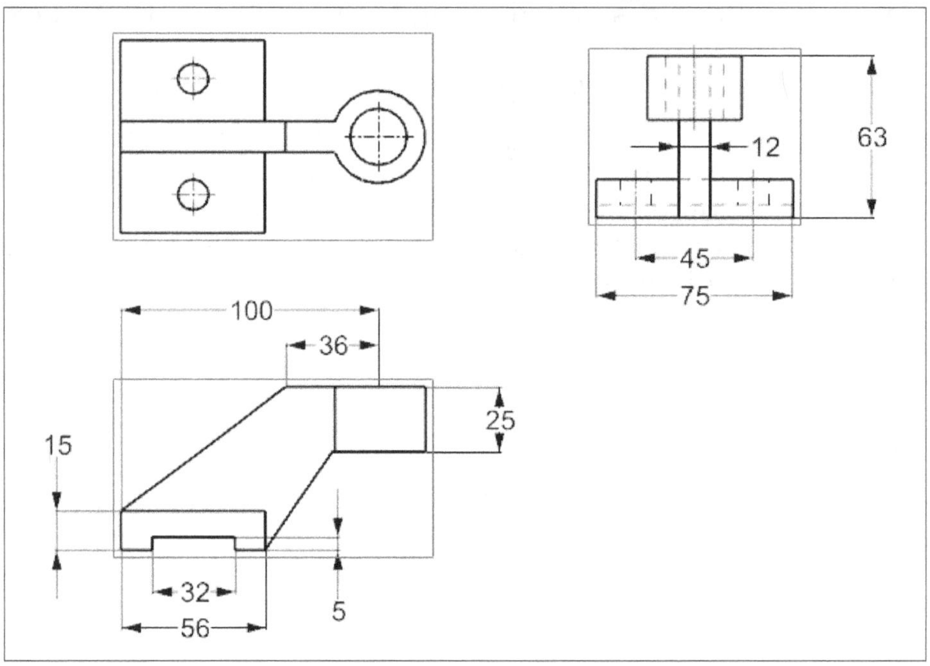

Figure-85. Applying linear dimensions

- Click on the **Radial** tool from **Dimension** group of the **Ribbon** and apply the radial dimensions as shown in Figure-86.

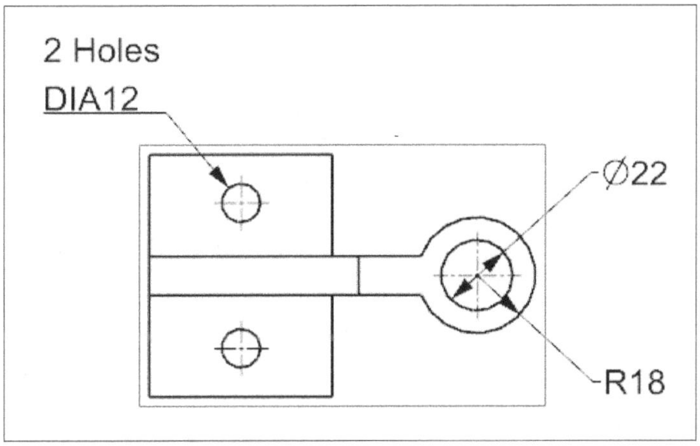

Figure-86. Applying radial dimensions

Printing Drawing

- Click on the **Plot** tool from the **File** menu. The **Plot** dialog box will be displayed.
- Specify desired parameters in the dialog box or as shown in Figure-87.

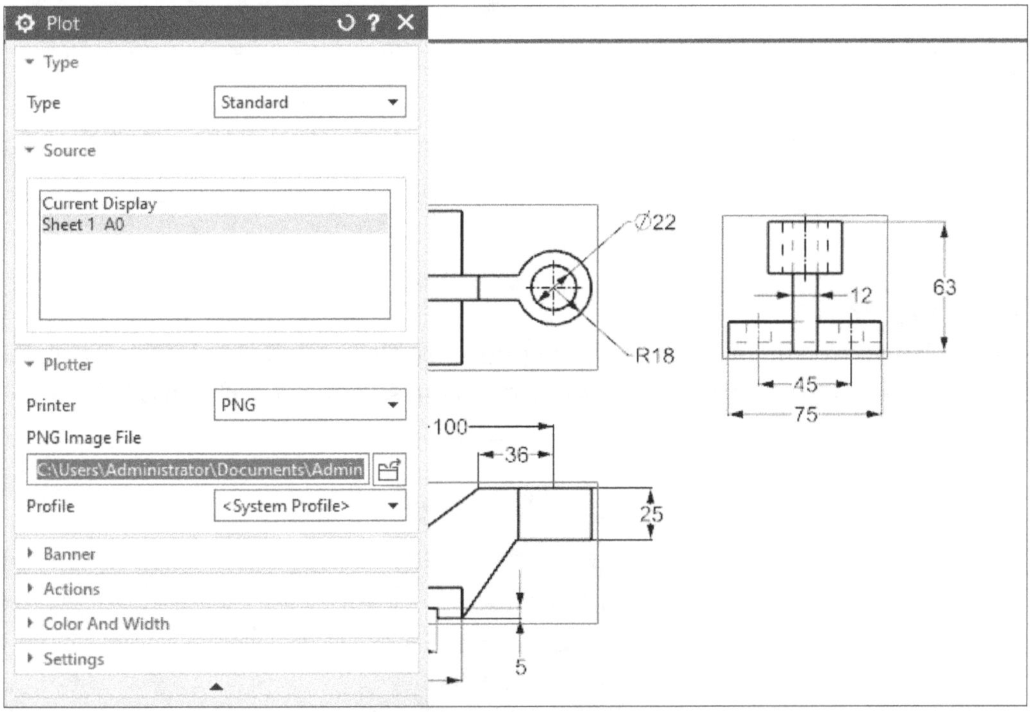

Figure-87. Specifying parameters in Plot dialog box

- After specifying desired parameters, click on **OK** button from the dialog box. The drawing will be plotted and saved.
- Open the saved drawing from the local directory, the drawing will be displayed as shown in Figure-88.

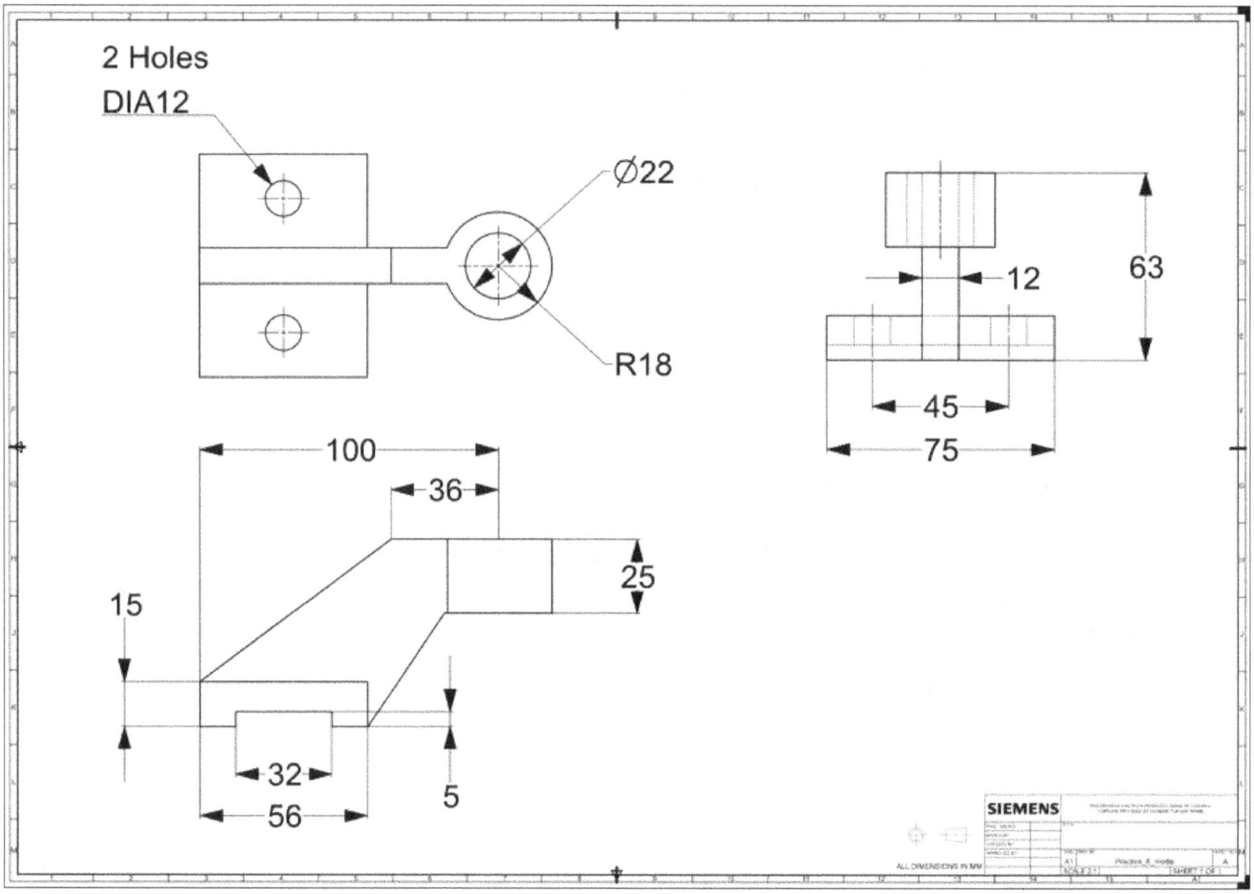

Figure-88. Drawing displayed

PRACTICAL 4

Create assembly drawing for assembly given in Practical 1 of Chapter 11; refer to Figure-89. Generate Bill of material with balloons; refer to Figure-90.

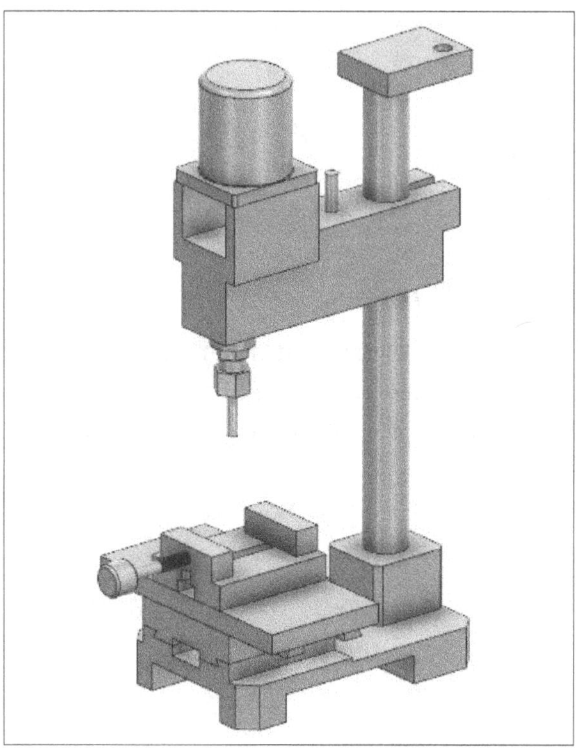

Figure-89. Assemble view of tiny milling machine

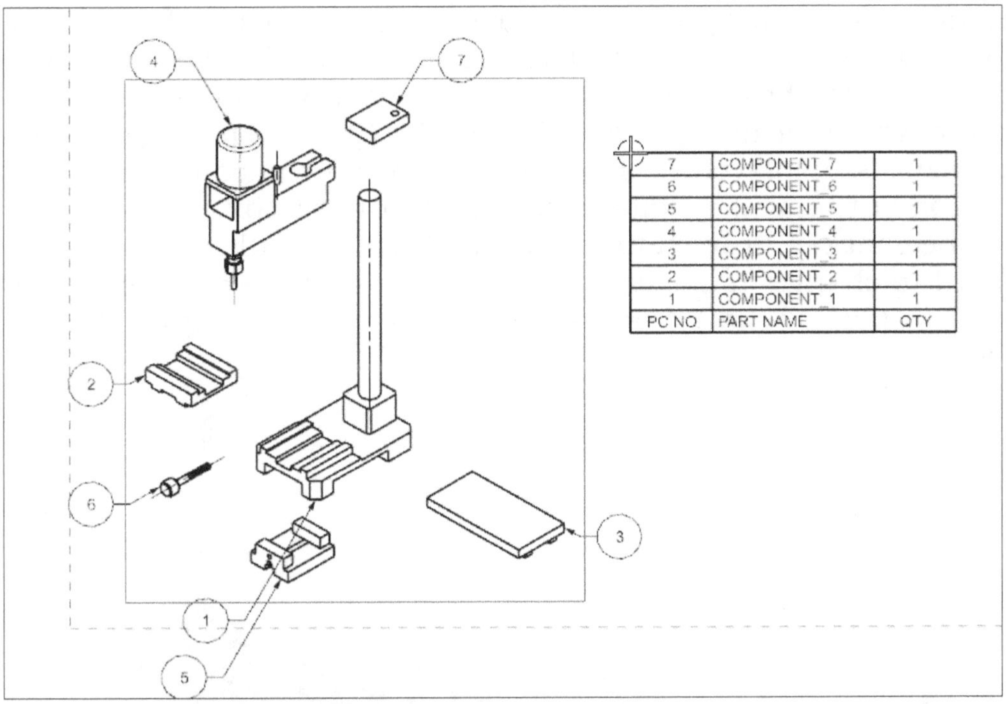

Figure-90. Exploded view with balloons and bill of materials table

Creating Exploded View

- Open the Assembly file of Tiny Milling machine created in Practical 1 of Chapter 11.
- Click on the **Explosions** tool from the **Explosions** group in the **Assemblies** tab of the **Ribbon**. The **Explosions** dialog box will be displayed.
- Click on the **New Explosions** button from the dialog box. The **Edit Explosion** dialog box will be displayed where you can specify parameters related to exploded view.
- Select the **Automatic** option from the **Explosion Type** drop-down and click on the **Auto-explode All** button to automatically separate the components assembled in the model; refer to Figure-91.

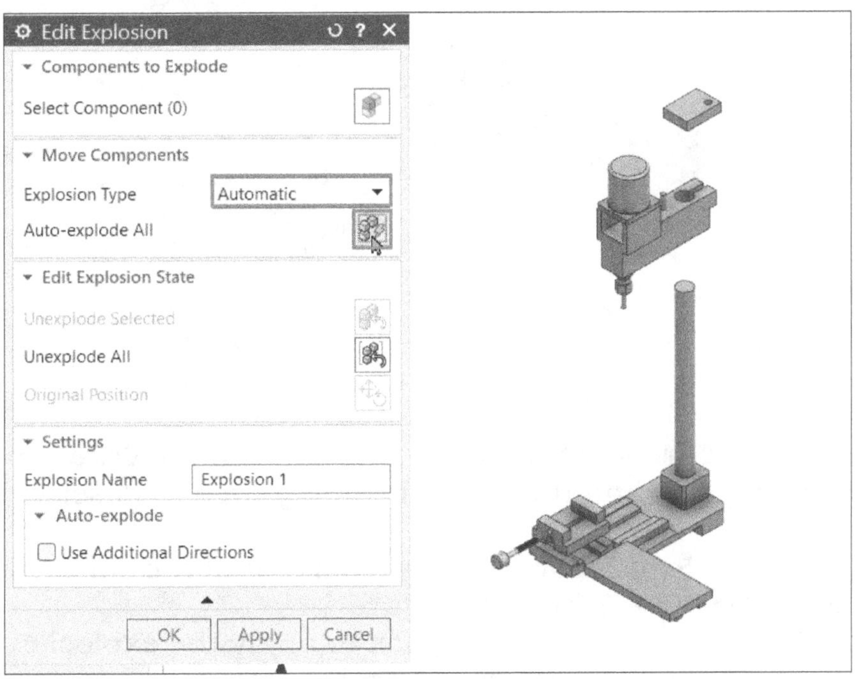

Figure-91. Performing Auto Explosion

- As you can see from the figure, there are some components that are not separated properly to be shown in exploded view in drawing. So, we will not use **Manual** method to separate those components. Select the **Manual** option from the **Explosion Type** drop-down in the dialog box and select **COMPONENT 3** from graphics area (Name of component is displayed on hovering cursor on the component). The **Specify Orientation** button will become active in the dialog box.
- Click on the **Specify Orientation** button. A drag handle will be displayed on the component to change its position in exploded view; refer to Figure-92.
- Drag the component away from rest of components using the handles; refer to Figure-93.

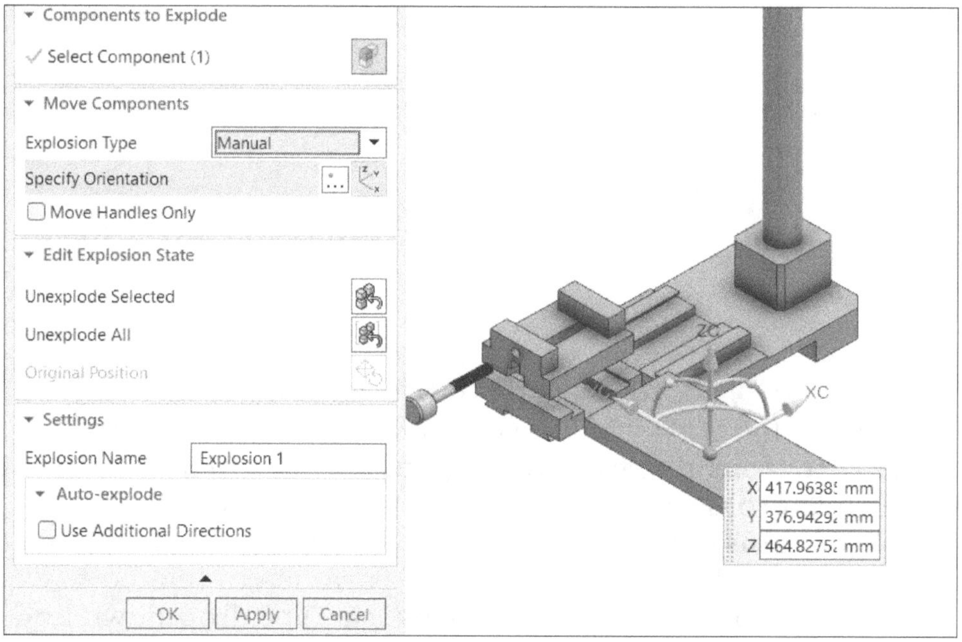

Figure-92. Drag handle for changing position of component

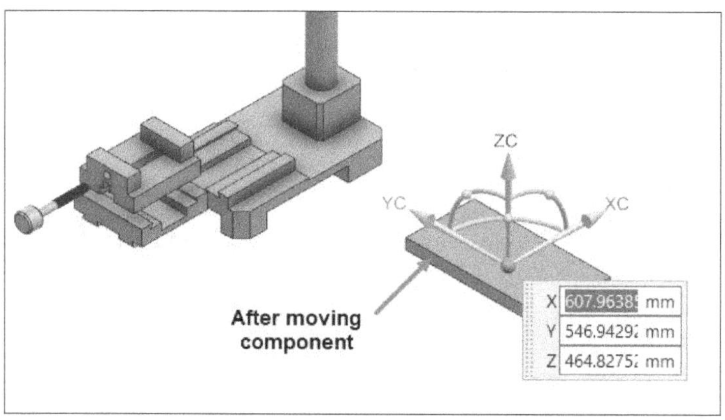

Figure-93. After moving component

- Click on the **Select Component** selection button from the **Components to Explode** section in the dialog box and then click in empty area to deselect earlier selected component.
- Select the **COMPONENT 5** and move it away from rest of the components. Similarly, move away the **COMPONENT 2**; refer to Figure-94.
- Click on the **OK** button from the dialog box to apply the explosion operation. The **Explosions** dialog box will be displayed again.
- Click on the **Close** button from the dialog box to exit.

- Now, we will create a new view of this exploded assembly so that it can be inserted in the drawing. To do so, right-click on **Model Views** node in the **Part Navigator** and select the **Add View** option from the shortcut menu; refer to Figure-95. A new view will be added in the model views list; refer to Figure-96. Right-click on newly added view and using **Rename** option from shortcut menu, change name of the view to "Exploded view".

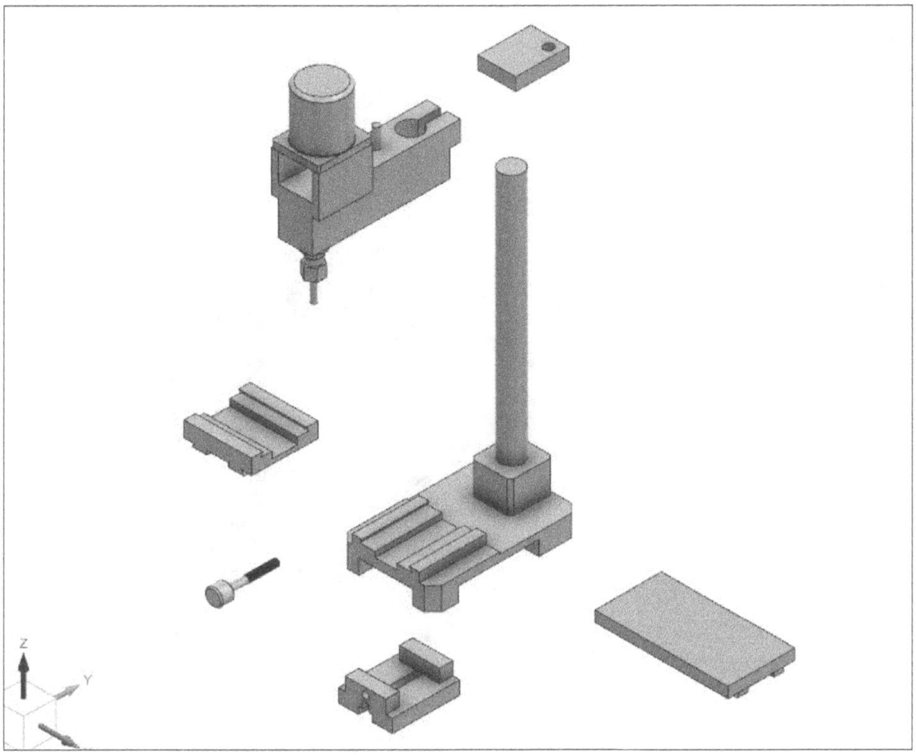

Figure-94. Components after moving components

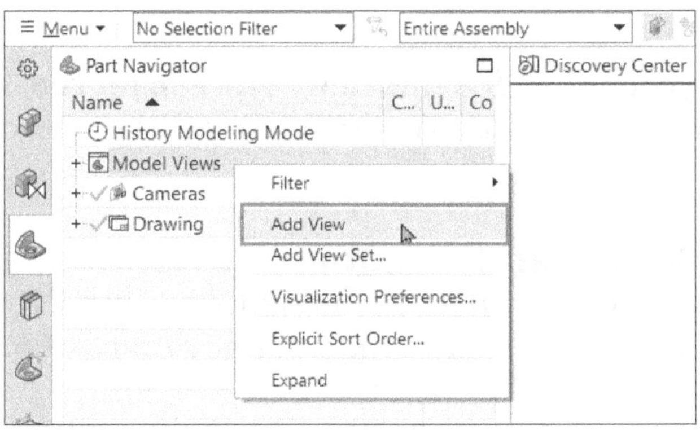

Figure-95. Add View option

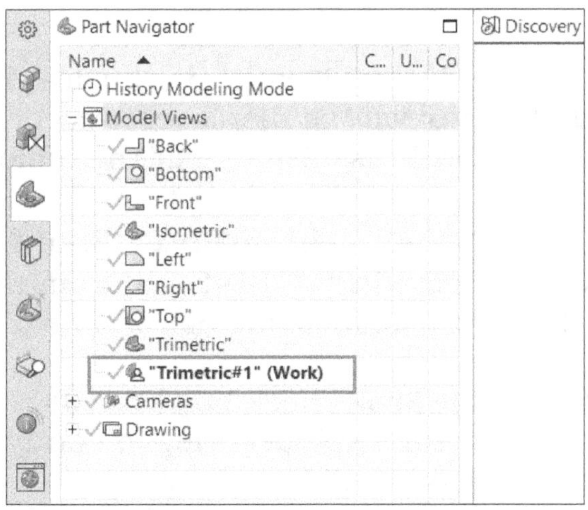

Figure-96. New view added in the list

Switching to Drawing

Switch from modeling to drawing environment by clicking on the **Drafting** tool from **Document** group of **Application** tab in the **Ribbon**. The **Drawing** environment will be displayed along with the **Sheet** dialog box.

Placing Views

- Set desired size of sheet for placing the drawing views. After selecting the sheet size, click on **OK** button from the dialog box. The **Base View** dialog box will be displayed along with the base view attached to the cursor.
- Select the **Exploded view** option from the **Model view to Use** drop-down in the **Model View** rollout of the dialog box and set desired value in **Scale** drop-down of **Scale** rollout to reduce the size of view to place it within sheet boundaries; refer to Figure-97.

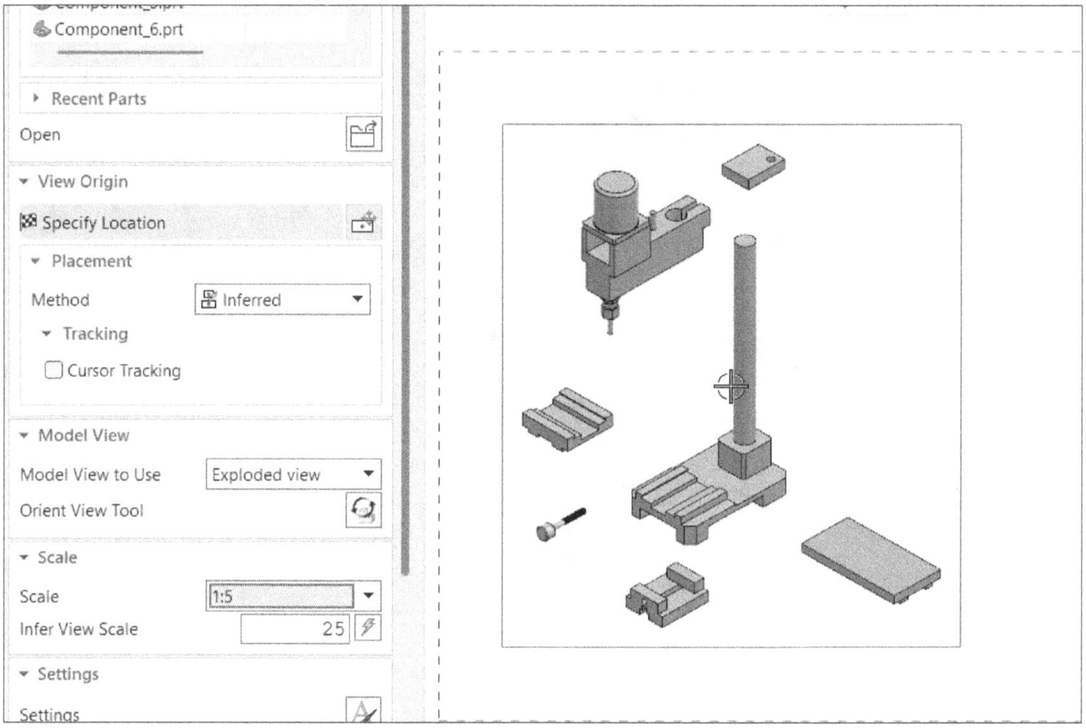

Figure-97. Placing exploded view

- Click at desired location in the drawing area to place the view. The **Projected View** dialog box will be displayed and projected view of current view will be attached to cursor. Press **ESC** to exit the dialog box.

Inserting Bill of Materials and Balloons

- Click on the **Parts List** tool from the **Table** group in the **Home** tab of the **Ribbon**. The **Parts List** dialog box will be displayed and bill of materials will be attached to cursor.
- Select the **Show** check box from **Balloons** rollout in the **Parts List** dialog box and click on the exploded view recently placed in the drawing area to define where the balloons will be created.
- Click on the **Specify Location** selection button at the top in the dialog box and click at desired location to place the bill of materials table; refer to Figure-98. Select and drag the balloons to reposition them.

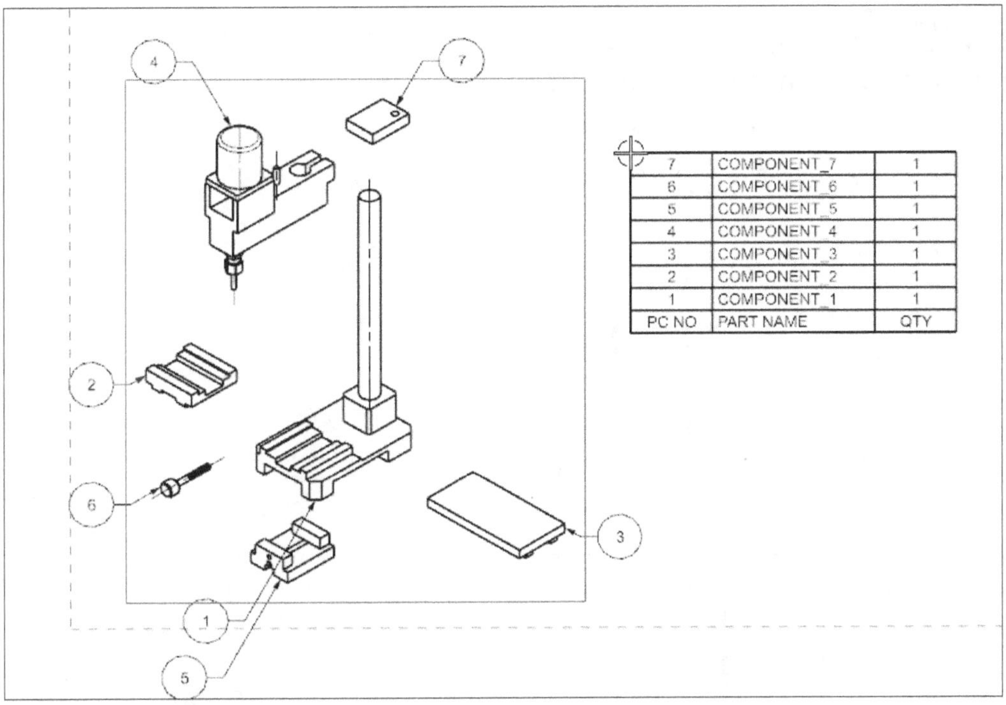

Figure-98. Exploded view with balloons and bill of materials table

PRACTICE 1

Generate the drawing views of all the solid models we have created in Practices and Practicals in the previous chapters.

PRACTICE 2

Generate the exploded views, bill of materials and balloons from all the assembly models we have worked on till this chapter.

PRACTICE 3

Create the model and drawing given in Figure-99.

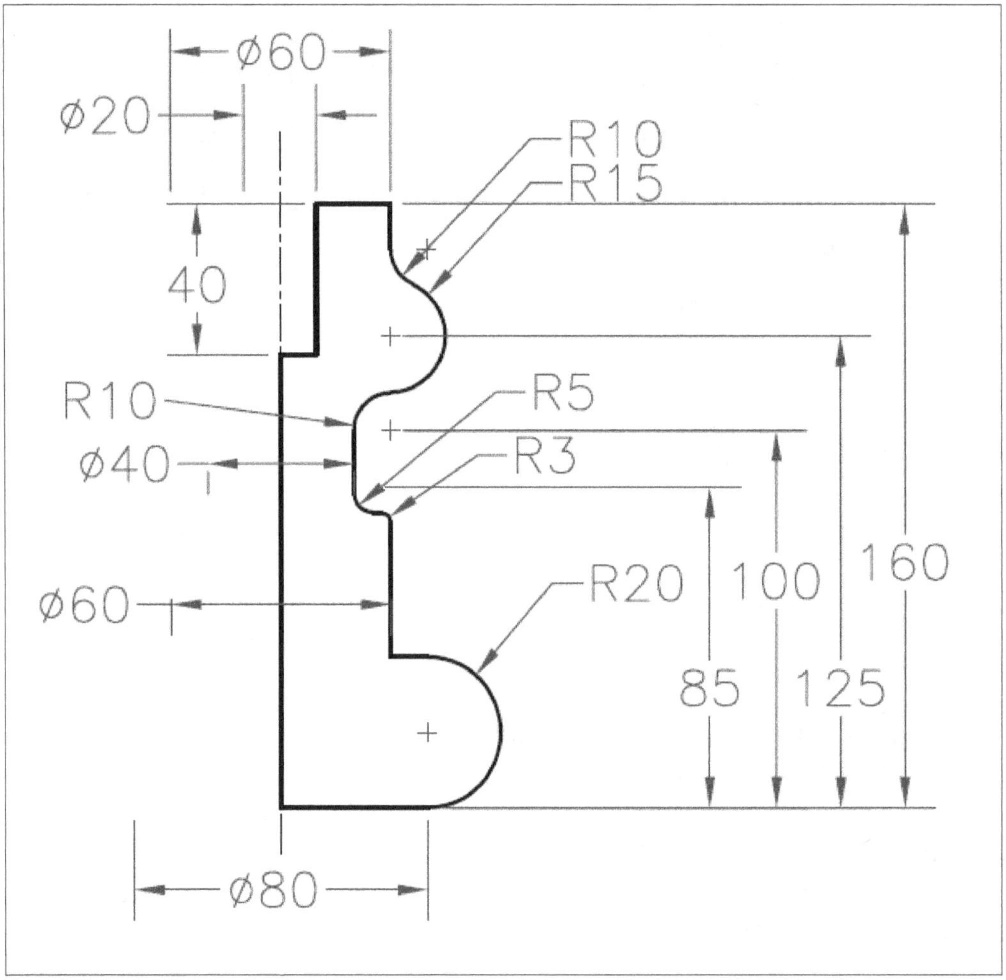

Figure-99. Practice 3

PRACTICE 4

Create the model and drawing given in Figure-100.

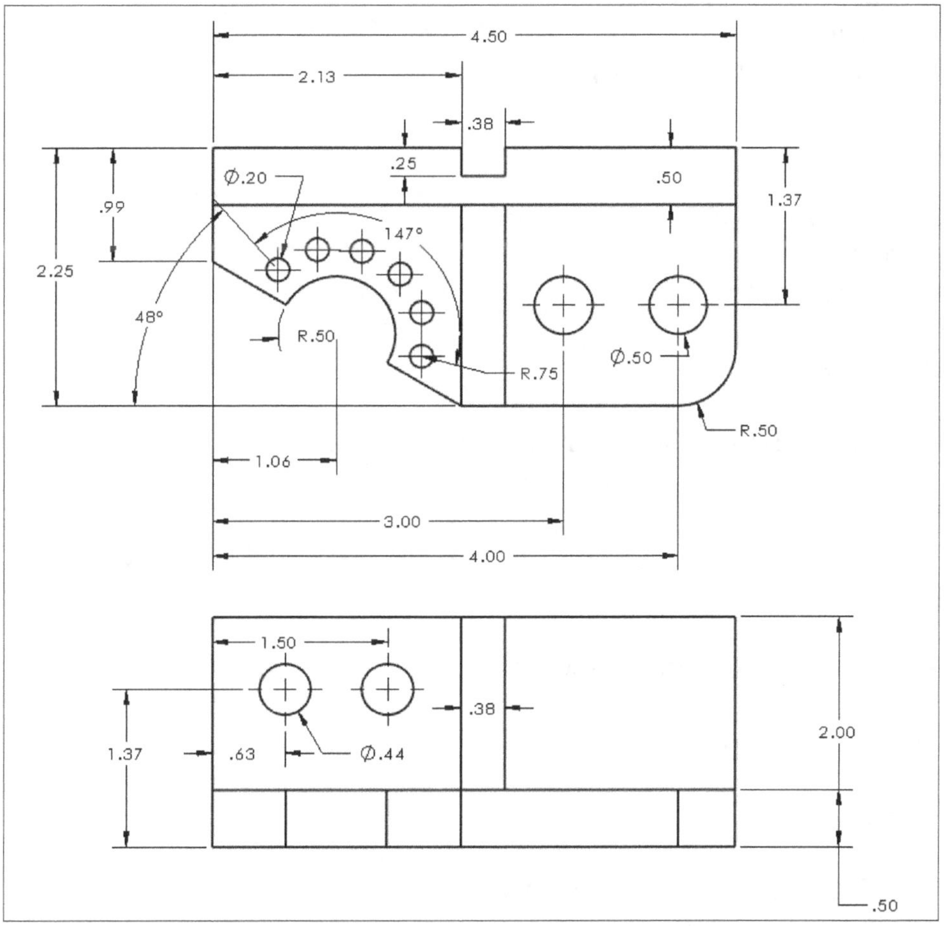

Figure-100. Practice 4

PRACTICE 5

Create the model and drawing given in Figure-101.

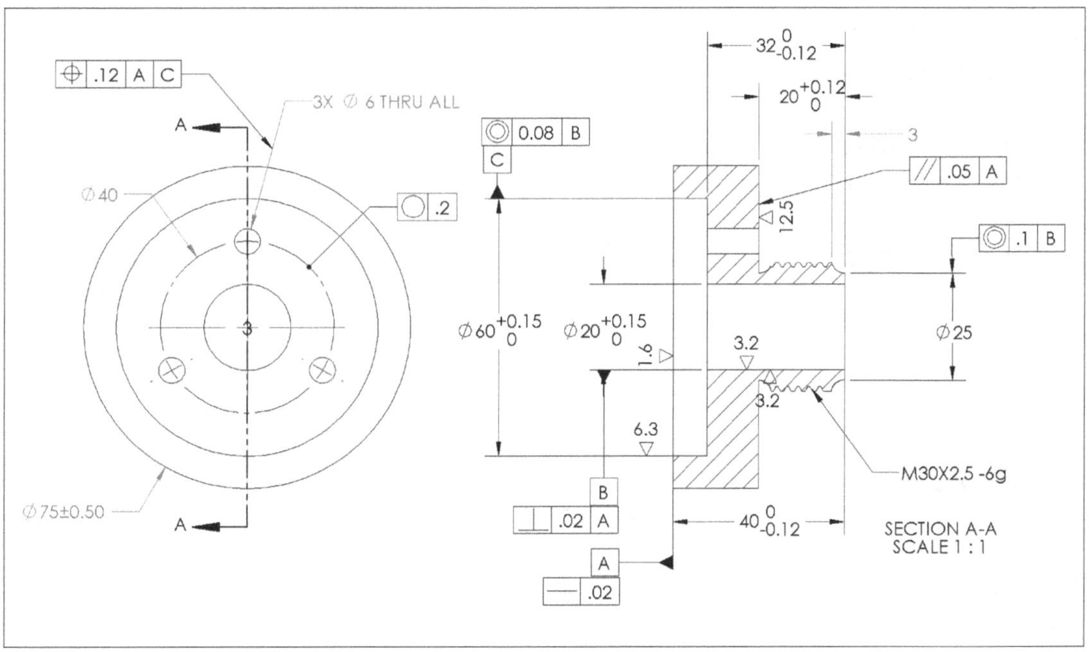

Figure-101. Practice 5

SELF ASSESSMENT

Q1. What is engineering drawing?
A. 3D representation
B. Representation of model on paper
C. Simulation
D. Animation

Q2. Drawings are used to:
A. Decorate models
B. Manufacture products
C. Store files
D. Run simulations

Q3. Which environment is used in NX for drawings?
A. Sketch
B. Modeling
C. Drawing
D. Assembly

Q4. "Stand-alone Part" option is used to:
A. Attach model
B. Create drawing without model
C. Edit model
D. Create assembly

Q5. "Reference Existing Part" is used to:
A. Delete model
B. Add reference 3D model
C. Create sketch
D. Modify template

Q6. Title block contains:
A. Only dimensions
B. Only material
C. Drawing information
D. Only views

Q7. Title block is located at:
A. Top left
B. Bottom right
C. Center
D. Top right

Q8. Drafting tool is used for:
A. Modeling
B. Switching environment
C. Rendering
D. Simulation

Q9. Sheet dialog box is used for:
A. Creating model
B. Setting sheet size
C. Editing geometry
D. Adding annotations

Q10. Standard Size option is used for:
A. Custom size
B. Predefined sheet size
C. Scaling
D. Rotation

Q11. Custom Size option allows:
A. Default size
B. User-defined dimensions
C. Automatic scaling
D. Fixed size

Q12. Scale 4:1 means:
A. Reduce size
B. Increase size
C. Same size
D. Rotate

Q13. Scale 1:2 means:
A. Double size
B. Half size
C. Same size
D. Rotate

Q14. First Angle Projection places views:
A. Same direction
B. Opposite direction
C. Random
D. Parallel

Q15. Third Angle Projection places views:
A. Opposite
B. Same as viewing direction
C. Random
D. Inverted

Q16. Base View tool is used to:
A. Delete views
B. Add base view
C. Align views
D. Scale view

Q17. Projected View depends on:
A. Sheet
B. Parent view
C. Title block
D. Annotation

Q18. Inferred option in projected view:
A. Manual
B. Automatic hinge line
C. Delete hinge
D. Rotate view

Q19. Detail View is used to:
A. Show full model
B. Zoom portion
C. Delete part
D. Scale view

Q20. Boundary type in detail view can be:
A. Only square
B. Circular or rectangular
C. Only circular
D. Triangle

Q21. Section Line tool creates:
A. Dimensions
B. Section lines
C. Notes
D. Views

Q22. Section View is created by:
A. Scaling
B. Cutting model
C. Rotating
D. Deleting

Q23. Dynamic option in section view:
A. Deletes line
B. Creates section line
C. Edits model
D. Rotates

Q24. Update Views tool updates:
A. Model
B. Outdated views
C. Sheet size
D. Scale

Q25. Move/Copy View tool is used to:
A. Delete
B. Move or copy
C. Rotate
D. Scale

Q26. View Alignment tool aligns:
A. Models
B. Views
C. Sheets
D. Dimensions

Q27. View Boundary tool defines:
A. Model
B. View boundary
C. Sheet size
D. Annotation

Q28. Automatic Rectangle boundary:
A. Fixed size
B. Updates automatically
C. Manual
D. Random

Q29. View Dependent Edit affects:
A. All views
B. Selected view only
C. Entire model
D. Sheet

Q30. Hole and Thread Callout is used for:
A. Surface finish
B. Hole parameters
C. Datum
D. Section

Q31. Linear option in callout shows:
A. Circular lines
B. Vertical lines
C. Horizontal lines
D. Diagonal

Q32. Ordinate dimension measures:
A. Radius
B. Distance from origin
C. Angle
D. Area

Q33. Multiple dimension option in ordinate:
A. One point
B. Multiple points
C. No points
D. Random

Q34. Thickness dimension measures:
A. Radius
B. Distance between curves
C. Area
D. Angle

Q35. Arc length dimension measures:
A. Straight line
B. Arc distance
C. Height
D. Width

Q36. Note tool is used for:
A. Views
B. Extra info
C. Dimensions
D. Sections

Q37. Feature Control Frame is used in:
A. CAD
B. GD&T
C. CAM
D. CAE

Q38. Leader arrow points to:
A. Sheet
B. Feature
C. Model
D. Dimension

Q39. Tolerance value defines:
A. Color
B. Limit
C. Size
D. Shape

Q40. Primary datum is fixed:
A. Last
B. First
C. Random
D. Never

Q41. Secondary datum is fixed:
A. First
B. After primary
C. Last
D. Never

Q42. Datum Feature Symbol defines:
A. Color
B. Reference
C. Size
D. Scale

Q43. Surface Finish Symbol shows:
A. Color
B. Roughness
C. Size
D. Weight

Q44. Waviness defines:
A. Roughness
B. Surface irregularities
C. Size
D. Color

Q45. Balloon tool creates:
A. Views
B. Text symbols
C. Sections
D. Models

Q46. Datum Target is:
A. Square
B. Circular divided frame
C. Triangle
D. Line

Q47. Crosshatch tool is used to:
A. Add text
B. Fill pattern
C. Create view
D. Scale

Q48. Area Fill tool is used to:
A. Section
B. Fill region
C. Rotate
D. Delete

Q49. Tabular Note tool creates:
A. Views
B. Tables
C. Models
D. Sections

Q50. Parts List tool creates:
A. Drawing
B. BOM
C. Section
D. Dimension

Q51. Include Subassemblies option:
A. Excludes parts
B. Includes sub-parts
C. Deletes parts
D. Rotates parts

Q52. Balloon rollout Show option:
A. Deletes
B. Adds callouts
C. Rotates
D. Scales

Q53. Select All Out-of-Date Views button:
A. Deletes views
B. Selects outdated views
C. Creates views
D. Aligns views

Q54. Reverse Direction button in section:
A. Deletes
B. Changes cut direction
C. Rotates
D. Scales

Q55. Specify Screen Position is used to:
A. Delete view
B. Move view
C. Rotate view
D. Scale

Q56. Cursor Tracking enables:
A. Rotation
B. Offset tracking
C. Scaling
D. Deletion

Q57. Infer View Scale determines:
A. Color
B. Suitable scale
C. Size of sheet
D. Model type

Q58. Always Start View Creation option:
A. Stops creation
B. Starts default view
C. Deletes view
D. Rotates view

Q59. Revision edit box defines:
A. Scale
B. Revision letter
C. Size
D. Color

Q60. Units area is used to:
A. Set dimensions
B. Set units
C. Rotate
D. Delete

FOR STUDENT NOTES

Index

Symbols

A

B

C

T

U

V

W

X

Z

Ethics of an Engineer

- Engineers shall hold paramount the safety, health, and welfare of the public and shall strive to comply with the principles of sustainable development in the performance of their professional duties.
- Engineers shall perform services only in areas of their competence.
- Engineers shall issue public statements only in an objective and truthful manner.
- Engineers shall act in professional manners for each employer or client as faithful agents or trustees, and shall avoid conflicts of interest.
- Engineers shall build their professional reputation on the merit of their services and shall not compete unfairly with others.
- Engineers shall act in such a manner as to uphold and enhance the honor, integrity, and dignity of the engineering profession and shall act with zero-tolerance for bribery, fraud, and corruption.
- Engineers shall continue their professional development throughout their careers, and shall provide opportunities for the professional development of those engineers under their supervision.

www.ingramcontent.com/pod-product-compliance
Lightning Source LLC
LaVergne TN
LVHW082000200926
848481LV00010B/2777
9781774592083